# COLORADO REVISED STATUTES
# TITLE 25
# PUBLIC HEALTH AND ENVIRONMENT

# 2018 EDITION

Updated as of May 15, 2018

THE LAW LIBRARY

# TABLE OF CONTENTS

# ADMINISTRATION

# ARTICLE 1. ADMINISTRATION

# PART 1. DEPARTMENT OF PUBLIC HEALTH AND ENVIRONMENT

## 25-1-101. Construction of terms.

(1) When any law of this state refers to the executive director of the state department of public health or of the department of health, said law shall be construed as referring to the executive director of the department of public health and environment.

(2) Whenever any law of this state refers to the state department of public health or to the department of health, said law shall be construed as referring to the department of public health and environment.

## 25-1-101.5. Authority of revisor of statutes to amend references to department - affected statutory provisions.

The revisor of statutes is hereby authorized to change all references in the Colorado Revised Statutes to the department of health from said reference to the department of public health and environment, as appropriate. In connection with such authority, the revisor of statutes is hereby authorized to amend or delete provisions of the Colorado Revised Statutes so as to make the statutes consistent with the renaming of the department to the department of public health and environment.

## 25-1-102. Department created - executive director - divisions.

(1) There is hereby created a department of public health and environment, referred to in this part 1 and article 1.5 of this title as the "department". The head of the department shall be the executive director of the department of public health and environment, which office is hereby created. The governor shall appoint said executive director, with the consent of the senate, and the executive director shall serve at the pleasure of the governor. The reappointment of an executive director after initial election of a governor shall be subject to the provisions of section 24-20-109, C.R.S. The executive director shall administer the department, subject to the authority of the state board of health, the air quality control commission, the state water quality control commission, and the solid and hazardous waste commission.

(2) The department shall consist of the following divisions:

(a) The division of administration, and such sections and units established as provided by law.

(b) (Deleted by amendment, L. 93, p. 1095, § 11, effective July 1, 1994.)

## 25-1-103. State board of health created.

(1) There is hereby created a state board of health, referred to in this part 1 as the "board", which shall consist of nine members, of which one member shall be appointed by the governor, with the consent of the senate, from each congressional district and the remainder from the state at large. A vacancy on the board occurs whenever any member moves out of the congressional district from

which he was appointed. A member who moves out of such congressional district shall promptly notify the governor of the date of such move, but such notice is not a condition precedent to the occurrence of the vacancy. The governor shall fill the vacancy by appointment for the unexpired term. No more than five members of the board shall be members of the same major political party. Appointments made to take effect on January 1, 1983, shall be made in accordance with section 24-1-135, C.R.S. Appointments thereafter shall be made, with the consent of the senate, for terms of four years each and shall be made so that no business or professional group shall constitute a majority of the board. In making appointments to the board, the governor is encouraged to include representation by at least one member who is a person with a disability, as defined in section 24-45.5-102 (2) , C.R.S., a family member of a person with a disability, or a member of an advocacy group for persons with disabilities if the other requirements of this subsection (1) are met.

(2) The first vacancy that occurs on the board after July 1, 1977, shall be filled by the appointment of a person who is then serving as a county commissioner. Thereafter, as vacancies occur and terms expire, there shall always be one county commissioner member on the board. Whenever a county commissioner ceases to hold the office of county commissioner, he ceases to hold his position as a member of the board. A county commissioner shall not vote on any matter coming before the board which affects his county in a manner significantly different from the manner in which it affects other counties.

## 25-1-104. State board - organization.

The board shall elect from its members a president, a vice-president, and such other board officers as it shall determine. The executive director of the department, in the discretion of the board, may serve as secretary of the board but shall not be eligible to appointment as a member. All board officers shall hold their offices at the pleasure of the board. Regular meetings of the board shall be held not less than once every three months at such times as may be fixed by resolution of the board. Special meetings may be called by the president, by the executive director of the department, or by a majority of the members of the board at any time on three days' prior notice by mail or, in case of emergency, on twenty-four hours' notice by telephone or other telecommunications device. The board shall adopt, and at any time may amend, bylaws in relation to its meetings and the transaction of its business. A majority shall constitute a quorum of the board. Members shall receive the same per diem compensation and reimbursement of expenses as those provided for members of boards and commissions in the division of professions and occupations pursuant to section 24-34-102 (13) , C.R.S. All meetings of the board, in every suit and proceeding, shall be taken to have been duly called and regularly held, and all orders and proceedings of the board to have been authorized, unless the contrary is proved.

## 25-1-105. Executive director - chief medical officer - qualifications - salary - office.

(1) The executive director of the department shall:

(a) Have a degree of doctor of medicine or doctor of osteopathy, be licensed to practice medicine in the state of Colorado, and have at least one of the following qualifications:

(I) One year of graduate study in a school of public health;

(II) Not less than two years' experience in an administrative capacity in a health care organization;

(III) Four years of said experience when one year of graduate study in a school of public health has not been completed; or

(b) Have, at a minimum, experience or education in public administration and public or environmental health.

(2) (a) If the governor appoints an executive director who does not have the qualifications specified in paragraph (a) of subsection (1) of this section, the executive director of the department shall, pursuant to the provisions of section 13 of article XII of the state constitution, upon consultation with the governor, and with the consent of a majority of the members of the senate, appoint a chief medical officer. The chief medical officer shall have the qualifications specified in

paragraph (a) of subsection (1) of this section and shall serve at the pleasure of the governor. The executive director shall initially appoint the chief medical officer no later than three months after the executive director's appointment has been confirmed by the senate.

(b) The chief medical officer shall provide independent medical judgment, guidance, and advice to the governor and to the executive director regarding medical and public health issues in all areas identified in article 1.5 of this title.

(c) The chief medical officer shall be afforded direct access to the governor and the governor's staff.

(3) The executive director shall receive such salary as may be fixed by the board subject to the state constitution and state laws and within the limits of funds made available to the department by appropriation of the general assembly or otherwise. The executive director shall be allowed traveling and subsistence expenses actually and necessarily incurred in the performance of the executive director's official duties when absent from his or her place of residence. The executive director shall be custodian of all property and records of the department.

## 25-1-106. Division personnel.

The executive director of the department shall appoint the director of the division of administration, pursuant to the provisions of section 13 of article XII of the state constitution. Each subdivision (and section) of the division of administration shall be under the management of a head, and such heads and all other subordinate personnel of the division shall be appointed by the director of the division, subject to the constitution and state personnel system laws of the state, and shall possess qualifications approved by the board. All personnel shall receive such compensation as fixed by the executive director with the approval of the board, subject to the constitution and state personnel system laws of the state and within the limits of funds made available to the department by appropriation of the general assembly or otherwise. With the approval of the executive director, employees shall also be allowed traveling and subsistence expenses actually and necessarily incurred in the performance of their official duties when absent from their places of residence.

## 25-1-107. Powers and duties of the department - repeal. (Repealed)

## 25-1-107.5. Additional authority of department - rules - remedies against nursing facilities - criteria for recommending assessments for civil penalties - cooperation with department of health care policy and financing - nursing home penalty cash fund - nursing home innovations grant board - reports - repeal.

(1) For the purposes of this section, unless the context otherwise requires:

(a) Repealed.

(b) "Federal regulations for participation" means the regulations found in part 442 of title 42 of the code of federal regulations, as amended, for participation under Title XIX of the federal "Social Security Act", as amended.

(b.5) "Benefit residents of nursing facilities" means that a grant has a direct impact on the residents of nursing facilities or has an indirect impact on the residents through education of nursing facility staff.

(b.7) "Board" means the nursing home innovations grant board, authorized by subsection (6) of this section.

(c) "Nursing facility" means any skilled or intermediate nursing care facility that receives federal and state funds under Title XIX of the federal "Social Security Act", as amended.

(2) The department, as the state agency responsible for certifying nursing facilities, is authorized to adopt rules necessary to establish a series of remedies in accordance with this section and the

federal "Omnibus Budget Reconciliation Act of 1987", Pub.L. 100-203, as amended, that may be imposed by the department of health care policy and financing when a nursing facility violates federal regulations for participation in the medicaid program. The remedies shall include any remedies required under federal law and the imposition of civil money penalties.

(3) (a) In accordance with rules promulgated under this section, the department is authorized to recommend to the department of health care policy and financing an appropriate civil money penalty based on the nature of the violation. Any penalties recommended shall not be less than one hundred dollars nor more than ten thousand dollars for each day the facility is found to be in violation of the federal regulations. Penalties assessed shall include interest at the statutory rate.

(b) The department shall adopt criteria for determining the amount of the penalty to be recommended for assessment. The criteria shall include, but need not be limited to, consideration of the following factors:

(I) The period during which the violation occurred;

(II) The frequency of the violation;

(III) The nursing facility's history concerning the type of violation for which the penalty is assessed;

(IV) The nursing facility's intent or reason for the violation;

(V) The effect, if any, of the violation on the health, safety, security, or welfare of the residents of the nursing facility;

(VI) The existence of other violations, in combination with the violation for which the penalty is assessed, that increase the threat to the health, safety, security, or welfare of the residents of the nursing facility;

(VII) The accuracy, thoroughness, and availability of records regarding the violation that the nursing facility is required to maintain; and

(VIII) The number of additional related violations occurring within the same period as the violation in question.

(c) (I) If the department finds that a violation is life threatening to one or more residents or creates a direct threat of serious adverse harm to the health, safety, security, rights, or welfare of one or more residents, the department of health care policy and financing shall impose a penalty for each day the deficiencies that constitute the violation are found to exist.

(II) Except as provided in subparagraph (I) of this paragraph (c) , the department of health care policy and financing shall not assess a penalty prior to the date a nursing facility receives written notice from the department of its recommendation to assess civil money penalties. The department shall provide the notice to the facility no later than five days after the last day of the inspection or survey during which the deficiencies that constitute the violation were found. The notice shall:

(A) Set forth the deficiencies that are the basis for the recommendation to assess a penalty;

(B) Provide instructions for responding to the notice; and

(C) Require the nursing facility to submit a written plan of correction. The department shall adopt criteria for the submission of written plans of correction by nursing facilities and approval of the plans by the department. If the facility acts in a timely and diligent manner to correct the violation in accordance with an approved plan of correction, the department may recommend to the department of health care policy and financing that it suspend or reduce the penalty during the period of correction specified in the approved plan of correction.

(d) Except as provided in sub-subparagraph (C) of subparagraph (II) of paragraph (c) of this subsection (3) , the department of health care policy and financing shall continue to assess any penalty recommended under this section until the department verifies to the department of health care policy and financing that the violation is corrected or until the nursing facility notifies the department that correction has occurred, whichever is earlier. If the penalty has been suspended or reduced pursuant to sub-subparagraph (C) of subparagraph (II) of paragraph (c) of this subsection (3) and the nursing facility has not corrected the violation, the department of health care policy and financing shall reinstate the penalty at an increased amount and shall retroactively assess the penalty to the date the penalty was suspended.

(4) (a) The department of health care policy and financing, after receiving a recommendation from

the department, is authorized to assess, enforce, and collect the civil money penalty pursuant to section 25.5-6-205, C.R.S., for credit to the nursing home penalty cash fund, created pursuant to section 25.5-6-205 (3) (a) , C.R.S.

(b) (I) The department of public health and environment and the department of health care policy and financing have joint authority for administering the nursing home penalty cash fund; except that final authority regarding the administration of moneys in the fund is in the department of health care policy and financing.

(II) The authority of both departments includes establishing circumstances under which funds may be distributed in order to protect the health or property of individuals residing in nursing facilities that the department of health care policy and financing has found to be in violation of federal regulations for participation in the medicaid program.

(III) The department of health care policy and financing shall promulgate rules necessary to ensure proper administration of the nursing home penalty cash fund.

(c) The departments shall consider, as a basis for distribution from the nursing home penalty cash fund, the following:

(I) The need to pay costs to:

(A) Relocate residents to other facilities when a nursing facility closes;

(B) Maintain the operation of a nursing facility pending correction of violations;

(C) Close a nursing facility;

(D) Reimburse residents for personal funds lost;

(II) Grants to be approved for measures that will benefit residents of nursing facilities by fostering innovation and improving the quality of life and care at the facilities, including:

(A) Consumer education to promote resident-centered care in nursing facilities;

(B) (Deleted by amendment, L. 2014.)

(C) Initiatives in nursing facilities related to the quality measures promoted by the federal centers for medicare and medicaid services and other national quality initiatives; and

(D) Education and consultation for purposes of identifying and implementing resident-centered care initiatives in nursing facilities.

(d) (I) The departments shall distribute the following amounts of moneys in the nursing home penalty cash fund for the purposes described in subparagraph (II) of paragraph (c) of this subsection (4) :

(A) For any fiscal year, two hundred fifty thousand dollars if the fund balance is greater than two million dollars on July 1 of that fiscal year;

(B) If the fund balance on July 1 of any fiscal year is less than two million dollars, the department shall distribute twenty-five percent of the moneys deposited in the fund in the immediately preceding fiscal year, not to exceed two hundred fifty thousand dollars in total fund distribution per fiscal year.

(II) The department of health care policy and financing, after receiving a recommendation from the board and approval from the federal centers for medicare and medicaid services, shall consider grants issued as sole source procurements that are not subject to the "Procurement Code", articles 101 to 112 of title 24, C.R.S.

(II.5) (A) The board shall make recommendations for the approval of grants that benefit residents of nursing facilities for at least one year and not more than three-year cycles. The projects awarded grants must be portable, sustainable, and replicable in other nursing facilities.

(B) The department of health care policy and financing and the board shall develop processes for grant payments, which processes may allow grant payments to be made in advance of the delivery of goods and services to grantees. Grantees receiving advance payments shall report progress to the board. No state agency nor any other governmental entity, with the exception of a facility that is owned or operated by a governmental agency and that is licensed as a nursing care facility under section 25-1.5-103 (1) (a) (I) (A) , may apply for or receive a grant under this subsection (4) .

(C) Any moneys remaining in the fund at the end of a fiscal year may be held over and used by the board in the next fiscal year. Unexpended and unencumbered moneys from an appropriation in the annual general appropriation act to the departments for the purpose of carrying out the nursing home innovation grant program under this section remain available for expenditure by the departments in the next fiscal year without further appropriation. This sub-subparagraph (C) applies to appropriations made by the general assembly for fiscal years ending on and after June 30, 2014. On or before June 30, 2014, and on or before June 30 of each year thereafter, the departments shall notify the state controller of the amount of the appropriation from the annual general appropriation act for the current fiscal year the departments need to remain available for expenditure in the next fiscal year. The departments may not expend more than the amount stated in the notice under this sub-subparagraph (C) .

(D) Other policies of the board must conform with practices of other granting organizations. The work product from grants funded through the nursing home penalty cash fund is the intellectual property of the department and must be made available without charge to all nursing homes in the state. The department of health care policy and financing shall adopt rules as necessary to govern the procedure for awarding grants under this section.

(II.7) The department of health care policy and financing shall adhere to all state and federal requirements for the encumbrance and payment of grants under this paragraph (d) . In addition, the department shall:

(A) Document necessary federal permissions for the use of moneys from the nursing home penalty cash fund, created under section 25.5-6-205, C.R.S., prior to making any payment or encumbrance; and

(B) Adhere to the written determination of the board under subsection (6) of this section in releasing state moneys for payment to grantees under this section. The department's adherence to the written determination of the board is sufficient evidence to ensure that work was completed fully and adequately.

(III) Notwithstanding subparagraph (I) of this paragraph (d) , the departments shall ensure that the balance of the nursing home penalty cash fund does not fall below one million dollars as a result of expenditures for the purposes described in subparagraph (II) of paragraph (c) of this subsection (4) and shall not distribute moneys pursuant to this paragraph (d) for such purposes if making a distribution would cause the fund balance to fall below the minimum balance required by this subparagraph (III) .

(IV) In determining how to allocate the moneys authorized to be distributed pursuant to this paragraph (d) , the departments shall take into consideration the recommendations of the board made pursuant to paragraph (c) of subsection (6) of this section. If the departments disagree with the recommendations of the board, they shall meet with the board to explain their rationale and shall seek to achieve a compromise with the board regarding the allocation of the moneys. If a compromise cannot be achieved with regard to all or a portion of the moneys to be distributed, the medical services board created pursuant to section 25.5-1-301, C.R.S., shall have the final authority regarding the distribution of moneys for which a compromise has not been reached.

(e) The departments shall not utilize moneys from the nursing home penalty cash fund for the purpose of paying their cost for administering the fund or for costs of administration associated with any specific movement, association, or organization; except that up to ten thousand dollars of the moneys distributed pursuant to paragraph (d) of this subsection (4) may be used to pay the cost to administer and operate the board, including expense reimbursement for board members.

(5) Repealed.

(6) (a) No later than September 1, 2014, the department of health care policy and financing shall establish the nursing home innovations grant board under the department of health care policy and financing either directly or by contract with or grant to any public agency or appropriate private nonprofit organization. The department of health care policy and financing, in consultation with stakeholders, shall determine the appropriate entity to administer the board. The board consists of ten members as follows:

(I) The state long-term care ombudsman or his or her designee;

(II) The executive director of the department of health care policy and financing or the executive director's designee;

(III) The executive director of the department of public health and environment or the executive director's designee;

(IV) Seven members appointed by the governor as follows:

(A) Four members currently employed in long-term care nursing facilities;

(B) One member who is or represents a consumer of long-term care;

(C) One member representing the disability community who is either a resident of a nursing facility or a family member of a nursing facility resident; and

(D) One member representing the business community.

(E) (Deleted by amendment, L. 2014.)

(b) The members of the board shall serve without compensation but may be reimbursed for expenses incurred while serving on the board.

(c) The board shall review all grant projects, determine whether the grantees completed their grant projects and grant objectives, and shall provide written recommendations to the department to make or withhold payment to grantees.

(d) By October 1 of each year, the departments, with the assistance of the board, shall jointly submit a report to the governor and the health and human services committee of the senate and the public health care and human services committee of the house of representatives of the general assembly, or their successor committees, regarding the expenditure of moneys in the nursing home penalty cash fund for the purposes described in subparagraph (II) of paragraph (c) of subsection (4) of this section. The report must detail the amount of moneys expended for such purposes, the recipients of the funds, the effectiveness of the use of the funds, and any other information deemed pertinent by the departments or requested by the governor or the committees. Notwithstanding the requirement in section 24-1-136 (11) , C.R.S., the report required in this paragraph (d) continues indefinitely.

(7) (a) Subparagraph (II) of paragraph (c) of subsection (4) of this section, subsection (6) of this section, and this subsection (7) are repealed, effective September 1, 2021.

(b) Prior to the repeal, the nursing home innovations grant board and its functions, and the use of moneys in the nursing home penalty cash fund for the purposes described in subparagraph (II) of paragraph (c) of subsection (4) of this section, shall be reviewed pursuant to section 24-34-104, C.R.S.

## 25-1-108. Powers and duties of state board of health.

(1) In addition to all other powers and duties conferred and imposed upon the state board of health by the provisions of this part 1, the board has the following specific powers and duties:

(a) To determine general policies to be followed by the division of administration in administering and enforcing the public health laws and the orders, standards, rules, and regulations of the board;

(b) To act in an advisory capacity to the executive director of the department on all matters pertaining to public health;

(c) (I) To issue from time to time such orders, to adopt such rules and regulations, and to establish such standards as the board may deem necessary or proper to carry out the provisions and purposes of this part 1 and to administer and enforce the public health laws of this state;

(II) To adopt rules and regulations and standards concerning building regulations and fire safety for skilled and intermediate health care facilities. The enforcement of these rules and regulations may be waived by the board for periods of time as recommended by the department if the rigid application thereof would result in demonstrated financial hardship to a skilled or intermediate facility, but only if the waiver will not adversely affect the health and safety of patients.

(III) All rules, regulations, and standards adopted prior to February 21, 1947, by the board concerning building regulations or fire safety for nursing homes which are more strict than those provided by the highest standards as set forth in this paragraph (c) are nullified by this section, but nothing contained in this paragraph (c) shall be construed to prevent the department from adopting and enforcing, with respect to projects for which federal assistance has been obtained or shall be requested, such higher standards as may be required by applicable federal laws or regulations of federal agencies responsible for the administration of such federal laws.

(IV) For the purpose of this part 1, all rules, regulations, and standards adopted prior to February 21, 1947, by the board or any board, office, or bureau whose duties are by virtue of this section transferred to the board or the department, in effect immediately prior to February 21, 1947, and not inconsistent with the authority of the board as provided in this part 1 shall remain in full force and effect until superseded by rules, regulations, or standards duly adopted pursuant to this paragraph (c) by the board in conformance with this part 1, to the same effect as though such rules, regulations, and standards were adopted subsequent to the passage of this part 1 in full conformance therewith.

(V) Repealed.

(VI) To adopt rules and to establish such standards as the board may deem necessary or proper to assure that hospitals, other acute care facilities, county, district, and municipal public health agencies, trauma centers, area trauma advisory councils, and managed care organizations are prepared for an emergency epidemic, as defined in section 24-33.5-703 (4) , C.R.S., that is declared to be a disaster emergency, including the immediate investigation of any case of a suspected emergency epidemic.

(d) To hold hearings, administer oaths, subpoena witnesses, and take testimony in all matters relating to the exercise and performance of the powers and duties vested in or imposed upon the board. The board may designate an administrative law judge appointed pursuant to part 10 of article 30 of title 24, C.R.S., to conduct hearings for the board, pursuant to section 24-4-105, C.R.S., and to carry out such administrative and other duties of the board as the board may require in the conduct of its hearings.

(e) To establish and appoint, as the board may deem necessary or advisable, special advisory committees to advise and confer with the board concerning the public health aspects of any business, profession, or industry within the state of Colorado. Any committee established and appointed under the provisions of this section shall act only in an advisory capacity to the board and shall meet with the board at least once each year at such regular meeting of the board as may be designated by the board and at such other times as such committee may be called into meeting by the president of the board. Members of any special advisory committee shall serve without compensation but may, in the discretion of the board, be allowed actual and necessary traveling and subsistence expenses when in attendance at meetings away from their places of residence.

(f) To accept and, through the division of administration, use, disburse, and administer all federal aid or other property, services, and moneys allotted to the department for state and local public works or public health functions, or allotted without designation of a specific agency for purposes which are within the functions of the department; and to prescribe, by rule or regulation not inconsistent with the laws of this state, the conditions under which such property, services, or moneys shall be accepted and administered. On behalf of the state, the board is empowered to make such agreements, with the approval of the attorney general, not inconsistent with the laws of this state, as may be required as a condition precedent to receiving such funds or other assistance.

(g) Repealed.

(h) To comply with the requirements of section 24-1-136.5, C.R.S., concerning the preparation of operational master plans, facilities master plans, and facilities program plans, as if the state board of health were the executive director of the department.

(2) The board shall act only by resolution adopted at a duly called meeting of the board, and no individual member of the board shall exercise individually any administrative authority with respect to the department.

(3) In the exercise of its powers, the department shall not promulgate any rule or standard that limits or interferes with the ability of an individual to enter into a contract with a private pay facility concerning the programs or services provided at the private pay facility. For the purposes of this subsection (3) , "private pay facility" means a skilled nursing facility or intermediate care facility subject to the requirements of section 25-1-120 or an assisted living residence licensed pursuant to section 25-27-105 that is not publicly funded or is not certified to provide services that are reimbursed from state or federal assistance funds.

(4) and (5) Repealed.

## 25-1-108.5. Additional powers and duties of state board of health and department - programs that receive tobacco settlement moneys - definitions - monitoring - annual report. (Repealed)

## 25-1-108.7. Health care credentials uniform application act - legislative declaration - definitions - state board of health rules.

(1) This section shall be known and may be cited as the "Health Care Credentials Uniform Application Act".

(2) The purpose of the "Health Care Credentials Uniform Application Act" is to make credentialing more efficient, less costly, and less duplicative by making it uniform through the use of a single application form for the collection of core credentials data for use by entities.

(3) As used in this section, unless the context otherwise requires:

(a) "Core credentials data" means data, information, or answers to questions that are collected and retained and that are common and necessary for the credentialing or recredentialing of a health care professional, but does not include additional nonduplicative credentials data deemed essential by a credentialing entity to complete credentialing.

(b) "Credentialing" means the process of assessing and validating the qualifications of a health care professional.

(c) "Credentialing entity" means any health care entity or health care plan that is engaged in the collection of information to be used in the process of credentialing or recredentialing of health care professionals.

(d) "Health care entity" means any of the following that require health professionals to submit credentials data:

(I) A health care facility or other health care organization licensed or certified to provide medical or health services in Colorado;

(II) A health care professional partnership, corporation, limited liability company, professional services corporation, or group practice;

(III) An independent practice association or physician-hospital organization;

(IV) A professional liability insurance carrier; or

(V) An insurance company, health maintenance organization, or other entity that contracts for the provision of health benefits.

(e) "Health care plan" means any entity that is licensed by the division of insurance as a prepaid health care plan, health maintenance organization, or insurer and that requires the submission of credentials data.

(f) "Health care professional" means a physician, dentist, dental hygienist, chiropractor, podiatrist, psychologist, advanced practice nurse, optometrist, physician assistant, licensed clinical social worker, child health associate, marriage and family therapist, or other health care professional who is registered, certified, or licensed pursuant to title 12, C.R.S.; who is subject to credentialing; and who practices, or intends to practice, in Colorado.

(g) "Nonspecific credentials data" means credentials data that is aggregated and reported without reference to the identity of the individual health care professional to whom it pertains.

(4) (a) Nothing in this section shall be construed to restrict the authority of any health care entity or health care plan to approve, suspend, or deny an application for insurance, staff membership, clinical privileges, or managed care network participation. This section shall not be construed to apply to the licensing activities of any board responsible for licensing health care professionals.

(b) Nothing in this section shall be construed to require a credentialing entity to use a particular credentialing process or to restrict or require such an entity from using a particular vendor in the credentialing process.

(5) Upon the effective date of the rule established by the state board of health pursuant to paragraph (e) of subsection (6) of this section, a credentialing entity shall collect core credentials

data through the use of the Colorado health care professional credentials application established pursuant to paragraph (a) of subsection (6) of this section. The form may be submitted electronically or by paper copy. The credentialing entity may require a health care professional to answer only select provisions of the application according to the needs of the entity. Questions that are prohibited by law shall not be included in the request for credentialing data by the credentialing entity.

(6) (a) There is hereby established the health care credentials application review committee to recommend to the state board of health, and to periodically review, a single application form for the collection of core credentials data in this state. The form shall be known as the "Colorado health care professional credentials application". The review committee shall consist of the following eight members, who shall serve for terms of four years and who shall be appointed by the state board of health:

(I) One member representing a statewide association or society of physicians;

(II) One member representing a statewide association or society of Colorado hospitals;

(III) One member representing a statewide association or society of health plans;

(IV) One member representing a professional liability insurance carrier domiciled in Colorado that provides professional liability insurance to health care professionals in Colorado;

(V) One member representing a statewide association or society of Colorado health care medical staff service specialists;

(VI) One advanced practice nurse;

(VII) Two members at large.

(b) Each board member may bring consultants and advisors to participate in board meetings. Consultants and advisors shall not have decision-making powers or voting privileges.

(c) The review committee shall be staffed by an entity approved by the Colorado medical board to collect medical license registration fees pursuant to section 12-36-123.5, C.R.S.

(d) Members of the review committee shall serve without compensation.

(e) Within one hundred twenty days after the time of appointment, the review committee shall make a recommendation to the state board of health regarding proposed contents of the Colorado health care professional credentials application. In accordance with section 24-4-103, C.R.S., the state board of health shall establish, by rule, the Colorado health care professional credentials application. The Colorado health care professional credentials application shall be the same as the provider application form developed by the council for affordable quality healthcare as of January 1, 2004, as modified, if necessary, to comply with Colorado law or as may be recommended by the majority of members of the review committee.

(f) The review committee shall meet at least annually to review and make any necessary recommendations for modifications to the Colorado health care professional credentials application to the state board of health.

(g) Initial appointments to the review committee shall be made on or before July 1, 2004. The state board of health shall appoint replacement members as necessary for a full committee.

(h) On or before September 1, 2008, the review committee shall make recommendations to the board concerning the feasibility of requiring all requests for additional credentials data deemed essential by a credentialing entity be uniform among all credentialing committees by July 1, 2009. On or before March 1, 2009, the review committee shall make recommendations to the board concerning the feasibility of requiring all Colorado health care professional credentials applications to be submitted through online electronic methods and that all health care entities required by this section to use the health care professional credentials application be required to accept and process the application through electronic means by January 1, 2010. If determined feasible by the board, the board shall establish by rule the standards, means, methods, and forms necessary to require the use of uniform supplemental questions and the submission, receipt, and processing of the health care professional credentials application electronically.

(7) Core credentials data collected and retained on behalf of a credentialing entity shall not be modified without the approval of the credentialing entity.

(8) The state board of health may promulgate rules as necessary to carry out the provisions of this

section.

(9) (Deleted by amendment, L. 2008, p. 688, § 1, effective July 1, 2008.)

## 25-1-109. Powers and duties of division of administration.

(1) In addition to the other powers and duties conferred and imposed in this part 1 upon the division of administration, the division, through the director or, upon the director's direction and under the director's supervision, through the other officers and employees of the division, has the following powers and duties:

(a) To administer and enforce the public health laws of the state of Colorado and the standards, orders, rules, and regulations established, issued, or adopted by the board;

(b) To exercise all powers and duties conferred and imposed upon the department not expressly delegated to the board by the provisions of this part 1;

(c) To hold hearings, administer oaths, subpoena witnesses, and take testimony in all matters relating to the exercise and performance of the powers and duties vested in or imposed upon the division of administration. The director may designate an administrative law judge appointed pursuant to part 10 of article 30 of title 24, C.R.S., to conduct hearings pursuant to section 24-4-105, C.R.S.

(d) Repealed.

(e) To supervise all subdivisions and boards of the department to determine that publications of the department and of any subdivisions thereof circulated in quantity outside the executive branch are issued in accordance with the provisions of section 24-1-136, C.R.S.;

(f) To appoint, pursuant to section 13 of article XII of the state constitution, a chief health inspector and such deputy inspectors as may be authorized. Such inspectors have the power to enter any workplace as provided in section 8-1-116, C.R.S. All expenses incurred by the division and its employees, pursuant to the provisions of this section, shall be paid from the funds appropriated for its use, upon approval of the director.

(g) Repealed.

(h) To administer and enforce the minimum general sanitary standards and regulations adopted pursuant to section 25-1.5-202.

## 25-1-110. Higher standards permissible.

Nothing in this part 1 shall prevent any incorporated city, city and county, town, county, or other political subdivision of the state from imposing and enforcing higher standards than are imposed under this part 1.

## 25-1-111. Revenues of department.

(1) Repealed.

(2) The department of the treasury of this state is designated as custodian of all funds allotted to the state for the purpose outlined by section 25-1-108 (1) (f) . Such funds and all other funds of the department shall be payable only on voucher signed by the executive director of the department and by the president of the board and shall be paid by warrant of the controller.

## 25-1-112. Legal adviser - actions.

The attorney general shall be the legal adviser for the department and shall defend it in all actions and proceedings brought against it. The district attorney of the judicial district in which a cause of action may arise shall bring any action, civil or criminal, requested by the executive director of the department to abate a condition which exists in violation of, or to restrain or enjoin any action which is in violation of, or to prosecute for the violation of or for the enforcement of the public health laws or the standards, orders, rules, and regulations of the department established by or issued under the provisions of this part 1. If the district attorney fails to act, the executive director may bring any such action and shall be represented by the attorney general or, with the approval of the board, by special counsel.

## 25-1-113. Judicial review of decisions.

(1) Any person aggrieved and affected by a decision of the board or the executive director of the department is entitled to judicial review by filing in the district court of the county of his residence, or of the city and county of Denver, within ninety days after the public announcement of the decision, an appropriate action requesting such review. The court may make any interested person a party to the action. The review shall be conducted by the court without a jury and shall be confined to the record, if a complete record is presented; except that, in cases of alleged irregularities in the record or in the procedure before the board or the division of administration, testimony may be taken in the court. The court may affirm the decision or may reverse or modify it if the substantial rights of the appellant have been prejudiced as a result of the findings and decisions of the board being: Contrary to constitutional rights or privileges; or in excess of the statutory authority or jurisdiction of the board or the executive director of the department; or affected by any error of law; or made or promulgated upon unlawful procedure; or unsupported by substantial evidence in view of the entire record as submitted; or arbitrary or capricious.

(2) Any party may have a review of the final judgment or decision of the district court by appellate review in accordance with law and the Colorado appellate rules.

## 25-1-114. Unlawful acts - penalties.

(1) It is unlawful for any person, association, or corporation, and the officers thereof:

(a) To willfully violate, disobey, or disregard the provisions of the public health laws or the terms of any lawful notice, order, standard, rule, or regulation issued pursuant thereto; or

(b) To fail to make or file reports required by law or rule of the board relating to the existence of disease or other facts and statistics relating to the public health; or

(c) To conduct any business or activity over which the department possesses the power to license and regulate without such license or permit as required by the department; or

(d) To willfully and falsely make or alter any certificate or license or certified copy thereof issued pursuant to the public health laws; or

(e) To knowingly transport or accept for transportation, interment, or other disposition a dead body without an accompanying permit issued in accordance with the public health laws or the rules of the board; or

(f) To willfully fail to remove from private property under his control at his own expense, within forty-eight hours after being ordered so to do by the health authorities, any nuisance, source of filth, or cause of sickness within the jurisdiction and control of the department, whether such person, association, or corporation is the owner, tenant, or occupant of such private property; except that, if such condition is due to an act of God, it shall be removed at public expense; or

(g) To pay, give, present, or otherwise convey to any officer or employee of the department any gift, remuneration, or other consideration, directly or indirectly, which such officer or employee is forbidden to receive by the provisions of this part 1; or

(h) To make, install, maintain, or permit any cross-connection between any water system supplying drinking water to the public and any pipe, plumbing fixture, or water system which contains water of a quality below the minimum general sanitary standards as to the quality of drinking water supplied to the public or to fail to remove such connection within ten days after being ordered in writing by the department to remove the same. For the purposes of this paragraph (h) , "cross-connection" means any connection which would allow water to flow from any pipe, plumbing fixture, or water system into a water system supplying drinking water to the public.

(i) To sell or offer for sale any raw milk, milk product, or unsanitary dairy product, as defined in section 25-5.5-104, for other than human consumption unless it has first been treated with a dye approved by the department.

(2) It is unlawful for any officer or employee of the department or member of the board to accept any gift, remuneration, or other consideration, directly or indirectly, for an incorrect or improper performance of the duties imposed upon him by or on behalf of the department.

(3) It is unlawful:

(a) For any officer or employee of the department to perform any work, labor, or services other than the duties assigned to him by or on behalf of the department during the hours such officer or employee is regularly employed by the department, or to perform his duties as an officer or employee of the department under any condition or arrangement that involves a violation of this or any other law of the state of Colorado;

(b) For any officer or employee of the department other than members of the board to perform any work, labor, or services which consist of the private practice of medicine, veterinary surgery, sanitary engineering, nursing, or any other profession which is or may be of special benefit to any private person, association, or corporation as distinguished from the department or the public generally, and which is performed by such officer or employee, directly or indirectly, for remuneration, whether done in an active, advisory, or consultative capacity or performed within or without the hours such officer or employee is regularly employed by the department.

(4) Except as provided in subsection (5) of this section, any person, association, or corporation, or the officers thereof, who violates any provision of this section is guilty of a misdemeanor and, upon conviction thereof, shall be punished by a fine of not more than one thousand dollars, or by imprisonment in the county jail for not more than one year, or by both such fine and imprisonment and, in addition to such fine and imprisonment, shall be liable for any expense incurred by health authorities in removing any nuisance, source of filth, or cause of sickness. Conviction under the penalty provisions of this part 1 or any other public health law shall not relieve any person from any civil action in damages that may exist for an injury resulting from any violation of the public health laws.

(5) (a) It is unlawful for any person, association, or corporation, or the officers thereof, to tamper, attempt to tamper, or threaten to tamper with a public water system or with drinking water after its withdrawal for or treatment by a public water system. For purposes of this subsection (5) , "tamper" means to introduce a contaminant into a public water system or into drinking water or to otherwise interfere with drinking water or the operation of a public water system with the intention of harming persons or the public water system. "Tamper" does not include the standardized and accepted treatment procedures performed by a supplier of water in preparing water for human consumption.

(b) (I) Any person, association, or corporation, or the officers thereof, who tampers with a public water system or with drinking water after its withdrawal for or treatment by a public water system commits a class 3 felony and shall be punished as provided in section 18-1.3-401, C.R.S.

(II) Any person, association, or corporation, or the officers thereof, who attempts to tamper or threatens to tamper with a public water system or with drinking water after its withdrawal for or treatment by a public water system commits a class 5 felony and shall be punished as provided in section 18-1.3-401, C.R.S.

(III) Conviction under this subsection (5) shall not relieve any person from a civil action initiated pursuant to section 25-1-114.1.

## 25-1-114.1. Civil remedies and penalties.

(1) The division of administration of the department may institute a civil action or administrative action, as described in subsection (2.5) of this section, against any person who violates a final enforcement order of the department issued for a violation of any minimum general sanitary standard or regulation adopted pursuant to section 25-1.5-202. Such civil action shall be brought in the district court of the county in which the violation of the standard or regulation is alleged to have occurred.

(2) Upon finding that a final enforcement order of the department has been violated and that the violation of the standard or regulation described in the order in fact occurred, the court shall:

(a) Impose a civil penalty on the violator of not more than one thousand dollars per day for each day the violation of the standard or regulation occurred if the court determines the violation was willful; or

(b) Enter such order as the public health may require, taking into consideration, where appropriate, the cost and time necessary to comply; or

(c) Impose such civil penalty and enter such order.

(2.5) (a) Any person who violates any minimum general sanitary standard and regulation promulgated pursuant to section 25-1.5-202 or 25-1-114 (1) (h) , or any final enforcement order issued by the department, shall be subject to an administrative penalty as follows:

(I) For systems that serve a population of more than ten thousand people, an amount not to exceed one thousand dollars per violation per day; or

(II) For systems that serve a population of ten thousand people or less, an amount not to exceed one thousand dollars per violation per day, but only in an amount, as determined by the division, that is necessary to ensure compliance.

(b) Penalties under this subsection (2.5) shall be determined by the executive director or the executive director's designee and may be collected by the division of administration by an action instituted in a court of competent jurisdiction for collection of such penalty. The final decision of the executive director or the executive director's designee may be appealed to the water quality control commission, created pursuant to section 25-8-201. A stay of any order of the division ending judicial review shall not relieve any person from any liability with respect to past or continuing violations of any minimum general sanitary standard or any regulation promulgated pursuant to section 25-1.5-202 or 25-1-114 (1) (h) , but the reason for the request for judicial review shall be considered in the determination of the amount of the penalty. In the event that such an action is instituted for the collection of such penalty, the court may consider the appropriateness of the amount of the penalty, if such issue is raised by the party against whom the penalty was assessed. Any administrative penalty collected under this section shall be credited to the general fund.

(3) The department may request the attorney general to bring a suit for a temporary restraining order or a preliminary or permanent injunction to prevent or abate any violation of a minimum general sanitary standard or regulation adopted pursuant to section 25-1.5-202 or to prevent or abate any release or imminent release that causes or is likely to cause contamination resulting in liability under section 25-1.5-207, and the department, in such a suit, may collect, on behalf of political subdivisions or public water systems, the damages incurred by such political subdivisions or public water systems under section 25-1.5-207. The department shall pay to such political subdivisions or public water systems all damages collected on their behalf. The department is not required to issue an enforcement order prior to institution of such a suit. Upon a de novo finding by the court that such a violation has occurred, is occurring, or is about to occur or that such release or imminent release exists, the court may enjoin such violation, release, or imminent release and enter such order as the public health may require, taking into consideration, where appropriate, the cost and time necessary to comply. An enforcement settlement with the state under the provisions of this subsection (3) shall bar a separate action by a political subdivision or public water system under section 25-1.5-207 whenever notice and adequate opportunity to comment on the proposed settlement have been given to the political subdivision or public water system, damages have been collected on behalf of and paid to such political subdivision or public water system by the state, and the release or imminent release has been prevented or abated by means of the settlement.

(4) Suits brought pursuant to subsection (3) of this section shall be brought in the district court of the county in which the violation is alleged to have occurred. The institution of such a suit by the division of administration shall confer upon such court exclusive jurisdiction to determine finally the subject matter of the proceeding; except that the exclusive jurisdiction of the court shall apply only to such proceeding and shall not preclude assessment of any civil penalties or any other enforcement action or sanction authorized by this section.

(4.5) An action for civil penalties under this section may be joined with a civil action to recover the state's costs pursuant to subsection (3) of this section.

(5) The powers of the department established by this section shall be in addition to, and not in derogation of, any powers of the department.

(6) (a) The attorney general, at the request of the department, or the district attorney of the county in which an affected public water system is located or the attorney of the supplier of water may institute a civil action against any person, association, or corporation, or the officers thereof, who tampers, attempts to tamper, or threatens to tamper with a public water system or with drinking water after its withdrawal for or treatment by a public water system. Such action shall be brought in the district court of the county in which the violation is alleged to have occurred. As used in this subsection (6) , "tamper" means to introduce a contaminant into a public water system or into drinking water or to otherwise interfere with drinking water or the operation of a public water system with the intention of harming persons or public water systems. "Tamper" does not include the standardized and accepted treatment procedures performed by a supplier of water in preparing water for human consumption.
(b) Upon finding that tampering, attempting to tamper, or threatening to tamper has occurred, the court shall have the authority to:
(I) Order appropriate injunctive relief;
(II) Impose a civil penalty on the violator of not more than fifty thousand dollars for each act of tampering or of not more than twenty thousand dollars for each act of attempting to tamper or threatening to tamper;
(III) Impose on the violator all costs incurred by the state and by the affected public water system in assessing and remedying all consequences of the tampering, attempting to tamper, or threatening to tamper; and
(IV) Impose on the violator all court costs associated with remedying consequences of the tampering, attempting to tamper, or threatening to tamper.
(7) Any person subject to an action brought pursuant to subsection (3) of this section or section 25-1.5-207 shall have an affirmative defense to such action if such person's potential liability results from a discharge of contaminants or substances authorized by and in substantial compliance with an existing federal or state permit which controls the quality of the release of the contaminant or substance.

## 25-1-114.5. Voluntary disclosure arising from self-evaluation - presumption against imposition of administrative or civil penalties.
(1) For the purposes of this section, a disclosure of information by a person or entity to any division or agency within the department of public health and environment regarding any information related to an environmental law is voluntary if all of the following are true:
(a) The disclosure is made promptly after knowledge of the information disclosed is obtained by the person or entity;
(b) The disclosure arises out of a voluntary self-evaluation;
(c) The person or entity making the disclosure initiates the appropriate effort to achieve compliance, pursues compliance with due diligence, and corrects the noncompliance within two years after the completion of the voluntary self-evaluation. Where such evidence shows the noncompliance is the failure to obtain a permit, appropriate efforts to correct the noncompliance may be demonstrated by the submittal of a complete permit application within a reasonable time.
(d) The person or entity making the disclosure cooperates with the appropriate division or agency in the department of public health and environment regarding investigation of the issues identified in the disclosure.
(2) For the purposes of paragraph (c) of subsection (1) of this section, upon application to and at the discretion of the department of public health and environment, the time period within which the noncompliance is required to be corrected may be extended if it is not practicable to correct the noncompliance within the two-year period. A request for a de novo review of the decision of the department of public health and environment may be made to the appropriate district court or administrative law judge.
(3) If a person or entity is required to make a disclosure to a division or agency within the department of public health and environment under a specific permit condition or under an order

issued by the division or agency, then the disclosure is not voluntary with respect to that division or agency.

(4) If any person or entity makes a voluntary disclosure of an environmental violation to a division or agency within the department of public health and environment, then there is a rebuttable presumption that the disclosure is voluntary and therefore the person or entity is immune from any administrative and civil penalties associated with the issues disclosed and is immune from any criminal penalties for negligent acts associated with the issues disclosed. The person or entity shall provide information supporting its claim that the disclosure is voluntary at the time that the disclosure is made to the division or agency.

(5) To rebut the presumption that a disclosure is voluntary, the appropriate division or agency shall show to the satisfaction of the respective commission in the department of public health and environment or the state board of health, if no respective commission exists, that the disclosure was not voluntary based upon the factors set forth in subsections (1), (2), and (3) of this section. A decision by the commission or the state board of health, whichever is appropriate, regarding the voluntary nature of a disclosure is final agency action. The division or agency may not include any administrative or civil penalty or fine or any criminal penalty or fine for negligent acts in a notice of violation or in a cease-and-desist order on any underlying environmental violation that is alleged absent a finding by the respective commission or the state board of health that the division or agency has rebutted the presumption of voluntariness of the disclosure. The burden to rebut the presumption of voluntariness is on the division or agency.

(6) The elimination of administrative, civil, or criminal penalties under this section does not apply if a person or entity has been found by a court or administrative law judge to have committed serious violations that constitute a pattern of continuous or repeated violations of environmental laws, rules, regulations, permit conditions, settlement agreements, or orders on consent and that were due to separate and distinct events giving rise to the violations, within the three-year period prior to the date of the disclosure. Such a pattern of continuous or repeated violations may also be demonstrated by multiple settlement agreements related to substantially the same alleged violations concerning serious instances of noncompliance with environmental laws that occurred within the three-year period immediately prior to the date of the voluntary disclosure.

(7) Except as specifically provided in this section, this section does not affect any authority the department of public health and environment has to require any action associated with the information disclosed in any voluntary disclosure of an environmental violation.

(8) Unless the context otherwise requires, the definitions contained in section 13-25-126.5 (2), C.R.S., apply to this section.

(9) This section applies to voluntary disclosures that are made and voluntary self-evaluations that are performed on or after June 1, 1994.

## 25-1-114.6. Implementation of environmental self-audit law - pilot project - legislative declaration.

(1) (a) The general assembly hereby finds and determines that, in order to encourage the regulated community to utilize the environmental self-audit provisions contained in this section and sections 25-1-114.5, 13-25-126.5, and 13-90-107 (1) (j), C.R.S., a pilot project is established. The general assembly hereby declares that the purpose of the environmental self-audit provisions contained in this section and sections 25-1-114.5, 13-25-126.5, and 13-90-107 (1) (j), C.R.S., is to encourage the regulated community to voluntarily identify environmental concerns and to address them expeditiously without fear of enforcement action by regulatory agencies. The general assembly recognizes that, due to concerns with the environmental self-audit provisions, the United States environmental protection agency has, in the past, taken direct action against entities in the regulated community that have made disclosures under the environmental self-audit provisions. The general assembly further declares that the pilot project enacted by this section is intended to allow entities to proceed under the environmental self-audit provisions with assurance that, if any such entity complies with such environmental self-audit provisions, the United States

environmental protection agency will forego any enforcement action based on the disclosures made and addressed under the environmental self-audit pilot project.

(b) The general assembly further recognizes that, under the pilot project enacted by this section, the department of public health and environment will have discretion to consider certain factors in assessing a regulated entity's eligibility for penalty immunity under the environmental laws. The general assembly intends that this additional flexibility to assess an entity's eligibility, along with the protection from federal overfiling that the pilot project provides, will encourage entities to participate in the project and allow the department of public health and environment to assess the effectiveness of the environmental self-audit provisions.

(c) The provisions of this section shall only apply to disclosures made under this section and sections 25-1-114.5, 13-25-126.5, and 13-90-107 (1) (j) , C.R.S., after the department of public health and environment and the United States environmental protection agency have entered into a memorandum of agreement binding Colorado and the federal government to enforce environmental laws in a manner consistent with the provisions of this section.

(2) Notwithstanding the provisions of sections 25-1-114.5 (4) and (5) , 13-25-126.5, and 13-90-107 (1) (j) , C.R.S., on and after May 30, 2000, the department of public health and environment may assess penalties for criminal negligence when available under federal environmental law.

(3) (a) In addition to the provisions of subsection (2) of this section, notwithstanding the provisions of sections 25-1-114.5 (4) and (5) , 13-25-126.5, and 13-90-107 (1) (j) , C.R.S., on and after May 30, 2000, in determining whether an entity is entitled to penalty immunity under the provisions of section 25-1-114.5, the department of public health and environment may consider:

(I) Whether the activities disclosed may create imminent and substantial endangerment of, or result in serious harm to, public health and the environment; and

(II) Whether the activities disclosed conferred an unfair or excessive economic benefit on the disclosing entity.

(b) Notwithstanding any provision of sections 25-1-114.5 (4) and (5) , 13-25-126.5, and 13-90-107 (1) (j) , C.R.S., the department of public health and environment has discretion to determine whether and to what degree the factors in paragraph (a) of this subsection (3) apply given the particular circumstances of each situation.

(4) The pilot project created by this section applies to voluntary disclosures made under this section and sections 25-1-114.5, 13-25-126.5, and 13-90-107 (1) (j) , C.R.S., on and after the effective dates of both this section (May 30, 2000) and the memorandum of agreement entered into under paragraph (c) of subsection (1) of this section.

(5) Pursuant to the procedures set forth in section 13-25-126.5, C.R.S., the department of public health and environment may obtain access to an environmental self-audit report where the department of public health and environment has independent evidence of any criminal violation of an environmental law. Evidence of a criminal violation constitutes "compelling circumstances" for purposes of section 13-25-126.5 (3) (c) , C.R.S., where the department of public health and environment seeks access to an environmental self-audit report. When a self-audit report is obtained, reviewed, or used in a criminal proceeding under this subsection (5) , the privilege provided in section 13-25-126.5, C.R.S., applicable to civil or administrative proceedings is not waived or eliminated.

(6) Repealed.

## 25-1-115. Treatment - religious belief.

Nothing in this part 1 shall authorize the department to impose any mode of treatment inconsistent with the religious faith or belief of any person.

## 25-1-116. Licensed healing systems not affected.

Nothing in this part 1 shall be construed or used to amend or restrict any statute in force pertaining to the scope of practice of any state licensed healing system.

## 25-1-117. Acquisition of federal surplus property.

The governor of the state of Colorado is authorized, for and on behalf of the state of Colorado, to make application for and secure the transfer to the state of Colorado of federal surplus property for the purpose of establishing state public health facilities in the state of Colorado; and to do and perform any acts and things which may be necessary to carry out the above, including the preparing, making, and filing of plans, applications, reports, and other documents, and the execution, acceptance, delivery, and recordation of agreements, deeds, and other instruments pertaining to the transfer of said property. The governor is further authorized to expend available general revenue funds, or such other funds as may be made available by the general assembly, for the purpose of making the above application and securing the transfer of said property in accordance with federal laws and with rules and regulations and requirements of the United States department of health, education, and welfare.

## 25-1-118. Rental properties - salvage - fund created - repeal. (Repealed)


## 25-1-119. Disposition and expenditures of moneys from fund. (Repealed)


## 25-1-120. Nursing facilities - rights of patients.

(1) The department shall require all skilled nursing facilities and intermediate care facilities to adopt and make public a statement of the rights and responsibilities of the patients who are receiving treatment in such facilities and to treat their patients in accordance with the provisions of said statement. The statement shall ensure each patient the following:

(a) The right to civil and religious liberties, including knowledge of available choices and the right to independent personal decisions, which will not be infringed upon, and the right to encouragement and assistance from the staff of the facility in the fullest possible exercise of these rights;

(b) The right to have private and unrestricted communications with any person of his choice;

(c) The right to present grievances on behalf of himself or others to the facility's staff or administrator, to governmental officials, or to any other person, without fear of reprisal, and to join with other patients or individuals within or outside of the facility to work for improvements in patient care;

(d) The right to manage his own financial affairs or to have a quarterly accounting of any financial transactions made in his behalf, should he delegate such responsibility to the facility for any period of time;

(e) The right to be fully informed, in writing, prior to or at the time of admission and during his stay, of services available in the facility and of related charges, including charges for services not covered under medicare or medicaid or not covered by the basic per diem rate;

(f) The right to be adequately informed of his medical condition and proposed treatment, unless otherwise indicated by his physician, and to participate in the planning of all medical treatment, including the right to refuse medication and treatment, unless otherwise indicated by his physician, and to know the consequences of such actions;

(g) The right to receive adequate and appropriate health care consistent with established and recognized practice standards within the community and with skilled and intermediate nursing care facility rules and regulations as promulgated by the department;

(h) The right to have privacy in treatment and in caring for personal needs, confidentiality in the treatment of personal and medical records, and security in storing and using personal possessions;

(i) The right to be treated courteously, fairly, and with the fullest measure of dignity and to receive a written statement of the services provided by the facility, including those required to be offered on an as-needed basis;

(j) The right to be free from mental and physical abuse and from physical and chemical restraints, except those restraints initiated through the judgment of the professional staff for a specified and limited period of time or on the written authorization of a physician;

(k) The right to be transferred or discharged only for medical reasons or his welfare, or that of other patients, or for nonpayment for his stay and the right to be given reasonable advance notice of any transfer or discharge, except in the case of an emergency as determined by the professional staff;

(l) The right to devolution of his or her rights and responsibilities upon a sponsor, guardian, or person exercising rights contained in a designated beneficiary agreement executed pursuant to article 22 of title 15, C.R.S., who shall see that he or she is provided with adequate, appropriate, and respectful medical treatment and care and all rights which he or she is capable of exercising should he or she be determined to be incompetent pursuant to law and not be restored to legal capacity;

(m) The right to freedom of choice in selecting a health care facility;

(n) The right to copies of the facility's rules and regulations and an explanation of his responsibility to obey all reasonable rules and regulations of the facility and to respect the personal rights and private property of the other patients.

(1.5) If a facility requires a lease agreement with a provision requiring in excess of a month-to-month tenancy and the lease agreement results in or requires forfeiture of more than thirty days of rent if a patient moves due to a medical condition or dies during the term of the lease agreement, then the lease agreement shall be deemed to be against public policy and shall be void; except that inclusion of such a provision shall not render the remainder of the contract or lease agreement void. A contract provision or lease agreement that requires forfeiture of rent for thirty days after the patient moves due to a medical condition or dies does not violate this section. The provisions regarding forfeiture of rent shall appear on the front page of the contract or lease agreement and shall be printed in no less than twelve-point bold-faced type. The provisions shall read as follows:

This lease agreement is for a month-to-month tenancy. The lessor shall not require the forfeiture of rent beyond a thirty-day period if the lessee moves due to a medical condition or dies during the term of the lease.

In circumstances in which the patient moves due to a medical condition or dies during the term of a contract or lease agreement, the facility shall return that part of the rent paid in excess of thirty days' rent after a patient moves or dies to the patient or the patient's estate. The facility may assess daily rental charges for any days in which the former or deceased patient's personal possessions remain in the patient's room after the period for which the patient has paid rent and for the usual time to clean the room after the patient's personal possessions have been removed. The facility shall have forty-five days after the date the patient's personal possessions have been removed from the patient's room to reconcile the patient's accounts and to return any moneys owed. This subsection (1.5) applies to any facility, or a distinct part of a facility, that meets the state nursing home licensing standards set forth in section 25-1.5-103 (1) (a) (I) and the licensing requirements specified in section 25-3-101. For purposes of this section, "daily rental charges" means an amount not to exceed one-thirtieth of thirty days' rental amount plus reasonable expenses.

(2) Each skilled nursing facility or intermediate care facility shall provide a copy of the statement required by subsection (1) of this section to each patient or his guardian at or before the patient's admission to a facility and to each staff member of a facility. Each such facility shall prepare a written plan and provide appropriate staff training to implement the provisions of this section.

(3) Each skilled nursing facility or intermediate care facility shall prepare a written plan and provide appropriate facilities to ensure that the rights guaranteed by subsection (1) of this section are enforced by a grievance procedure which contains the following procedures and rights:

(a) A resident of any facility, the residents' advisory council, or the sibling, child, spouse, parent, or person exercising rights contained in a designated beneficiary agreement executed pursuant to article 22 of title 15, C.R.S., of any resident may formally complain in the manner described in this subsection (3) about any conditions, treatment, or violations of his or her rights by the facility or its staff or about any treatment, conditions, or violations of the rights of any other resident, regardless of the consent of the victim of the alleged improper treatment, condition, or violation of rights by the facility or its staff.

(b) Each facility shall designate one full-time staff member, referred to in this subsection (3) as the "designee", to receive all grievances when they are first made.

(c) Each facility shall establish a grievance committee consisting of the chief administrator of the facility or his designee, a resident selected by the resident population of the facility, and a third person to be agreed upon by the administrator and the resident representative.

(d) If anyone designated in paragraph (a) of this subsection (3) wishes to complain about treatment, conditions, or violations of rights, he shall write or cause to be written his grievance or shall state it orally to the designee no later than fourteen days after the occurrence giving rise to the grievance. The designee shall confer with persons involved in the occurrence and with any other witnesses and, no later than three days after the grievance, give a written explanation of findings and proposed remedies, if any, to the complainant and to the aggrieved party, if someone other than the complainant. Where appropriate because of the mental or physical condition of the complainant or the aggrieved party, the written explanation shall be accompanied by an oral explanation.

(e) If the complainant or aggrieved party is dissatisfied with the findings and remedies or the implementation thereof, he may then make the same grievance orally or in writing, with any additional comments or information, to the grievance committee no later than ten days after the receipt of the explanation from the designee. Said committee shall confer with persons involved in the occurrence and with any other witnesses and, no later than ten days after the appeal from the designee, give a written explanation of its findings and proposed remedies, if any, to the complainant and to the aggrieved party, if someone other than the complainant. Where appropriate because of the mental or physical condition of the complainant or the aggrieved party, the written explanation shall be accompanied by an oral explanation.

(4) Each skilled nursing facility or intermediate care facility shall also establish a residents' advisory council which shall consist of not less than five members selected by and from the resident population of the facility. The council shall meet at least once a month with the administrator of the facility and a representative of the staff to make recommendations concerning policies of the facility. The council may also present grievances to the grievance committee on behalf of a resident.

(5) If a complainant or aggrieved party is dissatisfied with the findings and remedies of the grievance committee or implementation thereof, except for grievances against a physician or his prescribed treatment, he may file the same grievance in writing with the executive director of the department. The department shall investigate the facts and circumstances of the grievance and make findings of fact, conclusions, and recommendations, copies of which shall be transmitted to the complainant and the nursing home administrator. If the complainant or the nursing home administrator is aggrieved by the findings and the recommendations of the department, the aggrieved party may request a hearing to be conducted by the department pursuant to section 24-4-105, C.R.S. The board shall adopt rules and regulations to carry out the intent of this section.

(6) Implementation of this section shall be pursuant to section 25.5-6-204, C.R.S.

(7) Nothing in this section shall apply to any nursing institution conducted by or for the adherents of any well-recognized church or religious denomination for the purpose of providing facilities for the care and treatment of the sick who depend exclusively upon spiritual means through prayer for healing in the practice of the religion of such church or denomination.

(8) (a) A patient who is eligible to receive medicaid benefits pursuant to articles 4, 5, and 6 of title 25.5, C.R.S., and who qualifies for nursing facility care shall have the right to select any nursing care facility recommended for certification by the department of public health and environment under Title XIX of the federal "Social Security Act", as amended, as a provider of medicaid services and licensed by the department pursuant to article 3 of this title where space is available, and the department of health care policy and financing shall reimburse the selected facility for services pursuant to section 25.5-6-204, C.R.S., unless such nursing care facility shall have been

notified by the department of health care policy and financing that it may not qualify as a provider of medicaid services.

(b) A patient who is residing in such nursing care facility shall be assured the resident rights which are provided by section 4211 of Title IV of the federal "Omnibus Budget Reconciliation Act of 1987", as amended, Pub.L. 100-203. Failure to protect and promote those rights shall subject the violating facility to sanctions imposed by the department.

(9) A patient who is eligible to receive benefits from a skilled or intermediate nursing care facility certified by the department under Title XVIII of the federal "Social Security Act", as amended, as a provider of medicare services shall be assured the same rights as provided in paragraph (a) of subsection (8) of this section.

## 25-1-121. Patient grievance mechanism - institution's obligations to patient.

(1) As used in this section, "institution" means every hospital or related facility or institution having in excess of fifty beds and required to be licensed under part 1 of article 3 of this title or required to be certified pursuant to section 25-1.5-103 (1) (a) (II) , except skilled nursing facilities and intermediate care facilities which are subject to the provisions of section 25-1-120.

(2) The department shall require every institution to submit to the department a plan for a patient grievance mechanism and a policy statement with respect to the obligations of the institution to patients using the facilities of such institution. The plan and policy statement must meet with the approval of the department prior to certification of compliance or issuance or renewal of a license.

(3) A patient grievance mechanism plan shall include, but not be limited to:

(a) A provision for a patient representative to serve as a liaison between the patient and the institution;

(b) A description of the qualifications of the patient representative;

(c) An outline of the job description of the patient representative;

(d) A description of the amount of decision-making authority given to the patient representative;

(e) A method by which each patient will be made aware of the patient representative program and how the representative of the program may be contacted.

(4) The policy statement with respect to the obligations of the institution to patients using facilities of such an institution shall be posted conspicuously in a public place on its premises and made available to each patient upon admission. Such policy statement shall include, but need not be limited to, a clarification of a physician's duty to provide informed consent, admission procedures, staff identification, privacy, medical records, billing procedures, and the obligation of the physician to provide information regarding research, experimental, or educational projects relating to the patient's own case. Nothing in this section shall apply to any nursing institution conducted by or for the adherents of any well-recognized church or religious denomination for the purpose of providing facilities for the care and treatment of the sick who depend exclusively upon spiritual means through prayer for healing in the practice of the religion of such church or denomination.

## 25-1-122. Named reporting of certain diseases and conditions - access to medical records - confidentiality of reports and records.

(1) With respect to investigations of epidemic and communicable diseases, morbidity and mortality, cancer in connection with the statewide cancer registry, environmental and chronic diseases, sexually transmitted infections, tuberculosis, and rabies and mammal bites, the board has the authority to require reporting, without patient consent, of occurrences of those diseases and conditions by any person having knowledge of such to the state department of public health and environment and county, district, and municipal public health agencies, within their respective jurisdictions. Any required reports must contain the name, address, age, sex, and diagnosis and other relevant information as the board determines is necessary to protect the public health. The board shall set the manner, time period, and form in which the reports are to be made. The board may limit reporting for a specific disease or condition to a particular region or community or for a limited period of time.

(2) When investigating diseases and conditions pursuant to subsection (1) of this section, authorized personnel of the state department of public health and environment and county, district, and municipal public health agencies, within their respective jurisdictions, may, without patient consent, inspect, have access to, and obtain information from pertinent patient medical, coroner, and laboratory records in the custody of all medical practitioners, veterinarians, coroners, institutions, hospitals, agencies, laboratories, and clinics, whether public or private, which are relevant and necessary to the investigation. Review and inspection of records shall be conducted at reasonable times and with such notice as is reasonable under the circumstances. Under no circumstances may personnel of the state department of public health and environment or county, district, or municipal public health agencies, within their local jurisdictions, have access pursuant to this section to any medical record that is not pertinent, relevant, or necessary to the public health investigation.

(3) Any report or disclosure made in good faith pursuant to subsection (1) or (2) of this section shall not constitute libel or slander or a violation of any right of privacy or privileged communication.

(4) Reports and records resulting from the investigation of epidemic and communicable diseases, environmental and chronic diseases, reports of morbidity and mortality, reports of cancer in connection with the statewide cancer registry, and reports and records resulting from the investigation of sexually transmitted infections, tuberculosis, and rabies and mammal bites held by the state department of public health and environment or county, district, or municipal public health agencies shall be strictly confidential. Such reports and records shall not be released, shared with any agency or institution, or made public, upon subpoena, search warrant, discovery proceedings, or otherwise, except under any of the following circumstances:

(a) Release may be made of medical and epidemiological information in a manner such that no individual person can be identified.

(b) Release may be made of medical and epidemiological information to the extent necessary for the treatment, control, investigation, and prevention of diseases and conditions dangerous to the public health; except that every effort shall be made to limit disclosure of personal identifying information to the minimal amount necessary to accomplish the public health purpose.

(c) Release may be made to the person who is the subject of a medical record or report with written authorization from such person.

(d) An officer or employee of the county, district, or municipal public health agency or the state department of public health and environment may make a report of child abuse to agencies responsible for receiving or investigating reports of child abuse or neglect in accordance with the applicable provisions of the "Child Protection Act of 1987" set forth in part 3 of article 3 of title 19, C.R.S. However, in the event a report is made by the state department of public health and environment, only the following information shall be included in the report:

(I) The name, address, and sex of the child;

(II) The name and address of the person responsible for the child;

(III) The name and address of the person who is alleged to be responsible for the suspected abuse or neglect, if known; and

(IV) The general nature of the child's injury.

(e) Medical and epidemiological information may be released to a peace officer as described in section 16-2.5-101, C.R.S., the federal bureau of investigation, a federal law enforcement agency as designated by the United States attorney for the district of Colorado, or any prosecutor to the extent necessary for any investigation or prosecution related to bioterrorism; except that reasonable efforts shall be made to limit disclosure of personal identifying information to the minimal amount necessary to accomplish the law enforcement purpose. For purposes of this paragraph (e) , "bioterrorism" means the intentional use of, attempted use of, conspiracy to use, or solicitation to use microorganisms or toxins of biological origin or chemical or radiological agents to cause death or disease among humans or animals.

(5) No officer or employee or agent of the state department of public health and environment or county, district, or municipal public health agency shall be examined in any judicial, executive,

legislative, or other proceeding as to the existence or content of any individual's report obtained by such department pursuant to subsection (1) or (2) of this section without that individual's consent. However, this provision shall not apply to individuals who are under isolation or quarantine, school exclusion, or other restrictive action taken pursuant to section 25-1.5-102 (1) (c) or part 4, 5, 6, or 9 of article 4 of this title.

(6) Any officer or employee or agent of the state department of public health and environment or a county, district, or municipal public health agency who violates this section by releasing or making public confidential public health reports or records or by otherwise breaching the confidentiality requirements of subsection (4) or (5) of this section commits a class 1 misdemeanor and, upon conviction thereof, shall be punished as provided in section 18-1.3-501 (1) , C.R.S.

(7) Nothing in subsections (4) to (6) of this section applies to records and reports held by the state or local department of health pursuant to part 4 of article 4 of this title.

(8) Pursuant to section 25-1-113, any person may seek judicial review of a decision of the board or of the department affecting such person under this section.

(9) Notwithstanding any other provision of law to the contrary, the department shall administer the provisions of this section regardless of an individual's race, religion, gender, ethnicity, national origin, or immigration status.

## 25-1-122.5. Confidentiality of genetic testing records - "Uniform Parentage Act".

Notwithstanding any other law concerning public records, any records or information concerning the genetic testing of a person for purposes of the determination of parentage pursuant to article 4 of title 19, C.R.S., shall be confidential and shall not be disclosed except as otherwise provided in section 19-1-308, C.R.S.

## 25-1-123. Restructure of health and human services - development of plan - participation of department required.

The department, in cooperation with the department of health care policy and financing and the department of human services, shall develop a plan for the restructuring of the health and human services delivery system in the state in accordance with article 1.7 of title 24, C.R.S.

## 25-1-124. Health care facilities - consumer information - reporting - release.

(1) The general assembly hereby finds that an increasing number of people are faced with the difficult task of choosing a health care facility for themselves and their family members. This task may be made less difficult by improved access to reliable, helpful, and unbiased information concerning the quality of care and the safety of the environment offered by each health care facility. The general assembly further finds that it is appropriate that the department, in keeping with its role of protecting and improving the public health, solicit this information from health care facilities and disseminate it to the public in a form that will assist people in making informed choices among health care facilities.

(2) Each health care facility licensed pursuant to section 25-3-101 or certified pursuant to section 25-1.5-103 (1) (a) (II) shall report to the department all of the following occurrences:

(a) Any occurrence that results in the death of a patient or resident of the facility and is required to be reported to the coroner pursuant to section 30-10-606, C.R.S., as arising from an unexplained cause or under suspicious circumstances;

(b) Any occurrence that results in any of the following serious injuries to a patient or resident:

(I) Brain or spinal cord injuries;

(II) Life-threatening complications of anesthesia or life-threatening transfusion errors or reactions;

(III) Second- or third-degree burns involving twenty percent or more of the body surface area of an adult patient or resident or fifteen percent or more of the body surface area of a child patient or resident;

(c) Any time that a resident or patient of the facility cannot be located following a search of the facility, the facility grounds, and the area surrounding the facility and there are circumstances that place the resident's health, safety, or welfare at risk or, regardless of whether such circumstances exist, the patient or resident has been missing for eight hours;

(d) Any occurrence involving physical, sexual, or verbal abuse of a patient or resident, as described in section 18-3-202, 18-3-203, 18-3-204, 18-3-206, 18-3-402, 18-3-403, as it existed prior to July 1, 2000, 18-3-404, or 18-3-405, C.R.S., by another patient or resident, an employee of the facility, or a visitor to the facility;

(e) Any occurrence involving caretaker neglect of a patient or resident, as described in section 26-3.1-101 (2.3) , C.R.S.;

(f) Any occurrence involving misappropriation of a patient's or resident's property. For purposes of this paragraph (f) , "misappropriation of a patient's or resident's property" means a pattern of or deliberately misplacing, exploiting, or wrongfully using, either temporarily or permanently, a patient's or resident's belongings or money without the patient's or resident's consent.

(g) Any occurrence in which drugs intended for use by patients or residents are diverted to use by other persons. If the diverted drugs are injectable, the health care facility shall also report the full name and date of birth of any individual who diverted the injectable drugs, if known.

(h) Any occurrence involving the malfunction or intentional or accidental misuse of patient or resident care equipment that occurs during treatment or diagnosis of a patient or resident and that significantly adversely affects or if not averted would have significantly adversely affected a patient or resident of the facility.

(2.5) (a) In addition to the reports required by subsection (2) of this section, if the Colorado attorney general, the division for developmental disabilities in the department of human services, a community centered board, an adult protection service, or a law enforcement agency makes a report of an occurrence as described in subsection (2) of this section involving a licensed long-term care facility, that report shall be provided to the department and shall be made available for inspection consistent with the provisions of subsection (6) of this section. Any reports concerning an adult protection service shall be in compliance with the confidentiality requirements of section 26-3.1-102 (7) , C.R.S.

(b) For purposes of this subsection (2.5) , a "licensed long-term care facility" means a licensed community residential or group home, a licensed intermediate care facility for individuals with intellectual disabilities, and a licensed facility for persons with developmental disabilities.

(3) The board by rule shall specify the manner, time period, and form in which the reports required pursuant to subsection (2) of this section shall be made.

(4) Any report submitted pursuant to subsection (2) of this section shall be strictly confidential; except that information in any such report may be transmitted to an appropriate regulatory agency having jurisdiction for disciplinary or license sanctions. The information in such reports shall not be made public upon subpoena, search warrant, discovery proceedings, or otherwise, except as provided in subsection (6) of this section.

(5) The department shall investigate each report submitted pursuant to subsection (2) of this section that it determines was appropriately submitted. For each report investigated, the department shall prepare a summary of its findings, including the department's conclusions and whether there was a violation of licensing standards or a deficiency or whether the facility acted appropriately in response to the occurrence. If the investigation is not conducted on site, the department shall specify in the summary how the investigation was conducted. Any investigation conducted pursuant to this subsection (5) shall be in addition to and not in lieu of any inspection required to be conducted pursuant to section 25-1.5-103 (1) (a) with regard to licensing.

(6) (a) The department shall make the following information available to the public:

(I) Any investigation summaries prepared pursuant to subsection (5) of this section;

(II) Any complaints against a health care facility that have been filed with the department and that the department has investigated, including the conclusions reached by the department and whether there was a violation of licensing standards or a deficiency or whether the facility acted appropriately in response to the subject of the complaint; and

(III) A listing of any deficiency citations issued against each health care facility.

(b) The information released pursuant to this subsection (6) shall not identify the patient or resident or the health care professional involved in the report.

(7) Prior to the completion of an investigation pursuant to this section, the department may respond to any inquiry regarding a report received pursuant to subsection (2) of this section by confirming that it has received such report and that an investigation is pending.

(8) In addition to the report to the department for an occurrence described in paragraph (d) of subsection (2) of this section, the occurrence shall be reported to a law enforcement agency.

## 25-1-124.5. Nursing care facilities - employees - criminal history check - adult protective services data system check.

(1) On and after September 1, 1996, prior to employing any person, a nursing care facility or the person seeking employment at a nursing care facility shall make an inquiry to the director of the Colorado bureau of investigation or to private criminal background check companies authorized to do business in the state of Colorado to ascertain whether such person has a criminal history, including arrest and conviction records. The Colorado bureau of investigation or private criminal background check companies are authorized to utilize fingerprints to ascertain from the federal bureau of investigation whether such person has a criminal history record. The nursing care facility or the person seeking employment in a nursing care facility shall pay the costs of such inquiry. The criminal history check shall be conducted not more than ninety days prior to the employment of the applicant. For purposes of this section, criminal background check companies shall be approved by the state board of nursing. In approving such companies, approval shall be based upon the provision of lawfully available, accurate, and thorough information pertaining to criminal histories, including arrest and conviction records.

(2) As used in this section, "nursing care facility" includes:

(a) A nursing facility as defined in section 25.5-4-103 (14) , C.R.S.;

(b) An intermediate nursing facility for persons with intellectual and developmental disabilities as defined in section 25.5-4-103 (9) ;

(c) An adult day care facility as defined in section 25.5-6-303 (1) , C.R.S.;

(d) An alternative care facility as defined in section 25.5-6-303 (3) , C.R.S.;

(e) Any business that provides temporary nursing care services or that provides personnel who provide such services.

(3) In addition to the criminal history background check required pursuant to this section, on and after January 1, 2019, prior to employment, a nursing care facility shall submit the name of a person who will be providing direct care, as defined in section 26-3.1-101 (3.5) , to an at-risk adult, as defined in section 26-3.1-101 (1.5) , as well as any other required identifying information, to the department of human services for a check of the Colorado adult protective services data system pursuant to section 26-3.1-111, to determine if the person is substantiated in a case of mistreatment of an at-risk adult.

## 25-1-124.7. Health facilities - employees - adult protective services data system check.

On and after January 1, 2019, prior to employment, a health facility licensed pursuant to section 25-1.5-103 (1) (a) (I) (A) , including health facilities wholly owned and operated by any governmental unit or agency, shall submit the name of a person who will be providing direct care, as defined in section 26-3.1-101 (3.5) , to an at-risk adult, as defined in section 26-3.1-101 (1.5) , as well as any other required identifying information, to the department of human services for a check of the Colorado adult protective services data system pursuant to section 26-3.1-111, to determine if the person is substantiated in a case of mistreatment of an at-risk adult.

## 25-1-125. Applications for licenses - authority to suspend licenses - rules.

(1) Every application by an individual for a license issued by the department or any authorized

agent of the department shall require the applicant's name, address, and social security number.
(2) The department or any authorized agent of the department shall deny, suspend, or revoke any license pursuant to the provisions of section 26-13-126, C.R.S., and any rules promulgated in furtherance thereof, if the department or agent thereof receives a notice to deny, suspend, or revoke from the state child support enforcement agency because the licensee or applicant is out of compliance with a court or administrative order for current child support, child support debt, retroactive child support, child support arrearages, or child support when combined with maintenance or because the licensee or applicant has failed to comply with a properly issued subpoena or warrant relating to a paternity or child support proceeding. Any such denial, suspension, or revocation shall be in accordance with the procedures specified by rule of the department, rules promulgated by the state board of human services, and any memorandum of understanding entered into between the department or an authorized agent thereof and the state child support enforcement agency for the implementation of this section and section 26-13-126, C.R.S.
(3) (a) The department shall enter into a memorandum of understanding with the state child support enforcement agency, which memorandum shall identify the relative responsibilities of the department and the state child support enforcement agency in the department of human services with respect to the implementation of this section and section 26-13-126, C.R.S.
(b) The appropriate rule-making body of the department is authorized to promulgate rules to implement the provisions of this section.
(4) For purposes of this section, "license" means any recognition, authority, or permission that the department or any authorized agent of the department is authorized by law to issue for an individual to practice a profession or occupation or for an individual to participate in any recreational activity. "License" may include, but is not necessarily limited to, any license, certificate, certification, letter of authorization, or registration issued for an individual to practice a profession or occupation or for an individual to participate in any recreational activity.

## 25-1-126. County practitioner rural recruitment grant program - creation - legislative declaration - administration - report - definitions - repeal. (Repealed)

## 25-1-127. Medical equipment for rural communities grant program - creation - legislative declaration - administration - report - repeal. (Repealed)

## 25-1-128. Designation of caregiver - notice - instructions - definitions - rules.

(1) As used in this section:
(a) "Aftercare" means assistance provided by a caregiver to a patient in the patient's residence after the patient's discharge from a hospital, following an inpatient hospital stay, and may include: Assisting with basic activities of daily living; assisting with instrumental activities of daily living; and carrying out medical or nursing tasks such as managing wound care, assisting in administering medications, and operating medical equipment.
(b) "Caregiver" means a person eighteen years of age or older designated by a patient to provide aftercare to a patient living in his or her residence.
(c) "Hospital" means a facility currently licensed or certified by the department as a general hospital pursuant to the department's authority under sections 25-1.5-103 and 25-3-101.
(d) "Residence" means the patient's home. "Residence" does not include a rehabilitation facility, hospital, nursing home, assisted living facility, or licensed group home.
(2) (a) A hospital shall give each patient or the patient's legal guardian the opportunity to designate at least one caregiver no later than twenty-four hours after the patient's admission to the hospital

and prior to the patient's release from the hospital or nonemergency transfer to another facility.

(b) If a patient is unconscious or incapacitated upon his or her admission to the hospital, the hospital shall give the patient or the patient's legal guardian the opportunity to designate a caregiver as soon as practicable after the patient's recovery of consciousness or capacity.

(c) A patient or patient's legal guardian is not obligated to designate a caregiver at any time.

(d) If the patient or the patient's legal guardian declines to designate a caregiver, the hospital shall document this in the patient's medical record.

(3) (a) If the patient or the patient's legal guardian designates a caregiver, the hospital shall request consent from the patient or the patient's legal guardian to release medical information to the caregiver.

(b) The hospital shall record the designation of the caregiver, the relationship of the caregiver to the patient, and the name, telephone number, and address of the caregiver in the patient's medical record.

(c) A patient or the patient's legal guardian may change the caregiver designation at any time. The hospital shall record the change in the patient's medical record within twenty-four hours of the change.

(d) This section does not obligate a person designated as a caregiver to perform aftercare tasks for a patient.

(4) If a patient or the patient's legal guardian designates a caregiver, the hospital shall notify the patient's caregiver of the patient's discharge or transfer to another facility as soon as practicable, which may be after the patient's physician issues a discharge order. If the hospital is unable to contact the caregiver, the lack of contact shall not interfere with, delay, or otherwise affect the medical care provided to the patient or the appropriate discharge of the patient. The hospital shall promptly document the attempt in the patient's medical record.

(5) (a) As soon as possible and prior to the patient's release from the hospital, the hospital shall consult with the patient or the patient's legal guardian and the caregiver and issue a discharge plan that describes the patient's aftercare needs. The discharge plan must include:

(I) The name and contact information of the caregiver, as provided by the caregiver;

(II) A description of the aftercare tasks necessary to maintain the patient's ability to reside in his or her residence; and

(III) Contact information for any health care, community resources, and long-term services and support necessary to successfully carry out a patient's discharge plan.

(b) The hospital shall provide the caregiver with instructions concerning all aftercare tasks described in the discharge plan. The instructions shall include:

(I) A live demonstration of the aftercare tasks performed by a hospital employee or other authorized individual and provided in a culturally competent manner and in accordance with the hospital's requirements to provide language access services;

(II) An opportunity for the caregiver and the patient or the patient's legal guardian to ask questions about the aftercare tasks; and

(III) Answers to the caregiver's, patient's, and patient's legal guardian's questions in a culturally competent manner and in accordance with the hospital's requirements to provide language access services.

(c) The hospital shall document the instructions required in this subsection (5) in the patient's medical record, including the date, time, and contents of the instructions, and whether the caregiver accepted or refused the offer of instruction.

(6) Nothing in this section:

(a) Interferes with the rights of an agent acting under a valid health care directive;

(b) Creates a private right of action against a hospital, a hospital employee, or a person with whom the hospital has a contractual relationship;

(c) Creates additional civil or regulatory liability for a hospital or hospital employee;

(d) Supersedes or replaces existing rights or remedies under any other law; or

(e) Affects a license issued to a hospital pursuant to section 25-3-102.

(7) The board of health may promulgate rules to ensure compliance with this section.

# PART 2. ALCOHOL AND DRUG ABUSE

**25-1-201 to 25-1-217. (Repealed)**

# PART 3. ALCOHOLISM AND INTOXICATION TREATMENT

**25-1-301 to 25-1-316. (Repealed)**

# PART 4. STATE CHEMIST

### 25-1-401. Office of state chemist created.
The professor of food and drug chemistry in the department of chemistry at the university of Colorado shall be the state chemist of Colorado. The office and laboratory of the state chemist shall be in the department of chemistry at the university of Colorado. The office of state chemist shall be a section of the division of administration of the department of public health and environment.

### 25-1-402. Employment of assistants.
The state chemist has the power to employ such assistants as are necessary for the carrying out of this part 4. The appropriations for the office of state chemist shall be determined by each general assembly in the general appropriation bill. The state chemist and his assistant shall also be reimbursed for all legitimate and necessary expenses incurred in the performance of the duties of the office of state chemist.

### 25-1-403. Analyses of food and drugs.
It is the duty of the state chemist to make or cause to be made chemical analyses of all such samples of foods and drugs as may be collected for the purpose of analysis by the department of public health and environment. The state chemist shall make full and complete written reports, without unnecessary delay, of such analyses to the department of public health and environment.

### 25-1-404. Certificate presumptive evidence.
By the authority of this part 4, every certificate of analysis of foods or drugs duly signed by the state chemist shall be presumptive evidence of the facts therein stated.

# PART 5. PUBLIC HEALTH

SUBPART 1

## 25-1-501. Legislative declaration.

(1) The general assembly hereby finds and declares that:

(a) The public health system reduces health care costs by preventing disease and injury, promoting healthy behavior, and reducing the incidents of chronic diseases and conditions. Thus, the public health system is a critical part of any health care reform.

(b) Each community in Colorado should provide high-quality public health services regardless of its location. Thus, the state of Colorado and each local public health agency should have a comprehensive public health plan outlining how quality public health services will be provided.

(c) Each county should establish or be part of a local public health agency organized under a local board of health with a public health director and other staff necessary to provide public health services;

(d) A strong public health infrastructure is needed to provide essential public health services and is a shared responsibility among state and local public health agencies and their partners within the public health system; and

(e) Developing a strong public health infrastructure requires the coordinated efforts of state and local public health agencies and their public and private sector partners within the public health system to:

(I) Identify and provide leadership for the provision of essential public health services;

(II) Develop and support an information infrastructure that supports essential public health services and functions;

(III) Develop and provide effective education and training for members of the public health workforce;

(IV) Develop performance-management standards for the public health system that are tied to improvements in public health outcomes or other measures; and

(V) Develop a comprehensive plan and set priorities for providing essential public health services.

## 25-1-502. Definitions.

As used in this part 5, unless the context otherwise requires:

(1) "Agency" means a county or district public health agency established pursuant to section 25-1-506.

(2) "Core public health" shall be defined by the state board and shall include, but need not be limited to, the assessment of health status and health risks, development of policies to protect and promote health, and assurance of the provision of the essential public health services.

(3) "Essential public health services" means to:

(a) Monitor health status to identify and solve community health problems;

(b) Investigate and diagnose health problems and health hazards in the community;

(c) Inform, educate, and empower individuals about health issues;

(d) Mobilize public and private sector collaboration and action to identify and solve health problems;

(e) Develop policies, plans, and programs that support individual and community health efforts;

(f) Enforce laws and rules that protect health and promote safety;

(g) Link individuals to needed personal health services and ensure the provision of health care;

(h) Encourage a competent public health workforce;

(i) Evaluate effectiveness, accessibility, and quality of personal and population-based public health services; and

(j) Contribute to research into insightful and innovative solutions to health problems.

(4) "Medical officer" means a volunteer or paid licensed physician who contracts with or is employed by a county or district public health agency to advise the public health director on

medical decisions if the public health director is not a licensed physician.

(5) "Public health" means the prevention of injury, disease, and premature mortality; the promotion of health in the community; and the response to public and environmental health needs and emergencies and is accomplished through the provision of essential public health services.

(6) "Public health agency" means an organization operated by a federal, state, or local government or its designees that acts principally to protect or preserve the public's health. "Public health agency" includes a county public health agency or a district public health agency.

(7) "Public health director" means the administrative and executive head of each county or district public health agency.

(8) "Public health system" means state, county, and district public health agencies and other persons and organizations that provide public health services or promote public health.

(9) "State board" means the state board of health created pursuant to section 25-1-103.

(10) "State department" means the department of public health and environment created pursuant to section 25-1-102.

## 25-1-503. State board - public health duties.

(1) In addition to all other powers and duties conferred and imposed upon the state board, the state board has the following specific powers and duties:

(a) To establish, by rule, the core public health services that each county and district public health agency must provide or arrange for the provision of said services;

(b) To establish, by rule, the minimum quality standards for public health services;

(c) To establish, by rule, the minimum qualifications for county and district public health directors and medical officers;

(d) To ensure the development and implementation of a comprehensive, statewide public health improvement plan;

(e) To review all county and district public health agency public health plans, which review shall be based on criteria established by rule by the state board and against which each county or district public health plan shall be evaluated; and

(f) To establish, by rule, for the fiscal year beginning July 1, 2009, if practicable, and for each fiscal year thereafter, a formula for allocating moneys to county or district public health agencies based on input from the state department and from county or district public health agencies.
SUBPART 2

PUBLIC HEALTH PLANS

## 25-1-504. Comprehensive public health plan - development - approval - reassessment - cash fund.

(1) On or before December 31, 2009, and at a minimum on or before December 31 every five years thereafter, the state department shall develop a comprehensive, statewide public health improvement plan, referred to in this section as the "plan", that assesses and sets priorities for the public health system. The state board may appoint ad hoc or advisory committees as needed for the plan development process. The plan shall be developed in consultation with the state board and representatives from the state department, county or district public health agencies, and their partners within the public health system. The plan shall rely on existing or available data or other information acquired pursuant to this part 5, as well as national guidelines or recommendations concerning public health outcomes or improvements.

(2) (a) The plan shall assess and set priorities for the public health system and shall:

(I) Guide the public health system in targeting core public health services and functions through program development, implementation, and evaluation;

(II) Increase the efficiency and effectiveness of the public health system;

(III) Identify areas needing greater resource allocation to provide essential public health services;

(IV) Incorporate, to the extent possible, goals and priorities of public health plans developed by county or district public health agencies; and

(V) Consider available resources, including but not limited to state and local funding, and be subject to modification based on actual subsequent allocations.

(b) The plan shall include or address at a minimum the following elements:

(I) Core public health services and standards for county and district public health agencies;

(II) Recommendations for legislative or regulatory action, including but not limited to updating public health laws, eliminating obsolete statutory language, and establishing an effective and comprehensive state and local public health infrastructure;

(III) Identification and quantification of existing public health problems, disparities, or threats at the state and county levels;

(IV) Identification of existing public health resources at the state and local levels;

(V) Declaration of the goals of the plan;

(VI) Identification of specific recommendations for meeting these goals;

(VII) Development of public and environmental health infrastructure that supports core public health functions and essential public health services at the state and local levels;

(VIII) Explanation of the prioritization of one or more conditions of public health importance;

(IX) Detailed description of strategies to develop and promote culturally and linguistically appropriate services;

(X) Development, evaluation, and maintenance of, and improvements to, an information infrastructure that supports essential public health services;

(XI) Detailed description of the programs and activities that will be pursued to address existing public and environmental health problems, disparities, or threats;

(XII) Detailed description of how public health services will be integrated and public health resources shared to optimize efficiency and effectiveness of the public health system;

(XIII) Detailed description of how the plan will support county or district public health agencies in achieving the goals of their county or district public health plans;

(XIV) Estimation of costs of implementing the plan;

(XV) A timeline for implementing various elements of the plan;

(XVI) A strategy for coordinating service delivery within the public health system; and

(XVII) Measurable indicators of effectiveness and successes.

(c) The plan, including core public health services and standards, shall prospectively cover up to five years, subject to annual revisions and the implementation schedule established by the state board.

(3) The state department shall make the plan available to the governor, the general assembly, the state board, county and district public health agencies, and other partners.

(4) The state department is authorized to solicit and accept any gifts, grants, or donations to pay for the development of the plan. Any moneys received pursuant to this subsection (4) shall be transmitted to the state treasurer, who shall credit the same to the comprehensive public health plan cash fund, which is hereby created and referred to in this subsection (4) as the "fund". Any interest derived from the deposit and investment of moneys in the fund shall be credited to the fund. Any unexpended and unencumbered moneys remaining in the fund at the end of any fiscal year shall remain in the fund and shall not be credited or transferred to the general fund or another fund. Moneys in the fund may be expended by the state department, subject to annual appropriation by the general assembly, for the development of the plan described in this section.

(5) If the moneys received by the state department through gifts, grants, and donations are insufficient to cover the direct and indirect costs of complying with the provisions of section 25-1-503 and this section, the state department shall not be required to implement the provisions of said sections.

## 25-1-505. County and district public health plans - approval.

(1) As soon as practicable after the approval of each comprehensive, statewide public health

improvement plan pursuant to section 25-1-504, each county or district public health agency shall prepare a county or district public health plan, referred to in this section as the "local plan". Each local plan shall not be inconsistent with the comprehensive, statewide public health improvement plan required under section 25-1-504.

(2) Each local plan shall, at a minimum:

(a) Examine data about health status and risk factors in the local community;

(b) Assess the capacity and performance of the county or district public health system;

(c) Identify goals and strategies for improving the health of the local community;

(d) Describe how representatives of the local community develop and implement the local plan;

(e) Address how county or district public health agencies coordinate with the state department and others within the public health system to accomplish goals and priorities identified in the comprehensive, statewide public health improvement plan; and

(f) Identify financial resources available to meet identified public health needs and to meet requirements for the provision of core public health services.

(3) Subject to available appropriations, the state department shall encourage and provide technical assistance to county or district public health agencies that request such assistance and otherwise work with county or district public health agencies to generate their local plans.

SUBPART 3

COUNTY OR DISTRICT PUBLIC HEALTH AGENCIES

## 25-1-506. County or district public health agency.

(1) Each county, by resolution of its board of county commissioners, shall establish and maintain a county public health agency or shall participate in a district public health agency. Any two or more contiguous counties, by resolutions of the boards of county commissioners of the respective counties, may establish and maintain a district public health agency. An agency shall consist of a county or district board of health, a public health director, and all other personnel employed or retained under the provisions of this subpart 3.

(2) (a) (I) The jurisdiction of any agency shall extend over all unincorporated areas and over all municipal corporations within the territorial limits of the county or the counties comprising the district, but not over the territory of any municipal corporation that maintains its own public health agency. If the county has a county public health agency or a district board of health and if the county is within a district public health agency, any municipal corporation not otherwise within the jurisdiction of an agency, by agreement of its city council, board of trustees or other governing body, and the board of county commissioners of the county wherein the municipal corporation is situated may merge its department with the county or district public health agency.

(II) In the event of a merger between a health department of a municipal corporation with a county or district public health agency, the agreement of merger, among other things, shall provide that a member or members of the county or district board of health, as is specified in the agreement, shall be appointed by the city council or board of trustees of the municipal corporation rather than as provided in this section. The city council or board of trustees shall appoint the number of members specified in the agreement of merger, and the remaining members shall be appointed as provided in this section.

(III) The board of county commissioners, in order to give the municipal corporation representation on a county board of health previously established, may declare vacancies in the county board of health and permit the vacancies to be filled by the city council or board of trustees of the municipal corporation.

(b) All county or district boards of health existing within the county or district shall be dissolved upon the organization of a county or district public health agency under the provisions of this part 5 or upon the acceptance of a county into a district already established.

(c) In the event of the dissolution of any county or district public health agency, the withdrawal of a county from an established district, or the withdrawal of a municipal corporation that has voluntarily merged its health department or agency with a county or district public health agency, local boards of health shall be reestablished under the provisions of this part 5 and assume the powers and duties conferred upon such local boards.

(3) (a) Subject to available appropriations, an agency shall provide or arrange for the provisions of services necessary to carry out the public health laws and rules of the state board, the water quality control commission, the air quality control commission, and the solid and hazardous waste commission according to the specific needs and resources available within the community as determined by the county or district board of health or the board of county commissioners and as set out in both the comprehensive, statewide public health improvement plan developed pursuant to section 25-1-504 and the county or district public health plan developed pursuant to section 25-1-505.

(b) In addition to other powers and duties, an agency shall have the following duties:

(I) To complete a community health assessment and to create the county or district public health plan at least every five years under the direction of the county or district board and to submit the plan to the county or district board and state board for review;

(II) To advise the county or district board on public policy issues necessary to protect public health and the environment;

(III) To provide or arrange for the provision of quality, core public health services deemed essential by the state board and the comprehensive, statewide public health improvement plan; except that the agency shall be deemed to have met this requirement if the agency can demonstrate to the county or district board that other providers offer core public health services that are sufficient to meet the local needs as determined by the plan;

(IV) To the extent authorized by the provisions of this title or article 20 of title 30, C.R.S., to administer and enforce the laws pertaining to:

(A) Public health, air pollution, solid and hazardous waste, and water quality;

(B) Vital statistics; and

(C) The orders, rules, and standards of the state board and any other type 1 agency created pursuant to the provisions of this title;

(V) To investigate and control the causes of epidemic or communicable diseases and conditions affecting public health;

(VI) To establish, maintain, and enforce isolation and quarantine, and in pursuance thereof, and for this purpose only, to exercise physical control over property and over the persons of the people within the jurisdiction of the agency as the agency may find necessary for the protection of the public health;

(VII) To close schools and public places and to prohibit gatherings of people when necessary to protect public health;

(VIII) To investigate and abate nuisances when necessary in order to eliminate sources of epidemic or communicable diseases and conditions affecting public health;

(IX) To establish, maintain, or make available chemical, bacteriological, and biological laboratories, and to conduct such laboratory investigations and examinations as it may deem necessary or proper for the protection of the public health;

(X) To purchase and distribute to licensed physicians and veterinarians, with or without charge, as the county or district board may determine upon considerations of emergency or need, approved biological or therapeutic products necessary for the protection of public health;

(XI) To initiate and carry out health programs consistent with state law that are necessary or desirable by the county or district board to protect public health and the environment;

(XII) To collect, compile, and tabulate reports of marriages, dissolutions of marriage, and declarations of invalidity of marriage, births, deaths, and morbidity, and to require any person having information with regard to the same to make such reports and submit such information as is required by law or the rules of the state board;

(XIII) To make necessary sanitation and health investigations and inspections, on its own initiative or in cooperation with the state department, for matters affecting public health that are within the jurisdiction and control of the agency;

(XIV) To collaborate with the state department and the state board in all matters pertaining to public health, the water quality control commission in all matters pertaining to water quality, the air quality control commission and the division of administration of the state department in all matters pertaining to air pollution, and the solid and hazardous waste commission in all matters pertaining to solid and hazardous waste; and

(XV) To establish or arrange for the establishment of, by January 1, 2015, and subject to available appropriations, a local or regional child fatality prevention review team pursuant to section 25-20.5-404.

(c) If a county or district board of health does not receive sufficient appropriations to fulfill all the duties described in paragraph (b) of this subsection (3) , the county or district board shall set priorities for fulfilling the duties and shall include the list of priorities in its county or district public health plan submitted pursuant to section 25-1-505.

(4) Repealed.

## 25-1-507. Municipal board of health.

Except as otherwise provided by law, the mayor and council of each incorporated town or city, whether incorporated under general statutes or special charter in this state, may establish a municipal public health agency and appoint a municipal board of health. If appointed, the municipal board of health shall have all the powers and responsibilities and perform all the duties of a county or district board of health as provided in this part 5 within the limits of the respective city or town of which they are the officers.

## 25-1-508. County or district boards of public health - public health directors.

(1) Within ninety days after the adoption of a resolution to establish and maintain a county public health agency or to participate in a district public health agency, the respective board of county commissioners shall proceed to organize the agency by the appointment of a county or district board of health, referred to in this part 5 as a "county or district board".

(2) (a) (I) Each county board of health shall consist of at least five members to be appointed by the board of county commissioners for five-year terms; except that the board of county commissioners shall stagger the terms of the initial appointments. Thereafter, full-term appointments shall be for five years.

(II) Notwithstanding the provisions of subparagraph (I) of this paragraph (a) , a county with a population of less than one hundred thousand people may have a county board of health that consists of at least three members to be appointed by the board of county commissioners for five-year terms; except that the board of county commissioners shall stagger the terms of the initial appointments. Thereafter, full-term appointments shall be for five years.

(b) Each member of the county board of health shall be a resident of the county in which the county agency is located. Appointments shall be made to the board so that no business or professional group or governmental entity shall constitute a majority of the board. Any vacancy on the board shall be filled in the same manner as full-term appointments by the appointment of a qualified person for the unexpired term.

(c) In a county with a population of less than one hundred thousand people that, as of July 1, 2008, does not have a board of health that is separate from the board of county commissioners, the board of county commissioners may designate itself as the county board of health as of July 1, 2008. The terms of the members of the county board of health shall coincide with their terms as commissioners. Such county boards shall assume all the duties of appointed county boards.

(d) Notwithstanding the provisions of paragraphs (a) to (c) of this subsection (2) , a county board of health in a home-rule county shall comply with the requirements of its home-rule charter.

(3) (a) Each district board of health shall consist of a minimum of five members. The membership of each district board of health shall include at least one representative from each county in the district. The members of the board shall be appointed by an appointments committee composed of

one member of each of the boards of county commissioners of the counties comprising the district. The appointments committee for each district board shall designate the number of members of its district board and shall establish staggered terms for the initial appointments. Thereafter, full-term appointments shall be for five years.

(b) Each member of the district board shall be a resident of one of the counties comprising the district, and there shall be at least one member from each of the counties comprising the district. Appointments shall be made to the district board so that no business or professional group or governmental entity shall constitute a majority of the district board. The appointments committee shall fill any vacancy on the district board by the appointment of a qualified person for the remainder of the unexpired term.

(c) Upon establishment of a district board, all county boards previously existing within the county or district shall be dissolved. Upon the acceptance of a new county into an established district, the county or district board previously existing for the county being added shall be dissolved and the chair of the previous county or district board or the chair's designee shall represent the new county on the district board until a new member is appointed by the appointments committee.

(4) (a) A county or district board, at its organizational meeting, shall elect from its members a president and other officers as it shall determine. The public health director of the agency, at the discretion of the board, may serve as secretary but shall not be a member of the board. All officers and the public health director shall hold their positions at the pleasure of the board.

(b) (I) Regular meetings of a county or district board shall be held at least once every three months at such times as may be established by resolution of the board. Special meetings of a board may be called by the president, by the public health director, or by a majority of the members of the board at any time on three days' prior notice; except that, in case of emergency, twenty-four hours' notice shall be sufficient.

(II) A county or district board may adopt, and at any time may amend, bylaws in relation to its meetings and the transaction of its business. A majority of the board shall constitute a quorum. Members of the board shall serve without compensation but shall be reimbursed for their actual and necessary travel and subsistence expenses to attend meetings.

(5) In addition to all other powers and duties conferred and imposed upon a county board of health or a district board of health by the provisions of this subpart 3, a county board of health or a district board of health shall have and exercise the following specific powers and duties:

(a) To develop and promote the public policies needed to secure the conditions necessary for a healthy community;

(b) To approve the local public health plan completed by the county or district agency, and to submit the local plan to the state board for review;

(c) (I) To select a public health director to serve at the pleasure of the county or district board. The public health director shall possess such minimum qualifications as may be prescribed by the state board. A public health director may be a physician, physician assistant, public health nurse, or other qualified public health professional. A public health director may practice medicine, nursing, or his or her profession within his or her license and scope of practice, as necessary, to carry out the functions of the office of the public health director. The qualifications shall reflect the resources and needs of the county or counties covered by the agency. If the public health director is not a physician, the county or district board shall employ or contract with at least one medical officer to advise the public health director on medical decisions. The public health director shall maintain an office location designated by the county or district board and shall be the custodian of all property and records of the agency.

(II) A person employed or under contract to act as a medical officer pursuant to this paragraph (c) shall be covered by the "Colorado Governmental Immunity Act", article 10 of title 24, C.R.S., for duties performed for the agency.

(d) (I) In the event of a vacancy in the position of public health director or medical officer, to either employ or contract with a person deemed qualified to fill the position or to request temporary assistance from a public health director or a medical officer from another county. The county or district board may also request that an employee of the state department, such as a qualified executive director or the chief medical officer, serve on an interim basis with all the powers and duties of the position.

(II) A person filling a temporary vacancy as public health director or medical officer shall be covered by the "Colorado Governmental Immunity Act", article 10 of title 24, C.R.S., for duties performed for the agency.

(e) To provide, equip, and maintain suitable offices and all necessary facilities for the proper administration and provision of core public health services, as defined by the state board;

(f) To determine general policies to be followed by the public health director in administering and enforcing public health laws, orders, and rules of the county or district board, and orders, rules, and standards of the state board;

(g) To issue orders and to adopt rules not inconsistent with the public health laws of this state nor with the orders or rules of the state board as the county or district board may deem necessary for the proper exercise of the powers and duties vested in or imposed upon an agency or county or district board by this part 5;

(h) To act in an advisory capacity to the public health director on all matters pertaining to public health;

(i) To hold hearings, administer oaths, subpoena witnesses, and take testimony in all matters relating to the exercise and performance of the powers and duties vested in or imposed upon a county or district board;

(j) To provide environmental health services and to assess fees to offset the actual, direct cost of such services; except that no fee for a service shall be assessed against any person who has already paid a fee to the state or federal government for the service, and except that the only fee that shall be charged for annual retail food establishment inspections shall be the fee set forth in section 25-4-1607;

(k) To accept and, through the public health director, to use, disburse, and administer all federal aid, state aid, or other property, services, or moneys allotted to an agency for county or district public health functions or allotted without designation of a specific agency for purposes that are within the functions of an agency, and to prescribe, by rule consistent with the laws of this state, the conditions under which the property, services, or moneys shall be accepted and administered. The county or district board is empowered to make agreements that may be required to receive such moneys or other assistance.

(l) To approve, as provided for in section 25-1-520, a clean syringe exchange program proposed by an agency. A county board of health or district board of health shall not be required to approve a proposed program.

(6) Repealed.

## 25-1-509. County and district public health directors.

(1) (a) The director of each agency shall be the public health director.

(b) All other personnel required by an agency shall be selected by the public health director. All personnel shall perform duties as prescribed by the public health director.

(c) In the event of a public health emergency, the agency shall issue orders and adopt rules consistent with the laws and rules of the state as the public health director may deem necessary for the proper exercise of the powers and duties vested in or imposed upon the agency or county or district board.

(2) In addition to the other powers and duties conferred by this part 5 or by the agency, a public health director has the following powers and duties:

(a) To administer and enforce:

(I) The public health laws of the state and, as authorized by the provisions of this title or article 20 of title 30, C.R.S., the public health orders, rules, and standards of the state department or the state board; and

(II) The orders and rules of the county or district board;

(b) To exercise all powers and duties conferred and imposed upon agencies not expressly delegated by the provisions of this part 5 to a county or district board;

(c) To hold hearings, administer oaths, subpoena witnesses, and take testimony in all matters relating to the exercise and performance of his or her powers and duties;

(d) To act as the local registrar of vital statistics or to contract out the responsibility of registrar in the area over which the agency has jurisdiction;

(e) To direct the resources needed to carry out the county or district public health plan developed pursuant to section 25-1-505; and

(f) If requested by the county or district board, to serve as secretary to the board responsible for maintaining all records required by part 2 of article 72 of title 24, C.R.S., and ensuring public notice of all meetings in accordance with part 4 of article 6 of title 24, C.R.S. The director shall be the custodian of all properties and records for the agency.

## 25-1-510. County or district board unable or unwilling to act.

(1) If the county or district board is unable or unwilling to efficiently or promptly abate a nuisance or prevent the introduction or spread of a contagious or infectious disease, the county or district board or agency shall notify the state department and request assistance to take measures that will abate the nuisance or prevent the introduction or spread of disease.

(2) Upon receipt of the notice and request described in subsection (1) of this section, or upon determination that the county or district board is unable or unwilling to act, the state department has full power to take measures to ensure the abatement of the nuisance or prevent the introduction or spread of disease. The state department, for this purpose, may assume all powers conferred by law on the county or district board.

(3) The state department may reallocate state moneys from an agency that is not able to provide core public health services or standards to another entity to deliver services in that agency's jurisdiction.

## 25-1-511. County treasurer - agency funds.

(1) (a) In the case of a county public health agency, the county treasurer, as a part of his or her official duties as county treasurer, shall serve as treasurer of the agency, and the treasurer's official bond as county treasurer shall extend to and cover his or her duties as treasurer of the agency. In the case of a district public health agency, the county treasurer of the county in the district having the largest population as determined by the most recent federal census, as a part of his or her official duties as county treasurer, shall serve as treasurer of the district agency, and the treasurer's official bond as county treasurer shall extend to and cover his or her duties as treasurer of the district agency.

(b) Notwithstanding paragraph (a) of this subsection (1) , in a district where the combined population of the counties is four thousand or fewer, the boards of the county commissioners of the counties may, by consent of all counties in the district, select the county whose treasurer shall serve as treasurer of the district.

(2) The treasurer of an agency, upon organization of the agency, shall create a county or district public health agency fund, to which shall be credited:

(a) Any moneys appropriated from a county general fund; and

(b) Any moneys received from state or federal appropriations or any other gifts, grants, donations, or fees for local public health purposes.

(3) Any moneys credited to a fund created pursuant to subsection (2) of this section shall be expended only for the purposes of this part 5, and claims or demands against the fund shall be allowed only if certified by the public health director and the president of the county or district board or any other member of the county or district board designated by the president for such purpose.

(4) On or before September 1, 2008, and on or before September 1 of each year thereafter, a county board of health shall estimate the total cost of maintaining the county public health agency for the ensuing fiscal year, and the amount of moneys that may be available from unexpended

surpluses or from state or federal funds or other grants or donations. On or before September 1 of each year, the estimates shall be submitted in the form of a budget to the board of county commissioners. The board of county commissioners is authorized to provide any moneys necessary, over estimated moneys from surpluses, grants, and donations, to cover the total cost of maintaining the agency for the ensuing fiscal year by an appropriation from the county general fund.

(5) (a) On or before September 1, 2008, and on or before September 1 of each year thereafter, a district board of health shall estimate the total cost of maintaining the district public health agency for the ensuing fiscal year, and the amount of moneys that may be available from unexpended surpluses or from state or federal funds or other grants or donations. On or before September 1 of each year, the estimates shall be submitted in the form of a budget to a committee composed of the chairs of the boards of county commissioners of all counties comprising the district. The cost for maintaining the agency, over estimated moneys from surpluses, grants, or donations, shall be apportioned by the committee among the counties comprising the district in the proportion that the population of each county in the district bears to the total population of all counties in the district, population figures to be based on the most recent federal census. The boards of county commissioners of the respective counties are authorized to provide any moneys necessary to cover the proportionate shares of their counties by an appropriation from the county general fund.

(b) Notwithstanding paragraph (a) of this subsection (5) , in a district where the combined population of the counties is four thousand or fewer, the boards of the county commissioners of the counties may apportion the costs for each county maintaining the agency by consent of all the counties in the district.

## 25-1-512. Allocation of moneys - public health services support fund - created.

(1) (a) The state department shall allocate any moneys that the general assembly may appropriate for distribution to county or district public health agencies organized pursuant to this part 5 for the provision of local health services. The state board shall determine the basis for the allocation of moneys to the agencies. In determining the allocation of moneys, the state board shall take into account the population served by each agency, the additional costs involved in operating small or rural agencies, and the scope of services provided by each agency.

(b) (I) In order to qualify for state assistance, each county and city and county shall contribute a minimum of one dollar and fifty cents per capita for its local health services and may contribute additional amounts as it may determine to be necessary to meet its local health needs.

(II) Notwithstanding the provisions of subparagraph (I) of this paragraph (b) , for a district public health agency, the counties or cities and counties of the district in total shall contribute a minimum of one dollar and fifty cents per capita for local health services within the district.

(c) Federally funded and state-funded special projects and demonstrations shall be in addition to the allotments specified in paragraph (b) of this subsection (1) .

(2) Repealed.

## 25-1-513. Enlargement of or withdrawal from public health agency.

(1) Any county contiguous to a district maintaining a district public health agency may become a part of the district by agreement between its board of county commissioners and the boards of county commissioners of the counties comprising the district. The county, upon being accepted into the district, shall thereupon become subject to the provisions of this part 5.

(2) Any county in a district maintaining a district public health agency may withdraw from the district by resolution of its board of county commissioners. A county may not withdraw from a district within the two-year period following the establishment of the district or the county becoming a part of the district. A county may only withdraw from a district after one year's written notice given to the agency. In the event of withdrawal of a county from a district, any moneys that had been appropriated by the county before withdrawal to cover its proportionate share of

maintaining the district may be returned to the county. A county shall establish a county public health agency or join another district public health agency once the county withdraws from a district.

(3) A municipal corporation that has voluntarily merged its public health agency with a county or district public health agency under the authority of section 25-1-506 may withdraw from the county or district public health agency by resolution of its city council, board of trustees, or other governing body. A municipal corporation may not withdraw from an agency within the two-year period following the municipal corporation becoming a part of the agency. A county may only withdraw from a district ninety days after a written notice is given to the agency.

## 25-1-514. Legal actions - legal adviser.

The county attorney for the county or the district attorney of the judicial district in which a cause of action arises shall bring any civil or criminal action requested by a county or district public health director to abate a condition that exists in violation of, or to restrain or enjoin any action that is in violation of, or to prosecute for the violation of or for the enforcement of, the public health laws and the standards, orders, and rules of the state board or a county or district board of health. If the county attorney or the district attorney fails to act, the public health director may bring an action and be represented by special counsel employed by him or her with the approval of the county or district board. An agency, through its county or district board of health or through its public health director with the approval of the state board, may employ or retain and compensate an attorney to be the legal adviser of the agency and to defend all actions and proceedings brought against the agency or the officers and employees of the agency.

## 25-1-515. Judicial review of decisions.

(1) Any person aggrieved and affected by a decision of a county or district board of health or a public health director acting under the provisions of this part 5 shall be entitled to judicial review by filing, in the district court of any county over which the county or district board or public health director has jurisdiction, an appropriate action requesting the review within ninety days after the public announcement of the decision. The court may make any interested person a party to the action. The review shall be conducted by the court without a jury and shall be confined to the record, if a complete record is presented. In a case of alleged irregularities in the record or in the procedure before the county or district board or public health director, testimony may be taken in the court. The court may affirm the decision or may reverse or modify it if the substantial rights of the appellant have been prejudiced as a result of the findings and decision of the county or district board being:

(a) Contrary to constitutional rights or privileges;

(b) In excess of the statutory authority or jurisdiction of the county or district board or public health director;

(c) Affected by any error of law;

(d) Made or promulgated upon unlawful procedure;

(e) Unsupported by substantial evidence in view of the entire record as submitted; or

(f) Arbitrary or capricious.

(2) Any party may have a review of the final judgment or decision of the district court by appellate review in accordance with law and the Colorado appellate rules.

## 25-1-516. Unlawful acts - penalties.

(1) It is unlawful for any person, association, or corporation and the officers thereof to:

(a) Willfully violate, disobey, or disregard the provisions of the public health laws or the terms of any lawful notice, order, standard, or rule;

(b) Fail to make or file a report required by law or rule of the state board relating to the existence of disease or other facts and statistics relating to the public health;

(c) Willfully and falsely make or alter a certificate or certified copy of any certificate issued pursuant to the public health laws;

(d) Willfully fail to remove from private property under his or her control at his or her own expense, within forty-eight hours after being ordered to do so by the county or district public health agency, any nuisance, source of filth, or cause of sickness within the jurisdiction and control of the agency whether the person, association, or corporation is the owner, tenant, or occupant of the private property; except that, when the condition is due to an act of God, it shall be removed at public expense; or

(e) Pay, give, present, or otherwise convey to any officer or employee of an agency any gift, remuneration, or other consideration, directly or indirectly, that the officer or employee is forbidden to receive by the provisions of this part 5.

(2) It is unlawful for any officer or employee of any agency or member of any county or district board of health to accept any gift, remuneration, or other consideration, directly or indirectly, for an incorrect or improper performance of the duties imposed upon him or her by or on behalf of the agency or by the provisions of this part 5.

(3) Any person, association, or corporation, or the officers thereof, who violates any provision of this section is guilty of a class 1 misdemeanor and, upon conviction thereof, shall be punished pursuant to the provisions of section 18-1.3-501, C.R.S. In addition to the fine or imprisonment, the person, association, or corporation shall be liable for any expense incurred by health authorities in removing any nuisance, source of filth, or cause of sickness. Conviction under the penalty provisions of this part 5 or any other public health law shall not relieve any person from any civil action in damages that may exist for an injury resulting from any violation of the public health laws.

## 25-1-517. Mode of treatment inconsistent with religious creed or tenet.

Nothing in this part 5 authorizes a county or district board of health to impose on any person any mode of treatment inconsistent with the creed or tenets of any religious denomination of which he or she is an adherent if the person complies with sanitary and quarantine laws and rules.

## 25-1-518. Nuisances.

(1) Removal of nuisances. The county or district board of health shall examine all nuisances, sources of filth, and causes of sickness, which, in its opinion, may be injurious to the health of the inhabitants, within its town, city, county, city and county, or district, and it shall destroy, remove, or prevent the nuisance, source of filth, or cause of sickness, as the case may require.

(2) Unhealthy premises cleaned - structures removed. If any cellar, vault, lot, sewer, drain, place, or premises within any city is damp, unwholesome, offensive, or filthy, or is covered for any portion of the year with stagnant or impure water, or is in a condition as to produce unwholesome or offensive exhalations, the county or district board of health may cause the area to be drained, filled up, cleaned, amended, or purified; or may require the owner or occupant or person in charge of the lot, premises, or place to perform such duty; or may cause the removal to be done by the proper officers of the city.

(3) Expense for abating nuisance. If any person or company neglects to remove or abate any nuisance or to perform any requirement made by or in accordance with any ordinance or resolution of the county or district board of health for the protection of the health of the inhabitants and if any expense is incurred by the board in removing or abating the nuisance or in causing such duty or requirement to be performed, such expense may be recovered by the board in an action against such person or company. In all cases where the board incurs any expense for draining, filling, cleaning, or purifying any lot, place, or premises, or for removing or abating any nuisance found upon such lot or premises, the board, in addition to all other remedies, may provide for the recovery of such expense, charge the same or such part thereof as it deems proper to the lot or premises upon or on account of which such expense was incurred or from which such nuisance was removed or abated, and cause the same to be assessed upon such lot or premises and collected as a special assessment.

(4) Removal of nuisance on private property - penalty. Whenever any nuisance, source of filth, or cause of sickness is found on private property, the county or district board of health shall order the owner or occupant or the person who has caused or permitted such nuisance, at his or her own expense, to remove the same within twenty-four hours. In default thereof, he or she shall forfeit a sum not to exceed one hundred dollars at the suit of the board of county commissioners of the proper county or the board of the proper city, town, or village for the use of the county or district board of health of the city or town where the nuisance is found.

(5) Board to remove - when. If the owner or occupant does not comply with an order of the county or district board of health, the board may cause the nuisance, source of filth, or cause of sickness to be removed, and all expense incurred thereby shall be paid by the owner or occupant or by such other person who has caused or permitted the nuisance, source of filth, or cause of sickness.

(6) Conviction - nuisance to be abated. Whenever any person is convicted of maintaining a nuisance that may be injurious to the public health, the court, in its discretion, may order the nuisance abated, removed, or destroyed at the expense of the defendant under the direction of the county or district board of health of the town, city, county, or district where the nuisance is found, and the form of the warrant to the sheriff or other officer may be varied accordingly.

(7) Stay warrant of conviction. The court, on the application of the defendant, may order a stay of a warrant issued pursuant to subsection (6) of this section for such time as may be necessary, not exceeding six months, to give the defendant an opportunity to remove the nuisance upon giving satisfactory security to do so within the time specified in the order.

(8) Expense of abating. The expense of abating and removing the nuisance pursuant to a warrant issued pursuant to subsection (6) of this section shall be collected by the officer in the same manner as damages and costs are collected upon execution; except that the materials of any buildings, fences, or other things that may be removed as a nuisance may be sold by the officer in like manner as goods are sold on execution for the payment of debts. The officer may apply the proceeds of the sale to defray the expenses of the removal and shall pay over the balance thereof, if any, to the defendant upon demand. If the proceeds of the sale are not sufficient to defray the expenses incurred pursuant to this subsection (8) , the sheriff shall collect the residue thereof as provided in subsection (3) of this section.

(9) Refusal of admittance to premises. (a) Whenever a county or district board of health finds it necessary for the preservation of the lives or health of the inhabitants to enter any building, car, or train of cars in its town, city, county, or district for the purpose of examining and abating, removing, or preventing any nuisance, source of filth, or cause of sickness and is refused entry, any member of the board may make complaint under oath to the county court of his or her county stating the facts of the case as far as he or she has knowledge thereof.

(b) The court may thereupon issue a warrant directed to the sheriff commanding him or her to take sufficient aid and, being accompanied by any two or more members of the county or district board of health, during daylight hours, to return to the place where the nuisance, source of filth, or cause of sickness complained of may be and destroy, remove, or prevent the nuisance, source of filth, cause of sickness, or danger to life or limb under the direction of the members of the board of health.

(10) Damages occasioned by nuisance - action. Any person injured either in his or her comfort or in the enjoyment of his or her estate by any nuisance may have an action for damages sustained thereby.

## 25-1-519. Existing intergovernmental agreements.
Nothing in this part 5 shall void the terms of any intergovernmental agreement concerning public health entered into as of July 1, 2008, so long as all core and essential public health services continue to be provided.

## 25-1-520. Clean syringe exchange programs - approval - reporting requirements.

(1) A county public health agency or district public health agency may request approval from its county board of health or district board of health, referred to in this section as the "board", for a clean syringe exchange program operated by the agency or by a nonprofit organization with which the agency contracts to operate the clean syringe exchange program. Prior to approving or disapproving any such optional program, the board shall consult with the agency and interested stakeholders concerning the establishment of the clean syringe exchange program. Interested stakeholders must include, but need not be limited to, local law enforcement agencies, district attorneys, substance use disorder treatment providers, persons with a substance use disorder in remission, nonprofit organizations, hepatitis C and HIV advocacy organizations, and members of the community. The board and interested stakeholders shall consider, at a minimum, the following issues:

(a) The scope of the problem being addressed and the population the program would serve;

(b) Concerns of the law enforcement community; and

(c) The parameters of the proposed program, including methods for identifying program workers and volunteers.

(2) Each proposed clean syringe exchange program must, at a minimum, have the ability to:

(a) Provide an injection drug user with the information and the means to protect himself or herself, his or her partner, and his or her family from exposure to blood-borne disease through access to education, sterile injection equipment, voluntary testing for blood-borne diseases, and counseling;

(b) Provide thorough referrals to facilitate entry into substance use disorder treatment programs, including opioid substitution therapy;

(c) Encourage usage of medical care and mental health services as well as social welfare and health promotion;

(d) Provide safety protocols and classes for the proper handling and disposal of injection materials;

(e) Plan and implement the clean syringe exchange program with the clear objective of reducing the transmission of blood-borne diseases within a specific geographic area;

(f) Develop a timeline for the proposed program and for the development of policies and procedures; and

(g) Develop an education program regarding the legal rights under this section and section 18-18-428 (1) (b) , C.R.S., that encourages participants to always disclose their possession of hypodermic needles or syringes to peace officers or emergency medical technicians or other first responders prior to a search.

(3) The board may approve or disapprove the proposed clean syringe exchange program based on the results of the meetings held pursuant to subsection (1) of this section.

(4) If the board approves a clean syringe exchange program that is operated through a contract with a nonprofit organization, the contract shall be subject to annual review and shall be renewed only if the board approves the contract after consultation with the county or district public health agency and interested stakeholders as described in subsection (1) of this section.

(5) One or more counties represented on a district board of health may at any time opt out of a clean syringe exchange program proposed or approved pursuant to this section.

(6) Repealed.

# PART 6. LOCAL BOARDS OF HEALTH

## 25-1-601 to 25-1-667. (Repealed)

# PART 7. REGIONAL HEALTH DEPARTMENTS

**25-1-701 to 25-1-719. (Repealed)**

# PART 8. PATIENT RECORDS

## 25-1-801. Patient records in custody of health care facility - definitions.

(1) (a) Every patient record in the custody of a health facility licensed or certified pursuant to section 25-1.5-103 (1) or article 3 of this title, or both, or any entity regulated under title 10, C.R.S., providing health care services, as defined in section 10-16-102 (33) , C.R.S., directly or indirectly through a managed care plan, as defined in section 10-16-102 (43) , C.R.S., or otherwise shall be available for inspection to the patient or the patient's personal representative through the attending health care provider or the provider's designated representative at reasonable times and upon reasonable notice, except records withheld in accordance with 45 CFR 164.524 (a) . A summary of records pertaining to a patient's mental health problems may, upon written request and signed and dated authorization, be made available to the patient or the patient's personal representative following termination of the treatment program.

(b) (I) (A) A health facility licensed or certified pursuant to section 25-1.5-103 (1) or article 3 of this title, or both, or an entity regulated under title 10, C.R.S., providing health care services, as defined in section 10-16-102 (33) , C.R.S., directly or indirectly through a managed care plan, as defined in section 10-16-102 (43) , C.R.S., or otherwise, must provide copies of a patient's medical records, including X rays, to the patient or the patient's personal representative upon request and payment of the fee a covered entity may impose in accordance with the "Health Insurance Portability and Accountability Act of 1996", Pub.L. 104-191, as amended, and any rules promulgated pursuant to the act, or to a third person who requests the records upon submission of a HIPAA-compliant authorization, valid subpoena, or court order and upon the payment of the reasonable fees.

(B) The health care facility must deliver the medical records in electronic format if the person requests electronic format, the original medical records are stored in electronic format, and the medical records are readily producible in electronic format.

(II) In the event that a licensed health care professional determines that a copy of any X ray, mammogram, CT SCAN, MRI, or other film is not sufficient for diagnostic or other treatment purposes, the health facility or entity shall make the original of any such film available to the patient or another health care professional or facility as specifically directed by the patient pursuant to a written authorization-request for films and upon the payment of the reasonable costs for such film. If a health facility releases an original film pursuant to this subparagraph (II) , it shall not be responsible for any loss, damage, or other consequences as a result of such release. Any original X ray, mammogram, CT SCAN, MRI, or other film made available pursuant to this subparagraph (II) shall be returned upon request to the lending facility within thirty days.

(c) The hospital or related facility or institution shall post in conspicuous public places on the premises a statement of the requirements set forth in paragraphs (a) and (b) of this subsection (1) and shall make available a copy of said statement to each patient upon admission.

(d) Nothing in this section requires a person responsible for the diagnosis or treatment of sexually transmitted infections or addiction to or use of drugs in the case of minors pursuant to sections 13-22-102, C.R.S., and 25-4-409 to release patient records of such diagnosis or treatment to a parent, guardian, or person other than the minor or his or her designated representative.

(2) All requests by a patient or the patient's personal representative for inspection of the patient's

medical records made under this section shall be noted with the time and date of the request and the time and date of inspection noted by the attending health care provider or his or her designated representative. The patient or personal representative shall acknowledge the fact of the inspection by dating and signing the record file. A health care facility shall not charge a fee for the inspection of medical records.

(3) Nothing in this section shall apply to any nursing institution conducted by or for the adherents of any well-recognized church or religious denomination for the purpose of providing facilities for the care and treatment of the sick who depend exclusively upon spiritual means through prayer for healing and the practice of the religion of such church or denomination.

(4) For the purposes of this section, medical information transmitted during the delivery of health care via telemedicine, as defined in section 12-36-106 (1) (g) , C.R.S., is part of the patient's medical record maintained by the health care facility.

(5) As used in this part 8, unless the context otherwise requires:

(a) "HIPAA-compliant" means in compliance with the "Health Insurance Portability and Accountability Act of 1996", Pub.L. 104-191, as amended.

(b) "Personal representative" has the meaning set forth in 45 CFR 164.502.

(c) (I) "Reasonable fees" means an amount not to exceed:

(A) Eighteen dollars and fifty-three cents for the first ten pages, eighty-five cents per page for the next thirty pages, and fifty-seven cents per page for each additional page; except that, if the medical records are stored on microfilm, one dollar and fifty cents per page;

(B) For radiographic studies, actual reproduction costs for each copy of a radiograph;

(C) If the authorized person requests certification of the medical records, a fee of ten dollars;

(D) Actual postage and electronic media costs, if applicable; and

(E) Applicable taxes.

(II) Notwithstanding any other provision of this part 8:

(A) If a patient record is requested by a third-party entity that is performing duties under the "Laura Hershey Disability Support Act", part 22 of article 30 of title 24, C.R.S., the third party may obtain one free copy of the record for the application process or for an appeal or reapplication when required by the disability benefit administrator;

(B) If maximum rates have already been established by statute or rule for a state or local government entity, those rates prevail over the rates set forth in this part 8; and

(C) This part 8 does not apply to coroners requesting medical records pursuant to section 30-10-606, C.R.S.

## 25-1-802. Patient records in custody of individual health care providers.

(1) (a) Every patient record in the custody of a podiatrist, chiropractor, dentist, doctor of medicine, doctor of osteopathy, nurse, optometrist, occupational therapist, audiologist, acupuncturist, direct-entry midwife, or physical therapist required to be licensed under title 12, C.R.S., a naturopathic doctor required to be registered pursuant to article 37.3 of title 12, C.R.S., or a person practicing psychotherapy under article 43 of title 12, C.R.S., except records withheld in accordance with 45 CFR 164.524 (a) , must be available to the patient or the patient's personal representative upon submission of a valid authorization for inspection of records, dated and signed by the patient, at reasonable times and upon reasonable notice. A summary of records pertaining to a patient's mental health problems may, upon written request accompanied by a signed and dated authorization, be made available to the patient or the patient's personal representative following termination of the treatment program.

(b) (I) (A) A copy of the records, including radiographic studies, must be made available to the patient or the patient's personal representative, upon request and payment of the fee a covered entity may impose in accordance with the "Health Insurance Portability and Accountability Act of 1996", Pub.L. 104-191, as amended, or to a third person who requests the medical records upon submission of a HIPAA-compliant authorization, a valid subpoena, or a court order, and payment of reasonable fees.

(B) The health care provider must provide the medical records in electronic format if the person requests electronic format, the original medical records are stored in electronic format, and the medical records are readily producible in electronic format.

(II) If a licensed health care professional determines that a copy of a radiographic study, including an X ray, mammogram, CT scan, MRI, or other film is not sufficient for diagnostic or other treatment purposes, the podiatrist, chiropractor, dentist, doctor of medicine, doctor of osteopathy, nurse, optometrist, audiologist, acupuncturist, direct-entry midwife, or physical therapist required to be licensed under title 12, C.R.S., or, subject to the provisions of section 25-1-801 (1) (a) and paragraph (a) of this subsection (1) , the person practicing psychotherapy under article 43 of title 12, C.R.S., shall make the original of any radiographic study available to the patient, the patient's personal representative, a person authorized by the patient, or another health care professional or facility as specifically directed by the patient, personal representative, authorized person, or health care professional or facility pursuant to a HIPAA-compliant authorization and upon the payment of the reasonable fees for the radiographic study. If a practitioner releases an original radiographic study pursuant to this subparagraph (II) , the practitioner is not responsible for any loss, damage, or other consequences as a result of the release. Any original radiographic study made available pursuant to this subparagraph (II) must be returned upon request to the lending practitioner within thirty days.

(2) Nothing in this section requires a person responsible for the diagnosis or treatment of sexually transmitted infections or addiction to or use of drugs in the case of minors pursuant to sections 13-22-102, C.R.S., and 25-4-409 to release patient records of such diagnosis or treatment to a parent, guardian, or person other than the minor or his or her designated representative.

(3) For purposes of this section, "patient record" does not include a doctor's office notes.

(4) All requests by a patient or the patient's personal representative for inspection of his or her medical records made under this section shall be noted with the time and date of the request and the time and date of inspection noted by the health care provider or his or her designated representative. The patient or the patient's personal representative shall acknowledge the inspection by dating and signing the record file. A health care provider shall not charge a fee for the inspection of medical records.

(5) For the purposes of this section, medical information transmitted during the delivery of health care via telemedicine, as defined in section 12-36-106 (1) (g) , C.R.S., is part of the patient's medical record maintained by a health care provider.

### 25-1-803. Effect of this part 8 on similar rights of a patient.

(1) Nothing in this part 8:

(a) Limits the right of a patient, the patient's personal representative, or a person who requests the medical records upon submission of a HIPAA-compliant authorization, a valid subpoena, or a court order to inspect the patient's medical or mental health data pursuant to section 24-72-204 (3) (a) (I) , C.R.S.; or

(b) Limits or expands a right to inspect the patient's records that is otherwise granted by state statute to the patient, the patient's personal representative, or a person who requests the medical records upon submission of a HIPAA-compliant authorization, a valid subpoena, or a court order.

# PART 9. COMMISSION ON FAMILY MEDICINE

### 25-1-901 to 25-1-904. (Repealed)

# PART 10. CHILD CARE PROGRAMS IN NURSING HOME FACILITIES

### 25-1-1001. Legislative declaration.

The general assembly hereby finds that the operation of child care centers in nursing home facilities is desirable because the benefit to nursing home facility employees in having on-location child care will improve the quality of care in nursing home facilities by stabilizing the nursing home work force and because the general public, especially in rural areas, will benefit from the increased availability of day care centers in their communities. The general assembly also finds that the operation of child care centers in nursing home facilities is desirable because the intergenerational contact has been proven to be beneficial to the health and well-being of elderly persons and, therefore, will improve the quality of life of elderly residents in nursing home facilities and because the intergenerational contact will be beneficial to the children as well. The general assembly, therefore, declares that the intent of this part 10 is to encourage the development of child care centers in nursing home facilities by encouraging the creation of private grants to provide funds to start such centers and by requiring the state agencies which license nursing home facilities and child care centers to study and recommend statutory and regulatory changes to facilitate and encourage the development of child care centers in nursing home facilities.

### 25-1-1002. Definitions.

As used in this part 10, unless the context otherwise requires:
(1) "Nursing home facility" means a facility which provides skilled nursing home services or intermediate care nursing home services.

### 25-1-1003. Grant program - requirements - use of medical assistance funds prohibited.

(1) The department of public health and environment may encourage the development of a private grant program to provide start-up funds to nursing home facilities for the purpose of establishing child care centers located in such nursing home facilities.
(2) The state board of health, after consultation with the division in the department of human services involved in licensing child care centers and if the committee formed in section 25-1-1004 recommends the establishment of child care facilities in nursing homes, shall promulgate reasonable rules and regulations establishing any necessary requirements for operating a day care center in a nursing home facility. Such rules and regulations shall include, but need not be limited to, the following:
(a) Requirements for the operation of a safe and good-quality child care operation in the nursing home facility or upon the nursing home facility's grounds, which shall include:
(I) Precautions required to be taken to ensure that all staff and residents who will participate in the intergenerational programs have not been involved in incidents of sexual abuse or child abuse;
(II) Requirements relating to the ability to properly care for the children;
(III) Child care ratios of staff to children;
(IV) Requirements relating to the constant supervision of the children by staff members and not by nursing home residents;
(V) Life safety and fire regulations;
(b) Requirements on the amount and type of liability insurance necessary to insure the risks associated with the child care operation;
(c) Requirements on the ways in which the nursing home residents may be involved in the child care center and the requirement that the participation of nursing home residents in intergenerational activities with the children in the child care operation shall be on a voluntary basis;

(d) Requirements that any fees assessed to the employees of the nursing home facility whose children participate in the child care program will be based on a sliding scale;

(e) Requirements that the participation of employees of the nursing home facility in the enrollment of their children in the intergenerational day care program of the nursing home facility shall be on a voluntary basis.

(3) No medical assistance funds under the "Colorado Medical Assistance Act", articles 4, 5, and 6 of title 25.5, C.R.S., shall be used to subsidize the cost of operating a day care center or day care program in a nursing home facility.

### 25-1-1004. Study of statutes and rules and regulations pertaining to nursing home facilities and day care centers.

(1) The department of public health and environment and the department of human services, in conjunction with representatives of the nursing home industry, child care operators, and experts on child care programs in nursing home facilities, shall examine and study the existing statutes and rules and regulations concerning the licensing of child care centers and of nursing home facilities to determine what statutory or regulatory changes or both would make it easier for a nursing home facility to operate a child care center. The study shall also include an examination of the advantages and disadvantages of operating such intergenerational programs and the most appropriate and practical ways to design such intergenerational child care programs which are beneficial both to the children and to the elderly persons.

(2) The study conducted by the department of public health and environment and the department of human services shall include, but need not be limited to, consideration of the following:

(a) The establishment of new rules and regulations by the department of public health and environment and the department of human services which would allow nursing home facilities to operate a child care operation in the nursing home facilities;

(b) A coordinated licensure program to license a child care operation in a nursing home facility which would be based on rules and regulations designed specifically for the operation of a child care center in a nursing home facility.

(3) Repealed.

(4) The department of public health and environment and the department of human services shall comply with the requirements of this part 10 within the current appropriation established for each department. No request for appropriations shall be made to the general assembly for the implementation of this part 10.

# PART 11. DRUG ABUSE PREVENTION, EDUCATION, AND TREATMENT

### 25-1-1100.2 to 25-1-1112. (Repealed)

# PART 12. MEDICAL RECORD CONFIDENTIALITY

### 25-1-1201. Legislative declaration.

The general assembly hereby finds, determines, and declares that maintaining the confidentiality of medical records is of the utmost importance to the state and of critical importance to patient privacy for high quality medical care. Most people in the United States consider confidentiality of health information important and worry that the increased computerization of health records may result in inappropriate disclosure of such records. Patients have a strong interest in preserving the privacy of their personal health information, but they also have an interest in medical research and other efforts by health care organizations to improve the medical care they receive. How best to preserve confidentiality within a state health information infrastructure is an important discussion that is affected by recent regulations promulgated by the federal department of health and human services related to the electronic storage of health information. The purpose of this part 12 is to index the provisions that govern medical record confidentiality to facilitate locating the law concerning the confidentiality of medical records and health information. It is not intended to expand, narrow, or clarify existing provisions.

## 25-1-1202. Index of statutory sections regarding medical record confidentiality and health information.

(1) Statutory provisions concerning policies, procedures, and references to the release, sharing, and use of medical records and health information include the following:

(a) Section 10-16-1003, C.R.S., concerning use of information by health care cooperatives;

(b) Section 8-43-404, C.R.S., concerning examinations by a physician or chiropractor for the purposes of workers' compensation;

(c) Section 8-43-501, C.R.S., concerning utilization review related to workers' compensation;

(d) Section 8-73-108, C.R.S., concerning the award of benefits for unemployment compensation benefits;

(e) Section 10-3-1104.7, C.R.S., concerning the confidentiality and use of genetic testing information;

(f) Section 10-16-113, C.R.S., concerning the procedures related to the denial of health benefits by an insurer;

(g) Section 10-16-113.5, C.R.S., concerning the use of independent external review when health benefits have been denied;

(h) Section 10-16-423, C.R.S., concerning the confidentiality of medical information in the custody of a health maintenance organization;

(i) Section 12-32-108.3, C.R.S., concerning disciplinary actions against podiatrists;

(j) Section 12-33-126, C.R.S., concerning disciplinary actions against chiropractors;

(k) Section 12-35-129, C.R.S., concerning disciplinary actions against dentists and dental hygienists;

(l) Section 12-36-118, C.R.S., concerning disciplinary actions against physicians;

(m) Section 12-36-135 (1) , C.R.S., concerning reporting requirements for physicians pertaining to certain injuries;

(n) Section 12-36.5-104, C.R.S., concerning professional review committees for physicians;

(o) Section 12-36.5-104.4, C.R.S., concerning hospital professional review committees;

(p) Section 12-37.5-104, C.R.S., concerning reporting requirements by physicians related to abortions for minors;

(q) Section 12-38-116.5, C.R.S., concerning disciplinary proceedings against a practical nurse, a professional nurse, or a psychiatric technician;

(r) Section 12-43-218, C.R.S., concerning the disclosure of confidential communications by a mental health professional;

(s) Section 12-43-224 (4) , C.R.S., concerning disciplinary proceedings against a mental health professional;

(t) Section 13-21-110, C.R.S., concerning confidentiality of information, data, reports, or records of a utilization review committee of a hospital or other health care facility;

(u) Section 13-21-117, C.R.S., concerning civil liability of a mental health professional, mental health hospital, community mental health center, or clinic related to a duty to warn or protect;

(v) Sections 13-22-101 to 13-22-106, C.R.S., concerning the age of competence for certain medical procedures;

(w) Section 13-64-502, C.R.S., concerning civil liability related to genetic counseling and screening and prenatal care, or arising from or during the course of labor and delivery, or the period of postnatal care in a health institution;

(x) Section 13-80-103.7, C.R.S., concerning a limited waiver of medical information in civil actions related to sexual assault or sexual offenses against a child;

(y) Section 13-90-107 (1) (d) , C.R.S., concerning when a physician, surgeon, or registered professional nurse may testify related to the care and treatment of a person;

(z) Section 14-10-124, C.R.S., concerning the best interests of a child for the purposes of a separation or dissolution of marriage;

(aa) Section 14-10-127, C.R.S., concerning the allocation of parental responsibilities with respect to a child;

(bb) Section 17-27.1-101 (4) , C.R.S., concerning nongovernmental facilities for offenders and the waiver of confidential information;

(cc) Section 18-3-203 (1) (f.5) , C.R.S., concerning assault in the second degree and the availability of medical testing for certain circumstances;

(dd) Section 18-4-412, C.R.S., concerning theft of medical records or medical information;

(ee) Repealed.

(ee.5) Section 18-18-406.3, C.R.S., concerning medical marijuana patient records;

(ff) Section 18-18-503, C.R.S., concerning cooperative agreements to control substance abuse;

(gg) Section 19-3-304, C.R.S., concerning persons required to report child abuse or neglect;

(hh) Section 19-3-305, C.R.S., concerning postmortem investigation related to the death of a child;

(ii) Section 19-3-306, C.R.S., concerning evidence of abuse or neglect of a child;

(jj) Section 19-5-103 (2) , C.R.S., concerning relinquishment of rights concerning a child;

(kk) Section 19-5-305, C.R.S., concerning access to adoption records;

(ll) Section 22-1-123 (5) , C.R.S., concerning the protection of student data;

(mm) Sections 22-32-109.1 (6) and 22-32-109.3 (2) , C.R.S., concerning specific powers and duties of the state board of education;

(nn) Section 22-64-216, C.R.S., concerning confidentiality of records maintained by school district retirement plans;

(oo) Section 24-51-213, C.R.S., concerning confidentiality of records maintained by the public employees' retirement association;

(pp) Section 24-72-204 (3) , C.R.S., concerning public records not open to public inspection;

(qq) Section 25-1-122, concerning reporting of certain diseases and conditions for investigation of epidemic and communicable diseases, morbidity and mortality, cancer in connection with the statewide cancer registry, environmental and chronic diseases, sexually transmitted infections, tuberculosis, and rabies and mammal bites by the department of public health and environment;

(rr) Section 25-1-124 (2) , concerning health care facilities and reporting requirements;

(ss) Sections 27-81-110 and 27-81-113, C.R.S., concerning the treatment of intoxicated persons;

(tt) Section 25-1-801, concerning patient records in the care of a health care facility;

(uu) Section 25-1-802, concerning patient records in the care of individual health care providers;

(vv) Sections 27-82-106 and 27-82-109, concerning the treatment of persons with substance use disorders;

(vv.5) Section 25-1.5-106, concerning the medical marijuana program;

(ww) Section 25-2-120, concerning reports of electroconvulsive treatment;

(xx) Section 25-3-109, concerning quality management functions of health care facilities licensed by the department of public health and environment;

(yy) Section 25-3.5-501, concerning records maintained by ambulance services and emergency medical service providers;

(zz) Section 25-3.5-704 (2) (d) and (2) (f) , concerning the designation of emergency medical facilities and the statewide trauma system;

(aaa) Sections 25-4-406 and 25-4-409, concerning the reporting of sexually transmitted infections;

(bbb) Section 25-4-1003, concerning newborn screening programs and genetic counseling;

(ccc) Repealed.

(ddd) Section 25-4-1705, concerning immunization information;

(eee) Section 25-4-1905, concerning records collected related to Gulf War syndrome;

(fff) Section 25-32-106, concerning the release of medical information to a poison control service provider;

(ggg) Section 26-3.1-102 (2) , C.R.S., concerning reporting requirements related to at-risk adults;

(hhh) Section 26-11.5-108, C.R.S., concerning the long-term ombudsman program and access to medical records;

(iii) Section 27-65-103 (2) , C.R.S., concerning voluntary applications for mental health services;

(jjj) Sections 27-65-121 (2) and 27-65-122, C.R.S., concerning records related to mental health services for minor children;

(kkk) Section 30-10-606 (6) , C.R.S., concerning postmortem investigations and records;

(lll) Section 35-9-109, C.R.S., concerning confidentiality of information released to the commissioner of agriculture related to human exposure to pesticide applications;

(mmm) Section 42-2-112, C.R.S., concerning information supplied to the department of revenue for the purpose of renewing or obtaining a license to operate a motor vehicle; and

(nnn) Section 12-42.5-406, C.R.S., concerning information entered into the prescription drug monitoring program database.

## 25-1-1203. Electronic storage of medical records.

Health plans, health care clearinghouses, and health care providers shall develop policies, procedures, and systems to comply with federal regulations promulgated by the federal department of health and human services related to electronic storage and maintenance of medical record information pursuant to federal law.

## 25-1-1204. Online exchange of advanced directives forms permitted.

A public or private entity, including a nonprofit organization, that facilitates the exchange of health information among emergency medical service providers, doctors, hospitals, nursing homes, pharmacies, home health agencies, health plans, and local health information agencies through the use of health information technology may facilitate the voluntary, secure, and confidential exchange of forms containing advanced directives regarding a person's acceptance or rejection of life-sustaining medical or surgical treatment.

# PART 13. CLIMATE CHANGE MARKETS GRANT PROGRAM

## 25-1-1301. Short title.

This part 13 shall be known and may be cited as the "Colorado Climate Change Markets Act".

## 25-1-1302. Legislative declaration.

(1) The general assembly hereby finds and declares that:

(a) As the United States and other countries take action to address issues related to climate change, Colorado faces important policy choices.

(b) Emerging technologies and markets related to climate change promise significant economic opportunities for the state, particularly for agriculture and rural economies.

(c) The general assembly enacts the "Colorado Climate Change Markets Act" for the purpose of positioning Colorado at the forefront of emerging markets related to climate change and helping affected industries and economies benefit from these opportunities.

### 25-1-1303. Grants for research - reports to general assembly.

(1) The department of public health and environment shall administer a program to award grants pursuant to this section.

(2) (a) A grant of fifty thousand dollars shall be awarded to Colorado state university to conduct research on the potential for the use of terrestrial carbon sequestration in agricultural, rangeland, and forest soils as a technique for mitigating the emissions of greenhouse gases in the state.

(b) A grant of fifty thousand dollars shall be awarded to the Colorado school of mines to conduct research on the potential for the use of geologic carbon sequestration as a technique for mitigating the emissions of greenhouse gases in the state.

(c) A grant of thirty-five thousand dollars shall be awarded to the university of Colorado to conduct research on the emerging international and domestic markets in greenhouse gas emissions and to conduct research on private firms in various economic sectors that are reducing emissions of greenhouse gases.

(3) Each recipient of a grant awarded pursuant to this section shall report the results of the research conducted under the grant to the agriculture committees of the senate and the house of representatives no later than March 15, 2007.

# PART 14. HEALTH INFORMATION TECHNOLOGY

**25-1-1401 to 25-1-1403. (Repealed)**

# ARTICLE 1.5. POWERS AND DUTIES OF THE DEPARTMENT OF PUBLIC HEALTH AND ENVIRONMENT

# PART 1. GENERAL POWERS AND DUTIES

### 25-1.5-101. Powers and duties of department - laboratory cash fund.

(1) The department has, in addition to all other powers and duties imposed upon it by law, the powers and duties provided in this section as follows:

(a) To close theaters, schools, and other public places, and to forbid gatherings of people when necessary to protect the public health;

(b) (I) To establish and enforce minimum general sanitary standards as to the quality of wastes discharged upon land and the quality of fertilizer derived from excreta of human beings or from the sludge of sewage disposal plants.

(II) The phrase "minimum general sanitary standards" as used in this section means the minimum standards reasonably consistent with assuring adequate protection of the public health. The word "standards" as used in this section means standards reasonably designed to promote and protect the public health.

(c) (I) To collect, compile, and tabulate reports of marriages, dissolution of marriages, declaration of invalidity of marriages, births, deaths, and morbidity and to require any person having information with regard to the same to make such reports and submit such information as the board shall by rule or regulation provide.

(II) For the purposes of this paragraph (c) , the board is authorized to require reporting of morbidity and mortality in accordance with the provisions of section 25-1-122.

(d) To regulate the disposal, transportation, interment, and disinterment of the dead;

(e) (I) To establish, maintain, and approve chemical, bacteriological, and biological laboratories, and to conduct such laboratory investigations and examinations as it may deem necessary or proper for the protection of the public health.

(II) The department shall transmit all fees received by the department in connection with the laboratories established pursuant to this paragraph (e) , with the exception of fees received pursuant to part 10 of article 4 of this title that are credited to the newborn screening and genetic counseling cash funds created in section 25-4-1006 (1) , to the state treasurer, who shall deposit them in the laboratory cash fund, which is hereby created in the state treasury. The state treasurer shall credit all interest earned from the revenues in the fund to the fund. At the end of each fiscal year, the unencumbered balance of the fund remains in the fund. The revenues in the fund are subject to annual appropriation by the general assembly to the department to carry out its duties under this paragraph (e) .

(f) To make, approve, and establish standards for diagnostic tests by chemical, bacteriological, and biological laboratories, and to require such laboratories to conform thereto; and to prepare, distribute, and require the completion of forms or certificates with respect thereto;

(g) To purchase, and to distribute to licensed physicians and veterinarians, with or without charge, as the board may determine upon considerations of emergency or need, such vaccines, serums, toxoids, and other approved biological or therapeutic products as may be necessary for the protection of the public health;

(h) To establish and enforce sanitary standards for the operation and maintenance of orphanages, day care nurseries, foster homes, family care homes, summer camps for children, lodging houses, guest child care facilities as defined in section 26-6-102 (16) , C.R.S., public services short-term child care facilities as defined in section 26-6-102 (30) , C.R.S., hotels, public conveyances and stations, schools, factories, workshops, industrial and labor camps, recreational resorts and camps, swimming pools, public baths, mobile home parks, and other buildings, centers, and places used for public gatherings;

(i) (I) To establish sanitary standards and make sanitary, sewerage, and health inspections and examinations for charitable, penal, and other public institutions, and, with respect to the state institutions under the department of human services specified in section 27-90-104, C.R.S., or under the department of corrections specified in section 17-1-104.3 (1) (b) , C.R.S., such inspections and examinations shall be made at least once each year. Reports on such inspections of institutions under control of the department of human services or the department of corrections shall be made to the executive director of the appropriate department for appropriate action, if any.

(II) Notwithstanding the provisions of subparagraph (I) of this paragraph (i) , the standards adopted pursuant to subparagraph (I) of this paragraph (i) with regard to space requirements, furnishing requirements, required special use areas or special management housing, and environmental condition requirements, including but not limited to standards pertaining to light, ventilation, temperature, and noise level, shall not apply to any penal institution operated by or under contract with a county or municipality if the penal institution begins operations on or after August 30, 1999, and if the governing body of the jurisdiction operating the penal institution has adopted standards pertaining to such issues for the penal institution pursuant to section 30-11-104 (1) , C.R.S., or section 31-15-711.5, C.R.S., whichever is applicable.

(j) (I) To disseminate public health information;

(II) To provide poison control services, for the fiscal year beginning July 1, 2002, and fiscal years thereafter, on a statewide basis and to provide for the dissemination of information concerning the care and treatment of individuals exposed to poisonous substances pursuant to article 32 of this title;

(k) To establish and enforce standards for exposure to toxic materials in the gaseous, liquid, or solid phase that may be deemed necessary for the protection of public health;

(l) To establish and enforce standards for exposure to environmental conditions, including radiation, that may be deemed necessary for the protection of the public health;

(m) (I) To accept and expend on behalf of and in the name of the state, gifts, donations, and grants for any purpose connected with the work and programs of the department.

(II) Any such property so given shall be held by the state treasurer, but the department shall have the power to direct the disposition of any property so given for any purpose consistent with the terms and conditions under which such gift was created.

(n) To carry out the policies of the state as set forth in part 1 of article 6 of this title with respect to family planning;

(o) To carry out the policies of this state relating to the "Colorado Health Care Coverage Act" as set forth in parts 1 and 4 of article 16 of title 10, C.R.S.;

(p) To compile and maintain current information necessary to enable the department to answer any inquiry concerning the proper action to take to counteract, eliminate, or minimize the public health hazards of a hazardous substance incident involving any specific kind of hazardous substance. To make such information available and to facilitate the reporting of hazardous substance incidents, the department shall establish, maintain, and publicize an environmental emergency telephone service that shall be available to the public twenty-four hours each day. With respect to the powers and duties specified in this paragraph (p), the department shall have no rule-making authority and shall avail itself of all available private resources. As used in this paragraph (p), the terms "hazardous substance" and "hazardous substance incident" shall have the meanings ascribed to them in section 29-22-101, C.R.S. The department shall coordinate its activities pursuant to this section with the Colorado state patrol.

(q) (I) To establish and maintain a statewide cancer registry providing for compilation and analysis of appropriate information regarding incidence, diagnosis, treatment, and end results and any other data designed to provide more effective cancer control for the citizens of Colorado.

(II) For the purposes of this paragraph (q), the board is authorized to require reports relating to cancer in accordance with the provisions of section 25-1-122 and to have access to medical records relating to cancer in accordance with the provisions of section 25-1-122.

(r) To operate and maintain a program for children with disabilities to provide and expedite provision of health care services to children who have congenital birth defects or who are the victims of burns or trauma or children who have acquired disabilities;

(s) To annually enter into an agreement with a qualified person to perform necessary hazardous substance incident response actions when such actions are beyond the ability of the local and state response capabilities. Such response actions may include, but are not limited to, containment, clean-up, and disposal of a hazardous substance. Nothing in this article shall prevent the attorney general's office from pursuing cost recovery against responsible persons.

(t) To operate special health programs for migrant and seasonal farm workers and their dependent family members and to accept and employ federal and other moneys appropriated to implement such programs;

(u) To carry out the duties prescribed in article 11.5 of title 16, C.R.S., relating to substance abuse in the criminal justice system;

(v) To establish and maintain a statewide gulf war syndrome registry pursuant to part 19 of article 4 of this title providing for compilation and analysis of information regarding incidence, diagnosis, treatment, and treatment outcomes of veterans or family members of veterans suffering from gulf war syndrome;

(w) (I) To act as the coordinator for suicide prevention programs throughout the state, including the Colorado suicide prevention plan established in section 25-1.5-112.

(II) The department is authorized to accept gifts, grants, and donations to assist it in performing its duties as the coordinator for suicide prevention programs. All such gifts, grants, and donations shall be transmitted to the state treasurer who shall credit the same to the suicide prevention coordination cash fund, which fund is hereby created. The fund also consists of any money appropriated or transferred to the fund by the general assembly for the purposes of implementing section 25-1.5-112. Any moneys remaining in the suicide prevention coordination cash fund at the end of any fiscal year shall remain in the fund and shall not be transferred or credited to the general fund. The general assembly shall make appropriations from the suicide prevention coordination cash fund for expenditures incurred by the department in the performance of its duties under this paragraph (w) and section 25-1.5-112.

(III) (A) Notwithstanding section 24-1-136 (11) (a) (I) , as part of its duties as coordinator for suicide prevention programs, on or before each November 1, the department shall submit to the chairs of the senate health and human services committee and the house of representatives health, insurance, and environment committee, or their successor committees, and to the members of the joint budget committee, a report listing all suicide prevention programs in the state and describing the effectiveness of the department acting as the coordinator for suicide prevention programs. For the report submitted in 2013 and each year thereafter, the department shall include any findings and recommendations it has to improve suicide prevention in the state.

(B) (Deleted by amendment, L. 2012.)

(IV) In its role as coordinator for suicide prevention programs, the department may collaborate with each facility licensed or certified pursuant to section 25-1.5-103 in order to coordinate suicide prevention services, including relevant training and other services as part of the Colorado suicide prevention plan established in section 25-1.5-112. When a facility treats a person who has attempted suicide or exhibits a suicidal gesture, the facility may provide oral and written information or educational materials to the person or, in the case of a minor, to parents, relatives, or other responsible persons to whom the minor will be released, prior to the person's release, regarding warning signs of depression, risk factors of suicide, methods of preventing suicide, available suicide prevention resources, and any other information concerning suicide awareness and prevention. The department may work with facilities and the Colorado suicide prevention plan to determine whether and where gaps exist in suicide prevention programs and services, including gaps that may be present in:

(A) The information and materials being used and distributed in facilities throughout the state;

(B) Resources available to persons who attempt suicide or exhibit a suicidal gesture and, when the person is a minor, to parents, relatives, and other responsible persons to whom a minor is released; and

(C) The process for referring persons who attempt suicide or exhibit a suicidal gesture to suicide prevention services and programs or other appropriate health care providers for treatment.

(x) To implement the state dental loan repayment program created in article 23 of this title;

(y) To coordinate with the United States secretary of the interior and the United States secretary of agriculture to develop resource management plans consistent with this article for federal lands pursuant to 16 U.S.C. sec. 530, 16 U.S.C. sec. 1604, and 43 U.S.C. sec. 1712;

(z) To perform the duties specified in part 6 of article 10 of title 30, C.R.S., relating to the Colorado coroners standards and training board;

(aa) To determine if there is a shortage of drugs critical to the public safety of the people of Colorado and declare an emergency for the purpose of preventing the practice of unfair drug pricing as prohibited by section 6-1-714, C.R.S.;

(bb) To include on its public website home page a link to forms containing advanced directives regarding a person's acceptance or rejection of life-sustaining medical or surgical treatment, which forms are available to be downloaded electronically.

## 25-1.5-102. Epidemic and communicable diseases - powers and duties of department.

(1) The department has, in addition to all other powers and duties imposed upon it by law, the powers and duties provided in this section as follows:

(a) (I) To investigate and control the causes of epidemic and communicable diseases affecting the public health.

(II) For the purposes of this paragraph (a) , the board shall determine, by rule and regulation, those epidemic and communicable diseases and conditions that are dangerous to the public health. The board is authorized to require reports relating to such designated diseases in accordance with the provisions of section 25-1-122 and to have access to medical records relating to such designated diseases in accordance with the provisions of section 25-1-122.

(III) For the purposes of this paragraph (a) , "epidemic diseases" means cases of an illness or condition, communicable or noncommunicable, in excess of normal expectancy, compared to the usual frequency of the illness or condition in the same area, among the specified population, at the same season of the year. A single case of a disease long absent from a population may require immediate investigation.

(IV) For the purposes of this paragraph (a) , "communicable diseases" means an illness due to a specific infectious agent or its toxic products that arises through transmission of that agent or its products from an infected person, animal, or reservoir to a susceptible host, either directly or indirectly through an intermediate plant or animal host, vector, or the inanimate environment.

(b) (I) To investigate and monitor the spread of disease that is considered part of an emergency epidemic as defined in section 24-33.5-703 (4) , C.R.S., to determine the extent of environmental contamination resulting from the emergency epidemic, and to rapidly provide epidemiological and environmental information to the governor's expert emergency epidemic response committee, created in section 24-33.5-704 (8) , C.R.S.

(II) Except as otherwise directed by executive order of the governor, the department shall exercise its powers and duties to control epidemic and communicable diseases and protect the public health as set out in this section.

(III) The department may accept and expend federal funds, gifts, grants, and donations for the purposes of an emergency epidemic or preparation for an emergency epidemic.

(IV) When a public safety worker, emergency medical service provider, peace officer, or staff member of a detention facility has been exposed to blood or other bodily fluid which there is a reason to believe may be infectious with hepatitis C, the state department and county, district, and municipal public health agencies within their respective jurisdictions shall assist in evaluation and treatment of any involved persons by:

(A) Accessing information on the incident and any persons involved to determine whether a potential exposure to hepatitis C occurred;

(B) Examining and testing such involved persons to determine hepatitis C infection when the fact of an exposure has been established by the state department or county, district, or municipal public health agency;

(C) Communicating relevant information and laboratory test results on the involved persons to such persons' attending physicians or directly to the involved persons if the confidentiality of such information and test results is acknowledged by the recipients and adequately protected, as determined by the state department or county, district, or municipal public health agency; and

(D) Providing counseling to the involved persons on the potential health risks resulting from exposure and the available methods of treatment.

(V) The employer of an exposed person shall ensure that relevant information and laboratory test results on the involved person are kept confidential. Such information and laboratory results are considered medical information and protected from unauthorized disclosure.

(VI) For purposes of this paragraph (b) , "public safety worker" includes, but is not limited to, law enforcement officers, peace officers, and firefighters.

(c) To establish, maintain, and enforce isolation and quarantine, and, in pursuance thereof and for this purpose only, to exercise such physical control over property and the persons of the people within this state as the department may find necessary for the protection of the public health;

(d) To abate nuisances when necessary for the purpose of eliminating sources of epidemic and communicable diseases affecting the public health.

(2) Notwithstanding any other provision of law to the contrary, the department shall administer the provisions of this section regardless of an individual's race, religion, gender, ethnicity, national origin, or immigration status.

## 25-1.5-103. Health facilities - powers and duties of department - limitations

## on rules promulgated by department - definitions.

(1) The department has, in addition to all other powers and duties imposed upon it by law, the powers and duties provided in this section as follows:

(a) (I) (A) To annually license and to establish and enforce standards for the operation of general hospitals, hospital units as defined in section 25-3-101 (2) , psychiatric hospitals, community clinics, rehabilitation hospitals, convalescent centers, community mental health centers, acute treatment units, facilities for persons with intellectual and developmental disabilities, nursing care facilities, hospice care, assisted living residences, dialysis treatment clinics, ambulatory surgical centers, birthing centers, home care agencies, and other facilities of a like nature, except those wholly owned and operated by any governmental unit or agency.

(B) In establishing and enforcing such standards and in addition to the required announced inspections, the department shall, within available appropriations, make additional inspections without prior notice to the health facility, subject to sub-subparagraph (C) of this subparagraph (I) . Such inspections shall be made only during the hours of 7 a.m. to 7 p.m.

(C) The department shall extend the survey cycle or conduct a tiered inspection or survey of a health facility licensed for at least three years and against which no enforcement activity has been taken, no patterns of deficient practices exist, as documented in the inspection and survey reports issued by the department, and no substantiated complaint resulting in the discovery of significant deficiencies that may negatively affect the life, health, or safety of consumers of the health facility has been received within the three years prior to the date of the inspection. The department may expand the scope of the inspection or survey to an extended or full survey if the department finds deficient practice during the tiered inspection or survey. The department, by rule, shall establish a schedule for an extended survey cycle or a tiered inspection or survey system designed, at a minimum, to: Reduce the time needed for and costs of licensure inspections for both the department and the licensed health facility; reduce the number, frequency, and duration of on-site inspections; reduce the scope of data and information that health facilities are required to submit or provide to the department in connection with the licensure inspection; reduce the amount and scope of duplicative data, reports, and information required to complete the licensure inspection; and be based on a sample of the facility size. Nothing in this sub-subparagraph (C) limits the ability of the department to conduct a periodic inspection or survey that is required to meet its obligations as a state survey agency on behalf of the centers for medicare and medicaid services or the department of health care policy and financing to assure that the health facility meets the requirements for participation in the medicare and medicaid programs.

(D) In connection with the renewal of licenses issued pursuant to this subparagraph (I) , the department shall institute a performance incentive system pursuant to section 25-3-105 (1) (a) (I) (C) .

(E) The department shall not cite as a deficiency in a report resulting from a survey or inspection of a licensed health facility any deficiency from an isolated event identified by the department that can be effectively remedied during the survey or inspection of the health facility, unless the deficiency caused harm or a potential for harm, created a life- or limb-threatening emergency, or was due to abuse or neglect.

(F) Sections 24-4-104, C.R.S., and 25-3-102 govern the issuance, suspension, renewal, revocation, annulment, or modification of licenses. All licenses issued by the department must contain the date of issue and cover a twelve-month period. Nothing contained in this paragraph (a) prevents the department from adopting and enforcing, with respect to projects for which federal assistance has been obtained or is requested, higher standards as may be required by applicable federal laws or regulations of federal agencies responsible for the administration of applicable federal laws.

(II) To establish and enforce standards for the operation and maintenance of the health facilities named in subparagraph (I) of this paragraph (a) , wholly owned and operated by the state or any of its political subdivisions, and no such facility shall be operated or maintained without an annual certificate of compliance;

(b) To suspend, revoke, or refuse to renew any license issued to a health facility pursuant to subparagraph (I) or (II) of paragraph (a) of this subsection (1) if such health facility has committed abuse of health insurance pursuant to section 18-13-119, C.R.S., or if such health facility has advertised through newspapers, magazines, circulars, direct mail, directories, radio, television, or otherwise that it will perform any act prohibited by section 18-13-119 (3) , C.R.S., unless the health facility is exempted from section 18-13-119 (5) , C.R.S.;

(c) (I) To establish and enforce standards for licensure of community mental health centers and acute treatment units.

(II) The department of public health and environment has primary responsibility for the licensure of community mental health centers and acute treatments units. The department of human services has primary responsibility for program approval at these facilities. In performing their respective responsibilities pursuant to this subparagraph (II) , both departments shall take into account changes in health care policy and practice incorporating the concept and practice of integration of services and the development of a system that commingles and integrates health care services.

(2) For purposes of this section, unless the context otherwise requires:

(a) "Acute treatment unit" means a facility or a distinct part of a facility for short-term psychiatric care, which may include substance abuse treatment, and which provides a total, twenty-four-hour therapeutically planned and professionally staffed environment for persons who do not require inpatient hospitalization but need more intense and individual services than are available on an outpatient basis, such as crisis management and stabilization services.

(a.5) "Community clinic" has the same meaning as set forth in section 25-3-101 and does not include:

(I) A federally qualified health center, as defined in section 1861 (aa) (4) of the federal "Social Security Act", 42 U.S.C. sec. 1395x (aa) (4) ;

(II) A rural health clinic, as defined in section 1861 (aa) (2) of the federal "Social Security Act", 42 U.S.C. sec. 1395x (aa) (2) .

(b) "Community mental health center" means either a physical plant or a group of services under unified administration and including at least the following: Inpatient services; outpatient services; day hospitalization; emergency services; and consultation and educational services, which services are provided principally for persons with behavioral or mental health disorders residing in a particular community in or near which the facility is situated.

(b.5) "Enforcement activity" means the imposition of remedies such as civil money penalties; appointment of a receiver or temporary manager; conditional licensure; suspension or revocation of a license; a directed plan of correction; intermediate restrictions or conditions, including retaining a consultant, department monitoring, or providing additional training to employees, owners, or operators; or any other remedy provided by state or federal law or as authorized by federal survey, certification, and enforcement regulations and agreements for violations of federal or state law.

(c) "Facility for persons with developmental disabilities" means a facility specially designed for the active treatment and habilitation of persons with intellectual and developmental disabilities or a community residential home, as defined in section 25.5-10-202, C.R.S., which is licensed and certified pursuant to section 25.5-10-214, C.R.S.

(d) "Hospice care" means an entity that administers services to a terminally ill person utilizing palliative care or treatment.

(3) (a) In the exercise of its powers pursuant to this section, the department shall not promulgate any rule, regulation, or standard relating to nursing personnel for rural nursing care facilities, rural intermediate care facilities, and other rural facilities of a like nature more stringent than the applicable federal standards and regulations.

(b) For purposes of this subsection (3) , "rural" means:

(I) A county of less than fifteen thousand population; or

(II) A municipality of less than fifteen thousand population which is located ten miles or more from a municipality of over fifteen thousand population; or

(III) The unincorporated part of a county ten miles or more from a municipality of fifteen thousand population or more.

(c) A nursing care facility which is not rural as defined in paragraph (b) of this subsection (3) shall meet the licensing requirements of the department for nursing care facilities. However, if a registered nurse hired pursuant to department regulations is temporarily unavailable, a nursing care facility may use a licensed practical nurse in place of a registered nurse if such licensed practical nurse is a current employee of the nursing care facility.

(3.5) (a) (I) The department of public health and environment may establish life safety code and physical plant requirements for an occupancy that is contiguous with an acute treatment unit if the occupancy is operated by the acute treatment unit licensee and the services provided by the occupancy are outpatient services certified in accordance with article 65 of title 27, C.R.S., to determine appropriate placement or detoxification services licensed by the department of human services. The services provided by the occupancy shall benefit acute treatment unit clients, although the occupancy may also provide such services to other populations. It shall be at the discretion of the acute treatment unit licensee to either construct the necessary fire safety separations between the occupancy and the acute treatment unit or to assume fiscal and administrative responsibility for assuring that the occupancy meets the life safety code requirements as specified and verified by the department of public health and environment.

(II) The state board of health may promulgate rules authorizing the department of public health and environment to assess a penalty of up to one hundred dollars per day if the department finds that an occupancy does not comply with life safety code requirements. The department shall only assess the penalty after the acute treatment unit licensee has had an opportunity to correct the noncompliance.

(III) Nothing in this subsection (3.5) shall be construed to extend the life safety code authority of the department of public health and environment to an occupancy that is not subject to licensure by the department and that has the appropriate fire safety separations between the occupancy and the acute treatment unit.

(b) A licensee that is subject to life safety code oversight of one or more occupancies pursuant to paragraph (a) of this subsection (3.5) shall pay a fee or fees in accordance with rules promulgated by the state board of health.

(c) Any moneys collected pursuant to this subsection (3.5) shall be transmitted to the state treasurer, who shall credit the same to the health facilities general licensure cash fund created in section 25-3-103.1.

(4) In the exercise of its powers, the department shall not promulgate any rule, regulation, or standard that limits or interferes with the ability of an individual to enter into a contract with a private pay facility concerning the programs or services provided at the private pay facility. For the purposes of this subsection (4) , "private pay facility" means a skilled nursing facility or intermediate care facility subject to the requirements of section 25-1-120 or an assisted living residence licensed pursuant to section 25-27-105 that is not publicly funded or is not certified to provide services that are reimbursed from state or federal assistance funds.

(5) (a) This subsection (5) applies to construction, including substantial renovation, and ongoing compliance with article 33.5 of title 24, C.R.S., of a health care facility building or structure on or after July 1, 2013. All health facility buildings and structures shall be constructed in conformity with the standards adopted by the director of the division of fire prevention and control in the department of public safety.

(b) Except as provided in paragraph (c) of this subsection (5) but notwithstanding any other provision of law to the contrary, the department shall not issue or renew any license under this article unless the department has received a certificate of compliance from the division of fire prevention and control certifying that the building or structure of the health facility is in conformity with the standards adopted by the director of the division of fire prevention and control.

(c) The department has no authority to establish or enforce standards relating to building or fire codes. All functions, personnel, and property of the department as of June 30, 2013, that are principally directed to the administration, inspection, and enforcement of any building or fire codes or standards shall be transferred to the health facility construction and inspection section of the division of fire prevention and control pursuant to section 24-33.5-1201 (5) , C.R.S.

(d) Notwithstanding any provision of law to the contrary, all health facilities seeking certification pursuant to the federal insurance or assistance provided by Title XIX of the federal "Social Security Act", as amended and commonly known as "medicaid", or the federal insurance or assistance provided by Title XVIII of the federal "Social Security Act", as amended and commonly known as "medicare", or any successor code adopted or promulgated by the appropriate federal authorities, shall continue to meet such certification requirements.

(e) Nothing in this subsection (5) divests the department of the authority to perform health survey work or prevents the department from accessing related funds.

## 25-1.5-104. Regulation of standards relating to food - powers and duties of department.

(1) The department has, in addition to all other powers and duties imposed upon it by law, the powers and duties provided in this section as follows:

(a) To impound any vegetables and other edible crops and meat and animal products intended for and unfit for human consumption, and, upon five days' notice and after affording reasonable opportunity for a hearing to the interested parties, to condemn and destroy the same if deemed necessary for the protection of the public health;

(b) (I) To promulgate and enforce rules, regulations, and standards for the grading, labeling, classification, and composition of milk, milk products, and dairy products, including imitation dairy products; to establish minimum general sanitary standards of quality of all milk, milk products, dairy products, and imitation dairy products sold for human consumption in this state; to inspect and supervise, in dairy plants or dairy farms and in other establishments handling any milk, milk products, dairy products, or imitation dairy products, the sanitation of production, processing, and distribution of all milk, milk products, dairy products, and imitation dairy products sold for human consumption in this state and, to this end, to take samples of milk, milk products, dairy products, and imitation dairy products for bacteriological, chemical, and other analyses; and to enforce the standards for milk, milk products, dairy products, and imitation dairy products in processing plants, dairy farms, and other facilities and establishments handling, transporting, or selling such products; to certify persons licensed by the department under the provisions of section 25-5.5-107 as duly qualified persons for the purpose of collecting raw milk samples for official analyses in accordance with minimum qualifications established by the department; to issue, for the fees established by law, licenses and temporary permits to operate milk plants, dairy plants, receiving stations, dairy farms, and other facilities manufacturing any milk, milk products, dairy products, or imitation dairy products for human consumption.

(II) The phrase "minimum general sanitary standards" as used in this section means the minimum standards reasonably consistent with assuring adequate protection of the public health. The word "standards" as used in this section means standards reasonably designed to promote and protect the public health.

(c) To promulgate and enforce rules and regulations for the labeling and sale of oleomargarine and for the governing of milk- or cream-weighing-and-testing operations;

(d) To approve all oils used in reading tests of samples of cream and milk;

(e) To examine and license persons to sample or test milk, cream, or other dairy products for the purpose of determining the value of such products or to instruct other persons in the sampling and testing of such products and to cancel licenses issued by the department on account of incompetency or any violation of the provisions of the dairy laws or the rules and regulations promulgated by the board;

(f) To license manufacturers of oleomargarine;

(g) To establish and enforce sanitary standards for the operation of slaughtering, packing, canning, and rendering establishments and stores, shops, and vehicles wherein meat and animal products intended for human consumption may be offered for sale or transported, but this shall not be construed to authorize any state officer or employee to interfere with regulations or inspections

68

made by anyone acting under the laws of the United States.

## 25-1.5-105. Detection of diseases - powers and duties of department.

(1) The department has, in addition to all other powers and duties imposed upon it by law, the powers and duties provided in this section as follows:

(a) To establish and operate programs which the department determines are important in promoting, protecting, and maintaining the public's health by preventing, delaying, or detecting the onset of environmental and chronic diseases;

(b) To develop and maintain a system for detecting and monitoring environmental and chronic diseases within the state and to investigate and determine the epidemiology of those conditions which contribute to preventable or premature sickness and to death and disability;

(c) To establish programs of community and professional education relevant to the detection, prevention, and control of environmental and chronic diseases.

(2) For purposes of this section, "chronic disease" means impairment or deviation from the normal functioning of the human body which:

(a) Is permanent;

(b) Leaves residual disability;

(c) Is caused by nonreversible pathological alterations;

(d) Requires special patient education and instruction for rehabilitation; or

(e) May require a long period of supervision, observation, and care.

(3) For the purposes of this section, "environmental disease" means an impairment or deviation from the normal functioning of the human body which:

(a) May be either temporary or permanent;

(b) May leave residual disability;

(c) May result in birth defects, damage to tissues and organs, and chronic illness; and

(d) Is caused by exposure to hazardous chemical or radiological materials present in the environment.

(4) For the purposes of this section, the board shall determine, by rule and regulation, those environmental and chronic diseases that are dangerous to the public health. The board is authorized to require reports relating to such designated diseases in accordance with the provisions of section 25-1-122 and to have access to medical records relating to such designated diseases in accordance with the provisions of section 25-1-122.

## 25-1.5-106. Medical marijuana program - powers and duties of state health agency - rules - medical review board - medical marijuana program cash fund - subaccount - created - repeal.

(1) Legislative declaration. (a) The general assembly hereby declares that it is necessary to implement rules to ensure that patients suffering from legitimate debilitating medical conditions are able to safely gain access to medical marijuana and to ensure that these patients:

(I) Are not subject to criminal prosecution for their use of medical marijuana in accordance with section 14 of article XVIII of the state constitution, this section, and the rules of the state health agency; and

(II) Are able to establish an affirmative defense to their use of medical marijuana in accordance with section 14 of article XVIII of the state constitution, this section, and the rules of the state health agency.

(b) The general assembly hereby declares that it is necessary to implement rules to prevent persons who do not suffer from legitimate debilitating medical conditions from using section 14 of article XVIII of the state constitution as a means to sell, acquire, possess, produce, use, or transport marijuana in violation of state and federal laws.

(c) The general assembly hereby declares that it is necessary to implement rules to provide guidance for caregivers as defined in section 14 of article XVIII of the state constitution.

(d) The general assembly hereby declares that it is imperative to prevent the diversion of medical marijuana to other states. In order to do this the general assembly needs to provide clear guidance for law enforcement.

(2) Definitions. In addition to the definitions set forth in section 14 (1) of article XVIII of the state constitution, as used in this section, unless the context otherwise requires:

(a) "Authorized employees of the state health agency" includes independent contractors or other agencies with whom the state health agency contracts or is working under an intergovernmental agreement to provide services related to the administration of the medical marijuana program registry. These independent contractors are not state employees for the purposes of state employee benefits, including public employees' retirement association benefits.

(a.5) "Bona fide physician-patient relationship", for purposes of the medical marijuana program, means:

(I) A physician and a patient have a treatment or counseling relationship, in the course of which the physician has completed a full assessment of the patient's medical history, including reviewing a previous diagnosis for a debilitating or disabling medical condition, and current medical condition, including an appropriate personal physical examination;

(II) The physician has consulted with the patient with respect to the patient's debilitating medical condition or disabling medical condition before the patient applies for a registry identification card; and

(III) The physician is available to or offers to provide follow-up care and treatment to the patient, including patient examinations, to determine the efficacy of the use of medical marijuana as a treatment of the patient's debilitating medical condition or disabling medical condition.

(a.7) "Disabling medical condition" means post-traumatic stress disorder as diagnosed by a licensed mental health provider or physician.

(b) "Executive director" means the executive director of the state health agency.

(c) "In good standing", with respect to a physician's license, means:

(I) The physician holds a doctor of medicine or doctor of osteopathic medicine degree from an accredited medical school;

(II) The physician holds a valid license to practice medicine in Colorado that does not contain a restriction or condition that prohibits the recommendation of medical marijuana or for a license issued prior to July 1, 2011, a valid, unrestricted and unconditioned license; and

(III) The physician has a valid and unrestricted United States department of justice federal drug enforcement administration controlled substances registration.

(d) "Medical marijuana program" means the program established by section 14 of article XVIII of the state constitution and this section.

(d.3) "Patient" means a person who has a debilitating medical condition or disabling medical condition.

(d.5) "Primary caregiver" means a natural person, other than the patient or the patient's physician, who is eighteen years of age or older and has significant responsibility for managing the well-being of a patient who has a debilitating medical condition or disabling medical condition. A primary caregiver may have one or more of the following relationships:

(I) A parent of a child as described by subsection (6) (e) of section 14 of article XVIII of the Colorado constitution and anyone who assists that parent with caregiver responsibilities, including cultivation and transportation;

(II) An advising caregiver who advises a patient on which medical marijuana products to use and how to dose them and does not possess, provide, cultivate, or transport marijuana on behalf of the patient;

(III) A transporting caregiver who purchases and transports marijuana to a patient who is homebound; or

(IV) A cultivating caregiver who grows marijuana for a patient.

(e) "Registry identification card" means the nontransferable confidential registry identification card issued by the state health agency to patients and primary caregivers pursuant to this section.

(e.3) [Editor's note:Paragraph (e.3) is effective January 1, 2018.]"Residential property" means a single unit providing complete independent living facilities for one or more persons, including permanent provisions for living, sleeping, eating, cooking, and sanitation. "Residential property" also includes the real property surrounding a structure, owned in common with the structure, that includes one or more single units providing complete independent living facilities.

(e.5) "Significant responsibility for managing the well-being of a patient" means that the caregiver is involved in basic or instrumental activities of daily living. Cultivating or transporting marijuana and the act of advising a patient on which medical marijuana products to use and how to dose them constitutes a "significant responsibility".

(f) "State health agency" means the public health-related entity of state government designated by the governor by executive order pursuant to section 14 of article XVIII of the state constitution.

(2.5) (a) Except as otherwise provided in subsections (2.5) (h) and (2.5) (i) of this section and section 18-18-406.3, a patient with a disabling medical condition or his or her primary caregiver charged with a violation of the state's criminal laws related to the patient's medical use of marijuana will be deemed to have established an affirmative defense to such allegation where:

(I) The patient was previously diagnosed by a physician as having a disabling medical condition;

(II) The patient was advised by his or her physician, in the context of a bona fide physician-patient relationship, that the patient might benefit from the medical use of marijuana in connection with a disabling medical condition; and

(III) The patient and his or her primary caregiver were collectively in possession of amounts of marijuana only as permitted under this section.

(b) The affirmative defense in subsection (2.5) (a) of this section does not exclude the assertion of any other defense where a patient or primary caregiver is charged with a violation of state law related to the patient's medical use of marijuana.

(c) It is an exception from the state's criminal laws for any patient with a disabling medical condition or his or her primary caregiver in lawful possession of a registry identification card to engage or assist in the medical use of marijuana, except as otherwise provided in subsection (2.5) (h) of this section or section 18-18-406.3.

(d) It is an exception from the state's criminal laws for any physician to:

(I) Advise a patient whom the physician has diagnosed as having a disabling medical condition about the risks and benefits of the medical use of marijuana or that he or she might benefit from the medical use of marijuana, provided that such advice is based upon the physician's contemporaneous assessment of the patient's medical history and current medical condition and a bona fide physician-patient relationship; or

(II) Provide a patient with written documentation, based upon the physician's contemporaneous assessment of the patient's medical history and current medical condition and a bona fide physician-patient relationship, stating that the patient has a disabling medical condition and might benefit from the medical use of marijuana. No physician shall be denied any rights or privileges for the acts authorized by this section.

(e) Notwithstanding the foregoing provisions, no person, including a patient with a disabling medical condition or his or her primary caregiver, is entitled to the protection of this section for his or her acquisition, possession, manufacture, production, use, sale, distribution, dispensing, or transportation of marijuana for any use other than medical use.

(f) Any property interest that is possessed, owned, or used by a patient with a disabling medical condition or his or her primary caregiver in connection with the medical use of marijuana or acts incidental to such use shall not be harmed, neglected, injured, or destroyed while in the possession of state or local law enforcement officials where such property has been seized in connection with the claimed medical use of marijuana. Any such property interest shall not be forfeited under any provision of state law providing for the forfeiture of property other than as a sentence imposed after conviction of a criminal offense or entry of a plea of guilty to such offense.

(g) (I) A patient with a disabling medical condition may engage in the medical use of marijuana, with no more marijuana than is medically necessary to address a disabling medical condition. The medical use of marijuana by a patient with a disabling medical condition is lawful within the following limits:

(A) No more than two ounces of a usable form of marijuana; and

(B) No more than six marijuana plants, with three or fewer being mature, flowering plants that are producing a usable form of marijuana.

(II) For quantities of marijuana in excess of these amounts, a patient or his or her primary caregiver may raise as an affirmative defense to charges of violation of state law that such greater amounts were medically necessary to address the patient's disabling medical condition.

(h) (I) No patient with a disabling medical condition shall:

(A) Engage in the medical use of marijuana in a way that endangers the health or well-being of any person; or

(B) Engage in the medical use of marijuana in plain view of, or in a place open to, the general public.

(II) In addition to any other penalties provided by law, the state health agency shall revoke for a period of one year the registry identification card of any patient found to have willfully violated the provisions of this section.

(i) Notwithstanding the provisions of this subsection (2.5) , no patient with a disabling medical condition who is under eighteen years of age shall engage in the medical use of marijuana unless:

(I) Two physicians, one of whom must be a board-certified pediatrician, a board-certified family physician, or a board-certified child and adolescent psychiatrist and attest that he or she is part of the patient's primary care provider team, have diagnosed the patient as having a disabling medical condition;

(II) One of the physicians referred to in subsection (2.5) (i) (I) of this section has explained the possible risks and benefits of the medical use of marijuana to the patient and each of the patient's parents residing in Colorado;

(III) The physician referred to in subsection (2.5) (i) (II) of this section has provided the patient with the written documentation specifying that the patient has been diagnosed with a disabling medical condition and the physician has concluded that the patient might benefit from the medical use of marijuana;

(IV) Each of the patient's parents residing in Colorado consent in writing to the state health agency to permit the patient to engage in the medical use of marijuana;

(V) A parent residing in Colorado consents in writing to serve as the patient's primary caregiver;

(VI) A parent serving as a primary caregiver completes and submits an application for a registry identification card and the written consents referred to in subsections (2.5) (i) (IV) and (2.5) (i) (V) of this section to the state health agency;

(VII) The state health agency approves the patient's application and transmits the patient's registry identification card to the parent designated as a primary caregiver;

(VIII) The patient and primary caregiver collectively possess amounts of marijuana no greater than those specified in subsection (2.5) (g) of this section; and

(IX) The primary caregiver controls the acquisition of such marijuana and the dosage and frequency of its use by the patient with a disabling medical condition.

(3) Rule-making. (a) The state health agency shall, pursuant to section 14 of article XVIII of the state constitution, promulgate rules of administration concerning the implementation of the medical marijuana program that specifically govern the following:

(I) The establishment and maintenance of a confidential registry of patients who have applied for and are entitled to receive a registry identification card. The confidential registry of patients may be used to determine whether a physician should be referred to the Colorado board of medical examiners for a suspected violation of section 14 of article XVIII of the state constitution, paragraph (a) , (b) , or (c) of subsection (5) of this section, or the rules promulgated by the state health agency pursuant to this subsection (3) .

(II) The development by the state health agency of an application form and the process for making the form available to residents of this state seeking to be listed on the confidential registry of patients who are entitled to receive a registry identification card;

(III) The verification by the state health agency of medical information concerning patients who have applied for a registry identification card or for renewal of a registry identification card;

(IV) The development by the state health agency of a form that constitutes "written documentation" as defined and used in section 14 of article XVIII of the state constitution, which form a physician shall use when making a medical marijuana recommendation for a patient;

(V) The conditions for issuance and renewal, and the form, of the registry identification cards issued to patients, including but not limited to standards for ensuring that the state health agency issues a registry identification card to a patient only if he or she has a bona fide physician-patient relationship with a physician in good standing and licensed to practice medicine in the state of Colorado;

(VI) Communications with law enforcement officials about registry identification cards that have been suspended when a patient is no longer diagnosed as having a debilitating medical condition or disabling medical condition;

(VII) The manner in which the state health agency may consider adding debilitating medical conditions to the list of debilitating medical conditions contained in section 14 of article XVIII of the state constitution;

(VIII) A waiver process to allow a homebound patient who is on the registry to have a primary caregiver transport the patient's medical marijuana from a licensed medical marijuana center to the patient; and

(IX) Guidelines for primary caregivers to give informed consent to patients that the products they cultivate or produce may contain contaminants and that the cannabinoid levels may not be verified.

(b) The state health agency may promulgate rules regarding the following:

(I) Repealed.

(II) The development of a form for a primary caregiver to use in applying to the registry, which form shall require, at a minimum, that the applicant provide his or her full name, home address, date of birth, and an attestation that the applicant has a significant responsibility for managing the well-being of the patient for whom he or she is designated as the primary caregiver and that he or she understands and will abide by section 14 of article XVIII of the state constitution, this section, and the rules promulgated by the state health agency pursuant to this section;

(III) The development of a form that constitutes "written documentation", as defined and used in section 14 of article XVIII of the state constitution, which form a physician shall use when making a medical marijuana recommendation for a patient; and

(IV) The grounds and procedure for a patient to change his or her designated primary caregiver.

(c) Repealed.

(3.5) Marijuana laboratory testing reference library. (a) The state health agency shall develop and maintain a marijuana laboratory testing reference library. Laboratories licensed by the department of revenue shall be required to provide materials for the reference library; except that no licensee shall be required to provide testing protocols.

(b) The reference library must contain a library of methodologies for marijuana testing in the areas of potency, homogeneity, contaminants, and solvents consistent with the laboratory requirements set by the department of revenue pursuant to article 43.3 or 43.4 of title 12, C.R.S.

(c) The state health agency may also include in the reference library standard sample attainment procedures and standards related to sample preparation for laboratory analysis.

(d) The state health agency shall make reference library materials, including the methodologies, publicly available no later than December 31, 2015, and may continuously update the reference library as new materials become available.

(3.7) The state health agency shall convene a group of interested parties including representatives from the state licensing authority, primary caregivers, patients, marijuana testing laboratory licensees, and any other interested persons to explore laboratory testing options for medical marijuana not produced by someone licensed pursuant to article 43.3 of title 12, C.R.S.

(3.8) (a) The state health agency or an organization with whom the state health agency contracts shall be responsible for proficiency testing and remediating problems with laboratories licensed pursuant to article 43.3 or 43.4 of title 12, C.R.S.

(b) The state health agency shall convene a stakeholder process to discuss proposed models for sampling and proficiency testing. The stakeholder process shall be completed by September 1,

2015.

(4) Notwithstanding any other requirements to the contrary, notice issued by the state health agency for a rule-making hearing pursuant to section 24-4-103, C.R.S., for rules concerning the medical marijuana program shall be sufficient if the state health agency provides the notice no later than forty-five days in advance of the rule-making hearing in at least one publication in a newspaper of general distribution in the state and posts the notice on the state health agency's website; except that emergency rules pursuant to section 24-4-103 (6) , C.R.S., shall not require advance notice.

(5) Physicians. A physician who certifies a debilitating medical condition or disabling medical condition for an applicant to the medical marijuana program shall comply with all of the following requirements:

(a) The physician shall have a valid and active license to practice medicine, which license is in good standing.

(b) After a physician, who has a bona fide physician-patient relationship with the patient applying for the medical marijuana program, determines, for the purposes of making a recommendation, that the patient has a debilitating medical condition or disabling medical condition and that the patient may benefit from the use of medical marijuana, the physician shall certify to the state health agency that the patient has a debilitating medical condition or disabling medical condition and that the patient may benefit from the use of medical marijuana. If the physician certifies that the patient would benefit from the use of medical marijuana based on a chronic or debilitating disease or medical condition or disabling medical condition, the physician shall specify the chronic or debilitating disease or medical condition or disabling medical condition and, if known, the cause or source of the chronic or debilitating disease or medical condition or disabling medical condition.

(c) The physician shall maintain a record-keeping system for all patients for whom the physician has recommended the medical use of marijuana, and, pursuant to an investigation initiated pursuant to section 12-36-118, C.R.S., the physician shall produce such medical records to the Colorado state board of medical examiners after redacting any patient or primary caregiver identifying information.

(d) A physician shall not:

(I) Accept, solicit, or offer any form of pecuniary remuneration from or to a primary caregiver, distributor, or any other provider of medical marijuana;

(II) Offer a discount or any other thing of value to a patient who uses or agrees to use a particular primary caregiver, distributor, or other provider of medical marijuana to procure medical marijuana;

(III) Examine a patient for purposes of diagnosing a debilitating medical condition or a disabling medical condition at a location where medical marijuana is sold or distributed; or

(IV) Hold an economic interest in an enterprise that provides or distributes medical marijuana if the physician certifies the debilitating medical condition or disabling medical condition of a patient for participation in the medical marijuana program.

(6) Enforcement. (a) If the state health agency has reasonable cause to believe that a physician has violated section 14 of article XVIII of the state constitution, paragraph (a) , (b) , or (c) of subsection (5) of this section, or the rules promulgated by the state health agency pursuant to subsection (2) of this section, the state health agency may refer the matter to the state board of medical examiners created in section 12-36-103, C.R.S., for an investigation and determination.

(b) If the state health agency has reasonable cause to believe that a physician has violated paragraph (d) of subsection (5) of this section, the state health agency shall conduct a hearing pursuant to section 24-4-104, C.R.S., to determine whether a violation has occurred.

(c) Upon a finding of unprofessional conduct pursuant to section 12-36-117 (1) (mm) , C.R.S., by the state board of medical examiners or a finding of a violation of paragraph (d) of subsection (5) of this section by the state health agency, the state health agency shall restrict a physician's authority to recommend the use of medical marijuana, which restrictions may include the revocation or suspension of a physician's privilege to recommend medical marijuana. The restriction shall be in addition to any sanction imposed by the state board of medical examiners.

(d) When the state health agency has objective and reasonable grounds to believe and finds, upon a full investigation, that a physician has deliberately and willfully violated section 14 of article XVIII of the state constitution or this section and that the public health, safety, or welfare imperatively requires emergency action, and the state health agency incorporates those findings into an order, the state health agency may summarily suspend the physician's authority to recommend the use of medical marijuana pending the proceedings set forth in paragraphs (a) and (b) of this subsection (6) . A hearing on the order of summary suspension shall be held no later than thirty days after the issuance of the order of summary suspension, unless a longer time is agreed to by the parties, and an initial decision in accordance with section 24-4-105 (14) , C.R.S., shall be rendered no later than thirty days after the conclusion of the hearing concerning the order of summary suspension.

(7) Primary caregivers. (a) A primary caregiver may not delegate to any other person his or her authority to provide medical marijuana to a patient; nor may a primary caregiver engage others to assist in providing medical marijuana to a patient; except that a parent primary caregiver may use the services of an assistant for advisement, cultivation, or transportation.

(b) Two or more primary caregivers shall not join together for the purpose of cultivating medical marijuana.

(c) Only a medical marijuana center with an optional premises cultivation license, a medical marijuana-infused products manufacturing operation with an optional premises cultivation license, or a primary caregiver for his or her patients or a patient for himself or herself may cultivate or provide medical marijuana.

(d) A primary caregiver shall provide to a law enforcement agency, upon inquiry, the registry identification card number of each of his or her patients. The state health agency shall maintain a registry of this information and make it available twenty-four hours per day and seven days a week to law enforcement for verification purposes. Upon inquiry by a law enforcement officer as to an individual's status as a patient or primary caregiver, the state health agency shall check the registry. If the individual is not registered as a patient or primary caregiver, the state health agency may provide that response to law enforcement. If the person is a registered patient or primary caregiver, the state health agency may not release information unless consistent with section 14 of article XVIII of the state constitution. The state health agency may promulgate rules to provide for the efficient administration of this paragraph (d) .

(e) (I) (A) [Editor's note:This version of sub-subparagraph (A) is effective until January 1, 2018.]In order to be a primary caregiver who cultivates medical marijuana for his or her patients or transports medical marijuana for his or her patients, he or she shall also register with the state licensing authority. A person may not register as a primary caregiver if he or she is licensed as a medical marijuana business as described in part 4 of article 43.3 of title 12, C.R.S., or a retail marijuana business as described in part 4 of article 43.4 of title 12, C.R.S. An employee, contractor, or other support staff employed by a licensed entity pursuant to article 43.3 or 43.4 of title 12, C.R.S., or working in or having access to a restricted area of a licensed premises pursuant to article 43.3 or 43.4 of title 12, C.R.S., may be a primary caregiver.

(A) [Editor's note:This version of sub-subparagraph (A) is effective January 1, 2018.]In order to be a primary caregiver who cultivates medical marijuana for his or her patients or transports medical marijuana for his or her patients, he or she shall also register with the state licensing authority and comply with all local laws, regulations, and zoning and use restrictions. A person may not register as a primary caregiver if he or she is licensed as a medical marijuana business as described in part 4 of article 43.3 of title 12 or a retail marijuana business as described in part 4 of article 43.4 of title 12. An employee, contractor, or other support staff employed by a licensed entity pursuant to article 43.3 or 43.4 of title 12, or working in or having access to a restricted area of a licensed premises pursuant to article 43.3 or 43.4 of title 12, may be a primary caregiver.

(B) A cultivating primary caregiver, when registering, shall provide the cultivation operation location, the registration number of each patient, and any extended plant count numbers and their corresponding patient registry numbers.

(C) A transporting primary caregiver, when registering, shall provide the registration number of each homebound patient, the total number of plants and ounces that the caregiver is authorized to transport, if applicable, and the location of each patient's registered medical marijuana center or cultivating primary caregiver, as applicable. A transporting caregiver shall have on his or her person a receipt from the medical marijuana center or primary caregiver when transporting medical marijuana that shows the quantity of medical marijuana purchased by or provided to the transporting caregiver.

(D) The state licensing authority may verify patient registration numbers and extended plant count numbers with the state health agency to confirm that a patient does not have more than one primary caregiver, or does not have both a designated caregiver and medical marijuana center, cultivating medical marijuana on his or her behalf at any given time.

(E) If a peace officer makes a law enforcement contact with a primary caregiver who does not have proper documentation showing registration with the state licensing authority, the peace officer may report that individual to the state licensing authority or may take appropriate law enforcement action. The person may be subject to any chargeable criminal offenses.

(II) The state licensing authority shall share the minimum necessary information in accordance with applicable federal and state laws, such as patient and caregiver identification numbers, to verify that a patient has only one entity cultivating medical marijuana on his or her behalf at any given time.

(III) The information provided to the state licensing authority pursuant to this paragraph (e) shall not be provided to the public and is confidential. The state licensing authority shall verify the location of a primary caregiver cultivation operation to a local government or law enforcement agency upon receiving an address-specific request for verification. The location of the cultivation operation must comply with all applicable local laws, rules, or regulations.

(f) A cultivating primary caregiver shall only cultivate plants at the registered cultivation location as required pursuant to paragraph (e) of this subsection (7) and as permitted pursuant to subparagraphs (I) and (II) (B) of paragraph (a) of subsection (8.6) of this section. Nothing in this paragraph (f) shall be construed to limit the ability of the caregiver or person twenty-one years of age or older who makes permanent residence at the registered cultivation location from cultivating or possessing up to six plants pursuant to article XVIII, section 16, of the Colorado constitution. Notwithstanding these provisions, additional cultivation is not lawful at the premises registered by a caregiver to cultivate on behalf of patients.

(8) Patient - primary caregiver relationship. (a) (I) A person shall be listed as a cultivating or transporting primary caregiver for no more than five patients on the medical marijuana program registry at any given time; except that the state health agency may allow a primary caregiver to serve more than five patients in exceptional circumstances. In determining whether exceptional circumstances exist, the state health agency may consider the proximity of medical marijuana centers to the patient, as well as other factors.

(II) A cultivating or transporting primary caregiver shall maintain a list of his or her patients, including the registry identification card number of each patient and a recommended total plant count, at all times.

(b) A patient shall have only one primary caregiver at any given time.

(c) A patient who has designated a primary caregiver for himself or herself may not be designated as a primary caregiver for another patient.

(d) A primary caregiver may not charge a patient more than the cost of cultivating or purchasing the medical marijuana, but may charge for caregiver services.

(e) (I) The state health agency shall maintain a secure and confidential registry of available primary caregivers for those patients who are unable to secure the services of a primary caregiver.

(II) An existing primary caregiver may indicate at the time of registration whether he or she would be willing to handle additional patients and waive confidentiality to allow release of his or her contact information to physicians or registered patients only.

(III) An individual who is not registered but is willing to provide primary caregiving services may submit his or her contact information to be placed on the primary caregiver registry.

(IV) A patient-primary caregiver arrangement secured pursuant to this paragraph (e) shall be strictly between the patient and the potential primary caregiver. The state health agency, by providing the information required by this paragraph (e) , shall not endorse or vouch for a primary caregiver.

(V) The state health agency may make an exception, based on a request from a patient, to paragraph (a) of this subsection (8) limiting primary caregivers to five patients. If the state health agency makes an exception to the limit, the state health agency shall note the exception on the primary caregiver's record in the registry.

(f) At the time a patient applies for inclusion on the confidential registry, the patient shall indicate whether the patient intends to cultivate his or her own medical marijuana, both cultivate his or her own medical marijuana and obtain it from either a primary caregiver or licensed medical marijuana center, or obtain it from either a primary caregiver or a licensed medical marijuana center. If the patient elects to use a licensed medical marijuana center, the patient shall register the primary center he or she intends to use.

(g) Notwithstanding any other provision of law, a primary caregiver shall not grow, sell, or process marijuana for any person unless:

(I) The person is a patient holding a current and valid registry identification card; and

(II) The primary caregiver is currently identified on the medical marijuana registry as that patient's primary caregiver.

(8.5) Encourage patient voluntary registration - plant limits. (a) (I) All patients cultivating more than six medical marijuana plants for their own medical use are encouraged to register with the state licensing authority's registry created pursuant to subsection (7) of this section. A patient who chooses to register shall update his or her registration information upon renewal of his or her medical marijuana registry card.

(II) A patient who chooses to register shall register the following information with the state licensing authority: The location of his or her cultivation operation; his or her patient registration identification; and the total number of plants that the patient is authorized to cultivate.

(a.5) [Editor's note:Paragraph (a.5) is effective January 1, 2018.](I) Unless otherwise expressly authorized by local law, it is unlawful for a patient to possess at or cultivate on a residential property more than twelve marijuana plants regardless of the number of persons residing, either temporarily or permanently, at the property; except that it is unlawful for a patient to possess at or cultivate on or in a residential property more than twenty-four marijuana plants regardless of the number of persons residing, either temporarily or permanently, at the property if a patient:

(A) Lives in a county, municipality, or city and county that does not limit the number of marijuana plants that may be grown on or in a residential property;

(B) Registers pursuant to this subsection (8.5) with the state licensing authority's registry; and

(C) Provides notice to the applicable county, municipality, or city and county of his or her residential cultivation operation if required by the jurisdiction. A local jurisdiction shall not provide the information provided to it pursuant to this subsection (8.5) (a.5) (I) (C) to the public, and the information is confidential.

(II) A patient who cultivates more marijuana plants than permitted in subsection (8.5) (a.5) (I) of this section shall locate his or her cultivation operation on a property, other than a residential property, where marijuana cultivation is allowed by local law and shall comply with any applicable local law requiring disclosure about the cultivation operation. Cultivation operations conducted in a location other than a residential property are subject to any county and municipal building and public health inspection required by local law. A person who violates this subsection (8.5) (a.5) is subject to the offenses and penalties described in section 18-18-406.

(b) A patient shall not cultivate more than ninety-nine plants. Only a medical marijuana business licensed and properly authorized pursuant to article 43.3 of title 12, C.R.S., may cultivate more than ninety-nine plants.

(b.5) [Editor's note:Paragraph (b.5) is effective January 1, 2018.]A patient who cultivates his or her own medical marijuana plants shall comply with all local laws, regulations, and zoning and use restrictions.

(c) The information provided to the state licensing authority pursuant to this subsection (8.5) shall not be provided to the public and is confidential. The state licensing authority shall verify the location of a medical marijuana cultivation site for patient cultivation operations to a local government or law enforcement agency upon receiving a request for verification. The location of the cultivation operation shall comply with all applicable local laws, rules, or regulations.

(d) The state licensing authority shall provide cultivation information for patients who choose to register to state and local law enforcement through the Colorado crime information center. The Colorado bureau of investigation shall include proper use of medical marijuana information in audits of state and local law enforcement agencies.

(8.6) Primary caregivers plant limits - exceptional circumstances. (a) (I) A primary caregiver shall not cultivate, transport, or possess more than thirty-six plants unless the primary caregiver has one or more patients who, based on medical necessity, have an extended plant count.

(I.5) [Editor's note:Subparagraph (I.5) is effective January 1, 2018.]Unless otherwise expressly authorized by local law, it is unlawful for a primary caregiver to possess at or cultivate on a residential property more than twelve marijuana plants regardless of the number of persons residing, either temporarily or permanently, at the property; except that it is unlawful for a primary caregiver to possess at or cultivate on or in a residential property more than twenty-four marijuana plants regardless of the number of persons residing, either temporarily or permanently, at the property if a primary caregiver:

(A) Lives in a county, municipality, or city and county that does not limit the number of marijuana plants that may be grown on or in a residential property;

(B) Is registered pursuant to this subsection (8.6) with the state licensing authority's registry; and

(C) Provides notice to the applicable county, municipality, or city and county of his or her residential cultivation operation if required by the jurisdiction. A local jurisdiction shall not provide the information provided to it pursuant to this subsection (8.6) (a) (I.5) to the public, and the information is confidential.

(I.6) [Editor's note:Subparagraph (I.6) is effective January 1, 2018.]Any primary caregiver who cultivates more marijuana plants than permitted in subsection (8.6) (a) (I.5) of this section shall locate his or her cultivation operation on a property, other than a residential property, where marijuana cultivation is allowed by local law and shall comply with any applicable local law requiring disclosure about the cultivation operation. Cultivation operations conducted in a location other than a residential property are subject to any county and municipal building and public health inspection required by local law. A person who violates subsection (8.6) (a) (I) of this section is subject to the offenses and penalties described in section 18-18-406.

(II) (A) A primary caregiver who cultivates more than thirty-six plants shall register the information required in sub-subparagraph (B) of this subparagraph (II) with the state licensing authority's registry created pursuant to paragraph (e) of subsection (7) of this section. A primary caregiver shall update his or her registration information upon renewal of his or her primary caregiver registration.

(B) A primary caregiver subject to the registry in this subparagraph (II) shall register the following information with the state licensing authority: The location of his or her cultivation operation; the patient registration identification number for each of the primary caregiver's patients; and any extended plant count numbers and their corresponding patient registry numbers.

(b) A primary caregiver shall not cultivate more than ninety-nine plants. Only a medical marijuana business licensed and properly authorized pursuant to article 43.3 of title 12, C.R.S., may cultivate more than ninety-nine plants. The primary caregiver is not allowed to grow additional plants until he or she is licensed by the state licensing authority.

(c) The information provided to the state licensing authority pursuant to this subsection (8.6) shall not be provided to the public and is confidential. The state licensing authority shall verify the location of extended plant counts for primary caregiver cultivation operations and homebound patient registration for transporting caregivers to a local government or law enforcement agency upon receiving a request for verification. The location of the cultivation operation shall comply with all applicable local laws, rules, or regulations.

(d) The state licensing authority shall provide cultivation information for cultivating caregivers and transporting caregivers to state and local law enforcement through the Colorado crime information center. The Colorado bureau of investigation shall include proper use of medical marijuana information in audits of state and local law enforcement agencies.

(9) Registry identification card required - denial - revocation - renewal. (a) A person with a disabling medical condition may apply to the state health agency for a registry identification card. To be considered in compliance with the provisions of section 14 of article XVIII of the state constitution, this section, and the rules of the state health agency, a patient or primary caregiver shall have his or her registry identification card in his or her possession at all times that he or she is in possession of any form of medical marijuana and produce the same upon request of a law enforcement officer to demonstrate that the patient or primary caregiver is not in violation of the law; except that, if more than thirty-five days have passed since the date the patient or primary caregiver filed his or her medical marijuana program application and the state health agency has not yet issued or denied a registry identification card, a copy of the patient's or primary caregiver's application along with proof of the date of submission shall be in the patient's or primary caregiver's possession at all times that he or she is in possession of any form of medical marijuana until the state health agency issues or denies the registry identification card. A person who violates section 14 of article XVIII of the state constitution, this section, or the rules promulgated by the state health agency may be subject to criminal prosecution for violations of section 18-18-406.

(b) The state health agency may deny a patient's or primary caregiver's application for a registry identification card or revoke the card if the state health agency, in accordance with article 4 of title 24, determines that the physician who diagnosed the patient's debilitating medical condition or disabling medical condition, the patient, or the primary caregiver violated section 14 of article XVIII of the state constitution, this section, or the rules promulgated by the state health agency pursuant to this section; except that, when a physician's violation is the basis for adverse action, the state health agency may only deny or revoke a patient's application or registry identification card when the physician's violation is related to the issuance of a medical marijuana recommendation.

(c) A patient or primary caregiver registry identification card shall be valid for one year and shall contain a unique identification number. It shall be the responsibility of the patient or primary caregiver to apply to renew his or her registry identification card prior to the date on which the card expires. The state health agency shall develop a form for a patient or primary caregiver to use in renewing his or her registry identification card.

(d) If the state health agency grants a patient a waiver to allow a primary caregiver to transport the patient's medical marijuana from a medical marijuana center to the patient, the state health agency shall designate the waiver on the patient's registry identification card.

(e) A homebound patient who receives a waiver from the state health agency to allow a primary caregiver to transport the patient's medical marijuana to the patient from a medical marijuana center shall provide the primary caregiver with the patient's registry identification card, which the primary caregiver shall carry when the primary caregiver is transporting the medical marijuana. A medical marijuana center may provide the medical marijuana to the primary caregiver for transport to the patient if the primary caregiver produces the patient's registry identification card.

(10) Renewal of patient identification card upon criminal conviction. Any patient who is convicted of a criminal offense under article 18 of title 18, who is sentenced or ordered by a court to treatment for a substance use disorder, or sentenced to the division of youth services, is subject to immediate renewal of his or her patient registry identification card, and the patient shall apply for the renewal based upon a recommendation from a physician with whom the patient has a bona fide physician-patient relationship.

(11) A parent who submits a medical marijuana registry application for his or her child shall have his or her signature notarized on the application.

(12) Use of medical marijuana. (a) The use of medical marijuana is allowed under state law to the extent that it is carried out in accordance with the provisions of section 14 of article XVIII of the state constitution, this section, and the rules of the state health agency.

(b) A patient or primary caregiver shall not:

(I) Engage in the medical use of marijuana in a way that endangers the health and well-being of a person;

(II) Engage in the medical use of marijuana in plain view of or in a place open to the general public;

(III) Undertake any task while under the influence of medical marijuana, when doing so would constitute negligence or professional malpractice;

(IV) Possess medical marijuana or otherwise engage in the use of medical marijuana in or on the grounds of a school, in a school bus, or at a school-sponsored event except when the possession or use occurs pursuant to section 22-1-119.3, C.R.S.;

(V) Engage in the use of medical marijuana while:

(A) In a correctional facility or a community corrections facility;

(B) Subject to a sentence to incarceration; or

(C) In a vehicle, aircraft, or motorboat;

(VI) Operate, navigate, or be in actual physical control of any vehicle, aircraft, or motorboat while under the influence of medical marijuana; or

(VII) Use medical marijuana if the person does not have a debilitating medical condition or disabling medical condition as diagnosed by the person's physician in the course of a bona fide physician-patient relationship and for which the physician has recommended the use of medical marijuana.

(c) A person shall not establish a business to permit patients to congregate and smoke or otherwise consume medical marijuana.

(13) Repealed.

(13.5) Nothing herein shall reduce or eliminate the existing power of a statutory municipality or county through the "Local Government Land Use Control Enabling Act of 1974", article 20 of title 29, C.R.S., to regulate the growing of marijuana, commercially or otherwise.

(14) Affirmative defense. If a patient or primary caregiver raises an affirmative defense as provided in section 14 (4) (b) of article XVIII of the state constitution or subsection (2.5) (g) (II) of this section, the patient's physician shall certify the specific amounts in excess of two ounces that are necessary to address the patient's debilitating medical condition or disabling medical condition and why such amounts are necessary. A patient who asserts this affirmative defense shall waive confidentiality privileges related to the condition or conditions that were the basis for the recommendation. If a patient, primary caregiver, or physician raises an exception to the state criminal laws as provided in section 14 (2) (b) or (2) (c) of article XVIII of the state constitution or subsection (2.5) (c) or (2.5) (d) of this section, the patient, primary caregiver, or physician waives the confidentiality of his or her records related to the condition or conditions that were the basis for the recommendation maintained by the state health agency for the medical marijuana program. Upon request of a law enforcement agency for such records, the state health agency shall only provide records pertaining to the individual raising the exception, and shall redact all other patient, primary caregiver, or physician identifying information.

(15) (a) Except as provided in paragraph (b) of this subsection (15) , the state health agency shall establish a basic fee that shall be paid at the time of service of any subpoena upon the state health agency, plus a fee for meals and a fee for mileage at the rate prescribed for state officers and employees in section 24-9-104, C.R.S., for each mile actually and necessarily traveled in going to and returning from the place named in the subpoena. If the person named in the subpoena is required to attend the place named in the subpoena for more than one day, there shall be paid, in advance, a sum to be established by the state health agency for each day of attendance to cover the expenses of the person named in the subpoena.

(b) The subpoena fee established pursuant to paragraph (a) of this subsection (15) shall not be applicable to any federal, state, or local governmental agency.

(16) Fees. (a) The state health agency may collect fees from patients who, pursuant to section 14 of article XVIII of the state constitution or subsection (9) of this section, apply to the medical marijuana program for a registry identification card for the purpose of offsetting the state health

agency's direct and indirect costs of administering the program. The amount of the fees shall be set by rule of the state health agency. The amount of the fees set pursuant to this section shall reflect the actual direct and indirect costs of the state licensing authority in the administration and enforcement of this article so that the fees avoid exceeding the statutory limit on uncommitted reserves in administrative agency cash funds as set forth in section 24-75-402 (3) . The state health agency shall not assess a medical marijuana registry application fee to an applicant who demonstrates, pursuant to a copy of the applicant's state tax return certified by the department of revenue, that the applicant's income does not exceed one hundred eighty-five percent of the federal poverty line, adjusted for family size. All fees collected by the state health agency through the medical marijuana program shall be transferred to the state treasurer who shall credit the same to the medical marijuana program cash fund, which fund is hereby created.

(b) Repealed.

(17) Cash fund. (a) The medical marijuana program cash fund shall be subject to annual appropriation by the general assembly to the state health agency for the purpose of establishing, operating, and maintaining the medical marijuana program. All moneys credited to the medical marijuana program cash fund and all interest derived from the deposit of such moneys that are not expended during the fiscal year shall be retained in the fund for future use and shall not be credited or transferred to the general fund or any other fund.

(b) (Deleted by amendment, L. 2010, (HB 10-1284) , ch. 355, p. 1677, § 2, effective July 1, 2010.)

(b.5) (Deleted by amendment, L. 2014.)

(c) Repealed.

(d) (I) There is created a health research subaccount, referred to as "subaccount" in this section, in the medical marijuana program cash fund. The subaccount is established to support funding for medical marijuana health research. The department shall have continuous spending authority over the subaccount. The department may direct the state treasurer to transfer money from the medical marijuana program cash fund to the subaccount based on the cost of health research projects approved by the state board of health pursuant to section 25-1.5-106.5. The state treasurer shall not transfer more than ten million dollars in total to the subaccount.

(II) For the 2014-15 fiscal year and each fiscal year through 2018-19, the alternative maximum reserve for purposes of section 24-75-402, C.R.S., for the medical marijuana program cash fund is sixteen and five-tenths percent of the amount in the fund, excluding the ten million dollars available for transfer to the subaccount and any amount in the subaccount.

(III) This paragraph (d) is repealed, effective July 1, 2019. Any money remaining in the subaccount on June 30, 2019, must revert to the medical marijuana program cash fund.

(e) Notwithstanding any provision of paragraph (a) of this subsection (17) to the contrary, on July 1, 2014, and each July 1 through 2018, the state treasurer shall transfer two hundred thousand dollars from ten million dollars available for transfer pursuant to paragraph (d) of this subsection (17) in the medical marijuana program cash fund to the subaccount to be used for administrative purposes to administer the medical marijuana health research grant program created pursuant to section 25-1.5-106.5.

(18) (a) This section is repealed, effective September 1, 2019.

(b) Prior to the repeal of this section, the department of regulatory agencies shall conduct a sunset review as described in section 24-34-104 (5) , C.R.S.

## 25-1.5-106.5. Medical marijuana health research grant program.

(1) Legislative intent. There is a need for objective scientific research regarding the efficacy of marijuana and its component parts as part of medical treatment. It is the intent of the general assembly that the department gather objective scientific research regarding the efficacy of administering marijuana and its component parts as part of medical treatment.

(2) Medical marijuana research grant program - rules. (a) (I) The department shall be responsible for the administration of the Colorado medical marijuana research grant program created within the department and referred to in this section as the "grant program".

(II) The department shall coordinate the grant program to fund research intended to ascertain the general medical efficacy and appropriate administration of marijuana and its component parts. The grant program shall be limited to providing for objective scientific research to ascertain the efficacy of marijuana and its component parts as part of medical treatment and should not be construed as encouraging or sanctioning the social or recreational use of marijuana. The grant program shall fund observational trials and clinical trials.

(b) The state board of health shall promulgate rules for the administration of the grant program, including:

(I) The procedures and timelines by which an entity may apply for program grants;

(II) Grant application contents, including:

(A) Descriptions of key personnel, including clinicians, scientists, or epidemiologists and support personnel, demonstrating they are adequately trained to conduct this research;

(B) Procedures for outreach to patients with various medical conditions who may be suitable participants in research on marijuana and its component parts;

(C) Protocols suitable for research on marijuana and its component parts as medical treatment;

(D) For any research studies, demonstration that appropriate protocols for adequate patient consent and follow-up procedures are in place; and

(E) A process for a grant research proposal approved by the grant program to be reviewed and approved by an institutional review board that is able to approve, monitor, and review biomedical and behavioral research involving human subjects;

(III) Criteria for selecting entities to receive grants and determining the amount and duration of the grants, which shall include the following:

(A) The scientific merit of the research plan, including whether the research design and experimental procedures are potentially biased for or against a particular outcome; and

(B) The researchers' expertise in the scientific substance and methods of the proposed research and their lack of bias or conflict of interest regarding the topic of, and the approach taken in, the proposed research; and

(IV) Reporting requirements for entities that receive grants pursuant to this section.

(c) Program grants will be paid from the health research subaccount in the medical marijuana program cash fund created in section 25-1.5-106 (17) .

(d) In order to maximize the scope and size of the marijuana studies:

(I) The grant program may solicit, apply for, and accept moneys from foundations, private individuals, and all other funding sources that can be used to expand the scope or time frame of the marijuana studies that are authorized under this section; except that the program shall not accept any moneys that are offered with any conditions other than that the moneys be used to study the efficacy of marijuana and its component parts as part of medical treatment; and

(II) All donors shall be advised that moneys given for purposes of this section will be used to study both the possible medical benefits and detriments of marijuana and its component parts and that he or she will have no control over the use of these moneys.

(3) Review of applications. (a) (I) Scientific advisory council. In order to ensure objectivity in evaluating research proposals, the grant program shall establish a scientific advisory council, referred to in this section as the "council", to provide a peer review process that guards against funding research that is biased in favor of or against particular outcomes. The executive director of the department shall appoint at least six members and no more than thirteen members to the council to provide policy guidance in the creation and implementation of the grant program and in scientific oversight and review. The chief medical officer of the department, or his or her designee, is also a member of the council and is chair of the council. Except for the representative specified in sub-subparagraph (L) of this subparagraph (I) , the executive director shall choose members on the basis of their expertise in the scientific substance and methods of the proposed research and for their lack of bias or conflict of interest regarding the applicants or the topic of an approach taken in the proposed research and may choose members from around the country. Members of the council must include the following types of experts:

(A) At least one epidemiologist with expertise in designing and conducting large, observational

82

studies and clinical trials;

(B) At least one clinician with expertise in designing and conducting clinical trials;

(C) A clinician familiar with the prescription, dosage, and administration of medical marijuana under current state laws;

(D) A medical toxicologist;

(E) A neurologist;

(F) A pediatrician;

(G) A psychiatrist;

(H) An internal medicine physician or other specialist in adult medicine;

(I) A preventive medicine specialist or public health professional;

(J) A substance abuse specialist;

(K) An alternative medicine specialist with expertise in herbal or alternative medicine;

(L) A person who represents medical marijuana patient interests; and

(M) An ad hoc member with clinical expertise in the medical condition under study.

(II) Members of the council, other than the chief medical officer or his or her designee, shall serve on a voluntary basis for a two-year term and may be reappointed. Members shall be reimbursed for their travel expenses incurred in the course of their participation.

(III) Members of the council shall evaluate research proposals and submit recommendations to the department and the state board of health for recommended grant recipients, grant amounts, and grant duration.

(b) Grant approval. (I) The council shall submit recommendations for grants to the state board of health. The state board of health shall approve or disapprove of grants submitted by the council. If the state board of health disapproves a recommendation, the council may submit a replacement recommendation within thirty days.

(II) The state board of health shall award grants to the selected entities, specifying the amount and duration of the award. A grant awarded pursuant to this section shall not exceed three years without renewal. The size, scope, and number of studies funded shall be commensurate with the amount of appropriated and available grant program funding.

(4) Reporting. (a) No later than January 1, 2016, the grant program shall report to the state board of health on the progress of the medical marijuana studies.

(b) Thereafter, the grant program shall issue a report to the state board of health by January 1 of each year detailing the progress of the medical marijuana studies. The interim reports required under this paragraph (b) shall include data on all of the following:

(I) The names and number of diseases or conditions under study;

(II) The number of patients enrolled in each study by disease; and

(III) Any scientifically valid preliminary findings.

(5) Cultivation authority. [Editor's note:This version of subsection (5) is effective until January 1, 2018.]The attorney general shall seek authority from the federal government to permit Colorado institutions of higher education to contract with the national institute of drug abuse to cultivate marijuana and its component parts for use in research studies funded pursuant to this section.

(5) Sources of marijuana. [Editor's note:This version of subsection (5) is effective January 1, 2018.](a) The attorney general shall seek authority from the federal government to permit Colorado institutions of higher education to contract with the national institute of drug abuse to cultivate marijuana and its component parts for use in research studies funded pursuant to this section.

(b) A person who holds an optional premises cultivation license or medical marijuana-infused products manufacturing license issued pursuant to part 4 of article 43.3 of title 12 or a retail marijuana cultivation facility license or a retail marijuana products manufacturing license issued pursuant to part 4 of article 43.4 of title 12 may transfer marijuana to a medical research facility, including at an institution of higher education, for use in research studies funded pursuant to this section. Notwithstanding any other provision of law, a medical research facility authorized pursuant to this section to conduct medical research regarding marijuana is exempt from all otherwise applicable restrictions on the possession and use of marijuana; except that the facility shall use the marijuana only for the medical research authorized pursuant to this section, shall not possess at any time a quantity of medical marijuana or medical marijuana-infused product in excess of the limit established in rules promulgated by the state licensing authority, and shall destroy all marijuana remaining after the research has been completed. For the fiscal years beginning on or after July 1, 2017, the general assembly may annually appropriate up to one percent of the available money in the marijuana tax cash fund created in section 39-28.8-501 to the department to be used to award grants pursuant to this section to medical research facilities so that a facility may:

(I) Purchase marijuana from a licensee specified in this subsection (5) (b) that will be used in the research; and

(II) Conduct the medical research.

(6) Definition. For purposes of this section, "marijuana" means "usable form of marijuana" as that term is defined in section 14 (1) (i) of article XVIII of the Colorado constitution and also includes "industrial hemp" as that term is defined in section 16 (2) (d) of article XVIII of the Colorado constitution.

## 25-1.5-107. Pandemic influenza - purchase of antiviral therapy - definitions.

(1) The department may enter into partnerships with one or more authorized purchasers to purchase antiviral therapy in order to acquire a ready supply or stockpile of antiviral drugs in the event of an epidemic emergency, including pandemic influenza. If an entity wishes to purchase antiviral therapy through the department, the entity shall notify the department of its intent and shall demonstrate to the department, in a form and manner determined by the department, that the entity satisfies the criteria of an authorized purchaser. Upon a determination that an entity is an authorized purchaser, the department shall seek approval from the United States department of health and human services for the purchase of antiviral therapy by the authorized purchaser. Any purchase of antiviral therapy shall be approved by the United States department of health and human services, and antiviral therapy shall be stored and used in accordance with state and federal requirements.

(2) As used in this section, unless the context otherwise requires:

(a) "Authorized purchaser" means an entity licensed by the department pursuant to section 25-1.5-103 (1) (a) , a local public health agency, or a health maintenance organization, as defined in section 10-16-102 (35) , C.R.S., authorized to operate in this state pursuant to part 4 of article 16 of title 10, C.R.S., that:

(I) Is part of the state pandemic preparedness and response plan;

(II) Will purchase antiviral therapy with its own funds; and

(III) Agrees to stockpile the antiviral therapy for use in an epidemic emergency declared a disaster emergency pursuant to section 24-33.5-704, C.R.S., and to use the antiviral therapy only in accordance with state and federal requirements and for no other purpose.

(b) "Bioterrorism" means the intentional use of microorganisms or toxins of biological origin to cause death or disease among humans or animals.

(c) "Emergency epidemic" means cases of an illness or condition, communicable or noncommunicable, caused by bioterrorism, pandemic influenza, or novel and highly fatal infectious agents or biological toxins.

(d) "Pandemic influenza" means a widespread epidemic of influenza caused by a highly virulent strain of the influenza virus.

## 25-1.5-108. Regulation of dialysis treatment clinics - training for hemodialysis technicians - state board of health rules - definitions - repeal.

(1) As used in this section, unless the context otherwise requires:

(a) "Dialysis treatment clinic" means a health facility or a department or unit of a licensed hospital that is planned, organized, operated, and maintained to provide outpatient hemodialysis treatment or hemodialysis training for home use of hemodialysis equipment.

(b) "End-stage renal disease" means the stage of renal impairment that appears irreversible and permanent and that requires a regular course of dialysis or a kidney transplant to maintain life.

(c) "Hemodialysis technician" means a person who is not a physician or a registered nurse and who provides dialysis care.

(d) "National credentialing program" means any national program for credentialing or determining the competency of hemodialysis technicians that is recognized by the national association of nephrology technicians/technologists (NANT) , or a successor association.

(2) By January 1, 2008, the state board of health shall adopt rules to establish a process to verify that persons performing the duties and functions of a hemodialysis technician at or for a dialysis treatment clinic have been credentialed by a national credentialing program. The verification process shall be part of the department of public health and environment's licensing of dialysis treatment clinics and part of each routine survey of licensed dialysis clinics conducted by the department. As part of the rules adopted pursuant to this section, the state board shall establish fees consistent with section 25-3-105 to be assessed by the department against dialysis treatment clinics to cover the department's administrative costs in implementing this section.

(3) (a) On and after January 1, 2009, a person shall not act as, or perform the duties and functions of, a hemodialysis technician unless the person has been credentialed by a national credentialing program and is under the supervision of a licensed physician or licensed professional nurse experienced or trained in dialysis treatment.

(b) On and after January 1, 2009, a dialysis treatment clinic licensed by the department shall not allow a person to perform the duties and functions of a hemodialysis technician at or for the dialysis treatment clinic if the person has not been credentialed by a national credentialing program.

(c) Nothing in this subsection (3) shall prohibit:

(I) A person from providing dialysis care to himself or herself or in-home, gratuitous dialysis care provided to a person by a friend or family member who does not represent himself or herself to be a hemodialysis technician;

(II) A person participating in a hemodialysis technician training program from performing the duties and functions of a hemodialysis technician if:

(A) The person is under the direct supervision of a physician, or a registered nurse experienced or trained in dialysis treatment, who is on the premises and available for prompt consultation or treatment; and

(B) The person receives his or her credentials from a national credentialing program within eighteen months after the date the person enrolled in the training program.

(4) In connection with its regulation of dialysis treatment clinics pursuant to section 25-1.5-103 (1) (a) (I) and 25-3-101 (1) and rules adopted by the state board of health pursuant to subsection (2) of this section, on and after January 1, 2009, the department shall verify that a dialysis treatment clinic only employs hemodialysis technicians who have been credentialed by a national credentialing program. Compliance by a dialysis treatment clinic with this section shall be a condition of licensure by the department.

(5) Each dialysis treatment clinic licensed by the department and operating in this state shall post a clear and unambiguous notice in a public location in the clinic specifying that the clinic is licensed, regulated, and subject to inspection by the Colorado department of public health and environment. The dialysis treatment clinic shall also inform consumers, either in the public notice required by this subsection (5) or in written materials provided to consumers, about the ability to provide feedback to the clinic and to the department, including the method by which consumers can provide feedback. The state board may adopt rules, as necessary, to specify the contents of the notice or written materials required by this subsection (5) .

(5.5) A dialysis treatment clinic shall not provide outpatient hemodialysis treatment to a non-end-stage renal disease patient without a referral for treatment from a board-certified or board-eligible nephrologist licensed as a physician in Colorado. When making the referral, the nephrologist and other licensed physicians who cared for the patient in the hospital shall use their professional judgment to determine when the patient no longer requires hospitalization and may receive outpatient dialysis.

(6) This section is repealed, effective September 1, 2019. Prior to this repeal, the department of regulatory agencies shall review the functions of the state board of health and the department regarding hemodialysis technicians as provided in section 24-34-104, C.R.S.

## 25-1.5-109. Food allergies and anaphylaxis form for schools - powers and duties of department.

The department has, in addition to all other powers and duties imposed upon it by law, the duty to develop, maintain, and make available to school districts and institute charter schools a standard form to be used by school districts and institute charter schools to gather information from physicians and parents and guardians of students concerning students' risks of food allergies and anaphylaxis and the treatment thereof. The standard form shall include, at a minimum, fields for gathering the information described in section 22-2-135 (3) (b) , C.R.S.

## 25-1.5-110. Monitor health effects of marijuana.

(1) The department shall monitor changes in drug use patterns, broken down by county or region, as determined by the department, and race and ethnicity, and the emerging science and medical information relevant to the health effects associated with marijuana use.

(2) [Editor's note:This version of subsection (2) is effective until February 1, 2018.]The department shall appoint a panel of health care professionals with expertise in cannabinoid physiology to monitor the relevant information. The panel shall provide a report by January 31, 2015, and every two years thereafter to the state board of health, the department of revenue, and the general assembly. The department shall make the report available on its website. The panel shall establish criteria for studies to be reviewed, reviewing studies and other data, and making recommendations, as appropriate, for policies intended to protect consumers of marijuana or marijuana products and the general public.

(2) [Editor's note:This version of subsection (2) is effective February 1, 2018.]The department shall appoint a panel of health care professionals with expertise in cannabinoid physiology to monitor the relevant information. Notwithstanding section 24-1-136 (11) (a) (I) , the panel shall provide a report by January 31, 2015, and every two years thereafter to the state board of health, the department of revenue, and the general assembly. The department shall make the report available on its website. The panel shall establish criteria for studies to be reviewed, reviewing studies and other data, and making recommendations, as appropriate, for policies intended to protect consumers of marijuana or marijuana products and the general public.

(3) The department may collect Colorado-specific data that reports adverse health events involving marijuana use from the all-payer claims database, hospital discharge data, and behavioral risk factors.

## 25-1.5-111. Suicide prevention commission - created - responsibilities - gifts, grants, donations - repeal.

(1) The suicide prevention commission is hereby created for the purpose of:

(a) Providing public and private leadership for suicide prevention and intervention in Colorado;

(b) Setting statewide, data-driven, evidence-based, and clinically informed suicide prevention priorities in Colorado;

(c) Serving as an advisor to the office of suicide prevention;

(d) Establishing and leading subgroups to set strategy and implementation plans for each statewide suicide prevention priority for the office of suicide prevention;

(e) Providing a forum for government agencies, community members, business leaders, and lawmakers to examine the current status of suicide prevention and intervention policies, analyze the system's near-term opportunities and challenges, and make recommendations to the office of suicide prevention, the governor's office, and the general assembly regarding improvements and innovations in policies and programs to reduce the preventable occurrence of suicide in Colorado;

(f) Expanding local and national partnerships and resources for statewide suicide prevention activities;

(g) Promoting cooperation and coordination among suicide prevention programs and strategies across Colorado;

(h) Evaluating the distribution of state resources for suicide prevention;

(i) Ensuring that suicide prevention remains a state priority; and

(j) Encouraging the development of suicide prevention plans at the local level.

(2) (a) Within sixty days after May 29, 2014, the executive director of the department of public health and environment shall appoint to the committee no more than twenty-six members, including:

(I) A representative from the office of suicide prevention in the department, which office shall serve as the administrator and coordinator of the commission;

(II) A representative from the office of behavioral health in the department of human services;

(III) A representative from law enforcement;

(IV) A representative from higher education;

(V) A representative from K-12 education;

(VI) A representative from an employee assistance program or human resources in the private sector;

(VII) A representative from the suicide prevention coalition of Colorado;

(VIII) A licensed mental health professional;

(IX) A representative from the behavioral health transformation council;

(X) An active member or veteran of the United States military who has been affected by suicide;

(XI) A representative from the Colorado youth advisory council;

(XII) A family member of a person who died by suicide;

(XIII) A person who has attempted suicide, recovered, and is now thriving;

(XIV) A person representing a philanthropic foundation;

(XV) A representative of medical providers or first responders;

(XVI) A representative from a hospital with an on-site emergency department;

(XVII) A representative from the agricultural and ranching industry;

(XVIII) A representative from the oil and gas industry from a rural area;

(XIX) At least three members of the Colorado business community, one of whom represents a rural area;

(XX) One representative of the suicide prevention nonprofit community;

(XXI) A representative from a nonprofit community service club;

(XXII) A representative from an interfaith organization;

(XXIII) A representative from the school safety resource center with experience in bullying, including cyberbullying; and

(XXIV) A representative from the department of health care policy and financing.

(b) When appointing the commission members, the executive director shall ensure that persons of different ethnic backgrounds are represented and that the regions of the state with high suicide rates, including rural areas, are represented and that the commission includes members with expertise with groups associated with high suicide rates and suicide attempts, including: Persons with disabilities; working-age men; senior adults; veterans and active-duty military personnel; lesbian, gay, bisexual, and transgender youth and adults; and Coloradans of disproportionately affected diversities and genders.

(c) The members of the commission shall serve without compensation; except that the members may seek reimbursement for travel expenses to and from meetings of the commission.

(d) The executive director shall appoint one commission member who represents the public sector and one commission member who represents the private sector to serve as co-chairs of the commission.

(3) The department shall provide to the commission support that includes the coordination of all commission activities, including: Meeting logistics, agenda development, and follow-up; organizing and orienting commission members; working closely with the co-chairpersons to set

priorities, recruit members, oversee all commission initiatives, coordinate activities, and implement any commission-directed initiatives; and any other duties assigned by the co-chairpersons. The director of the office of behavioral health in the department of human services, a representative from the university of Colorado depression center, and a representative of the suicide prevention coalition of Colorado may also provide support to the commission.

(4) The office of suicide prevention shall include the recommendations of the commission in the report submitted annually to the general assembly pursuant to section 25-1.5-101 and shall present the recommendations as part of its annual presentation to the general assembly pursuant to the "State Measurement for Accountable, Responsive, and Transparent (SMART) Government Act" as enacted by House Bill 10-1119 in 2010.

(5) The department may accept gifts, grants, and donations from public and private sources for the direct and indirect costs associated with the implementation and duties associated with the commission. The department shall transmit any gifts, grants, and donations it receives to the state treasurer, who shall credit the moneys to the suicide prevention coordination cash fund created in section 25-1.5-101 (1) (w) (II) . The fund also consists of any moneys appropriated or transferred to the fund by the general assembly for the purposes of this section. The moneys in the fund are subject to annual appropriation by the general assembly.

(6) (a) This section is repealed, effective September 1, 2024.

(b) Prior to the repeal, the department of regulatory agencies shall review the commission pursuant to section 2-3-1203, C.R.S.

## 25-1.5-112. Colorado suicide prevention plan - established - goals - responsibilities - funding.

(1) The Colorado suicide prevention plan, referred to in this section as the "Colorado plan", is created in the office of suicide prevention within the department. The goal and purpose of the Colorado plan is to reduce suicide rates and numbers in Colorado through system-level implementation of the Colorado plan in criminal justice and health care systems, including mental and behavioral health systems.

(2) The suicide prevention commission, together with the office of suicide prevention, the office of behavioral health, the department, and the department of health care policy and financing, is strongly encouraged to collaborate with criminal justice and health care systems, mental and behavioral health systems, primary care providers, physical and mental health clinics in educational institutions, community mental health centers, advocacy groups, emergency medical services professionals and responders, public and private insurers, hospital chaplains, and faith-based organizations, to develop and implement:

(a) A plan to improve training to identify indicators of suicidal thoughts and behavior across criminal justice and health care systems;

(b) A plan to improve training on:

(I) The provisions of the emergency procedures for a seventy-two-hour mental health hold pursuant to section 27-65-105, C.R.S.;

(II) The provisions of the federal "Health Insurance Portability and Accountability Act of 1996", Pub.L. 104-191, as amended; and

(III) Other relevant patient privacy procedures; and

(c) Professional development resources and training opportunities regarding indicators of suicidal thoughts and behavior, risk assessment, and management, as developed in collaboration with the department of regulatory agencies, the department of corrections, and health care and mental health professional boards and associations.

(3) As a demonstration of their commitment to patient safety, criminal justice and health care systems, including mental and behavioral health systems, primary care providers, and hospitals throughout the state, are encouraged to contribute to and implement the Colorado plan.

(4) The following systems and organizations are encouraged to contribute to and implement the Colorado plan on or before July 1, 2019:

(a) Community mental health centers;

(b) Hospitals;

(c) The state crisis services system;

(d) Emergency medical services professionals and responders;

(e) Regional health and behavioral health systems;

(f) Substance use disorder treatment systems;

(g) Physical and mental health clinics in educational institutions;

(h) Criminal justice systems; and

(i) Advocacy groups, hospital chaplains, and faith-based organizations.

(5) The office of suicide prevention shall include a summary of the Colorado plan in a report submitted to the office of behavioral health, as well as the report submitted annually to the general assembly pursuant to section 25-1.5-101 (1) (w) (III) (A) and as part of its annual presentation to the general assembly pursuant to the "State Measurement for Accountable, Responsive, and Transparent (SMART) Government Act", part 2 of article 7 of title 2, C.R.S.

(6) The department may accept gifts, grants, and donations from public and private sources for the direct and indirect costs associated with the development and implementation of the Colorado plan. The department shall transmit any gifts, grants, and donations it receives to the state treasurer, who shall credit the money to the suicide prevention coordination cash fund created in section 25-1.5-101 (1) (w) (II) .

# PART 2. POWERS AND DUTIES OF THE DEPARTMENT WITH RESPECT TO WATER

### 25-1.5-201. Definitions.

As used in this part 2, unless the context otherwise requires:

(1) "Public water systems" means systems for the provision to the public of piped water for human consumption, if such system has at least fifteen service connections or regularly serves at least twenty-five individuals. The term includes systems that are owned or operated by private, nonprofit entities, as well as:

(a) Any collection, treatment, storage, and distribution facilities under control of the operator of such system and used primarily in connection with such system; and

(b) Any collection or pretreatment storage facilities not under such control which are used primarily in connection with such system.

(2) "Supplier of water" means any person who owns or operates a public water system.

### 25-1.5-202. Water - minimum general sanitary standards.

(1) The phrase "minimum general sanitary standards" as used in this part 2 and section 25-1-109 (1) (h) means the minimum standards reasonably consistent with assuring adequate protection of the public health, and, in the case of minimum general sanitary standards as to the quality of water supplied to the public, the same shall be established by rule and regulation and shall be appropriate to promote and protect the public health from endangerment presented by carcinogenic, mutagenic, teratogenic, pathogenic, or toxic contaminants or substances. Such standards shall be based on the best available endangerment assessment evidence and the best available treatment technology or methodology. The word "standards" as used in this part 2 and section 25-1-109 (1) (h) means standards reasonably designed to promote and protect the public health.

(2) Minimum general sanitary standards for the quality of water supplied to the public shall be no more stringent than the drinking water standards promulgated pursuant to the federal "Safe Drinking Water Act", if such standards exist. If no standards have been promulgated pursuant to the federal "Safe Drinking Water Act" regarding the permissible concentration of any contaminant

or any substance in drinking water, the department may recommend to the water quality control commission for promulgation minimum general sanitary standards regarding such contaminant or substance.

(3) (a) The department shall annually establish and revise a priority list of contaminants or substances for which standards may be considered and shall submit said list to the water quality control commission for review and approval.

(b) The priority list of contaminants or substances, together with the department's evaluation of the considerations listed in this paragraph (b) , shall be submitted to the water quality control commission for review and approval. The priority list shall be prepared according to a ranking process that incorporates the following considerations:

(I) The actual presence of a contaminant or substance in a drinking water supply system or the relative imminence of threat of contamination of a drinking water supply source;

(II) The identifiability of a potential pathway or continued pathway of contamination;

(III) The availability of analytical techniques for measuring and identifying the contaminant or substance in a reasonable manner;

(IV) Sufficient available information concerning the contaminant or substance to allow an appropriate standard to be developed, including information on the health effects of the contaminant or substance as well as available treatment technology;

(V) The magnitude of potential health risks of the contaminant or substance at reasonably anticipated exposure levels, utilizing the same exposure considerations, criteria for health risk, and criteria for data availability which are used by the criteria and standards division of the office of drinking water, United States environmental protection agency, in establishing the federal drinking water priority list;

(VI) The fact that the contaminant or substance will be the subject of a national primary drinking water regulation in the near future;

(VII) An analysis of the environmental fate and transport mechanisms within relevant environmental media;

(VIII) Identification, characterization, and analysis of the populations and drinking water supplies at risk; and

(IX) The level of effort and scope of work that will be necessary to develop sufficient data for the purpose of supporting an appropriate standard.

(4) (a) Following the department's submission of recommended standards to the water quality control commission, the commission may promulgate standards for contaminants or substances that are not the subject of a standard set pursuant to the federal "Safe Drinking Water Act".

(b) In the promulgation of such standards, the water quality control commission shall find that the standards are necessary to protect public health and have a demonstrated medical, technological, and scientific basis and that:

(I) Based on credible medical and toxicological evidence that has been subjected to peer review, there exists a substantial risk to the public health;

(II) The analytical techniques for measuring and identifying the contaminant or substance are reasonably available;

(III) The adverse health effects posed by the contaminant or substance are known to a reasonable degree of scientific certainty; and

(IV) Compliance with such standard is feasible utilizing the best technology or methodology which is generally available.

(5) All acts, orders, and rules adopted by the state board of health under the authority of this part 2 prior to July 1, 2006, that were valid prior to said date and not otherwise subject to judicial review shall, to the extent that they are not inconsistent with said provisions, be deemed and held to be legal and valid in all respects, as though issued by the water quality control commission under the authority of this part 2. No provision of this part 2 shall be construed to validate any actions, orders, or rules that were not valid when adopted by the board of health prior to such date.

## 25-1.5-203. Water - powers and duties of department - rules - repeal.

(1) The department has, in addition to all other powers and duties imposed upon it by law, the powers and duties provided in this section as follows:

(a) Construction of community water facilities. To examine plans, specifications, and other related data pertaining to the proposed construction of any publicly or privately owned community water facilities submitted for review of sanitary engineering features prior to construction of such facilities;

(b) Quality of drinking water. (I) To adopt and enforce minimum general sanitary standards and regulations to protect the quality of drinking water supplied to the public, including the authority to require disinfection and treatment of such water.

(II) Standards and regulations adopted pursuant to this paragraph (b) may also include such minimum standards and regulations as are necessary to assume enforcement of the federal "Safe Drinking Water Act" with regard to public water systems, including, but not limited to, requirements for:

(A) Review and approval by the department, prior to initiation of construction, of the technical plans and specifications, long-term financial plans, and operations and management plans for any new waterworks or technical plans and specifications for substantial modifications to existing waterworks. For the purposes of this subparagraph (II) , "waterworks" means the facilities that are directly involved in the production, treatment, or distribution of water for public water systems, as defined in section 141.2 of the national primary drinking water regulations. The department shall approve those new or substantially modified waterworks it determines are capable of complying with the Colorado primary drinking water regulations.

(B) Maintenance of records by the supplier of water relating to the results of tests and procedures required by the standards and regulations, including filing periodic reports with the department;

(C) Public notification by the supplier of water, pursuant to the provisions of the federal "Safe Drinking Water Act";

(D) Granting exemptions and variances from the minimum general sanitary standards to allow appropriate time for compliance, when such procedure can be effected without seriously jeopardizing the public health.

(c) Exemption of public water systems. (I) To exempt a water supplier from any further documentation requirements for purposes of establishing that it does not meet the definition of a public water system and is not subject to the requirements of the federal "Safe Drinking Water Act", where such water supplier has provided to the department evidence of the following:

(A) An ordinance, resolution, contractual provision, or other similarly enforceable enactment that prohibits connection to the system for the purpose of obtaining water for human consumption; and

(B) Either an annual visual inspection of the water supply system for the purpose of determining the presence of any unauthorized connections to the water supply system, or an annual written survey of those individuals or entities with whom the supplier has a contractual relationship governing the uses to which such water is placed by the contracting parties.

(II) Nothing in subparagraph (I) of this paragraph (c) shall be construed to eliminate from the provisions of the federal "Safe Drinking Water Act" any exclusion that may otherwise be available under federal law or regulation.

(d) Lab certification program for testing drinking water. (I) To establish and maintain a laboratory certification program for the purpose of ensuring competent testing of drinking water as required by the federal "Safe Drinking Water Act" and minimum general sanitary standards as set forth in section 25-1.5-202. Certification procedures shall, at a minimum, include water supply evaluation verification and on-site inspections. The laboratory certification program shall consist of certification levels which correspond to the testing capability and capacity of each laboratory. In addition to certifying laboratories for contaminants regulated as of May 11, 1988, the department shall adopt and implement a schedule for certifying sufficient laboratory capacity for the testing and analysis of contaminants for which reference methods are available and which are scheduled to be regulated under the federal "Safe Drinking Water Act".

(II) Upon request, the department shall refer a public water supplier to a laboratory, either the department's or one certified by the department, which is determined to be equipped to perform the required testing and analysis on a timely basis.

(III) To facilitate an effective laboratory certification program, the department shall work with local public water suppliers toward creating and maintaining a centralized data base which:

(A) Quantifies the current and expected demands for the monitoring, testing, and analysis of each supplier, grouped according to the size of the supply system, the source of its supply, and the requirements imposed on each supplier;

(B) Includes an updated list of laboratories certified and available for the testing and analysis of specific contaminants; and

(C) Tracks violations of drinking water standards for the purpose of facilitating an exchange among public water suppliers in addressing similar problems posed by specific contaminants.

(e) Drinking water list. To cooperate with and assist the Colorado water resources and power development authority in the administration of the drinking water revolving fund created by section 37-95-107.8, C.R.S., including adopting rules governing the drinking water project eligibility list provided by said section and modifications to the eligibility list for submission to the general assembly, and to take any other actions necessary to assist the authority in complying with the requirements of the federal "Safe Drinking Water Act".

(f) Public school lead testing grant program.(I) To establish a grant program to pay for testing to detect the presence and concentration of lead in drinking water in a public school, as that term is defined in section 22-1-101 (1) , that receives its drinking water from a public water system; except that, for purposes of this section, "public school" includes: A public school district; a charter school, as that term is defined in section 22-30.5-103 (2) , including an institute charter school, as that term is defined in section 22-30.5-502 (6) ; and a board of cooperative services, as that term is defined in section 22-5-103 (2) . The department may specify testing protocols and guidelines and may provide technical assistance, as necessary and feasible, to applicants and grant recipients regarding the grant application, sampling guidance, sampling plan review, and communication guidance. The commission may adopt rules to implement the grant program, which rules may include consideration of a public school's ability to pay for testing in administering the program.

(II) In administering the program, the department shall prioritize grant recipients in the following order: The oldest public elementary schools; the oldest public schools that are not elementary schools; and all other public schools. For purposes of this subsection (1) (f) (II) , an "elementary school" means a public school that includes any or all of the following: Preschool, kindergarten, and grades one through five. The department may also develop and apply secondary criteria as established through rules promulgated by the commission. A public school that is subject to the federal lead and copper rule, 40 CFR part 141, subpart I, or has already tested or is in the process of testing its drinking water for lead is not eligible for a grant pursuant to this subsection (1) (f) .

(III) The department shall apply its best efforts to complete all testing and analysis by June 30, 2020.

(IV) A public school that receives a grant pursuant to this subsection (1) (f) shall either enter into a contract that requires compliance with the department's testing protocols to have the testing conducted or follow the department's testing protocols and provide the test samples to the department's laboratory or a laboratory certified by the department that is equipped to perform the required testing and analysis on a timely basis. The public school shall provide the test results to its local public health agency, its supplier of water, its school board, and the department.

(V) The department shall use money from the water quality improvement fund created in section 25-8-608 (1.5) as authorized by section 25-8-608 (1.7) (d) to implement this subsection (1) (f) .

(VI) Notwithstanding section 24-1-136 (11) (a) (I) , the department shall annually report by February 1 of each year until February 1, 2021, to the general assembly's committees of reference with jurisdiction over public health regarding:

(A) The number, types, names, and locations of public schools that have applied for grants pursuant to this subsection (1) (f) ;

(B) The number of grants that have been issued; the individual amounts and total amount of grant money awarded; and the number, types, names, and locations of public schools that received the grants;

(C) A summary of the test results; and

(D) Any legislative proposals that the department believes to be warranted that would provide financial assistance to public schools to facilitate the testing for or remediation of high lead levels in drinking water.

(VII) This subsection (1) (f) is repealed, effective September 1, 2021.

## 25-1.5-204. Inspection for violations of minimum general sanitary standards relating to quality of drinking water.

(1) Upon presentation of proper credentials, authorized inspectors of the department may enter and inspect, at any reasonable time and in a reasonable manner, any property, premises, or place for the purpose of investigating any actual, suspected, or potential violations of minimum general sanitary standards adopted pursuant to section 25-1.5-202. Samples of drinking water may be obtained by such inspectors, and a portion of any samples to be used as evidence in an enforcement action shall be left with the owner, operator, or person in charge of the premises. A copy of the results of any analysis of such sample shall be furnished promptly to the owner, operator, or person in charge.

(2) If such entry or inspection is denied or not consented to, the department is empowered to and shall obtain, from the district or county court for the judicial district or county in which such property, premises, or place is located, a warrant to enter and inspect said property, premises, or place. The said district and county courts of the state are empowered to issue such warrants upon a proper showing of the need for such entry and inspection, and a copy of any inspection report shall be provided the court within a reasonable time after making the inspection.

## 25-1.5-205. Advice to other entities.

The department may advise municipalities, utilities, institutions, organizations, and individuals concerning the methods or processes believed best suited to provide the protection or purification of water to meet minimum general sanitary standards adopted pursuant to section 25-1.5-202.

## 25-1.5-206. Applicability.

(1) Except as otherwise provided in the federal "Safe Drinking Water Act", the provisions of this part 2 shall apply to each public water system in this state; except that the provisions of this part 2 shall not apply to a public water system that:

(a) Consists only of distribution and storage facilities (and does not have any collection and treatment facilities) ;

(b) Obtains all of its water from, but is not owned or operated by, a public water system to which such regulations apply;

(c) Does not sell water to any person;

(d) Does not authorize incidental use of untreated water; and

(e) Is not a carrier that conveys passengers in interstate commerce; or

(f) Prohibits, through ordinance, resolution, or other enforceable enactment, the use of its system, or connections thereto, for the delivery of water to the public for human consumption, except to the extent that such user is a public water system subject to the provisions of this part 2.

## 25-1.5-207. Damages and injunctive relief to prevent or abate release of contaminants in water.

(1) (a) Except as provided in section 25-1-114.1 (3) , any political subdivision or public water system which stores, releases, carries, conveys, supplies, or treats water for human consumption may bring suit to collect damages and for injunctive relief, in addition to all remedies otherwise

available to prevent or abate any release or imminent release of contaminants or substances which, in water withdrawn for use, results or would likely result in:

(I) A violation, at the point where the contaminant or substance enters or would enter the intake of the water treatment system of the same or another political subdivision or public water system, of any minimum general sanitary standard or regulation adopted pursuant to this part 2, and the existing treatment system cannot effectively treat the contaminant or substance in question so as to assure that treated water complies with such standard or regulation; or

(II) Significant impairment of the normal operational capability of a water treatment system which meets the applicable specifications of the department for water treatment; or

(III) Rendering the system's drinking water supply unfit for human consumption. Where there are no minimum general sanitary standards, water shall be deemed unfit for human consumption where it is shown that the risk of adverse human health effects from exposure to carcinogens in that water is greater than one times ten to the minus sixth power or greater than the acceptable levels of exposure to noncarcinogens as determined by the reference dose method.

(b) Such an action may be maintained against any person who owns or operates the source or sources of the release of the contaminants, but no such action may be maintained with regard to surface or underground agricultural return flows except as otherwise provided in the "Colorado Chemigation Act", article 11 of title 35, C.R.S. Damages, including the costs of any remedy ordered or approved by the court shall include, as appropriate, those incurred in providing an interim substitute drinking water supply and monitoring and responding to the release or imminent release of contaminants or substances.

(2) Other remedies. Except as provided in this subsection (2), nothing in this section shall be construed to restrict or preempt any right which the state, the department, any public water system, or any other person may have under any other law to seek enforcement, in any court or in any administrative proceeding, of any provision of this section or any other relief regarding contamination of any drinking water supply. In addition, nothing in this section shall be construed to condition, restrict, or prevent any other civil or criminal actions which may be brought by the state or any political subdivision pursuant to any other state or federal statute or regulation or any local ordinance or regulation; except that, with respect to any release or substantial threat of release of a hazardous substance, pollutant, or contaminant addressed in pleadings or otherwise in a lawsuit brought pursuant to the federal "Comprehensive Environmental Response, Compensation and Liability Act", 42 U.S.C. sec. 9601 et seq., or by the terms and conditions of a remedial action plan, removal order, consent decree, or other order or decree entered or issued by a court or administrative body of competent jurisdiction pursuant to such federal act, any person or entity which is a defendant in such a lawsuit or is subject to the terms and conditions of such a remedial action plan, removal order, consent decree, or other order or decree, shall not be subjected with respect to the same release or substantial threat of release of a hazardous substance, pollutant, or contaminant to any suit, action, or liability pursuant to section 25-1-114.1 (3) ; nor shall such person or entity be subject to any suit, action, or liability initiated or prosecuted by a political subdivision or a public water system pursuant to this section with respect to any release or substantial threat of release of a hazardous substance, pollutant, or contaminant which has been addressed by relief granted, or by measures implemented or legally required to be implemented, pursuant to a lawsuit brought pursuant to such federal act or the terms and conditions of a remedial action plan, removal order, consent decree, or other order or decree entered or issued by a court or administrative body of competent jurisdiction pursuant to such federal act. Nothing in this section shall be construed to bar a political subdivision or public water system from seeking to recover pursuant to applicable law its damages which have been reasonably incurred for the protection of the human health if enforceable arrangements to pay such damages have not otherwise been made.

## 25-1.5-208. Grant program for public water systems and domestic wastewater treatment works - small communities water and wastewater grant fund - rules.

(1) The department has, in addition to all other powers and duties imposed upon it by law, the powers and duties provided in this section as follows:

(a) To assist suppliers of water that serve a population of not more than five thousand people with meeting their responsibilities with respect to protection of public health, the department, in the name of the state and to the extent that state funds are appropriated therefor, may enter into contracts with both governmental agencies and not-for-profit public water systems, as defined in section 25-1.5-201 (1) , or with counties representing unincorporated areas that serve a population of not more than five thousand people, to grant moneys for the planning, design, and construction of public water systems.

(a.5) To assist domestic wastewater treatment works, as defined in section 25-8-103 (5) , that serve a population of not more than five thousand people with meeting their responsibilities with respect to the protection of public health and water quality, the department, in the name of the state and to the extent that state funds are appropriated therefor, may enter into contracts with governmental agencies, or with counties representing unincorporated areas that serve a population of not more than five thousand people, to grant moneys for eligible projects as defined in section 25-8-701 (2) .

(b) The department may use up to five percent of the appropriated funds for the administration and management of such project grants.

(2) The water quality control commission shall promulgate rules for the administration of any appropriated grant moneys pursuant to this section and for prioritizing proposed public water systems and domestic wastewater treatment works based upon public health impacts and water quality protection. The department shall authorize grants based on water quality needs and public health-related problems. The commission shall promulgate a project categorization system for use in determining the relative priority of proposed projects. The department shall review applications for state funds and may approve only those applications that are consistent with the project categorization system.

(3) During the grant application process, the department shall seek from the division of local government in the department of local affairs a fiscal analysis of the applying entity to determine financial need. Based upon its fiscal analysis, the division of local government shall issue or deny a certificate of financial need. If a certificate of financial need is issued, the department may authorize a state grant to the project in accordance with the project prioritization adopted by the department.

(4) (a) There is hereby created in the state treasury the small communities water and wastewater grant fund, referred to in this subsection (4) as the "fund". The fund shall consist of moneys transferred pursuant to section 39-29-109 (2) (a) (III) , C.R.S., and any other moneys transferred to the fund by the general assembly. The fund shall be used only for grants made pursuant to this section. All income derived from the deposit and investment of the moneys in the fund shall be credited to the fund. At the end of each fiscal year, all unexpended and unencumbered moneys in the fund shall remain in the fund and shall not revert to the general fund or to any other fund.

(b) The revenues in the fund are continuously appropriated to the department for the purposes of this section.

## 25-1.5-209. Drinking water fee - drinking water cash fund.

(1) Effective July 1, 2007, the division may assess an annual fee upon public water systems, and all such fees shall be in accordance with the following schedule:

Facility Categories and Subcategories for
Drinking Water FeesAnnual Fees

(a) Category 01Community surface water systems
 Subcategory 1Population from 25 - 250$75 Subcategory 2Population from 251 - 500$100
Subcategory 3Population from 501 - 1,000$310 Subcategory 4Population from 1,001 - 3,300$465

Subcategory 5Population from 3,301 - 10,000$865 Subcategory 6Population from 10,001 - 30,000$1,850 Subcategory 7Population from 30,001 - 100,000$4,940 Subcategory 8Population from 100,001 - 200,000$9,270 Subcategory 9Population from 200,001 - 500,000$15,450 Subcategory 10Population greater than 500,000$ 21,630
(b) Category 02Community groundwater systems
 Subcategory 1Population from 25 - 250$75 Subcategory 2Population from 251 - 500$100 Subcategory 3Population from 501 - 1,000$220 Subcategory 4Population from 1,001 - 3,300$310 Subcategory 5Population from 3,301 - 10,000$680 Subcategory 6Population from 10,001 - 30,000$1,545 Subcategory 7Population greater than 30,001$4,450
(c) Category 03Community-purchased surface water or groundwater systems
 Subcategory 1Population from 25 - 250$75 Subcategory 2Population from 251 - 500$100 Subcategory 3Population from 501 - 1,000$155 Subcategory 4Population from 1,001 - 3,300$250 Subcategory 5Population from 3,301 - 10,000$490 Subcategory 6Population from 10,001 - 30,000$865 Subcategory 7Population greater than 30,001$2,470
(d) Category 04Nontransient, noncommunity surface water systems
 Subcategory 1Population from 25 - 250$75 Subcategory 2Population from 251 - 500$100 Subcategory 3Population from 501 - 1,000$280 Subcategory 4Population from 1,001 - 3,300$400 Subcategory 5Population from 3,301 - 10,000$620 Subcategory 6Population from 10,001 - 30,000$1,670 Subcategory 7Population greater than 30,001$4,450 (e) Category 05Nontransient, noncommunity groundwater systems
 Subcategory 1Population from 25 - 250$75 Subcategory 2Population from 251 - 500$100 Subcategory 3Population from 501 - 1,000$155 Subcategory 4Population from 1,001 - 3,300$245 Subcategory 5Population from 3,301 - 10,000$495 Subcategory 6Population from 10,001 - 30,000$1,360 Subcategory 7Population greater than 30,001$3,650
(f) Category 06Nontransient, noncommunity-purchased surface water or groundwater systems
 Subcategory 1Population from 25 - 250$ 75 Subcategory 2Population from 251 - 500$100 Subcategory 3Population from 501 - 1,000$125 Subcategory 4Population from 1,001 - 3,300$185 Subcategory 5Population from 3,301 - 10,000$325 Subcategory 6Population from 10,001 - 30,000$805 Subcategory 7Population greater than 30,001$1,980
(g) Category 07Transient, noncommunity surface water systems
 Subcategory 1Population from 25 - 250$75 Subcategory 2Population from 251 - 500$100 Subcategory 3Population from 501 - 1,000$245 Subcategory 4Population from 1,001 - 3,300$310 Subcategory 5Population from 3,301 - 10,000$555 Subcategory 6Population from 10,001 - 30,000$620 Subcategory 7Population greater than 30,001$3,960
(h) Category 08Transient, noncommunity groundwater systems
 Subcategory 1Population from 25 - 250$75 Subcategory 2Population from 251 - 500$100 Subcategory 3Population from 501 - 1,000$125 Subcategory 4Population from 1,001 - 3,300$185 Subcategory 5Population from 3,301 - 10,000$495 Subcategory 6Population from 10,001 - 30,000$535 Subcategory 7Population greater than 30,001$2,970
(i) Category 09Transient, noncommunity-purchased surface water or groundwater systems
 Subcategory 1Population from 25 - 250$75 Subcategory 2Population from 251 - 500$100 Subcategory 3Population from 501 - 1,000$110 Subcategory 4Population from 1,001 - 3,300$125 Subcategory 5Population from 3,301 - 10,000$310 Subcategory 6Population from 10,001 - 30,000$435 Subcategory 7Population greater than 30,001$1,490

(2) All fees collected pursuant to this section shall be transmitted to the state treasurer, who shall credit them to the drinking water cash fund, which fund is hereby created in the state treasury. Moneys so collected shall be annually appropriated by the general assembly to the department for allocation to the division of administration to operate the drinking water program established in this part 2. The general assembly shall review expenditures of such moneys to assure that they are used only for such purposes. All interest earned on the investment or deposit of moneys in the cash fund and all unappropriated or unencumbered moneys in the cash fund shall remain in the cash fund and shall not revert to the general fund or any other fund at the end of any fiscal year or

any other time. Any funds remaining from fees collected prior to the repeal of former section 25-1.5-209, as it existed prior to July 1, 2005, shall be transmitted to the state treasurer, who shall credit the same to the cash fund.

### 25-1.5-210. Best practices for residential rooftop precipitation collection.
(1) With respect to the use of a rain barrel, as defined in section 37-96.5-102 (1) , C.R.S., to collect precipitation from a residential rooftop pursuant to section 37-96.5-103, C.R.S., the department, to the extent practicable within existing resources, shall develop best practices for:
(a) Nonpotable usage of the collected precipitation; and
(b) Disease and pest vector control.
(2) If the department develops best practices in accordance with subsection (1) of this section, the department shall:
(a) Post the best practices on the department's website; and
(b) Inform the state engineer of the best practices so that the state engineer can either post or link to the department's best practices on the state engineer's website.

# PART 3. ADMINISTRATION OF MEDICATIONS

### 25-1.5-301. Definitions.
As used in this part 3, unless the context otherwise requires:
(1) "Administration" means assisting a person in the ingestion, application, inhalation, or, using universal precautions, rectal or vaginal insertion of medication, including prescription drugs, according to the legibly written or printed directions of the attending physician or other authorized practitioner or as written on the prescription label and making a written record thereof with regard to each medication administered, including the time and the amount taken, but "administration" does not include judgment, evaluation, or assessments or the injections of medication, the monitoring of medication, or the self-administration of medication, including prescription drugs and including the self-injection of medication by the resident. "Administration" also means ingestion through gastrostomy tubes or naso-gastric tubes, if administered by a person authorized pursuant to sections 25.5-10-204 (2) (j) and 27-10.5-103 (2) (i) , C.R.S., as part of residential or day program services provided through service agencies approved by the department of health care policy and financing and supervised by a licensed physician or nurse.
(2) "Facility" means:
(a) The correctional facilities under the supervision of the executive director of the department of corrections including, but not limited to:
(I) Those facilities provided for in article 20 of title 17, C.R.S.;
(II) Minimum security facilities provided for in article 25 of title 17, C.R.S.;
(III) Jails provided for in article 26 of title 17, C.R.S.;
(IV) Community correctional facilities and programs provided for in article 27 of title 17, C.R.S.;
(V) The regimented inmate discipline and treatment program provided for in article 27.7 of title 17, C.R.S.; and
(VI) The Denver regional diagnostic center provided for in article 40 of title 17, C.R.S.;
(b) Institutions for juveniles provided for in part 4 of article 2 of title 19, C.R.S.;
(b.5) Assisted living residences as defined in section 25-27-102 (1.3) ;
(c) Adult foster care facilities provided for in section 26-2-122.3, C.R.S.;
(d) Alternate care facilities provided for in section 25.5-6-303 (3) , C.R.S.;
(e) Residential child care facilities for children as defined in section 26-6-102 (33) , C.R.S.;
(f) Secure residential treatment centers as defined in section 26-6-102 (35) , C.R.S.;
(g) Facilities that provide treatment for persons with mental health disorders as defined in section 27-65-102, except for those facilities that are publicly or privately licensed hospitals;

(h) All services funded through and regulated by the department of health care policy and financing pursuant to article 6 of title 25.5, C.R.S., in support of persons with intellectual and developmental disabilities; and

(i) Adult day care facilities providing services in support of persons as defined in section 25.5-6-303 (1) , C.R.S.

(3) "Monitoring" means:

(a) Reminding the resident to take medication or medications at the time ordered by the physician or other authorized licensed practitioner;

(b) Handing a resident a container or package of medication lawfully labeled previously for the individual resident by a licensed physician or other authorized licensed practitioner;

(c) Visual observation of the resident to ensure compliance;

(d) Making a written record of the resident's compliance with regard to each medication, including the time taken; and

(e) Notification to the physician or other authorized practitioner if the resident refuses to or is not able to comply with the physician's or other practitioner's instructions with regard to the medication.

(4) "Qualified manager" means a person who:

(a) Is the owner or operator of the facility or a supervisor designated by the owner or operator of the facility for the purpose of implementing section 25-1.5-303; and

(b) Has completed training in the administration of medications pursuant to section 25-1.5-303 or is a licensed nurse pursuant to article 38 of title 12, C.R.S., a licensed physician pursuant to article 36 of title 12, C.R.S., or a licensed pharmacist pursuant to article 42.5 of title 12, C.R.S. Every unlicensed person who is a "qualified manager" within the meaning of this subsection (4) shall successfully complete a competency evaluation pertaining to the administration of medications.

(5) "Self-administration" means the ability of a person to take medication independently without any assistance from another person.

## 25-1.5-302. Administration of medications - powers and duties of department - criminal history record checks.

(1) The department has, in addition to all other powers and duties imposed upon it by law, the power to establish and maintain by rule a program for the administration of medications in facilities. The department of human services, the department of health care policy and financing, and the department of corrections shall develop and conduct a medication administration program as provided in this part 3. A medication administration program developed pursuant to this subsection (1) must be conducted within the following guidelines:

(a) As a condition to authorizing or renewing the authorization to operate any facility that administers medications to persons under its care, the authorizing agency shall require that the facility have a staff member qualified pursuant to paragraph (b) of this subsection (1) on duty at any time that the facility administers such medications and that the facility maintain a written record of each medication administered to each resident, including the date, time, and amount of the medication and the signature of the person administering the medication. Such record is subject to review by the authorizing agency as a part of the agency's procedure in authorizing the continued operation of the facility. Notwithstanding any exemption enumerated in paragraph (b) of this subsection (1) , any facility may establish a policy that requires a person authorized to administer medication to report to, be supervised by, or be otherwise accountable for the performance of such administration to a registered nurse as defined in section 12-38-103, C.R.S.

(b) Any individual who is not otherwise authorized by law to administer medication in a facility shall be allowed to perform such duties only after passing a competency evaluation. An individual who administers medications in facilities in compliance with the provisions of this part 3 shall be exempt from the licensing requirements of the "Colorado Medical Practice Act", the "Nurse Practice Act", and the laws of this state pertaining to possession of controlled substances as contained in article 42.5 of title 12, C.R.S., part 2 of article 80 of title 27, C.R.S., or the "Uniform

Controlled Substances Act of 2013", article 18 of title 18, C.R.S.

(2) (a) The department shall establish by rule the minimum requirements for course content, including competency evaluations, for medication administration and to determine compliance with the requirements for facilities licensed under this title.

(b) The department shall approve training entities for facilities licensed under this title and maintain a list of approved training entities. The department shall establish by rule the minimum requirements for training entities, including instructor qualifications and the approval process. Approved training entities shall provide the department with a list of all persons who have successfully completed a competency evaluation.

(c) Training entities shall also provide the department with any other pertinent information reasonably requested by the department pursuant to the department's obligation and authority under this section.

(d) The department shall publish and maintain a current list of all persons who have passed a competency evaluation from an approved training entity and paid the fee required by paragraph (e) of this subsection (2) .

(e) The department shall set and collect a uniform fee for inclusion in the public competency listing. The department shall not include an individual on the public listing unless the individual has successfully completed a competency evaluation from an approved training entity and paid the fee established by the department. The revenue generated from the fee must approximate the direct and indirect costs incurred by the department in the performance of duties under this section.

(3) The department of human services, the department of health care policy and financing, and the department of corrections may develop and approve minimum requirements for course content, including competency evaluations, for individuals who administer medications in facilities whose operation is authorized by those departments. A department that administers competency evaluations shall maintain a public list of individuals who have successfully completed the competency evaluation.

(4) to (7) Repealed.

(8) Each owner, operator, or supervisor of a facility who employs a person who is not licensed to administer medications shall conduct a criminal background check on each employee prior to employment or promotion to a position in which the person has access to medications.

(9) Every unlicensed person and qualified manager described in this section, as a condition of employment or promotion to a position in which he or she has access to medications, shall sign a disclosure statement under penalty of perjury stating that he or she never had a professional license to practice nursing, medicine, or pharmacy revoked in this or any other state for reasons directly related to the administration of medications.

(10) A person who, on or before July 1, 2017, is authorized to administer medication pursuant to this section is not required to complete additional training but is otherwise subject to this section.

## 25-1.5-303. Medication reminder boxes or systems - medication cash fund.

(1) Medication reminder boxes or systems may be used if such containers have been filled and properly labeled by a pharmacist licensed pursuant to article 42.5 of title 12, C.R.S., a nurse licensed pursuant to article 38 of title 12, C.R.S., or an unlicensed person trained pursuant to this section or filled and properly labeled through the gratuitous care by members of one's family or friends. Nothing in this section authorizes or shall be construed to authorize the practice of pharmacy, as defined in section 12-42.5-102 (31) , C.R.S. An unlicensed person shall not fill and label medication reminder boxes pursuant to this section until the person has successfully completed a competency evaluation from an approved training entity or has been approved by an authorized agency, and no facility shall use an unlicensed person to perform such services unless the facility has a qualified manager to oversee the work of the unlicensed person or persons.

(2) The department has, in addition to all other powers and duties imposed upon it by law, the powers and duties provided in this section to develop and implement rules with respect to the provisions in subsection (1) of this section concerning the administration of medication reminder

boxes.

(3) The executive directors of the departments that control the facilities defined in section 25-1.5-301 (2) (a) and (2) (b) may direct the unlicensed staff of any such facility to monitor medications in any part of any such facility. Administration of medications in any such facility shall be allowed only in those areas of any such facility that have a licensed physician or other licensed practitioner on duty. Notwithstanding other training requirements established in this section, the operator or administrator of every facility that hires an unlicensed person to administer medications pursuant to this section shall provide on-the-job training for such person, and all such unlicensed persons hired on or after July 1, 2017, shall be adequately supervised until they have successfully completed the training. The on-the-job training must be appropriate to the job responsibilities of each trainee. Facility operators and administrators shall require each unlicensed person who administers medication in the facility to pass a competency evaluation pursuant to section 25-1.5-302 (2) as a condition of employment in that facility. Facility operators and administrators shall document each unlicensed person's satisfactory completion of on-the-job training and passage of the competency evaluation in his or her permanent personnel file.

(4) A person who self-administers medication is personally responsible for medication administration. No facility shall be responsible for observing or documenting the self-administration of medication. Compliance with the requirements for the training of unlicensed persons in medication administration pursuant to this section is not required when persons being cared for are self-administering.

(5) (a) All fees collected pursuant to this section shall be transmitted to the state treasurer, who shall credit the same to the medication administration cash fund, which fund is hereby created.

(b) The general assembly shall make annual appropriations from the medication administration cash fund for expenditures of the department incurred in the performance of its duties under this section.

(c) Repealed.

(d) In accordance with section 24-36-114, C.R.S., all interest derived from the deposit and investment of the medication administration cash fund created in paragraph (a) of this subsection (5) shall be credited to the general fund.

### 25-1.5-304. Repeal of part. (Repealed)

# PART 4. PRIMARY CARE OFFICE

### 25-1.5-401. Legislative declaration.

(1) The general assembly hereby finds and declares that:

(a) There is a shortage of qualified health care professionals in most areas of the state, particularly in rural and low-income communities;

(b) Lack of access to health care increases health inequities in Colorado and increases the overall cost of health care services;

(c) Communities designated as health professional shortage areas, medically underserved areas, or medically underserved populations may benefit from:

(I) Federal, state, and private programs that enhance reimbursement for medical services, provide grants for health service infrastructure, and create incentives for the placement of additional health care professionals in those communities; and

(II) The placement of physicians through federal waiver programs such as the national interest waiver program, the Conrad 30 J-1 visa waiver program, and the national health service corps; and

(d) Assessing the health service needs of the state and coordinating workforce programs to address those needs is an important strategy for increasing access to health services in Colorado.

(2) The general assembly therefore finds that it is in the best interests of the citizens of the state of Colorado to create the primary care office within the department of public health and environment for the purpose of identifying the areas within the state that lack sufficient health care resources and coordinating available resources to maximize medical reimbursements, grants, and placements of health care professionals within those areas.

## 25-1.5-402. Definitions.

As used in this part 4, unless the context otherwise requires:

(1) "Conrad 30 J-1 visa waiver program" means the program established in 8 U.S.C. sec. 1184 (l) (1) (D) (ii) , allowing foreign-trained physicians who meet certain criteria to practice in communities designated as medically underserved areas, medically underserved populations, or health professional shortage areas.

(2) "Department" means the department of public health and environment, created in section 25-1-102.

(3) "Executive director" means the executive director of the department.

(4) "Health care professional" means a licensed physician, an advanced practice nurse registered pursuant to section 12-38-111.5, C.R.S., a mental health practitioner, a licensed physician assistant, or any other licensed health care provider for which the federal government authorizes participation in a federally matched state loan repayment program to encourage health care professionals to provide services in underserved communities.

(5) "Health professional shortage area" has the same meaning as provided in 42 U.S.C. sec. 254e.

(6) "Medically underserved area" means a medically underserved community as defined in 42 U.S.C. sec. 295p.

(7) "Medically underserved population" has the same meaning as provided in 42 U.S.C. sec. 254b.

(8) "National health service corps" means the program established in 42 U.S.C. sec. 254d.

(9) "National interest waiver program" means the program established in 8 U.S.C. sec. 1153 (b) (2) (B) (ii) allowing foreign-trained physicians who meet certain criteria to practice in communities designated as medically underserved areas, medically underserved populations, or health professional shortage areas.

(10) "State board" means the state board of health created in section 25-1-103.

## 25-1.5-403. Primary care office - creation.

(1) There is hereby created in the department the primary care office for the purpose of assessing and addressing unmet needs concerning health care professionals, resources, and infrastructure across the state. The executive director of the department, subject to the provisions of section 13 of article XII of the state constitution, shall appoint the director of the primary care office, who is the head of the office.

(2) The primary care office and the director of the office shall exercise their powers and perform their duties and functions specified in this part 4 under the department as if the same were transferred to the department by a type 2 transfer, as such transfer is defined in the "Administrative Organization Act of 1968", article 1 of title 24, C.R.S.

(3) The primary care office includes the Colorado health service corps advisory council created in section 25-1.5-504.

## 25-1.5-404. Primary care office - powers and duties - rules.

(1) The primary care office has, at a minimum, the following powers and duties:

(a) To assess the health care professional needs of areas throughout the state;

(b) To apply to the United States department of health and human services, when appropriate, for designation of communities in the state as medically underserved areas, medically underserved populations, or health professional shortage areas or as any other designations necessary to participate in a federal program to address health care professional shortages;

(c) To maximize the placement of health care professionals who serve communities designated as medically underserved areas, medically underserved populations, or health professional shortage areas, or any other communities eligible for participation in a federal, state, or private program to address health care professional shortages, for the purpose of qualifying said communities for increased reimbursements, grants, and health care professional placements;

(d) To administer the Colorado health service corps pursuant to part 5 of this article;

(e) To administer or provide technical assistance to participants in applicable federal programs intended to address health care professional shortages, including the Conrad 30 J-1 visa waiver program, the national interest waiver program, and the national health service corps. The state board may promulgate rules as necessary for the administration of these programs and shall establish by rule application fees for the Conrad 30 J-1 visa waiver program and the national interest waiver program. The primary care office shall transfer the fee amounts collected to the state treasurer for crediting to the visa waiver program fund established in section 25-1.5-405.

(f) To seek and accept public or private gifts, grants, or donations to apply to the costs incurred in fulfilling the duties specified in this section and otherwise administering the programs within the office; and

(g) To administer nursing and health care professional faculty loan repayment pursuant to part 5 of this article.

### 25-1.5-405. Visa waiver program fund.

There is hereby created in the state treasury the visa waiver program fund, referred to in this section as the "fund", that consists of the application fees collected pursuant to section 25-1.5-404 (1) (e) and any additional moneys that the general assembly may appropriate to the fund. The moneys in the fund are subject to annual appropriation by the general assembly to the department for the direct and indirect costs incurred by the department in performing its duties under this part 4. Any moneys in the fund not expended for the purpose of this part 4 may be invested by the state treasurer as provided by law. All interest and income derived from the investment and deposit of moneys in the fund shall be credited to the fund. Any unexpended or unencumbered moneys remaining in the fund at the end of a fiscal year remain in the fund and shall not be credited or transferred to the general fund or another fund.

# PART 5. STATE HEALTH CARE PROFESSIONAL LOAN REPAYMENT PROGRAM

### 25-1.5-501. Legislative declaration.

(1) The general assembly hereby finds that there are areas of Colorado that suffer from a lack of health care professionals to serve, and a lack of nursing or other health care professional faculty to train health care professionals to meet, the medical needs of communities. The general assembly further finds that the state needs to implement incentives to encourage health care professionals to practice in these underserved areas and to encourage nursing faculty and other health care professional faculty to teach these health care professionals.

(2) It is therefore the intent of the general assembly in enacting this part 5 to create a state health service corps program that uses state moneys, federal moneys, when permissible, and contributions from communities and private sources to help repay the outstanding education loans that many health care professionals, nursing faculty, and health care professional faculty hold. In exchange for repayment of loans incurred for the purpose of obtaining education in their chosen health care professions, the health care professionals will commit to provide health care services in communities with underserved health care needs throughout the state, and the nursing and health care professional faculty will commit to providing a specified period of service in a qualified faculty position.

## 25-1.5-502. Definitions.

As used in this part 5, unless the context otherwise requires:

(1) "Advisory council" means the Colorado health service corps advisory council created pursuant to section 25-1.5-504.

(2) "Colorado health service corps" means the loan repayment program created and operated pursuant to this part 5.

(3) "Colorado health service corps fund" or "fund" means the Colorado health service corps fund created in section 25-1.5-506.

(4) "Federally designated health professional shortage area" means a health professional shortage area as defined in 42 U.S.C. sec. 254e.

(5) "Health care professional" means a licensed physician, an advanced practice nurse registered pursuant to section 12-38-111.5, C.R.S., a mental health practitioner, a licensed physician assistant, or any other licensed health care provider for which the federal government authorizes participation in a federally matched state loan repayment program to encourage health care professionals to provide services in underserved communities.

(6) "Health care professional faculty member" means a person who has an advanced degree in a health care professional field and is employed in a qualified faculty position.

(7) "National health service corps program" means the program established in 42 U.S.C. sec. 254d.

(8) "Nursing faculty member" means a person who has an advanced degree in nursing and is employed in a qualified faculty position.

(9) "Primary care office" means the primary care office created pursuant to part 4 of this article.

(10) "Primary health services" means health services regarding family medicine, general practice, general internal medicine, pediatrics, general obstetrics and gynecology, oral health, or mental health that are provided by health care professionals.

(11) "Qualified faculty position" means a part-time or full-time teaching position at an educational institution with accredited nursing or health care professional training programs, which position requires an advanced degree that meets national accreditation standards and is approved by the primary care office.

## 25-1.5-503. Colorado health service corps - program - creation - conditions.

(1) (a) (I) Beginning July 1, 2009, the primary care office shall maintain and administer, subject to available appropriations, the Colorado health service corps. Subject to available appropriations, the Colorado health service corps shall provide loan repayment for certain eligible health care professionals who provide primary health services. Beginning July 1, 2011, the Colorado health service corps shall also provide loan repayment for certain eligible nursing faculty or health care professional faculty members in qualified faculty positions.

(II) Under the Colorado health service corps, subject to the limitations specified in subsection (2) of this section, upon entering into a loan contract, the state may either:

(A) Make payments on the education loans of the health care professional, nursing faculty member, or health care professional faculty member; or

(B) Agree to make an advance payment in a lump sum of all or part of the principal, interest, and related expenses of the education loans of health care professionals, nursing faculty members, or health care professional faculty members, subject to the limitations specified in subsection (2) of this section.

(III) In consideration for receiving repayment of all or part of his or her education loan, the health care professional shall agree to provide primary health services in federally designated health professional shortage areas in Colorado.

(IV) In consideration for receiving repayment of all or part of his or her education loan, the nursing or other health care professional faculty member must agree to serve two or more consecutive academic years in a qualified faculty position.

(b) Repayment of loans under the Colorado health service corps may be made using moneys in the Colorado health service corps fund. The primary care office is authorized to receive and expend gifts, grants, and donations or moneys appropriated by the general assembly for the purpose of implementing the Colorado health service corps. In administering the Colorado health service corps, the primary care office shall collaborate with appropriate partners as needed to maximize the federal moneys available to the state for state loan repayment programs through the federal department of health and human services. The selection of health care professionals, nursing faculty members, and health care professional faculty members for participation in the Colorado health service corps is exempt from the competitive bidding requirements of the "Procurement Code", articles 101 to 112 of title 24, C.R.S.

(c) Health care professionals practicing in nonprimary care specialties or providing nonprimary health services are not eligible for loan repayments through the Colorado health service corps.

(d) (I) As a condition of receiving a loan repayment through the Colorado health service corps, a health care professional must enter into a contract pursuant to which the health care professional agrees to practice for at least two years in a community that is located in a federally designated health professional shortage area. The health care professional, the primary care office, and the community employer with which the health care professional is practicing must be parties to the contract.

(II) As a condition of receiving a loan repayment through the Colorado health service corps, a nursing faculty or health care professional faculty member must enter into a contract pursuant to which he or she agrees to serve at least two consecutive academic years or their equivalent in a qualified faculty position. The nursing faculty or health care professional faculty member, the primary care office, and the educational institution where the qualified faculty position is located must be parties to the contract.

(2) Subject to available appropriations, the primary care office shall annually select health care professionals, nursing faculty members, and health care professional members from the list provided by the advisory council pursuant to section 25-1.5-504 (6) to participate in the Colorado health service corps.

(3) The primary care office, after consulting with the advisory council and accredited health care professional training programs in the state, shall develop loan forgiveness criteria for nursing faculty and other health care professional faculty members. In determining whether to forgive the loan of a faculty member, the primary care office shall consider the following criteria:

(a) The faculty positions available at the educational institution at which the health care professional works;

(b) Documented recruiting efforts by the educational institution;

(c) The attributes of the educational or training program that are designed with the intent to address known shortages of health care professionals in Colorado;

(d) The type of programs offered at the educational institution, including associate, bachelor's, master's, or doctoral degrees in the health care professions, and the need for those programs in the state.

(4) In soliciting private grants to fund faculty loan repayments, the primary care office shall give priority to soliciting grants to fund repayments of loans for nursing faculty.

(5) A health care professional participating in the Colorado health service corps shall not practice with a for-profit private group or solo practice or at a proprietary hospital or clinic.

(6) A contract for loan repayment entered into pursuant to this part 5 must not include terms that are more favorable to health care professionals than the most favorable terms that the secretary of the federal department of health and human services is authorized to grant under the national health services corps program. In addition, each contract must include penalties for breach of contract that are at least as stringent as those available to the secretary of the federal department of health and human services. In the event of a breach of contract for a loan repayment entered into pursuant to this part 5, the primary care office shall enforce the contract and collect any damages or other penalties owed.

## 25-1.5-504. Colorado health service corps advisory council - creation - membership - duties.

(1) There is hereby created in the primary care office the Colorado health service corps advisory council to review applications for participation in the Colorado health service corps and make recommendations to the primary care office pursuant to section 25-1.5-503 (2) .

(2) The advisory council consists of thirteen members appointed by the governor as provided in this subsection (2) . In appointing members of the advisory council, the governor shall ensure that the advisory council includes at least one representative from each of the following organizations:

(a) The commission on family medicine created pursuant to part 6 of article 1 of title 25.5;

(b) A nonprofit statewide membership organization that provides programs and services to enhance rural health care in Colorado;

(c) A membership organization representing federally qualified health centers in Colorado;

(d) A foundation that funds a health care professional loan forgiveness program in Colorado;

(e) An economic development organization in Colorado;

(f) A membership organization representing community behavioral health care providers;

(g) An advanced practice nurse in a faculty position at an educational institution with health care professional programs, who is licensed to practice in Colorado;

(h) A physician who has experience in rural health, safety net clinics, or health equity;

(i) A nurse who has experience in rural health, safety net clinics, or health equity;

(j) A mental health provider who has experience in rural health, safety net clinics, or health equity;

(k) An oral health provider who has experience in rural health, safety net clinics, or health equity;

(l) A physician who is a faculty member of a medical school in Colorado; and

(m) A citizen representative who has knowledge in rural health, safety net clinics, or health equity.

(3) (a) Members appointed to the advisory council may serve terms of three years.

(b) The governor may appoint the same person to serve as a member of the advisory council for consecutive terms.

(4) (a) Advisory council members shall serve without compensation and without reimbursement for expenses.

(b) The primary care office shall provide staff assistance to the advisory council as necessary for the advisory council to complete the duties specified in this section.

(5) The advisory council shall review applications received from health care professionals, nursing faculty members, and health care professional faculty members to participate in the Colorado health service corps. Subject to available appropriations and federal requirements concerning eligibility for federal loan repayment matching funds, the advisory council shall annually select health care professionals, nursing faculty members, and health care professional faculty members to participate in the Colorado health service corps and shall forward its list of selected participants to the primary care office.

(6) Repealed.

## 25-1.5-505. Advisory council - report.

(1) On or before December 1, 2011, and on or before December 1 every two years thereafter, the advisory council shall submit to the governor, the health and human services committee of the senate, and the health and environment committee of the house of representatives, or any successor committees, a report that includes, at a minimum, the following information:

(a) Identification and a summary of successful loan forgiveness programs for health care professionals and best practices in health care professional loan forgiveness programs across the country;

(b) A description of the programmatic goals of the Colorado health service corps, including the present status of and any barriers to meeting those goals;

(c) Existing efforts and potential future projects to overcome any barriers to meeting the programmatic goals of the Colorado health service corps;

(d) An analysis of the impact of the Colorado health service corps program;

(e) If applicable, results of any surveys conducted of state health professional incentive programs in primary care and any recommendations to individually enhance, improve coordination among, and potentially consolidate existing or potential programs to better address Colorado's primary care workforce issues; and

(f) The number of nursing faculty or other health care professional faculty members who receive moneys from the Colorado health service corps and the number of educational institutions where the recipients teach.

### 25-1.5-506. Colorado health service corps fund - created - acceptance of grants and donations.

(1) The Colorado health service corps fund is hereby created in the state treasury, which fund consists of:

(a) All general fund moneys appropriated by the general assembly for the Colorado health service corps, the first five hundred thousand dollars of which shall be used solely for loan repayments for nursing faculty;

(b) Damages and penalties collected from breach of contract actions for loan repayment contracts; and

(c) For the 2016-17 fiscal year and each fiscal year thereafter, tobacco litigation settlement moneys transferred to the fund by the state treasurer pursuant to section 24-75-1104.5 (1.7) (n) , C.R.S.

(2) (a) The moneys in the fund, other than the moneys described in paragraph (c) of subsection (1) of this section, are hereby continuously appropriated to the primary care office for the Colorado health service corps. Any moneys in the fund not expended for the purpose of this part 5 may be invested by the state treasurer as provided by law. All interest and income derived from the investment and deposit of moneys in the fund shall be credited to the fund. Any unexpended and unencumbered moneys remaining in the fund at the end of a fiscal year remain in the fund and shall not be credited or transferred to the general fund or another fund.

(b) The moneys described in paragraph (c) of subsection (1) of this section are subject to annual appropriation by the general assembly to the primary care office for the Colorado health service corps.

(3) The primary care office is authorized to receive contributions, grants, and services from public and private sources to carry out the purposes of this part 5.

# PART 6. UNIFORM EMERGENCY VOLUNTEERHEALTH PRACTITIONERS ACT

### 25-1.5-601. Short title.

The short title of this part 6 is the "Uniform Emergency Volunteer Health Practitioners Act".

### 25-1.5-602. Definitions.

In this part 6:

(1) "Disaster management agency" means the department of public health and environment.

(2) "Disaster relief organization" means an entity that provides emergency or disaster relief services that include health or veterinary services provided by volunteer health practitioners and that:

(A) Is designated or recognized as a provider of those services pursuant to a disaster response and recovery plan adopted by an agency of the federal government or the disaster management agency; or

(B) Regularly plans and conducts its activities in coordination with an agency of the federal government or the disaster management agency.

(3) "Emergency" means an event or condition that is an emergency, disaster, incident of bioterrorism, emergency epidemic, pandemic influenza, or other public health emergency under section 24-33.5-704.

(4) "Emergency declaration" means a declaration of emergency issued by the governor pursuant to section 24-33.5-704.

(5) "Emergency management assistance compact" means the interstate compact approved by congress by Pub.L. 104-321, 110 Stat. 3877, part 29 of article 60 of title 24.

(6) "Entity" means a person other than an individual.

(7) "Health facility" means an entity licensed under the laws of this or another state to provide health or veterinary services.

(8) "Health practitioner" means an individual licensed under the laws of this or another state to provide health or veterinary services.

(9) "Health services" means the provision of treatment, care, advice or guidance, or other services, or supplies, related to the health or death of individuals or human populations, to the extent necessary to respond to an emergency, including:

(A) The following, concerning the physical or mental condition or functional status of an individual or affecting the structure or function of the body:

(i) Preventive, diagnostic, therapeutic, rehabilitative, maintenance, or palliative care; and

(ii) Counseling, assessment, procedures, or other services;

(B) Sale or dispensing of a drug, a device, equipment, or another item to an individual in accordance with a prescription; and

(C) Funeral, cremation, cemetery, or other mortuary services.

(10) "Host entity" means an entity operating in this state that uses volunteer health practitioners to respond to an emergency.

(11) "License" means authorization by a state to engage in health or veterinary services that are unlawful without the authorization. The term includes authorization under the laws of this state to an individual to provide health or veterinary services based upon a national certification issued by a public or private entity.

(12) "Person" means an individual, corporation, business trust, trust, partnership, limited liability company, association, joint venture, public corporation, government or governmental subdivision, agency, or instrumentality, or any other legal or commercial entity.

(13) "Scope of practice" means the extent of the authorization to provide health or veterinary services granted to a health practitioner by a license issued to the practitioner in the state in which the principal part of the practitioner's services are rendered, including any conditions imposed by the licensing authority.

(14) "State" means a state of the United States, the District of Columbia, Puerto Rico, the United States Virgin Islands, or any territory or insular possession subject to the jurisdiction of the United States.

(15) "Veterinary services" means the provision of treatment, care, advice or guidance, or other services, or supplies, related to the health or death of an animal or to animal populations, to the extent necessary to respond to an emergency, including:

(A) Diagnosis, treatment, or prevention of an animal disease, injury, or other physical or mental condition by the prescription, administration, or dispensing of vaccine, medicine, surgery, or therapy;

(B) Use of a procedure for reproductive management; and

(C) Monitoring and treatment of animal populations for diseases that have spread or demonstrate the potential to spread to humans.

(16) "Volunteer health practitioner" means a health practitioner who provides health or veterinary services, whether or not the practitioner receives compensation for those services. The term does not include a practitioner who receives compensation pursuant to a preexisting employment relationship with a host entity or affiliate that requires the practitioner to provide health services in this state, unless the practitioner is not a resident of this state and is employed by a disaster relief

organization providing services in this state while an emergency declaration is in effect.

## 25-1.5-603. Applicability to volunteer health practitioners.

This part 6 applies to volunteer health practitioners registered with a registration system that complies with section 25-1.5-605 and who provide health or veterinary services in this state for a host entity while an emergency declaration is in effect.

## 25-1.5-604. Regulation of services during emergency.

(a) While an emergency declaration is in effect, the disaster management agency, in consultation with the department of agriculture with regard to veterinary services, may limit, restrict, or otherwise regulate:

(1) The duration of practice by volunteer health practitioners;

(2) The geographical areas in which volunteer health practitioners may practice;

(3) The types of volunteer health practitioners who may practice; and

(4) Any other matters necessary to coordinate effectively the provision of health or veterinary services during the emergency.

(b) An order issued pursuant to subsection (a) of this section may take effect immediately, without prior notice or comment, and is not a rule within the meaning of the "State Administrative Procedure Act", article 4 of title 24.

(c) A host entity that uses volunteer health practitioners to provide health or veterinary services in this state shall:

(1) Consult and coordinate its activities with the disaster management agency and, with regard to veterinary services, the department of agriculture, to the extent practicable to provide for the efficient and effective use of volunteer health practitioners; and

(2) Comply with any laws other than this part 6 relating to the management of emergency health or veterinary services, including articles 29.1 to 43 of title 12.

## 25-1.5-605. Volunteer health practitioner registration systems.

(a) To qualify as a volunteer health practitioner registration system, a system must:

(1) Accept applications for the registration of volunteer health practitioners before or during an emergency;

(2) Include information about the licensure and good standing of health practitioners that is accessible by authorized persons;

(3) Be capable of confirming the accuracy of information concerning whether a health practitioner is licensed and in good standing before health services or veterinary services are provided under this part 6; and

(4) Meet one of the following conditions:

(A) Be an emergency system for advance registration of volunteer health-care practitioners established by a state and funded through the health resources services administration under section 319I of the "Public Health Service Act", 42 U.S.C. sec. 247d-7b, as amended;

(B) Be a local unit consisting of trained and equipped emergency response, public health, and medical personnel formed pursuant to section 2801 of the "Public Health Service Act", 42 U.S.C. sec. 300hh, as amended;

(C) Be operated by a:

(i) Disaster relief organization;

(ii) Licensing board;

(iii) National or regional association of licensing boards or health practitioners;

(iv) Health facility that provides comprehensive inpatient and outpatient health-care services, including a tertiary care and teaching hospital; or

(v) Governmental entity; or

(D) Be designated by the disaster management agency as a registration system for purposes of this part 6.

(b) While an emergency declaration is in effect, the disaster management agency, a person authorized to act on behalf of the disaster management agency, or a host entity, may confirm whether volunteer health practitioners utilized in this state are registered with a registration system that complies with subsection (a) of this section. Confirmation is limited to obtaining identities of the practitioners from the system and determining whether the system indicates that the practitioners are licensed and in good standing.

(c) Upon request of a person in this state authorized under subsection (b) of this section, or a similarly authorized person in another state, a registration system located in this state shall notify the person of the identities of volunteer health practitioners and whether the practitioners are licensed and in good standing.

(d) A host entity is not required to use the services of a volunteer health practitioner even if the practitioner is registered with a registration system that indicates that the practitioner is licensed and in good standing.

## 25-1.5-606. Recognition of volunteer health practitioners licensed in other states.

(a) While an emergency declaration is in effect, a volunteer health practitioner, registered with a registration system that complies with section 25-1.5-605 and licensed and in good standing in the state upon which the practitioner's registration is based, may practice in this state to the extent authorized by this part 6 as if the practitioner were licensed in this state.

(b) A volunteer health practitioner qualified under subsection (a) of this section is not entitled to the protections of this part 6 if the practitioner is licensed in more than one state and any license of the practitioner is suspended, revoked, or subject to an agency order limiting or restricting practice privileges, or has been voluntarily terminated under threat of sanction.

## 25-1.5-607. No effect on credentialing and privileging.

(a) In this section:

(1) "Credentialing" means obtaining, verifying, and assessing the qualifications of a health practitioner to provide treatment, care, or services in or for a health facility.

(2) "Privileging" means the authorizing by an appropriate authority, such as a governing body, of a health practitioner to provide specific treatment, care, or services at a health facility subject to limits based on factors that include license, education, training, experience, competence, health status, and specialized skill.

(b) This part 6 does not affect credentialing or privileging standards of a health facility and does not preclude a health facility from waiving or modifying those standards while an emergency declaration is in effect.

## 25-1.5-608. Provision of volunteer health or veterinary services - administrative sanctions.

(a) Subject to subsections (b) and (c) of this section, a volunteer health practitioner shall adhere to the scope of practice for a similarly licensed practitioner established by the licensing provisions, practice acts, or other laws of this state.

(b) Except as otherwise provided in subsection (c) of this section, this part 6 does not authorize a volunteer health practitioner to provide services that are outside the practitioner's scope of practice, even if a similarly licensed practitioner in this state would be permitted to provide the services.

(c) The disaster management agency may modify or restrict the health or veterinary services that volunteer health practitioners may provide pursuant to this part 6, and, with regard to emergencies that require only veterinary services, the department of agriculture may modify or restrict the veterinary services that volunteer health practitioners may provide pursuant to this part 6. An order under this subsection (c) may take effect immediately, without prior notice or comment, and is not a rule within the meaning of the "State Administrative Procedure Act", article 4 of title 24.

(d) A host entity may restrict the health or veterinary services that a volunteer health practitioner may provide pursuant to this part 6.

(e) A volunteer health practitioner does not engage in unauthorized practice unless the practitioner has reason to know of any limitation, modification, or restriction under this section or that a similarly licensed practitioner in this state would not be permitted to provide the services. A volunteer health practitioner has reason to know of a limitation, modification, or restriction or that a similarly licensed practitioner in this state would not be permitted to provide a service if:

(1) The practitioner knows the limitation, modification, or restriction exists or that a similarly licensed practitioner in this state would not be permitted to provide the service; or

(2) From all the facts and circumstances known to the practitioner at the relevant time, a reasonable person would conclude that the limitation, modification, or restriction exists or that a similarly licensed practitioner in this state would not be permitted to provide the service.

(f) In addition to the authority granted by law of this state other than this part 6 to regulate the conduct of health practitioners, a licensing board or other disciplinary authority in this state:

(1) May impose administrative sanctions upon a health practitioner licensed in this state for conduct outside of this state in response to an out-of-state emergency;

(2) May impose administrative sanctions upon a practitioner not licensed in this state for conduct in this state in response to an in-state emergency; and

(3) Shall report any administrative sanctions imposed upon a practitioner licensed in another state to the appropriate licensing board or other disciplinary authority in any other state in which the practitioner is known to be licensed.

(g) In determining whether to impose administrative sanctions under subsection (f) of this section, a licensing board or other disciplinary authority shall consider the circumstances in which the conduct took place, including any exigent circumstances, and the practitioner's scope of practice, education, training, experience, and specialized skill.

## 25-1.5-609. Relation to other laws.

(a) This part 6 does not limit rights, privileges, or immunities provided to volunteer health practitioners by laws other than this part 6. Except as otherwise provided in subsection (b) of this section, this part 6 does not affect requirements for the use of health practitioners pursuant to the emergency management assistance compact.

(b) The office of emergency management created in section 24-33.5-705, pursuant to the emergency management assistance compact, may incorporate into the emergency forces of this state volunteer health practitioners who are not officers or employees of this state, a political subdivision of this state, or a municipality or other local government within this state.

## 25-1.5-610. Rules.

The executive director of the department of public health and environment may promulgate rules to implement this part 6. In doing so, the executive director shall consult with and consider the recommendations of the department of agriculture with regard to veterinary services and the entity established to coordinate the implementation of the emergency management assistance compact and shall also consult with and consider rules promulgated by similarly empowered agencies in other states to promote uniformity of application of this part 6 and make the emergency response systems in the various states reasonably compatible.

## 25-1.5-611. Civil liability for volunteer health practitioners - vicarious liability.

A volunteer health practitioner's immunity from civil liability may be affected by section 13-21-115.5.

## 25-1.5-612. Workers' compensation coverage.

(Reserved)

## 25-1.5-613. Uniformity of application and construction.

In applying and construing this part 6, consideration must be given to the need to promote uniformity of the law with respect to its subject matter among states that enact it.

# VITAL STATISTICS

# ARTICLE 2. VITAL STATISTICS

## 25-2-101. Short title.

This article shall be known and may be cited as the "Vital Statistics Act of 1984".

## 25-2-102. Definitions.

As used in this article, unless the context otherwise requires:

(1) "Dead body" means a lifeless human body or parts of such body or bones thereof from the state of which it reasonably may be concluded that death recently occurred.

(2) "Fetal death" means death prior to the complete expulsion or extraction from its mother of a product of human conception, irrespective of the duration of pregnancy. The death is indicated by the fact that after such expulsion or extraction the fetus does not breathe or show any other evidence of life such as beating of the heart, pulsation of the umbilical cord, or definite movement of voluntary muscles.

(2.5) "Final disposition" means the burial, interment, cremation, removal from the state, or other authorized disposition of a dead body or fetus.

(2.7) "Induced termination of pregnancy" means the purposeful interruption of a pregnancy with an intention other than producing a live-born infant or removing a dead fetus and that does not result in a live birth.

(3) "Institution" means any establishment which provides inpatient medical, surgical, or diagnostic care or treatment or nursing, custodial, or domiciliary care to two or more unrelated individuals or to which persons are committed by law.

(3.5) "Physician" means a person licensed to practice medicine in Colorado pursuant to article 36 of title 12, C.R.S.

(4) "Regulations" means regulations duly adopted pursuant to section 25-2-103.

(4.5) "Stillborn death" or "stillbirth" means death prior to the complete expulsion or extraction from its mother of a product of human conception, occurring after the twentieth week of pregnancy, and does not include "induced termination of pregnancy", as defined by subsection (2.7) of this section. The death is indicated by the fact that after such expulsion or extraction the fetus does not breathe or show any other evidence of life such as beating of the heart, pulsation of the umbilical cord, or definite movement of voluntary muscles.

(5) "Vital statistics certificate" means any certificate required by section 25-2-110, 25-2-112, or 25-2-112.3.

(6) "Vital statistics report" means any report required by section 25-2-106 or 25-2-107.

## 25-2-103. Centralized registration system for all vital statistics - appointment of registrar - rules.

(1) In order to provide for the maintenance of a centralized registry of the vital statistics of this state, the office of state registrar of vital statistics, referred to in this article as the "state registrar", is hereby created in the department of public health and environment. The state registrar shall be

appointed by the state board of health and shall have such staff and clerical help as reasonably may be required in the performance of the state registrar's duties. The state registrar and the staff and clerical help of the state registrar shall be subject to the state constitution and state personnel system laws.

(2) The state board of health shall adopt, promulgate, amend, and repeal such rules and orders in accordance with the provisions of section 24-4-103, C.R.S., as are necessary and proper for carrying out the provisions of this article.

(3) (a) The state registrar shall direct and supervise the operation of the vital statistics system, prepare and publish annual reports of vital statistics, and administer and enforce the provisions of this article and all rules issued under this article.

(b) In conjunction with the requirements of paragraph (a) of this subsection (3) , the state registrar shall collect the name of the provider of prenatal care, if any, and the name of the provider of initial delivery services and shall require that such information be reported on all birth certificates. In addition, whenever an investigation or inquest is conducted pursuant to section 30-10-606, C.R.S., concerning the death of a child under one year of age, the coroner shall forward the information described in this paragraph (b) to the state registrar for inclusion on the death certificate of the subject of the inquest or investigation.

(4) Federal, state, local, and other public or private agencies may, upon request, be furnished copies of records of data for statistical purposes upon such terms and conditions as may be prescribed by regulation.

(4.5) Notwithstanding any other provision of law that limits the sharing of vital statistics, after receiving the list of names and social security numbers of individuals who received property tax exemptions as either qualifying seniors or disabled veterans for the prior year that is provided by the property tax administrator pursuant to section 39-3-207, C.R.S., the state registrar shall identify all individuals on the list who have died and transmit a list of the names and social security numbers of such individuals to the administrator.

(5) The state registrar shall designate organized county, district, or municipal public health agencies established pursuant to part 5 of article 1 of this title and may establish or designate additional offices throughout Colorado to aid in the efficient administration of the system of vital statistics.

(6) The state registrar may:

(a) Require departments or offices so designated or established to comply with performance and accounting standards as set forth in rules promulgated by the state board of health;

(b) Delegate such functions and duties to the staff and clerical help and to any offices established or designated by the state registrar pursuant to this section as deemed necessary or expedient;

(c) Conduct training programs to promote the uniformity of the administration of this article throughout Colorado.

## 25-2-104. Registration of vital statistics.

Promptly upon receipt of each vital statistics report or certificate, the state registrar shall examine it to determine that it has been properly completed. If the report has been properly completed, the state registrar shall register the statistical event described therein and shall note the date the report has been accepted as having been properly completed and shall place the same, or a reproduction thereof, made in accordance with section 25-2-117 (3) , in the permanent files of the office. If not properly completed, the state registrar shall take such action with respect thereto as may be required by applicable regulations.

## 25-2-105. Vital statistics, reports, and certificates - forms and information to be included.

(1) The state registrar shall prescribe, furnish, and distribute such forms as are required by this article and shall furnish and distribute such rules as are promulgated pursuant to section 25-2-103. The state registrar may also prescribe such other means for transmission of data as will accomplish

the purpose of complete and accurate reporting and registration.

(2) The state registrar shall prescribe, furnish, and distribute such forms as are required by this article with respect to civil union certificates, as defined in section 14-15-103 (2) , C.R.S.

## 25-2-106. Reports of marriage.

Each county clerk and recorder shall prepare a report containing such information and using such form as may be prescribed and furnished by the state registrar with respect to every duly executed marriage certificate that is returned in accordance with section 14-2-109, C.R.S. On or before the tenth day of each month, or more frequently if so requested by the state registrar, such clerk and recorder shall forward to the state registrar all such marriage reports for all marriage certificates returned in the preceding period. Certified copies of marriage certificates may be issued by any clerk and recorder.

## 25-2-106.5. Reports of civil unions.

Each county clerk and recorder shall prepare a report containing such information and using the form as may be prescribed and furnished by the state registrar with respect to every duly executed civil union certificate registered in accordance with section 14-15-112, C.R.S. On or before the tenth day of each month, or more frequently if requested by the state registrar, the county clerk and recorder shall forward to the state registrar all civil union reports for all civil union certificates registered in the preceding period. The county clerk and recorder may issue certified copies of civil union certificates.

## 25-2-107. Reports of adoption, dissolution of marriage, parentage, and other court proceedings affecting vital statistics - tax on court action affecting vital statistics.

(1) The clerk of each court or, for parentage proceedings, the clerk of the court or a delegate child support enforcement unit shall prepare a report containing such information and using such form as may be prescribed and furnished by the state registrar with respect to every decree entered by the court with respect to parentage, legitimacy, adoption, change of name, dissolution of marriage, legal separation, or declaration of invalidity of marriage and every decree amending or nullifying such a decree and also with respect to every decree entered pursuant to section 25-2-114. On or before the tenth day of each month, or more frequently if so requested by the state registrar, such clerk shall forward to the state registrar the reports for all such decrees entered during the preceding period.

(2) In order to help defray the maintenance of vital statistics records, there shall be levied, in addition to the tax levied under section 2-5-119, C.R.S., a tax of three dollars upon each action with respect to parentage, legitimacy, adoption, change of name, dissolution of marriage, legal separation, or declaration of invalidity of marriage that is filed in the office of each clerk of a court of record in this state on or after July 1, 1985. The tax shall be paid at the time of the filing of such action, and the clerk shall keep such tax in a separate fund and shall transmit such tax monthly to the state treasurer, who shall credit the same to the vital statistics records cash fund pursuant to section 25-2-121. A delegate child support enforcement unit acting pursuant to article 13 of title 26, C.R.S., shall be exempt from paying the tax authorized in this subsection (2) .

## 25-2-107.5. Reports of dissolution of civil unions, legal separation of civil unions, or declarations of invalidity of civil unions - fee.

(1) The clerk of each court shall prepare a report containing such information and using such form as may be prescribed and furnished by the state registrar with respect to every decree entered by the court for the dissolution of a civil union, legal separation of a civil union, or declaration of invalidity of a civil union, and every decree amending or nullifying such a decree. On or before the tenth day of each month, or more frequently if so requested by the state registrar, the clerk

shall forward to the state registrar the reports for all such decrees entered during the preceding period.

(2) In order to defray the costs of maintenance of vital statistics records, the clerk of the court shall assess a fee of three dollars upon each action filed for a dissolution of a civil union, legal separation of a civil union, or declaration of invalidity of a civil union that is filed in the office of each clerk of a court of record in this state on or after May 1, 2013. The clerk shall keep any fees so collected in a separate fund, and each month the clerk shall transmit those fees collected to the state treasurer, who shall credit the same to the vital statistics records cash fund created in section 25-2-121.

## 25-2-108. Reports and certificates as to births and deaths. (Repealed)

## 25-2-109. Local registration districts for processing of birth and death certificates. (Repealed)

## 25-2-110. Certificates of death.

(1) (a) A certificate of death for each death, including a stillborn death, that occurs in Colorado must be filed with the state registrar or as otherwise directed by the state registrar, within five days after the death occurs and prior to final disposition. The state registrar shall register the certificate if it has been completed in accordance with this section. Every certificate of death must identify the decedent's social security number, if available. If the place of death is unknown but the dead body is found in Colorado, the certificate of death must be completed and filed in accordance with this section. The place where the body is found must be shown as the place of death. If the date of death is unknown, the date must be determined by approximation.

(b) (I) The department of public health and environment shall create and the state registrar shall use an electronic death registration system for the purpose of collecting death information from funeral directors, coroners, physicians, local registrars, health facilities, and other authorized individuals, as determined by the department. Death information submitted electronically by a funeral director, coroner, physician, local registrar, health facility, or authorized individual, as determined by the department, to the electronic death registration system for purposes of fulfilling the requirements of this section satisfies the signature and filing requirements of this section and section 30-10-606, C.R.S.

(II) Repealed.

(c) Once a certificate of death has been filed pursuant to paragraph (a) of this subsection (1), a verification of death document may be used by local offices of vital statistics and the office of the state registrar of vital statistics when verifying a vital event to a person or organization that has requested a verification of fact-of-death. A verification of death document must include the name and address of the decedent, the date of death, the place of death, the date the document is filed, the state file number, and the name of any spouse of the decedent. A verification of death document is not required to contain a social security number of the deceased as is otherwise required of a certificate of death under paragraph (a) of this subsection (1).

(2) When a death occurs in a moving conveyance in the United States and the body is first removed from the conveyance in Colorado, the death shall be registered in Colorado, and the place where it is first removed shall be considered the place of death. When a death occurs on a moving conveyance while in international air space or in a foreign country or its air space and the body is first removed from the conveyance in Colorado, the death shall be registered in Colorado, but the certificate shall show the actual place of death insofar as can be determined.

(3) (a) The funeral director or person acting as such who first assumes custody of a dead body, stillborn fetus, or dead fetus shall be responsible for the filing of the death certificate required by subsection (1) of this section. He or she shall obtain the personal data required by the certificate

from the next of kin or the best qualified person or source available. He or she shall obtain the medical certification necessary to complete the portion of the certificate pertaining to the cause of death from the best qualified person or source available, pursuant to subsection (4) of this section.

(b) In the case of a stillborn fetus, notwithstanding the provisions of paragraph (a) of this subsection (3) , the physician, nurse, or other medical personnel attending to the stillborn death may assume responsibility for filing the death certificate required by paragraph (a) of this subsection (3) . The person filing the death certificate in the case of a stillborn fetus shall obtain the personal data required by the certificate from a parent and shall include a name on the death certificate if a parent desires to identify a name.

(c) If a death certificate is not filed in the case of a stillborn death as required by paragraph (a) of this subsection (3) , a parent may inform the state registrar of the information necessary to complete the death certificate. The state registrar shall confirm such information and complete the death certificate accordingly.

(4) Except when inquiry is required by section 30-10-606, C.R.S., the physician in charge of the patient's care for the illness or condition that resulted in death shall complete, sign, and return to the funeral director or person acting as such all medical certification within forty-eight hours after a death occurs. In the absence of said physician or with his or her approval, the certificate may be completed and signed by his or her associate physician, by the chief medical officer of the institution in which the death occurred, or by the physician who performed an autopsy upon the decedent, if such individual has access to the medical history of the case, if he or she views the decedent at or after the time of death, and if the death is due to natural causes. If an autopsy is performed, the certification shall indicate whether the decedent was pregnant at the time of death, and said information shall be reported on the death certificate as required by subsection (9) of this section.

(5) When inquiry is required by section 30-10-606, C.R.S., the coroner shall determine the cause of death and shall complete and sign the medical certification within forty-eight hours after taking charge of the case. If an autopsy is performed, the certification shall indicate whether the decedent was pregnant at the time of death, and said information shall be reported on the death certificate as required by subsection (9) of this section.

(6) If the cause of death cannot be determined within forty-eight hours after a death, the medical certification shall be completed as provided by rule. If an autopsy is performed, the certification shall indicate whether the decedent was pregnant at the time of death, and said information shall be reported on the death certificate as required by subsection (9) of this section. The attending physician or coroner shall give the funeral director or person acting as such notice of the reason for the delay, and final disposition of the body shall not be made until authorized by the office designated or established pursuant to section 25-2-103 in the county where the death occurred or, if such an office does not exist in the county where the death occurred, final disposition of the body shall not be made until authorized by the coroner or the coroner's designee.

(7) When a death is presumed to have occurred within Colorado but the body cannot be located, a death certificate may be prepared by the state registrar upon receipt of an order of a court of competent jurisdiction which shall include the finding of facts required to complete the death certificate. Such a death certificate shall be marked "presumptive" and shall show on its face the date of registration and shall identify the court and the date of decree.

(8) Every funeral establishment shall maintain registration with the office of the state registrar and shall act in accordance with the provisions of this article.

(9) (a) If an autopsy is performed, a certificate of death shall identify whether the decedent was pregnant at the time of death.

(b) The requirement in this subsection (9) and subsections (4) , (5) , and (6) of this section to indicate whether the decedent was pregnant at the time of death shall be complied with when the person required to make the designation has access to the certification form that permits compliance.

(10) Whenever in the Colorado Revised Statutes the terms "certificate of death" or "death certificate" are used, except as to the initial certificate of death required pursuant to paragraph (a)

of subsection (1) of this section, the same two terms include a verification of death document that is certified by the state registrar and issued pursuant to paragraph (c) of subsection (1) of this section.

## 25-2-110.5. Fetal deaths - treatment of remains.
(1) In every instance of fetal death, the pregnant woman shall have the option of treating the remains of a fetal death pursuant to article 54 of title 12, C.R.S.
(2) In every instance of fetal death, the health care provider, upon request of the pregnant woman, shall release to the woman or the woman's designee the remains of a fetal death for final disposition in accordance with applicable law. Such request shall be made by the pregnant woman or her authorized representative prior to or immediately following the expulsion or extraction of the fetal remains. Unless a timely request was made, nothing in this section shall require the health care provider to maintain or preserve the fetal remains.
(3) (a) Nothing in this section shall prohibit a health care provider from conducting or acquiring medical tests on the remains of a fetal death prior to release.
(b) Upon a request pursuant to subsection (2) of this section, whenever a medical test is conducted pursuant to paragraph (a) of this subsection (3) , the health care provider conducting the test shall, where medically permissible and otherwise permitted by law, release to the pregnant woman or the woman's designee the remains of a fetal death for final disposition.
(4) Nothing in this section shall prohibit the health care provider from requiring a release of liability for the release of the remains of a fetal death prior to such release.
(5) A health care provider shall be immune from all civil or criminal liability, suit, or sanction with regard to any action taken in good-faith compliance with the provisions of this section.

## 25-2-111. Dead bodies - disposition - removal from state - records.
(1) Any person requested to act as funeral director for a dead body or otherwise whoever first assumes custody of a dead body shall, prior to final disposition of the body, obtain authorization for final disposition of the body. The office designated or established pursuant to section 25-2-103 in the county where the death occurred or, if such an office does not exist in the county where the death occurred, the coroner or the coroner's designee shall authorize final disposition of the body on a form prescribed and furnished by the state registrar. No body shall be buried, cremated, deposited in a vault or tomb, or otherwise disposed of, nor shall any body be removed from this state, until such authorization has been obtained, completed, and approved. The coroner or the coroner's designee shall include in the authorization notice of the requirements of subsection (7) of this section.
(2) A disposition permit issued under the law of another state which accompanies a dead body or fetus brought into this state shall be authority for final disposition of the body or fetus in this state.
(3) Repealed.
(4) Any person who removes from the place of death or transports or finally disposes of a dead body or fetus, in addition to filing any certificate or other form required by this article, shall keep a record which shall identify the body and such information pertaining to his receipt, removal, and delivery of such body as may be prescribed in regulations. Such record shall be retained for a period of not less than seven years and shall be made available for inspection by the state registrar or his representative upon demand.
(5) No sexton or other person in charge of any place in which interment or other disposition of dead bodies is made shall inter or allow interment or other disposition of a dead body or fetus unless it is accompanied by authorization for final disposition.
(6) Authorization for disinterment and reinterment shall be required prior to disinterment of a dead body or fetus. Such authorization shall be issued by the state registrar to a funeral director or person acting as such upon proper application.
(7) (a) The owner of land that is used to inter a dead human body shall record the burial within thirty days after the burial with the county clerk and recorder of the county in which the land is

situated. The owner shall record the following:

(I) The dead person's name as it appears on the death certificate;

(II) The dead person's date of birth;

(III) The dead person's age at the time of death;

(IV) The cause of death;

(V) The name of the owner or owners of the property where the dead human body is interred;

(VI) The legal description of the property where the dead human body is interred if the person is interred on private property;

(VII) The reception number for the death certificate if recorded by the county clerk; and

(VIII) The latitude and longitude coordinates, such as those given by a global positioning system, that are verified by two witnesses or the county coroner, sheriff, or a designee of the county coroner or sheriff.

(b) This subsection (7) does not apply to dead human bodies interred in cemeteries, vaults, or tombs operated or maintained by public entities or businesses that inter people in the ordinary course of business and are available to the general public.

## 25-2-111.5. Transfer of fetal tissue from induced termination of pregnancy - legislative declaration.

(1) The general assembly hereby finds, determines, and declares that the United States congress enacted 42 U.S.C. sec. 289g-2, prohibiting the acquisition, receipt, or other transfer of human fetal tissue for valuable consideration if the transfer affects interstate commerce. The general assembly determines and declares that the acquisition, receipt, or other transfer of human fetal tissue for valuable consideration affects intrastate commerce and is not in the public interest of the residents of Colorado. Therefore, the general assembly finds, determines, and declares that the exchange for valuable consideration of human fetal tissue should be prohibited.

(2) (a) No physician or institution that performs procedures for the induced termination of pregnancy shall transfer such tissue for valuable consideration to any organization or person that conducts research using fetal tissue or that transplants fetal tissue for therapeutic purposes. For the purposes of this section, "valuable consideration" includes, but is not limited to:

(I) Any lease-sharing agreement in excess of the current market value for commercial rental property for the area in which the physician's or institution's place of business is located;

(II) Any lease-sharing agreement that is based on the term or number of induced terminations of pregnancy performed by such physician or institution;

(III) Any moneys, gifts in lieu of money, barter arrangements, or exchange of services that do not constitute reasonable payment associated with the transportation, implantation, processing, preservation, quality control, or storage of human fetal tissue as defined in 42 U.S.C. sec. 289g-2; or

(IV) Any agreement to purchase fetal tissue for a profit.

(b) Nothing in this subsection (2) shall prevent the disposition of fetal tissue from an induced termination of pregnancy pursuant to part 4 of article 15 of this title.

(3) Any physician or institution that violates subsection (2) of this section shall be fined by the state registrar not more than ten thousand dollars, depending upon the severity of the violation.

(4) The department of public health and environment may promulgate rules related to enforcement activities necessary to implement subsections (2) and (3) of this section.

## 25-2-112. Certificates of birth - filing - establishment of paternity.

(1) A certificate of birth for each live birth which occurs in this state shall be filed with the state registrar or as otherwise directed by the state registrar within ten days after such birth and shall be registered if it has been completed and filed in accordance with this section. When a birth occurs on a moving conveyance within the United States and the child is first removed from the conveyance in Colorado, the birth shall be registered in Colorado, and the place where the child is first removed shall be considered the place of birth. When a birth occurs on a moving conveyance

while in international air space or in a foreign country or its air space and the child is first removed from the conveyance in Colorado, the birth shall be registered in this state but the certificate shall show the actual place of birth insofar as can be determined. Either of the parents of the child shall verify the accuracy of the personal data entered thereon in time to permit its filing within such ten-day period.

(2) When a birth occurs in an institution, or upon order of any court with proper jurisdiction, the person in charge of the institution or such person's designated representative shall obtain the personal data, prepare the certificate, certify the authenticity of the birth registration either by signature or by an approved electronic process, and file it with the state registrar or as otherwise directed by the state registrar within the required ten days; the physician in attendance shall provide the medical information required by the certificate within five days after the birth. When the birth occurs outside an institution, the certificate shall be prepared and filed by the physician in attendance at or immediately after birth, or in the absence of such a physician by any person witnessing the birth, or in the absence of any such witness by the father or mother, or in the absence of the father and the inability of the mother by the person in charge of the premises where the birth occurred. The person who completes and files the certificate shall also be responsible for obtaining the social security account numbers of the parents and delivering those numbers to the state registrar along with the certificate.

(2.5) Repealed.

(2.7) For the purposes of a birth registration, the mother is deemed to be the woman who has given birth to the child, unless otherwise provided by law or determined by a court of competent jurisdiction prior to the filing of the birth certificate. The information about the father shall be entered as provided in subsection (3) of this section.

(3) (a) If the mother was married either at the time of conception or birth, the name of the husband shall be entered on the certificate as the father of the child unless:

(I) Paternity has been determined otherwise by a court of competent jurisdiction, in which case the name of the father as so determined shall be entered; or

(II) The mother and the mother's husband execute joint or separate forms prescribed and furnished by the state registrar reflecting the mother's and the husband's signatures individually witnessed and attesting that the husband is not the father of the child, in which case, information about the father shall be omitted from the certificate; or

(III) The mother executes a form prescribed and furnished by the state registrar attesting that the husband is not the father and that the putative father is the father, the putative father executes a form prescribed and furnished by the state registrar attesting that he is the father, and the husband executes a form prescribed and furnished by the state registrar attesting that he is not the father. Such forms may be joint or individual or a combination thereof, and each signature shall be individually witnessed. In such event, the putative father shall be shown as the father on the certificate.

(IV) A court of competent jurisdiction has determined the husband is not the presumed father and the putative father executes a form prescribed and furnished by the state registrar which is individually witnessed attesting that he is the father and the mother executes a form prescribed and furnished by the state registrar which is individually witnessed that the putative father is the father. In such event the putative father shall be shown as the father on the birth certificate.

(b) If the mother was not married at the time of conception or birth, the name of the father shall be entered if, but only if, the mother and the person to be named as the father so request in writing on a form prescribed and furnished by the state registrar or if paternity has been determined by a court of competent jurisdiction, in which case the name of the father as so determined shall be entered.

(c) For purposes of acknowledging paternity, the form prescribed and furnished by the state registrar shall contain the minimum requirements specified by the secretary of the federal department of health and human services.

(3.5) Upon the birth of a child to an unmarried woman in an institution, the person in charge of the institution or that person's designated representative shall provide an opportunity for the child's mother and natural father to complete a written acknowledgment of paternity on the form prescribed and furnished by the state registrar.

(4) Whoever assumes the custody of a living infant of unknown parentage shall report on a form and in the manner prescribed by the state registrar within ten days to the state registrar or as otherwise directed by the state registrar such information as the state registrar shall require, which report shall constitute the certificate of birth for the infant. The place where the child was found shall be entered as the place of birth, and the date of birth shall be determined by approximation. If the child is identified and a certificate of birth is found or obtained, any report registered under this section shall be sealed and filed and, except as provided in section 25-2-113.5, may be opened only by order of a court of competent jurisdiction or as provided by regulation.

(5) and (6) (Deleted by amendment, L. 93, p. 952, § 1, effective September 1, 1993.)

(7) The state registrar shall revise the birth certificate worksheet form used for the preparation of a certificate of live birth to include a statement that knowingly and intentionally misrepresenting material information on the worksheet form used for the preparation of a birth certificate is a misdemeanor.

## 25-2-112.3. Certificates of stillbirth - filing - delayed registration - rules.

(1) The state registrar shall create a certificate of stillbirth and shall furnish and distribute such form as necessary. The state board of health shall promulgate rules necessary to implement this section.

(2) (a) A certificate of stillbirth shall be offered to a mother after the occurrence of any stillbirth. If the mother decides to have a certificate of stillbirth filed, it shall be filed with the state registrar within three days after the stillbirth occurs and shall be registered by the state registrar if it has been completed and filed in accordance with the provisions of this section and section 25-2-112.

(b) If the mother decides not to place a name on the certificate of stillbirth, the person preparing the certificate of stillbirth shall leave this option on the certificate blank.

(3) Notwithstanding the provisions set forth in subsection (2) of this section, if a certificate of stillbirth is not registered after one year from the date the stillbirth occurs, a certificate marked "Delayed" may be filed and registered in accordance with the provisions of section 25-2-114.

## 25-2-112.5. Social security account numbers - acknowledgments of paternity - to be furnished.

(1) Regardless of the marital status of the mother, each parent shall furnish the social security account number or numbers, if the parent has more than one such number, issued to that parent, and the other parent's social security account number, if known, at the time of the child's birth to the person authorized under section 25-2-112 to obtain them for the state registrar, unless the state, in accordance with federal regulations, finds good cause for not requiring the parent to furnish such numbers to the state.

(2) The department of public health and environment shall make the birth certificate, the mother's and father's social security account numbers, and any written acknowledgments of paternity, including any notarized affidavits acknowledging paternity and any witnessed forms prescribed and furnished by the state registrar, furnished under this section and section 25-2-112 available to the state agency responsible for enforcing child support under Title IV-D of the federal "Social Security Act" upon request of that agency. The social security account numbers shall not be recorded on the birth certificate and may not be used for any purpose other than for the establishment and enforcement of child support orders.

## 25-2-112.7. Crime of misrepresentation of material information in the preparation of a birth certificate - definitions.

(1) As used in this section, unless the context otherwise requires:

(a) "Birth parent" means a natural parent, by birth, of a child born in this state. "Birth parent" also includes a presumed father or putative father in accordance with the presumptions for determination of paternity as set forth in section 25-2-112 (3) or a putative father who is not married to the mother who signs a voluntary acknowledgment of paternity.

(b) "Material information" means the legal name of a birth parent, the birth date of a birth parent, the mother's maiden name prior to a first marriage, if applicable, and the place of birth of a birth parent.

(2) A birth parent commits the crime of misrepresentation of material information in the preparation of a birth certificate if the birth parent knowingly and intentionally misrepresents material information that is used to create a child's birth certificate.

(3) A person who commits the crime of misrepresentation of material information in the preparation of a birth certificate is guilty of a misdemeanor and, upon conviction thereof, shall be punished by a fine of not more than one thousand dollars, or by imprisonment in the county jail for not more than one year, or by both such fine and imprisonment.

## 25-2-113. New certificates of birth following adoption - legitimation - parentage determination.

(1) (a) A new certificate of birth shall be prepared by the state registrar as to any person born in this state whenever he receives with respect to such a person any of the following: A report concerning adoption, legitimacy, or parentage as required by section 25-2-107; or a report or certified copy of a decree concerning the adoption, legitimacy, or parentage of such a person from a court of competent jurisdiction outside this state; or a certified copy of the marriage certificate of the parents, together with a statement of the husband, executed after such marriage, in which the husband acknowledges paternity; but with respect to adoptions no new certificate of birth shall be prepared if the state registrar is requested not to do so by the court that has decreed the adoption, by an adoptive parent, or by the adopted person. Each new certificate shall show all information shown on the original certificate of birth, except information for which substitute information is included as a result of the report or decree which prompts the preparation of the new certificate.

(b) A new certificate of birth shall be prepared by the state registrar as to any adopted person born in a foreign country and a resident of this state whenever the state registrar receives with respect to such person a certified copy of the final decree of adoption as required by section 19-5-212, C.R.S., and section 25-2-107 and findings of fact as required by this section. In proceedings for the adoption of a person who was born in a foreign country, the juvenile court having jurisdiction of adoptions, upon evidence from reliable sources, shall make findings of fact as to the date and place of birth and parentage of such person. The state registrar shall prepare a new birth certificate in the new name of the adopted person and shall seal the certified copy of the findings of the court and the certified copy of the final decree of adoption which shall be kept confidential except as otherwise provided in part 3 of article 5 of title 19, C.R.S. The birth certificate shall be labeled as a certificate of foreign birth and shall show specifically the true or probable country of birth and that the certificate is not evidence of United States citizenship. If the child was born in a foreign country but was a citizen of the United States at the time of birth, the state registrar shall not prepare a certificate of foreign birth but instead shall notify the adoptive parents of the procedures for obtaining a revised birth certificate for their child through the United States department of state. Any copy of a certificate of foreign birth issued shall indicate this policy, show the actual place of birth, and indicate the fact that the certificate is not proof of United States citizenship for the adopted child. A new certificate of birth in the new name of the adopted person prepared by the state registrar pursuant to this section is hereby legalized and made valid.

(c) Repealed.

(2) (a) The state registrar shall register each new certificate of birth prepared pursuant to subsection (1) of this section by marking thereon the words "new certificate", by marking thereon the date such certificate is completed, which date thereafter shall be the registration date, and by substituting such new certificate for the original certificate of birth for such person.

(b) A new certificate of birth issued pursuant to an adoption, and any copy of such certificate issued, shall be marked by the state registrar with the words "issued pursuant to adoption" if so requested by an adoptive parent or by an adopted person.

(c) The state registrar shall develop rules to ensure that the adoptive parent's decision to include such information, in paragraph (b) of this subsection (2) , is made knowingly, including having a separate signature line verifying such choice.

(3) Thereafter, the original certificate and evidence concerning adoption, legitimacy, or parentage shall be sealed and not be subject to inspection except as provided in section 25-2-113.5 or in part 3 of article 5 of title 19, C.R.S., by regulation, or upon order of a court of competent jurisdiction after the court has satisfied itself that the interests of the child or the child's descendants or the parents will best be served by opening said seal. The information obtained from opening said seal may be withheld from public view or from being presented as evidence at the discretion of the judge.

(4) In the event the decree which formed the basis for the new certificate of birth is annulled and if the state registrar receives either a certified copy of such decree of annulment or a report with respect to such decree as required by section 25-2-107, the state registrar shall return the original certificate to its place in the files. Thereafter the new certificate and evidence concerning the annulment shall not be subject to inspection except as provided in section 25-2-113.5, upon order of a court of competent jurisdiction, or as provided by regulation.

(5) If no certificate of birth is on file for the person for whom a new birth certificate is to be established under this section and the date and place of birth have not been determined in the adoption or paternity proceedings, a delayed certificate of birth shall be filed with the state registrar before a new certificate of birth is established. The new birth certificate shall be prepared on the delayed birth certificate form.

(6) When a new certificate of birth is established by the state registrar, all copies of the original certificate of birth in the custody of any other custodian of vital records in this state shall be sealed from inspection, except as otherwise provided in part 3 of article 5 of title 19, C.R.S., or forwarded to the state registrar, as the state registrar shall direct.

## 25-2-113.5. Limited access to information upon consent of all parties - voluntary adoption registry.

(1) Adoption is based upon the legal termination of parental rights and responsibilities of birth parents and the creation of the legal relationship of parent and child between an adoptee and his or her adoptive parents. Under current laws and the social premises underlying adoption, the general assembly has been charged with the duty to preserve the right to privacy and confidentiality of birth parents whose children were adopted, the adoptees, and the adoptive parents. The general assembly recognizes, however, that some adults who were adopted as children, their siblings who may or may not have been adopted, and some birth parents whose children were surrendered for adoption have a strong desire to obtain information about each other. The purpose of this section is to set up a voluntary adoption registry where qualified persons may register their willingness to the release of information to each other and to provide for the disclosure of such information.

(2) As used in this section, unless the context otherwise requires:

(a) "Adoptive parent" means an adult who has become a parent of a child through the legal process of adoption.

(b) "Consent" means a verified written statement which has been notarized.

(c) "Identifying information" includes the following information:

(I) The name of the qualified adoptee before placement in adoption;

(II) The name and address of each qualified birth parent as it appears in birth records;

(III) The current name, address, and telephone number of the qualified adult adoptee; and

(IV) The current name, address, and telephone number of each qualified birth parent.

(d) "Qualified adult adoptee" means an adopted person eighteen years of age or older who was born in Colorado and who meets the requirements of this section.

(e) "Qualified birth parent" means a genetic, biological, or natural parent whose rights were voluntarily or involuntarily terminated by a court or otherwise and who meets the requirements of this section. "Birth parent" includes a man who is the parent of a child as established in accordance with the provisions of the "Uniform Parentage Act", article 4 of title 19, C.R.S., prior to the termination of parental rights and who meets the requirements of this section.

(f) "Registrar" means the state registrar of vital statistics or his designated representative.

(g) "Relative" includes an individual's spouse, birth parent, adoptive parent, sibling, or child who is twenty-one years of age or older.

(g.5) "Sibling" shall have the same meaning as "biological sibling", section 19-1-103 (14) , C.R.S.

(h) "Voluntary adoption registry" or "registry" means a place where eligible persons, as described in this section, may indicate their willingness to have their identities and whereabouts disclosed to each other under conditions specified in this section.

(3) The registrar shall maintain a confidential list of qualified adult adoptees who have presented a consent regarding the release of identifying information about themselves. Any consent by a qualified adult adoptee shall be accompanied by the adoptee's desired method of notification in the event that a match occurs; however, the state shall not incur costs of notification in excess of that part of the fee charged to the applicant for the purpose of notification. Any consent shall also indicate whether the qualified adult adoptee desires release of his identifying information if a match occurs after his death. The qualified adult adoptee may revise his consent with respect to change of address or method of notification. Any name and accompanying information shall be removed from the list upon the verified written request of the listed adoptee. The registrar shall maintain a closed record of such list and accompanying information, except as provided in accordance with this section.

(4) The registrar shall maintain a confidential list of qualified birth parents who have presented a consent regarding the release of identifying information about themselves. Any consent by a qualified birth parent shall be accompanied by the birth parent's desired method of notification in the event that a match occurs; however, the state shall not incur costs of notification in excess of that part of the fee charged to the applicant for the purpose of notification. Any consent shall also indicate whether the qualified birth parent desires release of his identifying information if a match occurs after his death. The qualified birth parent may revise his consent with respect to change of address or method of notification. Any name and accompanying information shall be removed from the list upon the verified written request of the listed birth parent. The registrar shall maintain a closed record of such list and accompanying information, except as provided in accordance with this section. Any birth parent who in terminating his parental rights used an alias, and this alias is listed in the original sealed birth certificate, may also file a consent with the registry. A birth parent shall not be matched with the qualified adult adoptee without the consent of the other birth parent unless:

(a) There is only one birth parent listed on the birth certificate; or

(b) The other birth parent is deceased; or

(c) The other birth parent is unable to be located by the department of public health and environment after an exhaustive search, the cost of said search to be fully funded by the birth parent seeking a match, said search to be in accordance with the rules and regulations promulgated by the department.

(5) The registrar shall maintain a confidential list of relatives of deceased qualified adult adoptees and relatives of deceased qualified birth parents who have presented a consent regarding the release of identifying information about themselves. Any consent by such relative shall be accompanied by the person's desired method of notification in the event that a match occurs; however, the state shall not incur costs of notification in excess of that part of the fee charged to the applicant for the purpose of notification. Such relative may revise his consent with respect to change of address or method of notification. Any name and accompanying information shall be removed from the list upon the verified written request of the listed relative. The registrar shall maintain a closed record of such list and accompanying information, except as provided in accordance with this section.

(5.5) The registrar shall maintain a confidential list of former foster children who may or may not have been adopted, who are eighteen years of age or older, who have presented a consent regarding the release of identifying information about themselves and who are searching for a sibling who is also eighteen years of age or older, who may or may not have been adopted, and who may or may not have been in the foster care system. Any consent by such sibling shall be accompanied by the sibling's desired method of notification in the event that a match occurs. However, the state shall not incur costs of notification in excess of that part of the fee charged to the applicant for the purpose of notification. A sibling may revise his or her consent with respect to change of address or method of notification. Any name and accompanying information shall be removed from the list upon the verified written request of the listed sibling. The registrar shall maintain a closed record of the list and accompanying information except as provided for pursuant to this section.

(6) The registrar shall regularly review the lists provided for in subsections (3) , (4) , (5) , and (5.5) of this section and any other nonsealed administrative files or records within his or her office to determine if there is a match. If it appears that a match has occurred, then and only then is the registrar authorized to proceed to confirm the match through recourse to sealed documents on file in the office of the registrar. When a match is confirmed, the registrar shall notify each party, by his or her designated method only, prior to an exchange of identifying information. Nothing in this section shall be construed to allow any state or local governmental department, agency, or institution, or any employee thereof, to solicit any consent for the release of identifying information.

(7) Nothing in this section shall be construed to allow the registrar to issue a copy of the original birth certificate to any registrant.

(8) Any person who knowingly uses, publishes, or divulges information obtained through operation of the registry to any person in a manner not authorized by this section commits a class 2 petty offense and, upon conviction thereof, shall be punished by a fine of five hundred dollars.

(9) Notwithstanding any other provision of law, the information acquired by the registry shall not be disclosed under any public records law, sunshine or freedom of information legislation, rules, or practice.

(10) (a) The executive director of the department of public health and environment shall establish fees to be charged each person requesting that his name be placed on the list provided for in subsection (3) , (4) , or (5) of this section and for the services provided by the registrar in establishing and implementing the registry pursuant to this section. It is the intent of the general assembly that the fees shall cover all direct and indirect costs incurred pursuant to this section.

(b) The fees collected pursuant to this section shall be transmitted to the state treasurer, who shall credit the same to the general fund. The general assembly shall annually appropriate from the general fund to the department of public health and environment an amount sufficient to meet expenses incurred pursuant to this section.

## 25-2-114. Delayed registration of births and deaths.

(1) When a birth, foundling birth, death, or fetal death has occurred in this state but no certificate as to such event has been filed or registered in accordance with the provisions of section 25-2-110 or 25-2-112, a certificate as to such event may be accepted for filing or registration, or both, in accordance with applicable regulations concerning certificates that have not been timely or properly filed or registered. The state registrar shall endorse on the certificate a summary statement of the evidence submitted to substantiate the facts asserted in such certificate. If a certificate is not registered until more than a year after the event, the state registrar shall mark the word "Delayed" on the face thereof.

(2) When the state registrar finds the certificate or such supplementary evidence as may be required by regulations to be deficient or invalid, the certificate shall not be registered, and the person who requested the registration shall be advised in writing both as to the basis for the alleged deficiency or invalidity and also as to such person's right of appeal. Judicial review of the action of the state registrar may be had in accordance with the provisions of section 24-4-106, C.R.S., but an action for judicial review shall be commenced within sixty days after the date the

state registrar gives his notice in writing of his decision. If no action for judicial review is commenced within said period, the state registrar shall return the certificate and all documents submitted in support thereof to the person submitting the same if registration of the certificate has been refused.

## 25-2-115. Alteration of reports and certificates - amended reports and certificates.

(1) No vital statistics report or certificate shall ever be altered in any way except in accordance with this article and applicable regulations. The date of alteration and a summary description of the evidence submitted in support of the alteration shall be endorsed on or made a part of each vital statistics certificate that is altered. Every vital statistics report or certificate that is altered in any way shall be marked "Amended" except the birth report or certificate of any illegitimate child altered by the addition of a father's name pursuant to section 25-2-112 (3) , in which case, upon request of the parents, the surname of the child shall be changed on the report and certificate to that of the father, and also except additions and minor corrections made within one year after the date of the statistical event as may be specified by applicable regulations. A child's surname may be changed upon affidavit of the parent that the change is being made to conform such child's surname to the parent's legal surname.

(2) Upon receipt of a certified copy of a court order changing the name of a person born in this state and upon request of such person, or upon the request of his parent, guardian, or legal representative if he is under a legal disability, the original certificate of birth shall be amended to reflect the new name thereon.

(3) In the event the state registrar alters a birth certificate or death certificate, he shall promptly report the amendment to any other custodians of the vital statistics record and their records shall be amended accordingly.

(4) Upon receipt of a certified copy of an order of a court of competent jurisdiction indicating that the sex of an individual born in this state has been changed by surgical procedure and that such individual's name has been changed, the certificate of birth of such individual shall be amended as prescribed by regulation.

(5) When an applicant does not submit the minimum documentation required in the regulations for amending a vital statistics record or when the state registrar has reasonable cause to question the validity or adequacy of the applicant's sworn statements or documentary evidence, and if the deficiencies are not corrected, the state registrar shall not amend the vital statistics record and shall advise the applicant of the reason for this action and shall further advise the applicant of the right of appeal to a court of competent jurisdiction.

## 25-2-116. Institutions to keep records - persons to furnish information.

(1) Every person in charge of an institution shall keep a record of personal particulars and dates concerning each person admitted or confined to such institution. This record shall include such information as required by the standard certificate of birth, death, and fetal death forms issued under the provisions of this article. The record shall be made at the time of admission. The name and address of the person providing the information shall appear on the record.

(2) When a dead human body is released or disposed of by an institution, the person in charge of the institution shall record the name of the deceased, date of death, name and address of the person to whom the body is released, and date of removal from the institution, or, if finally disposed of by the institution, the date, place, and manner of disposition shall be recorded.

(3) Any person having knowledge of the facts shall furnish such information as he may possess regarding any birth, death, fetal death, adoption, marriage, or dissolution of marriage upon demand of the state registrar.

## 25-2-117. Certified copies furnished - fee.

(1) Vital statistics records shall be treated as confidential, but the department of public health and

environment shall, upon request, furnish to any applicant having a direct and tangible interest in a vital statistics record a certified copy of any record registered under the provisions of this article. Any copy of the record of a birth or death, when properly certified by the state registrar or as otherwise directed by the state registrar to be a true copy thereof, shall be prima facie evidence in all courts and places of the facts therein stated.

(2) An applicant shall pay fees established pursuant to section 25-2-121 for each of the following services:

(a) The reproduction and certification of birth or death records; except that an applicant shall not pay a fee:

(I) For the provision of a certified copy of such a record to:

(A) Another state agency;

(B) A county department of social services or human services; or

(C) An individual presenting a letter of referral from a county department of social services; or

(II) If the applicant is a delegate child support enforcement unit acting pursuant to article 13 of title 26, C.R.S.;

(b) Any search of the files and records of the state registrar when no certified copy is made, such fee to pertain to each hour or fractional hour of time of the search;

(c) The processing of new certificates, delayed certificates, or corrected certificates;

(d) The verification of marriage or divorce;

(e) The reproduction of various vital statistics, publications, reports, and data services; and

(f) The verification of a civil union or dissolution of a civil union.

(3) To preserve vital statistics records, the state registrar is authorized to prepare typewritten, photographic, electronic, or other reproductions of certificates or reports. When certified by the state registrar, such reproductions shall be accepted as the original records. The documents from which permanent reproductions have been made and verified may be disposed of as provided by regulation.

## 25-2-118. Penalties.

(1) Except as otherwise provided for in section 25-2-112.7 with respect to misrepresentation of material information in the preparation of a birth certificate, any person who knowingly and willfully makes any false statement in or supplies any false information for or for purposes of deception applies for, alters, mutilates, uses, attempts to use, applies for amendments thereto, or furnishes to another for deceptive use any vital statistics certificate, and any person who knowingly and willfully and for purposes of deception uses or attempts to use or furnishes for use by another any vital statistics certificate knowing that such certificate contains false information or relates to a person other than the person with respect to whom it purports to relate, and any person who manufactures, advertises for sale, sells, or alters any vital statistics certificate knowing or having reason to know that such document establishes or may be used to establish a false status, occupation, membership, license, privilege, or identity for himself or any other person, and any person who uses any such document to commit a crime is guilty of a misdemeanor and, upon conviction thereof, shall be punished by a fine of not more than one thousand dollars, or by imprisonment in the county jail for not more than one year, or by both such fine and imprisonment.

(2) Any person who willfully violates any of the provisions of this article or refuses or neglects to perform any of the duties imposed upon him by this article is guilty of a misdemeanor and, upon conviction thereof, shall be punished by a fine of not more than one hundred dollars, or by imprisonment in the county jail for not more than thirty days, or by both such fine and imprisonment.

## 25-2-119. Tax on court action affecting vital statistics. (Repealed)

## 25-2-120. Reports of electroconvulsive treatment.

(1) Any person who performs electroconvulsive treatment in the state of Colorado shall file a report with the department of public health and environment setting forth the data required by subsection (2) of this section. An institution in which electroconvulsive treatment is performed shall be the reporting entity for all electroconvulsive treatments performed at that institution.
(2) Such reports shall be made to the department of public health and environment on forms prescribed by the department within thirty days after January 1 and July 1 of each year on a semiannual basis and shall contain the following detailed information for each reporting period:
(a) The total number, broken down by inpatient and outpatient and exclusive of substance abuse, of adult psychiatric admissions, minor children psychiatric admissions, and readmissions of both;
(b) The number of patients within each category of paragraph (a) of this subsection (2) who received electroconvulsive treatment;
(c) Statistical information on each patient receiving electroconvulsive treatment including, but not limited to, the following:
(I) Diagnosis;
(II) Number of electroconvulsive treatments;
(III) Age;
(IV) Sex;
(V) Ethnicity;
(VI) Whether such patient was voluntary or involuntary;
(VII) Whether or not such patient was capable of giving his written informed consent;
(VIII) Whether or not any complications resulted from such electroconvulsive treatment, such as cardiac arrest, fracture, apnea, memory loss, or death (including autopsy results with particular attention to the brain) ;
(IX) The method of payment for such electroconvulsive treatment and, if applicable, the name of the insurance company making such payments.
(3) The name of the patient receiving electroconvulsive treatment shall remain confidential information and shall not be disclosed to the department, any other agency or individual. The forms prescribed by subsection (2) of this section shall not require any information which would disclose, directly or indirectly, the identity of the patient.

## 25-2-121. Fee adjustments - vital statistics records cash fund created.

(1) This section shall apply to all activities of the office of the state registrar in the department of public health and environment.
(2) (a) The office of the state registrar shall propose, as part of its annual budget request, an adjustment in the amount of each fee that the office of the state registrar is authorized by law to collect. The budget request and the adjusted fees for the office of the state registrar shall reflect its direct and indirect costs and the direct and indirect costs necessary to maintain and operate the Colorado responds to children with special needs program.
(b) (I) Based upon the appropriation made and subject to the approval of the executive director of the department of public health and environment, the office of the state registrar shall adjust its fees so that the revenue generated from said fees approximates its direct and indirect costs and the direct and indirect costs necessary to maintain and operate the Colorado responds to children with special needs program. Such fees shall remain in effect for the fiscal year for which the budget request applies. All fees collected by the office of the state registrar shall be transmitted to the state treasurer, who shall credit the same to the vital statistics records cash fund, which fund is hereby created. All moneys credited to the vital statistics records cash fund and all interest earned thereon shall be subject to appropriation by the general assembly to be used as provided in this section and shall not be deposited in or transferred to the general fund of this state or any other fund.
(II) For those services required by this article and those services provided by the Colorado responds to children with special needs program, each office designated or established pursuant to

section 25-2-103 shall charge fees as specified by the state registrar. Such fees shall be used for the purpose of paying the direct and indirect costs of the office and the office of the state registrar for compliance with the provisions of this article and the direct and indirect costs necessary to maintain and operate the Colorado responds to children with special needs program.

(c) Beginning July 1, 1985, and each July 1 thereafter, whenever moneys appropriated to the office of the state registrar for its activities for the prior fiscal year are unexpended, said moneys shall be made a part of the appropriation to the office of the state registrar for the next fiscal year, and such amount shall not be raised from fees collected by the office of the state registrar. If a supplemental appropriation is made to the office of the state registrar for its activities and the services provided by the Colorado responds to children with special needs program, the fees of the office of the state registrar, when adjusted for the fiscal year following that in which the supplemental appropriation was made, shall be adjusted by an additional amount that is sufficient to compensate for the supplemental appropriation. Moneys appropriated to the office of the state registrar in the annual general appropriation act shall be designated as cash funds and shall not exceed the amount anticipated to be raised from fees collected by the office of the state registrar.

(d) For purposes of this section, "Colorado responds to children with special needs program" means the program established within the department of public health and environment under the authority of section 25-1.5-105.

(3) Notwithstanding any provision of subsection (2) of this section to the contrary, on March 5, 2003, the state treasurer shall deduct seven hundred sixty-three thousand six hundred eighty dollars from the vital statistics records cash fund and transfer such sum to the general fund.

## 25-2-122. Heirloom birth and marriage certificates - funds created - report - rules - definitions.

(1) As used in this section, unless the context otherwise requires:

(a) "Heirloom birth certificate" means a birth certificate that is suitable for display and may bear the seal of the state and be signed by the governor.

(b) "Heirloom marriage certificate" means a marriage certificate that is suitable for display and may bear the seal of the state and be signed by the governor.

(2) (a) In addition to any other birth certificate issued pursuant to section 25-2-112, the state registrar shall issue, upon request and upon payment of a fee established by rule of the state board of health, an heirloom birth certificate representing the birth of the individual named on the original birth certificate. The state registrar may establish procedures for issuing heirloom birth certificates; except that an heirloom birth certificate shall be issued in a form consistent with the need to protect the integrity of vital records, including secure measures designed to prevent tampering, counterfeiting, or otherwise duplicating the birth certificate for fraudulent purposes, pursuant to the federal "Intelligence Reform and Terrorism Prevention Act of 2004", 5 U.S.C. sec. 301.

(b) An heirloom birth certificate shall have the same status as evidence as that of an original birth certificate.

(c) The fee established pursuant to paragraph (a) of this subsection (2) shall be sufficient to cover the direct and indirect costs of producing and issuing the heirloom birth certificate, plus an additional ten dollars. The state registrar shall transmit moneys generated pursuant to this subsection (2) , along with an explanation of the number of heirloom birth certificate sales that correspond to such moneys, to the state treasurer, who shall credit:

(I) For each sale of an heirloom birth certificate, ten dollars to the immunization fund created in section 25-4-1708; and

(II) The remainder of such moneys to the vital statistics records cash fund created in section 25-2-121.

(3) (a) In addition to any other marriage certificate issued pursuant to section 25-2-106, the state registrar shall issue, upon request and upon payment of a fee established by rule of the state board of health, an heirloom marriage certificate representing the marriage of the persons named on the

original marriage certificate recorded in the county clerk and recorder's office. The state registrar may establish procedures for issuing the heirloom marriage certificates; except that an heirloom marriage certificate shall be issued in a form consistent with the need to protect the integrity of vital records.

(b) An heirloom marriage certificate shall have the same status as evidence as that of an original marriage certificate.

(c) The fee established pursuant to paragraph (a) of this subsection (3) shall be sufficient to cover the direct and indirect costs of producing and issuing the heirloom marriage certificate, plus an additional ten dollars. The state registrar shall transmit moneys generated pursuant to this subsection (3) , along with an explanation of the number of heirloom marriage certificate sales that correspond to such moneys, to the state treasurer, who shall credit:

(I) For each sale of an heirloom marriage certificate, ten dollars to the Colorado domestic abuse program fund created in section 39-22-802, C.R.S.; and

(II) The remainder of such moneys to the vital statistics records cash fund created in section 25-2-121.

# HOSPITALS

# ARTICLE 3. HOSPITALS

# PART 1. HOSPITALS

## 25-3-100.5. Definitions.

As used in this article 3, unless the context otherwise requires:

(1) "Acute treatment unit" means a facility or a distinct part of a facility for short-term psychiatric care, which may include treatment for substance use disorders, that provides a total, twenty-four-hour, therapeutically planned and professionally staffed environment for persons who do not require inpatient hospitalization but need more intense and individual services than are available on an outpatient basis, such as crisis management and stabilization services.

(2) "Department" means the department of public health and environment.

(3) "Heart attack database" means a national registry designed for heart attack data.

(4) "Joint commission" means an independent, nonprofit organization that accredits and certifies health care organizations and programs in the United States, or its successor entity.

(5) "PCI center" means a hospital that performs percutaneous coronary intervention (PCI) , commonly known as coronary angioplasty, for acute myocardial infarction.

(6) "STEMI" means ST-elevation myocardial infarction.

## 25-3-101. Hospitals - health facilities - licensed - definitions.

(1) It is unlawful for any person, partnership, association, or corporation to open, conduct, or maintain any general hospital, hospital unit, psychiatric hospital, community clinic, rehabilitation hospital, convalescent center, community mental health center, acute treatment unit, facility for persons with developmental disabilities, as defined in section 25-1.5-103 (2) (c) , nursing care facility, hospice care, assisted living residence, except an assisted living residence shall be assessed a license fee as set forth in section 25-27-107, dialysis treatment clinic, ambulatory surgical center, birthing center, home care agency, or other facility of a like nature, except those wholly owned and operated by any governmental unit or agency, without first having obtained a

license from the department of public health and environment.

(2) As used in this section, unless the context otherwise requires:

(a) (I) "Community clinic" means a health care facility that provides health care services on an ambulatory basis, is neither licensed as an on-campus department or service of a hospital nor listed as an off-campus location under a hospital's license, and meets at least one of the following criteria:

(A) Operates inpatient beds at the facility for the provision of extended observation and other related services for not more than seventy-two hours;

(B) Provides emergency services at the facility; or

(C) Is not otherwise subject to health facility licensure under this section or section 25-1.5-103 but opts to obtain licensure as a community clinic in order to receive private donations, grants, government funds, or other public or private reimbursement for services rendered.

(II) "Community clinic" includes a prison clinic operated by the department of corrections.

(III) "Community clinic" does not include:

(A) A federally qualified health center, as defined in section 1861 (aa) (4) of the federal "Social Security Act", 42 U.S.C. sec. 1395x (aa) (4) ;

(B) A rural health clinic, as defined in section 1861 (aa) (2) of the federal "Social Security Act", 42 U.S.C. sec. 1395x (aa) (2) ;

(C) A facility that functions only as an office for the practice of medicine or the delivery of primary care services by other licensed or certified practitioners.

(b) "Hospital unit" means a physical portion of a licensed or certified general hospital, psychiatric hospital, maternity hospital, or rehabilitation hospital that is leased or otherwise occupied pursuant to a contractual agreement by a person other than the licensee of the host facility for the purpose of providing outpatient or inpatient services.

(3) Nothing in this section shall be construed to require the licensing of individual services provided by a licensed or certified provider on its own premises.

(4) A health care facility is not required to be licensed as a community clinic solely due to the facility's ownership status, corporate structure, or engagement of outside vendors to perform nonclinical management services. This section permits regulation of a physician's office only to the extent the office is a community clinic as defined in this section.

## 25-3-102. License - application - issuance - certificate of compliance required.

(1) (a) An applicant for a license described in section 25-3-101 shall apply to the department of public health and environment annually upon such form and in such manner as prescribed by the department; except that a community residential home shall make application for a license pursuant to section 25.5-10-214, C.R.S.

(b) The department has authority to administer oaths, subpoena witnesses or documents, and take testimony in all matters relating to issuing, denying, limiting, suspending, or revoking a license.

(c) The department shall issue licenses to applicants furnishing satisfactory evidence of fitness to conduct and maintain a health facility described in section 25-3-101 in accordance with this part 1 and the rules adopted by the department. The department shall not require, as satisfactory evidence of fitness, evidence as to whether an applicant has provided self declarations, affidavits, or other attestations as to its general compliance with statutory or regulatory licensing requirements. The department shall determine an applicant's fitness solely based on the specific fitness information or documentation submitted by the applicant upon the department's request or as otherwise acquired by the department through its own review or investigation of the applicant. The department may require the applicant to attest to the accuracy of the information provided as long as the attestation does not require the applicant's affirmation of its general compliance with statutory or regulatory licensing requirements.

(d) The license shall be signed by the president and attested by the secretary of the state board of health and have the state board's seal affixed to the license. The license expires one year from the date of issuance.

(e) (I) For a change of ownership, the department shall conduct a fitness review of a new owner based upon information compiled within the five years preceding the date of the application; except that the new owner shall disclose whether, within the ten years preceding the date of an application, the new owner:

(A) Has been convicted of a felony or misdemeanor involving moral turpitude;

(B) Had a state license or federal certification denied, revoked, or suspended by another jurisdiction;

(C) Had a civil judgment or criminal conviction against the new owner in a case brought by the federal, state, or local authorities that resulted from the operation, management, or ownership of a health facility or other entity related to substandard patient care or health care fraud.

(II) The new owner shall provide the information specified in subparagraph (I) of this paragraph (e) to the department regardless of whether action has been stayed during a judicial appeal or otherwise settled between the parties.

(III) The department may review an existing owner of a licensed health facility or entity only when the department has new information not previously available or disclosed that bears on the fitness of the existing owner to operate or maintain a licensed health facility or entity.

(IV) A conversion of the health facility's or entity's legal structure, or the legal structure of an entity that has a direct or indirect ownership interest in the health facility or entity, is not a change of ownership unless the conversion also includes a transfer of at least fifty percent of the licensed facility's direct or indirect ownership interest to one or more new owners.

(2) In the licensing of a community mental health center, acute treatment unit, or clinic, satisfactory evidence that the applicant is in compliance with the standards, rules, and regulations promulgated pursuant to section 27-66-102, C.R.S., shall be required for licensure.

(3) (a) Notwithstanding any provision of law to the contrary, the department of public health and environment shall not issue or renew any license described in section 25-3-101 for a facility covered by section 25-1.5-103 (5) unless the department receives a certificate of compliance for the applicant's building or structure from the division of fire prevention and control in the department of public safety in accordance with part 12 of article 33.5 of title 24, C.R.S.

(b) The department of public health and environment shall take action on an application for licensure within thirty days after the date that the department receives from the applicant all of the necessary information and documentation required for licensure, including a certificate of compliance from the division of fire prevention and control.

## 25-3-102.1. Deemed status for certain facilities.

(1) (a) In the licensing of an ambulatory surgical center following the issuance of initial licensure by the department of public health and environment, the voluntary submission of satisfactory evidence that the applicant is accredited by the joint commission, the American association for accreditation of ambulatory surgery facilities, inc., the accreditation association for ambulatory health care, the American osteopathic association, or any successor entities shall be deemed to meet certain requirements for license renewal so long as the standards for accreditation applied by the accrediting organization are at least as stringent as the licensure requirements otherwise specified by the department.

(b) (I) In the application for the renewal of a license for a health facility described in section 25-3-101, other than an ambulatory surgical center, the department of public health and environment shall deem health facilities that are currently accredited by an accrediting organization recognized by the federal centers for medicare and medicaid services as satisfying the requirements for renewal of the license.

(II) If the standards for national accreditation are less stringent than the state's licensure standards for a particular health facility, the department of public health and environment may conduct a survey that focuses on the more stringent state standards. Beginning one year after the department first grants deemed status to a health facility pursuant to this paragraph (b) , the department may conduct validation surveys, based on a valid sample methodology, of up to ten percent of the total number of accredited health facilities in the industry, excluding hospitals. If the department conducts a validation survey of a health facility, the validation survey is in lieu of a licensing renewal survey that the health facility would have undergone if the health facility did not have deemed status pursuant to this paragraph (b) .

(III) If the department of public health and environment takes an enforcement activity, as defined in section 25-1.5-103 (2) (b.5) , against a health facility to which it has granted deemed status pursuant to this paragraph (b) , the department may revoke the health facility's deemed status.

(c) Upon submission of a completed application for license renewal, the department of public health and environment shall accept proof of the accreditation in lieu of licensing inspections or other requirements. Nothing in this section exempts an accredited health facility from inspections or from other forms of oversight by the department as necessary to ensure public health and safety.

(2) In determining fees otherwise payable by a health facility for license renewal, the department of public health and environment shall give due consideration to efficiencies and savings generated in connection with the deemed status process in subsection (1) of this section and shall specifically provide an appropriate credit or reduced fee to a health facility that achieves license renewal through deemed status.

## 25-3-102.5. Nursing facilities - consumer satisfaction survey - pilot survey.

(1) (a) The department shall develop and implement a consumer satisfaction survey based on the results of the pilot survey implemented pursuant to paragraph (a.5) of this subsection (1) . The pilot survey and the resulting consumer satisfaction survey shall be implemented to determine the level of satisfaction among residents and residents' families regarding the quality of care and quality of living in nursing facilities. "Nursing facility", as used in this section, means a nursing facility as defined in section 25.5-4-103 (14) , C.R.S. The department shall appoint an advisory committee to develop the consumer satisfaction survey. The advisory committee shall include, but not be limited to, the state ombudsman, representatives of senior groups, representatives of the disabled community, representatives of providers of long term care services, and long term care consumers or their family members. The advisory committee shall develop recommendations for the development of an assessment tool for the consumer satisfaction survey and shall develop recommendations for the implementation of the pilot survey and the consumer satisfaction survey. The advisory committee shall ensure that a representative sample of participants are chosen and surveyed in a manner that will yield accurate and useful results. The department shall ensure that every nursing facility licensed by the department participates in the assessment of consumer satisfaction; except that any nursing facility that accepts exclusively private pay residents shall not be required to participate. Information about results of the most recent consumer satisfaction survey and how such survey was conducted shall be included by the facility in all informational materials provided to persons who inquire about the facility. The department shall assure confidentiality for residents during the survey process. The department shall make the results of consumer satisfaction surveys available to the public.

(a.5) (I) The department shall develop and implement a pilot consumer satisfaction survey to aid in the determination of the level of satisfaction among residents and residents' families regarding the quality of care and quality of living in nursing facilities. The pilot survey shall be used exclusively for the development of the consumer satisfaction survey to be implemented pursuant to paragraph (d) of this subsection (1) and shall not be used to penalize any participating facility. The pilot survey shall be used to assess:

(A) The validity of the questionnaire for use in the consumer satisfaction survey implemented pursuant to paragraph (d) of this subsection (1) ;

(B) The nursing facilities residents' cognition levels in order to determine the ability of the residents to complete the survey in a meaningful manner;

(C) The techniques employed to obtain the number of completed survey questionnaires needed to achieve a statistical validity of plus or minus ten percent on the final consumer satisfaction survey; and

(D) The survey data to ensure that such data is meaningful to consumers.

(II) The pilot survey shall involve the participation of no more than ten percent of all nursing facilities licensed by the department. The department shall select nursing facilities to participate in the pilot survey based on characteristics including, but not limited to, the rural or urban location of the facilities, and the cross-section of the resident population of the facilities. Facilities that volunteer to participate in the pilot survey shall be given priority in the selection process so long as the required characteristics are met.

(III) (A) The individual nursing facility results of the pilot survey shall be confidential and not made available to the public; except that each nursing facility shall be provided with the pilot survey results from its own facility.

(B) Aggregate statistical results of the pilot survey may be made available to the public.

(C) Repealed.

(IV) Repealed.

(b) The consumer satisfaction survey shall be easy to understand so that each resident or resident's family member or representative who participates may fill out the survey unassisted; except that the department or its designated representative may assist a resident or resident's family with filling out the survey. Nursing facility volunteers and employees shall be prohibited from assisting participants with the completion of the survey. The names of the participants in the survey shall be kept confidential, and all surveys shall be returned directly to the department.

(c) Repealed.

(d) The department shall administer the consumer satisfaction survey based on the recommendations of the advisory committee in all licensed nursing facilities that are required to participate in accordance with paragraph (a) of this subsection (1) . The department shall commence implementation of the survey on or before July 1, 2003. After the pilot survey is complete, the department shall evaluate the effectiveness of the pilot survey instruments, adopt any recommendations, and continue to survey all licensed facilities on a three-year cycle with one-third of the participating licensed nursing facilities completing the initial survey in one of the three years. Each participating licensed nursing facility shall perform a new consumer satisfaction survey every three years thereafter; except that the department may require, or a participating licensed nursing facility may request, that a new consumer satisfaction survey be performed more often if conditions warrant. If the licensed nursing facility requests such a survey, the department shall perform the survey if the licensed nursing facility pays the department for the costs associated with performing the survey. A licensed nursing facility may comment on the results of a consumer satisfaction survey and have such comments included in any publication or distribution of the results by the department.

(e) Hospice residents and their family members and transitional care unit residents and their family members, shall be exempt from participation in the pilot survey and consumer satisfaction survey conducted in each nursing facility.

(f) Nursing facilities shall release the name, address, and telephone number of each family member or party responsible for a nursing facility resident to the department for the sole use of conducting the pilot survey and the consumer satisfaction survey.

(2) (a) The department shall respond to a complaint from a nursing facility resident or resident's family member or representative within five working days after receipt of the complaint and, for sixty days after the date the department received the complaint, the department shall update the complainant on the status of the complaint investigation at least every fourteen days until the complaint is resolved and an investigation is finalized. If the complaint is not resolved within sixty days after the date the department received the complaint, the department shall continue to update the complainant on the status of the complaint every thirty days until the complaint is resolved and an investigation report is resolved and an investigation is finalized. At the request of the complainant, the department shall not maintain such contact.

(b) (I) The state and local long-term care ombudsman, established pursuant to article 11.5 of title 26, C.R.S., in compliance with the federal "Older Americans Act of 1965", ("ombudsman") shall refer to the state department for investigation and resolution all complaints received by the ombudsman involving possible licensure violations in nursing homes that are exclusively private pay facilities.

(II) Information about the ombudsman, including the ombudsman's role in dealing with resident complaints and all contact information and telephone numbers for the ombudsman, shall be included in the information provided to a resident upon admission to a facility that is not a private pay facility.

## 25-3-103. License denial or revocation - provisional license - rules.

(1) (a) The department of public health and environment may deny an application for a new or renewal license under this part 1 or revoke a license if the applicant or licensee has not satisfied the requirements of this part 1 or part 6 of this article and the rules of the department or the state board of health. If a license is denied or revoked, the department may grant the applicant or licensee a provisional license upon payment of a fee established by the state board of health by rule, subject to the limitations in paragraph (c) of this subsection (1). The provisional license is valid for no longer than ninety days and may be issued to allow the applicant or licensee time to comply with the requirements for a regular license. A second provisional license may be issued if the department determines it is necessary to effect compliance. The second provisional license must be issued for the same duration as the first provisional license upon payment of the fee established by the state board of health by rule, subject to the limitations in paragraph (c) of this subsection (1). No further provisional licenses may be issued for the then current year after the second issuance.

(b) The state board of health by rule or as otherwise provided by law may reduce the amount of the fee established pursuant to paragraph (a) of this subsection (1) if necessary pursuant to section 24-75-402 (3), C.R.S., to reduce the uncommitted reserves of the fund to which all or any portion of the fee is credited. After the uncommitted reserves of the fund are sufficiently reduced, the state board of health by rule or as otherwise provided by law may increase the amount of the fee as provided in section 24-75-402 (4), C.R.S.

(c) On or after June 4, 2012, the state board of health may increase the amount of a provisional license fee established pursuant to paragraph (a) of this subsection (1) that is in effect on June 4, 2012, by an amount not to exceed the annual percentage change in the United States department of labor, bureau of labor statistics, consumer price index for Denver-Boulder-Greeley for all urban consumers, all goods, or its successor index. Nothing in this paragraph (c) limits the ability of the state board of health to reduce the amount of a provisional license fee in effect on such date or to modify fees in accordance with paragraph (b) of this subsection (1) as necessary to comply with section 24-75-402, C.R.S.

(2) Upon a finding of reasonable compliance by an applicant holding a provisional license, a regular license shall be issued upon receipt of the regular license fee established pursuant to section 25-3-105.

(3) No denial of a renewal license shall be lawful unless, before institution of such proceedings by the department of public health and environment, said department has given the licensee notice in writing of facts on conduct that may warrant denial, has afforded the applicant opportunity to submit written data, views, and arguments with respect to such facts on conduct, and, except in cases of deliberate and willful violation, has given the applicant a reasonable opportunity to comply with all lawful requirements for licensure.

(4) No application for renewal of a license shall be denied by the department of public health and environment, and no previously issued license shall be revoked, suspended, annulled, limited, or modified until after a hearing as provided in section 24-4-105, C.R.S.

(5) The department of public health and environment may suspend or revoke the license for the operation of a nursing care facility or intermediate care facility of any licensee convicted of violating any provision of section 26-1-127 or section 25.5-6-206 (8), C.R.S., if the department finds such suspension or revocation necessary to safeguard the rights of patients in the future. No license or permit shall thereafter be issued to any person so convicted, except upon a specific

133

finding by the department that the rights of the patients will have adequate safeguards.

## 25-3-103.1. Health facilities general licensure cash fund.

(1) All fees collected pursuant to this article shall be transmitted to the state treasurer, who shall credit the same to the health facilities general licensure cash fund, which fund is hereby created. (2) The general assembly shall make annual appropriations from the health facilities general licensure cash fund to partially reimburse the department of public health and environment for the direct and indirect costs of the department incurred in the performance of its duties under this article and for the purposes of section 25-1.5-103 (3.5) . No appropriation shall be made out of the cash fund for expenditures incurred by the department pursuant to section 25-1.5-103 (1) (a) (II) in carrying out duties relating to health facilities wholly owned and operated by a governmental unit or agency.

## 25-3-103.5. Nondiscrimination - hospital surgical privileges - hospital rules and regulations.

(1) The bylaws of any hospital licensed pursuant to the provisions of part 3 of this article or established pursuant to section 32-1-1003, C.R.S., which does not limit staff privileges to employees or contracting physicians of such hospital, shall include provisions for the use of the facility by, and staff privileges for, duly licensed doctors of medicine, osteopathy, dentistry, and podiatry within the scope of their respective licenses. Such bylaws shall not discriminate on the basis of the staff member's holding a degree of doctor of medicine, doctor of osteopathy, doctor of dental science, or doctor of podiatric medicine within the scope of their respective licensure. Provision shall be made in the bylaws for the right to pursue and practice full surgical privileges for holders of a degree of doctor of medicine, doctor of osteopathy, doctor of dental science, or doctor of podiatric medicine within the scope of their respective licensure. Such rights and privileges may be limited or restricted upon the basis of an individual practitioner's demonstrated training, experience, current competence, professional ethics, health status, or failure to abide by the hospital's rules, regulations, and procedures.
(2) Nothing in this section shall be construed to require a hospital to offer a specific service or services not otherwise offered or to buy, construct, or renovate facilities, to purchase equipment, hire additional staff, or to comply with other requirements of law concerning its planning, financing, or operation. If a health service is offered, the hospital shall not discriminate between persons holding a degree of doctor of medicine, doctor of osteopathy, or doctor of podiatric medicine who are authorized by law to perform such services.
(3) A hospital may require the coadmittance by a medical doctor or doctor of osteopathy for any patient admitted for surgical treatment by a podiatrist or dentist. The responsibility for obtaining such coadmittance shall be that of the podiatrist or dentist admitting said patient and not of the hospital. Patients admitted for podiatric or dental care shall receive the same basic medical appraisal as patients admitted for other services. Such appraisal shall include an admission history and physical examination by a medical doctor, doctor of osteopathy, or qualified, hospital-credentialed and -privileged podiatrist, who is either on the medical staff or approved by the medical staff of such hospital. The findings of such appraisal shall be recorded on the patient's medical record. The admitting podiatrist or dentist shall be responsible for that part of the history and examination that is related to podiatry or dentistry. The medical doctor or doctor of osteopathy shall be responsible for the treatment of any medical problem that may be present on admission or arise during hospitalization of such podiatric or dental patient. Such doctor shall evaluate the general medical condition of the podiatric or dental patient and determine, after consultation if necessary, the overall risk of the pending surgical treatment to the patient's health.
(4) Within one hundred eighty days after May 25, 1983, the governing body of every hospital subject to the provisions of part 3 of this article or established pursuant to section 32-1-1003, C.R.S., which does not limit staff privileges to employees or contracting physicians of such hospital, shall provide in its bylaws reasonable standards and procedures to be applied by such

hospital and its staff in considering and acting upon applications for staff membership or privileges by a person holding a Colorado license to practice as a doctor of medicine, doctor of osteopathic medicine, podiatrist, or dentist in conformance with the requirements of any national accrediting body to which the hospital subscribes. Such standards and procedures shall be available for public inspection and shall be based on an applicant's individual training, experience, current competence, professional ethics, health status, and the hospital's rules of professional conduct applied equally to all persons holding a Colorado license to practice as a doctor of medicine, doctor of osteopathic medicine, podiatrist, or dentist.

(5) Hospital rules and regulations shall be reasonable, necessary, and applied in good faith equally and in a nondiscriminatory manner to all staff members, or applicants seeking to become staff members, holding a degree of doctor of medicine, doctor of osteopathic medicine, doctor of dental science, or doctor of podiatric medicine.

## 25-3-103.7. Employment of physicians - when permissible - conditions - definitions.

(1) For purposes of this section:

(a) "Community mental health center" means a community mental health center, as defined in section 25-1.5-103 (2) , that is currently licensed and regulated by the department pursuant to the department's authority under section 25-1.5-103 (1) (a) .

(b) "Department" means the department of public health and environment.

(c) "Federally qualified health center" or "FQHC" shall have the same meaning as set forth in section 1861(aa) (4) of the federal "Social Security Act", 42 U.S.C. sec. 1395x (aa) (4) .

(d) "Health care facility" means a hospital, hospice, community mental health center, federally qualified health center, school-based health center, rural health clinic, PACE organization, or long-term care facility.

(e) "Hospice" means an entity that administers services to a terminally ill person utilizing palliative care or treatment and that is currently licensed and regulated by the department pursuant to the department's authority under section 25-1.5-103 (1) (a) .

(f) "Hospital" means a hospital currently licensed or certified by the department pursuant to the department's authority under section 25-1.5-103 (1) (a) .

(f.3) "Long-term care facility" means:

(I) A nursing facility as defined by section 25.5-4-103, C.R.S., and licensed pursuant to section 25-1.5-103;

(II) An assisted living residence as defined by section 25-27-102 and licensed pursuant to section 25-27-103; or

(III) An independent living facility or a residence for seniors that provides assistance to its residents in the performance of their daily living activities.

(f.5) "PACE organization" means an organization providing a program of all-inclusive care for the elderly pursuant to section 25.5-5-412, C.R.S.

(g) "Physician" means a person duly licensed to practice under article 32, 35, or 36 of title 12, C.R.S.

(h) "Rural health clinic" shall have the same meaning as set forth in section 1861 (aa) (2) of the federal "Social Security Act", 42 U.S.C. sec. 1395x (aa) (2) .

(i) "School-based health center" shall have the same meaning as set forth in section 25-20.5-502.

(2) (a) A health care facility may employ physicians, subject to the limitations set forth in subsections (3) to (6) of this section. The employment of physicians at a long-term care facility may be direct or through a separate entity authorized to conduct business in this state that has common or overlapping ownership as an affiliate or subsidiary of an entity, including a foreign entity, that owns, controls, or manages the long-term care facility, subject to the limitations set forth in subsections (3) to (6) of this section.

(b) Nothing in this subsection (2) allows any person who is not licensed pursuant to article 36 of title 12, C.R.S., to practice or direct the practice of medicine at a long-term care facility.

(3) Nothing in this section shall be construed to allow any health care facility that employs a physician to limit or otherwise exercise control over the physician's independent professional judgment concerning the practice of medicine or diagnosis or treatment or to require physicians to refer exclusively to the health care facility or to the health care facility's employed physicians. Any health care facility that knowingly or recklessly so limits or controls a physician in such manner or attempts to do so shall be deemed to have violated standards of operation for the particular type of health care facility and may be held liable to the patient or the physician, or both, for such violations, including proximately caused damages. Nothing in this section shall be construed to affect any health care facility's decisions with respect to the availability of services, technology, equipment, facilities, or treatment programs, or as requiring any health care facility to make available to patients or physicians additional services, technology, equipment, facilities, or treatment programs.

(4) Nothing in this section shall be construed to allow a health care facility that employs a physician to offer the physician any percentage of fees charged to patients by the health care facility or other financial incentive to artificially increase services provided to patients.

(5) The medical staff bylaws or policies or the policies of any health care facility that employs physicians shall not discriminate with regard to credentials or staff privileges on the basis of whether a physician is an employee of, a physician with staff privileges at, or a contracting physician with, the health care facility. Any health care facility that discriminates with regard to credentials or staff privileges on the basis of whether a physician is an employee of, a physician with staff privileges at, or a contracting physician with, the health care facility shall be deemed to have violated standards of operation for the particular type of health care facility and may be held liable to the physician for such violations, including proximately caused damages. This subsection (5) shall not affect the terms of any contract or written employment arrangement that provides that the credentials or staff and clinical privileges of any practitioner are incident to or coterminous with the contract or employment arrangement or the individual's association with a group holding the contract.

(6) When applying for initial facility licensure and upon each application for license renewal, every health care facility licensed or certified by the department that employs a physician shall report to the department the number of physicians on the health care facility's medical staff. The report shall separately identify the number of those physicians who are employed by the health care facility under separate contract to the health care facility and independent of the health care facility.

(7) The medical staff bylaws or policies or the policies of any health care facility that employs physicians shall contain a procedure by which complaints by physicians alleging a violation of subsection (3) , (4) , or (5) of this section may be heard and resolved, which procedure shall ensure that the due process rights of the parties are protected. A physician who believes he or she has been the subject of a violation of subsection (3) , (4) , or (5) of this section has a right to complain and request review of the matter pursuant to such procedure.

(8) Nothing in this section shall preclude a physician or a patient from seeking other remedies available to the physician or to the patient at law or in equity.

## 25-3-104. Reports.

Any person, partnership, association, or corporation maintaining any hospital or other facility for the treatment or care of the sick or injured shall make a report to the department of public health and environment upon request but not more frequently than quarterly. The department of public health and environment shall have power to investigate and shall have free access to such facilities consistent with section 25-1.5-103 (1) (a) .

## 25-3-105. License - fee - rules - penalty.

(1) (a) (I) (A) Subject to the limitations in sub-subparagraph (B) of this subparagraph (I) , the state board of health shall establish a schedule of fees, which must be set at a level sufficient to meet the

direct and indirect costs of administration and enforcement of this article, as appropriated by the general assembly for each fiscal year, less any moneys appropriated for the same fiscal year by the general assembly from any other source to meet such costs. The fee schedule must also ensure that the reserve balance in the health facilities general licensure cash fund created in section 25-3-103.1 (1) is consistent with the limits specified in section 24-75-402 (3) , C.R.S., and must be modified, as necessary, to comply with said limits. The state board shall establish and modify, as necessary, the fee schedule by rules adopted in accordance with article 4 of title 24, C.R.S. Except as specified in subparagraph (II) of this paragraph (a) , the department of public health and environment may assess fees in accordance with the fee schedule established by the state board against health facilities licensed by the department. All fees collected pursuant to the fee schedule must be deposited in the health facilities general licensure cash fund created in section 25-3-103.1 (1) and are subject to appropriation by the general assembly in accordance with section 25-3-103.1 (2) .

(B) On or after June 4, 2012, the state board of health may increase the amount of any fee on the schedule of fees established pursuant to sub-subparagraph (A) of this subparagraph (I) that is in effect on June 4, 2012, by an amount not to exceed the annual percentage change in the United States department of labor, bureau of labor statistics, consumer price index for Denver-Boulder-Greeley for all urban consumers, all goods, or its successor index. Nothing in this sub-subparagraph (B) limits the ability of the state board of health to reduce the amount of any fee on the schedule of fees in effect on such date or to modify fees as necessary to comply with section 24-75-402, C.R.S.

(C) The department of public health and environment shall institute, by rule, a performance incentive system for licensed health facilities under which a licensed health facility would be eligible for a reduction in its license renewal fee if: The department's on-site relicensure inspection demonstrates that the health facility has no significant deficiencies that have negatively affected the life, safety, or health of its consumers; the licensed health facility has fully and timely cooperated with the department during the on-site inspection; the department has found no documented actual or potential harm to consumers; and, in the case where any significant deficiencies are found that do not negatively affect the life, safety, or health of consumers, the licensed health facility has submitted, and the department has accepted, a plan of correction and the health facility has corrected the deficient practice, as verified by the department, within the period required by the department.

(II) An acute treatment unit shall be assessed a fee as set forth in paragraph (c) of this subsection (1) , an assisted living residence shall be assessed a fee as set forth in section 25-27-107, and a separate fee shall be collected pursuant to section 25-3-704 to meet the costs incurred by the department in completing the requirements of part 7 of this article.

(III) A license issued by the department may be revoked at any time by the state board of health for any of the causes set forth in section 25-3-103 or for a licensee's failure to comply with any of the rules of the state board or to make the reports required by section 25-3-104. Any person, partnership, association, company, or corporation opening, conducting, or maintaining any facility for the treatment and care of the sick or injured who does not have a provisional or regular license authorizing such person or entity to open, conduct, or maintain the facility is guilty of a misdemeanor and, upon conviction thereof, shall be punished by a fine of not less than fifty dollars nor more than five hundred dollars.

(b) (Deleted by amendment, L. 2007, p. 953, § 2, effective May 17, 2007.)

(c) (I) On and after August 7, 2006, an applicant for licensure for an acute treatment unit shall submit to the department nonrefundable fees with an application for licensure as follows:

(A) A fee of one hundred dollars per available bed in addition to a fee of three thousand five hundred dollars for a license related to new facility operations; except that a facility that converts from a different licensure category to an acute treatment unit shall submit its application and initial licensure fee no later than July 1, 2008;

(B) A fee of twenty dollars per available bed in addition to a fee of one thousand seven hundred dollars to issue a new license when there has been a change of ownership of an existing licensed acute treatment unit;

(C) A fee of twenty dollars per available bed in addition to a fee of one thousand five hundred dollars when the licensee seeks annual renewal of an existing acute treatment unit license.

(II) A licensee shall submit a fee of one hundred dollars for an acute treatment unit in the following circumstances:

(A) When submitting a name change for approval by the department; or

(B) When submitting a request to increase the number of licensed beds for approval by the department.

(III) A licensee shall submit a fee of five hundred dollars for an acute treatment unit in the following circumstances:

(A) For remodeling plan review by the department when the licensee undergoes new construction or substantial remodeling of an acute treatment unit, as defined by rule of the state board of health; or

(B) For remodeling on-site review by the department when the licensee undergoes new construction or substantial remodeling of an acute treatment unit, as defined by rule of the state board of health. Fees for remodeling on-site review shall be in addition to the fees assessed for remodeling plan review.

(2) The department of public health and environment shall maintain a full, true, and accurate accounting of the costs of providing services under this article, including indirect costs, and, at least annually, shall provide a detailed cost accounting report to the health care facility stakeholder forum created in section 25-3-113. The department shall regularly evaluate and update its cost-accounting methods.

(3) Repealed.

(4) On July 1, 2013, any moneys remaining in the health facilities general licensure cash fund created in section 25-3-103.1 (1) from fees collected by the department of public health and environment for health facility building and structure code plan reviews and inspections are transferred to the health facility construction and inspection cash fund created in section 24-33.5-1207.8, C.R.S.

## 25-3-106. Unincorporated associations.

An unincorporated association organized and existing for the purpose of providing hospital services for its members shall be governed, managed, and controlled by a board of trustees selected in accordance with the provisions of the state constitution and bylaws of such association. Such board of trustees shall have the right to acquire, own, and hold, in the name of such association or in the name of persons who hold title in trust for said association, real property devoted to or connected with hospital purposes and to operate and manage the same in accordance with the laws of this state, and such board of trustees shall have the power and right from time to time to sell, convey, lease, or otherwise dispose of such property, including any hospital building of such association, whenever acquired, and to direct the sale, conveyance, lease, or other disposition of the same by persons who hold the title to such property in trust for said association to such purchaser, lessee, or other person or entity for such price and upon such terms and conditions as may be determined by resolution of the board of trustees of the association adopted by two-thirds vote of the entire board of trustees of such association at any regular or special meeting of said board. The sale, conveyance, lease, or other disposition of such property may be made in the manner provided in this section to any person, corporation, county, municipality, or other entity.

## 25-3-107. Disciplinary actions reported to Colorado medical board or podiatry board.

(1) Any disciplinary action to suspend, revoke, or otherwise limit the privileges of a licensed physician or podiatrist that is taken by the governing board of a hospital required to be licensed or certified pursuant to this part 1 or required to obtain a certificate of compliance pursuant to section

25-1.5-103 (1) (a) (I) or (1) (a) (II) shall be reported to the Colorado medical board or the Colorado podiatry board, whichever board is appropriate, in the form prescribed by said board.
(2) Said hospital shall provide such additional information as is deemed necessary by the Colorado medical board or the Colorado podiatry board to conduct a further investigation and hearing.

## 25-3-108. Receivership.

(1) It is the purpose of this section to establish a receivership mechanism that will be available as a remedy for such violations of applicable laws and regulations by a licensee of a long-term health care facility that require facility closure by the department of public health and environment in order to safeguard against potential transfer trauma resulting from relocation of its residents as a result of closure of the facility.
(2) The department of public health and environment, the licensee or owner of a long-term health care facility, or the lessee of such facility with the approval of the owner may apply to the district court for the appointment of a receiver to operate the long-term health care facility when:
(a) The department of public health and environment has refused to issue a renewal license or has revoked the license of such facility and the action of the department is final; or
(b) The department of public health and environment, through the executive director thereof, has taken summary action to suspend the license of any such facility in accordance with the provisions of section 24-4-104 (4) , C.R.S.
(3) The action of the department of public health and environment with respect to nonrenewal or revocation of a license and recommendation for certification for medicaid participation shall not be final for the purposes of paragraph (a) of subsection (2) of this section until all administrative hearings and judicial appeals sought by a licensee of a long-term health care facility have been exhausted or the time permitted for the same has expired and until the decisions resulting from any such appeals, if any, sustain the action of said department.
(4) Application for the appointment of a receiver pursuant to this section shall be to the district court for the county where the long-term health care facility is located. No hearing on such application shall be held sooner than seventy-two hours after the licensee of such facility has been served with notice thereof, as provided in the Colorado rules of civil procedure; except that when the department exercises its summary powers, an emergency receiver may be appointed upon agreement in writing between the department and licensee, with the approval of the owner, until a hearing for appointment of a receiver as provided in this section. Notice shall also be served upon any owner and any lessee of a long-term health care facility and any holder of a security interest of record in said facility. An application for appointment of a receiver pursuant to this section shall have precedence and priority over any civil or criminal case pending in the district court wherein the application is filed.
(5) For the purposes of this section the action of the department of public health and environment exercised pursuant to subsection (2) of this section shall become effective upon appointment of the receiver of the court.
(6) Prior to ordering the appointment of a receiver for the operation of a long-term health care facility, the district court must find:
(a) That grounds for the appointment of a receiver exist as provided in subsection (2) of this section; and
(b) That proper notice as required by subsection (4) of this section has been served; and
(c) That there is a necessity to continue care on a temporary basis at the facility to avoid potential transfer trauma which would serve the best interests of the residents of the facility pending arrangements for the lease, sale, or closure of the facility.
(7) The department of public health and environment shall grant the receiver a license pursuant to section 25-3-102 and shall recommend certification for medicaid participation, and the department of health care policy and financing shall reimburse the receiver for the long-term health care facility's medicaid residents pursuant to section 25.5-6-204, C.R.S.
(8) The appointment of the receiver shall be in accordance with and governed by the provisions of

rule 66 of the Colorado rules of civil procedure. The court shall enter an order of appointment and fix the fees and expenses of the receiver. The receiver shall be a licensed nursing home administrator and shall post a bond with adequate sureties as determined by the court, and the receiver may be sued upon the same in the name of the people of the state of Colorado at the instance and for the use of any party injured. The receiver shall perform duties, assume responsibilities, and preserve the long-term health care facility property in accordance with established principles of law for receivers of real property. Such duties and responsibilities shall be determined by the court following a hearing, at which time the parties may appear and be heard. The court shall specify the duties and responsibilities of the receiver in the order of appointment. No security interest in any real or personal property comprising said facility or contained within the facility nor any fixture of the facility shall be impaired or diminished by the receiver, but the receiver shall comply with the standards of the department of public health and environment in providing health care to patients.

(9) Nothing in this section shall prevent the court from altering or amending the terms and conditions of the receivership or the receiver's responsibilities and duties following a hearing, at which time the parties may appear and be heard; and nothing in this section shall prohibit the parties from stipulating to the terms and conditions of the receivership and the responsibilities and duties of the receiver, including the duration thereof, and such stipulation shall be submitted to the court for approval.

(10) A receivership established pursuant to this section may be terminated by the court upon application therefor by the licensee of a long-term health care facility, the department of public health and environment, or the receiver. The receivership may be terminated upon a finding by the court that the receivership is no longer necessary, but in no case shall the receivership continue for longer than one hundred eighty days from the date of the initial appointment of the receiver unless extended by written agreement of the parties as provided in subsection (9) of this section.

(11) Upon termination of the receivership, the court shall order a final accounting and finally fix the fees and expenses of the receiver following a hearing, at which time the parties may appear and be heard.

## 25-3-109. Quality management functions - confidentiality and immunity.

(1) The general assembly hereby finds and declares that the implementation of quality management functions to evaluate and improve patient and resident care is essential to the operation of health care facilities licensed or certified by the department of public health and environment pursuant to section 25-1.5-103 (1) (a) . For this purpose, it is necessary that the collection of information and data by such licensed or certified health care facilities be reasonably unfettered so a complete and thorough evaluation and improvement of the quality of patient and resident care can be accomplished. To this end, quality management information relating to the evaluation or improvement of the quality of health care services shall be confidential, subject to the provisions of subsection (4) of this section, and persons performing such functions shall be granted qualified immunity. It is the intent of the general assembly that nothing in this section revise, amend, or alter article 36 or part 1 of article 36.5 of title 12, C.R.S.

(2) For purposes of this section, a "quality management program" means a program which includes quality assurance and risk management activities, the peer review of licensed health care professionals not otherwise provided for in part 1 of article 36.5 of title 12, C.R.S., and other quality management functions which are described by a facility in a quality management program approved by the department of public health and environment. Nothing in this section shall revise, amend, or alter article 36 or part 1 of article 36.5 of title 12, C.R.S.

(3) Except as otherwise provided in this section, any records, reports, or other information of a licensed or certified health care facility that are part of a quality management program designed to identify, evaluate, and reduce the risk of patient or resident injury associated with care or to improve the quality of patient care shall be confidential information; except that such information shall be subject to the provisions of subsection (4) of this section.

(4) The records, reports, and other information described in subsection (3) and subsection (5.5) of this section shall not be subject to subpoena or discoverable or admissible as evidence in any civil or administrative proceeding. No person who participates in the reporting, collection, evaluation, or use of such quality management information with regard to a specific circumstance shall testify thereon in any civil or administrative proceeding. However, this subsection (4) shall not apply to:

(a) Any civil or administrative proceeding, inspection, or investigation as otherwise provided by law by the department of public health and environment or other appropriate regulatory agency having jurisdiction for disciplinary or licensing sanctions;

(b) Persons giving testimony concerning facts of which they have personal knowledge acquired independently of the quality management information program or function;

(c) The availability, as provided by law or the rules of civil procedure, of factual information relating solely to the individual in interest in a civil suit by such person, next friend or legal representative. In no event shall such factual information include opinions or evaluations performed as a part of the quality management program.

(d) Persons giving testimony concerning an act or omission which they have observed or in which they participated, notwithstanding any participation by them in the quality management program;

(e) Persons giving testimony concerning facts they have recorded in a medical record relating solely to the individual in interest in a civil suit by such person.

(5) Nothing in this section shall affect the voluntary release of any quality management record or information by a health care facility; except that no patient-identifying information shall be released without the patient's consent.

(5.5) (a) The confidentiality of information provided for in this section shall in no way be impaired or otherwise adversely affected solely by reason of the submission of the information to a nongovernmental entity to conduct studies that evaluate, develop, and analyze information about health care operations, practices, or any other function of health care facilities. The records, reports, and other information collected or developed by a nongovernmental entity shall remain protected as provided in subsections (3) and (4) of this section. In order to adequately protect the confidentiality of such information, no findings, conclusions, or recommendations contained in such studies conducted by any such nongovernmental entity shall be deemed to establish a standard of care for health care facilities.

(b) For purposes of this subsection (5.5) , "health care facility" includes a carrier as defined in section 10-16-102 (8) , C.R.S., and a health care practitioner licensed or certified pursuant to title 12, C.R.S.

(6) Any person who in good faith and within the scope of the functions of a quality management program participates in the reporting, collection, evaluation, or use of quality management information or performs other functions as part of a quality management program with regard to a specific circumstance shall be immune from suit in any civil action based on such functions brought by a health care provider or person to whom the quality information pertains. In no event shall this immunity apply to any negligent or intentional act or omission in the provision of care.

(7) and (8) (Deleted by amendment, L. 97, p. 507, § 2, effective April 24, 1997.)

(9) Nothing in this section shall be construed to limit any statutory or common law privilege, confidentiality, or immunity.

(10) Nothing in this section shall revise, amend, or alter the requirements of section 25-3-107.

(11) (Deleted by amendment, L. 97, p. 507, § 2, effective April 24, 1997.)

(12) Nothing in this section shall affect a person's access to his medical record as provided in section 25-1-801, nor shall it affect the right of any family member or any other person to obtain medical record information upon the consent of the patient or his authorized representative.

## 25-3-110. Emergency contraception - definitions.

(1) For purposes of this section, unless the context otherwise requires:

(a) "Emergency contraception" means a drug approved by the federal food and drug administration that prevents pregnancy after sexual intercourse, including but not limited to oral

contraceptive pills; except that "emergency contraception" shall not include RU-486, mifepristone, or any other drug or device that induces a medical abortion. Nothing in section 2-4-401 (1.5) , C.R.S., shall be construed to amend or alter the definition of "emergency contraception".
(b) "Sexual assault survivor" shall have the same meaning as "victim" as defined in section 18-3-401 (7) , C.R.S.
(2) Notwithstanding any other provision of law to the contrary, all health care facilities that are licensed pursuant to this part 1 and provide emergency care to sexual assault survivors shall amend their evidence-collection protocols for the treatment of sexual assault survivors to include informing the survivor in a timely manner of the availability of emergency contraception as a means of pregnancy prophylaxis and educating the survivor on the proper use of emergency contraception and the appropriate follow-up care.
(3) Nothing in this section shall be interpreted to require:
(a) A health care professional who is employed by a health care facility that provides emergency care to a sexual assault survivor to inform the survivor of the availability of emergency contraception if the professional refuses to provide the information on the basis of religious or moral beliefs; or
(b) A health care facility to provide emergency contraception to a sexual assault survivor who is not at risk of becoming pregnant as a result of the sexual assault or who was already pregnant at the time of the assault.
(4) If any licensed pharmacy does not have nonprescription emergency contraception in stock, the pharmacy shall place a conspicuous notice in the area where customers obtain prescription drugs that states "Plan B Emergency Contraception Not Available".
(5) The general assembly encourages health care facilities to provide training to emergency room staff concerning the efficacy of emergency contraception and the time-sensitive nature of the drug.
(6) Because emergency contraception is time-sensitive and a sexual assault survivor may seek information on or direct access to emergency contraception to prevent an unintended pregnancy resulting from the assault instead of or prior to seeking hospital treatment, it is critical that sexual assault survivors have accurate information about the availability and use of emergency contraception. Therefore, the general assembly encourages:
(a) Entities offering victim assistance or counseling and rape crisis hotlines to include information concerning the availability and use of emergency contraception; and
(b) Licensed or registered pharmacies in the state of Colorado to distribute information concerning the availability and use of emergency contraception.

## 25-3-111. Authentication of verbal orders - hospital policies or bylaws.

(1) A hospital licensed pursuant to part 3 of this article shall require that all verbal orders be authenticated by a physician or responsible individual who has the authority to issue verbal orders in accordance with hospital and medical staff policies or bylaws. The policies or bylaws shall require that:
(a) Authentication of a verbal order occurs within forty-eight hours after the time the order is made unless a read-back and verify process pursuant to paragraph (b) of this subsection (1) is used. The individual receiving a verbal order shall record in writing the date and time of the verbal order, and sign the verbal order in accordance with hospital policies or medical staff bylaws.
(b) A hospital policy may provide for a read-back and verify process for verbal orders. A read-back and verify process shall require that the individual receiving the order immediately read back the order to the physician or responsible individual, who shall immediately verify that the read-back order is correct. The individual receiving the verbal order shall record in writing that the order was read back and verified. If the read-back and verify process is followed, the verbal order shall be authenticated within thirty days after the date of the patient's discharge.
(2) Verbal orders shall be used infrequently. Nothing in this section shall be interpreted to encourage the more frequent use of verbal orders by the medical staff at a hospital.

## 25-3-112. Hospitals - charity care information - charges for the uninsured - reports to department - department review - collections protection - hospital financial assistance standards committee established - rules.

(1) Each hospital shall make information available to each patient about the hospital's financial assistance, charity care, and payment plan policies. Each hospital shall communicate this information in a clear and understandable manner and in languages appropriate to the communities and patients the hospital serves. The hospital shall:

(a) Post the information conspicuously on its website;

(b) Make the information available in patient waiting areas;

(c) Make the information available to each patient, when possible, before the patient's discharge from the hospital; and

(d) Inform each patient on each billing statement of his or her rights pursuant to this section and that financial assistance or charity care may be available and, where applicable, provide the website, e-mail address, and telephone number where the information may be obtained.

(2) (a) When possible, each hospital shall offer to screen each uninsured patient for eligibility for financial assistance as described by this subsection (2) . Each hospital shall offer financial assistance for qualified patients on a community-specific basis. In determining eligibility for financial assistance, each hospital shall, at a minimum, take into consideration federal, state, and local government requirements.

(b) For purposes of this section, a qualified patient is an individual:

(I) Who is uninsured;

(II) Whose annual family income is not more than two hundred fifty percent of the federal poverty guidelines; and

(III) Who received a service at a hospital for which the "Colorado Indigent Care Program" established in part 1 of article 3 of title 25.5, C.R.S., was not available.

(3) A hospital shall limit the amounts charged for emergency or other medically necessary care provided to individuals eligible for assistance under the financial assistance policy described in subsection (2) of this section to not more than the lowest negotiated rate from a private health plan.

(3.5) If a hospital discovers an omission of required information, incorrect billing, or other noncompliance with this section by the hospital, the hospital shall correct the error or omission, inform the patient, and provide a financial correction consistent with this section to the persons affected by the error or omission. The hospital shall inform the department of the errors, omissions, and corrective actions taken by the hospital in the same manner and form as the reports required in section 25-1-124. The department shall not investigate a hospital because that hospital has corrected an error, omission, or noncompliance with this section, unless there is good cause to open an investigation. If the department investigates a self-reported incident, the department shall investigate, document, and identify the self-reported errors, omissions, or noncompliance related to this section as a self-reported incident investigation, and not as a complaint investigation. The department shall make information concerning investigations and complaints available to the public in the same manner as section 25-1-124 (6) and (7) . The department shall make hospital self-reported incidents submitted to the department pursuant to this section available to the public upon request.

(3.7) (a) If the department receives a valid complaint regarding a hospital's compliance with this section, the department may conduct a review. In addition, the department shall periodically review hospitals to ensure compliance with this section.

(b) If the department finds that a hospital is not in compliance with this section, including the rules adopted pursuant to paragraph (c) of subsection (7) of this section, the department shall notify the hospital, and the hospital has ninety days to file with the department a corrective action plan that includes measures to inform the patient or patients, and provide a financial correction consistent with this section to the persons affected by the noncompliance. A hospital may request up to one hundred twenty days to submit a corrective action plan if necessary. The department may require a hospital that is not in compliance with this section, or with rules adopted pursuant to paragraph (c) of subsection (7) of this section, to develop and operate under a corrective action plan until the hospital is in compliance.

(c) If a hospital's noncompliance with this section is determined by the department to be knowing or willful, the department may fine the hospital up to five thousand dollars. In addition, if the hospital fails to take corrective action or fails to file a corrective action plan with the department within ninety days, or up to one hundred twenty days if approved by the department, the department may fine the hospital up to five thousand additional dollars. The department shall consider the size of the hospital and the seriousness of the violation in setting the fine amount.

(4) (a) Before initiating collection proceedings, a hospital shall:

(I) Offer a qualified patient a reasonable payment plan; and

(II) Allow for at least thirty days past the due date of any scheduled payment that is not paid in full. A hospital must allow the thirty-day period only for the first late payment.

(b) A hospital shall not initiate collections proceedings once the hospital is notified that it must submit a corrective action plan or when the hospital is operating pursuant to a corrective action plan pursuant to subsection (3.7) of this section.

(5) Nothing in this section limits or affects a hospital's right to pursue the collection of personal injury, bodily injury, liability, uninsured, underinsured, medical payment rehabilitation, disability, homeowner's, business owner's, workers' compensation, or fault-based insurance.

(6) For the purposes of this section, "hospital" means a hospital licensed pursuant to part 1 of article 3 of this title or certified pursuant to section 25-1.5-103 (1) (a) (II) .

(7) Repealed.

(8) The department shall make information available regarding any corrective actions for which fines were imposed pursuant to this section. Any information regarding the lowest negotiated rate provided to the department pursuant to this section is confidential and not a public record.

(9) Nothing in this section affects a license issued to a hospital pursuant to section 25-3-101. The department shall not charge a hospital an additional license fee for costs associated with this section.

## 25-3-113. Health care facility stakeholder forum - creation - membership - duties.

(1) There is hereby created in the department of public health and environment the health care facility stakeholder forum, referred to in this section as the "stakeholder forum". The stakeholder forum must consist of representatives from various types of provider facilities licensed by the department, consumers, consumer advocates, ombudsmen, and other interested parties. The department shall meet at least four times each year with the stakeholder forum to discuss and take into consideration the concerns and issues of interest to the forum members and other attendees regarding the development and implementation of rules and other matters that affect all health care facilities licensed by the department.

(2) The members of the stakeholder forum serve on a voluntary basis without compensation and are responsible for noticing, staffing, recording, and reporting the notes from the stakeholder forum meetings. The department shall consider the attendance of its representatives at meetings with the stakeholder forum to be within the normal course of business, with no additional appropriation to or resources from the department required.

(3) The stakeholder forum and the department shall work to coordinate with, and shall not duplicate the work being done by, established or statutorily authorized advisory committees or working groups on issues related to the development and implementation of rules.

(4) For purposes of section 24-4-103 (2) , C.R.S., as amended by House Bill 12-1008, enacted in 2012, the department may use the stakeholder forum described in this section, when appropriate, to serve as the representative group for the department of public health and environment.

## 25-3-114. STEMI task force - creation - membership - duties - report - notice

of funding through gifts, grants, and donations - definitions - repeal.
(Repealed)

## 25-3-115. Stroke advisory board - creation - membership - duties - report - definition - repeal.

(1) (a) There is hereby created in the department the stroke advisory board, the purpose of which is to evaluate potential strategies for stroke prevention and treatment and develop a statewide needs assessment identifying relevant resources. No later than August 1, 2013, the governor shall appoint eighteen members to the stroke advisory board as follows:

(I) Six physicians who are actively involved in stroke care and who satisfy the following criteria: One physician who is board-certified in primary care; one physician who is board-certified in vascular neurology; one physician who is privileged and actively practicing interventional neuroradiology; one physician who is board-certified in neurosurgery; one physician representing a statewide chapter of emergency physicians; and one physician who is a board-certified neurologist serving patients in a rural area of the state;

(II) One member representing a statewide association of physicians;

(III) One member representing a statewide hospital association;

(IV) One member who is an emergency medical service provider, as defined in section 25-3.5-103 (8) ;

(V) One member who is a registered nurse involved in stroke care;

(VI) One hospital administrator from a hospital located in a rural area of the state;

(VII) One hospital administrator from a hospital located in an urban area of the state;

(VIII) One representative from a stroke rehabilitation facility;

(IX) One member who is a Colorado resident representing a national association whose goal is to eliminate cardiovascular disease and stroke;

(X) One member who is a Colorado resident representing a national stroke association;

(XI) One member who is a physical or occupational therapist actively involved in stroke care;

(XII) One member of the public who has suffered a stroke or is the caregiver of a person who has suffered a stroke; and

(XIII) One member who is an expert in stroke database management.

(b) The executive director of the department or the executive director's designee shall serve as an ex officio member of the stroke advisory board.

(c) Members of the stroke advisory board serve without compensation and are not entitled to reimbursement of expenses incurred in serving on or performing duties of the advisory board.

(2) (a) The stroke advisory board shall study and make recommendations for developing a statewide plan to improve quality of care for stroke patients. In conducting the study, the stroke advisory board shall explore the following issues, without limitation:

(I) Creation of a state database or registry consisting of data on stroke care that mirrors the data hospitals submit to nationally recognized organizations;

(II) Access to aggregated stroke data, which must exclude any identifying or confidential information about the reporting hospital or patients treated by the hospital, from a state database that may be developed or from a nationally recognized organization by the advisory board, by any person who submits a written request for the data;

(III) Evaluation of currently available stroke treatments and the development of recommendations, based on medical evidence, for ways to improve stroke prevention and treatment;

(IV) A plan that would encourage rural and urban hospitals to coordinate services for the necessary referral or receipt of patients requiring stroke care in the state; and

(V) The criteria used by nationally recognized bodies for designating a hospital in stroke care and whether a designation is appropriate or needed to assure access to the best quality care for Colorado residents with stroke events.

(b) By January 31, 2014, and by each January 1 thereafter, the stroke advisory board shall submit a report specifying its findings and recommendations to the health and human services committee of the senate, the health, insurance, and environment committee of the house of representatives, or their successor committees, and the department. The stroke advisory board shall include in its report a recommendation on whether a designation of a hospital in stroke care is appropriate or needed to assure access to the best quality care for Colorado residents with stroke events.

(3) The department may accept and expend, subject to appropriation by the general assembly, gifts, grants, and donations to pay the direct expenses of the department in assisting and staffing the stroke advisory board. The department shall transmit any monetary gifts, grants, or donations it receives to the state treasurer for deposit in the health facilities general licensure cash fund, and those moneys may be used only to pay the direct expenses of the department.

(4) As used in this section, unless the context otherwise requires, "department" means the department of public health and environment.

(5) This section is repealed, effective September 1, 2018. Prior to the repeal, the department of regulatory agencies shall review the functions of the stroke advisory board in accordance with section 2-3-1203, C.R.S.

## 25-3-116. Department recognition of national certification - suspension or revocation of recognition.

(1) A hospital that has an accreditation, certification, or designation in stroke or STEMI care from a nationally recognized accrediting body, including a certification as a comprehensive stroke center or primary stroke center by the joint commission or an accreditation as a STEMI receiving center or STEMI referral center by the American College of Cardiology Accreditation Services or its successor organization, may send information and supporting documentation to the department. The department shall make a hospital's national accreditation, certification, or designation available to the public in a manner determined by the department.

(2) The department shall deem a hospital that is currently accredited, certified, or designated by a nationally recognized accrediting body as satisfying the requirements for recognition and publication by the department. The department may suspend or revoke a recognition and publication of a hospital's accreditation, certification, or designation if the department determines, after notice and hearing in accordance with the "State Administrative Procedure Act", article 4 of title 24, C.R.S., that the hospital no longer holds an active accreditation, certification, or designation from a nationally recognized certifying body.

(3) Whether a hospital attains a national accreditation, certification, or designation in stroke or STEMI care has no bearing on, or connection with, the licensing or certification of the hospital by the department pursuant to section 25-1.5-103 (1) (a) .

(4) Repealed.

## 25-3-117. Heart attack database - hospitals to report data on heart attack care.

(1) (a) A hospital that is accredited by the American College of Cardiology Accreditation Services or its successor organization or any nationally recognized accrediting body as a STEMI receiving center shall report to the heart attack database data that is consistent with nationally recognized guidelines on individuals with confirmed heart attacks within the state. Within thirty days after receiving a quarterly report of a hospital's heart attack data from the heart attack database, a hospital accredited as a STEMI receiving center shall submit the report to the department.

(b) Hospitals that are recognized as STEMI referral centers pursuant to section 25-3-116 and PCI centers that are not accredited as heart attack receiving centers are encouraged to report data to the heart attack database and provide quarterly database reports to the department.

(2) (a) Reports obtained by the department pursuant to this section are:

(I) Privileged and strictly confidential;

(II) Not subject to civil subpoena, not discoverable, and not admissible in a civil, criminal, or administrative proceeding against a health care facility or health care professional; and

(III) Not directly available to the public.

(b) With regard to reports obtained pursuant to this section, the department shall protect the confidentiality of patient records in accordance with state and federal laws and shall not disclose publicly any identifying or proprietary information of any hospital, hospital administrator, health care professional, or employee.

(3) The department shall sign a letter of commitment with any nationally recognized body whose reports are provided to the department pursuant to subsection (1) (a) of this section to ensure compliance with the confidentiality requirements and, as part of the letter of commitment, request reporting measures and metrics at the national level for benchmarking purposes.

# PART 2. MATERNITY HOSPITALS

## 25-3-201 to 25-3-207. (Repealed)

# PART 3. COUNTY HOSPITALS - ESTABLISHMENT

### 25-3-301. Establishment of public hospital.

(1) Whenever the board of county commissioners of any county which has a population of at least three thousand is presented with a petition signed by five hundred resident registered qualified electors, or by fifty percent of the resident registered qualified electors of such county, at least two hundred fifty of whom are residents of other than the county seat or town where it is proposed to locate such public hospital, asking that a public hospital board be appointed and that an annual tax be levied for the establishment and maintenance of a public hospital at a place in the county named therein, and which petition shall specify the maximum amount of money proposed to be expended in purchasing or building said hospital, such board of county commissioners shall have the power to create, by resolution, such public hospital board, to levy such tax, and to appropriate to such public hospital board the funds for purchasing or building such hospital and for maintaining the hospital, as well as the power to turn to the control and maintenance of such public hospital board any public or other hospital then being conducted by the board of county commissioners. Said tax shall not exceed three mills on the dollar for each year.

(2) If it is proposed in such petition, or in a petition later filed with like number of resident registered qualified elector signers, to create an indebtedness of the county for purchasing, erecting, or enlarging of buildings or equipment for such public hospital, then the board of county commissioners shall submit such question in the manner provided by law for creating debt for erecting public buildings and, if the vote authorizes it, shall issue such bonds, so authorized, as the public hospital board requests. In those counties having a population of less than three thousand, a public hospital board may be created by the petition of not less than fifty-one percent of the resident registered qualified electors or two hundred such resident registered qualified electors, regardless of where they live in the county. In such counties, an annual levy of not to exceed five mills on the dollar shall be assessed to purchase, build, and maintain such a county hospital.

### 25-3-302. Board of trustees.

(1) If the board of county commissioners decides to create such public hospital board, levy such annual tax, and appropriate funds to purchase, erect, and maintain or turn over to it control of such county hospital, the board of county commissioners shall proceed at once to appoint, for designated terms, a board of seven public hospital trustees chosen from the citizens at large with

147

reference to their fitness for such office, all of whom shall be residents of the county and none of whom shall be an elective or appointive state, county, or city official. Not more than four of said hospital trustees shall be residents of the city or town in which said hospital is to be located. Nothing in this article shall require that a licensed physician be appointed to the board of hospital trustees; however, should a licensed physician be appointed to the board, membership on that board shall be limited to one licensed physician at any given time. The seven appointees shall constitute the board of hospital trustees for said public hospital. Such board shall be a body corporate under the name "Board of Trustees for .............. Hospital", the name of the hospital being inserted in the blank.

(2) One of the trustees, so designated in such original appointment, shall hold office until the second Tuesday of January following his appointment, one until the second Tuesday of the second January following his appointment, two until the second Tuesday of the third January following their appointment, one until the second Tuesday of the fourth January following his appointment, and two until the second Tuesday of the fifth January from their appointment. Thereafter, the term of office of each appointee shall be five years from the end of the preceding term. At the expiration of the term of each of said trustees, the office shall be filled by appointment of the board of county commissioners.

(3) In those counties having a population of less than three thousand, the board of public hospital trustees shall consist of five citizens at large having the same requirements with reference to their fitness for such office as all other counties. One of said trustees, so designated in such original appointment, shall hold office until the second Tuesday of January following his appointment, one until the second Tuesday of the second January following his appointment, one until the second Tuesday of the third January following his appointment, one until the second Tuesday of the fourth January following his appointment, and one until the second Tuesday of the fifth January following his appointment. The term of office and the method of filling vacancies shall be the same as for all other counties.

## 25-3-303. Organization of trustees.

(1) The members of the board of public hospital trustees within ten days after their appointment shall qualify by taking the oath of office. On the second Tuesday of each January, they shall organize and operate as follows:

(a) Unless otherwise authorized under the provisions of paragraph (b) of this subsection (1) , they shall elect one of their number as president, one as vice-president, and one as secretary. No bond shall be required of them. The county treasurer of the county shall be treasurer of the board of trustees and shall receive and pay out all moneys under the control of said board as ordered by it but shall receive no compensation from such board. No trustee shall receive any compensation for services performed but may receive reimbursement for any cash expenditures actually made for personal expenses incurred as such trustee. An itemized statement of all such expenses and money paid out shall be made under oath by such trustee and filed with the secretary and allowed only by the affirmative vote of all the trustees present at a meeting of the board.

(b) If approved by resolution of the board of county commissioners, the board may organize and operate by electing one of their number as president, one as vice-president, and one as secretary-treasurer. The trustees may appoint an assistant secretary-treasurer from outside the membership of the board of trustees. No bond shall be required of the trustees, except of the secretary-treasurer and assistant secretary-treasurer who shall each file with the board of trustees, at the expense of the hospital, a corporate fidelity bond in an amount not less than ten thousand dollars, conditioned on the faithful performance of the duties of his office. The secretary-treasurer shall receive and pay out all the moneys under the control of the board of trustees as ordered by it. No trustee shall receive any compensation for services performed, but may receive reimbursement for any cash expenditures actually made for personal expenses incurred as such trustee. An itemized statement of all such expenses and money paid out shall be made under oath by such trustee and filed with the secretary-treasurer and allowed only by the affirmative vote of all the trustees present at a meeting of the board.

(2) For purposes of part 4 of article 6 of title 24, C.R.S., any board of public hospital trustees created pursuant to section 25-3-302 shall continue to be a local public body, as defined in section 24-6-402 (1) (a) , C.R.S., regardless of whether the hospital governed by such board of trustees is designated an enterprise pursuant to section 25-3-304 (3) .

## 25-3-304. Trustees - powers and duties.

(1) The board of public hospital trustees shall make and adopt such bylaws, rules, and regulations for its own guidance and for the government of the hospital as it deems expedient for the economic and equitable conduct thereof, not inconsistent with state law or the ordinances of the city or town wherein such public hospital is located. The public hospital board shall have the exclusive control of the use and expenditure of all moneys collected to the credit of the hospital, including the right to invest or have invested hospital moneys and funds held by the hospital or in the office of the county treasurer and to receive the interest and income therefrom, and of the purchase of sites, the purchase, construction, or enlargement of any hospital building, and the supervision, care, and custody of the grounds, rooms, or buildings purchased, constructed, leased, or set apart for that purpose. The hospital board may acquire by lease real and personal property subject to the approval of the board of county commissioners. All tax moneys received for hospital purposes shall be paid out of the county treasury only upon warrants drawn by the county commissioners upon sworn vouchers approved by the hospital board. All other moneys received for such hospital shall be deposited in the treasury of the hospital and paid out only upon order of said hospital board. Hospital property and facilities, including real and personal property, may be acquired and held by lease or conveyance on transfer of title, but if by conveyance title to all lands shall be in the name of the county. County hospitals situated in home rule counties shall have the additional borrowing authority as granted by section 30-35-201 (23) (b) , C.R.S.

(2) The board of public hospital trustees shall have power to hire, retain, and remove agents and employees, including administrative, nursing, and professional personnel, engineers, architects, and attorneys, and to fix their compensation; shall have the power to borrow money and incur indebtedness, and to issue bonds and other evidence of such indebtedness; except that no indebtedness shall be created, except as otherwise provided by statute, in excess of the revenue which may reasonably be expected to be available to the hospital for repayment thereof in the fiscal year in which such indebtedness is to be created, and except that no such indebtedness shall be incurred without the approval of the board of county commissioners; and shall in general carry out the spirit and intent of this part 3 in establishing and maintaining a county public hospital. Such board of public hospital trustees shall hold meetings at least once each month and shall keep a complete record of all its proceedings. Four members of the board shall constitute a quorum for the transaction of business. One of the trustees shall visit and examine said hospital at least twice each month, and the public hospital board, during the first week in each January and July, shall file with the board of county commissioners a report of their proceedings with reference to such hospital and a statement of all receipts and expenditures during the half year. On or before each October first, the board shall certify to the board of county commissioners the amount necessary to maintain and improve said hospital for the ensuing year. No trustee shall have a personal pecuniary interest, either directly or indirectly, in the purchase of any supplies for said hospital, unless the same are purchased by competitive bidding.

(3) (a) The board of public hospital trustees may, in accordance with the provisions of paragraph (b) of this subsection (3) , designate the hospital as an enterprise for purposes of section 20 of article X of the state constitution so long as said board of trustees retains authority to issue revenue bonds and the hospital receives less than ten percent of its total annual revenues in grants. So long as the hospital is designated as an enterprise pursuant to the provisions of this subsection (3) , the hospital shall not be subject to any of the provisions of section 20 of article X of the state constitution.

(b) (I) The board of public hospital trustees may, by resolution, designate the hospital as an enterprise as long as the hospital meets the requirements for an enterprise as stated in paragraph (a) of this subsection (3) . Such designation shall be effective beginning with the budget year immediately following the budget year in which such resolution is adopted. Such resolution shall be adopted no sooner than ninety days and no later than thirty days prior to the commencement of the budget year in which such designation becomes effective.

(II) The board of public hospital trustees may, by resolution, revoke the designation of the hospital as an enterprise. Such revocation shall be effective beginning with the budget year immediately following the budget year in which such resolution is adopted. Such resolution shall be adopted no sooner than ninety days and no later than thirty days prior to the commencement of the budget year in which such revocation becomes effective.

(III) Upon adoption of any resolution pursuant to the provisions of subparagraph (I) or (II) of this paragraph (b) , the board of public hospital trustees shall transmit a copy of the resolution to the division of local government in the department of local affairs and the appropriate board or boards of county commissioners.

(IV) The termination or revocation of the designation of the hospital as an enterprise shall not affect in any manner the validity of any revenue bonds issued by the board of public hospital trustees of such hospital pursuant to subsection (4) of this section.

(c) (I) For purposes of this subsection (3) , "grant" means any direct cash subsidy or other direct contribution of money from the state or any local government in Colorado which is not required to be repaid.

(II) "Grant" does not include:

(A) Any indirect benefit conferred upon a hospital from the state or any local government in Colorado;

(B) Any revenues resulting from rates, fees, assessments, or other charges imposed by a hospital for the provision of goods or services by such hospital;

(C) Any federal funds, regardless of whether such federal funds pass through the state or any local government in Colorado prior to receipt by a hospital.

(4) (a) Subject to the limitations set forth in paragraph (b) of this subsection (4) , the board of public hospital trustees shall have the power to issue revenue bonds, secured by any revenues of the hospital other than property tax revenues. Notwithstanding subsection (2) of this section to the contrary, such revenue bonds may provide for their repayment over a term greater than one fiscal year. The board shall authorize the issuance of revenue bonds by resolution, duly approved by no less than two-thirds of the entire membership of the board. All bonds shall be signed by the president of the board of trustees, countersigned by the secretary of the board of trustees, and shall be numbered and registered in a book kept by the secretary or the secretary-treasurer, as applicable. Each bond shall state upon its face the amount for which such bond is issued, to whom such bond is issued, and the date of its issuance.

(b) Except as otherwise provided in this paragraph (b) , the issuance of any revenue bonds pursuant to the provisions of this subsection (4) shall not become effective for a period of thirty days following the adoption of any resolution authorizing such issuance for the purpose of allowing the board of county commissioners to review such pending bond issue. Such review period shall commence upon the date of receipt by the board of county commissioners of written notice from the board of public hospital trustees of such pending revenue bond issue. During said thirty days, the board of county commissioners may file a written notice with the board of trustees stating that the board of county commissioners has no objection to such pending bond issue. Upon receipt of such notice of no objection, the issuance of such revenue bonds shall become effective. If, within said thirty days, the board of county commissioners does not file with the board of trustees either a written notice of no objection or a written objection, the issuance of such revenue bonds shall become effective. If the board of county commissioners files a written objection, the issuance of such revenue bonds shall be prohibited until such time as the board of county commissioners gives written notice to the board of trustees of withdrawal of the board's objection.

## 25-3-305. Vacancies - removal for cause.

Vacancies in the board of trustees occasioned by removals, resignations, or otherwise shall be reported to the board of county commissioners and be filled in like manner as original appointments. Any trustee may be removed for cause by the board of county commissioners.

## 25-3-306. Right of eminent domain.

If the board of public hospital trustees and the owners of any property desired by it for hospital purposes cannot agree as to the price to be paid therefor, said board shall report the facts to the board of county commissioners, and condemnation proceedings shall be instituted by the board of county commissioners and prosecuted in the name of the county wherein such public hospital is to be located.

## 25-3-307. Building requirements.

No hospital buildings shall be erected or constructed until the plans and specifications have been made therefor and adopted by the board of public hospital trustees and bids advertised for according to law as for other county public buildings. Such hospital may be in more than one unit or set of buildings within the same town or city, or in separate towns or cities, or within adjacent counties, and, if in adjacent counties, upon approval of the respective boards of county commissioners.

## 25-3-308. Improvements or enlargements.

In counties exercising the rights conferred by this part 3, the board of county commissioners may appropriate each year, in addition to the tax for hospital fund provided for in section 25-3-301, not more than five percent of its general fund for the improvement or enlargement of any public hospital so established.

## 25-3-309. Hospital fees.

Every hospital established under this part 3 shall be for the benefit of the inhabitants of such county and of any person falling sick or being injured or maimed within its limits. Every inhabitant or person who is not a pauper shall pay to the board of public hospital trustees or such officer as it shall designate for such county public hospital a reasonable compensation for occupancy, nursing, laboratories, care, medicine, or attendants according to the rules and regulations prescribed by said board in order to render the use of said hospital of the greatest benefit to the greatest number.

## 25-3-310. Rules and regulations.

(1) When such hospital is established, the physicians, nurses, attendants, persons sick therein, and persons approaching or coming within the limits of same and all buildings and grounds of such hospital and all furniture and other articles used or brought there shall be subject to such rules and regulations as said public hospital board may prescribe.
(2) Said public hospital board may exclude from the use of such hospital any inhabitants and persons who willfully violate such rules and regulations. The board may extend the privileges and use of such hospital to persons residing outside of such county upon such terms and conditions as said board may from time to time by its rules and regulations prescribe.

## 25-3-311. Donations permitted.

Any person, firm, organization, corporation, or society desiring to make donations of money, personal property, or real estate for the benefit of such public hospital shall have the right to vest title of the money, personal property, or real estate so donated in said county, to be controlled, when accepted, by the board of public hospital trustees according to the terms of the deed, gift, devise, or bequest of such property.

## 25-3-312. Training school for nurses.

The board of trustees of such county public hospital may establish and maintain, in connection therewith and as a part of said public hospital, a training school for nurses.

## 25-3-313. Lease of hospital.

The public hospital board having control of such hospital after its establishment and turning over to its management may in its discretion rent or lease the said hospital, for such rental and for such term as it deems reasonable and proper, to any corporation not for pecuniary profit duly organized under the laws of the state of Colorado for the purpose of conducting a hospital.

## 25-3-314. Charge for professional services.

Any hospital which is owned by a county, or by a city and county, having a population in excess of two hundred fifty thousand persons and which is a teaching hospital duly accredited as such by the joint commission on accreditation of hospitals and by the council on medical education of the American medical association may employ physicians and surgeons licensed to practice medicine in the state of Colorado for the performance of professional services in such hospital or in any related outpatient facility which is owned by such county or city and county. Charges for the services so rendered by any such physician or surgeon, excluding professional trainees, may be collected through the medium of such hospital in the name of the physician or surgeon and, upon collection, may be placed in a medical practice fund to be established, maintained, and used by such hospital solely for the purpose of payment of compensation to the physicians and surgeons so employed and for the payment of consultation fees to other physicians and surgeons not so employed, or directly to physicians and surgeons who are directly engaged in medical research or medical education.

## 25-3-315. Records of hospital.

For purposes of part 2 of article 72 of title 24, C.R.S., the records of any hospital established pursuant to this part 3 shall continue to be public records, as defined in section 24-72-202 (6) , C.R.S., regardless of whether such hospital is designated as an enterprise pursuant to section 25-3-304 (3) .

# PART 4. STATE PLAN FOR IMPLEMENTATION OF FEDERAL ACT FOR THE CONSTRUCTION OF HEALTH FACILITIES

## 25-3-401. Department to administer plan.

(1) The department of public health and environment is designated as the sole agency for carrying out the purposes of the federal "Hospital Survey and Construction Act", Public Law 79-725 of the 79th Congress of the United States, approved August 13, 1946, or any amendments thereto, and the successor provisions thereof of Public Law 93-641, and is authorized to formulate, submit, and administer a state plan for carrying out the provisions thereof and to accept on behalf of the state any funds allotted to the state under the provision of the said federal acts, or any amendments thereto. In carrying out the purposes of this section, the department of public health and environment is authorized to make such reports as may be required by the said federal acts, or any amendments thereto, and to do all things that may be required as a condition precedent to the proper application for the receipt of federal grants under the said federal acts, and any amendments thereto and regulations thereof, and to administer and supervise the expenditure of such grants for

the purposes of this section.

(2) The state plan established under subsection (1) of this section shall provide for adequate hospital facilities for the people residing in the state, without discrimination on account of race, creed, or color, and shall provide for adequate hospital facilities for persons unable to pay therefor. The department of public health and environment shall provide minimum standards for the maintenance and operation of hospitals which receive federal aid under this part 4, and compliance with such standards shall be required in the case of hospitals which have received federal aid under the provisions of said federal acts, or any amendments thereto.

### 25-3-402. State advisory hospital and mental retardation facilities and community mental health centers council. (Repealed)

### 25-3-403. Department to administer federal mental retardation and mental health construction funds.

The department of public health and environment is designated as the sole agency for carrying out the purposes of Part C of Title I and Title II of the federal "Mental Retardation Facilities and Community Mental Health Centers Construction Act of 1963", Public Law 88-164 of the 88th congress of the United States, approved October 31, 1963, or any amendments thereto, and is authorized to administer a state plan for carrying out the provisions thereof and to accept, on behalf of the state, all funds allotted to the state under the provisions of said federal act, or any amendments thereto. Such state plan shall be formulated by the state mental health and mental retardation authority. In carrying out the purposes hereof, the department of public health and environment is authorized to make such reports as may be required by said federal act, or any amendments thereto, and to do all things that may be required as a condition precedent to the proper application for the receipt of federal grants under said federal act, and any amendments thereto and regulations thereof, and to administer and supervise the expenditure of such grants for the purposes hereof in consultation with the mental health and mental retardation authority of the state of Colorado.

# PART 5. CERTIFICATE OF PUBLIC NECESSITY

### 25-3-501 to 25-3-521. (Repealed)

# PART 6. HOSPITAL-ACQUIRED INFECTIONS DISCLOSURE

### 25-3-601. Definitions.

As used in this part 6, unless the context otherwise requires:

(1) "Advisory committee" means the advisory committee created pursuant to section 25-3-602 (4).

(2) "Department" means the department of public health and environment.

(2.5) "Health-care-associated infection" means a localized or systemic condition that results from an adverse reaction to the presence of an infectious agent or its toxins that was not present or incubating at the time of admission to the health facility.

(3) "Health facility" means a hospital, a hospital unit, an ambulatory surgical center, a dialysis treatment clinic currently licensed or certified by the department pursuant to the department's authority under section 25-1.5-103 (1) (a) , or other state licensed or certified facility that submits data to the national healthcare safety network, or its successor.

(4) Repealed.

(5) "Infection" means the invasion of the body by pathogenic microorganisms that reproduce and multiply, causing disease by local cellular injury, secretion of a toxin, or antigen-antibody reaction in the host.

## 25-3-602. Health facility reports - repeal.

(1) (a) A health facility specified by the department shall collect data on health-care-associated infection rates for specific clinical procedures and health-care-associated infections as determined by the department.

(b) The advisory committee may define criteria to determine when data on a procedure or health-care-associated infection described in paragraph (a) of this subsection (1) shall be collected.

(c) An individual who collects data on health-care-associated infection rates shall take the test for the appropriate national certification for infection control and become certified within six months after the individual becomes eligible to take the certification test, as recommended by the Certification Board of Infection Control and Epidemiology, Inc., or its successor. Mandatory national certification requirements shall not apply to individuals collecting data on health-care-associated infections in hospitals licensed for fifty beds or less, licensed ambulatory surgical centers, licensed dialysis treatment centers, licensed long-term care facilities, and other licensed or certified health facilities specified by the department. Qualifications for these individuals may be met through ongoing education, training, experience, or certification, as defined by the department.

(2) Each health care provider who performs a clinical procedure subject to data collection as determined by the department pursuant to subsection (1) of this section shall report to the health facility at which the clinical procedure was performed a health-care-associated infection that the health care provider diagnoses at a follow-up appointment with the patient using standardized criteria and methods consistent with guidelines determined by the advisory committee. The reports made to the health facility under this subsection (2) shall be included in the reporting the health facility makes under subsection (3) of this section.

(3) (a) A health facility shall routinely submit its health-care-associated infection data to the national healthcare safety network in accordance with national healthcare safety network requirements and procedures. The data submissions shall begin on or before July 31, 2007, and continue thereafter.

(b) If a health facility is a division or subsidiary of another entity that owns or operates other health facilities or related organizations, the data submissions required under this part 6 shall be for the specific division or subsidiary and not for the other entity.

(c) Health facilities shall authorize the department to have access to health-facility-specific data contained in the national healthcare safety network database consistent with the requirements of this part 6.

(4) (a) The executive director of the department shall appoint an advisory committee. The advisory committee shall consist of:

(I) One representative from an urban hospital;

(II) One representative from a rural hospital;

(III) One board-certified or board-eligible physician licensed in the state of Colorado, who is affiliated with a Colorado hospital or medical school, who is an active member of a national organization specializing in health care epidemiology or infection control, and who has demonstrated an interest and expertise in health facility infection control;

(IV) Four infection control practitioners as follows:

(A) One from a stand-alone ambulatory surgical center;

(B) One health care professional certified by the Certification Board of Infection Control and Epidemiology, Inc., or its successor;

(C) One from a long-term care setting; and

(D) One other health care professional.

(V) Either one medical statistician with an advanced degree in such specialty or one clinical microbiologist with an advanced degree in such specialty;

(VI) One representative from a health consumer organization;

(VII) One representative from a health insurer; and

(VIII) One representative from a purchaser of health insurance.

(b) The advisory committee shall assist the department in development of the department's oversight of this article and the department's methodology for disclosing the information collected under this part 6, including the methods and means for release and dissemination.

(c) The department and the advisory committee shall evaluate on a regular basis the quality and accuracy of health-facility information reported under this part 6 and the data collection, analysis, and dissemination methodologies.

(d) The advisory committee shall elect a chair of the advisory committee annually. The advisory committee shall meet no less than four times per year in its first year of existence and no less than two times in each subsequent year. The chair shall set the meeting dates and times. The members of the advisory committee shall serve without compensation.

(5) (a) The advisory committee shall recommend additional clinical procedures based upon the criteria set forth in paragraph (c) of this subsection (5) and other health-care-associated infections that must be reported pursuant to subsection (1) of this section. The recommendations of the advisory committee must be consistent with information that may be collected by the national healthcare safety network.

(b) Repealed.

(c) In making its recommendations under paragraph (a) of this subsection (5) , the advisory committee shall recommend clinical procedures and other health-care-associated infections to monitor and report, using the following considerations:

(I) Whether the procedure contains a high risk for infection contraction;

(II) Whether the type or types of infection present a serious risk to the patient's health or life; and

(III) Any other factors determined by the advisory committee.

(d) Repealed.

(6) The advisory committee may recommend that health facilities report process measures to the advisory committee, in addition to those listed in subsections (1) and (5) of this section, to accommodate best practices for effective prevention of infection.

(7) (a) Subsections (4) , (5) , and (6) of this section and this subsection (7) are repealed, effective September 1, 2021.

(b) Prior to such repeal, the advisory committee and its functions shall be reviewed as provided for in section 2-3-1203, C.R.S.

## 25-3-603. Department reports.

(1) Notwithstanding section 24-1-136 (11) (a) (I) , on or before July 15, 2017, and each July 15 thereafter, the department shall submit to the health and human services committees of the house of representatives and of the senate a report summarizing the risk-adjusted health-facility data. The department shall post the report on its website.

(2) Repealed.

(3) (a) All data in reports issued by the department shall be risk-adjusted consistent with the standards of the national healthcare safety network.

(b) The annual report must compare the risk-adjusted, health-care-associated infection rates, collected under section 25-3-602 for health facilities specified by the department for each individual health facility in the state. The department, in consultation with the advisory committee, shall make this comparison as easy to comprehend as possible. The report must include an executive summary, written in plain language, that includes, but is not limited to, a discussion of findings, conclusions, and trends concerning the overall state of health-care-associated infections in the state, including a comparison to prior years when available. The report may include policy recommendations as appropriate.

(c) The department shall publicize the report and its availability as widely as practical to interested parties, including but not limited to health facilities, providers, media organizations, health insurers, health maintenance organizations, purchasers of health insurance, organized labor, consumer or patient advocacy groups, and individual consumers. The annual report shall be made available to any person upon request.

(d) A health-facility report or department disclosure may not contain information identifying a patient, employee, or licensed health care professional in connection with a specific infection incident.

## 25-3-604. Privacy.

Compliance with this part 6 shall not violate a patient's right to confidentiality. A patient's social security number and any other information that could be used to identify a patient shall not be released, notwithstanding any other provision of law.

## 25-3-605. Confidentiality.

(1) Except as provided by subsection (5) of this section, all information and materials obtained and compiled by the department under this part 6 or compiled by a health facility under this part 6, including all related information and materials, are confidential; are not subject to disclosure, discovery, subpoena, or other means of legal compulsion for release to any person, subject to subsection (2) of this section; and may not be admitted as evidence or otherwise disclosed in a civil, criminal, or administrative proceeding.

(2) The confidential protections under subsection (1) of this section shall apply without regard to whether the information or materials are obtained from or compiled by a health facility or an entity that has ownership or management interests in a health facility.

(3) The transfer of information or materials under this part 6 is not a waiver of a privilege or protection granted under law.

(4) Information reported by a health facility under this part 6 and analyses, plans, records, and reports obtained, prepared, or compiled by a health facility under this part 6 and all related information and materials are subject to an absolute privilege and shall not be used in any form against the health facility, its agents, employees, partners, assignees, or independent contractors in any civil, criminal, or administrative proceeding, regardless of the means by which a person came into possession of the information, analysis, plan, record, report, or related information or materials.

(5) The provisions of this section regarding the confidentiality of information or materials compiled or reported by a health facility in compliance with or as authorized under this part 6 shall not restrict access, to the extent authorized by law, by the patient or the patients' legally authorized representative to records of the patient's medical diagnosis or treatment or to other primary health records.

## 25-3-606. Penalties.

(1) A determination that a health facility has violated the provisions of this part 6 may result in the following:
(a) Termination of licensure or other sanctions related to licensure under part 1 of this article; or
(b) A civil penalty of up to one thousand dollars per violation for each day the health facility is in violation of this part 6.

## 25-3-607. Regulatory oversight.

The department shall be responsible for ensuring compliance with this part 6 as a condition of licensure under part 1 of this article and shall enforce compliance according to the provisions in part 1 of this article.

# PART 7. COLORADO HOSPITAL REPORT CARD ACT

### 25-3-701. Short title.
This part 7 shall be known and may be cited as the "Colorado Hospital Report Card Act".

### 25-3-702. Comprehensive hospital information system - executive director - duties - definitions.
(1) (a) The executive director shall approve a comprehensive hospital information system to provide for the collection, compilation, coordination, analysis, indexing, and utilization of both purposefully collected and extant hospital-related data and statistics to produce and report comparable and uniform health information and statistics that shall be utilized in the development and production of the report card described in section 25-3-703. The executive director shall designate or contract with any individual or entity he or she deems appropriate to carry out the purposes of this part 7.

(b) (I) The association selected pursuant to subsection (3) of this section shall review and prepare the nursing-sensitive quality measures set forth in this paragraph (b) for inclusion in the hospital information system and hospital report card developed pursuant to this part 7. In reviewing and preparing to implement the nursing-sensitive quality measures, the association shall determine whether the measures should be reported for the hospital as a whole or by unit level of a hospital. In making its determinations pursuant to this paragraph (b) , the association shall involve and seek input from no more than seven direct-care nurses who have been recommended by the governor.

(II) The association shall collect, review, and implement the following nursing-sensitive quality measures as soon as practicable:

(A) Practice environment scale or PES, as defined by the national quality forum, which is the nursing work index that measures the composite score and individual scores for the following subscales: Nurse participation in hospital affairs; nursing foundations for quality of care; nurse manager ability, leadership, and support of nurses; staffing and resource adequacy; and collegiality of nurse-physician relations; and

(B) Registered nurse education and certification.

(III) The association shall collect, review, and implement the following nursing-sensitive quality measures, as defined by the national quality forum, no later than November 30, 2010:

(A) Skill mix;

(B) The nursing hours per patient day;

(C) Voluntary turnover;

(D) Patient falls prevalence rate; and

(E) Patient falls with injury.

(IV) The association shall identify a process or mechanism to allow access to or use of the data collected pursuant to this paragraph (b) , as appropriate, for research purposes.

(V) The association may exempt from the requirements of this paragraph (b) a licensed or certified hospital that has not more than one hundred licensed beds.

(VI) As used in this paragraph (b) :

(A) "Direct-care nurse" means a registered nurse who is engaged in direct patient care responsibilities in an inpatient hospital unit setting for more than fifty percent of his or her working hours.

(B) (Deleted by amendment, L. 2010, (SB 10-217) , ch. 315, p. 1474, § 1, effective May 27,

2010.)

(C) "National quality forum" means the private, not-for-profit membership organization created to develop and implement a national strategy for healthcare quality measurement and reporting, or its successor organization.

(2) In order to implement this section the executive director or his or her designee shall:

(a) Develop and implement a long-range plan for making available clinical outcomes and data that will allow consumers to compare health care services;

(b) On or before May 15, 2007, submit an initial plan and an annual update to the plan and a report on the status of implementation to the governor and to the public, via a website. The plan shall identify the process and time frames for implementation, barriers to implementation, and recommendations of changes in the law that may be enacted by the general assembly to eliminate the barriers.

(c) Make available clinical outcomes measures from general hospitals licensed pursuant to this article and public hospitals certified pursuant to section 25-1.5-103 (1) (a) . When determining which data to report, the executive director or designee shall consider:

(I) Inclusion of data on all patients regardless of the payer source for Colorado hospitals and other information that may be required for either individual or group purchasers to assess the value of the product;

(II) Use of standardized clinical outcomes measures recognized by national organizations that establish standards to measure the performance of health care providers;

(III) Data that is severity and acuity adjusted using statistical methods that show variation in reported outcomes, where applicable, and data that has passed standard edits;

(IV) Reporting the results with separate documents containing the technical specification and measures;

(V) Standardization in reporting; and

(VI) Disclosure of the methodology of reporting.

(3) (a) The executive director shall select a duly constituted association of hospitals for assistance in carrying out the purposes of this part 7 and shall rely upon the advice and assistance of the selected association. The association shall provide the executive director with a copy of the association's organizational documents and any rules or regulations governing the association's activities and a list of the association's members. The association shall provide to the executive director a plan outlining the association's inclusion and consideration of the interests of health care consumers, including health plans and employers, in the process of carrying out the purposes of this part 7. The name and address of a representative of the organization, who is a resident of this state, upon whom notices or orders of the executive director may be served shall be provided to the executive director. The executive director shall have the authority to examine the collection, analysis, and validity of the data used as a basis for the reporting required in this part 7.

(b) The executive director may refuse to accept, or may suspend or revoke the acceptance of, an association for any of the following reasons:

(I) It reasonably appears that the association will not be able to carry out the purpose of this part 7.

(II) The association does not provide to the executive director a plan outlining the association's inclusion and consideration of the interests of health care consumers, including health plans and employers, in the process of carrying out the purposes of this part 7.

(III) On or before April 15, 2007, the association does not submit a plan to the executive director and report on the status of its implementation satisfactory to the executive director.

(IV) The association fails to meet other applicable requirements prescribed in this part 7.

(c) There shall not be liability on the part of, nor shall a cause of action of any nature arise against, the association or its agents, employees, directors, or authorized designees of the executive director for actions taken or omitted in the performance of their powers and duties under this section.

(4) (a) In the event the executive director refuses to accept, or suspends or revokes the acceptance of, an association previously accepted for assistance in carrying out the purposes of this part 7 for any of the reasons set forth in this part 7, there shall be created in the state department the

Colorado commission for hospital statistics, referred to in this subsection (4) as the "commission", to carry out the purposes of this part 7.

(b) The commission shall consist of nine members, who shall be appointed by the governor with the consent of the senate, as follows:

(I) Three members representing hospitals licensed under this article;

(II) Two members representing licensed health care providers; and

(III) Four members representing consumers or businesses without any direct interest in hospitals licensed under this article.

(c) At no time shall the commission have more than five members of any one political party. Members of the commission shall be compensated for actual and necessary expenses incurred in the conduct of official business.

(d) The commission shall annually elect the chairman of the commission from its members. A majority of the commission shall constitute a quorum.

(e) The commission shall meet at least once during each calendar quarter. Meeting dates shall be set upon written request by three or more members of the commission or by a call of the chairman upon five days' notice to the members.

(f) Action of the commission shall not be taken except upon the affirmative vote of a majority of a quorum of the commission.

(g) All meetings of the commission shall be open to the public pursuant to section 24-6-402, C.R.S.

## 25-3-703. Hospital report card.

(1) The executive director shall approve a Colorado hospital report card consisting of public disclosure of data assembled pursuant to this part 7. At a minimum, the data shall be made available on an internet website in a manner that allows consumers to conduct an interactive search that allows them to view and compare the information for specific hospitals. The website shall include such additional information as is determined necessary to ensure that the website enhances informed decision making among consumers and health care purchasers, which shall include, at a minimum, appropriate guidance on how to use the data and an explanation of why the data may vary from hospital to hospital. The data specified in this subsection (1) shall be released on or before November 30, 2007.

(2) Prior to the completion of the Colorado hospital report card, the executive director shall ensure that every hospital is allowed thirty days within which to examine the data and submit comments for consideration and inclusion in the final Colorado hospital report card.

## 25-3-704. Fees.

(1) The executive director shall annually determine the costs incurred by the department and the Colorado commission for hospital statistics in completing the requirements of this part 7.

(2) The executive director shall apportion, according to net patient service revenues, the costs annually among the hospitals who pay the annual registration fee required by this section and report the same to the state board of health. The state board of health by rule or as otherwise provided by law may increase the amount of the annual fee imposed by this section. At no time shall the fee be higher than what is necessary to implement the report required pursuant to this part 7.

(3) All fees collected pursuant to this part 7 shall be transmitted to the state treasurer, who shall credit the same to the health facilities general licensure cash fund created in section 25-3-103.1.

(4) Notwithstanding the amount specified for the fee in this section, the state board of health by rule or as otherwise provided by law may reduce the amount of the fee if necessary pursuant to section 24-75-402 (3), C.R.S., to reduce the uncommitted reserves of the fund to which all or any portion of the fee is credited. After the uncommitted reserves of the fund are sufficiently reduced, the state board of health by rule or as otherwise provided by law may increase the amount of the fee as provided in section 24-75-402 (4), C.R.S.

## 25-3-705. Health care charge transparency - hospital charge report.

(1) The commissioner of insurance shall work with the duly constituted association of hospitals selected by the executive director pursuant to section 25-3-702 for assistance in carrying out the purposes of this section.

(2) (a) On or before August 1, 2009, and on or before each August 1 thereafter, each hospital licensed pursuant to part 1 of this article shall report annually to the association of hospitals the information necessary to allow the association to determine the charges for the twenty-five most common inpatient diagnostic-related groups for which there are at least ten cases rendered by the hospital during the calendar year immediately preceding the release of the hospital charge report. If a hospital does not have twenty-five of the most common diagnostic-related groups with at least ten or more cases rendered, the hospital shall report only on those most common diagnostic-related groups that have at least ten cases rendered.

(b) A hospital that does not use diagnostic-related groups is exempt from paragraph (a) of this subsection (2) .

(3) (a) The commissioner of insurance shall work with the association of hospitals to incorporate the information reported pursuant to this section on the website.

(b) The commissioner of insurance shall require the association of hospitals to submit a plan to the commissioner on or before November 30, 2008, that states the implementation status of a plan to make the hospital charges reported pursuant to this section available to the public on the website. The plan shall identify the process and time periods for implementation, any barriers to implementation, and recommendations of changes in the law that may be enacted by the general assembly to eliminate the barriers.

(c) When developing the required plan, the association of hospitals shall consider:

(I) The method for hospitals to report charges to the association;

(II) Standards that provide for the validity and comparability of hospital charges; and

(III) The format for making hospital charges available to the public.

(4) (a) The association of hospitals shall make the information reported by the hospitals pursuant to this section available on the website on or before August 1, 2009, and on or before August 1 of each year thereafter. The information reported by the hospitals shall include disclaimers regarding factors including case severity ratings and individual patient variations that may affect actual charges to a patient for services provided.

(b) The information reported by the hospitals that is published in accordance with this section shall include:

(I) Volume of cases by diagnostic-related group required to be reported by the hospital;

(II) Rank by volume of the top twenty-five diagnostic-related groups required to be reported by the hospital;

(III) Mean charge for each of the top twenty-five diagnostic-related groups with more than ten occurrences by hospital;

(IV) Case severity rating by hospital by diagnostic-related group; and

(V) A general disclaimer statement regarding the hospital variations and patient variations that affect the actual charges to patients.

(c) Before publication of the information published pursuant to this section on the website, the commissioner shall ensure that every hospital is allowed thirty days within which to examine the data and submit comments for consideration and inclusion in the final hospital charge report.

(5) (a) The commissioner of insurance shall approve the publication of information on the website consisting of public disclosure of charge data assembled pursuant to this section. At a minimum, the information shall be made available on the website in a manner that allows consumers to conduct an interactive search to view and compare the information for specific hospitals. The website shall include any additional information necessary to ensure that the website information is available to consumers and health care purchasers. The information shall include, at a minimum, appropriate guidance on how to use the data and an explanation of why the data may vary from

hospital to hospital. The report specified in this subsection (5) shall be released on the website on or before August 1, 2009, and on or before each August 1 thereafter.

(b) The commissioner of insurance shall make the website available by hyperlink on the division of insurance website.

(c) The division of insurance shall review the information posted on the website to ensure that the website and information provided by the association is easy to navigate, contains consumer-friendly language, and fulfills the intent of this section. The division shall also ensure that the hyperlink from the division's website to the website is easily accessible.

(6) There shall be no liability on the association of hospitals or a cause of action against the association or its agents, employees, or directors or authorized designees of the commissioner for actions taken or omitted in the performance of duties pursuant to this section.

(7) Repealed.

(8) For purposes of this section:

(a) "Charge" means the amount that a hospital expects to charge for an inpatient diagnostic-related group. A charge that is required to be reported to the public shall be the mean charge for all cases of the diagnostic-related group occurring in the calendar year prior to the release of the hospital charge report.

(b) "Diagnostic-related group" means the classification assigned to an inpatient hospital service claim based on the patient's age and sex, the principal and secondary diagnoses, the procedures performed, and the discharge status.

(c) "Website" means a website established by the association of hospitals that links to the website created pursuant to section 25-3-703.

# ARTICLE 3.5. EMERGENCY MEDICAL AND TRAUMA SERVICES

# PART 1. GENERAL AND ADMINISTRATIVE

### 25-3.5-101. Short title.

This article shall be known and may be cited as the "Colorado Emergency Medical and Trauma Services Act".

### 25-3.5-102. Legislative declaration.

(1) The general assembly hereby declares that it is in the public interest to provide available, coordinated, and quality emergency medical and trauma services to the people of this state. It is the intent of the general assembly in enacting this article to establish an emergency medical and trauma services system, consisting of at least treatment, transportation, communication, and documentation subsystems, designed to prevent premature mortality and to reduce the morbidity that arises from critical injuries, exposure to poisonous substances, and illnesses.

(2) To effect this end, the general assembly finds it necessary that the department of public health and environment assist, when requested by local government entities, in planning and implementing any one of such subsystems so that it meets local and regional needs and requirements and that the department coordinate local systems so that they interface with an overall state system providing maximally effective emergency medical and trauma systems.

(3) The general assembly further finds that the provision of adequate emergency medical and trauma services on highways in all areas of the state is a matter of statewide concern and requires state financial assistance and support.

# 25-3.5-103. Definitions.

As used in this article, unless the context otherwise requires:

(1) "Air ambulance" means a fixed-wing or rotor-wing aircraft that is equipped to provide air transportation and is specifically designed to accommodate the medical needs of individuals who are ill, injured, or otherwise mentally or physically incapacitated and who require in-flight medical supervision.

(1.3) "Air ambulance service" means any public or private entity that uses an air ambulance to transport patients to a medical facility.

(1.5) "Ambulance" means any privately or publicly owned ground vehicle:

(a) Especially constructed or modified and equipped, intended to be used, and maintained or operated by an ambulance service for the transportation, upon the streets and highways in this state, of individuals who are sick, injured, or otherwise incapacitated or helpless; and

(b) That is required to be licensed pursuant to part 3 of this article.

(2) (Deleted by amendment, L. 2005, p. 1330, § 1, effective July 1, 2005.)

(3) "Ambulance service" means the furnishing, operating, conducting, maintaining, advertising, or otherwise engaging in or professing to be engaged in the transportation of patients by ambulance. Taken in context, it also means the person so engaged or professing to be so engaged. The person so engaged and the vehicles used for the emergency transportation of persons injured at a mine are excluded from this definition when the personnel utilized in the operation of said vehicles are subject to the mandatory safety standards of the federal mine safety and health administration, or its successor agency.

(3.5) "Board" means the state board of health created pursuant to section 25-1-103.

(4) "Board of county commissioners" includes the governing body of any city and county.

(4.3) "Community integrated health care service" means the provision of certain out-of-hospital medical services, as determined by rule, that a community paramedic may provide.

(4.5) "Community paramedic" means an emergency medical service provider who obtains an endorsement in community paramedicine pursuant to section 25-3.5-206.

(5) "Department" means the department of public health and environment.

(6) "Director" means the executive director of the department of public health and environment.

(7) "Emergency" means any actual or self-perceived event which threatens life, limb, or well-being of an individual in such a manner that a need for immediate medical care is created.

(7.5) "Emergency medical practice advisory council" or "advisory council" means the emergency medical practice advisory council created in section 25-3.5-206.

(8) "Emergency medical service provider" means an individual who holds a valid emergency medical service provider certificate issued by the department as provided in this article.

(9) "Patient" means any individual who is sick, injured, or otherwise incapacitated or helpless.

(10) "Permit" means the authorization issued by the governing body of a local government with respect to an ambulance used or to be used to provide ambulance service in this state.

(10.6) "Refresher course program" means a program establishing a course of instruction designed to keep emergency medical service providers abreast of developments or new techniques in their profession, which course includes an examination administered at any time during or following the course to facilitate continuing evaluation of emergency medical service providers.

(10.8) "Registered emergency medical responder" means an individual who has successfully completed the training and examination requirements for emergency medical responders, who provides assistance to the injured or ill until more highly trained and qualified personnel arrive, and who is registered with the department pursuant to part 11 of this article.

(11) "Rescue unit" means any organized group chartered by this state as a corporation not for profit or otherwise existing as a nonprofit organization whose purpose is the search for and the rescue of lost or injured persons and includes, but is not limited to, such groups as search and rescue, mountain rescue, ski patrols (either volunteer or professional) , law enforcement posses, civil defense units, or other organizations of governmental designation responsible for search and

rescue.

(11.5) "Service agency" means a fixed-base or mobile prehospital provider of emergency medical services that employs emergency medical service providers to render medical care to patients.

(12) "Volunteer emergency medical service provider" means an emergency medical service provider who does not receive direct remuneration for the performance of emergency medical services.

## 25-3.5-104. Emergency medical and trauma services advisory council - creation - duties.

(1) (a) There is hereby created, in the department of public health and environment, a state emergency medical and trauma services advisory council, referred to in this article as the "council", to be composed of thirty-two members, of whom twenty-five shall be appointed by the governor no later than January 1, 2001, and at least one of whom shall be from each of the regional emergency medical and trauma advisory council planning areas established in section 25-3.5-704. The other seven members shall be ex officio, nonvoting members. Not more than thirteen of the appointed members of the council shall be members of the same political party. A majority of the members shall constitute a quorum. The membership of the council shall reflect, as equally as possible, representation of urban and rural members.

(b) The appointed members of the council shall be from the following categories:

(I) A fire chief of a service that provides prehospital care in an urban area;

(II) A fire chief of a service that provides prehospital care in a rural area;

(III) An administrative representative of an urban trauma center;

(IV) An administrative representative of a rural trauma center;

(V) A licensed physician who is a prehospital medical director;

(VI) A board-certified physician certified in pediatrics or a pediatric subspecialty;

(VII) A board-certified emergency physician;

(VIII) A flight nurse of an emergency medical service air team or unit;

(IX) An officer or crew member of a volunteer organization who provides prehospital care;

(X) An officer or employee of a public provider of prehospital care;

(XI) An officer or employee of a private provider of prehospital care;

(XII) A representative of a government provider of prehospital care;

(XIII) Three county commissioners or council members from a city and county, two of whom shall represent rural counties and one of whom shall represent an urban county or city and county;

(XIV) A board-certified surgeon providing trauma care at a level I trauma center;

(XV) A board-certified surgeon providing trauma care at a level II trauma center;

(XVI) A board-certified surgeon providing trauma care at a level III trauma center;

(XVII) A board-certified neurosurgeon involved in providing trauma care at a level I or II trauma center;

(XVIII) A trauma nurse coordinator;

(XIX) A registered nurse involved in rural emergency medical and trauma services care;

(XX) A regional council chair;

(XXI) A county emergency manager; and

(XXII) Two representatives of the general public, one from a rural area and one from an urban area.

(c) Ex officio, nonvoting members of the council shall include members from the following categories:

(I) A representative of the state coroners' association, as selected by the association;

(II) The director of the state board for community colleges and occupational education or the director's designee;

(III) The manager of the telecommunication services of the Colorado information technology services in the department of personnel, general support services, or the manager's designee;

(IV) The executive director of the department of public health and environment or the director's designee;

(V) The director of the office of transportation safety in the department of transportation or the director's designee;

(VI) A representative from the state sheriffs' association; and

(VII) A representative from the Colorado state patrol.

(2) Members of the council shall serve for terms of three years each; except that, of the members first appointed, eight shall be appointed for terms of one year, nine shall be appointed for terms of two years, and eight shall be appointed for terms of three years. Members of the council shall be reimbursed for actual and necessary expenses incurred in the actual performance of their duties. All vouchers for expenditures shall be subject to approval by the director. A vacancy shall be filled by appointment by the governor for the remainder of the unexpired term. Any appointed member who has two consecutive unexcused absences from meetings of the council shall be deemed to have vacated the membership, and the governor shall fill such vacancy as provided in this subsection (2) .

(3) The council shall meet at least quarterly at the call of the chairperson or at the request of any seven members. At the first meeting after the appointment of new members, the members shall elect a chairperson who shall serve for a term of one year.

(4) The council shall:

(a) Advise the department on all matters relating to emergency medical and trauma services programs;

(b) Make recommendations concerning the development and implementation of statewide emergency medical and trauma services;

(c) Identify and make recommendations concerning statewide emergency medical and trauma service needs;

(d) Review and approve new rules and modifications to rules existing prior to July 1, 2000, prior to the adoption of such rules or modifications by the state board of health;

(e) Review and make recommendations concerning guidelines and standards for the delivery of emergency medical and trauma services, including:

(I) Establishing a list of minimum equipment requirements for ambulance vehicles operated by an ambulance service licensed in this state and making recommendations on the process used by counties in the licensure of ambulance services;

(II) Developing curricula for the training of emergency medical personnel;

(III) Making recommendations on the verification process used by the department to determine facility eligibility to receive trauma center designation; and

(IV) Making recommendations regarding the process used by the department to identify accrediting organizations for air ambulance licensing;

(f) Seek advice and counsel, up to and including the establishment of special ad hoc committees with other individuals, groups, organizations, or associations, when in the judgment of the council such is advisable to obtain necessary expertise for the purpose of meeting the council's responsibilities under this article. The council is authorized to establish special committees for the functions described in this paragraph (f) .

(g) Review and make recommendations to the department regarding the amount, allocation, and expenditure of funds for the development, implementation, and maintenance of the statewide emergency medical and trauma system.

## 25-3.5-104.3. State trauma advisory council - duties. (Repealed)

## 25-3.5-104.5. Joint advisory council - duties. (Repealed)

## 25-3.5-105. Rules and regulations.

All rules and regulations adopted pursuant to the provisions of this article shall be adopted in accordance with the provisions of article 4 of title 24, C.R.S.

### 25-3.5-106. Local standards - uninterrupted service.

(1) Nothing in this article shall be construed to prevent a municipality or special district from adopting standards more stringent than those provided in this article.

(2) In no event shall the providing of service to sick or injured persons be interrupted, between point of origin and point of destination, when an ambulance run traverses one or more jurisdictions whose adopted standards are more stringent than those adopted in the jurisdiction where such ambulance run originates.

### 25-3.5-107. Religious exception.

Nothing in this article or the rules and regulations adopted pursuant to this article shall be construed to authorize any medical treatment or transportation to any hospital or other emergency care center of an adult who objects thereto on religious grounds and signs a written waiver to that effect.

# PART 2. TREATMENT SUBSYSTEM

### 25-3.5-201. Training programs.

(1) The department shall design and establish specialized curricula for personnel who respond routinely to emergencies. The board of county commissioners may select from the various curricula available those courses meeting the minimum requirements established by said board.

(2) The department shall distribute the curricula and teaching aids to training institutions and hospitals upon request from a recognized training group or hospital. If a county is unable to arrange for necessary training programs, the department shall arrange a training program within the immediate vicinity of the agency requesting the program. The department shall issue emergency medical service provider certificates in accordance with section 25-3.5-203 (1) and may issue certificates of successful course completion to those individuals who successfully complete other emergency medical services training programs of the department. The programs may provide for the training of emergency medical dispatchers, emergency medical services instructors, emergency medical services coordinators, and other personnel who provide emergency medical services. The receipt of the certificate of course completion is not deemed state licensure, approval, or a determination of competency.

### 25-3.5-202. Personnel - basic requirements.

Emergency medical personnel employed or utilized in connection with an ambulance service shall meet the qualifications established, by resolution, by the board of county commissioners of the county in which the ambulance is based in order to be certified. For ambulance drivers, the minimum requirements include the possession of a valid driver's license and other requirements established by the board by rule under section 25-3.5-308; for any person responsible for providing direct emergency medical care and treatment to patients transported in an ambulance, the minimum requirement is possession of an emergency medical service provider certificate issued by the department. In the case of an emergency in an ambulance service area where no person possessing the qualifications required by this section is present or available to respond to a call for the emergency transportation of patients by ambulance, any person may operate the ambulance to transport any sick, injured, or otherwise incapacitated or helpless person in order to stabilize the medical condition of the person pending the availability of medical care.

## 25-3.5-203. Emergency medical service providers - certification - renewal of certificate - duties of department - rules - criminal history record checks - definitions.

(1) (a) Repealed.

(a.5) The executive director or chief medical officer shall regulate the acts emergency medical service providers are authorized to perform subject to the medical direction of a licensed physician. The executive director or chief medical officer, after considering the advice and recommendations of the advisory council, shall adopt and revise rules, as necessary, regarding the regulation of emergency medical service providers and their duties and functions.

(b) The department shall certify emergency medical service providers. The board shall adopt rules for the certification of emergency medical service providers. The rules must include the following:

(I) A statement that a certificate is valid for a period of three years after the date of issuance;

(II) A statement that the certificate shall be renewable at its expiration upon the certificate holder's satisfactory completion of the training requirements established pursuant to subsection (2) of this section;

(III) Provisions governing the use of results of national and state criminal history record checks by the department to determine the action to take on a certification application pursuant to subsection (4) of this section. Notwithstanding the provisions of section 24-5-101, C.R.S., these provisions shall allow the department to consider whether the applicant has been convicted of a felony or misdemeanor involving moral turpitude and the pertinent circumstances connected with the conviction and to make a determination whether any such conviction disqualifies the applicant from certification.

(IV) Disciplinary sanctions, which shall include provisions for the denial, revocation, and suspension of certificates and the suspension and probation of certificate holders; and

(V) An appeals process pursuant to sections 24-4-104 and 24-4-105, C.R.S., that is applicable to department decisions in connection with certifications and sanctions.

(c) (I) The department may issue a provisional certification to an applicant for certification as an emergency medical service provider who requests issuance of a provisional certification and who pays any fee authorized under rules adopted by the board. A provisional certification is valid for not more than ninety days.

(II) The department shall not issue a provisional certification unless the applicant satisfies the requirements for certification in accordance with this section and rules adopted by the board under this subsection (1) . If the department finds that an emergency medical service provider that has received a provisional certification has violated any requirements for certification, the department may impose disciplinary sanctions under subparagraph (IV) of paragraph (b) of this subsection (1)
.

(III) The department may issue a provisional certification to an applicant whose fingerprint-based criminal history record check has not yet been completed. The department shall require the applicant to submit a name-based criminal history record check prior to issuing a provisional certification.

(IV) The board shall adopt rules as necessary to implement this paragraph (c) , including rules establishing a fee to be charged to applicants seeking a provisional certification. Any fee collected for a provisional certification shall be deposited in the emergency medical services account created in section 25-3.5-603.

(d) (I) The department shall exempt certified emergency medical service providers who have been called to federally funded active duty for more than one hundred twenty days to serve in a war, emergency, or contingency from the payment of certification fees and from continuing education or professional competency requirements of this article for a renewal date during the service or the six months after the completion of service.

(II) Upon presentation of satisfactory evidence by an applicant for renewal of certification, the department may accept continuing medical education, training, or service completed by an individual as a member of the armed forces or reserves of the United States, the National Guard of any state, the military reserves of any state, or the naval militia of any state toward the qualifications to renew the individual's certification.

(III) (A) A veteran, active military service member, or member of the National Guard and reserves separating from an active duty tour or the spouse of a veteran or member may apply for certification under this article while stationed or residing within this state. The veteran, member, or spouse is exempt from the initial certification requirements in this article, except for those in subsection (4) of this section, if the veteran, member, or spouse holds a current, valid, and unrestricted certification from the National Registry of Emergency Medical Technicians (NREMT) at or above the level of state certification being sought.

(B) The department shall expedite the processing of a certification application submitted by a veteran, active military service member, or member of the National Guard and reserves separating from an active duty tour or the spouse of a veteran or member.

(IV) The board shall promulgate rules to implement this paragraph (d) , including the criteria and evidence for acceptable continuing medical education and training or service.

(2) The council shall advise the department and the board in establishing the training requirements for certificate renewal. Such training requirements shall consist of not more than fifty classroom hours and not less than thirty-six classroom hours.

(3) Repealed.

(4) (a) The department may, with reasonable cause, acquire a fingerprint-based criminal history record check from the Colorado bureau of investigation to investigate the holder of or applicant for an emergency medical service provider certificate. The department may acquire a name-based criminal history record check for a certificate holder or an applicant who has twice submitted to a fingerprint-based criminal history record check and whose fingerprints are unclassifiable.

(b) (I) Any government entity that employs a person as or allows a person to volunteer as an emergency medical service provider in a position requiring direct contact with patients shall require all volunteer and employed emergency medical service providers, who have lived in the state for three years or less at the time of the initial certification or certification renewal, to submit to a federal bureau of investigation fingerprint-based national criminal history record check to determine eligibility for employment. Each emergency medical service provider required to submit to a federal bureau of investigation fingerprint-based national criminal history record check shall obtain a complete set of fingerprints taken by a local law enforcement agency, another entity designated by the department, or any third party approved by the Colorado bureau of investigation. If an approved third party takes the person's fingerprints, the fingerprints may be electronically captured using Colorado bureau of investigation-approved livescan equipment. Third-party vendors shall not keep the person's information for more than thirty days unless requested to do so by the person. The approved third party or government entity shall transmit the fingerprints to the Colorado bureau of investigation, which shall in turn forward them to the federal bureau of investigation for a national criminal history record check. The department or other authorized government entity is the authorized agency to receive and disseminate information regarding the result of a national criminal history record check. Each entity handling the national criminal history record check shall comply with Pub.L. 92-544, as amended. Each government entity acting as the authorized recipient of the result of a national criminal history record check shall forward the result of the initial national criminal history record check and any subsequent notification of activity on the record to the department to determine the individual's eligibility for initial certification or certification renewal.

(II) Notwithstanding the provisions of subparagraph (I) of this paragraph (b) , the government entity may acquire a name-based criminal history record check for an individual who has twice submitted to a fingerprint-based criminal history record check and whose fingerprints are unclassifiable.

(c) (I) (A) A government entity or private, not-for-profit, or for-profit organization that employs a person or allows a person to volunteer as an emergency medical service provider in a position requiring direct contact with patients shall require all volunteer and employed emergency medical service providers, who have lived in the state for more than three years at the time of initial certification or certification renewal, to submit to a fingerprint-based criminal history record check by the Colorado bureau of investigation to determine eligibility for employment. The organization shall forward the result of the criminal history record check and any subsequent notification of activity on the record to the department to determine eligibility for initial certification or certification renewal.

(B) Notwithstanding the provisions of sub-subparagraph (A) of this subparagraph (I) , the government entity or private, not-for-profit, or for-profit organization may acquire a name-based criminal history record check for an individual who has twice submitted to a fingerprint-based criminal history record check and whose fingerprints are unclassifiable.

(II) Notwithstanding the provisions of subparagraph (I) of this paragraph (c) , if a person submitted to a fingerprint-based criminal history record check at the time of initial certification or certification renewal, the person shall not be required to submit to a subsequent fingerprint-based criminal history record check.

(d) (I) If an applicant for initial certification or certification renewal is not employed at the time of application, the department shall require the applicant to submit to a fingerprint-based criminal history record check by the Colorado bureau of investigation as defined in rule by the board of health, if the applicant has lived in the state for more than three years; except that the department may acquire a state name-based criminal history record check for an applicant who has twice submitted to a fingerprint-based criminal history record check and whose fingerprints are unclassifiable.

(II) Notwithstanding the provisions of subparagraph (I) of this paragraph (d) , if a person submitted to a fingerprint-based criminal history record check at the time of initial certification or certification renewal, the person shall not be required to submit to a subsequent fingerprint-based criminal history record check.

(e) If the applicant is not employed or is employed by a nongovernmental entity at the time of application and has lived in the state for three years or less, the department shall require the applicant to submit to a federal bureau of investigation fingerprint-based national criminal history record check; except that the department may acquire a national name-based criminal history record check for an applicant who has twice submitted to a fingerprint-based criminal history record check and whose fingerprints are unclassifiable. The department shall be the authorized agency to receive and disseminate information regarding the result of any national criminal history record check. Any such national criminal history record check shall be handled in accordance with Pub.L. 92-544, as amended.

(4.5) (a) As used in this subsection (4.5) , unless the context otherwise requires:

(I) "Cat" means a small, domesticated feline animal that is kept as a pet. "Cat" does not include a nondomesticated wild animal.

(II) "Dog" means any canine animal owned for domestic, companionship, service, therapeutic, or assistance purposes.

(III) "Emergency medical service provider" means an emergency medical service provider that is certified or licensed by the department of public health and environment, created under section 25-1-102.

(IV) "Employer" means an entity or organization that employs or enlists the services of an emergency medical service provider, regardless of whether the provider is paid or is a volunteer. The employer may be a public, private, for-profit, or nonprofit organization or entity; or a special district.

(V) "Preveterinary emergency care" means the immediate medical stabilization of a dog or cat by an emergency medical service provider, in an emergency to which the emergency medical service provider is responding, through means including oxygen, fluids, medications, or bandaging, with the intent of enabling the dog or cat to be treated by a veterinarian. "Preveterinary emergency care" does not include care provided in response to an emergency call made solely for the purpose of tending to an injured dog or cat, unless a person's life could be in danger attempting to save the life of a dog or cat.

(b) Notwithstanding any other provision of law, an emergency medical service provider may provide preveterinary emergency care to dogs and cats to the extent the provider has received commensurate training and is authorized by the employer to provide the care. Requirements governing the circumstances under which emergency medical service providers may provide preveterinary emergency care to dogs and cats may be specified in the employer's policies governing the provision of care.

(c) Notwithstanding any other provision of law, nothing in this subsection (4.5) imposes upon an emergency medical service provider any obligation to provide care to a dog or cat, or to provide care to a dog or cat before a person.

(5) For the purposes of this article, unless the context otherwise requires, "medical direction" includes, but is not limited to, the following:

(a) Approval of the medical components of treatment protocols and appropriate prearrival instructions;

(b) Routine review of program performance and maintenance of active involvement in quality improvement activities, including access to dispatch tapes as necessary for the evaluation of procedures;

(c) Authority to recommend appropriate changes to protocols for the improvement of patient care; and

(d) Provide oversight for the ongoing education, training, and quality assurance for providers of emergency care.

## 25-3.5-203.5. Community paramedic endorsement - rules.

(1) On or before January 1, 2018, the board shall adopt rules in accordance with article 4 of title 24, C.R.S., for community paramedics including standards for:

(a) The department's issuance of an endorsement in community paramedicine to an emergency medical service provider;

(b) Verifying an emergency medical service provider's competency to be endorsed as a community paramedic. The standards must include a requirement that the emergency medical service provider has obtained from an accredited paramedic training center or an accredited college or university a certificate of completion for a course in community paramedicine with competency verified by a passing score on an examination offered nationally and recognized in Colorado for certifying competency to serve as a community paramedic.

(c) Continuing competency to maintain a community paramedic endorsement.

(2) Rules adopted under this section supersede any rules of the Colorado medical board regarding the matters set forth in this part 2.

## 25-3.5-204. Emergency medical services for children.

(1) The department is authorized to establish a program to improve the quality of emergency care to pediatric patients throughout the state, including a component to address public awareness of pediatric emergencies and injury prevention.

(2) The department is authorized to receive contributions, grants, donations, or funds from any public or private entity to be expended for the program authorized pursuant to this section.

## 25-3.5-205. Emergency medical service providers - investigation - discipline.

(1) (a) The department may administer oaths, take affirmations of witnesses, and issue subpoenas to compel the attendance of witnesses and the production of all relevant records and documents to investigate alleged misconduct by certified emergency medical service providers.

(b) Upon failure of a witness to comply with a subpoena, the department may apply to a district court for an order requiring the person to appear before the department or an administrative law judge, to produce the relevant records or documents, or to give testimony or evidence touching the matter under investigation or in question. When seeking an order, the department shall apply to the district court of the county in which the subpoenaed person resides or conducts business. The court may punish such failure as a contempt of court.

(2) An emergency medical service provider, the employer of an emergency medical service provider, a medical director, and a physician providing medical direction of an emergency medical service provider shall report to the department any misconduct that is known or reasonably believed by the person to have occurred.

(3) A person acting as a witness or consultant to the department, a witness testifying, and a person or employer who reports misconduct to the department under this section shall be immune from liability in any civil action brought for acts occurring while testifying, producing evidence, or reporting misconduct under this section if such individual or employer was acting in good faith and with a reasonable belief of the facts. A person or employer participating in good faith in an investigation or an administrative proceeding pursuant to this section shall be immune from any civil or criminal liability that may result from such participation.

(4) All records, documents, testimony, or evidence obtained under this section shall remain confidential except to the extent necessary to support the administrative action taken by the department, to refer the matter to another regulatory agency, or to refer the matter to a law enforcement agency for criminal prosecution.

(5) For the purposes of this section:

(a) "Medical director" means a physician who supervises certified emergency medical service providers consistent with the rules adopted by the executive director or chief medical officer, as applicable, under section 25-3.5-206.

(b) "Misconduct" means an activity meeting the good cause for disciplinary sanctions standard, as defined by the board.

## 25-3.5-206. Emergency medical practice advisory council - creation - powers and duties - emergency medical service provider scope of practice - rules.

(1) There is hereby created within the department, as a type 2 entity under the direction of the executive director of the department, the emergency medical practice advisory council, referred to in this part 2 as the "advisory council". The advisory council is responsible for advising the department regarding the appropriate scope of practice for emergency medical service providers certified under section 25-3.5-203.

(2) (a) The emergency medical practice advisory council consists of the following eleven members:

(I) Eight voting members appointed by the governor as follows:

(A) Two physicians licensed in good standing in Colorado who are actively serving as emergency medical service medical directors and are practicing in rural or frontier counties;

(B) Two physicians licensed in good standing in Colorado who are actively serving as emergency medical service medical directors and are practicing in urban counties;

(C) One physician licensed in good standing in Colorado who is actively serving as an emergency medical service medical director in any area of the state;

(D) One emergency medical service provider certified at an advanced life support level who is actively involved in the provision of emergency medical services;

(E) One emergency medical service provider certified at a basic life support level who is actively involved in the provision of emergency medical services; and

(F) One emergency medical service provider certified at any level who is actively involved in the provision of emergency medical services;

(II) One voting member who, as of July 1, 2010, is a member of the state emergency medical and trauma services advisory council, appointed by the executive director of the department; and

(III) Two nonvoting ex officio members appointed by the executive director of the department.

(b) Members of the advisory council shall serve four-year terms; except that, of the members initially appointed to the advisory council by the governor, four members shall serve three-year terms. A vacancy on the advisory council shall be filled by appointment by the appointing authority for that vacant position for the remainder of the unexpired term. Members serve at the pleasure of the appointing authority and continue in office until the member's successor is appointed.

(c) Members of the advisory council shall serve without compensation but shall be reimbursed from the emergency medical services account, created in section 25-3.5-603, for their actual and necessary travel expenses incurred in the performance of their duties under this article.

(d) The advisory council shall elect a chair and vice-chair from its members.

(e) The advisory council shall meet at least quarterly and more frequently as necessary to fulfill its obligations.

(f) The department shall provide staff support to the advisory council.

(g) As used in this subsection (2) , "licensed in good standing" means that the physician holds a current, valid license to practice medicine in Colorado that is not subject to any restrictions.

(3) The advisory council shall provide general technical expertise on matters related to the provision of patient care by emergency medical service providers and shall advise or make recommendations to the department in the following areas:

(a) The acts and medications that certified emergency medical service providers at each level of certification are authorized to perform or administer under the direction of a physician medical director;

(b) Requests for waivers to the scope of practice rules adopted pursuant to this section and section 25-3.5-203 (1) (a.5) ;

(c) Modifications to emergency medical service provider certification levels and capabilities; and

(d) Criteria for physicians to serve as emergency medical service medical directors.

(4) (a) The director or, if the director is not a physician, the chief medical officer shall adopt rules in accordance with article 4 of title 24, C.R.S., concerning the scope of practice of emergency medical service providers for prehospital care. The rules must include the following:

(I) Allowable acts for each level of emergency medical service provider certification and the medications that each level of emergency medical service provider certification can administer;

(II) Defining the physician medical direction required for appropriate oversight of an emergency medical service provider by an emergency medical services medical director;

(III) Criteria for requests to waive the scope of practice rules and the conditions for such waivers;

(IV) Minimum standards for physicians to be emergency medical services medical directors; and

(V) (A) Standards for the issuance by the department of a critical care endorsement for emergency medical service providers. An emergency medical service provider with a critical care endorsement is authorized to perform the tasks and procedures specified by rule. The endorsement is valid as long as the emergency medical service provider maintains certification by the department.

(B) The director or, if the director is not a physician, the chief medical officer, shall adopt rules implementing this subparagraph (V) by August 1, 2014.

(a.5) (I) On or before January 1, 2018, the director, or, if the director is not a physician, the chief medical officer shall adopt rules in accordance with article 4 of title 24, C.R.S., concerning the scope of practice of a community paramedic. An emergency medical service provider's endorsement as a community paramedic, issued pursuant to the rules adopted under section 25-3.5-203.5, is valid for as long as the emergency medical service provider maintains his or her certification by the department.

(II) The rules must establish the tasks and procedures that an emergency medical service provider with a community paramedic endorsement is authorized to perform in addition to an emergency medical service provider's scope of practice, including:

(A) An initial assessment of the patient and any subsequent assessments, as needed;

(B) Medical interventions;

(C) Care coordination;

(D) Resource navigation;

(E) Patient education;

(F) Inventory, compliance, and administration of medications; and

(G) Gathering of laboratory and diagnostic data.

(b) Rules adopted pursuant to this subsection (4) supersede any rules of the Colorado medical board regarding the matters set forth in this subsection (4) .

# PART 3. TRANSPORTATION SUBSYSTEM

## 25-3.5-301. License required - exceptions.

(1) After January 1, 1978, no person shall provide ambulance service publicly or privately in this state unless that person holds a valid license to do so issued by the board of county commissioners of the county in which the ambulance service is based, except as provided in subsection (5) of this section. Licenses, permits, and renewals thereof, issued under this part 3, shall require the payment of fees in amounts to be determined by the board to reflect the direct and indirect costs incurred by the department in implementing such licensure, but the board may waive payment of such fees for ambulance services operated by municipalities or special districts.

(2) (a) (I) Each ambulance operated by an ambulance service shall be issued a permit and, in order to be approved, shall bear evidence that its equipment meets or is equivalent to the minimum requirements set forth in the minimum equipment list established by the council and approved by the state board of health. The board of county commissioners of any county may impose by resolution additional requirements for ambulances based in such county.

(II) Repealed.

(a.1) Repealed.

(b) The council shall make available to the board of county commissioners guidelines for ambulance design criteria for use in developing standards for vehicle replacement.

(3) No patient shall be transported in an ambulance in this state after January 1, 1978, unless there are two or more individuals, including the driver, present and authorized to operate said ambulance except under unusual conditions when only one authorized person is available.

(4) (Deleted by amendment, L. 2002, p. 696, § 1, effective May 29, 2002.)

(5) The provisions of subsections (1) to (3) of this section shall not apply to the following:

(a) The exceptional emergency use of a privately or publicly owned vehicle, including search and rescue unit vehicles, or aircraft not ordinarily used in the formal act of transporting patients;

(b) A vehicle rendering services as an ambulance in case of a major catastrophe or emergency when ambulances with permits based in the localities of the catastrophe or emergency are insufficient to render the services required;

(c) Ambulances based outside this state which are transporting a patient in Colorado;

(d) Vehicles used or designed for the scheduled transportation of convalescent patients, individuals with disabilities, or persons who would not be expected to require skilled treatment or care while in the vehicle;

(e) Vehicles used solely for the transportation of intoxicated persons or persons incapacitated by alcohol as defined in section 27-81-102, C.R.S., but who are not otherwise disabled or seriously injured and who would not be expected to require skilled treatment or care while in the vehicle.

## 25-3.5-302. Issuance of licenses and permits - term - requirements.

(1) (a) After receipt of an original application for a license to provide ambulance service, the board of county commissioners shall review the application and the applicant's record and provide for the inspection of equipment to determine compliance with the provisions of this part 3.

(b) The board of county commissioners shall issue a license to the applicant to provide ambulance service and a permit for each ambulance used, both of which shall be valid for twelve months following the date of issue, upon a finding that the applicant's staff, vehicle, and equipment comply with the provisions of this part 3 and any other requirement established by said board.

(2) Any such license or permit, unless revoked by the board of county commissioners, may be renewed by filing an application as in the case of an original application for such license or permit. Applications for renewal shall be filed annually but not less than thirty days before the date the

license or permit expires.

(3) No license or permit issued pursuant to this section shall be sold, assigned, or otherwise transferred.

### 25-3.5-303. Vehicular liability insurance required.

No ambulance shall operate in this state unless it is covered by a complying policy as defined in section 10-4-601 (2) , C.R.S.

### 25-3.5-304. Suspension - revocation - hearings.

(1) Upon a determination by the board of county commissioners that any person has violated or failed to comply with any provisions of this part 3, the board may temporarily suspend, for a period not to exceed thirty days, any license or permit issued pursuant to this part 3. The licensee shall receive written notice of such temporary suspension, and a hearing shall be held no later than ten days after such temporary suspension. After such hearing, the board may suspend any license or permit, issued pursuant to this part 3, for any portion of or for the remainder of its life. At the end of such period, the person whose license or permit was suspended may apply for a new license or permit as in the case of an original application.

(2) Upon a second violation or failure to comply with any provision of this part 3 by any licensee, the board of county commissioners may permanently revoke such license or permit.

### 25-3.5-305. Alleged negligence.

(1) In any legal action filed against a person who has been issued a license pursuant to this part 3 in which it is alleged that the plaintiff's injury, illness, or incapacity was exacerbated or that he was otherwise injured by the negligence of the licensee, an act of negligence shall not be presumed based on the fact of the allegation.

(2) In the event a judgment is entered against any such licensee, he shall, within thirty days thereof, file a copy of the findings of fact, conclusions of law, and order in such case with the clerk and recorder of the county issuing the license. Said board shall take note of such judgment for purposes of investigation and appropriate action if a violation of this part 3 is present. Any and all complaints received directly by said board shall be subject to review.

### 25-3.5-306. Violation - penalty.

Any person who violates any provision of this part 3 commits a class 3 misdemeanor and shall be punished as provided in section 18-1.3-501, C.R.S.

### 25-3.5-307. Licensure of fixed-wing and rotor-wing air ambulances - cash fund created - rules.

(1) (a) Except as provided in paragraph (b) of this subsection (1) , prior to beginning air ambulance operations in this state, an air ambulance service must be licensed by the department. Except as otherwise provided in paragraph (d) of this subsection (1) , compliance with rules promulgated by the board or successful completion of an accreditation process through an accrediting organization approved by the department as having standards equivalent to or exceeding the standards established in rules of the board is required for full licensure and renewal of such license by the department for an air ambulance service.

(b) (I) Upon a showing of exigent circumstances, as defined by the board, the department may authorize an unlicensed air ambulance service to provide a particular transport.

(II) The department may recognize the license issued by another jurisdiction for an air ambulance service that makes a limited number of flights per calendar year into or out of Colorado, and the department shall impose an annual fee upon an air ambulance service whose license is so recognized. The department may rescind such recognition, without refunding or prorating the fee, if rescission is necessary to protect public health and safety.

(b.5) The board shall allow the department to grant a waiver of a rule adopted by the board if the applicant for the waiver satisfactorily demonstrates:

(I) (A) The waiver will not adversely affect the health and safety of patients; and

(B) In the particular situation, the requirement serves no beneficial public purpose; or

(II) Circumstances indicate that the public benefit of waiving the requirement outweighs the public benefit to be gained by strictly adhering to the requirement.

(c) In addition to its rule-making authority granted under section 25-3.5-307.5, the board shall promulgate rules specifying minimum licensure requirements and standards for air ambulance services necessary to ensure public health and safety, including governing the issuance of initial and renewal licenses, conditional licenses, provisional licenses, and other necessary licenses; establishing reasonable fees for licensure and for on-site inspections, investigations, changes of ownership, and other activities related to licensure; defining exigent circumstances for purposes of the exception in subparagraph (I) of paragraph (b) of this subsection (1) ; and specifying the procedure and grounds for the suspension, revocation, or denial of a license. The rules must include the process used to investigate complaints against an air ambulance service and procedures for data collection and reporting to the department by an air ambulance service; except that complaints that are related to the requirements of an accrediting organization approved by the department in accordance with paragraph (a) of this subsection (1) may be referred to the organization for investigation if the department determines that referral is appropriate. The department shall consider the results of such investigations in making licensure decisions concerning air ambulance services.

(d) The department may issue a provisional license to an applicant for an initial license to operate an air ambulance service if the applicant is temporarily unable to conform to all the minimum standards required under this article and rules of the board; except that a license shall not be issued to an applicant if the operation of the applicant's air ambulance service will adversely affect patient care or the health, safety, and welfare of the public. As a condition of obtaining a provisional license, the applicant must demonstrate to the department that the applicant is making its best efforts to achieve compliance with applicable standards. The department may issue the applicant a second provisional license for the same duration and shall charge the same fee as for the first provisional license, but the department shall not issue a third or subsequent provisional license to the applicant.

(2) (a) The board shall establish the amount of the licensure fee to reflect the direct and indirect costs incurred by the department in implementing such licensure. The department shall transmit all fees collected pursuant to this section to the state treasurer who shall credit the same to the fixed-wing and rotary-wing ambulances cash fund, which fund is hereby created in the state treasury.

(b) Any interest derived from the deposit and investment of moneys in the fixed-wing and rotary-wing ambulances cash fund shall be credited to such fund. Any unexpended or unencumbered moneys remaining in such fund at the end of any fiscal year shall remain in the fund and shall not revert or be transferred to the general fund or any other fund of the state. Moneys in such fund shall be subject to annual appropriation by the general assembly to the department for the costs incurred by the department in implementing this section.

## 25-3.5-307.5. Standards for air ambulance services - rules - civil penalties - disciplinary actions - transitional provisions - repeal.

(1) The board shall promulgate rules in accordance with section 24-4-103, C.R.S., to establish minimum standards for an air ambulance service. The rules must include minimum requirements or standards for:

(a) Approval of an accrediting organization;

(b) Recognizing another jurisdiction's license, including a restriction on the number of allowable flights per year in Colorado under that license, a fee for such recognition, and a process to rescind the recognition upon a showing of good cause;

(c) Malpractice and liability insurance for injuries to persons, in amounts determined by the board, and workers' compensation coverage as required by Colorado law;

(d) Medical crew qualifications and training;

(e) Qualifications, training, and roles and responsibilities for a medical director for an air ambulance service;

(f) Communication equipment, reporting capabilities, patient safety, and crew safety and staffing;

(g) Medical equipment in an air ambulance;

(h) Data collection and submission, including reporting requirements as determined by the department;

(i) Maintaining program quality; and

(j) Management of patient and medical staff safety with regard to clinical staffing and shift time.

(2) Rules promulgated by the board must not include activities preempted by the federal aviation administration or 49 U.S.C. sec. 41713.

(3) Civil penalties. An air ambulance operator, service, or provider or other person who violates this section, section 25-3.5-307, or a rule of the board promulgated pursuant to this part 3 or who operates without a current and valid license is subject to a civil penalty of up to five thousand dollars per violation or for each day of a continuing violation. The department shall assess and collect these penalties. Before collecting a penalty, the department shall provide the alleged violator with notice and the opportunity for a hearing in accordance with the "State Administrative Procedure Act", article 4 of title 24, C.R.S., and all applicable rules of the board. The department shall transmit all penalties collected pursuant to this section to the state treasurer, who shall credit them to the general fund.

(4) Disciplinary actions. For violation of any provision of this section, section 25-3.5-307, or a rule of the board promulgated pursuant to this part 3 or for operating without a license, the department may take any one or more of the following actions:

(a) Deny, suspend, or revoke a license issued pursuant to this part 3;

(b) Impose a civil penalty as provided in subsection (3) of this section;

(c) Issue a cease-and-desist order if the department has determined that a violation has occurred and immediate enforcement is deemed necessary. The cease-and-desist order must set forth the provisions alleged to have been violated, the facts alleged to have constituted the violation, and the requirement that all violations cease forthwith.

(d) Summarily suspend a license issued pursuant to this part 3 in accordance with article 4 of title 24, C.R.S.

(5) Transitional provisions - repeal. (a) On or before December 30, 2017, the board shall adopt rules to implement this section. Before the rules become effective, the department may:

(I) Authorize an air ambulance service to treat and transport patients if the air ambulance service is licensed by another state or accredited by an organization approved by the department;

(II) Investigate complaints against an air ambulance service; and

(III) Take disciplinary action as necessary to protect the public health, safety, and welfare in a manner consistent with the rules in effect on June 1, 2016.

(b) This subsection (5) is repealed, effective July 1, 2018.

## 25-3.5-308. Rules.

(1) The board shall adopt rules establishing the minimum requirements for ground ambulance service licensing, including but not limited to:

(a) Minimum equipment to be carried on an ambulance pursuant to section 25-3.5-104;

(b) Staffing requirements for ambulances as required in section 25-3.5-104;

(c) Medical oversight and quality improvement of ambulance services pursuant to section 25-3.5-704 (2) (h) ;

(d) The process used to investigate complaints against an ambulance service; and

(e) Data collection and reporting to the department by an ambulance service.

# PART 4. TELECOMMUNICATIONS SUBSYSTEM

## 25-3.5-401. Responsibility for coordination.

(1) The telecommunications subsystem shall be used to maintain effective interface with the other components of the system, which shall include but not be limited to the following:

(a) To dispatch the ambulance;

(b) To maintain contact while en route to the scene of the emergency;

(c) To provide for triage at the scene of the emergency;

(d) To provide for treatment while en route to the primary emergency care center;

(e) To arrange for transfer to advanced emergency care centers.

(2) (a) The department of personnel, in consultation with the office of information technology created in the office of the governor, shall coordinate the telecommunications subsystem with the existing state telecommunications network to the extent possible.

(b) Repealed.

## 25-3.5-402. Local government participation.

The department of personnel shall consult with local government entities to ensure that provision is made for their entry into the statewide telecommunications subsystem and that their present resources are being fully utilized.

## 25-3.5-403. Poison information center - state funding. (Repealed)

# PART 5. DOCUMENTATION SUBSYSTEM

## 25-3.5-501. Records.

(1) Each ambulance service shall prepare and transmit copies of uniform and standardized records, as specified by regulation adopted by the department, concerning the transportation and treatment of patients in order to evaluate the performance of the emergency medical services system and to plan systematically for improvements in said system at all levels.

(2) The record forms adopted by the department may distinguish between rural ambulance service and urban ambulance service and between mobile intensive care units and basic ambulance service.

## 25-3.5-502. Forms and reports.

The department shall provide the necessary forms and copies of quarterly statistical report forms for local and state evaluation of ambulance service unless specifically exempted by the board of county commissioners of a particular county for that county.

# PART 6. LOCAL EMERGENCY MEDICAL SERVICES

## 25-3.5-601. Legislative declaration.

(1) The general assembly recognizes that an efficient and reliable statewide emergency medical and trauma network would serve not only to promote the health, safety, and welfare of Colorado residents, but would also, by increasing safety throughout the state, indirectly serve to facilitate

tourism and economic development in the state.

(2) The general assembly also finds that accident victims are often transported over state highways and that an improved response to accidents through an efficient and reliable statewide emergency medical and trauma network impacts both directly and indirectly on the maintenance and supervision of the public highways of this state.

(3) Therefore, it is the purpose of this part 6 to enhance emergency medical and trauma services statewide by financially assisting local emergency medical and trauma service providers who operate or wish to operate in the counties in their efforts to improve the quality and effectiveness of local emergency medical and trauma services, including emergency medical and trauma equipment and communications, and by supporting the overall coordination of such efforts by the department.

## 25-3.5-602. Definitions.

As used in this part 6, unless the context otherwise requires:

(1) "Council" means the state emergency medical and trauma services advisory council created in section 25-3.5-104.

(2) "Department" means the department of public health and environment.

(3) "EMTS" means emergency medical and trauma services.

(4) "Local emergency medical and trauma service providers" includes, but is not limited to, local governing boards, training centers, hospitals, special districts, and other private and public service providers that have as their purpose the provision of emergency medical and trauma services.

## 25-3.5-603. Emergency medical services account - creation - allocation of funds.

(1) (a) There is hereby created a special account within the highway users tax fund established under section 43-4-201, C.R.S., to be known as the emergency medical services account, which consists of all moneys transferred thereto in accordance with section 42-3-304 (21) , C.R.S., fees collected under section 25-3.5-203 for provisional certifications of emergency medical service providers, and fees collected under section 25-3.5-1103 for provisional registration of emergency medical responders.

(b) All moneys in and state FTE funded by the emergency medical services account shall be subject to annual appropriation by the general assembly.

(c) At the end of any fiscal year, all unexpended and unencumbered moneys in the emergency medical services account shall remain therein and shall not be credited or transferred to the general fund or any other fund. Any interest earned on the investment or deposit of moneys in the account shall also remain in the account and shall not be credited to the general fund.

(2) (Deleted by amendment, L. 2005, p. 280, § 13, effective August 8, 2005.)

(3) On and after July 1, 2002, the general assembly shall appropriate moneys in the emergency medical services account:

(a) (I) To the department for distribution as grants to local emergency medical and trauma service providers pursuant to the emergency medical and trauma services (EMTS) grant program set forth in section 25-3.5-604.

(II) Of the amount appropriated under subparagraph (I) of this paragraph (a) for grants:

(A) One hundred thousand dollars shall remain in the account for unexpected emergencies that arise after the deadline for grant applications has passed. The department and the council shall promulgate any rules necessary to define the expenditures of such emergency funds.

(B) The department shall award a minimum of one hundred fifty thousand dollars to offset the training costs of emergency medical service providers, emergency medical dispatchers, emergency medical services instructors, emergency medical services coordinators, and other personnel who provide emergency medical services. Of said one hundred fifty thousand dollars, no less than eighty percent shall be used in the training of emergency medical service providers.

(b) (I) To the department for distribution for each Colorado county within a RETAC no less than fifteen thousand dollars and seventy-five thousand dollars to each RETAC, in accordance with section 25-3.5-605 for planning and, to the extent possible, coordination of emergency medical and trauma services in the county and between counties when such coordination would provide for better service geographically. In the event that a RETAC is composed of less than five counties as of July 1, 2002, the council shall recommend that for each Colorado county within such RETAC, the RETAC shall receive fifteen thousand dollars in accordance with section 25-3.5-605 for planning and, to the extent possible, coordination of emergency medical and trauma services in the county and between counties when such coordination would provide for better service geographically. Any RETAC may apply for additional moneys and may receive such moneys if the request is approved by the council, so long as the moneys are used in accordance with section 25-3.5-605 for planning and, to the extent possible, coordination of emergency medical and trauma services in the county and between counties when such coordination would provide for better service geographically.

(II) A county may request to the council that the county's representative fifteen thousand dollars be divided between two different RETACs pursuant to section 25-3.5-704 (2) (c) (IV) (B) .

(c) To the direct and indirect costs of planning, developing, implementing, maintaining, and improving the statewide emergency medical and trauma services system. These costs include:

(I) Providing technical assistance and support to local governments, local emergency medical and trauma service providers, and RETACs operating a statewide data collection system, coordinating local and state programs, providing assistance in selection and purchasing of medical and communication equipment, administering the EMTS grant program, establishing and maintaining scope of practice for certified medical service providers, and administering a registration program for emergency medical responders; and

(II) The costs of the department of revenue in collecting the additional motor vehicle registration fee pursuant to section 42-3-304 (21) , C.R.S.

## 25-3.5-604. EMTS grant program - EMS account - role of council and department - rules - awards.

(1) (a) The council shall make recommendations to the department concerning the application for and distribution of moneys from the EMS account for the development, maintenance, and improvement of emergency medical and trauma services in Colorado and for the establishment of priorities for emergency medical and trauma services grants.

(b) Any rules that relate to the distribution of grants shall provide that awards shall be made on the basis of a substantiated need and that priority shall be given to those applicants that have underdeveloped or aged emergency medical and trauma services equipment or systems.

(c) The department, upon recommendations from the council, shall allocate moneys pursuant to section 25-3.5-603.

(2) (a) Applications for grants shall be made to the department commencing January, 2001, and each January thereafter, except as otherwise provided in section 25-3.5-603 (3) .

(b) The department shall review each application and make awards in accordance with the rules promulgated pursuant to subsection (1) of this section.

(c) Grants awarded under this section shall require local matching funds, unless such requirement is waived by the council upon demonstration that local sources of matching funds are not available.

(3) Grants shall be awarded July 1 of each year.

(4) The council shall review the adequacy of funding for each RETAC for the period beginning July 1, 2002. The review shall be completed by December 31, 2005. The council may recommend any necessary changes to the department as a result of the review conducted pursuant to this subsection (4) .

## 25-3.5-605. Improvement of county emergency medical and trauma services - eligibility for county funding - manner of distributing funds.

(1) Moneys in the emergency medical services account shall be apportioned pursuant to subsection (2.5) of this section.

(2) In order to qualify for moneys under this section, a county must:

(a) Comply with all provisions of part 3 of this article regarding the inspection and licensing of ambulances that are based in the county;

(b) Require all licensed ambulance services to utilize the statewide emergency medical and trauma services uniform prehospital care reporting system operated by the department;

(c) Repealed.

(d) Ensure that all moneys received under this section are expended on developing and updating the emergency medical and trauma services plan and other emergency medical and trauma services needs of the county such as:

(I) Training and certification of emergency medical service providers;

(II) Assisting local emergency medical and trauma providers in applying for grants under section 25-3.5-604;

(III) Improving the emergency medical and trauma services system on a county wide or regional basis and implementing the county emergency medical and trauma services plan;

(e) Repealed.

(2.5) (a) On or before October 1, 2003, and on or before October 1 each year thereafter, each RETAC shall submit to the council an annual financial report that details the expenditure of moneys received. Such report shall be in a format specified by the council and the department. In instances where the council finds such report inadequate, the RETAC shall resubmit the report to the council by December 1 of the same year.

(b) On or before July 1, 2003, and on or before July 1 each odd-numbered year thereafter, each RETAC shall submit to the council a biennial plan that details the RETAC's EMTS plan and any revisions pursuant to section 25-3.5-704 (2) (c) (I) (B) . If the RETAC includes a county that has been divided geographically pursuant to section 25-3.5-704 (2) (c) (IV) , the plan shall include an evaluation of such division. Such plan shall be in a format specified by the council and the department. In instances where the council finds such plan inadequate, the RETAC shall resubmit the plan to the council by September 14 of the same year.

(c) On or before October 15, 2003, and on or before October 15 each odd-numbered year thereafter, the council shall submit to the department a plan for all RETACs in the state. On or before November 1, 2003, and on or before November 1 each odd-numbered year thereafter, the department, in consultation with the council, shall approve a plan for all RETACs in the state.

(3) Funds distributed to counties and RETACs pursuant to this section shall be used in planning the improvement of existing county emergency medical and trauma service programs and shall not be used to supplant moneys already allocated by the county for emergency medical and trauma services.

(4) (a) Failure to comply with the requirements of subsection (2) of this section shall render a county ineligible to receive moneys from the emergency medical services account until the following January.

(b) At the end of any fiscal year, moneys which are not distributed to a county shall remain in the emergency medical services account until the following January.

## 25-3.5-606. Annual report.

No later than January 1, 1991, and prior to November 1 of each year thereafter, the department, in cooperation with the council, shall submit a report to the health, environment, welfare, and institutions committees and the joint budget committee of the general assembly on the moneys credited to the emergency medical services account and on the expenditure of such moneys during the preceding fiscal year. Such report shall contain a listing of the grant recipients, proposed projects, and a statement of the short-term and long-term planning goals of the department and the council to further implement the provisions of this part 6.

**25-3.5-607. Repeal of part. (Repealed)**

# PART 7. STATEWIDE TRAUMA SYSTEM

## 25-3.5-701. Short title.
This part 7 shall be known and may be cited as the "Statewide Trauma Care System Act".

## 25-3.5-702. Legislative declaration.
(1) The general assembly hereby finds and declares that trauma is the greatest single cause of death and disability in Colorado for persons under the age of forty-five years and that trauma care is a unique type of emergency medical service.

(2) The general assembly further finds that a trauma system task force made up of various emergency health and trauma care entities submitted a report to the general assembly in 1993 indicating a compelling need to develop and implement a statewide trauma care system in order to assure that appropriate resources are available to trauma victims from the point of injury through rehabilitative care. In addition, a statewide system is essential to provide Colorado residents and visitors with a greater probability of surviving a life-threatening injury and to reduce trauma-related morbidity and mortality in this state.

(3) The general assembly, therefore, declares that it is necessary to enact legislation directing the board of health to adopt rules that govern the implementation and oversight of the trauma care system. The general assembly further declares that to ensure the availability and coordination of resources necessary to provide essential care, it is necessary to enact legislation that directs the department of public health and environment to collaborate with existing agencies and organizations, including governing bodies for counties and cities and counties, in implementing and monitoring a statewide trauma care system.

## 25-3.5-703. Definitions.
As used in this article, unless the context otherwise requires:

(1) (Deleted by amendment, L. 2000, p. 537, § 16, effective July 1, 2000.)

(2) "Board" means the state board of health.

(3) Repealed.

(3.5) "Council" means the state emergency medical and trauma services advisory council created by section 25-3.5-104.

(4) "Designation" means the process undertaken by the department to assign a status to a health care facility based on the level of trauma services the facility is capable of and committed to providing to injured persons. Facilities may be designated at one of the following levels:

(a) Nondesignated, which is for facilities that do not meet the criteria required for level I to V facilities, but that receive and are accountable for injured persons, which accountability includes having a transfer agreement to transfer persons to level I to V facilities as determined by rules promulgated by the board;

(a.5) Level V, which is for basic trauma care in rural areas, including resuscitation, stabilization, and arrangement for the transfer of all patients with potentially life- or limb-threatening injuries, consistent with triage and transport protocols as recommended by the council and adopted by the board. Level V facilities shall transfer patients within their own region or to a higher level facility in another region, as described in paragraphs (c) , (d) , and (e) of this subsection (4) .

(b) Level IV, which is for basic trauma care, including resuscitation, stabilization, and arrangement for appropriate transfer of persons requiring a higher level of care based upon patient criticality and triage practices within each facility, which are consistent with triage criteria and transport protocols as recommended by the council and adopted by the board. These facilities must transfer appropriate patients to a higher level facility within their own region or to a higher level facility in another region, as described in paragraphs (d) and (e) of this subsection (4) .

(c) Level III, which is for general trauma care, including resuscitation, stabilization, and assessment of injured persons, and either the provision of care for the injured person or arrangement for appropriate transfer based upon patient criticality and triage practices within each facility, which are consistent with triage criteria and transport protocols as recommended by the council and adopted by the board. The facilities must transfer appropriate patients to a higher level facility within its own region or to a higher level facility in another region, as described in paragraphs (d) and (e) of this subsection (4) .

(d) Level II, which is for major trauma care based upon patient criticality and triage practices within each facility, which are consistent with triage criteria and transport protocols as recommended by the council and adopted by the board. This type of facility may serve as a resource for lower level facilities when a level I facility, as described in paragraph (e) of this subsection (4) , is not available within its region, but it is not a facility required to conduct research or provide comprehensive services through subspecialty units such as, but not limited to, burn units, spinal cord injury centers, eye trauma centers, and reimplantation centers.

(e) Level I, which is for comprehensive trauma care, including the acute management of the most severely injured patients, which is a facility that may serve as the ultimate resource for lower level facilities or as the key resource facility for a trauma area and which is a facility that provides education in trauma-related areas for health care professionals and performs trauma research;

(f) Regional pediatric trauma center, which is a facility that provides comprehensive pediatric trauma care, including acute management of the most severely injured pediatric trauma patients, and is a facility that may serve as an ultimate resource for lower level facilities on pediatric trauma care, and which is a facility that performs pediatric trauma research and provides pediatric trauma education for health care professionals. No facility shall be deemed a regional pediatric trauma center unless the facility predominately serves children and is a facility where at least eighty-five percent of hospital admissions are for individuals who are under eighteen years of age. A separate administrative unit within a general hospital or hospital system shall not be deemed a regional pediatric trauma center.

(5) (Deleted by amendment, L. 2000, p. 537, § 16, effective July 1, 2000.)

(6) "Interfacility transfer" means the movement of a trauma victim from one facility to another.

(6.5) "Key resource facility" means a level I or level II certified trauma facility that provides consultation and technical assistance to a RETAC, as such term is defined in subsection (6.8) of this section, regarding education, quality, training, communication, and other trauma issues described in this part 7 that relate to the development of the statewide trauma care system.

(6.8) "Regional emergency medical and trauma services advisory council" or "RETAC" means the representative body appointed by the governing bodies of counties or cities and counties for the purpose of providing recommendations concerning regional area emergency medical and trauma service plans for such counties or cities and counties.

(7) Repealed.

(8) "Statewide trauma registry" means a statewide data base of information concerning injured persons and licensed facilities receiving injured persons, which information is used to evaluate and improve the quality of patient management and care and the quality of trauma education, research, and injury prevention programs. The data base integrates medical and trauma systems information related to patient diagnosis and provision of care. Such information includes epidemiologic and demographic information.

(9) "Trauma" means an injury or wound to a living person caused by the application of an external force or by violence. Trauma includes any serious life-threatening or limb-threatening situations.

(10) "Trauma care system" means an organized approach to providing quality and coordinated care to trauma victims throughout the state on a twenty-four-hour per day basis by transporting a trauma victim to the appropriate trauma designated facility.

(11) "Trauma transport protocols" means written standards adopted by the board that address the

use of appropriate resources to move trauma victims from one level of care to another on a continuum of care.

(12) "Triage" means the assessment and classification of an injured person in order to determine the severity of trauma injury and to prioritize care for the injured person.

(13) "Verification process" means a procedure to evaluate a facility's compliance with trauma care standards established by the board and to make recommendations to the department concerning the designation of a facility.

## 25-3.5-704. Statewide emergency medical and trauma care system - development and implementation - duties of department - rules adopted by board.

(1) The department shall develop, implement, and monitor a statewide emergency medical and trauma care system in accordance with the provisions of this part 7 and with rules adopted by the state board. The system shall be implemented statewide no later than July 1, 1997. In addition, the board shall cooperate with the department of personnel in adopting criteria for adequate communications systems that counties shall be required to identify in regional emergency medical and trauma system plans in accordance with subsection (2) of this section. Pursuant to section 24-50-504 (2) , C.R.S., the department may contract with any public or private entity in performing any of its duties concerning education, the statewide trauma registry, and the verification process as set forth in this part 7.

(2) The board shall adopt rules for the statewide emergency medical and trauma care system, including but not limited to the following:

(a) Minimum services in rendering patient care. These rules ensure the appropriate access through designated centers to the following minimum services:

(I) Prehospital care;

(II) Hospital care;

(III) Rehabilitative care;

(IV) Injury prevention;

(V) Disaster medical care;

(VI) Education and research; and

(VII) Trauma communications.

(b) Transport protocols. The board shall set forth trauma transport protocols in these rules, which include but are not limited to a requirement that a facility that receives an injured person provide the appropriate available care, which may include stabilizing an injured person before transferring that person to the appropriate facility based on the person's injury. These rules ensure that when the most appropriate trauma facility for an injured person is not easily accessible in an area, that person will be transferred as soon as medically feasible to the nearest appropriate facility, which may be in or out of the state. These rules shall conform with applicable federal law governing the transfer of patients.

(c) Regional emergency medical and trauma advisory councils - plans established - process. (I) These rules provide for the implementation of regional emergency medical and trauma system plans that describe methods for providing the appropriate service and care to persons who are ill or injured in areas included under a regional emergency medical and trauma system plan. In these rules, the board shall specify that:

(A) The governing body of each county or city and county throughout the state shall establish a regional emergency medical and trauma advisory council (RETAC) with the governing body of four or more other counties, or with the governing body of a city and county, to form a multicounty RETAC. The number of members on a RETAC shall be defined by the participating counties. Membership shall reflect, as equally as possible, representation between hospital and prehospital providers and from each participating county and city and county. There shall be at least one member from each participating county and city and county in the RETAC. Each county within a RETAC shall be located in reasonable geographic proximity to the other counties and city and counties within the same RETAC. In establishing a RETAC, the governing body shall obtain input from health care facilities and providers within the area to be served by the RETAC. If the governing body for a county or city and county fails to establish a RETAC by July 1, 2002, two counties with a combined population of at least seven hundred fifty thousand residents may apply to the council for establishment of a RETAC of fewer than four counties. The council shall conduct a hearing with all counties that may be affected by the establishment of a RETAC with fewer than four counties before deciding whether to grant such application. The decision on such an application shall be completed within sixty days after the date of application. For all other counties that do not qualify as a two-county RETAC and that have not established a RETAC by July 1, 2002, the council shall designate an established RETAC to serve as the county's or city and county's RETAC.

(B) No later than July 1, 2003, each RETAC with approval from the governing bodies for a multicounty RETAC shall submit a regional emergency medical and trauma system plan to the council for approval by the department. If the governing body for a county or city and county fails to submit a plan, if a county or city and county is not included in a multicounty plan, or, if a multicounty plan is not approved pursuant to a procedure established by the board for approving plans, the department shall design a plan for the county, city and county, or multicounty area.

(II) In addition to any issues the board requires to be addressed, every regional emergency medical and trauma system plan shall address the following issues:

(A) The provision of minimum services and care at the most appropriate facilities in response to the following factors: Facility-established triage and transport plans; interfacility transfer agreements; geographical barriers; population density; emergency medical services and trauma care resources; and accessibility to designated facilities;

(B) The level of commitment of counties and city and counties under a regional emergency medical and trauma system plan to cooperate in the development and implementation of a statewide communications system and the statewide emergency medical and trauma care system;

(C) The methods for ensuring facility and county or city and county adherence to the regional emergency medical and trauma system plan, compliance with board rules and procedures, and commitment to the continuing quality improvement system described in paragraph (h) of this subsection (2) ;

(D) A description of public information, education, and prevention programs to be provided for the area;

(E) A description of the functions that will be contracted services; and

(F) The identification of regional emergency medical and trauma system needs through the use of a needs assessment instrument developed by the department; except that the use of such instrument shall be subject to approval by the counties and city and counties included in a RETAC.

(III) The board shall specify in regional emergency medical and trauma system plan rules the time frames for approving regional emergency medical and trauma system plans and for resubmitting plans, as well as the number of times the plans may be resubmitted by a governing body before the department designs a plan for a multicounty area. The department shall provide technical assistance to any RETAC for preparation, implementation, and modification, as necessary, of regional emergency medical and trauma system plans.

(IV) (A) A county may request that the county be included in two separate RETACs because of geographical concerns. The council shall review and approve any request that a county be divided prior to inclusion within two separate RETACs if the county demonstrates such a division will not adversely impact the emergency medical and trauma needs for the county, that such a division is beneficial to both RETACs, and that such division does not create a RETAC with fewer than five contiguous counties, except for RETACs that contain two counties with a combined population of at least seven hundred fifty thousand residents pursuant to sub-subparagraph (A) of subparagraph (I) of this paragraph (c) .

(B) A county that is included in two separate RETACs may request that the council allocate any portion of the fifteen thousand dollars received by a RETAC, pursuant to section 25-3.5-603, between the two separate RETACs.

(d) Designation of facilities. The designation rules shall provide that every facility in this state required to be licensed in accordance with article 3 of this title and that receives ambulance patients shall participate in the statewide emergency medical and trauma care system. Each such facility shall submit an application to the department requesting designation as a specific level trauma facility or requesting nondesignation status. A facility that is given nondesignated status shall not represent that it is a designated facility, as prohibited in section 25-3.5-707. The board shall include provisions for the following:

(I) The criteria to be applied for designating and periodically reviewing facilities based on level of care capability providing trauma care. In establishing such criteria, the board shall take into consideration recognized national standards including, but not limited to, standards on trauma resources for optimal care of the injured patient adopted by the American college of surgeons' committee and the guidelines for trauma care systems adopted by the American college of emergency physicians.

(II) A verification process;

(III) The length of a designation period;

(IV) The process for evaluating, reviewing, and designating facilities, including an ongoing periodic review process for designated facilities, which process shall take into account the national standards referenced in subparagraph (I) of this paragraph (d) . Each facility shall be subject to review in accordance with rules adopted pursuant to this paragraph (d) . In the event a certified facility seeks to be designated at a different level or seeks nondesignation status, the facility shall comply with the board's procedures for initial designation.

(V) Disciplinary sanctions, which shall be limited to the revocation of a designation, temporary suspension while the facility takes remedial steps to correct the cause of the discipline, redesignation, or assignment of nondesignation status to a facility;

(VI) A designation fee established in accordance with section 25-3.5-705; and

(VII) An appeals process concerning department decisions in connection with evaluations, reviews, designations, and sanctions.

(e) Communications system. (I) The communications system rules shall require that a regional emergency medical and trauma system plan ensure citizen access to emergency medical and trauma services through the 911 telephone system or its local equivalent and that the plan include adequate provisions for:

(A) Public safety dispatch to ambulance service and for efficient communication from ambulance to ambulance and from ambulance to a designated facility;

(B) Efficient communications among the trauma facilities and between trauma facilities and other medical care facilities;

(C) Efficient communications among service agencies to coordinate prehospital, day-to-day, and disaster activities; and

(D) Efficient communications among counties and RETACs to coordinate prehospital, day-to-day, and disaster activities.

(II) In addition, the board shall require that a regional emergency medical and trauma system plan identify the key resource facilities for the area. The key resource facilities shall assist the RETAC in resolving trauma care issues that arise in the area and in coordinating patient destination and interfacility transfer policies to assure that patients are transferred to the appropriate facility for treatment in or outside of the area.

(f) Statewide trauma registry. (I) The registry rules shall require the department to establish and oversee the operation of a statewide trauma registry. The rules shall allow for the provision of technical assistance and training to designated facilities within the various trauma areas in connection with requirements to collect, compile, and maintain information for the statewide central registry. Each licensed facility, clinic, or prehospital provider that provides any service or care to or for persons with trauma injury in this state shall collect the information described in this subparagraph (I) about any such person who is admitted to a hospital as an inpatient or transferred from one facility to another or who dies from trauma injury. The facility, clinic, or prehospital provider shall submit the following information to the registry:

(A) Admission and readmission information;

(B) Number of trauma deaths;

(C) Number and types of transfers to and from the facility or the provider; and

(D) Injury cause, type, and severity.

(II) In addition to the information described in subparagraph (I) of this paragraph (f) , facilities designated as level I, II, or III shall provide such additional information as may be required by board rules.

(III) The registry rules shall include provisions concerning access to information in the registry that does not identify patients or physicians. Any data maintained in the registry that identifies patients or physicians shall be strictly confidential and shall not be admissible in any civil or criminal proceeding.

(g) Public information, education, and injury prevention. The department and county, district, and municipal public health agencies may operate injury prevention programs, but the public information, education, and injury prevention rules shall require the department and county, district, and municipal public health agencies to consult with the state and regional emergency medical and trauma advisory councils in developing and implementing area and state-based injury prevention and public information and education programs including, but not limited to, a pediatric injury prevention and public awareness component. In addition, the rules shall require that regional emergency medical and trauma system plans include a description of public information and education programs to be provided for the area.

(h) (I) Continuing quality improvement system (CQI) . These rules require the department to oversee a continuing quality improvement system for the statewide emergency medical and trauma care system. The board shall specify the methods and periods for assessing the quality of regional emergency medical and trauma systems and the statewide emergency medical and trauma care system. These rules must include the following requirements:

(A) That RETACs assess periodically the quality of their respective regional emergency medical and trauma system plans and that the state assess periodically the quality of the statewide emergency medical and trauma care system to determine whether positive results under regional emergency medical and trauma system plans and the statewide emergency medical and trauma care system can be demonstrated;

(B) That all facilities comply with the trauma registry rules;

(C) That reports concerning regional emergency medical and trauma system plans include results for the emergency medical and trauma area, identification of problems under the regional emergency medical and trauma system plan, and recommendations for resolving problems under the plan. In preparing these reports, the RETACs shall obtain input from facilities, counties included under the regional emergency medical and trauma system plan, and service agencies.

(D) That the names of patients or information that identifies individual patients shall be kept confidential and shall not be publicly disclosed without the patient's consent;

(E) That the department be allowed access to prehospital, hospital, and coroner records of emergency medical and trauma patients to assess the continuing quality improvement system for the area and state-based injury prevention and public information and education programs pursuant to subsection (2) (g) of this section. All information provided to the department shall be confidential pursuant to this subsection (2) (h) . To the greatest extent possible, patient-identifying information shall not be gathered. If patient-identifying information is necessary, the department shall keep such information strictly confidential, and such information may only be released outside of the department upon written authorization of the patient. The department shall prepare an annual report that includes an evaluation of the statewide emergency medical and trauma services system. Such report shall be distributed to all designated trauma centers, ambulance services, and service agencies.

(II) Any data or information related to the identification of individual patient's, provider's, or facility's care outcomes collected as a result of the continuing quality improvement system and any records or reports collected or compiled as a result of the continuing quality improvement system are confidential and are exempt from the open records law in part 2 of article 72 of title 24, C.R.S. Such data, information, records, or reports shall not be subject to subpoena or discovery and shall not be admissible in any civil action, except pursuant to a court order that provides for the protection of sensitive information about interested parties. Nothing in this subparagraph (II) shall preclude the patient or the patient's representative from obtaining the patient's medical records as provided in section 25-1-801. Nothing in this subparagraph (II) shall be construed to allow access to confidential professional review committee records or reviews conducted under article 36.5 of title 12, C.R.S.

(III) That reports concerning regional emergency medical and trauma system plans include results for the emergency medical and trauma area, identification of problems under the regional emergency medical and trauma system plan, and recommendations for resolving problems under the plan. In preparing these reports, the RETACs shall obtain input from facilities, counties included under the regional emergency medical and trauma system plan, and service agencies.

(i) Trauma care for pediatric patients. The trauma care for pediatric patient rules shall provide for the improvement of the quality of care for pediatric patients.

(3) The board shall adopt rules that take into consideration recognized national standards for emergency medical and trauma care systems, such as the standards on trauma resources for optimal care of the injured patient adopted by the American college of surgeons' committee on trauma and the guidelines for emergency medical and trauma care systems adopted by the American college of emergency physicians and the American academy of pediatrics.

(4) The board shall adopt and the department shall use only cost-efficient administrative procedures and forms for the statewide emergency medical and trauma care system.

(5) In adopting its rules, the board shall consult with and seek advice from the council, as defined in section 25-3.5-703 (3.5), where appropriate, and from any other appropriate agency. In addition, the board shall obtain input from appropriate health care agencies, institutions, facilities, and providers at the national, state, and local levels and from counties and city and counties.

## 25-3.5-705. Creation of fee - creation of trauma system cash fund.

(1) The board is authorized, by rule, to establish a schedule of fees based on the direct and indirect costs incurred in designating facilities. In addition, the department is authorized to collect the appropriate fee on the schedule. The board may adjust fees in amounts necessary to cover such costs. The fees collected pursuant to this section shall be deposited in the trauma system cash fund created by subsection (2) of this section.

(2) There is hereby created in the state treasury a statewide trauma care system cash fund. All moneys in the fund shall be subject to appropriation by the general assembly for allocation to the department to administer the trauma system. Any moneys in the fund not appropriated shall remain in the fund and shall not be transferred or revert to the general fund at the end of any fiscal year. All interest derived from the deposit and investment of moneys in the fund shall remain in the fund.

## 25-3.5-706. Immunity from liability.

The department, the board, the council as defined in section 25-3.5-703 (3.5), a RETAC as defined in section 25-3.5-703 (6.8), the emergency medical practice advisory council created in section 25-3.5-206, key resource facilities, any other public or private entity acting on behalf of or under contract with the department, and counties and cities and counties shall be immune from civil and criminal liability and from regulatory sanction for acting in compliance with the provisions of this part 7. Nothing in this section shall be construed as providing any immunity to such entities or any other person in connection with the provision of medical treatment, care, or services that are governed by the medical malpractice statutes, article 64 of title 13, C.R.S.

## 25-3.5-707. False representation as trauma facility - penalty.

(1) No facility, or agent or employee of a facility, shall represent that the facility functions as a

level I, II, III, IV, or V trauma facility unless the facility possesses a valid certificate of designation issued pursuant to section 25-3.5-704 (2) (d) . In addition, no facility, provider, or person shall violate any rule adopted by the board.

(2) Any facility, provider, or person who violates the provisions of subsection (1) of this section is subject to a civil penalty, which the board shall establish by rule, but which shall not exceed five hundred dollars. The penalty shall be assessed and collected by the department. Before a fee is collected, a facility, provider, or person shall be provided an opportunity for review of the assessed penalty. The procedures for review shall be in accordance with the "State Administrative Procedure Act", article 4 of title 24, C.R.S., and board rules. Any penalty collected pursuant to this section shall be transmitted to the state treasurer, who shall credit the same to the statewide trauma care system cash fund created in section 25-3.5-705.

## 25-3.5-708. Financing for statewide trauma system.

(1) The implementation of the statewide trauma system shall be subject to the availability of:
(a) Federal transportation highway safety seed moneys that the department of transportation transfers to the department of public health and environment pursuant to an intergovernmental agreement between the two agencies;
(b) Moneys from the emergency medical services account within the highway users tax fund that are unexpended portions of state administrative funds that may be allocated pursuant to section 25-3.5-603 (2) (c) . Nothing in this paragraph (b) shall be construed to authorize moneys that may be allocated pursuant to section 25-3.5-603 (2) (a) (I) or (2) (b) to be used for the financing of the administration of the statewide trauma system.
(c) Moneys from the statewide trauma care system cash fund created in section 25-3.5-705.
(2) In addition to any funds available pursuant to subsection (1) of this section, the executive director of the department of public health and environment is hereby authorized to accept any grants, donations, gifts, or contributions from any other private or public entity for the purpose of implementing this part 7.

## 25-3.5-709. Annual report.

No later than January 1, 1999, and prior to November 1 of each year thereafter, the department, in cooperation with the council, as defined in section 25-3.5-703 (3.5) , shall submit a report to the health, environment, welfare, and institutions committees and the joint budget committee of the general assembly on the quality of the statewide emergency medical and trauma care system. Such report shall include an evaluation of each component of the statewide emergency medical and trauma care system and any recommendation for legislation concerning the statewide emergency medical and trauma care system or any component thereof.

# PART 8. TOBACCO EDUCATION, PREVENTION, AND CESSATION PROGRAMS

## 25-3.5-801. Short title.

This part 8 shall be known and may be cited as the "Tobacco Education, Prevention, and Cessation Act".

## 25-3.5-802. Legislative declaration.

(1) The general assembly hereby finds that:
(a) The use of all types of tobacco products, including smokeless tobacco, results in a high incidence of addiction, disease, illness, and death;
(b) Persons who begin using and become addicted to tobacco products in their youth often face a

lifetime of struggle and recurring illness in coping with and attempting to overcome addiction to tobacco products;

(c) Experimentation with tobacco products by youth is often a first step toward more serious drug experimentation and creates a greater likelihood that the youth who experiment with tobacco will at some point be addicted to even more harmful substances;

(d) Implementation of aggressive tobacco and substance abuse prevention, education, and cessation programs for school-age children is necessary to assist young people in avoiding and ending tobacco use;

(e) School districts, schools, and other entities that provide tobacco and substance abuse prevention, education, and cessation programs for school-age children should reach out to parents and encourage them to participate, either as students or role models, in implementing said programs.

(2) The general assembly finds that persons with behavioral or mental health disorders are more likely to abuse tobacco products than any other segment of society. The general assembly further finds that the unusually heavy pattern of tobacco abuse engaged in by persons with behavioral or mental health disorders requires special treatment strategies that are not provided by other alcohol, drug, or tobacco abuse programs or substance use disorder treatment programs. It is therefore the general assembly's intent that the programs funded pursuant to this part 8 include comprehensive programs to prevent and treat tobacco addiction among persons with behavioral or mental health disorders.

(3) The general assembly also finds that:

(a) Each year, thousands of people in this state die from diseases that have been clinically proven to be caused by or directly related to tobacco use;

(b) Once a person starts using tobacco, he or she usually becomes addicted to the nicotine contained in the tobacco, which makes it terribly difficult for the person to quit using tobacco even when the person is aware of the significant health risks that accompany tobacco use;

(c) Studies show that a child is at a substantially greater risk of starting to use tobacco if the child's parents or older siblings use tobacco. Therefore, reducing tobacco use by adults may significantly reduce the risk that children will begin using tobacco.

(d) Annual direct medical costs from tobacco use in Colorado currently exceed one billion dollars;

(e) Comprehensive tobacco education, prevention, and cessation programs may result in millions of dollars in savings to the state and individual residents of the state for generations.

## 25-3.5-803. Definitions.

As used in this part 8, unless the context otherwise requires:

(1) "Division" means the division within the department of public health and environment responsible for prevention services.

(2) "Entity" means any local government, county, district, or municipal public health agency, political subdivision of the state, county department of social services, state agency, state institution of higher education that offers a teacher education program, school, school district, or board of cooperative services or any private nonprofit or not-for-profit community-based organization. "Entity" also means a for-profit organization that applies for a grant for the sole purpose of providing a statewide public information campaign concerning tobacco use prevention and cessation.

(3) "Master settlement agreement" means the master settlement agreement, the smokeless tobacco master settlement agreement, and the consent decree approved and entered by the court in the case denominated State of Colorado, ex rel. Gale A. Norton, Attorney General v. R.J. Reynolds Tobacco Co.; American Tobacco Co., Inc.; Brown & Williamson Tobacco Corp.; Liggett & Myers, Inc.; Lorillard Tobacco Co., Inc.; Philip Morris, Inc.; United States Tobacco Co.; B.A.T. Industries, P.L.C.; The Council For Tobacco Research--U.S.A., Inc.; and Tobacco Institute, Inc., Case No. 97 CV 3432, in the district court for the city and county of Denver.

(4) "Program" means the tobacco education, prevention, and cessation grant program created in

section 25-3.5-804.

(5) "State board" means the state board of health created in section 25-1-103.

## 25-3.5-804. Tobacco education, prevention, and cessation programs - review committee - grants.

(1) There is hereby created the tobacco education, prevention, and cessation grant program to provide funding for community-based and statewide tobacco education programs designed to reduce initiation of tobacco use by children and youth, promote cessation of tobacco use among youth and adults, and reduce exposure to secondhand smoke. Any such tobacco programs may be presented in combination with other substance abuse programs. The program shall be administered by the division within the department and coordinated with efforts pursuant to part 5 of article 35 of title 24, C.R.S. The state board shall award grants to selected entities from moneys appropriated to the department from the tobacco education programs fund created in section 24-22-117, C.R.S.

(2) The state board shall adopt rules that specify, but are not necessarily limited to, the following:

(a) The procedures and timelines by which an entity may apply for program grants;

(b) Grant application contents;

(c) Criteria for selecting those entities that shall receive grants and determining the amount and duration of said grants;

(d) Reporting requirements for entities that receive grants pursuant to this part 8.

(3) (a) The division shall review the applications received pursuant to this part 8 and make recommendations to the state board regarding those entities that may receive grants and the amounts of said grants. On and after October 1, 2005, the review committee shall review the applications received pursuant to this part 8 and submit to the state board and the director of the department recommended grant recipients, grant amounts, and the duration of each grant. Within thirty days after receiving the review committee's recommendations, the director shall submit his or her recommendations to the state board. The review committee's recommendations regarding grantees of the Tony Grampsas youth services program, section 26-6.8-102, pursuant to section 25-3.5-805 (5) shall be submitted to the state board and the Tony Grampsas youth services board. Within thirty days after receiving the review committee's recommendations, the Tony Grampsas youth services board shall submit its recommendations to the state board. The state board has the final authority to approve the grants under this part 8. If the state board disapproves a recommendation for a grant recipient, the review committee may submit a replacement recommendation within thirty days. In reviewing grant applications for programs to provide tobacco education, prevention, and cessation programs for persons with behavioral or mental health disorders, the division or the review committee shall consult with the programs for public psychiatry at the university of Colorado health sciences center, the national alliance for the mentally ill, the mental health association of Colorado, and the department of human services.

(b) The state board shall award grants to the selected entities, specifying the amount and duration of the award. No grant awarded pursuant to this part 8 shall exceed three years without renewal. Of the amount awarded each year pursuant to the provisions of this part 8, the state board shall award at least one-third of the amount to entities that provide tobacco education, prevention, and cessation programs, solely or in combination with substance abuse programs, to school-age children.

(4) In implementing the program, the division shall survey the need for trained teachers, health professionals, and others involved in providing tobacco education, prevention, and cessation programs. To the extent the division determines there is a need, the division may provide technical training and assistance to entities that receive program grants pursuant to this part 8.

(5) (a) There is hereby created the tobacco education, prevention, and cessation grant program review committee, referred to in this part 8 as the "review committee". The review committee is established in the division. The review committee is responsible for ensuring that program priorities are established consistent with the Colorado tobacco prevention and control strategic plan, overseeing program strategies and activities, and ensuring that the program grants are in

compliance with section 25-3.5-805.

(b) The review committee shall consist of the following sixteen members:

(I) The director of the department or the director's designee;

(II) Five members who shall be appointed by the director of the department, one of whom shall include the director of the tobacco education, prevention, and cessation program within the division and four of whom shall be staff of the program with expertise in tobacco prevention among youth, reducing exposure to secondhand smoke, tobacco cessation, or public education.

(III) Eight members who shall be appointed by the state board as follows:

(A) One member who is a member of the state board;

(B) One member who is a representative of a local public health agency;

(C) One member who is a representative of a statewide association representing physicians;

(D) One member who is a representative of an association representing family physicians;

(E) One member who is a representative of the Colorado department of education;

(F) One member who is a representative of the university of Colorado health sciences center who has expertise in evaluation;

(G) One member who represents a socio-demographic disadvantaged population in Colorado; and

(H) One member who is a representative of a statewide nonprofit organization with a demonstrated expertise in and commitment to tobacco control.

(IV) The president of the senate shall appoint one member of the senate.

(V) The speaker of the house of representatives shall appoint one member of the house of representatives.

(c) (I) Except as provided in subparagraph (II) of this paragraph (c) , members of the review committee shall serve three-year terms; except that of the members initially appointed to the review committee, five members appointed by the state board shall serve two-year terms. Members of the review committee appointed pursuant to subparagraph (III) of paragraph (b) of this subsection (5) shall not serve more than two consecutive terms.

(II) The terms of the members appointed by the speaker of the house of representatives and the president of the senate and who are serving on March 22, 2007, shall be extended to and expire on or shall terminate on the convening date of the first regular session of the sixty-seventh general assembly. As soon as practicable after such convening date, the speaker and the president shall appoint or reappoint members in the same manner as provided in subparagraphs (IV) and (V) of paragraph (b) of this subsection (5) . Thereafter, the terms of members appointed or reappointed by the speaker and the president shall expire on the convening date of the first regular session of each general assembly, and all subsequent appointments and reappointments by the speaker and the president shall be made as soon as practicable after such convening date. The person making the original appointment or reappointment shall fill any vacancy by appointment for the remainder of an unexpired term. Members shall serve at the pleasure of the appointing authority and shall continue in office until the member's successor is appointed.

(d) The composition of the review committee shall reflect, to the extent practical, Colorado's ethnic, racial, and geographic diversity.

(e) Except as otherwise provided in section 2-2-326, C.R.S., members of the review committee shall serve without compensation but shall be reimbursed from moneys deposited in the tobacco education programs fund created in section 24-22-117, C.R.S., for their actual and necessary expenses incurred in the performance of their duties pursuant to this part 8.

(f) The review committee shall elect from its membership a chair and a vice-chair of the committee.

(g) The division shall provide staff support to the review committee.

(h) If a member of the review committee has an immediate personal, private, or financial interest in any matter pending before the review committee, the member shall disclose the fact and shall not vote upon such matter.

## 25-3.5-805. Tobacco education, prevention, and cessation programs -

**requirements.**

(1) An entity that applies for a grant pursuant to the provisions of this part 8 shall in the application demonstrate that the tobacco education, prevention, or cessation program provides at least one of the following:

(a) Education designed for school-age children that, at a minimum, addresses tobacco use prevention and cessation strategies and the dangers of tobacco use; or

(b) Education programs, including but not limited to school, work site, mass media, and health-care setting programs, designed to prevent or reduce the use of all types of tobacco products or help reduce exposure to secondhand smoke; or

(c) Counseling regarding the use of all types of tobacco products; or

(d) Programs that address prevention and cessation of the abuse of various types of drugs, with an emphasis on prevention and cessation of tobacco use; or

(e) (Deleted by amendment, L. 2005, p. 935, § 25, effective June 2, 2005.)

(f) Tobacco use and substance abuse prevention and cessation services addressed to specific population groups such as adolescents and pregnant women and provided within specific ethnic and low-income communities; or

(g) Training of teachers, health professionals, and others in the field of tobacco use and prevention; or

(h) Tobacco addiction prevention and treatment strategies that are designed specifically for persons with behavioral or mental health disorders; or

(i) Activities to prevent the sale or furnishing by other means of cigarettes or tobacco products to minors; or

(j) Programs that are designed to eliminate health disparities among segments of the population that have higher than average tobacco burdens.

(1.5) Notwithstanding the requirements of subsection (1) of this section, an entity may apply for a grant for the purpose of evaluating the entire statewide program or individual components of the program.

(2) If the entity applying for a grant pursuant to the provisions of this part 8 is a school district or board of cooperative services, in addition to the information specified in subsection (1) of this section, the entity shall demonstrate in the application that the tobacco education, prevention, and cessation program to be operated with moneys received from the grant is a program that has not been previously provided by the school district or board of cooperative services. The entity shall also demonstrate that the program is specifically designed to appeal to and address the concerns of the age group to which the program will be presented.

(3) In adopting criteria for awarding grants, the state board shall adopt such criteria as will ensure that the implementation of a comprehensive program is consistent with the Colorado tobacco prevention and control strategic plan, that tobacco education, prevention, and cessation programs are available throughout the state, and that the programs are available to serve persons of all ages.

(4) At least fifteen percent of the moneys annually awarded to grantees pursuant to this section shall be for the purposes of providing funding to eliminate health disparities among minority populations and high-risk populations that have higher-than-average tobacco burdens.

(5) Up to fifteen percent of the moneys annually awarded pursuant to this section shall be allocated to grantees of the Tony Grampsas youth services program, section 26-6.8-102, C.R.S., for proven tobacco prevention and cessation programs.

(6) The majority of moneys annually awarded to grantees that qualify pursuant to subsections (1) , (2) , and (5) of this section shall be for evidence-based programs and programs that prevent and reduce tobacco use among youth and young adults.

## 25-3.5-806. Tobacco education, prevention, and cessation programs - reporting requirements.

(1) In adopting rules specifying the reporting requirements for entities that receive grants pursuant to this part 8, the state board shall ensure that such reports, at a minimum, include:

(a) An evaluation of the implementation of the program, including but not limited to the number of persons served and the services provided;

(b) The results achieved by the program, specifying the goals of the program and the criteria used in measuring attainment of the goals;

(c) An explanation of how the results achieved by the program contribute to the achievement of the program goals as stated in section 25-3.5-802.

(2) The division shall compile the annual reports received from entities pursuant to this section.

(3) (a) The division shall annually review the reports received from entities receiving grants pursuant to this part 8 and shall make recommendations to the state board concerning whether the amount received by an entity should be continued, reduced, or increased. The division may also recommend that the grant for an entity be immediately terminated or not renewed if the tobacco education, prevention, and cessation program funded by the grant does not demonstrate a sufficient level of success, as determined by the division.

(b) The division may contract with one or more public or private entities to review and compile the reports received pursuant to this section and prepare the recommendations pursuant to paragraph (a) of this subsection (3) .

## 25-3.5-807. Tobacco program fund - created. (Repealed)


## 25-3.5-807.5. Transfer of balance of tobacco program fund - repeal. (Repealed)


## 25-3.5-808. Administration - limitation.

The prevention services division of the department may receive up to five percent of the moneys annually appropriated by the general assembly from the tobacco education programs fund created in section 24-22-117, C.R.S., for the actual costs incurred in administering the program, including the hiring of sufficient staff within the division to effectively administer the program and reimbursement of review committee members pursuant to section 25-3.5-804 (5) .

## 25-3.5-809. Tobacco education, prevention, and cessation programs - funding.

The programs under this part 8 shall be funded by moneys annually appropriated by the general assembly to the department from the tobacco education programs fund created in section 24-22-117, C.R.S.

# PART 9. QUALITY MANAGEMENT


## 25-3.5-901. Short title.

This part 9 shall be known and may be cited as the "Carol J. Shanaberger Act".

## 25-3.5-902. Legislative declaration.

The general assembly hereby finds and declares that the implementation of quality management functions to evaluate and improve prehospital emergency medical service patient care is essential to the operation of emergency medical services organizations. For this purpose, it is necessary that the collection of information by prehospital medical directors and emergency medical services organizations be reasonably unfettered so that a complete and thorough evaluation and improvement of the quality of patient care can be accomplished. To this end, quality management information relating to the evaluation or improvement of the quality of prehospital emergency medical services is confidential, subject to section 25-3.5-904 (3) , and persons performing quality management functions are granted qualified immunity as specified in section 25-3.5-904 (4) . It is the intent of the general assembly that nothing in this section revise, amend, or alter article 36 or part 1 of article 36.5 of title 12, C.R.S.

## 25-3.5-903. Definitions.

As used in this part 9, unless the context otherwise requires:

(1) "Emergency medical services organization" means:

(a) Local emergency medical and trauma service providers, as defined in section 25-3.5-602 (4) , excluding a health care facility licensed or certified by the department pursuant to section 25-1.5-103 (1) (a) that has a quality management program pursuant to section 25-3-109;

(b) Regional emergency medical and trauma services advisory councils, as defined in section 25-3.5-703 (6.8) and established under section 25-3.5-704 (2) (c) ; and

(c) Public safety answering points, as defined in section 29-11-101 (6.5) , C.R.S., performing emergency medical dispatch.

(2) "Prehospital medical director" or "medical director" means a licensed physician who supervises certified emergency medical service providers who provide prehospital care.

(3) "Quality management assessment" means a review and assessment of the performance of prehospital care provided by emergency medical service providers operating under a medical director.

(4) (a) "Quality management program" means a program established under this part 9 that is designed to perform quality management assessments for the purpose of improving patient care and includes:

(I) Quality assurance and risk management activities;

(II) Peer review of emergency medical service providers; and

(III) Other quality management functions.

(b) "Quality management program" does not include review or assessment of the licensing, use, or maintenance of vehicles used by an emergency medical services organization.

## 25-3.5-904. Quality management programs - creation - assessments - confidentiality of information - exceptions - immunity for good-faith participants.

(1) Each emergency medical services organization that institutes a quality management program to conduct quality management assessments shall include in that program at least the following components:

(a) Periodic review of treatment protocols, compliance with treatment protocols, and prehospital emergency medical care provided to patients;

(b) Peer review of emergency medical service providers, including review of their qualifications and competence and quality and appropriateness of patient care;

(c) The collection of data if required pursuant to section 25-3.5-704 (2) (h) (II) ;

(d) A general description of the types of cases, problems, or risks to be reviewed and the process used for identifying potential risks;

(e) Identification of the personnel or committees responsible for coordinating quality management activities and the means of reporting within the quality management program;

(f) A description of the method for systematically reporting information to the organization's medical director;

(g) A description of the method for investigating and analyzing causes of individual problems and patterns of problems;

(h) A description of possible corrective actions to address the problems, including education, prevention, and minimizing potential problems or risks; and

(i) A description of the method for following up in a timely manner on corrective action to determine the effectiveness of the action.

(2) (a) Except as provided in paragraph (b) of this subsection (2) or subsection (3) of this section, information required to be collected and maintained, including information from the prehospital care reporting system that identifies an individual, and records, reports, and other information obtained and maintained in accordance with a quality management program established pursuant to this section are confidential and shall not be released except to the department in cases of an alleged violation of board rules pertaining to emergency medical service provider certification or except in accordance with section 25-3.5-205 (4) .

(b) (I) An emergency medical services organization or prehospital medical director may share quality management records related to peer review of an emergency medical service provider with another emergency medical services organization or a licensed or certified health care facility that has a quality management program under this section or section 25-3-109, as applicable, without violating the confidentiality requirements of paragraph (a) of this subsection (2) and without waiving the privilege specified in subsection (3) of this section, if the emergency medical service provider seeks to subject himself or herself to, or is currently subject to, the authority of the emergency medical services organization or health care facility.

(II) A health care facility licensed or certified by the department pursuant to section 25-1.5-103 (1) (a) that has a quality management program pursuant to section 25-3-109 may share quality management records related to peer review of an emergency medical service provider with an emergency medical services organization or prehospital medical director if the emergency medical service provider seeks to subject himself or herself to, or is currently subject to, the authority of the emergency medical services organization or prehospital medical director without violating the confidentiality requirements of this subsection (2) and section 25-3-109 (3) and without waiving the privilege specified in subsection (3) of this section and section 25-3-109 (4) .

(c) The confidentiality of information provided for in this section is not impaired or otherwise adversely affected solely because the prehospital medical director or emergency medical services organization submits the information to a nongovernmental entity to conduct studies that evaluate, develop, and analyze information about emergency medical care operations, practices, or any other function of emergency medical care organizations. The records, reports, and other information collected or developed by a nongovernmental entity remain protected as provided in paragraph (a) of this subsection (2) . In order to adequately protect the confidentiality of the information, the findings, conclusions, or recommendations contained in the studies conducted by a nongovernmental entity are not deemed to establish a standard of care for emergency medical care organizations.

(3) (a) The records, reports, and other information described in subsection (2) of this section are not subject to subpoena and are not discoverable or admissible as evidence in any civil or administrative proceeding. A person who participates in the reporting, collection, evaluation, or use of quality management information with regard to a specific circumstance shall not testify about his or her participation in any civil or administrative proceeding.

(b) This subsection (3) does not apply to:

(I) Any civil or administrative proceeding, inspection, or investigation as otherwise provided by law by the department or other appropriate regulatory agency having jurisdiction for disciplinary or licensing sanctions;

(II) A person giving testimony concerning facts of which he or she has personal knowledge acquired independently of the quality management program or function;

(III) The availability, as provided by law or the rules of civil procedure, of factual information relating solely to the individual in interest in a civil suit by the person, next friend, or legal representative, but factual information does not include opinions or evaluations performed as a part of the quality management program;

(IV) A person giving testimony concerning an act or omission that he or she observed or in which he or she participated, notwithstanding any participation by him or her in the quality management program;

(V) A person giving testimony concerning facts he or she had recorded in a medical record relating solely to the individual in interest in a civil suit.

(4) A person, acting in good faith, within the scope and functions of a quality management program, and without violating any applicable laws, who participates in the reporting, collection, evaluation, or use of quality management information or performs other functions as part of a quality management program with regard to a specific circumstance is immune from liability in any civil action based on his or her participation in the quality management program brought by an emergency medical service provider or person to whom the quality management information pertains. This immunity does not apply to any negligent or intentional act or omission in the provision of care.

(5) Nothing in this section:

(a) Affects or prevents the voluntary release of any quality management record or information by a prehospital medical director or emergency medical services organization; except that no patient-identifying information may be released without the patient's consent;

(b) Limits any statutory or common-law privilege, confidentiality, or immunity; or

(c) Affects a person's ability to access his or her medical records as provided in section 25-1-801 or the right of any family member or other person to obtain medical record information upon the consent of the patient or his or her authorized representative.

# PART 10. STATEWIDE MARIJUANA EDUCATION CAMPAIGN

### 25-3.5-1001. Legislative declaration.

(1) The general assembly hereby finds and declares that:

(a) Many substance abuse, public health, education, regulatory, and law enforcement professionals are concerned about the impact that the legalization of retail marijuana will have on children, youth, and adults in the state;

(b) Many of these professionals believe that the legalization of retail marijuana may result in:

(I) An increase in the abuse of marijuana by adults and youth;

(II) A greater need for early intervention services due to increased use of marijuana by youth and adults;

(III) A belief among children and youth that the risks associated with marijuana use are low;

(IV) Health impacts in connection with exposure to secondhand smoke;

(V) An increase in the instances of impaired driving and the associated increase in crashes;

(VI) New health concerns regarding pregnant or nursing women who use marijuana or who are exposed to secondhand smoke from marijuana; and

(VII) Other potential concerns that have not yet been identified.

(c) Mass-reach health communications strategies have been found to be effective in reducing tobacco and alcohol use among adults and youth, in increasing the use of cessation services, and in limiting tobacco and alcohol initiation by youth; and

(d) There is substantial evidence that mass media campaigns and community coalitions are effective in preventing marijuana use.

(2) The general assembly further finds and declares that to protect and improve the health of the citizens of the state, it is a prudent use of state resources to require the Colorado department of public health and environment to implement a campaign to increase the awareness of and education about the impacts of marijuana use.

### 25-3.5-1002. Definitions.

As used in this part 10, unless the context otherwise requires:

(1) "Division" means the division within the department of public health and environment responsible for prevention services.

(2) "Retail marijuana" means marijuana that is legal for adults to purchase and use pursuant to section 16 of article XVIII of the state constitution.

## 25-3.5-1003. Eighteen-month public awareness and education campaign - legalization of marijuana - repeal. (Repealed)

## 25-3.5-1004. Ongoing prevention and education campaign - training - marijuana.

(1) Subject to available appropriations, beginning in the 2014-15 state fiscal year, the division shall develop, implement, and evaluate an ongoing statewide prevention and education campaign to address the long-term marijuana education needs in the state. In the prevention and education messaging, the division shall provide information to:

(a) The general public regarding the law surrounding the legal use of retail marijuana;

(b) People in the retail marijuana industry regarding restricting youth access to retail marijuana;

(c) Retail marijuana users and other relevant populations identified as high-risk regarding the potential risks associated with the use of marijuana; and

(d) The general public regarding the dangers associated with the over-consumption of marijuana-infused products.

(2) In furtherance of the goals of the ongoing marijuana prevention and education campaign, the division may use television messaging, radio broadcasts, print media, digital strategies, or any other form of messaging deemed necessary and appropriate by the division to reach the target audiences of the campaign.

(3) In furtherance of the goals of the ongoing marijuana prevention and education campaign, the department of public health and environment shall provide at least five regional training sessions during the 2014-15 fiscal year for community partners to implement youth health development strategies.

## 25-3.5-1005. Website - primary state resource for information.

(1) In furtherance of the goals of the eighteen-month public awareness and education campaign created in section 25-3.5-1003, as it existed prior to its repeal in 2016, and the ongoing prevention and education campaign created in section 25-3.5-1004, the division shall create a website that will serve as the state portal for the most accurate and timely information regarding the health effects of marijuana use and the laws regarding marijuana use. The division shall ensure that the website links to the information made available by local governments that have passed additional restrictions on the use of retail marijuana and links to the website of every state agency that contains relevant information regarding retail marijuana, including any youth prevention campaign managed by a state agency.

(2) The division shall implement a marketing campaign to generate public awareness of the website as the primary state resource for information regarding the legalization and use of retail marijuana in the state.

## 25-3.5-1006. Align marijuana messaging - integration of information across state agencies.

(1) The division shall integrate information from each state agency involved in providing retail marijuana information, including the department of human services, the department of transportation, the department of revenue, the department of law, the department of public safety, and the department of education, to align the messaging, branding, and education provided by each agency for the eighteen-month public education and awareness campaign required pursuant

to section 25-3.5-1003, as it existed prior to its repeal in 2016, the ongoing prevention and education campaign required pursuant to section 25-3.5-1004, and the website required pursuant to section 25-3.5-1005.

(2) The division shall provide data, training, educational materials, and resources on effective prevention strategies to local community coalitions and programs addressing marijuana prevention.

### 25-3.5-1007. Evaluation of marijuana campaigns.

(1) The department shall contract with a respected evaluation partner to develop and implement a three-year evaluation plan assessing the reach and impact of the eighteen-month public education and awareness campaign required pursuant to section 25-3.5-1003, as it existed prior to its repeal in 2016, and the ongoing prevention and education campaign required pursuant to section 25-3.5-1004. The evaluation must also assess the department's success in educating the citizens of the state regarding the legal parameters of the use of retail marijuana and preventing negative health impacts from the legalization of retail marijuana.

(2) (Deleted by amendment, L. 2017.)

# PART 11. EMERGENCY MEDICAL RESPONDERS

### 25-3.5-1101. Legislative declaration.

(1) The general assembly hereby finds that:

(a) The department of public health and environment has responsibility for oversight of the emergency medical and trauma services system and the certification of emergency medical service providers. Emergency medical service providers are certified by the department to provide treatment and transport to the sick and injured.

(b) Emergency medical responders are the part of the emergency medical and trauma services system who answer emergency calls, provide effective and immediate care to ill and injured patients, prepare the scene for the arrival of the ambulance and emergency medical service providers, and provide assistance to emergency medical service providers as directed;

(c) Most emergency medical responders perform their duties in an ethical and professional manner;

(d) It is in the interests of the citizens of this state that a voluntary process exists whereby individuals may register their training and status as an emergency medical responder with the state; and

(e) It is in the public interest to place the voluntary registration of emergency medical responders within the state department that has statutory responsibility for the statewide emergency medical and trauma services system.

(2) Therefore, it is the intent of the general assembly to:

(a) Transfer the oversight of emergency medical responders, formerly known as first responders, from the department of public safety to the department of public health and environment; and

(b) Fund the oversight of the voluntary registration program through the highway users tax fund established in section 42-3-304 (21) , C.R.S., in order to avoid cost-prohibitive registration fees.

### 25-3.5-1102. Definitions.

As used in this part 11:

(1) "Emergency medical responder" means an individual who has successfully completed the training and examination requirements for emergency medical responders and who provides assistance to the injured or ill until more highly trained and qualified personnel arrive.

(2) "Physician" means a person licensed pursuant to article 36 of title 12, C.R.S., in good standing,

who authorizes and directs, through protocols and standing orders, the performance of students-in-training enrolled in department-recognized emergency medical responder education programs.

(3) "Registered emergency medical responder" means an individual who has successfully completed the training and examination requirements for emergency medical responders, who provides assistance to the injured or ill until more highly trained and qualified personnel arrive, and who is registered with the department pursuant to this part 11.

## 25-3.5-1103. Registration - rules - funds.

(1) On and after July 1, 2017, the department shall administer a voluntary registration program for emergency medical responders. A person shall not hold himself or herself out as a registered emergency medical responder, providing care or services as identified in national guidelines for emergency medical response as approved by the department, unless the person meets the requirements set forth in this part 11; except that a person may function as a good samaritan pursuant to section 13-21-116, C.R.S.

(2) The board shall adopt rules for the administration of the emergency medical responder registration program, which rules shall include, at a minimum, the following:

(a) Requirements for emergency medical responder registration, which include certification of the applicant through a nationally recognized emergency responder certification organization approved by the department;

(b) The period of time for which the registration as an emergency medical responder is valid;

(c) Registration renewal requirements;

(d) Training requirements for new and renewing registrants;

(e) Provisions governing national and state criminal history record checks for new and renewing registrants and the use of the results of the checks by the department to determine the action to take on a registration application. Notwithstanding section 24-5-101, C.R.S., these provisions must allow the department to consider whether the applicant has been convicted of a felony or misdemeanor involving moral turpitude and the pertinent circumstances connected with the conviction and to make a determination whether any such conviction disqualifies the applicant from registration.

(f) Disciplinary sanctions, which may include provisions for the denial, revocation, probation, and suspension, including summary suspension, of registration and of education program recognition; and

(g) An appeal process consistent with sections 24-4-104 and 24-4-105, C.R.S., that is applicable to department decisions in connection with sanctions.

(3) Rules promulgated by the department of public safety remain in effect until superceded by rules duly adopted pursuant to this part 11.

(4) (a) The department may issue a provisional registration to an applicant for registration as an emergency medical responder who requests issuance of a provisional registration and who pays a fee authorized under rules adopted by the board. A provisional registration is valid for not more than ninety days.

(b) The department may not issue a provisional registration unless the applicant satisfies the requirements for registration established in rules of the board. If the department finds that an emergency medical responder who has received a provisional registration has violated any requirements for registration, the department may revoke the provisional registration and prohibit the registration of the emergency medical responder.

(c) The department may issue a provisional registration to an applicant whose fingerprint-based criminal history record check has not yet been completed. The department shall require the applicant to submit a name-based criminal history record check prior to issuing a provisional registration.

(d) The board shall adopt rules as necessary to implement this subsection (4), including rules establishing a fee to be charged to applicants seeking a provisional registration. The department shall deposit any fee collected for a provisional registration in the emergency medical services account created in section 25-3.5-603.

(5) (a) The department shall acquire a fingerprint-based criminal history record check from the Colorado bureau of investigation to investigate the holder of or applicant for an emergency medical responder registration. The department may acquire a name-based criminal history record check for a registrant or an applicant who has twice submitted to a fingerprint-based criminal history record check and whose fingerprints are unclassifiable. Notwithstanding paragraph (b) of this subsection (5), if a person submitted to a fingerprint-based criminal history record check at the time of initial registration or registration renewal, the person shall not be required to submit to a subsequent fingerprint-based criminal history record check.

(b) If, at the time of application for registry or for renewal, an individual has lived in the state for three years or less, the department shall require the applicant to submit to a federal bureau of investigation fingerprint-based national criminal history record check; except that the department may acquire a national name-based criminal history record check for an applicant who has twice submitted to a fingerprint-based criminal history record check and whose fingerprints are unclassifiable. The department shall be the authorized agency to receive and disseminate information regarding the result of any national criminal history record check.

## 25-3.5-1104. Training programs - rules.

(1) The board shall adopt rules regarding the recognition by the department of education programs that provide initial training and continued competency education for emergency medical responders.

(2) The receipt of a certificate or other document of course completion issued by an education program or national certification organization is not deemed state licensure, approval, or registration.

## 25-3.5-1105. Investigation and discipline.

(1) The department may administer oaths, take affirmations of witnesses, and issue subpoenas to compel the attendance of witnesses and the production of all relevant records and documents to investigate alleged misconduct by registered emergency medical responders.

(2) Upon failure of a witness to comply with a subpoena, the department may apply to a district court for an order requiring the person to appear before the department or an administrative law judge, to produce the relevant records or documents, or to give testimony or evidence touching the matter under investigation or in question. When seeking an order, the department shall apply to the district court of the county in which the subpoenaed person resides or conducts business. The court may punish such failure as a contempt of court.

(3) A registered emergency medical responder, the employer of a registered emergency medical responder, or a physician shall report to the department any misconduct by a registered emergency medical responder that is known or reasonably believed by the person to have occurred.

(4) A person acting as a witness or consultant to the department, a witness testifying, and a person or employer who reports misconduct to the department under this section is immune from liability in any civil action brought for acts occurring while testifying, producing evidence, or reporting misconduct under this section if the individual or employer was acting in good faith and with a reasonable belief of the facts. A person or employer participating in good faith in an investigation or an administrative proceeding pursuant to this section is immune from any civil or criminal liability that may result from such participation.

(5) Records, documents, testimony, or evidence obtained under this section are confidential except to the extent necessary to support the administrative action taken by the department, to refer the matter to another regulatory agency, or to refer the matter to a law enforcement agency for criminal prosecution.

# PART 12. COMMUNITY ASSISTANCE REFERRAL AND EDUCATION SERVICES (CARES) PROGRAM

## 25-3.5-1201. Short title.
The short title of this part 12 is the "Community Assistance Referral and Education Services (CARES) Program Act".

## 25-3.5-1202. Definitions.
As used in this part 12, unless the context otherwise requires:
(1) "Authorized entity" means:
(a) A licensed ambulance service;
(b) A fire department of a town, city, or city and county;
(c) A fire protection district, ambulance district, health assurance district, health service district, or metropolitan district or a special district authority; or
(d) A health care business entity, including a licensed or certified health care facility that is subject to regulation under article 3 of this title.
(2) "Medical direction" means the supervision over and direction of individuals who perform acts on behalf of a CARES program by a physician or advanced practice registered nurse who is licensed in Colorado and in good standing and who is identified as being responsible for assuring the competency of those individuals in the performance of acts on behalf of the CARES program.
(3) "Program" or "CARES program" means a community assistance referral and education services program established in accordance with this part 12.

## 25-3.5-1203. Community assistance referral and education services programs - authorization - scope - repeal.
(1) To improve the health of residents within its jurisdiction, prevent illness and injury, or reduce the incidence of 911 calls and hospital emergency department visits made for the purpose of obtaining nonemergency, nonurgent medical care or services, an authorized entity may establish a community assistance referral and education services program to provide community outreach and health education to residents within the authorized entity's jurisdiction.
(2) (a) On or after July 1, 2018, an authorized entity that operates or plans to operate a CARES program in Colorado shall notify the department of its CARES program in the form and manner required by the department.
(b) The department shall maintain a list of all authorized entities that operate a CARES program and make the list accessible to the public.
(c) An authorized entity operating a CARES program shall not assert that it is licensed or certified by the department.
(3) Subject to medical direction, an authorized entity operating a program may, within the scope of practice of its practitioners:
(a) Provide the following services:
(I) Health education and information available on relevant services; and
(II) Referrals for and information concerning low-cost medication programs and alternative resources to the 911 system;
(b) To provide services in accordance with paragraph (a) of this subsection (3) and to ensure nonduplication of the services, collaborate with appropriate community resources, including:
(I) Health care facilities licensed or issued a certificate of compliance pursuant to section 25-1.5-103 or subject to regulation by the department pursuant to article 1 or 3 of this title;
(II) Primary care providers;
(III) Other health care professionals; or
(IV) Social services agencies.

(4) (a) An authorized entity operating a CARES program shall not provide services that would require a license or certification pursuant to part 13 of this article or article 3 or 3.5 of this title.

(b) In the form and manner prescribed by the department and before referring a service or provider to a recipient of a CARES program service, an authorized entity operating a CARES program shall disclose, at a minimum, in writing, the following information to the recipient:

(I) Any relationship that the CARES program has with an individual or entity to which it refers a recipient of CARES program service; and

(II) Whether the authorized entity directs, controls, schedules, or trains any provider to which it refers a recipient of CARES program services.

(5) The department may investigate an authorized entity as it deems necessary to ensure:

(a) The protection of the health, safety, and welfare of a recipient of CARES program services; and

(b) That the authorized entity is not providing services through its CARES program that require a license or certification pursuant to part 13 of this article or article 3 or 3.5 of this title.

(6) A person working directly or indirectly for a CARES program, whether as an employee or a contractor, may only provide services consistent with the requirements of subsection (3) of this section; except that nothing in this section prohibits a licensed, certified, or registered health care or mental health provider or certified emergency medical service provider from acting or providing services within his or her scope of practice if necessary to respond to an emergent situation.

(7) (a) If an entity offered community outreach and health education before January 1, 2015, the entity may continue and need not comply with the requirements of this part 12. The entity may voluntarily provide reports consistent with the requirements of section 25-3.5-1204.

(b) This subsection (7) is repealed, effective July 1, 2021.

## 25-3.5-1204. Reports.

(1) (a) If an authorized entity develops a program under this article, the authorized entity shall report to the department, in the form and manner determined by the department, on the progress of the program on or before December 31 in the year following the year in which the program commenced and on or before December 31 of each subsequent year in which the program continues to operate.

(b) An authorized entity's report must include:

(I) The number of residents who have used program services and the types of program services used;

(II) A measurement of any reduction in the use of the 911 system for nonemergency, nonurgent medical assistance by residents within the authorized entity's jurisdiction; and

(III) A measurement of any reduction in visits to the emergency department in a hospital for nonemergency, nonurgent medical assistance by residents within the authorized entity's jurisdiction.

(c) An authorized entity's report pursuant to this section must not include any personally identifiable information concerning a program client or prospective client.

(2) On or before March 31 of each year, the department shall compile annual reports received from authorized entities in the previous year into a single report and post the report on its website.

# PART 13. COMMUNITY INTEGRATED HEALTH CARE SERVICE AGENCIES

## 25-3.5-1301. Definitions.

As used in this part 13, unless the context otherwise requires:

(1) "Community integrated health care service agency" or "agency" means a sole proprietorship, partnership, corporation, nonprofit entity, special district, governmental unit or agency, or licensed or certified health care facility that is subject to regulation under article 1.5 or 3 of this title that manages and offers, directly or by contract, community integrated health care services.

(2) "Manager" or "administrator" means any person who controls and supervises or offers or attempts to control and supervise the day-to-day operations of a community integrated health care service agency.

(3) "Medical direction" means the supervision over and direction of individuals who perform acts on behalf of an agency by a physician or advanced practice registered nurse who is licensed in Colorado, is in good standing, and is identified as being responsible for assuring the competency of those individuals in the performance of acts on behalf of the agency; except that, if the agency hires or contracts with a community paramedic, only a licensed physician in good standing may provide medical direction.

(4) "Owner" means an officer, director, general partner, limited partner, or other person having a financial or equity interest of twenty-five percent or greater.

## 25-3.5-1302. Community integrated health care service agency license required - rules - civil and criminal penalties - liability insurance.

(1) On or after July 1, 2018, a person shall not operate or maintain a community integrated health care service agency unless the person has submitted to the department a completed application for licensure as a community integrated health care service agency. On or after December 31, 2018, a person shall not operate or maintain an agency without a community integrated health care service agency license issued by the department.

(2) (a) A person who violates subsection (1) of this section:

(I) Is guilty of a misdemeanor and, upon conviction thereof, shall be punished by a fine of not less than fifty dollars nor more than five hundred dollars; and

(II) May be subject to a civil penalty assessed by the department, after conducting a hearing in accordance with section 24-4-105, C.R.S., of up to ten thousand dollars for each violation of this section. The department shall transmit all fines collected pursuant to this subparagraph (II) to the state treasurer, who shall credit the moneys to the general fund.

(b) An owner, manager, or administrator of an agency is subject to the penalties in this subsection (2) for any violation of subsection (1) of this section.

(3) A license applicant shall submit to the department, in the manner determined by the board by rule, proof that the agency and any staff that it employs or contracts is covered by general liability insurance in an amount determined by the board by rule, but not less than the amount calculated in accordance with section 24-10-114 (1) (a) (I) and (1) (b) , C.R.S.

## 25-3.5-1303. Minimum standards for community integrated health care service agencies - adult protective services data system check - rules.

(1) In addition to the services that the board, by rule, authorizes a community integrated health care service agency to perform, an agency may perform any of the services that may be provided through a CARES program pursuant to section 25-3.5-1203 (3) and the tasks and procedures that a community paramedic is authorized to perform within his or her scope of practice in accordance with section 25-3.5-206 and rules promulgated pursuant to that section. On or before January 1, 2018, the board shall promulgate rules providing minimum standards for the operation of an agency within the state. The rules must include the following:

(a) A requirement that the agency have medical direction;

(b) Inspection of agencies by the department or the department's designated representative;

(c) Minimum educational, training, and experience standards for the administrator and staff of an agency, including a requirement that the administrator and staff be of good moral character;

(d) (I) Fees for agency applications and licensure based on the department's direct and indirect costs in implementing this part 13. The department shall transmit the fees to the state treasurer, who shall credit the fees to the community integrated health care service agencies cash fund created in section 25-3.5-1304.

(II) The department shall collect fees from any entity that applies to operate a community integrated health care service agency, including an agency wholly owned and operated by a governmental unit or agency. The department shall transmit the fees to the state treasurer who shall credit the fees to the community integrated health care service agencies cash fund created in section 25-3.5-1304.

(e) The amount of general liability insurance coverage that an agency shall maintain and the manner in which an agency shall demonstrate proof of insurance to the department. The board may establish by rule that an agency may obtain a surety bond in lieu of liability insurance coverage.

(f) Establishing occurrence reporting requirements pursuant to section 25-1-124;

(g) Requirements for retaining records, including the time that agencies must maintain records for inspection by the department; and

(h) A requirement that agencies report to the department on an annual basis.

(2) On and after January 1, 2019, prior to employment, a community integrated health care service agency shall submit the name of a person who will be providing direct care, as defined in section 26-3.1-101 (3.5) , to an at-risk adult, as defined in section 26-3.1-101 (1.5) , as well as any other required identifying information, to the department of human services for a check of the Colorado adult protective services data system, pursuant to section 26-3.1-111, to determine if the person is substantiated in a case of mistreatment of an at-risk adult.

## 25-3.5-1304. Community integrated health care service agencies cash fund - created.

There is created the community integrated health care service agencies cash fund, referred to in this section as the "fund". The department shall transmit fees collected pursuant to this part 13 to the state treasurer for deposit in the fund. The money in the fund is subject to annual appropriation by the general assembly to the department for the department's direct and indirect costs in implementing and administering this part 13. Any unencumbered or unexpended money in the fund at the end of a fiscal year remains in the fund and shall not be credited or transferred to the general fund or any other fund.

## 25-3.5-1305. License - application - inspection - criminal history record check - issuance.

(1) A community integrated health care service agency license expires after one year. The department shall determine the form and manner of initial and renewal license applications.

(2) (a) The department shall inspect an agency as it deems necessary to ensure the health, safety, and welfare of agency consumers. An agency shall submit in writing, in a form and manner prescribed by the department, a plan detailing the measures that the agency will take to correct any violations found by the department as a result of an inspection.

(b) The department shall keep all medical records and personally identifying information obtained during an inspection of an agency confidential. All records and information obtained by the department through an inspection are exempt from disclosure pursuant to sections 24-72-204, C.R.S., and 25-1-124.

(3) (a) (I) With the submission of an application for a license pursuant to this section, each owner, manager, and administrator of an agency applying for an initial or renewal license shall submit a complete set of his or her fingerprints to the Colorado bureau of investigation for the purpose of conducting a state and national fingerprint-based criminal history record check utilizing the records of the Colorado bureau of investigation and the federal bureau of investigation. The Colorado bureau of investigation shall forward the results of a criminal history record check to the department.

(II) Each owner, manager, or administrator of an agency is responsible for paying the fee established by the Colorado bureau of investigation for conducting the fingerprint-based criminal history record check to the bureau.

(III) The department may acquire a name-based criminal history record check for an owner, manager, or administrator who has twice submitted to a fingerprint-based criminal history record check and whose fingerprints are unclassifiable.

(b) The department may deny a license or renewal of a license if the results of a criminal history record check of an owner, manager, or administrator demonstrates that the owner, manager, or administrator has been convicted of a felony or a misdemeanor involving conduct that the department determines could pose a risk to the health, safety, or welfare of community integrated health care service consumers.

(c) If an agency applying for an initial license is temporarily unable to satisfy all of the requirements for licensure, the department may issue a provisional license to the agency; except that the department shall not issue a provisional license to an agency if operation of the agency will adversely affect the health, safety, or welfare of the agency's consumers. The department may require an agency applying for a provisional license to demonstrate to the department's satisfaction that the agency is taking sufficient steps to satisfy all of the requirements for full licensure. A provisional license is valid for ninety days and may be renewed one time at the department's discretion.

## 25-3.5-1306. License denial - suspension - revocation.

(1) Upon denial of an application for an initial license, the department shall notify the applicant in writing of the denial by mailing a notice to the applicant at the address shown on the application. If an applicant, within sixty days after receiving the notice of denial, petitions the department to set a date and place for a hearing, the department shall grant the applicant a hearing to review the denial in accordance with article 4 of title 24, C.R.S.

(2) The department may suspend, revoke, or refuse to renew the license of a community integrated health care service agency that is out of compliance with the requirements of this part 13 or rules promulgated pursuant to this part 13. Before taking final action to suspend, revoke, or refuse to renew a license, the department shall conduct a hearing on the matter in accordance with article 4 of title 24, C.R.S. The department may implement a summary suspension before a hearing in accordance with section 24-4-104 (4) (a) , C.R.S.

(3) After conducting a hearing on the matter in accordance with article 4 of title 24, C.R.S., the department may revoke or refuse to renew an agency license where the owner, manager, or administrator of the agency has been convicted of a felony or misdemeanor involving conduct that the department determines could pose a risk to the health, safety, or welfare of the agency's consumers.

(4) The department may impose intermediate restrictions or conditions on an agency that may require the agency to:

(a) Retain a consultant to address corrective measures;

(b) Be monitored by the department for a specific period;

(c) Provide additional training to its employees, owners, managers, or administrators;

(d) Comply with a directed written plan to correct the violation, in accordance with the procedures established under section 25-27.5-108 (2) (b) ; or

(e) Pay a civil penalty of up to ten thousand dollars per violation. The department, after providing the agency with the opportunity for a hearing in accordance with section 24-4-105, C.R.S., on any penalties assessed, shall transmit all penalties collected pursuant to this paragraph (e) to the state treasurer, who shall credit the money to the general fund. The agency may request, and the department shall grant, a stay in payment of a civil penalty until final disposition of the restriction or condition.

## 25-3.5-1307. Repeal of part - review of functions.

This part 13 is repealed, effective September 1, 2025. Before the repeal, the department's functions under this part 13 shall be reviewed as provided for in section 24-34-104, C.R.S.

# DISEASE CONTROL

# ARTICLE 4. DISEASE CONTROL

# PART 1. SANITARY REGULATIONS

### 25-4-101. Premises sanitation - food defined.
Every building, room, basement, enclosure, or premises occupied, used, or maintained as a bakery, confectionery, cannery, packing house, slaughterhouse, creamery, cheese factory, restaurant, hotel, grocery, meat market factory, shop, or warehouse, or any public place or manufacturing place used for the preparation, manufacture, packing, storage, sale, or distribution of any food, as defined in this section, which is intended for sale shall be properly and adequately lighted, drained, plumbed, and ventilated and shall be conducted with strict regard to the influence of such conditions upon the health of operatives, employees, clerks, or other persons therein employed and the purity and wholesomeness of the food therein produced, prepared, manufactured, packed, stored, sold, or distributed. For the purposes of this part 1, "food" includes all articles used for food, drink, confectionery, or condiment, whether simple, mixed, or compound, and all substances or ingredients used in the preparation thereof.

### 25-4-102. Sanitary regulations.
The floors, sidewalls, ceilings, furniture, receptacles, utensils, dishes, implements, and machinery of every restaurant, hotel kitchen, and establishment or place where such food intended for sale is produced, prepared, manufactured, packed, stored, sold, or distributed and all cars, trucks, and vehicles used in the transportation of such food products shall at no time be kept or permitted to remain in an unclean, unhealthful, or unsanitary condition. For the purpose of this part 1, unclean, unhealthful, and unsanitary conditions shall be deemed to exist if food in the process of production, preparation, manufacture, packing, storage, sale, distribution, or transportation is not securely protected from flies, dust, dirt, and all other foreign or injurious contamination, as far as may be necessary by all reasonable means; or if the refuse, dirt, or waste products incident to the manufacture, preparation, packing, selling, distributing, or transportation of such food are not removed daily; or if all trucks, trays, boxes, buckets, or other receptacles or the chutes, platforms, racks, tables, shelves, and knives, saws, cleavers, or other utensils, or the machinery used in moving, handling, cutting, chopping, mixing, canning, or other processes are not thoroughly cleaned daily; or if the clothing of operatives, employees, clerks, or other persons therein employed is unclean; or if all dishes, cups, glasses, knives, forks, and spoons are not thoroughly washed in hot or running water and rinsed after each usage; or if dishes, cups, or glasses are used which are so cracked, chipped, or broken as to be detrimental to health; or if all ice-cream cones and straws are not securely covered.

### 25-4-103. Construction requirements.
The sidewalls, floors, and ceilings of every bakery, confectionery, creamery, cheese factory, and hotel or restaurant kitchen and every building, room, basement, or enclosure occupied or used for the preparation, manufacture, packing, storage, sale, or distribution of food shall be so constructed that they can easily be kept clean.

## 25-4-104. Protection from dirt.

All such factories, buildings, and other places containing food shall be provided with proper doors and screens necessary and adequate to protect against the contamination of the product from flies, dust, or dirt.

## 25-4-105. Toilet rooms and lavatories.

Every such building, room, basement, enclosure, or premises occupied, used, or maintained for the production, preparation, manufacture, canning, packing, storage, sale, or distribution of such food shall have adequate and convenient toilet rooms or lavatories. The toilet rooms shall be separate and apart from the rooms where the process of production, preparation, manufacture, packing, storing, canning, selling, and distributing is conducted. The floors of such toilet rooms shall be of cement, tile, wood, brick, or other nonabsorbent material and shall be washed and scoured daily. Such toilets shall be furnished with separate ventilating flues and pipes discharging into soil pipes or shall be on the outside of and well removed from the building. Lavatories and washrooms shall be maintained in a sanitary condition.

## 25-4-106. Nuisances - misdemeanor.

If any such building, room, basement, enclosure, or premises occupied, used, or maintained for the purposes stated in sections 25-4-101 to 25-4-105 or if the floors, sidewalls, ceilings, furniture, receptacles, utensils, implements, appliances, or machinery of any such establishment shall be constructed, kept, maintained, or permitted to remain in a condition contrary to any of the provisions of sections 25-4-101 to 25-4-105, the same is declared a nuisance. Any toilet room, lavatory, or washroom which shall be constructed, kept, maintained, or permitted to remain in a condition contrary to the requirements of section 25-4-105 is declared a nuisance. Any car, truck, or vehicle used in the moving or transportation of any food product which shall be kept or permitted to remain in an unclean, unhealthful, or unsanitary condition is declared a nuisance. Whoever unlawfully maintains, or allows or permits to exist, a nuisance as defined in this section is guilty of a misdemeanor and, upon conviction thereof, shall be punished as provided in section 25-4-111.

## 25-4-107. Rooms not used for sleeping.

It is unlawful for any person to sleep or to allow or permit any person to sleep in any workroom of a bakeshop, kitchen, dining room, confectionery, creamery, cheese factory, or other place where food is prepared for sale, served, or sold unless all foods therein handled are at all times in hermetically sealed packages.

## 25-4-108. Work by diseased persons forbidden.

It is unlawful for any employer to permit any person who works in food preparation and is affected with any contagious or infectious disease that is spread by food to work, or for any person so affected to work, in any capacity in which there is a likelihood that the employee would contaminate food or food-contact surfaces with pathogenic organisms or transmit disease to other persons.

## 25-4-109. Enforcement.

(1) It is the duty of the department of public health and environment to enforce this part 1, and, for that purpose, the department has full power at all times to enter every such building, room, basement, enclosure, or premises occupied or used or suspected of being occupied or used for the production, preparation, or manufacture for sale, or the storage, sale, distribution, or transportation of such food, to inspect the premises and all utensils, fixtures, furniture, and machinery used pursuant to the provisions of this subsection (1). Any refusal to permit such inspection shall be

deemed a violation of this part 1. If upon inspection any such food producing or distributing establishment, conveyance, or employer, employee, clerk, driver, or other person is found to be violating any of the provisions of this part 1, or if the production, preparation, manufacture, packing, storage, sale, distribution, or transportation of such food is being conducted in a manner detrimental to the health of the employees and operatives or to the character or quality of the food therein produced, prepared, manufactured, packed, stored, sold, distributed, or conveyed, the department of public health and environment shall issue a written order to the person, firm, or corporation responsible for the violation or condition to abate such condition or violation or to make such changes or improvements as may be necessary to abate them within a reasonable time. Notice of such order may be served by delivering a copy thereof to said person, firm, or corporation or by sending a copy thereof by registered mail, and the receipt thereof through the post office shall be prima facie evidence that notice of said order has been received.

(2) Such person, firm, or corporation has the right to appear in person or by attorney before the department of public health and environment, or the person appointed by it for such purpose, within the time limited in the order and shall be given an opportunity to be heard and to show why such order or instructions should not be obeyed. Such hearing shall be under such rules and regulations as may be prescribed by the department. If after such hearing it appears that the provisions or requirements of this part 1 have not been violated, said order shall be rescinded. If it appears that the requirements or provisions of this part 1 are being violated and that the person, firm, or corporation notified is responsible therefor, said previous order shall be confirmed or amended, as the facts shall warrant, and shall thereupon be final, but such additional time as is necessary may be granted within which to comply with said final order. If such person, firm, or corporation is not present or represented when such final order is made, notice thereof shall be given as provided in subsection (1) of this section. Upon failure of the parties to comply with the first order of the department within the time prescribed when no hearing is demanded or upon failure to comply with the final order within the time specified, the department of public health and environment shall certify the facts to the district attorney of the county in which such violation occurred, and such district attorney shall proceed against the parties for the fines and penalties provided by this part 1 and also for the abatement of the nuisance. The proceedings prescribed in this section for the abatement of nuisance as defined in section 25-4-106 shall not in any manner relieve the violator from prosecution in the first instance for any such violation or from the penalties for such violation prescribed by section 25-4-111.

## 25-4-110. Prosecutions - disposition of fines.

All fines collected under the provisions of this part 1 shall be paid to the county treasurer of the county in which the prosecution is brought, and it is the duty of the district attorneys in the respective counties to prosecute all persons violating or refusing to obey the provisions of this part 1.

## 25-4-111. Penalty.

Any person who violates any of the provisions of this part 1 or refuses to comply with any lawful order or requirement of the department of public health and environment, duly made in writing as provided in section 25-4-109, is guilty of a misdemeanor and, upon conviction thereof, shall be punished for the first offense by a fine of not more than two hundred dollars and for the second and subsequent offenses by a fine of not more than two hundred dollars, or by imprisonment in the county jail for not more than ninety days, or by both such fine and imprisonment. Each day of noncompliance after the expiration of the time limit for abating unsanitary conditions and completing improvements to abate such conditions, as ordered by the department of public health and environment, constitutes a separate offense.

## 25-4-112. Rules.

The state board of health, created in section 25-1-103, may adopt rules as necessary for the implementation of this article.

# PART 2. PRENATAL EXAMINATIONS

## 25-4-201. Pregnant woman to take blood test.

(1) Every licensed health care provider authorized to provide care to a pregnant woman in this state for conditions relating to her pregnancy during the period of gestation or at delivery shall take or cause to be taken a sample of blood of the woman at the time of the first professional visit or during the first trimester for testing pursuant to this section. The blood specimen obtained shall be submitted to an approved laboratory for a standard serological test for syphilis and HIV. Every other person permitted by law to attend pregnant women in this state but not permitted by law to take blood samples shall cause a sample of blood of each pregnant woman to be taken by a licensed health care provider authorized to take blood samples and shall have the sample submitted to an approved laboratory for a standard serological test for syphilis and HIV. A pregnant woman may decline to be tested as specified in this subsection (1) , in which case the licensed health care provider shall document that fact in her medical record.

(2) If a pregnant woman entering a hospital for delivery has not been tested for HIV during her pregnancy, the hospital shall notify the woman that she will be tested for HIV unless she objects and declines the test. If the woman declines to be tested, the hospital shall document that fact in the pregnant woman's medical record.

## 25-4-202. Tests approved by department. (Repealed)

## 25-4-203. Birth certificate - blood test.

In reporting every birth and stillbirth, physicians and others required to make such reports shall state on the certificate whether a blood test for syphilis and HIV has been made upon a specimen of blood taken from the woman who bore the child for which a birth or stillbirth certificate is filed and the approximate date when the specimen was taken. In no event shall the birth certificate state the result of the test.

## 25-4-204. Penalty.

Any licensed physician and surgeon or other person engaged in attendance upon a pregnant woman during the period of gestation or at delivery or any representative of a laboratory who violates the provisions of this part 2 is guilty of a misdemeanor and, upon conviction thereof, shall be punished by a fine of not more than three hundred dollars. Every licensed physician and surgeon or other person engaged in attendance upon a pregnant woman during the period of gestation or at delivery who requests such specimen in accordance with the provisions of section 25-4-201 and whose request is refused is not guilty of a misdemeanor.

## 25-4-205. District attorneys to prosecute.

The district attorneys in the several districts in the state shall prosecute for violation of this part 2 as for other crimes and misdemeanors.

# PART 3. BLINDNESS IN NEWLY BORN

### 25-4-301. Inflammation of eyes.

(1) Any inflammation, swelling, or unusual redness in either one or both eyes of any infant, either apart from or together with any unnatural discharge from the eyes of such infant, independent of the nature of the infection, if any, occurring at any time within two weeks after the birth of such infant shall be known as "inflammation of the eyes of the newly born" (ophthalmia neonatorum) .

(2) It is the duty of any physician, nurse, or other person who assists or is in charge at the birth of an infant or is charged with the care of the infant after birth to treat the eyes of the infant with a prophylaxis in accordance with current standard of care. Such treatment shall be given as soon as practicable after the birth of the infant and always within one hour. If any redness, swelling, inflammation, or gathering of pus appears in the eyes of such infant, or upon the lids or about the eyes, within two weeks after birth, any person charged with care of the infant shall report the same to some competent practicing physician or advanced practice nurse within six hours after its discovery.

(3) Nothing in this section requires medical treatment for the minor child of any person who is a member of a well-recognized church or religious denomination and whose religious convictions, in accordance with the tenets or principles of his or her church or religious denomination, are against medical treatment for disease.

### 25-4-302. Duties of department. (Repealed)


### 25-4-303. Duty to treat eyes. (Repealed)


### 25-4-304. Duties of county, district, or municipal public health director. (Repealed)


### 25-4-305. Penalty. (Repealed)


# PART 4. SEXUALLY TRANSMITTED INFECTIONS


### 25-4-401. Legislative declaration.

(1) The general assembly declares that:

(a) Sexually transmitted infections, regardless of the mode of transmission, impact the public health of the state and are a matter of statewide concern;

(b) Coloradans have a right to receive accurate, confidential, and timely information to make informed decisions that promote their individual physical and mental health and well-being. This right applies to all Coloradans, regardless of geographic location, ethnic or racial background, income, ability, gender, gender identity, or sexual orientation;

(c) Positive, stigma-free messages and comprehensive, evidence-based information must be available to create healthy, safe relationships and a healthier Colorado; and

(d) It is the responsibility of any individual who has knowledge or reasonable grounds to suspect that he or she has a sexually transmitted infection to not intentionally transmit the infection to another individual.

(2) The general assembly further declares that:

(a) Reporting sexually transmitted infections to public health agencies is essential to enable a better understanding of the scope of exposure and the impact of the exposure on the community and to optimize means of sexually transmitted infection control;

(b) Efforts to control sexually transmitted infections include public education, counseling, voluntary testing, linkage to treatment, prevention, and access to services;

(c) Restrictive enforcement measures may be used only when necessary to protect the public health;

(d) Having a sexually transmitted infection, being presumed to have one, or seeking testing for the presence of such an infection must not serve as the basis for discriminatory actions or prevent access to services; and

(e) It is the policy of the state to encourage voluntary testing for sexually transmitted infections and promote linkage to care without perpetuating stigma.

(3) Therefore, the general assembly further declares that the purpose of this part 4 is to protect the public health, empower individuals to take personal responsibility for their sexual health, and to prevent infections that may be sexually transmitted.

## 25-4-402. Definitions.

As used in this part 4:

(1) "Executive director" means the executive director of the state department.

(2) "Health care provider" means a person whose vocation or profession is related to the maintenance of individuals' health or anyone who provides diagnostic screening tests, medical treatment, or other medical services.

(3) "Health officer" means the executive director of the state department, the chief medical officer appointed pursuant to section 25-1-105, or a local director.

(4) "HIV" means human immunodeficiency virus.

(5) "Local director" has the same meaning as set forth in section 25-1-502 for "public health director".

(6) "Local public health agency" means a county or district public health agency established pursuant to section 25-1-506 or a local department of public health.

(7) "Medical emergency" means an acute injury, illness, or exposure that poses an immediate risk to a person's life or long-term health, such that the absence of immediate medical attention could reasonably be expected to result in placing the person's health in serious jeopardy, including a serious impairment to bodily function or a serious dysfunction of any bodily organ or part.

(8) "Minor", unless otherwise specified, means a person who is under eighteen years of age.

(9) "Public safety workers" includes law enforcement officers, peace officers, emergency service providers, and firefighters.

(10) "Sexually transmitted infection" refers to chlamydia, syphilis, gonorrhea, HIV, and relevant types of hepatitis, as well as any other sexually transmitted infection, regardless of mode of transmission, as designated by the state board by rule upon making a finding that the particular sexually transmitted infection is contagious.

(11) "State board" means the state board of health created in section 25-1-103.

(12) "State department" means the state department of public health and environment established in section 25-1-102.

(13) "Test" means any diagnostic, screening, or other test that may be provided in a health care or community-based environment.

(14) "Victim" has the same meaning as defined in section 24-4.1-302 (5) , C.R.S.

## 25-4-403. Eligibility - nondiscrimination.

Notwithstanding any other provision of this part 4 to the contrary, programs and services that provide for the investigation, identification, testing, preventive care, and treatment of sexually transmitted infections are available regardless of a person's actual or perceived race, creed, color, ancestry, national origin, religion, age, sex, sexual orientation, gender identity, mental or physical disability, familial status, marital status, or immigration status.

## 25-4-404. Rules.

(1) The state board, with sufficient involvement and consultation from the state department, the community, and other interested stakeholders, shall adopt rules it deems necessary to carry out the provisions of this part 4, including rules addressing the control and treatment of sexually transmitted infections. The rules are binding on all public health agencies, health officers, and other persons affected by this part 4. The rules must include, at a minimum:

(a) The information that must be reported pursuant to section 25-4-405 and the form, manner, and time frame in which it must be reported; and

(b) The performance standards for anonymous and confidential HIV counseling and testing sites established pursuant to section 25-4-411. Standards must include performance standards for notifying and counseling a person who is diagnosed with a sexually transmitted infection and for notification of his or her partner or partners.

(2) The state department shall create and maintain guidelines, subject to approval by the state board, concerning the public health procedures described in sections 25-4-412 and 25-4-413.

## 25-4-405. Reporting requirements - immunity.

(1) In accordance with the provisions of sections 25-1-122, 25-4-404, 25-4-406, and 12-36-135, C.R.S., for every individual known to the person or entity to have a diagnosis of a sexually transmitted infection or have a positive test for a sexually transmitted infection, the following persons and entities shall report any information required by rule of the state board to the state department or local public health agency, in a form and within a time period designated by rule of the state board:

(a) Every health care provider in the state;

(b) Persons who test, diagnose, or treat sexually transmitted infections in a hospital, clinic, correctional institution, community-based organization, nonclinical setting, or other private or public institution; or

(c) A laboratory or a person performing a test for a case of a sexually transmitted infection.

(2) The reports submitted pursuant to subsection (1) of this section must include the name, date of birth, sex at birth, gender identity, address, and phone number of the individual with the sexually transmitted infection, and the name, address, and phone number of the person making the report. The report must also include any test results and the name, address, and phone number of the health care provider and any other person or agency that referred the specimen for testing.

(3) (a) A person who, in good faith, complies with the reporting and treatment requirements of this part 4 is immune from civil and criminal liability for such actions.

(b) Immunity from liability pursuant to paragraph (a) of this subsection (3) does not apply to a negligent act or omission on the part of the health care provider.

## 25-4-406. Reports - confidentiality.

(1) The public health reports required pursuant to section 25-4-405 and any records resulting from compliance with that section held by the state department and local public health agencies, or any health care provider, facility, third-party payor, physician, clinic, laboratory, blood bank, health records database, or other agency, are confidential information. The information may only be released, shared with any agency or institution, or made public, upon subpoena, search warrant, discovery proceedings, or otherwise, under the following circumstances:

(a) For statistical purposes, but only in a manner such that an individual cannot be identified from the information released;

(b) To the extent necessary to enforce the provisions of this part 4 and related rules concerning the treatment, control, prevention, and investigation of sexually transmitted infections by public health officers;

(c) To health care providers and medical personnel in a medical emergency to the extent necessary to protect the health or life of the named party;

(d) To agencies responsible for receiving or investigating reports of child abuse or neglect in accordance with the provisions of the "Child Protection Act of 1987", part 3 of article 3 of title 19, C.R.S., if an officer or employee of the state department or a local public health agency makes a report of child abuse or neglect; or

(e) Pursuant to section 18-3-415.5, C.R.S., to a district attorney for the information specified in said section, or, for the purposes of a sentencing hearing, oral and documentary evidence limited to whether a person who has been bound over for trial for any sexual offense, as described in section 18-3-415.5, C.R.S., was provided with notice or discussion that he or she had tested positive for a sexually transmitted infection and the date of such notice or discussion.

(2) An officer or employee of the state department or a local public health agency must not be examined in any judicial, executive, legislative, or other proceedings as to the existence or content of any individual's report by such department pursuant to this part 4 or as to the existence of the content of the reports received pursuant to section 25-4-405 or the result of an investigation conducted pursuant to section 25-4-408. The provisions of this subsection (2) do not apply to administrative or judicial proceedings held pursuant to section 25-4-412 or 25-4-413.

(3) Information in medical records concerning the diagnosis and treatment of a sexually transmitted infection is considered medical information, is not part of public health reports, and is protected from unauthorized disclosure pursuant to the provisions of section 18-4-412, C.R.S.

## 25-4-407. Reporting requirements - research exemption.

(1) The state board shall approve an exemption from the reporting requirements of section 25-4-405 for a research activity that meets all of the following criteria:

(a) The research activity is fully described by a research protocol;

(b) The research activity is subject to review by and is governed by the federal department of health and human services;

(c) The research activity has as protocol objectives either:

(I) The investigation of the effectiveness of a medical therapy or vaccine to prevent infection; or

(II) Basic medical research into the cellular mechanisms that cause sexually transmitted infections;

(d) The research activity is reviewed and approved by a duly constituted institutional review board in accordance with the regulations established by the secretary of the federal department of health and human services;

(e) The research for the research activity has provided information that demonstrates that the research will be facilitated by an exemption specified in this section; and

(f) The research activity has been determined to have a potential health benefit.

(2) The research exemption authorized in this section does not alter the reporting requirements of persons and researchers who are otherwise required to make reports when engaged in any treatment or testing outside the scope of or prior to enrollment in an approved research protocol, including required reporting of other reportable diseases.

## 25-4-408. Infection control - duties.

(1) It is the duty of the executive director, health officers, or local directors to investigate sexually transmitted infections and to use appropriate means to prevent the spread of such sexually transmitted infections.

(2) As part of infection control efforts, it is the duty of the executive director, health officers, and local directors to provide public information; risk-reduction education; voluntary testing; counseling; age-appropriate, medically accurate, and culturally responsive educational materials for school use; and professional education for public safety workers and health care providers.

(3) The state department shall provide current, evidence-based, and medically accurate programs under which the state department and local public health agencies may perform the following tasks:

(a) Provide and disseminate to health care providers digital, written, and verbal presentations describing the epidemiology, prevention, testing, diagnosis, treatment, medical services, counseling, and other aspects of sexually transmitted infections;

(b) Provide consultation to agencies and organizations, including those employing public safety workers, regarding appropriate policies for prevention, testing, education, confidentiality, and control of sexually transmitted infections;

(c) Conduct health information programs to inform the general public of the medical and psychosocial aspects of sexually transmitted infections, including updated information on how these infections are transmitted and may be prevented. The state department shall provide and distribute to the residents of the state, at no charge, printed and electronic information and instructions concerning the risks from sexually transmitted infections, the prevention of sexually transmitted infections, and the necessity for testing.

(d) Update and provide educational information concerning sexually transmitted infections that employers may use in the workplace;

(e) Provide and implement medically accurate and culturally appropriate educational risk-reduction programs for specific populations at higher risk for infection; and

(f) Update and provide accurate, age-appropriate, and culturally responsive sexually transmitted infection prevention curricula for use at the discretion of secondary and middle schools in the state.

(4) When investigating sexually transmitted infections, the state department and local public health agencies, within their respective jurisdictions, may inspect and have access to medical and laboratory records relevant to their investigation.

(5) Every person who is confined, detained, or imprisoned in a state, county, or city hospital; an institution for persons with behavioral or mental health disorders; a home for dependent children; a correctional facility; or any other private or charitable institution where a person may be confined, detained, or imprisoned by order of a court of this state must be examined for and, if diagnosed with a sexually transmitted infection, referred for treatment of such sexually transmitted infection, in accordance with current standards of care, by the health authorities having jurisdiction over the given institution. The managing authorities of any such institution shall make available to the health authorities whatever portion of their respective institution as may be necessary for a clinic or hospital for treatment of a person's sexually transmitted infection with current and evidence-based standards of care in a professional manner.

(6) (a) When a public safety worker, emergency or other health care provider, first responder, victim of crime, or a staff member of a correctional facility, the state department, or a local public health agency has been exposed to blood or other bodily fluids for which there is an evidence-based reason to believe it may result in exposure to a sexually transmitted infection, the state department or local public health agency, within their respective jurisdictions, shall assist in the evaluation and treatment of any involved persons by:

(I) Accessing information on the incident and any persons involved to determine whether a potential exposure to infection occurred;

(II) When the potential for exposure has been determined by the state department or a local public health agency, examining and testing any involved persons to determine infection;

(III) Communicating relevant information and laboratory test results on involved persons directly to the involved person or to his or her attending health care provider, if the confidentiality of such information and test results are acknowledged by the recipient and adequately protected, as provided for in section 25-4-406; and

(IV) Providing timely counseling to any involved persons on the potential health risks resulting from exposure to infection; prophylaxis and treatment of infections until cured, where possible; treatment to prevent progression of such infections; measures for preventing transmission to others; and the necessity of regular medical evaluations.

(b) For the purposes of this subsection (6) , the employer of an involved person shall comply with the provisions of section 25-4-406 and ensure that relevant information and laboratory test results on the involved person are kept confidential.

## 25-4-409. Minors - treatment - consent.

(1) (a) A health care provider or facility, if consulted by a patient who is a minor, shall perform, at the minor's request, a diagnostic examination for a sexually transmitted infection. The health care provider or facility shall treat the minor for a sexually transmitted infection, if necessary; discuss prevention measures, where applicable; and include appropriate therapies and prescriptions.
(b) If a minor requests a diagnostic examination, care, prevention services, or treatment for a sexually transmitted infection, the health care provider who provides such services is not civilly or criminally liable for performing the service, but the immunity from liability does not apply to any negligent act or omission by the health care provider.
(2) The consent of a parent or legal guardian is not a prerequisite for a minor to receive a consultation, examination, or treatment for sexually transmitted infections. For the purposes of this section, health care provided to a minor is confidential, and information related to that care must not be divulged to any person other than the minor; except that the reporting required pursuant to the "Child Protection Act of 1987", part 3 of article 3 of title 19, C.R.S., still applies. If the minor is thirteen years of age or younger, the health care provider may involve the minor's parent or legal guardian. A health care provider shall counsel the minor on the importance of bringing his or her parent or legal guardian into the minor's confidence regarding the consultation, exam, or treatment.

## 25-4-410. Patient consent - rights of patients, victims, and pregnant women.

(1) (a) Except as provided in paragraph (b) of this subsection (1) , a health care provider, hospital, clinic, laboratory, or other private or public institution shall not test, or cause by any means to have tested, any specimen of a patient for a sexually transmitted infection without the knowledge and consent of the patient, which is satisfied as follows:
(I) The patient signs a general consent form for treatment;
(II) The patient is provided with a verbal consultation about sexually transmitted infections, testing, and reporting requirements; and
(III) The patient is provided with the opportunity to opt out of testing, following the verbal consultation.
(b) Knowledge and consent for testing need not be given in the following circumstances:
(I) When a public safety worker, emergency or other health care provider, first responder, victim of crime, or a staff member of a correctional facility, the state department, or a local public health agency is exposed to blood or other bodily fluids under circumstances that pose an evidence-based risk of transmission of a sexually transmitted infection;
(II) When a patient's medical condition is such that knowledge and consent cannot be obtained;
(III) When the testing is done as part of a seroprevalence survey, but only if all personal identifiers are removed from the specimens prior to the laboratory testing;
(IV) When the patient to be tested is sentenced to and in the custody of the department of corrections or is committed to the Colorado mental health institute at Pueblo and confined to the forensic ward or the minimum or maximum security ward of the institute; and
(V) Notwithstanding the provisions of section 25-4-201, when a pregnant woman presents in labor in a hospital, and the results of syphilis and HIV tests are not on record, a rapid test will be performed to determine whether to provide prophylaxis to prevent transmission of sexually transmitted infections to the infant.
(c) A health care provider shall notify a patient who was tested for a sexually transmitted infection without his or her knowledge and consent pursuant to section 25-4-408. The notification must be prompt, personal, and confidential and inform the individual that a test sample was taken and that the results of the test may be obtained upon his or her request.
(2) It is the duty of every health care provider in the state who, during the course of an examination, discovers the existence of a sexually transmitted infection, or who treats a patient for such an infection, to inform the person of the interpretations of laboratory results and counsel the person on measures for preventing transmission to others; prophylaxis and treatment of infections until cured, where possible; treatment to prevent progression of such infections; and the necessity

of regular medical evaluations. Such information and laboratory test results are considered medical information and are protected from unauthorized disclosure.

(3) A pregnant woman seeking prenatal care must be informed that syphilis and HIV testing are part of standard prenatal testing and given the opportunity to decline such tests pursuant to section 25-4-201. A pregnant woman must be informed that test results inform the decision as to whether to provide prophylaxis and prevent transmission of a sexually transmitted infection to her infant.

(4) When an adult or minor has been exposed to blood or other bodily fluids as a result of a sexual offense involving sexual penetration, as defined in section 18-3-401 (6) , C.R.S., for which there is an evidence-based reason to believe that the sexual offense may have resulted in exposure to a sexually transmitted infection, the state department or local public health agency, within their respective jurisdictions, shall assist in the evaluation and treatment of any involved person by:

(a) Accessing information on the incident and any persons involved to determine whether a potential exposure to a sexually transmitted infection occurred;

(b) When potential for exposure has been confirmed by the state department or a local public health agency, examining and testing any involved person to determine whether or not an involved person has been infected;

(c) Communicating relevant information and laboratory test results on the involved person to his or her attending health care provider or directly to the involved person if the confidentiality of the information and test results are acknowledged by the recipient and adequately protected, as determined by the state department or local public health agency; and

(d) Providing immediate counseling to any involved person on the potential health risks and available post-exposure treatment.

## 25-4-411. Confidential counseling and testing sites - legislative declaration.

(1) Confidential HIV counseling and testing services are the preferred screening services for the detection of a possible infection. However, the state department shall, consistent with generally accepted practices for the protection of the public health and safety, conduct an anonymous HIV counseling and testing program at selected sites. The state department may operate sites or separately contract through local public health agencies to conduct HIV testing in conjunction with counseling and testing sites, subject to maintaining standards for performance as set by rule of the state board pursuant to section 25-4-404.

(2) (a) The disclosure of a person's name, address, phone number, birth date, or other personally identifying information is not required as a condition to be tested for HIV at an anonymous testing site. Any provision of this part 4 that requires or can be construed as requiring a person seeking testing to report or disclose such information does not apply to persons seeking to be tested at an anonymous testing site created pursuant to this section.

(b) Notwithstanding the provisions of subsection (2) (a) of this section, the age, gender, or gender identity of a person seeking to be tested at a testing site may be required.

## 25-4-412. Public safety - public health procedures - orders for compliance - petitions - hearings.

(1) An order or restrictive measure directed to a person with a sexually transmitted infection must only be used as the last resort when other measures to protect the public health have failed, including all reasonable efforts, which must be documented, to obtain the voluntary cooperation of the person who may be subject to the order or restrictive measure. The order or restrictive measure must be applied serially with the least intrusive measures used first. The state department or local public health agency has the burden of proof to show that specified grounds exist for the issuance of the order or restrictive measure and that the terms and conditions imposed are no more restrictive than necessary to protect the public health.

(2) When the executive director or the local director, within his or her respective jurisdiction, knows or has reason to believe, because of evidence-based, medical, or epidemiological information, that a person has a sexually transmitted infection and poses a credible risk to the

public health, he or she may issue an order to:

(a) Require the person to be examined and tested to determine whether he or she has acquired a sexually transmitted infection;

(b) Require him or her to report to a qualified health care provider for counseling regarding sexually transmitted infections, information on treatment, and how to avoid transmitting sexually transmitted infections to others; or

(c) Direct a person with a sexually transmitted infection to cease and desist from specific conduct that poses risks to the public health, but only if the executive director or local director has determined that clear and convincing evidence exists to believe that such person has been ordered to report for counseling or has received counseling by a qualified health care provider and continues to demonstrate behavior that poses an evidence-based risk to the public health.

(3) (a) If a person violates a cease-and-desist order issued pursuant to paragraph (c) of subsection (2) of this section and it is shown that the person poses an evidence-based risk to the public health, the executive director or the local director may enforce the cease-and-desist order by imposing such restrictions upon the person as are necessary to prevent the specific conduct that risks the public health. Restrictions may include required participation in evaluative, therapeutic, and counseling programs.

(b) Any restriction must be in writing, setting forth the name of the person to be restricted; the initial period of time that the restrictive order is effective, not to exceed three months; the terms of the restrictions; and any other conditions necessary to protect the public health. Restrictions must be imposed in the least restrictive manner necessary to protect the public health.

(c) The executive director or local director who issues an order pursuant to this subsection (3) shall review petitions for reconsideration from the person affected by the order. Restriction orders issued by local directors shall be submitted for review and approval by the executive director.

(4) (a) (I) Upon the issuance of an order by the state department or a local public health agency pursuant to subsection (2) or (3) of this section, the state department or local public health agency shall give notice promptly, personally, and confidentially to the person who is the subject of the order. The notice must state the grounds and provisions of the order and notify the person who is the subject of the order that he or she has the right to refuse to comply with the order, that he or she has the right to be present at a judicial hearing in the district court to review the order, and that he or she may have an attorney appear on his or her behalf at the hearing. If a respondent to any such action cannot afford an attorney, one shall be appointed for him or her at the commencement of the court process.

(II) If the person who is the subject of the order refuses to comply with the order and refuses to voluntarily cooperate with the executive director or local director, the executive director or local director may petition the district court for an order of compliance with the order. The executive director or local director shall request that the county or city and county attorney, or district public health agency, file such petition in the district court. However, if the county or city and county attorney, or district public health agency, refuses to act, the executive director may file such petition and be represented by the attorney general.

(III) If an order of compliance is requested, the court shall hear the matter within fourteen days following the request. Notice of the place, date, and time of the hearing must be by personal service or, if the person who is the subject of the order is not available, mailed by prepaid certified mail, return receipt requested, at the person's last-known address. Proof of mailing by the state department or local public health agency is sufficient notice under this section. The state department or local public health agency has the burden of proof to show by clear and convincing evidence that the specified grounds exist for the issuance of the order, the need for compliance, and the terms and conditions imposed in the order are no more restrictive than necessary to protect the public health.

(IV) An officer or employee of the state department or a local public health agency must not be examined in any judicial, legislative, executive, or other proceedings as to the existence or content of any individual's report, other than the respondent in a proceeding authorized by this section, made by such department or agency pursuant to this part 4; the existence of the content of the reports received pursuant to section 25-4-405; or the result of an investigation conducted pursuant to section 25-4-408.

(V) Upon the conclusion of the hearing, the court shall issue appropriate orders affirming, modifying, or dismissing the original order.

(b) If the executive director or local director does not petition the district court for an order of compliance within thirty days after the person who is the subject of the order refuses to comply, the person may petition the district court for dismissal of the order. If the district court dismisses the order, the fact that the order was issued must be expunged from the records of the state department or the local public health agency.

(5) Any hearing conducted pursuant to this section must be closed and confidential, and any transcripts or records related to the hearing are also confidential.

## 25-4-413. Emergency public health procedures - injunctions.

(1) When the procedures set forth in section 25-4-412 have been exhausted or cannot be satisfied and the executive director or a local director, within his or her respective jurisdiction, knows or has reason to believe, based on accurate, evidence-based, and medical and epidemiological information, that a person has acquired a sexually transmitted infection and that the person presents an imminent risk to the public health, the executive director or the local director may bring an action in district court, pursuant to rule 65 of the Colorado rules of civil procedure, to enjoin the person from engaging in or continuing to engage in specific conduct that poses an evidence-based risk to the public health. The executive director or the local director shall request the district attorney to file such an action in the district court. However, if the district attorney refuses to act, the executive director may file the action and be represented by the attorney general. The court is authorized to hold an ex parte proceeding when necessary.

(2) (a) Under the circumstances outlined in subsection (1) of this section, in addition to the injunction order, the district court may issue other appropriate court orders, including an order to take the person into custody for a period not to exceed seventy-two hours and place him or her in a facility designated or approved by the executive director. A custody order issued for the purpose of counseling and testing to determine whether the person has a sexually transmitted infection must provide for the immediate release from custody of a person who tests negative and may provide for counseling or other appropriate measures to be imposed on a person who tests positive.

(b) The state department or local public health agency shall give notice of the order, promptly, personally, and confidentially, to the person who is the subject of the order. The order must state the grounds and provisions of the order and notify the person that he or she has the right to refuse to comply with the order, that he or she has the right to be present at a hearing to review the order, and that he or she may have an attorney appear on his or her behalf at the hearing. If a respondent to any such action cannot afford an attorney, one shall be appointed for him or her at the commencement of the proceedings.

(c) If the person contests testing or treatment, invasive medical procedures shall not be carried out prior to a hearing held pursuant to subsection (3) of this section.

(3) An order issued by a district court pursuant to subsection (2) of this section is subject to review in a court hearing. Notice of the place, date, and time of the court hearing shall be given promptly, personally, and confidentially to the person who is the subject of the court order. The court shall conduct the hearing no later than forty-eight hours after the issuance of the order. The person has the right to be present at the hearing and have an attorney appear on his or her behalf at the hearing. If a respondent to any such action cannot afford an attorney, one shall be appointed for him or her at the beginning of the injunction process. Upon the conclusion of the hearing, the court shall issue appropriate orders affirming, modifying, or dismissing the original order.

(4) The state department or local public health agency has the burden of proof to show by clear and convincing evidence that evidence-based grounds exist for the issuance of any court order made pursuant to subsection (2) or (3) of this section.

(5) A hearing conducted by the district court pursuant to this section must be closed and confidential, and any transcripts or records relating to the hearing are also confidential.
(6) An order entered by the district court pursuant to subsection (2) or (3) of this section must impose terms and conditions no more restrictive than necessary to protect the public health.

## 25-4-414. Penalties.

(1) A health care provider, laboratory employee, or other person who is required to make a report pursuant to section 25-4-405 and who fails to make such a report commits a class 2 petty offense and, upon conviction, shall be punished by a fine of not more than three hundred dollars.
(2) A health care provider; officer or employee of the state department; officer or employee of a local public health agency; or a person, firm, or corporation that violates section 25-4-406 by breaching the confidentiality requirements of such section is guilty of a misdemeanor and, upon conviction, shall be punished by a fine of not less than five hundred dollars but not more than five thousand dollars or by imprisonment in the county jail for not less than six months but not more than twenty-four months or by both fine and imprisonment as ordered by a court.

# PART 5. TUBERCULOSIS

## 25-4-500.3. Definitions.

As used in this part 5, unless the context otherwise requires:
(1) "Active tuberculosis" means a diagnosis of tuberculosis demonstrated by clinical, bacteriologic, or diagnostic imaging evidence, or a combination thereof. A person who has been diagnosed as having active tuberculosis and has not completed a course of antituberculosis treatment is still considered to have active tuberculosis and may be infectious.
(2) "Board of health" means the state board of health created in section 25-1-103.
(3) "Contact" means a person who has shared the same air space with a person who has active tuberculosis.
(4) "Contagious" means having a disease that may be transmitted from one living person to another through direct or indirect contact.
(5) "Department" means the department of public health and environment.
(6) "Health officer" means the executive director of the department, the state chief medical officer, and county or district public health directors.
(7) "Infectious" means contagious.
(8) "Isolation" means separation of a person infected, or suspected to be infected, with tuberculosis from other persons to prevent the spread of tuberculosis.
(9) "Latent tuberculosis infection" means that tuberculosis organisms are present in a person's body, but the person does not have tuberculosis or symptoms, nor is the person infectious. Such a person usually has a positive reaction to the tuberculin skin test.
(10) "Local health officer" means the chief medical health officer of a county, district, or municipal public health agency or the health officer for a public health nursing service.
(11) "Multidrug-resistant tuberculosis" means tuberculosis caused by tuberculosis organisms that are resistant to at least the drugs isoniazid and rifampin.
(12) "Screening" means measures used to identify persons who have active tuberculosis or latent tuberculosis infection.
(13) "State chief medical officer" means the chief medical officer of the department, as described in section 25-1-105, or the executive director of the department.
(14) "Suspected case of active tuberculosis", "suspected case of tuberculosis", "suspected tuberculosis", or "suspected tuberculosis case" means a diagnosis of tuberculosis is being considered for a person, whether or not antituberculosis therapy has been started.
(15) "Tubercle bacilli" means tuberculosis organisms.

(16) "Tuberculosis" means a potentially fatal contagious disease caused by the bacterial microorganisms of the mycobacterium tuberculosis complex that can affect almost any part of the body but most commonly affects the lungs.

## 25-4-501. Tuberculosis declared to be an infectious and communicable disease.

It is hereby declared that tuberculosis is an infectious and communicable disease, that it endangers the population of this state, and that the treatment and control of such disease is a state and local responsibility. It is further declared that the emergence of multidrug-resistant tuberculosis requires that this threat be addressed with a coherent and consistent strategy in order to protect the public health. To the end that tuberculosis may be brought better under control and multidrug-resistant tuberculosis prevented, it is further declared that the department and local public health agencies shall, within available resources, cooperatively promote control and treatment of persons suffering from tuberculosis.

## 25-4-502. Tuberculosis to be reported.

(1) Every attending physician and other persons either treating or having knowledge of active or suspected tuberculosis in this state shall make a report to the department in accordance with section 25-1-122 (1) on every person known by said physician or other person to have active or suspected tuberculosis.

(2) Any health care facility or other similar private or public institution in this state shall make a report to the department in accordance with section 25-1-122 (1) on every person having active or suspected tuberculosis who comes into its care or observation.

(3) All clinical laboratories rendering diagnostic service shall report to the department in accordance with section 25-1-122 (1) , within twenty-four hours after diagnosis, the full name and other available data relating to the person whose sputa or other specimens submitted for examination reveal the presence of tubercle bacilli.

## 25-4-503. Examination of sputum.(Deleted by amendment)

## 25-4-504. Statistical case register.(Deleted by amendment)

## 25-4-505. Laboratories to report.(Deleted by amendment)

## 25-4-506. Investigation and examination of suspected or known tuberculosis cases.

(1) The state chief medical officer and all local health officers are directed to use every available means to investigate immediately and ascertain the existence of all reported or suspected cases of active tuberculosis within the health officer's jurisdiction, to determine the sources of such infections, and to identify and evaluate the contacts of such cases and offer treatment as appropriate. In carrying out such investigations, such health officer is invested with full powers of inspection and examination of all persons known to be infected with active tuberculosis and is directed to make or cause to be made such examinations as are deemed necessary of persons who, on reasonable grounds, are suspected of having active tuberculosis in an infectious form.

(2) Whenever a health officer determines on reasonable grounds that an examination of any person is necessary for the preservation and protection of the public health, the health officer shall issue a written order directing medical examination, setting forth the name of the person to be examined, the time and place of the examination, and such other terms and conditions as the health officer

may deem necessary. A copy of such order shall be served upon the person. Such an examination may be made by a licensed physician or advanced practice nurse of the person's own choice under such terms and conditions as the health officer shall specify.

(3) Any person who depends exclusively on prayer for healing in accordance with the teachings of any well-recognized religious sect, denomination, or organization, and claims exemptions on such grounds, shall nevertheless be subject to examination, and the provisions of this part 5 regarding compulsory reporting of communicable diseases and isolations shall apply where there is probable cause to suspect that such person has active tuberculosis. Such person shall not be required to submit to any medical treatment or to go to or be confined in a hospital or other medical institution if the person can safely be isolated in the person's own home or other suitable place of the person's choice.

(4) A health officer may conduct screening programs of populations that are at increased risk of developing tuberculosis or having latent tuberculosis infection and offer treatment as appropriate. Such screening programs may be implemented by a local health officer with the approval of the state chief medical officer.

## 25-4-507. Isolation order - enforcement - court review.

(1) (a) Whenever a health officer determines that isolation of a person in a particular tuberculosis case is necessary for the preservation and protection of the public health, the health officer shall make an isolation order in writing.

(b) When a health officer is determining whether to issue an isolation order for a person, the health officer shall consider, but is not limited to, the following factors:

(I) Whether the person has active tuberculosis;

(II) If the person is violating the rules promulgated by the board of health or the orders issued by the appropriate health officer to comply with rules or orders; and

(III) Whether the person presents a substantial risk of exposing other persons to an imminent danger of infection.

(c) All isolation orders shall set forth the name of the person to be isolated and the initial period, not to exceed six months, during which the order shall remain effective, the place of isolation, and such other terms and conditions as may be immediately necessary to protect the public health. The isolation order shall advise the person being detained that he or she has the right to request release from detention by contacting a person designated in the order and that the detention shall not continue for more than five business days after the request for release, unless the detention is authorized by court order. The health officer shall serve a copy of the isolation order upon the person. The person shall be reexamined at the time the initial order expires to ascertain whether or not the tuberculous condition continues to be infectious. When it has been medically determined that the person no longer has active tuberculosis, the person shall be relieved from all further liability or duty imposed by this part 5, and the health officer shall rescind the order.

(d) A health officer may detain a person who is the subject of an isolation order issued pursuant to this subsection (1) without a prior court order. The health officer may detain the person in a hospital or other appropriate place for examination or treatment.

(2) In a case of a person with multidrug-resistant tuberculosis, the health officer may issue an isolation order to such person if it is determined that the person has ceased taking prescribed medications against medical advice. Such order may be issued even if the person is no longer contagious so long as the person has not completed an entire course of therapy.

(3) (a) If a person detained pursuant to an isolation order requests to be released, the detaining authority shall release the person not later than five business days after the person requests the release, absent a court order authorizing detention. Upon receipt of a request for release, the detaining authority shall apply for a court order authorizing continued detention of the person. The detaining authority shall make the application within seventy-two hours after the person requests release or, if the seventy-two-hour period ends on a Saturday, Sunday, or legal holiday, by the end of the first business day following the Saturday, Sunday, or legal holiday. The application shall

include a request for an expedited hearing.

(b) In any court proceeding to enforce an isolation order, the health officer shall prove the particular circumstances constituting the necessity for the detention by clear and convincing evidence. Any person who is subject to an isolation order has the right to be represented by counsel and, upon request, counsel shall be provided to the person.

(c) The request for release or filing of an application for a court order to continue an isolation order shall not stay the isolation order.

(d) In reviewing the application to continue the isolation order, the court shall not conduct a de novo review. The court shall consider the existing administrative record and any supplemental evidence the court deems relevant.

(e) Upon completion of the hearing, the court shall issue an order continuing, modifying, or dismissing the isolation order.

(f) A hearing conducted pursuant to this section shall be closed and confidential, and any transcripts relating to the hearing shall be confidential.

## 25-4-508. Inspection of records.

Authorized department personnel may inspect and have access to all medical records of all medical practitioners, hospitals, institutions, and clinics, both public and private, where persons with known or suspected tuberculosis are treated and shall provide consultation services regarding the control of tuberculosis and the care of persons having tuberculosis to health care providers or any other persons having responsibility for the care of persons with tuberculosis. Authorized department personnel shall also have access to laboratory records of persons tested for tuberculosis.

## 25-4-509. Violations - penalty.

(1) Any person who, after service upon him or her of an order of a health officer directing his or her isolation or examination as provided in sections 25-4-506 and 25-4-507, violates or fails to comply with the order is guilty of a misdemeanor and, upon conviction thereof, in addition to any and all other penalties that may be imposed by law upon such convictions, the court may make an appropriate order providing for examination, isolation, or treatment.

(2) Any person, firm, or corporation that fails to make the reports required by this part 5 or knowingly makes any false report is guilty of a misdemeanor and, upon conviction thereof, shall be punished by a fine of not more than five hundred dollars.

(3) Upon the receipt of information that any examination, isolation, or treatment order made and served as provided in this part 5 has been violated, the health officer shall advise the district attorney of the judicial district in which such violation occurred of the pertinent facts relating to the violation.

## 25-4-510. Jurisdiction.

District courts shall have original jurisdiction under this part 5.

## 25-4-511. Duties of board of health and department - confidentiality of records - rules.

(1) The board of health is authorized to adopt such rules as are deemed necessary, appropriate, and consistent with good medical practice in the state of Colorado for the treatment and control of persons with tuberculosis.

(2) Subject to available appropriations, the department may contract with local public health agencies to provide assistance with tuberculosis treatment and control. The department shall retain the authority to, when necessary:

(a) Direct any program of investigation and examination of suspected tuberculosis cases, including persons who have had contact with a person who has suspected or confirmed active tuberculosis, and the administration of antituberculosis chemotherapy or the treatment of a latent tuberculosis infection on an outpatient basis where appropriate;

(b) Perform such other duties and have such other powers with relation to the provisions, objects, and purposes of this part 5 as the board of health shall prescribe.

(3) Except as otherwise provided by law, all records kept by the department and by local public health agencies and all records retained in a county coroner's office in accordance with section 30-10-606 (4) (c) , C.R.S., as a result of the investigation of tuberculosis shall be kept strictly confidential and shall only be shared to the extent necessary for the investigation, treatment, control, and prevention of tuberculosis; except that every effort shall be made to limit disclosure of personal identifying information to the minimal amount necessary to accomplish the public health purpose.

## 25-4-512. Nondiscrimination in the provision of general services.

Notwithstanding any other provision of this part 5 to the contrary, programs and services that provide for the investigation, identification, testing, preventive care, or treatment of tuberculosis shall be available to a person regardless of his or her race, religion, gender, ethnicity, national origin, or immigration status.

## 25-4-513. Funding.

The department shall provide funding to local public health agencies for tuberculosis treatment and control and shall consider the number of active, suspected, and latent tuberculosis cases undergoing therapy in each agency's jurisdiction when determining funding levels.

# PART 6. RABIES CONTROL

## 25-4-601. Definitions.

As used in this part 6, unless the context otherwise requires:

(1) "County board of health" means the body acting as the county or district board of health under the provisions of section 25-1-508.

(2) "Health department" means the department of public health and environment or any county or district public health agency organized and maintained under the provisions of part 5 of article 1 of this title.

(3) "Health officer" means the person appointed as the public health director of a district, county, city, or town under the provisions of section 25-1-509.

(4) "Inoculation against rabies" means the administration of the antirabies vaccine as approved by the department of public health and environment or the county or district department of health.

(5) "Owner" means any person who has a right of property in a dog, cat, other pet animal, or other mammal, or who keeps or harbors a dog, cat, other pet animal, or other mammal, or who has it in his care or acts as its custodian.

## 25-4-602. Notice to health department or officer if animal affected or suspected of being affected by rabies.

Whenever a dog, cat, other pet animal, or other mammal is affected by rabies or suspected of being affected by rabies or has been bitten by an animal known or suspected to be affected by rabies, the owner of the dog, cat, other pet animal, or other mammal, or any person having knowledge thereof, shall forthwith notify the health department or health officer in the county, city, or town in which such animal is located, stating precisely where such animal may be found.

## 25-4-603. Report of person bitten by animal to health department or health officer.

Every physician after his first professional attendance upon a person bitten by a dog, cat, other pet animal, or other mammal, or any person having knowledge thereof, shall report to the health department or health officer in accordance with the provisions of section 25-1-122 (1) .

## 25-4-604. Animal attacking or biting person to be confined - examination.

The health department or health officer shall serve notice upon the owner of a dog, cat, other pet animal, or other mammal which has attacked or bitten a person to confine the animal at the expense of the owner upon his premises or at a pound or other place designated in the notice for a period designated by the department of public health and environment. The health department, health officer, or his representative shall be permitted by the owner of such dog, cat, other pet animal, or other mammal to examine the animal at any time within the period of confinement to determine whether such animal shows symptoms of rabies. No person shall obstruct or interfere with the authorized person in making such examination.

## 25-4-605. Animals bitten by animals known or suspected of having rabies to be confined.

The health department or health officer shall serve notice in writing upon the owner of a dog, cat, other pet animal, or other mammal known to have been bitten by an animal known or suspected of having rabies requiring the owner to immediately treat and confine such animal by procedures outlined by the department of public health and environment.

## 25-4-606. Animals to be confined to prevent spread of rabies.

Whenever the board of health of a health department or the county board of health has reason to believe or has been notified by the department of public health and environment that there is imminent danger that rabies may spread within that county or district, such board shall serve public notice by publication in a newspaper of general circulation in such county or district covered by such department requiring the owners of dogs, cats, other pet animals, or other mammals specified to confine such dogs, cats, pet animals, or mammals for such period as may be necessary to prevent the spread of rabies in such county or district.

## 25-4-607. Order of board of health requiring inoculation of animals - veterinarian waiver of order.

(1) (a) When it is deemed advisable in the interest of public health and safety, the board of health of an organized health department or a county board of health may order that all dogs, cats, other pet animals, or other mammals in the county or district be vaccinated against rabies, such vaccination to be performed by a licensed veterinarian.

(b) Notwithstanding the provisions of paragraph (a) of this subsection (1) , a board of health of an organized health department or a county board of health shall not order the inoculation of dogs, cats, or ferrets against rabies any more frequently than is recommended in the "Compendium of Animal Rabies Control" as promulgated by the national association of state public health veterinarians.

(2) A veterinarian, with the written consent of an animal's owner, may issue a written waiver pursuant to the rules of the health department, exempting an animal from a rabies vaccination order if the veterinarian, in his or her professional opinion, determines that the rabies inoculation is contraindicated due to the animal's medical condition.

(3) (a) The executive director of the health department shall enact rules allowing for the exemption of an animal from a rabies vaccination due to the medical condition of the animal.

(b) The owner of an animal seeking an exemption from a rabies vaccination for his or her animal must provide the veterinarian with written consent for the exemption.

(c) A veterinarian supplying a waiver exempting an animal from a rabies vaccination, county, district, and municipal health departments, their assistants and employees, the health department, health officers, and anyone enforcing this part 6 shall not be liable for any subsequent accident, disease, injury, or quarantine that may occur as a result of an animal exempted from a rabies vaccination pursuant to the rules of the health department.

(4) A waiver executed pursuant to this section shall be accepted and recognized by any local or regional authority issuing licenses for the ownership of animals.

## 25-4-608. Notice of order requiring inoculation of animals.

The order of a board of health of a health department or a county board of health requiring inoculation of all dogs, cats, other pet animals, or other mammals shall not become effective until twenty-four hours after notice of adoption of the order requiring inoculation of all dogs, cats, other pet animals, or other mammals has been published in a newspaper of general circulation in the county or district.

## 25-4-609. Effect of order requiring inoculation of animals.

Sections 25-4-610 and 25-4-611 shall be in force and effect only in those counties, districts, or portions of counties or districts where an order requiring inoculation of all dogs, cats, other pet animals, or other mammals is in effect.

## 25-4-610. Uninoculated animals not to run at large - impounding and disposition of animals.

It is unlawful for any owner of any dog, cat, other pet animal, or other mammal which has not been inoculated as required by the order of the county board of health or board of health of a health department to allow it to run at large. The health department or health officer may capture and impound any such dog, cat, other pet animal, or other mammal found running at large and dispose of such animal in accordance with local program policy. Such power to impound and dispose shall extend to any and all animals unclaimed and found or suspected to be affected by rabies, whether wild or domestic. The division of parks and wildlife shall cooperate with and aid the health department or health officer in the enforcement of this section as it affects animals found or suspected to be affected by rabies when such animals are in its care, jurisdiction, or control.

## 25-4-611. Report to state department.

Each health department or health officer shall furnish information to the department of public health and environment concerning all cases of rabies and the prevalence of rabies within the county at any time such information is requested by the department of public health and environment.

## 25-4-612. Enforcement of part 6.

The health officer or health department shall enforce the provisions of this part 6, and the sheriff and his deputies and the police officers in each incorporated municipality and the division of parks and wildlife shall be aides and are instructed to cooperate with the health department or health officer in carrying out the provisions of this part 6.

## 25-4-613. Liability for accident or subsequent disease from inoculation.

The health departments, their assistants and employees, the department of public health and environment, health officers, or anyone enforcing the provisions of this part 6 shall not be held responsible for any accident or subsequent disease that may occur in connection with the administration of this part 6.

## 25-4-614. Penalties.

Any person who refuses to comply with or who violates any of the provisions of this part 6 is guilty of a misdemeanor and, upon conviction thereof, shall be punished by a fine of not more than one hundred dollars or by imprisonment in the county jail for not more than thirty days for each offense.

### 25-4-615. Further municipal restrictions not prohibited.

(1) Nothing in this part 6 shall be construed to limit the power of any municipality within this state to prohibit dogs from running at large, whether or not they have been inoculated as provided in this part 6; and nothing in this part 6 shall be construed to limit the power of any municipality to regulate and control and to enforce other and additional measures for the restriction and control of rabies.

(2) Notwithstanding subsection (1) of this section, a municipality shall not require a dog, cat, or ferret to be inoculated against rabies any more frequently than is recommended in the "Compendium of Animal Rabies Control" as promulgated by the national association of state public health veterinarians, and a veterinarian may issue a written waiver exempting an animal from a rabies vaccination order as provided in section 25-4-607.

# PART 7. PET ANIMAL AND PSITTACINE BIRD FACILITIES

### 25-4-701. Definitions.

As used in this part 7, unless the context otherwise requires:

(1) "Board" means the state board of health.

(2) "Department" means the department of public health and environment.

(3) "Pet animal facility" means any place or premises used in whole or in part for the keeping of pet animals for the purpose of adoption, breeding, boarding, grooming, handling, selling, sheltering, trading, or transferring such animals.

(4) "Psittacine birds" includes all birds of the order psittaciformes.

### 25-4-702. Board to establish rules - department to administer.

(1) The board may establish rules that are necessary to carry out the provisions of this part 7. Such rules shall set forth procedures to be followed by pet animal facilities in the event of an outbreak of disease or quarantine. Such rules may include provisions pertaining to the breeding and sale of psittacine birds that are necessary to prevent or minimize the danger of transmission of psittacosis to handlers, the general public, and other pet birds.

(2) This part 7 shall be administered by the department; except that county, district, and municipal public health agencies and animal control personnel may be authorized by the department to assist it in performing its powers and duties pursuant to this part 7.

(3) (Deleted by amendment, L. 94, p. 1296, § 2, effective July 1, 1994.)

### 25-4-703. License required - fee. (Repealed)

### 25-4-704. Hobby breeders of psittacine birds. (Repealed)

### 25-4-705. Importation for resale prohibited - when. (Repealed)

## 25-4-706. Pet animal and psittacine bird dealers - duties. (Repealed)

## 25-4-707. Psittacine birds - sale or transfer - requirements. (Repealed)

## 25-4-708. Nonpsittacine birds - when regulated. (Repealed)

## 25-4-709. Quarantine.
If at any time it appears to the department that any pet animal is, or was during its lifetime, infected with a disease dangerous to the public health, it may place an embargo on said pet animal and may trace, or cause to be traced, the whereabouts of said animal and determine the identity and whereabouts of any other animals which may have been exposed to such disease. If the department determines that the interest of the public health requires, it may: Cause any pet animal facility to be quarantined for such time as the department determines to be necessary to protect the public health; prohibit the sale or importation into this state of such pet animals from such places or areas where such danger exists; and require the euthanasia and the proper disposal of infected animals.

## 25-4-710. Right of entry - inspections.
It is lawful for any employee of the department, any employee of any county, district, or municipal public health agency or animal control agency authorized by the department, or any authorized official of the United States department of agriculture when conducting an official disease investigation of a pet animal facility to enter such facility and to inspect the same, any animals, or any health or transaction records relating to the investigation.

## 25-4-711. Suspension or revocation of license. (Repealed)

## 25-4-712. Unlawful acts.
(1) It is unlawful for any person:
(a) To make a material misstatement or provide false information to the department during an official disease investigation;
(b) To violate a provision of this part 7 or a rule promulgated pursuant to this part 7;
(c) To aid or abet another in a violation of this part 7 or a rule promulgated pursuant to this part 7;
(d) To refuse to permit entry or inspection in accordance with section 25-4-710.
(e) to (k) (Deleted by amendment, L. 94, p. 1298, § 5, effective July 1, 1994.)

## 25-4-713. Penalty for violations - assessments.
(1) Any person who violates any of the provisions of this part 7 is guilty of a class 2 misdemeanor and shall be punished as provided in section 18-1.3-501, C.R.S.
(2) (Deleted by amendment, L. 94, p. 1299, § 6, effective July 1, 1994.)

## 25-4-714. Exemptions from part 7. (Repealed)

## 25-4-715. Repeal of sections - review of functions. (Repealed)

# PART 8. PHENYLKETONURIA

## 25-4-801. Legislative declaration.
The general assembly declares that, as a matter of public policy of this state and in the interest of public health, every newborn infant should be tested for phenylketonuria and other metabolic defects in order to prevent mental retardation resulting therefrom and that the people of this state should be extensively informed as to the nature and effects of such defects.

## 25-4-802. Tests for metabolic defects.
(1) It is the duty of either the chief medical staff officer or other person in charge of each institution caring for newborn infants or, if a newborn infant is not born in an institution or is discharged therefrom prior to the time prescribed for the taking of the specimen designated in this section, the person responsible for the signing of the birth certificate of such child to cause to be obtained from every such infant a specimen of the type designated by the state board of health, which specimen shall be forwarded to the department of public health and environment or other laboratory approved by it for testing for phenylketonuria and testing for such other metabolic defects which may be prescribed from time to time by the state board of health to be conducted with respect to such specimen.
(2) The state board of health has the duty to prescribe from time to time effective tests and examinations designed to detect phenylketonuria and such other metabolic disorders or defects likely to cause mental retardation as accepted medical practice indicates.
(3) The performance of such tests and the reporting of results shall be done at such times and places and in such manner as may be prescribed by the department of public health and environment.
(4) It is the duty of the department of public health and environment to contact as soon as possible all cases suspected of having any such disorders or defects and to do any additional testing required to confirm or disprove the suspected disorder or defect.

## 25-4-803. Rules and regulations.
(1) The state board of health shall promulgate rules and regulations concerning the obtaining of samples or specimens from newborn infants required for the tests prescribed by the state board of health for the handling and delivery of the same and for the testing and examination thereof to detect phenylketonuria or other metabolic disorders found likely to cause mental retardation.
(2) The department of public health and environment shall furnish all physicians, public health nurses, hospitals, maternity homes, county departments of social services, and the state department of human services available medical information concerning the nature and effects of phenylketonuria and other metabolic disorders and defects found likely to cause mental retardation.

## 25-4-804. Exceptions.
Nothing in the provisions of this part 8 shall be construed to require the testing or medical treatment for the minor child of any person who is a member of a well-recognized church or religious denomination and whose religious convictions in accordance with the tenets or principles of his church or religious denomination are against medical treatment for disease or physical defects.

# PART 9. SCHOOL ENTRY IMMUNIZATION

## 25-4-901. Definitions.

As used in this part 9, unless the context otherwise requires:

(1) "Certificate of immunization" means one of the following forms of documentation that include the dates and types of immunizations administered to a student:

(a) A paper document that includes information transferred from the records of a licensed physician, registered nurse, or public health official; or

(b) An electronic file or a hard copy of an electronic file provided to the school directly from the immunization tracking system, established pursuant to section 25-4-2403.

(1.5) "Child" means any student less than eighteen years of age.

(2) (a) "School" means, except as otherwise provided in paragraph (b) of this subsection (2), a public, private, or parochial nursery school, day care center, child care facility or child care center as defined in section 26-6-102 (5), C.R.S., family child care home, foster care home, head start program, kindergarten, elementary or secondary school through grade twelve, or college or university.

(b) "School" does not include:

(I) A public services short-term child care facility as defined in section 26-6-102 (30), C.R.S.;

(I.5) A guest child care facility as defined in section 26-6-102 (16), C.R.S., or a ski school as defined in section 26-6-103.5 (6), C.R.S.; or

(II) College or university courses of study that are offered off-campus, or are offered to nontraditional adult students, as defined by the governing board of the institution, or are offered at colleges or universities that do not have residence hall facilities.

(3) "Student" means any person enrolled in a Colorado school or child care center as defined in subsection (2) of this section. "Student" does not include a child who enrolls and attends a licensed child care center, as defined in section 26-6-102 (5), C.R.S., which is located at a ski area, for up to fifteen days or less in a fifteen-consecutive-day period, no more than twice in a calendar year, with each fifteen-consecutive-day period separated by at least sixty days.

## 25-4-902. Immunization prior to attending school - standardized immunization information.

(1) Except as provided in section 25-4-903, a student shall not attend any school in the state of Colorado on or after the dates specified in section 25-4-906 (4) unless he or she has presented the following to the appropriate school official:

(a) An up-to-date certificate of immunization from a licensed physician, a licensed advanced practice nurse, or authorized representative of the department of public health and environment or county, district, or municipal public health agency stating that the student has received immunization against communicable diseases as specified by the state board of health, based on recommendations of the advisory committee on immunization practices of the United States department of health and human services or the American academy of pediatrics; or

(b) A written authorization signed by one parent or guardian or an authorization signed by the emancipated student requesting that local health officials administer the immunizations.

(2) If the student's certificate of immunization is not up-to-date according to the requirements of the state board of health, the parent or guardian or the emancipated student or the student eighteen years of age or older shall submit to the school, within fourteen days after receiving direct personal notification that the certificate is not up-to-date, documentation that the next required immunization has been given and a written plan for completion of all required immunizations. The scheduling of immunizations in the written plan shall follow medically recommended minimum intervals approved by the state board of health. If the student begins but does not continue or complete the written plan, he or she shall be suspended or expelled pursuant to this part 9.

(3) Notwithstanding the provisions of subsection (1) of this section, a school shall enroll a student who is in out-of-home placement within five school days after receiving the student's education information and records as required in section 22-32-138, C.R.S., regardless of whether the school has received the items specified in subsection (1) of this section. Upon enrolling the student, the

school shall notify the student's legal guardian that, unless the school receives the student's certificate of immunization or a written authorization for administration of immunizations within fourteen days after the student enrolls, the school shall suspend the student until such time as the school receives the certificate of immunization or the authorization.

(4) On or before March 1, 2011, the department of public health and environment shall develop and provide to the department of education a standardized document regarding childhood immunizations. The department of education shall post the standardized immunization document on its website on or before January 15, 2011, and each year thereafter. The standardized document shall be updated annually and shall include, but need not be limited to:

(a) A list of the immunizations required for enrollment in a school and the age at which the immunization is required; and

(b) A list of immunizations currently recommended for children by the center for disease control advisory committee on immunization practices and the recommended age at which each immunization should be given.

(5) The document created pursuant to subsection (4) of this section shall comply with the provisions of section 25-4-903 (4) regarding allowable exemptions from required immunizations.

## 25-4-902.5. Immunization prior to attending a college or university - tuberculosis screening process development.

(1) Except as provided in section 25-4-903, no student shall attend any college or university in the state of Colorado on or after the dates specified in section 25-4-906 (4) unless the student can present to the appropriate official of the school a certificate of immunization from a licensed physician, licensed physician assistant authorized under section 12-36-106 (5) , C.R.S., licensed advanced practice nurse, or authorized representative of the department of public health and environment or county, district, or municipal public health agency stating that the student has received immunization against communicable diseases as specified by the state board of health or a written authorization signed by one parent or guardian or the emancipated student or the student eighteen years of age or older requesting that local health officials administer the immunizations or a plan signed by one parent or guardian or the emancipated student or the student eighteen years of age or older for receipt by the student of the required inoculation or the first or the next required of a series of inoculations within thirty days.

(2) (Deleted by amendment, L. 94, p. 695, §2, effective April 19, 1994.)

(3) (a) Each college and university in Colorado may work to create a tuberculosis screening process with the goal of making the process as uniform as possible for all colleges and universities in the state. The department of public health and environment may attend and participate in any meetings held by the universities and colleges regarding the screening process. The screening process may include a tuberculosis risk questionnaire, a tuberculosis education policy, a clinical review process for each completed questionnaire, and follow-up testing procedures for students who are determined to be at risk for tuberculosis. On or before January 1, 2009, the colleges and universities that work to create a tuberculosis screening process pursuant to this subsection (3) shall report to the health and human services committees of the senate and the house of representatives, or their successor committees, regarding any legislative recommendations necessary regarding a tuberculosis screening process.

(b) This subsection (3) shall not apply to a university or college that provides course work solely online.

## 25-4-903. Exemptions from immunization - rules.

(1) (Deleted by amendment, L. 97, p. 409, § 2, effective July 1, 1997.)

(2) It is the responsibility of the parent or legal guardian to have his or her child immunized unless the child is exempted pursuant to this section. A student shall be exempted from receiving the required immunizations in the following manner:

(a) By submitting to the student's school certification from a licensed physician, physician assistant authorized under section 12-36-106 (5) , C.R.S., or advanced practice nurse that the physical condition of the student is such that one or more specified immunizations would endanger his or her life or health or is medically contraindicated due to other medical conditions; or

(b) By submitting to the student's school a statement of exemption signed by one parent or guardian or the emancipated student or student eighteen years of age or older that the parent, guardian, or student is an adherent to a religious belief whose teachings are opposed to immunizations or that the parent or guardian or the emancipated student or student eighteen years of age or older has a personal belief that is opposed to immunizations.

(2.5) The state board of health shall promulgate rules regarding:

(a) Immunization information, including exemption rates, that is available to the public through the department, including evidence-based research, resources and information from credible scientific and public health organizations, peer-reviewed studies, and an online learning module; and

(b) The frequency of submission of exemption forms.

(3) The state board of health may provide, by regulation, for further exemptions to immunization based upon sound medical practice.

(4) All information distributed to parents by school districts regarding immunization shall inform them of their rights under subsection (2) of this section.

(5) Each school shall make the immunization and exemption rates of their enrolled student population publicly available upon request.

## 25-4-904. Rules and regulations - immunization rules - rule-making authority of state board of health.

(1) The state board of health shall establish rules and regulations for administering this part 9. Such rules and regulations shall establish which immunizations shall be required and the manner and frequency of their administration and shall conform to recognized standard medical practices. Such rules and regulations may also require the reporting of statistical information and names of noncompliers by the schools. The department of public health and environment shall administer and enforce the immunization requirements.

(2) All rule-making authority granted to the state board of health under the provisions of this article is granted on the condition that the general assembly reserves the power to delete or rescind any rule of the board. All rules promulgated pursuant to this subsection (2) shall be subject to sections 24-4-103 (8) (c) and (8) (d) and 24-4-108, C.R.S.

## 25-4-905. Immunization of indigent children.

(1) The county, district, or municipal public health agency; a public health or school nurse under the supervision of a licensed physician or physician assistant authorized under section 12-36-106 (5) , C.R.S.; or the department of public health and environment, in the absence of a county, district, or municipal public health agency or public health nurse, shall provide, at public expense to the extent that funds are available, immunizations required by this part 9 to each child whose parents or guardians cannot afford to have the child immunized or, if emancipated, who cannot himself or herself afford immunization and who has not been exempted. The department of public health and environment shall provide all vaccines necessary to comply with this section as far as funds will permit. Nothing in this section precludes the department of public health and environment from distributing vaccines to physicians, advanced practice nurses, or others as required by law or the rules of the department. No indigent child shall be excluded, suspended, or expelled from school unless the immunizations have been available and readily accessible to the child at public expense.

(2) Notwithstanding any other provision of this part 9 to the contrary, programs and services that provide immunizations to children for communicable diseases shall be available to a child regardless of his or her race, religion, gender, ethnicity, national origin, or immigration status.

## 25-4-906. Certificate of immunization - forms.

(1) The department of public health and environment shall provide official certificates of immunization to the schools, private physicians, and county, district, and municipal public health agencies. Upon the commencement of the gathering of epidemiological information pursuant to section 25-4-2403 to implement the immunization tracking system, such form shall include a notice that informs a parent or legal guardian that he or she has the option to exclude his or her infant's, child's, or student's immunization information from the immunization tracking system created in section 25-4-2403. Any immunization record provided by a licensed physician, registered nurse, or public health official may be accepted by the school official as certification of immunization if the information is transferred to the official certificate of immunization and verified by the school official.

(2) Each school shall maintain on file an official certificate of immunization for every student enrolled. The certificate shall be returned to the parent or guardian or the emancipated student or student eighteen years of age or older when a student withdraws, transfers, is promoted, or otherwise leaves the school, or the school shall transfer the certificate with the student's school record to the new school. Upon a college or university student's request, the official certificate of immunization shall be forwarded as specified by the student.

(3) The department of public health and environment may examine, audit, and verify the records of immunizations maintained by each school.

(4) All students enrolled in any school in Colorado on and after August 15, 1979, shall furnish the required certificate of immunization or shall be suspended or expelled from school. Students enrolling in school in Colorado for the first time on and after July 1, 1978, shall provide a certificate of immunization or shall be excluded from school except as provided in section 25-4-903.

## 25-4-907. Noncompliance.

(1) A school official of each school shall suspend or expel from school, pursuant to the provisions of section 22-33-105, C.R.S., or the provisions established by the school official of a college or university or private school, any student not otherwise exempted under this part 9 who fails to comply with the provisions of this part 9. No student shall be suspended or expelled for failure to comply with the provisions of this part 9 unless there has been a direct personal notification by the appropriate school authority to the student's parent or guardian or to the emancipated student or the student eighteen years of age or older of the noncompliance with this part 9 and of such person's rights under sections 25-4-902, 25-4-902.5, and 25-4-903.

(2) In the event of suspension or expulsion of a student, school officials shall notify the state department of public health and environment or the county, district, and municipal public health agency. An agent of said department shall then contact the parent or guardian or the emancipated student or student eighteen years of age or older in an effort to secure compliance with this part 9 in order that the student may be reenrolled in school.

(3) Any student expelled for failure to comply with the provisions of this part 9 shall not be included in calculating the dropout rate for the school from which such student was expelled or the school district in which such student was enrolled prior to being expelled. Such student shall be included in the annual report of the number of expelled students prepared pursuant to section 22-33-105, C.R.S.

## 25-4-908. When exemption from immunization not recognized.

If at any time there is, in the opinion of the state department of public health and environment or the county, district, or municipal public health agency, danger of an epidemic from any of the communicable diseases for which an immunization is required pursuant to the rules and regulations promulgated pursuant to section 25-4-904, no exemption or exception from immunization against such disease shall be recognized. Quarantine by the state department of public health and environment or the county, district, or municipal public health agency is hereby authorized as a legal alternative to immunization.

### 25-4-909. Vaccine-related injury or death - limitations on liability.
(1) The general assembly finds, determines, and declares that immunization of the population of this state is vital to the health of Colorado citizens and has demonstrated such finding by requiring such immunization pursuant to the provisions of sections 25-4-901 to 25-4-908.
(2) No person who administers a vaccine which is required under the provisions of this part 9 to an infant or child whose age is greater than twenty days shall be held liable for injuries sustained pursuant to such vaccine if:
(a) The vaccine was administered using generally accepted clinical methods;
(b) The vaccine was administered according to the schedule of immunization as published by the communicable disease control administration of the federal government; and
(c) There were no clinical symptoms nor clinical history present under which prudent health care professionals would not have administered such vaccine.
(3) An action shall not be maintained for a vaccine-related injury or death until action for compensation for such alleged injury has been exhausted under the terms of the "National Childhood Vaccine Injury Act of 1986", 42 U.S.C. secs. 300aa-10 to 300aa-33, as such law is from time to time amended.
(4) If the injury or death which is sustained does not fall within the parameters of the vaccine injury table as defined in 42 U.S.C. sec. 300aa-14, as enacted on November 14, 1986, a rebuttable presumption is established that the injury sustained or the death was not due to the administration of vaccine. Such presumption shall be overcome by a preponderance of the evidence.

### 25-4-910. Immunization data collection.
(1) The department of public health and environment, in consultation with other state departments, shall establish a joint policy on immunization data collection and sharing.
(2) The department of public health and environment shall provide assistance to schools with the analysis and interpretation of the immunization data.

# PART 10. NEWBORN SCREENING AND GENETIC COUNSELING AND EDUCATION ACT

### 25-4-1001. Short title.
This part 10 shall be known and may be cited as the "Newborn Screening and Genetic Counseling and Education Act".

### 25-4-1002. Legislative declaration.
(1) The general assembly hereby finds and declares that:
(a) State policy regarding newborn screening and genetic counseling and education should be made with full public knowledge, in light of expert opinion, and should be constantly reviewed to consider changing medical knowledge and ensure full public protection;
(b) Participation of persons in genetic counseling programs in this state should be wholly voluntary and that all information obtained from persons involved in such programs or in newborn screening programs in the state should be held strictly confidential.

### 25-4-1003. Powers and duties of executive director - newborn screening programs - genetic counseling and education programs - rules.

(1) The executive director of the department of public health and environment shall have the authority to:

(a) Establish and administer state programs for newborn screening and genetic counseling and education;

(b) Promulgate rules, regulations, and standards for the provision of newborn screening programs and genetic counseling and education programs;

(c) Designate such personnel as are necessary to carry out the provisions of this part 10, disburse and collect such funds as are available to the administration of this part 10, and fix reasonable fees to be charged for services pursuant to this part 10;

(d) Gather and disseminate information to further the public's understanding of newborn screening and genetic counseling and education programs;

(e) Establish systems for recording information obtained in newborn screening and genetic counseling and education programs.

(2) The executive director of the department of public health and environment shall comply with the following provisions:

(a) Newborn screening shall be provided in the most efficient and cost-effective manner possible and newborn screening and diagnostic services should be carried out under adequate standards of supervision and quality control;

(b) No program for genetic counseling shall require mandatory participation, restriction of childbearing, or be a prerequisite to eligibility for, or receipt of, any other service or assistance from, or to participation in, any other program;

(c) Genetic counseling services shall be available to persons in need, such counseling shall be nondirective, and such counseling shall emphasize informing the client and not require restriction of childbearing;

(d) The extremely personal decision to bear children shall remain the free choice and responsibility of the individual, and such free choice and responsibility shall not be restricted by any of the genetic services of the state;

(e) All information gathered by the department of public health and environment, or by other agencies, entities, and individuals conducting programs and projects on newborn screening and genetic counseling and education, other than statistical information and information which the individual allows to be released through his informed consent, shall be confidential. Public and private access to individual patient data shall be limited to data compiled without the individual's name.

(f) Information on the operation of all programs on newborn screening and genetic counseling and education within the state, except for confidential information obtained from participants in such programs, shall be open and freely available to the public;

(g) All participants in programs on genetic counseling and education shall be informed of the nature of possible risks involved in participation in such a program or project, and shall be informed of the nature and cost of available therapies or maintenance programs for those affected by hereditary disorders, and shall be informed of the possible benefits and risks of such therapies and programs;

(h) Nothing in this section shall be construed to require any hospital or other health facility or any physician or other health professional to provide genetic counseling beyond the usual and customary and accepted practice nor shall any hospital or other health facility be held liable for not providing such genetic counseling.

## 25-4-1004. Newborn screening.

(1) (a) Repealed.

(b) On or after April 1, 1989, all infants born in the state of Colorado shall be tested for the following conditions: Phenylketonuria, hypothyroidism, abnormal hemoglobins, galactosemia, cystic fibrosis, biotinidase deficiency, and such other conditions as the board of health may determine meet the criteria set forth in paragraph (c) of this subsection (1) . Appropriate specimens

233

for such testing shall be forwarded by the hospital in which the child is born to the laboratory operated or designated by the department of public health and environment for such purposes. The physician, nurse, midwife, or other health professional attending a birth outside a hospital shall be responsible for the collection and forwarding of such specimens. The results of the testing shall be forwarded directly to the physician or other primary health care provider for the provision of such information to the parent or parents of the child. The results of any testing or follow-up testing pursuant to section 25-4-1004.5 may be sent to the immunization tracking system authorized by section 25-4-2403 and accessed by the physician or other primary health care provider. The state board of health may discontinue testing for any condition listed in this paragraph (b) if, upon consideration of criteria set forth in paragraph (c) of this subsection (1) , the board finds that the public health is better served by not testing infants for that condition.

(c) The board of health shall use the following criteria to determine whether or not to test infants for conditions which are not specifically enumerated in this subsection (1) :

(I) The condition for which the test is designed presents a significant danger to the health of the infant or his family and is amenable to treatment;

(II) The incidence of the condition is sufficiently high to warrant screening;

(III) The test meets commonly accepted clinical standards of reliability, as demonstrated through research or use in another state or jurisdiction; and

(IV) The cost-benefit consequences of screening are acceptable within the context of the total newborn screening program.

(2) The executive director of the department of public health and environment shall assess a fee which is sufficient to cover the costs of such testing and to accomplish the other purposes of this part 10. Hospitals shall assess a reasonable fee to be charged the parent or parents of the infant to cover the costs of handling the specimens, the reimbursement of laboratory costs, and the costs of providing other services necessary to implement the purposes of this part 10.

## 25-4-1004.3. Newborn heart defect screening - pulse oximetry - rules - definition.

(1) (a) On and after January 1, 2016, a birthing facility that is below seven thousand feet of elevation shall test all infants born in the facility for critical congenital heart defects using pulse oximetry.

(b) Upon receipt of the confirmation of the appropriate algorithm for the pulse oximetry reading from the newborn screening committee, the newborn screening committee shall evaluate whether pulse oximetry testing in birthing facilities at or above seven thousand feet elevation meets the criteria in section 25-4-1004. Upon confirmation from the committee that the criteria have been met, the state board of health shall promulgate rules to ensure that all newborns born at or above seven thousand feet elevation are screened for critical congenital heart defects.

(c) The critical congenital heart defect screening using pulse oximetry must be performed on every newborn prior to the newborn's release from the birthing facility.

(2) Each birthing facility shall report the results of the pulse oximetry screenings to the department of public health and environment. The state board of health may promulgate rules for the implementation of this section.

(3) As used in this section, a "birthing facility" means a general hospital or birthing center licensed or certified pursuant to section 25-1.5-103 and that provides birthing and newborn care services.

## 25-4-1004.5. Follow-up testing and treatment - second screening - legislative declaration - fee - rules.

(1) The general assembly finds that:

(a) Newborn screening authorized by section 25-4-1004 is provided for every newborn in the state;

(b) Newborn testing is designed to identify metabolic disorders that cause mental retardation and other health problems unless they are diagnosed and treated early in life;

(c) In order to ensure that children with metabolic disorders are able to lead as normal a life as possible and to minimize long-term health care costs for such children, it is necessary to provide centralized follow-up testing and treatment services;

(d) For over twenty-five years the follow-up testing and treatment services were provided by a federal grant that was discontinued June 30, 1993. Since that time, follow-up testing and treatment services have been limited. If alternative sources of funding are not provided, those services will be eliminated.

(e) A nominal increase of the fee on newborn screening to cover the costs of providing follow-up and referral services would allow for those services to be continued;

(f) Over the past ten years, many children with serious health conditions have received timely diagnosis and treatment as a result of the newborn screening required by this part 10. Such screening has averted the possibility of life-long institutionalization of some children and substantial related health care costs. The general assembly further finds, however, that many infants who are screened early in life may exhibit false or inaccurate results on certain newborn screening tests. The general assembly therefore finds and declares that subsequent newborn screening will provide more accurate and reliable test results for the timely and effective diagnosis and treatment of certain health conditions in newborn infants and the best interests of children in Colorado will be served by a new screening program that routinely tests all newborns twice.

(2) (a) Repealed.

(b) On and after July 1, 1994, the executive director of the department of public health and environment shall increase the newborn screening fee as provided in section 25-4-1004 (2) so that the fee is sufficient to include the costs of providing follow-up and referral services to families with a newborn whose test results under a newborn screening indicate a metabolic disorder. Follow-up services include comprehensive diagnostic testing. The increase shall not exceed five dollars; except that it may be adjusted annually to reflect any change in the Denver-Boulder consumer price index. Any fees collected shall be subject to the provisions of section 25-4-1006.

(3) (a) On and after July 1, 1996, all infants born in the state of Colorado who receive newborn screening pursuant to section 25-4-1004 (1) shall have a second specimen taken to screen for the following conditions:

(I) Phenylketonuria;

(II) Hypothyroidism;

(III) Galactosemia;

(IV) Cystic fibrosis; and

(V) Such other conditions as the state board of health may determine meet the criteria set forth in section 25-4-1004 (1) (c) and require a second screening for accurate test results.

(b) The executive director of the department of public health and environment is authorized to promulgate rules, regulations, and standards for the implementation of the second specimen testing specified in this subsection (3) , including but not limited to the following:

(I) Identification of those conditions for which a second specimen shall be required;

(II) The age of the infant at which the second screening may be administered;

(III) The method by which the parent or parents of a newborn shall be advised of the necessity for a second specimen test;

(IV) The procedure to be followed in administering the second specimen test;

(V) Any exceptions to the necessity for a second specimen test and the procedures to be followed in such cases; and

(VI) The standards of supervision and quality control that shall apply to second specimen testing.

(c) On and after July 1, 1996, the executive director of the department of public health and environment may adjust the newborn screening fee set forth in section 25-4-1004 (2) so that the fee is sufficient to cover the costs associated with the second screening described in this subsection (3) . Any increase shall be in addition to the fee described in subsection (2) of this section and shall not initially exceed five dollars and seventy-five cents but may be adjusted annually to reflect any actual cost increase associated with the administration of the second screening. Any fees collected pursuant to this paragraph (c) shall be subject to the provisions of section 25-4-1006.

(4) The provisions of section 25-4-1003 (2) shall apply to second newborn screenings.

## 25-4-1004.7. Newborn hearing screening - legislative declaration - advisory committee - report - rules.

(1) (a) The general assembly finds, determines, and declares:

(I) That hearing loss occurs in newborn infants more frequently than any other health condition for which newborn infant screening is required;

(II) That eighty percent of the language ability of a child is established by the time the child is eighteen months of age and that hearing is vitally important to the healthy development of such language skills;

(III) That early detection of hearing loss in a child and early intervention and treatment has been demonstrated to be highly effective in facilitating a child's healthy development in a manner consistent with the child's age and cognitive ability;

(IV) That children with hearing loss who do not receive such early intervention and treatment frequently require special educational services and that such services are publicly funded for the vast majority of children with hearing needs in the state;

(V) That appropriate testing and identification of newborn infants with hearing loss will facilitate early intervention and treatment and may therefore serve the public purposes of promoting the healthy development of children and reducing public expenditure; and

(VI) That consumers should be entitled to know whether the hospital at which they choose to deliver their infant provides newborn hearing screening.

(b) For these reasons the general assembly hereby determines that it would be beneficial and in the best interests of the development of the children of the state of Colorado that newborn infants' hearing be screened.

(2) (a) (I) There is hereby established an advisory committee on hearing in newborn infants for the purpose of collecting the informational data specified in paragraph (b) of subsection (3) of this section, and for the purpose of providing recommendations to hospitals, other health care institutions, the department of public health and environment, and the public concerning, but not necessarily limited to, the following:

(A) Appropriate methodologies to be implemented for hearing screening of newborn infants, which methodologies shall be objective and physiologically based and which shall not include a requirement that the initial newborn hearing screening be performed by an audiologist;

(B) The number of births sufficient to qualify a hospital or health institution to arrange otherwise for hearing screenings; and

(C) Guidelines for reporting and the means to assure that identified children receive referral for appropriate follow-up services.

(II) The advisory committee on hearing in newborn infants shall consist of at least seven members who shall be appointed by the executive director of the department of public health and environment. Members appointed to the committee shall have training, experience, or interest in the area of hearing conditions in children.

(III) The members of the advisory committee on hearing in newborn infants shall serve without compensation.

(IV) Repealed.

(b) Repealed.

(3) (a) It is the intent of the general assembly that newborn hearing screening be conducted on no fewer than ninety-five percent of the infants born in hospitals, using procedures recommended by the advisory committee on hearing in newborn infants, created in subsection (2) of this section. Toward that end, every licensed or certified hospital shall educate the parents of infants born in such hospitals of the importance of screening the hearing of newborn infants and follow-up care. Education shall not be considered a substitute for the hearing screening described in this section. Every licensed or certified hospital shall report annually to the advisory committee concerning the following:

(I) The number of infants born in the hospital;

(II) The number of infants screened;

(III) The number of infants who passed the screening, if administered; and

(IV) The number of infants who did not pass the screening, if administered.

(b) The advisory committee on hearing in newborn infants shall determine which hospitals or other health care institutions in the state of Colorado are administering hearing screening to newborn infants on a voluntary basis and the number of infants screened.

(I) to (IV) Repealed.

(c) Repealed.

(4) (a) If the number of infants screened falls below eighty-five percent, the board of health shall promulgate rules requiring hearing screening of newborn infants pursuant to section 24-4-103, C.R.S., of the "State Administrative Procedure Act".

(b) Such rules, if promulgated, shall address those hospitals with a low volume of births, as determined by the state board of health based upon recommendations by the advisory committee on hearing in newborn infants, which may arrange otherwise for newborn infant hearing screening.

(5) A physician, nurse, midwife, or other health professional attending a birth outside a hospital or institution shall provide information, as established by the department, to parents regarding places where the parents may have their infants' hearing screened and the importance of such screening.

(6) The department shall encourage the cooperation of county, district, and municipal public health agencies, health care clinics, school districts, and any other appropriate resources to promote the screening of newborn infants' hearing for those infants born outside a hospital or institution.

## 25-4-1005. Exceptions.

Nothing in the provisions of this part 10 shall be construed to require the testing or medical treatment for the minor child of any person or of any person who is a member of a well-recognized church or religious denomination and whose religious convictions in accordance with the tenets or principles of his church or religious denomination are against medical treatment for disease or physical defects or has a personal objection to the administration of such tests or treatment.

## 25-4-1006. Cash funds.

(1) All moneys received from fees collected pursuant to this part 10 shall be transmitted to the state treasurer who shall credit the same to the newborn screening and genetic counseling cash funds, which funds are hereby created. Such moneys shall be utilized for expenditures authorized or contemplated by and not inconsistent with the provisions of this part 10 relating to newborn screening, follow-up care, and genetic counseling and education programs and functions. All moneys credited to the newborn screening and genetic counseling cash funds shall be used as provided in this part 10 and shall not be deposited in or transferred to the general fund of this state or any other fund.

(2) Repealed.

# PART 11. KENNELS

## 25-4-1101 to 25-4-1111. (Repealed)

# PART 12. STREPTOCOCCUS CONTROL

### 25-4-1201. Powers and duties of executive director.
(1) The executive director of the department of public health and environment shall have the authority to:
(a) Establish and administer a culture-testing program to test for streptococcus;
(b) Designate such personnel as are necessary to carry out the provisions of this part 12, disburse and collect such funds as are available for the administration of this part 12, and fix reasonable fees to be charged for services pursuant to this part 12.

### 25-4-1202. Streptococcus cash fund.
(1) The executive director of the department of public health and environment shall establish the fees to be collected for any streptococcus culture test performed by the department.
(2) (a) All moneys collected pursuant to this part 12 shall be transmitted to the state treasurer, who shall credit the same to the streptococcus cash fund, which fund is hereby created. All moneys credited to the streptococcus cash fund shall be subject to appropriation by the general assembly to be used as provided in this section and shall not be deposited in or transferred to the general fund of this state or to any other fund.
(b) Repealed.
(3) (a) The executive director of the department of public health and environment shall propose, as part of the annual budget request of the department of public health and environment, an adjustment in the amount of the fee for the streptococcus culture test which the department is authorized by law to collect. The budget request and the adjusted fees for the streptococcus culture test shall reflect direct and indirect costs.
(b) Based upon the appropriation made by the general assembly, the executive director of the department of public health and environment shall adjust the streptococcus fee so that the revenue generated from said fee approximates the department's direct and indirect costs. Such fee shall remain in effect for the fiscal year for which the budget request applies.
(c) Beginning July 1, 1984, and each July 1 thereafter, whenever moneys appropriated to the department of public health and environment for its activities pursuant to this part 12 for the prior fiscal year are unexpended, said moneys shall be made a part of the appropriation to the department for the next fiscal year, and such amount shall not be raised from fees collected by such department. If a supplemental appropriation is made to the department for such activities, the streptococcus fee of the department, when adjusted for the fiscal year next following the year in which the supplemental appropriation was made, shall be adjusted by an additional amount which is sufficient to compensate for such supplemental appropriation. Moneys to be appropriated annually to the department in the general appropriation bill for the purposes of this part 12 shall be designated as cash funds and shall not exceed the amount anticipated to be raised from such fee collected by the department.

# PART 13. RETAIL FOOD STORE SANITATION ACT

### 25-4-1301. Legislative declaration.
The general assembly hereby declares that the sanitary protection of bulk foods and the sanitary maintenance of equipment used to display and dispense bulk foods are matters of statewide concern and are affected with a public interest and that the provisions of this part 13 are enacted in the exercise of the police powers of this state for the purpose of protecting the health, peace, safety, and general welfare of the people of this state.

## 25-4-1302. Definitions.

As used in this part 13, unless the context otherwise requires:

(1) "Bulk foods" means unpackaged or unwrapped foods, either processed or unprocessed, in aggregate containers from which quantities desired by the consumer are withdrawn. "Bulk foods" does not include fresh fruits, fresh vegetables, nuts in the shell, salad bars, bulk pet foods, potentially hazardous foods, and bulk nonfood items.

(2) "Department" means the department of public health and environment.

(3) "Display area" means a location, including physical facilities and equipment, where bulk foods are offered for customer self-service.

(4) "Potentially hazardous foods" includes any food that consists in whole or in part of milk or milk products, eggs, meat, poultry, fish, shellfish, edible crustacea, or other food products or ingredients, including synthetic ingredients, in a form capable of supporting rapid and progressive growth of infectious or toxigenic microorganisms. This term does not include refrigerated, clean, whole, uncracked, odor-free shell eggs.

(5) "Product module" means a food-contact container (multiuse or single-service) designed for customer self-service of bulk foods by either direct or indirect means.

(6) "Servicing area" means a designated location equipped for cleaning, sanitizing, drying, or refilling product modules or for preparing bulk foods.

## 25-4-1303. Labeling - product modules - take-home containers.

(1) Product modules shall be labeled with either:

(a) The manufacturer's or processor's bulk food container labeling plainly in view; or

(b) A counter card, a counter sign, or any other appropriate device bearing prominently and conspicuously the common name of the product, a list of ingredients in their proper order of predominance, and a declaration of artificial color or flavor and chemical preservatives if contained in the product.

(2) Any unpackaged bulk food need not comply with the labeling requirements of this section if the unpackaged bulk food is manufactured on the premises of a store or manufactured by the same store at a different location and if the manufactured bulk food is offered for retail sale on the store's premises and if there are no state requirements.

(3) Labels or marking pens shall be available to customers to identify their take-home containers with the common name of the product unless the product is readily identifiable on sight.

## 25-4-1304. Bulk food protection.

(1) Bulk foods and product modules shall be protected from contamination during display, customer self-service, refilling, and storage.

(2) Containers of bulk pet foods and bulk nonfood items shall be separated from product modules by a barrier or open space.

(3) Bulk foods returned to stores by customers shall not be offered for resale.

(4) Only containers provided by stores in their display areas shall be filled with bulk foods; except that any customer may fill or refill his own container with vended or dispensed water; however, the risk that the customer's own container is unsafe, unpure, contaminated, or in a nonsterile condition when it is filled or refilled by the customer, shall be borne solely by the customer, and, except for warranties, no liability shall attach thereto to the manufacturer, seller, or dispenser of such container.

## 25-4-1305. Bulk food display.

(1) Bulk foods shall be dispensed only from product modules which are protected by close-fitting, individual covers. If any product module is to be opened by customers, the cover shall be self-closing and shall remain closed when not in use.

(2) Customer access to bulk foods in product modules shall be limited and controlled to avoid the

introduction of contaminants. All product modules shall have an access height of thirty inches or more above the floor and a depth of eighteen inches or less.

(3) Potentially hazardous foods shall not be made available for customer self-service.

## 25-4-1306. Dispensing utensils.

(1) Manual handling of bulk foods by customers during dispensing shall be discouraged. Mechanical dispensing devices shall be used, including gravity dispensers, pumps, extruders, and augers. Manual dispensing utensils shall also be used, including tongs, scoops, ladles, and spatulas.

(2) If the dispensing devices and utensils listed in subsection (1) of this section do not discourage manual customer handling of bulk foods, such bulk foods must be wrapped or sacked prior to display.

(3) Manual dispensing utensils shall be protected against becoming contaminated and serving as vehicles for introducing contamination into bulk foods. A tether of easily cleanable material shall be attached to such a utensil and shall be of such length that the utensil cannot contact the floor. A sleeve or protective housing attached or adjacent to the display unit shall be available for storing a utensil when not in use.

(4) Ladles and spatulas shall be stored in bulk foods with handles extending to the outside of product modules. Handles shall not prevent lids from being self-closing.

## 25-4-1307. Materials.

Product modules and utensils shall be constructed of safe materials and shall be corrosion resistant, nonabsorbent, smooth, easily cleanable, and durable under conditions of normal use. Wood shall not be used as a food-contact surface.

## 25-4-1308. Food-contact surfaces.

Product modules, lids, dispensing units, and utensils shall be designed and fabricated to meet the requirements for food-contact surfaces, as provided in section 25-4-1307.

## 25-4-1309. Non-food-contact surfaces.

Surfaces of product module display units, tethers, and display equipment which are not intended for food contact but which are exposed to splash, food debris, or other soiling shall be designed and fabricated to be smooth, cleanable, durable under conditions of normal use, and free of unnecessary ledges, projections, and crevices. The materials for non-food-contact surfaces shall be nonabsorbent or made nonabsorbent by being finished and sealed with a cleanable coating.

## 25-4-1310. Accessibility.

Individual product modules shall be designed to be easily removable from a display unit for servicing unless the product modules are so designed and fabricated that they can be effectively cleaned and sanitized when necessary through a manual in-place cleaning procedure that will not contaminate or otherwise adversely affect bulk foods or equipment in any adjoining display areas.

## 25-4-1311. Equipment sanitization.

(1) Tongs, scoops, ladles, spatulas, and other appropriate utensils and tethers used by customers shall be cleaned and sanitized at least daily or at more frequent intervals based on the type of bulk food and the amount of food particle accumulation or soiling.

(2) When soiled, product modules, lids, and other equipment shall be cleaned and sanitized prior to restocking or at intervals of a schedule based on the type of bulk food and the amount of food particle accumulation.

(3) Food-contact surfaces shall be cleaned and sanitized immediately if contamination is observed or suspected.

(4) Facilities and equipment shall be available, either in a servicing area or in place, to provide for the proper cleaning and sanitizing of all food-contact surfaces, including product modules, lids, and dispensing utensils.

(5) Take-home containers, including but not limited to bags, cups, and lids, which are provided in a display area for customer use shall be stored and dispensed in a sanitary manner.

### 25-4-1312. Violation - penalty.

Any retail food store owner violating any of the provisions of this part 13 is guilty of a misdemeanor and, upon conviction thereof, shall be punished by a fine of not more than five hundred dollars, or by imprisonment in the county jail for not more than ninety days, or by both such fine and imprisonment. It is the duty of the district attorneys of the several districts of this state to prosecute for violations of this part 13 as for other crimes and misdemeanors.

### 25-4-1313. Rules and regulations.

The department has the power to promulgate rules and regulations for the implementation of this part 13.

### 25-4-1314. Limitation.

The provisions of this part 13 shall be expressly limited to retail food store outlets.

# PART 14. HIV INFECTION AND ACQUIRED IMMUNE DEFICIENCY SYNDROME ASSISTANCE

### 25-4-1401. Drug assistance program - program fund - created - legislative declaration - no entitlement created.

(1) (a) The general assembly recognizes that:

(I) Medical science is making strides in treating individuals who have AIDS or HIV;

(II) There are effective biomedical strategies to reduce new HIV infections;

(III) Individuals at risk of HIV may also be at risk of other infectious diseases that can exacerbate the outcomes of an HIV infection;

(IV) Individuals of lower income face barriers accessing biomedical interventions, particularly if they lack health insurance coverage or if their health insurance includes unaffordable premiums or cost-sharing requirements; and

(V) Both the public health and quality of life would benefit from providing assistance with such costs and encouraging prompt and sustained treatment, eventually preventing further transmission of HIV, viral hepatitis, and sexually transmitted infections through prevention, cure, or viral suppression.

(b) Therefore, the general assembly declares that the purpose of this section is to implement the drug assistance program for qualifying individuals of lower income who have medical or preventive needs concerning AIDS or HIV, viral hepatitis, or a sexually transmitted infection.

(c) Nothing in this section shall be construed to establish any entitlement to services from the department of public health and environment.

(2) (a) Subject to available appropriations, the department of public health and environment is authorized to implement and administer a drug assistance program, referred to in this section as the "state program", to provide assistance with indicated screening, general medical, preventive, and pharmaceutical costs for eligible individuals.

(b) The general assembly may annually appropriate moneys from the general fund to assist with indicated screening, general medical, preventive, and pharmaceutical costs for individuals participating in the state program.

(c) The state program is also funded with federal funds available under the federal "Ryan White C.A.R.E. Act of 1990", as amended.

(d) Any moneys received in excess of a federal price agreement are a donation.

(e) For activities of the state program funded by the drug assistance program fund that exceed the appropriation from the drug assistance program fund, if there are sufficient uncommitted moneys in the AIDS and HIV prevention fund, the program may use moneys appropriated for the implementation and administration of the state program from the AIDS and HIV prevention fund as authorized by section 25-4-1405.

(3) To be eligible to participate in the state program, an individual must:

(a) Have a medical indication for treatment or prevention of HIV or AIDS, viral hepatitis, or another sexually transmitted infection;

(b) Have a prescription from an authorized provider for a pharmaceutical product or combination of pharmaceutical products, as applicable, that are included on the drug formulary for the state program; and

(c) Meet income eligibility requirements as determined by the department of public health and environment in consultation with the subcommittee of the advisory group on AIDS policy established in subsection (5) of this section.

(4) Notwithstanding any other provision of this part 14 to the contrary, if a person meets the eligibility requirements set forth in subsection (3) of this section, he or she is eligible for programs and services that provide for the investigation, identification, testing, preventive care, or treatment of HIV infection or AIDS regardless of his or her race, religion, gender, ethnicity, national origin, or immigration status.

(5) A subcommittee of an advisory group convened by the governor to make recommendations for HIV and AIDS policy in the state shall serve in an advisory role to the department of public health and environment in implementing the state program and shall provide advice and recommendations to the department of public health and environment concerning:

(a) Which pharmaceutical products should be listed on the drug formulary for the state program;

(b) Income and other eligibility requirements for the state program; and

(c) The uses of funding for the state program pursuant to paragraphs (a) to (e) of subsection (2) of this section.

(6) If at any time the department of public health and environment, in consultation with the subcommittee of the advisory group on HIV and AIDS policy established in subsection (5) of this section, determines that the drug assistance program is reaching the program's fiscal limitations, the department, in consultation with the subcommittee, shall implement a policy of giving preference to the highest-priority applicants of lower income, who otherwise meet the eligibility requirements in subsection (3) of this section, for enrollment into the program in the following rank order:

(a) Individuals diagnosed with HIV or AIDS;

(b) Individuals in need of treatment to prevent HIV infection;

(c) Individuals diagnosed with other sexually transmitted infections that can be prevented or cured through currently available pharmaceutical treatments;

(d) Individuals diagnosed with viral hepatitis;

(e) Individuals with emerging care, treatment, or prevention needs concerning HIV, viral hepatitis, or other sexually transmitted infections.

(7) (a) The drug assistance program fund is created in the state treasury. The principal of the fund consists of tobacco litigation settlement moneys transferred by the state treasurer to the fund pursuant to section 24-75-1104.5 (1.7) (f) , C.R.S. Subject to annual appropriation by the general assembly, the department of public health and environment may expend moneys from the fund for the state program. Any unexpended or unencumbered money remaining in the fund at the end of any fiscal year remains in the fund and shall not be credited or transferred to the general fund or any other fund.

(b) The department of public health and environment and the advisory group shall determine how the moneys appropriated for the state program pursuant to this subsection (7) are to be used.

## 25-4-1402. Definitions.

As used in this section and sections 25-4-1403 to 25-4-1405, unless the context otherwise requires:

(1) "Program" means the Colorado HIV and AIDS prevention grant program created in section 25-4-1403.

(2) "State board" means the state board of health created in section 25-1-103.

## 25-4-1403. Colorado HIV and AIDS prevention grant program.

(1) There is hereby created in the department the Colorado HIV and AIDS prevention grant program to address local community needs in the areas of medically accurate HIV and AIDS prevention and education through a competitive grant process. The department shall administer the program.

(2) Grant applicants must be nonprofit organizations that are governed by a board of directors and have the benefit of tax-exempt status pursuant to section 501 (c) (3) of the federal "Internal Revenue Code of 1986", or are county, district, or municipal public health agencies.

(3) (a) Preference shall be given to grant applicants that have as one of their primary purposes HIV and AIDS prevention and education.

(b) Grants may be given to organizations that conduct HIV prevention in conjunction with other comorbidities secondary to HIV infections.

(4) Grant applications must include, but need not be limited to:

(a) A statement of the local HIV and AIDS prevention or education issue to be addressed, a description of the constituency that shall be served or targeted, and how the constituency will benefit;

(b) A description of the goals and objectives of the grant applicant in submitting an application under the program; and

(c) A description of the activities planned to accomplish the goals and objectives of the grant applicant and of the outcome measures that will be used by the grant applicant.

(5) Grants must only be given for medically accurate HIV and AIDS prevention and education programs that are based in behavioral and social science theory and research and shall not be used to contribute to existing scholarships, directly to endowments, fund-raising events, annual fund drives, or debt reduction.

## 25-4-1404. Grant program - rules - conflict of interest.

(1) (a) The program shall fund medically accurate HIV and AIDS prevention and education programs through a competitive grant process that is overseen by the HIV and AIDS prevention grant program advisory committee, which is hereby created and referred to in this section as the "advisory committee". The advisory committee consists of seven members appointed by the executive director of the department as follows:

(I) One member who is recommended by the department's minority health advisory commission;

(II) Four members who are recommended by a statewide collaborative group that assists the department in the department's comprehensive plan for HIV and AIDS prevention;

(III) One member who has expertise in HIV and AIDS prevention and education; and

(IV) One member who represents a clinic that receives moneys under part 3 of the federal "Ryan White C.A.R.E. Act of 1990", as amended.

(b) The composition of the advisory committee shall reflect, to the extent practical, Colorado's ethnic, racial, and geographic diversity.

(c) The grants administered pursuant to section 25-4-1403 are only subject to the restrictions provided for in this section and section 25-4-1403 and are not subject to the same restrictions as grants provided with federal moneys for HIV and AIDS prevention. The state board, upon recommendations of the advisory committee, shall adopt rules that specify, but need not be limited to, the following:

(I) The procedures and timelines by which an entity may apply for program grants;

(II) Grant application contents, in addition to those specified in section 25-4-1403 (4) ;

(III) Criteria for selecting the entities that receive grants and determining the amount and duration of the grants;

(IV) Reporting requirements for entities that receive grants pursuant to this section; and

(V) The qualifications of an adequate proposal.

(2) The advisory committee shall review the applications received pursuant to this section and submit to the state board and the executive director of the department recommended grant recipients, recommended grant amounts, and the duration of each recommended grant. In making recommendations for grants, the advisory committee shall consider the distribution of federal funds in the areas of HIV and AIDS prevention, education, and treatment. Within thirty days after receiving the advisory committee's recommendations, the executive director shall submit his or her recommendations to the state board. The state board has the final authority to approve the grants administered under this section and section 25-4-1403. If the state board disapproves a recommendation for a grant recipient, the advisory committee may submit a replacement recommendation within thirty days after disapproval. In making grant recommendations, the advisory committee shall follow the purpose of the program as outlined in section 25-4-1403. The state board shall award grants to the entities selected by the advisory committee, specifying the amount and duration of each grant award. In reviewing and approving grant applications, the advisory committee and the state board shall ensure that grants are distributed statewide and address the needs of both urban and rural residents of Colorado.

(3) If a member of the advisory committee has an immediate personal, private, or financial interest in any matter pending before the advisory committee, the member shall disclose the fact and shall not vote upon the matter.

## 25-4-1405. AIDS and HIV prevention fund - administration - limitation.

(1) There is hereby created in the state treasury the AIDS and HIV prevention fund, referred to in this section as the "fund", which consists of moneys that may be appropriated to the fund by the general assembly. The moneys in the fund are subject to annual appropriation by the general assembly for the direct and indirect costs associated with the implementation of the program. Any moneys in the fund not expended for the purpose of the program may be invested by the state treasurer as provided by law. All interest and income derived from the investment and deposit of moneys in the fund must be credited to the fund. Any unexpended and unencumbered moneys remaining in the fund at the end of a fiscal year remain in the fund and shall not be credited or transferred to the general fund or another fund.

(2) Pursuant to section 24-75-1104.5 (1.7) (g) , C.R.S., and except as otherwise provided in section 24-75-1104.5 (5) , C.R.S., for the 2016-17 fiscal year and for each fiscal year thereafter so long as the state receives moneys pursuant to the master settlement agreement, the state treasurer shall annually transfer to the fund three and one-half percent of the total amount of the moneys received by the state pursuant to the master settlement agreement, not including attorney fees and costs, during the preceding fiscal year. The state treasurer shall transfer the amount specified in this subsection (2) from moneys credited to the tobacco litigation settlement cash fund created in section 24-22-115, C.R.S.

(3) The department may receive up to five percent of the moneys annually appropriated by the general assembly to the department from the fund created in subsection (1) of this section for the actual costs incurred in administering the program.

# PART 15. BREAST CANCER SCREENING

## 25-4-1501. Legislative declaration.

The general assembly hereby finds and declares that the incidence of breast cancer in women of this state is a significant health problem that can and should be reduced through early detection and treatment. Accordingly, it is the intention of the general assembly in enacting this part 15 to provide breast cancer screening where it is not otherwise readily available for reasons of cost or distance to suitable medical facilities.

## 25-4-1502. Definitions.

As used in this part 15, unless the context otherwise requires:

(1) (Deleted by amendment, L. 95, p. 487, § 2, effective July 1, 1995.)

(2) "Board" means the state board of health.

(3) "Department" means the department of public health and environment.

(3.5) "Diagnostic screening" means the use of procedures including physical examinations, radiologic imaging, surgical techniques, and any new technologies approved by the board for detecting whether abnormalities of the breast are malignant or benign.

(4) "Fund" means the breast cancer screening fund established in section 25-4-1503.

(5) "Screening" means the conduct of physical examinations, visual inspections, or other medical tests exclusively for the purpose of ascertaining the existence of any physiological abnormality which might be indicative of the presence of disease. "Screening" includes diagnostic screening services.

## 25-4-1503. Fund created.

(1) There is hereby established in the state treasury a fund to be known as the breast cancer screening fund, which shall be subject to annual appropriation to the department for the purposes of this part 15. The fund shall be credited with such appropriations as the general assembly may make from the general fund for the purposes of this part 15, as well as any moneys received by the department pursuant to section 25-4-1505 (2) and (4) . In accordance with section 24-36-114, C.R.S., all interest derived from the deposit and investment of this fund shall be credited to the general fund.

(2) All moneys credited to the breast cancer screening fund which are not expended during the fiscal year shall be retained in the fund for its future use and shall not be credited or transferred to the general fund or any other fund.

## 25-4-1504. Allocation of fund.

(1) All moneys in the fund shall be used by the department for the following purposes:

(a) The creation and development of a breast cancer screening program, undertaken by private contract for services or operated by the department, that will improve the availability of breast cancer screening and which may include the purchase, maintenance, and staffing of a truck, a van, or any other vehicle suitably equipped to perform breast cancer screening;

(a.5) To provide such further breast cancer diagnostic screening services, as may be indicated;

(b) The creation and operation of a referral service for the benefit of women for whom further examination or treatment is indicated by the breast cancer screening.

## 25-4-1505. Powers and duties of department and advisory board.

(1) The executive director of the department shall appoint an advisory board which shall recommend guidelines for the services of the program and such rules and regulations as may be necessary to effect the purposes of this part 15. Members of the advisory board shall be persons interested in health care and the promotion of breast cancer screening drawn from both the private and public sectors. The board of health shall have the authority to approve recommendations of the advisory board and the authority to promulgate rules and regulations recommended by the advisory board.

(2) The department is authorized to accept any grant or award of funds from the federal government or private sources for the furtherance of the purposes of this part 15. Any moneys thus

received shall be credited to the fund. Any expenses incurred in the solicitation of donations to the fund shall be paid from the fund.

(3) Any program of breast cancer screening conducted pursuant to this part 15 shall be conducted so as to make such screening available to persons who are at or below two hundred fifty percent of the federal poverty line and who are at least forty years of age but less than sixty-five years of age.

(4) The department may adopt a schedule of fees to be charged for breast cancer screening. The schedule of fees shall be determined so as to make such screening available to the largest possible number of women. The department shall, where practical, collect any available insurance proceeds or other reimbursement payable on behalf of any recipient of a breast cancer screening under this part 15 and may adjust the schedule of fees to reflect insurance contributions. All fees collected shall be credited to the fund.

## 25-4-1506. Repeal of part. (Repealed)

# PART 16. FOOD PROTECTION ACT

## 25-4-1601. Legislative declaration.

(1) The general assembly hereby finds, determines, and declares that it is in the public interest for the department of public health and environment to establish minimum standards and rules for retail food establishments in Colorado and to provide authority for the uniform statewide administration, implementation, interpretation, and enforcement of such minimum standards and rules. Such standards and rules are established to:

(a) Ensure the safety of food prepared, sold, or served in retail food establishments;

(b) Maximize public health protection;

(c) Identify hazards and potential sources of contamination and take measures to prevent, reduce, or eliminate the physical, chemical, or biological agents in food prepared, sold, or served in retail food establishments; and

(d) Improve the sanitary condition of all retail food establishments, reduce food-borne illness outbreaks, and control the spread of food-borne disease from retail food establishments.

(2) This part 16 is deemed an exercise of the police powers of the state for the protection of the health and social welfare of the people of the state of Colorado.

## 25-4-1602. Definitions.

As used in this part 16, unless the context otherwise requires:

(1) "Automated food merchandising enterprise" means the collective activity of the supplying or preparing of food or drink for automated food merchandising machines.

(2) "Certificate of license" means a grant to operate a retail food establishment without a fee, under the conditions set forth in section 25-4-1607 (9) .

(2.5) "County or district public health agency" means a county or district health department or a county or municipal board of health.

(3) "Department" means the department of public health and environment, and its authorized employees.

(4) "Food" means any raw, cooked, or processed edible substance, ice, beverage, or ingredient used or intended for use or for sale in whole or in part for human consumption.

(5) "Fund" means the food protection cash fund created in section 25-4-1608.

(6) "HACCP plan" means a written document setting forth the formal procedures for following hazard analysis critical control point principles.

(6.5) "Imminent health hazard" means a significant threat or danger to health that is considered to exist when there is evidence sufficient to show that a product, practice, circumstance, or event creates a situation that requires immediate correction or cessation of operation to prevent injury or illness based on the number of potential injuries or illnesses and the nature, severity, and duration of the anticipated injury or illness.

(7) "Inspection" means an inspection of a retail food establishment conducted by the department or a county or district board of health to ensure compliance by such establishment with rules promulgated by the department pursuant to this part 16.

(8) "License" means a grant to a licensee to operate a retail food establishment.

(9) "Licensee" means a person that is licensed or who holds a certificate of license pursuant to this part 16 and is responsible for the lawful operation of a retail food establishment.

(10) (Deleted by amendment, L. 2009, (SB 09-223), ch. 255, p. 1151, § 2, effective May 15, 2009.)

(11) "Modified atmosphere packaging" means the reduction of the amount of oxygen in a package by mechanically evacuating the oxygen, displacing the oxygen with another gas or combination of gases, or otherwise controlling the oxygen content to a level below that normally found in the surrounding atmosphere, which is twenty-one percent oxygen.

(12) "Nonpotentially hazardous" means any food or beverage that, when stored under normal conditions without refrigeration, will not support the rapid and progressive growth of microorganisms that cause food infections or food intoxications.

(13) "Person" means a natural person, partnership, association, company, corporation, or organization or a manager, agent, servant, officer, or employee of any of such entities.

(14) "Retail food establishment" means a retail operation that stores, prepares, or packages food for human consumption or serves or otherwise provides food for human consumption to consumers directly or indirectly through a delivery service, whether such food is consumed on or off the premises or whether there is a charge for such food. "Retail food establishment" does not mean:

(a) Any private home;

(b) Private boarding houses;

(c) Hospital and health facility patient feeding operations licensed by the department;

(d) Child care centers and other child care facilities licensed by the department of human services;

(e) Hunting camps and other outdoor recreation locations where food is prepared in the field rather than at a fixed base of operation;

(f) Food or beverage wholesale manufacturing, processing, or packaging plants, or portions thereof, that are subject to regulatory controls under state or federal laws or regulations;

(g) Motor vehicles used only for the transport of food;

(h) Establishments preparing and serving only hot coffee, hot tea, instant hot beverages, and nonpotentially hazardous doughnuts or pastries obtained from sources complying with all laws related to food and food labeling;

(i) Establishments that handle only nonpotentially hazardous prepackaged food and operations serving only commercially prepared, prepackaged foods requiring no preparation other than the heating of food within its original container or package;

(j) Farmers markets and roadside markets that offer only uncut fresh fruit and vegetables for sale;

(k) Automated food merchandising enterprises that supply only prepackaged nonpotentially hazardous food or drink or food or drink in bottles, cans, or cartons only, and operations that dispense only chewing gum or salted nuts in their natural protective covering;

(l) The donation, preparation, sale, or service of food by a nonprofit or charitable organization in conjunction with an event or celebration if such donation, preparation, sale, or service of food:

(I) Does not exceed the duration of the event or celebration or a maximum of fifty-two days within a calendar year; and

(II) Takes place in the county in which such nonprofit or charitable organization resides or is principally located.

(m) A home, commercial, private, or public kitchen in which a person produces food products sold directly to consumers pursuant to the "Colorado Cottage Foods Act", section 25-4-1614.

(15) "Safe food" means food that does not contain any poisonous, deleterious, or disease-causing substance or microorganisms that may render such food injurious to human health.

(16) "Special event" means an organized event or celebration at which retail food establishments prepare, serve, or otherwise provide food for human consumption.

(17) "Uniform statewide administration, implementation, interpretation, and enforcement" means the application of the rules adopted by the state board of health and the policy guidance of the department by state and county or district public health agencies responsible for implementation of the rules and policies. The uniform application shall not preclude county or district public health agencies from implementing administrative efficiencies or practices if the practices do not conflict with the state board of health rules or department policies.

## 25-4-1603. Licensing, certification, and food protection agency.

The department is hereby designated the state licensing, certification, and food protection agency for the purpose of protecting the public health and ensuring a safe food supply in this state. In addition to such designation, the department is hereby authorized to regulate and control retail food establishments, promulgate rules governing the operation of such establishments, and uniformly enforce and administer this part 16.

## 25-4-1604. Powers and duties of department - rules.

(1) The department shall have the following powers and duties:

(a) To grant or refuse licenses and certificates of license pursuant to section 25-4-1606, or to suspend or revoke licenses and certificates of license pursuant to section 25-4-1609;

(b) (I) To promulgate rules for adoption by the state board of health pursuant to article 4 of title 24, C.R.S., for the uniform statewide administration, implementation, interpretation, and enforcement of this part 16 and, as necessary, to ensure a safe food supply in retail food establishments. Such rules may include provisions for the initial and periodic medical examination by the department or other competent medical authority of all employees of retail food establishments and shall include provisions specifying and regulating the places and conditions under which food shall be prepared for consumption, a uniform code of sanitary rules, and such other rules as the department deems necessary. Such rules may be modified and changed from time to time.

(II) For purposes of this paragraph (b), a uniform code of sanitary rules means rules for the preparation, sale, and serving of food, including but not be limited to general overall retail food establishment and equipment design and construction; sanitary maintenance of equipment, utensils, and facilities for food preparation, service, and storage; wholesomeness of food and drink; source and protection of food and water; disposal of liquid and solid wastes; and other rules for the effective administration and enforcement of this part 16.

(c) To hear and determine all complaints against licensees or grantees of certificates of license and to administer oaths and issue subpoenas to require the presence of any person necessary to the determination of any such hearing;

(d) To uniformly enforce this part 16 and the rules promulgated pursuant to this section;

(e) To enter retail food establishments during business hours and at other times during which activity is evident to conduct inspections and other interventions related to food safety and the protection of public health;

(f) To develop and enforce uniform statewide standards of program conduct and performance to be followed and adhered to by employees of the department and county or district boards of health;

(g) To provide technical assistance, equipment and product review, training and standardization, program evaluation, and other services necessary to assure the uniform statewide administration, implementation, interpretation, and enforcement of this part 16 and rules promulgated under this part 16;

(h) To review and approve HACCP plans submitted for evaluation to verify and ensure that food handling risks are reduced to prevent food-borne illness outbreaks;

(i) To delegate to any county or district board of health the powers and duties described in paragraphs (a) , (c) , (d) , (e) , and (h) of this subsection (1) at the request of such county or district board of health.

(2) Subsection (1) of this section shall not apply to the city and county of Denver, which, by ordinance, may provide for the licensure of retail food establishments.

## 25-4-1605. Submission of plans for approval - required.

(1) An owner or operator of a retail food establishment shall submit plans and specifications to the department or a county or district board of health in the jurisdiction in which a retail food establishment is to be constructed or extensively remodeled before such construction or extensive remodeling is begun or any existing structure is converted for use as a retail food establishment. Such plans and specifications shall be submitted for review and approval, in such form as the department requires or approves, to ensure that the retail food establishment layout, equipment, and food handling procedures are conducive to providing a safe food product. Each plan and specification submission shall be accompanied by the fees set forth in section 25-4-1607. The department and a county or district board of health shall treat the plans and specifications as confidential trade secret information. The plans and specifications shall indicate the proposed layout, arrangement, mechanical plants, construction materials of work areas, and the location, type, and model of proposed fixed equipment and facilities.

(2) The construction, extensive remodeling, or conversion of any retail food establishment shall be in accordance with the plans and specifications submitted to and approved by the department or a county or district board of health. The department or a county or district board of health shall conduct preopening inspections of retail food establishments to assure compliance with the approved plans, as circumstances require.

(3) An owner or operator of a retail food establishment shall submit an HACCP plan to the department or a county or district board of health for review and approval before beginning a modified atmosphere packaging process or other food preparation method that does not meet rules promulgated by the department. HACCP plans shall be submitted in such form as the department requires or approves. The submission shall ensure that food handling risks are reduced to prevent food-borne illness and outbreaks. The department and any county or district board of health shall treat HACCP plans as confidential trade secret information.

(4) The department or a county or district board of health shall respond to any plans and specifications submitted pursuant to subsection (1) of this section and to any HACCP plan submitted pursuant to subsection (3) of this section within fourteen working days after receipt. If a submitted HACCP plan or other plan or specification is deemed inadequate, the department or a county or district board of health shall respond in writing to the submitter of the plans or specifications with a statement describing how such deficiencies may be corrected.

## 25-4-1606. Licensure - exception.

(1) An application for a license or a certificate of license shall be filed with the department or a county or district board of health before any person may operate a retail food establishment in this state. The application shall be on a form supplied by the department and shall include such information as the department may require.

(2) Before granting any license or certificate of license, the department or a county or district board of health may conduct an inspection of the retail food establishment to determine compliance with the rules promulgated by the department. If the applicant appears to be in compliance with the rules and with the applicable provisions of this part 16, the department or a county or district board of health shall approve the application for a license or certificate of license.

(2.5) If a critical violation or a noncritical violation that is significant in nature is documented during a preoperational inspection, and the retail food establishment is unable to correct the violation while the inspector is on site, follow-up activities shall be conducted for the purpose of

249

granting a license or certificate of license.

(3) Every license and certificate of license granted pursuant to this section shall specify the date granted, the period of coverage, the name of the licensee, and the name and address of the licensed establishment. All licenses shall be conspicuously displayed at all times in the licensed establishment.

(4) Licenses and certificates of license shall be valid for one calendar year or such portion thereof as remains after the granting of a license or certificate. When a license or certificate is valid for only a portion of a calendar year, there shall be no reduction of the fees required by section 25-4-1607. All licenses and certificates of license shall expire December 31 of the year in which they were granted and renewal applications shall be filed with the department during December of each year. Once a license or certificate of license has been granted, the department or a county or district board of health shall not refuse to renew such license or certificate unless the licensee has engaged in an unlawful act set forth in section 25-4-1610 or is in violation of any rules promulgated pursuant to this part 16.

(5) Subsections (1) and (2) of this section shall not apply in the city and county of Denver, which, by ordinance, may provide for the licensure of retail food establishments.

## 25-4-1607. Fees.

(1) Except as provided in subsections (1) (d.5) and (14) of this section, effective January 1 of the year following the increases specified in subsection (1.5) (a) of this section, each retail food establishment in this state shall be assessed an annual license fee as follows:

(a) A retail food establishment preparing or serving food in individual portions for immediate on- or off-premises consumption shall be assessed an annual fee based on the following schedule:
Seating Capacity Fee
0 to 100$385 101 to 200430 Over 200465

(a.5) A retail food establishment limited to preparing or serving food that does not require time or temperature control for safety, providing self-service beverages, offering prepackaged commercially prepared food and beverages requiring time or temperature control, or only reheating commercially prepared foods that require time or temperature control for safety for retail sale to consumers shall be assessed an annual fee of two hundred seventy dollars.

(b) A retail food establishment only offering prepackaged commercially prepared food and beverages, including those that are required to be held at refrigerated or frozen time or temperature control for safety for retail sale to consumers for off-premises consumption, shall be assessed an annual fee based on the following schedule:
Square Footage Fee
Less than 15,001$195 over 15,000353

(c) A retail food establishment offering food for retail sale to consumers for off-premises consumption and preparing or serving food in individual portions for immediate consumption either on- or off-premises shall be assessed an annual fee based on the following schedule:
Square Footage Fee
Less than 15,001$375 over 15,000715

(c.5) A retail food establishment offering food at a temporary living quarter for workers associated with oil and gas shall be assessed an annual fee of eight hundred fifty-five dollars.

(d) A retail food establishment is subject to only one of the fees established in this subsection (1) ; except that effective September 1, 2016, the license fees established for retail food establishments at a special event, as defined in section 25-4-1602 (16) , must be established by the county or district public health agency.

(d.5) The fees established in this subsection (1) are effective September 1, 2018, for any new retail food establishment that was not licensed and in operation prior to that date.

(e) (I) Retail food establishment license fees shall be established pursuant to this subsection (1) ; except that:

(A) The city and county of Denver may establish such fees by ordinance; and

(B) A county or district board of health may establish fees that are lower than the fees listed in subsection (1.5) of this section if the county or district board of health is in compliance with this part 16;

(II) Notwithstanding subparagraph (I) of this paragraph (e) , the fees established in this subsection (1) or by ordinance of the city and county of Denver shall be the only annual license fees charged by the state or any county, district, local, or regional inspection authority and shall cover all inspections of a retail food establishment pursuant to this subsection (1) throughout an annual license period.

(1.5) (a) Except as provided in subparagraph (VI) of this paragraph (a) and subsection (14) of this section, effective January 1, 2018, to December 31, 2018, each retail food establishment in this state shall be assessed an annual license fee as follows:

(I) A retail food establishment preparing or serving food in individual portions for immediate on- or off-premises consumption shall be assessed an annual fee based on the following schedule:
Seating Capacity Fee
0 to 100$ 360 101 to 200400 Over 200435

(II) A retail food establishment preparing or serving food that does not require time or temperature control for safety, providing self-service beverages, offering prepackaged commercially prepared food and beverages requiring time or temperature control or only reheating commercially prepared foods that require time or temperature control for safety for retail sale to consumers shall be assessed an annual fee of two hundred fifty-three dollars.

(III) A retail food establishment only offering prepackaged commercially prepared food and beverages, including those that are required to be held at refrigerated or frozen time or temperature control for safety for retail sale to consumers for off-premises consumption, shall be assessed an annual fee based on the following schedule:
Square Footage Fee
Less than 15,001$183 Over 15,000330

(IV) A retail food establishment offering food for retail sale to consumers for off-premises consumption and preparing or serving food in individual portions for immediate consumption either on- or off-premises shall be assessed an annual fee based on the following schedule:
Square Footage Fee
Less than 15,001$350 Over 15,000665

(V) A retail food establishment offering food at a temporary living quarter for workers associated with oil and gas shall be assessed an annual fee of eight hundred dollars.

(VI) The fees established in this subsection (1.5) are effective September 1, 2017, for any new retail food establishment that was not licensed and in operation prior to that date.

(b) Effective January 1, 2017, to December 31, 2017, each retail food establishment in this state shall be assessed an annual license fee as follows:

(I) A retail food establishment preparing or serving food in individual portions for immediate on- or off-premises consumption shall be assessed an annual fee based on the following schedule:
Seating Capacity Fee
0 to 100$330 101 to 200370 Over 200405

(II) A retail food establishment limited to preparing or serving food that does not require time or temperature control for safety, providing self-service beverages, offering prepackaged commercially prepared food and beverages requiring time or temperature control or only reheating commercially prepared foods that require time or temperature control for safety for retail sale to consumers shall be assessed an annual fee of two hundred thirty-five dollars.

251

(III) A retail food establishment only offering prepackaged commercially prepared food and beverages, including those that are required to be held at refrigerated or frozen time or temperature control for safety for retail sale to consumers for off-premises consumption, shall be assessed an annual fee based on the following schedule:

Square Footage Fee
Less than 15,001 $170 Over 15,000 305

(IV) A retail food establishment offering food for retail sale to consumers for off-premises consumption and preparing or serving food in individual portions for immediate consumption either on- or off-premises shall be assessed an annual fee based on the following schedule:

Square Footage Fee
Less than 15,001 $325 Over 15,000 620

(V) A retail food establishment offering food at a temporary living quarter for workers associated with oil and gas shall be assessed an annual fee of seven hundred forty dollars.

(VI) Repealed.

(c) A retail food establishment is subject to only one of the fees established in this subsection (1.5) per year.

(d) Retail food establishment license fees shall be established pursuant to this subsection (1.5) ; except that:

(I) The city and county of Denver may establish such fees by ordinance; and

(II) A county or district board of health may establish fees that are lower than the fees listed in this subsection (1.5) if the county or district board of health is in compliance with this part 16.

(2) At the time a plan is submitted for review, an application fee of one hundred dollars shall be paid to the department or a county or district board of health. The fee for plan review and preopening inspection of a new or remodeled retail food establishment shall be the actual cost of such review, which shall not exceed five hundred eighty dollars. Such costs shall be payable at the time the plan is approved and an inspection is completed to determine compliance.

(3) At the time an equipment review is submitted, an application fee of one hundred dollars shall be paid to the department. The fee for equipment review by the department to determine compliance with applicable standards shall be the actual cost of such review, which shall not exceed five hundred dollars. Such costs shall be payable when the review is completed.

(4) The fee for an HACCP plan review of a specific written process shall be the actual cost of such review, which shall not exceed one hundred dollars. The review of an HACCP plan for a process already conducted at a facility shall be the actual cost of such review, which shall not exceed four hundred dollars. Costs shall be paid at the time the plan is approved and an inspection is completed.

(5) The fee for services requested by any person seeking department or county or district board of health review of a potential retail food establishment site shall be seventy-five dollars or the actual cost of such review, whichever is greater. Seventy-five dollars of such fee shall be billed at the time the review is requested, and the remainder shall be payable when services are completed.

(6) The fee for food protection services provided to special events shall not exceed the actual cost of such services and shall be paid by the organizer of such special event when services are completed.

(7) The fee for any requested service not specifically set forth in this section shall not exceed the actual cost of such service.

(8) The actual cost of a service shall be established by the department or a county or district board of health, whichever provided the service.

(9) (a) A certificate of license may be issued to and in the name and address of any:

(I) Public or nonpublic school for students in kindergarten through twelfth grade or any portion thereof;

(II) Penal institution;

(III) Nonprofit organization that provides food solely to people who are food insecure, including, but not limited to, a soup kitchen, food pantry, or home delivery service; and

(IV) Local government entity or nonprofit organization that donates, prepares, or sells food at a special event, including, but not limited to, a school sporting event, firefighters' picnic, or church supper, that takes place in the county in which the local government entity or nonprofit organization resides or is principally located.

(b) No institution or organization listed in paragraph (a) of this subsection (9) shall pay any fee imposed on a retail food establishment pursuant to this section.

(10) County or district boards of health created in part 5 of article 1 of this title shall collect fees under this section if the county or district boards of health are authorized by the department to enforce this part 16 and any rules promulgated pursuant to this part 16.

(11) (Deleted by amendment, L. 2009, (SB 09-223) , ch. 255, p. 1155, § 7, effective May 15, 2009.)

(12) Notwithstanding the amount specified for any fee in this section, the state board of health by rule or as otherwise provided by law may reduce the amount of one or more of the fees if necessary pursuant to section 24-75-402 (3) , C.R.S., to reduce the uncommitted reserves of the fund to which all or any portion of one or more of the fees is credited. After the uncommitted reserves of the fund are sufficiently reduced, the state board of health by rule or as otherwise provided by law may increase the amount of one or more of the fees as provided in section 24-75-402 (4) , C.R.S.

(13) Legislative declaration - disposition of fee revenue. (a) The general assembly does not intend for the fees paid by retail food establishments as outlined in subsections (1) and (1.5) of this section to subsidize inspection or other costs associated with entities exempt from fees under paragraph (a) of subsection (9) of this section.

(b) Counties may only spend the increased revenue from the increase of retail food establishment fees on retail food health-related activities. Prior to January 1, 2019, supplanting funds for other county programs is prohibited.

(14) (a) The fee increase in subsection (1.5) of this section does not take effect until the department and all local public health agencies contracted by the department to perform inspections and enforce regulations regarding retail food establishments prove compliance with section 25-4-1607.7 (2) . If the department and all local public health agencies are not in compliance on January 1, 2018, the increase does not take effect until January 1 in the year following proven compliance.

(b) The fee increase in subsection (1) of this section does not take effect until the department proves compliance with section 25-4-1607.9 (1) . If the department is not in compliance on January 1 following the fee increase specified in subsection (1.5) of this section, the increase in subsection (1) does not take effect until January 1 in the year following proven compliance.

(c) The executive director of the department shall notify the revisor of statutes, in writing, when the conditions specified in paragraphs (a) and (b) of this subsection (14) have been satisfied.

## 25-4-1607.5. Retail food establishment regulation - fees - investigations - stakeholder process.

(1) The executive director of the department or his or her designee shall convene a stakeholder group, including representatives from Colorado associations representing county or district public health agencies, county commissioners, retail food establishments, and any other party that represents a retail food establishment and expresses interest in participating.

(2) The department shall keep and maintain a list of stakeholders.

(3) The department shall convene the first meeting with the stakeholders no later than June 15, 2015, and as needed thereafter. After submission of the report described in subsection (5) of this section, the department shall meet with the stakeholders at least once every three years.

(4) The department shall meet with the stakeholders to study retail food establishments, retail food establishment license fees, and retail food inspection programs, including:

(a) Incidents of, and trends in, food-borne illnesses, including the correlation to inspections;

(b) Uniform statewide administration, implementation, interpretation, and enforcement of the inspection program to include, at a minimum:

(I) Training;

(II) Application;

(III) Communication to the public;

(IV) Guidance documents; and

(V) Inspection frequency, including compliance strategies;

(c) Potential regulatory changes;

(d) Collaboration with the industry;

(e) A requested annual license fee adjustment with appropriate documentation, including costs of providing an inspection;

(f) An annual license fee charged for parochial, public, or private schools; charitable organizations and benevolent, nonprofit retail food establishments that assist elderly, incapacitated, or disadvantaged persons; and nonprofit or charitable organizations that donate, prepare, sell, or serve food in conjunction with an event or celebration;

(g) Alternative administrative actions;

(h) The current annual license fee structure and license categories;

(i) The review of risk-based inspection schedules; and

(j) The actual cost of inspections.

(5) On or before December 1, 2015, and every three years thereafter, the executive director of the department or his or her designee shall prepare a report of the findings and conclusions of the study and shall present the report to all stakeholders and others upon request.

## 25-4-1607.7. Health inspection results - development of a uniform system - communication to the public.

(1) On or before January 1, 2017, the department shall solicit input from retail food establishments, contracted local public health agencies, county commissioners, and others with a vested interest in the retail food inspection program to establish a uniform system to communicate health inspection results to the public. The uniform system established pursuant to this section must provide meaningful and reasonably detailed information to the public and must not summarize the results of the inspection with a letter, number, or symbol grading system, or a similar, oversimplified method of quantifying results.

(2) After July 1, 2017, the department or a local public health agency contracted by the department to perform inspections and enforce regulations regarding retail food establishments shall only utilize the system developed and approved by the department to communicate inspection results.

## 25-4-1607.9. Department targets - audits - reporting.

(1) On or before April 1, 2017, the department shall respond to all plans and specifications and HACCP plan reviews within fourteen working days after receipt, as required by section 25-4-1605 (4) .

(2) On or before December 31, 2019, the department shall ensure significant statewide compliance with the federal food and drug administration's voluntary national retail food regulatory program standards by verifying that:

(a) At least seventy percent of Colorado's retail food program staff meet the national criteria for appropriate training and education to adequately perform required inspections; and

(b) At least seventy percent of Colorado's retail food program staff meet the national criteria regarding the focus of inspections on critical item risk factors, the correction of documented deficiencies, and the focus of inspections on the highest-risk establishments.

(3) To verify compliance with this section:

(a) The department shall audit any local public health agency that conducts inspections within its jurisdiction; and

(b) Local public health agencies shall audit the department regarding the jurisdictions where the department conducts inspections.

(4) The results of the audits conducted pursuant to subsection (3) of this section must be documented and reported during each stakeholder process held pursuant to section 25-4-1607.5.

## 25-4-1608. Food protection cash fund - creation.

(1) Fees collected by the department pursuant to section 25-4-1607 shall be transmitted to the state treasurer who shall credit the same to the food protection cash fund, which fund is hereby created in the state treasury. The general assembly shall appropriate the moneys in the fund to the department for the payment of salaries and expenses necessary for the administration of this part 16.

(2) Forty-three dollars of each fee collected by the department and a county or district board of health pursuant to section 25-4-1607 (1) (a) , (1) (a.5) , (1) (b) , (1) (c) , (1) (c.5) , (1) (e) (I) (B) , (1.5) (a) (I) , (1.5) (a) (II) , (1.5) (a) (III) , (1.5) (a) (IV) , (1.5) (a) (V) , (1.5) (b) (I) , (1.5) (b) (II) , (1.5) (b) (III) , (1.5) (b) (IV) , (1.5) (b) (V) , and (1.5) (d) (II) shall be transmitted to the state treasurer, who shall credit the fee to the food protection cash fund created in subsection (1) of this section. This portion of the fee shall be used by the department to conduct the duties and responsibilities set forth in section 25-4-1604 (1) (a) , (1) (b) , (1) (c) , (1) (f) , (1) (g) , and (1) (i) . The remainder of the fee shall be retained by the county or district board of health for deposit in the appropriate county or district public health agency fund in accordance with section 25-1-511 or, if the fee is collected by the department, it shall be deposited pursuant to subsection (1) of this section, and used to pay a portion of the cost of conducting a retail food establishment protection program.

(3) Any interest derived from the deposit and investment of moneys in the food protection cash fund shall be credited to such fund. Any unexpended or unencumbered moneys remaining in such fund at the end of a fiscal year shall remain in the fund and shall not revert or be transferred to the general fund or any other fund of the state.

## 25-4-1609. Disciplinary actions - closure - revocation - suspension - review.

(1) The department or a county or district board of health may, on its own motion or complaint and after an investigation and hearing at which the licensee is afforded an opportunity to be heard, suspend or revoke a license or certificate of license for any violation of this part 16, any rule adopted pursuant to this part 16, or any of the terms, conditions, or provisions of such license or certificate of license. A written notice of suspension or revocation, as well as any required notice of hearing, shall be sent to the licensee by certified mail, or by one or more other methods that assure receipt, at the address contained in the license or certificate of license.

(2) Except in cases of closure due to an imminent health hazard, proceedings for the revocation or suspension of a license or certificate of license may not be commenced until after the imposition of the penalties prescribed by section 25-4-1611. The maximum period of suspension is one month. When a license or certificate of license is suspended or revoked, no part of the fees paid for a license may be returned to the licensee.

(2.5) The department or a county or district board of health may issue a cease-and-desist administrative order if a person or licensee has been issued a civil penalty in accordance with section 25-4-1611 (1) and remains in noncompliance.

(3) Any suspension or revocation of a license or certificate of license may be reviewed by any court of general jurisdiction having jurisdiction over the retail food establishment for which the application for license or certificate of license was made. If such court determines that such suspension or revocation was without good cause, it shall order the department to reinstate such license or certificate of license.

## 25-4-1609.5. Grievance process.

(1) If a licensee believes that a county or district public health agency is taking regulatory action outside the scope of its authority, the licensee may file a written complaint with the department

within thirty days after the licensee's knowledge of the regulatory action.

(2) Within forty-five days after receipt of a written complaint pursuant to subsection (1) of this section, the department shall convene a dispute resolution panel that consists of one person from the department, one person from the retail food industry, and one person from a county or district public health agency who is not within the jurisdiction of the licensee requesting resolution. The dispute resolution panel shall allow the licensee and the county or district public health agency to provide information related to the grievance. The dispute resolution panel shall make findings concerning the grievance and shall recommend to the county or district public health agency a resolution to the dispute. The county or district public health agency shall implement the recommendations within thirty days after receipt of the findings and recommendations from the dispute resolution panel. If the parties to the grievance resolve the complaint prior to review by the dispute resolution panel, the parties shall notify the department in writing and the grievance shall be dismissed.

(3) If the county or district public health agency fails to implement the recommendations of the dispute resolution panel within thirty days after receipt of the recommendations, the county or district public health agency shall provide the licensee with the opportunity to request an administrative hearing in accordance with section 24-4-105, C.R.S.

## 25-4-1610. Unlawful acts.

(1) It is unlawful for:

(a) Any person to begin the construction or extensive remodeling of a retail food establishment unless such person has received department or county or district board of health approval of plans and specifications for such construction or remodeling pursuant to section 25-4-1605;

(b) Any person to operate a retail food establishment without a valid license or certificate of license from the department or a county or district board of health having jurisdiction over such establishment;

(c) Any person to violate this part 16 and any rules promulgated pursuant to this part 16;

(d) Any person or retail food establishment to refuse to permit entry to such establishment in accordance with sections 25-4-1604 (1) (e) and 25-4-1606 (2) ;

(e) Any retail food establishment to sell or serve food prepared in a private home to any person;

(f) Any person to fail to pay a civil penalty assessed by the department or a county or district board of health.

## 25-4-1611. Violation - penalties.

(1) If the department or a county or district board of health finds that a licensee or other person operating a retail food establishment was provided with written notification of a violation of section 25-4-1610 (1) (a) , (1) (b) , (1) (d) , (1) (e) , or (1) (f) and was given a reasonable time to comply but remained in noncompliance, such person shall be subject to a civil penalty of not less than two hundred fifty dollars and not more than one thousand dollars, assessed by the department or a county or district board of health.

(2) (a) Upon a finding by the department or a county or district board of health that a retail food establishment is in violation of this part 16 or the rules promulgated pursuant to this part 16, and that the violation is sufficient to permit the department or a county or district board of health to establish a date and time for correction, the department or county or district board of health shall, in writing, advise the licensee or other person operating the establishment of the violation, provide the person with a reasonable time to comply, and conduct a follow-up inspection. If, at the time of the follow-up inspection, the establishment is found to be in violation of the same provisions, the department or a county or district board of health shall issue the person a written notification of noncompliance, provide the person with a reasonable time to comply, and conduct a second follow-up inspection.

(b) (I) If, at a second follow-up inspection, a retail food establishment is found to be in compliance with the same provisions as were cited in the written notification issued pursuant to paragraph (a) of this subsection (2) , the department or a county or district board of health shall advise the licensee or other person operating the establishment that noncompliance with such provisions at the next regular inspection shall result in the issuance of a second written notification of noncompliance.

(II) If, at a second follow-up inspection, a retail food establishment is found to be in violation of the same provisions as were cited in the written notification of noncompliance issued pursuant to paragraph (a) of this subsection (2) , the department or a county or district board of health shall issue a second written notification of noncompliance, advising the licensee or other person operating the establishment of the violation and potential civil penalties that may be assessed if the noncompliance continues. The department or a county or district board of health shall conduct a third follow-up inspection.

(c) (I) If, at a third follow-up inspection, a retail food establishment is found to be in compliance with the same provisions as were cited in the second written notification of noncompliance issued pursuant to paragraph (b) of this subsection (2) , the department or a county or district board of health may assess a civil penalty of not less than two hundred fifty dollars nor more than five hundred dollars and shall advise the person operating the establishment in writing that future noncompliance with the cited provisions in the second notification of noncompliance shall result in the issuance of a third written notification of noncompliance and subject the establishment to an additional civil penalty of not less than two hundred fifty dollars nor more than five hundred dollars.

(II) If, at a third follow-up inspection, a retail food establishment is found to be in violation of the same provisions as were cited in the second written notification of noncompliance issued pursuant to paragraph (b) of this subsection (2) , the department or a county or district board of health may assess a civil penalty of not less than five hundred dollars nor more than one thousand dollars. When compliance with the provisions cited in the second written notification of noncompliance is obtained, the department or a county or district board of health shall notify the licensee or other person operating the establishment in writing that noncompliance with the cited provisions in the second notification of noncompliance at the next regular inspection will result in the issuance of a third written notification of noncompliance and may result in an additional civil penalty of not less than five hundred dollars nor more than one thousand dollars.

(3) A maximum of three civil penalties may be assessed against a licensee or other person operating a retail food establishment in any twelve-month period. Whenever a third civil penalty is assessed in a twelve-month period, the department or a county or district board of health may initiate proceedings to suspend or revoke the license of the licensee pursuant to section 25-4-1609.

(4) Neither the department nor a county or district board of health shall assess a civil penalty pursuant to this section if a disciplinary action is pending against the same licensee under section 25-4-1609.

(5) (a) All penalties collected by the department pursuant to this section shall be transmitted to the state treasurer, who shall credit the same to the food protection cash fund created in section 25-4-1608.

(b) Penalties collected by a county or district board of health shall be deposited in the appropriate county or district public health agency fund in accordance with section 25-4-1608, and shall be used to pay expenses related to the inspection of retail food establishments.

(6) To obtain compliance with this part 16, the department or a county or district board of health may allow the owner of a retail food establishment to use any assessed penalty fee to pay for employee training or the cost of needed improvements to the establishment.

(7) In addition to the remedies provided in this part 16 and other remedies provided by law, the department or a county or district board of health is authorized to apply to the county or district court of the county or district where a retail food establishment is located for a temporary or permanent injunction, and such court shall have jurisdiction to issue an injunction restraining any person from violating section 25-4-1610.

## 25-4-1612. Judicial review.

Any person adversely affected or aggrieved by a department decision to refuse to grant a license or certificate of license may seek judicial review in the district court having jurisdiction over the retail food establishment for which the application for license or certificate of license was made. Any other final order or determination by the department or a county or district board of health pursuant to this part 16 shall be subject to judicial review in accordance with article 4 of title 24, C.R.S.

## 25-4-1613. General fund moneys - repeal. (Repealed)

## 25-4-1614. Home kitchens - exemption - food inspection - short title - definitions - rules.

(1) This section shall be known and may be cited as the "Colorado Cottage Foods Act". The purposes of this section are to allow for the sale and consumption of homemade foods and to encourage the expansion of agricultural sales by farmers' markets, farms, and home-based producers and accessibility of these resources to informed end consumers by:

(a) Facilitating the purchase and consumption of fresh and local agricultural products;

(b) Enhancing the agricultural economy; and

(c) Providing Colorado citizens with unimpeded access to healthy food from known sources.

(2) (a) A producer may use his or her home kitchen or a commercial, private, or public kitchen to produce foods for sale only if the producer sells the foods directly to informed end consumers.

(b) (I) A producer is permitted under this section to sell only a limited range of foods that have been produced, processed, or packaged that are nonpotentially hazardous and do not require refrigeration. These foods include pickled fruits and vegetables, spices, teas, dehydrated produce, nuts, seeds, honey, jams, jellies, preserves, fruit butter, flour, and baked goods, including candies, fruit empanadas, and tortillas, and other nonpotentially hazardous foods.

(II) A person may sell whole eggs under this section; except that a person may not sell more than two hundred fifty dozen whole eggs per month under this section. A person selling whole eggs must meet the requirements of section 35-21-105, C.R.S.

(c) A producer must take a food safety course that includes basic food handling training and is comparable to, or is a course given by, the Colorado state university extension service or a state, county, or district public health agency, and must maintain a status of good standing in accordance with the course requirements, including attending any additional classes if necessary.

(d) The foods produced under this section must:

(I) Be delivered directly from a producer to an informed end consumer;

(II) Be sold only in Colorado; and

(III) Not involve interstate commerce.

(e) This section applies only to producers who earn net revenues of ten thousand dollars or less per calendar year from the sale of each eligible food product produced in the producer's home kitchen or a commercial, private, or public kitchen.

(3) (a) A food product sold under this section must have an affixed label that includes at least:

(I) Identification of the product;

(II) The producer's name, the address at which the food was prepared, and the producer's current telephone number or electronic mail address;

(III) The date on which the food was produced;

(IV) A complete list of ingredients; and

(V) The following disclaimer: "This product was produced in a home kitchen that is not subject to state licensure or inspection and that may also process common food allergens such as tree nuts, peanuts, eggs, soy, wheat, milk, fish, and crustacean shellfish. This product is not intended for resale."

(b) A food product sold under this section and not labeled in accordance with paragraph (a) of this subsection (3) is misbranded and is subject to food sampling and inspection pursuant to subsection (4) of this section.

(c) A producer operating under this section shall conspicuously display a placard, sign, or card at the point of sale with the following disclaimer: "This product was produced in a home kitchen that is not subject to state licensure or inspection. This product is not intended for resale."

(4) A food product produced pursuant to this section is subject to food sampling and inspection by the department or a county, district, or regional health agency pursuant to section 25-5-406 if it is determined that the food product is misbranded pursuant to subsection (3) of this section or if a consumer complaint has been received or if the product is suspected in an injury or food-borne illness outbreak.

(5) A person who purchases a product made by a producer shall not resell the product.

(6) A person who sells foods pursuant to this act is encouraged to maintain home bakery liability insurance or other adequate liability insurance.

(7) Sections 25-4-1604 to 25-4-1613 do not apply to this section.

(8) The department or a county, district, or regional health agency may create a voluntary electronic registry of producers if it determines that a registry would be of value to producers and consumers.

(9) As used in this section:

(a) "Home" means a primary residence occupied by the producer producing the food under this section.

(a.5) "Homemade" means food that is prepared in a private home kitchen, or a commercial, private, or public kitchen, when the kitchen is not licensed, inspected, or regulated.

(a.7) "Informed end consumer" means a person who is the last person to purchase any product, who does not resell the product, and who has been informed that the product is not licensed, regulated, or inspected.

(b) "Nonpotentially hazardous" has the meaning set forth in section 25-4-1602 (12) .

(c) "Producer" means a person who prepares nonpotentially hazardous foods in a home kitchen or similar venue for sale directly to consumers pursuant to this section and includes that person's designated representative. A producer may only be:

(I) An individual who is a resident of Colorado; or

(II) A limited liability company formed in Colorado, consisting of two or fewer members, and of which all members are residents of Colorado.

(10) Repealed.

# PART 17. INFANT IMMUNIZATION ACT

## 25-4-1701. Short title.
This part 17 shall be known and may be cited as the "Infant Immunization Act".

## 25-4-1702. Legislative declaration.
(1) The general assembly hereby finds, determines, and declares that vaccine preventable diseases represent a serious public health threat to the people of this state. It has been well documented that vaccines are an effective way to save lives and prevent debilitating disease. Vaccines are among the most cost-effective components of preventive medical care because for every dollar spent on immunization, ten dollars are saved in later medical expenses.

(2) The general assembly further finds, determines, and declares that the rate of routine immunization among preschool children appears to be falling steadily. Therefore, it is the purpose of this part 17 to fully immunize all infants, subject to available appropriations, at a level that is age-appropriate as determined by the board of health.

(3) The general assembly further finds, determines, and declares that the inability of some parents

to personally take their children to health care professionals for the purpose of immunization contributes to the significant number of children who have not been immunized on a timely basis in accordance with this part 17. Therefore, it is the further purpose of this part 17 to provide an alternative method by which such children may be immunized without circumventing parental authority and control.

## 25-4-1703. Definitions.
As used in this part 17, unless the context otherwise requires:
(1) "Board of health" means the state board of health.
(2) "Department" means the state department of public health and environment.
(3) "Infant" means any child up to twenty-four months of age or any child eligible for vaccination and enrolled under the "Colorado Medical Assistance Act", articles 4, 5, and 6 of title 25.5, C.R.S.
(3.5) "Minor" means any child under eighteen years of age.
(4) "Practitioner" means a duly licensed physician or other person who is permitted and otherwise qualified to administer vaccines under the laws of this state.
(5) "Vaccine" means such vaccines as are determined by the board of health to be necessary to conform to recognized standard medical practices. Such term includes, but is not limited to, the following vaccines:
(a) Diphtheria-tetanus-pertussis (DTP) ;
(b) Polio: Oral polio vaccine (OPV) or inactivated polio vaccine (IPV) ;
(c) Measles-mumps-rubella (MMR) ;
(d) Haemophilus influenzae type B conjugate vaccines (HIB) .

## 25-4-1704. Infant immunization program - delegation of authority to immunize minor.
(1) There is hereby created in the department an infant immunization program which is established to immunize infants against vaccine preventable disease. Such program shall be implemented on and after January 1, 1993.
(2) Every parent, legal guardian, or person vested with legal custody or decision-making responsibility for the medical care of a minor, or person otherwise responsible for the care of an infant residing in this state, shall be responsible for having such infant vaccinated in compliance with the schedule of immunization established by the board of health; except that, failure to vaccinate a child in accordance with this subsection (2) shall not constitute sufficient grounds for any insurance company to deny a claim submitted on behalf of a child who develops a vaccine preventable disease.
(2.5) (a) Subject to the provisions of this subsection (2.5) , a parent, legal guardian, person vested with legal custody of a minor or decision-making responsibility for the medical care of a minor, or such other adult person responsible for the care of a minor in this state, other than any employee of a licensed child care center in which the minor is enrolled, may delegate, verbally or in writing, that person's authority to consent to the immunization of a minor to a stepparent, an adult relative of first or second degree of kinship, or an adult child care provider who has care and control of the minor. Any immunization administered pursuant to a delegation of authority under this subsection (2.5) shall be administered only at a health care clinic, hospital, office of a private practitioner, or county public health clinic.
(b) If a parent, legal guardian, person vested with legal custody of a minor or decision-making responsibility for the medial care of a minor, or other adult person responsible for the care of a minor in this state verbally delegates his or her authority to consent to the immunization of a minor under this subsection (2.5) , the person to whom such authority is thereby delegated shall confirm the verbal delegation in writing and shall verbally relay any relevant health history to the administering practitioner. The practitioner administering the vaccination shall include the written confirmation in the minor's medical record. If a parent, legal guardian, person vested with legal custody of a minor or decision-making responsibility for the medical care of a minor, or other

adult person responsible for the care of a minor in this state delegates his or her authority to consent to the immunization of a minor under this subsection (2.5) in writing, such writing shall include the relevant health history, and the practitioner administering the vaccination shall include a copy of the written delegation of authority in the minor's medical record.

(c) A person who consents to the immunization of a minor pursuant to a delegation of authority under this subsection (2.5) shall provide the practitioner with sufficient and accurate health information about the minor for whom the consent is given and, if necessary, sufficient and accurate health information about the minor's family to enable the practitioner to assess adequately the risks and benefits inherent in the proposed immunization and to determine whether the immunization is advisable.

(d) A person may not consent to the immunization of a minor pursuant to this subsection (2.5) if:

(I) The person has actual knowledge that the parent, legal guardian, person vested with legal custody of a minor or decision-making responsibility for the medical care of a minor, or other adult person responsible for the care of a minor in this state has expressly refused to give consent to the immunization; or

(II) The parent, legal guardian, person vested with legal custody of a minor or decision-making responsibility for the medical care of a minor, or other adult person responsible for the care of a minor in this state has told the person that the person may not consent to the immunization of the minor or, in the case of a written authorization, has withdrawn the authorization in writing.

(3) In addition to the immunization obligations set forth in section 25-4-905, relating to the immunization of indigent children, and except as provided in subsection (4) of this section, the department shall provide at public expense, subject to available appropriations, systematic immunizations to those infants that are not exempt from such immunization pursuant to paragraph (a) or (b) of subsection (4) of this section. The manner and frequency of vaccine administration shall conform to recognized standards of medical practice which are necessary for the protection of public health.

(4) An infant shall be exempted from receiving the required immunizations:

(a) Upon submitting certification from a licensed physician or advanced practice nurse that the physical condition of the infant is such that one or more specified immunizations would endanger the infant's life or health; or

(b) Upon submitting a statement signed by one parent or guardian that such parent or guardian adheres to a religious belief whose teachings are opposed to immunizations, or that such parent or guardian has a personal belief that is opposed to immunization.

## 25-4-1705. Department of public health and environment - powers and duties - rules.

(1) The department shall negotiate for the purchase of and shall purchase vaccines to achieve the purposes of this part 17.

(2) The department shall secure and maintain such facilities as may be necessary for the safe and adequate preservation and storage of such vaccines.

(3) The department shall distribute such vaccines, in accordance with rules promulgated by the board of health, without purchase, shipping, handling, or other charges to practitioners who agree not to impose a charge for such vaccine on the infant recipient, the child's parent or guardian, third-party payor, or any other person; except that a practitioner may charge a reasonable administrative fee in connection with the administration of a vaccine. The board of health shall determine the amount of such administrative fee that a practitioner may charge.

(4) The department shall collect epidemiological information and shall establish a system for recording such information pursuant to rules and regulations adopted by the board of health.

(5) The board of health, in consultation with the medical services board in the state department of health care policy and financing, and such other persons, agencies, or organizations that the board of health deems advisable, shall formulate, adopt, and promulgate rules governing the implementation and operation of the infant immunization program. Such rules shall address the

following:

(a) The purchase, storage, and distribution of the vaccines by the department;

(b) Requirements that providers, hospitals, and health care clinics must meet before entering into a contract with the department, making such provider, hospital, or clinic an agent of the department for the purposes of the infant immunization program;

(c) Which vaccines shall be required to be administered;

(d) The route and frequency of the vaccine's administration;

(e) (Deleted by amendment, L. 2007, p. 655, § 3, effective April 26, 2007.)

(f) The issuance of immunization records to parents or guardians;

(g) The assessment of the vaccination status of infants;

(h) The dissemination of information about the operation of the infant immunization program, including the requirement that such information be distributed by hospitals to parents of newborns.

(6) The department is authorized to accept any gifts or grants or awards of funds from the federal government or private sources for the implementation and operation of the infant immunization program.

(7) The department is authorized to enter into contracts which are necessary for the implementation and operation of the infant immunization program.

(8) County, district, or municipal public health agencies and the department shall use the birth certificate of any infant to enroll such infant in an immunization tracking system established in section 25-4-2403. Such use of the infant's birth certificate shall be considered an official duty of county, district, and municipal public health agencies and the department.

(9) (a) (Deleted by amendment, L. 2003, p. 2198, § 1, effective August 6, 2003.)

(b) The department or any person who contracts with the department pursuant to subsection (7) of this section may establish a purchase system as described in section 25-4-2403 for the procurement of vaccines for privately insured persons under federal government contracts.

(10) Physicians, licensed health care practitioners, clinics, schools, licensed child care providers, hospitals, managed care organizations or health insurers in which a student, as defined in section 25-4-901 (3) , or an infant is enrolled as a member or insured, persons that have contracted with the department pursuant to subsection (7) of this section, and public health officials may release any immunization records in their possession, whether or not such records are in the immunization tracking system established in section 25-4-2403, to the persons or entities specified in section 25-4-2403 (1) to provide an accurate and complete immunization record for the child in order to verify compliance with state immunization law.

## 25-4-1706. Infant immunization program - eligibility.

Any infant shall be eligible for participation in the infant immunization program; except that, for fiscal year 1992-93, only infants born on or after January 1, 1993, shall be eligible for participation in the infant immunization tracking program.

## 25-4-1707. Moneys targeted for medical assistance for infants - reimbursement.

The state department of health care policy and financing shall reimburse the department of public health and environment for the costs of vaccinating infants under the infant immunization program who are medicaid eligible pursuant to the "Colorado Medical Assistance Act", articles 4, 5, and 6 of title 25.5, C.R.S. Such moneys received from the state department of health care policy and financing shall be credited to the immunization fund.

## 25-4-1708. Fund created.

(1) (a) There is hereby established in the state treasury a fund to be known as the immunization fund, which fund is subject to annual appropriation by the general assembly to the department of public health and environment for the purposes of:

(I) Purchasing vaccines, including purchasing vaccines through a vaccine purchasing system, if such a system is developed pursuant to section 25-4-2403 (1) and (1.3) , which system may include vaccines for privately insured individuals;

(II) Assisting users of the immunization tracking system established in section 25-4-2403 to connect to the system;

(III) Utilizing the reminder and recall process of the immunization tracking system; and

(IV) Implementing, developing, and operating immunization programs.

(b) The fund consists of:

(I) Moneys appropriated by the general assembly from the general fund for immunization programs;

(II) Any gifts, grants, or awards received pursuant to sections 25-4-1705 (6) and 25-4-2403 (9) (c) or for purposes of expanding access to childhood immunizations; and

(III) Moneys received from the state department of health care policy and financing as reimbursement pursuant to section 25-4-1707.

(c) The state treasurer shall credit to the fund all income from the investment of moneys in the fund.

(d) The department shall use the moneys in the immunization fund to pay the department's direct and indirect costs of administering the programs described in paragraph (a) of this subsection (1) .

(2) If federal funds are not received to implement and operate the immunization programs created in this part 17 and part 24 of this article, no additional general fund moneys shall be appropriated for such purposes.

(3) All moneys credited to the immunization fund that are not expended during the fiscal year shall be retained in the fund for its future use and shall not be credited or transferred to the general fund or any other fund.

(4) (Deleted by amendment, L. 2007, p. 658, § 5, effective April 26, 2007.)

## 25-4-1709. Limitations on liability.

(1) No person who administers a vaccine required under the provisions of this part 17 shall be held liable for injuries sustained pursuant to such vaccine if:

(a) The vaccine was administered according to the schedule of immunization established by the board of health;

(b) There were no medical contraindications for administering such vaccine; and

(c) The vaccine was administered using generally accepted clinical methods.

(2) An action shall not be maintained for a vaccine-related injury or death until action for compensation for such alleged injury has been exhausted under the terms of the federal "National Childhood Vaccine Injury Act of 1986", 42 U.S.C. secs. 300aa-10 to 300aa-33, as such law is from time to time amended, provided the federal "National Childhood Vaccine Injury Act of 1986" applies to the particular vaccine administered.

(3) If the injury or death which is sustained does not fall within the parameters of the vaccine injury table as defined in 42 U.S.C. sec. 300aa-14, as enacted on November 14, 1986, a rebuttable presumption is established that the injury sustained or the death was not due to the administration of the vaccine. Such presumption shall be overcome by a preponderance of the evidence.

(4) Where a claim against a hospital, clinic, or provider arises from injuries resulting from the handling, storage, or distribution of vaccines required by this part 17, such hospital, clinic, or provider shall not be liable unless such injuries are the result of the negligent failure of an employee of such hospital, clinic, or provider to conform to recognized standards of practice which are necessary for the protection of public health.

(5) A practitioner licensed to practice medicine pursuant to article 36 of title 12, C.R.S., or nursing pursuant to article 38 of title 12, C.R.S., or the health care clinic, hospital, office of a private practitioner, or county public health clinic at which the immunization was administered that relies on the health history and other information given by a person who has been delegated the authority to consent to the immunization of a minor pursuant to section 25-4-1704 (2.5) is not liable for damages related to an immunization resulting from factual errors in the health history or

information given to the practitioner or the health care clinic, hospital, office of a private practitioner, or county public health clinic at which the immunization was administered by the person when such practitioner or health care clinic, hospital, office of a private practitioner, or county public health clinic reasonably relies upon the health history information given and exercises reasonable and prudent care in administering the immunization.

### 25-4-1710. Report to the general assembly. (Repealed)

### 25-4-1711. Infant immunization advisory committee - creation. (Repealed)

# PART 18. SHELLFISH DEALER CERTIFICATION ACT

### 25-4-1801. Short title.
This part 18 shall be known and may be cited as the "Shellfish Dealer Certification Act".

### 25-4-1802. Legislative declaration.
The general assembly finds, determines, and declares that the certification of shellfish dealers and the regulation of premises or places wherein shellfish are handled, stored, and processed for distribution in accordance with the guidelines of the national shellfish sanitation program administered by the United States food and drug administration is necessary to protect the public health; will benefit consumers by ensuring that the sale and distribution of shellfish is from safe sources; will assist retailers by ensuring that shellfish have not been adulterated during processing, shipping, or handling; and will contribute to the economic health of the state by assuring that Colorado certified dealers are permitted to ship their product in interstate commerce.

### 25-4-1803. Definitions.
As used in this part 18, unless the context otherwise requires:
(1) "Certification" means the issuance of a numbered certificate to a person for a particular activity or group of activities that indicates:
(a) Permission from the department to conduct the activity; and
(b) Compliance with the requirements of the department.
(2) "Certification number" means the unique identification number issued by the department to each dealer for each location.
(3) "Dealer" means a person to whom certification is issued for the activities of shell stock shipper, shucker-packer, repacker, reshipper, depuration processor, or wet storage.
(4) "Department" means the Colorado department of public health and environment and its authorized agents and employees.
(5) "Depuration processor" or "DP" means a person who receives shell stock from approved or restricted growing areas and submits such shell stock to an approved, controlled purification process.
(6) "FDA" means the United States food and drug administration.
(7) "Person" means any individual, receiver, trustee, guardian, personal representative, fiduciary, or representative of any kind, and any partnership, association, corporation, or other entity. "Person" also includes the federal or state government and any other public or private entity.
(8) "Repacker" or "RP" means any person, other than the original certified shucker-packer, who

repackages shucked shellfish into other containers.

(9) "Reshipper" or "RS" means a person who purchases shucked shellfish or shell stock from other certified shippers and sells the product without repacking or relabeling to other certified shippers, wholesalers, or retailers.

(10) "Shellfish" means all species of:

(a) Oysters, clams, or mussels, whether:

(I) Shucked or in the shell;

(II) Fresh or frozen; and

(III) Whole or in part; and

(b) Scallops in any form, except when the final product form is the adductor muscle only.

(11) "Shell stock" means live shellfish in the shell.

(12) "Shell stock shipper" or "SS" means a person who grows, harvests, buys, or repacks and sells shell stock. A shell stock shipper is not authorized to shuck shellfish nor to repack shucked shellfish, but may ship shucked shellfish.

(13) "Shucker-packer" or "SP" means a person who shucks and packs shellfish. A shucker-packer may act as a shell stock shipper or reshipper or may repack shellfish originating from other certified dealers.

(14) "Wet storage" means the temporary storage of shell stock from growing areas in the approved classification or in the open status of the conditionally approved classification in containers or floats in natural bodies of water or in tanks containing natural or synthetic seawater.

## 25-4-1804. Department designated as certifying and inspecting agency.

For the purpose of regulating and controlling shellfish dealers, establishing sanitary conditions therein, and the enforcement and administration of this part 18, the department is hereby authorized as the state certifying and inspection agency pursuant to applicable federal law and rules.

## 25-4-1805. Powers and duties of department - rules.

(1) The department is hereby authorized to enforce this part 18 and to adopt and enforce reasonable rules and standards to implement this part 18. Such rules and standards shall be consistent with, and no more stringent than, standards adopted pursuant to the national shellfish sanitation program and may include, but shall not be limited to:

(a) Rules governing applications for initial certification and for annual renewal of certifications;

(b) Requirements for comprehensive on-site inspections of the premises and facilities of applicants for certification;

(c) Standards concerning the form and manner of submission of records required for certification and record keeping pursuant to this part 18;

(d) Establishment of fees required for certification and renewal of certification; and

(e) Grounds for denial, suspension, or revocation of a certificate.

(2) This part 18 shall be administered by the department; except that county, district, and municipal public health agencies may be authorized by the department to assist it in performing its powers and duties pursuant to this part 18.

(3) The department is authorized to conduct hearings in accordance with article 4 of title 24, C.R.S., and to use administrative law judges to conduct such hearings when the use of administrative law judges would result in a net saving of costs to the department.

(4) The department is authorized to enter into cooperative agreements with and to accept grants from any agency or political subdivision of this state or any other state, or with any agency of the United States government, subject to limitations set forth elsewhere in law and the state constitution, to carry out the provisions of this part 18.

(5) (a) When the department determines that a dealer's activity constitutes a major public health threat, the department shall:

(I) Suspend or withdraw certification; and

(II) Immediately notify the FDA and the authorities in known states that receive the dealer's shellfish.

(b) The department shall prohibit any dealer whose certification has been suspended or withdrawn from shipping in interstate or intrastate commerce.

(c) When the department recertifies any dealer, the department shall notify the FDA and the authorities in known states that receive the shellfish.

## 25-4-1806. Shellfish dealers - certificate required - application - fees.

(1) Any person desiring to do business as a shellfish dealer in Colorado shall apply for and obtain a valid shellfish dealer certification issued by the department pursuant to this part 18 and any rules adopted pursuant thereto. Any such application shall be accompanied by the appropriate fee, if any, set by the department.

(2) Each shellfish dealer certification shall expire on June 30 in the year following the year of issuance.

(3) Each certificated shellfish dealer shall report to the department, in the form and manner required by the department, any change in the information provided in the dealer's application or in such reports previously submitted, within thirty days of such change.

(4) Certifications issued pursuant to this part 18 are not transferable.

(5) An application for renewal of a shellfish dealer certification shall be in the form and manner prescribed by the department.

(6) The department shall issue only one certification number to any dealer for any location. A dealer may maintain more than one certification if each business is operated as a separate entity and is not found at the same location.

(7) The certification number issued to any dealer by the department shall be unique. Each certification number shall consist of a one- to five-digit Arabic number preceded by the two-letter state postal abbreviation ("CO") and followed by a two-letter abbreviation for the type of activity or activities the dealer is qualified to perform in accordance with the following terms as defined in section 25-4-1802:

(a) Shell stock shipper (SS) ;

(b) Shucker-packer (SP) ;

(c) Repacker (RP) ;

(d) Reshipper (RS) ;

(e) Depuration processor (DP) ; or

(f) Wet storage (WS) .

(8) All fees collected pursuant to this section shall be transmitted to the state treasurer, who shall credit the same to the wholesale food manufacturing and storage protection cash fund created in section 25-5-426.

## 25-4-1807. Record-keeping requirements.

(1) Each certificated shellfish dealer shall keep and maintain records in the form and manner designated by the department.

(2) Records maintained pursuant to subsection (1) of this section shall be retained at the dealer's address of record for at least one year or for such different period as the department may specify by rule.

## 25-4-1808. Unlawful acts.

(1) Unless otherwise authorized by law, it is unlawful and a violation of this part 18 for any person to:

(a) Perform any of the acts for which certification as a shellfish dealer is required without possessing a valid certification;

(b) Hold oneself out as being so qualified to perform any of the acts for which certification pursuant to this part 18 is required without possessing a valid certification;

(c) Solicit, advertise, or offer to perform any of the acts for which certification under this part 18 is required without possessing a valid certification to perform such acts;

(d) Refuse or fail to comply with the provisions of this part 18;

(e) Refuse or fail to comply with any rules adopted by the department pursuant to this part 18 or to any lawful order issued by the department;

(f) Refuse to comply with a cease-and-desist order issued pursuant to section 25-4-1810;

(g) Willfully make a material misstatement in the application for a certification or in the application for renewal thereof or to the department during an official investigation;

(h) Impersonate any federal, state, county, city and county, or municipal official or inspector;

(i) Aid or abet another in any violation of this part 18 or of any rule adopted pursuant thereto;

(j) Refuse to permit entry or inspection in accordance with section 25-4-1809;

(k) Allow a certification issued pursuant to this part 18 to be used by an uncertificated person; or

(l) Make any misrepresentation or false promise, through advertisements, employees, agents, or otherwise, in connection with the business operations certificated pursuant to this part 18 or for which an application for a certification is pending.

## 25-4-1809. Inspections - investigations - access - subpoena.

(1) The department, upon its own motion or upon the complaint of any person, may make any and all investigations necessary to ensure compliance with this part 18.

(2) The department shall have the right of access, at any reasonable time, during regular working hours and at other times during which activity is evident, to any premises for the purpose of any examination or inspection necessary to enforce any of the provisions of this part 18 or the rules or standards adopted thereunder.

(3) Complaints of record made to the department and the results of the department's investigations may, in the discretion of the department, be closed to public inspection, except to the person in interest, as defined in section 24-72-202 (4) , C.R.S., or as provided by court order, during the investigatory period and until dismissed or until notice of hearing and charges are served on the person in interest.

(4) (a) The department shall have full authority to administer oaths and take statements, to issue subpoenas requiring the attendance of witnesses and the production of books, memoranda, papers, and other documents, articles, or instruments, and to compel the disclosure by such witnesses of all facts known to them relative to the matters under investigation.

(b) Upon failure or refusal of any witness to obey any subpoena, the department may petition the district court, and, upon a proper showing, the court may enter an order compelling the witness to appear and testify or produce documentary evidence. Failure to obey such an order of the court shall be punishable as a contempt of court.

## 25-4-1810. Enforcement.

(1) The department or its designee shall enforce the provisions of this part 18.

(2) (a) If the department has reasonable cause to believe a violation of any provision of this part 18 or any rule adopted pursuant to this part 18 has occurred and immediate enforcement is deemed necessary, it may issue a cease-and-desist order, which shall require a person to cease violating any provision of this part 18 or any rule promulgated pursuant to this part 18.

(b) A cease-and-desist order shall set forth the provisions alleged to have been violated, the facts constituting the violation, and the requirement that all violating actions immediately cease.

(c) (I) At any time after service of the order to cease and desist, the person for whom such order was served may request, at such person's discretion, a prompt hearing to determine whether or not such violation has occurred.

(II) A hearing held pursuant to this paragraph (c) shall be conducted in conformance with the provisions of article 4 of title 24, C.R.S., and shall be determined promptly.

(3) If the department possesses sufficient evidence to indicate that a person has engaged in any act or practice constituting a violation of this part 18 or of any rule adopted under this part 18, the

department may apply to any court of competent jurisdiction to temporarily or permanently restrain or enjoin the act or practice in question and to enforce compliance with this part 18 or any rule or order under this part 18. In any such action, the department shall not be required to plead or prove irreparable injury or the inadequacy of the remedy at law. The court shall not require the department to post a bond.

## 25-4-1811. Disciplinary actions - denial of certification.
(1) The department, pursuant to the provisions of article 4 of title 24, C.R.S., may issue letters of admonition or may deny, suspend, refuse to renew, restrict, or revoke any certification authorized under this part 18 if the applicant or certificated person has:
(a) Refused or failed to comply with any provision of this part 18, any rule adopted under this part 18, or any lawful order of the department;
(b) Had an equivalent certification denied, revoked, or suspended by any authority;
(c) Refused to provide the department with reasonable, complete, and accurate information when requested by the department; or
(d) Falsified any information requested by the department.
(2) In any proceeding held under this section, the department may accept as prima facie evidence of grounds for disciplinary action any disciplinary action taken against a dealer in another jurisdiction if the violation which prompted the disciplinary action in that jurisdiction would be grounds for disciplinary action under this section.

## 25-4-1812. Civil penalties.
(1) Any person who violates any provision of this part 18 or any rule adopted pursuant to this part 18 is subject to a civil penalty, as determined by the department. The maximum penalty shall not exceed fifty dollars per violation.
(2) No civil penalty may be imposed unless the person charged is given notice and opportunity for a hearing pursuant to article 4 of title 24, C.R.S.
(3) If the department is unable to collect such civil penalty or if any person fails to pay all or a set portion of the civil penalty as determined by the department, the department may bring suit to recover such amount plus costs and attorney fees by action in any court of competent jurisdiction.
(4) Before imposing any civil penalty, the department may consider the effect of such penalty on the ability of the person charged to stay in business.
(5) All penalties collected pursuant to this section by the department shall be transmitted to the state treasurer who shall credit the same to the food protection cash fund created in section 25-4-1605.

## 25-4-1813. Criminal penalties.
Any person who violates any of the provisions of section 25-4-1808 commits a class 3 misdemeanor and shall be punished as provided in section 18-1.3-501 (1) , C.R.S.

# PART 19. GULF WAR SYNDROME REGISTRY

## 25-4-1901. Short title.
This part 19 shall be known and may be cited as the "Gulf War Syndrome Registry Act".

## 25-4-1902. Definitions.
As used in this part 19, unless the context otherwise requires:
(1) "Birth defect" means any physical or mental disability, disorder, or condition, including any susceptibility to any illness, disorder, or condition other than normal childhood illnesses,

disorders, or conditions.

(2) "Department" means the department of public health and environment.

(3) "Family member" means a spouse or a child of a veteran who served in the gulf war.

(4) "Gulf war syndrome" means the wide range of physical and mental conditions, disorders, problems, and illnesses, including birth defects, experienced by veterans and family members that are connected with a veteran's service in the armed forces of the United States during the gulf war.

(5) "Registry" means the gulf war syndrome registry created in section 25-4-1903.

(6) "Veteran" means a person who is a resident of this state, who served on and after August 2, 1990, but prior to December 31, 1991, during the gulf war in the southwest Asia theater of operations, which includes Iraq, Kuwait, Saudi Arabia, the neutral zone between Iraq and Saudi Arabia, Bahrain, Qatar, the United Arab Emirates, Oman, the Gulf of Aden, the Gulf of Oman, the Persian Gulf, the Arabian Sea, the Red Sea, and the airspace above these locations.

## 25-4-1903. Gulf war syndrome registry - creation - reporting.

(1) There is hereby created a statewide gulf war syndrome registry that shall be established and maintained by the department. The registry shall contain the names of veterans and family members of veterans who have been affected by gulf war syndrome as reported by physicians, health care professionals, hospitals, or medical facilities as provided in subsection (2) of this section or as reported by veterans on forms prescribed by the department. The registry shall also contain the names of children with cancer or birth defects who have at least one parent that is a veteran of the gulf war, and who submit information to the registry as provided in subsection (4) of this section.

(2) A physician or other qualified health care professional who has primary responsibility for treating a veteran or a family member of a veteran and who believes the veteran may have been exposed to certain causative agents while serving in the armed forces of the United States during the gulf war shall submit a report to the department on a form provided by the department. If there is no physician or other qualified health care professional having primary responsibility for treating the veteran or the veteran's family member, the hospital or other medical facility treating the veteran or family member shall submit the report to the department. No report shall be submitted pursuant to this subsection (2) unless consent of the veteran or, if the report involves a family member of the veteran, of the affected family member has been obtained. If the report involves a person who is under the age of eighteen years, consent shall be obtained from a parent or legal guardian of the child.

(3) The form provided by the department to veterans and to physicians or other qualified health care professionals, hospitals, or other medical facilities shall request the following information:

(a) Symptoms of the veteran or family member of the veteran that may be related to exposure to causative agents during the gulf war;

(b) Diagnoses of the veteran or family member of the veteran;

(c) Methods of treatment prescribed;

(d) Outcome or results of any treatment prescribed.

(4) The department shall contact the families of any child born after August 2, 1990, who is on the state cancer registry or who has been reported to the department as having birth defects to determine whether either of the two biological parents of such child is a veteran of the gulf war. If either parent did serve, the department shall inform the family of the child about the registry. If the family consents, the child's name and any symptoms, diagnoses, methods of treatment, and treatment outcomes shall be listed in the registry.

## 25-4-1904. Gulf war syndrome advisory committee - creation. (Repealed)

## 25-4-1905. Confidentiality of information collected.

(1) The department shall compile, analyze, and evaluate the information and data submitted to the

registry.

(2) All information obtained from or concerning a veteran or an individual on the registry shall be confidential; except that release may be made of such information for statistical purposes in a manner such that no individual person can be identified.

(3) A physician or other qualified health care professional, a hospital, or medical facility that complies with the provisions of this part 19 shall not be held civilly or criminally liable for providing information required by this part 19.

### 25-4-1906. Gulf war syndrome registry fund.

The department is authorized to accept and expend grants, donations, and gifts-in-kind from private and public sources for the purposes of maintaining and publicizing the registry created in this part 19; except that the registry shall not be implemented until sufficient grants, donations, and gifts are obtained to support its implementation. Once sufficient funds are obtained to implement the registry, the department shall contract with a private entity to perform any of its duties concerning the registry. Any grants, donations, and gifts shall be credited to the gulf war syndrome registry fund, which fund is hereby created in the state treasury. The moneys in said fund shall be subject to annual appropriation by the general assembly for the purpose of implementing the gulf war syndrome registry. All interest derived from the deposit and investment of moneys in the fund shall be credited to the fund. Any moneys not appropriated shall remain in the fund and shall not be transferred or revert to the general fund of the state at the end of any fiscal year.

# PART 20. HEPATITIS C EDUCATION AND SCREENING PROGRAM

### 25-4-2001. Short title.

This part 20 shall be known and may be cited as the "Hepatitis C Program Act".

### 25-4-2002. Legislative declaration.

(1) The general assembly hereby finds, determines, and declares that:

(a) Hepatitis C is a silent killer, being largely asymptomatic until irreversible liver damage may have occurred;

(b) Hepatitis C has been characterized by the world health organization as a disease of primary concern to humanity;

(c) Currently, approximately four million five hundred thousand Americans are infected with hepatitis C, and there are approximately thirty thousand new infections occurring each year in the United States;

(d) The center for disease control estimates that approximately twelve thousand individuals die each year due to the consequences of hepatitis C, and this number continues to grow each year;

(e) Hepatitis C is considered such a public health threat that the United States department of health and human services has launched a comprehensive plan to address it, beginning with the identification and notification of the hundreds of thousands of persons inadvertently exposed to hepatitis C through blood transfusion; and

(f) In the absence of a vaccine for hepatitis C, emphasis must be placed on other means of disease awareness and prevention, including but not limited to education of police officers, firefighters, health care professionals, and the general public. This approach may be the only means of halting the spread of this devastating disease.

(2) The general assembly further declares that the purpose of this part 20 is to create and develop a program that will:

(a) Heighten awareness and enhance knowledge and understanding of hepatitis C by disseminating educational materials and information about services and strategies for detection and treatment to patients and the general public;

(b) Promote public awareness and knowledge about the risk factors, the value of early detection, and the options available for the treatment of hepatitis C;

(c) Utilize any available technical assistance from and any educational and training resources and services that have been developed by organizations with appropriate expertise and knowledge of hepatitis C;

(d) Design a model screening process to provide guidelines for health care professionals to use to prevent further transmission of the hepatitis C virus and prevent onset of chronic liver disease caused by hepatitis C by detecting and treating chronic hepatitis C virus infection;

(e) Evaluate existing hepatitis C support services in the community and assess the need for improving the quality and accessibility of these services; and

(f) Provide easy access to clear, complete, and accurate hepatitis C and patient referral services information.

(3) The general assembly further finds, determines, and declares that it is the intent of the general assembly to provide funding for the hepatitis C program created in this part 20 for the fiscal year beginning July 1, 1999, and to review the effectiveness of and the necessity for the hepatitis C program in determining the reasonableness and the amount of future funding, if any.

## 25-4-2003. Definitions.

As used in this part 20, unless the context otherwise requires:

(1) "CDC" means the centers for disease control and prevention.

(2) "Department" means the department of public health and environment.

(3) "Health care professional" means any person licensed in this state or any other state to practice medicine, chiropractic, nursing, physical therapy, podiatry, dentistry, pharmacy, optometry, or other healing arts. The term includes any professional corporation or other professional entity comprised of such health care providers as permitted by the laws of this state, as well as certified addiction counselors.

(4) "Hepatitis C" means a liver disease caused by the hepatitis C virus and is also known as non-A-non-B hepatitis.

(5) "Outreach service" means services including, but not limited to, provision of educational materials and information on screening and provision of counseling services.

(6) "Program" means the hepatitis C program created in this part 20.

(7) "Screening" means administration of an examination or test exclusively for the purpose of ascertaining the existence of any physiological abnormality that might be indicative of the presence of disease.

## 25-4-2004. Powers and duties of executive director - hepatitis C program.

(1) The executive director of the department shall design and implement a hepatitis C program to:

(a) Coordinate with local public health officials, health care professionals, public institutions, and community organizations to identify high risk populations, including those associated with currently understood means of transmission, to assist in implementing a model screening process, and to provide information on referral services or to otherwise assist in obtaining treatment for those with hepatitis C infection;

(b) Educate and provide outreach services related to hepatitis C to the general public. At a minimum, public education on these issues shall be designed to:

(I) Provide basic information about the prevalence, transmission, risks, care, and treatment of hepatitis C;

(II) Provide information about co-infection with hepatitis C and the implications of co-infection for other similarly transmitted diseases;

(III) Provide information on screening services available in the community;

(IV) Coordinate with national public education efforts related to the identification and notification of recipients of blood from hepatitis C virus positive donors;

(V) Stimulate interest among and coordinate with community-based organizations to sponsor community forums and to undertake other appropriate community outreach activities; and

(VI) Employ public communication strategies, including the print media, radio, television, video, internet, and any other appropriate form of communication.

(2) The program described in subsection (1) of this section shall be implemented within available appropriations. If available appropriations are inadequate to fund the entire program described in subsection (1) of this section, the program shall be implemented in stages, commencing with the coordination with local public health officials, health care professionals, public institutions and community organizations, as described in paragraph (a) of subsection (1) of this section, and followed by the education of the general public, as described in paragraph (b) of subsection (1) of this section.

(3) The department is authorized to enter into contracts that are necessary for the implementation and operation of the program.

(4) After implementation of subsection (1) of this section, if funding is available, the executive director of the department shall have the authority to implement a system to:

(a) Collect and analyze reports of cases of hepatitis C, without regard to the distinction between chronic and acute;

(b) Investigate all reported cases of hepatitis C and maintain records of possible sources of transmission;

(c) Prepare a statistical report on the numbers and types of reported hepatitis C cases; and

(d) Report cases to the CDC to the extent permitted by the CDC.

(5) Repealed.

## 25-4-2005. Hepatitis C testing - recommendations - definitions.

(1) The department recommends that each primary health care provider or physician, physician assistant, or nurse practitioner who treats a patient in an inpatient or outpatient setting offer a person born between the years of 1945 and 1965 a hepatitis C screening test or hepatitis C diagnostic test unless the health care provider providing such services reasonably believes that:

(a) The patient is being treated for a life-threatening emergency;

(b) The patient has previously been offered or has been the subject of a hepatitis C screening; or

(c) The patient lacks capacity to consent to a hepatitis C screening test.

(2) If a patient accepts the offer of a hepatitis C screening test and the screening test is reactive, the health care provider may either offer the patient follow-up health care or refer the individual to a health care provider who can provide follow-up health care, including a hepatitis C diagnostic test.

(3) The health care provider shall make the offer of a hepatitis C screening to the patient in a linguistically and culturally appropriate manner, as determined by rules promulgated by the department.

(4) Nothing in this section affects the scope of practice of a health care provider or diminishes any authority or legal or professional obligation of a health care provider to offer a hepatitis C screening test or hepatitis C diagnostic test or to provide services or care for the subject of a hepatitis C screening test or hepatitis C diagnostic test.

(5) As used in this section, unless the context otherwise requires:

(a) "Hepatitis C diagnostic test" means a laboratory test or tests that detect the presence of hepatitis C virus in the blood and provide confirmation of whether the patient has a hepatitis C infection.

(b) "Hepatitis C screening test" means a federal food and drug administration-approved rapid point of care test or other food and drug administration-approved tests that detect the presence of hepatitis C virus antibodies in the blood.

# PART 21. BODY ARTISTS

### 25-4-2101. Powers and duties of department - rules.
In addition to any other powers and duties, the department of public health and environment shall promulgate rules governing the safe and sanitary practice of body art, the safe and sanitary physical environment where body art is performed, and the safe and sanitary conditions of equipment utilized in body art procedures. Nothing in this section shall be construed to prohibit a city, county, or district board of health established pursuant to part 5 of article 1 of this title, or a county or district public health agency established pursuant to part 5 of article 1 of this title, from adopting or enforcing ordinances, resolutions, or rules that impose standards for body art that are at least as stringent as the standards imposed by the rules adopted by the department of public health and environment.

### 25-4-2102. Penalties for violations.
Upon a finding by the department of public health and environment or a local board of health that a body art facility is in violation of any rule adopted pursuant to section 25-4-2101, the department or local board of health may assess a penalty not to exceed two hundred fifty dollars for each day of a violation. Each day of a violation shall be considered a separate offense. The department or local board of health shall consider the degree of danger to the public caused by the violation, the duration of the violation, and whether such facility has committed any similar violations.

### 25-4-2103. Parental consent for minors.
No body artist shall perform a body art procedure upon a minor unless the body artist has received express consent from the minor's parent or guardian. Failure to obtain such permission before performing body art procedures on a minor shall constitute a petty offense punishable by a fine of two hundred fifty dollars.

# PART 22. HEALTH DISPARITIES GRANT PROGRAM

### 25-4-2201. Legislative declaration.
(1) The general assembly hereby finds that:
(a) Although Colorado as a whole is a healthy state, African Americans, Hispanics, and Native Americans, who represent over twenty-five percent of the population, are disproportionately impacted by disease, injury, disability, and death;
(b) Compared to the state average:
(I) African Americans have a twenty-five percent higher death rate from heart disease, a twenty-eight percent higher death rate from stroke, a thirty percent higher death rate from breast cancer, a fifty percent higher death rate from colon cancer, and nearly twice the death rate from diabetes;
(II) Hispanics have approximately twice the incidence of cervical cancer, a fifty percent higher death rate from cervical cancer, and approximately twice the death rate from diabetes;
(III) Hispanics are fourteen and one-half percent less likely to be screened for cervical cancer and both African Americans and Hispanics are, respectively, twenty-eight percent and thirty-nine percent less likely to be screened for colon cancer.
(1.5) The general assembly hereby determines and declares that:
(a) Understanding the root causes of health disparities includes recognizing that health starts in our homes, schools, and communities;

(b) Vulnerable populations that are currently identified by race, ethnicity, sexual orientation, gender identity, disability status, aging population, and socioeconomic status, among others, experience poorer health status outcomes; and

(c) Mounting evidence demonstrates that factors such as economic, physical, and social environment play a significant role in health, and if addressed, can create better health outcomes.

(2) Therefore, the general assembly hereby declares that it is in the best interests of the state to establish a health disparities grant program to provide prevention, early detection, and treatment of cancer and cardiovascular and pulmonary diseases to under-represented populations.

(3) The general assembly finds that modifying the duties and structure of the office of health disparities to become the office of health equity reflects the recent advancements in the field of health by broadening the scope of the office to include the economic, physical, and social environment, and offers a more inclusive approach to eliminating health disparities for all Coloradans.

## 25-4-2202. Definitions.

As used in this part 22, unless the context otherwise requires:

(1) "Commission" means the health equity commission created in section 25-4-2206.

(2) Repealed.

(3) "Department" means the department of public health and environment.

(3.5) "Health disparities" means differences in health status, access to care, and quality of care as determined by race, ethnicity, sexual orientation, gender identity, disability status, aging population, socioeconomic status, and other factors.

(3.7) "Health equity" means achieving the highest level of health for all people and entails focused efforts to address avoidable inequalities by equalizing those conditions for health for all groups, especially for those that have experienced socioeconomic disadvantages or historical injustices.

(4) "Office" means the office of health equity created in section 25-4-2204.

(4.5) "Social determinants of health" means life-enhancing resources, such as food, housing, economic and social relationships, transportation, education, and health care, whose distribution across populations effectively determines the length and quality of life.

(5) "State board" means the state board of health created in section 25-1-103.

## 25-4-2203. Health disparities grant program - rules.

(1) There is hereby created in the department the health disparities grant program, referred to in this section as the "grant program", to provide financial support for statewide initiatives that address prevention, early detection, and treatment of cancer and cardiovascular and pulmonary diseases in underrepresented populations. The office shall administer the grant program. The state board shall award grants to selected entities from moneys transferred to the health disparities grant program fund created in section 24-22-117 (2) (f) , C.R.S.

(2) The state board shall adopt rules that specify, but are not necessarily limited to, the following:

(a) The procedures and timelines by which an entity may apply for program grants;

(b) Grant application contents, including but not limited to how the program meets at least one of the program criteria specified in section 25-20.5-302 (1) ;

(c) Criteria for selecting the entities that shall receive grants and determining the amount and duration of the grants;

(d) Reporting requirements for entities that receive grants pursuant to this section;

(e) Criteria for the office and the state board to determine the effectiveness of the programs that receive grants pursuant to this section.

(3) The commission shall appoint a review committee to review the applications received pursuant to this section and make recommendations to the commission regarding the entities that may receive grants and the amounts of the grants. The commission shall finalize the recommendations for funding and provide them to the state board. Within thirty days after receiving the commission's recommendations, the state board shall award grants to the selected entities,

specifying the amount and duration of each award. A grant awarded pursuant to this section shall not exceed three years without renewal.

## 25-4-2204. Office of health equity - creation.

(1) There is hereby created in the department of public health and environment the office of health equity. The executive director of the department, subject to the provisions of section 13 of article XII of the state constitution, shall appoint the director of the office, who shall be the head of the office.

(2) The office and the director of the office shall exercise their powers and perform their duties and functions specified in this part 22 under the department as if the same were transferred to the department by a type 2 transfer, as such transfer is defined in the "Administrative Organization Act of 1968", article 1 of title 24, C.R.S.

## 25-4-2205. Powers and duties of office of health equity.

(1) The purpose of the office is to serve in a coordinating, educating, and capacity-building role for state and local public health programs and community-based organizations promoting health equity in Colorado by implementing strategies tailored to address the varying complex causes of health disparities, including the economic, physical, and social environment. The office shall work collaboratively within the department and with affected stakeholders to set priorities, collect and disseminate data, and align resources within the department and across other state agencies.

(2) The office has the following powers, duties, and functions:

(a) Administering and coordinating the health disparities grant program created in section 25-4-2203;

(b) Leading and coordinating the department's health equity efforts;

(c) Publishing data reports documenting health disparities;

(d) Providing education to the public on health equity, health disparities, and the social determinants of health;

(e) Coordinating the interpretation and translation services within the department and offering technical assistance to other state and local agencies;

(f) Building capacity within communities to offer or expand public health programs to better meet the needs of a diverse population;

(g) Conducting state-level strategic planning on minority health improvement;

(h) Providing technical assistance to the department in carrying out its programs and to county, district, and municipal public health agencies, community-based organizations, and communities in the state;

(i) Promoting workforce diversity within public health systems;

(j) Coordinating and staffing the health equity commission created in section 25-4-2206;

(k) Repealed.

(l) Building collaborative partnerships with communities to identify and promote health equity strategies; and

(m) Developing communications strategies regarding health equity.

(3) The office shall report to the executive director of the department or his or her designee, at the discretion of the executive director.

## 25-4-2206. Health equity commission - creation - repeal.

(1) There is hereby created in the office the health equity commission. The purpose of the commission is to serve as an advisor to the office on health equity issues, specifically focusing on alignment, education, and capacity-building for state and local health programs and community-based organizations. The commission shall be dedicated to promoting health equity and eliminating health disparities.

(2) (a) The commission consists of the following fifteen members, who are as follows:

(I) The speaker of the house of representatives shall appoint one member of the house of representatives;

(II) The president of the senate shall appoint one member of the senate;

(III) The executive director of the department shall appoint ten members who represent, to the extent practical, Colorado's diverse ethnic, racial, sexual orientation, gender identity, disability, aging population, socioeconomic, and geographic backgrounds. Each person appointed to the commission must have demonstrated expertise in at least one, and preferably two, of the following areas:

(A) African-American, black, Asian-American, Pacific Islander, Native American, Hispanic, Latino, aging population, lesbian, gay, bisexual, transgender, disabled, low socioeconomic status, and geographic community health issues;

(B) Data collection, aggregation, or dissemination;

(C) Education;

(D) Housing;

(E) Healthy community design;

(F) Community engagement;

(G) Local public health;

(H) Nonprofits, foundation, or grant-making;

(I) Environmental health;

(J) Behavioral health; or

(K) The provision of health care services.

(IV) The executive director of the department, or his or her designee, shall serve as an ex officio member of the commission;

(V) The executive director of the department of human services, or his or her designee; and

(VI) The executive director of the department of health care policy and financing, or his or her designee.

(b) The members of the commission shall serve at the pleasure of the appointing authority. Except as otherwise provided in section 2-2-326, C.R.S., the members of the commission shall serve without compensation, but shall be reimbursed by the department for their actual and necessary expenses incurred in the performance of their duties pursuant to this part 22.

(c) The members of the commission shall elect a chair and vice-chair from among its membership.

(3) The commission has the following powers and duties:

(a) Providing a formal mechanism for the public to give input to the office;

(b) Advising the department through the office on:

(I) Determining innovative data collection and dissemination strategies;

(II) Aligning the department's health equity efforts and the health disparities grant program created in section 25-4-2203;

(III) Strengthening collaborative partnerships with communities impacted by health disparities to identify and promote health equity strategies; and

(IV) Promoting workforce diversity;

(c) Repealed.

(d) Making recommendations to the office and the department on the health disparities grant program created in section 25-4-2203, regarding financial support for local and statewide initiatives that address prevention, early detection, needs assessment, and treatment of cancer, cardiovascular disease, including diabetes, and pulmonary disease in minority populations.

(4) The office shall provide staff to the commission.

(5) This section is repealed, effective September 1, 2023. Prior to the repeal of this section, the commission is subject to review as provided in section 2-3-1203, C.R.S.

## 25-4-2207. Interagency health disparities leadership council - creation. (Repealed)

### 25-4-2208. Necessary document program - definition - repeal.

(1) As used in this section, "necessary document" means:

(a) A social security card issued pursuant to 42 U.S.C. sec. 405 (c) (2) (G) ;

(b) One of the following documents issued in Colorado or analogous documents issued in another jurisdiction:

(I) A driver's license issued pursuant to part 1 of article 2 of title 42, C.R.S.;

(II) An identification card issued pursuant to part 3 of article 2 of title 42, C.R.S.; and

(III) A vital statistics certificate or vital statistics report issued pursuant to article 2 of this title; or

(c) Any document required as a condition of issuance of a document specified in paragraph (a) or (b) of this subsection (1) .

(2) The office shall administer a necessary document program. The office shall make one or more grants per fiscal year to, enter into one or more vendor contracts with, or both, a nonprofit entity or collection of nonprofit entities that conduct a collaborative identification project to assist Colorado residents who are victims of domestic violence, impacted by a natural disaster, low-income, disabled, homeless, or elderly and who are seeking documentation of their identity, status, or citizenship by paying the fees to acquire a necessary document.

(3) The general assembly shall annually appropriate to the office up to three hundred thousand dollars from the general fund. The office shall expend the money for the purposes specified in this section, including up to fifteen thousand dollars for the office's direct and indirect costs in administering the necessary document program.

(4) This section is repealed, effective September 1, 2021.

# PART 23. COLORADO IMMUNIZATION FUND

### 25-4-2301. Colorado immunization fund - supplemental tobacco litigation settlement moneys account - creation.

There are hereby created in the state treasury the Colorado immunization fund and an account within the fund to be known as the supplemental tobacco litigation settlement moneys account. The principal of the portion of the fund that is not the account consists of general fund appropriations made by the general assembly to the fund and gifts, grants, or awards received by the department of public health and environment from the federal government or private sources for the fund. The principal of the account consists of tobacco litigation settlement moneys transferred by the state treasurer to the account in accordance with section 24-75-1104.5 (1.7) (h) , C.R.S. All interest and income earned on the deposit and investment of moneys in the portion of the fund that is not the account shall be credited to that portion of the fund. All interest and income earned on the deposit and investment of moneys in the account shall be credited to and remain in the account until transferred as required by this section. Except as otherwise provided in this section, and subject to annual appropriation by the general assembly to the department, the department shall expend the principal of the fund and the account only for the purpose of immunization and immunization strategies; except that, at the end of the 2007-08 fiscal year and at the end of any fiscal year thereafter, any unexpended and unencumbered moneys in the portion of the fund that is not the account shall remain in that portion of the fund and may be used by the department through the state immunization program to support infant, child, and adolescent vaccination. All unexpended and unencumbered moneys in the account at the end of any fiscal year remain in the account and shall not be transferred to the general fund or any other fund.

# PART 24. IMMUNIZATION REGISTRY ACT

## 25-4-2401. Short title.

This part 24 shall be known and may be cited as the "Immunization Registry Act".

## 25-4-2402. Legislative declaration.

(1) The general assembly hereby finds and declares that:

(a) Immunization is one of the most important ways to protect individuals and communities against serious infectious diseases and their consequences, and widespread immunization has virtually eliminated many serious diseases that were once responsible for millions of infections and thousands of deaths each year.

(b) Although immunization rates of infants, children, adolescents, and adults in Colorado have improved over the last several years, there is a need to continue to improve the rates so that fewer individuals are put at risk from vaccine-preventable diseases.

(c) Timely vaccination of children, adolescents, and adults not only protects them against common, sometimes serious, and potentially fatal diseases, but also serves the community as one of the most successful and cost-effective public health tools available for the prevention and spread of these infections, and the vaccines are safe and highly protective, particularly when administered according to recommended schedules.

(d) More than twenty percent of preschool-aged children in Colorado are not fully vaccinated and are at increased risk of contracting and spreading vaccine-preventable diseases.

(e) It is unnecessary for children, adolescents, and adults to be subjected to suffering or death from diseases that are immunization preventable.

(f) In 2005, hospital charges for the care of children with vaccine-preventable diseases exceeded twenty-five million dollars. Additionally, tens of millions of dollars were spent on the costs of the outpatient care of affected children, in addition to the costs of the loss of productivity and absences from work for caregivers due to the absences of children from school.

(g) Over the past three decades, the recommended vaccination schedules for children and adults have become increasingly more complex as vaccines have been combined, new vaccines have been added, and the delivery system has incorporated more manufacturers, distributors, and providers. Additionally, local and national vaccine shortages and distribution errors have resulted in compromised vaccination initiatives.

(h) For Colorado to be consistent with the healthy people 2010 initiative and reach the goal of immunizing ninety percent of all children in the state in a timely and expeditious manner, the Colorado immunization information system must be funded and sustained. The Colorado immunization information system may also provide a secure method for authorized individuals and entities to access information collected by public agencies.

(2) Therefore, the general assembly supports the expansion of the Colorado immunization registry and supports increased access to immunizations for persons in Colorado.

## 25-4-2403. Department of public health and environment - powers and duties - immunization tracking system - definitions.

(1) In order to expand the immunization registry and increase access to immunizations, the department may address:

(a) Mechanisms for:

(I) Maximizing federal funds to purchase, distribute, and deliver vaccines for individuals in Colorado; and

(II) Statewide purchase, distribution, and prioritization of vaccines, including childhood immunizations and the seasonal influenza vaccine;

(b) Methods to reduce the administrative burden of providing immunizations to individuals in Colorado by reviewing current immunization activities and strategies and epidemiological data related to vaccine-preventable diseases and identifying opportunities to implement best practices for immunizations throughout Colorado using innovative strategies that are population-specific, culturally sensitive, and inclusive; address safety issues; and enhance current services;

(c) Options for Colorado to more effectively purchase, distribute, and deliver vaccines to insured, underinsured, and uninsured individuals;

(d) The pursuit of private and public partnerships for funding for the immunization registry infrastructure;

(e) Options for the most effective and cost-effective use of funds that may be available to the department of public health and environment to address vaccine delivery in the state; and

(f) The ability of the department of health care policy and financing to purchase vaccines recommended by ACIP through a purchasing system, if developed pursuant to this subsection (1) and subsection (1.3) of this section, for children who are enrolled in the children's basic health plan created in article 8 of title 25.5, C.R.S.

(1.3) (a) The department shall convene a task force of interested stakeholders to consider the issues identified in subsection (1) of this section. The task force must consist of at least the following persons or groups:

(I) Primary care providers, including essential community providers, pediatricians, family physicians, mid-level providers, and practice managers;

(II) Pharmacists from both independent and chain pharmacies;

(III) Local public health providers;

(IV) Child health advocates;

(V) Health insurers and other persons who pay for health care services;

(VI) A representative from a Colorado-based innovative vaccine company;

(VII) Pharmaceutical manufacturers; and

(VIII) Representatives from the departments of public health and environment and health care policy and financing.

(b) The task force shall make recommendations to the department and the board on the financing, ordering, and delivery of childhood immunizations, including through any of the following methods:

(I) A public-private model of vaccine purchase and delivery;

(II) Just-in-time delivery;

(III) Inventory management, including vaccine choices, combination vaccines, and equivalent vaccines;

(IV) Outbreak response;

(V) Linkage between the immunization tracking system established pursuant to subsection (2) of this section and vaccine inventory;

(VI) Vaccine shortage response;

(VII) Preservation of vaccine delivery in a medical home model of care;

(VIII) Mechanisms for local public health entities to bill health insurance carriers; and

(IX) Continuation and preservation of current models of vaccine purchase, financing, and delivery and the ability of health care providers to use those current models or any new models that may be developed pursuant to this subsection (1.3) and subsection (1) of this section.

(c) The board may adopt rules as necessary to implement the recommendations of the task force.

(d) No health care provider is compelled to participate in a vaccine purchasing system, if such system is developed pursuant to this section.

(2) To enable the gathering of epidemiological information and investigation and control of communicable diseases, the department of public health and environment may establish a comprehensive immunization tracking system with immunization information gathered by state and local health officials from the following sources:

(a) Practitioners;

(b) Clinics;

(c) Schools;

(d) Parents, legal guardians, or persons authorized to consent to immunization pursuant to section 25-4-1704;

(e) Individuals;

(f) Managed care organizations or health insurance plans in which an individual is enrolled as a member or insured, if such managed care organization or health insurer reimburses or otherwise financially provides coverage for immunizations;

(g) Hospitals;

(h) The department of health care policy and financing with respect to individuals who are eligible for coverage under the "Colorado Medical Assistance Act", articles 4, 5, and 6 of title 25.5, C.R.S.; and

(i) Persons and entities that have contracted with the state pursuant to paragraph (d) of subsection (9) of this section.

(3) Records in the immunization tracking system shall be strictly confidential and shall not be released, shared with any agency or institution, or made public upon subpoena, search warrant, discovery proceedings, or otherwise, except under the following circumstances:

(a) Medical and epidemiological information may be released in a manner such that no individual person can be identified.

(b) Immunization records and epidemiological information may be released to the extent necessary for the treatment, control, investigation, and prevention of vaccine-preventable diseases; except that every effort shall be made to limit disclosure of personal identifying information to the minimum amount necessary to accomplish the public health purpose.

(c) Immunization records and epidemiological information may be released to the individual who is the subject of the record, to a parent of a minor individual, to a guardian or person authorized to consent to immunization under section 25-4-1704, to the physician, clinic, hospital, or licensed health care practitioner treating the person who is the subject of an immunization record, to a school in which such person is enrolled, or any entity or person described in paragraph (f) , (h) , or (i) of subsection (2) of this section.

(4) An officer, employee, or agent of the department of public health and environment or a county, district, or municipal public health agency shall not be examined in any judicial, executive, legislative, or other proceeding as to the existence or content of any individual's report obtained by such department without consent of the individual or the individual's parent or guardian. However, this subsection (4) shall not apply to individuals who are under isolation, quarantine, or other restrictive action taken pursuant to section 25-1.5-102 (1) (c) .

(5) (a) An officer, employee, or agent of the department of public health and environment or any other person who violates this section by releasing or making public confidential immunization records or epidemiological information in the immunization tracking system or by otherwise breaching the confidentiality requirements of this section or releasing such information without authorization commits a class 1 misdemeanor and, upon conviction thereof, shall be punished as provided in section 18-1.3-501 (1) , C.R.S. The unauthorized release of each record shall constitute a separate offense.

(b) A natural person who, in exchange for money or any other thing of value, violates this section by wrongfully releasing or making public confidential immunization records or epidemiological information in the immunization tracking system or by otherwise breaching the confidentiality requirements of this section or releasing such information without authorization commits a class 1 misdemeanor and, upon conviction thereof, shall be punished as provided in section 18-1.3-501 (1) , C.R.S.

(c) A business entity who, in exchange for money or any other thing of value, violates this section by wrongfully releasing or making public confidential immunization records or epidemiological information in the immunization tracking system or by otherwise breaching the confidentiality requirements of this section or releasing such information without authorization shall be assessed a civil penalty of ten thousand dollars per sale of information per subject of such information.

(6) (a) The department of public health and environment or the department's contractor may directly contact the individual who is the subject of immunization records or the individual's parent or legal guardian for the purpose of notifying the individual, parent, or legal guardian if immunizations are due or overdue as indicated by the advisory committee on immunization practices of the United States department of health and human services or the American academy

of pediatrics. The department or the department's contractor shall contact the individual, parent, or legal guardian if it is necessary to control an outbreak of or prevent the spread of a vaccine-preventable disease pursuant to section 25-1.5-102 (1) (a) or 25-4-908.

(b) A notice given to an individual or a parent or legal guardian of an individual under eighteen years of age pursuant to this subsection (6) shall also inform the individual, parent, or legal guardian of the option to refuse an immunization on the grounds of medical, religious, or personal belief considerations pursuant to section 25-4-903.

(7) An individual or a parent or legal guardian who consents to the immunization of an infant, child, or student pursuant to part 9 or 17 of this article or this part 24 may exclude immunization information from the immunization tracking system. The individual, parent, or legal guardian may remove such immunization information from the immunization tracking system at any time. The department of public health and environment shall ensure that the process to exclude immunization information from the system is readily available and not burdensome. The physician, licensed health care practitioner, clinic, hospital, or county, district, or municipal public health agency shall inform the individual, parent, or legal guardian of the option to exclude such information from such system and the potential benefits of inclusion in such system. In addition, the physician, licensed health care practitioner, clinic, hospital, or county, district, or municipal public health agency shall inform such parent or legal guardian of a minor individual of the option to refuse an immunization on the grounds of medical, religious, or personal belief considerations pursuant to section 25-4-903. Neither refusing an immunization on the grounds of medical, religious, or personal belief considerations pursuant to section 25-4-903 nor opting to exclude immunization notification information from the immunization tracking system shall, by itself, constitute child abuse or neglect by a parent or legal guardian.

(8) A person licensed to practice medicine pursuant to article 36 of title 12, C.R.S.; a person licensed to practice nursing pursuant to article 38 of title 12, C.R.S.; any other licensed health care practitioner as defined in section 25-4-1703; providers of county nursing services; staff members of health care clinics, hospitals, and offices of private practitioners; county, district, and municipal public health agencies; and all persons and entities listed in subsection (2) of this section are authorized to report to the immunization tracking system and to use the reminder and recall process established by the immunization tracking system.

(9) The department of public health and environment may:

(a) Issue immunization records to individuals, parents, or guardians authorized to consent to immunizations;

(b) Assess the vaccination status of individuals;

(c) Accept any gifts or grants or awards of funds from the federal government or private sources for the implementation and operation of the immunization tracking system, which shall be credited to the immunization fund created in section 25-4-1708; and

(d) Enter into contracts that are necessary for the implementation and operation of the immunization tracking system. A person who enters into a contract pursuant to this paragraph (d) shall only use the information gathered from the immunization tracking system in accordance with this part 24 and shall be subject to all applicable state and federal laws regarding the confidentiality of information.

(10) County, district, and municipal public health agencies and the department of public health and environment shall use the birth certificate of any person to enroll the person in an immunization tracking system. The use of the birth certificate shall be considered an official duty of local health departments and the department of public health and environment.

(11) Physicians, licensed health care practitioners, clinics, schools, licensed child care providers, hospitals, managed care organizations or health insurance plans in which an individual is enrolled as a member or insured, persons that have contracted with the department of public health and environment pursuant to paragraph (d) of subsection (9) of this section, and public health officials may release any immunization records in their possession, whether or not such records are in the immunization tracking system, to the persons or entities specified in subsection (2) of this section to provide treatment for such individual or to provide an accurate and complete immunization

record for the individual.

(12) The department of public health and environment shall disseminate information about the immunization tracking system, including providing notification pursuant to subsection (7) of this section to birthing hospitals. The hospitals shall provide the notices to the parents of newborns.

(13) As used in this section:

(a) "ACIP" means the advisory committee on immunization practices to the centers for disease control and prevention in the federal department of health and human services, or its successor entity.

(b) "Board" means the state board of health created in section 25-1-103.

(c) "Department" means the department of public health and environment created in section 25-1-102.

(d) "Equivalent vaccines" means two or more vaccines that:

(I) Protect a recipient of the vaccine against the same infection;

(II) Have similar safety and efficacy profiles; and

(III) Are recommended for comparable populations by the federal centers for disease control and prevention.

# PART 25. CERVICAL CANCER IMMUNIZATION ACT

## 25-4-2501. Short title.

This part 25 shall be known and may be cited as the "Cervical Cancer Immunization Act".

## 25-4-2502. Definitions.

As used in this part 25, unless the context otherwise requires:

(1) "Board of health" means the state board of health.

(2) "Cervical cancer vaccine" or "cervical cancer immunization" means the series of vaccines to prevent cervical cancer as determined by the board of health to be necessary to conform to recognized standard medical practices.

(3) "Department" means the department of public health and environment.

(4) "FQHC" means a provider designated as a federally qualified health center pursuant to the provisions of 42 U.S.C. sec. 1396d (l) (2) (B) .

(5) "Local public health agency" means a county or district public health agency established pursuant to section 25-1-506.

(6) "Program" means the cervical cancer immunization program, created in section 25-4-2503.

## 25-4-2503. Cervical cancer immunization program - rules.

(1) There is hereby created in the department the cervical cancer immunization program. The department is directed to investigate manners in which the cervical cancer vaccine may be administered in an economical fashion. The state board is authorized to promulgate rules to assist the department in making the vaccine available.

(2) FQHCs are encouraged to enter into agreements with local public health agencies to administer vaccinations to underinsured female minors through a federally recognized vaccination program for children. If a local public health agency enters into an agreement, the agency shall administer vaccinations, including but not limited to cervical cancer vaccinations, pursuant to the agreement with the FQHC. The department shall pay to a local public health agency the agency's administrative cost for administering a cervical cancer vaccination to an underinsured female entering the sixth grade.

### 25-4-2504. Public awareness campaign - fund.

(1) Subject to the moneys being available in the fund created in subsection (2) of this section, on and after January 1, 2008, the department shall conduct a public awareness campaign on cervical cancer immunization and the benefits, disadvantages, and possible side effects of receiving cervical cancer immunization.

(2) There is hereby created in the state treasury the cervical cancer immunization awareness campaign fund, referred to in this section as the "fund". The fund shall consist of any gifts, grants, or donations received by the department pursuant to paragraph (a) of subsection (3) of this section and any moneys appropriated to the fund by the general assembly. Moneys in the fund shall be subject to annual appropriation by the general assembly for the direct and indirect costs associated with the implementation of this section. Interest and income derived from the deposit and investment of moneys in the fund shall be credited to the fund. Any unexpended and unencumbered moneys remaining in the fund at the end of a fiscal year shall remain in the fund and shall not be credited or transferred to the general fund or any other fund.

(3) (a) The department is authorized to seek and accept gifts, grants, or donations from private or public sources for the purposes of this section.

(b) Repealed.

# PRODUCTS CONTROL AND SAFETY

# ARTICLE 5. PRODUCTS CONTROL AND SAFETY

# PART 1. PROPHYLACTICS

**25-5-101 to 25-5-112. (Repealed)**

# PART 2. ENRICHMENT OF FLOUR AND BREAD

### 25-5-201. Legislative declaration.

The purpose of this part 2 is to protect so far as may be possible the health and well-being of the people of this state by providing for the enrichment of certain kinds of flour and bread in order to increase their content of certain essential vitamins and minerals. There will continue to be widespread deficiencies in the diets of our people unless such nutrients are contained in flour, bread, and rolls as provided in this part 2.

### 25-5-202. Definitions.

As used in this part 2, unless the context otherwise requires:

(1) "Department" means the department of public health and environment of the state of Colorado.

(2) "Flour" includes and is limited to the foods commonly known in the milling and baking industries as:

(a) White flour, also known as wheat flour or plain flour;

(b) Bromated flour;

(c) Self-rising flour, also known as self-rising white flour or self-rising wheat flour; and

(d) Phosphated flour, also known as phosphated white flour or phosphated wheat flour, which includes whole wheat flour but excludes special flours not used for bread, roll, bun, or biscuit baking, such as specialty cake, pancake, and pastry flours.

(3) "Person" means an individual, a corporation, a partnership, an association, a joint-stock company, a trust, or any group of persons, whether incorporated or not, engaged in the commercial manufacture or sale of flour, white bread, or rolls.

(4) "Rolls" includes plain white rolls and buns of the semibread dough type, namely: Soft rolls, such as hamburger rolls, hot dog rolls, and parker house rolls; and hard rolls, such as Vienna rolls and kaiser rolls. It does not include yeast-raised sweet rolls or sweet buns made with fillings or coatings, such as cinnamon rolls or buns and butterfly rolls.

(5) "White bread" means any bread made with flour, as defined in paragraph (a) of subsection (2) of this section, whether baked in a pan or on a hearth or screen, which is commonly known or usually represented and sold as white bread, including Vienna bread, French bread, and Italian bread.

## 25-5-203. Content of flour.

(1) It is unlawful for any person to manufacture, mix, compound, sell, or offer for sale flour for human consumption in this state unless the following vitamins and minerals are contained in each pound of such flour: Not less than two milligrams and not more than two and five-tenths milligrams of thiamine; not less than one and two-tenths milligrams and not more than one and five-tenths milligrams of riboflavin; not less than sixteen milligrams and not more than twenty milligrams of niacin or niacin amide; not less than thirteen milligrams and not more than sixteen and five-tenths milligrams of iron (Fe) , except in the case of self-rising flour which in addition to the above ingredients shall contain not less than five hundred milligrams and not more than one thousand five hundred milligrams of calcium (Ca) .

(2) The terms of this section shall not apply to flour sold to distributors, bakers, or other processors if the purchaser furnishes to the seller a certificate, in such form as the department by regulation shall prescribe, certifying that such flour will be:

(a) Resold to a distributor, baker, or other processor;

(b) Used in the manufacture, mixing, or compounding of flour, white bread, or rolls enriched to meet the requirements of this part 2;

(c) Used in the manufacture of products other than flour, white bread, or rolls.

(2.5) Notwithstanding any provision of this section to the contrary, the department shall promulgate rules and regulations which shall establish standards for the production, manufacture, distribution, and sale of flour, white flour, wheat flour, and plain flour. Such rules shall include the requirement that all such flour sold be clearly and distinctly labeled "Flour", "White Flour", "Wheat Flour", or "Plain Flour". All such flour shall be produced, manufactured, distributed, and sold in accordance with such rules and standards; except that the department shall allow the distribution and sale in this state of such flour produced and manufactured in another state if such flour has been produced and manufactured under rules and standards similar to those of the department.

(3) It is unlawful for any purchaser to use or resell the flour so purchased in any manner other than as prescribed in this section.

## 25-5-204. Content of white bread or rolls.

It is unlawful for any person to manufacture, bake, sell, or offer for sale any white bread or rolls for human consumption in this state unless the following vitamins and minerals are contained in each pound of such bread or rolls: Not less than one and one-tenth milligrams and not more than one and eight-tenths milligrams of thiamine; not less than seven-tenths milligrams and not more than one and six-tenths milligrams of riboflavin; not less than ten milligrams and not more than fifteen milligrams of niacin or niacin amide; and not less than eight milligrams and not more than twelve and five-tenths milligrams of iron (Fe) .

## 25-5-205. Enforcement of part 2.

(1) The department is charged with the duty of enforcing the provisions of this part 2, and it is authorized to make, amend, or rescind rules, regulations, and orders for the efficient enforcement of this part 2.

(2) Whenever the vitamin and mineral requirements set forth in sections 25-5-203 and 25-5-204 are no longer in conformity with the legally established standards governing the interstate shipment of enriched flour and enriched white bread or enriched rolls, the department, in order to maintain uniformity between intrastate and interstate vitamin and mineral requirements for the foods within the provisions of this part 2, is authorized to modify or revise such requirements to conform with amended standards governing interstate shipments.

(3) (a) In the event of findings by the department that there is an existing or imminent shortage of any ingredient required by sections 25-5-203 and 25-5-204 and that because of such shortage the sale and distribution of flour or white bread or rolls may be impeded by the enforcement of this part 2, the department shall issue an order, to be effective immediately upon issuance, permitting the omission of such ingredient from flour or white bread or rolls and, if it is found necessary or appropriate, excepting such foods from labeling requirements until further order of the department. Any such findings may be made without hearing on the basis of factual information supplied to or obtained by the department. Furthermore, the department, on its own motion, may hold a public hearing and, upon receiving the sworn statements of ten or more persons subject to this part 2 that they believe such a shortage exists or is imminent, within twenty days thereafter, shall hold a public hearing with respect thereto at which any interested person may present evidence; and it shall make findings based upon the evidence presented. The department shall publish notice of any such hearing at least ten days prior thereto.

(b) Whenever the department has reason to believe that such shortage no longer exists, it shall hold a public hearing, after at least ten days' notice has been given, at which any interested person may present evidence, and it shall make findings based upon the evidence so presented. If its findings are that such shortage no longer exists, it shall issue an order, to become effective not less than thirty days after publication thereof, revoking such previous order; but undisposed floor stocks of flour on hand at the effective date of such revocation order or flour manufactured prior to such effective date for sale in this state may thereafter be lawfully sold or disposed of.

(4) All orders, rules, and regulations adopted by the department pursuant to this part 2 shall be published in the manner prescribed in subsection (5) of this section and, within the limits specified by this part 2, shall become effective upon such date as the department shall fix.

(5) Whenever under this part 2 publication of any notice, order, rule, or regulation is required, such publication shall be made at least once in at least one daily newspaper of general circulation printed and published in this state.

(6) For the purpose of this part 2, the department, or such officers or employees under its supervision as it may designate, is authorized to take samples for analysis; and to conduct examinations and investigations; and to enter, at reasonable times, any factory, mill, bakery, warehouse, shop, or establishment where flour, white bread, or rolls are manufactured, processed, packed, sold, or held, or any vehicle being used for the transportation thereof; and to inspect any such place or vehicle and any flour, white bread, or rolls therein and all pertinent equipment, materials, containers, and labeling.

## 25-5-206. Penalty.

Any person who violates any of the provisions of this part 2 or the orders, rules, or regulations promulgated by the department under authority thereof is guilty of a misdemeanor and, upon conviction thereof, shall be punished by a fine for each offense of not more than one hundred dollars or by imprisonment in the county jail for not more than thirty days.

# PART 3. MATTRESSES AND BEDDING

## 25-5-301. Short title.
This part 3 shall be known and may be cited as the "Bedding Act".

## 25-5-302. Definitions.
As used in this part 3, unless the context otherwise requires:

(1) "Bedding" means any quilted pad, packing pad, mattress pad, hammock pad, mattress, comforter, bunk quilt, sleeping bag, box spring, studio couch, pillow, or cushion, any bag or container made of leather, cloth, or any other material, or any other device that is stuffed or filled in whole or in part with any concealed material in addition to the structural units and filling material used therein and its container, all of which can be used by any human being for sleeping or reclining purposes.

(2) "New material" means any material which has not been formerly used in the manufacture of another article or used for any other purpose.

(3) "Person" means any individual, corporation, partnership, or association.

(4) "Previously used material" means any material which has been used in the manufacture of another article or previously used for any other purpose.

(5) "Secondhand" means any article of bedding which has been previously used but not remade before it is offered for resale.

(6) "Sell" and "sold", in the corresponding tense, include: Sell, offer to sell, or deliver or consign in sale, or possess with intent to sell, deliver or consign in sale, including bedding stored in warehouses for ultimate purpose of sale.

## 25-5-303. Restrictions.
No person shall sell or distribute any bedding or bedding materials which are not clean or which may be deemed injurious to the public's health.

## 25-5-304. Sale of bedding exposed to contagion. (Repealed)

## 25-5-305. Disinfection.
(1) No person engaged in manufacturing, remaking, or renovating bedding for sale or distribution shall use any previously used material which since last used has not been disinfected by a method approved by the department of public health and environment.

(2) No person shall knowingly sell any bedding containing animal material, including but not limited to hair, feathers, down, or wool, which has not been disinfected by a method approved by the department of health prior to being incorporated into such bedding.

(3) Repealed.

## 25-5-306. Receiving bedding to be remade. (Repealed)

## 25-5-307. Tagging.
(1) No person shall sell bedding or materials therefor to which is not securely sewn by at least one edge a cloth or clothbacked tag at least two inches by three inches in size.

(2) Upon said tag shall be legibly stamped or printed in English in letters at least one-eighth of an inch high:

(a) If the materials used in the manufacture of the article of bedding to which the label is to be attached are entirely new, the label shall be as follows: "The materials used in the manufacture of this mattress (or other article of bedding) are entirely new."

(b) If the materials used in the manufacture of the article to which the label is to be attached are partially or wholly previously used materials, the label shall be as follows: "The materials used in the manufacture of this mattress (or other article of bedding) are previously used materials and have been disinfected."

(c) If the article to which the label is to be attached is secondhand, the label shall be as follows: "This mattress (or other article of bedding) is secondhand."

(3) In addition to the requirements of subsections (1) and (2) of this section, every label shall bear the name and address of the manufacturer or vendor of the article of bedding to which it is attached and the name of the material used to fill such article of bedding.

(4) Nothing likely to mislead shall appear on said tag. The tag shall contain all statements required by this section, and it shall be sewn to the outside covering of every article of bedding sold, manufactured, or remade.

(5) The tagging requirement of this section shall not apply to any individual selling his own personal articles of bedding to another individual.

## 25-5-308. Removing or defacing tag or stamp. (Repealed)

## 25-5-309. Administered by department.

(1) The department of public health and environment is charged with the administration and enforcement of this part 3.

(2) Repealed.

## 25-5-310. License. (Repealed)

## 25-5-311. Disposition of moneys. (Repealed)

## 25-5-312. Appropriation. (Repealed)

## 25-5-313. Posting of license. (Repealed)

## 25-5-314. Enforcement.

The department of public health and environment shall enforce this part 3 upon complaint or upon request by a consumer. The department of public health and environment, as often as necessary, may inspect any place where bedding is made, remade, renovated, or sold or where material is disinfected under this part 3. If the department has reason to believe that any article of bedding is not tagged as required by this part 3, the department has the authority to open the same and examine the materials therein to determine if said filling is as stated on said tag; except that, in opening such bedding, the department shall use reasonable means not to damage the same or destroy the value thereof. The department also has the power to examine any purchase records necessary to determine definitely the kind of material used in said bedding, and the department has the power to seize and hold for evidence any article or material therein possessed or offered for sale contrary to this part 3. The department of public health and environment may thereafter commence an action against any violator pursuant to section 25-5-316.

## 25-5-315. Violation - what constitutes. (Repealed)

## 25-5-316. Penalty for violation.
Any person who violates any provision of this part 3 shall be subject to a civil penalty of not more than one thousand dollars. Such penalty shall be determined and collected by the district court for the judicial district in which such violation occurs upon an action instituted by the department of public health and environment. In determining the amount of any such penalty, the court shall take into account the seriousness of the violation, whether the violation was willful or due to a mistake, the economic impact of the penalty upon the violator, and any other relevant factors. All penalties collected pursuant to this section shall be transmitted to the state treasurer and credited to the general fund. The court may also order that the violator pay any court costs of such action, and the court may order that the violator pay restitution to any person damaged by such violation. Any person damaged by a violation of this part 3 may maintain a civil suit for damages against any violator responsible for such damages.

## 25-5-317. Rules and regulations.
The department of public health and environment shall have the right to promulgate rules and regulations deemed necessary for the proper enforcement of this part 3 and not inconsistent therewith.

# PART 4. PURE FOOD AND DRUG LAW

## 25-5-401. Short title.
This part 4 shall be known and may be cited as the "Colorado Food and Drug Act".

## 25-5-402. Definitions.
As used in this part 4, unless the context otherwise requires:
(1) "Advertisement" means all representations disseminated in any manner or by any means, other than by labeling, for the purpose of inducing, or which are likely to induce, directly or indirectly, the purchase of food, drugs, devices, or cosmetics.
(2) "Color" includes black, white, and intermediate grays.
(3) (a) "Color additive" means a material which:
(I) Is a dye, pigment, or other substance made by a process of synthesis or similar artifice or extracted, isolated, or otherwise derived, with or without intermediate or final change of identity, from a vegetable, animal, mineral, or other source; and
(II) When added or applied to a food, drug, or cosmetic or to the human body or any part thereof, is capable (alone or through reaction with other substance) of imparting color thereto; except that such term does not include any material which is exempted under the federal act.
(b) Nothing in this subsection (3) shall be construed to apply to any pesticide chemical, soil or plant nutrient, or other agricultural chemical solely because of its effect in aiding, retarding, or otherwise affecting, directly or indirectly, the growth or other natural physiological process or produce of the soil and thereby affecting its color, whether before or after harvest.
(4) "Consumer commodity", except as otherwise specifically provided in this subsection (4) , means any food, drug, cosmetic, or device. Such term does not include:
(a) Any tobacco or tobacco product;
(b) Any commodity subject to packaging or labeling requirements imposed under article 9 of title 35, C.R.S., being known as the "Pesticide Act", or imposed by the secretary of agriculture under the "Federal Insecticide, Fungicide, and Rodenticide Act", as amended (7 U.S.C. secs. 135-135k) ,

or under the federal "Animal Virus, Serum, Toxin, Antitoxin Act" (21 U.S.C. secs. 151-158) ;

(c) Any drug subject to the provisions of section 25-5-415 (1) (m) or of 21 U.S.C. sec. 353 (b) (1) or 356;

(d) Any beverage subject to or complying with packaging or labeling requirements imposed under the "Federal Alcohol Administration Act" (27 U.S.C. secs. 201-211) ; or

(e) Any commodity subject to the provisions of article 27 of title 35, C.R.S., concerning seeds.

(5) "Contaminated with filth" applies to any food, drug, cosmetic, or device not securely protected from dust, dirt, and, as far as may be necessary by all reasonable means, from all foreign or injurious contaminations.

(6) "Cosmetic" means articles intended to be rubbed, poured, sprinkled, or sprayed on, introduced into, or otherwise applied to the human body or any part thereof for cleansing, beautifying, promoting attractiveness, or altering the appearance or articles intended for use as a component of any such articles; except that such term does not include soap.

(7) "Department" means the department of public health and environment.

(8) "Device", except when used in subsection (23) of this section and in sections 25-5-403 (1) (j) , 25-5-411 (1) (g) , 25-5-415 (1) (d) , and 25-5-417 (1) (d) , means instruments, apparatus, and contrivances, including their components, parts, and accessories, intended for use in the diagnosis, cure, mitigation, treatment, or prevention of disease in man or other animals or to affect the structure or any function of the body of man or other animals.

(9) "Drug" means:

(a) Articles recognized in the official United States pharmacopoeia, official homeopathic pharmacopoeia of the United States, official national formulary, or any supplement to any of them;

(b) Articles intended for use in the diagnosis, cure, mitigation, treatment, or prevention of disease in man or other animals;

(c) Articles, other than food, intended to affect the structure or any function of the body of man or other animals;

(d) Articles intended for use as a component of any article specified in paragraph (a) , (b) , or (c) of this subsection (9) but does not include devices or their components, parts, or accessories.

(10) "Federal act" means the "Federal Food, Drug, and Cosmetic Act" (21 U.S.C. sec. 301 et seq., 52 Stat. 1040 et seq.) .

(11) "Food" means articles used for food or drink for man or other animals, chewing gum, and articles used for components of any such article.

(12) "Food additive" means any substance, the intended use of which results or may be reasonably expected to result, directly or indirectly, in its becoming a component or otherwise affecting the characteristics of any food (including any substance intended for use in producing, manufacturing, packing, processing, preparing, treating, packaging, transporting, or holding food and including any source of radiation intended for any such use) if such substance is not generally recognized among experts qualified by scientific training and experience to evaluate its safety as having been adequately shown through scientific procedures (or, in the case of a substance used in a food prior to January 1, 1958, through either scientific procedures or experience based on common use in food) to be safe under the conditions of its intended use. The term does not include:

(a) A pesticide chemical in or on a raw agricultural commodity;

(b) A pesticide chemical to the extent that it is intended for use or is used in the production, storage, or transportation of any raw agricultural commodity;

(c) A color additive; or

(d) Any substance used in accordance with a sanction or approval granted prior to the enactment of the amendment to the federal act known as the "Food Additives Amendment of 1958", the "Poultry Products Inspection Act" (21 U.S.C. secs. 451-470) , or the "Meat Inspection Act of March 4, 1907", as amended and extended (21 U.S.C. secs. 71-91) .

(13) "Immediate container" does not include package liners.

(14) "Label" means a display of written, printed, or graphic matter upon the immediate container of any article; and by or under the authority of this part 4 a requirement that any word, statement, or other information appear on the label shall not be considered to be complied with unless such

word, statement, or other information also appears on the outside container or wrapper, if any, of the retail package of such article or is easily legible through the outside container or wrapper.

(15) "Labeling" means all labels and other written, printed, or graphic matter upon an article or any of its containers or wrappers, or accompanying such article.

(16) "Official compendium" means the official United States pharmacopoeia, official homeopathic pharmacopoeia of the United States, official national formulary, or any supplement to any of them.

(17) "Package" means any container or wrapping in which any consumer commodity is enclosed for use in the delivery or display of that consumer commodity to retail purchasers. The term does not include:

(a) Shipping containers or wrappings used solely for the transportation of any consumer commodity in bulk or in quantity to manufacturers, packers, or processors, or to wholesale or retail distributors thereof; or

(b) Shipping containers or outer wrappings used by retailers to ship or deliver any commodity to retail customers if such containers or wrappers bear no printed matter pertaining to any particular commodity.

(18) "Person" includes an individual, partnership, corporation, and association.

(19) "Pesticide chemical" means any substance which alone, in chemical combination, or in formulation with one or more other substances is a pesticide within the meaning of section 35-9-102 (21) , C.R.S., and which is used in the production, storage, or transportation of raw agricultural commodities.

(20) "Principal display panel" means that part of a label that is most likely to be displayed, presented, shown, or examined under normal and customary conditions of display for retail sale.

(21) "Raw agricultural commodity" means any food in its raw or natural state, including all fruits that are washed, colored, or otherwise treated in their unpeeled natural form prior to marketing.

(22) "Safe", as used in subsection (12) of this section, has reference to the health of man or animal.

(23) If an article is alleged to be misbranded because the labeling is misleading or if an advertisement is alleged to be false because it is misleading, then, in determining whether the labeling or advertisement is misleading, there shall be taken into account all representations made or suggested by statement, work, design, device, sound, or any combination thereof, and also the extent to which the labeling or advertisement fails to reveal facts material in the light of such representations or material with respect to consequences which may result from the use of the article to which the labeling or advertisement relates under the conditions of use prescribed in the labeling or advertisement thereof or under such conditions of use as are customary or usual.

(24) The representation of a drug, in its labeling or advertisement, as an antiseptic shall be considered to be a representation that it is a germicide, except in the case of a drug purporting to be, or represented as being, an antiseptic for inhibitory use which involves prolonged contact with the body.

(25) The provisions of this part 4 regarding the selling of food, drugs, devices, or cosmetics shall be considered to include the manufacture, production, processing, packing, exposure, offer, possession, and holding of any such article for sale; and the sale, dispensing, and giving of any such article; and the supplying or applying of any such articles in the conduct of any food, drug, or cosmetic establishment.

## 25-5-403. Offenses.

(1) The following acts and the causing thereof within this state are prohibited:

(a) The manufacture, sale, or delivery or the holding or offering for sale of any food, drug, device, or cosmetic that is adulterated or misbranded;

(b) The adulteration or misbranding of any food, drug, device, or cosmetic;

(c) The receipt in commerce of any food, drug, device, or cosmetic that is adulterated or misbranded and the delivery or proffered delivery thereof for pay or otherwise;

(d) The sale, delivery for sale, holding for sale, or offering for sale of any article in violation of section 25-5-412;

(e) The dissemination of any false or misleading advertisement;

(f) The refusal to permit entry, inspection, or the taking of a sample, as authorized by section 25-5-421;

(g) The giving of a false guaranty or undertaking except by a person who relied on a guaranty or undertaking to the same effect signed by and containing the name and address of the person residing in the United States from whom he received in good faith the food, drug, device, or cosmetic;

(h) The removal or disposal of a detained or embargoed article in violation of section 25-5-406;

(i) The alteration, mutilation, destruction, obliteration, or removal of the whole or any part of the labeling of or the doing of any other act with respect to a food, drug, device, or cosmetic which results in such article being adulterated or misbranded, if such act is done while such article is being stored or held for sale;

(j) Forging, counterfeiting, simulating, falsely representing, or without proper authority using any mark, stamp, tag, label, or other identification device required by this part 4 or by regulations promulgated under the provisions of this part 4;

(k) The distribution or causing to be distributed in commerce of any consumer commodity if such commodity is contained in a package or if there is affixed to that commodity a label which does not conform to the provisions of this part 4 and of regulations promulgated pursuant to this part 4; except that this prohibition shall not apply to persons engaged in business as wholesale or retail distributors of consumer commodities except to the extent that such persons:

(I) Are engaged in the packaging or labeling of such commodities; or

(II) Prescribe or specify by any means the manner in which such commodities are packaged or labeled;

(l) The using by any person to his own advantage or the revealing, other than to the executive director of the department or his authorized representative or to the courts, when relevant in any judicial proceeding under this part 4, of any information acquired under authority of this part 4 concerning any method or process which as a trade secret is entitled to protection.

(2) It is prohibited for any person to sell, give, or in any way furnish to another person who is under the age of twenty-one years any confectionery which contains alcohol in excess of one-half of one percent by volume.

(3) The provisions of this section shall not apply to a medical marijuana center or a medical-marijuana-infused products manufacturer licensed pursuant to article 43.3 of title 12, C.R.S., that manufactures or sells a food product that contains medical marijuana so long as the food product is labeled as containing medical marijuana and the label specifies that the product is manufactured without any regulatory oversight for health, safety, or efficacy, and that there may be health risks associated with the consumption or use of the product.

## 25-5-404. Injunction.

In addition to the remedies provided in this part 4, the department is authorized to apply to the district court of the district wherein the defendant resides or has his place of business for, and such court shall have jurisdiction upon hearing and for cause shown to grant, a temporary or permanent injunction restraining any person from violating any provision of section 25-5-403, irrespective of whether or not there exists an adequate remedy at law.

## 25-5-405. Penalties.

(1) Any person who violates any of the provisions of section 25-5-403 (1) is guilty of a misdemeanor and, upon conviction thereof, shall be punished by a fine of not more than one thousand dollars, or by imprisonment in the county jail for not more than six months, or by both such fine and imprisonment; but, if the violation is committed after a conviction of such person under this section has become final, such person shall be subject to a fine of not more than two thousand dollars, or to imprisonment for not more than one year, or to both such fine and imprisonment for each succeeding offense. Each violation shall be considered a separate offense.

(2) No person shall be subject to the penalties of subsection (1) of this section for having violated section 25-5-403 (1) (a) or (1) (c) if he establishes a valid guaranty or undertaking signed by and containing the name and address of the person residing in the United States from whom he received in good faith the article to the effect that such article is not adulterated or misbranded within the meaning of this part 4, designating this part 4.

(3) No publisher, radio-broadcast licensee, television licensee, or agency or medium for the dissemination of an advertisement, except the manufacturer, packer, distributor, or seller of the article to which a false advertisement relates, shall be liable under this section by reason of the dissemination by him of such false advertisement unless he refuses, on the request of the department, to furnish the department the name and post-office address of the manufacturer, packer, distributor, seller, or advertising agency residing in the United States who caused him to disseminate such advertisement.

(4) Any person who violates section 25-5-403 (2) is guilty of a misdemeanor and, upon conviction thereof, shall be punished by a fine of not more than seven hundred fifty dollars.

## 25-5-406. Tagging articles misbranded or adulterated.

(1) Whenever a duly authorized agent of the department finds or has probable cause to believe that any food, drug, device, or cosmetic is adulterated or misbranded within the meaning of this part 4, he shall affix to such article a tag or other appropriate marking giving notice that such article is, or is suspected of being, adulterated or misbranded and has been detained or embargoed and warning all persons not to remove or dispose of such article by sale or otherwise until provision for removal or disposal is given by the department or such agent or the court. No person shall remove or dispose of such embargoed article by sale or otherwise without the permission of the department or its agent or, after summary proceedings have been instituted, without permission from the court. If the embargo is removed by the department or by the court, neither the department nor the state shall be held liable for damages because of such embargo in the event that the court finds that there was probable cause for the embargo.

(2) When an article detained or embargoed under subsection (1) of this section has been found by such agent to be adulterated or misbranded, he shall petition the judge of the district court in whose jurisdiction the article is detained or embargoed for an order for condemnation of such article. When such agent finds that an article so detained or embargoed is not adulterated or misbranded, he shall remove the tag or other marking.

(3) If the court finds that a detained or embargoed article is adulterated or misbranded, such article shall, after entry of the decree, be destroyed at the expense of the claimant thereof, under the supervision of such agent, and all court costs and fees and storage and other proper expense shall be taxed against the claimant of such article or his agent; except that, when the adulteration or misbranding can be corrected by proper labeling or processing of the article, the court, after entry of the decree and after such costs, fees, and expenses have been paid and a good and sufficient bond, conditioned that such article shall be so labeled or processed, has been executed, may by order direct that such article be delivered to the claimant thereof for such labeling or processing under the supervision of an agent of the department. The expense of such supervision shall be paid by the claimant. Such bond shall be returned to the claimant of the article on representation to the court by the department that the article is no longer in violation of this part 4 and that the expenses of such supervision have been paid.

(4) Whenever the department or any of its authorized agents find in any room, building, vehicle of transportation, or other structure any meat, seafood, poultry, vegetable, fruit, or other perishable articles which are unsound or contain any filthy, decomposed, or putrid substance or which may be poisonous or deleterious to health or otherwise unsafe, the same being hereby declared to be a nuisance, the department or its authorized agent shall forthwith condemn or destroy the same or in any other manner render the same unsalable as human food.

## 25-5-407. Duties of district attorney.

It is the duty of each district attorney to whom the department reports any violation of this part 4 to cause appropriate proceedings to be instituted in the proper courts without delay and to be prosecuted in the manner required by law.

## 25-5-408. Discretion as to warning.

Nothing in this part 4 shall be construed as requiring the department to report, for the institution of proceedings under this part 4, minor violations of this part 4 whenever the department believes that the public interest will be adequately served in the circumstances by a suitable written notice or warning.

## 25-5-409. Regulations.

(1) Definitions and standards of identity, quality, and fill of container for any food adopted under authority of the federal act are the definitions and standards of identity, quality, and fill of container in this state. However, when, in its judgment, such action will promote honesty and fair dealing in the interest of consumers, the department may promulgate additional regulations establishing definitions and standards of identity, quality, and fill of container for foods which are not subject to any federal regulations. Any definition or standard of identity, quality, or fill of container promulgated under this subsection (1) which is in addition to federal definitions and standards shall constitute a regulation of the department, and it shall be subject to the requirements of section 25-5-420 concerning the procedures for promulgating such regulations. The department may promulgate amendments to any federal or state regulations which set definitions and standards of identity, quality, and fill of container for foods in the same manner as is provided for their adoption.

(2) Temporary permits granted under the federal act for interstate shipment of experimental packs of food varying from the requirements of federal definitions and standards of identity are automatically effective in this state under the conditions provided in such permits. The department may issue additional permits if they are necessary to the completion or conclusiveness of an otherwise adequate investigation and if the interests of consumers are safeguarded. Such permits are subject to the terms and conditions the department may prescribe by regulation.

## 25-5-410. Definitions of "adulterated".

(1) A food is deemed to be adulterated:

(a) If it bears or contains any poisonous or deleterious substance which may render it injurious to health; but, in case the substance is not an added substance, such food shall not be considered adulterated under this paragraph (a) if the quantity of such substance in such food does not ordinarily render it injurious to health;

(b) (I) If it bears or contains any added poisonous or added deleterious substance which is unsafe within the meaning of section 25-5-413; except that a pesticide chemical in or on a raw agricultural commodity, a food additive, or a color additive shall not be deemed a poisonous or deleterious substance within the meaning of this paragraph (b) ;

(II) If it is a raw agricultural commodity and it bears or contains a pesticide chemical which is unsafe within the meaning of section 25-5-413 (1) ; but, if a pesticide chemical has been used in or on a raw agricultural commodity in conformity with an exemption granted or tolerance prescribed under section 25-5-413 (2) and such raw agricultural commodity has been subjected to processing such as canning, cooking, freezing, dehydrating, or milling, the residue of such pesticide chemical remaining in or on such processed food, notwithstanding the provisions of section 25-5-413 (1) and this subparagraph (II) , shall not be deemed unsafe if such residue in or on the raw agricultural commodity has been removed to the extent possible in good manufacturing practice and the concentration of such residue in the processed food when ready to eat is not greater than the tolerance prescribed for the raw agricultural commodity; or

(III) If it is, or it bears or contains any food additive which is, unsafe within the meaning of section 25-5-413 (1) ;

(c) If it consists in whole or in part of a diseased, contaminated, filthy, putrid, or decomposed substance or if it is otherwise unfit for food;

(d) If it is produced, prepared, packed, or held under unsanitary conditions whereby it may be contaminated with filth or rendered diseased, unwholesome, or injurious to health;

(e) If it is, in whole or in part, the product of a diseased animal or an animal which has died otherwise than by slaughter or which has been fed upon the uncooked offal from a slaughterhouse;

(f) If its container is composed, in whole or in part, of any poisonous or deleterious substance which may render the contents injurious to health;

(g) If it has been intentionally subjected to radiation unless the use of the radiation was in conformity with a regulation or exemption in effect pursuant to section 25-5-413 or 21 U.S.C. sec. 348;

(h) (I) If any valuable constituent has been in whole or in part omitted or abstracted therefrom;

(II) If any substance has been substituted wholly or in part therefor;

(III) If damage or inferiority has been concealed in any manner;

(IV) If any substance has been added thereto or mixed or packed therewith so as to increase its bulk or weight, or reduce its quality or strength, or make it appear better or of greater value than it is;

(i) If it is confectionery and:

(I) Has partially or completely imbedded therein any nonnutritive object; but this subparagraph (I) shall not apply in the case of any nonnutritive object if, in the judgment of the department as provided by regulations, such object is of practical functional value to the confectionery product and does not render the product injurious or hazardous to health;

(II) Bears or contains any alcohol other than alcohol not in excess of six and twenty-five hundredths percent by volume or five percent by weight; or

(III) Bears or contains any nonnutritive substance; but this subparagraph (III) shall not apply to a safe nonnutritive substance which is in or on confectionery by reason of its use for some practical functional purpose in the manufacture, packaging, or storage of such confectionery if the use of the substance does not promote deception of the consumer or otherwise result in adulteration or misbranding in violation of any provision of this part 4; and, furthermore, the department, for the purpose of avoiding or resolving uncertainty as to the application of this subparagraph (III), may issue regulations allowing or prohibiting the use of particular nonnutritive substances;

(j) If it is, or it bears or contains a color additive which is, unsafe within the meaning of section 25-5-413 (1) or the federal act;

(k) If it is chopped or ground beef or hamburger and it contains any meat other than the voluntary striated muscle of beef, or the total fat content, derived solely from beef, is in excess of thirty percent, or it contains any substance other than those which the department has by regulation declared to be permitted optional ingredients;

(l) If it is fresh meat or a fresh meat product, or fresh poultry, parts thereof, or fresh poultry products, and contains any antiseptic or chemical preservative;

(m) If it is meat or a meat product and contains any artificial coloring or if it is contained in an artificially colored casing or wrapper; except that the department may by regulation establish the conditions of the use of artificial color in casings and wrappers;

(n) If it is pork sausage or pork breakfast sausage and the total fat content is in excess of fifty percent.

## 25-5-411. Definitions of "misbranding".

(1) A food shall be deemed to be misbranded:

(a) If its labeling is false or misleading in any particular;

(b) If its labeling or packaging fails to conform to the requirements of section 25-5-419;

(c) If it is offered for sale under the name of another food;

(d) If it is an imitation of another food, unless its label bears, in type of uniform size and prominence, the word "imitation" and, immediately thereafter, the name of the food imitated;

(e) If its container is so made, formed, or filled as to be misleading;

(f) If in package form, unless it bears a label containing:

(I) The name and place of business of the manufacturer, packer, or distributor; and

(II) An accurate statement of the net quantity of the contents in terms of weight, measure, or numerical count, which statement shall be separately and accurately stated in a uniform location upon the principal display panel of the label; but, as to such terms of quantity, reasonable variations shall be permitted, and exemptions as to small packages shall be established by regulation prescribed by the department;

(g) If any word, statement, or other information required by or under authority of this part 4 to appear on the label or labeling is not prominently placed thereon with such conspicuousness (as compared with other words, statements, designs, or devices in the labeling) and in such terms as to render it likely to be read and understood by the ordinary individual under customary conditions of purchase and use;

(h) If it purports to be or is represented as a food for which a definition and standard of identity is prescribed by regulations as provided by section 25-5-409, unless it conforms to such definition and standard and its label bears the name of the food specified in the definition and standard and, insofar as may be required by such regulations, the common names of optional ingredients (other than spices, flavoring, and coloring) present in such food;

(i) If it purports to be or is represented as:

(I) A food for which a standard of quality has been prescribed by regulations as provided by section 25-5-409 and its quality falls below such standard, unless its label bears, in such manner and form as regulations specify, a statement that it falls below such standard; or

(II) A food for which a standard of fill of container is prescribed by regulations as provided by section 25-5-409 and it falls below the standard of fill of container applicable thereto, unless its label bears, in such manner and form as such regulations specify, a statement that it falls below such standard;

(j) If it is not subject to the provisions of paragraph (h) of this section, unless it bears labeling clearly giving the common or usual name of the food, if any, and, if it is fabricated from two or more ingredients, the common or usual name of each such ingredient; except that spices, flavorings, and colorings, other than those sold as such, may be designated as spices, flavorings, and colorings without naming each; but, to the extent that compliance with the requirements as to such multiple names is impractical or results in deception or unfair competition, exemptions shall be established by regulations promulgated by the department. The requirements of this paragraph (j) shall not apply to food products which are packaged at the direction of purchasers at retail at the time of sale whose ingredients are disclosed to the purchasers by other means in accordance with regulations promulgated by the department.

(k) If it purports to be or is represented for special dietary uses, unless its label bears such information concerning its vitamin, mineral, and other dietary properties as the department determines to be and by regulations prescribes as necessary in order to fully inform purchasers as to its value for such uses;

(l) If it bears or contains any artificial flavoring, artificial coloring, or chemical preservative, unless it bears labeling stating that fact; but, to the extent that compliance with the requirements of this paragraph (l) is impracticable, exemptions shall be established by regulations promulgated by the department. The provisions of this paragraph (l) and paragraphs (h) and (j) of this subsection (1) with respect to artificial coloring do not apply to butter, cheese, or ice cream. The provisions of this paragraph (l) with respect to chemical preservatives do not apply to a pesticide chemical when used in or on a raw agricultural commodity which is the produce of the soil.

(m) If it is a product intended as an ingredient of another food and, when used according to the directions of the purveyor, will result in the final food product being adulterated or misbranded;

(n) If it is meat imported from without the boundaries of the United States or if it is a meat product containing such meat, unless it bears labeling stating the fact that it is imported meat or that it contains imported meat. Any person who sells or offers for sale in this state any meat imported from without the boundaries of the United States, or any meat product containing such imported meat, without labeling such meat or meat product stating that it is imported, or contains imported meat, is guilty of a misdemeanor and, upon conviction thereof, shall be punished by a fine of not less than one hundred dollars nor more than one thousand dollars, or by imprisonment in the county jail for not less than thirty days nor more than ninety days, or by both such fine and imprisonment.

(o) If it is a raw agricultural commodity which is the produce of the soil, bearing or containing a pesticide chemical applied after harvest, unless the shipping container of such commodity bears labeling which declares the presence of such chemical in or on such commodity and the common or usual name and the function of such chemical; except that no such declaration shall be required while such commodity, having been removed from the shipping container, is being held or displayed for sale at retail out of such container in accordance with the custom of the trade;

(p) If it is a color additive, unless its packaging and labeling are in conformity with such packaging and labeling requirements applicable to such color additive as may be contained in regulations issued pursuant to the provisions of the federal act.

(2) Foods which, in accordance with the practice of the trade, are to be processed, labeled, or repacked in substantial quantities at establishments other than those where originally processed or packed shall be exempt from any labeling requirements under this section if such food is not adulterated or misbranded under any provision of this part 4 upon removal from such processing, labeling, or repacking establishment. Regulations adopted under authority of the federal act (21 U.S.C. sec. 345) relating to such exemptions are automatically effective in this state. The department may promulgate additional regulations or amendments to existing regulations concerning such exemptions, but the department may not promulgate any regulation which has the effect of allowing any food which is subject to federal labeling requirements to be exempt from labeling requirements under the law of this state.

## 25-5-412. Issuance of permits.

(1) Whenever the department finds after investigation that the distribution in this state of any class of food may, by reason of contamination with microorganisms during manufacture, processing, or packing thereof in any locality, be injurious to health and that such injurious nature cannot be adequately determined after such articles have entered commerce, it, then and in such case only, shall promulgate regulations providing for the issuance to manufacturers, processors, or packers of such class of food in such locality of permits to which shall be attached such conditions governing the manufacture, processing, or packing of such class of food for such temporary period of time as may be necessary to protect the public health; and, after the effective date of such regulations and during such temporary period, no person shall introduce or deliver for introduction into commerce any such food manufactured, processed, or packed by any such manufacturer, processor, or packer, unless such manufacturer, processor, or packer holds a permit issued by the department as provided by such regulations.

(2) The department is authorized to suspend immediately upon notice any permit issued under authority of this section if it is found that any of the conditions of the permit have been violated. The holder of a permit so suspended shall be privileged to apply at any time for the reinstatement of such permit, and the department shall, immediately after prompt hearing and inspection of the establishment, reinstate such permit if it is found that adequate measures have been taken to comply with and maintain the conditions of the permit as originally issued or as amended.

(3) Any officer or employee duly designated by the department shall have access to any factory or establishment, the operator of which holds such a permit from the department, for the purpose of ascertaining whether or not the conditions of the permit are being complied with, and denial of access for such inspection shall be grounds for suspension of the permit until such access is freely given by the operator.

## 25-5-413. Limit of adulteration - rule or regulation.

(1) Any added poisonous or deleterious substance, food additive, pesticide chemical in or on a raw

agricultural commodity, or color additive, with respect to any particular use or intended use, shall be deemed unsafe for the purpose of application of section 25-5-410 (1) (b) with respect to any food, section 25-5-414 (1) (a) to (1) (f) with respect to any drug or device, or section 25-5-416 (1) (a) with respect to any cosmetic, unless there is in effect a regulation pursuant to section 25-5-419 or subsection (2) of this section limiting the quantity of such substance and the use or intended use of such substance is within the limits prescribed by such regulation. While such a regulation relating to such substance is in effect, a food, drug, or cosmetic, by reason of bearing or containing such substance in accordance with the regulations, shall not be considered adulterated within the meaning of section 25-5-410 (1) (b) , 25-5-414 (1) (a) to (1) (f) , or 25-5-416 (1) (a) .

(2) The department, whenever public health or other considerations so require, is authorized to adopt, amend, or repeal regulations upon its own motion or upon the petition of any interested party, whether or not in accordance with regulations promulgated under the federal act. Such regulations may prescribe tolerances for any added poisonous or deleterious substances, food additives, pesticide chemicals in or on raw agricultural commodities, or color additives, including but not limited to zero tolerances. The department may prescribe exemptions from tolerances in the case of pesticide chemicals in or on raw agricultural commodities. The department may also promulgate regulations prescribing the conditions under which a food additive or a color additive may be safely used and exemptions if such food additive or color additive is to be used solely for investigational or experimental purposes. It shall be incumbent upon any petitioner to establish that a necessity exists for such regulation and that its effect will not be detrimental to the public health. If the data furnished by the petitioner are not sufficient to allow the department to determine whether such regulation should be promulgated, the department may require additional data to be submitted, and failure to comply with the request shall be sufficient grounds for denial of the request. In adopting, amending, or repealing regulations under this section, the department shall consider, among other relevant factors, the following, which the petitioner, if any, shall furnish:

(a) The name and all pertinent information concerning such substance, including, where available, its chemical identity and composition; a statement of the conditions of the proposed use, including directions, recommendations, suggestions, and specimens of proposed labeling; all relevant data bearing on the physical or other technical effects; and the quantity required to produce such effect;

(b) The probable composition of any substance formed in or on a food, drug, or cosmetic resulting from the use of such substance;

(c) The probable consumption of such substance in the diet of man and animals taking into account any chemically or pharmacologically related substance in such diet;

(d) Safety factors which, in the opinion of experts qualified by scientific training and experience to evaluate the safety of such substances for the uses for which they are proposed to be used, are generally recognized as appropriate for the use of animal experimentation data;

(e) The availability of any needed practicable methods of analysis for determining the identity and quantity of:

(I) Such substance in or on an article;

(II) Any substance formed in or on such article because of the use of such substance; and

(III) The pure substance and all intermediates and impurities;

(f) Facts supporting a contention that the proposed use of such substance will serve a useful purpose.

## 25-5-414. Adulterations.

(1) A drug or device shall be deemed to be adulterated:

(a) If it consists in whole or in part of any filthy, putrid, or decomposed substance;

(b) If it has been produced, prepared, packed, or held under unsanitary conditions under which it may have been contaminated with filth or rendered injurious to health;

(c) If it is a drug and the methods used in, or the facilities or controls used for, its manufacture, processing, packing, or holding do not conform to or are not operated or administered in conformity with current good manufacturing practice to assure that such drug meets the requirements of this part 4 as to safety and that such drug has the identity and strength and meets the quality and purity characteristics which it purports or is represented to possess;

(d) If it is a drug and its container is composed, in whole or in part, of any poisonous or deleterious substance which may render the contents injurious to health;

(e) If it is a drug and it bears or contains, for purposes of coloring only, a color additive which is unsafe within the meaning of the federal act or section 25-5-413 (1) ;

(f) If it is a color additive, the intended use of which in or on drugs is for purposes of coloring only, and is unsafe within the meaning of the federal act or section 25-5-413 (1) ;

(g) If it purports to be or is represented as a drug, the name of which is recognized in an official compendium, and its strength differs from, or its quality or purity falls below, the standard set forth in such compendium. Such determination as to strength, quality, or purity shall be made in accordance with the tests or methods of assay set forth in such compendium or, in case of the absence or inadequacy of such tests or methods of assay, those prescribed under authority of the federal act. No drug defined in an official compendium shall be deemed to be adulterated under this paragraph (g) because it differs from the standard of strength, quality, or purity therefor set forth in such compendium if its difference in strength, quality, or purity from such standard is plainly stated on its label. Whenever a drug is recognized in both the United States pharmacopoeia and the homeopathic pharmacopoeia of the United States, it shall be subject to the requirements of the United States pharmacopoeia unless it is labeled and offered for sale as a homeopathic drug, in which case it shall be subject to the provisions of the homeopathic pharmacopoeia of the United States and not to those of the United States pharmacopoeia.

(h) If it is not subject to the provisions of paragraph (g) of this subsection (1) and its strength differs from, or its purity or quality falls below, that which it purports or is represented to possess;

(i) If it is a drug and any substance has been mixed or packed therewith so as to reduce its quality or strength or substituted wholly or in part therefor.

## 25-5-415. Misbranding.

(1) A drug or device shall be deemed to be misbranded:

(a) If its labeling is false or misleading in any particular;

(b) If its labeling or packaging fails to conform with the requirements of section 25-5-419;

(c) If in package form, unless it bears a label containing:

(I) The name and place of business of the manufacturer, packer, or distributor; and

(II) An accurate statement of the quantity of the contents in terms of weight, measure, or numerical count, which statement shall be separately and accurately stated in a uniform location upon the principal display panel of the label, except as exempted by section 25-5-402 (4) (c) ; but, as to such terms of quantity, reasonable variations shall be permitted, and exemptions as to small packages shall be established, by regulation prescribed by the department or issued under the federal act;

(d) If any word, statement, or other information required by or under authority of this part 4 to appear on the label or labeling is not prominently placed thereon with such conspicuousness (as compared with other words, statements, designs, or devices in the labeling) and in such terms as to render it likely to be read and understood by the ordinary individual under customary conditions of purchase and use;

(e) (I) If it is a drug, unless:

(A) Its label bears, to the exclusion of any other nonproprietary name (except the applicable systematic chemical name or the chemical formula) , the established name, as defined in subparagraph (II) of this paragraph (e) , of the drug, if such there be; and, in case it is fabricated from two or more ingredients, the established name and quantity of each active ingredient, including the kind and quantity or proportion of any bromides, ether, chloroform, acetanilid, acetophenetidin, amidopyrine, antipyrine, atropine, hyoscine, hyoscyamine, arsenic, digitalis, digitalis glucosides, mercury, ouabain, strophanthin, strychnine, thyroid, or any derivative or preparation of any such substances contained therein; except that the requirement for stating the quantity of the active ingredients, other than the quantity of those specifically named in this sub-subparagraph (A) , shall apply only to prescription drugs; and

(B) For any prescription drug, the established name of such drug or ingredient, as the case may be, on such label (and on any labeling on which a name for such drug or ingredient is used) is printed prominently and in type at least half as large as that used thereon for any proprietary name or designation for such drug or ingredient. To the extent that compliance with the requirements of this sub-subparagraph (B) and sub-subparagraph (A) of this subparagraph (I) as to fabricated drugs is impracticable, exemptions shall be established by regulations promulgated by the department or under the federal act.

(II) As used in this paragraph (e) , the term "established name", with respect to a drug or ingredient thereof, means:

(A) The applicable official name designated pursuant to the federal act; or

(B) If there is no such name and such drug or such ingredient is an article recognized in an official compendium, then the official title thereof in such compendium; or

(C) If neither sub-subparagraph (A) nor sub-subparagraph (B) of this subparagraph (II) applies, then the common or usual name, if any, of such drug or of such ingredient;

(D) Where sub-subparagraph (B) of this subparagraph (II) applies to an article recognized in the United States pharmacopoeia and in the homeopathic pharmacopoeia under different official titles, the official title used in the United States pharmacopoeia shall apply unless it is labeled and offered for sale as a homeopathic drug, in which case the official title used in the homeopathic pharmacopoeia shall apply.

(f) Unless its labeling bears adequate directions for use and such adequate warnings against use in those pathological conditions or by children where its use may be dangerous to health or against unsafe dosage or methods or duration of administration or application, in such manner and form as are necessary for the protection of users; but, where any requirement as to such adequate directions for use, as applied to any drug or device, is not necessary for the protection of the public health, the department shall promulgate regulations exempting such drug or device from such requirement, and articles exempted under regulations issued under the federal act shall also be exempt;

(g) If it purports to be a drug, the name of which is recognized in an official compendium, unless it is packaged and labeled as prescribed therein; but the method of packing may be modified with the consent of the department or if consent is obtained under the federal act. Whenever a drug is recognized in both the United States pharmacopoeia and the homeopathic pharmacopoeia of the United States, it shall be subject to the requirements of the United States pharmacopoeia with respect to packaging and labeling unless it is labeled and offered for sale as a homeopathic drug, in which case it shall be subject to the provisions of the homeopathic pharmacopoeia of the United States and not to those of the United States pharmacopoeia. In the event of inconsistency between the requirements of this paragraph (g) and those of paragraph (e) of this subsection (1) as to the name by which the drug or its ingredients are designated, the requirements of paragraph (e) of this subsection (1) shall prevail.

(h) If it is found by the department or under the federal act to be a drug liable to deterioration, unless it is packaged in such form and manner and its label bears a statement of such precautions as the regulations issued by the department or under the federal act require as necessary for the protection of public health. No such regulation shall be established for any drug recognized in an official compendium until the department has informed the appropriate body charged with the revision of such compendium of the need for such packaging or labeling requirements and such body has failed within a reasonable time to prescribe such requirements.

(i) (I) If it is a drug and its container is so made, formed, or filled as to be misleading; or

(II) If it is an imitation of another drug; or

(III) If it is offered for sale under the name of another drug;

(j) If it is dangerous to health when used in the dosage or with the frequency or duration prescribed, recommended, or suggested in the labeling thereof;

(k) If its labeling represents it to have any effect in albuminuria, appendicitis, arteriosclerosis, arthritis, baldness, blood poison, bone disease, Bright's disease, cancer, carbuncles, cholecystitis, diabetes, diphtheria, dropsy, erysipelas, gallstones, heart and vascular diseases, high blood pressure, mastoiditis, measles, meningitis, mumps, nephritis, otitis media, paralysis, pneumonia, poliomyelitis (infantile paralysis) , prostate gland disorders, pyelitis, rheumatism, scarlet fever, sexual impotence, sexually transmitted infection, sinus infection, smallpox, tuberculosis, tumors, typhoid, or uremia, and shall also be deemed to be false; except that no labeling in violation of paragraphs (a) and (b) of this subsection (1) shall be deemed to be false under this paragraph (k) if it is disseminated only to members of the medical, dental, chiropractic, or veterinary professions or is disseminated only for the purpose of public health education by persons not commercially interested, directly or indirectly, in the sale of such drugs or devices; but, if the department determines that an advance in medical science has made any type of self-medication safe as to any of the diseases named in this paragraph (k) , the department shall by regulation authorize the labeling of drugs having curative or therapeutic effect for such disease, subject to such conditions and restrictions as the department may deem necessary in the interests of public health; except that this paragraph (k) shall not be construed as indicating that self-medication for any disease is safe or efficacious;

(l) If it is for use by man and contains any quantity of the narcotic or hypnotic substance alpha eucaine, barbituric acid, betaeucaine, bromal, cannabis, carbromal, chloral, coca, cocaine, codeine, heroin, marijuana, morphine, opium, paraldehyde, peyote, or sulphonmethane, or any chemical derivative of such substance, which derivative, after investigation, has been found to be and designated as habit-forming by rules issued by the department or pursuant to the federal act, unless its label bears the name and quantity or proportion of the substance or derivative and in juxtaposition therewith the statement "Warning - May be habit-forming";

(m) If it is, or purports to be, or is represented as a drug composed wholly or partly of insulin, unless:

(I) It is from a batch with respect to which a certificate or release has been issued pursuant to the federal act; and

(II) Such certificate or release is in effect with respect to such drug;

(n) If it is, or purports to be, or is represented as a drug composed wholly or partly of any kind of penicillin, streptomycin, chlortetracycline, chloramphenicol, bacitracin, or any other antibiotic drug, or any derivative thereof, unless:

(I) It is from a batch with respect to which a certificate or release has been issued pursuant to the federal act; and

(II) Such certificate or release is in effect with respect to such drug; but this subparagraph (II) shall not apply to any drug or class of drugs exempted by regulations promulgated under the federal act. For the purpose of this paragraph (n) , "antibiotic drug" means any drug intended for use by man containing any quantity of any chemical substance which is produced by microorganisms and which has the capacity to inhibit or destroy microorganisms in dilute solution (including the chemically synthesized equivalent of any such substance) .

(o) If it is a color additive, the intended use of which in or on drugs is for the purpose of coloring only, unless its packaging and labeling are in conformity with such packaging and labeling requirements applicable to such color additive prescribed under the provisions of section 25-5-413 (2) or of the federal act;

(p) In the case of any prescription drug distributed or offered for sale in this state, unless the manufacturer, packer, or distributor thereof includes, in all advertisements and other descriptive printed matter issued or caused to be issued by the manufacturer, packer, or distributor with respect to that drug, a true statement of:

(I) The established name, as defined in paragraph (e) (II) of this subsection (1) , printed prominently and in type at least half as large as that used for any trade or brand name thereof;

(II) The formula showing quantitatively each ingredient of such drug to the extent required for labels under the federal act; and

(III) Such other information in brief summary relating to side effects, contraindications, and effectiveness as shall be required in regulations issued under the federal act;

(q) If a trademark, trade name, or other identifying mark, imprint, or device of another or any likeness of the foregoing has been placed thereon or upon its container with intent to defraud.

(2) A drug sold on a prescription given by a member of the medical, dental, or veterinary profession (except a drug sold in the course of the conduct of a business of selling drugs pursuant to diagnosis by mail) shall be exempt from the requirements of this section if such member of the medical, dental, or veterinary profession is authorized by law to administer such drug or if such drug bears a label containing the name and place of business of the seller, the serial number and date of such prescription, the name of such member of the medical, dental, or veterinary profession, and, if stated in the prescription, the name of the patient, the directions for use, and any cautionary statements contained in such prescription.

(3) Drugs and devices which, in accordance with the practice of the trade, are to be processed, labeled, or repacked in substantial quantities at establishments other than those where originally processed or packed shall be exempt from any labeling or packaging requirements of this part 4 if such drugs and devices are being delivered, manufactured, processed, labeled, repacked, or otherwise held in compliance with regulations issued by the department or under the federal act.

## 25-5-416. Adulteration of cosmetics.

(1) A cosmetic shall be deemed to be adulterated:

(a) If it bears or contains any poisonous or deleterious substance which may render it injurious to users under the conditions of use prescribed in the labeling or advertisement thereof or under such conditions of use as are customary or usual. This provision shall not apply to coal-tar hair dye, the label of which bears the following legend conspicuously displayed thereon: "Caution - This product contains ingredients which may cause skin irritations on certain individuals and a preliminary test according to accompanying directions should first be made. This product must not be used for dyeing the eyelashes or eyebrows; to do so may cause blindness." The label shall also bear adequate directions for such preliminary testing. For the purposes of this paragraph (a) and paragraph (e) of this subsection (1) , "hair dye" does not include eyelash dyes or eyebrow dyes.

(b) If it consists in whole or in part of any filthy, putrid, or decomposed substance;

(c) If it is produced, prepared, packed, or held under unsanitary conditions under which it may become contaminated with filth or rendered injurious to health;

(d) If its container is composed, in whole or in part, of any poisonous or deleterious substance which may render the contents injurious to health;

(e) If it is not a hair dye and it is, or it bears or contains, a color additive which is unsafe within the meaning of the federal act or section 25-5-413 (1) .

## 25-5-417. Misbranding of cosmetics.

(1) A cosmetic shall be deemed to be misbranded:

(a) If its labeling is false or misleading in any particular;

(b) If its labeling or packaging fails to conform with the requirements of section 25-5-419;

(c) If in package form, unless it bears a label containing the name and place of business of the manufacturer, packer, or distributor and an accurate statement of the quantity of the contents in terms of weight, measure, or numerical count, which statement shall be separately and accurately stated in a uniform location upon the principal display panel of the label; but, as to such terms of quantity required, reasonable variations shall be permitted and exemptions as to small packages shall be established by regulation prescribed by the department or under the federal act;

(d) If any word, statement, or other information required by or under authority of this part 4 to appear on the label or labeling is not prominently placed thereon with such conspicuousness (as compared with other words, statements, designs, or devices in the labeling) and in such terms as to render it likely to be read and understood by the ordinary individual under customary conditions of purchase and use;

(e) If its container is so made, formed, or filled as to be misleading;

(f) If it is a color additive, unless its packaging and labeling are in conformity with such packaging and labeling requirements applicable to such color additive prescribed in regulations under the provisions of the federal act. This paragraph (f) shall not apply to packages of color additives which, with respect to their use for cosmetics, are marketed and intended for use only in or on hair dyes as defined in section 25-5-416 (1) (a) .

(2) A cosmetic which is, in accordance with the practice of the trade, to be processed, labeled, or repacked in substantial quantities at an establishment other than the establishment where it was originally processed or packed is exempted from the affirmative labeling requirements of this part 4 while it is in transit in commerce from one establishment to the other if such transit is made in good faith for such completion purposes only; but such cosmetic is otherwise subject to all applicable provisions of this part 4.

## 25-5-418. Advertisements.

(1) An advertisement of a food, drug, device, or cosmetic is deemed to be false if it is false or misleading in any particular.

(2) For the purpose of this part 4, the advertisement of a drug or device representing it to have any effect in albuminuria, appendicitis, arteriosclerosis, arthritis, baldness, blood poison, bone disease, Bright's disease, cancer, carbuncles, cholecystitis, diabetes, diphtheria, dropsy, erysipelas, gallstones, heart and vascular diseases, high blood pressure, mastoiditis, measles, meningitis, mumps, nephritis, otitis media, paralysis, pneumonia, poliomyelitis (infantile paralysis) , prostate gland disorders, pyelitis, rheumatism, scarlet fever, sexual impotence, sexually transmitted infections, sinus infection, smallpox, tuberculosis, tumors, typhoid, or uremia shall also be deemed to be false; except that no advertisement not in violation of subsection (1) of this section shall be deemed to be false under this subsection (2) if it is disseminated only to members of the medical, dental, chiropractic, or veterinary professions, or appears only in the scientific periodicals of these professions, or is disseminated only for the purpose of public health education by persons not commercially interested, directly or indirectly, in the sale of such drugs or devices; but, if the department determines that an advance in medical science has made any type of self-medication safe as to any of the diseases named in this subsection (2) , the department shall by regulation authorize the advertisement of drugs having curative or therapeutic effect for such disease, subject to such conditions and restrictions as the department may deem necessary in the interests of public health; except that this subsection (2) shall not be construed as indicating that self-medication for any diseases is safe or efficacious.

## 25-5-419. Packaging and labeling of consumer commodities.

(1) All labels of consumer commodities, as defined in section 25-5-402 (4) , shall conform with the requirements for the declaration of net quantity of contents of the federal "Fair Packaging and Labeling Act" (15 U.S.C. sec. 1453) and the regulations promulgated pursuant thereto; but consumer commodities exempted from such requirements of the federal "Fair Packaging and Labeling Act" (15 U.S.C. secs. 1451-1461) shall also be exempt from this subsection (1) .

(2) The label of any package of a consumer commodity which bears a representation as to the number of servings of such commodity contained in such package shall bear a statement of the net quantity (in terms of weight, measure, or numerical count) of each such serving.

(3) No person shall distribute or cause to be distributed in commerce any packaged consumer commodity if any qualifying words or phrases appear in conjunction with the separate statement of the net quantity of contents required by subsection (1) of this section, but nothing in this subsection (3) shall prohibit supplemental statements, at other places on the package, describing in nondeceptive terms the net quantity of contents; but such supplemental statements of net quantity of contents shall not include any term qualifying a unit of weight, measure, or count that tends to exaggerate the amount of the commodity contained in the package.

(4) (a) Whenever the department determines that regulations containing prohibitions or requirements other than those prescribed by subsection (1) of this section are necessary to prevent

the deception of consumers or to facilitate value comparisons as to any consumer commodity, the department shall promulgate with respect to that commodity regulations effective to:

(I) Establish and define standards for the characterization of the size of a package enclosing any consumer commodity, which may be used to supplement the label statement of net quantity of contents of packages containing such consumer commodity, but this subparagraph (I) shall not be construed as authorizing any limitation on the size, shape, weight, dimensions, or number of packages which may be used to enclose any consumer commodity;

(II) Regulate the placement upon any package containing any consumer commodity, or upon any label affixed to such consumer commodity, of any printed matter stating or representing by implication that such consumer commodity is offered for retail sale at a price lower than the ordinary and customary retail sale price or that a retail sale price advantage is accorded to purchasers thereof by reason of the size of that package or the quantity of its contents;

(III) Require that the label on each package of a consumer commodity bear the common or usual name of such consumer commodity, if any, and, in case such consumer commodity consists of two or more ingredients, the common or usual name of each such ingredient listed in order of decreasing predominance, and, with respect to any confectionery containing alcohol in excess of one-half of one percent by volume, but within the limits prescribed by section 25-5-410 (1) (i) (II) , a statement that the content of alcohol does not exceed six and twenty-five hundredths percent by volume or five percent by weight, and that the product is unlawful for any person under twenty-one years of age, but nothing in this subparagraph (III) shall be deemed to require that any trade secret be divulged; or

(IV) Prevent the nonfunctional slack-fill of packages containing consumer commodities.

(b) For the purposes of subparagraph (IV) of paragraph (a) of this subsection (4) , a package shall be deemed to be nonfunctionally slack-filled if it is filled to substantially less than its capacity for reasons other than protection of the contents of such package or the requirements of machines used for enclosing the contents in such package; except that the department may adopt any regulations promulgated pursuant to the federal "Fair Packaging and Labeling Act" (15 U.S.C. secs. 1451-1461) which shall have the force and effect of law in this state.

## 25-5-420. Enforcement.

(1) The authority to promulgate regulations for the efficient enforcement of this part 4 is vested in the department. The department is authorized to make the regulations promulgated under this part 4 conform, insofar as practicable, with those promulgated under the federal act, the federal "Fair Packaging and Labeling Act" (15 U.S.C. secs. 1451-1461) , and the federal "Meat Inspection Act of March 4, 1907", as amended (21 U.S.C. secs. 71-91) . All regulations promulgated under this part 4 shall be promulgated in accordance with the provisions of article 4 of title 24, C.R.S.

(2) Hearings authorized or required by this part 4 or by article 4 of title 24, C.R.S., shall be conducted by the department or such officer, agent, or employee as the department may designate for the purpose.

(3) All pesticide chemical regulations and their amendments adopted under authority of the federal act are the pesticide chemical regulations in this state. However, the department may adopt regulations which prescribe tolerances for pesticides in finished foods in this state which are no less stringent than regulations promulgated under the federal act.

(4) All food additive regulations and their amendments adopted under authority of the federal act are the food additive regulations in this state. However, the department may adopt regulations which prescribe conditions under which a food additive may be used in this state which are no less stringent than regulations promulgated under the federal act.

(5) All color additive regulations and their amendments adopted under authority of the federal act are the color additive regulations in this state. However, the department may adopt regulations which prescribe conditions under which a color additive may be used in this state which are no less stringent than regulations promulgated under the federal act.

(6) All special dietary use regulations and their amendments adopted under authority of the federal

act are the special dietary use regulations in this state. However, the department may, if it finds it necessary to inform purchasers of the value of a food for special dietary use, prescribe special dietary use regulations which are no less stringent than regulations promulgated under the federal act.

(7) All regulations and their amendments adopted under the federal "Fair Packaging and Labeling Act" shall be the regulations in this state. However, the department may, if it finds it necessary in the interest of consumers, prescribe packaging and labeling regulations for consumer commodities which are no less stringent than regulations promulgated under such "Fair Packaging and Labeling Act", but no such regulations shall be promulgated which are contrary to the labeling requirements for the net quantity of contents required pursuant to the "Fair Packaging and Labeling Act" (15 U.S.C. sec. 1453) and the regulations promulgated thereunder.

(8) All regulations establishing standards of identity and composition for meat and meat food products and their amendments adopted under the federal "Meat Inspection Act of March 4, 1907", as amended (21 U.S.C. secs. 71-91) , are the established standards of identity and composition for meat and meat food products in this state. However, the department may, if it finds it necessary in the interest of consumers, adopt additional regulations establishing standards of identity and composition for meat and meat food products which are no less stringent than regulations promulgated under the federal "Meat Inspection Act".

(9) (a) A federal regulation automatically adopted pursuant to this part 4 takes effect in this state on the date it becomes effective as a federal regulation. The department shall publish all other proposed regulations thirty days prior to hearing thereon. A person who may be adversely affected by a regulation may file with the department, in writing, objections and a request for a hearing. The timely filing of substantial objections to a federal regulation automatically adopted stays the effect of the regulation in this state.

(b) If no substantial objections are received and no hearing is requested within thirty days after publication of a proposed regulation, it shall take effect on a date set by the department. The effective date shall be at least sixty days after the time for filing objections has expired.

(c) If substantial objections are made to a federal regulation within thirty days after it is automatically adopted or to a proposed regulation within thirty days after it is published, the department, after notice, shall conduct a public hearing to receive evidence on the issues raised by the objections. Any interested person or his representative may be heard. The department shall act upon objections by order and shall mail the order to objectors by certified mail as soon after the hearing as practicable. The order shall be based on substantial evidence in the record of the hearing. If the order concerns a federal regulation, it may reinstate, rescind, or modify such regulation. If the order concerns a proposed regulation, it may withdraw it or set an effective date for the regulation as published or as modified by the order. The effective date shall be at least sixty days after publication of the order.

## 25-5-421. Inspections.

(1) (a) For purposes of enforcement of this part 4, the authorized agents of the department, upon presenting appropriate credentials to the owner, operator, or agent in charge, are authorized to enter, at reasonable times, any factory, warehouse, or establishment in which food, drugs, devices, or cosmetics are manufactured, processed, packed, or held for introduction into commerce, or are held after such introduction, or to enter any vehicle being used to transport or hold such food, drugs, devices, or cosmetics in commerce; and to inspect, at reasonable times and within reasonable limits and in a reasonable manner, such factory, warehouse, establishment, or vehicle and all pertinent equipment, finished and unfinished materials, containers, and labeling therein and to obtain samples necessary to the enforcement of this part 4.

(b) (I) In the case of any factory, warehouse, establishment, or consulting laboratory in which prescription drugs are manufactured, processed, packed, or held, the inspection shall extend to all things therein (including records, files, papers, processes, controls, and facilities) bearing on whether prescription drugs which are adulterated or misbranded within the meaning of this part 4 or which may not be manufactured, introduced into commerce, or sold or offered for sale by reason of any provision of this part 4 have been or are being manufactured, processed, packed, transported, or held in any such place or otherwise bearing on violation of this part 4.

(II) No inspection authorized for prescription drugs by subparagraph (I) of this paragraph (b) shall extend to financial data, sales data other than shipment data, pricing data, personnel data (other than data as to qualifications of technical and professional personnel performing functions subject to this article) , and research data (other than data, relating to new drugs and antibiotic drugs, subject to reporting and inspection under regulations lawfully issued pursuant to 21 U.S.C. sec. 355 (i) or (j) and data, relating to other drugs, which in the case of a new drug would be subject to reporting or inspection under regulations issued pursuant to 21 U.S.C. sec. 355 (j) ) . Each such inspection shall be commenced and completed with reasonable promptness.

(III) The provisions of subparagraph (I) of this paragraph (b) shall not apply to pharmacies which maintain establishments in conformance with the laws of this state regulating the practice of pharmacy and medicine and which are regularly engaged in dispensing prescription drugs upon prescriptions of practitioners licensed to administer such drugs to patients under the care of such practitioners in the course of their professional practice and which do not, either through a subsidiary or otherwise, manufacture, prepare, propagate, compound, or process drugs for sale other than in the regular course of their business of dispensing or selling drugs at retail; to practitioners licensed by law to prescribe or administer drugs and who manufacture, prepare, propagate, compound, or process drugs solely for use in the course of their professional practice; to persons who manufacture, prepare, propagate, compound, or process drugs solely for use in research, teaching, or chemical analysis and not for sale; nor to such other classes of persons as the department may by regulation exempt from the application of this section upon a finding that inspection as applied to such classes of persons in accordance with this section is not necessary for the protection of the public health.

(c) The authorized agents of the department, upon presenting appropriate credentials to the owner, operator, or agent in charge, are authorized to have access to and to copy all records of carriers in commerce showing the movement in commerce of any food, drug, device, or cosmetic, or the holding thereof during or after such movement, and the quantity, shipper, and consignee thereof; but evidence obtained under this paragraph (c) shall not be used in a criminal prosecution of the person from whom obtained, and carriers shall not be subject to the other provisions of this part 4 by reason of their receipt, carriage, holding, or delivery of food, drugs, devices, or cosmetics in the usual course of business as carriers.

(2) Upon completion of any such inspection of a factory, warehouse, consulting laboratory, or other establishment, and prior to leaving the premises, the authorized agent making the inspection shall give to the owner, operator, or agent in charge a report in writing setting forth any conditions or practices observed by him which, in his judgment, indicate that any food, drug, device, or cosmetic in such establishment consists in whole or in part of any filthy, putrid, or decomposed substance or has been prepared, packed, or held under unsanitary conditions under which it may become contaminated with filth or rendered injurious to health. A copy of such report shall be sent promptly to the department.

(3) If the authorized agent making any such inspection of a factory, warehouse, or other establishment has obtained any sample in the course of the inspection, upon completion of the inspection and prior to leaving the premises, he shall give to the owner, operator, or agent in charge a receipt describing the samples obtained.

(4) Whenever, in the course of any such inspection of a factory or other establishment where food is manufactured, processed, or packed, the officer or employee making the inspection obtains a sample of any such food, and an analysis is made of such sample for the purpose of ascertaining whether such food consists in whole or in part of any filthy, putrid, or decomposed substance, or is otherwise unfit for food, a copy of the results of such analysis shall be furnished promptly to the owner, operator, or agent in charge.

## 25-5-422. Reports and information.

(1) The department may cause to be published from time to time reports summarizing all judgments, decrees, and court orders which have been rendered under this part 4, including the nature of the charge and the disposition thereof.

(2) The department may also cause to be disseminated such information regarding food, drugs, devices, and cosmetics as the department deems necessary in the interest of public health and the protection of the consumer against fraud. Nothing in this section shall be construed to prohibit the department from collecting, reporting, and illustrating the results of the investigations of the department.

## 25-5-423. Cooperation with federal agencies.

The department is authorized to confer and cooperate with the federal food and drug administration in the enforcement of the federal act and the United States department of agriculture in the enforcement of the federal "Meat Inspection Act of 1907", as amended, as they may apply to foods, drugs, devices, and cosmetics received in this state from other states, territories, or foreign countries.

## 25-5-424. Review.

Any person aggrieved by a decision of the department, and affected thereby, is entitled to judicial review pursuant to section 25-1-113.

## 25-5-425. Application of part 4.

The powers in this part 4 vested in the department are declared to be cumulative and in addition to and not in exclusion nor derogation nor limitation of the powers vested by law in the department, or in any other department of this state, or in any board or commission established by law, or in any law enforcement authority of this state.

## 25-5-426. Wholesale food manufacturing and storage - definitions - legislative declaration - fees - cash fund.

(1) The general assembly hereby finds, determines, and declares that the registration of wholesale food manufacturers and the regulation of premises or places wherein manufactured foods are produced, manufactured, packed, processed, prepared, treated, packaged, transported, or held for distribution in accordance with the "Colorado Food and Drug Act", the "Shellfish Dealer Certification Act", and the sanitary regulations administered by the department pursuant to part 1 of article 4 of this title and any rules promulgated thereunder:

(a) Is necessary to protect the public health;

(b) Will benefit consumers by ensuring that the sale and distribution of manufactured food is from safe sources;

(c) Will assist retailers by ensuring that manufactured foods have not been adulterated during manufacturing, packing, processing, preparing, treating, packaging, transporting, and storage; and

(d) Will contribute to the economic health of the state by assuring that Colorado wholesale food manufacturers are permitted to ship their product in interstate commerce.

(2) As used in this section, unless the context otherwise requires:

(a) "Brew pub" has the same meaning as set forth in section 12-47-103 (4) .

(b) "Brewery" has the same meaning as set forth in section 12-47-103 (5) .

(c) "Dietary ingredient" means one or any combination of a vitamin, mineral, herb or other botanical, amino acid, and a substance such as an enzyme, organ tissue, glandular, or metabolite.

(d) "Dietary supplement" means a product taken by mouth that contains a dietary ingredient or a new dietary ingredient intended to supplement the diet.

(e) "Distillery" or "distiller" has the same meaning as set forth in section 12-47-103 (7) .

(f) "Grain" means a small hard fruit or seed produced by a cereal grass and the seeds of such plants as a whole.

(g) "Grain storage facility" means any establishment, structure, or structures under one management at one general physical location that holds grain without further manufacturing or processing after harvest.

(h) "Manufacturing or processing" means making food from one or more ingredients, or synthesizing, preparing, treating, modifying, or manipulating food, including food crops or ingredients. Examples include: Cutting, peeling, trimming, washing, waxing, eviscerating, rendering, cooking, baking, freezing, cooling, pasteurizing, homogenizing, mixing, formulating, bottling, milling, grinding, extracting juices, distilling, labeling, or packaging.

(i) "New dietary ingredient" means a dietary ingredient that was not sold in the United States as a dietary supplement before October 15, 1994.

(j) "Nonprofit facility" means a charitable entity that provides food to the public, including food banks and nonprofit food facilities. To qualify as a nonprofit facility, the entity shall be exempt from paying federal income tax under the federal internal revenue code.

(k) "Spirituous liquors" has the same meaning as set forth in section 12-47-103 (36) .

(l) "Wholesale food manufacturer" and "storage facility" mean a facility that manufactures, produces, packs, processes, treats, packages, transports, or holds human food, including dietary supplements. These terms include, without limitation, any repacker, reshipper, shell stock shipper, and shucker-packer, as defined in section 25-4-1803 (8) , (9) , (12) , and (13) , respectively.

(m) "Winery" has the same meaning as set forth in section 12-47-103 (40) .

(3) The department has the following powers and duties:

(a) To grant or refuse to grant registration pursuant to subsection (4) of this section and to grant or refuse to grant the annual renewal of a registration;

(b) To deny, suspend, or revoke a registration;

(c) To issue a certificate of free sale; and

(d) To review any records of a wholesale food manufacturer or storage facility necessary to verify compliance with the provisions of this section.

(4) (a) Beginning July 1, 2003, and on or before July 1 of each year thereafter, the owner of any wholesale food manufacturer or storage facility shall submit an application to the department. Each wholesale food manufacturer or storage facility shall pay an annual application fee of one hundred dollars, plus any additional registration fee specified in subsection (4) (b) of this section; except that an application fee is not required for a nonprofit facility. The application for registration is valid for one year or for the portion of the fiscal year that remains if an application is submitted after July 1 of any fiscal year. If an application is valid for only a portion of a fiscal year, an application fee reduction is not required by this section. Each application expires on June 30 of the state fiscal year in which the application is submitted.

(b) In addition to the application fee a facility is required to pay pursuant to subsection (4) (a) of this section, the schedule for annual registration fees for wholesale food manufacturers or storage facilities is as follows:

(I) A registration fee is not required for a nonprofit facility, grain storage facility, brewery, brew pub, winery, or a distiller of spirituous liquors.

(II) A wholesale food manufacturer or storage facility with gross annual sales of less than one hundred fifty thousand dollars shall pay the department a registration fee of sixty dollars.

(III) A wholesale food manufacturer or storage facility with gross annual sales of one hundred fifty thousand dollars or more shall pay the department a registration fee of three hundred dollars.

(c) Upon issuing a certificate of free sale, the department shall collect a fee of one hundred fifty dollars.

(5) Fees collected by the department pursuant to subsection (4) of this section shall be transmitted to the state treasurer, who shall credit such fees to the wholesale food manufacturing and storage protection cash fund, which is hereby created in the state treasury. The general assembly shall annually appropriate the moneys in such fund to the department for the payment of expenses necessary for the administration of this section. Any unexpended and unencumbered moneys remaining in the fund at the end of any fiscal year shall remain in the fund and shall not revert to

the general fund or any other fund.

(6) Repealed.

# PART 5. HAZARDOUS SUBSTANCES

## 25-5-501. Short title.
This part 5 shall be known and may be cited as the "Colorado Hazardous Substances Act of 1973".

## 25-5-502. Definitions.
As used in this part 5, unless the context otherwise requires:

(1) "Banned hazardous substance" means:

(a) (I) Any toy, or other article intended for use by children, which is a hazardous substance, or which bears or contains a hazardous substance in such manner as to be susceptible of access by a child to whom such toy or other article is entrusted.

(II) The department shall exempt by regulation articles, such as chemical sets, which by reason of their functional purpose require the inclusion of the hazardous substance involved or necessarily present an electrical, mechanical, or thermal hazard, and which bear labeling giving adequate directions and warnings for safe use and are intended for use by children who have attained sufficient maturity, and may reasonably be expected, to read and heed such directions and warnings. Proceedings for the issuance, amendment, or repeal of exemption regulations shall be governed by the provisions of section 25-5-508.

(b) Any hazardous substance intended, or packaged in a form suitable, for use in the household which the department by regulation classifies as a banned hazardous substance on the basis of a finding that, notwithstanding such cautionary labeling as is or may be required under this article for that substance, the degree or nature of the hazard involved in the presence or use of such substance in households is such that the objective of the protection of the public health and safety can be adequately served only by keeping such substance, when so intended or packaged, out of the channels of commerce.

(2) "Combustible" means any substance which has a flash point above eighty degrees Fahrenheit to and including one hundred and fifty degrees, as determined by the Tagliabue open cup tester. This definition shall not apply to the flammability or combustibility of solids and of the contents of self-pressurized containers which shall be determined by methods generally applicable to such materials or containers and established by regulations issued by the department.

(3) "Commerce" means any and all commerce within the state of Colorado, and subject to the jurisdiction thereof, and includes the operation of any business or service establishment.

(4) "Corrosive substance" means any substance which, in contact with living tissue, will cause destruction of tissue by chemical action but shall not refer to action on inanimate surfaces.

(5) "Department" means the department of public health and environment.

(6) "Electrical hazard" means an article, the design or manufacture of which, in normal use or when subjected to reasonably foreseeable damage or abuse, may cause personal injury or illness by electric shock.

(7) "Executive director" means the executive director of the department of public health and environment.

(8) "Extremely flammable substance" is a substance which has a flash point at or below twenty degrees Fahrenheit as determined by the Tagliabue open cup tester. This definition shall not apply to the flammability or combustibility of solids and of the contents of self-pressurized containers which shall be determined by methods generally applicable to such materials or containers and established by regulations issued by the department.

(9) "Flammable substance" is a substance which has a flash point above twenty degrees Fahrenheit to and including eighty degrees Fahrenheit as determined by the Tagliabue open cup tester. This

definition shall not apply to the flammability or combustibility of solids and of the contents of self-pressurized containers which shall be determined by the methods generally applicable to such materials or containers and established by regulation issued by the department.

(10) (a) "Hazardous substance" means any substance or mixture of substances which:

(I) Is toxic;

(II) Is corrosive;

(III) Is an irritant;

(IV) Is a strong sensitizer;

(V) Is flammable or combustible; or

(VI) Generates pressure through decomposition, heat, or other means, if such substance or mixture of substances may cause substantial personal injury or substantial illness during or as a proximate result of any customary or reasonably foreseeable handling or use, including reasonably foreseeable ingestion by children.

(b) "Hazardous substance" also means:

(I) Any substances which the department by regulation finds, pursuant to the provisions of section 25-5-508, meet the requirements of paragraph (a) of this subsection (10) ;

(II) Any radioactive substance, if, with respect to such substance as used in a particular class of article or as packaged, the department determines by regulation that the substance is sufficiently hazardous to require labeling in accordance with this article in order to protect the public health;

(III) Any toy or other article intended for use by children which the department by regulation determines, in accordance with section 25-5-508, presents an electrical, mechanical, or thermal hazard.

(c) The term "hazardous substance" shall not apply to an economic poison subject to regulation by the federal government; to a substance regulated by the "Pesticide Act"; to food, drugs, and cosmetics subject to regulation by the federal government or the "Colorado Food and Drug Act"; or to anhydrous ammonia as an agricultural fertilizer as regulated by article 13 of title 35, C.R.S. "Hazardous substance" shall not include a substance intended for use as fuels when stored in containers and used in the heating, cooking, or refrigeration system of a house or any source material, special nuclear material, or byproduct material as defined in the federal "Atomic Energy Act of 1954", as amended, and regulations issued pursuant thereto by the atomic energy commission.

(11) (a) "Highly toxic" means any substance which falls within any of the following categories:

(I) Produces death within fourteen days in one-half or more than one-half of a group of ten or more laboratory white rats each weighing between two hundred and three hundred grams, at a single dose of fifty milligrams or less per kilogram of body weight, when orally administered; or

(II) Produces death within fourteen days in one-half or more than one-half of a group of ten or more laboratory white rats each weighing between two hundred and three hundred grams when inhaled continuously for a period of one hour or less at an atmospheric concentration of two hundred parts per million by volume or less of gas or vapor or two milligrams per liter by volume or less of mist or dust, provided such concentration is likely to be encountered by man when the substance is used in any reasonably foreseeable manner; or

(III) Produces death within fourteen days in one-half or more than one-half of a group of ten or more rabbits tested in a dosage of two hundred milligrams or less per kilogram of body weight when administered by continuous contact with the bare skin for twenty-four hours or less.

(b) If the department finds that available data on human experience with any substance indicate results different from those obtained on animals in the above-named dosages or concentrations, the human data shall take precedence.

(12) "Irritant" means any substance not corrosive within the meaning of subsection (4) of this section which on immediate, prolonged, or repeated contact with normal living tissue will induce a local inflammatory reaction.

(13) "Label" means a display of written, printed, or graphic matter upon the immediate container (not including package liners) of any substance or, in the case of an article which is unpackaged or is not packaged in an immediate container intended or suitable for delivery to the ultimate

consumer, a display of such matter directly upon the article involved or upon a tag or other suitable material affixed thereto. A requirement made by or under authority of this part 5 that any word, statement, or other information appear on the label shall not be considered to be complied with unless such word, statement, or other information also appears on the outside container or wrapper, if any there be, unless it is easily legible through the outside container or wrapper and on all accompanying literature where there are directions for use, written or otherwise.

(14) "Mechanical hazard" means an article, the design or manufacture of which, in normal use or when subjected to reasonably foreseeable damage or abuse, presents an unreasonable risk of personal injury or illness from fracture, fragmentation, or disassembly of the article; from propulsion of the article or any part or accessory thereof; from points or other protrusions, surfaces, edges, openings, or closures of the article; from moving parts of the article; from lack or insufficiency of controls to reduce or stop the motion of the article; as a result of self-adhering characteristics of the article; because the article, or any part or accessory thereof, may be aspirated or ingested; because of the instability of the article; or because of any other aspect of the article's design or manufacture.

(15) "Misbranded hazardous substance" means a hazardous substance (including a toy, or other article intended for use by children, which is a hazardous substance, or which bears or contains a hazardous substance in such manner as to be susceptible of access by a child to whom such toy or other article is entrusted) intended, or packaged in a form suitable, for use in the household or by children, which substance, except as otherwise provided by or pursuant to section 25-5-508, fails to bear a label:

(a) Which states conspicuously:

(I) The name and place of business of the manufacturer, packer, distributor, or seller;

(II) The common or usual name or the chemical name (if there be no common or usual name) of the hazardous substance or of each component which contributes substantially to its hazard, unless the department by regulation permits or requires the use of a recognized generic name;

(III) The signal word "DANGER" on substances which are extremely flammable, corrosive, or highly toxic;

(IV) The signal word "WARNING" or "CAUTION" on all other hazardous substances;

(V) An affirmative statement of the principal hazard or hazards, such as "Flammable", "Combustible", "Vapor Harmful", "Causes Burns", "Absorbed Through Skin", or similar wording descriptive of the hazard;

(VI) Precautionary measures describing the action to be followed or avoided, except when modified by regulation of the department pursuant to section 25-5-508;

(VII) Instruction, when necessary or appropriate, for first-aid treatment;

(VIII) The word "poison" for any hazardous substance which is highly toxic;

(IX) Instructions for handling and storage of packages which require special care in handling or storage; and

(X) The statement "Keep out of the reach of children" or its practical equivalent or, if the article is intended for use by children and is not a banned hazardous substance, adequate directions for the protection of children from the hazard.

(b) On which any statement required under paragraph (a) of this subsection (15) is located prominently and is in the English language in conspicuous and legible type in contrast by typography, layout, or color with other printed matter on the label.

(16) "Person" means an individual, partnership, corporation, or association or its legal representative or agent.

(17) "Radioactive substance" means a substance which emits ionizing radiation.

(18) "Strong sensitizer" means a substance which will cause, on normal living tissue, through an allergic or photodynamic process, a hypersensitivity which becomes evident on reapplication of the same substance and which is designated as such by the department. Before designating any substance as a strong sensitizer, the department, upon consideration of frequency of occurrence and severity of the reaction, shall find that the substance has significant potential for causing hypersensitivity.

(19) "Thermal hazard" means an article, the design, or manufacture of which, in normal use or when subjected to reasonably foreseeable damage or abuse, presents an unreasonable risk of personal injury or illness because of heat, as from heated parts, substances, or surfaces.

(20) "Toxic" shall apply to any substance (other than a radioactive substance) which has the capacity to produce personal injury or illness to man through ingestion, inhalation, or absorption through any body surface.

## 25-5-503. Prohibited acts.

(1) The following acts and the causing thereof are hereby prohibited:

(a) The introduction or delivery for introduction into commerce of any misbranded hazardous substance or banned hazardous substance;

(b) The alteration, mutilation, destruction, obliteration, or removal of the whole or any part of the label of, or the doing of any other act with respect to, a hazardous substance if such act is done while the substance is in commerce, or while the substance is held for sale (whether or not the first sale) after shipment in commerce, and results in the hazardous substance being a misbranded hazardous substance or a banned hazardous substance;

(c) The receipt in commerce of any misbranded hazardous substance or banned hazardous substance and the delivery or proffered delivery thereof for pay or otherwise;

(d) The giving of a guarantee or undertaking referred to in section 25-5-504 (2) , which guarantee or undertaking is false, except by a person who relied upon a guarantee or undertaking to the same effect signed by, and containing the name and address of, the person residing in the United States from whom he received in good faith the hazardous substance;

(e) The failure to permit entry, inspection, or sampling as authorized by section 25-5-509 or to permit access to and copying of any record as authorized by section 25-5-510;

(f) The removing or disposing of a detained or embargoed article by sale or otherwise without permission of an authorized agent or court;

(g) The introduction or delivery for introduction into commerce or the receipt in commerce and subsequent delivery or proffered delivery, for pay or otherwise, of a hazardous substance in a reused food, drug, or cosmetic container or in a container which, though not a reused container, is identifiable as a food, drug, or cosmetic container by its labeling or by other identification. The reuse of a food, drug, or cosmetic container as a container for a hazardous substance shall be deemed to be an act which results in the hazardous substance being a misbranded hazardous substance. As used in this paragraph (g) , the terms "food", "drug", and "cosmetic" shall have the same meanings as in the "Colorado Food and Drug Act".

(h) The use by any person to his own advantage or the revealing, other than to the executive director or officers or employees of the department or to the courts when relevant in any judicial proceeding under this part 5, of any information acquired under authority of section 25-5-509 concerning any method or process which as a trade secret is entitled to protection.

## 25-5-504. Penalties.

(1) Any person who violates any of the provisions of section 25-5-503 is guilty of a misdemeanor and, upon conviction thereof, shall be punished by a fine of not more than five hundred dollars, or by imprisonment in the county jail for not more than ninety days, or by both such fine and imprisonment; but, for offenses committed with intent to defraud or mislead, or for second and subsequent offenses, the penalty shall be imprisonment for not more than one year, or a fine of not more than three thousand dollars, or both such imprisonment and fine. Each violation shall be considered a separate offense.

(2) No person shall be subject to the penalties of this section for having violated section 25-5-503 (1) (c) if the receipt, delivery, or proffered delivery of the hazardous substance was made in good faith, unless he refuses to furnish on request of an officer or employee duly designated by the executive director, the name and address of the person from whom he purchased or received such hazardous substance and copies of all documents, if any there be, pertaining to the delivery of the

hazardous substance to him; or for having violated section 25-5-503 (1) (a) if he establishes a guarantee or undertaking signed by, and containing the name and address of, the person residing in the United States from whom he received in good faith the hazardous substance to the effect that the hazardous substance is not a misbranded hazardous substance or a banned hazardous substance within the meaning of those terms in this part 5.

## 25-5-505. Injunction proceedings.

In addition to the remedies provided in this part 5, the executive director is authorized to apply to the district court for a temporary or permanent injunction restraining any person from violating any provision of section 25-5-503, irrespective of whether or not there exists an adequate remedy at law.

## 25-5-506. Embargo and seizure.

(1) Whenever a duly authorized agent of the department finds or has probable cause to believe that any hazardous substance is misbranded or is a banned hazardous substance within the meaning of this part 5, he shall affix to such article a tag or other appropriate marking, giving notice that such article is, or is suspected of being, misbranded or is a banned hazardous substance and has been detained or embargoed and warning all persons not to remove or dispose of such article by sale or otherwise until permission for removal or disposal is given by such agent or the district court.

(2) When an article detained or embargoed under subsection (1) of this section has been found by such agent to be misbranded or a banned hazardous substance, he shall petition the district court in whose jurisdiction the article is detained or embargoed for an order for condemnation of such article. When such agent has found that an article so detained or embargoed is not misbranded or is not a banned hazardous substance, he shall remove the tag or other marking.

(3) If the court finds that a detained or embargoed article is misbranded or is a banned hazardous substance, such article shall, after entry of the decree, be destroyed at the expense of the claimant thereof, under supervision of the agent, and all court costs and fees and storage and other proper expenses shall be taxed against the claimant of such article or his agent; except that, when the misbranding can be corrected by proper labeling of the article, the court, after entry of the decree and after such costs, fees, and expenses have been paid and a good and sufficient bond, conditioned that such article shall be so labeled, has been executed, may by order direct that such article be delivered to the claimant thereof for such labeling under the supervision of an agent of the department. The expense of such supervision shall be paid by the claimant. The article shall be returned to the claimant on the representation to the court by the executive director that the article is no longer in violation of this part 5 and that the expenses of such supervision have been paid.

## 25-5-507. Duties of district attorney.

(1) It is the duty of each district attorney to whom the executive director reports any violation of this part 5 to cause appropriate proceedings to be instituted in the proper courts without delay and to be prosecuted in the manner required by law.

(2) Before any violation of this part 5 is reported to any such district attorney for the institution of a criminal proceeding, the person against whom such proceeding is contemplated shall be given appropriate notice and an opportunity to present his views before the executive director or his designated agent, either orally or in writing, or by attorney, with regard to such contemplated proceeding.

## 25-5-508. Regulations.

(1) All regulations adopted now or hereafter under the "Federal Hazardous Substances Act", as amended, shall be the hazardous substances regulations in this state. However, the department is authorized to promulgate regulations for the efficient enforcement of this part 5, which regulations shall be no less stringent than the regulations established pursuant to the "Federal Hazardous Substances Act", as amended; except that regulation relating to the precautionary labeling or

exemptions thereto shall not differ from the requirements of the "Federal Hazardous Substances Act", as amended, and the regulations promulgated pursuant thereto.

(2) (a) Whenever in the judgment of the executive director such action will promote the objectives of this part 5 by avoiding or resolving uncertainty as to its application, the executive director may by regulation declare to be a hazardous substance, for the purposes of this part 5, any substance or mixture of substances which he finds meets the definition in section 25-5-502 (10) .

(b) If the executive director finds that the hazard of an article subject to this part 5 is such that labeling adequate to protect the public health and safety cannot be devised or the article presents an imminent danger to the public health and safety, the executive director may declare such article to be a banned hazardous substance and require its removal from commerce.

(c) (I) A determination by the executive director that a toy or other article intended for use by children presents an electrical, mechanical, or thermal hazard shall be made by regulation in accordance with article 4 of title 24, C.R.S.

(II) If, before or during a proceeding pursuant to subparagraph (I) of this paragraph (c) , the executive director finds that, because of an electrical, mechanical, or thermal hazard, distribution of the toy or other article involved presents an imminent hazard to the public health and he gives notice of such finding, such toy or other article shall be deemed to be a banned hazardous substance for purposes of this part 5 until the proceeding has been completed. If not yet initiated when such notice is given, such proceeding shall be initiated as soon as possible.

(d) In the case of any toy, substance, or other article intended for use by children which is determined by the executive director to present an electrical, mechanical, or thermal hazard, any person who will be adversely affected by such a determination may, at any time prior to the sixtieth day after the regulation making such determination is issued by the executive director, ask for judicial review as provided in section 24-4-106, C.R.S.

(3) All regulations promulgated under this part 5 shall be promulgated in accordance with the provisions of article 4 of title 24, C.R.S.

(4) Hearings authorized or required by this article shall be conducted according to the provisions of article 4 of title 24, C.R.S.

(5) A federal regulation automatically adopted pursuant to this part 5 takes effect in this state on the date it becomes effective as a federal regulation. The department shall publish all other proposed regulations thirty days prior to hearing thereon. A person who may be adversely affected by a regulation may file with the department, in writing, objections and a request for a hearing. The timely filing of substantial objections to a federal regulation automatically adopted stays the effect of the regulation in this state.

(6) If no substantial objections are received and no hearing is requested within thirty days after publication of a proposed regulation, it shall take effect on a date set by the department. The effective date shall be at least sixty days after the time for filing objections has expired.

(7) If substantial objections are made to a federal regulation within thirty days after it is automatically adopted or to a proposed regulation within thirty days after it is published, the department, after notice, shall conduct a public hearing to receive evidence on the issues raised by the objections. Any interested person or his representative may be heard. The department shall act upon objections by order and shall mail the order to objectors by certified mail as soon after the hearing as practicable. The order shall be based on substantial evidence in the record of the hearing. If the order concerns a federal regulation, it may reinstate, rescind, or modify such regulation. If the order concerns a proposed regulation, it may withdraw it or set an effective date for the regulation as published or as modified by the order. The effective date shall be at least sixty days after publication of the order.

## 25-5-509. Examinations - investigations.

(1) For the purposes of enforcement of this part 5, officers or employees duly designated by the executive director, upon presenting appropriate credentials to the owner, operator, or agent in charge, are authorized to enter, at reasonable times, any factory, warehouse, or establishment in

which hazardous substances are manufactured, processed, packed, or held for introduction into commerce or are held after such introduction or to enter any vehicle being used to transport or hold such hazardous substances in commerce; to inspect, at reasonable times, and within reasonable limits and in a reasonable manner, such factory, warehouse, establishment, or vehicle and all pertinent equipment, finished and unfinished materials, and labeling therein; and to obtain samples of such materials, or packages thereof, and of such labeling.

(2) If the officer or employee obtains any sample prior to leaving the premises, he shall pay or offer to pay the owner, operator, or agent in charge for such sample and give a receipt describing the sample obtained. If analysis is made of such sample, a copy of the results of such analysis shall be furnished promptly to the owner, operator, or agent in charge.

### 25-5-510. Records of shipment.

For the purpose of enforcing the provisions of this part 5, carriers engaged in commerce and persons receiving hazardous substances in commerce or holding such hazardous substances so received shall, upon the request of an officer or employee duly designated by the executive director, permit such officer or employee, at reasonable times, to have access to and to copy all records showing the movement in commerce of any such hazardous substances, or the holding thereof during or after such movement, and the quantity, shipper, and consignee thereof; and it is unlawful for any such carrier or person to fail to permit such access to and copying of any record so requested when such request is accompanied by a statement in writing specifying the nature or kind of such hazardous substance to which such request relates. Evidence obtained under this section shall not be used in a criminal prosecution of the person from whom obtained; and carriers shall not be subject to the other provisions of this part 5 by reason of their receipt, carriage, holding, or delivery of hazardous substances in the usual course of business as carriers.

### 25-5-511. Publicity.

(1) The executive director may cause to be published from time to time reports summarizing any judgments, decrees, or court orders which have been rendered under this part 5, including the nature of the charge and the disposition thereof.

(2) The executive director may also cause to be disseminated information regarding hazardous substances in situations involving, in the opinion of the executive director, imminent danger to health. Nothing in this section shall be construed to prohibit the executive director from collecting, reporting, and illustrating the results of the investigations of the department.

### 25-5-512. Exception - discretion as to reporting.

(1) Nothing in this part 5 shall be construed as:

(a) Applicable to any person or corporation if the safety of his or its product or service is already regulated by any agency of the state of Colorado;

(b) Requiring the executive director to report minor violations of this part 5 for the institution of proceedings under this part 5 whenever the executive director believes that the public interest will be adequately served in the circumstances by a suitable written notice or warning.

# PART 6. SALE OF EYEGLASSES AND SUNGLASSES

### 25-5-601 to 25-5-604. (Repealed)

# PART 7. PASSENGER TRAMWAY SAFETY

## 25-5-701. Legislative declaration.

In order to assist in safeguarding life, health, property, and the welfare of this state, it is the policy of the state of Colorado to establish a board empowered to prevent unnecessary mechanical hazards in the operation of passenger tramways and to assure that reasonable design and construction are used for, that accepted safety devices and sufficient personnel are provided for, and that periodic inspections and adjustments are made which are deemed essential to the safe operation of, passenger tramways.

## 25-5-702. Definitions.

As used in this part 7, unless the context otherwise requires:

(1) "Area operator" means a person who owns, manages, or directs the operation and maintenance of a passenger tramway. "Area operator" may apply to the state or any political subdivision or instrumentality thereof.

(1.5) "Board" means the passenger tramway safety board created by section 25-5-703.

(1.7) "Commercial recreational area" means an entity using passenger tramways to provide recreational opportunities to the public for a fee.

(2) "Industry" means the activities of all those persons in this state who own, manage, or direct the operation of passenger tramways.

(3) "License" means the formal, legal, written permission of the board to operate a passenger tramway.

(4) "Passenger tramway" means a device used to transport passengers uphill on skis, or in cars on tracks, or suspended in the air by the use of steel cables, chains, or belts, or by ropes, and usually supported by trestles or towers with one or more spans. "Passenger tramway" includes, but is not limited to, the following devices:

(a) Fixed-grip lifts. "Fixed-grip lift" means an aerial lift on which carriers remain attached to a haul rope. The tramway system may be either continuously or intermittently circulating, and may be either monocable or bicable.

(b) Detachable-grip lifts. "Detachable-grip lift" means an aerial lift on which carriers alternately attach to and detach from a moving haul rope. The tramway system may be monocable or bicable.

(c) Funiculars. "Funicular" means a device in which a passenger car running on steel or wooden tracks is attached to and propelled by a steel cable, and any similar devices.

(d) Chair lifts. "Chair lift" means a type of transportation on which passengers are carried on chairs suspended in the air and attached to a moving cable, chain, or link belt supported by trestles or towers with one or more spans, and any similar devices.

(e) Surface lifts. "Surface lift" means a J-bar, T-bar, or platter pull and any similar types of devices or means of transportation which pull skiers riding on skis by means of an attachment to a main overhead cable supported by trestles or towers with one or more spans.

(f) Rope tows. "Rope tow" means a type of transportation which pulls the skier riding on skis as the skier grasps the rope manually, and any similar devices.

(g) Portable aerial tramway devices. "Portable aerial tramway device" means any device designed for temporary use and operation, without permanent foundations, in changing or variable locations, with a capacity of less than five persons, which transports equipment or personnel, and is not used or intended to be used by the general public.

(h) Portable tramway devices. "Portable tramway device" means any device designed to be used and operated as a rope tow or surface lift without permanent foundations and intended for temporary use in changing or variable locations, when used within the boundary of a recognized ski area.

(i) Private residence tramways. "Private residence tramway" means a device installed at a private residence or installed in multiple dwellings as a means of access to a private residence in such multiple dwelling buildings, so long as the tramway is so installed that it is not accessible to the general public or to other occupants of the building.

(j) Reversible aerial tramways. "Reversible aerial tramway" means a device on which passengers are transported in cable-supported carriers and are not in contact with the ground or snow surface, and in which the carriers reciprocate between terminals.

(k) Conveyors. "Conveyor" means a type of transportation by which skiers, or passengers on recreational devices, are transported uphill on top of a flexible, moving element such as a belt or a series of rollers.

(4.5) "Program administrator" means the person who manages the board's offices on a day-to-day basis and works with the supervisory tramway engineer and the board in implementing the policies, decisions, and orders of the board.

(5) "Qualified tramway design engineer" or "qualified tramway construction engineer" means an engineer licensed by the state board of licensure for architects, professional engineers, and professional land surveyors pursuant to part 1 of article 25 of title 12, C.R.S., to practice professional engineering in this state.

(6) "Staff" means the program administrator, the supervisory tramway engineer, and their clerical staff.

(7) "Supervisory tramway engineer" means the tramway engineer who works with the program administrator and the board in implementing the policies, decisions, and orders of the board.

## 25-5-703. Passenger tramway safety board - composition - termination.

(1) There is hereby created a passenger tramway safety board of six appointive members and one member designated by the United States forest service. The appointive members shall be appointed by the governor from persons representing the following interests: Two members to represent the industry or area operators; two members to represent the public at large; one member who is a licensed professional engineer not employed by a ski area or related industry; and one member familiar with or experienced in the tramway industry who may represent the passenger tramway manufacturing or design industry or an area operator. No person shall be so appointed or designated except those who, by reason of knowledge or experience, shall be deemed to be qualified. Such knowledge or experience shall be either from active and relevant involvement in the design, manufacture, or operation of passenger tramways or as a result of extensive and relevant involvement in related activities. The governor, in making such appointments, shall consider recommendations made to him or her by the membership of the particular interest from which the appointments are to be made.

(2) Each of the appointed members shall be appointed for a term of four years and until a successor is appointed and qualified and no board member shall serve more than two consecutive four-year terms. A former board member may be reappointed to the board after having vacated the board for one four-year term. Vacancies on the board, for either an unexpired term or for a new term, shall be filled through prompt appointment by the governor. The member of the board designated by the United States forest service shall serve for such period as such federal agency shall determine and shall serve without compensation or reimbursement of expenses.

(3) The governor may remove any member of the board for misconduct, incompetence, or neglect of duty.

(4) Board members appointed by the governor shall have been residents of this state for at least three years.

(5) No member of the board who has any form of conflict of interest or the potential thereof shall participate in consideration of the deliberations on matters to which such conflict may relate; such conflicts may include, but are not limited to, a member of the board having acted in any consulting relationship or being directly or indirectly involved in the operation of the tramway in question.

(6) A majority of the board shall constitute a quorum. When necessary, the board may conduct business telephonically during a public meeting for purposes of obtaining a quorum, facilitating the participation of members in remote locations, or both.

(7) The provisions of section 24-34-104, C.R.S., concerning the termination schedule for regulatory bodies of the state unless extended as provided in that section, are applicable to the passenger tramway safety board created by this section.

## 25-5-703.5. Board subject to termination - repeal of article. (Repealed)

## 25-5-704. Powers and duties of board.

(1) The board has the following powers and duties in addition to those otherwise described by this part 7:

(a) To promulgate, amend, and repeal such rules as may be necessary and proper to carry out the provisions of this article. In adopting such rules, the board may use as general guidelines the standards contained in the "American National Standard for Passenger Ropeways - Aerial Tramways and Aerial Lifts, Surface Lifts, Tows, and Conveyors - Safety Requirements", as adopted by the American national standards institute, incorporated, as amended from time to time. Such rules shall not be discriminatory in their application to area operators and procedures of the board with respect thereto shall be as provided in section 24-4-103, C.R.S., with respect to rule-making.

(b) To investigate matters relating to the exercise and performance of the powers and duties of the board;

(c) To receive complaints concerning violations of this part 7;

(d) To conduct meetings, hold hearings, and take evidence in all matters relating to the exercise and performance of the powers and duties of the board, subpoena witnesses, administer oaths, and compel the testimony of witnesses and the production of books, papers, and records relevant to the subject inquiry. The program administrator may issue subpoenas on behalf of the board at the board's direction. If any person refuses to obey any subpoena so issued, the board may petition the district court, setting forth the facts, and thereupon the court in a proper case shall issue its subpoena. The board may appoint an administrative law judge pursuant to part 10 of article 30 of title 24, C.R.S., to take evidence and to make findings and report them to the board. The board may elect to hear the matter itself with the assistance of an administrative law judge, who shall rule on the evidence and otherwise conduct the hearing in accordance with the "State Administrative Procedure Act", article 4 of title 24, C.R.S.

(e) To discipline area operators in accordance with this part 7;

(f) To approve and renew licenses in accordance with this part 7;

(g) To elect officers;

(h) To establish standing or temporary technical and safety committees composed of persons with expertise in tramway-related fields to review, as the board deems necessary, the design, construction, maintenance, and operation of passenger tramways and to make recommendations to the board concerning their findings. Committees established pursuant to this paragraph (h) shall meet as deemed necessary by the board or the supervisory tramway engineer.

(i) To collect fees, established pursuant to section 24-34-105, C.R.S., for any application for a new construction or major modification, for any application for licensing, and for inspection and accident investigations;

(j) To cause the prosecution and enjoinder of all persons violating such provisions and to incur the necessary expenses thereof;

(k) To delegate duties to the program administrator;

(l) To keep records of its proceedings and of all applications.

## 25-5-705. Responsibilities of area operators.

The primary responsibility for design, construction, maintenance, operation, and inspection rests with the area operators of passenger tramway devices.

## 25-5-706. Disciplinary action - administrative sanctions - grounds.

(1) Disciplinary action of the board pursuant to this section shall be taken in accordance with the "State Administrative Procedure Act", article 4 of title 24, C.R.S.

(2) Disciplinary action of the board may be imposed as an alternative to or in conjunction with the issuance of orders or the pursuit of other remedies provided by section 25-5-707 or 25-5-716, and may consist of any of the following:

(a) Denial, suspension, revocation, or refusal to renew the license of any passenger tramway. The board may summarily suspend a license pursuant to the authority granted by this part 7 or article 4 of title 24, C.R.S.

(b) (I) When a complaint or investigation discloses an instance of misconduct that, in the opinion of the board, does not warrant formal action by the board but that should not be dismissed as being without merit, issuance and sending of a letter of admonition, by certified mail, to the area operator.

(II) When a letter of admonition is sent by the board, by certified mail, to an area operator such area operator shall be advised that he or she has the right to request in writing, within twenty days after receipt of the letter, that formal disciplinary proceedings be initiated to adjudicate the propriety of the conduct upon which the letter of admonition is based.

(III) If the request for adjudication is timely made, the letter of admonition shall be deemed vacated and the matter shall be processed by means of formal disciplinary proceedings.

(c) Assessment of a fine, not to exceed ten thousand dollars per act or omission or, in the case of acts or omissions found to be willful, fifty thousand dollars per act or omission, against any area operator;

(d) Imposition of reasonable conditions upon the continued licensing of a passenger tramway or upon the suspension of further disciplinary action against an area operator.

(3) The board may take disciplinary action for any of the following acts or omissions:

(a) Any violation of the provisions of this part 7 or of any rule or regulation of the board promulgated pursuant to section 25-5-704 when the act or omission upon which the violation is based was known to, or reasonably should have been known to, the area operator;

(b) Violation of any order of the board issued pursuant to provisions of this part 7;

(c) Failure to report any incident or accident to the board as required by any provision of this part 7 or any rule or regulation of the board promulgated pursuant to section 25-5-704 when the incident or accident was known to, or reasonably should have been known to, the area operator;

(d) Willful or wanton misconduct in the operation or maintenance of a passenger tramway;

(e) Operation of a passenger tramway while a condition exists in the design, construction, operation, or maintenance of the passenger tramway which endangers the public health, safety, or welfare, which condition was known, or reasonably should have been known, by the area operator;

(f) Operation of a passenger tramway by an operator whose license has been suspended;

(g) Failure to comply with an order issued under section 25-5-707 or 25-5-716.

## 25-5-707. Orders - enforcement.

(1) If, after investigation, the board finds that a violation of any of its rules or regulations exists or that there is a condition in passenger tramway design, construction, operation, or maintenance endangering the safety of the public, it shall forthwith issue its written order setting forth its findings and the corrective action to be taken and fixing a reasonable time for compliance therewith. Such order shall be served upon the area operator involved in accordance with the Colorado rules of civil procedure or the "State Administrative Procedure Act", article 4 of title 24, C.R.S., and shall become final unless the area operator applies to the board for a hearing in the manner provided in section 24-4-105, C.R.S.

(2) If any area operator fails to comply with a lawful order of the board issued under this section within the time fixed thereby, the board may take further action as permitted by sections 25-5-706 and 25-5-716 and may commence an action seeking injunctive relief in the district court of the judicial district in which the relevant passenger tramway is located.

(3) Any person who violates an order issued pursuant to this section shall be subject to a civil penalty of not more than five thousand dollars for each day during which such violation occurs.

(4) Any area operator who operates a passenger tramway which has not been licensed by the board or the license of which has been suspended, or who fails to comply with an order issued under this section or section 25-5-716, commits a class 3 misdemeanor and shall be punished as provided in section 18-1.3-501, C.R.S. Fines collected pursuant to this section shall be deposited in the general fund of the state.

## 25-5-708. Disciplinary proceedings.

(1) The board may investigate all matters which present grounds for disciplinary action as specified in this part 7.

(2) Disciplinary hearings shall be conducted by the board or by an administrative law judge in accordance with section 25-5-704 (1) (d) .

(3) Any person aggrieved by a final action or order of the board may appeal such action to the Colorado court of appeals in accordance with section 24-4-106 (11) , C.R.S.

## 25-5-709. Passenger tramway licensing required.

(1) The state, through the board, shall license all passenger tramways, unless specifically exempted by law, establish reasonable standards of design and operational practices, and cause to be made such inspections as may be necessary in carrying out the provisions of this section.

(2) A passenger tramway shall not be operated in this state unless it has been licensed by the board. No new passenger tramway shall be initially licensed in this state unless its design and construction have been certified to this state as complying with the rules and regulations of the board promulgated pursuant to section 25-5-704. Such certification shall be made by a qualified tramway design engineer or a qualified tramway construction engineer, whichever the case requires.

(3) The board shall have no jurisdiction over the construction of a new private residence tramway or over any modifications to an existing private residence tramway when such tramway is not used, or intended to be used, by the general public.

(4) The board shall have no jurisdiction over a portable aerial tramway device.

(5) The board shall have no jurisdiction over a portable tramway device when such tramway device is not used, or intended to be used, by the general public.

## 25-5-710. Application for new construction or major modification.

Any new construction of a passenger tramway or any major modification to an existing installation shall not be initiated unless an application for such construction or major modification has been made to the board and a permit therefor has been issued by the board.

## 25-5-711. Application for licensing.

Each year, every area operator of a passenger tramway shall apply to the board, in such form as the board shall designate, for licensing of the passenger tramways which such area operator owns or manages or the operation of which such area operator directs. The application shall contain such information as the board may reasonably require in order for it to determine whether the passenger tramway sought to be licensed by such area operator complies with the intent of this part 7 as specified in section 25-5-701 and the rules and regulations promulgated by the board pursuant to section 25-5-704.

## 25-5-712. Licensing of passenger tramways.

(1) The board shall issue to the applying area operator without delay licensing certificates for each passenger tramway owned, managed, or the operation of which is directed by such area operator when the board is satisfied:

(a) That the facts stated in the application are sufficient to enable the board to fulfill its duties under this part 7; and

(b) That each such passenger tramway sought to be licensed has been inspected by an inspector designated by the board according to procedures established by the board and that such inspection disclosed no unreasonable safety hazard and no violations of the provisions of this part 7 or the rules and regulations of the board promulgated pursuant to section 25-5-704.

(2) In order to satisfy itself that the conditions described in subsection (1) of this section have been fulfilled, the board may cause to be made such inspections described in section 25-5-715 as it may reasonably deem necessary.

(3) Repealed.

(4) Licenses shall expire on dates established by the board.

(5) Each area operator shall cause the licensing certificate, or a copy thereof, for each passenger tramway thus licensed to be displayed prominently at the place where passengers are loaded thereon.

## 25-5-713. Licensing and certification fees.

The application for new construction or major modification and the application for licensing shall be accompanied by a fee established pursuant to section 24-34-105, C.R.S.

## 25-5-714. Disposition of fees and fines.

(1) All fees collected by the board under the provisions of this part 7 shall be transmitted to the state treasurer, who shall credit the same pursuant to section 24-34-105, C.R.S., and the general assembly shall make annual appropriations pursuant to said section for expenditures of the board incurred in the performance of its duties under this part 7, which expenditures shall be made from such appropriations upon vouchers and warrants drawn pursuant to law.

(2) Fines collected pursuant to section 25-5-707 shall be deposited in the general fund of the state.

## 25-5-715. Inspections and investigations - costs - reports.

(1) The board may cause to be made such inspection of the design, construction, operation, and maintenance of passenger tramways as the board may reasonably require.

(2) Such inspections shall include, at a minimum, two inspections per year or per two thousand hours of operation, whichever occurs first, of each passenger tramway, one of which inspections shall be during the high use season and shall be unannounced, and shall be carried out under contract by independent contractors selected by the board or by the supervisory tramway engineer. Additional inspections may be required by the board if the area operator does not, in the opinion of the board, make reasonable efforts to correct any deficiencies identified in any prior inspection or if the board otherwise deems such additional inspections necessary. The board shall provide in its rules and regulations that no facility shall be shut down for the purposes of a regular inspection during normal operating hours unless sufficient daylight is not available for the inspection.

(3) The board may employ independent contractors to make such inspections for reasonable fees plus expenses. The expenses incurred by the board in connection with the conduct of inspections provided for in this part 7 shall be paid in the first instance by the board, but each area operator of the passenger tramway which was the subject of such inspection shall, upon notification by the board of the amount due, reimburse the board for any charges made by such personnel for such services and for the actual expenses of each inspection.

(4) The board may cause an investigation to be made in response to an accident or incident involving a passenger tramway, as the board may reasonably require. The board may employ independent contractors to make such investigations for reasonable fees plus expenses. The expenses incurred by the board in connection with the conduct of investigations provided for in this part 7 shall be paid in the first instance by the board, and thereafter one or more area operators may be billed for work performed pursuant to subsection (3) of this section.

(5) If, as the result of an inspection, it is found that a violation of the board's rules and regulations exists, or a condition in passenger tramway design, construction, operation, or maintenance exists,

endangering the safety of the public, an immediate report shall be made to the board for appropriate investigation and order.

## 25-5-716. Emergency shutdown.

When facts are presented tending to show that an unreasonable hazard exists in the continued operation of a passenger tramway, after such verification of said facts as is practical under the circumstances and consistent with the public safety, the board, any member thereof, or the supervisory tramway engineer may, by an emergency order, require the area operator of said tramway forthwith to cease using the same for the transportation of passengers. Such emergency order shall be in writing and signed by a member of the board or the supervisory tramway engineer, and notice thereof may be served by the supervisory tramway engineer, any member of the board, or as provided by the Colorado rules of civil procedure or the "State Administrative Procedure Act", article 4 of title 24, C.R.S. Such service shall be made upon the area operator or the area operator's agent immediately in control of said tramway. Such emergency shutdown shall be effective for a period not to exceed seventy-two hours from the time of service. The board shall conduct an investigation into the facts of the case and shall take such action under this part 7 as may be appropriate.

## 25-5-717. Provisions in lieu of others.

The provisions for regulation, registration, and licensing of passenger tramways and the area operators thereof under this part 7 shall be in lieu of all other regulations or registration or licensing requirements, and passenger tramways shall not be construed to be common carriers within the meaning of the laws of this state.

## 25-5-718. Governmental immunity - limitations on liability.

The board, any member of the board, any person on the staff of the board, any technical advisor appointed by the board, any member of an advisory committee appointed by the board, and any independent contractor hired to perform or acting as a state tramway inspector on behalf of the board with whom the board contracts for assistance shall be provided all protections of governmental immunity provided to public employees by article 10 of title 24, C.R.S., including but not limited to the payment of judgments and settlements, the provision of legal defense, and the payment of costs incurred in court actions. These protections shall be provided to the board, board members, staff, technical advisors, committee members, and independent contractors hired to perform or acting as a state tramway inspector on behalf of the board only with regard to actions brought because of acts or omissions committed by such persons in the course of official board duties.

## 25-5-719. Independent contractors - no general immunity.

The provisions of section 25-5-718 shall be construed as a specific exception to the general exclusion of independent contractors hired to perform or acting as a state tramway inspector on behalf of the board from the protections of governmental immunity provided in article 10 of title 24, C.R.S.

## 25-5-720. Confidentiality of reports and other materials.

(1) Reports of investigations conducted by an area operator or by a private contractor on an area operator's behalf and filed with the board or the board's staff shall be presumed to be privileged information exempt from public inspection under section 24-72-204 (3) (a) (IV) , C.R.S., except as may be ordered by a court of competent jurisdiction.

(2) Except as otherwise provided in subsection (1) of this section, all information in the possession of the board's staff and all final reports to the board shall be open to public inspection in accordance with part 2 of article 72 of title 24, C.R.S.

## 25-5-721. Repeal of part.

(1) This part 7 is repealed, effective July 1, 2019.

(2) Prior to such repeal, the passenger tramway safety board shall be reviewed as provided for in section 24-34-104, C.R.S.

# PART 8. SWIMMING AREAS

## 25-5-801. Definitions.

As used in this part 8, unless the context otherwise requires:

(1) "Natural swimming area" means a designated portion of a natural or impounded body of water in which the designated portion is devoted to swimming, recreative bathing, or wading and for which an individual is charged a fee for the use of such area for such purposes. Appurtenances used in connection with the natural swimming area shall also be included.

(2) "Swimming area" means a designated body of water of such volume and depth that one or more persons can swim in it and which is used for the purpose of swimming, recreative bathing, or wading and includes natural swimming areas and swimming pools.

(3) "Swimming pool" means a body of water, other than a natural swimming area, maintained exclusively for swimming, recreative bathing, or wading and includes appurtenances used in connection with the swimming pool.

## 25-5-802. Submission of plans and specifications.

Prior to the construction, extension, enlarging, remodeling, or modification of a swimming area, the plans and specifications for the work to be done shall be submitted for review and recommendation to the department of public health and environment by the owner of the swimming area. The department of public health and environment may direct that such plans and specifications be submitted to the municipality or other political subdivision in which the swimming area is or may be located rather than to the department of public health and environment. This section does not prohibit any municipality from requiring that the plans also be submitted to the proper authority of the municipality.

## 25-5-803. Sanitation of swimming areas.

(1) A swimming area shall be kept clean and free of all accumulations of trash, garbage, filth, and debris. Concentrations of any other matter in the water shall not be injurious to health.

(2) All swimming areas shall provide separate toilet facilities for both males and females, and swimming pools shall also provide separate shower and locker room facilities; except that swimming pools used in connection with hotels, motels, apartment houses, and private clubs shall not be required to furnish separate shower, toilet, and locker room facilities. All such facilities shall be kept clean and free from dirt, refuse, soiled toweling, or other noxious material.

(3) A swimming pool shall have an apparatus for the continuous removal from the water of suspended, floating, and settleable substances. Equipment for the disinfection of water shall be provided that shall be capable of either maintaining a minimum concentration of not less than twenty-five hundredths part per million of free chlorine residual or maintaining the minimum standards for drinking water in effect on January 1, 1969, as specified by the public health service of the United States department of health, education, and welfare. The water shall be kept clear enough to permit the bottom of the pool to be visible from the surface.

## 25-5-804. Safety standards for swimming areas.

(1) All natural swimming areas shall have a sanded beach the slope of which shall not be steeper than one foot of fall to ten feet of horizontal distance and shall be posted with warning signs,

buoys, or other markers located not more than one hundred feet apart and visible to a person of ordinary visual acuity at a distance of not less than one hundred feet to mark water over three feet in depth and to mark the exterior limits of the designated swimming area. There shall also be provided not less than one life ring fifteen inches in diameter with seventy-five feet of three-sixteenths inch manila line attached which shall be hung in a conspicuous place on the beach where it shall be kept readily available for use. Each natural swimming area shall also have not less than one square-sterned boat with oars and oarlocks which shall be used only for lifesaving purposes. All other floating craft shall be excluded from the swimming areas except for enforcement craft when necessary to provide adequate supervision. When night swimming is permitted in the natural swimming area, the beach shall be fully illuminated.

(2) The diving tower or springboard, when provided, shall be rigidly constructed and securely anchored.

(3) Swimming pools shall be equipped with not less than one lightweight reaching pole of not less than twelve feet in length and not less than one life ring fifteen inches in diameter with seventy-five feet of three-sixteenths inch manila line attached, both of which shall be kept in a conspicuous place readily available to persons in the pool. When night swimming is permitted, the pool, adjacent area, and all appurtenances shall be fully illuminated.

## 25-5-805. Connection with potable water.
All potable water supply sources connected to the swimming pool or pool appurtenances shall be protected against contamination by means of an air gap or equivalent device, and such device shall be placed between the source of the potable water supply and the pool or pool appurtenance.

## 25-5-806. Inspection.
All swimming areas shall be open to inspection at any time they are in use and at any other reasonable time by agents of the department of public health and environment.

## 25-5-807. Injunctive relief.
The operation of a swimming area in violation of any provision of this part 8 may be restrained by the executive director of the department of public health and environment; by any city, county, city and county, or district health officer; or by any of their authorized agents in an action brought in a court of competent jurisdiction pursuant to the Colorado rules of civil procedure.

## 25-5-808. Municipalities may regulate.
Any city, town, or city and county may by ordinance regulate swimming areas. Any such ordinance may include standards which are the same or more restrictive than the standards set forth in this part 8 but shall not supersede the state law except insofar as they are more restrictive than the state standards.

## 25-5-809. Applicability of part 8.
This part 8 shall not apply to any swimming pool constructed in connection with or appurtenant to a single-family dwelling, condominium, or apartment house, which pool is used solely by the persons living within such dwelling, condominium, or apartment house and the guests of such persons.

## 25-5-810. Rules and regulations.
The department of public health and environment may adopt any rules and regulations necessary for the proper administration and enforcement of this part 8.

# PART 9. DANGEROUS DRUGS - THERAPEUTIC USE

## 25-5-901 to 25-5-907. (Repealed)

# PART 10. ARTIFICIAL TANNING DEVICES

## 25-5-1001. Short title.
This part 10 shall be known and may be cited as the "Artificial Tanning Device Operation Act".

## 25-5-1002. Legislative declaration.
(1) The general assembly hereby finds, determines, and declares that injuries may result from improperly supervised use of artificial tanning devices which expose the human body to ultraviolet radiation. Artificial tanning devices may emit more than ten times the amount of ultraviolet radiation than normal exposure to the sun. Injuries from intense exposure may result in cases of premature aging, adverse reactions to medication, skin burns, eye burns, retinal damage, formation of cataracts, precancers, and the promotion of several types of skin cancers including, but not limited to, melanoma.
(2) The general assembly further finds, determines, and declares that artificial tanning device users may be unaware of and lack access to information that they may experience a heightened photosensitivity to artificial tanning as a result of the use of medications such as birth control pills, antibiotics, high blood pressure medications, diuretics, antihistamines, and oral diabetes medications; commonly available cosmetics; and certain citrus products such as limes.
(3) The general assembly further finds, determines, and declares that establishments which provide users with access to artificial tanning devices may fail to establish basic sanitary precautions against the transmission of communicable skin disorders, may fail to protect the user from either direct contact with bulbs or from shards of glass if a bulb explodes, and may fail to provide users with appropriate health or physical safety information.

## 25-5-1003. Definitions.
As used in this part 10, unless the context otherwise requires:
(1) "Artificial tanning device" means any equipment that emits ultraviolet radiation with wavelengths in the air between two hundred and four hundred nanometers and that is used for the tanning of human skin, including, but not limited to, sunlamps, tanning beds, and tanning booths. "Artificial tanning device" does not include phototherapy devices.
(2) "Board" means the state board of health.
(3) "Department" means the department of public health and environment.
(4) "Fund" means the artificial tanning device education fund created in section 25-5-1004.
(5) "Phototherapy device" means a piece of equipment that emits ultraviolet radiation and that is used by or under the supervision of a licensed health care professional in the treatment of disease.
(6) "Tanning facility" means any location, premises, place, area, structure, or business, whether permanent or mobile, which provides persons access to artificial tanning devices.
(7) "Ultraviolet radiation" means electromagnetic radiation with wavelengths in the air between two hundred and four hundred nanometers.

## 25-5-1004. Registration required - fee - artificial tanning device education fund - creation.

(1) Commencing January 1, 1993, and on each January 1 thereafter, the owner of any artificial tanning facility which makes artificial tanning devices available for public use shall register said facility with the department.

(2) (a) The registration of each artificial tanning facility as required in subsection (1) of this section shall be accompanied by an annual registration fee for each artificial tanning facility in the amount of one hundred twenty dollars for each calendar year. The annual registration fee shall be prorated on a monthly basis for any initial registration received after January 1 of any year.

(b) Notwithstanding the amount specified for the fee in paragraph (a) of this subsection (2) , the board by rule or as otherwise provided by law may reduce the amount of the fee if necessary pursuant to section 24-75-402 (3) , C.R.S., to reduce the uncommitted reserves of the fund to which all or any portion of the fee is credited. After the uncommitted reserves of the fund are sufficiently reduced, the board by rule or as otherwise provided by law may increase the amount of the fee as provided in section 24-75-402 (4) , C.R.S.

(3) All fees shall be collected by the department and transmitted to the state treasurer, who shall credit the same to the artificial tanning device education fund, which fund is hereby created. The fund shall be comprised of the annual registration fees. In accordance with section 24-36-114, C.R.S., all interest derived from the deposit and investment of moneys in the fund shall be credited to the general fund. At the end of any fiscal year, all unexpended and unencumbered moneys in the fund shall remain therein and shall not be credited or transferred to the general fund or any other fund. The moneys in the fund shall be annually appropriated by the general assembly to the department for the direct and indirect costs of the administration and implementation of the provisions of this part 10.

## 25-5-1005. Exemptions.

(1) The following devices are exempt from the requirements of this part 10:

(a) Artificial tanning devices which are used exclusively for personal, noncommercial purposes by the owner, members of the owner's family, or persons authorized by the owner to use the device;

(b) Phototherapy devices used by or under the supervision of a licensed physician or other licensed health care professional within the scope of such person's practice for the purposes of treating diseases; and

(c) Artificial tanning devices which are in transit or storage and are not made available for use during such transit or storage.

(2) Nothing in this section shall be construed to mean that the department endorses any type of artificial tanning device, any location of such devices, any business which provides artificial tanning devices for use by the public, or the use of any such devices.

## 25-5-1006. Rule-making authority - board.

(1) The standards established by the United States food and drug administration shall be the minimum standards for exposure to radiation through an artificial tanning device in this state; except that the board may establish rules adopting standards for exposure to radiation through artificial tanning devices which are no less stringent than the federal standards.

(2) (a) The board may, by rule, adopt any further standards or regulations necessary to protect the public from unsafe artificial tanning devices or other unsafe equipment, and from unsafe operational methods, and any such other rules and regulations as are necessary for the implementation of this part 10.

(b) The board shall formulate, adopt, and promulgate rules and regulations concerning on-site inspections of tanning facilities, and the department shall conduct such on-site inspections in accordance with the rules and regulations promulgated under this paragraph (b) .

## 25-5-1007. Owner responsibilities.

(1) The owner of each registered artificial tanning device shall provide to the department such information concerning the safe and proper operation of the owner's artificial tanning device as is

required by this part 10.

(2) The owner shall post a sign on the premises where the artificial tanning device is located which notifies operators and potential users of the safety and health risks associated with the use of such devices. The board shall establish standards concerning the information to be contained in said notice and the size and location of posting the notice on the premises. Said notice shall be of a size and in a location on the premises which allows it to be easily read by users before being exposed to the artificial tanning device.

(3) The owner shall provide each user with a written handout as specified by the board containing, at a minimum, the following information:

(a) The risks of potential negative health effects as a result of improperly supervised exposure to ultraviolet radiation and the general health and sanitation risks associated with the use of such devices;

(b) The risks of potential negative health effects as a result of exposure to ultraviolet radiation while in poor health or on certain medications; and

(c) Specific safety and operation information on the artificial tanning device which is to be used.

(4) The owner shall provide to users the safety equipment required by the board.

(5) The owner shall provide and maintain such general sanitation and cleaning of equipment as required by the board.

(6) The owner shall inform the department of any accident or adverse reaction to the use of an artificial tanning device and provide such detailed information as required by the department. A written report in the format required by the department shall be submitted within fifteen days after discovery of the event. Any records, reports, or information obtained from a person pursuant to the provisions of this subsection (6) shall be closed and confidential.

(7) No owner, employee, or operator of any artificial tanning device or tanning facility shall advertise or promote that the use of any artificial tanning device is safe or without risk to the user or that registration with the department constitutes approval or endorsement of either the use of the device or the use of artificial tanning in general.

## 25-5-1008. Complaints - investigation.

The department shall have the authority to investigate complaints regarding any injury, accident, or the unsafe operation of an artificial tanning device.

## 25-5-1009. Penalties.

(1) Upon a finding by the board that an owner or lessee of a tanning facility is in violation of any of the provisions of this part 10, or the standards, rules, or regulations adopted by the board pursuant to this part 10, the board may assess a penalty of up to two hundred dollars for each day of violation, and each day of violation shall be considered a separate offense. Actions may be brought by the attorney general in the district court of the district within which the tanning device is located. In determining the amount of the penalty, the board shall consider the degree of danger to the public caused by the violation, the duration of the violation, and whether the owner or lessee has committed any similar violations. Any penalty fees collected by the board shall be remitted to the state treasurer, who shall credit the same to the tanning device education fund, created in section 25-5-1004.

(2) An owner or lessee subject to a penalty assessment pursuant to this section may appeal the penalty to the board by requesting a hearing before the board. Such a request shall be filed within thirty days after the penalty assessment is issued. A hearing before the board shall be conducted in accordance with article 4 of title 24, C.R.S.

## 25-5-1010. Enforcement.

(1) (a) Whenever the department has reasonable cause to believe a violation of this part 10 or any rule made pursuant to this part 10 has occurred and immediate enforcement is deemed necessary, the department may issue a cease-and-desist order, which may require any person to cease

violating any provision of this part 10 or any rule made pursuant to this part 10. Such cease-and-desist order shall set forth the provisions alleged to have been violated, the facts alleged to have constituted the violation, and the requirement that all actions be ceased forthwith.

(b) In the event that any person fails to comply with a cease-and-desist order within twenty-four hours, the department may apply to the district court of the district within which the tanning device is located for a temporary or permanent injunction restraining any person from violating any provision of this part 10 regardless of whether there is an adequate remedy at law.

(c) No stay of a cease-and-desist order shall be issued before a hearing thereon involving both parties.

(2) Whenever it appears to the department, upon evidence satisfactory to the department, that any person has engaged in or is about to engage in any act or practice constituting a violation of any provision of this part 10 or of any rule or of any order promulgated under this part 10, the department may apply to the district court of the district within which the tanning device is located to temporarily or permanently restrain or enjoin the act or practice in question and to enforce compliance with this part 10 or any rule or order promulgated under this part 10. In any such action, the department shall not be required to plead or prove irreparable injury or the inadequacy of the remedy at law. Under no circumstances shall the court require the department to post a bond.

(3) It is a violation of this part 10 for:

(a) Any person to knowingly operate a tanning facility without having registered said facility with the department in accordance with the provisions of this part 10;

(b) Any person to offer for use to the public any artificial tanning device which is not registered with the department as required by the provisions of this part 10;

(c) Any person to violate any provision of this part 10 or any provision of any standards, rules, or regulations adopted by the board;

(d) Any person to refuse to permit entry for the purpose of inspection of a tanning facility during normal business hours.

### 25-5-1011. Assumption of risk inapplicable.
In any civil action for damages for an injury sustained as the result of the use of an artificial tanning device, it shall be presumed that the defense of assumption of risk as set forth in section 13-21-111.7, C.R.S., shall not apply if the owner has failed to provide the injured party with the written handout or the safety equipment as required by section 25-5-1007, or if the owner has failed to provide a safe artificial tanning device.

# PART 11. PREVENTION, INTERVENTION, AND REDUCTION OF LEAD EXPOSURE

### 25-5-1101. Legislative declaration.
(1) (a) The general assembly hereby declares that this part 11 is enacted for the purpose of reducing exposure of children to lead hazards and reducing the prevalence of elevated blood lead levels in children under seven years of age. The general assembly finds and determines that:

(I) Exposure of children to lead represents a significant environmental health problem in the state that is preventable;

(II) The existence of elevated blood lead levels in children is of great concern to the citizens of Colorado because lead poisoning in children may necessitate large expenditures of public funds for health care and special education, which expenditures could be avoided if exposure of children to lead is reduced;

(III) A comprehensive lead hazard reduction program is needed to prevent elevated blood lead levels in children and, if implemented, such program could prevent hundreds of Colorado's children, many of whom currently go undiagnosed or untreated, from being exposed to lead at levels believed to be harmful.

(b) Therefore, it is the intent of the general assembly to establish and fund a statewide lead hazard prevention, intervention, and reduction program within the department of public health and environment for the purposes of:

(I) Compiling information concerning the prevalence, causes, and geographic occurrence of elevated levels of lead in children's blood;

(II) Identifying areas of the state where children's lead exposures are significant;

(III) Analyzing lead information and, where indicated, designing and implementing a program of medical monitoring and follow-up and environmental intervention that will reduce the incidence of excessive exposure of children to lead in residences and child-occupied facilities in Colorado; and

(IV) Providing comprehensive educational materials that are targeted to health care providers, child care providers, schools, parents of young children, the real estate industry, and owners of rental properties.

## 25-5-1102. Definitions.

As used in this part 11, unless the context otherwise requires:

(1) "Child-occupied facility" has the same meaning as that set forth in section 25-7-1102 (2) .

(2) "Department" means the department of public health and environment.

(3) "Lead-based paint" has the same meaning as that set forth in section 25-7-1102 (5) .

## 25-5-1103. Lead hazard reduction program.

There is hereby created the lead hazard reduction program in the department of public health and environment to perform prevention, intervention, and general hazard reduction activities needed to reduce exposure of children to lead-based paint hazards. As part of the program, the department shall coordinate actions between the department and the departments of education, human services, health care policy and financing, and local affairs to produce a comprehensive plan and program to prevent elevated blood lead levels in children and to control exposure to lead-based paint hazards in residences and child-occupied facilities in Colorado. The provisions of this part 11 apply only to lead-based paint hazards.

## 25-5-1104. Comprehensive plan.

(1) On or before July 1, 1998, the department shall establish a comprehensive plan to prevent elevated blood lead levels in children and to control exposure of children to lead-based paint hazards in residences and child-occupied facilities. The plan shall include:

(a) Development of standards by the state board of health concerning the method and frequency of screening of young children for elevated blood lead levels. The state board of health shall consult with recognized medical, public health, and environmental professionals and appropriate professional organizations in the development of such standards.

(b) Development of a comprehensive education program regarding lead contamination that makes appropriate educational materials available to health care providers, child care providers, schools, owners and tenants of residential dwellings built prior to 1978, and parents of young children;

(c) Case management and environmental follow-up services by state or local health agencies to ensure that all cases of elevated blood lead levels in children receive service appropriate for the severity of the lead exposure;

(d) Recommendations concerning further legislative actions to address lead exposure, including, but not limited to, requiring third-party insurers or payers, including medicaid, to provide coverage for screening, treatment, environmental investigations, and environmental intervention;

(e) Proposed regulations governing the requirement, timing, and conduct of environmental investigations and interventions; and

(f) A detailed fiscal analysis of the lead hazard reduction program.

## 25-5-1105. Report. (Repealed)

## 25-5-1106. Acceptance of gifts, grants, and donations - lead hazard reduction cash fund.

(1) The department is authorized to accept gifts, grants, and donations for the purpose of implementing this part 11 and part 11 of article 7 of this title.

(2) There is hereby established in the state treasury the lead hazard reduction cash fund, referred to in this part 11 as the "fund". The fund shall consist of any fees, gifts, grants, and donations received from any person or entity. Any interest derived from the deposit and investment of moneys in the fund shall remain in the fund and may not be credited or transferred to the general fund or any other fund.

(3) The general assembly shall make appropriations from the fund to the department for the implementation of this part 11 and the implementation of part 11 of article 7 of this title.

# PART 12. PERSONAL CARE PRODUCTS CONTAINING MICROBEADS

## 25-5-1201. Preemption.

The prohibition against producing, manufacturing, selling, and promoting personal care products that contain synthetic plastic microbeads is a matter of statewide concern, and, accordingly, this part 12 preempts any conflicting county or municipal ordinance, rule, or order.

## 25-5-1202. Definitions.

As used in this part 12:

(1) "Over-the-counter drug" means a drug that is a personal care product that contains a label that identifies the product as a drug, as required by and meeting the labeling requirements of 21 CFR 201.66.

(2) (a) "Personal care product" means:

(I) Any article intended to be rubbed, poured, sprinkled, sprayed on, introduced into, or otherwise applied to the human body for cleansing, beautifying, promoting attractiveness, or altering the appearance of a person; and

(II) Any item intended to be used as a component of an article listed in subparagraph (I) of this paragraph (a) .

(b) "Personal care product" does not include prescription drugs.

(3) "Plastic" means a synthetic material made by linking monomers through a chemical reaction to create an organic polymer chain that can be molded or extruded at high heat into various solid forms that retain their defined shapes during the life cycle and after disposal.

(4) "Synthetic plastic microbead" means an intentionally added, nonbiodegradable, solid plastic particle measuring less than five millimeters in size intended to aid in exfoliating or cleansing as part of a rinse-off product.

## 25-5-1203. Personal care products containing microbeads - production, manufacture, and sale prohibited.

(1) On and after January 1, 2018, a person shall not produce or manufacture in this state a personal care product containing synthetic plastic microbeads, except for an over-the-counter drug.

(2) On and after January 1, 2019, a person shall not:

(a) Accept for sale in this state a personal care product that contains synthetic plastic microbeads, except for an over-the-counter drug; or

(b) Produce or manufacture in this state an over-the-counter drug that contains synthetic plastic microbeads.

(3) On and after January 1, 2020, a person shall not accept for sale in this state an over-the-counter drug that contains synthetic plastic microbeads.

### 25-5-1204. Penalty for violation.

A person who violates any provision of this part 12 is subject to a civil penalty of not less than one thousand dollars and not more than ten thousand dollars for each offense. The penalty is determined and collected by the district court for the judicial district in which the violation occurs upon an action instituted by the department of public health and environment. The district court shall transmit penalties collected pursuant to this section to the state treasurer, who shall credit the moneys to the general fund.

# ARTICLE 5.5. DAIRY PRODUCTS, IMITATION DAIRY PRODUCTS, AND FROZEN DESSERTS

# PART 1. DAIRY PRODUCTS

### 25-5.5-101. Definitions.

As used in this part 1, unless the context otherwise requires:

(1) "Cheese" means the fresh or matured product obtained by the draining, after coagulation, of milk, cream, skimmed or partly skimmed milk, or a combination of some or all of these products, including any cheese that conforms to the provisions of the definitions and standards of identity for cheese and cheese products, a regulation of the food and drug administration, 21 CFR 133.3.

(2) "Cream" means the liquid milk product which is high in fat and separated from milk and which may have been adjusted by adding milk, concentrated milk, dry whole milk, or nonfat dry milk and which contains not less than eighteen percent milk fat.

(3) "Dairy farm" means the place or premises on which one or more lactating hooved animals are kept and from which a part or all of the milk produced thereon is delivered, sold, or offered for sale to a dairy plant for manufacturing purposes.

(4) (a) "Dairy plant" means any place, premises, or establishment where milk or dairy products are received or handled for processing or manufacturing and where they are prepared for distribution.

(b) For the purposes of this subsection (4) , "dairy plant", when used in connection with the requirements therefor or the licensing thereof, means any establishment that manufactures dairy products; except that any "dairy plant" that is located in an establishment licensed pursuant to part 16 of article 4 of this title is exempt from the licensing requirements of this article if such establishment sells or serves dairy products exclusively and directly to the final consumer of the product.

(5) "Dairy products" means food products manufactured from milk or cream or from any combination of milk and cream with other food ingredients intended for human consumption, including, but not limited to, butter, natural or processed cheese, dry whole milk, nonfat dry milk, dry buttermilk, dry whey, evaporated whole milk or skim milk, condensed whole milk, condensed skim milk, or ice cream or other frozen desserts specified in part 3 of this article. "Dairy products" does not include milk or milk products as defined in the grade A pasteurized milk ordinance, 1978

recommendations of the United States public health service, food and drug administration, superintendent of documents number HE 20.4002:M59-3.

(6) "Department" means the department of public health and environment or its authorized representative.

(7) "Goat milk" means the lacteal secretion, practically free from colostrum, which is obtained by the complete milking of healthy goats.

(8) "HTST method" means the high temperature short-time method of pasteurization.

(9) "Manufacturing milk" means milk produced for processing and manufacturing into dairy products for human consumption but not subject to grade A or comparable requirements.

(10) "Milk" means the lacteal secretion, practically free from colostrum, which is obtained by the complete milking of healthy cows, excluding that milk obtained less than eight days before and less than four days after calving or for such longer period as may be necessary to render the milk practically colostrum free, and which contains not less than eight and one-quarter percent nonfat milk solids and not less than three percent milk fat; except that, in those instances where the normal secretion of the cows is less than three percent milk fat, this product shall be accepted as milk for manufacturing purposes.

(11) "Milk sampler" means a person licensed by the department who is qualified and trained to sample or test milk or cream for the purpose of payment and includes a bulk milk hauler that collects milk from dairy farms.

(12) "Official methods" means official methods of analysis of the association of official analytical chemists, 13th edition, 1980, a publication of the association of official analytical chemists, as amended, supplemented, or republished.

(13) "Pasteurization" means the process of heating every particle of milk or milk product in properly designed and operated equipment to one of the temperatures provided in the following table and held continuously at or above that temperature for at least the corresponding specified time.


TemperatureTime


*145degrees F (63 degrees C) 30minutes
*161degrees F (72 degrees C) 15seconds
191degrees F (89 degrees C) 1second
194degrees F (90 degrees C) 0.5second
201degrees F (94 degrees C) 0.1second
204degrees F (96 degrees C) 0.05second
212degrees F (100 degrees C) 0.01second


*If the fat content of the milk product is ten percent or more or if it contains added sweeteners, the specified temperature shall be increased by five degrees Fahrenheit (three degrees Celsius) .


(14) "Pasteurized" means treated pursuant to the pasteurization process specified in subsection (13) of this section.

(15) "Person" means any individual, firm, association, corporation, or partnership doing business in this state, in whole or in part, and any officer, agent, servant, and employee thereof.

(16) "Producer" means the person who exercises control over the production of the milk delivered to a processing plant or receiving station and who receives payment for this product.

(17) To "sanitize" means to treat a clean surface with any effective method or substance acceptable to the department for the destruction of pathogens and other organisms as far as is practical without adversely affecting the equipment, the milk or milk product, or the health of consumers.

(18) "Standard methods" means the standard methods for the examination of dairy products, 13th edition, 1972, a publication of the American public health association, as amended, supplemented, or republished.

(19) "Test" means the process of determining the milkfat content of milk and milk products for the purpose of buying or selling milk or milk products. All tests shall be conducted and samples shall be collected in accordance with the standard methods specified in subsection (18) of this section or any other method approved by the department.

(20) "Transfer or receiving station" means any place, premises, or establishment where milk or milk products are transferred directly from one milk tank truck to another or where raw milk is received, collected, handled, stored, or cooled and prepared for further transporting. The term "transfer or receiving station" shall not include a dairy farm.

## 25-5.5-102. Butter defined - standards.

(1) (a) Butter is a food product which is made exclusively from milk, from cream, or from both milk and cream, with or without common salt and with or without additional coloring matter, and which contains not less than eighty percent by weight of milk fat, with all tolerances having been allowed for.

(b) Cream for butter-making shall be pasteurized at a temperature of not less than one hundred sixty-five degrees Fahrenheit and held continuously in a vat at such temperature for not less than thirty minutes or pasteurized by the HTST method at a minimum temperature of not less than one hundred eighty-five degrees Fahrenheit for not less than fifteen seconds or pasteurized by any other equivalent temperature and holding time which will assure adequate pasteurization.

(c) Whipped butter is butter that has been stirred or whipped to incorporate air or inert gas until its volume has been increased up to a range of fifty percent to one hundred percent.

(2) The standards for butter are as follows: The proteolytic count of not more than one hundred per gram, the yeast and mold count of not more than twenty per gram, and the coliform count of not more than ten per gram.

## 25-5.5-103. Powers and duties.

(1) The department shall cause to be enforced the provisions of this part 1 and all other state laws and regulations regarding the production, manufacture, and sale of dairy products. The department shall inspect or cause to be inspected any milk, butter, or cheese or any other dairy product which it suspects or has reason to believe is unsanitary, adulterated, or counterfeit and shall inspect or cause to be inspected any cow, building, dairy farm, dairy plant, vehicle, or premises used for the production, manufacture, sale, or transportation of any dairy product when it suspects or has reason to believe that such product is unsanitary, adulterated, or counterfeit. Unsanitary or adulterated dairy products shall be subject to condemnation by the department and, when condemned, must be so treated that it cannot be manufactured or renovated for human food.

(2) For the purpose of enforcing this part 1, the department shall have free access to any barn or stable where any cow is kept or milked or to any factory, building, dairy farm, dairy plant, premises, or place in which it has reason to believe that any dairy product or counterfeit dairy product is manufactured, handled, prepared, sold, or offered for sale and may enforce such measures as may be necessary to secure perfect cleanliness in and around the same, and of any utensil used therein, and to prevent the sale of any unsanitary, adulterated, or counterfeit dairy product.

(3) For the purpose of enforcing this part 1, the department may open any package or receptacle of any kind which contains, or which is supposed to contain, any dairy product or counterfeit dairy product and examine or analyze the contents thereof. Any such article or sample thereof may be seized or taken for the purpose of having it analyzed; but, if the person from whom it is taken so requests at the time of taking, the officer shall then, and in the presence of that person, securely seal two samples of such article, one of which shall be for analysis under the direction of the department and the other for delivery to the person from whom the sample or article was obtained.

## 25-5.5-104. Unsanitary dairy products.

(1) The following types of dairy products are declared to be unsanitary: Milk drawn within eight days before or four days after calving; milk drawn from cows that are kept in barns or stables which are not reasonably well-lighted and well-ventilated or that are kept in barns or stables that are filthy from an accumulation of animal feces and excreta or from any other cause; milk which is drawn from cows which are themselves filthy or in an unhealthy condition; milk kept or transported in dirty, rusty, or open seamed cans, tanks, or other containers; cream produced from any such milk, or milk, cream, butter, or any other dairy product that is stale or putrid, or milk, cream, butter, or any other dairy product which has been exposed to foul or noxious air or gases in barns occupied by animals or drawn or kept exposed in dirty, foul, or unclean places or under unclean conditions or where transmissible human disease exists; cream containing less than sixteen percent butterfat; cream produced by the use of a cream separator, which separator has not been thoroughly washed, cleansed, and sanitized after previous use in the separation of cream from milk; cream produced by the use of a separator placed or stationed in any unclean or filthy room or place or in any building containing a stable wherein cattle or other animals are kept, unless said cream separator is so separated and shielded by partition from the stable portion of such building as to be free from all foul or noxious air or gases which issue or may issue from such place or stable; cream which when delivered at the point of shipment is more than three days old during the months of May to October inclusive or more than four days old during the months of November to April inclusive; milk or cream to which has been added, in any quantity, any foreign substance or coloring matter, chemical or preservative, or butter or butterfat, whether for the purpose of increasing the quantity of milk or for preserving the condition of sweetness thereof or for any purpose whatever.

(2) Nothing in this part 1 shall be construed to prohibit the sale of homogenized cream made from butter and milk, if such product is labeled or stamped as imitation cream according to the requirements of the department, or the sale of standardized milk which otherwise meets with the requirements of this part 1.

(3) No person shall sell or offer for sale, or furnish or deliver or have in his possession or under his control with intent to sell or offer for sale, or furnish or deliver to any other person as food for man or to any creamery, cheese factory, milk-condensing factory, or milk or cream dealer any unsanitary milk, cream, or butter or any adulterated dairy product.

(4) No person shall manufacture for sale any article of food for man from any unsanitary milk or from any unsanitary cream.

## 25-5.5-105. Unsanitary utensils, equipment, and premises - prohibited.

It is unlawful for any person using such premises, equipment, or utensils, or causing them to be used, to maintain them in an unsanitary condition.

## 25-5.5-106. Containers of dairy products - prompt delivery - removal of products.

Any person who receives in cans, tanks, or other containers any milk, cream, or other dairy products intended as food for man which has been transported by any private or common carrier, when such cans, tanks, or containers are to be returned, shall cause the said cans, tanks, or other containers to be thoroughly washed, cleansed, and sanitized before return shipment. It is unlawful for any common or private carrier to neglect or fail to remove or ship from any transportation facility, on the day of its arrival there for shipment, any milk, cream, or other dairy products left at such facility for transportation unless a refrigerated facility is provided for holding such products. It is unlawful for any person, firm, or corporation using cans, tanks, or other containers in which milk or cream is shipped to allow the same to remain at a transportation facility longer than one day from the date of their arrival unless such product is maintained in a refrigerated facility at a temperature not exceeding forty-five degrees Fahrenheit.

## 25-5.5-107. Testing and sampling of dairy products - unlawful acts - licensing - dairy protection cash fund - created.

(1) It is unlawful for any person engaged in buying, selling, testing, or handling, or engaged in determining the value of, milk, cream, or any other dairy product by the use of an approved test to give, by himself or his agent, any false reading of the test, or to manipulate the test in any way so as to give a higher or lower percent of butterfat than the milk, cream, or other dairy product actually contains, or to cause any inaccuracy in reading the percent of butterfat by securing from any quantity of the milk, cream, or other dairy product to be tested an inaccurate sample for the test. It is unlawful for any person to use any test tube, bottle, pipette, or instrument in connection with such test which is not perfectly clean; and any such unclean glassware is declared to be inaccurate.

(2) It is unlawful for any person to sample or test milk, cream, or any other dairy product to determine the value of such product when bought and sold or to instruct another person for such purpose without first having a license granted by the department, which license shall be conspicuously displayed in the person's place of business. Licenses shall be granted to those persons who have completed a course in milk and cream testing in any recognized college or dairy school or to those persons who have passed a satisfactory examination under the direction of the department. Payment of a yearly fee of fifty dollars is required, and the license shall be issued for a period of one year from the July 1 next preceding the actual date of issue; however, the license shall be subject to cancellation by the department at any time if it finds that the person holding the license is incompetent or guilty of violating this part 1.

(3) Every person engaged in receiving, buying, selling, or otherwise handling milk or cream for sale, shipment, manufacture, or distribution, except public transportation companies, is required to hold a license to be known as a dairy plant license for the operation of each receiving station, skimming station, concentrating station, milk plant condensary, creamery, cheese factory, ice-cream factory, or other dairy plant being so operated.

(4) (a) (I) A temporary permit to operate the following dairy plants may be issued by the department upon application and upon the payment of a yearly license fee in the amount specified in subparagraph (II) of this paragraph (a) for each condensary, cheese factory, ice-cream factory, or other place of business where dairy products are manufactured or put in containers for sale or distribution.

(II) Except for a transfer or receiving station, which shall be charged the fee set forth in sub-subparagraph (A) of this subparagraph (II) , the fee for a license issued under this subsection (4) shall be determined and paid according to the annual average daily amount of milk received for manufacturing by the dairy plant, as follows:
Annual average dailyFee amount of milk received

(A) Under 1,000 pounds$300
(B) 1,000 to 19,999 pounds$600
(C) 20,000 to 449,999 pounds$1,000
(D) 450,000 or more pounds$1,600

(b) A temporary permit is valid until an inspection has been made by an agent of the department; whereupon, if the applicant has complied with the requirements of the dairy laws, the department shall issue a license for a period of one year from the July 1 next preceding the actual date of issue.

(5) The department has the power to issue necessary regulations for the government of licensed dairy plants and licensed milk samplers covering such points as disposal of sewage, location with regard to living rooms and other possible sources of contamination, and other points not specifically mentioned in the dairy laws.

(6) These regulations shall have the force and effect of law, and the department has the power to cancel a license for a period not exceeding ninety days when it finds that the holder thereof has

violated the law or regulations. Suit may be brought against the state to establish the reasonableness of a regulation, and, if the decision affirms the reasonableness of the regulation, it shall be enforced.

(7) All moneys collected by the department for the license fees provided for in this section shall be transmitted to the state treasurer, who shall credit the same to the dairy protection cash fund, referred to in this subsection (7) as the "fund",which is hereby created in the state treasury. The general assembly shall annually appropriate the moneys in the fund to the department for the payment of expenses necessary to administer this section. Any unexpended and unencumbered moneys remaining in the fund at the end of any fiscal year shall not revert to the general fund or any other fund.

## 25-5.5-108. Condensed milk and cream.

(1) No person shall manufacture for sale within this state or offer or expose for sale or have in his possession with intent to sell or exchange any sweetened condensed milk, unless the same contains not less than twenty-eight percent by weight of milk solids and not less than seven and five-tenths percent butterfat, or any unsweetened condensed milk, unless the same contains not less than seven and five-tenths percent butterfat. Nothing in this part 1 shall be construed to prohibit the handling, manufacture, or sale of bulk condensed or evaporated skim milk when properly tagged and labeled in accordance with rulings of the department.

(2) No person shall manufacture for sale within this state or offer or expose for sale, have in his possession with intent to sell, or sell or exchange for evaporated or condensed cream any substance except the product obtained by the evaporation of a portion of water from cream containing not less than eighteen percent by weight of butterfat. Nothing in this part 1 shall apply to goods manufactured within this state for sale and shipment outside of the state.

## 25-5.5-109. Brands and marks - defacement.

(1) Any person engaged in the transportation or manufacture of any dairy product or ice cream or in bottling milk and cream for sale and use may adopt a brand or mark of ownership to be stamped or marked on any can, bottle, or other receptacle used in the handling and transportation of any of said products and may file in the office of the secretary of state a description of the brand or mark so used by them and the use to be made of any such can, bottle, or other receptacle. The brand or mark so selected and adopted may consist of a name, design, or mark or some particular color of paint or enamel used upon the can, bottle, or other receptacle or any part thereof.

(2) It is unlawful for any person to adopt or use any brand or mark which has already been designed, appropriated, or obtained under the provisions of this section. It is unlawful for any person, other than the rightful owner thereof, to use any can, bottle, or other receptacle marked or branded for any purpose or for the transportation or handling of any other article or dairy product than the one designed or provided for by such brand or mark. It is unlawful for any person, other than the rightful owner thereof, to deface or remove any such brand or mark put upon any such can, bottle, or other receptacle.

(3) To prevent the use of said cans, bottles, or other receptacles for any purpose other than those provided for in this part 1 and to insure the wholesomeness and high quality of the dairy products and the sanitary conditions of the receptacles in which the same are transported, it is the duty of the department to enforce the provisions of this section.

## 25-5.5-110. Milk, cream, and cheese - standards.

(1) Whole milk sold or offered for retail sale shall contain not less than three and one-fourth percent butterfat. Cream for the same use shall contain not less than eighteen percent butterfat.

(2) Full cream cheese shall contain not less than fifty percent butterfat in comparison with the total solids. Cheese containing less than the said amount of fat shall be branded "skim" cheese or "part skim" cheese, as the case may be.

## 25-5.5-111. Treated milk to be labeled.

It is unlawful for any milk or cream to be sold or offered for sale which has been homogenized, viscolized, emulsified, or treated in any manner which will give it the appearance of containing more butterfat than it actually contains, unless it is so labeled as such.

## 25-5.5-112. Weight ticket to be furnished.

An itemized daily weight ticket covering every shipment of milk or cream shall be furnished with each settlement to the producer or his agent.

## 25-5.5-113. Sample taken upon arrival.

At any plant where a bacterial test is used as a basis of price-fixing, the sample for such test shall be taken at the dairy farm or immediately upon arrival of the milk at the receiving plant.

## 25-5.5-114. Interference with officer - penalty.

Any person who refuses to allow the inspections provided for in this part 1 or in any way hinders or obstructs the proper officers from performing their duties under this part 1 is guilty of a misdemeanor and, upon conviction thereof, shall be punished by a fine of not more than one hundred dollars or by imprisonment in the county jail for not more than thirty days.

## 25-5.5-115. Analyses prima facie evidence.

Reports of analyses and tests signed by the department shall be accepted in all courts and places as prima facie evidence of the properties, constituency, or condition of the article analyzed.

## 25-5.5-116. Penalty.

Any person or any agent or servant thereof who violates any of the provisions of this part 1, if the punishment for the violation is not elsewhere prescribed in this part 1, is guilty of a misdemeanor and, upon conviction thereof, shall be punished by a fine of not less than ten dollars nor more than two hundred dollars and by imprisonment in the county jail for not more than sixty days for each such offense.

## 25-5.5-117. Raw milk.

(1) The acquisition of raw milk from cows or goats by a consumer for use or consumption by the consumer shall not constitute the sale of raw milk and shall not be prohibited if all of the following conditions are met:

(a) The owner of a cow, goat, cow shares, or goat shares shall receive raw milk directly from the farm or dairy where the cow, goat, or dairy herd is located and the farm or dairy is registered pursuant to subsection (2) of this section. A person who is the owner of a cow share or goat share in a cow, goat, or dairy herd may receive raw milk on behalf of another owner of the same cow, goat, or dairy herd. A person who is not an owner of a cow share or goat share in the same cow, goat, or dairy herd shall not receive raw milk on behalf of the owner of a cow share or goat share.

(b) The milk is obtained pursuant to a cow share or a goat share. A cow share or a goat share is an undivided interest in a cow, goat, or herd of cows or goats, created by a written contractual relationship between a consumer and a farmer that includes a legal bill of sale to the consumer for an interest in the cow, goat, or dairy herd and a boarding contract under which the consumer boards the cow, goat, or dairy herd in which the consumer has an interest with the farmer for care and milking, and under which the consumer is entitled to receive a share of milk from the cow, goat, or dairy herd.

(c) A prominent warning statement that the milk is not pasteurized is delivered to the consumer with the milk or is displayed on a label affixed to the milk container; and

(d) Information describing the standards used by the farm or dairy with respect to herd health, and in the production of milk from the herd, is provided to the consumer by the farmer together with results of tests performed on the cows or goats that produced the milk, tests performed on the milk, and an explanation of the tests and test results.

(2) Registration of a farm or dairy as required by paragraph (a) of subsection (1) of this section shall be accomplished by delivering to the Colorado department of public health and environment a written statement containing:

(a) The name of the farmer, farm, or dairy;

(b) A valid, current address of the farmer, farm, or dairy; and

(c) A statement that raw milk is being produced at the farm or dairy.

(3) Retail sales of raw, unpasteurized milk shall not be allowed. Resale of raw milk obtained from a cow share or goat share is strictly prohibited. Raw milk that is not intended for pasteurization shall not be sold to, or offered for sale at, farmers' markets, educational institutions, health care facilities, nursing homes, governmental organizations, or any food establishment.

(4) No person who, as a consumer, obtains raw milk in accordance with this section shall be entitled to sell or redistribute the milk.

(5) No producer of raw milk shall publish any statement that implies approval or endorsement by the Colorado department of public health and environment.

# PART 2. IMITATION DAIRY PRODUCTS

### 25-5.5-201. Short title.
This part 2 shall be known and may be cited as the "Colorado Imitation Dairy Products Act".

### 25-5.5-202. Purpose.
(1) The purpose of this part 2 is to prevent fraud in sales and to protect the public health by informing the public of the ingredients making up imitation dairy products.

(2) Even though imitation dairy products are manufactured and sold on the basis of reduced costs to the consumer and certain nutritional advantages of some or all of the ingredients, they should be sampled and inspected on the same basis as the product imitated for sanitary quality and composition.

### 25-5.5-203. Definitions.
As used in this part 2, unless the context otherwise requires:

(1) "Department" means the department of public health and environment or its authorized representative.

(2) (a) "Imitation dairy product" means any milk, cream, skimmed milk, or any combination thereof, whether or not condensed, evaporated, concentrated, frozen, powdered, dried, or desiccated, or any food product made or manufactured therefrom to which is added, or which is blended or compounded with, any fat or oil other than milk fat so that the resulting product is in imitation or semblance of any dairy product, including but not limited to milk, cream, sour cream, butter cream, skimmed milk, ice cream, whipped or whipping cream, flavored milk or skim milk drink, dried or powdered milk, cheese, cream cheese, cottage cheese, creamed cottage cheese, ice-cream mix, sherbet or other frozen desserts, condensed milk, evaporated milk, or concentrated milk. "Imitation dairy product" also means any food product that does not contain milk or dairy products but which is made in imitation or semblance of any milk or dairy product defined in part 1 of this article and, on the basis of its appearance, flavor, and texture, closely resembles such product.

(b) "Imitation dairy product" does not mean or include:

(I) Any distinctive proprietary food compound not readily mistaken for a dairy product, if such product is customarily used on the order or prescription of a physician, is prepared or designed for medicinal or special dietary use, and is prominently so labeled;

(II) Any dairy product which is flavored with chocolate or cocoa, or the vitamin content of which has been increased, or which is both so flavored and which contains such increased vitamin content, if the fats or oils other than milk fat contained in such product do not exceed the amount of cacao fat naturally present in the chocolate or cocoa used and the food oil, in no event in excess of one-hundredth of one percent of the weight of the finished product, is used as a carrier of such vitamins; or

(III) Oleomargarine.

(3) "Person" includes an individual, firm, partnership, association, trust, estate, and corporation, any other business unit, device, arrangement, or organization, and any officer, agent, servant, and employee thereof.

## 25-5.5-204. Imitation dairy products - labeling.

(1) It is unlawful for a person to manufacture, sell, or exchange, to offer for sale or exchange, or to transport or possess any imitation dairy product unless the imitation dairy product is properly labeled, branded, or otherwise marked for identification. The department is authorized to evaluate and rule upon compliance with this requirement.

(2) Ingredients shall be listed by the common or usual name in the order of descending predominance. The declaration shall be presented on any appropriate information panel in adequate type size without obscuring design or vignettes and without crowding. The entire ingredient statement shall appear on a single panel of the label.

## 25-5.5-205. Enforcement and power - rules.

(1) The department is authorized to administer and supervise the enforcement of this part 2. To this end, the department shall:

(a) Provide for and have complete power to make such periodic inspections and investigations as may be deemed necessary to disclose violations of this part 2;

(b) Receive and provide for the investigation of complaints of violations of this part 2;

(c) To carry out the terms and provisions of this part 2, have the power to promulgate rules and regulations for the enforcement of this part 2, not inconsistent with or violative of the terms and provisions thereof, and to publish the same.

## 25-5.5-206. Enforcement by injunction.

The provisions of this part 2 may be enforced by injunction in any court having jurisdiction to grant injunctive relief at the suit and upon the petition of the department or any other person, and it shall not be requisite in such action for an injunction that the plaintiff plead, prove, or show pecuniary loss, damage, or injury or personal damage or injury.

## 25-5.5-207. Subpoena of defendant.

Any defendant, in an action brought under the provisions of section 25-5.5-205, may be required to testify under a subpoena duly issued or in pursuance of the Colorado rules of civil procedure; and the books and records of any such defendant may be brought into court and introduced into evidence; but no information so obtained may be used against the defendant as the basis for a misdemeanor prosecution under the provisions of this part 2.

## 25-5.5-208. Seizure of products.

Imitation dairy products illegally held or otherwise involved in a violation of this part 2 shall be subject to seizure and disposition in accordance with an appropriate order of court.

## 25-5.5-209. Penalty.

Any person who violates any of the provisions of this part 2 or who directs or knowingly permits such violation or aids or assists therein is guilty of a misdemeanor and, upon conviction thereof, shall be punished by a fine of not more than one thousand dollars, or by imprisonment in the county jail for not more than ninety days, or by both such fine and imprisonment.

# PART 3. FROZEN DESSERTS

### 25-5.5-301. Short title.
This part 3 shall be known and may be cited as the "Colorado Frozen Desserts Act".

### 25-5.5-302. Definitions.
As used in this part 3, unless the context otherwise requires:
(1) "Confectionery" means candy, cakes, cookies, and glazed fruit.
(2) "Department" means the department of public health and environment or its authorized representative.
(3) "Mix" means the pasteurized unfrozen combination of all ingredients of a frozen dairy dessert with or without fruits, fruit juices, chocolate, cocoa, confectionery, nut meats, flavor, or harmless color.

### 25-5.5-303. Ice cream - standards.
(1) Ice cream is a food which is prepared by freezing or partially freezing, while stirring, a pasteurized mix composed of one or more of the optional dairy ingredients specified in subsection (2) of this section, which is sweetened with one or more of the optional sweetening ingredients specified in subsection (3) of this section, and which is flavored with one or more of the optional flavoring ingredients specified in subsection (4) of this section. One or more of the optional egg ingredients specified in subsection (5) of this section, one or more of the optional stabilizing ingredients specified in subsection (6) of this section, and one or more of the optional pH adjusting and protein stabilizing ingredients specified in subsection (7) of this section may be used, subject to the conditions set forth in subsections (5) , (6) , and (7) of this section. Harmless coloring may be added. The mix may be seasoned with salt and may be homogenized. Water may be added. The kind and quantity of optional dairy ingredients used and the content of milk fat and total milk solids shall be such that the weights of milk fat and total milk solids are not less than ten percent and twenty percent respectively of the weight of the finished ice cream; but, when one or more of the optional flavoring ingredients specified in paragraphs (d) to (k) of subsection (4) of this section are used, then the weights of milk fat and total milk solids shall not be less than ten percent and twenty percent respectively, except for such reduction in milk fat and in total milk solids as is due to the addition of one or more of the optional ingredients specified in paragraphs (d) to (k) of subsection (4) of this section, but in no case shall it contain less than eight percent of milk fat nor less than eighteen percent of total milk solids. Ice cream shall contain not less than one and six-tenths pounds of total food solids per gallon and shall weigh not less than four and one-half pounds per gallon.
(2) The optional dairy ingredients referred to in subsection (1) of this section are cream, dried cream, butter, butter oil, concentrated milk fat, milk, concentrated milk, evaporated milk, sweetened condensed milk, superheated condensed milk, dried milk, skim milk, concentrated (evaporated or condensed) skim milk, superheated condensed skim milk, sweetened condensed skim milk, sweetened condensed partly skimmed milk, nonfat dry milk solids, liquid or condensed or dried sweet cream buttermilk, or dried whey solids or any of such products from which all or a portion of the lactose has been removed by crystallization or the lactose has been converted to simple sugars by hydrolysis if such products are approved as suitable optional dairy ingredients by the department. Citric acid, ascorbic acid, lecithin, tocopherols, or other harmless optional

ingredients, which are approved by the department for the purpose of preventing fat oxidation in any of such optional dairy ingredients, may be added in amounts not to exceed five-thousandths of one percent of the weight of the butterfat present in such dairy ingredients.

(3) The optional sweetening ingredients referred to in subsection (1) of this section are sugar (sucrose) , sugar syrup, dextrose, invert sugar (paste or syrup) , lactose, corn sugar, dried or liquid corn syrup, glucose syrup, maple syrup, maple sugar, honey, brown sugar, maltose syrup, malt syrup, dried malt syrup, dried maltose syrup, malt extracts in liquid or dried form, refiners' syrup, and molasses other than blackstrap.

(4) The optional flavoring ingredients referred to in subsection (1) of this section are:

(a) Harmless natural food flavoring, including, but not limited to, ground spice, ground vanilla beans, and infusion of coffee or tea;

(b) Harmless artificial food flavoring;

(c) Fruit juice, which may be fresh, frozen, canned, concentrated, or dried and which may be sweetened and thickened with one or more of the optional stabilizing ingredients specified in subsection (6) of this section;

(d) Chocolate;

(e) Cocoa;

(f) Fruit, including cocoanut, which may be fresh, frozen, canned, concentrated, shredded, pureed, comminuted, or dried and which may be sweetened, thickened with stabilizer, and acidulated with citric, tartaric, malic, lactic, or ascorbic acid;

(g) Nut meats;

(h) Confectionery;

(i) Malted milk;

(j) Properly prepared and cooked cereal;

(k) Any distilled alcoholic beverage, including a liqueur, or any wine or any mixture of two or more thereof.

(5) The optional egg ingredients referred to in subsection (1) of this section are liquid eggs, frozen eggs, dried eggs, egg yolks, frozen yolks, and dried yolks; but the total weight of egg yolk solids in any of such ingredients used singly or used in any combination of two or more of such ingredients shall be less than the minimum prescribed in section 25-5.5-304 for French ice cream.

(6) The optional stabilizing ingredients specified in subsection (1) of this section are gelatin, algin, sodium carboxymethycellulose, extract of Irish moss, psyllium seed husk, agar-agar, gum acacia, gum karaya, locust bean gum, gum tragacanth, oat gum, guar seed gum, calcium sulfate, monoglycerides or diglycerides or both of fat forming fatty acids except lauric acid, or other harmless stabilizers or emulsifiers (surface active agents) approved by the department; but the total weight of the active material contained in the solids of any of such ingredients used singly or used in any combination of two or more of such ingredients shall not be more than one-half of one percent of the weight of the finished ice cream.

(7) (a) The following optional harmless ingredients or combinations thereof may be added to control viscosity, adjust protein stability, and adjust the pH of the combined mix ingredients:

(I) Neutralizers which are approved by the department;

(II) Sodium citrate;

(III) Sodium phosphates.

(b) The total of ingredients included in subparagraph (I) of paragraph (a) of this subsection (7) shall not exceed one-tenth of one percent by weight of the finished mix; nor shall the weight of ingredients included in subparagraphs (II) and (III) of paragraph (a) of this subsection (7) exceed two-tenths of one percent by weight of the finished mix.

(8) It is further provided that the percentage of developed lactic acid in the mix prior to the addition of the optional ingredients listed in subsections (6) and (7) of this section shall not exceed three-thousandths of one percent by weight for each one percent of milk-solids-non-fat present in the mix.

## 25-5.5-304. French ice cream and custards - standards.

French ice cream, frozen custard, and French custard ice cream shall conform to the definition and standard of identity prescribed for ice cream by section 25-5.5-303 if one or more of the optional egg ingredients permitted by section 25-5.5-303 are used in such quantity that the total weight of egg yolk solids therein is not less than one and four-tenths percent of the weight of the finished French ice cream, except when any of the optional flavoring ingredients specified in section 25-5.5-303 (4) (d) to (4) (k) is used, in which case the weight of egg yolk solids shall not be less than one and twelve-hundredths percent of the weight of the finished French ice cream.

## 25-5.5-305. Ice milk - standards.

Ice milk shall conform in all respects to the definition and standard of identity for ice cream prescribed in section 25-5.5-303; except that it shall contain not less than two percent nor more than seven percent of milk fat, not less than eleven percent of total milk solids, and not less than one and three-tenths pounds of food solids per gallon. When ice milk is packaged in containers of greater than one-half gallon capacity, it shall not contain color or any of the optional flavoring ingredients specified in section 25-5.5-303 (4) .

## 25-5.5-305.5. Low-fat frozen dairy dessert - standards.

Low-fat frozen dairy dessert shall conform in all respects to the definition and standard of identity for ice cream prescribed in section 25-5.5-303; except that it shall contain not less than one and five-tenths percent nor more than one and nine-tenths percent of milk fat and not less than twelve percent total milk-solids-non-fat and except that it shall contain not less than one and three-tenths pounds of food solids per gallon.

## 25-5.5-306. Sherbet - standards.

Sherbet is the food prepared by freezing or partially freezing, while stirring, a pasteurized mix composed of one or a combination of the optional dairy ingredients specified in section 25-5.5-303 (2) , one or more of the optional sweetening ingredients specified in section 25-5.5-303 (3) , fruit, fruit juice, or flavoring as provided in this section. It may contain one or more of the optional stabilizing ingredients specified in section 25-5.5-303 (6) or pectin if the weight of such stabilizer is not more than one-half of one percent of the weight of the finished sherbet. The kind and quantity of optional dairy ingredients used is such that the total milk solids content is not more than five percent by weight of the finished sherbet and the milk fat content is not more than two percent nor less than one percent by weight of the finished sherbet. It shall contain fruit or fruit juice, as described in section 25-5.5-303 (4) (c) and (4) (f) , and may contain natural food flavoring. It may contain citric, tartaric, malic, lactic, or ascorbic acid. The acidity of the finished sherbet shall be not less than thirty-five hundredths of one percent of acid as determined by titrating with standard alkali and expressed as lactic acid. It may contain the optional egg ingredients specified in section 25-5.5-303 (5) in amounts not to exceed one-half of one percent of the weight of the finished sherbet. Harmless coloring may be added. The mix may be seasoned with salt and may be homogenized. It shall weigh not less than six pounds per gallon.

## 25-5.5-307. Water ice - standards.

Water ice conforms in all respects to the definition and standard of identity for sherbet prescribed in section 25-5.5-306; except that the mix need not be pasteurized and, since it does not contain any of the optional dairy ingredients, it does not meet the provision respecting total milk solids and butterfat.

## 25-5.5-308. Adulterated and misbranded - when.

Any food product which is made in semblance of or in imitation of any food for which a definition and standard of identity is established in sections 25-5.5-303 to 25-5.5-307 or any food which purports to be or is represented as a food for which a definition and standard of identity is established in said sections shall be deemed to be adulterated and misbranded if such food does not conform to such standard, notwithstanding the employment of any fanciful name or the use of the word "imitation" to designate the product.

## 25-5.5-309. Administration and enforcement.

The department is authorized to administer and supervise the enforcement of this part 3; to provide for such periodic inspections and investigations as may be deemed necessary to disclose violations; to collect samples of optional ingredients, mixes, and finished products for analysis; to receive and provide for the investigation of complaints; and to provide for the institution and prosecution of civil actions. The provisions of this part 3 and the rules and regulations issued in connection therewith may be enforced by injunction in any court having jurisdiction to grant injunctive relief, and adulterated or misbranded articles illegally held or otherwise involved in a violation of this part 3 or of said rules and regulations shall be subject to seizure and disposition in accordance with an order of court.

## 25-5.5-310. Regulations.

Whenever, in the judgment of the department, such action will promote honesty and fair dealing in the interest of consumers, the department shall promulgate regulations fixing and establishing, for any class of frozen desserts, a reasonable definition and standard of identity. The department may, for the purpose of promoting honesty and fair dealing in the interest of consumers, designate harmless optional ingredients which may be used in a mix as permitted by this part 3 but which may not have been specifically identified in this part 3 by any chemical or trade name.

## 25-5.5-311. Products detained or embargoed - when.

Whenever any duly authorized agent of the department finds or has probable cause to believe that any frozen dessert specified in this part 3 is adulterated or misbranded within the meaning of this part 3, he shall affix to such product container a tag or other appropriate marking, giving notice that such frozen dessert is or is suspected of being adulterated or misbranded and that it is being detained or embargoed and warning all persons not to remove or dispose of such product by sale or otherwise until provision for removal or disposal is given by the department. No person shall remove or dispose of such embargoed product by sale or otherwise without permission of the department or its agent or, after summary proceedings have been instituted, without permission from the court having jurisdiction. If the embargo is removed by the department or by the court, neither the department nor the state shall be held liable for damages because of such embargo in the event that the court finds that there was probable cause for the embargo.

## 25-5.5-312. Violations - penalty.

Any person, firm, or corporation that willfully violates any of the provisions of this part 3 and any officer, agent, or employee thereof who directs or knowingly permits such violation or who aids or assists therein is guilty of a misdemeanor and, upon conviction thereof, shall be punished by a fine of not more than one thousand dollars, or by imprisonment in the county jail for not more than ninety days, or by both such fine and imprisonment.

# FAMILY PLANNING

# ARTICLE 6. FAMILY PLANNING

# PART 1. FAMILY PLANNING

## 25-6-101. Legislative declaration.
(1) Continuing population growth either causes or aggravates many social, economic, and environmental problems, both in this state and in the nation.
(2) Contraceptive procedures, supplies, and information are not available as a practical matter to many persons in this state.
(3) It is desirable that inhibitions and restrictions be eliminated so that all persons desiring contraceptive procedures, supplies, and information shall have ready and practicable access thereto.
(4) Section 25-6-102 sets forth the policy and authority of this state, its political subdivisions, and all agencies and institutions thereof, including prohibitions against restrictions with respect to contraceptive procedures, supplies, and information.

## 25-6-102. Policy, authority, and prohibitions against restrictions.
(1) All medically acceptable contraceptive procedures, supplies, and information shall be readily and practicably available to each person desirous of the same regardless of sex, sexual orientation, race, color, creed, religion, disability, age, income, number of children, marital status, citizenship, national origin, ancestry, or motive.
(2) Medical evaluation and advice is encouraged for all persons seeking any contraceptive procedures, supplies, and information.
(3) No hospital, clinic, medical center, institution, or pharmacy shall subject any person to any standard or requirement as a prerequisite for any contraceptive procedures, supplies, or information, including sterilization, other than referral to a physician.
(4) No hospital, clinic, medical center, or pharmacy licensed in this state, nor any agency or institution of this state, nor any unit of local government shall have any policy which interferes with either the physician-patient relationship or any physician or patient desiring to use any medically acceptable contraceptive procedures, supplies, or information.
(5) Contraceptive procedures, including medical procedures for permanent sterilization, when performed by a physician on a requesting and consenting patient, are consistent with public policy.
(6) Notwithstanding any other provision of this part 1, no unmarried person under eighteen years of age may consent to permanent sterilization procedures without the consent of parent or guardian.
(7) Nothing in this part 1 shall inhibit a physician from refusing to furnish any contraceptive procedures, supplies, or information for medical reasons.
(8) Dissemination of medically acceptable contraceptive information by duly authorized persons at schools, in state, district, and county health and welfare departments or public health agencies, in medical facilities at institutions of higher education, and at other agencies and instrumentalities of this state is consistent with public policy.
(9) No private institution or physician, nor any agent or employee of such institution or physician, shall be prohibited from refusing to provide contraceptive procedures, supplies, and information when such refusal is based upon religious or conscientious objection, and no such institution, employee, agent, or physician shall be held liable for such refusal.
(10) To the extent family planning funds are available, each agency and institution of this state and each of its political subdivisions shall provide contraceptive procedures, supplies, and information, including permanent sterilization procedures, to indigent persons free of charge and to other persons at cost.

## 25-6-103. Department of public health and environment - powers and duties.
The department of public health and environment is authorized to receive and disburse such funds

as may become available to it for family planning programs to any organization, public or private, engaged in providing contraceptive procedures, supplies, and information. Any family planning program administered by the department of public health and environment shall be developed in consultation and coordination with other family planning agencies in this state, including but not limited to the department of human services.

# PART 2. FAMILY PLANNING AND BIRTH CONTROL

### 25-6-201. This part 2 to be liberally construed.
This part 2 shall be liberally construed to protect the rights of all individuals to pursue their religious beliefs, to follow the dictates of their own consciences, to prevent the imposition upon any individual of practices offensive to the individual's moral standards, to respect the right of every individual to self-determination in the procreation of children, and to insure a complete freedom of choice in pursuance of constitutional rights.

### 25-6-202. Services to be offered by the county.
The governing body of each county and each city and county or any county or district public health agency thereof or any welfare department thereof may provide and pay for, and each county and each city and county or any public health agency or county or district public health agency thereof or any welfare department thereof may offer, family planning and birth control services to every parent who is a public assistance recipient and to any other parent or married person who might have interest in, and benefit from, such services; except that no county or city and county or public health agency thereof is required by this section to seek out such persons.

### 25-6-203. Extent of services.
Family planning and birth control services shall include: Interview with trained personnel; distribution of literature; referral to a licensed physician or advanced practice nurse for consultation, examination, tests, medical treatment, and prescription; and, to the extent so prescribed, the distribution of rhythm charts, drugs, medical preparations, contraceptive devices, and similar products.

### 25-6-204. Counties may charge for services.
The governmental unit making provision for and offering such services may charge those persons to whom family planning and birth control services are rendered a fee sufficient to reimburse the county or city and county all or any portion of the costs of the services rendered.

### 25-6-205. Services may be refused.
The refusal of any person to accept family planning and birth control services shall in no way affect the right of such person to receive public assistance or to avail himself of any other public benefit, and every person to whom such services are offered shall be so advised initially both orally and in writing. County and city and county employees engaged in the administration of this part 2 shall recognize that the right to make decisions concerning family planning and birth control is a fundamental personal right of the individual, and nothing in this part 2 shall in any way abridge such individual right, nor shall any individual be required to state his reason for refusing the offer of family planning and birth control services.

### 25-6-206. Interviews conducted in language recipient understands.

In all cases where the recipient does not speak or read the English language, the services shall not be given unless the interviews are conducted and all literature is written in a language which the recipient understands.

## 25-6-207. County employee exemption.

Any county employee or city and county employee may refuse to accept the duty of offering family planning and birth control services to the extent that such duty is contrary to his personal religious beliefs, and such refusal shall not be grounds for any disciplinary action, for dismissal, for any interdepartmental transfer, for any other discrimination in his employment, for suspension from employment with the county or city and county, or for any loss in pay or other benefits.

# PART 3. BREAST-FEEDING

## 25-6-301. Legislative declaration.

(1) The general assembly hereby finds and declares that:

(a) The American academy of pediatrics recommends breast-feeding exclusively for the first six months of an infant's life but continuing with other forms of nutrition for at least the first twelve months of an infant's life and as long thereafter as is mutually desired.

(b) The American academy of pediatrics has continuously endorsed breast-feeding as the optimal form of nutrition for infants and as a foundation for good feeding practices. Extensive research indicates that there are diverse and compelling advantages to breast-feeding for infants, mothers, families, and society.

(c) Epidemiologic research shows that breast-feeding of infants provides benefits to their general health, growth, and development and results in significant decreases in risk for numerous acute and chronic diseases.

(d) Research in developed countries provides strong evidence that breast-feeding decreases the incidence and severity of diarrhea, lower respiratory infection, otitis media, and urinary tract infection.

(e) Research studies have also shown that human milk and breast-feeding have possible protective effects against the development of a number of chronic diseases, including allergic diseases and some chronic digestive diseases. In addition, human milk and breast-feeding may prevent obesity.

(f) In addition, breast-feeding has been related to the possible enhancement of cognitive development.

(g) Breast-feeding has been shown to have numerous health benefits for mothers, including an earlier return to prepregnant weight, delayed resumption of ovulation with increased child spacing, improved bone remineralization postpartum with reduction in hip fractures in the postmenopausal period, and reduced risk of ovarian cancer and premenopausal breast cancer, as well as increased levels of oxytocin, resulting in less postpartum bleeding and more rapid uterine involution.

(h) In addition to individual health benefits, breast-feeding results in substantial benefits to society, including reduced health care costs, reduced environmental damage, reduced governmental spending on the women, infants, and children supplementary feeding programs, and reduced employee absenteeism for care attributable to infant illness.

(i) Breast-feeding is a basic and important act of nurturing that should be encouraged in the interests of maternal and infant health.

(2) The general assembly further declares that the purpose of this part 3 is for the state of Colorado to become involved in the national movement to recognize the medical importance of breast-feeding, within the scope of complete pediatric care, and to encourage removal of societal boundaries placed on breast-feeding in public.

## 25-6-302. Breast-feeding.
A mother may breast-feed in any place she has a right to be.


# ENVIRONMENTAL CONTROL


# ARTICLE 6.5. ENVIRONMENTAL CONTROL


# PART 1. PROVISIONS FOR RULES AND REGULATIONS CONCERNING ENVIRONMENTAL CONTROL


### 25-6.5-101. Legislative declaration.
(1) The general assembly hereby finds and determines that the protection of the natural environment of this state is important to the public health and welfare of the citizens of Colorado.
(2) The general assembly further finds and determines that the environmental laws of this state relating to air quality control in article 7 of this title, water quality control in article 8 of this title, hazardous waste in article 15 of this title, and solid waste in article 20 of title 30, C.R.S., may be highly technical, complex, and subject to varying interpretation.
(3) The general assembly, therefore, declares that the provisions of this article are enacted to enhance public notice and awareness of rules, regulations, and interpretations of the environmental laws of this state and to ensure public confidence in the fairness of the enforcement of any agency requirements.


### 25-6.5-102. Requirements for environmental rules - publication.
(1) All agency policies and guidance, including any amendments or revisions thereto, relating to the implementation, administration, and enforcement of article 7, 8, 11, or 15 of this title, article 20.5 of title 8, C.R.S., or article 20 of title 30, C.R.S., except for policies relating to personnel or other internal administrative matters not directly related to enforceable requirements under such articles, shall be reduced to writing and published. Three copies shall be filed with the state librarian for the state publications depository and distribution center. Copies of each such policy or guidance issued under article 7, 8, 11, or 15 of this title, article 20.5 of title 8, C.R.S., or article 20 of title 30, C.R.S., shall be made available to the public upon request. Interpretive rules issued under article 15 of this title shall also be made available to the public upon request. Each affected agency shall maintain and make available to the public a current index of all such policies, guidance, and interpretive rules in effect. Copies of any policy, guidance, interpretive rule, or index shall be provided to the public at cost.
(2) No policy or guidance referred to in subsection (1) of this section shall have the force and effect of a rule unless it has been promulgated by the relevant commission pursuant to the provisions of the "State Administrative Procedure Act", article 4 of title 24, C.R.S., and applicable provisions of article 7, 8, 11, or 15 of this title, article 20.5 of title 8, C.R.S., or article 20 of title 30, C.R.S., pertaining to rule-making procedures or authorizing the promulgation of rules, and made available to the public in accordance with section 24-4-103, C.R.S.
(3) (a) Any policy or guidance, including any amendments or revisions thereto, may be brought to the attention of the relevant division director and thereafter may be brought to the relevant commission for review. The review shall determine whether such policy or guidance is within the

statutory authority of the relevant agency, is consistent with applicable statutes and any applicable regulations, including the provisions of subsection (1) of this section, and is appropriate for the relevant commission to undertake rule-making with respect to the subject matter of the policy or guidance and shall consider other questions within the scope of the relevant commission's authority related to such policy or guidance.

(b) Following such review, the commission shall take action or, if appropriate, refer the matter to the relevant division director to take action within a specified period of time in accordance with its determination.

(4) Any obligation to submit payment of any monetary penalty arising from an enforcement action that concerns a matter under review by the relevant commission shall be stayed until the relevant commission completes its review.

(5) The commission review regarding the policy or guidance shall not constitute an adjudication of any facts of a specific enforcement action.

(6) Failure to request a review under this section shall not be considered in any permit appeal or enforcement action.

(7) As used in this section:

(a) "Relevant commission" means the commission or agency responsible for the promulgation of rules for the environmental program under which the guidance or policy is issued.

(b) "Relevant division director" means the director of the division within the department of public health and environment, responsible for the subject matter of the guidance or policy at issue.

# PART 2. POLLUTION CONTROL EQUIPMENT CERTIFICATION

## 25-6.5-201. Definitions.

As used in this part 2, unless the context otherwise requires:

(1) "Division" means the division of administration of the department of public health and environment.

(2) "Pollution control equipment" means any personal property, including, but not limited to, equipment, machinery, devices, systems, buildings, or structures, that is installed, constructed, or used in or as a part of a facility that creates a product in a manner that generates less pollution by the utilization of an alternative manufacturing or generating technology. "Pollution control equipment" includes, but is not limited to, gas or wind turbines and associated compressors or equipment or solar, thermal, or photovoltaic equipment.

## 25-6.5-202. Certification of pollution control equipment.

(1) Within twelve months after the date of acquisition of an ownership or lease interest, a person owning or leasing property may file a request for certification of such property as pollution control equipment with the division on forms prescribed by the division.

(2) At any time after the filing of a request for certification pursuant to subsection (1) of this section and prior to a determination, the division may schedule a conference with the applicant to obtain further information relevant to the determination of eligibility for certification as pollution control equipment.

(3) Within six months after the filing of a request pursuant to subsection (1) of this section, the division shall determine the eligibility of such property as pollution control equipment and shall certify its determination to the applicant and the executive director of the department of revenue. The division may certify as pollution control equipment all of the property for which a request has been filed pursuant to subsection (1) of this section, specified portions of the property, or none of the property. In making its determination, the division shall consider any available and pertinent

information.

(4) If the division denies a request for certification in whole or in part, the applicant may file with the division a written objection to the determination within thirty days after receipt of written notice of the determination. If a written objection is filed, the division shall grant the applicant a hearing in accordance with section 24-4-105, C.R.S., within thirty days after receipt of the written objection and shall make a final determination based on the hearing.

(5) If the final determination of the division denies the request for certification in whole or in part, the final determination shall be subject to judicial review in accordance with the provisions of section 24-4-106, C.R.S.

(6) The division may assess against an applicant a fee sufficient to cover the actual and direct cost incurred by the division in making a determination pursuant to this section, including, but not limited to, the actual and direct cost of any hearing or appeal related to the denial of certification if the denial is upheld. Any fee assessed by the division pursuant to this subsection (6) shall be credited to the pollution control equipment certification fund created in section 25-6.5-203.

### 25-6.5-203. Pollution control equipment certification fund - creation - purpose.

(1) There is hereby established in the state treasury the pollution control equipment certification fund, which shall consist of all moneys collected by the division pursuant to section 25-6.5-202. All interest derived from the deposit and investment of moneys in the fund shall be credited to the fund. Any unexpended or unencumbered moneys in the fund at the end of any fiscal year shall remain in the fund and shall not be transferred to the general fund.

(2) The moneys in the pollution control equipment certification fund shall be subject to annual appropriation by the general assembly to the department of public health and environment to defray the costs incurred by the division in performing its obligations pursuant to section 25-6.5-202.

# ARTICLE 6.6. ENVIRONMENTAL MANAGEMENT SYSTEM PERMIT PROGRAM

### 25-6.6-101. Short title.

This article shall be known and may be cited as the "Environmental Management System Permit Program".

### 25-6.6-102. Legislative declaration.

(1) The general assembly finds that while Colorado's existing environmental laws play an important role in protecting the environment, environmental protection could be further enhanced by authorizing innovative advances in environmental regulatory methods and approaches. The general assembly finds that Colorado should promote and develop environmental regulatory approaches that:

(a) Encourage facility owners and operators to assess the environmental impact of their operations;

(b) Encourage innovation by and measure success through facility owners and operators setting measurable goals;

(c) Provide facility owners and operators with flexibility to implement the most effective pollution prevention, source reduction, or other pollution reduction strategies for their particular facilities, while complying with verifiable and enforceable pollution limits;

(d) Encourage superior environmental performance, continuous improvement toward sustainable levels of resource usage, and minimal levels of pollution discharges, emissions, and releases;

(e) Recognize facility owners and operators that are considered environmental leaders and that reduce pollution to levels below what is required by applicable law, through participation in the environmental management system permit program;

(f) Consolidate environmental requirements into one permit, while respecting local agency jurisdiction and encouraging local agencies to participate, and allow facility owners and operators to make environmental decisions based upon all environmental considerations;

(g) Reduce the time and money spent by agencies and facility owners and operators on paperwork and other administrative tasks that do not benefit the environment, including streamlining permit, record-keeping, and reporting requirements;

(h) Increase public participation and encourage stakeholder consensus in the development of innovative environmental regulatory approaches and methods for monitoring the environmental performance of projects pursuant to this title;

(i) Encourage groups of facilities and communities to work together to reduce pollution to levels below what is required by applicable law;

(j) Provide reasonable assistance to facilitate meaningful stakeholder participation; and

(k) Increase understanding and transparency of environmental laws and promote communication among agencies, regulated entities, and the public.

## 25-6.6-103. Definitions.

As used in this article, unless the context otherwise requires:

(1) "Department" means the state department of public health and environment.

(2) "Environmental permit" means a permit issued pursuant to article 20.5 of title 8, C.R.S., articles 7, 8, 11, and 15 of this title or article 20 of title 30, C.R.S., or rules promulgated under such provisions, and may also include permits issued pursuant to local government authority, with the consent of such local government authority.

(3) "Environmental requirement" means a requirement in a law administered by the department, a rule adopted by a statutorily designed state board or commission, a permit or order issued by the department, or an agreement entered into with the department.

## 25-6.6-104. Powers and duties of department - rules.

(1) The department is authorized to implement a voluntary environmental management system permit program, which shall be a pilot program until May 15, 2007, that allows a limited number of participants as determined by the department to obtain an environmental management system permit. The environmental management system permit shall allow participants to meet existing environmental standards of a law, rule, order, or permit related to the control or abatement of pollution through the use of alternative methods and procedures while ensuring compliance with an established ambient air or water standard. Nothing in this section shall be construed to authorize a participant to exceed an established ambient air or water standard.

(2) Notwithstanding the provisions of section 25-1-102, the executive director of the department has the sole authority to promulgate and amend rules, to the extent that such rules and amendments to the rules are consistent with federal law, in order to specify the procedures and other necessary requirements for issuing, implementing, revoking, and enforcing an environmental management system permit and to establish alternative methods or procedures for meeting environmental standards. The procedures outlined in the rules shall include the opportunity for public notice and comment.

(3) The department shall include, but not be limited to, the following elements in the environmental management system permit:

(a) The elements of an environmental management system;

(b) A requirement and criteria for audits of the environmental management system;

(c) A requirement and criteria for environmental compliance audits;

(d) A requirement and criteria for reporting a summary of the results of the environmental compliance audits;

(e) Environmental performance standards and limits;

(f) A requirement that program participants commit to measurable environmental benefits and continual environmental improvement;

(g) Monitoring, reporting, and record-keeping requirements;

(h) The ability for an analysis and consideration of all environmental impacts in developing environmental requirements;

(i) A requirement for community involvement and a communications plan; and

(j) Procedures that reduce otherwise required permit modification procedural requirements.

(4) (a) An entity may apply to participate in the voluntary environmental management system permit program if the entity meets the requirements for any of the following tiers:

(I) Platinum tier. The department shall establish the criteria for the platinum tier by rule, which criteria shall be more stringent than the gold tier criteria and shall include that the entity has assisted the department in developing proposals for streamlining environmental requirements and easing the regulatory burden on businesses of environmental compliance.

(II) Gold tier. The criteria are as follows:

(A) The entity has no serious violations of applicable local, state, or federal environmental requirements or environmental permits for a period of three years prior to the date of submission of the application for participation in the program;

(B) The entity has no convictions or out-of-court settlements of formal charges of a criminal violation of an environmental requirement or environmental permit within a five-year period prior to the date of submission of the application for participation in the program; and

(C) The entity has not entered into a settlement agreement and no compliance or consent order has been issued for a serious violation of an environmental requirement or environmental permit for three years prior to the date of submission of the application for participation in the program.

(III) Silver tier. The criteria are as follows:

(A) The entity has no serious violations of applicable local, state, or federal environmental requirements or environmental permits for a period of one year prior to the date of submission of the application for participation in the program;

(B) The entity has no convictions or out-of-court settlements of formal charges of a criminal violation of an environmental requirement or environmental permit within a two-year period prior to the date of submission of the application for participation in the program;

(C) The entity has not entered into a settlement agreement and no compliance or consent order has been issued for serious violations of an environmental requirement or environmental permit for a one-year period prior to the date of submission of the application for participation in the program; and

(D) No permit shall be issued to silver tier applicants pursuant to this article until the applicant achieves compliance with gold or platinum tier requirements.

(b) Any facility that will be subject to the program and that is part of a corporation, partnership, sole proprietorship, municipality, county, city and county, special district, or state or federal agency or department that has other Colorado facilities shall not be eligible for the program unless all of such facilities located in Colorado are in compliance with applicable local, state, and federal environmental requirements and environmental permits. The department shall determine the applicability of this paragraph (b) on a case-by-case basis.

(5) The department shall develop and make available to the public information on any alternative monitoring, record keeping, reporting, method, or condition that the environmental management system permit prescribes and any other incentive provided to the applicant within the environmental management system permit.

(6) An entity subject to an environmental management system permit shall be subject to the same fee provisions as other existing permits, unless the department reduces the fee as an operational flexibility incentive. The department is authorized to exercise such flexibility.

(7) The department shall establish performance measures, including public notice and comment, to assess the pilot program's performance after public notice and comment.

## 25-6.6-105. Enforcement - self-audit - review.

(1) The department is authorized to enter and inspect any property, premises, or place, and all facilities, on- or off-site, that is or are covered by an environmental management permit or where relevant documents may be located, for the purpose of investigating any actual, suspected, or potential source of pollution or ascertaining compliance or noncompliance with any requirement of this article, any rule promulgated pursuant to this article, or any permit issued pursuant to this article. The department may, at reasonable times, have access to and copy any record, inspect any monitoring equipment or method, or sample any emissions or wastes, including mixtures of waste with environmental media or other materials required pursuant to this article; except that, if the permit holder denies or does not consent to such entry or inspection, the department has the authority to seek a warrant from a court of competent jurisdiction in the county in which the property, premises, or place is located prior to inspection. The court shall issue such a warrant upon a proper showing of the need for such entry and inspection. Any trade secrets and proprietary information obtained in the course of the inspection or investigation shall be kept confidential unless the permit holder consents to the release of the information; except that information required to be made available to the department pursuant to any other law shall not be confidential. The department shall provide a permit holder with a duplicate of any analytical report or observation of a pollutant made by the department. If samples are taken, the permittee shall be entitled to a receipt for such samples. Upon request of the permit holder, the department shall provide the permit holder with a sufficient sample so that the permit holder may perform its own test.

(2) In addition to the rights of entry and inspection by the department pursuant to subsection (1) of this section, the terms and conditions of the environmental management system permit shall be enforced in any manner provided by law for the enforcement of permits issued pursuant to department rules. Appeals of initial determinations shall be made to the executive director or a designated hearing officer in accordance with the "State Administrative Procedure Act", article 4 of title 24, C.R.S.

(3) This section shall not be interpreted to exclude a participant in the environmental management system permit program that performs an audit as required by the program from exercising or applying any rights or privileges granted in section 13-25-126.5, C.R.S., and sections 25-1-114.5 and 25-1-114.6.

(4) The department, in consultation with interested parties, including applicable environmental boards and commissions, shall review the pilot permit program to assess its effectiveness in improving, enhancing, and protecting the environment of the state, garnering resource efficiencies, and decreasing administrative burdens. The department shall report the results of the review to the general assembly and the governor on or before January 1, 2007. The report shall include recommendations concerning whether the pilot project should be allowed to continue, and, if so, the recommended form and structure of the program.

## 25-6.6-106. Repeal of article.

This article is repealed, effective July 1, 2018. Prior to such repeal, the environmental management system permit program shall be reviewed as provided for in section 24-34-104, C.R.S.

# ARTICLE 6.7. ENVIRONMENTAL LEADERSHIP ACT

## 25-6.7-101 to 25-6.7-110. (Repealed)

# ARTICLE 7. AIR QUALITY CONTROL

# PART 1. AIR QUALITY CONTROL PROGRAM

## 25-7-101. Short title.
This article shall be known and may be cited as the "Colorado Air Pollution Prevention and Control Act".

## 25-7-102. Legislative declaration.
In order to foster the health, welfare, convenience, and comfort of the inhabitants of the state of Colorado and to facilitate the enjoyment and use of the scenic and natural resources of the state, it is declared to be the policy of this state to achieve the maximum practical degree of air purity in every portion of the state, to attain and maintain the national ambient air quality standards, and to prevent the significant deterioration of air quality in those portions of the state where the air quality is better than the national ambient air quality standards. To that end, it is the purpose of this article to require the use of all available practical methods which are technologically feasible and economically reasonable so as to reduce, prevent, and control air pollution throughout the state of Colorado; to require the development of an air quality control program in which the benefits of the air pollution control measures utilized bear a reasonable relationship to the economic, environmental, and energy impacts and other costs of such measures; and to maintain a cooperative program between the state and local units of government. It is further declared that the prevention, abatement, and control of air pollution in each portion of the state are matters of statewide concern and are affected with a public interest and that the provisions of this article are enacted in the exercise of the police powers of this state for the purpose of protecting the health, peace, safety, and general welfare of the people of this state. The general assembly further recognizes that a current and accurate inventory of actual emissions of air pollutants from all sources is essential for the proper identification and designation of attainment and nonattainment areas, the determination of the most cost-effective regulatory strategy to reduce pollution, the targeting of regulatory efforts to achieve the greatest health and environmental benefits, and the achievement of a federally approved clean air program. In order to achieve the most accurate inventory of air pollution sources possible, this article specifically provides incentives to achieve the most accurate and complete inventory possible and to provide for the most accurate enforcement program achievable based upon that inventory.

## 25-7-103. Definitions.
As used in this article, unless the context otherwise requires:
(1) "Administrator" means the administrator of the federal environmental protection agency.
(1.3) "Adverse environmental effect", as a term used in the context of regulating hazardous air pollutants, means any significant and widespread adverse effect, which may reasonably be anticipated, to wildlife, aquatic life, or other natural resources, including adverse impacts on populations of endangered or threatened species or significant degradation of environmental quality over broad areas.
(1.5) "Air pollutant" means any fume, smoke, particulate matter, vapor, or gas or any combination thereof which is emitted into or otherwise enters the atmosphere, including, but not limited to, any physical, chemical, biological, radioactive (including source material, special nuclear material, and byproduct material) substance or matter, but "air pollutant" does not include water vapor or steam condensate or any other emission exempted by the commission consistent with the federal act.

Such term includes any precursors to the formation of any air pollutant, to the extent the administrator of the United States environmental protection agency or the commission has identified such precursor or precursors for the particular purpose for which the term "air pollutant" is used.

(2) "Air pollution control authority" means the division, or any person or agency given authority by the division, or a local governmental unit duly authorized with respect to air pollution control.

(3) "Air pollution source" means any source whatsoever at, from, or by reason of which there is emitted or discharged into the atmosphere any air pollutant.

(4) "Allowable emissions" means the emission rate calculated for a stationary source using the maximum rated capacity of the source (unless the source is subject to enforceable permit conditions which limit the operating rate or hours of operation, or both) and the most stringent of the following:

(a) The applicable standards promulgated pursuant to the federal act for new source performance or hazardous air pollutants;

(b) The applicable Colorado emission control regulation; or

(c) The emission rate specified as a permit condition.

(5) "Ambient air" means that portion of the atmosphere, external to the sources, to which the general public has access.

(5.5) "Appliance" means any device which contains and uses as a refrigerant a class I or class II ozone depleting compound as defined by the administrator and which is used for household or commercial purposes, including any air conditioner, refrigerator, chiller, or freezer.

(5.7) "Approved motor vehicle refrigerant recycling equipment" means any equipment models certified by the administrator, or any independent standards testing organization approved by such administrator, to meet the standards established by the administrator which are applicable to equipment for the extraction of refrigerants from motor vehicle air conditioners. Equipment for such purpose purchased prior to the promulgation of regulations pursuant to section 25-7-105 (11) (c) shall be considered certified if it is substantially identical to equipment which is certified by the administrator.

(6) Repealed.

(6.5) "CFC" means any of the chlorofluorocarbon chemicals CFC-11, CFC-12, CFC-112, CFC-113, CFC-114, CFC-115, or CFC-502.

(6.7) "Colorado generally available control technology" or "Colorado GACT" means standards imposed pursuant to section 25-7-109.3 (3) utilizing principles of sound engineering judgment in applying the criteria set forth in section 112 (d) of the federal act respecting the creation of standards or requirements utilizing generally available control technologies or management practices by area sources for the reduction of emissions of hazardous air pollutants considering a cost-benefit analysis, economics, the cost and availability of control technology, and the location, nature, and size of the source involved, and the actual or potential impacts on the public health, welfare, and the environment.

(6.8) "Colorado maximum achievable control technology" or "Colorado MACT" means standards imposed pursuant to section 25-7-109.3 (3) utilizing principles of sound engineering judgment in applying the criteria set forth in section 112 (d) of the federal act respecting the creation of standards or requirements which provide for the maximum degree of emissions reduction that has been demonstrated to be achievable for the control of hazardous air pollutants, considering a cost-benefit analysis, economics, the cost and availability of control technology, and the location, nature, and size of the source involved, and the actual or potential impacts on the public health, welfare, and the environment.

(7) "Commission" means the air quality control commission created by section 25-7-104.

(8) "Construction" means fabrication, erection, installation, or modification of an air pollution source.

(9) "Division" means the division of administration of the department of public health and environment.

(9.5) "Effects on public welfare" means all language referring to effects on public welfare, which

353

includes, but is not limited to, effects on soils, water, crops, vegetation, manmade materials, animals, wildlife, weather, visibility, climate, damage to and deterioration of property, and hazards to transportation, as well as effects on economic values and on personal comfort and well-being, whether caused by transformation, conversion, or combination with other air pollutants.

(10) "Emission" means the discharge or release into the atmosphere of one or more air pollutants.

(11) "Emission control regulation" means and includes any standard promulgated by regulation which is applicable to all air pollution sources within a specified area and which prohibits or establishes permissible limits for specific types of emissions in such area, and also any regulation which by its terms is applicable to a specified type of facility, process, or activity for the purpose of controlling the extent, degree, or nature of pollution emitted from such type of facility, process, or activity, any regulation adopted for the purpose of preventing or minimizing emission of any air pollutant in potentially dangerous quantities, and also any regulation that adopts any design, equipment, work practice, or operational standard. Emission control regulations shall not include standards which describe maximum ambient air concentrations of specifically identified pollutants or which describe varying degrees of pollution of ambient air. Emission control regulations pertaining to hazardous air pollutants, as defined in subsection (13) of this section, shall be consistent with the emission standards promulgated under section 112 of the federal act or section 25-7-109.3 in reducing or preventing emissions of hazardous air pollutants, and may include application of measures, processes, methods, systems, or techniques, including, but not limited to, measures which:

(a) Reduce the volume of, or eliminate emissions of, such pollutants through process changes, substitution of materials, or other modifications;

(b) Enclose systems or processes to eliminate emissions;

(c) Collect, capture, or treat such pollutants when released from a process, stack, storage, or fugitive emissions point;

(d) Are design, equipment, or work practice standards (including requirements for operator training or certification) ; or

(e) Are a combination of the provisions of paragraphs (a) to (d) of this subsection (11) .

(11.5) "Emission data" means, with reference to any source of emission of any substance into the air:

(a) Information necessary to determine the identity, amount, frequency, concentration, or other characteristics (to the extent related to air quality) of any emission which has been, or will be, emitted by the source (or of any pollutant resulting from any emission by the source) , or any combination thereof;

(b) Information necessary to determine the identity, amount, frequency, concentration, or other characteristics (to the extent related to air quality) of the emission which, under an applicable standard or limitation, the source was authorized to emit (including, to the extent necessary for such purposes, a description of the manner or rate of operation of the source) , or any combination thereof;

(c) A general description of the location or nature, or both, of the source to the extent necessary to identify the source and to distinguish it from other sources (including, to the extent necessary for such purposes, a description of the device, installation, or operation constituting the source) .

(12) "Federal act" means the federal "Clean Air Act", 42 U.S.C. sec. 7401 et seq. (1970) , as the same is in effect on November 15, 1990.

(12.1) "Generally available control technology" or "GACT" means standards promulgated pursuant to section 112 of the federal act which provide for the use of generally available control technologies or management practices for the control of hazardous air pollutants for area sources, as defined in section 112 of the federal act, including equivalent emission limitations by permit pursuant to section 112 (j) of the federal act.

(13) "Hazardous air pollutant" means an air pollutant which presents through inhalation or other routes of exposure, a threat of adverse human health effects (including, but not limited to, substances which are known to be, or may reasonably be anticipated to be carcinogenic, mutagenic, teratogenic, neurotoxic, which cause reproductive dysfunction, or which are acutely or

chronically toxic) or adverse environmental effects whether through ambient concentrations, bioaccumulation, deposition, or otherwise and which has been listed pursuant to section 112 of the federal act or section 25-7-109.3.

(14) "Indirect air pollution source" means any facility, building, structure, or installation, or any combination thereof, excluding dwellings, which can reasonably be expected to cause or induce substantial mobile source activity which results in emissions of air pollutants which might reasonably be expected to interfere with the attainment and maintenance of national ambient air standards.

(15) "Issue" or "issuance" means the mailing of any order, permit, determination, or notice, other than notice by publication, by certified mail to the last address furnished to the agency by the person subject thereto or personal service on such person, and the date of issuance of such order, permit, determination, or notice shall be the date of such mailing or service or such later date as is stated in the order, permit, determination, or notice.

(16) "Local air pollution law" means any law, ordinance, resolution, code, rule, or regulation adopted by the governing body of any city, town, county, or city and county, pertaining to the prevention, control, and abatement of air pollution.

(16.5) "Maximum achievable control technology" or "MACT" means emission standards promulgated under section 112 of the federal act requiring the maximum degree of emissions reduction that has been demonstrated to be achievable for the control of hazardous air pollutants, including equivalent emission limitations by permit pursuant to section 112 (j) of the federal act.

(17) "Malfunction" means any sudden and unavoidable failure of air pollution control equipment or process equipment or unintended failure of a process to operate in a normal or usual manner. Failures that are primarily caused by poor maintenance, careless operation, or any other preventable upset condition or preventable equipment breakdown shall not be considered malfunctions.

(18) "Motor vehicle" means any self-propelled vehicle which is designed primarily for travel on the public highways and which is generally and commonly used to transport persons and property over the public highways.

(18.3) "Motor vehicle air conditioner" means any air conditioner designed for installation in a motor vehicle which uses as a refrigerant any class I or class II ozone depleting compound as defined by the administrator.

(18.4) "Owner or operator" means any person who owns, leases, operates, controls, or supervises a stationary source.

(18.5) "Ozone depleting compound" means any substance on the list of class I and class II ozone depleting compounds as defined by the administrator and as referenced in section 602 of the federal "Clean Air Act Amendments of 1990".

(19) "Person" means any individual, public or private corporation, partnership, association, firm, trust, estate, the United States or the state or any department, institution, or agency thereof, any municipal corporation, county, city and county, or other political subdivision of the state, or any other legal entity whatsoever which is recognized by law as the subject of rights and duties.

(19.5) "Refrigeration system" includes refrigerators, freezers, cold storage warehouse refrigeration systems, and air conditioners, any of which hold more than one hundred pounds of refrigerant or more than one hundred pounds total if more than one refrigeration unit or system exists at the same location.

(20) "Shutdown" means the cessation of operation of any air pollution source for any purpose.

(21) "Start-up" means the setting in operation of any air pollution source for any purpose.

(22) "State implementation plan" means the plan required by and described in section 110(a) of the federal act.

(23) "Stationary source" means any building, structure, facility, or installation which emits or may emit any air pollutant.

## 25-7-104. Air quality control commission created.

(1) There is hereby created in the department of public health and environment the air quality control commission, which shall consist of nine citizens of this state who shall be appointed by the governor with the consent of the senate.

(2) Appointments to the commission shall be made so as to include persons with appropriate scientific, technical, industrial, labor, agricultural, and legal training or with experience on the commission; although no specific number of its members shall be required to be so trained or experienced, three members shall have appropriate private sector, technical, or industrial employment experience. No more than five commissioners shall be members of one political party.

(3) Terms of members shall be for three years, and said terms shall commence on February 1 of the year of appointment. Any vacancy occurring during the term of office of any member shall be filled by appointment by the governor of a qualified person for the unexpired portion of the regular term.

(4) The governor may remove any member of the commission for malfeasance in office, failure to regularly attend meetings, or any cause that renders such a member incapable or unfit to discharge the duties of his office, and any such removal, when made, shall not be subject to review. If any member of the commission is absent from two consecutive meetings, the chairman of the commission shall determine whether the cause of such absences was reasonable. If he determines that the cause of the absences was unreasonable, he shall so notify the governor, who shall appoint a qualified person for the unexpired portion of the regular term.

(5) Each member of the commission not otherwise in full-time employment of the state shall receive a per diem of forty dollars for each day actually and necessarily spent in the discharge of official duties, but not to exceed twelve hundred eighty-four dollars in any one year; and all members shall receive traveling and other necessary expenses actually incurred in the performance of official duties.

(6) Each year the commission shall select from its own membership a chairman, vice-chairman, and secretary. The secretary of the commission shall keep a record of its proceedings. The commission shall hold regular public monthly meetings and may hold special meetings on the call of the chairman or vice-chairman at such other times as deemed necessary. Written notice of the time and place of all meetings shall be mailed by the secretary at least five days in advance of any such meetings to each member.

(7) All members shall have a vote. Two-thirds of the commission shall constitute a quorum, and the concurrence of a majority of the commission in any matter within its powers and duties shall be required for any determination made by the commission.

(8) The commission shall have at least a majority of members who represent the public interest and do not derive a significant portion of their income from persons subject to permits or enforcement orders under this article or under the federal act. The members of the commission shall disclose any potential conflicts of interest to the governor and the committee of reference of the general assembly prior to confirmation and shall disclose any potential conflicts of interest which arise during their terms of membership to the governor and to the other commission members in a public meeting of the commission.

(9) (Deleted by amendment, L. 92, p. 1169, § 6, effective July 1, 1992.)

## 25-7-105. Duties of commission - rules.

(1) Except as provided in sections 25-7-130 and 25-7-131, the commission shall promulgate such rules and regulations as are consistent with the legislative declaration set forth in section 25-7-102 and necessary for the proper implementation and administration of this article, including but not limited to:

(a) (I) A comprehensive state implementation plan which will assure attainment and maintenance of national ambient air quality standards and which will prevent significant deterioration of air quality, all in conformity with the provisions of this article. The comprehensive plan shall meet all requirements of the federal act and shall be revised whenever necessary or appropriate.

(II) The comprehensive state implementation plan of the commission shall, wherever feasible, include local or regional air pollution plans and programs adopted or enforceable by municipal or county governments. Before making any changes to those portions of the state implementation plan which include such air pollution plans and programs or to such plans and programs which are suggested for inclusion in the state implementation plan, the commission shall give thirty days' notice of the proposed changes to the affected municipal or county government to allow a reasonable opportunity to prepare comments on the proposed changes. The commission shall consider such comments in its action on the state implementation plan and shall document in the record of the hearing its reasons for any changes to such plans and programs. Any such plans and programs which are approved by the commission and formally submitted as a part of the state implementation plan shall be deemed a part of the comprehensive program of the commission and shall be enforced as such.

(III) The revisions to the Denver element of the PM-10 state implementation plan adopted by the commission on February 16, 1995, which contain a sixty tons-per-day PM-10 mobile source emissions budget which expires January 1, 1998, and reverts to a forty-four tons-per-day budget, are amended to provide that such forty-four tons-per-day reversion shall not be a part of the state implementation plan and shall only apply as a regulation adopted exclusively under reserved state authority pursuant to the provisions of section 25-7-105.1. The sixty tons-per-day emissions budget shall, unless modified by the commission through rule-making, apply for federal transportation conformity and is included in the state implementation plan only as required by the federal act. Any entity with authority to adopt a transportation plan required under section 43-1-1103, C.R.S., shall consider any mobile source emissions budgets in effect under this article in the development of transportation improvement programs for federal purposes.

(IV) Notwithstanding the provisions of section 25-7-133, the expiration of the state implementation plan for ozone maintenance and related rules of the air quality control commission, and the amendments to commission regulations number 3 and 7, which state implementation plan and rules, and amendments to regulations number 3 and 7, were adopted or amended by the commission on March 21, 1996, and which are therefore scheduled for expiration May 15, 1997, is postponed until December 31, 2005, and the provisions of section 24-4-108, C.R.S., shall apply.

(b) Emission control regulations in conformity with section 25-7-109;

(c) A prevention of significant deterioration program in conformity with part 2 of this article and federal requirements; except that definitions used in the program shall not differ from any definitions pertaining to the prevention of significant deterioration program which appear in section 169 of the federal act or in federal regulations promulgated thereunder, and an attainment program in conformity with part 3 of this article;

(d) A satisfactory process of consultation with general purpose local governments and any federal land manager having authority over federal land to which the state implementation plan applies, effective with respect to measures adopted after August 7, 1978, pertaining to transportation controls, air quality maintenance plan requirements, preconstruction review of stationary sources of air pollution, or any measure referred to in the prevention of significant deterioration program established pursuant to part 2 of this article or the attainment program established pursuant to part 3 of this article, or granting delayed compliance orders pursuant to section 25-7-118.

(2) The commission shall provide forms of application and shall receive all such applications for review of the classification of any attainment, nonattainment, or unclassifiable area within the state made pursuant to section 25-7-106 (1) or 25-7-107 (2) , all applications for designation or redesignation made pursuant to section 25-7-208, and all applications for any revision of general application of the state implementation plan and shall set such applications for hearing and determination by the commission in accordance with the provisions of section 25-7-119.

(3) The commission shall employ a technical secretary and shall delegate to such secretary such duties and responsibilities as it may deem necessary; except that no authority shall be delegated to such secretary to adopt, promulgate, amend, or repeal standards or regulations, or to make determinations, or to issue or countermand orders of the commission. Such secretary shall have

appropriate practical, educational, and administrative experience related to air pollution control and shall be employed pursuant to the state personnel system laws.

(4) (a) The commission and the state board of health shall hold a joint public hearing during the month of October of each year in order to hear public comment on air pollution problems within the state, alleged sources of air pollution within the state, and the availability of practical remedies therefor; and at such hearing the technical secretary shall answer reasonable questions from the public concerning administration and enforcement of the various provisions of this article, as well as rules and regulations promulgated under the authority of this article.

(b) On or before September 30, 1993, the commission shall publish and revise from time to time thereafter, as is necessary, a regulatory agenda which includes its schedule for future rule-making and its schedule for implementing section 25-7-109.3 and other air quality programs.

(5) Prior to the hearing required under subsection (4) of this section, the commission shall prepare and make available to the public a report, which shall contain the following specific information:

(a) A description of the pollution problem in each of the polluted areas of the state, described separately for each such area;

(b) To the extent possible, the identification of the sources of air pollution in each separate area of the state, such as motor vehicles, industrial sources, and power-generating facilities;

(c) A list of all alleged violations of emission control regulations showing the status of control procedures in effect with respect to each such alleged violation; and

(d) Stationary industrial sources permitting information as follows:

(I) The total number of permits issued;

(II) The total number of hours billed for permitting;

(III) The average number of hours billed per permit; and

(IV) The number of general permits issued.

(6) and (7) Repealed.

(8) (Deleted by amendment, L. 92, p. 1170, § 7, effective July 1, 1992.)

(9) The commission shall adopt exhaust emissions standards for motor vehicles purchased for state use and shall assist the executive director of the department of personnel in determining those vehicles which meet or exceed such standards.

(10) The commission shall promulgate such rules and regulations as are necessary to implement the provisions of part 5 of this article concerning asbestos control.

(11) The commission shall promulgate rules concerning CFC and ozone-depleting compounds as follows:

(a) Regulations requiring the recycling or reuse of any refrigerant containing CFC which is removed from the refrigeration system of a retail store, cold storage warehouse, or commercial or industrial building by any person who installs, services, repairs, or disposes of such system as a result of service to or disposal of such system;

(b) Regulations prohibiting the intentional venting or disposal of any refrigerant containing CFC by the owner or operator of a retail store, cold storage warehouse, or commercial or industrial building and requiring the recycling or reuse of such refrigerant;

(c) Regulations requiring the use of approved motor vehicle refrigerant recycling equipment during the repair or servicing of a motor vehicle air conditioner, requiring that such repair or servicing be done by a person certified in accordance with federal regulations, and including requirements for reclamation of refrigerants during the disposal of a vehicle;

(d) Repealed.

(e) Regulations which establish requirements for recycling;

(f) Regulations which conform with the requirements of section 608 of the federal "Clean Air Act Amendments of 1990" to establish standards and requirements regarding the use and disposal of class I and class II ozone depleting compounds during the service, repair, or disposal of appliances and industrial process refrigeration. If federal training and certification requirements are adopted under section 609 of the federal "Clean Air Act Amendments of 1990" as of January 1, 1993, no state training and certification requirements shall be adopted. If the federal regulations are not adopted, then such state regulations shall contain training and certification requirements substantially similar to those required under section 609 of the federal "Clean Air Act Amendments of 1990". Such regulations shall also include provisions for the imposition and collection of a certification fee sufficient to implement the training, certification, and enforcement requirements of this paragraph (f) .

(g) Repealed.

(h) Rules that are necessary for the imposition and collection of a fee for registering as stationary sources refrigeration systems and other appliances that contain a minimum of one hundred pounds or use a drive system of one hundred horsepower or more and use ozone-depleting compounds. The fee set by the commission shall reflect the direct and indirect costs of registering refrigeration systems and appliances; however, such fee shall not exceed seventy-five dollars per unit and shall not exceed a maximum of three hundred dollars per facility.

(12) The commission shall promulgate such rules and regulations as are necessary to implement the provisions of the emission notice and construction permit programs and the minimum elements of a permit program provided in Title V of the federal act.

(13) (a) The commission shall promulgate rules and regulations requiring motor vehicles which have manufacturer-installed diagnostic systems for emission controls to have such diagnostic systems inspected and maintained consistent with section 202 of the federal act as part of the periodic inspection of vehicle emission control systems required pursuant to this article.

(b) This subsection (13) shall take effect July 1, 1994.

(14) The commission shall repeal the clean vehicle fleet program mandated by section 246 of the federal act and shall replace such program if required by federal law. Nothing in this subsection (14) shall be deemed to impair the availability of the income tax credit established pursuant to section 39-22-516, C.R.S.

(15) The commission shall promulgate rules and regulations as are necessary to provide an emission reduction incentive permit fee credit program which provides for a permit fee reduction in the year following the year in which a permittee achieves an early reduction in emissions of hazardous air pollutants, consistent with the provisions of section 112 of the federal act and section 25-7-114.3.

(16) The commission shall give priority to and take expeditious action upon consideration of the following:

(a) A request by a unit of local government to investigate and resolve air quality problems associated with a source;

(b) A request by a unit of local government for inclusion of a locally developed air pollution control measure in a state implementation plan;

(c) A request by a unit of local government that the commission consider local concerns respecting environmental and economic effects in the context of a proceeding where the state is targeting a source for imposition of additional air pollution controls.

(17) (a) Not later than December 31, 2002, and no less frequently than every five years thereafter, the commission shall conduct rule-making hearings to approve an update to the emission inventories from state and federal public land management agency activities on public lands resulting in emissions of any criteria pollutant, including surrogates or precursors for that pollutant, that affect any mandatory class I federal areas in Colorado by reducing visibility in such areas. At a minimum, such inventories shall report on emissions from the sources set forth in paragraph (d) of this subsection (17) .

(b) The commission shall ensure that the division prepares inventories for all state land management agencies with jurisdiction over state lands, including, without limitation, the state land board, the department of agriculture, and the department of natural resources, to provide an inventory of emissions from land management activities that are sources of pollutant emissions that may affect any mandatory class I federal area in Colorado by reducing visibility in such areas; except that the commission shall exempt from the inventory requirement any sources or categories of sources that it determines to be of minor significance.

(c) The commission shall use the emission inventories provided under this subsection (17) to develop control strategies for reducing emissions within the state as a component of the visibility long-term strategies for inclusion in the state implementation plan and for inclusion in any environmental impact statement or environmental assessment required to be performed under the federal "National Environmental Policy Act of 1969", 42 U.S.C. secs. 4321 to 4347.

(d) The rule-making hearing held to approve the inventories provided under this subsection (17) shall require public participation and shall require the reporting of both current emissions and projected future emissions, over at least a five-year period, from the following sources on public land that affect any mandatory class I federal areas in Colorado:

(I) Stationary source emissions, based on existing air pollution emission notices filed with the division;

(II) Mobile sources utilizing state lands, excluding state and federal highways;

(III) Paved and unpaved roads;

(IV) Fires on public lands from all sources;

(V) Biogenic sources, including emissions from flora and fauna.

(e) Each inventory provided under this subsection (17) shall state the basis and methodology used to accumulate the data and shall be based upon data that are:

(I) Developed no later than three years prior to the submittal; and

(II) No more than five years old.

(18) Upon petition by any person or on its own motion, for good cause shown, the commission may determine that the emission inventory of any criteria pollutant, including a surrogate or precursor for that pollutant, for a region of the state is inadequate for purposes of commission rule-making or adjudications in connection with development of the state implementation plan, selection of pollution control strategies, attribution of emissions to sources or categories of sources, or findings of adverse impacts. If, after conducting a public hearing in accordance with the rule-making provisions of the "State Administrative Procedure Act", article 4 of title 24, C.R.S., the commission finds that the emission inventory should be revised to take into consideration existing credible studies or scientific data in order to reasonably attribute emissions to source categories, it shall direct that such revision be performed prior to a final rule-making or adjudication.

(19) The commission may coordinate with the United States secretary of the interior and the United States secretary of agriculture to develop air quality management plans consistent with this article for federal lands pursuant to 16 U.S.C. sec. 530, 16 U.S.C. sec. 1604, and 43 U.S.C. sec. 1712.

(20) The commission may, within existing resources:

(a) Analyze a range of residential, commercial, and industrial biomass equipment for air emissions standards;

(b) Identify biomass equipment that meets the emissions standards; and

(c) Publicly post a statement of the parameters for equipment fueled by biomass that is smaller than one million British thermal units, as defined in section 8-20-201 (1.3) , C.R.S., per hour and include a list of biomass equipment that meets the emissions standards.

## 25-7-105.1. Federal enforceability.

(1) To the extent that any provision of this article or any standard or regulation promulgated pursuant thereto is not required by Part C (prevention of significant deterioration) , Part D (nonattainment) , or Title V (minimum elements of a permit program) of the federal act, or is not required by section 111 of the federal act, or is not required for sources to participate in the early reduction program of section 112 of the federal act, or is not required for sources to be excluded as a major source under this article, or is otherwise more stringent than other requirements of the federal act, such provision, standard, or regulation is hereby declared to be adopted under powers reserved to the state of Colorado pursuant to section 116 of the federal act. Any such provision, standard, or regulation adopted exclusively under state authority shall not constitute part of the state implementation plan.

(2) Whenever the division or commission grants relief to an owner or operator of a new or

modified stationary source from that part of a state standard or regulation which is not required by Part C (prevention of significant deterioration) , Part D (nonattainment) , or Title V (minimum elements of a permit program) of the federal act, or is not required by section 111 of the federal act, or is not required for sources to participate in the early reduction program of section 112 of the federal act, or is not required for sources to be excluded as a major source under this article, or which is otherwise more stringent than other requirements of the federal act and is not included as part of the state implementation plan, such relief shall be governed exclusively by the laws of this state and the regulations of the commission.

(3) To the extent any term or condition contained in any permit issued pursuant to this article is not required by Part C (prevention of significant deterioration) , Part D (nonattainment) , or Title V (minimum elements of a permit program) of the federal act, or is not required by section 111 of the federal act, or is not required for sources to participate in the early reduction program of section 112 of the federal act, or is not required for sources to be excluded as a major source under this article, or is otherwise more stringent than other requirements of the federal act, such term or condition shall be subject to enforcement exclusively under the laws of this state and the regulations of the commission.

## 25-7-106. Commission - additional authority.

(1) Except as provided in sections 25-7-130 and 25-7-131, the commission shall have maximum flexibility in developing an effective air quality control program and may promulgate such combination of regulations as may be necessary or desirable to carry out that program; except that such program and regulations shall be consistent with the legislative declaration set forth in section 25-7-102. Such regulations may include, but shall not be limited to:

(a) Classification and, as appropriate, reclassification of the state into attainment, nonattainment, and unclassifiable areas, and division of the state into such control regions or areas as may be necessary or desirable for effective administration of this article;

(b) Classification and definition of different degrees or types of air pollution;

(c) Emission control regulations that are applicable to the entire state, that are applicable only within specified areas or zones of the state, or that are applicable only when a specified class of pollution is present;

(d) Development of a high altitude performance adjustment program for motor vehicles to the extent authorized by section 215 of the federal act;

(e) Development of a control or prohibition respecting the use of a fuel or fuel additives in a motor vehicle or motor vehicle engine to the extent authorized by section 211(c) of the federal act if, based on sound scientific data, the commission finds that a measurable reduction in ambient concentrations of criteria pollutants or other pollutants shall occur.

(2) The commission may hold public hearings, issue notice of hearings, issue subpoenas requiring the attendance of witnesses and the production of evidence, administer oaths, and take such testimony as it deems necessary, all in conformity with article 4 of title 24, C.R.S., and with sections 25-7-110 and 25-7-119.

(3) The commission may adopt such rules and regulations in conformity with article 4 of title 24, C.R.S., governing procedures before the commission as may be necessary to assure that hearings before the commission will be fair and impartial.

(4) (a) In the event the commission, after hearing, finds and determines that a particular style or model of automobile air pollution control device is not sufficiently effective to justify the continued connection and operation of such device, the commission shall so notify the department of revenue; thereafter, all devices of such particular style or model shall be exempt from the provisions of section 42-4-314, C.R.S.

(b) Repealed.

(4.1) Repealed.

(5) The commission may exercise all incidental powers necessary to carry out the purposes of this article.

(6) The commission may require the owner or operator, or both, of any air pollution source to:

(a) Establish and maintain reports as prescribed by the commission;

(b) Install, use, and maintain monitoring equipment or methods as prescribed by the commission;

(c) Record, monitor, and sample emissions in accordance with such methods, at such locations, at such intervals, and in such manner as the commission shall prescribe;

(d) Provide such other information as the commission may require.

(7) (a) The commission is specifically authorized and directed to develop a program to apply and enforce every relevant provision of the state implementation plan and every relevant emission control strategy to minimize emissions, including the impacts of actions by significant users of prescribed fire, including federal, state, and local government, and private land managers that are significant users of prescribed fire. The program developed by the commission under this subsection (7) shall include, but not be limited to, the imposition of any fees necessary to administer the program, including the recovery of costs by the state for the evaluation of planning documents pursuant to subsection (8) of this section, and the imposition of penalties pursuant to section 25-7-122.

(b) The general assembly hereby finds, determines, and declares that the Grand Canyon visibility transport commission's recommendations for improving western vistas report identified the emissions from fire, both wildfire and prescribed fires, as likely to have the single greatest impact on visibility at class I areas through the year 2040. The emissions from fire, both wildfire and prescribed fire, are an important episodic contributor to visibility impairing aerosols. The Grand Canyon visibility transport commission report identified that significant amounts of visibility impairment result from activities on federal lands, from mobile sources, and from Mexico.

(c) The general assembly further finds, determines, and declares that emissions from grassland and forest fires have substantial episodic impacts on ambient air quality throughout the state and are a major source of visibility impairment over which this state has jurisdiction but has not yet developed a comprehensive program to reduce such impairment.

(d) The general assembly further finds, determines, and declares that the standard in its statement of legislative purpose in section 25-7-102 of the "Colorado Air Pollution Prevention and Control Act" requiring the use of all practical methods that are technologically feasible and economically reasonable so as to reduce, prevent, and control air pollution is an appropriate standard to apply in relation to air pollution emissions resulting from the use of prescribed fire in grassland and forest management.

(e) This subsection (7) and subsection (8) of this section are adopted pursuant to section 118 of the federal act and shall be construed to exercise the full extent of the state's authority as granted by the provisions of said federal act. The federal government, as the only landowner of its size in the state and the only landowner in the state other than the state government itself that routinely prepares plans involving the management of grassland and forest lands using prescribed fire, is appropriately subject to the requirements of this section pertaining to review and approval of planning documents.

(f) Persons owning or managing large parcels of land who significantly use prescribed fire as a grassland or forest management tool shall prepare plans addressing the use and role of prescribed fire and the air quality impacts resulting therefrom, and such plans are appropriately subject to the review requirements of this section. The state, by reviewing these types of plans, can achieve significant progress towards cooperatively reducing emissions from those lands that impact visibility in Colorado.

(g) As used in this subsection (7) and in subsection (8) of this section, the term "significant user of prescribed fire" means a federal, state, or local agency or significant management unit thereof or person that collectively manages or owns more than ten thousand acres of grasslands or forest lands within the state of Colorado and that uses prescribed fire. The adoption of a fire management plan by a local or county unit of government pursuant to section 30-11-124, C.R.S., does not constitute management for purposes of this section unless the county or local unit of government owns or manages more than ten thousand acres and is a significant user of prescribed fire. "Prescribed fire" means fire that is intentionally used for grassland or forest management,

362

regardless of whether the fire is caused by natural or human sources. Prescribed fire does not include open burning in the course of agricultural operations and does not include open burning for the purpose of maintaining water conveyance structures, unless the commission acts pursuant to section 25-7-123. The commission shall by rule exempt from the program developed pursuant to this subsection (7) those sources that have an insignificant impact on visibility and air quality.

(8) (a) The commission, in exercising the powers conferred by subsection (7) of this section and this subsection (8) , shall require all significant users of prescribed fire, including federal agencies for activities directly conducted by or on behalf of federal agencies on federal lands, to minimize emissions using all available, practicable methods that are technologically feasible and economically reasonable in order to minimize the impact or reduce the potential for such impact on both the attainment and maintenance of national ambient air quality standards and the achievement of federal and state visibility goals.

(b) (I) In order to ensure compliance with the requirements of paragraph (a) of this subsection (8) , significant users of prescribed fire shall submit planning documents to the commission. The commission shall then conduct a public hearing to review each planning document submitted relevant to achieving the goal of minimizing emissions and impacts as set forth in paragraph (a) of this subsection (8) . Only one hearing shall be held for each planning document. The commission shall hold a hearing and complete its review of the planning documents submitted by any significant user of prescribed fire within forty-five days of their receipt by the commission, unless otherwise agreed to by the significant user of prescribed fire.

(II) As used in this paragraph (b) , "planning documents" means documents that summarize the use of prescribed fire as a grassland or forest management tool and the associated discharge or release of air pollution and that demonstrate how compliance with the state standard expressed in section 25-7-102 shall be achieved. "Planning documents" shall include land management plans or a summary of the equivalent information that explains and supports the land management criteria evaluated and the decision to use prescribed fire as the fuel treatment method. Planning documents shall include a discussion of the alternatives considered and a discussion of how prescribed fire, if selected, minimizes the risk of wildfire.

(III) The commission shall have discretion to adopt rules governing the resubmission of planning documents to prevent such plans from becoming outdated.

(c) Following a public hearing, the commission shall comment and make recommendations to the significant user of prescribed fire regarding any changes to elements of the plan relating to the discharge or release of air pollutants that the commission finds necessary to comply with the state standard expressed in section 25-7-102.

## 25-7-106.1. Commission - duties - visibility standard - report. (Repealed)

## 25-7-106.3. Commission - duties - wood-burning stoves - episodic no-burn days - rules.

(1) The commission shall promulgate, no later than March 1, 1990, such combination of regulations as it may find to be cost-effective and consistent with the legislative declaration set forth in section 25-7-102 in order to establish limitations on the use of wood-burning stoves and fireplaces during those periods of time declared by the Colorado department of health to be a high pollution day. The department may declare a high pollution day based on experienced or anticipated excessive levels of carbon monoxide or particulates when air pollution standards are exceeded for particulates, carbon monoxide, or visibility. The limitations on the use of wood-burning stoves and fireplaces imposed pursuant to this section may include no-burn days, and such no-burn days shall be specific to the separate airsheds within the Denver-Boulder metropolitan area. Such limitations shall be applicable only in those portions of the counties of Adams, Arapahoe, Boulder, Denver, Douglas, and Jefferson which are located in the AIR program area, as such area is defined in section 42-4-304 (20) , C.R.S. Such regulations shall exclude areas above

seven thousand feet unless the commission determines that particulates from wood burning in such areas are contributing to the brown cloud. Such regulations shall not apply to any person who utilizes wood-burning stoves or fireplaces as the primary source of heat in such person's place of residence. Such regulations shall permit exemptions for wood-burning stoves that meet Phase III emissions standards. For the purposes of this section, "Phase III" means wood stove standards adopted by the commission which are more strict than existing wood stove standards. The regulations promulgated pursuant to this subsection (1) shall not be effective until July 1, 1990. (2) No regulation promulgated by the commission pursuant to subsection (1) of this section shall apply within any municipality which has in effect on January 1, 1990, an ordinance mandating restricted use of wood-burning stoves and fireplaces during those periods of time declared by the Colorado department of health to be high pollution days.

## 25-7-106.5. Commission - duties - alternative fuels - street-cleaning - time-shifting - reports. (Repealed)

## 25-7-106.7. Regulations - studies - AIR program area.

The authority of the commission to promulgate regulations pursuant to section 25-7-106.3 is limited to the program area, as defined in section 42-4-304 (20) , C.R.S., and such regulations shall not apply outside the program area.

## 25-7-106.8. Colorado clean vehicle fleet program.

(1) As used in this section, unless the context otherwise requires:
(a) "Alternative fuel" means compressed natural gas, propane, ethanol, or any mixture of ethanol containing eighty-five percent or more ethanol by volume with gasoline or other fuels, electricity, or any other fuels, which fuels may include, but are not limited to, clean diesel and reformulated gasoline so long as these other fuels make comparable reductions in carbon monoxide emissions and brown cloud pollutants as determined by the air quality control commission. "Alternative fuel" does not include any fuel product, as defined in section 25-7-139 (3) , that contains or is treated with methyl tertiary butyl ether (MTBE) .
(b) to (f) Repealed.
(2) to (7) Repealed.

## 25-7-106.9. Alternative fuels financial incentive program. (Repealed)

## 25-7-107. Commission - area classification.

(1) The commission shall, within one hundred eighty days after June 20, 1979, and thereafter from time to time, if evidence indicates a need, review the current classification of any attainment, nonattainment, or unclassifiable area within the state and shall revise the classification of any such area or part thereof which is calculated by air quality modeling or shown by monitored data or other reliable methods to be invalid.
(2) The commission shall, upon application by the owner or operator of any existing or proposed stationary source, review the designation of any attainment, nonattainment, or unclassifiable area within the state and shall revise the designation of any such area or part thereof which is calculated by air quality modeling or shown by monitored data or other reliable methods to be invalid.
(2.5) Whenever monitoring data for any pollutant for which an area is designated nonattainment demonstrate that the national ambient air quality standard for that pollutant has been attained in accordance with the criteria required under the federal act, the division and commission shall take expeditious action to redesignate the area as attainment for that pollutant.
(3) In making any determination regarding the attainment, nonattainment, or unclassifiable

designation of any area within the state with regard to particulate matter, the commission shall consider and, if consistent with the requirements of Part D of the federal act, discount the effects of particulate matter not of a size or substance to adversely affect public health or welfare.

(4) All revisions of designations shall be submitted to the administrator of the United States environmental protection agency.

## 25-7-108. Commission to promulgate ambient air quality standards.

(1) In addition to the other powers and duties enumerated in this article, the commission shall have the power to adopt, promulgate, amend, and modify such standards for the quality of ambient air as may be appropriate or necessary to carry out the purposes of this article, including, but not limited to:

(a) Standards which describe the maximum concentrations of specifically described pollutants that can be tolerated, consistent with the protection of the good health of the public at large; such standards may differ for different parts of the state as may be necessitated by variations in altitude, topography, climate, or meteorology;

(b) Standards which describe the air quality goals that are to be achieved by control programs within specified periods of time; such standards may be either statewide or restricted to specified control areas; and

(c) Standards which describe varying degrees of pollution of ambient air.

(2) Ambient air standards shall include such requirements for test methods and procedures as will assure that the samples of ambient air tested are representative of the ambient air.

(3) Notwithstanding any provision of this article to the contrary, no provision of this article shall preclude the commission from adopting ambient air quality standards which are more stringent than the national ambient air quality standards.

(4) Ambient standards may only be implemented and enforced through permit terms and conditions or regulations promulgated to meet requirements for state implementation plans.

## 25-7-109. Commission to promulgate emission control regulations.

(1) (a) Except as provided in sections 25-7-130 and 25-7-131, as promptly as possible, the commission shall adopt, promulgate, and from time to time modify or repeal emission control regulations which require the use of effective practical air pollution controls:

(I) For each significant source or category of significant sources of air pollutants;

(II) For each type of facility, process, or activity which produces or might produce significant emissions of air pollutants.

(b) The requirements and prohibitions contained in such regulations shall be set forth with as much specificity and clarity as is practical. Upon adoption of an emission control regulation under subparagraph (II) of paragraph (a) of this subsection (1) for the control of a specific facility, process, or activity, such regulation shall apply to the exclusion of other emission control regulations adopted pursuant to subparagraph (I) of paragraph (a) of this subsection (1) ; prior to such adoption, the general regulations adopted pursuant to subparagraph (I) of paragraph (a) of this subsection (1) shall be applicable to such facility, process, or activity. In the formulation of each emission control regulation, the commission shall take into consideration the following:

(I) The state policy regarding air pollution, as set forth in section 25-7-102;

(II) Federal recommendations and requirements;

(III) The degree to which altitude, topography, climate, or meteorology in certain portions of the state require that emission control regulations be more or less stringent than in other portions of the state;

(IV) The degree to which any particular type of emission is subject to treatment, and the availability, technical feasibility, and economic reasonableness of control techniques;

(V) The extent to which the emission to be controlled is significant;

(VI) The continuous, intermittent, or seasonal nature of the emission to be controlled;

(VII) The economic, environmental, and energy costs of compliance with such emission control regulation;

(VIII) Whether an emission control regulation should be applied throughout the entire state or only within specified areas or zones of the state, and whether it should be applied only when a specified class or type of pollution is concerned.

(2) Such emission control regulations may include, but shall not be limited to, regulations pertaining to:

(a) Visible pollutants;

(b) Particulates;

(c) Sulfur oxides, sulfuric acids, hydrogen sulfide, nitrogen oxides, carbon oxides, hydrocarbons, fluorides, and any other chemical substance;

(d) Odors, except for livestock feeding operations that are not housed commercial swine feeding operations as defined in section 25-8-501.1 (2) (b) ;

(e) Open burning activity;

(f) Organic solvents;

(g) Photochemical substances;

(h) Hazardous air pollutants.

(3) Emission control regulations adopted pursuant to this section shall include, but shall not be limited to, regulations pertaining to the following facilities, processes, and activities:

(a) Incinerator and incinerator design;

(b) Storage and transfer of petroleum products and any other volatile organic compounds;

(c) Activities which frequently result in particulate matter becoming airborne, such as construction and demolition operations;

(d) Specifications, prohibitions, and requirements pertaining to fuels and fuel additives, such as tetraethyl lead;

(e) Wigwam waste burners, pulp mills, alfalfa dehydrators, asphalt plants, and any other industrial or commercial activity which tends to emit air pollutants as a by-product;

(f) Industrial process equipment;

(g) Industrial spraying operations;

(h) Airplanes;

(i) Diesel-powered machines, vehicles, engines, and equipment;

(j) Storage and transfer of volatile compounds and hazardous or toxic gases or other hazardous substances which may become airborne.

(4) The commission shall promulgate appropriate regulations pertaining to hazardous air pollutants.

(5) The commission shall promulgate appropriate regulations setting conditions and time limitations for periods of start-up, shutdown, or malfunction or other conditions which justify temporary relief from controls. Operations of any air pollution source during periods of start-up, shutdown, and malfunction shall not constitute representative conditions for the purpose of a performance or compliance test.

(6) The commission shall establish test methods and procedures for determining compliance with emission control regulations promulgated under this section and, in so doing, shall, to the maximum degree consistent with the purposes of this article, consider the test methods and procedures established by the United States environmental protection agency and shall adopt such test methods and procedures as shall minimize the possibility of inconsistency or duplication of effort.

(7) All regulations promulgated pursuant to this section shall conform with the provisions of part 5 of this article concerning asbestos control.

(8) (a) Notwithstanding any other provision of this section, the commission shall not regulate emissions from agricultural, horticultural, or floricultural production such as farming, seasonal crop drying, animal feeding operations that are not housed commercial swine feeding operations as defined in section 25-8-501.1 (2) (b) , and pesticide application; except that the commission shall regulate such emissions if they are "major stationary sources", as that term is defined in 42 U.S.C. sec. 7602 (j) , or are required by Part C (prevention of significant deterioration) , Part D

(nonattainment) , or Title V (minimum elements of a permit program) , or are participating in the early reduction program of section 112 of the federal act, or is not required by section 111 of the federal act, or is not required for sources to be excluded as a major source under this article.

(b) Nothing in paragraph (a) of this subsection (8) , as amended by House Bill 05-1180, as enacted at the first regular session of the sixty-fifth general assembly, shall be construed as changing the property tax classification of property owned by a horticultural or floricultural operation.

(9) (a) The commission shall adopt a procedure consistent with the federal environmental protection agency requirements for determining when there has been a net significant emissions increase which results in a major modification that subjects a source to the permitting requirements of the prevention of significant deterioration program or the nonattainment area new source review. The commission's procedure shall also prohibit sources from circumventing the new source review requirements in a manner consistent with the federal environmental protection agency guidance. Such procedure shall be the same for both the prevention of significant deterioration program and the nonattainment area new source review program and shall not apply to hazardous air pollutants. Such net emissions increase procedure shall be as described in paragraph (b) of this subsection (9) , unless and until the federal environmental protection agency requires otherwise or unless after January 1, 1998, the commission:

(I) Undertakes a collaborative process with the affected industries to determine the cost and emission impacts associated with any proposed changes in this procedure;

(II) Reviews at least three years of emissions increases and decreases under the procedures described in paragraph (b) of this subsection (9) ;

(III) Delivers reports on the matters required in subparagraphs (I) and (II) of this paragraph (a) to the general assembly for its review;

(IV) Determines through rule-making that an applicability procedure for major modifications more stringent than that described in paragraph (b) of this subsection (9) is equitable when considering minor, area, and mobile source controls; and

(V) Determines through rule-making that such more stringent applicability procedure is necessary to attain and to maintain the national ambient air quality standards.

(b) The procedure for determining when there has been a net significant emissions increase shall be consistent with requirements of the federal environmental protection agency and:

(I) Such requirements shall apply only if there is, in the first instance, a significant emissions increase from an individual proposed project or modification. If the individual proposed project or modification will not result in a significant emissions increase, it shall be exempt from the prevention of significant deterioration program and the nonattainment area new source review requirements.

(II) If a project or modification is not exempt under subparagraph (I) of this paragraph (b) , each pollutant for which the project results in a significant emissions increase shall be subject to the prevention of significant deterioration program or the nonattainment area new source review requirements only if the sum of all source-wide, non-de minimis, contemporaneous, and creditable emissions increases and decreases of that pollutant or that regulated precursor exceed applicable significance levels. Each specific regulated precursor shall be considered independently in determining applicable significance levels.

(III) In determining the non-de minimis net emissions increase during the contemporaneous period, the commission's procedures shall be consistent with the federal environmental protection agency's review procedure for determining net emissions increases and decreases. Non-de minimis increases shall exclude all increases which would be exempt under commission rules from a requirement to obtain a construction permit under section 25-7-114.2.

## 25-7-109.1. Emergency rule-making.

In addition to all other powers of the commission, the commission, pursuant to section 24-4-103 (6) , C.R.S., shall have the authority to conduct emergency rule-making for the purpose of adopting an interim emission control regulation to apply for a specified period of time in place of an existing emission control regulation or to create an emission control regulation whenever federal regulations have been adopted and become effective pursuant to section 111 of the federal act and which add to the list of categories of stationary sources, or add new or more restrictive standards of performance for new sources, or whenever federal regulations are adopted and effective pursuant to section 112 of the federal act and which modify or adopt MACT or GACT for new or existing sources, and such regulations are required to be implemented by the states. Interim emission control regulations adopted pursuant to this section shall not be effective for a period greater than twelve months from the date of adoption.

## 25-7-109.2. Small business stationary source technical and environmental compliance assistance program - repeal.

(1) The commission shall promulgate such rules, regulations, and procedures as are necessary to establish and administer the Colorado small business stationary source technical and environmental compliance assistance program consistent with the requirements of the federal act.

(2) There is hereby created a compliance advisory panel, which shall:

(a) Render advisory opinions concerning the effectiveness of the small business stationary source technical and environmental compliance assistance program, difficulties encountered, degree of enforcement, and severity of penalties;

(b) Make periodic reports to the governor and the administrator of the United States environmental protection agency;

(c) Review information for small business stationary sources to assure such information is understandable by the layperson; and

(d) Advise the small business stationary source technical and environmental compliance assistance program, which shall serve as the secretariat for the development and dissemination of such reports and advisory opinions.

(3) The panel shall consist of:

(a) Two members who are not owners or representatives of owners of small business stationary sources, appointed by the governor to represent the general public;

(b) Two members who are owners or who represent owners of small business stationary sources, one appointed by the speaker of the house of representatives and one appointed by the minority leader of the house of representatives;

(c) Two members who are owners or who represent owners of small business stationary sources, one appointed by the president of the senate and one appointed by the minority leader of the senate; and

(d) One member appointed by the executive director of the department of public health and environment to represent such department.

(4) The terms of those members of the panel initially appointed by the governor, the speaker of the house of representatives, and the minority leader of the house of representatives shall expire on January 31, 1994. The terms of those members initially appointed by the president of the senate, the minority leader of the senate, and the executive director of the department of public health and environment shall expire on January 31, 1995. Thereafter, members of the panel shall serve for terms of three years, such terms to commence on February 1 of the year of appointment. Vacancies occurring during the term of office of any member of the panel shall be filled for the unexpired portion of the regular term in the same manner as for the original appointment.

(5) In furtherance of the small business stationary source technical and environmental compliance assistance program established as provided in subsection (1) of this section, the department of public health and environment shall serve as ombudsman for small business stationary sources. The department shall carry out the ombudsman duties using personnel outside of the air pollution control division.

(6) The general assembly finds, determines, and declares that this section is enacted for purposes of compliance with the provisions of section 507 of the federal act, 42 U.S.C. sec. 7661f. Subsections (2) , (3) , and (4) of this section and this subsection (6) are repealed, effective

September 1, 2026. Prior to said repeal, the compliance advisory panel shall be reviewed by a legislative committee of reference, designated pursuant to section 2-3-1201, C.R.S., to conduct the review pursuant to section 2-3-1203, C.R.S.

## 25-7-109.3. Colorado hazardous air pollutant control and reduction program - rules.

(1) The commission shall promulgate appropriate regulations pertaining to hazardous air pollutants as defined in section 25-7-103 (13) which are consistent with this section and the requirements of and emission standards promulgated pursuant to section 112 of the federal act, including any standard required to be imposed under section 112(r) of the federal act. The commission shall monitor the progress and results of the risk studies performed under section 112 of the federal act to show that Colorado's hazardous air pollutant control and reduction program is consistent with the national strategy.

(2) The commission may only promulgate regulations pertaining to hazardous air pollutants as defined in section 25-7-103 (13) in accordance with this section. In order to minimize additional regulatory and compliance costs to the state's economy, any program created by the commission pursuant to this section shall contain a provision which exempts those sources or categories of sources which it determines to be of minor significance from the requirements of the program. Consistent with the provisions of section 25-7-105.1, the commission shall authorize synthetic minor sources of hazardous air pollutants by the issuance of construction permits or prohibitory rules or other regulations. Such permits, rules, or regulations shall only be as stringent as necessary to establish synthetic minor status. The commission shall expeditiously implement this subsection (2) to assure that all sources may be able to timely qualify as a synthetic minor source, thereby avoiding the costs of the operating permit program.

(3) (a) (I) As soon as adequate scientific, technological, and hazardous air pollutant emissions information is available, the commission may promulgate regulations for the control of hazardous air pollutants utilizing Colorado GACT or Colorado MACT technology-based emission reduction requirements, as defined in section 25-7-103 (6.7) and (6.8) .

(II) The division may establish schedules of compliance of up to five years leading to final compliance for any such regulation, which shall be enforced through regulations or conditions in construction permits issued pursuant to section 25-7-114.2 or 25-7-114.5. In determining any schedule of compliance, the division shall consider the current availability of technology, costs of compliance, and the consequence of delay to the public health or environment or economy.

(III) The division shall issue its determination of Colorado GACT or Colorado MACT and the compliance schedule in writing.

(IV) Within thirty calendar days after receipt of a determination by the division requiring installation of Colorado GACT or Colorado MACT and the compliance schedule, pursuant to this subsection (3) , a source may appeal such a determination or compliance schedule by filing with the commission a written petition requesting a hearing to review the determination on a de novo basis.

(V) Such hearing shall allow the parties to present evidence and argument on all issues and to conduct cross-examination required for full disclosure of the facts and shall otherwise be conducted in accordance with section 25-7-119.

(b) This section shall only apply to sources emitting a hazardous air pollutant identified in the list established or amended pursuant to subsection (5) of this section which:

(I) Are not included in categories or subcategories of sources listed or proposed to be listed by the environmental protection agency under section 112 of the federal act and thus will not be required to comply with GACT or MACT under the federal act, as defined in section 25-7-103 (12.1) and (16.5) ; or

(II) Are included in categories or subcategories of sources listed or proposed to be listed under section 112 of the federal act and which have:

(A) Levels of emissions of hazardous air pollutants listed under section 112 (b) of the federal act

369

which are below thresholds established under the federal act and thus will not be required to comply with GACT and MACT under the federal act and as defined in section 25-7-103 (12.1) and (16.5) ; except that this section shall not apply to a source included in a category or subcategory for which a lesser quantity emission rate has been proposed or adopted under section 112 of the federal act; or

(B) Hazardous air pollutant emissions above a threshold level of the substance listed under subparagraph (II) of paragraph (a) and paragraph (b) of subsection (5) of this section.

(b.1) The commission may recognize similarities among regulated sources or apply, when appropriate, previous control requirements established by the commission in making a determination about the need for such regulation under this subsection (3) . The commission shall also consider fundamentally different factors between sources in making these determinations.

(c) The commission shall designate by regulation those classes of minor or insignificant sources of emissions of hazardous air pollutants which are exempt from the requirements of this section because their emissions of hazardous air pollutants will result in an inconsequential risk to public health.

(d) (I) A source subject to the requirements of this section may be exempt from installation of Colorado MACT or Colorado GACT or any Colorado health-based requirement if the division makes a determination that an alternative level of control, including no emission controls, will result in an inconsequential risk to public health.

(II) The division shall issue its determination of a source's request for exemption under this paragraph (d) in writing within sixty days of receipt of a complete application for an exemption and shall publish notice of its determination by at least one publication in a newspaper of general distribution in the area of the source requesting the exemption.

(III) Within thirty calendar days after receipt of a determination by the division of a request for exemption by a source under this paragraph (d) , the source or any person may appeal such determination by filing with the commission a written petition requesting a hearing to review the exemption request on a de novo basis.

(IV) Such hearing shall allow the parties to present evidence and argument on all issues and to conduct cross-examination required for full disclosure of the facts and shall otherwise be conducted in accordance with section 25-7-119.

(e) Any source as defined in section 112(i) of the federal act, and regulations promulgated thereunder, that participates in the early reduction program pursuant to section 112(i) of the federal act, or this article, shall be exempt from the requirements of this section for the same period of time exemptions from federal requirements or requirements under this article are allowed under the early reduction program.

(f) This section shall not apply to sources subject to national emission standards for hazardous air pollutants (NESHAP) established by the administrator pursuant to the federal act, but only for those emissions for which a NESHAP is established.

(g) This section shall not impose requirements on sources included in categories or subcategories of sources which are listed in section 112(n) of the federal act which are inconsistent with the timing of studies or assessments conducted under or definitions set forth in section 112(n) of the federal act.

(4) (a) (I) On or after the risk-based studies required under sections 112(k) (3) , 112(o) , and 112(f) of the federal act are completed and received by the commission, the commission may adopt regulations pertaining to those sources identified as emitting hazardous air pollutants regulated under this section which may include additional emission reduction requirements to address any residual risk of health effects with respect to actual persons living in the vicinity of sources after installation of technology-based controls. Imposition of such requirements may be made upon a determination by the commission that operation of sources without health-based controls does not or will not represent an inconsequential threat to public health. Regulations as finally adopted pursuant to this subsection (4) may apply on a source-specific basis.

(II) Repealed.

(b) Repealed.

(c) Subject to paragraph (a) of this subsection (4) , for existing sources not subject to regulation under section 25-7-114.3, or not subject to regulation as a modified source, the commission may promulgate health-based regulations on a source-by-source basis, with the exceptions specified in paragraph (d) of this subsection (4) .

(d) The commission may recognize similarities among regulated sources or apply, when appropriate, previous control requirements established by the commission pursuant to paragraph (a) of this subsection (4) in making a determination about the need for such regulation under this subsection (4) . The commission shall also consider fundamentally different factors between sources in making these determinations.

(e) The commission may establish schedules of compliance leading to final compliance for any regulation promulgated pursuant to this subsection (4) .

(f) A hearing conducted by the commission under this subsection (4) shall be conducted in accordance with section 25-7-110 or 25-7-119 or article 4 of title 24, C.R.S., as applicable.

(g) In reaching a determination under this subsection (4) , the commission shall give consideration to the technical availability of methods of compliance, the costs of compliance, and the consequences of delay. The commission shall also consider cost-benefit analysis and risk-benefit analysis pursuant to section 24-4-103 (4.5) , C.R.S.

(h) Temporary exceptional authority. (I) (A) This subparagraph (I) shall apply until such time as the commission is authorized to act pursuant to paragraph (a) of this subsection (4) . If the executive director of the department of public health and environment finds that a source in a category or subcategory of sources listed or proposed to be listed under section 112 of the federal act for which MACT or GACT is not scheduled for proposal until after 1997 and presents an unacceptable threat of actual health effects, then the executive director may direct the commission to evaluate and, as necessary, study such actual health effects. If the commission finds by a preponderance of the evidence that waiting until the source would be required to install GACT or MACT under section 112 of the federal act will cause an unacceptable incremental threat of actual health effects to persons living in the vicinity of such source, the commission may promulgate regulations for the control of hazardous air pollutants for the source. The control regulations may include the least restrictive control that will adequately protect the public, including but not limited to: Chemical substitution, pollution prevention, work process modifications, additional control technologies, or Colorado MACT or GACT. In promulgating Colorado GACT or MACT for the source, the commission shall consider and be as consistent as possible with GACT or MACT under section 112 of the federal act, minimization of duplicative capital expenditures and minimization of substantial reconstruction time. The commission shall provide a schedule of compliance leading to final compliance which considers matters identified in paragraphs (c) , (e) , (f) , and (g) of this subsection (4) .

(B) Any source which is required to install Colorado MACT or GACT under regulations promulgated pursuant to sub-subparagraph (A) of this subparagraph (I) only and which subsequently is required to install federal MACT or GACT that is significantly different than Colorado MACT or GACT and imposes a significant capital cost on the source, then the general assembly shall study and consider whether an operating permit fee credit or a state tax credit for the capital costs, or a percentage of the costs, is appropriate.

(II) Until such time as the commission is authorized to act pursuant to paragraph (a) of this subsection (4) and upon the recommendation of the executive director of the department of public health and environment, the governor may find, as expressed in an executive order, that after an existing source has installed Colorado or federal MACT or GACT, or Colorado MACT or GACT has been proposed for a new source or a modification of an existing source, the source presents an unacceptable threat of actual health effects. The governor may then direct the commission to evaluate and, as necessary, conduct studies on actual health effects. If the commission determines by a preponderance of the evidence that emissions of hazardous air pollutants by the source will cause an unacceptable threat of actual health effects to persons living in the vicinity of such source, the commission may then promulgate additional technology-based control regulations, pollution prevention, or health-based measures to protect the public health. The commission shall provide a schedule of compliance leading to final compliance which considers matters identified in paragraphs (c) , (e) , (f) , and (g) of this subsection (4) .

(III) This paragraph (h) shall remain effective only until such time as the commission acts pursuant to its authority under paragraph (a) of this subsection (4) .

(5) (a) The substances listed in or pursuant to section 112(b) of the federal act, and the following substances, are declared to be hazardous air pollutants and are subject to regulation by the commission under this section:

ChemicalAbstract

ServiceNumberChemical

(I) 50-18-0Cyclophosphamide
(II) 50-32-8Benzo(a) pyrene
(III) 52-24-4Tris(aziridinyl) -phosphinc sulfide
(IV) 52-24-4Thio-tepa
(V) 53-70-3Dibenz[a,h]anthracene
(VI) 55-98-11,4-butanediol dimethanesulphonate
(VII) 56-53-1Dirthylstulresterol
(VIII) 56-55-3Benz[a]anthracene
(IX) 70-25-7N-methyl-n-nitro-n-nitrosoguanidine
(X) 78-98-8Methylglyoxol
(XI) 115-28-6Chlorendic acid
(XII) 117-10-2Chrysazin
(XIII) 122-60-1Phenyl glycidyl ether
(XIV) 132-27-42-biphenylol sodium salt
(XV) 154-93-8Bischloroethyl nitrosourea
(XVI) 298-81-78-methoxypsoralen
(XVII) 299-75-2Treosulphan
(XVIII) 305-03-3Clorambucil
(XIX) 370-67-2Azactidine
(XX) 366-70-1Procarbazine hydrochloride
(XXI) 446-86-6Azathioprine
(XXII) 484-20-85-methoxypsoralen
(XXIII) 494-03-1Chlornaphazine
(XXIV) 590-96-5Methanol, (methyl-onn-azoxy)
(XXV) 607-57-82-nitrofluorene
(XXVI) 615-53-2N-nitroso-n-methylurethane
(XXVII) 817-09-4Trichlormethine
(XXVIII) 1188-47-2Nitrilotriacetic
acid, copper(2+) salt(1:1)
(XXIX) 1188-48-3Nitrilotriacetic
acid, magnesium salt(1:1)
(XXX) 1309-64-4Antimony oxide
(XXXI) 1317-98-2Valentinite
(XXXII) 1402-68-2Aflatoxins
(XXXIII) 2399-81-7Nitrilotriacetic acid,
beryllium salt(1:1)
(XXXIV) 2399-83-9Nitrilotriacetic acid,
barium salt(1:1)

(XXXV) 2399-85-1Nitrilotriacetic acid,
tripotassium salt
(XXXVI) 2399-86-2Nitrilotriacetic acid,
dipotassium salt
(XXXVII) 2399-87-3Nitrilotriacetic acid,
beryllium potassium salt(1:1)
(XXXVIII) 2399-88-4Nitrilotriacetic acid,
potassium magnesium salt(1:1:1)
(XXXIX) 2399-89-5Nitrilotriacetic acid,
potassium strontium salt(1:1:1)
(XL) 2399-94-2Nitrilotriacetic acid,
calcium salt(1:1)
(XLI) 2455-08-5Nitrilotriacetic acid,
calcium potassium salt(1:1:1)
(XLII) 2475-45-8Disperse blue 1
(XLIII) 2646-17-5C1 solvent orange2


(XLIV) 3130-95-8Nitrilotriacetic acid,
scandium (3+) salt (1:1)
(XLV) 3438-06-0Nitrilotriacetic acid,
neodymium (3+) salt (1:1)
(XLVI) 5064-31-3Nitrilotriacetic acid,
trisodium salt
(XLVII) 5522-43-01-nitropyrene
(XLVIII) 5798-43-6Nitrilotriacetic acid,
disodium salt, compound
with oxo (dihydrogen nit)
(XLIX) 7496-02-86-nitrochrysene
(L) 10042-84-9Nitrilotriacetic acid,
sodium salt (unspecified)
(LI) 10043-92-2Radon decay products
(LII) 10413-71-5Nitrilotriacetic acid,
erbium(3+) salt (3:1)
(LIII) 12412-52-1Senarmontite
(LIV) 12510-42-8Erionite
(LV) 13010-47-41-(2-chloroethyl) -3-
cyclohexyl-1-nitrosourea
(LVI) 13909-09-61,(2-chloroethyl) -3-(4
methyl-cyclohexyl) -1
nitrosourea
(LVII) 14695-88-6Nitrilotriacetic acid,
compound with iron
chloride, as /fecl3/
(LVIII) 14807-96-6Talc (containing
asbestos fibers)
(LIX) 14981-08-9Nitrilotriacetic acid,
calcium salt
(LX) 15414-25-2Nitrilotriacetic acid,
yttrium (3+) salt (1:1)
(LXI) 15467-20-6Nitrilotriacetic acid,
disodium salt
(LXII) 15663-27-1Cisplatin

(LXIII) 15844-52-7Nitrilotriacetic acid, copper (2+) complex

(LXIV) 15934-02-8Nitrilotriacetic acid, monoammonium salt

(LXV) 16448-54-7Nitrilotriacetic acid, iron (3+) complex

(LXVI) 16568-02-8Gyromitrin

(LXVII) 18105-03-8Nitrilotriacetic acid, mercury (2+) salt (2:3)

(LXVIII) 18432-54-7Nitrilotriacetic acid, cadmium (2+) complex

(LXIX) 18540-29-9Chromium compounds, hexavalent

(LXX) 18662-53-8Nitrilotriacetic acid, trisodium salt monohydrate

(LXXI) 18946-94-6Nitrilotriacetic acid, neodymium (3+) salt (1:1)

(LXXII) 18983-72-7Nitrilotriacetic acid, beryllium potassium salt (1:1)

(LXXIII) 18994-66-6Nitrilotriacetic acid, monosodium salt

(LXXIV) 19010-73-2Nitrilotriacetic acid, aluminium (3+) complex


(LXXV) 19456-58-7Nitrilotriacetic acid, inidium (3+) complex

(LXXVI) 22965-60-2Nitrilotriacetic acid, nickel (3+) complex

(LXXVII) 23214-92-8Adrianmycin

(LXXVIII) 23255-03-0Nitrilotriacetic acid, disodium salt, monohydrate

(LXXIX) 23319-51-9Nitrilotriacetic acid, cobalt (3+) complex

(LXXX) 23555-96-6Nitrilotriacetic acid, potassium strontium salt
(2:4:1)

(LXXXI) 23555-98-8Nitrilotriacetic acid, calcium potassium salt
(2:1:4)

(LXXXII) 25817-24-7Nitrilotriacetic acid, potassium salt

(LXXXIII) 28444-53-3Nitrilotriacetic acid, monopotassium salt

(LXXXIV) 28027-38-0Nitrilotriacetic acid, holmium salt

(LXXXV) 29027-90-5Nitrilotriacetic acid, cerium salt

(LXXXVI) 29507-58-2Nitrilotriacetic acid, zinc (3+) complex sodium salt

(LXXXVII) 32685-17-9Nitrilotriacetic acid, triammonium salt

(LXXXVIII) 34831-02-2Nitrilotriacetic acid,

copper (2+) hydrogen complex
(LXXXIX) 34831-03-3Nitrilotriacetic acid,
nickel (2+) hydrogen
complex
(XC) 36711-58-7Nitrilotriacetic acid,
manganese salt
(XCI) 42397-64-81,6-dinitropyrene
(XCII) 42397-65-91,8-dinitropyrene
(XCIII) 46242-44-8Nitrilotriacetic acid,
antimony (3+) complex
(XCIV) 50618-02-7Nitrilotriacetic acid,
tricadium (2+) complex
(XCV) 53108-47-7Nitrilotriacetic acid,
copper (2+) complex sodium
salt
(XCVI) 53108-50-2Nitrilotriacetic acid,
cobalt (3+) hydrogen
complex
(XCVII) 53818-84-1Nitrilotriacetic acid,
tin (2+) salt
(XCVIII) 54749-90-5Chlorozotocin
(XCIX) 57835-92-44-nitropyrene
(C) 59865-13-3Cyclosporin A
(CI) 60034-45-9Nitrilotriacetic acid,
calcium sodium salt
(1:1:1)
(CII) 60153-49-33-(n-nitrosomethylamino)
propionitrile


(CIII) 61017-62-7Nitrilotriacetic acid,
iron (2+) complex sodium
salt (1:1:1)
(CIV) 62450-06-0trp-p-1
(CV) 62450-07-1trp-p-2
(CVI) 64091-91-4Ketone, 3-pyridyl3-
(n-methyl-n-nitrosoamino)
propyl
(CVII) 67730-10-32-aminodipyrido[1,2-a3,2-
d]imidazole
(CVIII) 66730-11-42-amino-6-
methyldipyrido[1,2-a32-
d]imidazole
(CIX) 68006-83-72-amino-3-methyl-
9h-pyrido[2,3-b]indole
(CX) 69679-89-6Nitrilotriacetic acid,
calcium salt (2:3)
(CXI) 71484-80-5Nitrilotriacetic acid,
copper (2+) complex
ammonium salt
(CXII) 72629-49-3Nitrilotriacetic acid,
dilithium salt
(CXIII) 73772-91-5Nitrilotriacetic acid,

magnesium salt
(CXIV) 76180-96-62-amino-3-
methylimadazo[4,5-
f]quinoline
(CXV) 79217-60-0Cyclosporine
(CXVI) 79849-02-8Nitrilotriacetic acid,
lead (2+) salt (1:1)
(CXVII) 79915-08-5Nitrilotriacetic acid,
lead (2+) potassium salt
(1:1:1)
(CXVIII) 79915-09-6Nitrilotriacetic acid,
lead (2+) salt (2:3)
(CXIX) 80508-23-2N-nitrosonornicotine
(CXX) 86892-89-9Nitrilotriacetic acid,
disodium ammonium salt
(CXXI) 92474-39-0Nitrilotriacetic acid,
trisilver salt
(CXXII) 92988-11-9Nitrilotriacetic acid,
strontium sodium salt
(CXXIII) 108171-26-2Chlorinated paraffins
(c12, 60% chlorine)
(CXXIV) 309-00-2 Aldrin
(CXXV) 60-57-1Dieldrin
(CXXVI) 55-18-5N-nitrosodiethylamine
(CXXVII) 319-84-6 L-hexachlorocyclohexane
(CXXVIII) 608-73-1Hexachlorocyclohexane-tech
(CXXIX) 7644-41-01,4 dichloro-2-butene
(CXXX) 924-16-3N-nitroso-d-n-butyl-amine


(b) The commission may promulgate a regulation which amends by adding to, or deleting from, the list of hazardous air pollutants subject to regulation under this section within the state which are not listed as hazardous air pollutants under the federal act. In amending the list of hazardous air pollutants in paragraph (a) of this subsection (5) , the commission shall utilize the same standards and criteria which section 112 of the federal act requires the administrator to utilize in amending the list of hazardous air pollutants under the federal act.
(c) The commission shall by regulation establish de minimis emission levels for each hazardous air pollutant beneath which levels emissions are considered to be of minor significance.
(d) The rule-making authorized under paragraphs (b) and (c) of this subsection (5) shall include a hearing to allow the parties to present evidence and argument on all issues and to conduct cross-examination required for full disclosure of the facts and shall otherwise be conducted in accordance with section 25-7-119.
(e) Proceedings of the commission to amend the list of hazardous air pollutants under paragraph (b) of this subsection (5) shall be conducted on a substance-by-substance basis and there shall not be a consolidation of proceedings wherein more than five substances are considered for listing as a hazardous air pollutant in one proceeding.

## 25-7-109.4. Air quality science advisory board - created - repeal. (Repealed)

## 25-7-109.6. Accidental release prevention program.
(1) The commission may promulgate such rules, regulations, and procedures as are necessary to

establish and implement an accidental release prevention program consistent with and no sooner than the requirements of section 112 (r) of the federal act, including release prevention, detection, and correction requirements which may include monitoring, record-keeping, reporting, training, vapor recovery, secondary containment, and other design, equipment, work practice, and operational requirements.

(2) For purposes of this section:

(a) "Accidental release" means an unanticipated emission of a regulated substance or other extremely hazardous substance, defined pursuant to the federal act, into the ambient air from a stationary source;

(b) "Regulated substance" means those substances listed by the administrator pursuant to section 112 (r) (3) of the federal act;

(c) "Stationary source" means any buildings, structures, equipment, installations, or substance emitting stationary activities:

(I) Which belong to the same industrial group;

(II) Which are located on one or more contiguous properties;

(III) Which are under the control of the same person (or persons under common control) ; and

(IV) From which an accidental release may occur.

(d) "Threshold quantity" shall have the same meaning as defined in section 112 (r) of the federal act.

(3) As appropriate, rules, regulations, and procedures promulgated pursuant to this section shall:

(a) Consider the use, operation, repair, replacement, and maintenance of equipment to monitor, detect, inspect, and control such releases, including training of persons in the use and maintenance of such equipment and the conduct of periodic inspections;

(b) Include procedures and measures for emergency response after an accidental release of a regulated substance in order to protect human health and the environment;

(c) Cover storage, as well as operations;

(d) As appropriate, recognize differences in size, operations, processes, classes, and categories of sources and the voluntary actions of such sources to prevent accidental releases and respond to such releases;

(e) Require the owner or operator of stationary sources at which a threshold quantity of a regulated substance is present to prepare and implement a risk management plan to detect and prevent or minimize accidental releases of such substances from the stationary source, and to provide a prompt emergency response to any such releases in order to protect human health and the environment. Such plan shall provide for compliance with the requirements of this subsection (3) and shall also include each of the following:

(I) A hazard assessment, to be updated periodically and registered with the division, the United States environmental protection agency, and other appropriate local agencies, to assess the potential effects of an accidental release of any regulated substance;

(II) A program for preventing accidental releases of regulated substances, including safety precautions and maintenance, monitoring, and employee training measures to be used at the sources; and

(III) A response program providing for specific actions to be taken in response to an accidental release of a regulated substance so as to protect human health and the environment, including procedures for informing the public and local agencies responsible for responding to accidental releases, emergency health care, and employee training measures.

(f) Coordinate notification, reporting, and response requirements between federal, state, and local agencies to avoid duplicate notification and reporting requirements and to integrate emergency response plans.

(4) In addition to any other action taken, when the division determines that there may be an imminent and substantial endangerment to the human health or welfare or the environment because of an actual or threatened accidental release of a regulated substance, the division may take action pursuant to sections 25-7-112 and 25-7-113.

(5) The implementation and effectiveness of this section shall be contingent on the receipt of

funding from the federal government in sufficient amount to totally fund the division's costs in implementing this section; except that the small business stationary source technical and environmental compliance assistance program shall be funded as provided in section 25-7-114.7.

## 25-7-110. Commission - procedures to be followed in setting standards and regulations.

(1) Prior to adopting, promulgating, amending, or modifying any ambient air quality standard authorized in section 25-7-108, or any emission control regulation authorized in section 25-7-109, or any other regulatory plans or programs authorized by sections 25-7-105 (1) (c) or 25-7-106, the commission shall conduct a public hearing thereon as provided in section 24-4-103, C.R.S. Notice of any such hearing shall conform to the requirements of section 24-4-103, C.R.S., but such notice shall be given at least sixty days prior to the hearing, and shall include each proposed regulation, and shall be mailed to all persons who have filed with the commission a written request to receive such notices.

(2) Any person desiring to propose a regulation differing from the regulation proposed by the commission or to propose a revision of limited applicability, pursuant to section 25-7-117, to the commission's proposal shall file such other proposal with the commission not less than twenty days prior to the hearing, and, when on file, such proposal shall be open for public inspection.

(3) Witnesses at the hearing shall be subject to cross-examination by or on behalf of the commission and by or on behalf of persons who have proposed regulations pursuant to subsection (2) of this section.

(4) Rules and regulations promulgated pursuant to this article shall not take effect until after they have been published in accordance with section 24-4-103, C.R.S., or on such later date as is stated in such rules and regulations.

## 25-7-110.5. Required analysis of proposed air quality rules.

(1) In addition to the requirements of section 25-7-110.8, whenever the commission proposes a rule, the technical secretary of the commission shall provide to the public upon request at cost, at the time the notice for public rule-making is published, a proposed rule-making packet containing:

(a) A memorandum of notice, as required by subsection (3) of this section;

(b) The actual language of the proposed rule;

(c) A statement describing the fiscal and economic impact of the proposed rule, as required by subsection (4) of this section;

(d) A statement describing the potential justification for terms differing from federal requirements, as required by subsection (5) of this section;

(e) On or before July 1, 1997, a statement describing the risk analysis, if required by the general assembly under subsection (6) of this section;

(f) The range of regulatory alternatives, including the no-action alternative, to be considered in adopting the proposed rule; and

(g) Any other concise background material that would assist the interested and affected public in understanding the impact of the proposed rule.

(1.5) As used in this section, "rule" includes an amendment to an existing rule.

(2) The requirements of subsections (1) (c) to (1) (f) , (3) (g) , and (4) of this section shall not apply to any rule-making packet for any commission rule, and the requirements of subsections (3) (g) and (4) of this section shall not apply to any commission rule, which adopts by reference applicable federal rules or which rule is adopted to implement prescriptive state statutory requirements, where the commission is allowed no significant policy-making options, or which rule will have no regulatory impact on any person, facility, or activity.

(3) Whenever the commission proposes a rule, the technical secretary of the commission, in cooperation with the proponent of the rule, shall provide a memorandum of notice containing:

(a) An explanation of the proposed rule;

(b) A disclosure of materials contained in the proposed rule;

(c) A preliminary plan for meetings with the commission staff on the proposed rule;

(d) An explanation of the problem sought to be remedied by the proposed rule;

(e) An analysis of how the proposed rule solves the problem delineated in paragraph (d) of this subsection (3) ;

(f) An explanation of the process that was used to develop the proposed rule;

(g) An initial analysis of the economic effects of the proposed rule pursuant to subsection (4) of this section;

(h) An explanation of the substantive differences with federal requirements and the requirements of Utah, Arizona, and New Mexico, where relevant;

(i) An explanation of how the proposed rule may be implemented;

(j) Whether there will be any time constraints on the regulated community and state agencies as a result of implementation or a delay in implementation of the proposed rule;

(k) A contact person or persons who may provide additional information on the proposed rule to interested persons; and

(l) A no-action analysis.

(4) (a) Before any permanent rule is proposed pursuant to this section, an initial economic impact analysis shall be conducted in compliance with this subsection (4) of the proposed rule or alternative proposed rules. Such economic impact analysis shall be in writing, developed by the proponent, or the division in cooperation with the proponent and made available to the public at the time any request for hearing on a proposed rule is heard by the commission. A final economic impact analysis shall be in writing and delivered to the technical secretary and to all parties of record five working days prior to the prehearing conference or, if no prehearing conference is scheduled, at least ten working days before the date of the rule-making hearing. The proponent of an alternative proposal will provide, in cooperation with the division, a final economic impact analysis five working days prior to the prehearing conference. The economic impact analyses shall be based upon reasonably available data. Except where data is not reasonably available, or as otherwise provided in this section, the failure to provide an economic impact analysis of any noticed proposed rule or any alternative proposed rule will preclude such proposed rule or alternative proposed rule from being considered by the commission. Nothing in this section shall be construed to restrict the commission's authority to consider alternative proposals and alternative economic impact analyses that have not been submitted prior to the prehearing conference for good cause shown and so long as parties have adequate time to review them.

(b) Before any emergency rule is adopted, any person may request that a regulatory analysis, as defined in section 24-4-103 (4.5) , C.R.S., be prepared and made available to the public five working days prior to the hearing, unless there is an imminent and serious hazard to health, welfare, or the environment.

(c) The proponent and the division shall select one or more of the following economic impact analyses. The commission may ask affected industry to submit information with regard to the cost of compliance with the proposed rule, and, if it is not provided, it shall not be considered reasonably available. The economic impact analysis required by this subsection (4) shall be based upon reasonably available data and shall consist of one or more of the following:

(I) Cost-effectiveness analyses for air pollution control that identify:

(A) The cumulative cost including but not limited to the total capital, operation, and maintenance costs of any proposed controls for affected business entity or industry to comply with the provisions of the proposal;

(B) Any direct costs to be incurred by the general public to comply with the provisions of the proposal;

(C) Air pollution reductions caused by the proposal;

(D) The cost per unit of air pollution reductions caused by the proposal; and

(E) The cost for the division to implement the provisions of the proposal; or

(II) Industry studies that examine the direct costs of the proposal on directly affected entities that may be either in the form of a business analysis (The regulatory impacts on the general business climate or subsets thereof) or an industry analysis (the regulatory impacts on specific industries) , including:

(A) The characteristics and current economic conditions of the impacted business or industry sector; and

(B) The projected impacts on the growth of the affected industry sectors with and without implementation of the proposal; and

(C) How the proposal may effect or alter the growth of the affected industry sector; and

(D) The direct cost of the proposal on the affected industry sector; or

(III) An economic impact analysis that:

(A) Identifies the industrial and business sectors that will be impacted by the proposal; and

(B) Quantifies the direct cost to the primary affected business or industrial sector; and

(C) Incorporates an estimate of the economic impact of the proposal on the supporting business and industrial sectors associated with the primary affected business or industry sectors.

(d) Repealed.

(e) The economic impact analysis required by this subsection (4) shall not consist of an analysis of any nonmarket costs or external costs asserted to occur notwithstanding compliance by a source with applicable environmental regulations.

(5) (a) Whenever the commission proposes any rule that exceeds the requirements of the federal act or differs from the federal act or rules thereunder, the commission shall make available in writing a copy of any such proposed rule and a detailed, footnoted explanation of the differences between the rule and the federal requirements.

(b) The written explanation required pursuant to paragraph (a) of this subsection (5) shall contain an explanation of the following information:

(I) Any federal requirements that are applicable to this situation with a commentary on those requirements;

(II) Whether the applicable federal requirements are performance-based or technology-based and whether there is any flexibility in those requirements, and if not, why not;

(III) Whether the applicable federal requirements specifically address the issues that are of concern to Colorado and whether data or information that would reasonably reflect Colorado's concern and situation was considered in the federal process that established the federal requirements;

(IV) Whether the proposed requirement will improve the ability of the regulated community to comply in a more cost-effective way by clarifying confusing or potentially conflicting requirements (within or cross-media) , increasing certainty, or preventing or reducing the need for costly retrofit to meet more stringent requirements later;

(V) Whether there is a timing issue which might justify changing the time frame for implementation of federal requirements;

(VI) Whether the proposed requirement will assist in establishing and maintaining a reasonable margin for accommodation of uncertainty and future growth;

(VII) Whether the proposed requirement establishes or maintains reasonable equity in the requirements for various sources;

(VIII) Whether others would face increased costs if a more stringent rule is not enacted;

(IX) Whether the proposed requirement includes procedural, reporting, or monitoring requirements that are different from applicable federal requirements and, if so, why and what the "compelling reason" is for different procedural, reporting, or monitoring requirements;

(X) Whether demonstrated technology is available to comply with the proposed requirement;

(XI) Whether the proposed requirement will contribute to the prevention of pollution or address a potential problem and represent a more cost-effective environmental gain; and

(XII) Whether an alternative rule, including a no-action alternative, would address the required standard.

(6) Repealed.

## 25-7-110.8. Additional requirements for commission to act under section 25-

# 7-110.5.

(1) In issuing any final rule intended to reduce air pollution, except for any rule that adopts by reference applicable federal rules, if the commission has no discretion under state law not to adopt the rules or to adopt any alternative rule, the commission shall make a determination that:

(a) Any rule promulgated under section 25-7-110.5 is based on reasonably available, validated, reviewed, and sound scientific methodologies and that all validated, reviewed, and sound scientific methodologies and information made available by interested parties has been considered. Such review may include internal organizational review and not peer review.

(b) Evidence in the record supports the finding that the rule shall result in a demonstrable reduction in air pollution to be addressed by the rule unless such rule is administrative in nature;

(c) On and after July 1, 1997, and in conformance with guidance from the general assembly to incorporate the recommendations of the task force established in section 25-7-110.5 (6) , evidence in the record supports the finding that the rule shall bring about reductions in risks to human health or the environment or provide other benefits that will justify the cost to government, the regulated community, and to the public to implement and comply with the rule;

(d) The commission shall choose an alternative that is the most cost-effective under the analysis required by section 25-7-110.5 (4) , provides the regulated community flexibility, and which achieves the necessary reduction in air pollution. The commission may reject the most cost-effective alternative and shall provide findings of fact detailing why the most cost-effective alternative is unacceptable.

(e) The selection of the regulatory alternative by the commission will maximize the air quality benefits of regulation pursuant to this article in the most cost-effective manner. For purposes of the required analyses under this section, prior to the completion of the rule-making required pursuant to section 25-7-110.5, no benefit (except for air pollution reductions) can be attributed to regulating a facility already operating in compliance with a permit issued pursuant to applicable law.

(1.5) As used in this section, "rule" includes an amendment to an existing rule.

(2) In the event that the commission and division fail to reasonably comply with requirements of section 25-7-110.5 or this section, the rule shall be void and unenforceable. Judicial review of agency action under this section or section 25-7-110.5 may only be obtained by parties to the rule-making hearing and can only be brought regarding deficiencies or issues alleging a failure to comply with the requirements in section 25-7-110.5 or this section raised during or before the hearing to afford the commission, its staff, or interested parties an opportunity to address the deficiencies or issues raised.

## 25-7-111. Administration of air quality control programs - directive - prescribed fire - review.

(1) The division shall administer and enforce the air quality control programs adopted by the commission. In furtherance of such responsibility of the division, the executive director of the department of public health and environment shall establish within the division a separate air quality control agency, the head of which shall be a licensed professional engineer or shall have a graduate degree in engineering or other specialty dealing with the problems of air quality control. Such person shall also have appropriate practical and administrative experience related to air quality control. Such person shall not be the technical secretary employed pursuant to section 25-7-105 (3) . Any potential conflict of interest of such person shall be adequately disclosed prior to appointment and as may from time to time arise. All policies and procedures followed in the administration and enforcement of the air quality control programs that have been adopted by the commission shall be subject to supervision by the state board of health.

(2) In addition to authority specified elsewhere in this article, the division has the power to:

(a) Conduct or cause to be conducted studies and research with respect to air pollution and the control, abatement, or prevention thereof, as requested by the commission;

(b) Collect data, by means of field studies and air monitoring conducted by the division or by individual stationary sources or individual indirect air pollution sources, and determine the nature and quality of existing ambient air throughout the state;

(c) Enter and inspect any property, premises, or place for the purpose of investigating any actual, suspected, or potential source of air pollution or ascertaining compliance or noncompliance with any requirement of this article or any order or permit, or term or condition thereof, issued or promulgated pursuant to this article; and the division may, at reasonable times, have access to and copy any record, inspect any monitoring equipment or method, or sample any emissions required pursuant to section 25-7-106 (6) or part 5 of this article; except that, if such entry or inspection is denied or not consented to and no emergency exists, the division is empowered to and shall obtain from the district or county court for the district or county in which such property, premises, or place is located a warrant to enter and inspect any such property, premises, or place prior to entry and inspection. The district and county courts of this state are empowered to issue such warrants upon a proper showing of the need for such entry and inspection. Any information relating to secret processes or methods of manufacture or production obtained in the course of the inspection or investigation shall be kept confidential; except that emission data shall not be withheld from the division as confidential. A duplicate of any analytical report or observation of an air pollutant by the division shall be furnished promptly to the person who is suspected of causing such air pollution.

(d) Furnish technical advice and services relating to air pollution problems and control techniques;

(e) Inform the appropriate governmental agency of the results of atmospheric tests conducted in its jurisdiction and notify the affected city, town, county, or city and county whenever tests establish that the ambient air or source of emission of smoke or air pollution fails to meet the standards established under this article;

(f) Designate one or more persons or agencies in any area of the state as an air pollution control authority as agent of the division to exercise and perform such powers and duties of the division as may be specified in such designation;

(g) Furnish such personnel to the commission as the commission may reasonably require to carry out its duties and responsibilities under this article;

(h) Certify, or otherwise designate, to any other agency or department of this state or of any other state or of the federal government that any facility, land, building, machinery, or equipment, or any part thereof, has been constructed, erected, installed, or acquired in conformity with the requirements of this state or of this article for control of air pollution or in conformity with the requirements for control of air pollution of any other state or the federal government;

(i) Require any source to furnish information which the division may reasonably require relating to emissions of the source or to any investigation authorized by this article. If such request for information is refused, the division is empowered to and may obtain from the district or county court for the district or county in which the source is located a subpoena to compel production of such information.

(3) Repealed.

(4) The division shall assure that any information obtained by the division which is entitled to protection as a trade secret under federal or Colorado law is kept confidential and protected against disclosure, except as required by the federal act.

(5) Repealed.

## 25-7-112. Air pollution emergencies endangering public health anywhere in this state.

(1) Whenever the division determines, after an investigation initiated either independently by the division or upon the request of an affected member of the public living or working in the vicinity of a suspected discharge, that any person is either engaging in any activity involving a significant risk of air pollution or is discharging or causing to be discharged into the atmosphere, directly or indirectly, any air pollutants and such activity or discharge constitutes a clear, present, and immediate danger to the environment or to the health of the public, or that any such activity or

discharge of air pollutants, if permitted to continue unabated, will result in a condition of clear, present, and immediate danger to the health of the public, the division shall:

(a) Issue a written cease-and-desist order to said person requiring immediate discontinuance of such activity or the discharge of such pollutant into the atmosphere, and, upon receipt of such order, such person shall immediately discontinue such activity or discharge; or

(b) Apply to any district court of this state for the district in which the said activity or discharge is occurring for a temporary restraining order, temporary injunction, or permanent injunction as provided for in the Colorado rules of civil procedure. Any such action in a district court shall be given precedence over all other matters pending in such district court. The institution of such injunction proceedings by the division shall confer upon said district court exclusive jurisdiction to determine finally the subject matter of the proceeding; or

(c) Both issue such a cease-and-desist order and apply for any such restraining order or injunction.

(1.5) (a) If, upon the request of a member of the public as described in subsection (1) of this section, the division chooses to investigate a suspected discharge, the division shall report the result of its investigation to the person who made the request and shall make such result public no later than sixty days after the completion of the investigation. If the person who made the request is dissatisfied with the result of the investigation, or if no investigation was made, such person may complain to the commission by petition.

(b) Upon receipt of a petition filed under paragraph (a) of this subsection (1.5), the commission shall promptly give notice of receipt of the petition to the owner or operator of the source of the alleged discharge, and, after considering the petition, the response, if any, of such owner or operator, and the response of the division, the commission shall respond to the petition within forty-five days after receipt by:

(I) Ordering the division to proceed with a new or further investigation under this section or section 25-7-113; or

(II) Denying the petition and stating the reasons for denial, which may include, but are not limited to, the lack of a substantial factual basis, the allegation of facts substantially similar to those at issue in a previous or currently pending investigation, or a finding that the petition was interposed for purposes of harassment or delay; or

(III) Providing an opportunity to submit additional factual information in support of, or in response to, the petition. The commission may require any new information to be submitted in writing, or it may convene an informal hearing as soon as is practicable.

(c) A hearing held pursuant to subparagraph (III) of paragraph (b) of this subsection (1.5) shall be subject to the following procedural requirements:

(I) The hearing shall be conducted as an informal hearing, and, in particular, no sworn testimony shall be taken except as the commission deems necessary to clarify the factual basis of the petition;

(II) Parties may represent themselves or be represented by agents who need not be attorneys;

(III) Notice of such hearing shall be given at least twenty days prior to the hearing;

(IV) The purpose of the hearing shall be to enable the commission to decide whether to order an investigation as provided in subparagraph (I) of paragraph (b) of this subsection (1.5); and

(V) To preserve the commission's role as an appellate body, the hearing shall not be used as a forum for determining the merits of the petition.

(2) (a) Whenever the division determines, after investigation, that the condition of the ambient air in any portion of this state constitutes a clear, present, and immediate danger to the environment or to the health of the public, or that any activity or discharge of air pollutants, if permitted to continue unabated, will result in a condition of clear, present, and immediate danger to the health of the public, and that the procedures available to the division under subsection (1) of this section will not adequately protect the public, it shall immediately notify the governor of its determination of either of such conditions, and it shall request the governor to declare a state of air pollution emergency in such portion of this state.

(b) Upon such notification and request by the division, the governor is empowered to declare a state of air pollution emergency in such portion of the state and to take any and all actions necessary to protect the health of the public in such portion of the state, including, but not limited to:

(I) Ordering a halt or curtailment of the movement of all motor vehicles except emergency vehicles; and

(II) Ordering a halt or curtailment of all operations, activities, processes, or conditions which he reasonably believes to be contributing to such emergency.

(c) From time to time, whenever appropriate, the governor, in cooperation with his department heads, shall develop or modify such plans as will be necessary or appropriate to control and abate the air pollution conditions most likely to require the exercise of the powers granted in paragraph (b) of this subsection (2) .

## 25-7-113. Air pollution emergencies endangering public welfare anywhere in this state.

(1) Whenever the division determines, after investigation, that any person is either engaging in any activity involving a significant risk of air pollution or is discharging or causing to be discharged into the atmosphere, directly or indirectly, any air pollutants and such activity or discharge does not constitute a clear, present, and immediate danger to the health of the public, but is of such a nature as to cause extreme discomfort or that it is an immediate danger to the welfare of the public because such pollutants make habitation of residences or the conduct of businesses subjected to the pollutants extremely unhealthy or disruptive, the division shall:

(a) Issue a written cease-and-desist order to said person requiring immediate discontinuance of such activity or the discharge of such pollutant into the atmosphere, and, upon receipt of such order, such person shall immediately discontinue such activity or discharge; or

(b) Apply to any district court of this state for the district in which the said activity or discharge is occurring for a temporary restraining order, temporary injunction, or permanent injunction as provided for in the Colorado rules of civil procedure. Any such action in a district court shall be given precedence over all other matters pending in such district court. The institution of such injunction proceedings by the division shall confer upon said district court exclusive jurisdiction to determine finally the subject matter of the proceeding; or

(c) Both issue such a cease-and-desist order and apply for any such restraining order or injunction.

## 25-7-114. Permit program - definitions.

As used in sections 25-7-114 to 25-7-114.7, unless the context otherwise requires:

(1) "Affected source" means a source that includes one or more fossil-fuel-fired combustion devices subject to emission reduction requirements or limitations under subchapter IV of the federal act or this article.

(2) "Construction permit" means the same as an "emission permit" as required under this section as it existed prior to July 1, 1992, and is the permit required under section 25-7-114.2 after July 1, 1992.

(3) "Major source" means any stationary source (or group of stationary sources which have the same two-digit standard industrial code, are located on one or more contiguous or adjacent properties, and are under common control) that:

(a) Subject to the provisions of section 112 (n) (4) of the federal act, emits or has the potential to emit considering enforceable controls, in the aggregate, ten tons per year or more of any hazardous air pollutant or twenty-five tons per year or more of any combination of hazardous air pollutants, or such lesser quantity of hazardous air pollutants as may be established pursuant to the federal act; or

(b) Directly emits, or has the potential to emit, one hundred tons per year or more of any air pollutant; or

(c) Meets any of the definitions of major source set forth in Part D of subchapter I of the federal act.

(4) "Potential to emit" means the maximum capacity of a stationary source to emit a pollutant

under its physical and operational design. Any physical or operational limitations on the capacity of the source to emit a pollutant, including air pollution control equipment and restrictions on hours of operation or on the type or amount of material combusted, stored, or processed, shall be treated as part of its design if the limitation or the effect it would have on emissions is enforceable and federally enforceable. Secondary emissions do not count in determining the potential to emit of a stationary source.

(5) "Schedule of compliance" means a schedule of required measures, including an enforceable sequence of actions or operations, leading to compliance with an applicable implementation plan, emission standard, emission limitation, emission prohibition, or emission control regulation.

(6) "Synthetic minor source" means, for purposes of this article, any source which would otherwise meet the definition of major source for any pollutants but for the existence of enforceable emission limitations contained in the permit or regulation applicable to that source.

## 25-7-114.1. Air pollutant emission notices.

(1) No person shall permit emission of air pollutants from, or construction or alteration of, any facility, process, or activity except residential structures from which air pollutants are, or are to be, emitted unless and until an air pollutant emission notice has been filed with the division with respect to such emission. An air pollutant emission notice shall be valid for a period of five years.

(2) All sources existing on or before December 31, 1992, shall file an updated air pollutant emission notice with the division on or before December 31, 1992. In addition, a revised emission notice shall be filed whenever a significant change in emissions, in processes, or in the facility is anticipated or has occurred. The revised air pollutant emission notice shall be valid for five years or until the underlying permit expires. The commission shall exempt those sources or categories of sources which it determines to be of minor significance from the requirement that an air pollutant emission notice be filed.

(3) The commission shall promulgate a list of air pollutants which are required to be reported in an air pollutant emission notice. Prior to the commission's promulgation of such a list of air pollutants to be reported in an air pollutant emission notice, sources shall report any emissions of the following which are in excess of de minimis quantities:

(a) Volatile organic compounds or precursors of air quality problems in Colorado as determined by the commission by regulation;

(b) Any pollutant regulated under section 25-7-109.3 or under section 112(b) of the federal act;

(c) Any pollutant for which a national primary ambient air quality standard has been promulgated under section 109 of the federal act;

(d) All extremely hazardous substances listed pursuant to section 302(a) (2) of the federal "Superfund Amendments and Reauthorization Act of 1986", 42 U.S.C. sec. 11002 (a) (2) .

(4) Each such notice shall specify the location at which the proposed emission will occur, the name and address of the person operating or owning such facility, process, or activity, the nature of such facility, process, or activity, and an estimate of the quantity and composition of the expected emission. The division shall make available at all air pollution control authority offices appropriate forms on which the information required by this section shall be furnished.

(5) (Deleted by amendment, L. 2001, p. 640, § 2, effective May 30, 2001.)

(6) (a) The fee for filing an air pollutant emission notice or amendment thereto under this section shall be one hundred fifty-two dollars and ninety cents. The moneys collected pursuant to this section shall be transmitted to the state treasurer, who shall credit the same to the stationary sources control fund created in section 25-7-114.7 (2) (b) (I) .

(b) Notwithstanding the amount specified for the fee in paragraph (a) of this subsection (6) , the commission by rule or as otherwise provided by law may reduce the amount of the fee if necessary pursuant to section 24-75-402 (3) , C.R.S., to reduce the uncommitted reserves of the fund to which all or any portion of the fee is credited. After the uncommitted reserves of the fund are sufficiently reduced, the commission by rule or as otherwise provided by law may increase the amount of the fee as provided in section 24-75-402 (4) , C.R.S.

## 25-7-114.2. Construction permits.

No person shall construct or substantially alter any building, facility, structure, or installation, except single-family residential structures, or install any machine, equipment, or other device, or commence the conduct of any such activity, or commence performance of any combinations thereof, or commence operations of any of the same which will or do constitute a new stationary source or a new indirect air pollution source without first obtaining or having a valid construction permit therefor from the division or commission, as the case may be; except that no construction permit shall be required for new indirect air pollution sources until regulations regarding construction permits for such sources have been promulgated by the commission, but in no event shall regulations governing indirect air pollution sources be more stringent than those required for compliance with the federal act and final rules and regulations adopted pursuant thereto. Any emission permit validly issued prior to July 1, 1992, pursuant to section 25-7-114, as said section existed prior to July 1, 1992, and in effect on or after July 1, 1992, shall be deemed to be a valid construction permit issued pursuant to this section. The commission shall designate by regulation those classes of minor or insignificant sources of air pollution which are exempt from the requirement for a permit because of their negligible impact on air quality.

## 25-7-114.3. Operating permits required for emission of pollutants.

(1) No person shall operate any of the following sources without first obtaining a renewable operating permit from the division for such source in a manner consistent with the requirements of this article and the federal act:

(a) Any affected source;

(b) Any major source;

(c) Any source required to comply with standards of performance for new stationary sources under section 111 of the federal act, unless otherwise exempted from permitting requirements pursuant to federal rules adopted in accordance with section 502 of the federal act;

(d) Any source subject to emission standards or regulations for hazardous air pollutants under section 112 of the federal act, unless otherwise exempted from federal permitting requirements pursuant to federal rules adopted in accordance with section 502 of the federal act;

(e) Any source required to have a permit pursuant to part 2 (prevention of significant deterioration program) or part 3 (attainment program) of this article, or Part C (prevention of significant deterioration of air quality) or Part D (plan requirements for nonattainment area) of subchapter I of the federal act;

(f) Any other source designated under federal law as requiring an operating permit.

(2) For those sources located in the state and participating in the federal early reductions program as specified in section 112 (i) (5) of the federal act, or the United States environmental protection agency's 33/50 program, or the state early reductions program as set forth in subsection (3) of this section, or any of such programs, the commission and division shall establish a system to credit emission permit fees to be established pursuant to sections 25-7-114.6 and 25-7-114.7 and to be assessed against such sources at a ratio of at least two-for-one for every ton of emissions reduced pursuant to the federal early reductions program, the United States environmental protection agency's 33/50 program, or the state early reductions program. A participating source shall be offered a one-time permit fee credit of two tons for each corresponding ton of its reduced emissions that are verified by the division. The permit fee credit shall be available in the year following the year in which the early reduction in emissions is achieved.

(3) The commission shall adopt the federal early reductions program specified in section 112 (i) (5) of the federal act and promulgate a state early reductions program which shall include the following elements:

(a) The state early reductions program shall be consistent with the federal early reductions program; and

(b) A six-year extension of compliance for existing sources with emission standards promulgated pursuant to section 112 (d) of the federal act if the source has achieved an emission reduction of ninety percent or more of hazardous air pollutants (ninety-five percent or more for hazardous air pollutants which are particulates) ; and

(c) If a source is granted a compliance extension, an alternative limitation to be established by permit to ensure continued achievement of the emission reduction; and

(d) Sources subject to and in compliance with an enforceable commitment under the federal and state early reductions programs shall be considered in compliance with all state regulations and requirements for hazardous air pollutants for the period of such commitment.

(4) For affected sources under Title V of the federal act:

(a) Operating permits and requirements for permit applications, compliance plans, and monitoring and reporting requirements shall be consistent with the provisions of Title IV as well as Title V of the federal act;

(b) In order to ensure reliability of electric power, nothing in the requirements pertaining to renewable operating permits required by this article shall be construed as requiring termination of operations of an electric utility steam generating unit for failure to have an approved permit or compliance plan;

(c) Nothing in this article shall be construed as affecting SO2 allowances given to sources affected under Title IV of the federal act.

## 25-7-114.4. Permit applications - contents - rules.

(1) The commission shall promulgate such regulations as may be necessary and proper for the orderly and effective administration of construction permits and renewable operating permits. Such regulations shall be in conformity with the provisions of this article and with federal requirements, shall be in furtherance of the policy contained in section 25-7-102, and shall implement, where applicable, permit and permit application contents, procedures, requirements, and restrictions with respect to the following:

(a) Identification and address of the owner and operator of the source or facility from which the emission or emissions are to be permitted;

(b) Location, quantity, and quality characteristics of the permitted emissions;

(c) Inspection, monitoring, record-keeping, and reporting requirements consistent with standard procedures, methods, and requirements established by the division;

(d) Deadlines for submitting permit applications and compliance plans, which, for applications for renewable operating permits, shall be no later than twelve months after the source becomes subject to an approved permit program. Deadlines for submitting permit applications for renewal of renewable operating permits shall be consistent with the requirements for filing such applications promulgated under the federal act but in no event earlier than required under the federal act.

(e) Contents of compliance plans to be submitted with renewable operating permit applications, which shall include schedules of compliance and progress reports at least every six months;

(f) Annual certifications of facility compliance with permit requirements, with prompt reporting of deviations from permit requirements;

(g) Submission of pertinent plans and specifications for the facility or source from which the emission is to be permitted;

(h) Restrictions on transfers of the permit;

(i) Procedures to be followed in the event of expansion or modification of the source or facility from which the emission occurs, or change in the quality, quantity, or frequency of the emission;

(j) Duration of the permit and renewal procedures. The duration of construction permits shall be until the renewable operating permit is issued. The duration of renewable operating permits is five years.

(k) Procedures to terminate, modify, or revoke and reissue permits for cause; procedures to revise permits, prior to renewal or termination, to incorporate applicable standards and regulations adopted after the issuance of such permit as expeditiously as practicable, but not later than eighteen months after promulgation of the applicable requirement, or to incorporate otherwise applicable standards and regulations in the permit; except that no such revision shall be required if the effective date of the standards or regulation occurs after the permit term expires, such revision shall be treated as a permit renewal, and the defense established under subsection (3) of this section shall apply until the permit amendment is complete;

(l) Procedures for incorporating emission limitations and other requirements from an applicable implementation plan, and other applicable requirements, into new or renewed permits;

(m) Procedures for notifying other contiguous states whose air quality may be affected by the emissions or that are within fifty miles of the source and for submitting comments and recommendations regarding the proposed permit;

(n) Procedures for modifying or amending permits, and procedures for authorizing any change within a permitted facility without requiring a permit revision, so long as any such change is not a modification under any provision of subchapter I of the federal act, and any such change does not exceed the emissions allowable under the permit, and advance notice is given to the division and the administrator. Such advance notice shall be no earlier than that required under regulations promulgated pursuant to the federal act. Failure of the division to respond by the day following the last day of such advance notice period allows the source to proceed with any such change.

(o) Procedures to make available to the public any permit application, compliance plan, permit, and monitoring or compliance report, subject to the provisions of section 25-7-119 (4) . If an applicant is required to submit information entitled to protection from disclosure, the applicant may submit such information separately.

(p) Procedures for issuing general permits after notice and an opportunity for hearing, covering numerous similar sources;

(q) Procedures for issuing single permits for a facility with multiple sources; and

(r) Requirements for permit applications, including a standard application form and criteria for determining in a timely fashion the completeness of applications.

(2) The division shall examine applications for and may issue, suspend, revoke, modify, deny, and otherwise administer all permits required under this article. Such administration shall be in accordance with the provisions of this article and regulations promulgated by the commission.

(3) (a) Compliance with all renewable operating permit terms and conditions shall be deemed compliance with section 25-7-114.3 and shall be deemed compliance with other applicable provisions of this article if:

(I) The permit includes the applicable requirements of such provisions; or

(II) The division or commission, in acting on the permit application, makes a determination that such other provisions are not applicable, and the permit includes the determination or a concise summary thereof. Such other provisions as are not applicable in each permit shall be identified upon the request of the permittee.

(b) Nothing in paragraph (a) of this subsection (3) shall alter or affect:

(I) The provisions of section 25-7-112 or 25-7-113 or section 303 of the federal act;

(II) The liability of an owner or operator of a source for any violation of applicable requirements prior to or at the time of permit issuance.

(4) For any permitted sand and gravel operation or crushed stone quarry or oil and gas well operation, if a breakdown of equipment or changes in market conditions require any additional crusher or screen or skid-mounted compressor or glycol dehydrator to be brought onto a site, the air pollutant emission notice filed under section 25-7-114.1 shall also serve as an application for a permit under the provisions of this section to continue operations at such a site with alternative or additional equipment until such permit is issued stating emission limitations.

## 25-7-114.5. Application review - public participation.

(1) Prior to submitting an application for a permit, the applicant may request and, if so requested, the division shall grant a planning meeting with the applicant. At such meeting, the division shall advise the applicant of the applicable permit requirements, including the information, plans, specifications, and data required to be furnished with the permit application.

(2) The division shall evaluate permit applications to determine, for construction permits, whether operation of the proposed new source at the date of start-up and for operating permits, whether the permitted emissions, will comply with all applicable emission control regulations, regulations for the control of hazardous pollutants, and requirements of part 2 or 3 of this article.

(3) The division shall also determine whether applications are for a new source activity that may have an impact upon areas which, as of the projected new source start-up date, are in compliance with national ambient air quality standards as of the date of the permit application, or for new source activity that may have an impact upon areas which, as of the projected new source start-up date, are not in compliance with national ambient air quality standards as of the date of the permit application.

(4) The division shall prepare its preliminary analysis regarding compliance, as set forth in subsection (2) of this section, and regarding the impact on attainment or nonattainment areas, as set forth in subsection (3) of this section, as expeditiously as possible. For construction permits not subject to part 2 of this article, such preliminary analysis shall be completed no later than sixty calendar days after receipt of a completed permit application. Applicants must be advised within sixty calendar days after receipt of any application, or supplement thereto, if and in what respects the subject application is incomplete. Upon failure of the division to so notify the applicant within sixty calendar days of its filing, the application shall be deemed complete. Applications for construction permits subject to part 2 of this article shall be approved or disapproved within twelve months of receipt of a complete application. Applications for renewable operating permits shall be approved or disapproved within eighteen months after the receipt of the completed permit application; except that those applications submitted within the first year after the effective date of the operating permit program shall be subject to a phased schedule for acting on such permit applications established by the division. The phased schedule shall assure that at least one-third of such permits will be acted on by the division annually over a three-year period. The commission may establish a phased schedule for acting on applications for which a deferral has been granted pursuant to the federal act. A timely and complete permit application operates as a defense to enforcement action for operating without a permit for the period of time during which the division or the commission is reviewing the application and until such time as the division or the commission makes a final determination on the permit application; except that this defense to an enforcement action shall not be available to an applicant which files a fraudulent application.

(5) For those types of projects or activities for which a construction permit application has been filed, defined, or designated by the commission as warranting public comment with respect thereto, the division shall, within fifteen calendar days after it has prepared its preliminary analysis, give public notice of the proposed project or activity by at least one publication in a newspaper of general distribution in the area in which the proposed project or activity, or a part thereof, is to be located or by such other method that is reasonably designed to ensure effective general public notice. The division shall also during such period of time maintain in the office of the county clerk and recorder of the county in which the proposed project or activity, or a part thereof, is located a copy of its preliminary analysis and a copy of the application with all accompanying data for public inspection. The division shall receive and consider public comment thereon for a period of thirty calendar days thereafter.

(6) (a) For any construction permit application subject to the requirements of a new or modified major source in a nonattainment area, or for prevention of significant deterioration as provided in part 2 of this article, or for any application for a renewable operating permit, within fifteen calendar days after the issuance of its preliminary analysis, the division shall:

(I) Forward to the applicant written notice of the applicant's right to a formal hearing before the commission with respect to the application; and

(II) Give public notice of the proposed source or modification and the division's preliminary analysis thereof by at least one publication in a newspaper of general distribution in the area of the proposed source or modification, or by such other method that is reasonably designed to ensure effective general public notice. Such notice shall advise of the opportunity for a public hearing for interested persons to appear and submit written or oral comments to the commission on the air quality impacts of the source or modification, the alternatives to the source or modification, the control technology required, if applicable, and other appropriate considerations. Any such notice shall be printed prominently in at least ten-point bold-faced type. The division shall receive and consider any comments submitted.

(b) If within thirty calendar days of publication of such public notice the applicant or an interested person submits a written request for a public hearing to the division, the division shall transmit such request to the commission along with the application, the division's preliminary analysis, and any written comments received by the division, within five calendar days of the end of such thirty-day period. The commission shall, within sixty calendar days after receipt of the application, comments, and analysis, unless such greater time is agreed to by the applicant and the division, hold a public hearing to elicit and record the comment of any interested person regarding the sufficiency of the preliminary analysis and whether the permit application should be approved or denied. At least thirty calendar days prior to such public hearing, notice thereof shall be mailed by the commission to the applicant, printed in a newspaper of general distribution in the area of the proposed source or modification, and submitted for public review with the county clerk and recorder of the county wherein the project or activity is proposed.

(7) (a) Within thirty calendar days following the completion of the division's preliminary analysis for applications for construction permits not subject to part 2 of this article, or within thirty calendar days following the period for public comment provided for in subsection (5) of this section, or for applications for construction permits subject to part 2 of this article and for renewable operating permits, if a hearing is held, within the appropriate time period established pursuant to this article, the division or the commission, as the case may be, shall grant or deny the permit application. Any permit required pursuant to this article shall be granted by the division or the commission, as the case may be, if it finds that:

(I) The source or activity will meet all applicable emission control regulations and regulations for the control of hazardous air pollutants;

(II) The source or activity will meet the requirements of part 2 or 3 of this article, if applicable;

(III) For construction permits, the source or activity will meet any applicable ambient air quality standards and all applicable regulations;

(III.5) For renewable operating permits, the source or activity will meet all applicable regulations; and

(IV) For renewable operating permits, the United States environmental protection agency has not made a timely objection to issuance of such permit pursuant to the federal act.

(b) Failure of the division or commission, as the case may be, to grant or deny the permit application or permit renewal application within the time prescribed shall be treated as a final permit action for purposes of obtaining judicial review in the district court in which the source is located, to require that action be taken on such application by the commission or division, as appropriate, without additional delay.

(c) If an applicant has submitted a timely and complete application for a renewable operating permit required by this article, including renewals, but final action has not been taken on such application, and, if required to have a construction permit, such construction permit is in place and valid, the source's failure to have a renewable operating permit shall not be a violation of this article, unless the delay in final action was due to the failure of the applicant to timely submit information required or requested by the division to process the application.

(8) If the division denies a permit or imposes conditions upon the issuance of a permit which are contested by the applicant or if the division revokes a permit pursuant to subsection (12) of this section, the applicant may request a hearing before the commission. The hearing shall be held in accordance with sections 25-7-119 and 24-4-105, C.R.S. The commission may, after review of the evidence presented at the hearing, affirm, reverse, or modify the decision of the division but shall, in any event, assure that all the requirements of subsections (6) and (7) of this section are met.

(9) Renewable operating permits shall summarize existing operating restrictions pursuant to section 25-7-114.4 (3) .

(10) A permit amendment will not be required to authorize a change in practice which is otherwise

permitted pursuant to this article, the state implementation plan, or the federal act merely because an existing permit does not address the practice. Changes in industrial practices and procedures that are not inconsistent with the terms of a renewable operating permit can be made without seeking any change to the terms of said permit.

(11) An order of the division or commission shall be final upon issuance. Any participant in the public comment process and any other person who could obtain judicial review under applicable law shall have standing for purposes of seeking review of any final order of the commission or division regarding applications, renewals, or revisions of any permits. The public participation requirements of subsections (5) and (6) of this section shall apply to all renewable operating permit applications, revisions, and renewals.

(12) (a) A permitted entity shall notify the division within fifteen days after the commencement of any activity for which a construction permit has been issued. Within one hundred eighty days after commencement of operation for which a construction permit has been issued, the source shall demonstrate to the division compliance with the terms and conditions of the construction permit or the division may, pursuant to rules that are adopted by the commission based upon the results of the study conducted under section 25-7-114.7 (2) (a) (V) , inspect the project or activity to determine whether or not the terms and conditions of the construction permit have been properly satisfied. At the end of one hundred eighty days after the commencement of operation, the division must:

(I) Revoke the construction permit; or

(II) Continue the construction permit, if applicable; or

(III) Notify the owner or operator that the source has demonstrated compliance with the construction permit.

(b) For those sources subject to the renewable operating permit program, a renewable operating permit will be issued within the appropriate time periods if all requirements for a renewable operating permit are met by the source. The construction permit requirements shall remain in effect until the renewable operating permit is issued.

(12.5) (a) (I) Except for sources involved in agricultural, horticultural, or floricultural production such as farming, seasonal crop drying, animal feeding, or pesticide application, upon determination by the division that the criteria set forth in paragraph (b) of this subsection (12.5) applies to a source that is not required to obtain a renewable operating permit, the division may reopen such construction permit for the purpose of imposing any or all of the following additional terms and conditions:

(A) Enhanced record-keeping requirements;

(B) Enhanced emissions and ambient monitoring requirements;

(C) Operating and maintenance requirements; and

(D) Emission control requirements pursuant to section 25-7-109.3.

(II) Any such condition which is contested by the permittee may be reviewed by the commission in accordance with the provisions of subsection (7) of this section.

(b) With the exception of those sources involved in agricultural, horticultural, or floricultural production such as farming, seasonal crop drying, animal feeding, and pesticide application, a source's construction permit may be reopened for cause for the purposes of paragraph (a) of this subsection (12.5) only upon a determination by the division that the location of the source is significant in terms of its proximity to residential or business areas, and one or more of the following criteria apply to the permitted source:

(I) The control equipment utilized by the source requires an unusually high degree of maintenance or operational sensitivity when compared to control equipment in general; or

(II) The design characteristics of the source require an unusually high degree of maintenance or operational sensitivity when compared to the design characteristics of all sources in general; or

(III) The application of the control equipment utilized is unique or untested; or

(IV) The operational variability of the source may impact the effectiveness of the controls; or

(V) The emissions from the source will threaten public health, as determined pursuant to section 25-7-109.3.

(c) Nothing in paragraph (a) or (b) of this subsection (12.5) , as amended by House Bill 05-1180, as enacted at the first regular session of the sixty-fifth general assembly, shall be construed as changing the property tax classification of property owned by a horticultural or floricultural operation.

(13) The commission shall, wherever practicable, promulgate regulations for renewable operating permit application requirements that combine requirements for construction permits with renewable operating permits to avoid duplicative efforts by the source and the division.

(14) (Deleted by amendment, L. 2010, (HB 10-1042) , ch. 209, p. 909, § 3, effective September 1, 2010.)

(15) Repealed.

(16) (a) If the division experiences a backlog in processing air quality permit applications caused by an occasional need that is seasonal, irregular, or fluctuating in nature, and the department determines or reasonably expects that, as a result, permits would not be issued within statutory time frames, the division shall make available to sources that are not subject to permitting under part C of the federal act the option to have the air quality modeling that is submitted with the applicant's air permit application reviewed for acceptance as demonstrating compliance by a contract consultant selected by the division in lieu of the review being conducted by division staff.

(b) The division shall select and contract with nongovernmental air quality modeling engineers to perform air quality modeling reviews of applicants who choose contract consultant review of their air quality permit modeling. The division is not subject to the requirements of the "Procurement Code", articles 101 to 112 of title 24, C.R.S., in selecting and contracting with the consultants. The division shall review and exclude from consideration as a contract air quality modeling consultant any contractors with a conflict of interest regarding air quality permit applications. Applicants that choose consultant review of their air quality modeling are responsible for both the consultant's costs associated with the air modeling review as well as the division's costs associated with the review and determination of the air permit application, to be paid to the division. The division shall transfer the money to the state treasurer, who shall credit it to the stationary sources control fund created in section 25-7-114.7 (2) (b) (I) .

(c) The division shall use the results of the modeling conducted pursuant to paragraph (b) of this subsection (16) for purposes of the division's permit application analysis.

## 25-7-114.6. Emission notice - fees.

(1) The commission shall designate by regulations those classes of minor or insignificant sources of air pollution which are exempt from the requirement for an emission notice or the payment of an emission notice filing fee because of their negligible impact upon air quality.

(2) An air pollution emission notice shall be deemed to run with the land. The moneys collected pursuant to this section and sections 25-7-403 and 25-7-510 shall be remitted to the state treasurer, who shall credit the same to the stationary sources control fund created in section 25-7-114.7 and subject to the provisions of said section.

(3) The general assembly shall direct the commission to adjust any fees imposed by this section so that the revenues approximate the annual appropriations to the division to carry out its duties under this subsection (3) with respect to stationary sources.

## 25-7-114.7. Emission fees - fund.

(1) As used in this section, unless the context otherwise requires:

(a) Indirect and direct costs include, but are not limited to:

(I) Reviewing and acting upon any application for such a permit;

(II) Implementing and enforcing the terms and conditions of any such permit (not including court costs or other legal costs associated with any enforcement action) ;

(III) Emissions and ambient monitoring;

(IV) Preparing generally applicable regulations or guidance;

(V) Modeling, analyses, and demonstrations;

(VI) Preparing inventories and tracking emissions; and

(VII) Establishing and administering a small business stationary source technical and environmental compliance program, pursuant to section 25-7-109.2.

(b) (I) "Regulated pollutant" means:

(A) A volatile organic compound;

(B) Each pollutant regulated under section 25-7-109 or section 111 of the federal act;

(C) Each pollutant regulated under section 112 (b) of the federal act;

(D) Each pollutant for which a national primary ambient air quality standard has been promulgated, except for carbon monoxide;

(II) The term "regulated pollutant", for the purpose of assessing fees, shall not include fugitive dust or any fraction thereof.

(2) (a) (I) The commission shall designate by rule those classes of sources of air pollution that are exempt from the requirement to pay an annual emission fee. Every owner or operator of an air pollution source not otherwise exempt in accordance with such commission rules shall pay an annual fee as follows:

(A) For fiscal years 2008-09 and thereafter, twenty-two dollars and ninety cents per ton of regulated pollutant reported in the most recent air pollution emission notice on file with the division;

(A.5) A late payment fee. Such fee shall be assessed at the rate of one percent per month for accounts more than sixty days past due; except that no late payment fee may be assessed during a period in which an account is under administrative review by the division in order to respond to a reasonable request by the owner or operator of a source for allocation of the fees among multiple sources or to resolve a good-faith claim by the owner or operator of a source that there has been an error in calculation of the amount of fees due. At the end of the administrative review, the division shall inform the owner or operator of the source in writing of any findings.

(B) For fiscal years 2008-09 and thereafter, in addition to the annual fee set forth in sub-subparagraph (A) of this subparagraph (I) , for hazardous air pollutants, including ozone-depleting compounds, an annual fee of one hundred fifty-two dollars and ninety cents per ton;

(C) Every local air pollution control authority that adopts any air pollution resolution or ordinance that is more stringent than corresponding state provisions shall pay for the state's enforcement costs;

(II) In no event shall an owner or operator of a major source pay more than a fee based upon total annual emissions of four thousand tons of each regulated pollutant per source.

(III) Every owner or operator subject to the requirements of paying fees set forth in subparagraph (I) of this paragraph (a) shall also pay a processing fee for the costs of processing any application other than an air pollution emission notice under this article. Every significant user of prescribed fire, including federal facilities, submitting a planning document to the commission pursuant to section 25-7-106 (8) (b) shall pay a fee for costs of evaluating such documents. The division shall assess a fee for work it performs, up to a maximum of thirty hours at a rate of seventy-six dollars and forty-five cents per hour. If the division requires more than thirty hours to process the application or evaluate the prescribed fire-related planning documents, the fee paid by the applicant shall not exceed three thousand dollars unless the division has informed the source that the respective billings may exceed three thousand dollars and has provided the source with an estimate of what the actual charges may be prior to commencing the work.

(IV) and (V) Repealed.

(VI) Notwithstanding subparagraph (III) of this paragraph (a) , the division shall not assess a fee for work performed to negotiate a voluntary agreement under part 12 of this article above a maximum of one hundred hours at a rate of fifty-nine dollars and ninety-eight cents per hour unless the owner or operator proposing the voluntary agreement consents to a greater fee in writing.

(b) (I) The moneys collected pursuant to this section shall be remitted to the state treasurer, who shall credit the same to the stationary sources control fund, which fund is hereby created. From such fund, the general assembly shall appropriate to the department of public health and environment, at least annually, such moneys as may be necessary to cover the division's direct and indirect costs required to develop and administer the programs established pursuant to parts 1 to 4 and 10 of this article for the control of air pollution from stationary sources. Any permit fee moneys not appropriated by the general assembly and any appropriated funds not spent by the division shall remain in the stationary sources control fund and shall not revert to the general fund of the state at the end of any fiscal year. Any such moneys shall be separately accounted for. All interest earned on moneys in the stationary sources control fund shall remain in the fund and shall not revert to the general fund or to any other fund.

(II) Of the portion of fee revenue attributable to the increases enacted during the first regular session of the sixty-third general assembly, the department shall allocate one hundred fifty thousand dollars per year for the purpose of modernizing and maintaining the computer system used for the administration of the stationary source program so as to make the overall system more efficient, and seventy thousand dollars for the purpose of enhancing county and district public health agency participation in air quality control activities. The department may reallocate moneys between these two purposes as reasonably necessary so long as the total amount devoted to such purposes remains at two hundred twenty thousand dollars annually.

(c) The general assembly by bill may annually adjust the fees established in this section and in section 25-7-114.1 as necessary to cover the reasonable costs, both direct and indirect, of the stationary source program and to assure that adequate personnel and funding will be available to administer the permit program.

(d) No permit will be issued if the administrator objects to its issuance in a timely manner under this title.

(e) Repealed.

(f) Notwithstanding the amount specified for any fee in this subsection (2) , the commission by rule or as otherwise provided by law may reduce the amount of one or more of the fees if necessary pursuant to section 24-75-402 (3) , C.R.S., to reduce the uncommitted reserves of the fund to which all or any portion of one or more of the fees is credited. After the uncommitted reserves of the fund are sufficiently reduced, the commission by rule or as otherwise provided by law may increase the amount of one or more of the fees as provided in section 24-75-402 (4) , C.R.S.

## 25-7-114.8. Permit fee credits. (Repealed)

## 25-7-115. Enforcement.

(1) (a) The division shall enforce compliance with the emission control regulations of the commission, the requirements of the state implementation plan, and the provisions of parts 1 to 4 and part 11 of this article, including terms and conditions of any permit required pursuant to this article.

(b) The division shall enforce the provisions of part 5 of this article pursuant to sections 25-7-112, 25-7-113, and 25-7-511.

(2) If a written and verified complaint is filed with the division alleging that, or if the division itself has cause to believe that, any person is violating or failing to comply with any regulation of the commission issued pursuant to parts 1 to 4 of this article, order issued pursuant to section 25-7-118, requirement of the state implementation plan, provision of parts 1 to 4 of this article, including any term or condition of a permit required pursuant to this article, the division shall cause a prompt investigation to be made; and, if the division investigation determines that any such violation or failure to comply exists, the division shall act expeditiously and within the period prescribed by law in formally notifying the owner or operator of such air pollution source after the discovery of the alleged violation or noncompliance. Such notice shall specify the provision alleged to have been violated or not complied with and the facts alleged to constitute the violation or noncompliance.

(3) (a) Within thirty calendar days after notice has been given, the division shall confer with the owner or operator of the source to determine whether a violation or noncompliance did or did not occur and, if such violation or noncompliance occurred, whether a noncompliance penalty must be assessed under subsection (5) of this section. The division shall provide an opportunity to the owner or operator at such conference, and may provide further opportunity thereafter, to submit data, views, and arguments concerning the alleged violation or noncompliance or the assessment of any noncompliance penalty.

(b) If, after any such conference, a violation or noncompliance is determined to have occurred, the division shall issue an order requiring the owner or operator or any other responsible person to comply, unless the owner or operator demonstrates that such violation occurred during a period of start-up, shutdown, or malfunction, and timely notice was given to the division of such condition. Such order may include termination, modification, or revocation and reissuance of the subject permit and the assessment of civil penalties in accordance with section 25-7-122. Such order may also require the calculation of a noncompliance penalty under subsection (5) of this section. Unless enforcement of its order has been stayed as provided in paragraph (b) of subsection (4) of this section, the division may seek enforcement, pursuant to section 25-7-121 or 25-7-122, of the applicable regulation of the commission, order issued pursuant to section 25-7-121 or 25-7-122 of the applicable regulation of the commission, order issued pursuant to section 25-7-118, requirement of the state implementation plan, provision of this article, or terms or conditions of a permit required pursuant to this article in the district court for the district where the affected air pollution source is located. The court shall issue an appropriate order, which may include a schedule for compliance by the owner or operator of the source.

(c) The order for compliance shall set forth with specificity the final determination of the division regarding the nature and extent of the violation or noncompliance by the named persons and facilities and shall also include, by reference, a summary of the proceedings at the conference held after the notice of violation and an evaluation of the evidence considered by the division in reaching its final determinations. Any order issued under this subsection (3) which is not reviewed by the commission in accordance with the provisions of subsection (4) of this section shall become final agency action.

(4) (a) (I) Within twenty calendar days after receipt of an order issued pursuant to subsection (3) of this section, the recipient thereof may file with the commission a written petition requesting a hearing to determine all or any of the following:

(A) Whether the alleged violation or noncompliance exists or did exist;

(B) Whether a revision of the state implementation plan or revision of a regulation or standard which is not part of the state implementation plan should be implemented with respect to such violation or noncompliance;

(C) Whether the owner or operator is subject to civil or noncompliance penalties under subsection (5) of this section.

(II) Such hearing shall allow the parties to present evidence and argument on all issues and to conduct cross-examination required for full disclosure of the facts and shall otherwise be conducted in accordance with section 25-7-119.

(b) Except with respect to actions taken pursuant to section 25-7-112 or 25-7-113, upon the filing of such petition, the order and the provisions of the state implementation plan which relate to the alleged violation or noncompliance shall be stayed pending determination of the petition by the commission. Any stay pursuant to this paragraph (b) shall be effective only as to the specific source covered by the order and such petition.

(5) (a) (I) Any order issued pursuant to subsection (3) of this section which pertains to an alleged violation described in section 120(a) (2) (A) of the federal act shall also require each person who is subject to such order, within forty-five calendar days after the issuance of such order, to calculate the penalty owed in accordance with paragraph (b) of this subsection (5) and submit the calculation, together with a payment schedule and all information necessary for an independent verification thereof, to the division. If the order has been stayed pursuant to subsection (4) of this section, the penalty calculation shall be submitted by the owner or operator to the division within

forty-five calendar days after issuance of a final determination of the commission that:

(A) A violation or noncompliance occurred;

(B) If a revision to the state implementation plan has been requested, all or part of such request should be denied; except that, if only part of such request is denied, the penalty calculation shall not be submitted for any aspect of the violation or noncompliance which is excused by reason of approval of a requested revision of the state implementation plan;

(C) The violation is one described in section 120(a) (2) (A) of the federal act; and

(D) If an exemption pursuant to subsection (7) of this section has been claimed, the owner or operator is not entitled thereto.

(II) The division shall review the penalty calculation and schedule submitted pursuant to subparagraph (I) of this paragraph (a) and shall issue an order assessing the noncompliance penalty and providing a payment schedule therefor.

(b) (I) The amount of the penalty which shall be assessed under this subsection (5) shall be equal to:

(A) The amount, determined in accordance with section 120 of the federal act and rules and regulations promulgated under said act by the United States environmental protection agency, which shall be no less than the sum of the quarterly equivalent of the capital costs of compliance and debt service over a normal amortization period of not longer than ten years, operation and maintenance costs foregone as a result of noncompliance, and any additional value which a delay in compliance beyond July 1, 1979, may have for the owner or operator of such stationary source; less

(B) The amount of any expenditure made by the owner or operator of such stationary source during any such quarter for the purpose of bringing the source into, and maintaining compliance with, such requirement to the extent that such expenditure has not been taken into account in the calculation of the penalty under sub-subparagraph (A) of this subparagraph (I) .

(II) To the extent that any expenditure under sub-subparagraph (B) of subparagraph (I) of this paragraph (b) made during any quarter is not subtracted for such quarter from the costs under sub-subparagraph (A) of subparagraph (I) of this paragraph (b) , such expenditure may be subtracted for any subsequent quarter from such costs; except that in no event shall the amount paid be less than the quarterly payment minus the amount attributed to the actual cost of construction.

(c) Any penalty assessed pursuant to subsections (5) to (11) of this section shall be paid in equal quarterly installments (except as provided in sub-subparagraph (B) of subparagraph (I) of paragraph (b) of this subsection (5) ) for the period which begins either August 7, 1979, if notice pursuant to subsection (2) of this section is issued on or before such date or which begins on the date of issuance of notice pursuant to subsection (2) of this section if such notice is issued after August 7, 1979, and which period ends on the date on which such stationary source is estimated to come into compliance.

(d) Any person who fails to pay the amount of any penalty with respect to any stationary source under this subsection (5) on a timely basis shall be required to pay, in addition, a quarterly nonpayment penalty for each quarter during which such failure to pay persists. Such nonpayment penalty shall be in an amount equal to twenty percent of the aggregate amount of such person's penalties and nonpayment penalties with respect to such stationary source which are unpaid as of the beginning of such quarter.

(6) Within twenty calendar days after issuance of an order under subparagraph (II) of paragraph (a) of subsection (5) of this section, the owner or operator may file with the commission a written petition requesting a hearing to review such order. Within sixty calendar days after the filing of such petition, the commission shall hold a hearing and issue a decision thereon.

(7) (a) The owner or operator of any stationary source shall be exempt from the duty to pay a noncompliance penalty pursuant to this section if after notice the owner or operator demonstrates at a hearing that the failure of such stationary source to comply is due solely to:

(I) The conversion by such stationary source from the burning of petroleum products or natural gas, or both, as the primary energy source to the burning of coal pursuant to an order under section 119 of the federal act;

(II) In the case of a coal-burning source granted an extension under section 119 of the federal act, a prohibition from using petroleum products or natural gas, or both, by reason of an order under the provisions of section 2 (a) and (b) of the federal "Energy Supply and Environmental Coordination Act of 1974" or under any legislation which amends or supersedes those provisions;

(III) The use of innovative technology sanctioned by an enforcement order under section 113 (d) (4) of the federal act;

(IV) An inability to comply with such requirements for which the stationary source has received an order pursuant to section 25-7-118, which inability results from reasons entirely beyond the control of the owner or operator of such stationary source or of any entity controlling, controlled by, or under common control with the owner or operator of such stationary source; or

(V) The conditions by reason of which a temporary emergency suspension is authorized under section 110 (f) or (g) of the federal act;

(b) The division may, after notice and opportunity for a public hearing, exempt any stationary source from the duty to pay a noncompliance penalty pursuant to this section with respect to a particular instance of noncompliance if it finds that such instance of noncompliance is inconsequential in nature and duration. Any instance of noncompliance occurring during a period of start-up, shutdown, or malfunction shall be deemed to be inconsequential. If a public hearing is requested by an interested person, the request shall be transmitted to the commission within twenty calendar days of its receipt by the division. The commission shall, within sixty calendar days of its receipt of the request, hold a public hearing with respect thereto and within thirty calendar days of such hearing issue its decision.

(c) An exemption under this subsection (7) shall cease to be effective if the stationary source fails to comply with the interim emission control requirements or schedules of compliance, including increments of progress, under any such extension, order, or suspension.

(8) If the owner or operator of a stationary source who receives an order pursuant to subsection (5) of this section fails to submit a calculation of the penalty, a schedule for payment, and the information necessary for an independent verification thereof, the division may enter into a contract with a person who has no financial interest in the ownership or operation of the stationary source or in any person controlling, controlled by, or under common control with such stationary source to assist in determining the penalty assessment or payment schedule with respect to such stationary source. The cost of such contract may be added to the penalty to be assessed against the owner or operator of such stationary source.

(9) (a) The division or the commission may adjust the amount of the penalty assessment or the payment schedule proposed by the owner or operator if the administrator of the United States environmental protection agency determines that the penalty or schedule does not meet the requirements of the federal act.

(b) Upon making a determination that a stationary source which is subject to a penalty assessment pursuant to this section is in compliance, the division shall review the actual expenditures made by the owner or operator of such stationary source for the purpose of attaining and maintaining compliance and, within one hundred eighty days after such stationary source comes into compliance, shall either provide reimbursement with interest at appropriate prevailing rates for any overpayment by such person or assess and collect any additional payment with interest at prevailing rates for any underpayment by such person.

(10) Any orders, payments, sanctions, or other requirements under this section shall be in addition to any other orders, payments, sanctions, or other requirements of this article.

(11) The division or the commission may request the district attorney for the district in which the alleged violation or noncompliance, or any part thereof, occurred or may request the attorney general to bring, and if so requested it is his or her duty to bring, a suit for recovery of any penalty or nonpayment penalty, with interest, imposed pursuant to subsection (5) of this section if the penalty is not paid when due.

## 25-7-116. Air quality hearings board. (Repealed)

## 25-7-117. State implementation plan - revisions of limited applicability.

(1) The commission, upon application by the owner or operator of a stationary or mobile source or as provided in section 25-7-110 (2) , may revise the state implementation plan or any regulation or standard that is not part of the state implementation plan pursuant to this section if it determines that:

(a) Control techniques are not available, compliance with applicable emission control regulations would cause an unreasonable economic burden, compliance with applicable emission control regulations through new or improved technology is economically and technologically beneficial, or compliance with applicable emission control regulations would result in an arbitrary and unreasonable taking of property;

(b) The adoption of such revision would be consistent with, and aid in, implementing the legislative policy set forth in section 25-7-102; and

(c) In any event, adoption of such revision would be consistent with the requirements of section 110 of the federal act.

(2) Any revision of the state implementation plan or of a regulation or standard which is not part of the state implementation plan pursuant to the provisions of subsection (1) of this section may be adopted for such period of time as shall be specified by the commission.

## 25-7-118. Delayed compliance orders.

(1) The division may, after notice and an opportunity for a public hearing, issue an order for any stationary source which specifies a date for final compliance with any requirement of the state implementation plan not later than the date for attainment of any national ambient air quality standard specified in such plan and in no event longer than one year after the date the order was issued, if the requirements of this section are met. If a public hearing is requested by an interested person, the request shall, within twenty days of its receipt, be transmitted to the commission. The commission shall, within sixty days of its receipt of the request, hold a public hearing with respect thereto and, within thirty days of such hearing, issue its decision and order.

(2) An order pursuant to this section may be issued if the order:

(a) Is issued after notice to the public containing the content of the proposed order and after an opportunity for a public hearing thereon;

(b) Contains a schedule and timetable for compliance which requires final compliance as expeditiously as practical, but in no event later than July 1, 1979, or three years after the date for final compliance with such requirement that is specified in the state implementation plan, whichever is later;

(c) In the case of a major stationary source, notifies the source that it will be required to pay a penalty under section 25-7-115 in the event such stationary source fails to achieve final compliance by July 1, 1979, or by such later date as is specified in the order in accordance with section 25-7-115;

(d) Requires emission monitoring and reporting by the stationary source;

(e) Requires the stationary source to use the best practical system of emission reduction for the period during which such order is in effect and requires the stationary source to comply with such interim requirements as the division or commission determines are reasonable and practical.

(3) If any stationary source not in compliance with any requirement of the state implementation plan gives notice to the division or commission that such stationary source intends to comply by means of replacement of the facility, a complete change in its production process, or a termination of its operations, the division or commission may issue an order under this section permitting the stationary source to operate until July 1, 1979, without any interim schedule of compliance. As a condition of the issuance of any such order, the owner or operator of such stationary source shall post a bond or other surety in an amount equal to the cost of actual compliance by such facility and any economic value which may accrue to the owner or operator of such stationary source by

reason of the failure to comply. If the owner or operator of a stationary source for which the bond or other surety required by this subsection (3) has been posted fails to replace the facility, change the production process, or terminate the operations as specified in the order by the required date, the owner or operator shall immediately forfeit on the bond or other surety, and the commission shall have no discretion to modify the order under this subsection (3) or to compromise the bond or other surety.

(4) Any order pursuant to this section shall be terminated if the commission determines, after notice and a hearing, that the inability of the stationary source to comply no longer exists. If the owner or operator of the stationary source to which the order is issued demonstrates that prompt termination of such order would result in undue hardship, the termination shall become effective at the earliest practicable date on which such undue hardship would not result but in no event later than the date required under this section.

(5) (a) If, on the basis of any information available to it, the division has reason to believe that a stationary source to which an order has been issued pursuant to this section is in violation of any requirement of such order or of any provision of this section, it shall notify the commission and the owner or operator of the alleged violation and may revoke such order or may commence an appropriate enforcement action pursuant to this article, or both.

(b) The owner or operator shall respond as provided in section 25-7-115, and, within sixty days after receipt of such notice, the division shall issue a determination thereon. If the division determines that the stationary source is in violation of any requirement of such order or of any provision of this section, it shall revoke such order and enforce compliance with the requirement with respect to which such order was granted or shall order payment of a penalty as provided in section 25-7-115, or both.

(6) During the period of the order issued under this section and when the owner or operator is in compliance with the terms of such order, no other enforcement action pursuant to this article shall be taken against such owner or operator based upon noncompliance during the period the order is in effect with the requirement for the stationary source covered by such order.

(7) Nothing in this section, and no delayed compliance order granted pursuant to this section, shall be construed to prevent or limit the application of the emergency provisions of section 25-7-112 or 25-7-113. No order issued under this subsection (7) shall prevent the state from assessing penalties nor otherwise affect or limit the state's authority to enforce under other provisions of this article.

## 25-7-119. Hearings.

(1) Not less than fifteen calendar days after a hearing has been requested as provided in this article, the commission shall grant such request and set a time and place therefor not more than ninety calendar days following receipt of such request, unless a shorter period is otherwise specifically provided for in this article. Notice of such hearing shall be printed in a newspaper of general circulation in the area in which the proposed project or activity is located at least thirty days prior to the date of said hearing.

(2) The division shall appear as a party in any hearing before the commission and shall have the same rights to judicial review as any other party.

(2.5) The division or the federal environmental protection agency, or both, may appear as parties pursuant to subsection (5) of this section in any hearing before the commission. The federal environmental protection agency is encouraged to participate in the hearing process early and often so that its interpretations are heard. If the federal environmental protection agency does not comply with the provisions of this subsection (2.5), the commission may not receive evidence from such agency in any hearing related to stationary sources conducted pursuant to this section, and any subsequent opinions by such agency shall carry no weight before the commission or in any judicial proceeding.

(3) All testimony taken at any such hearing before the commission shall be under oath or affirmation. A full and complete record of all proceedings and testimony presented shall be taken and filed. The stenographer shall furnish, upon payment and receipt of any fees allowed therefor, a

certified transcript of the whole or any part of the record to any party in such hearing requesting the same.

(4) Any information relating to secret processes or methods of manufacture or production which may be required, ascertained, or discovered shall not be publicly disclosed in public hearings or otherwise and shall be kept confidential by any member, officer, or employee of the commission or the division. Any person seeking to invoke the protection of this subsection (4) in any hearing shall bear the burden of proving its applicability. Except as provided in the federal act, information claimed to be related to secret processes or methods of manufacture or production but which constitutes emission data may not be withheld as confidential; except that such information may be submitted under a claim of confidentiality, and the division shall not disclose any such information to the public unless required under the federal act.

(5) At any hearing, any person who is affected by the proceeding and whose interests are not already adequately represented shall have the opportunity to be a party thereto upon prior application to and approval by the commission in its sole discretion, as deemed reasonable and proper by said commission, and such person shall have the right to be heard and to cross-examine any witness.

(6) After due consideration of the written and oral statements, the testimony, and the arguments presented at any such hearing, the commission shall make its findings and order, based upon evidence in the record, or make such determination of the matter as it shall deem appropriate, consistent with the provisions of this article and any rule, regulation, or determination promulgated by the commission pursuant thereto. Unless a time period is otherwise specifically provided for in this article, such finding and order or determination shall be made within thirty calendar days after the completion of such hearing.

(7) In all proceedings before the commission with respect to any alleged violation of any provision of this article, regulation of the commission, order or permit or terms or conditions thereof, or requirement of the state implementation plan, the burden of proof shall be upon the division.

(8) The applicant for a permit or delayed compliance order, or any modification thereof, and the petitioner for any amendment to the state implementation plan shall bear the burden of proof with respect to the justification therefor and the information, data, and analysis supportive thereof or required with respect to such application or petition.

(9) Repealed.

(10) Every hearing granted by the commission shall be conducted by the commission, and every hearing shall comply with the provisions of this article and the provisions of article 4 of title 24, C.R.S.

## 25-7-120. Judicial review.

(1) Any final order or determination by the division or the commission shall be subject to judicial review in accordance with the provisions of this article and the provisions of article 4 of title 24, C.R.S.

(2) Any party may move the court to remand the case to the division or the commission in the interests of justice for the purpose of adducing additional specified and material evidence and findings thereon; but such party shall show reasonable grounds for the failure to adduce such evidence previously before the division or the commission.

(3) Any proceeding for judicial review of any final order or determination of the division or the commission shall be filed in the district court for the district in which is located the air pollution source affected.

## 25-7-121. Injunctions.

(1) In the event any person fails to comply with a final order of the division or the commission that is not subject to stay pending administrative or judicial review or in the event any person violates any emission control regulation of the commission, the requirements of the state implementation plan, or any provision of parts 1 to 4 of this article, including any term or condition contained in

any permit required under this article, the division or the commission, as the case may be, may request the district attorney for the district in which the alleged violation occurs or the attorney general to bring, and if so requested it is his or her duty to bring, a suit for an injunction to prevent any further or continued violation.

(2) In any proceedings brought pursuant to this section to enforce an order of the division or the commission, a temporary restraining order or preliminary injunction, if sought, shall not issue if there is probable cause to believe that granting such temporary restraining order or preliminary injunction will cause serious harm to the affected person or any other person and:

(a) That the alleged violation or activity to which the order pertains will not continue or be repeated; or

(b) That granting such temporary restraining order or preliminary injunction would be without sufficient corresponding public benefit.

(3) Notwithstanding any other provision in this section, no action for injunction may be taken where the source has obtained a renewable operating permit and conducts its operations in compliance with the permit terms, as provided in section 25-7-114.4 (3) .

## 25-7-122. Civil penalties.

(1) Upon application of the division, penalties as determined under this article may be collected by the division by action instituted in the district court for the district in which is located the air pollution source affected in accordance with the following provisions:

(a) (Deleted by amendment, L. 92, p. 1220, § 23, effective July 1, 1992.)

(b) Any person who violates any requirement or prohibition of an applicable emission control regulation of the commission, the state implementation plan, a construction permit, any provision for the prevention of significant deterioration under part 2 of this article, any provision related to attainment under part 3 of this article, or any provision of section 25-7-105, 25-7-106, 25-7-106.3, 25-7-106.8, 25-7-106.9, 25-7-108, 25-7-109, 25-7-111, 25-7-112, 25-7-113, 25-7-114.2, 25-7-114.5, 25-7-118, 25-7-206, 25-7-403, 25-7-404, 25-7-405, 25-7-407, 42-4-403, 42-4-404, 42-4-405, 42-4-406, 42-4-407, 42-4-409, 42-4-410, or 42-4-414, C.R.S., shall be subject to a civil penalty of not more than fifteen thousand dollars per day for each day of such violation; except that there shall be no civil penalties assessed or collected against persons who violate emission regulations promulgated by the commission for the control of odor until a compliance order issued pursuant to section 25-7-115 and ordering compliance with the odor regulation has been violated.

(c) Any person failing to comply with the provisions of section 25-7-114.1 shall be subject to a civil penalty of not more than five hundred dollars.

(d) Any person who violates any requirement, prohibition, or order respecting an operating permit issued pursuant to section 25-7-114.3, including but not limited to failure to obtain such a permit or to operate in compliance with any term or condition thereof or to pay the permit fee required under section 25-7-114.7 (2) or commits a violation of section 25-7-109.6 shall be subject to a civil penalty of not more than fifteen thousand dollars per day for each violation.

(e) Any person who violates any provision of section 25-7-139 shall be subject to a civil penalty of not more than one thousand dollars.

(2) (a) In determining the amount of any civil penalty, the following factors shall be considered:

(I) The violator's compliance history;

(II) Good-faith efforts on behalf of the violator to comply;

(III) Payment by the violator of penalties previously assessed for the same violation;

(IV) Duration of the violation;

(V) Economic benefit of noncompliance to the violator;

(VI) Impact on, or threat to, the public health or welfare or the environment as a result of the violation;

(VII) Malfeasance; and

(VIII) Whether legal and factual theories were advanced for purposes of delay.

(b) In addition to the factors set forth in paragraph (a) of this subsection (2) , the following circumstances shall be considered as grounds for reducing or eliminating civil penalties:

(I) The voluntary and complete disclosure by the violator of such violation in a timely fashion after discovery of the noncompliance;

(II) Full and prompt cooperation by the violator following disclosure of the violation including, when appropriate, entering into a legally enforceable commitment to undertake compliance and remedial efforts;

(III) The existence and scope of a regularized and comprehensive environmental compliance program or an environmental audit program;

(IV) Substantial economic impact of a penalty on the violator;

(V) Nonfeasance; and

(VI) Other mitigating factors.

(c) The imposition of civil penalties may be deferred or suspended where appropriate based on consideration of the factors set forth in this subsection (2) .

(3) Notwithstanding any other provision in this section, no action for civil enforcement of this article may be taken where the source has obtained a renewable operating permit and conducts its operations in compliance with the permit terms, as provided in section 25-7-114.4 (3) .

## 25-7-122.1. Criminal penalties.

(1) General provisions. (a) Whenever the division has reason to believe that a person has knowingly, as defined in section 18-1-501 (6) , C.R.S., violated any requirement or prohibition of an applicable emission control regulation of the commission, state implementation plan, permit required under this article, or any provision for the prevention of significant deterioration under part 2 of this article, any provision related to attainment under part 3 of this article, or any provision of section 25-7-105, 25-7-106, 25-7-106.3, 25-7-106.8, 25-7-106.9, 25-7-108, 25-7-109, 25-7-111, 25-7-112, 25-7-113, 25-7-114.2, 25-7-114.5, 25-7-118, 25-7-206, 25-7-403, 25-7-404, 25-7-405, 25-7-407, 42-4-403, 42-4-404, 42-4-405, 42-4-406, 42-4-407, 42-4-409, or 42-4-410, C.R.S., the division may request either the attorney general or the district attorney for the district in which the alleged violation occurs to pursue criminal penalties under this section.

(b) Except for those violations identified in paragraph (c) of this subsection (1) and subsections (2) and (3) of this section, any person who knowingly, as defined in section 18-1-501 (6) , C.R.S., violates any requirement or prohibition of an applicable emission control regulation of the commission, state implementation plan, permit required under this article, or any provision for the prevention of significant deterioration under part 2 of this article, any provision related to attainment under part 3 of this article, or any provision of section 25-7-105, 25-7-106, 25-7-106.3, 25-7-106.8, 25-7-106.9, 25-7-108, 25-7-109, 25-7-109.6, 25-7-111, 25-7-112, 25-7-113, 25-7-114.2, 25-7-114.5, 25-7-118, 25-7-206, 25-7-403, 25-7-404, 25-7-405, 25-7-407, 42-4-403, 42-4-404, 42-4-405, 42-4-406, 42-4-407, 42-4-409, or 42-4-410, C.R.S., is guilty of a misdemeanor, and upon conviction thereof, may be punished by a fine of not more than twenty-five thousand dollars per day for each day of violation. Upon a second conviction for a violation of this paragraph (b) within two years, the maximum punishment shall be doubled.

(c) Except for those violations identified in paragraph (b) of this subsection (1) and subsections (2) and (3) of this section, any person who knowingly, as defined in section 18-1-501 (6) , C.R.S., violates any requirement, prohibition, or order respecting an operating permit issued pursuant to section 25-7-114.3, including but not limited to failure to obtain such a permit or to operate in compliance with any term or condition thereof or to pay the permit fee required under section 25-7-114.7 (2) is guilty of a misdemeanor, and upon conviction thereof, may be punished by a fine of not more than twenty-five thousand dollars per violation per day. Upon a second conviction for a violation of this paragraph (c) within two years, the maximum punishment shall be doubled.

(2) False statements. Any person who knowingly, as defined in section 18-1-501 (6) , C.R.S., makes any false material statement, representation, or certification in, or omits material information from, or knowingly alters or conceals any notice, application, record, report, plan, or other document required pursuant to this article to be either filed or maintained or falsifies,

tampers with, or renders inaccurate any monitoring device or method required to be maintained or followed under this article is guilty of a misdemeanor, and upon conviction thereof, may be punished by a fine of not more than twelve thousand five hundred dollars for each instance of violation. Upon a second conviction for a violation of this subsection (2) within two years, the maximum punishment shall be doubled.

(3) (a) Knowing endangerment. Any person who knowingly, as defined in section 18-1-501 (6) , C.R.S., releases into the ambient air any hazardous air pollutant listed pursuant to section 112 of the federal act, or any other hazardous air pollutant as defined by this article, and who knows at the time that such action thereby places another person in imminent danger of death or serious bodily injury is guilty of a felony, and upon conviction thereof, may be punished by a fine of not more than fifty thousand dollars per day for each day of violation, or by imprisonment for not more than four years, or by both such fine and imprisonment. Any person committing such violation which is an organization shall, upon conviction under this subsection (3) , be subject to a fine of not more than one million dollars for each such violation. Upon a second conviction for a violation of this subsection (3) , the maximum punishment shall be doubled. For any air pollutant for which an emissions standard has been set, or for any source for which an operating permit has been issued under this article, a release of such pollutant in accordance with that standard or permit shall not constitute a violation of this subsection (3) .

(b) In determining whether a defendant who is an individual knew that the violation placed another person in imminent danger of death or serious bodily injury:

(I) The defendant is responsible only for actual awareness or actual belief possessed; and

(II) Knowledge possessed by a person other than the defendant, but not by the defendant, may not be attributed to the defendant.

(c) (I) It is an affirmative defense to a prosecution that the conduct charged was freely consented to by the person endangered and that the danger and conduct charged were reasonably foreseeable hazards of:

(A) An occupation, a business, or a profession; or

(B) Medical treatment or medical or scientific experimentation conducted by professionally approved methods and such other person had been made aware of the risks involved prior to giving consent.

(II) The defendant may establish an affirmative defense under this paragraph (c) by a preponderance of the evidence.

(d) Any person who negligently, as defined in section 18-1-501 (3) , C.R.S., violates any requirement or prohibition of an applicable emission control regulation of the commission, state implementation plan, permit required under this article, or any provision for the prevention of significant deterioration under part 2 of this article, is guilty of a misdemeanor and, upon conviction thereof, may be punished by a fine of not more than twelve thousand five hundred dollars per day for each day of violation.

(4) All general defenses, affirmative defenses, and bars to prosecution that may apply with respect to other criminal offenses may apply under this section and shall be determined by the courts of this state according to the principles of common law as they may be interpreted in the light of reason and experience. Concepts of justification and excuse applicable under this section may be developed in the light of reason and experience.

(5) For purposes of this section, unless the context otherwise requires:

(a) "Organization" means a legal entity, other than a government, established or organized for any purpose, and such term includes a corporation, company, association, firm, partnership, joint-stock company, foundation, institution, trust, society, union, or any other association of persons.

(b) "Person" includes, in addition to the entities referred to in section 25-7-103 (19) , any responsible corporate officer.

(c) "Serious bodily injury" means bodily injury which involves a substantial risk of death, unconsciousness, extreme physical pain, protracted and obvious disfigurement, or protracted loss or impairment of the function of a bodily member, organ, or mental faculty.

## 25-7-122.5. Enforcement of chlorofluorocarbon regulations.

(1) Whenever the division has reason to believe that any person has violated the rules and regulations promulgated pursuant to section 25-7-105 (11), the division may issue a notice of violation or a cease-and-desist order. Such notice or order shall set forth the rule or regulation alleged to have been violated, the facts constituting such violation, and any measures which the person is required to take. In addition, if the division finds that a person is in violation of any rule or regulation promulgated pursuant to section 25-7-105 (11), it may assess a fine of up to one thousand dollars for each violation.

(2) Any person who has been issued a notice of violation or a cease-and-desist order or who has been ordered to pay a fine may request a hearing before the commission to contest the notice, order, or fine. Such request shall be filed within thirty days after the notice or order has been issued or the fine has been assessed. Upon such request, a hearing shall be held before the commission within a reasonable time.

(3) After a hearing pursuant to subsection (2) of this section, any person aggrieved by the determination of the commission may seek judicial review of the commission's order within thirty days after entry thereof in the district court for the judicial district in which the violation occurred.

(4) All fines collected pursuant to this section shall be transmitted to the state treasurer, who shall credit the same to the general fund.

## 25-7-122.6. Administrative and judicial stays.

(1) Except with respect to emergency orders issued pursuant to sections 25-7-112 and 25-7-113, and delayed compliance orders issued pursuant to section 25-7-118, any person to whom an order has been issued by the division or the commission, or against whom an adverse determination has been made, may petition the commission or the district court for the district in which is located the air pollution source affected, as appropriate, for a stay of the effectiveness of such order or determination.

(2) Such petitions may be filed prior to any such order or determination becoming final or during any period in which such order or determination is under judicial review.

(3) Such stay shall be granted if there is probable cause to believe:

(a) That the movant will suffer irreparable harm if the motion is denied;

(b) That there will be no irreparable harm to human health, welfare, or the environment if the motion is granted; and

(c) That the movant will succeed on the merits of its case.

(4) Such order shall be stayed pending a final determination of the petition.

## 25-7-123. Open burning - penalties.

(1) (a) The commission shall adopt a program to control open burning in each portion of the state in which such control is necessary in order to carry out the policies of this article, as set forth in section 25-7-102, and to comply with the requirements of the federal act. Such program shall include emission control regulations and the designation, after public hearing and from time to time, of such portions by legal description.

(b) Open burning in the course of agricultural operations may be regulated only where the absence of regulations would substantially impede the commission in carrying out the objectives of this article. In adopting any program applicable to agricultural operations, the commission shall take into consideration the necessity of conducting open burning. For purposes of this section, "agricultural operations" does not include grassland, forest, or habitat management activities of significant users of prescribed fire conducted on lands the primary purpose of which is nonagricultural, unless a person asserts and the commission finds that the absence of regulation would substantially impede the objectives of this article. Such activities shall be deemed "commercial purposes" within the meaning of paragraph (b) of subsection (3) of this section.

(c) No permit shall be issued by the division pursuant to paragraph (a) of subsection (2) of this section after July 1, 2002, unless such permit is consistent with the comments and recommendations of the commission concerning the planning document, as defined in section 25-7-106 (8) (b) (II) , applicable to the area to be burned; except that permit conditions may be excluded from a permit if a significant user of prescribed fire demonstrates and the state finds that such conditions are inconsistent with applicable law. The division shall report all such exclusions, within thirty days after they are granted, to the governor and to the director of the legislative council. In no event shall a permit be issued unless a planning document for the area to be burned has been submitted to the commission for review, public hearing, and comment in accordance with section 25-7-106 (8) . The commission shall adopt rules to provide for exceptions from the requirements of section 25-7-106 (8) when immediate issuance of a permit is necessary to protect the public health and safety.

(2) (a) Within such designated portions of the state, no person shall burn or permit to be burned on any open premises owned or controlled by such person, or on any public street, alley, or other land adjacent to such premises any rubbish, wastepaper, wood, or other flammable material, unless a permit therefor has first been obtained from the division. In granting or denying the issuance of any such permit, the division shall base its action on the location and proximity of such burning to any building or other structure, the potential contribution of such burning to air pollution in the area, climatic conditions on the day of such burning, and compliance by the applicant for the permit with applicable fire protection and safety requirements of the local authority or area.

(b) In all or any part of any portion of the state designated pursuant to subsection (1) of this section, the prohibition contained in this subsection (2) may be suspended by the commission with respect to any particular type or category of open burning upon a finding that enforcement of the prohibition would neither significantly assist in the prevention, abatement, and control of air pollution nor significantly enhance the quality of the ambient air in such designated area.

(3) (a) Any person who violates paragraph (a) of subsection (2) of this section by burning or permitting any burning for noncommercial purposes without first having obtained a permit as required shall be subject to a civil penalty of up to five hundred dollars per day for each day during which such a violation occurs. For a second violation, the civil penalty shall be up to one thousand dollars per day for each day during which such a violation occurs. For a third or subsequent violation, the civil penalty shall be up to one thousand five hundred dollars per day for each day during which such a violation occurs.

(b) Any person who violates paragraph (a) of subsection (2) of this section by burning or permitting any burning for commercial purposes without first having obtained a permit as required shall be subject to a civil penalty of not more than ten thousand dollars per day for each day during which such a violation occurs.

## 25-7-123.1. Statute of limitations - penalty assessment - criteria.

(1) (a) Any action pursuant to this section not commenced within five years of occurrence of the alleged violation is time barred.

(b) Without expanding the statute of limitations contained in paragraph (a) of this subsection (1) , any action pursuant to this article, except those commenced pursuant to section 25-7-122 (1) (d) or 25-7-122.1 (1) (c) , which is not commenced within eighteen months of the date upon which the division discovers the alleged violation is time barred. For purposes of this section, the division discovers the alleged violation when it learns of the alleged violation or should have learned of the alleged violation by the exercise of reasonable diligence, including by receipt of actual or constructive notice.

(c) The five-year period of limitation contained in this section does not apply where information regarding the alleged violation is knowingly or willfully concealed by the alleged violator.

(2) A penalty may be assessed for each day of violation. For purposes of determining the number of days of violation for which a penalty may be assessed under sections 25-7-122 and 25-7-122.1 (1) , or an assessment may be made under section 25-7-115 (5) , where the division has notified the source of the violation, and the division makes a prima facie showing that the conduct or events giving rise to the violation are likely to have continued or recurred past the date of notice,

the days of violation shall be presumed to include the date of such notice and each and every day thereafter until the violator establishes that continuous compliance has been achieved, except to the extent that the violator can prove by a preponderance of the evidence that there were intervening days during which no violation occurred or that the violation was not continuing in nature.

(3) The division may request the district attorney for the district in which the alleged violation or noncompliance, or any part thereof, occurred or may request the attorney general to bring, and if so requested, it is the duty of such official to bring a suit for recovery or any penalty or nonpayment penalty, with interest, imposed pursuant to section 25-7-122 (civil penalties) or 25-7-122.1 (criminal penalties) , if the penalty is not paid when due. The division may not revoke a permit issued pursuant to parts 1 to 4 of this article or certification issued pursuant to part 5 of this article solely for failure to pay penalties when due, unless an order is first issued and all administrative and judicial remedies are pursued unsuccessfully.

## 25-7-124. Relationship with federal government, regional agencies, and other states.

(1) The commission shall serve as the state agency for all purposes of the federal act and regulations promulgated under said act; except that the department of public health and environment shall accept and supervise the administration of loans and grants from the federal government and from other sources, public or private, which are received by the state for air pollution control purposes.

(2) Repealed.

(3) The department of public health and environment may enter into agreements with any air pollution control agencies of the federal government or other states and with regional air pollution control agencies, but any such agreement involving, authorizing, or requiring compliance in this state with any ambient air quality standard or emission control regulation shall not be effective unless or until the commission has held a hearing with respect to such standard or regulation and has adopted the same in compliance with section 25-7-110.

## 25-7-125. Organization within department of public health and environment.

The air quality control commission, together with the technical secretary under said commission, shall exercise its powers and perform its duties and functions specified in this article in the department of public health and environment as if the same were transferred to the department by a type 1 transfer, as such transfer is defined in the "Administrative Organization Act of 1968", article 1 of title 24, C.R.S.

## 25-7-126. Application of article.

(1) The factual or legal basis for proceedings or other actions that shall result from a violation of any emission control regulation inure solely to and shall be for the benefit of the people of the state generally, and it is not intended to create by this article, in any way, new or enlarged private rights, or to enlarge existing private rights, or to diminish private rights. A determination that air pollution exists or that any standard has been disregarded or violated, whether or not a proceeding or action may be brought by the state, shall not create by reason thereof any presumption of law or finding of fact which shall inure to or be for the benefit of any person other than the state.

(2) Other than section 25-7-112 or 25-7-113, the provisions of this article and regulations adopted under this article shall not apply to air pollution insofar as such pollution exists within the confines of a particular commercial or industrial plant, works, or shop which is the source of air pollution and shall not apply or affect the relations between employers and employees with respect to or arising out of any condition of air pollution.

(3) It is the purpose of this article to provide additional and cumulative remedies to prevent and abate air pollution. Nothing in this article shall abridge or alter rights of action or remedies existing on June 20, 1979, or after said date, nor shall any provision of this article or anything

done by virtue of this article be construed as estopping individuals, cities, towns, counties, cities and counties, or duly constituted political subdivisions of the state from the exercise of their respective rights to suppress nuisances.

## 25-7-127. Continuance of existing rules and orders.

(1) All rules or amendments to existing rules adopted by the commission on or after June 20, 1979, shall be subject to sections 24-4-103 (8) (c) and (8) (d) and 24-4-108, C.R.S.

(2) All actions, orders, and determinations by the division and the state board of health pursuant to article 29 of chapter 66, C.R.S. 1963, as that article existed on January 1, 1970, shall remain in full force and effect until countermanded or modified by the division.

(3) All actions, orders, and determinations of the air pollution variance board created by article 29 of chapter 66, C.R.S. 1963, as that article existed on January 1, 1970, shall remain in full force and effect unless countermanded or modified by said board prior to July 1, 1984, or until countermanded or modified by the commission created by this article.

(4) All actions, orders, and determinations of the air pollution variance board created by this article as it existed prior to June 20, 1979, shall remain in full force and effect unless countermanded or modified by said board prior to July 1, 1984, or until countermanded or modified by the commission created by this article.

(5) All actions, orders, and determinations of the air quality hearings board created by this article as this article existed prior to July 1, 1984, shall remain in full force and effect until countermanded or modified by the commission created by this article.

## 25-7-128. Local government - authority - penalty.

(1) Home rule cities, cities, towns, counties, and cities and counties are hereby authorized to enact local air pollution resolutions or ordinances. Every such resolution or ordinance shall provide for hearings, judicial review, and injunctions consistent with sections 25-7-118 to 25-7-121 and shall include emission control regulations which are at least the same as, or may be more restrictive than, the emission control regulations adopted pursuant to this article; except that nothing in this article shall prohibit any such local law from controlling any air pollution or air pollution source which is not subject to control under the provisions of this article and except that no permit issued under any local air pollution law with respect to any facility, activity, or process shall ever be construed to relieve any holder thereof from the duty to maintain such facility, activity, or process in compliance with the emission standards and emission control regulations adopted pursuant to this article nor to relieve the division from its duty to enforce such emission standards and emission control regulations with respect to such facility, activity, or process. Any local air pollution standards or regulations submitted and approved as revisions to the state implementation plan shall be enforced as such by the division. In order to assure coordination of efforts to control and abate air pollution, local governmental entities are encouraged to submit their adopted plans and regulations as revisions to the state implementation plan for Colorado.

(2) All local air pollution resolutions and ordinances and orders issued pursuant thereto in existence on March 1, 1979, are validated as though adopted pursuant to the authority of subsection (1) of this section; except that, if any such local resolution, ordinance, or order fails to meet the requirements of this article, the governing body under whose authority such resolution, ordinance, or order was promulgated shall have until July 1, 1979, to amend, modify, or repeal the same so that it will meet the requirements of this article, but, if not so amended, modified, or repealed, the same shall be superseded by this article.

(3) To the extent that a local air pollution resolution adopted by a county is more restrictive than an ordinance adopted by any city or town within such county, the county resolution shall apply in lieu of the city or town ordinance to the extent of the inconsistency.

(4) Any local governmental authority enforcing air pollution control regulations which shall issue any enforcement order or grant any permit shall, at the time of such issuance or granting, transmit to the commission a copy of such order or permit.

(5) Application, operation, and enforcement of valid local air pollution laws shall be completely independent of, but may be concurrent with, the application, operation, and enforcement of this article. The appointment of an air pollution control authority by the division shall in no way affect the duties and responsibilities given the same person or agency under a local air pollution law, and the appointment of an air pollution control authority by a local governmental unit shall in no way affect the duties and responsibilities given the same person or agency by the division.

(6) In order to assure coordination of efforts to control and abate air pollution, at least semiannually the commission and each air pollution control authority created by a local air pollution law shall confer and review each other's records concerning the area subject to such local law and coordinate their respective plans and programs for such area.

(7) No local air pollution control authority shall institute any system or program that:

(a) Conflicts with, or is in any way inconsistent with, air pollution emergency plans promulgated by the governor pursuant to section 25-7-112 (2) ;

(b) Is more stringent than a corresponding state provision with respect to measures to preserve the stratospheric ozone layer;

(c) Is more stringent than a corresponding state provision with respect to hazardous air pollutants; except that this paragraph (c) shall not limit local zoning powers and ordinances enacted pursuant to other authorities under state law;

(d) Does not contain provisions to ensure adequate reimbursement of state compliance and administrative expenses as required by section 25-7-114.7 (2) (a) (I) (C) ;

(e) Is more stringent than a corresponding state provision with respect to asphalt and concrete plants and crushing equipment;

(f) Imposes less restrictive requirements on its own stationary sources than those imposed on similar nongovernmental sources.

(8) Any person who violates any emission standard or emission control regulation adopted by a local governmental entity, where such local government has not submitted its standards or regulations as revisions to the state implementation plan, shall be subject to a civil penalty of not more than three hundred dollars. Each day during which such a violation occurs shall be deemed a separate offense.

## 25-7-129. Disposition of fines and penalties.

All receipts from penalties or fines collected under the provisions of sections 25-7-115, 25-7-122, and 25-7-123 shall be credited to the general fund of the state.

## 25-7-130. Motor vehicle emission control studies.

(1) The department of public health and environment, motor vehicle emission control section of the air pollution control division, and the department of revenue shall develop a continuing joint program for the study of the control of motor vehicle exhaust emissions, including emissions from model year 1975 and later models. Such emission control studies shall include such investigations and evaluations of existing and available motor vehicle emission control equipment and technology and the social problems, economic impacts, effectiveness, and costs involved in the use of such technology in motor vehicle emissions inspections and maintenance programs as they may jointly recommend.

(2) (a) The department of public health and environment, motor vehicle emission control section of the air pollution control division, shall develop a pilot program for the purpose of testing a representative sample of motor vehicles with various vehicle emission control alternatives which may include emission testing and maintenance, air pollution control tune-up, and vehicle modification alternatives as determined by the commission.

(b) Based upon the results of the pilot program and emission control studies, the commission shall develop recommendations for implementing programs of emission testing or mandatory maintenance, or both; air pollution control tune-ups; and vehicle modifications, including altitude modifications and retrofit control systems, for the control of motor vehicle emissions. Such recommendations shall include information on the costs and air pollution control effectiveness of alternate control measures and legislative and regulatory measures necessary to implement an effective program. Any program recommended shall be based upon establishing statewide minimum standards and shall include more stringent standards for motor vehicles registered in air quality control basins defined by the commission.

(3) (Deleted by amendment, L. 96, p. 1259, § 156, effective August 7, 1996.)

(4) and (5) Repealed.

## 25-7-131. Training programs - emission controls.

(1) (a) State-employed investigators shall complete a training course and pass qualification tests as developed and approved by the commission, after conferring with the department of revenue, as related to the orientation and basic maintenance procedures on air pollution control systems installed by manufacturers. The commission may waive the requirement for completion of such a training course under such circumstances as the commission deems appropriate. Only inspectors passing said qualification tests shall perform emissions inspections. The commission may require that inspection stations have on hand any equipment necessary to complete emissions inspections as provided for in this section.

(b) Repealed.

(1.1) Repealed.

(2) The training programs provided for by this section shall be oriented toward basic motor vehicle air pollution control systems installed in motor vehicles by the manufacturers and shall be made available to motor vehicle mechanics on a voluntary basis in such air quality control areas as the commission may designate in coordination with educational facilities throughout the state in which it may certify to conduct such training.

(3) and (4) Repealed.

## 25-7-132. Emission data - public availability.

Notwithstanding any other provisions of this article or any other law to the contrary, all emission data received or obtained by the commission or the division shall be available to the public to the extent required by the federal act.

## 25-7-133. Legislative review and approval of state implementation plans and rules - legislative declaration.

(1) Notwithstanding any other provision of law but subject to subsection (7) of this section, by January 15 of each year the commission shall certify in a report to the chairperson of the legislative council in summary form any additions or changes to elements of the state implementation plan adopted during the prior year that are to be submitted to the administrator for purposes of federal enforceability. Such report shall be written in plain, nontechnical language using words with common and everyday meaning that are understandable to the average reader. Copies of such report shall be available to the public and shall be made available to each member of the general assembly. The provisions of this section shall not apply to control measures and strategies that have been adopted and implemented by the enacting jurisdiction of a local unit of government if such measures and strategies do not result in mandatory direct costs upon any entity other than the enacting jurisdiction.

(2) (a) By the February 15 following submission of the certified report under subsection (1) of this section, any member of the general assembly may make a request in writing to the chairperson of the legislative council that the legislative council hold a hearing or hearings to review any addition or change to elements of the SIP contained in the report submitted pursuant to subsection (1) of this section. Upon receipt of such request, the chairperson of the legislative council shall forthwith schedule a hearing to conduct such review. Any review by the legislative council shall determine whether the addition or change to the SIP element accomplishes the results intended by enactment of the statutory provisions under which the addition or change to the SIP element was adopted.

The legislative council, after allowing a public hearing preceded by adequate notice to the public and the commission, may recommend the introduction of a bill or bills based on the results of such review. If the legislative council does not recommend introduction of a bill under this subsection (2) , the addition or change to the SIP element may be submitted under paragraph (b) of this subsection (2) . Any bill recommended for consideration under this subsection (2) shall not be counted against the number of bills to which members of the general assembly are limited by law or joint rule of the senate and the house of representatives. If the legislative council does not recommend the introduction of a bill under this paragraph (a) , and the member or members of the general assembly that requested such review will be introducing a bill under the provisions of paragraph (c) of this subsection (2) , any such member shall provide written notice to the chairperson of the legislative council within three days after the action by the legislative council not to recommend introduction of a bill. If such member or members provide such written notice, the addition or change to the SIP or any element thereof that is the subject of any such bill may not be submitted to the administrator of the federal environmental protection agency until the expiration of the addition or change to the SIP has been postponed by the general assembly acting by bill or the member or members provide written notice to the chairperson of the executive committee of the legislative council that no bill will be introduced.

(b) Unless a written request for legislative council review of an addition or change to a SIP element is submitted by the February 15 following submission of the report under subsection (1) of this section, or a notice is provided by a member or members that they are introducing a bill under paragraph (c) of this subsection (2) within three days after legislative council action not to introduce a bill under paragraph (a) of this subsection (2) , all other additions or changes to a SIP element described in such report shall be submitted to the administrator for final approval and incorporation into the SIP.

(c) Until such February 15 as provided in paragraph (b) of this subsection (2) , the commission may only submit an addition or change to the SIP or any element thereof, as defined in section 110 of the federal act, any rule which is a part thereof, or any revision thereto as specified in subsection (1) of this section to the administrator for conditional approval or temporary approval. If legislative council review is requested as to any addition or change to a SIP element under paragraph (a) of this subsection (2) , then no such SIP, revision, rule required by the SIP or revision, or rule related to the implementation of the SIP or revision so submitted to the administrator may take effect for purposes of federal enforceability, or enforcement of any kind at the state level against any person or entity based only on the commission's general authority to adopt a SIP under section 25-7-105 (1) , unless expiration of the SIP, rule required for the SIP, or addition or change to a SIP element has been postponed by the general assembly acting by bill in the same manner as provided in section 24-4-103 (8) (c) and (8) (d) , C.R.S. Any member of the general assembly may introduce a bill to modify or delete all or a portion of the SIP or any rule or additions or changes to SIP elements which are a component thereof. Any bill introduced under this paragraph (c) shall not be counted against the number of bills to which members of the general assembly are limited by law or joint rule of the senate and the house of representatives. Any committee of reference of the senate or the house of representatives to which a bill introduced under this paragraph (c) is referred shall conduct as part of consideration of any such bill on the merits the review provided for under paragraph (a) of this subsection (2) . If any bill is introduced under paragraph (a) of this subsection (2) or under this paragraph (c) to postpone the expiration of any addition or change to a SIP element described in a report submitted under subsection (1) of this section, and any such bill does not become law, the addition or change to a SIP element addressed in such bill may be submitted to the administrator of the federal environmental protection agency for final approval and incorporation into the SIP under paragraph (b) of this subsection (2) .

(d) Repealed.

(3) In order to further the goals of section 25-7-105.1 in assuring that nonfederally required rules or policies are not submitted to the administrator for inclusion in a SIP, the commission shall, effective July 1, 1995, with respect to any rule or any portion thereof not required by the federal

act or which is otherwise more stringent in whole or in part than requirements of the federal act, ensure that the public notice and the general statement of such rule's basis, specific statutory authority, and purpose required by section 24-4-103, C.R.S., in connection with the commission's proposal and promulgation of such rule shall also specifically identify what portion of such rule is not required by provisions of the federal act or is otherwise more stringent than requirements of the federal act.

(4) (a) The general assembly recognizes that the commission must exercise discretion in selecting from available options in developing a cost effective SIP which attains or maintains national ambient air quality standards.

(b) On or before November 15 of each year, the commission, in coordination with designated organizations for air quality planning in local areas, shall provide the legislative council:

(I) A comprehensive listing of additions or changes to elements of the SIP that the commission and local areas will consider during the following calendar year;

(II) The projected schedule for local action and commission consideration of such measures;

(III) (Deleted by amendment, L. 2000, p. 187, § 1, effective March 22, 2000.)

(IV) The statutory deadline, if any, for submittal to the administrator of the change or addition to elements of the SIP and the corresponding federal sanctions or consequences for failure to submit the change or addition to elements of the SIP by the deadline under the federal act; and

(V) A brief description of the principal technical and policy issues and available options presented for decision in each addition or change to elements of the SIP.

(c) The commission, in coordination with designated organizations for air quality planning in local areas, shall communicate regularly with the legislative council regarding each of the SIP elements or revisions thereto scheduled for adoption and submission to the administrator of the United States environmental protection agency.

(5) The information required by paragraph (b) of subsection (4) of this section shall be submitted to the legislative council in the form and manner and accompanied by supporting materials prescribed by the legislative council.

(6) This section is exempt from the provisions of section 24-1-136 (11) , C.R.S., and the periodic reporting requirement of this section shall remain in effect until changed by the general assembly acting by bill.

(7) (a) (Deleted by amendment, L. 2003, p. 1973, § 1, effective May 22, 2003.)

(b) Any revisions to the automobile inspection and readjustment program area pursuant to section 42-4-304 (20) (d) , C.R.S., that delete specific regions within that portion of the AIR program area that is approved for incorporation into the state implementation plan shall be submitted to the federal environmental protection agency as expeditiously as possible and shall not be subject to further review and approval pursuant to this section; except that the commission shall submit a report pursuant to subsection (1) of this section.

(c) Repealed.

(d) (I) The commission shall request the governor to submit the plan adopted by the commission on March 12, 2004, to reduce the amount of pollutants emitted that create ozone pollution to the federal environmental protection agency for approval and incorporation into the state implementation plan. Passage of this paragraph (d) is in lieu of, and said plan shall be deemed to have satisfied, all review requirements under this section.

(II) A regulated entity that is required to comply with the amendments to regulation number 7 adopted by the air quality control commission on March 12, 2004, to reduce emissions of volatile organic compounds from atmospheric condensate storage tanks shall:

(A) Provide advance notice of the location where it intends to install an emission control unit; and

(B) Indicate whether such unit exceeds the height of the existing equipment at the facility.

(III) The regulated entity shall deliver the notice required pursuant to subparagraph (II) of this paragraph (d) to the local government designee, if any, registered with the Colorado oil and gas conservation commission for receipt of information relating to oil and gas operations within a local jurisdiction, and shall include a phone number for a contact person. If the local jurisdiction does not have a local government designee, the notice shall be provided to the municipal clerk.

(IV) The local government shall, within ten business days after receipt of the notice, notify the regulated entity whether the local government objects to the intended installation of the emission control unit. The objection shall be based on site-specific land use issues and may not be made on a blanket basis to every proposed emission control unit installation within a local jurisdiction. If the local government fails to object within ten business days after submission of the notice, the local jurisdiction is presumed to have approved the installation of the specified emission control unit, and the regulated entity may commence such installation.

(V) If a local government designee notifies a regulated entity of its objection within ten business days after receipt of the notice of installation of an emission control unit, the regulated entity and the local jurisdiction shall endeavor to informally resolve the matter within an additional ten business days. If such attempt fails, the local jurisdiction shall have ten business days to petition the air quality control commission for an adjudicatory hearing pursuant to section 24-4-105, C.R.S., which petition shall be granted by the commission. The hearing shall be held and the matter decided by the commission or a hearing officer designated by the commission within forty-five calendar days after receipt of the petition by the commission. In ruling on the objection, the commission shall have the authority only to uphold or deny the objection.

(VI) The commission shall determine the procedures and criteria that govern its review of local government objections to the installation of emission control units at atmospheric condensate storage tank facilities, and the process provided thereby shall be the exclusive procedure for such disputes. No other local permit or land use approval shall be required for the installation of such emission control units.

## 25-7-133.5. Approval or rescission of specific revisions to state implementation plan (SIP) after 1996.

(1) Consistent with the provisions of section 25-7-105.1, to the extent senate bill 96-129 and senate bill 96-236, enacted at the second regular session of the sixtieth general assembly, approved submitting portions of air quality control commission regulation 1, section VI, to the federal environmental protection agency for inclusion in the state implementation plan, such approval is hereby rescinded. The inclusion of said regulation 1 in the Denver metropolitan nonattainment area state implementation plan for particulate matter (PM-10) is not affected by this rescission.

(2) Pursuant to section 25-7-133, the following revisions to the state implementation plan (SIP) , which were adopted by the air quality control commission on the dates indicated and received by the legislative council for review, are approved for incorporation into the state implementation plan:

(a) The 1993 periodic emissions inventory update to the Denver metropolitan, Colorado Springs, Longmont, and Fort Collins carbon monoxide nonattainment area elements of the SIP, adopted by the air quality control commission on December 21, 1995;

(b) The emergency episode plan revisions as a part of the Denver PM-10 nonattainment area element of the SIP, adopted by the air quality control commission on January 18, 1996;

(c) Amendments adopted by the air quality control commission on September 19, 1996, to the Greeley carbon monoxide nonattainment area element of the SIP;

(d) Amendments adopted by the air quality control commission on October 17, 1996, to the Cañon City PM-10 nonattainment area element of the SIP;

(e) Amendments adopted by the air quality control commission on October 17, 1996, to the Steamboat Springs PM-10 nonattainment area element of the SIP;

(f) Amendments adopted by the air quality control commission on March 21, 1996, and June 20, 1996, to regulation number 3, concerning air pollution emission notice deferral, insignificant activities, and fugitive emissions;

(g) Amendments adopted by the air quality control commission on June 20, 1996, to regulation number 3, concerning prevention of significant deterioration permits, total suspended particulates, and hydrogen sulfide;

(h) Amendments adopted by the air quality control commission on October 14, 1996, to regulation number 10, concerning general conformity;

(i) Amendments adopted by the air quality control commission on March 21, 1996, to regulation number 11, concerning the inspection and maintenance program;

(j) Repealed.

(k) Amendments adopted by the air quality control commission on October 24, 1996, to regulation number 5, concerning the generic banking emissions/trading rules and conforming revisions to regulation number 3, part 4, section V;

(l) Amendments adopted by the air quality control commission on December 21, 1995, to regulations number 1 and 7, and the common provisions concerning negligibly reactive volatile organic compounds and delisting of acetone;

(m) Amendments adopted by the air quality control commission on December 23, 1996, to regulation number 1, concerning opacity limitations and sulfur dioxide averaging provisions for coal-fired electric utility boilers during periods of startup, shutdown, and upset;

(n) Repealed.

(o) Amendments adopted by the air quality control commission on April 17, 1997, to the motor vehicle emissions inspection program in all carbon monoxide nonattainment areas in the state (Boulder, Colorado Springs, Denver, and Greeley) under the carbon monoxide nonattainment area element of the SIP;

(p) Amendments adopted by the air quality control commission on January 15, 1998, redesignating Colorado Springs as an attainment area for carbon monoxide and adopting a corresponding maintenance plan;

(q) Amendments adopted by the air quality control commission on December 18, 1997, to the Longmont carbon monoxide maintenance plan;

(r) Amendments adopted by the air quality control commission on April 17, 1997, concerning long-term strategy for the element of the SIP relating to visibility in class I areas;

(s) Amendments adopted by the air quality control commission on November 21, 1996, to regulations number 3, 7, and 8 and common provisions, concerning negligibly reactive volatile organic compounds and regulated hazardous air pollutants;

(t) Amendments adopted by the air quality control commission on September 17, 1998, to regulation number 1, section II. D., concerning military smokes and obscurants training exercises;

(u) Amendments adopted by the air quality control commission on October 15, 1998, to regulation number 7, concerning emissions of volatile organic compounds;

(v) Amendments adopted by the air quality control commission on October 15, 1998, to regulation number 10, concerning conformity of federally funded or approved transportation plans with air quality implementation plans;

(w) Amendments adopted by the air quality control commission on November 19, 1998, to regulation number 11, part F (III), concerning the motor vehicle emissions inspection program for the Denver-Boulder area;

(x) Amendments adopted by the air quality control commission on January 16, 1998, to regulation number 12, concerning reduction of diesel vehicle emissions;

(y) Repealed.

(z) Amendments adopted by the air quality control commission on January 16, 1998, to section 1.11.0 of the procedural rules of the air pollution control division;

(aa) Amendments adopted by the air quality control commission on September 17, 1998, concerning ambient air quality standards for suspended particulate matter; and

(bb) (I) The "Colorado Visibility and Regional Haze State Implementation Plan for the Twelve Mandatory Class I Federal Areas in Colorado", adopted by the air quality control commission on January 7, 2011.

(II) The automatic expiration of the rules contained in the plan specified in subparagraph (I) of this paragraph (bb) that were adopted on January 7, 2011, and that are therefore scheduled for expiration on May 15, 2012, is postponed, effective May 15, 2011.

(3) Revisions to the SIP that are adopted solely to conform the SIP to prior actions of the general assembly under section 25-7-133 and this section may be submitted to the federal environmental

protection agency for final approval under section 25-7-133 (2) without further approval by the general assembly under section 25-7-133 or this section.

(4) If the division and the designated organization for air quality planning in the Colorado Springs area request removal of mandatory control measures that have been adequately demonstrated to be unnecessary to achieve and maintain compliance with the federal ambient air quality standards and request corresponding modifications to the mobile source emission budget, the commission shall adopt such revisions to the carbon monoxide maintenance plan for the Colorado Springs area approved pursuant to paragraph (p) of subsection (2) of this section. Notwithstanding section 25-7-133, such revisions shall be submitted to the federal environmental protection agency for incorporation into the state implementation plan as expeditiously as possible and shall not be subject to further review and approval pursuant to section 25-7-133.

(5) Revisions to the visibility component of the SIP that implement and enforce a control strategy that meets the following requirements may be submitted to the United States environmental protection agency for incorporation into the SIP as expeditiously as possible without further review and approval pursuant to section 25-7-133:

(a) On or before November 1, 2001, one or more sources have entered into a consent decree in which such sources make a judicially enforceable commitment to adopt such control strategy; and

(b) The division determines that such control strategy provides for reasonable progress:

(I) Toward the national visibility goal stated in federal rules set forth at 40 CFR part 51, subpart P, and in rules of the division set forth at 5 CCR 1001-5, as said rules provided on January 1, 2001; and

(II) In reducing any present or future impairment of an air-quality-related value.

(6) Notwithstanding the provisions of section 25-7-133, revisions to the Denver metropolitan area element of the PM-10 state implementation plan adopted by the commission on April 19, 2001, are approved for incorporation into the state implementation plan, shall be submitted to the federal environmental protection agency as expeditiously as possible, and shall not be subject to further review and approval pursuant to section 25-7-133.

## 25-7-134. Study of air quality control programs. (Repealed)


## 25-7-135. Ozone protection fund created.

(1) There is hereby created in the state treasury an ozone protection fund, which shall consist of fees collected pursuant to section 25-7-105 (11) . In accordance with section 24-36-114, C.R.S., all interest derived from the deposit and investment of moneys in the fund shall be credited to the general fund. Any moneys not appropriated by the general assembly shall remain in the ozone protection fund and shall not be transferred or revert to the general fund of the state at the end of any fiscal year.

(2) (Deleted by amendment, L. 2003, p. 723, § 2, effective July 1, 2003.)

## 25-7-136. Air pollution data collection and technical evaluation - repeal. (Repealed)


## 25-7-137. Requirements for legislative approval of Grand Canyon visibility transport commission or successor body advisory recommendations, reports, and interpretations.

(1) The general assembly hereby finds, determines, and declares:

(a) That the Grand Canyon visibility transport commission (GCVTC) was created pursuant to section 169B of the federal act to issue a report directed toward protecting visibility in the Grand Canyon national park;

(b) That the GCVTC's tasks assigned under the federal act have been completed, and a successor body is being proposed;

(c) That protecting visibility is important to the people of Colorado, is an interstate issue, and is highly technical, complex, and subject to varying interpretations; and

(d) That the provisions of this section are enacted to preserve Colorado sovereignty and to enhance public notice and awareness of the GCVTC or its successor bodies' advisory recommendations, reports, or interpretations, and to ensure public confidence in the fairness of the implementation of any Colorado requirements.

(2) The governor or the governor's designee is encouraged to attend and participate in the successor body to the GCVTC. A stakeholder process shall be implemented to include representatives of the general assembly. The governor shall provide an annual report of the activities of the GCVTC or its successor bodies to the general assembly until such time as the governor has forwarded to the federal environmental protection agency notification that the state shall comply with the provisions of Title 40, code of federal regulations, part 51.308, adopted in accordance with the federal act. The goal of this process is to protect the interest of Colorado over air quality issues.

(3) No final recommendation or report or other action of the GCVTC or its successor bodies may impose any new or different requirements upon the regulated community or citizens of the state of Colorado unless approved or enacted by the general assembly acting by bill.

## 25-7-138. Housed commercial swine feeding operations - waste impoundments - odor emissions - fund created.

(1) All new or expanded anaerobic process wastewater vessels and impoundments, including, but not limited to, treatment or storage lagoons, constructed or under construction for use in connection with a housed commercial swine feeding operation as defined in section 25-8-501.1 (2) (b) shall be covered, or operated with technologies or practices that are as effective as covers at minimizing odor from the operation, to capture, recover, incinerate, or otherwise manage odorous gases to minimize, to the greatest extent practicable, the emission of such gases into the atmosphere. The housed commercial swine feeding operation shall submit to the department of public health and environment information sufficient to demonstrate that the technologies and practices used are as effective as covers at minimizing odor from the operation. The housed commercial swine feeding operation shall manage odor emissions such that odor emissions from the operation shall not be detected at or beyond the property boundary after the odorous air has been diluted with seven volumes of odor-free air. The housed commercial swine feeding operation shall manage odor emissions such that odor emissions from the operation shall not be detected at any off-site receptor after the odorous air has been diluted with two volumes of odor-free air. For purposes of this section, "receptor" means any occupied dwelling used as a primary dwelling or its curtilage, a public or private school, or a place of business. As used in this section, "anaerobic" means a waste treatment method that, in whole or in part, does not utilize air or oxygen. All new aerobic impoundments shall employ technologies to ensure maintenance of aerobic conditions or otherwise to minimize the emission of odorous gases to the greatest extent practicable. As used in this section, "aerobic" means a waste treatment method that utilizes air or oxygen.

(2) All existing anaerobic process wastewater vessels and impoundments, including, but not limited to, aeration tanks and treatment or storage lagoons, owned or operated for use in connection with a housed commercial swine feeding operation as defined in section 25-8-501.1 (2) (b) shall be covered, or operated with technologies or practices that are as effective as covers at minimizing odor from the operation, to capture, recover, incinerate, or otherwise manage odorous gases to minimize, to the greatest extent practicable, the emission of such gases into the atmosphere. The housed commercial swine feeding operation shall submit to the department of public health and environment information sufficient to demonstrate that the technologies and practices used are as effective as covers at minimizing odor from the operation. The housed commercial swine feeding operation shall manage odor emissions such that odor emissions from

the operation shall not be detected at or beyond the property boundary after the odorous air has been diluted with seven volumes of odor-free air. The housed commercial swine feeding operation shall manage odor emissions such that odor emissions from the operation shall not be detected at any off-site receptor after the odorous air has been diluted with two volumes of odor-free air. For purposes of this section, "receptor" means any occupied dwelling used as a primary dwelling or its curtilage, a public or private school, or a place of business. All existing aerobic impoundments shall employ technologies to ensure maintenance of aerobic conditions or otherwise to minimize the emission of odorous gases to the greatest extent practicable.

(3) The commission shall, by rules promulgated on or before March 1, 1999, require that all housed commercial swine feeding operations employ technology to minimize to the greatest extent practicable off-site odor emissions from all aspects of its operations, including odor from its swine confinement structures, manure and composting storage sites, and odor and aerosol drift from land application equipment and sites.

(4) No new land waste application site or new waste impoundment used in connection with a housed commercial swine feeding operation, shall be located less than:

(a) One mile from an occupied dwelling without the written consent of the owner of the dwelling;

(b) One mile from a public or private school without the written consent of the school's board of trustees or board of directors; and

(c) One mile from the boundaries of any incorporated municipality without the consent of the governing body of the municipality by resolution. As used in this subsection (4), a new land waste application site and new waste impoundment are those that were not in use as of June 1, 1998.

(5) The division shall enforce the provisions of this section. The division may delegate enforcement of the provisions of this section to any county or district public health agency. If the division delegates enforcement of this section, the division shall monitor the actions of any county or district public health agency as such actions pertain to enforcement of this section. The division shall assess a housed commercial swine feeding operation an annual fee, not to exceed seven cents per animal, based on the operation's working capacity, to offset the division's direct and indirect costs of enforcement, compliance, and regulation pursuant to this section. This fee shall be designated to fund an inspection and complaint response and enforcement program. By mutual agreement, any county or district public health agency that assists in enforcement of this section shall receive funding to conduct inspections and respond to complaints. As used in this subsection (5), "working capacity" means the number of swine the housed commercial swine feeding operation is capable of housing at any one time. In addition, any person who may be adversely affected by a housed commercial swine feeding operation may enforce these provisions directly against the operation by filing a civil action in the district court in the county in which the person resides.

(6) All moneys collected pursuant to this section shall be transmitted to the state treasurer, who shall credit the same to the housed commercial swine feeding operation fund, which fund is hereby created in the state treasury. The moneys in such fund shall be subject to annual appropriation by the general assembly for the purposes of this section, including the reimbursement of county or district public health agencies for assistance in the enforcement of this section. Any interest earned on moneys in the fund shall remain in the fund and shall not revert to the general fund at the end of any fiscal year.

## 25-7-139. Methyl tertiary butyl ether - prohibition - phase-out - civil penalty.

(1) The general assembly finds and declares that methyl tertiary butyl ether ("MTBE") is an oxygenate used in gasoline and other fuel products in this state and in the United States. The general assembly also finds that MTBE may leak into and contaminate groundwater supplies, and that MTBE is water soluble and therefore is difficult and costly to remove from water. MTBE is colorless, tastes and smells like turpentine, and can be tasted and detected by smell at extremely low concentrations. MTBE may be a human carcinogen and poses other potential health risks, including but not limited to memory loss, asthma, and skin irritation.

(2) The general assembly further finds and declares that water is precious and vital to this state's growing population, agricultural industry, and unique environment. Therefore it is the intent of the general assembly in enacting this section to halt further contamination and pollution of this state's groundwater supplies by MTBE.

(3) (a) (I) Except as otherwise provided in this paragraph (a) , a person may not sell, offer for sale, or store any fuel product containing or treated with MTBE.

(II) The provisions of this paragraph (a) shall not apply if the presence of MTBE in a fuel product is caused solely by incidental commingling of MTBE with the fuel product during storage or transfer of the fuel product. In no event shall the provisions of this subsection (3) be construed to permit the knowing or willful addition of MTBE to any fuel product.

(b) (Deleted by amendment, L. 2005, p. 283, § 21, effective August 8, 2005.)

(c) For purposes of this section, "fuel product" means gasoline, reformulated gasoline, benzine, benzene, naphtha, benzol, and kerosene and any other volatile and inflammable liquid that is produced, compounded, and offered for sale or used for the purpose of generating power in internal combustion engines or generating heat or light or used for cleaning or for any other similar usage.

(4) Any person who violates the provisions of this section shall be subject to a civil penalty as provided in section 25-7-122 (1) (e) .

# PART 2. PREVENTION OF SIGNIFICANT DETERIORATION PROGRAM

### 25-7-201. Prevention of significant deterioration program.

(1) It is the policy of this state to prevent the significant deterioration of air quality in those portions of the state where the air quality is better than the national ambient air quality standards by means including, but not limited to, the following:

(a) Except as provided in section 25-7-209, in areas designated as Class I, II, or III, pursuant to this article and in accordance with the federal act, increases allowed in air pollutant concentrations over the baseline concentration from the construction of major stationary sources or from major modifications shall, in the case of particulate matter and sulfur dioxide, be the same as those increases established by section 163(b) of the federal act and shall, in the case of any other air pollutants, be the same as those increases established pursuant to section 166(a) of the federal act. For any period other than an annual period, the applicable maximum allowable increase may be exceeded during one such period per year at any one location.

(b) No concentration of an air pollutant shall exceed a national ambient air quality standard.

(c) No major stationary source or major modification shall be constructed unless the requirements of this part 2, as applicable, have been met.

### 25-7-202. Definitions. (Repealed)

### 25-7-203. State implementation plan - contents.

In accordance with Part C (Prevention of Significant Deterioration) of the federal act and this part 2, the commission shall incorporate in the state implementation plan emission limitations, requirements for employment of best available control technology, and such other measures as may be necessary to prevent significant deterioration of ambient air quality in each region, or portion thereof, of the state identified pursuant to section 107(d) (1) (D) or (E) of the federal act.

### 25-7-204. Exclusions.

(1) The requirements of the state implementation plan for prevention of significant deterioration of ambient air quality shall not apply to a major stationary source or major modification with respect to a particular pollutant if the owner or operator demonstrates that:

(a) As to the pollutant, the source or modification is subject to part 3 of this article, and the source or modification would impact no area attaining the national ambient air quality standards (either internal or external to areas designated as nonattainment under section 107 of the federal act) ; or

(b) (Deleted by amendment, L. 92, p. 1229, § 27, effective July 1, 1992.)

(c) Such emissions would be from a temporary activity which will not have an adverse impact on air quality in any class I area or an area where an allowable increase over the baseline concentration is known to be violated; except that such temporary activities shall be subject to requirements related to the employment of best available control technology; or

(d) Such emissions would not be significant.

(2) The following pollutant concentrations shall be excluded in determining compliance with maximum allowable increases:

(a) Concentrations attributable to the increase in emissions from sources which have converted from the use of petroleum products, natural gas, or both, by reason of an order in effect under sections (2) (a) and (b) of the federal "Energy Supply and Environmental Coordination Act of 1974" (or any superseding legislation) over the emissions from such sources before the effective date of such an order, but not more than five years after the effective date of such an order;

(b) Concentrations attributable to the increase in emissions from sources which have converted from using natural gas by reason of a natural gas curtailment plan in effect pursuant to the federal "Power Act" over the emissions from such sources before the effective date of such plan but not more than five years after the effective date of the plan; and

(c) (Deleted by amendment, L. 92, p. 1229, § 27, effective July 1, 1992.)

(d) Concentrations of particulate matter attributable to an increase in emissions from temporary activity.

## 25-7-205. Innovative technology - waivers.

The division or the commission may grant a waiver from the best available control technology requirements of this part 2 for proposed new or modified sources in order to encourage the use of an innovative technological system or systems of continuous emission reduction if the administrator of the United States environmental protection agency has delegated such authority and if the division or the commission determines, after notice and opportunity for public hearing, and after securing the consent of the governor of an affected state, to the extent that such consent may be lawfully required by the federal act, that such innovative technological system or systems of continuous emission reduction have a substantial likelihood of achieving greater continuous emission reduction than the means of emission limitation which, but for such waiver, would be required, or of achieving continuous emission reduction equivalent to that which, but for such waiver, would be required, at a lower cost in terms of energy or economic or nonair quality environmental impact. If a public hearing is requested by an interested person, the request shall, within twenty days after its receipt, be transmitted to the commission. The commission shall, within sixty days after its receipt of the request, hold a public hearing with respect thereto and shall, within thirty days after such hearing, issue its decision.

## 25-7-206. Procedure - permits.

(1) Applications for a proposed new or modified source subject to the requirements of this part 2, or any additions to such applications, shall be processed by the division and the commission as provided in sections 25-7-114 to 25-7-114.7.

(2) The owner or operator of a proposed source or modification shall submit all information determined by the division to be reasonably necessary to perform any analysis or make any determination required under this part 2.

(3) The division shall transmit to the administrator of the United States environmental protection

agency a copy of each permit application relating to a major stationary source or major modification. Thereafter, the division and the commission shall provide notice to the administrator of the United States environmental protection agency of every action related to the consideration of such permit.

## 25-7-207. Exemptions. (Repealed)

## 25-7-208. Area designations.

(1) Except as provided in section 25-7-209, all areas of the state shall initially be designated as provided in section 162 of the federal act.

(2) To the extent permitted by section 164 of the federal act, the commission may redesignate any area in the state as a Class I, Class II, or Class III area. The commission shall promulgate rules and regulations in conformity with article 4 of title 24, C.R.S., establishing the procedures for such redesignations; except that:

(a) Such procedures shall be uniform for all redesignations;

(b) Any redesignation may be adopted by the commission only after reasonable notice and public hearing;

(c) All redesignations, except any established by an Indian governing body, shall be specifically approved by the governor, after consultation with the appropriate committees of the general assembly if it is in session or with the leadership of the general assembly if it is not in session, and by resolutions or ordinances enacted by the general purpose unit of local government representing a majority of the residents of the area to be redesignated;

(d) Any redesignation shall constitute a revision to the state implementation plan and shall be submitted to the administrator of the United States environmental protection agency.

(3) Any redesignations or any denial of an application for redesignation made pursuant to subsection (2) of this section shall be subject to judicial review in accord with section 25-7-120.

## 25-7-209. Colorado designated pristine areas for sulfur dioxide.

(1) In the following areas which were designated Colorado category I for sulfur dioxide by the commission on October 27, 1977, the increase allowed in sulfur dioxide concentrations over the baseline concentration shall be the same as the increase established by section 163(b) of the federal act for Class I areas:

(a) National parks:

(I) Rocky mountain;

(II) Mesa Verde;

(III) Great sand dunes;

(IV) Black canyon of the Gunnison;

(b) National monuments:

(I) Florissant fossil beds;

(II) (Deleted by amendment, L. 2009, (SB 09-292) , ch. 369, p. 1971, § 87, effective August 5, 2009.)

(III) Colorado;

(IV) Dinosaur;

(V) (Deleted by amendment, L. 2009, (SB 09-292) , ch. 369, p. 1971, § 87, effective August 5, 2009.)

(c) Forest service wilderness areas:

(I) Eagles nest;

(II) Flattops;

(III) La Garita;

(IV) Maroon bells - Snowmass;

(V) Mount Zirkel;

(VI) Rawah;

(VII) Weminuche;

(VIII) West elk;

(d) Forest service primitive areas:

(I) Uncompahgre mountain;

(II) Wilson mountain;

(e) Lands administered by the federal bureau of land management in the Gunnison gorge recreation area as of October 27, 1977.

## 25-7-210. Applicability.

Sections 25-7-201 and 25-7-203 to 25-7-206 shall apply only to applications for proposed new major stationary sources and major modifications which are submitted on or after the date of approval by the United States environmental protection agency of the program for prevention of significant deterioration embodied in the state implementation plan.

## 25-7-211. Visibility impairment attribution studies.

(1) Any visibility impairment reasonable attribution study pertaining to class I areas shall be subject to balanced peer review by a panel including scientists with appropriate expertise who do not have any substantive involvement with any party, shall be site-specific with respect to any suspected source of impairment and to any impacted area, shall be conducted under the oversight of the division, including, but not limited to, determination of deadlines for such study, and shall utilize study design and data collection and analytical techniques, including, but not limited to, contemporaneous ambient air quality, visibility, and meteorological sampling that allows correlation of the data relevant to any such study. With the exception of emissions from agricultural, horticultural, or floricultural activities that are exempted under section 25-7-109 (8) , relevant data shall include a reasonable assessment of the contributions of emissions from reasonably identifiable sources, including natural sources, within the state and region. Any remedy selection must include relevant economic impact data. In order to minimize delay in the process, the study shall proceed as expeditiously as sound science will allow. The cost of any such study shall not be required to be paid by the department of public health and environment.

(2) Nothing in subsection (1) of this section, as amended by House Bill 05-1180, as enacted at the first regular session of the sixty-fifth general assembly, shall be construed as changing the property tax classification of property owned by a horticultural or floricultural operation.

## 25-7-212. Actions of federal government affecting visibility - evaluation report.

(1) As a part of the state's ongoing development and implementation of a long-term strategy in connection with visibility and air quality related values within class I areas, the division shall evaluate the extent to which the activities of the federal government are directly adversely impacting visibility and air quality related values within a class I area and make a determination whether such entities have taken or are taking all reasonable steps necessary to remedy that impact. At any time, the division may make, and a federal land manager shall respond to, reasonable requests for information necessary for the division to perform such regulation.

(2) The joint public hearing required under section 25-7-105 (4) (a) shall report on the results of the evaluation required under subsection (1) of this section.

(3) (a) The general assembly hereby finds, determines, and declares, after reviewing the factors that contribute to regional haze and visibility impairment in Colorado, that significant contributions to regional haze and visibility impairment emanate from federal lands within the state of Colorado and from federal lands in other parts of the west. For the purpose of addressing regional haze visibility impairment in Colorado's mandatory class I federal areas, the federal land manager of each such area shall develop a plan for evaluating visibility in that area by visual observation or other appropriate monitoring technique approved by the federal environmental

protection agency and shall submit such plan for approval to the division for incorporation by the commission as part of the state implementation plan. Such submittal and compliance by the federal land managers shall be done in a manner and at a time so as to meet all present or future federal requirements for the protection of visibility in any mandatory class I federal area. Such plan shall only be approved by the commission if the expense of implementing such a plan is borne by the federal government.

(b) (I) In addition to the plan submitted by each federal land manager pursuant to paragraph (a) of this subsection (3) , the responsible federal land management agency shall provide an emission inventory to the commission of all federal land management activities in Colorado or other states that result in the emission of criteria pollutants, including surrogates or precursors for such pollutants, that affect any mandatory class I federal area in Colorado by reducing visibility in such an area. Such emission inventory shall be submitted to the commission no later than December 31, 2001, and no less frequently than every five years thereafter.

(II) Each emission inventory submitted to the commission shall be subject to approval by the commission pursuant to section 25-7-105 (17) . The commission shall exempt from the inventory requirement any sources or categories of sources that it determines to be of minor significance.

(III) The commission shall adopt rules to fully implement the general assembly's intention to exercise state powers to the maximum extent allowed under section 118 of the federal act in requiring each federal land management agency with any presence in the state of Colorado to develop and submit to the division an inventory of emissions from lands, wherever situated, which could have any effect on visibility within mandatory class I federal areas located in Colorado. The commission and the division shall use the information from these emission inventories:

(A) To develop control strategies for reducing emissions within the state of Colorado as a primary component of the visibility long-term strategies for inclusion in the state implementation plan;

(B) In any environmental impact statement or environmental assessment required to be performed under the federal "National Environmental Policy Act of 1969", 42 U.S.C. secs. 4321 to 4347; and

(C) To exercise all powers and processes that exist to seek reductions in emissions outside the state of Colorado that reduce visibility in Colorado mandatory class I federal areas.

(IV) The cost of preparing and submitting inventories pursuant to subparagraph (I) of this paragraph (b) shall be borne by the federal government.

## 25-7-213. Visibility and air quality related values policy task force. (Repealed)

## 25-7-214. Visibility impairment subcommittee. (Repealed)

# PART 3. ATTAINMENT PROGRAM

## 25-7-301. Attainment program.

(1) The commission shall develop a program providing for the attainment and maintenance of each national ambient air quality standard in each nonattainment area of the state, in conformity with and as provided in Part D (Nonattainment Program) of the federal act.

(2) Subject to the requirement of subsection (1) of this section:

(a) The attainment program shall be designed to account for and regulate all significant sources of air pollution, including stationary, mobile, and indirect sources, and shall assure that air quality benefits of the control measures utilized bear a reasonable relationship to economic, environmental, and energy impacts and other costs of such measures; and

(b) Control measures required pursuant to the attainment program shall take into consideration the respective contributions of different categories of sources to air pollution, existing control measures, and the availability and feasibility of additional control measures.

### 25-7-302. State implementation plan - contents.
The attainment program embodied in the state implementation plan may, with respect to proposed new or modified major stationary sources within nonattainment areas which would cause or contribute to a violation of a national ambient air quality standard, provide an allowance for growth while providing reasonable further progress toward attainment, and new sources may be allowed that do not result, individually or in the aggregate, in emissions that exceed the allowance. Particulate matter not of a size or substance to adversely affect public health or welfare shall not be considered in determining whether any applicable growth allowance has been consumed. Modifications to an existing facility within a source may be allowed which are accompanied by emission reduction offsets within the same source sufficient to provide no net increase in emissions of an air pollutant from the source. If an applicable growth allowance has been consumed, the attainment program shall permit sources to be constructed only if emission reduction offsets providing a greater than one-for-one emission reduction are obtained from existing sources sufficient to provide reasonable further progress toward attaining the applicable national ambient air quality standards by the attainment date prescribed under Part D (Nonattainment Program) of the federal act. Any emission offsets required for sulfur dioxide, particulates, and carbon monoxide shall provide a positive net air quality benefit in the area affected by the proposed source.

### 25-7-303. Exemptions. (Repealed)

### 25-7-304. Emission reduction offsets.
The attainment program shall provide that emission reduction offsets which exceed those otherwise necessary to the granting of a permit under this part 3 may be preserved for sale or use in the future. Any emission reduction offset so preserved for future use and credit shall be specifically identified either in the state implementation plan or in the permit for the source as to which such offset was originally obtained. Any offsets so preserved and identified shall not in any way be condemned or taken under the provisions of articles 1 to 7 of title 38, C.R.S.

### 25-7-305. Alternative emission reduction.
The attainment program shall provide that upon application of the owner or operator of a stationary source, the commission may approve as a revision to the state implementation plan a proposal to meet the applicable requirements of the state implementation plan for a given air pollutant for two or more facilities or operations within such source through a combination of different requirements which separately may be more or less stringent than the applicable requirements of the state implementation plan; except that the total emissions from such facilities or operations shall not exceed the total emissions allowed by the applicable requirements of the state implementation plan.

# PART 4. CONTROL OF POLLUTION CAUSED BY WOOD SMOKE

### 25-7-401. Legislative declaration.

The general assembly hereby declares that it is in the interest of the state to control, reduce, and prevent air pollution caused by wood smoke. It is therefore the intent of this part 4 to significantly reduce particulate and carbon monoxide emissions caused by burning wood by developing an evaluation and certification program, in the department of public health and environment, for the sale of wood stoves in Colorado and by encouraging the air quality control commission to continue efforts to educate the public about the effects of wood smoke and the desirability of achieving reduced wood smoke emissions. The general assembly hereby finds that it is beneficial to the state to implement a program of voluntary no-burn days whenever the air quality control division determines that the anticipated level of wood smoke will or is likely to have an adverse impact on the air quality in any nonattainment area in the state.

## 25-7-402. Definitions.

As used in this part 4, unless the context otherwise requires:

(1) "Evaluate" means to review wood-burning appliances' emission levels, as determined by an independent testing laboratory, and compare the emission levels to the emission performance standards established by the commission under section 25-7-403.

(2) and (3) Repealed.

## 25-7-403. Commission - rule-making for wood-burning stoves.

(1) The commission shall promulgate rules and regulations to carry out the provisions of this part 4 relating to wood-burning stoves in conformity with the provisions and procedures specified in article 4 of title 24, C.R.S., and which shall become effective only as provided in said article.

(2) (a) In promulgating such rules and regulations, the commission shall:

(I) Set emission performance standards for new wood stoves;

(II) Establish criteria and procedures for testing new wood stoves for compliance with the emission performance standards;

(III) Prescribe the form and content of the emission performance label to be attached to a new wood stove meeting the emission performance standards;

(IV) Establish procedures for administering the program and for collecting fees for the certification of new wood stoves;

(V) Establish fees for certifying new wood stoves at a level such that said fees reflect the direct and indirect costs of administering the program less any general fund or federal grant moneys appropriated to cover the start-up costs of the program;

(VI) Repealed.

(VII) Establish a definition for new wood stoves; and

(VIII) Establish exemptions from the provisions of this subsection (2) of the extent that such exemptions are appropriate.

(b) The moneys collected under this subsection (2) shall be transmitted to the state treasurer, who shall credit the same to the stationary sources control fund established in section 25-7-114.7 (2)

(b) . Any moneys not appropriated by the general assembly shall be retained in the stationary sources control fund and shall not revert to the general fund at the end of any fiscal year.

## 25-7-404. Wood stove testing program established.

(1) There is hereby established, in the department of health, an evaluation and certification program for the control of air pollution caused by wood stove emissions, which is designed to significantly reduce particulate and carbon monoxide emissions, referred to in this part 4 as the "program".

(2) The program as implemented by rules and regulations as set forth in section 25-7-403 shall be administered by the air quality control division. The said division shall establish a program that:

(a) Determines whether or not any new wood stove complies with the emission performance standards set by the commission when tested by an independent testing laboratory;

(b) If such new wood stove complies with the emission performance standards, certifies such compliance.

(3) On or after July 1, 1985, a wood stove manufacturer or dealer may request the air quality control division to evaluate the emissions performance of any new wood stove.

(4) Repealed.

## 25-7-405. Certification required for sale.

(1) On or after January 1, 1987, a person shall not advertise to sell, offer to sell, or sell a new wood stove in Colorado unless:

(a) The particular model of wood stove or the particular configuration of wood stove appliance has been evaluated to determine its emission performance and has been certified by the air quality control division under the program established under this part 4; and

(b) An emission performance label is attached to the wood stove.

## 25-7-405.5. Resale of used noncertified wood-burning devices - prohibited.

On and after January 1, 1993, no used wood-burning device shall be sold or installed in the program area unless such device meets the most stringent standards adopted by the commission pursuant to section 25-7-106.3 (1) .

## 25-7-406. Fireplace design program.

The air pollution control division shall establish a program to study the ways that differences in the structural design of fireplaces affect emissions. The objective of this program will be to determine those structural designs of fireplaces which effectively minimize emissions. The division shall conduct performance tests of different fireplace designs to identify those designs that minimize emissions.

## 25-7-407. Commission - rule-making for fireplaces.

(1) to (7) Repealed.

(8) On and after January 1, 1993, any new or remodeled fireplace to be installed in any dwelling in an area subject to wood-burning limitations provided for in section 25-7-106.3 shall be one of the following:

(a) A gas appliance;

(b) An electric device; or

(c) A fireplace or fireplace insert that meets the most stringent emissions standards for wood stoves established by the commission, or any other clean burning device that is approved by the commission.

(9) No regulation promulgated by the commission in accordance with subsection (8) of this section shall apply to any municipality or a county in the AIR program that has in effect, on and after January 1, 1993, an ordinance or building code provision substantially equivalent to the requirement set forth in subsection (8) of this section, as determined by the commission.

(10) Repealed.

## 25-7-407.5. Certification required for sale. (Repealed)

## 25-7-408. Required compliance in building codes.

(1) (a) Repealed.

(b) On and after January 1, 1993, every board of county commissioners of a county in the AIR program area which has enacted a building code, and thereafter every board of county commissioners of a county in the AIR program area which enacts a building code, shall, pursuant to section 30-28-201 (2) , C.R.S., adopt a building code provision requiring any person who installs or constructs any fireplace to comply with section 25-7-407 (8) .

(2) (a) Repealed.

(b) On and after January 1, 1993, every governing body of a municipality in the AIR program area which has enacted a building code, and thereafter every governing body of a municipality in the AIR program area which enacts a building code, shall, pursuant to section 31-15-601 (2) , C.R.S., adopt a building code provision requiring any person who installs or constructs any fireplace to comply with section 25-7-407 (8) .

(3) Nothing in this article shall prevent a board of county commissioners or a governing body of a municipality from enacting a building code which requires more stringent standards for wood stoves and for fireplaces, if such standards are necessary and reflect technology suitable for commercial application within the meaning of section 25-7-407 (1) .

## 25-7-409. Voluntary no-burn days.

Whenever the air quality control division determines, after investigation, that the level of wood stove emissions anticipated will contribute adversely or is likely to have an adverse impact on the air quality in any nonattainment area in the state, the commission should implement and announce a program of voluntary no-burn days.

## 25-7-410. Applicability.

The provisions of this part 4 do not apply to a used wood stove and shall not apply to any fireplace constructed prior to the date established in section 25-7-407.

## 25-7-411. Legislative declaration.

(1) The general assembly hereby finds, determines, and declares that air pollution in the state of Colorado is a threat to the health and welfare of its citizens and that a major contributor to said pollution is wood smoke, which accounts for twenty-five to forty percent of the brown cloud, fifteen to thirty percent of small particulate matter, hereafter referred to as PM 10, up to ten percent of carbon monoxide, and a portion of toxic, cancer-causing chemicals.

(2) The general assembly further finds, determines, and declares that PM 10 particulates created by wood burning threaten the public health in that said particulates are so small that they lodge in persons' lungs and inhibit the body's pulmonary function. Such pollutant is particularly damaging to persons with lung disease, cardiovascular disease, and chronic upper respiratory conditions, to the very young and elderly, and to pregnant women. The brown cloud is a threat to the economic health of the state because it discourages businesses and tourists from coming to Colorado. Wood burning is one of the most easily controllable sources of air pollution. New technologies can dramatically reduce pollution caused by wood burning. In addition, the reduction of wood burning can reduce the amount of fine particulate emissions into the air.

(3) Therefore, the general assembly finds that it is necessary to implement a plan to further reduce wood smoke emissions in the AIR program area and, therefore, enacts sections 25-7-411 to 25-7-413 to encourage and promote the reduction of wood-burning devices and the use of less polluting devices by taking advantage of new technology.

## 25-7-412. Definitions.

As used in sections 25-7-411 to 25-7-413, unless the context otherwise requires:

(1) "Fireplace insert" means any wood-burning device designed to be installed in an existing fireplace which meets the Phase III standard, as such term is defined in subsection (2) of this section.

(2) "Phase III wood stove" means any wood-burning device that meets the most stringent standards adopted by the commission pursuant to section 25-7-106.3 (1) or any nonaffected wood-burning device that is approved by the commission.

(3) "Program area" means the portions of the six counties in the AIR program area, including Adams, Arapahoe, Boulder, Denver, Douglas, and Jefferson counties.

# 25-7-413. Methods for reducing wood smoke in program area.

(1) Methods for reducing wood smoke in the program area may be implemented, as follows:

(a) Voluntary financial incentives. The lead air quality planning agency for the Denver metropolitan area shall work with other organizations to establish a program of financial incentives to encourage and defray the costs associated with conversions to Phase III wood stoves or to gas or electric devices. The program shall include incentives to use energy efficient devices.

(b) Educational program. The lead air quality planning agency for the Denver metropolitan area shall work with public and private organizations to promote the following: The voluntary upgrade of conventional wood-burning stoves to Phase III stoves and the conversion of existing conventional fireplaces to fireplace inserts or to gas or electric devices;

(c) Voluntary conversions. (I) The commission shall establish goals for voluntary conversion of wood-burning units to cleaner burning technology to be met by December 31, 1994, and by December 31, 1997. The primary objective of the goals shall be to attain and maintain standards for particulate matter established pursuant to the federal "Clean Air Act", taking into account other strategies adopted in the state implementation plan. The goals established by the commission may not exceed the following maximum levels:

(A) The conversion or nonuse of one hundred thousand conventional wood-burning fireplaces to clean technology by December 31, 1994, and one hundred fifty thousand by December 31, 1997;

(B) The conversion or nonuse of twenty thousand conventional wood stoves to Phase III wood stoves by December 31, 1994, and thirty thousand conversions by December 31, 1997.

(II) The goals established pursuant to subparagraph (I) of this paragraph (c) may be less than the maximum levels if the commission determines that such nonuse or conversions are not necessary to attain and maintain federal particulate matter standards.

(d) Contingency plan. (I) In the event that goals established in paragraph (c) of this subsection (1) are not met, or the commission determines that wood-burning controls are necessary to either attain or maintain the standards for particulate matter established pursuant to the 1990 amendments to the federal "Clean Air Act", taking into account other strategies, the commission shall develop and implement a contingency plan.

(II) Prior to the development of the contingency plan, the commission shall contract with an independent contractor to conduct a random survey of the program area to determine public preferences for various wood smoke reduction strategies and shall hold a public hearing before adopting any recommendations concerning wood smoke reduction strategies, which recommendations shall be submitted to the general assembly for action.

(III) Strategies surveyed for public preference and considered by the commission for inclusion in the contingency plan shall include, but need not be limited to, the following:

(A) Charging a fee for residents of dwellings who wish to burn wood in a conventional stove or fireplace and using the fee for conversion incentives, enforcement of rules against burning wood without having paid a fee, and monitoring for compliance with rules;

(B) Conversion to clean burning devices upon the sale of a dwelling unit containing a conventional fireplace or non-Phase III wood stove;

(C) Removal of the exemption for primary heat sources on no-burn days;

(D) A permit-to-burn program with a maximum number of permits determined by the commission and issued in a random but proportional manner throughout the program area.

(2) Verifying voluntary conversions. To measure and verify progress in regard to the provisions of subsection (1) of this section, the commission shall do the following:

(a) The commission shall develop measures for obtaining from consumers in the program area pledges not to use any device other than a Phase III wood stove, fireplace insert, or a gas or electric fireplace; and

(b) The department of revenue shall adopt a procedure for tracking conversions of non-Phase III wood stoves and fireplaces and, if applicable, the number of non-Phase III wood stoves permanently destroyed, which procedure shall include a requirement that retailers regularly submit to the commission the number of consumer purchases of Phase III wood stoves or inserts or gas or electric fireplaces.

(3) Wood smoke reduction fee - termination. (a) On and after July 1, 1992, any retailer who sells a new wood stove or insert or a gas or electric fireplace or fireplace that uses a gas or electric device in the program area shall obtain from the purchaser a signed conversion form, which form shall be provided by the department of revenue, or an entity with which the department is hereby authorized to contract, affirming the purchase of such device and indicating whether the purchase is in connection with a conversion to a cleaner burning device. In addition to obtaining the signed conversion form, the retailer shall submit to the department of revenue in accordance with paragraph (b) of this subsection (3) a fee in the amount of one dollar.

(b) On and after July 1, 1992, and in accordance with paragraph (c) of this subsection (3) , the retailer shall submit to the department of revenue the conversion form along with the fee described in paragraph (a) of this subsection (3) . The department of revenue shall transmit the fee to the state treasurer who shall credit the same to the wood smoke reduction fund, which fund is hereby created. The moneys in the fund shall be subject to annual appropriation by the general assembly to the department of revenue to cover the direct and indirect costs of developing a conversion form in accordance with paragraph (a) of this subsection (3) , tracking conversion in accordance with paragraph (a) of this subsection (3) and paragraph (b) of subsection (2) of this section, and for the department of public health and environment to conduct a survey in connection with the implementation of a contingency plan in accordance with paragraph (d) of subsection (1) of this section; except that no moneys shall be used for conducting a survey in connection with the implementation of a contingency plan in accordance with paragraph (d) of subsection (1) of this section without specific approval by the joint budget committee. In accordance with section 24-36-114, C.R.S., all interest derived from the deposit and investment of this fund shall be credited to the general fund. The department of revenue, or the entity with which the department has contracted pursuant to paragraph (a) of this subsection (3) , shall submit a report to the commission on the number of conversions no later than thirty days after receiving reports from retailers in accordance with paragraph (c) of this subsection (3) .

(c) The retailer shall submit semi-annual reports to the department of revenue no later than on the twentieth day of the month after the close of the preceding six-month period together with the conversion forms and the remittance for all fees collected for the preceding six-month period. If no fees are submitted by the retailer, no report is necessary.

(d) Effective July 1, 1997, the wood smoke reduction fund and the wood smoke reduction fee are eliminated, and the following provisions shall apply:

(I) A retailer within the program area that sells a new wood stove or insert, or a gas or electric fireplace that uses a gas or electric device, between January 1, 1997, and June 30, 1997, shall submit a final semi-annual report to the department of revenue no later than July 20, 1997, together with:

(A) Signed conversion forms indicating whether such purchases were made in connection with a conversion to a cleaner burning device; and

(B) A remittance of the wood smoke reduction fees collected during such period.

(II) A retailer who does not have fees to remit pursuant to sub-subparagraph (B) of subparagraph (I) of this paragraph (d) need not file a final semi-annual report.

(III) Moneys held by the state treasurer in the wood smoke reduction fund on July 1, 1997, and any moneys credited to the fund on or after such date shall be transferred to the general fund.

(4) Commission - rule-making. The commission may promulgate rules necessary for the effectuation of this section.

(5) Repealed.

# PART 5. ASBESTOS CONTROL

# 25-7-501. Legislative declaration.

(1) The general assembly hereby declares that it is in the interest of the general public to control the exposure of the general public to friable asbestos. It is the intent of the general assembly to ensure the health, safety, and welfare of the public by regulating the practice of asbestos abatement in locations to which the general public has access for the purpose of ensuring that such abatement is performed in a manner which will minimize the risk of release of asbestos. However, it is not the intent of the general assembly to regulate occupational health practices which are regulated pursuant to federal laws or to grant any authority to the department of public health and environment to enter and regulate work areas where general public access is limited. It is the intent of the general assembly that the commission may adopt regulations to permit the enforcement of the national emission standards for hazardous air pollutants as set forth in 42 U.S.C. sec. 7412.
(2) Therefore, the general assembly determines and declares that the enactment of this part 5 is a matter of statewide concern to achieve statewide uniformity in the regulation of such asbestos abatement practices and uniformity in the qualifications for and certification of persons who perform such abatement.

# 25-7-502. Definitions.

As used in this part 5, unless the context otherwise requires:
(1) (a) "Area of public access" means any building, facility, or property, or only that portion thereof, that any member of the general public can enter without limitation or restriction by the owner or lessee under normal business conditions; except that "area of public access" includes a single-family residential dwelling and any facility that charges the general public a fee for admission, such as any theater or arena. For purposes of this subsection (1) , "general public" does not include employees of the entity that owns, leases, or operates such building, facility, or property, or such portion thereof, or any service personnel or vendors connected therewith.
(b) Repealed.
(c) Notwithstanding the provisions of paragraph (a) of this subsection (1) , a single family residential dwelling shall not be considered an area of public access for purposes of this part 5 if the homeowner who resides in the single family dwelling that is the homeowner's primary residence requests, on a form provided by the division, that the single family dwelling not be considered an area of public access.
(2) "Asbestos" means asbestiform varieties of chrysotile, amosite, crocidolite, anthophyllite, tremolite, and actinolite.
(3) "Asbestos abatement" means any of the following:
(a) The wrecking or removal of structural members that contain friable asbestos-containing material;
(b) The following practices intended to prevent the escape of asbestos fibers into the atmosphere:
(I) Coating, binding, or resurfacing of walls, ceilings, pipes, or other structures for the purpose of minimizing friable asbestos-containing material from becoming airborne;
(II) Enclosing friable asbestos-containing material to make it inaccessible;
(III) Removal of friable asbestos-containing material from any pipe, duct, boiler, tank, reactor, furnace, or other structural member.
(4) "Commission" means the air quality control commission created by section 25-7-104.
(5) "Division" means the division of administration in the department of public health and environment.
(6) "Friable asbestos-containing material" means any material that contains asbestos and when dry can be crumbled, pulverized, or reduced to powder by hand pressure and that contains more than one percent asbestos by weight, area, or volume. The term includes nonfriable forms of asbestos after such previously nonfriable material becomes damaged to the extent that when dry it can be crumbled, pulverized, or reduced to powder by hand pressure.
(7) "Person" means any individual, any public or private corporation, partnership, association, firm, trust, or estate, the state or any department, institution, or agency thereof, any municipal

corporation, county, city and county, or other political subdivision of the state, or any other legal entity which is recognized by law as the subject of rights and duties.

(7.5) "Project manager" means a person who has satisfied the experience and academic training requirements set forth by the commission.

(8) (a) "School" means any institution that provides elementary or secondary education.

(b) and (c) Repealed.

(9) "State-owned or state-leased buildings" means structures occupied by any person which are either owned by the state or utilized by the state through leases of one year's duration or longer.

(10) "Structural member" means any beam, ceiling, floor, or wall.

(11) "Trained supervisor" means an individual certified by the division to supervise asbestos abatement pursuant to section 25-7-506.

## 25-7-503. Powers and duties of commission - rules - delegation of authority to division.

(1) The commission has the following powers and duties:

(a) To promulgate rules pursuant to section 24-4-103, C.R.S., regarding the following, as are necessary to implement the provisions of this part 5 only for areas of public access:

(I) Performance standards and practices for asbestos abatement which are not more stringent than 29 CFR 1910.1001 and 1926.58;

(II) (A) Determination of a maximum allowable asbestos level, which shall be the highest level of airborne asbestos under normal conditions that allows for protection of the general public; except that, until the commission adopts by rule a level, the maximum allowable asbestos level for the protection of the general public shall be 0.01 fibers per cubic centimeter of air, measured during normal occupancy and calculated as an eight-hour time-weighted average, in accord with 29 CFR 1910.1000 (d) (1) (i) .

(B) If airborne asbestos fiber levels exceed such a level, a second test of samples may be collected during normal occupancy, analyzed by transmission electron microscopy (TEM) analysis, and calculated as an eight-hour time-weighted average in accord with 29 CFR 1910.1000 (d) (1) (i) , before any order of abatement is issued.

(C) Notwithstanding the provisions of sub-subparagraph (A) of this subparagraph (II) , if the asbestos level in the outside ambient air which is adjacent to an asbestos project site or area of public access exceeds 0.01 fibers per cubic centimeter of air, the existing asbestos level in such air shall be the maximum allowable asbestos level.

(III) Exemptions in emergency situations from the requirements of section 25-7-505 regarding the certificate to perform asbestos abatement;

(IV) Requirements for air pollution permits. Permits shall be required for asbestos abatement projects in any building, facility, or structure, or any portion thereof, having public access; except that the requirements of this subparagraph (IV) shall not apply to asbestos abatement projects performed by an individual on a single-family residential dwelling.

(V) Fees for air pollution permits, site inspections, and any necessary monitoring for compliance with this part 5;

(VI) Fees for certification as a trained supervisor;

(VII) Fees for certification which is required under federal law to engage in the inspection of schools, the preparation of asbestos management plans for schools, and the performance of asbestos abatement services for schools;

(VIII) Fees for a certificate to perform asbestos abatement;

(IX) Assessment procedures which determine the need for response actions for friable asbestos-containing materials. Such procedures shall include, but not be limited to, visual inspection and air monitoring which shows an airborne concentration of asbestos during normal occupancy conditions in excess of the maximum allowable level established by the commission in state-owned or state-leased buildings. Nothing in this subparagraph (IX) shall be construed to require that such assessments be made in state-owned or state-leased buildings; however, such procedures

429

shall be followed in the event any such assessment is made.

(X) Requirements for asbestos management plans to be submitted and implemented by schools;

(XI) Fees to be collected from schools for review and evaluation of asbestos management plans;

(b) To promulgate rules pursuant to section 24-4-103, C.R.S., regarding the following, as are necessary to implement the provisions of this part 5, as required by the federal "Clean Air Act", 42 U.S.C. sec. 7412 et seq., as amended:

(I) Determination of the minimum scope of asbestos abatement to which the provisions of this part 5 shall apply, but not less than:

(A) With regard to asbestos abatement projects on a single-family residential dwelling, fifty linear feet on pipes or thirty-two square feet on other materials or the equivalent of a fifty-five-gallon drum;

(B) With regard to asbestos abatement projects not subject to sub-subparagraph (A) of this subparagraph (I) , two hundred sixty linear feet on pipes or one hundred sixty square feet on other materials or the equivalent of a fifty-five-gallon drum;

(II) Requirements of notification, as consistent with the federal act, to demolish, renovate, or perform asbestos abatement in any building, structure, facility, or installation, or any portion thereof, which contains asbestos, except within such minimum scope of asbestos abatement or when otherwise exempt;

(III) (A) Procedures for the inspection and monitoring of sites where demolition, renovation, or the performance of asbestos abatement is taking place, including rules assuring that aggressive air monitoring shall be utilized only in the context of conducting final clearance of an abatement project as outlined in the federal "Asbestos Hazardous Emergency Response Act of 1986", 42 U.S.C. sec. 2641 et seq., and pursuant to the regulations found at 40 CFR 763. Specifications as listed in "measuring airborne asbestos following an abatement action", published by the environmental protection agency in 1985, shall be adopted by the commission as criteria for aggressive sampling.

(B) The division shall provide information to local governments to be used in connection with the issuance of a building permit regarding the need for an inspection for the presence of asbestos-containing materials prior to renovation or demolition of any building, structure, facility, or installation that may contain asbestos.

(IV) (A) Fees for notifications to demolish, renovate, or perform asbestos abatement and for any associated site inspections or necessary monitoring for compliance with this part 5.

(B) Fees pursuant to this subparagraph (IV) shall be paid on an annual basis for large contiguous facility complexes and on an individual notification basis for small noncontiguous facilities.

(V) Requirements to prevent any real or potential conflict of interest between the identification of asbestos-containing materials and the abatement of such materials, including requirements that project managers be used on projects of a certain size, that project managers be independent of the abatement contractor and work strictly on behalf of the building owner to the extent feasible, and that building owners may seek waivers from the project manager requirements.

(c) To approve the examination administered to applicants for certification as a trained supervisor pursuant to section 25-7-506;

(d) To authorize the division to:

(I) Establish procedures regarding applications, examinations, and certifications required under this part 5;

(II) Enforce compliance with the provisions of this part 5, the rules and regulations promulgated thereunder, and any order issued pursuant thereto.

(e) To promulgate rules setting minimum standards for sampling the asbestos in the air and standards for persons engaging in such sampling and to seek injunctive relief under section 25-7-511.5, including relief against any asbestos air sampler who acts beyond his or her level of competency. In promulgating rules setting such standards, the commission shall not use the term "air sampling professional" in such standards.

(f) (I) To adopt rules pursuant to section 24-4-103, C.R.S., setting out required training for persons applying for certification, recertification, or renewal of certificates as required by regulations promulgated by the federal environmental protection agency or the occupational safety and health administration.

(II) Training required pursuant to this paragraph (f) shall not be unduly duplicative or excessive.

(III) Refresher courses shall be required annually.

(2) Notwithstanding any other provisions of this section to the contrary, neither the commission nor the division shall have the authority to enforce standards more restrictive than the federal standards set forth in the "Occupational Safety and Health Act", on asbestos abatement projects which are subject to such federal standards; except that, nothing in this subsection (2) shall be construed to prevent the application and enforcement of the maximum allowable asbestos level prescribed in subparagraph (II) of paragraph (a) of subsection (1) of this section as a clearance level and a condition of reentry by the general public upon completion of the project.

## 25-7-504. Asbestos abatement project requirements - certification required for schools - certificate to perform asbestos abatement - certified trained persons.

(1) (a) Any person who inspects schools for the presence of friable asbestos, prepares asbestos management plans for schools, or conducts asbestos abatement services in schools shall obtain certification pursuant to section 25-7-507.

(b) Any person who inspects public or commercial buildings for the presence of asbestos, prepares management plans for public and commercial buildings, designs abatement actions in public and commercial buildings, or conducts abatement actions in public and commercial buildings shall obtain certification pursuant to section 25-7-507.

(2) (a) Any person who conducts asbestos abatement in any building, other than a school, shall obtain a certificate to perform asbestos abatement pursuant to section 25-7-505 unless such abatement project is exempt from the requirement for certification pursuant to rules and regulations promulgated by the commission.

(b) Unless otherwise exempt, asbestos abatement shall be performed under the supervision of an individual certified by the division as a trained supervisor pursuant to section 25-7-506, who shall be at the project site at all times that work is in progress.

(3) The requirements of this section shall apply to asbestos abatement on a single-family residential dwelling; except that the requirements of this section shall not apply to any individual who performs asbestos abatement on a single-family residential dwelling that is the individual's primary residence.

## 25-7-505. Certificate to perform asbestos abatement - application - approval by division - suspension or revocation of certificate.

(1) Any person may apply to the division for a certificate to perform asbestos abatement by submitting an application in the form specified by the division and by paying a fee set by the commission. Such application shall include, but shall not be limited to:

(a) A description of the applicant's employee training program for asbestos abatement;

(b) A statement identifying all individuals employed by the applicant who are certified as trained supervisors pursuant to section 25-7-506.

(2) No applicant shall be certified to perform asbestos abatement unless the applicant, or at least one of the applicant's employees, is certified as a trained supervisor pursuant to section 25-7-506.

(3) Within fifteen days after receiving an application pursuant to this section, the division shall acknowledge its receipt and notify the applicant as to whether the application is complete. Within thirty days after receiving a completed application, the division shall issue a certificate to the applicant if the division finds that, in addition to all other requirements, the employee training program for asbestos abatement described in the application is acceptable. A certificate issued by the division pursuant to this section shall be valid for three years from the date of issuance.

(4) A certificate issued pursuant to this section may be suspended or revoked for the failure to implement the employee training program for asbestos abatement described in the application

submitted pursuant to this section.

## 25-7-505.5. Testing for certification under part 5.

(1) The division shall develop or purchase the examinations administered pursuant to this part 5 for certification under sections 25-7-506, 25-7-506.5, and 25-7-507 and shall set the passing scores on all such examinations based on a minimum level of competency in the procedures to be followed in asbestos abatement. The division shall administer such examinations at least twice each year or more frequently if demand so warrants and shall administer such examinations at various locations in the state if demand so warrants. The purpose of the examinations required pursuant to this section is to ensure minimum competency in asbestos abatement procedures. If a person fails to achieve a passing score on any such examination, retesting of such person shall be with a different examination and after such person has completed remedial training as determined to be satisfactory to the division for minimum competency in asbestos abatement procedures. Prior to such reexamination, an applicant shall file a new application and pay a fee set by the division. Such fee shall be no greater than the amount paid for the original examination.

(2) Notwithstanding the provisions of sections 25-7-506, 25-7-506.5, and 25-7-507, the division may certify an individual under this part 5 by endorsement if such individual possesses in good standing a valid license, certificate, or other registration from any other state or territory of the United States or from the District of Columbia, if the applicant presents proof satisfactory to the division that at the time of application for a Colorado certificate by endorsement the applicant possesses qualifications substantially equivalent to those of this part 5 as determined by the division.

## 25-7-506. Certificate of trained supervisors - application - approval by division - rules - responsibilities of trained supervisors - renewal of certificate.

(1) Any individual may apply to the division to be certified as a trained supervisor by submitting an application in the form specified by the division and paying a fee set by the commission. Within fifteen days after receiving an application, the division shall notify the applicant as to whether the application is complete.

(2) Within thirty days after receiving a completed application and the results of the examination administered pursuant to paragraph (b) of this subsection (2) , the division shall issue a certification valid for a period not to exceed five years as established by the commission by rule from the date of issuance upon a finding:

(a) That the applicant has, within twelve months prior to the date of the application, completed a training course on safe asbestos abatement procedures which has been approved by the division; and

(b) That the applicant has passed an examination administered by the division pursuant to section 25-7-505.5 on the procedures to be followed in asbestos abatement.

(3) An individual acting as a trained supervisor pursuant to this section shall be responsible for supervising a specific asbestos abatement project in such a manner as to assure that asbestos abatement is performed in compliance with the provisions of this part 5 and the rules and regulations promulgated thereunder.

(4) (Deleted by amendment, L. 92, p. 1232, § 37, effective July 1, 1992.)

(5) (Deleted by amendment, L. 95, p. 22, § 3, effective July 1, 1995.)

## 25-7-506.5. Certification of air monitoring specialist - rules.

(1) No person may perform air monitoring or air monitoring specialist activities for asbestos, as set forth in rules promulgated by the commission, including visual clearance inspections of an asbestos abatement project, without first obtaining a certificate pursuant to this section.

(2) Any individual may apply to the division to be certified as an air monitoring specialist by submitting an application in the form specified by the division and paying a fee set by the

commission. Within fifteen days after receiving an application, the division shall notify the applicant as to whether the application is complete.

(3) Within thirty days after receiving a completed application, the division shall issue a certification valid for a period not to exceed five years as established by the commission by rule from the date of issuance upon a finding that the applicant has successfully met the experience, education, examination, and training requirements and has paid a fee, as set forth in rules promulgated by the commission.

## 25-7-507. Certification required under federal law for asbestos projects in schools and public and commercial buildings.

Pursuant to the federal "Asbestos Hazard Emergency Response Act of 1986" (Public Law 99-519) and the federal "Asbestos School Hazard Abatement Reauthorization Act of 1990" (Public Law 101-637) , the division shall certify, in the manner required under the federal law, all persons engaged in the inspection of schools or public or commercial buildings, the preparation of management plans for schools or public or commercial buildings, the design of abatement actions in schools or public or commercial buildings, or the conduct of abatement actions in schools or public or commercial buildings.

## 25-7-507.5. Renewal of certificates - rules - recertification.

(1) Any certificate issued pursuant to this part 5 that has lapsed shall be deemed to have expired.

(2) (a) A certificate issued pursuant to this part 5 may be renewed prior to expiration upon payment of a renewal fee set by the commission.

(b) Renewal of a certificate may be made for a period not to exceed five years as established in rules promulgated by the commission.

(3) An individual may reinstate an expired certificate within one year after such expiration upon payment of a reinstatement fee in an amount set by the commission.

(4) An individual whose certificate has lapsed for a period longer than one year after expiration shall apply to the division for certification as required by this part 5 and shall not be recertified until the division determines that such individual has fully complied with the requirements of this part 5 and any rules promulgated pursuant thereto.

(5) (a) Any individual whose certificate has lapsed because such individual has not completed the refresher course required pursuant to section 25-7-503 (1) (f) may complete such refresher course within one year after the date the certificate lapses.

(b) Completion of the refresher course shall be a requirement for recertification.

(c) (I) The commission shall promulgate rules governing refresher training programs for persons in both school and nonschool asbestos abatement. Such programs shall not exceed the requirements of refresher training mandated under the federal "Asbestos Hazard Emergency Response Act of 1986" (Public Law 99-519) and any rules promulgated pursuant to such federal law.

(II) In adopting rules the commission shall ensure that refresher training requirements are related to ensuring continuing competency in asbestos abatement procedures.

(III) The division shall implement a system of testing to measure the knowledge obtained by certified persons attending the refresher training programs. Such testing shall not exceed the requirements of refresher training mandated pursuant to federal law.

## 25-7-508. Grounds for disciplinary action - letters of admonition - denial of certification - suspension, revocation, or refusal to renew - requirement for corrective education - administrative fines.

(1) When an application for certification pursuant to section 25-7-505, 25-7-506, 25-7-506.5, 25-7-507, or 25-7-507.5 is denied by the division, the applicant may contest the decision of the division by requesting a hearing before the office of administrative courts. A request for a hearing

433

must be made within thirty calendar days after the division has issued a denial of the application in writing to the applicant. The hearing shall be held pursuant to section 25-7-119.

(2) (a) The division may take disciplinary action in the form of the issuance of a letter of admonition or, in conformity with the provisions of article 4 of title 24, C.R.S., the suspension, revocation, or refusal to renew certification pursuant to section 25-7-505, 25-7-506, 25-7-506.5, 25-7-507, or 25-7-507.5, should the division find that a person certified under this part 5:

(I) Has violated or has aided and abetted in the violation of any provision of this part 5 or any rule or regulation or order of the division or commission promulgated or issued under this part 5;

(II) (A) Has been subject to a disciplinary action relating to a certification or other form of registration or license to practice asbestos abatement under this part 5 or any related occupation in any other state, territory, or country for disciplinary reasons, which action shall be deemed to be prima facie evidence of grounds for disciplinary action, including denial of certification by the division.

(B) This subparagraph (II) shall apply only to disciplinary actions based upon acts or omissions in such other state, territory, or country substantially similar to those set out as grounds for disciplinary action pursuant to this part 5.

(C) A plea of nolo contendere or its equivalent to a charge of violating a law or regulation governing the practice of asbestos removal in another state, territory, or country that is accepted by the disciplining body of such other state, territory, or country may be considered to be the same as a finding of guilt for purposes of a hearing conducted by the division pursuant to this subsection (2).

(III) Has been convicted of a felony or has had accepted by a court a plea of guilty or nolo contendere to a felony if the felony is related to the ability to engage in activities regulated pursuant to this part 5. A certified copy of the judgment of a court of competent jurisdiction of such conviction or plea shall be conclusive evidence of such conviction or plea. In considering the disciplinary action, the division shall be governed by the provisions of section 24-5-101, C.R.S.

(IV) Has failed to report to the division a disciplinary action specified in subparagraph (II) of this paragraph (a) or a felony conviction for an act specified in subparagraph (III) of this paragraph (a);

(V) Has failed to meet any permit and notification requirement or failed to correct any violations cited by the division during any inspection within a reasonable period of time;

(VI) Has used misrepresentation or fraud in obtaining or attempting to obtain a certificate under this part 5;

(VII) Has failed to adequately supervise an asbestos abatement project as a certified trained supervisor;

(VIII) Has committed any act or omission which does not meet generally accepted standards of the practice of asbestos abatement;

(IX) Has engaged in any false or misleading advertising.

(b) When a complaint or an investigation discloses an instance of misconduct which, in the opinion of the division, does not warrant suspension or revocation by the division but which should not be dismissed as being without merit, a letter of admonition may be sent by certified mail to the certified person against whom a complaint was made and a copy thereof to the person making the complaint, but, when a letter of admonition is sent by certified mail by the division to a certified person complained against, such certified person shall be advised that such person has the right to request in writing, within twenty days after proven receipt of the letter, that formal disciplinary proceedings be initiated against such person to adjudicate the propriety of the conduct upon which the letter of admonition is based. If such request is timely made, the letter of admonition shall be deemed vacated, and the matter shall be processed by means of formal disciplinary proceedings.

(3) A person aggrieved by an action taken by the division pursuant to subsection (2) of this section may contest the action by requesting a hearing before the office of administrative courts within thirty days after the applicant is notified in writing of the division's action. The hearing shall be held pursuant to section 25-7-119. Any person aggrieved by an action taken by the office of

administrative courts pursuant to subsection (2) of this section may appeal the action to the court of appeals in accordance with section 24-4-106 (11) , C.R.S.

(4) In addition to or in lieu of the forms of disciplinary action authorized in subsection (2) of this section, the division, in its discretion, may require corrective education in the area of asbestos abatement as a disciplinary action against a certified person when the situation so warrants, such corrective education to be directed toward weak or problematic areas of a certified person's practice.

(5) Any certified person who violates any provision of this section, in addition to any other enforcement action available under this article, may be disciplined upon a finding of misconduct by the division as follows:

(a) In any first administrative proceeding against a certified person, a fine of not less than one hundred dollars nor more than one thousand dollars;

(b) In a second or subsequent administrative proceeding against a certified person for transactions occurring after a final agency action determining that a violation of this part 5 has occurred, a fine of not less than one thousand dollars nor more than ten thousand dollars.

(6) If a certification is revoked by the division, the person against whom such action was taken shall not apply for recertification for a period of one year after such revocation and shall be required to demonstrate compliance with any disciplinary action imposed by the division and to demonstrate competency in asbestos abatement procedures prior to receiving a new certificate.

## 25-7-509. Prohibition against local certification regarding asbestos abatement.

Inasmuch as uniformity in the regulation of asbestos abatement practices and uniformity in the qualifications and certification of persons performing asbestos abatement is a matter of statewide concern, no certification or licensing of asbestos abatement projects nor any examination or certification of persons certified under this part 5 shall be required by any city, town, county, or city and county; however, any such local governmental authority may impose reasonable registration requirements on any person performing asbestos abatement as a condition of performing such activity within the jurisdiction of such authority. Registration fees charged by any such local governmental authority to any such person shall not exceed those costs associated with such registration requirements and functions.

## 25-7-509.5. Building permits.

(1) Except as otherwise provided in subsection (2) of this section, a local government entity with authority to issue building permits shall require a property owner applying for either a permit to renovate property or a permit to demolish property to disclose, on the permit application form, whether the property owner knows if the property has been inspected for asbestos.

(2) (a) A local government entity with authority to issue building permits need not update its application forms to include the disclosure required by subsection (1) of this section until the entity otherwise creates and disseminates updated application forms pursuant to its standard practice. The local government entity need not require a property owner applying for a permit to renovate or demolish property to make the disclosure required by subsection (1) of this section until it has updated its application forms.

(b) When updating the application form for a permit to renovate property or a permit to demolish property, the local government entity shall include on the application form substantially the following information:

&squ;I DO NOT KNOW IF AN ASBESTOS INSPECTION HAS BEEN CONDUCTED ON THE BUILDING MATERIALS THAT WILL BE DISTURBED BY THIS PROJECT.

&squ;AN ASBESTOS INSPECTION HAS BEEN CONDUCTED ON THE BUILDING MATERIALS THAT WILL BE DISTURBED BY THIS PROJECT ON OR ABOUT:

&squ;AN ASBESTOS INSPECTION HAS NOT BEEN CONDUCTED ON THE BUILDING
MATERIALS THAT WILL BE DISTURBED BY THIS PROJECT.

## 25-7-510. Fees.

(1) (a) The fees required pursuant to this part 5 shall be established pursuant to rules and
regulations promulgated by the commission.

(b) The commission shall adjust the fees so that the revenue generated from such fees is sufficient
to cover the division's direct and indirect costs in implementing the provisions of this part 5.

(2) All fees collected by the division pursuant to this part 5 shall be transmitted to the state
treasurer, who shall credit the same to the stationary sources control fund established pursuant to
section 25-7-114.7 (2) (b) . The general assembly shall appropriate to the department of public
health and environment, at least annually, from the fund, an amount sufficient to implement the
provisions of this part 5.

## 25-7-511. Enforcement.

(1) Whenever the division has reason to believe that any person has violated any of the provisions
of this part 5 or the rules and regulations promulgated thereunder, the division may issue a notice
of violation and cease-and-desist order. The notice of violation shall set forth the provision, rule,
or regulation alleged to have been violated and the facts constituting such violation. The cease-
and-desist order shall set forth the measures which the person shall take to eliminate the violation
and the time within which these measures shall be performed. The order may require that the
person stop work at the asbestos abatement project until the violation has been eliminated or may
require a school to submit and implement an asbestos management plan by a date specified by the
division.

(2) If the recipient of a cease-and-desist order issued pursuant to subsection (1) of this section fails
to comply with the terms of the order within the time specified, the division may file an action in
the district court of the county where the violation is alleged to have occurred requesting that the
court order the person to comply with the cease-and-desist order. When the division alleges that
the violation poses a significant danger to the health of any person, the court shall grant such
action priority.

(3) Unless the division has filed an action in the district court pursuant to subsection (2) of this
section, a recipient of a cease-and-desist order may request a hearing before the commission to
contest the cease-and-desist order. Such request shall be filed within thirty days after the cease-
and-desist order has been issued. A hearing on the cease-and-desist order shall be held pursuant to
section 25-7-119.

(4) Upon a finding by the division that a person is in violation of any of the provisions of this part
5 or the rules and regulations promulgated thereunder, the division may assess a penalty of up to
twenty-five thousand dollars per day of violation or such lesser amount as may be required by
applicable federal law or regulation. In determining the amount of the penalty to be assessed, the
division shall consider the seriousness of the danger to the public's health caused by the violation,
whether or not the violation was willful, the duration of the violation, and the record of the person
committing such violation.

(5) A person subject to a penalty assessed pursuant to subsection (4) of this section may appeal the
penalty to the commission by requesting a hearing before the commission. Such request shall be
filed within thirty days after the penalty assessment is issued. A hearing pursuant to this
subsection (5) shall be conducted pursuant to section 25-7-119.

(6) All penalties collected pursuant to this section shall be transmitted to the state treasurer, who
shall credit the same to the general fund.

## 25-7-511.5. Injunctive proceedings.

(1) The division may, in the name of the people of the state of Colorado, through the attorney

general of the state of Colorado, apply for an injunction in any court of competent jurisdiction:
(a) To enjoin any person from committing any act prohibited by the provisions of this part 5;
(b) To enjoin a certified person from practicing the profession for which he is certified under this part 5.
(2) If it is established that the defendant has been or is committing any act prohibited by this part 5, the court shall enter a decree perpetually enjoining said defendant from further committing said act or from practicing asbestos abatement.
(3) Such injunctive proceedings shall be in addition to and not in lieu of all penalties and other remedies provided in this part 5.
(4) When seeking an injunction under this section, the division shall not be required to allege or prove either that an adequate remedy at law does not exist or that substantial or irreparable damage would result from a continued violation.

### 25-7-511.6. Refresher training - authorization.
The commission shall promulgate rules and regulations governing refresher training programs for persons in both school and nonschool asbestos abatement. Such programs shall not exceed the requirements of refresher training mandated under the federal "Asbestos Hazard Emergency Response Act of 1986" (Public Law 99-519) , as amended, and any rules and regulations promulgated under such federal law. In adopting such rules and regulations, the commission shall ensure that refresher training requirements are related to ensuring continuing competency in asbestos abatement procedures. The division shall implement a system of testing to measure the knowledge obtained by certified persons attending such programs.

### 25-7-512. Repeal of part.
This part 5 is repealed, effective September 1, 2022. Before the repeal, the department of regulatory agencies shall review the functions of the division under this part 5 as provided for in section 24-34-104, C.R.S.

# PART 6. DIESEL INSPECTION PROGRAM

**25-7-601 to 25-7-610. (Repealed)**

# PART 7. TRAVEL REDUCTION TASK FORCE

**25-7-701 to 25-7-706. (Repealed)**

# PART 8. TRAVEL REDUCTION PROGRAM

**25-7-801 to 25-7-806. (Repealed)**

# PART 9. CLEAN AIR TRANSIT OPTIONS

### 25-7-901. Legislative declaration.
The general assembly hereby declares that the state's effort to mitigate traffic congestion and promote clean air will be served by providing clean air transit options to state employees.

### 25-7-902. Definitions.
(1) "State agency" means any department, board, bureau, commission, institution, or other agency of the state, including institutions of higher education.
(2) "State employees" means the employees of any state agency.

### 25-7-903. Clean air transit options for state employees.
Any state agency may provide clean air transit options to state employees of that agency, including, but not limited to, the use of available mass transit. The financing of any transit option offered by a state agency to state employees shall be from existing appropriations to that state agency. A transit option shall be considered a perquisite that is subject to the state controller's fiscal rules controlling perquisites under section 24-30-202 (22) , C.R.S.

# PART 10. AIR QUALITY RELATED VALUES - CLASS I FEDERAL AREAS

### 25-7-1001. Legislative declaration.
In order to establish a fair, practical, and cost-effective process for evaluating and, where appropriate, responding to assertions that air quality related values within Colorado's class I federal areas are being significantly and adversely affected by air pollution, such as air pollution that is causing biological harm, the general assembly hereby institutes the procedures set forth in this part 10.

### 25-7-1002. Air quality related values program.
(1) In addition to maintaining a program that complies with the requirements of the federal act for prevention and remediation of significant deterioration of visibility in class I federal areas, the commission, in consultation with the general assembly, the governor, and affected federal, state, and local governmental entities, shall maintain a state-retained authority program in conformance with section 25-7-105.1 for nonvisibility air quality related values, referred to in this part 10 as the "program".
(2) The commission shall develop a program under which, except for grant funds secured from other sources, the federal government undertakes the responsibility for the funding of air quality related value baseline data collection and the verification studies needed to substantiate an assertion of significant impairment, and the commission is encouraged to conduct the activities specified in this part 10 in coordination with interested state and local governmental entities and affected citizens and businesses.

### 25-7-1003. Definitions.
As used in this part 10:
(1) "Air quality related value (AQRV) " means a feature or property of a class I federal area other than visibility that the state of Colorado finds may be affected by air pollution. General categories of air quality related values include odor, flora, fauna, soil, water, geologic features, and cultural

resources.

(2) "Air quality related value baseline data" means research data based on site-specific measurements and samplings of air quality related values within a class I federal area needed to substantiate a determination of whether or not a particular observation is within the range of naturally occurring changes or fluctuations.

(3) "Best available retrofit technology" means a control strategy for addressing emissions of a stationary source developed on a case-by-case basis after taking into consideration the costs of compliance, the energy and nonair quality environmental impacts of compliance, any existing pollution control technology in use at the source, the remaining useful life of the source, and the degree of improvement in the air quality related value that may reasonably be anticipated to result from the use of such technology.

(4) "Peer review" means a review of scientific or technical information by a balanced objective panel of experienced scientists qualified to review the subject matter involved in verifying the existence of or attributing the cause of an AQRV impairment.

(5) "Reasonably available control measure" means a control strategy for addressing emissions of a nonstationary source developed on a case-by-case basis after taking into consideration the options available to achieve emission reductions that a particular source or source category is capable of meeting as appropriate to an air quality related value if such steps may be feasibly and practicably taken considering technical and economic constraints.

(6) "Significant impairment of an air quality related value" means a measurable change in an air quality related value that is outside the probability of natural variability, that is caused by human activities, and that is causing a significant adverse effect to flora, fauna, soil, geologic features, cultural resources, or a beneficial use of water recognized under Colorado law.

## 25-7-1004. Administration of program by division.

(1) In administering the program, the division shall:

(a) Conduct or oversee program activities and scientific studies and determine an appropriate scope, sequence, and timetable for such studies and activities;

(b) Subject assertions by a federal land manager of air quality related value impairment in a class I federal area and studies concerning source attribution and source apportionment to peer review;

(c) Utilize the study design and data collection and analytical techniques set forth in section 25-7-211 that are relevant and appropriate to the activity or study;

(d) Assure that studies proceed as expeditiously as sound science will allow in order to minimize any delay in the process.

(2) As necessary or appropriate, the division may:

(a) Enter into memoranda of understanding for participation in the studies and activities required by this part 10;

(b) Create cooperative public-private partnerships with various entities; and

(c) Perform any other appropriate activity to carry out the intent of the program.

(3) The division shall not be required to pay the cost of any studies that are discretionary as set forth in this part 10 other than as set forth in this section. If the division determines that an air quality related value of a class I federal area has the potential to be significantly threatened by air pollution, or is being impacted by air pollution, then the division shall apply for grants or act as a catalyst to secure financial support from available funding sources in federal, state, or local governments and private entities, to identify the threat by funding the necessary air quality related value baseline data collection, or to assist in remedying the threat by funding necessary attribution or apportionment studies. The division is also authorized to act as a catalyst to secure financial support from other sources for such studies. The results of such studies and data collection shall be made available to the appropriate federal land manager and interested members of the public to assist in the management of these scenic resources and to cooperate in any needed air quality related values assessments.

## 25-7-1005. Verification of federal land manager's assertion of air quality related value impairment.

(1) The federal land manager of a class I federal area may initiate the procedures of this part 10 by submitting to the governor and division an assertion of significant impairment of an air quality related value, referred to in this part 10 as an "assertion". To be adequate to support a verification of impairment, the assertion shall be supported by sufficient air quality related value baseline data and site-specific evidence of impairment. The assertion may be supported in part by information that concerns other areas with a similar environment to the class I federal area asserted to be impaired, provided such information is relevant to the class I federal area asserted to be impaired and significant site-specific data is also available.

(2) Upon receipt of an assertion, the division shall initiate the following actions concurrently:

(a) Inform the commission at its next regularly scheduled monthly meeting of the receipt of an assertion, at which time the commission shall schedule the matter for a formal report from the division at the regular commission meeting that is scheduled to occur six months subsequent. All such informational briefings and formal reports on the subject shall be noticed on the published agenda of the commission.

(b) Within sixty days of receipt of the assertion, the division shall convene a peer review panel to review the assertion, its supporting documentation, including the adequacy of the baseline data and the adequacy of the site-specific and other evidence of impairment, and any other relevant information submitted to the division by the public. The requirement for peer review as specified in this paragraph (b) is waived with respect to any peer reviewer who has not submitted peer review comments within sixty days of the date on which the division certifies that the assertion, documentation, and other information has been transmitted to the individual peer reviewers.

(c) Convene a consultation process that is open to the public in order to apprise the public and potentially affected sources and source categories of all stages of the program and to solicit the scientific, technical, economic, and managerial views and assistance of the public and the potentially affected sources and source categories; and

(d) Initiate a review by division staff of the assertion and the supporting documentation submitted by the federal land manager to assess whether the federal land manager has demonstrated a significant impairment of an air quality related value in a class I federal area within Colorado.

(3) At the commission meeting required by paragraph (a) of subsection (2) of this section, the division shall report to the commission. The division's report shall include, but is not limited to, the conclusions of the peer review panel concerning verification of the assertion and the division's determination of whether the federal land manager has demonstrated a significant impairment of an air quality related value in a class I area within Colorado. If the division determines that the assertion has not been verified, it shall so notify the commission and the federal land manager of its findings and the fact that the proceedings authorized under this part 10 have been completed. If the division determines that the assertion has been verified, it shall proceed in accordance with the provisions of section 25-7-1006.

## 25-7-1006. Source attribution and control strategy development.

(1) If the division determines that the assertion has been verified, it shall:

(a) Compile a comprehensive inventory of the sources of the pollutants that are suspected to be causing the impairment;

(b) Subject the development, conduct, and results of the attribution and apportionment studies to appropriate peer review; and

(c) Perform attribution and apportionment studies to the extent feasible in order to develop for the division and the commission the identity and relative contribution of the significant contributors to air quality related value impairment, including, but not limited to, stationary sources, natural sources, wood smoke, agriculture, mining, roads, mobile source categories, and other area sources. The general assembly recognizes that the ability to attribute the cause of air pollution effects and apportion the air pollution effects among sources and source categories identified by attribution studies is an area of evolving science.

(2) (a) The funding of source attribution and apportionment studies shall be derived as provided in this subsection (2) . Contributions to support the funding of such studies shall be requested from sources and source categories identified by the division as potentially contributing to the impairment.

(b) If a potential contribution to impairment is identified from federal lands or state lands, the division shall request a funding contribution for such studies from the appropriate federal or state land manager.

(c) If a potential contribution to impairment is identified from stationary sources or source categories, the division shall request a funding contribution for such studies from such sources or source categories.

(d) If a potential contribution to impairment is identified from mobile sources, the division shall seek an appropriation by the general assembly of excess funds in the AIR account in the highway users tax fund for funding contributions to such studies.

(e) The division shall annually report to the legislative council on the adequacy of funding derived pursuant to this subsection (2) . If funding derived pursuant to this subsection (2) is inadequate, the legislative council may recommend that the general assembly appropriate funds from available sources for purposes of this section.

(3) Following its review and analysis of the reasonable attribution and source apportionment studies and the reports thereon from the members of the peer review panel, the division shall identify those sources and source categories within the state and region significantly contributing to air quality related value impairment.

(4) The division shall identify the sources and source categories significantly contributing to air quality related value impairment that are located outside the state and report this list to the commission, governor, and general assembly for their consideration in identifying options for remedying such impacts.

(5) The division shall issue an order to the sources and source categories significantly contributing to air quality related value impairment located within the state that have not made a voluntary enforceable commitment under section 25-7-1008.

(6) (a) An order issued pursuant to subsection (5) of this section shall require:

(I) Such sources and source categories to submit a report within a reasonable period of time;

(II) A stationary source to identify the best available retrofit technology; and

(III) Other sources and source categories to identify reasonably available control measures.

(b) After considering the responses to an order issued pursuant to subsection (5) of this section, the division shall issue a public report to the commission concerning its recommendations on air quality related value impairment, source attribution, source apportionment, and control strategy options.

## 25-7-1007. Commission to consider control strategies in rule-making proceeding.

(1) Upon receipt of a report under section 25-7-1006 (6) (b) from the division, and after the division has made the report available to all significant source or source categories identified pursuant to section 25-7-1006, the commission shall give notice that it is to conduct a rule-making hearing concerning the implementation of control strategies recommended in the report.

(2) In addition to other applicable rule-making provisions, the rule-making hearing shall be conducted:

(a) In reasonable proximity to the affected class I federal area;

(b) To allow sufficient time for comment and testimony by all interested persons; and

(c) To allow reasonable discovery pursuant to section 24-4-103 (13) and (14) , C.R.S.

(3) (a) The commission shall order by rule implementation within a reasonable time of a practical and cost-effective control strategy or strategies that will provide reasonable progress toward remedying the impairment, if the commission finds that:

(I) The evidence in the record shows the existence of a significant impairment of an air quality related value in a class I federal area;

(II) An identifiable source or source category is responsible for significantly causing or contributing to the impairment;

(III) The best available retrofit technology exists for any such stationary source;

(IV) Reasonably available control measures exist for any such other sources or source categories;

(V) Implementation of the control strategies would make significant improvement in the impairment;

(VI) Taking into account that the ability to attribute the cause of air pollution effects and to apportion the air pollution effects among sources and source categories identified by attribution studies is an area of evolving science, a correlation of the extent of improvement in air quality related value impairment can reasonably be expected to result from imposition of a control strategy or strategies for each significant source or source category identified by the division.

(b) Within fourteen days after having received the division's report under section 25-7-1006 (6) (b) , a source or source category may petition the commission, as part of its rule-making hearing conducted pursuant to this subsection (3) , to make a determination that the benefits of phasing, segmenting, or excusing the control strategy or strategies outweigh the benefits of imposing the control strategy or strategies. In making such determination, the commission shall consider all economic and related costs associated with the implementation of the control strategy or strategies involving the source or source category. The burden of proof shall be on the petitioner.

## 25-7-1008. Voluntary agreements.

(1) The division may convene, at any appropriate time, an informal voluntary negotiation process, with appropriate public participation, to seek voluntary enforceable commitments from sources and source categories to achieve emissions reductions sufficient to make reasonable further progress in reducing any portion of the impairment.

(2) A voluntary enforceable commitment becomes enforceable through a commission rule, local ordinance or resolution, judicially enforceable consent decree, or division permit condition, as appropriate to the circumstances.

(3) If subsequent to January 15, 1996, a source or source category agrees to an enforceable commitment to adopt a control strategy that the division determines is as effective or is more effective than best available retrofit technology for stationary sources or reasonably available control measures for nonstationary sources, the division shall exempt that source or source category from the imposition of further controls pursuant to this part 10 for a period of ten years from the date established for achieving the emission reductions as specified in the voluntary enforceable agreement.

(4) If subsequent to January 15, 1996, and prior to January 15, 1998, a source or source category agrees to an enforceable commitment contained in a judicially enforceable consent decree to adopt a control strategy that the division determines provides both for reasonable progress toward the national visibility goal under 40 CFR Part 51, Subpart P and 5 CCR 1001-4 and for reasonable progress in reducing any present or future impairment of an air quality related value, the division shall exempt that source or source category from the imposition of further controls pursuant to this part 10 for a period of ten years from the date established for achieving the emission reductions as specified in the judicially enforceable consent decree. The provisions of section 25-7-133 shall not apply to that portion of an amendment to the visibility component of the state implementation plan that implements and enforces the control strategy covered by this subsection (4) .

(5) If a source or source category agrees to an enforceable commitment to adopt a control strategy that the division determines is not as effective as best available retrofit technology for stationary sources or reasonably available control measures for nonstationary sources but that the division determines will assist in making reasonable further progress in reducing impairment of an air quality related value, the commission may, after public hearing, exempt that source or source category from the imposition of further controls pursuant to this part 10 with respect to those

pollutants that the source or source category has agreed to control for a period of up to ten years from the date established for achieving the emission reductions as specified in the voluntary enforceable agreement.

(6) A source that, prior to June 1, 1996, has received a permit under the federal prevention of significant deterioration program, 42 U.S.C. secs. 7470 to 7479 or sections 25-7-201 to 25-7-210, and installed pollution control measures comparable to the best available control technology pursuant to that program shall not be required to install additional control measures pursuant to this part 10 for a period of ten years from June 1, 1996, but may be required to operate pollution control equipment to its maximum efficiency. This section shall not apply to any source that is not subject to compliance with the requirements of 42 U.S.C. sec. 7651 (f) , which establishes schedules and emission limitations for the control of nitrogen oxide emissions from certain stationary sources. Nothing in this subsection (6) shall be construed to modify the terms of any permit applicable to such source or excuse compliance with respect to any other requirement under this article or the federal act. Except for the exemption for a period of ten years provided in this subsection (6) , nothing in this subsection (6) shall excuse such sources from responding to reasonable requests by the division for information required to complete inventories and attribution and apportionment studies.

# PART 11. LEAD-BASED PAINT ABATEMENT

## 25-7-1101. Legislative declaration.

(1) The general assembly hereby declares that:

(a) Exposure of children to lead represents a significant environmental health problem that is preventable;

(b) According to the federal "Residential Lead-based Paint Hazard Reduction Act of 1992", 15 U.S.C. secs. 2682 and 2684, et seq., as amended, home buyers and renters must be properly informed of the risks of lead exposure to children, especially children under seven years of age;

(c) Trained and qualified individuals are needed in order to advise consumers about lead hazards in general and about specific measures that may be needed to control such hazards; and

(d) The state seeks to adopt the concept of "lead-safe" housing units and child-occupied facilities, rather than "lead-free" housing and facilities. The goal of the state should not be the removal of all lead-based paint, but the creation of housing and facilities where no significant lead-based paint hazard is present. This goal includes the removal, enclosure, or encapsulation of lead-based paint to remove lead hazards from target housing and child-occupied facilities.

(2) The general assembly declares that the enforcement of the lead-based paint abatement standards may be delegated to local health and building departments in Colorado.

(3) Therefore, the general assembly determines and declares that the enactment of this part 11 is a matter of statewide concern to achieve uniformity in the regulation of lead abatement practices and uniformity in the qualifications for and certification of persons who perform such abatement.

## 25-7-1102. Definitions.

As used in this part 11, unless the context otherwise requires:

(1) "Abatement" means any measure or set of measures that will contain or permanently eliminate lead-based paint hazards, including:

(a) The removal of lead-based paint and lead-contaminated dust;

(b) The permanent containment of lead-based paint;

(c) The encapsulation of lead-based paint;

(d) The replacement or enclosure of lead-painted surfaces or fixtures;

(e) The removal or covering of lead-contaminated soil; and

(f) All preparation, cleanup, disposal, monitoring, and clearance testing activities associated with the measures described in this subsection (1) .

(2) (a) "Child-occupied facility" means a building or portion of a building that:

(I) Was constructed prior to 1978;

(II) Is visited regularly by the same child who is under seven years of age;

(III) Is visited by such child on two or more days within any week, consisting of the period from Sunday through the following Saturday, with each such visit totaling six or more hours; and

(IV) Is visited by such child a total of at least sixty hours in one year.

(b) "Child-occupied facility" includes, but is not limited to, any day-care center, preschool, or kindergarten classroom constructed prior to 1978.

(3) "Commission" means the air quality control commission created by section 25-7-104.

(4) "Division" means the air pollution control division in the department of public health and environment.

(5) "Lead-based paint" means any paint containing more than six one-hundredths of one per cent by wet weight of lead metal, more than five-tenths of one percent by dry weight of lead metal, or more than one milligram per square centimeter of lead metal.

(6) "Lead-based paint hazard" means any condition that causes exposure to lead from lead-contaminated dust, lead-contaminated soil, or lead-based paint.

(7) "Target housing" means housing constructed prior to 1978 other than any zero-bedroom dwelling or any housing for the elderly or a person with a disability; except that "target housing" includes housing for the elderly or a person with a disability if a child under seven years of age resides or is expected to reside in the housing.

## 25-7-1103. Powers and duties of air quality control commission - rules.

(1) The commission shall promulgate rules pursuant to section 24-4-103, C.R.S., as necessary to implement this part 11 under the requirements of the federal "Residential Lead-Based Paint Hazard Reduction Act of 1992", 15 U.S.C. secs. 2682, 2684, and 2686, as amended, including the following:

(a) Procedures for a training and certification program for persons and companies involved in inspection, risk assessment, planning, project design, supervision, or conduct of the abatement of surfaces containing lead-based paint, as such actions are defined in the federal "Residential Lead-based Paint Hazard Reduction Act of 1992", in target housing or child-occupied facilities;

(b) Performance standards and practices for lead abatement;

(c) Procedures for the approval of persons or companies who provide training or accreditation for workers, supervisors, inspectors, risk assessors, or project designers performing lead-based paint activities in target housing or child-occupied facilities;

(d) Procedures for notification to appropriate persons regarding lead-based paint projects in target housing or child-occupied facilities;

(e) Establishment of fees for certification of persons under paragraph (a) of this subsection (1) , for any necessary monitoring of such persons to ensure compliance with this part 11, and for approval of persons or companies involved in the training or accreditation under paragraph (c) of this subsection (1) ; and

(f) (I) Requirements for each person who performs for compensation a renovation of target housing to provide a lead hazard information pamphlet to the owner and occupant of such housing prior to commencing the renovation.

(II) If the federal funding necessary to comply with this paragraph (f) is revoked, the division shall not be required to comply with this paragraph (f) until such funding is restored.

(2) (a) The requirements for the training and certification program established by the commission under paragraph (a) of subsection (1) of this section shall not be more stringent than:

(I) The training and certification requirements established by the federal "Residential Lead-based Paint Hazard Reduction Act of 1992" or federal rules promulgated pursuant to such act; or

(II) The training and certification requirements of any program that has been established under the federal "Residential Lead-based Paint Hazard Reduction Act of 1992" and that has been approved by the federal environmental protection agency.

(b) The commission shall consider prior experience in abatement of lead-based paint hazards when establishing training and certification requirements.

(3) The provisions of this part 11 apply only to lead-based paint hazards.

### 25-7-1104. Duties of air pollution control division - certification of trained individuals.

(1) Pursuant to the federal "Residential Lead-based Paint Hazard Reduction Act of 1992", 15 U.S.C. secs. 2682 and 2684, et seq., as amended, the division shall implement, coordinate, and oversee the implementation of the rules promulgated by the commission, including, but not limited to:

(a) Certifying any person or company involved in inspection, risk assessment, planning, project design, supervision, or conduct of the abatement of surfaces containing lead-based paint, as such actions are defined in the federal "Residential Lead-based Paint Hazard Reduction Act of 1992", in target housing or child-occupied facilities; and

(b) Taking actions necessary to enforce such rules of the commission.

(2) Other than training and certification requirements, which are deemed to be matters of statewide concern, the division may delegate the implementation or enforcement of standards under this part 11 to local health or building departments, as appropriate, if requested by such a local department. The air quality control commission shall establish standards regarding such delegations to local health and building departments.

### 25-7-1105. Fees.

(1) (a) The commission shall promulgate rules to establish the fees required under this part 11.

(b) The commission shall adjust the fees so that the revenue generated from such fees is sufficient to cover the direct and indirect costs to implement the lead hazard reduction program under this part 11 and part 11 of article 5 of this title.

(2) All fees collected by the division or its designee pursuant to this part 11 shall be transmitted to the state treasurer, who shall credit the same to the lead hazard reduction cash fund established pursuant to section 25-5-1106. The general assembly shall appropriate from such fund to the department of public health and environment sufficient moneys to implement the provisions of this part 11 and part 11 of article 5 of this title.

### 25-7-1106. Enforcement.

Whenever the division or its designee has reason to believe that any person has violated any of the provisions of this part 11 or the rules promulgated thereunder, the division or its designee may commence an enforcement action pursuant to section 25-7-115.

### 25-7-1107. Applicability of article - child-occupied facilities and target housing.

Nothing in this article shall be interpreted to affect any facility or location other than a child-occupied facility or target housing.

# PART 12. VOLUNTARY EMISSION LIMITATIONS

### 25-7-1201. Legislative declaration.

The general assembly hereby finds, determines, and declares that voluntary emission limitations are an effective and efficient way to reduce emissions of air pollutants. However, the uncertainty of future control requirements impedes an owner or operator of a stationary source or group of stationary sources from making the investments necessary to voluntarily reduce emissions. The department of public health and environment should encourage all owners and operators of stationary sources or groups of stationary sources to voluntarily reduce emissions by providing, to the extent possible, certainty with respect to future control requirements.

## 25-7-1202. Definitions.

The definitions contained in section 25-7-103 shall apply to this part 12. In addition, the following definitions shall apply to this part 12:

(1) "Actual emissions" means the average amount of emissions, calculated in tons per year, that the stationary source or group of stationary sources emitted during the three-year period immediately prior to the date the proposed voluntary agreement was submitted to the division for review so long as the three-year time period is representative of normal unit operation. A different time period may be used to calculate actual emissions if such time period is more representative of normal unit operation than the three-year period immediately prior to the date the proposed voluntary agreement was submitted to the division.

(2) "Actual emission rate" means the average rate of emissions, calculated in pounds per million BTU or a comparable measure of the mass of emissions per unit of production, that the stationary source or group of stationary sources emitted during the three-year period immediately prior to the date the proposed voluntary agreement was submitted to the division for review so long as the three-year time period is representative of normal unit operation. A different time period may be used to calculate the actual emission rate if such time period is more representative of normal unit operation than the three-year period immediately prior to the date the proposed voluntary agreement was submitted to the division.

## 25-7-1203. Voluntary agreements.

(1) The owner or operator of any stationary source or group of stationary sources may obtain regulatory assurance, as described in section 25-7-1204, by entering into a voluntary agreement pursuant to this part 12. The parties to the proposed voluntary agreement shall negotiate in good faith to reach a voluntary agreement as expeditiously as possible. The owner or operator shall provide the division with any information necessary to evaluate the terms and conditions of the proposed voluntary agreement. The parties to the proposed voluntary agreement shall structure the emission limitations or emission reductions contained in a voluntary agreement so as to minimize costs and maximize the operational flexibility available to the owner or operator of the stationary source or group of stationary sources by using, among other things, numeric emission limits, annual emission limits, or emissions averaging across several emission points or sources, as appropriate.

(2) The division shall evaluate the emission limitations contained in a proposed voluntary agreement to determine whether they will result in reductions in actual emissions or actual emission rates, will result in emission reductions earlier than would be required by existing laws or regulations, will result in emission reductions significantly greater than required by existing laws or regulations, and will protect human health or the environment. The division shall also evaluate the assurance period proposed in the voluntary agreement based on the following factors:

(a) The environmental benefits of the emission limitations and their significance;

(b) The time necessary to achieve the emission limitations;

(c) The capital, operating, and other costs associated with achieving the emission limitations; and

(d) The energy impacts and environmental impacts not related to air quality of achieving the emission limitations.

(3) After conducting the evaluation required in subsection (2) of this section, the division may reject any proposed voluntary agreement that does not meet the requirements of this section. If the division rejects the proposed voluntary agreement, the owner or operator of the stationary source or group of stationary sources may petition the commission for review of the proposed voluntary agreement and the division's rejection thereof in accordance with the rules promulgated by the

commission.

(4) If the division finds that the emission limitations and the assurance period proposed in a voluntary agreement meet the requirements of this section, the division shall submit the proposed voluntary agreement to the commission for approval. The commission shall provide the public with notice and an opportunity to comment on the proposed voluntary agreement. The commission shall act upon the voluntary agreement as expeditiously as possible. The commission shall approve the voluntary agreement unless it finds by substantial evidence that the proposed voluntary agreement is inconsistent with the requirements of this part 12. In no event shall the commission adopt emission limitations or an assurance period different than proposed in the voluntary agreement without the express written approval of the owner or operator of the stationary source or group of stationary sources subject to the agreement.

(5) If the commission approves the proposed voluntary agreement, the emission limitations and other provisions contained in the voluntary agreement shall be enforceable under this article against the stationary source or group of stationary sources in accordance with the terms and conditions contained in the voluntary agreement. Such enforcement may include any appropriate mechanism, including rule, permit condition, or consent order.

(6) No voluntary agreement or the underlying emission limitations under subsection (1) of this section shall be made federally enforceable without the written consent of the owner or operator of the stationary source or group of stationary sources.

(7) Except as provided in this part 12 or other applicable law, no voluntary agreement entered into under this part 12 shall alter any existing federal or state requirement otherwise applicable to the stationary source or group of stationary sources subject to such agreement.

(8) The commission may adopt any rules, procedures, or combination thereof necessary to implement this part 12. Notwithstanding this authority, the division may negotiate and evaluate proposed voluntary agreements, and the commission may approve proposed voluntary agreements and review the division's rejection of a proposed voluntary agreement as of July 1, 1998.

## 25-7-1204. Regulatory assurances.

(1) Except as provided in this section and in section 25-7-1205, the owner or operator of a stationary source or group of stationary sources who enters into a voluntary agreement pursuant to section 25-7-1203 shall be granted the regulatory assurances provided in this section. For the assurance period set forth in the voluntary agreement, not to exceed fifteen years, a stationary source or group of stationary sources subject to the voluntary agreement shall not be required to install additional pollution control equipment or implement additional pollution control strategies to reduce emissions of the air pollutant subject to the emission limitations contained in the voluntary agreement in order to comply with:

(a) State regulatory requirements that are based exclusively on state authority and that, either directly or indirectly, necessitate reductions in the air pollutant subject to the voluntary agreement; or

(b) Federal regulatory requirements that:

(I) Either directly or indirectly necessitate reductions in emissions of the air pollutant subject to the voluntary agreement;

(II) Establish generally applicable goals for the reductions of ambient concentrations of the air pollutant subject to the voluntary agreement or its chemical products; and

(III) Do not establish requirements that apply specifically to the stationary source or group of stationary sources.

(2) Notwithstanding subsection (1) of this section, the owner or operator of the stationary source or group of stationary sources may be required to comply with federal regulatory requirements if:

(a) The owner or operator has agreed in writing to abide by the requirements; or

(b) The commission promulgates the requirements in regulations that first require all other sources, including mobile sources, of the air pollutant within the affected region within Colorado to implement all available cost-effective measures to reduce emissions of the air pollutant. Such regulations, including the requirements contained therein applicable to the stationary source or group of stationary sources subject to the voluntary agreement, shall not apply to any stationary source or group of stationary sources unless and until the general assembly acts to postpone the expiration of the regulations in accordance with section 24-4-103, C.R.S.

## 25-7-1205. Exceptions.

(1) The regulatory assurances provided in section 25-7-1204 shall not apply to the following permit requirements, emission control requirements, or emission limitations:

(a) Additional requirements provided under section 111 of the federal act, as defined in section 25-7-103 (12) , or parts 2 and 3 of this article by any modification or reconstruction of a stationary source after the date of the voluntary agreement;

(b) Emission limitations established for hazardous air pollutants identified in section 112 of the federal act;

(c) Requirements established to implement Title VI and section 112 (r) of the federal act; and

(d) Requirements applicable to mobile sources.

## 25-7-1206. Coal-fired power plants.

(1) (a) If the owner or operator of a coal-fired power plant or group of coal-fired power plants reduces the uncontrolled sulfur dioxide emission rate, measured in either pounds per million BTU or tons per year, by an average of at least seventy percent and the actual emission rate of sulfur dioxide by an average of at least fifty percent from one or more units located within the same airshed, regardless of whether the units are located on the same plant site, and such reductions are pursuant to a voluntary agreement entered into under section 25-7-1203, the assurance period for such units shall be a period ending fifteen years after the date established for achieving the voluntary emission limitations under the agreement.

(b) If the owner or operator of any coal-fired power plant that includes one or more units, each of which already has emission control technologies in place to reduce sulfur dioxide emissions by at least sixty-five percent from uncontrolled levels, significantly reduces the actual emission rate of sulfur dioxide and such reduction is pursuant to a voluntary agreement entered into under section 25-7-1203, the assurance period for such units shall be no more than fifteen years from the date the emissions reductions are achieved. Such a coal-fired power plant that is the subject of a certification of visibility impairment in a federally designated class 1 area as of July 1, 1998, may not enter into a voluntary agreement addressing the pollutants subject to the certification of visibility of impairment under section 25-7-1203 unless:

(I) The owner or operator of the plant has negotiated a settlement with the division that resolves all matters related to such certification of visibility impairment; and

(II) The voluntary agreement is fully consistent with the terms and conditions of the negotiated settlement.

(c) A coal-fired power plant or group of plants may achieve the emission reductions required by this section through a voluntary agreement that allows the plant or group of plants to control emissions by methods other than the installation and operation of pollution control equipment. Such methods may include but are not limited to burning low-sulfur coal, reducing the operation of units, retiring units, and changing fuels. If such methods are included in a voluntary agreement, the agreement shall include the procedure by which the division shall calculate the emission reductions to be obtained by such methods.

(2) It is the intent of the general assembly that the commission should consider any coal-fired power plant or power plants located within the same airshed that are achieving the emission limitations described in this section under a voluntary agreement to be in compliance with any emission limitation that is based on a technology requirement in the federal act. Such consideration should continue for a period of fifteen years after the date established in the voluntary agreement for achieving the emission limitations that are contained in the voluntary agreement. During the fifteen-year period, the commission, by rule, may require the coal-fired

power plant to meet a different emission limitation based on a technology requirement in the federal act if:

(a) The commission finds that a different emission limitation is necessary to comply with the federal act; and

(b) The owner or operator of the coal-fired power plant is not required to begin installation of the required emission control technology unless and until the general assembly has acted to postpone the expiration of the commission's rule in accordance with section 24-4-103, C.R.S.

(3) The general assembly further intends that nothing in subsection (2) of this section shall be construed to create a precedent for the application or interpretation of either the "Colorado Air Pollution Prevention and Control Act", article 7 of title 25, C.R.S., or the federal act in any circumstance other than the execution of voluntary agreements between the state of Colorado and the owners and operators of coal-fired power plants in accordance with this part 12.

### 25-7-1207. Allowances.

Notwithstanding any other provision of this part 12, no owner or operator of a stationary source or group of stationary sources shall lose the benefits of regulatory assurances granted under this part 12 by transferring, selling, banking, or otherwise using allowances established under Title IV of the federal act or by any other federally required trading program of regional or national applicability as a result of entering into a voluntary agreement.

### 25-7-1208. Economic or cost-effectiveness analyses not required.

Notwithstanding section 25-7-110.5, the commission shall not conduct an economic impact analysis, cost-effectiveness analysis, or any other analyses required by section 25-7-110.5 in considering a voluntary agreement or the emission limitations contained therein.

# PART 13. THE SOUTHERN UTE INDIAN TRIBE/STATE OF COLORADO ENVIRONMENTAL COMMISSION

### 25-7-1301. Legislative declaration.

(1) The general assembly hereby finds and declares that:

(a) The Southern Ute Indian tribe and the state of Colorado have entered into an intergovernmental agreement, as set forth in House Bill 00-1324, enacted at the second regular session of the sixty-second general assembly and found at 24-62-101, C.R.S.;

(b) Pursuant to said intergovernmental agreement, the tribe and the state have agreed to create a tribal/state environmental commission with the authority to promulgate rules and regulations for one air quality program for all lands, all persons, and all air pollution sources within the exterior boundaries of the Southern Ute Indian reservation;

(c) As governments that share contiguous physical boundaries, it is in the interest of the environment and all residents of the reservation and the state of Colorado to work together to ensure consistent and comprehensive air quality regulation on the reservation;

(d) The establishment of a single collaborative authority for all lands within the exterior boundaries of the reservation best advances rational, sound, air quality management and will minimize duplicative efforts and expenditures of monetary and program resources by the tribe and the state;

(e) Pursuant to the intergovernmental agreement, the tribe will seek delegation from the United States environmental protection agency to administer certain programs under the federal "Clean Air Act", 42 U.S.C. sec. 7401 et seq. (1970) , as the same is in effect on November 15, 1990, such delegation being contingent upon the existence of the tribal/state commission and the intergovernmental agreement.

(2) It is the intent of the general assembly in enacting this part 13 to establish state authority for the creation of a commission that will establish a separate reservation air program for all lands within the exterior boundaries of the Southern Ute Indian reservation, as provided in the intergovernmental agreement. Therefore, for the duration of the intergovernmental agreement, all lands within the exterior boundaries of the reservation shall be subject to the authority of the commission and the provisions of the reservation air program, as described in this part 13 and in the intergovernmental agreement, and shall not be subject to the authority of the Colorado air quality control commission or the provisions of parts 1 to 12 of this article, except as otherwise provided in the intergovernmental agreement and in this part 13.

(3) In article IV of the intergovernmental agreement, the tribe and the state agreed that neither party intended to alter the existing sovereignty or jurisdiction of any party, and by approving the intergovernmental agreement, neither party conceded or agreed to any jurisdiction of the other party that would not otherwise exist. To the extent the state has jurisdiction over non-Indians on fee lands within the exterior boundaries of the reservation, it is the intent of the general assembly in enacting this part 13 that the commission shall exercise such authority for the purposes set forth in this part 13.

(4) The general assembly enacts this part 13 with the understanding that the tribe has also adopted tribal legislation that will carry out the terms of the intergovernmental agreement with respect to persons, air pollution sources, and lands within the reservation that are subject to the jurisdiction of the tribe.

(5) The general assembly hereby declares that its intent in enacting senate bill 02-235 is to ratify the continued existence of the Southern Ute Indian tribe/state of Colorado environmental commission after December 13, 2001.

## 25-7-1302. Definitions.

(1) "Commission" means the Southern Ute Indian tribe/state of Colorado environmental commission established by this part 13.

(2) "Division" means the division in the department of public health and environment that pertains to air pollution control.

(3) "EPA" means the United States environmental protection agency.

(4) "Fee land" means real property located within the reservation that is owned in fee by non-Indians.

(5) "Intergovernmental agreement" means the agreement entered into by the Southern Ute Indian tribe and the state of Colorado, as set forth in House Bill 00-1324, enacted at the second regular session of the sixty-second general assembly.

(6) "Reservation" means the Southern Ute Indian reservation, the exterior boundaries of which were confirmed in the act of May 21, 1984, Pub.L. 98-290, 98 Stat. 201, 202 (found at "other provisions" note to 25 U.S.C. sec. 668) .

(7) "Reservation air program" means the regulatory air quality program established by the commission for all persons, lands, and air pollution sources within the exterior boundaries of the reservation.

(8) "State" means the state of Colorado.

(9) "Tribe" means the Southern Ute Indian tribe.

(10) "Trust land" means land within the reservation held in trust by the United States of America for the benefit of the tribe or individual Indians.

## 25-7-1303. Southern Ute Indian tribe/state of Colorado environmental commission created.

(1) There is hereby created the Southern Ute Indian tribe/state of Colorado environmental commission. The commission is not an agency of the state, but is an authority created pursuant to

the intergovernmental agreement. The commission's actions are not subject to the provisions of the "State Administrative Procedure Act", article 4 of title 24, C.R.S., but rather are subject to procedural rules adopted by the commission.

(2) The commission shall have authority to adopt air quality standards, promulgate rules and regulations, and review appealable administrative actions pertaining to the reservation air program.

(3) It is the intent of the general assembly that the commission's rules, regulations, and orders shall be effective against all persons located within the reservation over whom the state would otherwise have jurisdiction as provided by state or federal law.

(4) The commission shall consist of three members appointed by the tribe and three members appointed by the governor. The initial members appointed by the governor shall serve terms as follows: One member shall serve until July 1, 2001, one member shall serve until July 1, 2002, and one member shall serve until July 1, 2003. All subsequent appointments by the governor shall be for terms of three years. The governor's appointees shall be residents of the state of Colorado. At least two of such appointees shall be residents of either Archuleta or La Plata county and at least one of such appointees shall reside on fee land.

(5) The governor may remove any member appointed by the governor at any time. The governor may not remove any member appointed by the tribe.

(6) Except as provided in section 25-7-1307, commission members shall not receive any compensation from the state of Colorado for their services in the conduct of commission business. Commission members may be reimbursed for necessary travel and other reasonable expenses incurred in the performance of their official duties out of funds collected or received by the tribe.

(7) Each member shall have one vote. The affirmative vote of a majority of all members of the commission on any matter within its powers and duties shall be required for any final determination made by the commission.

(8) The commission shall annually elect a member to preside as chair. The chair shall alternate annually between a tribal and a state member.

## 25-7-1304. Commission - powers and duties - rules.

(1) The commission shall be the air quality policy-making and the administrative review entity for the reservation air program.

(2) The duties of the commission shall include the responsibility to:

(a) Determine the specific air quality programs under the federal "Clean Air Act", or other air quality programs, that should apply to the reservation, taking into account the specific environmental, economic, geographic, and cultural needs of the reservation;

(b) Promulgate rules and regulations that are necessary for the proper implementation and administration of those programs, including determining which administrative actions are appealable to the commission;

(c) Establish procedures the commission will follow in promulgating rules and regulations and for administrative review of actions taken by the tribe;

(d) Review and approve of a long-term plan, initially prepared by the tribe, to improve and maintain air quality within the reservation, which also takes into account regional planning in the La Plata and Archuleta county region;

(e) Monitor the relationships among the state and tribal environmental protection agencies to facilitate cooperation, information sharing, technical assistance, and training;

(f) Review enforcement actions according to the commission's adopted administrative procedures;

(g) Approve and adopt fees for permits and other regulatory services conducted by the tribe or the state, after considering a proposed fee schedule prepared by the tribe, and direct payment by air pollution sources to the tribe;

(h) Ensure consistency and adherence to applicable standards and resolving disputes involving third parties;

(i) Review emission inventories as developed by the tribe and state;

(j) Conduct public hearings pertaining to the adoption of rules and regulations, or relating to enforcement and permit appeals, and to issue orders resulting from those proceedings;

(k) Request tribal staff to perform any administrative or clerical functions necessary to issue orders and conduct commission business, or the commission, at its option, may appoint a technical secretary to perform such duties; except that no authority shall be delegated to adopt, promulgate, amend, or repeal standards or regulations, or to make determinations, or to issue or countermand orders of the commission;

(l) Any other duties necessary to accomplish the purposes of the intergovernmental agreement and as authorized by the state and tribe enabling legislation.

## 25-7-1305. Administration of reservation air program.

(1) After the commission has adopted rules and regulations for the reservation air program and after the EPA has delegated to the tribe administration of programs under the federal "Clean Air Act", the tribe shall administer and enforce the standards, rules, and regulations adopted by the commission for the reservation air program. The actions of the tribe pursuant to this section and this part 13 shall apply to any non-Indian air pollution source within the reservation as if the state had taken the same action.

(2) Until the EPA delegates to the tribe the authority to administer federal "Clean Air Act" programs, the Colorado air quality control commission and the division shall have authority under this article to continue to enforce any state program or permits, laws, and regulations for any non-Indian owned air pollution sources on fee land within the reservation. The division shall afford the tribe the opportunity to participate in its regulatory activities involving such sources, including the review of permit applications, notices of violations, or other orders, inspections, and other enforcement actions.

## 25-7-1306. Agencies of state to cooperate.

(1) Agencies of the state, including but not limited to the division, may provide technical assistance, training, and consultation to the tribe to carry out the purposes of the intergovernmental agreement and this part 13.

(2) The general assembly authorizes state agencies to perform duties on behalf of the commission to administer the reservation air program. State agencies may contract with the tribe to receive payment for the reasonable cost of the services state employees perform for the tribe or the commission.

## 25-7-1307. Funding for staff and program costs.

(1) The commission shall establish fees for permits and other regulatory services provided by the division or the tribe under this part 13. The commission shall direct air pollution sources to pay said fees to the tribe. The tribe may also apply for and receive EPA grants for the administration of the reservation air program.

(2) From the fees and grants, the tribe shall fund the staff and program costs necessary to perform the tribe's duties under the intergovernmental agreement and this part 13. The tribe shall pay the state for the personal services costs, at a rate of compensation determined by contract, of any state employee who participates in the administration of the reservation air program pursuant to the intergovernmental agreement or this part 13.

(3) It is the intent of the general assembly that fees and grants shall pay the necessary expenses of the commission. If the fees and grants are not sufficient to pay the commission's expenses, then the state and the tribe shall be responsible for funding associated with the participation of their respective representatives on the commission. State funding for its expenses must come from either a separate appropriation to the division or from funds otherwise available that the state is authorized to use for such a purpose.

(4) Prior to the establishment and collection of fees from air pollution sources under the reservation air program, the tribe may have expenses associated with its administration of permits

for non-Indian owned sources on fee land. If the state continues to collect fees under section 25-7-114.7 from air pollution sources on fee lands, and if the tribe has expenses associated with the administration of a state-issued permit, then the division is authorized to use such permit and other fees to pay for the tribe's personal services costs. The state is authorized to contract with the tribe setting forth the reasonable cost for such services performed by the tribe.

### 25-7-1308. Administrative and judicial review of commission actions.

(1) Prior to the formation of the commission, the adoption of the federal legislation contemplated in the intergovernmental agreement, and actual EPA delegation of federal "Clean Air Act" programs:

(a) The state, through the Colorado air quality control commission and the division, shall exercise civil and criminal enforcement jurisdiction over non-Indians on fee lands within reservation boundaries for violations of applicable air quality permits, laws, and regulations.

(b) Appeals of state air enforcement action and other air quality-related decisions may be brought in state court consistent with state law and regulation.

(c) The tribe shall exercise jurisdiction over Indians, on all lands within the boundaries of the reservation, and over non-Indians on trust land, for violations of applicable tribal air quality regulations.

(d) Nothing in this part 13 is intended to restrict, diminish, or define the jurisdiction of the EPA.

(2) Following the adoption of the federal legislation and the EPA delegation of federal "Clean Air Act" programs:

(a) The tribe shall exercise civil enforcement jurisdiction over all persons and air pollution sources on all lands within reservation boundaries for violations of the reservation air program, subject to administrative review by the commission; and

(b) Consistent with the federal legislation provided in the intergovernmental agreement, the general assembly intends that final decisions of the commission shall be subject to review in federal district court in accordance with the provisions of the federal "Administrative Procedure Act".

(3) Following the formation of the commission and the adoption of the federal legislation provided in the intergovernmental agreement, it is the intent of the general assembly that the EPA will exercise criminal enforcement jurisdiction over any persons on all lands within reservation boundaries for criminal violations of the reservation air program.

### 25-7-1309. Repeal of part.

(1) This part 13 shall be repealed on the occurrence of any one of the following events:

(a) Termination of the intergovernmental agreement by either the tribe or the state; or

(b) Enactment of an explicit repeal by the general assembly, acting by separate bill.

(c) (Deleted by amendment, L. 2010, (SB 10-082) , ch. 182, p. 655, § 2, effective April 29, 2010.)

# ARTICLE 8. WATER QUALITY CONTROL

# PART 1. GENERAL PROVISIONS

### 25-8-101. Short title.

This article shall be known and may be cited as the "Colorado Water Quality Control Act".

### 25-8-102. Legislative declaration.

(1) In order to foster the health, welfare, and safety of the inhabitants of the state of Colorado and

to facilitate the enjoyment and use of the scenic and natural resources of the state, it is declared to be the policy of this state to prevent injury to beneficial uses made of state waters, to maximize the beneficial uses of water, and to develop waters to which Colorado and its citizens are entitled and, within this context, to achieve the maximum practical degree of water quality in the waters of the state consistent with the welfare of the state. It is further declared that pollution of state waters may constitute a menace to public health and welfare, may create public nuisances, may be harmful to wildlife and aquatic life, and may impair beneficial uses of state waters and that the problem of water pollution in this state is closely related to the problem of water pollution in adjoining states.

(2) It is further declared to be the public policy of this state to conserve state waters and to protect, maintain, and improve, where necessary and reasonable, the quality thereof for public water supplies, for protection and propagation of wildlife and aquatic life, for domestic, agricultural, industrial, and recreational uses, and for other beneficial uses, taking into consideration the requirements of such uses; to provide that no pollutant be released into any state waters without first receiving the treatment or other corrective action necessary to reasonably protect the legitimate and beneficial uses of such waters; to provide for the prevention, abatement, and control of new or existing water pollution; and to cooperate with other states and the federal government in carrying out these objectives.

(3) It is further declared that protection of the quality of state waters and the prevention, abatement, and control of water pollution are matters of statewide concern and affected with a public interest, and the provisions of this article are enacted in the exercise of the police powers of this state for the purpose of protecting the health, peace, safety, and general welfare of the people of this state.

(4) This article and the agencies authorized under this article shall be the final authority in the administration of water pollution prevention, abatement, and control. Notwithstanding any other provision of law, no department or agency of the state, and no municipal corporation, county, or other political subdivision, having jurisdiction over water pollution prevention, abatement, and control, shall issue any authorization for the discharge of pollutants into state waters unless authorized to do so in accordance with this article.

(5) It is further declared that the general assembly intends that this article shall be construed to require the development of a water quality program in which the water quality benefits of the pollution control measures utilized have a reasonable relationship to the economic, environmental, energy, and public health costs and impacts of such measures, and that before any final action is taken, with the exception of any enforcement action, consideration be given to the economic reasonableness of the action. Such consideration shall include evaluation of the benefits derived from achieving the goals of this article and of the economic, environmental, public health, and energy impacts to the public and affected persons.

## 25-8-103. Definitions.

As used in this article 8, unless the context otherwise requires:

(1) "Agricultural chemical" means any of the following:

(a) A pesticide as defined in section 35-10-103, C.R.S.; or

(b) A commercial fertilizer as defined in section 35-12-103, C.R.S.

(1.1) "Agricultural management area" means a designated geographic area defined by the commissioner of agriculture that includes natural or man-made features where there is a significant risk of contamination or pollution of groundwater from agricultural activities conducted at or near the land surface.

(1.2) "Agricultural management plan" means any activity, procedure, or practice adopted as a rule by the commissioner of agriculture pursuant to article 4 of title 24, C.R.S., in consultation with the Colorado cooperative extension service and the water quality control division, to prevent or remedy the introduction of agricultural chemicals into groundwater to the extent technically and economically practical.

(1.3) "Best management practices" means any voluntary activity, procedure, or practice established by the department of agriculture, in consultation with the Colorado cooperative extension service and the water quality control division, to prevent or remedy the introduction of agricultural chemicals into groundwater to the extent technically and economically practical.

(1.4) "Biosolids" means the accumulated residual product resulting from a domestic wastewater treatment works or other domestic sources. "Biosolids" does not include grit or screenings from a wastewater treatment works or commercial and industrial septage or on-site wastewater treatment systems regulated by article 10 of this title.

(1.5) "Commission" means the water quality control commission created by section 25-8-201.

(1.7) "Commissioner" means the commissioner of agriculture.

(2) "Control regulation" means any regulation promulgated by the commission pursuant to section 25-8-205.

(3) "Discharge of pollutants" means the introduction or addition of a pollutant into state waters.

(4) "Division" means the division of administration of the department of public health and environment.

(5) "Domestic wastewater treatment works" means a system or facility for treating, neutralizing, stabilizing, or disposing of domestic wastewater which system or facility has a designed capacity to receive more than two thousand gallons of domestic wastewater per day. The term "domestic wastewater treatment works" also includes appurtenances to such system or facility, such as outfall sewers and pumping stations, and to equipment related to such appurtenances. The term "domestic wastewater treatment works" does not include industrial wastewater treatment plants or complexes whose primary function is the treatment of industrial wastes, notwithstanding the fact that human wastes generated incidentally to the industrial processes are treated therein.

(6) "Effluent limitation" means any restriction or prohibition established under this article or federal law on quantities, rates, and concentrations of chemical, physical, biological, and other constituents which are discharged from point sources into state waters, including, but not limited to, standards of performance for new sources, toxic effluent standards, and schedules of compliance.

(7) "Executive director" means the executive director of the department of public health and environment.

(8) "Federal act" means the "Federal Water Pollution Control Act", commonly referred to as the "Clean Water Act".

(8.3) (a) "Graywater" means that portion of wastewater that, before being treated or combined with other wastewater, is collected from fixtures within residential, commercial, or industrial buildings or institutional facilities for the purpose of being put to beneficial uses authorized by the commission in accordance with section 25-8-205 (1) (g) ; except that graywater use for purposes of scientific research must comply with the requirements of section 25-8-205.3, but need not comply with the commission's control regulations established under section 25-8-205 (1) .

(b) Sources of graywater may include discharges from bathroom and laundry room sinks, bathtubs, showers, laundry machines, and other sources authorized by rule. Graywater does not include the wastewater from toilets, urinals, kitchen sinks, dishwashers, or nonlaundry utility sinks. Graywater must be collected in a manner that minimizes household wastes, human excreta, animal or vegetable matter, and chemicals that are hazardous or toxic, as determined by the commission; except that a person may collect, treat, and use graywater in a manner that departs from the commission's control regulations established under section 25-8-205 (1) if the person collects, treats, and uses graywater for purposes of scientific research in accordance with the requirements of section 25-8-205.3.

(8.4) "Graywater treatment works" means an arrangement of devices and structures used to:

(a) Collect graywater from within a building or a facility; and

(b) Treat, neutralize, or stabilize graywater within the same building or facility to the level necessary for its authorized uses.

(8.5) "Industrial discharger" means any entity which introduces pollutants into a domestic wastewater treatment works from any nondomestic source subject to regulation under section 307

(b) , (c) , or (d) of the federal act.

(9) "Irrigation return flow" means tailwater, tile drainage, or surfaced groundwater flow from irrigated land.

(10) "Issue" or "issuance" means the mailing to all parties of any order, permit, determination, or notice, other than notice by publication, by certified mail to the last address furnished to the agency by the person subject thereto or personal service on such person, and the date of issuance of such order, permit, determination, or notice shall be the date of such mailing or service or such later date as is stated in the order, permit, determination, or notice.

(11) "Municipality" means any regional commission, county, metropolitan district offering sanitation service, sanitation district, water and sanitation district, water conservancy district, metropolitan sewage disposal district, service authority, city and county, city, town, Indian tribe or authorized Indian tribal organization, or any two or more of them which are acting jointly in connection with a sewage treatment works.

(12) "Permit" means a permit issued pursuant to part 5 of this article.

(13) "Person" means an individual, corporation, partnership, association, state or political subdivision thereof, federal agency, state agency, municipality, commission, or interstate body.

(14) "Point source" means any discernible, confined, and discrete conveyance, including, but not limited to, any pipe, ditch, channel, tunnel, conduit, well, discrete fissure, container, rolling stock, concentrated animal feeding operation, or vessel or other floating craft, from which pollutants are or may be discharged. "Point source" does not include irrigation return flow.

(15) "Pollutant" means dredged spoil, dirt, slurry, solid waste, incinerator residue, sewage, sewage sludge, garbage, trash, chemical waste, biological nutrient, biological material, radioactive material, heat, wrecked or discarded equipment, rock, sand, or any industrial, municipal, or agricultural waste.

(16) "Pollution" means the man-made, man-induced, or natural alteration of the physical, chemical, biological, and radiological integrity of water.

(16.5) "Pretreatment requirement and standard" means any requirement, prohibition, standard, concentration, or effluent limitation described in enforceable pretreatment requirements by the commission pursuant to section 25-8-205 (1) (b) , (1) (c) , or (1) (d) .

(17) "Promulgate" means and includes authority to adopt, and from time to time amend, repeal, modify, publish, and put into effect.

(17.5) "Reclaimed domestic wastewater" means wastewater that has received treatment that enables the wastewater to meet the requirements, prohibitions, standards, and concentration limitations adopted by the commission for subsequent reuses other than drinking.

(18) "Schedule of compliance" means a schedule of remedial measures and times including an enforceable sequence of actions or operations leading to compliance with any control regulation or effluent limitation.

(19) "State waters" means any and all surface and subsurface waters which are contained in or flow in or through this state, but does not include waters in sewage systems, waters in treatment works of disposal systems, waters in potable water distribution systems, and all water withdrawn for use until use and treatment have been completed.

(20) "Water quality standard" means any standard promulgated pursuant to section 25-8-204.

## 25-8-104. Interpretation and construction of water quality provisions.

(1) No provision of this article shall be interpreted so as to supersede, abrogate, or impair rights to divert water and apply water to beneficial uses in accordance with the provisions of sections 5 and 6 of article XVI of the constitution of the state of Colorado, compacts entered into by the state of Colorado, or the provisions of articles 80 to 93 of title 37, C.R.S., or Colorado court determinations with respect to the determination and administration of water rights. Nothing in this article shall be construed, enforced, or applied so as to cause or result in material injury to water rights. The general assembly recognizes that this article may lead to dischargers choosing consumptive types of treatment techniques in order to meet water quality requirements. Under

such circumstances, the discharger must comply with all of the applicable provisions of articles 80 to 93 of title 37, C.R.S., and shall be obliged to remedy any material injury to water rights to the extent required under the provisions of articles 80 to 93 of title 37, C.R.S. The question of whether such material injury to water rights exists and the remedy therefor shall be determined by the water court. This section shall not be interpreted so as to prevent the issuance of a permit pursuant to sections 25-8-501 to 25-8-503 which is necessary to protect public health. Nothing in this article shall be construed to allow the commission or the division to require minimum stream flows or minimum water levels in any lakes or impoundments.

(2) The following criteria, in addition to those otherwise prescribed by law, shall apply to any policy, rule-making, adjudicatory, administrative, or executive decision of the water quality control commission or to any judicial decision related thereto:

(a) All state waters shall be presumed to be available for beneficial uses under and in accordance with the constitution and laws of the state; and a water right includes the right to divert as defined in section 37-92-103 (7), C.R.S., the waters of the state for application to beneficial use.

(b) The commission or division shall not require an instream flow for any purpose.

(c) Mixing zones in state waters shall be allowed in accordance with other provisions of this article in calculating the necessary degree of source pollutant control, so long as water rights are not materially injured.

(d) The commission and division shall consult with the state engineer and the water conservation board or their designees before making any decision or adopting any rule or policy which has the potential to cause material injury to water rights.

(e) Underground water may be extracted from state waters in order to treat or remove pollutants from the water extracted; except that any material injury to water rights resulting therefrom shall be remedied as required by law.

(3) The state engineer shall issue well permits pursuant to section 37-90-137 (2), C.R.S., necessary to accomplish the purposes of paragraph (e) of subsection (2) of this section. Well construction shall be in accordance with article 91 of title 37, C.R.S.

## 25-8-105. Regional wastewater management plans - amendments.

(1) (a) Regional wastewater management plans which include plans known for purposes of the federal act as "208 plans" may be developed by designated planning agencies or by the state for nondesignated areas or for statewide purposes.

(b) Before submitting a proposed plan or amendment to the division, the designated planning agency shall hold a hearing on the proposed plan or amendment.

(c) The division shall consider any proposed plan or amendment developed by the state.

(d) Notice of a hearing to be held pursuant to this subsection (1) shall be given by at least one publication in a newspaper of general distribution in the area of the proposed plan, and actual notice shall be given to anyone requesting such notice. Such notice shall advise of the opportunity for interested persons to appear and submit written or oral comments on the proposed plan or amendment. The agency holding the hearing shall receive and consider all comments submitted on the proposed plan or amendment.

(2) Each regional wastewater management plan and each amendment to such a plan must be either developed or reviewed by the division.

(3) (a) The commission, after notice and hearing, shall approve or reject proposed regional wastewater management plans and amendments thereto. The commission shall approve, conditionally approve, or reject a plan or an amendment developed by a management or planning agency within one hundred eighty days after submittal of the plan or amendment by the management or planning agency to the division. Only those portions of a regional wastewater management plan which are adopted as a regulation by the commission pursuant to section 24-4-103, C.R.S., shall be binding on regulatory decisions, including, but not limited to, site approvals, construction grants, or point or nonpoint source control decisions. Only those plans or portions thereof which are adopted by the commission as regulations shall be binding for purposes of any

federal law, regulation, or action.

(b) Notwithstanding the provisions of paragraph (a) of this subsection (3) , the commission may delegate to the division the authority to approve, conditionally approve, or reject nonrule-making amendments to regional wastewater management plans. If the commission delegates such authority, the division shall give notice of its decision on an amendment to the commission and to anyone who has requested notice of amendments to the affected plan. Notice of such decision shall also be included on the next commission agenda. Upon a request by any affected person, the commission shall review the division's decision. The decision of the division shall be final within forty-five days after agenda notice of the decision has been given unless review is requested by an affected person.

(4) The governor may certify to the federal environmental protection agency a regional wastewater management plan or an amendment thereto which has been approved by the commission or an amendment thereto which has become final after approval by the division. The governor may designate planning agencies for the purposes of the federal act.

### 25-8-106. Study - organizational placement of water quality control programs. (Repealed)

# PART 2. WATER QUALITY CONTROL COMMISSION

### 25-8-201. Water quality control commission created.

(1) (a) There is hereby created in the department of public health and environment a water quality control commission which shall exercise its powers and perform its duties and functions as if it were transferred to said department by a type 1 transfer. The commission shall consist of nine citizens of the state who shall be appointed by the governor, with the consent of the senate, for terms of three years each; except that, of the members appointed to take office in 1984, one shall be appointed for a one-year term, one shall be appointed for a two-year term, and three shall be appointed for three-year terms. Members of the commission shall be appointed so as to achieve geographical representation and to reflect the various interests in water in the state. At least two members shall reside in that portion of the state which is west of the continental divide.

(b) Repealed.

(c) Whenever a vacancy exists, the governor shall appoint a member for the remaining portion of the unexpired term created by the vacancy, subject to confirmation by the senate.

(2) (a) The governor may remove any appointed member of the commission for malfeasance in office, failure to regularly attend meetings, or for any cause that renders such a member incapable or unfit to discharge the duties of his office.

(b) If any member of the commission is absent from two consecutive meetings, the chairman of the commission shall determine whether the cause of such absences was reasonable. If he determines that the cause of the absences was unreasonable, he shall so notify the governor who may remove such member and appoint a qualified person for the unexpired portion of the regular term, subject to confirmation by the senate.

(3) Each member of the commission not otherwise in full-time employment of the state shall receive a per diem which shall be the same amount paid to the general assembly for attendance at interim committees for each day actually and necessarily spent in the discharge of official duties, not to exceed twelve hundred dollars in any one year; and each member shall receive traveling and other necessary expenses actually incurred in the performance of his official duties as a member of the commission.

(4) The commission shall select from its own membership a chairman, a vice-chairman, and a secretary. The commission shall keep a record of its proceedings.

(5) The commission shall hold regular public meetings and may hold special meetings on the call of the chairman or vice-chairman at such other times as deemed necessary. Written notice of the time and place of each meeting shall be mailed to each member at least five days in advance.

(6) All members shall have a vote. Two-thirds of the commission shall constitute a quorum, and the concurrence of a majority of the quorum in any matter within its powers and duties shall be required for any determination made by the commission.

## 25-8-202. Duties of commission - rules.

(1) The commission shall develop and maintain a comprehensive and effective program for prevention, control, and abatement of water pollution and for water quality protection throughout the entire state and, to ensure provision of continuously safe drinking water by public water systems, and, in connection therewith, shall:

(a) Classify state waters in accordance with section 25-8-203;

(b) Promulgate water quality standards in accordance with section 25-8-204;

(c) Promulgate control regulations in accordance with section 25-8-205;

(d) Promulgate permit regulations in accordance with sections 25-8-501 to 25-8-504;

(e) Perform duties assigned to the commission in part 7 of this article with respect to the location, design, construction, financing, and operation of domestic wastewater treatment plants;

(f) Review from time to time, at intervals of not more than three years, classification of waters, water quality standards, and control regulations which it has promulgated;

(g) Promulgate rules and adopt priority ranking for the administration of federal and other public source construction loans or grants, and grants from the water quality improvement fund, which the commission or the division administers and which shall not be expended for any purpose other than that for which they were provided;

(h) Advise and consult and cooperate with other agencies of the state, the federal government, and other states, and with groups, political subdivisions, and industries affected by the provisions of this article and the policies or regulations of the commission;

(i) Exercise all incidental powers necessary or proper for carrying out the purposes of this article including the powers to issue and enforce rules and orders;

(i.5) Promulgate rules and regulations to govern the division's certification activities pursuant to section 401 of the federal act;

(j) Perform such other duties as may lawfully be assigned to it by Colorado statutes;

(k) Act as an appellate body to review all determinations by the division except those determinations dealing with surface water discharge permits or portions thereof;

(l) Coordinate with the United States secretary of the interior and the United States secretary of agriculture to develop water quality management plans for federal lands pursuant to 16 U.S.C. sec. 530, 16 U.S.C. sec. 1604, and 43 U.S.C. sec. 1712;

(m) Adopt rules providing minimum standards for the location, construction, performance, installation, alteration, and use of on-site wastewater treatment systems within the state of Colorado, in accordance with section 25-10-104;

(n) Adopt minimum general sanitary standards for drinking water systems in accordance with section 25-1.5-202;

(o) Develop additions or modifications to the drinking water project eligibility list in accordance with section 37-95-107.8, C.R.S.;

(p) Establish, and revise as necessary, a schedule of nonrefundable fees to cover the reasonable costs of implementing a program for the beneficial use of biosolids, in accordance with section 30-20-110.5, C.R.S.; and

(q) Hear appeals of penalties imposed pursuant to section 25-1-114.1 (2.5) for a violation of minimum general sanitary standards and regulations for drinking water.

(2) The commission shall have authority to implement the legislative declaration as prescribed in

section 25-8-102.

(3) The commission shall hold a public hearing during the month of October of each year in order to hear public comment on water pollution problems within the state, alleged sources of water pollution within this state, and the availability of practical remedies therefor; and at such hearing the commission, administrator, and division personnel shall answer reasonable questions from the public concerning administration and enforcement of the various provisions of this article, as well as rules and regulations promulgated under the authority of this article.

(4) The commission shall employ an administrator and shall delegate to such administrator such duties and responsibilities as it may deem necessary, including acting as a hearing officer for the commission; but no authority shall be delegated to such administrator to promulgate standards or regulations, or to make determinations, or to issue or countermand orders of the commission. Such administrator shall have appropriate practical, educational, and administrative experience related to water quality control and shall be employed pursuant to section 13 of article XII of the state constitution.

(5) Repealed.

(6) The commission is hereby designated as the state water pollution control agency for this state for all purposes of the federal act. The commission shall maintain a program which does not conflict with the provisions of the federal act and is hereby authorized to take all action necessary and appropriate to secure to this state, its municipalities, or intermunicipal or interstate agencies the benefits of said act.

(7) The commission and the division shall recognize water quality responsibilities of the following state agencies, referred to in this subsection (7) as the "implementing agencies": The office of mined land reclamation; the state engineer; the oil and gas conservation commission; and the state agency responsible for activities related to the federal "Resource Conservation and Recovery Act of 1976", as amended, and related state programs. Activities subject to the jurisdiction of the implementing agencies that result in discharge to state waters shall be regulated as follows:

(a) The commission shall be solely responsible for the adoption of water quality standards and classifications for state waters affected by such discharges. Except as set forth in paragraph (b) of this subsection (7) , such classifications and standards shall be implemented by the implementing agencies, after consultation with the division and the commission, through their own programs. For the purpose of subsection (7) , water quality standards and classifications under this section for state waters other than surface waters shall not specify applicable points of compliance, but such points of compliance shall be adopted, in accordance with criteria established through rule-making after public hearing and consultation with the commission and division, by the appropriate agency with jurisdiction as specified in paragraph (b) of this subsection (7) so as to protect present and future beneficial uses of water.

(b) (I) The division shall be solely responsible for the issuance and enforcement of permits authorizing point source discharges to surface waters of the state affected by such discharges.

(II) Neither the commission nor the division shall require permits for, or otherwise regulate, other activities subject to the jurisdiction of the implementing agencies, unless the commission finds, after notice and public hearing, that:

(A) Such regulation is necessary to assure compliance with the federal act, the provisions of articles 80 to 93 of title 37, C.R.S., or water quality standards and classifications adopted for state waters or to protect present and future beneficial uses of water; or

(B) Such regulation is necessary to avoid the imposition of a disproportionate burden on other dischargers or classes of dischargers to the affected state waters who are subject to the requirements of this article; or

(C) The implementing agency fails to provide reasonable assurance that compliance with this subsection (7) has been obtained through its own programs.

(III) Regulation by the commission under this paragraph (b) shall be undertaken solely through the adoption of control regulations under section 25-8-205, or permit regulations under section 25-8-501, and the division may enforce such regulations as provided in this article.

(c) Nothing in this subsection (7) shall relieve any activity from participation in waste load allocation proceedings under this article or limit the emergency authority of the division pursuant to section 25-8-307.

(d) This subsection (7) is intended to restate and clarify existing law and to provide a procedure for coordination between state agencies which have responsibilities to implement water quality protection of state waters. It is not intended either to grant additional jurisdiction to any agency or to curtail the jurisdiction of any agency to fulfill its statutory responsibilities, including jurisdiction to maintain a program consistent with the requirements of the federal "Resource Conservation and Recovery Act of 1976", as amended.

(8) (a) The commission may adopt rules more stringent than corresponding enforceable federal requirements only if it is demonstrated at a public hearing, and the commission finds, based on sound scientific or technical evidence in the record, that state rules more stringent than the corresponding federal requirements are necessary to protect the public health, beneficial use of water, or the environment of the state. Those findings shall be accompanied by a statement of basis and purpose referring to and evaluating the public health and environmental information and studies contained in the record which form the basis for the commission's conclusion.

(b) The existing policies, rules, and regulations of the commission and division shall be applied in conformance with section 25-8-104 and this section.

## 25-8-203. Classification of state waters.

(1) The commission may classify state waters.

(2) The types of classes shall be determined by regulations and may be based upon or intended to indicate or describe any relevant characteristic, such as:

(a) The existing extent of pollution or the maximum extent of pollution to be tolerated as a goal;

(b) Whether or not pollution arises from natural sources;

(c) Present beneficial uses of the water, or the beneficial uses that may be reasonably expected in the future for which the water is suitable in its present condition, or the beneficial uses for which it is to become suitable as a goal;

(d) The character and uses of the land area bordering the water;

(e) The need to protect the quality of the water for beneficial uses such as domestic, agricultural, municipal, and industrial uses, the protection and propagation of fish and wildlife, recreation, drinking water, or such beneficial uses as the commission deems consistent with the policies of section 25-8-102 and the need to minimize negative impacts on water rights;

(f) The type and character of the water, such as surface or subsurface, lake or stream, together with volume, flow, depth, stream gradient, temperature, surface area involved, and daily or seasonal variability of any of such characteristics. Waters in ditches and other man-made conveyance structures shall not be classified, and water quality standards shall not be applied to them but may be utilized for purposes of discharge permits.

(3) The particular class into which any particular segment of state waters is placed shall be determined by regulation.

## 25-8-204. Water quality standards.

(1) Water quality standards shall be promulgated by the commission by regulations which describe water characteristics or the extent of specifically identified pollutants for state waters.

(2) Water quality standards may be promulgated with respect to any measurable characteristic of water, including, but not limited to:

(a) Toxic substances;

(b) Suspended solids, colloids, and combinations of solids with other suspended substances;

(c) Bacteria, fecal coliform, fungi, viruses, and other biological constituents and characteristics;

(d) Dissolved oxygen, and the extent of oxygen demanding substances;

(e) Phosphates, nitrates, and other dissolved nutrients;

(f) pH and hydrogen compounds;

(g) Chlorine, heavy metals, and other chemical constituents;

(h) Salinity, acidity, and alkalinity;

(i) Trash, refuse, oil and grease, and other foreign material;

(j) Taste, odor, color, and turbidity;

(k) Temperature.

(3) Water quality standards may be promulgated for use in connection with any one or more of the classes of state waters established by the commission pursuant to section 25-8-203 and may be made applicable with respect to any designated portion of state water or to all state waters.

(4) In promulgating water quality standards, the commission shall consider:

(a) The need for standards which regulate specified pollutants;

(b) Such information as may be available to the commission as to the degree to which any particular type of pollutant is subject to treatment; the availability, practicality, and technical and economic feasibility of treatment techniques; the impact of treatment requirements upon water quantity; and the extent to which the discharge to be controlled is significant;

(c) The continuous, intermittent, or seasonal nature of the pollutant to be controlled;

(d) The existing extent of pollution or the maximum extent of pollution to be tolerated as a goal;

(e) Whether the pollutant arises from natural sources;

(f) Beneficial uses of water; and

(g) Such information as may be available to the commission regarding the risk associated with the pollutants including its persistence, degradability, the usual or potential presence of the affected organism in any waters, the importance of the affected organisms, and the nature and extent of the effect of the pollutant on such organisms.

(5) In establishing water quality standards using statistical methodologies or in requiring the use of statistical methodologies for permit or enforcement purposes, statistical methodologies used must be based on assumptions that are compatible with the water quality data.

(6) For the purpose of implementing section 303(c) (2) (B) of the federal act, the commission may adopt numerical water quality standards for toxic pollutants listed pursuant to section 307(a) (1) of the federal act for which criteria have been published under section 304(a) of the federal act, and these standards may be applied in accordance with this article to discharges of pollutants to specified portions or segments of surface waters where such pollutants may be discharged or are present in the affected surface waters and could reasonably be expected to interfere with classified uses. Monitoring requirements for discharges of such pollutants shall be reasonably related to the potential for the presence of such pollutants in the discharge at levels inconsistent with water quality standards and shall be imposed to the maximum extent practical on those responsible for the presence of the pollutants. This subsection (6) does not in any way limit the commission's authority to adopt water quality standards in order to comply with provisions of the federal act.

(7) If, after full application of publicly owned treatment work authority pursuant to section 307(b) (1) of the federal act, stream standards or effluent limitations established pursuant to subsection (6) of this section are exceeded as a result of a discharge from a publicly owned treatment work, the commission, upon request of a publicly owned treatment work, shall conduct a public hearing to investigate the source of pollution causing such exceedance.

## 25-8-205. Control regulations.

(1) The commission may promulgate control regulations for the following purposes:

(a) To describe prohibitions, standards, concentrations, and effluent limitations on the extent of specifically identified pollutants, including, but not limited to, those mentioned in section 25-8-204, that any person may discharge into any specified class of state waters;

(b) To describe pretreatment requirements, prohibitions, standards, concentrations, and effluent limitations on wastes any person may discharge into any specified class of state water from any specified type of facility, process, activity, or waste pile including, but not limited to, all types specified in section 306 (b) (1) (A) of the federal act;

(c) To describe precautionary measures, both mandatory and prohibitory, that must be taken by any person owning, operating, conducting, or maintaining any facility, process, activity, or waste pile that does cause or could reasonably be expected to cause pollution of any state waters in violation of control regulations or that does cause the quality of any state waters to be in violation of any applicable water quality standard;

(d) To adopt toxic effluent standards and pretreatment standards for pollutants which interfere with, pass through, or are otherwise incompatible with sewage treatment works;

(e) To describe requirements, prohibitions, standards, and concentration limitations on the use and disposal of biosolids to protect public health and to prevent the discharge of pollutants into state waters, except as authorized by permit. The commission requirements described pursuant to this paragraph (e) shall be no more restrictive than the requirements adopted for solid wastes disposal sites and facilities pursuant to part 1 of article 20 of title 30, C.R.S., except as necessary to be consistent with section 405 of the federal act. Fees shall be established as set forth in section 30-20-110.5, C.R.S., and the commission shall have no authority to levy additional or duplicative fees.

(f) To describe requirements, prohibitions, standards, and concentration limitations on the reuse of reclaimed domestic wastewater for purposes other than drinking that will protect public health and encourage the reuse of reclaimed domestic wastewater;

(g) (I) To describe requirements, prohibitions, and standards for the use of graywater for nondrinking purposes, to encourage the use of graywater, and to protect public health and water quality.

(II) Except as authorized in section 25-8-205.3, graywater may be used only in areas where the local city, city and county, or county has adopted an ordinance or resolution approving the use of graywater pursuant to section 30-11-107 (1) (kk) or 31-15-601 (1) (m) . The city, city and county, or county that has adopted an ordinance or resolution approving the use of graywater pursuant to section 30-11-107 (1) (kk) or 31-15-601 (1) (m) has exclusive enforcement authority regarding compliance with the ordinance or resolution.

(III) Use of graywater shall be allowed only in accordance with the terms and conditions of the decrees, contracts, and well permits applicable to the use of the source water rights or source water and any return flows therefrom, and no use of graywater shall be allowed that would not be allowed under such decrees, contracts, or permits if the graywater ordinance or resolution did not exist.

(IV) A local city, city and county, or county may only authorize the use of graywater in accordance with federal, state, and local requirements.

(2) In the formulation of each control regulation, the commission shall consider the following:

(a) The need for regulations that control discharges of specified pollutants that are the subject of water quality standards for the receiving state waters;

(b) The need for regulations that specify treatment requirements for various types of discharges;

(c) The degree to which any particular type of discharge is subject to treatment, the availability, practicality, and technical and economic feasibility of treatment techniques, and the extent to which the discharge to be controlled is significant;

(d) Control requirements promulgated by agencies of the federal government;

(e) The continuous, intermittent, or seasonal nature of the discharge to be controlled;

(f) Whether a regulation that is to be applicable to discharges into flowing water should be written in such a way that the degree of pollution tolerated or treatment required will be dependent upon the volume of flow of the receiving water or the extent to which the discharge is diluted therein, or the capacity of the receiving water to assimilate the discharge; and

(g) The need for specification of safety precautions that should be taken to protect water quality including, but not limited to, requirements for the keeping of logs and other records, requirements to protect subsurface waters in connection with mining and the drilling and operation of wells, and requirements as to settling ponds, holding tanks, and other treatment facilities for water that will or might enter state waters.

(3) Control regulations may be promulgated for use in connection with any one or more of the classes of state waters authorized pursuant to section 25-8-203 and may be made applicable with respect to any designated portion of state waters or to all state waters.

(4) The commission shall coordinate and cooperate with the state engineer, the Colorado water conservation board, the oil and gas conservation commission, the state board of health, and other state agencies having regulatory powers in order to avoid adopting control regulations that would be either redundant or unnecessary.

(5) The commission shall not adopt control regulations that require agricultural nonpoint source dischargers to utilize treatment techniques that require additional consumptive or evaporative use which would cause material injury to water rights. With regard to nonpoint source water pollution control related to agricultural practices, the commission and division shall pursue incentive, grant, and cooperative programs in preference to the promulgation of control regulations. When interested water conservation districts, water conservancy districts, and conservation districts recommend nonpoint source control activities related to agricultural practices to the division and commission, the division and commission, after consultation with such districts, shall give substantial weight to the recommendations of such districts into the approved program. Except as provided by section 25-8-205.5, control regulations related to agricultural practices shall be promulgated only if incentive, grant, and cooperative programs are determined by the commission to be inadequate and such regulations are necessary to meet state law or the federal act. This subsection (5) does not allocate wasteloads or relieve any source from participation in wasteload allocations determined necessary under any duly promulgated regulations established by the water quality control commission under this section.

(6) The division may issue a variance from a control regulation of general applicability, based upon a determination that the benefits derived from meeting the control regulation do not bear a reasonable relationship to the economic, environmental, or energy impacts or other factors which are particular to the applicant in complying with the control regulation; except that such variance shall be consistent with the purposes of this article including the protection of existing beneficial uses. No variance shall be issued for longer than five years. Variances shall be granted or renewed according to the procedure established in section 25-8-401 (5) .

## 25-8-205.3. Exemption from control regulations for graywater research - definition.

(1) Subject to the conditions set forth in subsection (2) of this section, a water utility, an institution of higher education in Colorado, or a public or private entity that a water utility or an institution of higher education in Colorado contracts with to conduct graywater research on the utility's or institution's behalf, may collect, treat, and use graywater in a manner that departs from the requirements of the commission's control regulations, as promulgated pursuant to section 25-8-205 (1) (g) , for the purpose of conducting scientific research on the collection, treatment, and use of graywater.

(2) A person collecting, treating, or using graywater pursuant to this section:

(a) Shall collect and use the graywater in accordance with the terms and conditions of the decrees, contracts, and well permits applicable to the use of the source water rights or source water and any return flows;

(b) Shall utilize a graywater treatment works system that incorporates a secondary water supply, such as a municipal water supply, to provide an alternative source of water if any portion of the system does not function properly; however, this subsection (2) (b) does not apply to scientific research involving the use of graywater exclusively for irrigation purposes;

(c) May collect, treat, and use the graywater in an area that is not within the jurisdiction of any city, city and county, or county that has adopted an ordinance or resolution authorizing graywater use pursuant to section 25-8-205 (1) (g) (II) ;

(d) May use the graywater for a nonpotable beneficial use including irrigation or toilet flushing if such use is tied to the purpose of the person's scientific research;

(e) Must comply with 45 CFR 46 and other applicable statutes and regulations for scientific research involving human exposure to graywater; and

(f) On an annual basis, shall report to the water resources review committee, created in section 37-

98-102, the results of periodic monitoring of the project conducted to assess:

(I) The functioning of the graywater treatment works system used to collect graywater; and

(II) For scientific research involving human exposure, the project's continued compliance with the requirements of the federal department of health and human services' regulations concerning the protection of human research subjects, codified in 45 CFR 46.

(3) Only an institution of higher education or a person contracting with an institution of higher education may collect, treat, and use graywater for research involving human exposure.

(4) As used in this section, "scientific research involving human exposure" means a research study in which:

(a) Empirical data is collected and analyzed about collection, treatment, or use of graywater; and

(b) Humans participate as subjects in the study.

## 25-8-205.5. Pollution from agricultural chemicals - rules.

(1) Legislative declaration. The general assembly hereby declares that the public policy of this state is to protect groundwater and the environment from impairment or degradation due to the improper use of agricultural chemicals while allowing for their proper and correct use, in particular, to provide for the management of agricultural chemicals to prevent, minimize, and mitigate their presence in groundwater and to provide for the education and training of agricultural chemical applicators and the general public regarding groundwater protection, agricultural chemical use, and the use of other agricultural methods.

(2) Definition. For the purpose of this section only, "groundwater" means any subsurface water in a zone of saturation which is or can be brought to the surface of the ground or to surface waters through wells, springs, seeps, or other discharge areas.

(3) Powers and duties of the commissioner of agriculture. (a) The commissioner of agriculture shall identify agricultural management areas in the state.

(b) The commissioner shall promulgate rules for the following:

(I) Facilities for the storage of pesticides in bulk, except for facilities storing pesticides used for water treatment at public water systems, which are systems used to provide the public with piped water for human consumption, and domestic wastewater treatment works;

(II) Mixing and loading areas where any of the following are handled in any one-year period:

(A) Five hundred gallons or more, in the aggregate, of formulated product or combination of formulated products of liquid pesticides;

(B) Three thousand pounds or more, in the aggregate, of formulated product or combination of formulated products of dry pesticides;

(C) One thousand five hundred pounds or more, in the aggregate, of active ingredients of pesticides;

(III) Storage facilities where any liquid fertilizer is stored in any container or series of interconnected containers having a capacity greater than five thousand gallons;

(IV) Storage facilities where fifty-five thousand pounds or more, in the aggregate, of formulated product or combination of formulated products of bulk dry fertilizer are stored;

(V) Mixing and loading areas at any storage facility subject to the provisions of this section.

(b.1) No rule promulgated pursuant to paragraph (b) of this subsection (3) shall apply to any field mixing and loading of agricultural chemicals.

(b.2) Every rule promulgated pursuant to paragraph (b) of this subsection (3) shall include a three-year phase-in period after promulgation of the rule for persons subject to the rule.

(b.3) Pursuant to paragraph (h) of this subsection (3) , the commissioner is authorized to enforce rules promulgated pursuant to paragraph (b) of this subsection (3) .

(c) The commissioner may, in his discretion, develop best management practices for any other activity relating to the use of any agricultural chemical.

(d) If the commissioner determines that the use of best management practices is ineffective or insufficient to prevent or mitigate the pollution of groundwater, the commissioner may require, by rule and regulation adopted pursuant to article 4 of title 24, C.R.S., the use of agricultural management plans.

(e) The commissioner is authorized to adopt, pursuant to article 4 of title 24, C.R.S., any other reasonable rules and regulations for the administration and implementation of this section.

(f) The commissioner is authorized to enter into an agreement with the Colorado cooperative extension service to provide training and education as specified in subsection (4) of this section.

(g) The commissioner shall perform the monitoring specified in subsection (5) of this section. The commissioner shall enter into an agreement with the department of public health and environment to assist in the identification of agricultural management areas and to perform analysis, interpretation, and reporting of groundwater monitoring data supplied by the commissioner.

(h) With respect to any rule or regulation adopted pursuant to paragraph (b) of this subsection (3) only, the commissioner shall have the following investigation and enforcement powers:

(I) At any reasonable time during regular business hours, the commissioner shall have free and unimpeded access upon consent or upon obtaining an administrative search warrant:

(A) To all areas, buildings, yards, warehouses, and storage facilities in which any agricultural chemicals are kept, stored, handled, processed, or transported; and

(B) To all records, if any, required to be kept and to make copies of such records.

(II) The commissioner shall have full authority to administer oaths and take statements, to issue administrative subpoenas requiring the attendance of witnesses before him and the production of all books, memoranda, papers, and other documents, articles, or instruments, and to compel the disclosure by such witnesses of all facts known to them relative to the matters under investigation. Upon the failure or refusal of any witness to obey any subpoena, the commissioner may petition the district court, and, upon a proper showing, the court may enter an order compelling the witness to appear and testify or produce documentary evidence. Failure to obey such an order of the court shall be punishable as a contempt of court.

(III) Any complaints of record made to the commissioner and the results of his investigations may, in the discretion of the commissioner, be closed to public inspection, except as provided by court order, during the investigatory period and until dismissed or until notice of hearing and charges are served on any such person subject to a rule or regulation adopted pursuant to paragraph (b) of this subsection (3) .

(IV) (A) Whenever the commissioner has reasonable cause to believe that a violation of any rule or regulation adopted pursuant to paragraph (b) of this subsection (3) has occurred and immediate enforcement is deemed necessary, he may issue a cease-and-desist order, which may require any person to cease violating any such rule or regulation. Such cease-and-desist order shall set forth the rule or regulation alleged to have been violated, the facts alleged to have constituted the violation, and the requirement that all actions be ceased forthwith.

(B) At any time after the date of the service of the order to cease and desist, the person may request a hearing on the question of whether or not such violation has occurred. Such hearing shall be concluded in not more than ten days after such request, excluding Saturdays, Sundays, and any legal holidays, and shall be conducted pursuant to the provisions of article 4 of title 24, C.R.S.

(C) In the event that any person fails to comply with a cease-and-desist order within twenty-four hours, the commissioner may bring a suit for a temporary restraining order and injunctive relief to prevent any further or continued violation of such order.

(D) No stay of a cease-and-desist order shall be issued before a hearing thereon involving both parties.

(E) Matters brought before a court pursuant to this section shall have preference over other matters on the court's calendar.

(V) Whenever the commissioner possesses evidence satisfactory to him that any person has engaged in or is about to engage in any act or practice constituting a violation of any rule or regulation adopted pursuant to paragraph (b) of this subsection (3) , he may apply to any court of competent jurisdiction to temporarily or permanently restrain or enjoin the act or practice in question and to enforce compliance with the rule or regulation. In any such action, the commissioner shall not be required to plead or prove irreparable injury or the inadequacy of the remedy at law. Under no circumstances shall the court require the commissioner to post a bond.

(VI) (A) Any person who violates any rule or regulation adopted pursuant to paragraph (b) of this subsection (3) is subject to a civil penalty, as determined by the commissioner. The maximum penalty shall not exceed one thousand dollars per violation. Each day the violation occurs shall constitute a separate violation.

(B) No civil penalty may be imposed unless the person charged is given notice and opportunity for a hearing pursuant to article 4 of title 24, C.R.S.

(C) If the commissioner is unable to collect such civil penalty or if any person fails to pay all or a set portion of the civil penalty as determined by the commissioner, the commissioner may recover such amount plus costs and attorney fees by action in any court of competent jurisdiction.

(D) Before imposing any civil penalty, the commissioner may consider the effect of such penalty on the ability of the person charged to stay in business.

(4) Training and education. The Colorado cooperative extension service, acting in cooperation with the commissioner of agriculture and pursuant to any contract authorized in paragraph (f) of subsection (3) of this section, shall disseminate information and provide training regarding agricultural management areas, best management practices, and agricultural management plans.

(5) Monitoring. Pursuant to the commissioner's duties as set forth in any contract authorized in paragraph (g) of subsection (3) of this section, the commissioner shall identify agricultural management areas as defined in section 25-8-103 (1.1) and shall conduct monitoring programs to determine:

(a) The presence of any agricultural chemical in groundwater at a level which meets or exceeds any water quality standard applicable under this article or which has a reasonable likelihood of meeting or exceeding any such standard; or

(b) The likelihood that an agricultural chemical will enter the groundwater, based upon the existence of sufficient, valid scientific data which reasonably predict the behavior of a particular agricultural chemical in the soil.

(6) Reporting of monitoring results - regulation. (a) If the division determines that any agricultural chemical exists at a level which meets or exceeds any water quality standard or which has a reasonable likelihood of meeting or exceeding any such standard, it shall so notify the commissioner of agriculture and shall provide him with any written reports it deems necessary or desirable to define the extent of such occurrence. When the commissioner has been notified of such an occurrence related to an agricultural chemical which is registered as a pesticide, he shall take reasonable steps to notify the registrant of any such pesticide. When the commissioner has been notified of such an occurrence related to any other agricultural chemical, he shall take reasonable steps to notify the distributors of such chemical in the area affected by such occurrence.

(b) Unless such occurrence is determined by the commissioner of agriculture and the water quality control commission to require a control regulation as set forth in paragraph (c) of this subsection (6) , the commissioner of agriculture may promulgate rules and regulations regarding the use of any agricultural chemical giving rise to the occurrence.

(c) If continued monitoring reveals that rules and regulations adopted by the commissioner pursuant to this section are not preventing or mitigating the presence of the subject agricultural chemical to the extent necessary, the commissioner of agriculture and the water quality control commission shall confer and determine whether an amendment to such rules and regulations may be sufficient to prevent or mitigate the occurrence to the extent necessary. Only if the commissioner of agriculture and the water quality control commission determine that such rules and regulations have been or will be insufficient to meet the requirements of state law or the federal act shall the occurrence be referred to the water quality control commission for the promulgation of a control regulation. In the event that the commissioner of agriculture and the water quality control commission fail to agree on such a determination, the authority of the water quality control commission shall be final.

(7) Promulgation of control regulations. (a) With respect to the regulation of pollutants from agricultural chemicals, the water quality control commission is authorized to promulgate control regulations only when:

(I) Any occurrence has been referred to the commission pursuant to subsection (6) of this section;

467

or

(II) Incentive, grant, and cooperative programs are determined by the water quality control commission to be inadequate as set forth in section 25-8-205 (5) .

(b) Any such control regulations shall be promulgated in consultation with the commissioner of agriculture.

(8) Groundwater protection fund - transfer of moneys to the plant health, pest control, and environmental protection cash fund - fees. The fees as specified and collected pursuant to sections 35-9-118 (3) (a) and 35-12-106 (1) , C.R.S., and any civil fines imposed pursuant to subparagraph (VI) of paragraph (h) of subsection (3) of this section shall be transmitted to the state treasurer, who shall credit the same to the plant health, pest control, and environmental protection cash fund created in section 35-1-106.3, C.R.S. Within sixty days after July 1, 2009, the unexpended and unencumbered balance of the groundwater protection fund, as that fund existed prior to July 1, 2009, shall be transferred to the plant health, pest control, and environmental protection cash fund.

(9) Repealed.

## 25-8-206. Prior acts validated.

(1) All acts, hearings, orders, rules, regulations, and standards adopted by the water pollution control commission as constituted and empowered by the laws of this state prior to July 6, 1973, which were valid prior to said date, shall be deemed and held to be legal and valid in all respects, as though issued by the commission under the authority of this article, and no provision of this article shall be construed to repeal or in any way invalidate any actions, orders, rules, regulations, or water quality standards adopted by said commission prior to said date.

(2) All acts, hearings, orders, rules, regulations, and standards adopted by the water quality control commission as constituted and empowered by the laws of this state prior to July 1, 1981, which were valid prior to said date, shall be deemed and held to be legal and valid in all respects, as though issued by the commission under the authority of this article, and no provision of this article shall be construed to repeal or in any way invalidate any actions, orders, rules, regulations, or water quality standards adopted by said commission prior to said date.

(3) All acts, orders, and rules adopted by the state board of health under the authority of part 2 of article 1.5 of this title, part 1 of article 10 of this title, and section 30-20-110.5, C.R.S., prior to July 1, 2006, that were valid prior to said date and not otherwise subject to judicial review shall, to the extent that they are not inconsistent with said provisions, be deemed and held to be legal and valid in all respects, as though issued by the commission under the authority of such provisions of law. No provision of this article shall be construed to validate any actions, orders, or rules that were not valid when adopted by the board of health prior to such date.

## 25-8-207. Review of classifications and standards.

(1) The commission, upon petition or upon its own motion, shall review, pursuant to section 24-4-103, C.R.S., any classification, standard, designation, or regulation adopted pursuant to sections 25-8-203, 25-8-204, and 25-8-209 for consistency with this subsection (1) and consistency with the policies set forth in sections 25-8-102 and 25-8-104. Rule-making hearings on petitions filed under this subsection (1) shall be held expeditiously with respect to such classifications, standards, designations, or regulations adopted prior to July 1, 1992. The commission shall make a finding of inconsistency where:

(a) Use classifications and water quality standards for aquatic life are more stringent than is necessary to protect fish life, shellfish life, and wildlife in water body segments which are reasonably capable of sustaining such fish life, shellfish life, and wildlife from the standpoint of physical, streambed, flow, habitat, climatic, and other pertinent characteristics;

(b) Any use classifications or water quality standards were adopted based upon material assumptions that were in error or no longer apply; or

(c) Any designation does not conform with the provisions of section 25-8-209.

(2) Where the commission determines that an inconsistency exists, it shall declare the inconsistent

classifications or standards void ab initio and shall simultaneously establish appropriate classifications or standards.

## 25-8-208. Emergency rule-making.

In addition to all other powers of the commission, the commission, pursuant to section 24-4-103 (6) , C.R.S., shall have the authority to conduct emergency rule-making for the purpose of adopting an interim standard to apply for a specified period of time in place of an existing water quality standard. The commission shall hold emergency rule-making hearings to consider the adoption of such an interim standard whenever it finds, in its discretion, that the petitioner requesting such rule-making has established exigent circumstances which warrant the emergency action.

## 25-8-209. Water quality designations.

(1) The commission may adopt the following water quality designations:

(a) Outstanding waters;

(b) Use-protected waters.

(2) The commission shall promulgate criteria governing the designations provided in subsection (1) of this section. Such criteria shall be consistent with the provisions of this section and sections 25-8-102 and 25-8-104.

(3) (a) Outstanding waters. Outstanding waters shall be maintained and protected at their existing quality. Segments shall not be designated as outstanding waters unless the commission determines that:

(I) The quality of the waters is better than necessary to support propagation of fish, shellfish, and wildlife and recreation in and on the water based upon water quality standards for indicator parameters identified by the commission in the criteria promulgated under the provisions of subsection (2) of this section;

(II) The waters constitute an outstanding natural resource; and

(III) Protection of such resource requires protection in addition to that provided by the combination of water quality classifications and standards and the protection afforded reviewable waters under the provisions of subsection (5) of this section.

(b) All waters that were designated as high quality 1 by the commission prior to July 1, 1992, are hereby designated as outstanding waters.

(4) Use-protected waters. Use-protected waters shall be those waters with existing quality that is not better than necessary to support propagation of fish, shellfish, and wildlife and recreation in and on the water. The quality of waters designated as use-protected may be altered if that quality provided for in applicable water quality classifications and standards is maintained.

(5) Reviewable waters. Waters that are not designated as outstanding waters or use-protected waters shall be referred to as reviewable waters. The existing quality of reviewable waters shall be maintained and protected unless it is determined that allowing lower water quality is necessary to accommodate important economic or social development in the area in which the waters are located, which shall include all areas directly impacted by the proposed activity. Notwithstanding any other provisions of this subsection (5) , that quality which is provided for in applicable water quality classifications and standards shall be maintained for reviewable waters.

(6) Water quality designations and reviewable waters provisions shall not be utilized by the commission or by any other state, federal, or local agency in a manner that is contrary to the provisions of section 25-8-104.

# PART 3. ADMINISTRATION

## 25-8-301. Administration of water quality control programs.

(1) The department of public health and environment shall administer and enforce the water quality control programs adopted by the commission.

(2) In furtherance of such responsibility of the department, the executive director shall maintain within the division a separate water quality control agency.

(3) The director of said water quality control agency shall be employed pursuant to section 13 of article XII of the state constitution. He or she shall be a licensed professional engineer or have a graduate degree in engineering or other specialty dealing with the problems of pollution and shall also have appropriate practical and administrative experience related to such problems. Such person shall not be the administrator employed pursuant to section 25-8-202 (4) .

(4) The division shall act as staff to the commission in commission proceedings other than adjudicatory or appellate proceedings in which the division is a party.

## 25-8-302. Duties of division.

(1) The division shall:

(a) Carry out the enforcement provisions of this article, including the seeking of criminal prosecution of violations and such other judicial relief as may be appropriate;

(b) Administer the permit system as provided in part 5 of this article;

(c) Monitor waste discharges and the state waters as provided in section 25-8-303;

(d) Submit an annual report to the commission as provided in section 25-8-305;

(e) Maintain a mailing list of persons requesting notice of actions by the division or by the commission and notify persons on the list of such actions, for which service the division shall assess a fee to cover the costs thereof;

(f) Review and certify, conditionally certify, or deny requests for certifications under the provisions of section 401 of the federal act and this article, known as "401 certificates". Conditions attached to the division's certification shall only implement rules which the commission has made applicable to 401 certifications. General or nationwide permits under section 404 of the federal act shall be certified for use in Colorado without the imposition of any additional state conditions. Appeals by an affected entity of a final 401 certification decision of the division shall be heard in accordance with section 24-4-105, C.R.S., of the "State Administrative Procedure Act".

(g) Perform such other duties as may lawfully be assigned to it.

## 25-8-303. Monitoring.

(1) The division shall take such samplings as may be necessary to enable it to determine the quality of every reasonably accessible segment of state waters, wherever practical. In sampling such waters the division shall give consideration to characteristics such as those listed in section 25-8-204 (2) , but if pollution is suspected the sampling shall not be limited or restricted by reason of the fact that no water quality standard has been promulgated for the suspected type of pollution.

(2) As to every segment of state waters so sampled, the division shall endeavor to determine the nature and amount of each pollutant, whether a new or different water quality standard is needed, the source of each pollutant, the place where each such pollutant enters the water, and the names and addresses of each person responsible for or in control of each entry.

(3) As to each separate pollution source identified, the division shall:

(a) Determine what control regulations are applicable, if any;

(b) Determine whether the discharge is covered by a permit and whether or not any condition of the permit is being violated;

(c) Determine what further control measures with respect to such pollution source are practicable.

(4) The division shall inform the commission of any unusual problem which creates difficulties in abating pollution.

## 25-8-304. Monitoring, recording, and reporting.

(1) The owner or operator of any facility, process, or activity from which a discharge of pollutants is made into state waters or into any municipal domestic wastewater treatment works shall, according to standard procedures and methods prescribed by the division:

(a) Establish and maintain records;

(b) Make reports;

(c) Install, calibrate, use, and maintain monitoring methods and equipment, including biological and indicator pollutant monitoring methods;

(d) Sample discharges;

(e) Provide additional reasonably available information relating to discharges into domestic wastewater treatment works.

## 25-8-305. Annual report.

Notwithstanding section 24-1-136 (11) (a) (I) , on or before October 1 of each year, the division through the executive director shall report to the commission on the effectiveness of this article and shall include in such report any recommendations it may have with respect to any regulatory or legislative changes that may be needed or desired. The report must include the then-current information that has been obtained pursuant to section 25-8-303 and information concerning the status of the division's implementation of the discharge permit program established in part 5 of this article. The report shall be filed with the house agriculture, livestock, and natural resources committee and the senate agriculture, natural resources, and energy committee, or any successor committees.

## 25-8-306. Authority to enter and inspect premises and records.

(1) The division has the power, upon presentation of proper credentials, to enter and inspect at any reasonable time and in a reasonable manner any property, premise, or place for the purpose of investigating any actual, suspected, or potential source of water pollution, or ascertaining compliance or noncompliance with any control regulation or any order promulgated under this article. Such entry is also authorized for the purpose of inspecting and copying records required to be kept concerning any effluent source.

(2) In the making of such inspections, investigations, and determinations, the division, insofar as practicable, may designate as its authorized representatives any qualified personnel of the department of agriculture. The division may also request assistance from any other state or local agency or institution.

(3) If such entry or inspection is denied or not consented to, the division is empowered to and shall obtain, from the district or county court for the judicial district or county in which such property, premise, or place is located, a warrant to enter and inspect any such property, premise, or place prior to entry and inspection. The district and county courts of the state of Colorado are empowered to issue such warrants upon a proper showing of the need for such entry and inspection.

## 25-8-307. Emergencies.

Whenever the division determines, after investigation, that any person is discharging or causing to be discharged or is about to discharge into any state waters, directly or indirectly, any pollutant which in the opinion of the division constitutes a clear, present, and immediate danger to the health or livelihood of members of the public, the division shall issue its written order to said person that he must immediately cease or prevent the discharge of such pollutant into such waters and thereupon such person shall immediately discontinue such discharge. Concurrently with the issuance of such order, the division may seek a restraining order or injunction pursuant to section 25-8-607.

## 25-8-308. Additional authority and duties of division - penalties.

(1) In addition to the authority specified elsewhere in this article, the division has the power to:

(a) Conduct or cause to be conducted studies, research, and demonstrations with respect to water pollution and the control, abatement, or prevention thereof, as requested by the commission;

(b) Furnish technical advice and services relating to water pollution problems and control techniques;

(c) Designate one or more persons or agencies in any area of the state as a water quality control authority, as agent of the division, to exercise and perform such powers and duties of the division as may be specified in such designation;

(d) Administer, in compliance with regulations and the priority ranking adopted by the commission, loans and grants from the federal government and from other public sources;

(e) Advise, consult, cooperate, and enter into agreements with other agencies of the state, the federal government, other states, and interstate agencies, and with groups, political subdivisions, and industries affected by the provisions of this article and the policies of the commission; but any such agreement involving, authorizing, or requiring compliance in this state with any standard or regulation shall not be effective unless or until the commission has held a hearing with respect to such standard or regulation and has adopted the same in compliance with this article;

(f) Certify, when requested, the existence of any facility, land, building, machinery, equipment, treatment works, or sewage or disposal systems as have been acquired, constructed, or installed in conformity with the purposes of this article;

(g) Take such action in accordance with rules and orders promulgated by the commission as may be necessary to prevent, abate, and control pollution;

(h) Implement a program, in accordance with rules and orders of the commission, for the reuse of reclaimed domestic wastewater for purposes other than drinking.

(2) Except as provided in section 25-8-608, all fines and penalties for violations of this article 8 must be transmitted to the state treasurer for deposit to the credit of the general fund.

## 25-8-309. Study of classification and standard issues. (Repealed)

## 25-8-310. Education program - storm water.

(1) The division may develop education programs for use by state and local governmental entities.

(2) The educational programs developed in accordance with subsection (1) of this section shall be designed to inform the public about storm water quality problems resulting from:

(a) The washing of motor vehicles on nonpermeable surfaces and the advantages of washing motor vehicles at car wash facilities that comply with recognized industry water conservation and water quality control standards;

(b) The disposal of leaves, litter, pet wastes, and debris in street gutters and storm drains;

(c) The disposal of used oil, antifreeze, paints, and other household chemicals in storm sewers or drains; and

(d) Soil erosion on property due to lack of planting of ground cover and stabilization of erosion-prone areas.

(3) The division may obtain gifts, grants, and donations to fund the costs of developing the education programs described in subsection (1) of this section. If the funding necessary to comply with said subsection (1) is not obtained, the division shall not be required to comply with said subsection (1) until such funding is obtained.

# PART 4. PROCEDURES

## 25-8-401. Authority and procedures for hearings.

(1) The commission or the division may hold public hearings, which shall be held pursuant to and

in conformity with article 4 of title 24, C.R.S., and with this article.

(2) The commission may adopt such rules and regulations governing procedures and hearings before the commission or division as may be necessary to assure that such procedures and hearings will be fair and impartial. Such rules and regulations shall be consistent with the pertinent provisions of article 4 of title 24, C.R.S.

(3) In all proceedings before the commission or the division with respect to any alleged violation of any control regulation, permit, or order, the burden of proof shall be upon the division.

(4) Except for classification and water quality standard-setting proceedings, the commission or the department of public health and environment may designate a hearing officer or an administrative law judge pursuant to part 10 of article 30 of title 24, C.R.S., subject to appropriations made to the department of public health and environment. When appropriate, the hearing officer may be an employee of the department of public health and environment or a member of or the administrator of the commission.

(5) (a) Any request for a variance with respect to a permit condition shall be made within thirty days after issuance by the division of the final permit. Requests for variances from any other application of a control regulation shall be made within thirty days of legal notice by the division of the regulation or prior to operation of any new or expanded facility which would be affected by the control regulations. A variance may also be sought within thirty days of facts becoming available which had not been reasonably available to the applicant prior to that time or upon application to the commission for good cause shown.

(b) The division shall approve or disapprove any variance request and issue its decision within ninety days after receipt of the variance request. Notice of a variance request shall be sent to anyone who has requested such notice and shall be included on the next commission agenda. In the case of a variance being granted prior to the final permit being issued, the division shall publish for public notice and comment the entire draft permit with the variance incorporated therein. In the case of a variance granted after a final permit has been issued, the division shall publish for public notice and comment the variance as a proposed modification to the permit. Within forty-five days of issuance of a variance decision by the division which does not involve discharge permit conditions required by the federal act, the commission on its own motion or on the motion of the division or any interested person may decide to review the variance decision. In such event, a hearing pursuant to section 24-4-105, C.R.S., shall be held, and the commission may affirm, modify, or deny the decision. Variance decisions of the division which involve discharge permit conditions required by the federal act shall be subject to review by an administrative law judge of the department of personnel pursuant to section 24-4-105, C.R.S., as part of any challenge to the conditions of a final discharge permit issued by the division.

## 25-8-402. Procedures to be followed in classifying state waters and setting standards and control regulations.

(1) Prior to the classification of state waters and promulgating any water quality standard or any control regulation authorized in this article, the commission shall conduct a public hearing thereon as provided in section 24-4-103, C.R.S. Notice of any such hearing shall conform to the requirements of section 24-4-103, C.R.S., but such notice shall be given at least sixty days prior to the hearing and shall include each proposed standard or regulation.

(2) Any person desiring to propose a standard or regulation differing from the standard or regulation proposed by the commission shall file such other written proposal with the commission not less than twenty days prior to the hearing, and, when on file, such proposal shall be open for public inspection.

(3) Witnesses at the hearing shall be subject to cross-examination by or on behalf of the commission, by or on behalf of persons who have proposed standards or regulations pursuant to subsection (2) of this section, and by or on behalf of persons who have obtained party status to the proceeding.

(4) Standards or regulations promulgated pursuant to this section shall take effect as provided in

section 24-4-103 (5) , C.R.S.

(5) Any emergency rule-making proceedings by the commission shall be conducted pursuant to section 24-4-103 (6) , C.R.S., and not pursuant to this section. Any rule adopted pursuant to such proceedings may be effective for a specified period longer than one hundred twenty days, but not later than one year, if the commission determines that such longer period is necessary to complete rule-making pursuant to section 24-4-103, C.R.S., to reconsider the emergency rule.

## 25-8-403. Administrative reconsideration.

During the time permitted for seeking judicial review of any final order or determination of the commission or division, any party directly affected by such order or determination may apply to the commission or division, as appropriate, for a hearing or rehearing with respect to, or reconsideration of, such order or determination. The determination by the commission or division of whether to grant or deny the application for a hearing, rehearing, or reconsideration shall be made within ten days after receipt by the commission or division of such application. Such determination by the commission may be made by telephone or mail or at a meeting, but in any event shall be confirmed at the next meeting of the commission. If the application for a hearing, rehearing, or reconsideration is granted, the order or determination to which such application pertains shall not be considered final for purposes of judicial review, and the commission or the division may affirm, reverse, or modify, in whole or in part, the pertinent order or determination; thereafter such order or determination shall be final and not subject to stay or reconsideration under this section.

## 25-8-404. Judicial review.

(1) Any final rule, order, or determination by the division or the commission, including but not limited to classification of state waters, approval of areawide waste treatment management plans, water quality standards, site approvals, permits, control regulations, enforcement orders, cease-and-desist orders, and clean-up orders, shall be subject to judicial review in accordance with the provisions of this article and article 4 of title 24, C.R.S. All regulations, orders, and determinations of the commission or division shall be adopted, promulgated, or issued in accordance with the provisions of said article 4 of title 24.

(2) Any proceeding for judicial review of any final order or determination of the commission or division shall be filed in the district court for the district in which the pollution source affected is located.

(3) Any proceeding for judicial review of any final rule, order, or determination of the commission or division shall be filed within thirty days after said rule, order, or determination has become final. Rule-making determinations shall become final in accordance with the "State Administrative Procedure Act". Quasi-judicial determinations shall become final upon issuance of such determinations to those parties to the proceedings. The period for filing the action for judicial review shall be stayed while any application for a hearing, rehearing, or reconsideration is pending pursuant to section 25-8-403, and the period during which any such application is pending shall extend the time for filing a proceeding for judicial review an equal length of time.

(4) (a) Except with respect to emergency orders issued pursuant to section 25-8-307, any person to whom a cease-and-desist order, clean-up order, or other order has been issued by the division or commission, or against whom an adverse determination has been made, may petition the district court for a stay of the effectiveness of such order or determination. Such petition shall be filed in the district court in which the pollution source affected is located.

(b) Such petitions may be filed prior to any such order or determination becoming final or during any period in which such order or determination is under judicial review.

(c) Such stay shall be granted by the court if there is probable cause to believe that refusal to grant a stay will cause serious harm to the affected person or any other person, and:

(I) That the alleged violation or activity to which the order or determination pertains will not continue, or if it does continue, any harmful effects on state waters will be alleviated promptly after the cessation of the violation or activity; or

(II) That the refusal to grant a stay would be without sufficient corresponding public benefit.

(5) Any party may move the court to remand the case to the division or the commission in the interests of justice, for the purpose of adducing additional specified and material evidence, and findings thereon; but such party shall show reasonable grounds for the failure to adduce such evidence previously before the division or the commission.

(6) If the court does not stay the effectiveness of an order of the commission or division, the court shall enforce compliance with that order by issuing a temporary restraining order or injunction at the request of the commission or division.

### 25-8-405. Samples - secret processes.

(1) If samples of water or water pollutants are taken for analysis, the person believed to be responsible for any suspected violation or who is or will be subject to any remedial action shall be notified immediately of the collection of the samples and a representative portion of the sample shall be furnished immediately upon request to said person. A representative portion of such sample shall be furnished to any suspected violator whenever any remedial action is taken with respect thereto by the division. A duplicate of every analytical report pertaining to such sample shall also be furnished as soon as practicable to such person. Any request for a sample split shall be made within six months of the notification of the collection of samples.

(2) Any information relating to any secret process, method of manufacture or production, or sales or marketing data which may be acquired, ascertained, or discovered, whether in any sampling investigation, emergency investigation, or otherwise, shall not be publicly disclosed by any member, officer, or employee of the commission or the division, but shall be kept confidential. Any person seeking to invoke the protection of this subsection (2) shall bear the burden of proving its applicability. This section shall never be interpreted as preventing full disclosure of effluent data.

### 25-8-406. Administrative stays - renewal permits.

If a permittee requests a hearing pursuant to section 24-4-105, C.R.S., challenging final action by the division in regard to any terms and conditions of a renewal permit, said permit shall become effective in its entirety unless a stay is granted pursuant to this section. The division may stay any contested terms and conditions of a permit for good cause shown. The division shall act on any stay request within ten days of receipt thereof. Any stay granted under this section shall expire when a final determination is made after the conclusion of the hearing held pursuant to section 24-4-105, C.R.S. During the period of any such stay, the corresponding terms and conditions of the prior permit shall be in effect. Action by the division granting or denying a stay pursuant to this section shall be final agency action subject to de novo determination pursuant to section 25-8-404.

# PART 5. PERMIT SYSTEM

### 25-8-501. Permits required for discharge of pollutants - administration.

(1) No person shall discharge any pollutant into any state water from a point source without first having obtained a permit from the division for such discharge, and no person shall discharge into a ditch or man-made conveyance for the purpose of evading the requirement to obtain a permit under this article. No person covered by this article shall use or dispose of biosolids, except as authorized by regulations that shall not be more restrictive than the requirements adopted for solid wastes disposal sites and facilities pursuant to part 1 of article 20 of title 30, C.R.S., except as necessary to be consistent with section 405 of the federal act. Existing authorization for the use or disposal of biosolids shall continue until permits are issued in accordance with this part 5. Each

application for a permit duly filed under the federal act shall be deemed to be a permit application filed under this article, and each permit issued pursuant to the federal act shall be deemed to be a temporary permit issued under this article which shall expire upon expiration of the federal permit. (2) The division shall examine applications for and may issue, suspend, revoke, modify, deny, and otherwise administer permits for the discharge of pollutants into state waters and for the use and disposal of biosolids. Such administration shall be in accordance with the provisions of this article and regulations promulgated by the commission. Until modified pursuant to this article, final permits shall be governed by their existing limitations.

(3) The commission shall promulgate such regulations as may be necessary and proper for the orderly and effective administration of permits for the discharge of pollutants, which regulations shall include, but not be limited to, procedures for the issuance of a variance pursuant to section 25-8-503 (4) , and shall also require that, in appropriate circumstances, the effluent limitations contained in a permit shall be adjusted to account for the pollutants contained in the discharger's intake water. Such regulations shall be consistent with the provisions of this article and with federal requirements and shall be in furtherance of the policy contained in section 25-8-102. Such regulations shall establish a permit process that allows permit conditions to remain in effect as long as circumstances dictate those conditions. In order to comply with federal requirements, but not to lessen compliance with federal standards, such permit process may require periodic renewal of permits even where minimal or no changes in the permit conditions are necessary. Renewal shall be required where more than minimal changes in permit conditions are necessary. The regulations may pertain to and implement, among other matters, permit and permit application contents, procedures, requirements, and restrictions with respect to the following:

(a) Identification and address of the owner and operator of the activity, facility, or process from which the discharge is to be permitted;

(b) Location and quantity and quality characteristics of the permitted discharge;

(c) Effluent limitations and conditions for treatment prior to discharge to a publicly owned treatment works;

(d) Monitoring as well as record-keeping and reporting requirements consistent with standard procedures and methods established by the division;

(e) Schedules of compliance;

(f) Procedures to be followed by division personnel for entering and inspecting premises;

(g) Submission of pertinent plans and specifications for the facility, process, or activity which is the source of a waste discharge;

(h) Restrictions on transfers of the permit;

(i) Procedures to be followed in the event of expansion or modification of the process, facility, or activity from which the discharge occurs or the quality, quantity, or frequency of the discharge;

(j) Duration of the permit and renewal procedures using a risk-based approach that limits the amount of work required to renew permits that have minimal or no changes in the permit conditions to streamline the renewal process;

(k) Authority of the division to require changes in plans and specifications for control facilities as a condition for the issuance of a permit;

(l) Identification of control regulations over which the permit takes precedence and identification of control regulations over which a permit may never take precedence;

(m) Notice requirements of any intent to construct, install, or alter any process, facility, or activity that is likely to result in a new or altered discharge;

(n) Effectiveness under this article of permit applications submitted to and permits issued by the federal government under the federal act.

(4) Nothing in any permit shall ever be construed to prevent or limit the application of any emergency power of the division.

(5) Every permit issued for a domestic wastewater treatment works shall contain such terms and conditions as the division determines to be necessary or desirable to assure continuing compliance with applicable control regulations. Such terms and conditions may require that whenever deemed necessary by the division to assure such compliance the permittee shall:

(a) Require pretreatment of effluent from industrial, governmental, or commercial facilities, processes, and activities before such effluent is received into the gathering and collection system of the permittee;

(b) Prohibit any connection to any municipal permittee's interceptors and collection system that would result in receipt by such municipal permittee of any effluent other than sewage required by law to be received by such permittee;

(c) Include specified terms and conditions of its permit in all contracts for receipt by the permittee of any effluent not required to be received by a municipal permittee;

(d) Initiate engineering and financial planning for expansion of the domestic wastewater treatment works whenever throughput and treatment reaches eighty percent of design capacity;

(e) Commence construction of such domestic wastewater treatment works expansion whenever throughput and treatment reaches ninety-five percent of design capacity or, in the case of a municipality, either commence such construction or cease issuance of building permits within such municipality until such construction is commenced; except that building permits may continue to be issued for any construction which would not have the effect of increasing the input of domestic wastewater to the sewage treatment works of the municipality involved. The term "commence construction", as used in this paragraph (e) , includes execution of, and commencement of work under, contracts for engineering design, plans, and specifications for erection, building, alteration, remodeling, improvement, or extension of treatment works and commitment to the completion of construction of such treatment works prior to exceeding permit effluent limitations based upon facility design and capacity or execution of a contract for the construction thereof.

(6) Inclusion of the requirements authorized by paragraph (d) of subsection (5) of this section shall be presumed unnecessary to assure compliance upon a showing that the area served by a domestic wastewater treatment works has a stable or declining population; but this provision shall not be construed as preventing periodic review by the division should it be felt that growth is occurring or will occur in the area.

## 25-8-501.1. Permit required for point source water pollution control - definitions - housed commercial swine feeding operations - legislative declaration.

(1) The people of the state of Colorado hereby find, determine, and declare that the advent of large housed commercial swine feeding operations in Colorado has presented new challenges to ensuring that the quality of the state's environment is preserved and protected. As distinguished from more traditional operations that historically have characterized Colorado's livestock industry, large housed swine feeding operations use significant amounts of process water for flushing and disposing of swine waste, commonly store this waste in large impoundments, and dispose of it through land application. The waste storage, handling and disposal by such operations are particularly odorous and offensive. The people further find that it is necessary to ensure that the storage and land application of waste by housed commercial swine feeding operations is done in a responsible manner, so as not to adversely impact Colorado's valuable air, land and water resources.

(2) As used in this section, unless the context otherwise requires:

(a) "Agronomic rate of application" means the rate of application of nutrients to plants that is necessary to satisfy the plants' nutritional requirements while strictly minimizing the amount of nutrients that run off to surface waters or which pass below the root zone of the plants, as specified by the most current published fertilizer suggestions of the Colorado state university cooperative extension service for the plants, or most closely related plant type, to which the nutrients are applied.

(b) "Housed commercial swine feeding operation" means a housed swine feeding operation that is capable of housing eight hundred thousand pounds or more of live animal weight of swine at any one time or is deemed a commercial operation under local zoning or land use regulations. Two or more housed swine confined feeding operations shall be considered to comprise a single housed commercial swine feeding operation if they are under common or affiliated ownership or management, and are adjacent to or utilize a common area or system for manure disposal, are integrated in any way, are located or discharge within the same watershed or into watersheds that are hydrologically connected, or are located on or discharge onto land overlying the same groundwater aquifer.

(c) "Housed swine feeding operation" means the practice of raising swine in buildings, or other enclosed structures wherein swine of any size are fed for forty-five days or longer in any twelve-month period, and crop or forage growth or production is not sustained in the area of confinement.

(d) "Process wastewater" means any process-generated wastewater used in a housed commercial swine feeding operation, including water used for feeding, flushing, or washing, and any water or precipitation that comes into contact with any manure, urine, or any product used in or resulting from the production of swine.

(3) No person shall operate, construct, or expand a housed commercial swine feeding operation without first having obtained an individual discharge permit from the division.

(4) On or before March 31, 1999, the commission shall promulgate rules necessary to ensure the issuance and effective administration and enforcement of permits under this section by July 1, 1999. Such rules shall incorporate the preceding subsection (3) and shall, at a minimum, require:

(a) That the owner or operator of a housed commercial swine feeding operation must obtain division approval of construction, operations and swine waste management plans that, for any land waste application, includes a detailed agronomic analysis. Said plans shall employ the best available waste management practices, provide for remediation of residual soil and groundwater contamination, and ensure that disposal of solid or liquid waste to the soil not exceed agronomic rates of application.

(b) That appropriate setbacks for maintaining water quality be established for land waste application areas and waste impoundments;

(c) That waste impoundments or manure stock piles shall not be located within a one-hundred-year floodplain unless proper flood proofing measures are designed and constructed;

(d) That the owner or operator of the housed commercial swine feeding operation shall provide financial assurances for the final closure of the housed commercial swine feeding operation, the conduct of any necessary postclosure activities, the undertaking of any corrective action made necessary by migration of contaminants from the housed commercial swine feeding operation into the soil and groundwater, or cleanup of any spill or breach;

(e) That the owner or operator of a housed commercial swine feeding operation shall ensure that no solid or liquid waste generated by it shall be applied to land by any person at a rate that exceeds, in amount or duration, the agronomic rate of application; and

(f) That, because waste storage and disposal by housed commercial swine feeding operations pose particular jeopardy for state trust lands, in light of the mandate in the Colorado constitution, article IX, section 10, that state land board trust lands be held in trust and be protected and enhanced to promote long-term productivity and sound stewardship, the construction, operations and waste management plans approved for housed commercial swine feeding operations on such lands, shall not permit the degradation of the physical attributes or value of any state trust lands.

(5) Any spill or contamination by a housed commercial swine feeding operation shall be reported immediately to the division and the county or district public health agency for the county in which the housed commercial swine feeding operation is conducted, and, within twenty-four hours after the spill or contamination, a written report shall be filed with the division and the county or district public health agency for the county in which the housed commercial swine feeding operation is conducted.

(6) Housed commercial swine feeding operations shall submit to the division and the county or district public health agency quarterly, comprehensive monitoring reports and agronomic analyses that demonstrate that the operation has land-applied solid and liquid waste at no greater than agronomic rates. The division shall require the sampling and monitoring of chemical and appropriate biological parameters to protect the quality and existing and future beneficial uses of

groundwater including, at a minimum, nitrogen, phosphorus, heavy metals, and salts. At a minimum, the monitoring program shall include quarterly samples, analysis, and reporting of the groundwater, soils within the root zone, and soils beneath the root zone within each waste application site, and shall also include monitoring to ensure that no excessive seepage occurs from any waste impoundments.

(7) Repealed.

(8) The division shall enforce the provisions of this section and shall take immediate enforcement action against any housed commercial swine feeding operation that has exceeded the agronomic rate limit of this section. In addition, any person who may be adversely affected by a housed commercial swine feeding operation may enforce these provisions directly against the operation by filing a civil action in the district court in the county in which the person resides.

(9) These provisions shall not preclude any local government from imposing requirements more restrictive than those contained in this section.

## 25-8-502. Application - definitions - fees - funds created - public participation - repeal.

(1) For the purposes of this section:

(a) "Animal feeding operation" or "CAFO" means a lot or facility, other than an aquatic animal production facility, where:

(I) Animals, other than aquatic animals, have been, are, or will be stabled or confined and fed or maintained for a total of forty-five days or more in any twelve-month period; and

(II) Crops, vegetation, forage growth, or post-harvest residues are not sustained in the normal growing season over any portion of the lot or facility.

(b) "Categorical effluent standards" means those standards established by the federal environmental protection agency pursuant to section 307 (b) of the federal act.

(c) "Discharge" means the discharge of pollutants, and includes land application.

(d) "Gallons per day" is based on design capacity of the facility, not flow.

(e) "Land application" is any discharge being applied to the land for treatment purposes.

(f) "Municipal separate storm sewer system" or "MS4" means a conveyance or system of conveyances, including roads with drainage systems, municipal streets, catch basins, curbs, gutters, ditches, man-made channels, or storm drains, that is:

(I) Owned or operated by a state, city, town, county, district, association, or other public body created by or pursuant to state law having jurisdiction over disposal of sewage, industrial wastes, storm water, or other wastes, including special districts under state law such as a sewer district, flood control district, drainage district, or similar entity, or a designated and approved management agency under section 208 of the federal act that discharges to state waters;

(II) Designed or used for collecting or conveying storm water;

(III) Not a combined sewer; and

(IV) Not part of a publicly owned treatment works.

(g) "Significant industrial discharger" means an industrial discharger that meets one or more criteria established by the federal environmental protection agency pursuant to section 307 (b) of the federal act.

(1.1) For each regulated activity listed in this subsection (1.1) , the division may assess an annual permit fee and a nonrefundable permit application fee for new permits that must equal fifty percent of the annual permit fee. The full amount of the application fee is credited toward the annual permit fee. All such fees must be in accordance with the following schedules:

(a) The animal agriculture sector includes annual fee schedules for regulated activities associated with animal feeding operations as follows:

(I) General permit: The division shall assess a CAFO an annual permit fee not to exceed two hundred fifty dollars plus four cents per animal unit, based on the CAFO's permitted capacity; except that, from July 1, 2009, through June 30, 2018, the division shall assess a CAFO an annual permit fee not to exceed seven hundred fifty dollars plus nine cents per animal unit, based on the

CAFO's permitted capacity.

(II) Individual permit: The division shall assess a CAFO an annual permit fee not to exceed five hundred dollars plus eight cents per animal unit, based on the CAFO's permitted capacity; except that, from July 1, 2009, through June 30, 2018, the division shall assess a CAFO an annual permit fee not to exceed one thousand five hundred dollars plus nine cents per animal unit, based on the CAFO's permitted capacity.

(III) (A) Effective July 1, 2009, through June 30, 2018, the division shall assess an unpermitted CAFO an annual administrative fee, not to exceed six cents per animal unit based upon the CAFO's registered capacity, to cover the direct and indirect costs associated with the environmental agriculture program, including inspections, compliance assurance, compliance assistance, and associated regulatory interpretation and review.

(B) This subparagraph (III) is repealed, effective July 1, 2018.

(IV) (A) Except as otherwise provided in this subparagraph (IV) , the division shall assess on each housed commercial swine feeding operation an annual permit fee, not to exceed twenty cents per animal, based on the operation's working capacity, to offset the direct and indirect costs of the program created in section 25-8-501.1.

(B) From July 1, 2009, through June 30, 2018, the division shall assess on each housed commercial swine feeding operation an annual permit fee that shall not exceed twenty-six cents per animal, based on the operation's working capacity, to offset the direct and indirect costs of the program created in section 25-8-501.1. This sub-subparagraph (B) is repealed, effective July 1, 2018.

(C) As used in this subparagraph (IV) , "working capacity" means the number of swine the housed commercial swine feeding operation is capable of housing at any one time.

(b) [Editor's note:This version of paragraph (b) is effective until July 1, 2018.]The commerce and industry sector includes annual fee schedules for regulated activities associated with mining, hydrocarbon refining, sugar processing, industrial storm water, utilities not included in the private and public utilities sector, manufacturing activities, commercial activities, and all other industrial activities as follows:

Facility Categories and Subcategoriesfor Permit Fees within the Commerce and Industry Sector

Annual Fees

(I) Sand and gravel and placer mining:
(A) Pit dewatering only$500
(B) Pit dewatering or wash-water discharge$570
(C) Mercury use with discharge impact$640
(D) Storm water discharge only$435
(II) Coal mining:
(A) Sedimentation ponds, surface runoff only$980
(B) Mine water, preparation plant discharge$1,320
(III) Hardrock mining:
(A) Mine dewatering from 0 up to 49,999 gallons
per day$1,140
(B) Mine dewatering from 50,000 up to 999,999 gallons
per day$2,150
(C) Mine dewatering, 1,000,000 gallons
per day or more$3,280
(D) Mine dewatering and milling with no discharge$3,280
(E) Mine dewatering and milling with discharge$9,880
(F) No discharge$1,140
(G) Milling with discharge from 0 up to 49,999 gallons
per day$3,350
(H) Milling with discharge, 50,000 gallons

per day or more$6,680

(IV) Oil shale:

(A) Sedimentation ponds, surface runoff only$1,990

(B) Mine water from 0 up to 49,999 gallons
per day$2,150

(C) Mine water from 50,000 up to 999,999
gallons per day$2,670

(D) Mine water from 1,000,000 gallons
per day or more$2,600

(E) Mine water and process water discharge$9,880

(F) No discharge$1,830

(V) General permits:

(A) Sand and gravel with process discharge
and storm water$270

(B) Sand and gravel without process discharge
- storm water only$75

(C) Placer mining$520

(D) Coal mining$780

(E) Industrial - single municipal industrial
- storm water only$185

(F) Active mineral mines less than ten acres - storm water only$125

(G) Active mineral mines - ten acres or more
- storm water only$375

(H) Inactive mineral mines - storm water only$75

(I) Department of transportation - sand and
gravel storm-water permit$4,360

(J) Coal degasification - process water
from 0 up to 49,999 gallons per day$2,150

(K) Coal degasification - process water from
50,000 up to 99,999 gallons per day$3,280

(L) Coal degasification - process water,
100,000 gallons per day or more$9,880

(M) Minimal discharge of industrial or
commercial waste waters - general permit$630

(VI) Power plants:

(A) Cooling water only, no discharge$1,140

(B) Process water from 0 up to 49,999
gallons per day$2,150

(C) Process water from 50,000 up to 999,999
gallons per day$3,280

(D) Process water from 1,000,000 up to 4,999,999
gallons per day$9,880

(E) Process water, 5,000,000 gallons per day or more$9,880

(VII) Sugar processing:

(A) Cooling water only, no discharge$1,210

(B) Process water from 0 up to 49,999
gallons per day$1,480

(C) Process water from 50,000 up to 999,999
gallons per day$3,700

(D) Process water from 1,000,000 up to 4,999,999
gallons per day$9,880

(E) Process water, 5,000,000 gallons
per day or more$9,880

481

(VIII) Petroleum refining:
(A) Cooling water only, no discharge$1,140
(B) Process water from 0 up to 49,999 gallons
per day$2,560
(C) Process water from 50,000 up to 999,999
gallons per day$3,285
(D) Process water from 1,000,000 up to 4,999,999
gallons per day$9,880
(E) Process water, 5,000,000 gallons per day or more$9,880
(IX) Fish hatcheries$820
(X) Manufacturing and other industry:
(A) Cooling water only$1,140
(B) Process water from 0 up to 49,999
gallons per day$2,150
(C) Process water from 50,000 up to 999,999
gallons per day$3,280
(D) Process water from 1,000,000 up to 4,999,999
gallons per day$9,880
(E) Process water from 5,000,000 up to 19,999,999
gallons per day$12,140
(F) Process water, 20,000,000 gallons
per day or more$19,760
(G) No discharge$1,480
(H) Amusement and recreation services$1,480
(XI) Individual industrial storm-water permits:
(A) Individual industrial - less than ten acres$295
(B) Individual industrial - ten acres or more$375
(C) Individual industrial - storm water only
- international airports$6,220
(b) [Editor's note:This version of paragraph (b) is effective July 1, 2018.]The commerce and
industry sector includes annual fee schedules for regulated activities associated with mining,
hydrocarbon refining, sugar processing, industrial storm water, utilities not included in the private
and public utilities sector, manufacturing activities, commercial activities, and all other industrial
activities as follows:
Facility Categories and Subcategoriesfor Permit Fees within the Commerce and Industry Sector

Annual Fees

(I) Sand and gravel and placer mining:
(A) Pit dewatering only$805
(B) Pit dewatering or wash-water discharge$918
(C) Mercury use with discharge impact$1,030
(D) Storm water discharge only$700
(II) Coal mining:
(A) Sedimentation ponds, surface runoff only$1,578
(B) Mine water, preparation plant discharge$2,125
(III) Hardrock mining:
(A) Mine dewatering from 0 up to 49,999 gallons
per day$1,835
(B) Mine dewatering from 50,000 up to
999,999 gallons per day$3,462
(C) Mine dewatering, 1,000,000 gallons
per day or more$5,281

(D) Mine dewatering and milling with
no discharge$5,281
(E) Mine dewatering and milling
with discharge$15,907
(F) No discharge$1,835
(G) Milling with discharge from 0 up to 49,999 gallons
per day$5,394
(H) Milling with discharge, 50,000 gallons
per day or more$10,755
(IV) Oil shale:
(A) Sedimentation ponds, surface runoff only$3,204
(B) Mine water from 0 up to 49,999
gallons per day$3,462
(C) Mine water from 50,000 up to 999,999
gallons per day$4,299
(D) Mine water from 1,000,000 gallons
per day or more$4,186
(E) Mine water and process water discharge$15,907
(F) No discharge$2,946
(V) General permits:
(A) Sand and gravel with process discharge
and storm water$435
(B) Sand and gravel without process discharge
- storm water only$121
(C) Placer mining$837
(D) Coal mining$1,256
(E) Industrial - single municipal industrial
- storm water only$298
(F) Active mineral mines less than ten acres
- storm water only$201
(G) Active mineral mines - ten acres or more
- storm water only$604
(H) Inactive mineral mines - storm water only$121
(I) Department of transportation - sand and
gravel storm-water permit$7,020
(J) Coal degasification - process water
from 0 up to 49,999 gallons per day$3,462
(K) Coal degasification - process water from
50,000 up to 99,999 gallons per day$5,281
(L) Coal degasification - process water,
100,000 gallons per day or more$15,907
(M) Minimal discharge of industrial or
commercial waste waters - general permit$630
(VI) Power plants:
(A) Cooling water only, no discharge$1,835
(B) Process water from 0 up to 49,999
gallons per day$3,462
(C) Process water from 50,000 up to 999,999
gallons per day$5,281
(D) Process water from 1,000,000 up to 4,999,999
gallons per day$15,907
(E) Process water, 5,000,000 gallons per
day or more$15,907

(VII) Sugar processing:
(A) Cooling water only, no discharge$1,948
(B) Process water from 0 up to 49,999
gallons per day$2,383
(C) Process water from 50,000 up to 999,999
gallons per day$5,957
(D) Process water from 1,000,000 up to 4,999,999
gallons per day$15,907
(E) Process water, 5,000,000 gallons
per day or more$15,907
(VIII) Petroleum refining:
(A) Cooling water only, no discharge$1,835
(B) Process water from 0 up to 49,999 gallons
per day$4,122
(C) Process water from 50,000 up to 999,999
gallons per day$5,289
(D) Process water from 1,000,000 up to 4,999,999
gallons per day$15,907
(E) Process water, 5,000,000 gallons per
day or more$15,907
(IX) Fish hatcheries$1,320
(X) Manufacturing and other industry:
(A) Cooling water only$1,835
(B) Process water from 0 up to 49,999
gallons per day$3,462
(C) Process water from 50,000 up to 999,999
gallons per day$5,281
(D) Process water from 1,000,000 up to 4,999,999
gallons per day$15,907
(E) Process water from 5,000,000 up to 19,999,999
gallons per day$19,545
(F) Process water, 20,000,000 gallons
per day or more$31,814
(G) No discharge$2,383
(H) Amusement and recreation services$2,383
(XI) Individual industrial storm-water permits:
(A) Individual industrial - less than ten acres$475
(B) Individual industrial - ten acres or more$604
(C) Individual industrial - storm water only
- international airports$10,014
(c) The construction sector includes annual fee schedules for regulated activities associated with construction activities as follows:
Facility Categories and Subcategories for Permit Fees within the Construction Sector

Annual Fees

(I) Repealed.
(II) [Editor's note:This version of subparagraph (II) is effective until July 1, 2018.]General permits:
(A) to (D) Repealed.
(E) Department of transportation (DOT) -
storm-water construction discharges from
projects where DOT is the permittee -

statewide permit$9,400

(F) Minimal discharge of industrial or
commercial wastewater$630

(G) Low complexity, effective on and after
July 1, 2016$820

(H) High complexity, effective on
and after July 1, 2016$2,000

(I) Construction - storm water only; less than
1 acre of disturbed area,
effective on and after July 1, 2016$165

(J) Construction - storm water only;
from 1 acre to less than 30 acres,
effective on and after July 1, 2016$350

(K) Construction - storm water only;
30 acres or more of disturbed area,
effective on and after July 1, 2016$540

(II) [Editor's note:This version of subparagraph (II) is effective July 1, 2018.]General permits:

(A) to (D) Repealed.

(E) Department of transportation (DOT) -
storm-water construction discharges from
projects where DOT is the permittee -
statewide permit$9,400

(F) Minimal discharge of industrial or
commercial wastewater$630

(G) Low complexity$820

(H) High complexity$2,000

(I) Construction - storm water only; less than
1 acre of disturbed area$165

(J) Construction - storm water only;
from 1 acre to less than 30 acres$350

(K) Construction - storm water only;
30 acres or more of disturbed area$540

(III) [Editor's note:This version of subparagraph (III) is effective until July 1, 2018.]Effective on and after July 1, 2016, the fee for an individual permit for construction activity is four thousand four hundred dollars; and

(III) [Editor's note:This version of subparagraph (III) is effective July 1, 2018.]The fee for an individual permit for construction activity is four thousand four hundred dollars; and

(IV) [Editor's note:This version of the introductory portion to subparagraph (IV) is effective until July 1, 2018.]The division shall use the revenue generated by the fees set forth in subsections (1.1) (c) (II) (G) to (1.1) (c) (II) (K) and (1.1) (c) (III) of this section to continue to fund the administration and oversight of the construction sector and shall use the increased revenue, when compared with the revenue generated by the fees contained in subcategories 2, 8, 9A, and 9B of sub-subparagraph (G) and sub-subparagraphs (H) , (I) , (J) , and (L) of subparagraph (I) of paragraph (b) of subsection (1) of this section as they existed on June 30, 2015, to fund new services provided under the alternative compliance assurance model. The division shall not use the increased revenue to fund additional enforcement staff. The division may use the increased revenue for the following purposes:

(IV) [Editor's note:This version of the introductory portion to subparagraph (IV) is effective July 1, 2018.]The division shall use the revenue generated by the fees set forth in subsections (1.1) (c) (II) (G) to (1.1) (c) (II) (K) and (1.1) (c) (III) of this section to continue to fund the administration and oversight of the construction sector and shall use the increased revenue, when compared with the revenue generated by the corresponding fees as they existed on June 30, 2015, to fund new services provided under the alternative compliance assurance model. The division shall not use the increased revenue to fund additional enforcement staff. The division may use the increased revenue for the following purposes:

(A) Increasing inspections of the construction sector to meet compliance objectives identified by the federal environmental protection agency;

(B) Implementing a compliance strategy that relies on increased assistance and follow-up to obtain an overall increase in compliance instead of increased reliance on enforcement;

(C) Targeting additional compliance assistance towards permittees to seek increased compliance, including: Streamlined site visits that provide initial assistance consultations and increased assistance resources such as guidance documents, presentations, and online resources; review and response to the inspected entity's written response to the inspection; follow-up inspections and additional inspections for owners and operators with systemic violations; and increased overall inspection frequency;

(D) Maintaining and increasing current service levels of administration and oversight for the division's storm water management system administrator program; and

(E) Targeting enforcement towards operators that show chronic violations, significant violations, or recalcitrant response actions.

(d) [Editor's note:This version of paragraph (d) is effective until July 1, 2018.]The pesticide sector includes annual fee schedules for regulated activities associated with pesticide applications that are regulated under the federal act as follows: For a general permit, decision makers with pesticide application on or over waters of the state that are subject to annual reporting requirements under the pesticide general permit, an annual fee of two hundred seventy-five dollars.

(d) [Editor's note:This version of paragraph (d) is effective July 1, 2018.]The pesticide sector includes annual fee schedules for regulated activities associated with pesticide applications that are regulated under the federal act as follows: For a general permit, decision makers with pesticide application on or over waters of the state that are subject to annual reporting requirements under the pesticide general permit, an annual fee of two hundred eighty-one dollars.

(e) [Editor's note:This version of paragraph (e) is effective until July 1, 2018.]The public and private utilities sector includes annual fee schedules for regulated activities associated with the operation of domestic wastewater treatment works, water treatment facilities, reclaimed water systems, and industrial operations that discharge to a domestic wastewater treatment works as follows:

Facility Categories and Subcategories for Permit Fees within the Public and Private Utilities Sector

Annual Fees

(I) Water treatment plants:
(A) Intermittent discharge$570
(B) Routing discharge$820
(II) General permits:
(A) Water treatment plants - intermittent discharge$475
(B) Water treatment plants - routine discharge$715
(C) Discharges associated with treated water distribution systems for a population of 3,300 or fewer$105
(D) Discharges associated with treated water distribution systems for a population from 3,301 up to 9,999$210
(E) Discharges associated with treated water distribution systems for a population of 10,000 or more$315
(III) Domestic wastewater - lagoons:

(A) Sewage from 0 up to 49,999 gallons per day$525

(B) Sewage from 50,000 up to 99,999 gallons
per day$845

(C) Sewage from 100,000 up to 499,999 gallons
per day$1,230

(D) Sewage from 500,000 up to 999,999 gallons
per day$2,120

(E) Sewage from 1,000,000 up to 1,999,999 gallons
per day$3,170

(F) Sewage, 2,000,000 gallons per day or more$6,460

(IV) Domestic wastewater - mechanical plants:

(A) Sewage from 0 up to 19,999 gallons per day$615

(B) Sewage from 20,000 up to 49,999 gallons
per day$980

(C) Sewage from 50,000 up to 99,999 gallons
per day$1,440

(D) Sewage from 100,000 up to 499,999 gallons
per day$2,240

(E) Sewage from 500,000 up to 999,999 gallons
per day$3,720

(F) Sewage from 1,000,000 up to 2,499,999 gallons
per day$6,090

(G) Sewage from 2,500,000 up to 9,999,999 gallons
per day$11,410

(H) Sewage from 10,000,000 up to 49,999,999 gallons per day$19,780

(I) Sewage from 50,000,000 up to 99,999,999
gallons per day$22,820

(J) Sewage, 100,000,000 gallons per day or more$25,100

(V) Domestic facilities discharge to unclassified waters - general permit:

(A) Sewage from 0 up to 49,999 gallons per day$455

(B) Sewage from 50,000 up to 199,999 gallons
per day$800

(C) Sewage from 200,000 up to 599,999 gallons
per day$1,170

(D) Sewage from 600,000 up to 999,999 gallons
per day$1,860

(VI) Industrial dischargers subject to categorical effluent standards discharging to publicly owned treatment works with pretreatment programs, not including categorical industries subject to zero-discharge standards:

(A) Very low flow - less than 100 gallons per day$292

(B) 100 up to 9,999 gallons per day$699

(C) 10,000 up to 50,000 gallons per day$1,047

(D) More than 50,000 gallons per day$1,397

(VII) All other significant industrial dischargers discharging to publicly owned treatment works with pretreatment, including categorical industries subject to zero-discharge standards:

(A) Less than 10,000 gallons per day$175

(B) 10,000 up to 50,000 gallons per day$349

(C) More than 50,000 gallons per day$465

(D) Pit dewatering only$270

(VIII) Industrial dischargers subject to categorical effluent standards discharging to publicly owned treatment works without pretreatment programs, not including categorical industries subject to zero discharge standards:

(A) Less than 10,000 gallons per day$815

(B) 10,000 up to 50,000 gallons per day$1,280

(C) More than 50,000 gallons per day$1,746

(IX) All other significant industrial dischargers discharging to publicly owned treatment works without pretreatment programs, including categorical industries subject to zero-discharge standards:

(A) Less than 10,000 gallons per day$349

(B) 10,000 up to 50,000 gallons per day$524

(C) More than 50,000 gallons per day$699

(X) Domestic wastewater - lagoons:

(A) Sewage from 0 up to 49,999 gallons per day$75

(B) Sewage from 50,000 up to 99,999 gallons
per day$75

(C) Sewage from 100,000 up to 499,999 gallons
per day$75

(D) Sewage from 500,000 up to 999,999 gallons
per day$75

(E) Sewage from 1,000,000 up to 2,499,999 gallons
per day$81

(F) Sewage, 2,500,000 gallons per day or more$94

(XI) Domestic wastewater - mechanical plants:

(A) Sewage from 0 up to 19,999 gallons per day$75

(B) Sewage from 20,000 up to 49,999 gallons per day$75

(C) Sewage from 50,000 up to 99,999 gallons per day$75

(D) Sewage from 100,000 up to 499,999 gallons
per day$75

(E) Sewage from 500,000 up to 999,999 gallons per day$75

(F) Sewage from 1,000,000 up to 2,499,999 gallons
per day$81

(G) Sewage from 2,500,000 up to 9,999,999 gallons
per day$94

(H) Sewage from 10,000,000 up to 49,999,999
gallons per day$105

(I) Sewage from 50,000,000 up to 99,999,999
gallons per day$117

(J) Sewage, 100,000,000 gallons per day or more$128

(XII) Wastewater reuse authorizations:

(A) Facility capacity of less than 100,000
gallons per day$450

(B) Facility capacity from 100,000 gallons to
499,999 gallons per day$840

(C) Facility capacity from 500,000 gallons to
999,999 gallons per day$1,400

(D) Facility capacity from 1,000,000 gallons to
2,499,999 gallons per day$2,300

(E) Facility capacity from 2,500,000 gallons to
9,999,999 gallons per day$4,300

(F) Facility capacity, 10,000,000 gallons per
day or more$6,300

(XIII) and (XIV) Repealed.

(e) [Editor's note:This version of paragraph (e) is effective July 1, 2018.]The public and private utilities sector includes annual fee schedules for regulated activities associated with the operation of domestic wastewater treatment works, water treatment facilities, reclaimed water systems, and industrial operations that discharge to a domestic wastewater treatment works as follows:

Facility Categories and Subcategories for Permit Fees within the Public and Private Utilities Sector

Annual Fees

(I) Water treatment plants:
(A) Intermittent discharge$695
(B) Routing discharge$1,000
(II) General permits:
(A) Water treatment plants - intermittent
discharge$580
(B) Water treatment plants - routine discharge$872
(C) Discharges associated with treated water
distribution systems for a population of
3,300 or fewer$128
(D) Discharges associated with treated
water distribution systems for
a population from 3,301 up to 9,999$256
(E) Discharges associated with treated
water distribution systems for a
population of 10,000 or more$384
(III) Domestic wastewater - lagoons:
(A) Sewage from 0 up to 49,999 gallons per day$641
(B) Sewage from 50,000 up to 99,999 gallons
per day$1,031
(C) Sewage from 100,000 up to 499,999 gallons
per day$1,501
(D) Sewage from 500,000 up to 999,999 gallons
per day$2,586
(E) Sewage from 1,000,000 up to 1,999,999 gallons
per day$3,867
(F) Sewage, 2,000,000 gallons per day or more$7,881
(IV) Domestic wastewater - mechanical plants:
(A) Sewage from 0 up to 19,999 gallons per day$750
(B) Sewage from 20,000 up to 49,999 gallons
per day$1,196
(C) Sewage from 50,000 up to 99,999 gallons
per day$1,757
(D) Sewage from 100,000 up to 499,999 gallons
per day$2,733
(E) Sewage from 500,000 up to 999,999 gallons
per day$4,538
(F) Sewage from 1,000,000 up to 2,499,999 gallons
per day$7,430
(G) Sewage from 2,500,000 up to 9,999,999 gallons
per day$13,920
(H) Sewage from 10,000,000 up to 49,999,999
gallons per day$24,132
(I) Sewage from 50,000,000 up to 99,999,999
gallons per day$27,840
(J) Sewage, 100,000,000 gallons per day or more$30,622
(V) Domestic facilities discharge to unclassified waters - general permit:
(A) Sewage from 0 up to 49,999 gallons per day$555

(B) Sewage from 50,000 up to 199,999 gallons
per day$976
(C) Sewage from 200,000 up to 599,999 gallons
per day$1,427
(D) Sewage from 600,000 up to 999,999 gallons
per day$2,269
(VI) Industrial dischargers subject to categorical effluent standards discharging to publicly owned treatment works with pretreatment programs, not including categorical industries subject to zero-discharge standards:
(A) Very low flow - less than 100 gallons per day$356
(B) 100 up to 9,999 gallons per day$853
(C) 10,000 up to 50,000 gallons per day$1,277
(D) More than 50,000 gallons per day$1,704
(VII) All other significant industrial dischargers discharging to publicly owned treatment works with pretreatment, including categorical industries subject to zero-discharge standards:
(A) Less than 10,000 gallons per day$214
(B) 10,000 up to 50,000 gallons per day$426
(C) More than 50,000 gallons per day$567
(D) Pit dewatering only$329
(VIII) Industrial dischargers subject to categorical effluent standards discharging to publicly owned treatment works without pretreatment programs, not including categorical industries subject to zero discharge standards:
(A) Less than 10,000 gallons per day$994
(B) 10,000 up to 50,000 gallons per day$1,562
(C) More than 50,000 gallons per day$2,130
(IX) All other significant industrial dischargers discharging to publicly owned treatment works without pretreatment programs, including categorical industries subject to zero-discharge standards:
(A) Less than 10,000 gallons per day$426
(B) 10,000 up to 50,000 gallons per day$639
(C) More than 50,000 gallons per day$853
(X) Domestic wastewater - lagoons:
(A) Sewage from 0 up to 49,999 gallons per day$92
(B) Sewage from 50,000 up to 99,999 gallons
per day$92
(C) Sewage from 100,000 up to 499,999 gallons
per day$92
(D) Sewage from 500,000 up to 999,999 gallons
per day$92
(E) Sewage from 1,000,000 up to 2,499,999 gallons
per day$99
(F) Sewage, 2,500,000 gallons per day or more$115
(XI) Domestic wastewater - mechanical plants:
(A) Sewage from 0 up to 19,999 gallons per day$92
(B) Sewage from 20,000 up to 49,999 gallons per day$92
(C) Sewage from 50,000 up to 99,999 gallons per day$92
(D) Sewage from 100,000 up to 499,999 gallons
per day$92
(E) Sewage from 500,000 up to 999,999 gallons
per day$92
(F) Sewage from 1,000,000 up to 2,499,999 gallons
per day$99
(G) Sewage from 2,500,000 up to 9,999,999 gallons

490

per day$115
(H) Sewage from 10,000,000 up to 49,999,999
gallons per day$128
(I) Sewage from 50,000,000 up to 99,999,999
gallons per day$143
(J) Sewage, 100,000,000 gallons per day or more$156
(XII) Wastewater reuse authorizations:
(A) Facility capacity of less than 100,000
gallons per day$549
(B) Facility capacity from 100,000 gallons to
499,999 gallons per day$1,025
(C) Facility capacity from 500,000 gallons to
999,999 gallons per day$1,708
(D) Facility capacity from 1,000,000 gallons to
2,499,999 gallons per day$2,806
(E) Facility capacity from 2,500,000 gallons to
9,999,999 gallons per day$5,246
(F) Facility capacity, 10,000,000 gallons per
day or more$7,686
(XIII) and (XIV) Repealed.
(f) [Editor's note:This version of paragraph (f) is effective until July 1, 2018.]The municipal
separate storm sewer systems sector includes annual fees for regulated activities associated with
the operation of municipal separate storm sewer systems, as follows:
Facility Categories and Subcategories for Permit Fees within the Municipal Separate Storm Sewer
System Sector

Annual Fees

(I) MS4 general permits:
(A) Storm water municipal for a population
of 10,000 or fewer$355
(B) Storm water municipal for a population
from 10,000 up to 49,999$810
(C) Storm water municipal for a population
from 50,000 up to 99,999$2,020
(D) Storm water municipal for a population
of 100,000 or more$4,050
(II) MS4 individual permits:
(A) Municipalities with a population from
10,000 up to 49,999$1,245
(B) Municipalities with a population from
50,000 up to 99,999$3,110
(C) Municipalities with a population from
100,000 up to 249,999$6,225
(D) Municipalities with a population of
250,000 or more$10,580
(E) Statewide permit for municipal separate
storm water systems, owned or
operated by the department of
transportation, in municipal areas
where storm water permits are required$4,360
(f) [Editor's note:This version of paragraph (f) is effective July 1, 2018.]The municipal separate
storm sewer systems sector includes annual fees for regulated activities associated with the

operation of municipal separate storm sewer systems, as follows:
Facility Categories and Subcategories for Permit Fees within the Municipal Separate Storm Sewer System Sector

Annual Fees

(I) MS4 general permits:
(A) Storm water municipal for a population
of 10,000 or fewer$462
(B) Storm water municipal for a population
from 10,000 up to 49,999$1,053
(C) Storm water municipal for a population
from 50,000 up to 99,999$2,626
(D) Storm water municipal for a population
of 100,000 or more$5,265
(II) MS4 individual permits:
(A) Municipalities with a population from
10,000 up to 49,999$1,619
(B) Municipalities with a population from
50,000 up to 99,999$4,043
(C) Municipalities with a population from
100,000 up to 249,999$8,093
(D) Municipalities with a population of
250,000 or more$13,754
(E) Statewide permit for municipal separate
storm water systems, owned or
operated by the department of
transportation, in municipal areas
where storm water permits are required$5,668
(1.2) (a) [Editor's note:This version of the introductory portion to paragraph (a) is effective until July 1, 2018.]For the activities listed in this subsection (1.2) associated with reviewing requests for certifications under section 401 of the federal act and this article, known as "401 certificates", the division may assess a fee for the review. There is hereby created in the state treasury the water quality certification sector fund, which consists of fees collected pursuant to this subsection (1.2) . The division shall transmit the fees to the state treasurer, who shall credit them to the water quality certification sector fund. All such fees must be in accordance with the following schedules:
(a) [Editor's note:This version of the introductory portion to paragraph (a) is effective July 1, 2018.]For the activities listed in this subsection (1.2) associated with reviewing requests for certifications under section 401 of the federal act and this article 8, known as "401 certificates", the division may assess a fee for the review. There is hereby created in the state treasury the water quality certification sector fund, which consists of fees collected pursuant to this subsection (1.2) . The division shall transmit the fees to the state treasurer, who shall credit them to the water quality certification sector fund. All such fees must be in accordance with the following schedules:
(I) [Editor's note:This version of the introductory portion to subparagraph (I) is effective until July 1, 2018.]The fee for a tier 1 project is one thousand one hundred dollars, which must be submitted with the certification application. Tier 1 projects are projects that incur minimal costs and minimal water quality impacts. Tier 1 includes certifications of channel stabilization projects and single drainage improvement projects. Typical characteristics of tier 1 projects may include all or some of the following:
(I) [Editor's note:This version of the introductory portion to subparagraph (I) is effective July 1, 2018.]The fee for a tier 1 project is one thousand one hundred twenty-two dollars, which must be submitted with the certification application. Tier 1 projects are projects that incur minimal costs and minimal water quality impacts. Tier 1 includes certifications of channel stabilization projects

and single drainage improvement projects. Typical characteristics of tier 1 projects may include all or some of the following:

(A) The potential for minimal impacts to water quality;

(B) A low level of public participation;

(C) No more than standard coordination with federal, state, or local agencies may be required;

(D) Limited technical assistance may be needed.

(II) [Editor's note:This version of the introductory portion to subparagraph (II) is effective until July 1, 2018.]The fee for a tier 2 project is three thousand eight hundred dollars, which must be submitted with the certification application. Tier 2 projects are projects that incur moderate costs and potential water quality impacts. Tier 2 includes certifications of projects that affect multiple drainages. Typical characteristics of tier 2 projects may include all or some of the following:

(II) [Editor's note:This version of the introductory portion to subparagraph (II) is effective July 1, 2018.]The fee for a tier 2 project is three thousand eight hundred seventy-six dollars, which must be submitted with the certification application. Tier 2 projects are projects that incur moderate costs and potential water quality impacts. Tier 2 includes certifications of projects that affect multiple drainages. Typical characteristics of tier 2 projects may include all or some of the following:

(A) The potential for minimal impacts to water quality;

(B) A basic to high level of public participation may be required with potential for participation in public meetings or hearings held by outside parties;

(C) More than the standard level of coordination with multiple federal, state, or local agencies may be required, including one or more meetings or pre-application site visits;

(D) A moderate and ongoing level of technical assistance may be needed;

(E) Compensatory mitigation review may be required;

(F) Review of a full evaluation and findings report if needed; or

(G) If the certification is appealed, addressing an appeal of the division's water quality certification to the commission pursuant to sections 25-8-202 (1) (k) , 25-8-302 (1) (f) , and 25-8-401.

(III) The fee for a tier 3 project is calculated on an hourly rate based on the actual costs of division staff and contractor time. Tier 3 projects are projects that involve a large watershed area, a high degree of complexity, or high potential for water quality impacts. Tier 3 includes certifications of federal energy regulatory commission relicensing projects or projects involving more long-term water quality impacts. Typical characteristics of tier 3 projects may include all or some of the following:

(A) The potential for greater, permanent water quality impacts if one or more of the following occurs: The water body is identified as not attaining water quality standards; or multiple stream or lake segments as established by section 25-8-203 are affected;

(B) A high level of public participation, including extensive public comments and the potential for one or more public meetings or hearings conducted by the division or outside parties;

(C) Substantially more than standard coordination with multiple federal, state, or local agencies may be required, including one or more meetings;

(D) A high level of iterative technical assistance may be required or substantive project revisions may be received;

(E) The potential for complex compensatory mitigation review;

(F) A site visit may be needed to understand impacts and advise on potential alternatives;

(G) The review of a full evaluation and findings report if needed; or

(H) If the certification is appealed, addressing an appeal of the division's water quality certification to the commission pursuant to sections 25-8-202 (1) (k) , 25-8-302 (1) (f) , and 25-8-401.

(IV) The fee for a tier 4 project is calculated on an hourly rate based on the actual costs of division staff and contractor time. Tier 4 projects are projects that involve multiple or large watershed areas, a very high degree of complexity, a very high potential for water quality impacts, or a high level of public participation. Tier 4 includes transmountain water supply projects. Typical characteristics of tier 4 projects may include all or some of the following:

(A) The potential for greater water quality impacts if one or more of the following occurs: The water body is identified as not attaining water quality standards; or multiple stream or lake segments as established by section 25-8-203 are affected;

(B) A high level of public participation, including extensive public comments and the potential for one or more public meetings or hearings conducted by the division or outside parties;

(C) Substantially more coordination than is standard with multiple federal, state, or local agencies may be required, including one or more meetings;

(D) A high level of iterative technical assistance may be required or substantive project revisions may be received;

(E) The potential for complex compensatory mitigation review;

(F) A site visit may be needed to understand impacts and advise on potential alternatives;

(G) Coordination with the governor's office in conjunction with other state agencies, tribal nations, and the federal government may be required;

(H) To the extent pertinent, review of additional documents, such as federal "National Environmental Policy Act" resource reports, environmental assessments, and environmental impact statements;

(I) If needed, to the extent not addressed in the documents addressed in sub-subparagraph (H) of this subparagraph (IV) and consistent with the requirements of this article and of the rules promulgated pursuant to this article, review and use of a full evaluation and findings report; or

(J) If the certification is appealed, addressing an appeal of the division's water quality certification to the commission pursuant to sections 25-8-202 (1) (k) , 25-8-302 (1) (f) , and 25-8-401.

(b) For tier 3 and tier 4 projects, the division may assess fees for services provided by the division prior to the applicant submitting a formal water quality certification application, which fees must reflect the actual cost of division staff and contractor time.

(c) For tier 3 and tier 4 projects, the division may assess fees for services provided by the division to monitor the projects certified with conditions, which fees must reflect the actual cost of division staff and contractor time.

(1.3) For each service listed below, the division may assess a fee for the service, and all such fees must be in accordance with the following schedules:

(a) Amendments to permits associated with the commerce and industry sector, construction sector, pesticides application, public and private utility sector under subsection (1.1) of this section, and amendments to permits issued through June 30, 2018, associated with regulated activities in subparagraph (IV) of the animal agriculture sector in paragraph (a) of subsection (1.1) of this section:

(I) Minor amendment: An amount equal to twenty-five percent of the annual fee for the permit being amended, not to exceed two thousand eight hundred ten dollars;

(II) Major amendment: An amount equal to fifty-five percent of the annual fee for the permit being amended, not to exceed five thousand nine hundred fifty dollars;

(b) Preliminary effluent limitations:

(I) In accordance with section 25-8-702, the division may assess a fee, as set forth in the schedules in this paragraph (b) , for the determination of preliminary effluent limitations upon a domestic wastewater treatment works pursuant to the site location approval process. All such fees shall be paid in advance of any work done.

(II) At the request of an entity that is not a domestic wastewater treatment works, and upon payment of the appropriate fee as set forth in the schedules in this paragraph (b) , the division may determine preliminary effluent limits for a proposed discharge as described by the requester.

(III) Fees set forth in the schedules established in this paragraph (b) are increased by an amount equal to seventy-five percent of the applicable fee for each set of preliminary effluent limitations requested by domestic wastewater treatment works for discharges to second or additional receiving water bodies.

(IV) The division may, where an entity requests modification of existing division-approved preliminary effluent limitations, complete the modification for a fee equal to twenty-five percent of the applicable fee as set forth in the schedules in this paragraph (b) .

Facility Categories and Subcategories for Preliminary Effluent Limitations

Fees

(V) [Editor's note:This version of subparagraph (V) is effective until July 1, 2018.]Preliminary effluent limitations for individual permits:
(A) Less than 100,000 gallons per day$2,100
(B) 100,000 to 999,999 gallons per day$4,200
(C) 1,000,000 to 9,999,999 gallons per day$6,300
(D) 10,000,000 or more gallons per day$8,400
(V) [Editor's note:This version of subparagraph (V) is effective July 1, 2018.]Preliminary effluent limitations for individual permits:
(A) Less than 100,000 gallons per day$2,562
(B) 100,000 to 999,999 gallons per day$5,124
(C) 1,000,000 to 9,999,999 gallons per day$7,686
(D) 10,000,000 or more gallons per day$10,248
(VI) [Editor's note:This version of subparagraph (VI) is effective until July 1, 2018.]Preliminary effluent limitations for
general permits from 0 up to 1,000,000
gallons per day$1,050
(VI) [Editor's note:This version of subparagraph (VI) is effective July 1, 2018.]Preliminary effluent limitations for
general permits from 0 up to 1,000,000
gallons per day$1,281
(VII) [Editor's note:This version of subparagraph (VII) is effective until July 1, 2018.]Preliminary effluent limitations for discharges to groundwater:
(A) Minor facilities, less than 1,000,000 gallons
per day$525
(B) Major facilities, 1,000,000 gallons
per day or more$840
(VII) [Editor's note:This version of subparagraph (VII) is effective July 1, 2018.]Preliminary effluent limitations for discharges to groundwater:
(A) Minor facilities, less than 1,000,000 gallons
per day$641
(B) Major facilities, 1,000,000 gallons
per day or more$1,025
(VIII) [Editor's note:This version of subparagraph (VIII) is effective until July 1, 2018.]Review of preliminary effluent limitations for individual permits professionally prepared by others:
(A) Minor facilities, less than 1,000,000 gallons
per day$1,575
(B) Major facilities, 1,000,000 gallons
per day or more$3,150
(VIII) [Editor's note:This version of subparagraph (VIII) is effective July 1, 2018.]Review of preliminary effluent limitations for individual permits professionally prepared by others:
(A) Minor facilities, less than 1,000,000 gallons
per day$1,922
(B) Major facilities, 1,000,000 gallons
per day or more$3,843

(c) [Editor's note:This version of paragraph (c) is effective until July 1, 2018.]Wastewater site applications and design reviews:
Facility Categories and Subcategories for Wastewater Site Applications and Design Reviews

Fees

(I) Wastewater site applications:
(A) Wastewater treatment plants, less than 100,000 gallons per day:
New$7,738
Expansion$6,191
(B) Wastewater treatment plants from 100,000 to 999,999 gallons per day:
New$15,477
Expansion$12,381
(C) Wastewater treatment plants from 1,000,000 to 9,999,999 gallons per day:
New$23,215
Expansion$18,572
(D) Wastewater treatment plants, 10,000,000 gallons per day or more:
New$30,953
Expansion$24,763
(E) Lift stations, less than 100,000 gallons per day:
New$1,935
Expansion$1,548
(F) Lift stations from 100,000 to 999,999 gallons per day:
New$3,869
Expansion$3,095
(G) Lift stations from 1,000,000 to 9,999,999 gallons per day:
New$5,804
Expansion$4,643
(H) Lift stations, 10,000,000 gallons per day or more:
New$7,738
Expansion$6,191
(I) Amendments to site applications concerning
a change from gas chlorination to liquid
chlorination or from any form of
chlorination to ultraviolet light
disinfection, less than 100,000
gallons per day$451
(J) Amendments to site applications concerning
a change from gas chlorination to liquid chlorination
or from any form of chlorination to ultraviolet light
disinfection from 100,000 to 999,999 gallons per day$903
(K) Amendments to site applications concerning a change
from gas chlorination to liquid chlorination or from any
form of chlorination to ultraviolet light disinfection
from 1,000,000 to 9,999,999 gallons per day$1,354
(L) Amendments to site applications concerning a change
from gas chlorination to liquid chlorination or from any
form of chlorination to ultraviolet light disinfection,
10,000,000 gallons per day or more$1,806
(M) Other amendments to site application, less than
100,000 gallons per day$645
(N) Other amendments to site applications from
100,000 to 999,999 gallons per day$1,290
(O) Other amendments to site applications
from 1,000,000 to 9,999,999 gallons per day$1,935
(P) Other amendments to site applications,
10,000,000 gallons per day or more$2,579
(Q) On-site wastewater treatment systems$4,500

(R) Extension$650

(S) Interceptor site applications$1,300

(T) Interceptor certifications$300

(U) Outfall sewers$1,300

(II) Wastewater design review:

(A) Wastewater treatment plants, less than 100,000 gallons per day:
New$4,900
Expansion$3,900

(B) Wastewater treatment plants from 100,000 to 999,999 gallons per day:
New$9,900
Expansion$7,900

(C) Wastewater treatment plants from 1,000,000 to 9,999,999 gallons per day:
New$14,800
Expansion$11,800

(D) Wastewater treatment plants, 10,000,000 gallons per day or more:
New$19,700
Expansion$15,800

(E) Lift stations, less than 100,000 gallons per day:
New$1,200
Expansion$1,000

(F) Lift stations from 100,000 to 999,999 gallons per day:
New$2,500
Expansion$2,000

(G) Lift stations from 1,000,000 to 9,999,999 gallons per day:
New$3,700
Expansion$3,000

(H) Lift stations, 10,000,000 gallons per day or more:
New$4,900
Expansion$3,900

(I) Amendments to site applications concerning a change
from gas chlorination to liquid chlorination or from any
form of chlorination to ultraviolet light disinfection,
less than 100,000 gallons per day$500

(J) Amendments to site applications concerning a change
from gas chlorination to liquid chlorination or from any
form of chlorination to ultraviolet light disinfection
from 100,000 to 999,999 gallons per day$1,000

(K) Amendments to site applications concerning a change
from gas chlorination to liquid chlorination or from any
form of chlorination to ultraviolet light disinfection
from 1,000,000 to 9,999,999 gallons per day$1,500

(L) Amendments to site applications concerning a change
from gas chlorination to liquid chlorination or from any
form of chlorination to ultraviolet light disinfection,
10,000,000 gallons per day or more$2,000

(M) Other amendments to site application,
less than 100,000 gallons per day$700

(N) Other amendments to site applications,
from 100,000 to 999,999 gallons per day$1,400

(O) Other amendments to site applications,
from 1,000,000 to 9,999,999 gallons per day$2,100

(P) Other amendments to site applications,
10,000,000 gallons per day or more$2,800

(Q) On-site wastewater treatment systems$3,000

(R) Interceptor site applications$1,400

(S) Outfall sewers$1,400

(c) [Editor's note:This version of paragraph (c) is effective July 1, 2018.]Wastewater site applications and design reviews:
Facility Categories and Subcategories for Wastewater Site Applications and Design Reviews

Fees

(I) Wastewater site applications:
(A) Wastewater treatment plants, less than 100,000 gallons per day:
New$9,440 Expansion$7,553
(B) Wastewater treatment plants from 100,000 to 999,999 gallons per day:
New$18,882
Expansion$15,105
(C) Wastewater treatment plants from 1,000,000 to 9,999,999 gallons per day:
New$28,322
Expansion$22,658
(D) Wastewater treatment plants, 10,000,000 gallons per day or more:
New$37,763
Expansion$30,211
(E) Lift stations, less than 100,000 gallons per day:
New$2,361
Expansion$1,889
(F) Lift stations from 100,000 to 999,999 gallons per day:
New$4,720
Expansion$3,776
(G) Lift stations from 1,000,000 to 9,999,999 gallons per day:
New$7,081
Expansion$5,664
(H) Lift stations, 10,000,000 gallons per day or more:
New$9,440
Expansion$7,553
(I) Amendments to site applications concerning
a change from gas chlorination to liquid
chlorination or from any form of
chlorination to ultraviolet light
disinfection, less than 100,000
gallons per day$550
(J) Amendments to site applications concerning
a change from gas chlorination to liquid chlorination
or from any form of chlorination to ultraviolet light
disinfection from 100,000 to 999,999 gallons per day$1,102
(K) Amendments to site applications concerning a change
from gas chlorination to liquid chlorination or from any
form of chlorination to ultraviolet light disinfection
from 1,000,000 to 9,999,999 gallons per day$1,652
(L) Amendments to site applications concerning a change
from gas chlorination to liquid chlorination or from any
form of chlorination to ultraviolet light disinfection,
10,000,000 gallons per day or more$2,203
(M) Other amendments to site application, less than

100,000 gallons per day$787

(N) Other amendments to site applications from
100,000 to 999,999 gallons per day$1,574

(O) Other amendments to site applications
from 1,000,000 to 9,999,999 gallons per day$2,361

(P) Other amendments to site applications,
10,000,000 gallons per day or more$3,146

(Q) On-site wastewater treatment systems$5,490

(R) Extension$793

(S) Interceptor site applications$1,586

(T) Interceptor certifications$366

(U) Outfall sewers$1,586

(II) Wastewater design review:

(A) Wastewater treatment plants, less than 100,000 gallons per day:
New$5,978
Expansion$4,758

(B) Wastewater treatment plants from 100,000 to 999,999 gallons per day:
New$12,078
Expansion$9,638

(C) Wastewater treatment plants from 1,000,000 to 9,999,999 gallons per day:
New$18,056
Expansion$14,396

(D) Wastewater treatment plants, 10,000,000 gallons per day or more:
New$24,034
Expansion$19,276

(E) Lift stations, less than 100,000 gallons per day:
New$1,464
Expansion$1,220

(F) Lift stations from 100,000 to 999,999 gallons per day:
New$3,050
Expansion$2,440

(G) Lift stations from 1,000,000 to 9,999,999 gallons per day:
New$4,514
Expansion$3,660

(H) Lift stations, 10,000,000 gallons per day or more:
New$5,978
Expansion$4,758

(I) Amendments to site applications concerning a change
from gas chlorination to liquid chlorination or from any
form of chlorination to ultraviolet light disinfection,
less than 100,000 gallons per day$610

(J) Amendments to site applications concerning a change
from gas chlorination to liquid chlorination or from any
form of chlorination to ultraviolet light disinfection
from 100,000 to 999,999 gallons per day$1,220

(K) Amendments to site applications concerning a change
from gas chlorination to liquid chlorination or from
any form of chlorination to ultraviolet light
disinfection from 1,000,000 to
9,999,999 gallons per day$1,830

(L) Amendments to site applications concerning a change
from gas chlorination to liquid chlorination or from any
form of chlorination to ultraviolet light disinfection,

10,000,000 gallons per day or more$2,440
(M) Other amendments to site application,
less than 100,000 gallons per day$854
(N) Other amendments to site applications,
from 100,000 to 999,999 gallons per day$1,708
(O) Other amendments to site applications, from
1,000,000 to 9,999,999 gallons per day$2,562
(P) Other amendments to site applications,
10,000,000 gallons per day or more$3,416
(Q) On-site wastewater treatment systems$3,660
(R) Interceptor site applications$1,708
(S) Outfall sewers$1,708
(1.4) The division may establish an interim fee that must be consistent and equitable with the fees contained in subsection (1.1) of this section in any case where a facility other than those listed must be permitted. This interim fee applies until the date of adjournment sine die of the next regular session of the general assembly following imposition of the interim fee.
(1.5) (a) (I) There is hereby created in the state treasury the commerce and industry sector fund, which consists of all annual fees for regulated activities associated with the commerce and industry sector collected pursuant to subsection (1.1) of this section; all fees for services performed by the division associated with the commerce and industry sector collected pursuant to subsection (1.3) of this section; and all interim fees associated with the commerce and industry sector collected pursuant to subsection (1.4) of this section. The division shall transmit the fees to the state treasurer, who shall credit them to the commerce and industry sector fund.
(II) There is hereby created in the state treasury the construction sector fund, which consists of all annual fees collected for regulated activities associated with the construction sector pursuant to subsection (1.1) of this section; all fees for services performed by the division associated with the construction sector collected pursuant to subsection (1.3) of this section; and all interim fees associated with the construction sector collected pursuant to subsection (1.4) of this section. The division shall transmit the fees to the state treasurer, who shall credit them to the construction sector fund.
(III) There is hereby created in the state treasury the pesticides sector fund, which consists of all annual fees collected for regulated activities associated with the pesticides sector pursuant to subsection (1.1) of this section; all fees for services performed by the division associated with the pesticides sector collected pursuant to subsection (1.3) of this section; and all interim fees associated with the pesticides sector collected pursuant to subsection (1.4) of this section. The division shall transmit the fees to the state treasurer, who shall credit them to the pesticides sector fund.
(IV) There is hereby created in the state treasury the municipal separate storm sewer system sector fund, which consists of all annual fees collected for regulated activities associated with the municipal separate storm sewer system sector pursuant to subsection (1.1) of this section; all fees for services performed by the division associated with the municipal separate storm sewer system sector collected pursuant to subsection (1.3) of this section; and all interim fees associated with the municipal separate storm sewer system sector collected pursuant to subsection (1.4) of this section. The division shall transmit the fees to the state treasurer, who shall credit them to the municipal separate storm sewer system sector fund.
(V) There is hereby created in the state treasury the public and private utilities sector fund, which consists of all annual fees collected for regulated activities associated with the public and private utilities sector pursuant to subsection (1.1) of this section; all fees for services performed by the division associated with the public and private utilities sector collected pursuant to subsection (1.3) of this section; and all interim fees associated with the public and private utilities sector collected pursuant to subsection (1.4) of this section. The division shall transmit the fees to the state treasurer, who shall credit them to the public and private utilities sector fund.
(b) (I) The general assembly shall annually appropriate the money in the funds created in

paragraph (a) of this subsection (1.5) and in subsection (1.2) of this section to the department of public health and environment for its direct and indirect costs in administering the appropriate sector. The department shall review expenditures of the money to ensure that it is used only to fund the expenses of the discharge permit system and other activities included in subsections (1.1) , (1.2) , (1.3) , and (1.4) of this section and that, except as specified in subparagraph (II) of this paragraph (b) :

(A) Money derived from a particular sector is used only for that sector; and

(B) Money derived from subsection (1.2) of this section is used only to provide water quality certifications.

(II) (A) If the money derived from a particular sector is inadequate to cover the department's direct and indirect costs in administering that sector, the general assembly may, during fiscal years 2016-17 and 2017-18, appropriate money from any of the funds created in paragraph (a) of this subsection (1.5) and in subsection (1.2) of this section for the department's direct and indirect costs in administering that sector.

(B) During the 2016 interim, the department shall conduct a stakeholder process regarding the appropriate and necessary fees that each subcategory of each sector should pay to enable each sector to be adequately funded by fees collected from that sector. The department shall submit a legislative proposal to the joint budget committee by November 1, 2016, concerning its conclusions regarding the fees.

(C) This subparagraph (II) is repealed, effective September 1, 2018.

(III) All interest earned on the investment or deposit of money in each fund and all unencumbered or unappropriated balances in each fund remain in each individual fund, shall be appropriated only for the expenses of the discharge permit system, and shall not be transferred or revert to the general fund or any other fund at the end of any fiscal year or any other time.

(c) [Editor's note:This version of paragraph (c) is effective until July 1, 2018.]It is the intent of the general assembly that a portion of the expenses of the discharge permit system be funded from the general fund, reflecting the benefit derived by the general public; except that the general assembly may determine, in any given fiscal year, that general fund revenues are inadequate to meet general fund demands and that, as a consequence, it is necessary to forego, subject to future reconsideration, all or some portion of such general fund contribution to the discharge permit program pursuant to this part 5.

(c) [Editor's note:This version of paragraph (c) is effective July 1, 2018.](I) It is the intent of the general assembly that:

(A) A portion of the expenses of the discharge permit system be funded from the general fund, reflecting the benefit derived by the general public; except that the general assembly may determine, in any given fiscal year, that general fund revenues are inadequate to meet general fund demands and that, as a consequence, it is necessary to forego, subject to future reconsideration, all or some portion of such general fund contribution to the discharge permit program pursuant to this part 5; and

(B) The fees established in this section should not be adjusted until at least 2023 and, before the general assembly adjusts the fees, the department of public health and environment shall engage stakeholders in a process to review the total funding for the discharge permit system, including federal money, money from the general fund, and all sector fees.

(II) In furtherance of this policy, in future fee and funding changes, the ratios described in this subsection (1.5) (c) (II) should be maintained except as may be revised by the general assembly by bill:

(A) Commerce and industry sector: Fifty percent general fund and fifty percent cash funds;

(B) Construction sector: Twenty percent general fund and eighty percent cash funds;

(C) Municipal separate storm sewer: Fifty percent general fund and fifty percent cash funds;

(D) Pesticides sector: Ninety-four percent general fund and six percent cash funds;

(E) Public and private utilities sector: Fifty percent general fund and fifty percent cash funds; and

(F) Water quality certifications sector: Five percent general fund and ninety-five percent cash funds.

(d) Notwithstanding the amount specified for any fee in subsection (1.1) or (1.3) of this section, the commission by rule or as otherwise provided by law may reduce the amount of one or more of the fees if necessary pursuant to section 24-75-402 (3) , C.R.S., to reduce the uncommitted reserves of the fund to which all or any portion of one or more of the fees is credited. After the uncommitted reserves of the fund are sufficiently reduced, the commission by rule or as otherwise provided by law may increase the amount of one or more of the fees as provided in section 24-75-402 (4) , C.R.S.

(1.6) There is hereby created the animal feeding operations fund, which consists of all fees collected for regulated activities associated with the animal agriculture sector in paragraph (a) of subsection (1.1) of this section, as well as all fees collected for services provided by the division associated with the animal agriculture sector in subsection (1.3) of this section. The division shall transmit the fees to the state treasurer, who shall credit them to the animal feeding operations fund. Any unexpended and unencumbered moneys remaining in the animal feeding operations fund at the end of any fiscal year remain in the animal feeding operations fund and shall not be transferred or revert to the general fund or any other fund. The general assembly shall annually appropriate the moneys in the animal feeding operations fund to the department of public health and environment for the direct and indirect costs associated with the permitting and oversight of animal feeding operations under this article.

(1.7) (a) The department of public health and environment shall report annually to:

(I) The senate agriculture and natural resources committee and the house of representatives agriculture, livestock, and natural resources committee, or their successor committees, on:

(A) The environmental agriculture program. The report must include the number of permits processed, the number of inspections conducted, the number of enforcement actions taken, and the costs associated with all program activities during the preceding year. The department shall submit the report on or before March 31 of each year.

(B) The clean water program. The report must include the number of permits processed, the number of applications pending for new and amended permits, the length of time the permits remain in the system prior to issuance, the number of inspections conducted, the number of site application and design reviews completed, the number of enforcement actions taken, the costs associated with each sector specified in subsections (1.1) , (1.2) , and (1.3) of this section, the number of full-time equivalents assigned to and actively processing permits, the number of full-time equivalents assigned to and actively conducting inspections, the number of full-time equivalents assigned to and actively conducting site application and design reviews, the number of full-time equivalents assigned to and actively conducting enforcement actions, and the number of full-time equivalents assigned to and actively developing rules and standards. The department shall inform the committees regarding all new standards and rules to be proposed within the subsequent year. The department shall submit the report on or before March 31 of each year. Commencing in 2017, the department shall develop baseline information for reporting. Commencing in 2018, the department shall provide information on improvements that have been made in comparison to the baseline information and information on the barriers to making improvements.

(II) The joint budget committee by November 1 of each year regarding the fee revenue received from each sector specified in subsections (1.1) , (1.2) , and (1.3) of this section, including expenditures by fund source and revenues by fund and sector source based on the November 1 request.

(b) The reporting required by this section is exempt from section 24-1-136, C.R.S.

(2) (a) A complete and accurate application for all discharges shall be filed with the division not less than one hundred eighty days prior to the date proposed for commencing the discharge.

(b) The application shall contain such relevant plans, specifications, water quality data, and other information related to the proposed discharge as the division may reasonably require. Prior to submitting an application for a permit, the applicant may request and, if so requested, the division shall grant a planning meeting with the applicant. At such meeting, the division shall advise the applicant of the applicable permit requirements, including the information, plans, specifications, and data required to be furnished with the permit application.

(c) The division shall begin the review of an application within forty-five days after the receipt of the application and shall notify the applicant within ninety days after receipt of the application whether the application is complete. If the division determines that an application is incomplete, the division may request that the applicant submit additional information. If additional information is requested by the division and submitted by the applicant, the division shall have fifteen days after the date the additional information is submitted to determine whether the additional information satisfies the request and to advise the applicant if, and in what respects, the additional information does not satisfy the request. A final decision that an application is not complete shall be considered final agency action upon issuance of such decision to the applicant and shall be subject to judicial review. A petition for review of such decision shall be given priority scheduling by the court.

(3) (a) The division shall evaluate complete permit applications to determine whether the proposed discharge will comply with all applicable federal and state statutory and regulatory requirements.

(b) The division shall give public notice of a complete permit application and the division's preliminary analysis of the application as provided in subsection (4) of this section. The notice shall advise of the opportunity for interested persons to submit written comments on the permit application and the division's preliminary analysis or to request, for good cause shown, a public meeting on the application and analysis. A request for a public meeting shall be made within thirty days after the initial public notice of the permit application and the division's preliminary analysis. If a public meeting is requested and the division, in its discretion and for good cause shown, grants the request, the division shall hold the public meeting not more than seventy-five days after the initial public notice. The division shall provide notice as provided in subsection (4) of this section of the public meeting not less than thirty days prior to the date of the meeting.

(c) The period for public comment shall close thirty days from the date of notice of the permit application and the division's preliminary analysis thereof; except that, if a public meeting is held on the application and analysis, the period for public comment shall close sixty days from the date of notice of the application.

(4) Public notice of every complete permit application and the division's preliminary analysis thereof shall be circulated in a manner designed to inform interested and potentially interested persons of the application and analysis. Procedures for the circulation of such public notice or a notice regarding a public meeting concerning an application and analysis shall be established by the commission and shall include at least the following:

(a) Notice shall be given by at least one publication in a newspaper of general circulation which is distributed within the geographical areas of the proposed discharge.

(b) Notice shall be mailed to any person or group upon request.

(c) The division shall add the name of any person or group upon request to a mailing list to receive copies of notices for all discharge permit applications within the state or within a certain geographical area.

(d) The division shall also, during the period from the date of the initial public notice of the application and analysis to the close of the public comment period, maintain in the office of the county clerk and recorder of the county in which the proposed discharge, or a part thereof, is to occur a copy of its preliminary analysis and a copy of the permit application with all accompanying data for public inspection.

(5) (a) (I) Except as provided in this subsection (5) , if the division has not finally issued or denied a permit within one hundred eighty days after receipt of the permit application, unless this time limit is waived or extended by the applicant or if the division determines at any time after receiving an application that it cannot issue a permit prior to the expiration of an existing permit, the division shall issue a temporary permit or the existing permit shall be extended pursuant to the operation of section 24-4-104, C.R.S.

(II) The deadlines established pursuant to subparagraph (I) of this paragraph (a) for a determination on a permit application shall be extended by:

(A) The number of days which an applicant takes to submit information requested by the division pursuant to paragraph (c) of subsection (2) of this section plus the fifteen days provided for the division to evaluate such additional information; and

(B) Forty-five days, if a public meeting is held pursuant to subsection (3) of this section.

(b) All temporary permits shall contain such conditions as are necessary to protect public health and shall not be less restrictive than required by state and federal effluent guidelines unless a schedule of compliance or a variance is set forth therein. A temporary permit shall be issued for a period not to exceed two years and shall expire as provided in the issuance or denial of the final permit. Issuance of a temporary permit shall be final agency action for the purposes of section 24-4-106, C.R.S.

(6) Repealed.

## 25-8-503. Permits - when required and when prohibited - variances.

(1) (a) The division shall issue a permit in accordance with regulations promulgated under this article when the division has determined that the provisions of this article and the federal act and regulations thereunder have been met with respect to both the application and proposed permit.

(b) When necessary for compliance with the federal act for the achievement of technology-based effluent limitations, the division may exercise best professional judgment in establishing effluent limitations on a case-by-case basis for permits as granted pursuant to paragraph (a) of this subsection (1) . Technology-based effluent limitations based on best professional judgment shall be made only for good cause and in the absence of federally promulgated effluent guidelines or effluent limitation regulations promulgated by the commission and shall be subject to review as provided for in paragraph (c) of this subsection (1) . Any effluent limitations established according to this paragraph (b) shall be made after considering the availability of appropriate technology, its economic reasonableness, the age of equipment and facilities involved, the process employed, and any increase in water or energy consumption.

(c) Review by a hearing officer or an administrative law judge of the department of personnel of technology-based effluent limitations based on best professional judgment shall be on request of the permit applicant or permittee or any aggrieved person and shall take place in an adjudicatory hearing to be held pursuant to section 24-4-105, C.R.S. The necessity of effluent limitations based on best professional judgment, as well as the reasonableness of the effluent limitation, considering all factors enumerated in paragraph (b) of this subsection (1) , must be supported by substantial evidence. If such hearing is requested, it shall be held as part of a hearing requested to challenge the conditions of the permit.

(d) Repealed.

(2) No permit shall be issued which is inconsistent with any duly promulgated and controlling state, regional, or local land use plan or any portion of an approved regional wastewater management plan which has been adopted as a regulation pursuant to this article, unless all other requirements and conditions of this act have been met or will be met pursuant to a schedule of compliance or a variance specifying treatment requirements as determined by the division.

(3) No permit shall be issued which allows a violation of a control regulation unless the waste discharge permit contains effluent limitations and a schedule of compliance or a variance specifying treatment requirements as determined by the division.

(4) No permit shall be issued which allows a discharge that by itself or in combination with other pollution will result in pollution of the receiving waters in excess of the pollution permitted by an applicable water quality standard unless the permit contains effluent limitations and a schedule of compliance specifying treatment requirements. Effluent limitations designed to meet water quality standards shall be based on application of appropriate physical, chemical, and biological factors reasonably necessary to achieve the levels of protection required by the standards.

(5) Activities such as diversion, carriage, and exchange of water from or into streams, lakes, reservoirs, or conveyance structures, or storage of water in or the release of water from lakes, reservoirs, or conveyance structures, in the exercise of water rights shall not be considered to be point source discharges of pollution under this article. Water quality standards may apply to

discharges from such activities only if the commission has adopted appropriate control regulations pursuant to section 25-8-205. Nothing in this article shall supersede the provisions of articles 80 to 93 of title 37, C.R.S.

(6) Nothing in subsection (5) of this section shall exempt any point source discharger which generates wastewater effluent from the requirement of obtaining a permit pursuant to this article. All permits for such discharges shall apply at the point where wastewater effluent is released from the control of the discharger. All permits for discharges into ditches or other man-made conveyance structures shall contain such provisions as are necessary for the protection of agricultural, domestic, industrial, and municipal beneficial uses made of the waters of the ditch or other man-made conveyance structures, which use or uses were decreed and in existence prior to the inception of the discharge.

(7) Repealed.

(8) Where a permit requires treatment to levels necessary to protect water quality standards and beyond levels required by technology-based effluent limitation requirements, the division must determine whether or not any or all of the water-quality-standard-based effluent limitations are reasonably related to the economic, environmental, public health, and energy impact to the public and affected persons, and are in furtherance of the policies set forth in sections 25-8-102 and 25-8-104. The division's determination shall be based upon information available to it including information provided during the public comment period on the draft permit or in response to specific requests for information. Such determinations shall be included as a part of the written record of the issuance of the final permit, whether or not a variance is available under subsection (9) of this section to alter the water quality standard based effluent limitations.

(9) The division may grant a variance from otherwise applicable requirements only to the extent authorized in the federal act or implementing regulations. Variances may be granted for no longer than the duration of the permit. Variances shall be granted or renewed according to the procedure established in section 25-8-401 (5) . Any variances granted prior to June 4, 1985, which were validly granted under the provisions then in effect shall be valid according to their original terms.

## 25-8-503.5. General permits - process for changing permit requirements.

(1) With respect to a general permit listed in section 25-8-502 (1) (b) (I) (G) , when proposing new or amended permit requirements for dischargers to meet, to obtain, or to maintain authorization for discharges under the permit, the division shall:

(a) Prepare a statement of basis and purpose explaining the need for the proposed requirements;

(b) Present evidence supporting the need for the proposed requirements, including information regarding pollutant potential and available controls, incidents of environmental damage, and permit violations;

(c) Before implementing the proposed requirements, provide public notice of, and consider comments received from affected parties about, the proposed requirements; and

(d) Upon request by an affected party, consider and give due weight to a cost-benefit analysis:

(I) Received by the division during the comment phase set forth in paragraph (c) of this subsection (1) ;

(II) Concerning one or more proposed requirements that are not already required by federal or state statute or rule;

(III) Prepared by a third party chosen from an approved list of analysts, as developed by the division in consultation with representatives of the industries that are subject to general permitting; and

(IV) Paid for by the affected party.

(2) Nothing in subsection (1) of this section confers rule-making authority on the division.

(3) A party may appeal a general permit issued under section 25-8-502 (1) (b) (I) (G) pursuant to the appeals process set forth in section 24-4-105, C.R.S.

## 25-8-504. Agricultural wastes.

(1) Neither the commission nor the division shall require any permit for any flow or return flow of irrigation water into state waters except as may be required by the federal act or regulations. The provisions of any permit that are so required shall not be any more stringent than, and shall not contain any condition for monitoring or reporting in excess of, the minimum required by the federal act or regulations.

(2) (a) Neither the commission nor the division shall require any permit for animal or agricultural waste on farms, ranches, and horticultural or floricultural operations, except as may be required by the federal act or regulations. The provisions of any permit that are so required shall not be any more stringent than, and shall not contain any condition for monitoring or reporting in excess of, the minimum required by the federal act or regulations.

(b) Nothing in paragraph (a) of this subsection (2), as amended by House Bill 05-1180, as enacted at the first regular session of the sixty-fifth general assembly, shall be construed as changing the property tax classification of property owned by a horticultural or floricultural operation.

(3) No permit or fee shall ever be required pursuant to this part 5 for the diversion of water from natural surface streams.

(4) Nothing in this section shall be construed to affect the requirement of permits for housed commercial swine feeding operations pursuant to section 25-8-501.1.

## 25-8-505. Permit conditions concerning publicly owned wastewater treatment works.

The division is authorized to impose, as conditions in permits for the discharge of pollutants from publicly owned wastewater treatment works, appropriate measures to establish and insure compliance by industrial users with any system of user charges or industrial cost recovery.

## 25-8-506. Nuclear and radioactive wastes.

(1) It is unlawful for any person to discharge, deposit, or dispose of any radioactive waste underground in liquid, solid, or explosive form unless the division, upon application of the person desiring to undertake such activity and after investigation and hearing, has first found, based upon a preponderance of the evidence, that there will be no significant pollution resulting therefrom or that the pollution, if any, will be limited to waters in a specified limited area from which there is no significant migration.

(2) (a) In such case the division shall issue a permit for the proposed activity, upon the payment of a fee of one thousand dollars. The division may include in such permit issued under this subsection (2) such reasonable terms and conditions as it may from time to time require to implement this section in a manner consistent with the purposes of this article. The terms or conditions which may be imposed shall include, without limitation, those with respect to duration of use or operation; monitoring; reporting; volume of discharge or disposal; treatment of wastes; and the deposit with the state treasurer of a bond, with or without surety as the division may in its discretion require, or other security, to assure that the permitted activities will be conducted in compliance with the terms and conditions of the permit, and that upon abandonment, cessation, or interruption of the permitted activities or facilities, appropriate measures will be taken to protect the waters of the state. Other than relief from provisions of this article to the extent specified in this subsection (2), no permit issued pursuant to this subsection (2) shall relieve any person of any duty or liability to the state or to any other person existing or arising under any statute or under common law.

(b) Notwithstanding the amount specified for the fee in paragraph (a) of this subsection (2), the commission by rule or as otherwise provided by law may reduce the amount of the fee if necessary pursuant to section 24-75-402 (3), C.R.S., to reduce the uncommitted reserves of the fund to which all or any portion of the fee is credited. After the uncommitted reserves of the fund are sufficiently reduced, the commission by rule or as otherwise provided by law may increase the amount of the fee as provided in section 24-75-402 (4), C.R.S.

(3) No permit for the discharge, deposit, or disposal of nuclear or radioactive waste underground

shall be required in any case where groundwater quality regulation is conducted under article 11 of this title, or under the uranium mill tailings radiation control act of 1978 (Pub.L. 95-604) or a successor statute, where such regulation is determined by the division to comply with the standard set forth in subsection (1) of this section.

(4) (a) The provisions of this section revise and replace, in part, section 25-8-505 of this article, the "Colorado Water Quality Control Act", as said article existed prior to July 1, 1981. All permits issued pursuant to said section 25-8-505 prior to July 1, 1981, shall be deemed a permit issued pursuant to this section and subject to the standards of subsection (1) of this section unless or until:

(I) Such permitted activities are exempted by the provisions of subsection (3) of this section. In such case, all permits issued pursuant to said section 25-8-505 shall terminate and have no effect whatsoever; or

(II) Such permitted activities are the subject of a new permit issued pursuant to this section.

(b) Repealed.

### 25-8-507. Program repeal.

If final federal agency action is taken revoking or withdrawing prior federal approval of all or any part of the state permit program, sections 25-8-203, 25-8-204, 25-8-501, 25-8-502, 25-8-503, and 25-8-505 and regulations adopted to implement such provisions are repealed as of the date of that final federal action.

### 25-8-508. Industrial pretreatment program - creation - fees.

(1) The division shall establish an industrial pretreatment program for the state which is designed to eliminate problems that occur when pollutants from industrial wastewaters are discharged into publicly owned treatment works, including health hazards caused to the public and to workers in sewers and treatment plants, pollution of state waters, interference with the operation of treatment plants or increased expense to dispose of sludges, damage to the pipes and equipment that may occur from pollutants, and the potential for explosion caused by highly volatile wastes. The program shall be adopted by the commission pursuant to section 25-8-205 and shall be adequate to comply with requirements set forth in section 307 (a) , (b) , and (c) of the federal act.

(2) The division is authorized to require compliance with applicable pretreatment requirements and standards by any domestic wastewater treatment works or by any industrial user of such treatment works. The division may grant a variance from applicable requirements only to the extent authorized in the federal act or implementing regulations.

### 25-8-509. Permit conditions concerning use and disposal of biosolids.

The division is authorized to impose, as conditions to the issuance of permits, requirements, prohibitions, standards, and concentration limitations on the use and disposal of biosolids in accordance with the regulations promulgated by the commission pursuant to section 25-8-205 (1) (e) . The requirements, prohibitions, standards, and concentration limitations imposed by the division shall not be more restrictive than the requirements adopted for the solid wastes disposal sites and facilities pursuant to part 1 of article 20 of title 30, C.R.S., except as necessary to be consistent with section 405 of the federal act.

# PART 6. VIOLATIONS, REMEDIES, AND PENALTIES

### 25-8-601. Division to be notified of suspected violations and accidental discharges - penalty.

(1) Any person or any agency of the state or federal government may apply to the division to investigate and take action upon any suspected or alleged violation of any provision of this article or of any order, permit, or regulation issued or promulgated under authority of this article.

(2) Any person engaged in any operation or activity which results in a spill or discharge of oil or other substance which may cause pollution of the waters of the state contrary to the provisions of this article, as soon as he has knowledge thereof, shall notify the division of such discharge. Any person who fails to notify the division as soon as practicable is guilty of a misdemeanor and, upon conviction thereof, shall be punished by a fine of not more than ten thousand dollars, or by imprisonment in the county jail for not more than one year, or by both such fine and imprisonment. Notification received pursuant to this subsection (2) or information obtained by the exploitation of such notification shall not be used against any such person in a criminal case except prosecution for perjury, for false swearing, or for failure to comply with a clean-up order issued pursuant to section 25-8-606.

(3) Any penalty collected under this section shall be credited to the general fund.

## 25-8-602. Notice of alleged violations.

(1) Whenever the division has reason to believe that a violation of an order, permit, or control regulation issued or promulgated under authority of this article has occurred, the division shall cause written notice to be served personally or by certified mail, return receipt requested, upon the alleged violator or his agent for service of process. The notice shall state the provision alleged to be violated and the facts alleged to constitute a violation, and it may include the nature of any corrective action proposed to be required.

(2) Each cease-and-desist and clean-up order issued pursuant to sections 25-8-605 and 25-8-606 shall be accompanied by or have incorporated in it the notice provided for in subsection (1) of this section unless such notice has been given prior to issuance of such cease-and-desist or clean-up order.

## 25-8-603. Hearing procedures for alleged violations.

(1) In any notice given under section 25-8-602, the division shall require the alleged violator to answer each alleged violation and may require the alleged violator to appear before it for a public hearing to provide such answer. Such hearing shall be held no sooner than fifteen days after service of the notice; except that the division may set an earlier date for hearing if it is requested by the alleged violator.

(2) If the division does not require an alleged violator to appear for a public hearing, the alleged violator may request the division to conduct such a hearing. Such request shall be in writing and shall be filed with the division no later than thirty days after issuance of a notice under section 25-8-602. If such a request is filed, a hearing shall be held within a reasonable time.

(3) If a hearing is held pursuant to the provisions of this section, it shall be public and, if the division deems it practicable, shall be held in any county in which the violation is alleged to have occurred. The division shall permit all parties to respond to the notice served under section 25-8-602, to present evidence and argument on all issues, and to conduct cross-examination required for full disclosure of the facts.

(4) Hearings held pursuant to this section shall be conducted in accordance with section 24-4-105, C.R.S.

## 25-8-604. Suspension, modification, and revocation of permit.

Upon a finding and determination, after hearing, that a violation of a permit provision has occurred, the division may suspend, modify, or revoke the pertinent permit or take such other action with respect to the violation as may be authorized pursuant to regulations promulgated by the commission.

## 25-8-605. Cease-and-desist orders.

If the division determines, with or without hearing, that a violation of any provision of this article or of any order, permit, or control regulation issued or promulgated under authority of this article exists, the division may issue a cease-and-desist order. Such order shall set forth the provision alleged to be violated, the facts alleged to constitute the violation, and the time by which the acts or practices complained of must be terminated.

## 25-8-606. Clean-up orders.

The division may issue orders to any person to clean up any material which he, his employee, or his agent has accidentally or purposely dumped, spilled, or otherwise deposited in or near state waters which may pollute them. The division may also request the district attorney to proceed and take appropriate action under section 16-13-305 and sections 16-13-307 to 16-13-315, C.R.S., or section 18-4-511, C.R.S.

## 25-8-607. Restraining orders and injunctions.

(1) The division may request the district attorney for the judicial district with jurisdiction pursuant to subsection (2) of this section or the attorney general to bring, and if so requested it shall be the duty of such district attorney or the attorney general to bring, a suit for a temporary restraining order, preliminary injunction, or permanent injunction to prevent any threatened violation of this article or any order, permit, or control regulation issued or promulgated pursuant to this article which violation poses imminent and substantial endangerment to the beneficial uses of state waters and which cannot be timely prevented by a permit modification or permit enforcement action, or any continued violation of this article, or any order, permit, or control regulation issued or promulgated pursuant to this article. In any suit for a violation of an order, the final findings of the division, after opportunity for a hearing, based upon evidence in the record, shall be prima facie evidence of the facts found in such record.

(2) Suits under this section shall be brought in the district or county court for the district or county in which the violation or threatened violation occurs. Emergencies shall be given precedence over all other matters pending in such court. The institution of such injunction proceeding by the division shall confer upon such court exclusive jurisdiction to determine finally the subject matter of the proceeding; except that the exclusive jurisdiction of the court shall apply only to such injunctive proceeding and shall not preclude assessment of civil penalties or any other enforcement action or sanction authorized by this article.

## 25-8-608. Civil penalties - rules - fund created - temporary moratorium on penalties for minor violations - definitions - repeal.

(1) Except as otherwise provided in subsection (3) of this section, any person who violates any provision of this article or of any permit issued under this article, or any control regulation promulgated pursuant to this article, or any final cease-and-desist order or clean-up order shall be subject to a civil penalty of not more than ten thousand dollars per day for each day during which such violation occurs. In determining the amount of a penalty under this part 6, the following factors shall be considered:

(a) The potential damage from the violation;

(b) The violator's compliance history;

(c) Whether the violation was intentional, reckless, or negligent;

(d) The impact upon or threat to the public health or environment as a result of the violation;

(e) The duration of the violation; and

(f) The economic benefit realized by the violator as a result of the violation.

(1.5) All penalties collected pursuant to subsection (1) of this section shall be transmitted to the state treasurer, who shall credit the same to the water quality improvement fund, which is hereby created. The moneys in such fund shall be subject to annual appropriation. Any interest earned on moneys in the fund shall remain in the fund to be used for purposes of this section.

(1.7) (a) The department shall expend moneys in the water quality improvement fund for the following purposes:

(I) Improving the water quality in the community or water body impacted by the violation;

(II) Providing grants for storm water projects or to assist with planning, design, construction, or repair of domestic wastewater treatment works;

(III) Providing the nonfederal match funding for nonpoint source projects under 33 U.S.C. sec. 1329; or

(IV) Providing grants for storm water management training and best practices training to prevent or reduce the pollution of state waters.

(b) The division may retain five percent of the moneys in the water quality improvement fund to cover the cost of administering the projects or grants under paragraph (a) of this subsection (1.7) .

(c) The commission shall promulgate rules as may be necessary to administer this subsection (1.7) , including, but not limited to, rules defining who is eligible for grants, and what criteria shall be used in awarding grants. Any rules shall be promulgated in accordance with article 4 of title 24, C.R.S.

(d) (I) If there is money still available after fully funding all purposes specified in subsection (1.7) (a) of this section, the department shall expend the following amounts:

(A) Up to three hundred thousand dollars for fiscal year 2017-18, three hundred thousand dollars for fiscal year 2018-19, and three hundred thousand dollars for fiscal year 2019-20 for grants for lead testing as authorized by the public school lead testing grant program established in section 25-1.5-203 (1) (f) ; and

(B) One hundred forty thousand dollars for fiscal year 2017-18, one hundred thousand dollars for fiscal year 2018-19, and one hundred thousand dollars for fiscal year 2019-20 to implement the public school lead testing grant program established in section 25-1.5-203 (1) (f) , including technical support for schools, grant administration, and reporting.

(II) This subsection (1.7) (d) is repealed, effective September 1, 2021.

(1.8) Notwithstanding any provision of subsection (1.5) or (1.7) of this section to the contrary, on April 20, 2009, the state treasurer shall deduct seven hundred thousand dollars from the water quality improvement fund and transfer such sum to the general fund.

(1.9) The division shall include in a separate section of the annual report required pursuant to section 25-8-305 a full accounting of all projects funded pursuant to this section for the preceding year.

(2) The division may institute a civil action or administrative action to impose and collect penalties under this section. Upon application of the division, penalties shall be determined by the executive director or his or her designee. The final decision of the executive director or his or her designee may be appealed to the commission. The final decision of the commission is subject to judicial review in accordance with article 4 of title 24, C.R.S. Any penalty may be collected by the division by action instituted in a court of competent jurisdiction for collection of such penalty. A stay of any order of the division pending judicial review shall not relieve any person from any liability under subsection (1) of this section, but the reason for the request for judicial review shall be considered in the determination of the amount of the penalty. In the event that such an action is instituted for the collection of such penalty, the court may consider the appropriateness of the amount of the penalty, if such issue is raised by the party against whom the penalty was assessed.

(3) and (4) Repealed.

## 25-8-608.5. Nutrients grant fund - rules - repeal. (Repealed)

## 25-8-608.7. Natural disaster grant fund - creation - rules.

(1) The natural disaster grant fund is hereby created in the state treasury. Moneys in the fund, including interest earned on the investment of moneys in the fund, are continuously appropriated to the department of public health and environment for the purpose specified in subsection (2) of this section.

(2) (a) The division shall expend moneys in the fund to award grants to local governments, including local governments accepting grants on behalf of and in coordination with not-for-profit public water systems, for the planning, design, construction, improvement, renovation, or reconstruction of domestic wastewater treatment works or public drinking water systems that have been impacted, damaged, or destroyed in connection with a natural disaster, as defined in section 24-33.5-703 (3) , C.R.S. The division may also award grants to local governments to assist with the repair and restoration of on-site wastewater treatment systems, as defined in section 25-10-103 (12) , that have been impacted, damaged, or destroyed in connection with a natural disaster. The division may only award grants to be used in counties for which the governor has declared a disaster emergency by executive order or proclamation under section 24-33.5-704, C.R.S.
(b) Grant recipients may use the grant moneys to provide a portion of any matching funds required to secure federal or state funding for the planning, design, construction, improvement, renovation, or reconstruction of drinking water and wastewater infrastructure.
(c) For the 2014-15 fiscal year and, as needed, the 2015-16 fiscal year, the division shall award grants to local governments that are eligible under paragraph (a) of this subsection (2) and have domestic wastewater treatment works, public drinking water systems, or on-site wastewater treatment systems that have been impacted, damaged, or destroyed in connection with the flood of September 2013 to restore the facilities' compliance with this article or the Colorado primary drinking water regulations.
(d) The division may retain up to one hundred thousand dollars per fiscal year of the moneys in the fund to cover the cost of administering projects or grants under this section.
(e) Repealed.
(3) The commission shall promulgate rules in accordance with article 4 of title 24, C.R.S., as necessary to administer this section, including rules defining who is eligible to apply for grants and the criteria to be used in awarding grants. The criteria must give priority to applicants that have the lowest financial ability to pay for the necessary construction, improvements, renovation, or reconstruction.

## 25-8-609. Criminal pollution - penalties.
(1) Any person who recklessly, knowingly, intentionally, or with criminal negligence discharges any pollutant into any state waters or into any domestic wastewater treatment works commits criminal pollution if such discharge is made:
(a) In violation of any permit issued under this article; or
(b) In violation of any cease-and-desist order or clean-up order issued by the division which is final and not stayed by court order; or
(c) Without a permit, if a permit is required by the provisions of this article for such discharge; or
(d) Repealed.
(e) In violation of any pretreatment regulations promulgated by the commission.
(2) Prosecution under paragraph (a) of subsection (1) of this section shall be commenced only upon complaint filed by the division or a peace officer.
(3) Any person who commits criminal pollution of state waters shall be fined, for each day the violation occurs, as follows:
(a) If the violation is committed with criminal negligence or recklessly, as defined in section 18-1-501, C.R.S., the maximum fine shall be twelve thousand five hundred dollars.
(b) If the violation is committed knowingly or intentionally, as defined in section 18-1-501, C.R.S., the maximum fine shall be twenty-five thousand dollars.
(c) If two separate offenses under this article occur in two separate occurrences during a period of two years, the maximum fine for the second offense shall be double the amounts specified in paragraph (a) or (b) of this subsection (3) , whichever is applicable.
(d) (Deleted by amendment, L. 2009, (SB 09-119) , ch. 223, p. 1009, § 1, effective August 5, 2009.)
(4) Any criminal penalty collected under this section shall be credited to the general fund.

(5) No provision of this article shall be interpreted to supersede, limit, abrogate, or impair the ability to enforce:

(a) Civil or criminal penalties pursuant to article 22 of title 29, C.R.S., if the pollutant discharged into state waters or domestic wastewater treatment works is a "hazardous substance" as defined in section 29-22-101, C.R.S.; or

(b) Civil penalties pursuant to section 25-15-309 or criminal penalties pursuant to section 25-15-310 if the pollutant discharged into state waters or domestic wastewater treatment works is a "hazardous waste" as defined in section 25-15-101.

### 25-8-610. Falsification and tampering.

(1) Any person who knowingly makes any false statement, representation, or certification in any application, record, report, plan, or other document filed or required to be maintained under this article or who falsifies, tampers with, or knowingly renders inaccurate any monitoring device or method required to be maintained under this article is guilty of a misdemeanor and, upon conviction thereof, shall be punished by a fine of not more than ten thousand dollars, or by imprisonment in the county jail for not more than six months, or by both such fine and imprisonment.

(2) Any penalty collected under this section shall be credited to the general fund.

### 25-8-611. Proceedings by other parties.

(1) The factual or legal basis for proceedings or other actions that result from a violation of any control regulation inure solely to, and shall be for the benefit of the people of, the state generally, and it is not intended by this article, in any way, to create new private rights or to enlarge existing private rights. A determination that water pollution exists or that any standard has been disregarded or violated, whether or not a proceeding or action may be brought by the state, shall not create any presumption of law or finding of fact which shall inure to or be for the benefit of any person other than the state.

(2) A permit issued pursuant to this article may be introduced in any court of law as evidence that the permittee's activity is not a public or private nuisance. Introduction into evidence of such permit and evidence of compliance with the permit conditions shall constitute a prima facie case that the activity to which the permit pertains is not a public or private nuisance.

### 25-8-612. Remedies cumulative.

(1) It is the purpose of this article to provide additional and cumulative remedies to prevent, control, and abate water pollution and protect water quality.

(2) No action pursuant to section 25-8-609 shall bar enforcement of any provision of this article or of any rule or order issued pursuant to this article by any authorized means.

(3) Nothing in this article shall abridge or alter rights of action or remedies existing on or after July 1, 1981, nor shall any provision of this article or anything done by virtue of this article be construed as estopping individuals, cities, towns, counties, cities and counties, or duly constituted political subdivisions of the state from the exercise of their respective rights to suppress nuisances.

# PART 7. DOMESTIC WASTEWATER TREATMENT WORKS

### 25-8-701. Definitions.

As used in this part 7, unless the context otherwise requires:

(1) "Construction" means entering into a contract for the erection or physical placement of materials, equipment, piping, earthwork, or buildings which are to be part of a domestic

wastewater treatment works.

(2) "Eligible project" means a project for the planning, design, or construction of domestic wastewater treatment works or of facilities for the discharge of wastewater or backwash water from public water treatment plants that is, in the judgment of the division, necessary for the accomplishment of the state water quality control program and that conforms with applicable rules of the commission.

(3) Repealed.

## 25-8-702. Approval for commencement of construction.

(1) No person shall commence the construction of any domestic wastewater treatment works or the enlargement of the capacity of an existing domestic wastewater treatment works, unless the site location and the design for the construction or expansion have been approved by the division.

(2) In evaluating the suitability of a proposed site location for a domestic wastewater treatment works, the division shall:

(a) Consider the local long-range comprehensive plan for the area as it affects water quality and any approved regional wastewater management plan for the area;

(b) Determine that the plant on the proposed site will be managed to minimize the potential adverse impacts on water quality; and

(c) Encourage the consolidation of wastewater treatment facilities whenever feasible.

(3) Ninety days prior to commencement of construction of an interceptor line, the entity responsible for that line shall notify the planning agency and the division of such construction. This notification shall be accompanied with a certification by the agency receiving the wastewater for treatment that it has or will have the capacity to treat the projected wastewater from that interceptor line in accordance with the treatment agency's site approval and discharge permit. Within thirty days of receipt of notification, the planning agency, or the division, if a planning agency does not exist, shall certify that the proposed interceptor line has the capacity to carry the projected flow. In the event the entity responsible for an interceptor line does not have the said certification from the treatment agency and the planning agency, the entity shall be required to apply for a site location approval prior to commencement of construction.

(4) The decision of the division concerning approval of the site location or design may be appealed to the commission. The commission shall hold a hearing on the site location or design in accordance with the provisions of section 24-4-105, C.R.S., and the decision of the commission shall be final administrative action for the purposes of section 24-4-106, C.R.S.

## 25-8-703. State contracts for construction of domestic wastewater treatment works. (Repealed)

# PART 8. STORM WATER MANAGEMENT SYSTEM ADMINISTRATORS

## 25-8-801. Definitions.

As used in this part 8, unless the context otherwise requires:

(1) "Administrator" or "storm water management system administrator" means a nonprofit entity designated by the division to conduct the activities required under this part 8.

(2) "Advisory board" means an oversight group, established as a required element within each storm water management system administrator's program, that is made up of volunteers representing industry sector stakeholders active in the program, including nonprofit administrator representatives, participants, participating MS4s, and third-party auditors. While acting in the

capacity of a board of directors, the advisory board has the authority to establish all program policies and procedures, collect and maintain program records, compile annual participant performance summary reports, and take all necessary actions to maintain the department's designation of the administrator.

(3) "CDPS" means the Colorado discharge permit system.

(4) "CDPS MS4 permit" means a CDPS permit for storm water discharges associated with an MS4.

(5) "CDPS storm water construction permit" means a CDPS permit for storm water discharges associated with construction activities.

(6) "MS4" means a municipal separate storm sewer system.

(7) "MS4 permittee" means a governmental entity with a CDPS permit for storm water discharges associated with an MS4.

(8) "Participant" means a person that is required to obtain a CDPS storm water construction permit from the division and that volunteers to participate in a storm water management system program administered by a storm water management system administrator.

(9) "SWMP" means a storm water management plan as defined in the CDPS permit for storm water discharges associated with construction activities.

(10) "Third-party auditor" means a person who meets the professional qualifications defined in the administrator's written program and who operates independently from, and is not an employee of, any participant or MS4 in the administrator's program.

## 25-8-802. Storm water management system administrator.

(1) A nonprofit entity may apply to be a storm water management system administrator by completing an application in such form as the division may require. The division may designate one or more storm water management system administrators. To be designated as an administrator, the applicant must demonstrate to the satisfaction of the division that:

(a) The applicant has in place a standardized compliance assistance and assurance program that contains processes, procedures, and associated training for participants that, when fully implemented by the program participants, would result in full compliance with the requirements of the applicable CDPS storm water construction permit. The compliance assistance and assurance program shall assure, at a minimum, that each participant:

(I) Maintains a qualified permit compliance manager in accordance with the CDPS storm water construction permit and the administrator's written policies;

(II) Maintains complete and updated permit documentation available for inspection at the permitted facility;

(III) Completes established minimum requirements for training to maintain permit compliance manager status; and

(IV) Complies with all applicable terms and conditions required by any MS4 permittee with jurisdiction over the participant's construction activities.

(b) The applicant ensures that a third-party audit of each participant facility operating under a CDPS storm water construction permit is completed on a monthly basis using standardized inspection reporting forms and procedures approved by the division. Third-party audit reports must include standardized compliance performance measurement and scoring clearly demonstrating the following:

(I) The adequacy of implementation of each aspect of the administrator's storm water management systems;

(II) The adequacy of the SWMP in meeting all applicable permit requirements defined in this part 8; and

(III) The adequacy of each storm water management practice used to implement the SWMP.

(c) The applicant maintains records of its compliance assistance and assurance program, including a list of participants and each participant facility, and monthly required third-party audits, in a form approved by the division;

(d) The applicant has fully implemented the compliance assistance and assurance program with a sufficient number of participants to demonstrate the adequacy of the program for one year prior to submittal of an application for designation as an administrator;

(e) The applicant maintains an advisory board that meets regularly, but not less than quarterly, and such meetings are open to the public; and

(f) The applicant has a written storm water management program that includes:

(I) An organizational chart defining relationships among stakeholders, including the roles and responsibilities of each;

(II) Advisory board make-up and associated policies and procedures;

(III) Participant policies and procedures, including performance standards and measurement methodology;

(IV) Third-party auditor policies and procedures; and

(V) Other policies and procedures the division may require to demonstrate a complete and functional program.

(2) Upon the division's approval of the application, the division shall designate the applicant as a storm water management system administrator. The applicant shall maintain a compliance assistance and assurance program, including requiring third-party audits and record keeping, consistent with the requirements of this part 8.

(3) A storm water management system administrator shall provide to the division on at least a yearly basis a summary report that describes in detail significant program accomplishments and changes and that adequately demonstrates the overall performance of the administrator's program in improving participant compliance with the participants' storm water permits. The division shall make the yearly administrator summary report available to the public.

(4) To the extent permitted by federal law, the division may reduce compliance oversight activities for facilities authorized to discharge under a CDPS storm water construction permit participating in a storm water management system administrator program based on a determination by the division that the participants or the participant facilities have a demonstrated record of reduced potential for occurrences of noncompliance and reduced risk of negative impacts on receiving waters. This part 8 does not prohibit or restrict any compliance oversight, including inspections, by the division.

(5) The division may revoke the designation of an administrator for evidence of repeated failure to meet the requirements of this part 8.

(6) The disclosure of any information related to a participant's third-party audit to an administrator is not a disclosure under section 25-1-114.5.

(7) Participation in a storm water management system administrator program by a holder of a CDPS storm water construction permit is strictly voluntary, and a participant may end its participation at any time upon written notice to the administrator.

(8) The administrator may work with the division to establish reporting requirements acceptable to the division that would allow participants in the administrator's program to participate in environmental performance recognition programs, including the department's environmental leadership program.

## 25-8-803. Storm water management system administrator audits to support MS4 permittees' programs.

(1) MS4 permittees may choose to work with any administrator to assist the MS4 permittee in complying with the terms and conditions of the MS4 permittee's CDPS MS4 permit. An MS4 permittee may utilize all, or portions of, the storm water management system administrator's program as part of the MS4 permittee's program for oversight of construction sites to demonstrate compliance with the requirements of the MS4 permittee's CDPS permit for storm water discharges associated with an MS4.

(2) The division may consider third-party audits conducted pursuant to a storm water management system administrator's program to be part of the MS4 permittee's compliance oversight program

required by its CDPS MS4 permit if the MS4 permittee formally utilizes the storm water management system administrator's program that conducted the audit, and the MS4 permittee implements procedures to demonstrate and report to the division, upon division request, that the administrator's program is meeting the requirements for third-party audits in section 25-8-802 (1) and (3) for participant construction activities located within the jurisdiction of the MS4 permittee.

(3) An MS4 permittee may reduce compliance oversight activities for facilities authorized to discharge under a CDPS storm water construction permit that are operated by participants in a storm water management system administrator's program based on a determination by the MS4 permittee that the participants or participant facilities have a demonstrated record of reduced potential for occurrences of noncompliance and reduced risk of negative impacts on receiving waters. This part 8 does not prohibit or restrict any compliance oversight, including inspections, by an MS4 permittee.

(4) Modification of the MS4 permittee's program is subject to division approval in accordance with the requirements of the applicable CDPS MS4 permit.

(5) An MS4 permittee's use of a storm water management system administrator's program is strictly voluntary, and an MS4 permittee may end its use of the program at any time upon written notice to the administrator.

(6) Nothing in this part 8 grants regulatory authority to a storm water management system administrator or the authority to impose any fine.

(7) Nothing in this part 8 preempts or supersedes any authority of an MS4 permittee or any other local agency.

(8) Nothing in this part 8 removes, reduces, or transfers the responsibility for compliance with an MS4 permit from the MS4 permittee.

# ARTICLE 8.5. CHERRY CREEK BASIN WATER QUALITY AUTHORITY

## 25-8.5-101. Legislative declaration.

(1) The general assembly hereby finds and declares that the organization of a Cherry Creek basin water quality authority will:

(a) Be for the public benefit and advantage of the people of the state of Colorado;

(b) Benefit the inhabitants and landowners within the authority by preserving water quality in Cherry Creek and Cherry Creek reservoir;

(c) Benefit the people of the state of Colorado by preserving waters for recreation, fisheries, water supplies, and other beneficial uses;

(d) Promote the health, safety, and welfare of the people of the state of Colorado.

(2) It is further declared that the authority will provide for effective efforts by the various counties, municipalities, special districts, and landowners within the boundaries of the authority in the protection of water quality.

(3) It is further declared that the authority should provide that new developments and construction activities pay their equitable proportion of costs for water quality preservation and facilities.

(4) This article, being necessary to secure the public health, safety, convenience, and welfare, shall be liberally construed to effect its purposes.

## 25-8.5-102. Definitions.

As used in this article, unless the context otherwise requires:

(1) "Agricultural lands" means all lands except land rezoned by a county or municipality for business, commercial, residential, or similar uses or subdivided lands. Those include property consisting of a lot one acre or more in size which contains a dwelling unit.

(2) "Authority" means the Cherry Creek basin water quality authority created pursuant to section 25-8.5-103.

(3) "Board" means the governing body of the authority provided for in section 25-8.5-106.

(3.5) "Conservation district" means any conservation district created pursuant to article 70 of title 35, C.R.S.

(4) "County" means any county enumerated in article 5 of title 30, C.R.S.

(5) "Municipality" means a municipality as defined in section 31-1-101 (6) , C.R.S.

(6) "Publication" means three consecutive weekly advertisements in a newspaper or newspapers of general circulation within the boundaries of the authority. It shall not be necessary that an advertisement be made on the same day of the week in each of the three weeks, but not less than twelve days, excluding the day of first publication, shall intervene between the first publication and the last publication. Publication shall be complete on the date of the last publication.

(7) "Resolution" means an ordinance as passed by a member municipality or a resolution as passed by a member county or special district.

(8) (Deleted by amendment, L. 2002, p. 517, § 12, effective July 1, 2002.)

(9) "Special district" means any district created pursuant to article 1 of title 32, C.R.S., which has the power to provide sanitation services or water and sanitation services and has wastewater treatment facilities within the boundaries of the authority.

(10) "Wastewater treatment facility" means a facility providing wastewater treatment services which has a designed capacity to receive sewage for treating, neutralizing, stabilizing, and reducing pollutants contained therein prior to the disposal or discharge of the treated sewage. "Wastewater treatment facility" does not include any pretreatment facilities, lift stations, interceptor lines, or other transmission facilities to transmit sewage effluent outside the boundaries of the authority.

## 25-8.5-103. Creation and organization.

The Cherry Creek basin water quality authority is hereby created. The authority shall be a quasi-municipal corporation and political subdivision of the state, with the powers provided in this article.

## 25-8.5-104. Boundaries of authority.

(1) The boundaries of the authority shall be determined by the authority, subject to the following:

(a) The boundaries shall be limited to the drainage basin of Cherry Creek from its headwaters to the dam at Cherry Creek reservoir, which the general assembly hereby finds to be:

(I) Arapahoe county: Portions of sections thirty-five and thirty-six, township four south, range sixty-seven west of the sixth principal meridian; a portion of section thirty-one, township four south, range sixty-six west of the sixth principal meridian; portions of sections one, two, three, ten, fifteen, twenty-two, twenty-three, twenty-seven, and thirty-four, and all of sections eleven, twelve, thirteen, fourteen, twenty-four, twenty-five, twenty-six, thirty-five and thirty-six, township five south, range sixty-seven west of the sixth principal meridian; all of sections seven, seventeen, eighteen, nineteen, twenty, twenty-one, twenty-two, twenty-five, twenty-six, twenty-seven, twenty-eight, twenty-nine, thirty, thirty-one, thirty-two, thirty-three, thirty-four, thirty-five, thirty-six and portions of sections five, six, eight, nine, fourteen, fifteen, sixteen, twenty-three and twenty-four, township five south, range sixty-six west of the sixth principal meridian; all of section thirty-one and portions of sections nineteen, twenty-nine, thirty, and thirty-two, township five south, range sixty-five west of the sixth principal meridian;

(II) Douglas county: Portions of sections four, nine, sixteen, twenty-one, twenty-eight and thirty-three, and all of sections five, six, seven, eight, seventeen, eighteen, nineteen, twenty, twenty-nine, thirty, thirty-one, and thirty-two, township six south, range sixty-five west of the sixth principal meridian; township six south, range sixty-six west of the sixth principal meridian; portions of sections three, ten, fifteen, twenty-one, twenty-two, twenty-eight, thirty-one, thirty-two and thirty-three, and all of sections one, two, eleven, twelve, thirteen, fourteen, twenty-three, twenty-four, twenty-five, twenty-six, twenty-seven, thirty-four, thirty-five and thirty-six, township six south, range sixty-seven west of the sixth principal meridian; portions of sections four, nine, sixteen, and twenty-one, and all of sections five, six, seven, eight, seventeen, eighteen, nineteen, twenty, twenty-eight, twenty-nine, thirty, thirty-one, thirty-two, and thirty-three, township seven south, range sixty-five west of the sixth principal meridian; township seven south, range sixty-six west of the sixth principal meridian; portions of sections four, five, nine, fourteen, fifteen, sixteen, twenty-three, twenty-five, twenty-six, and thirty-six, and all of sections one, two, three, ten, eleven, twelve, thirteen, and twenty-four, township seven south, range sixty-seven west of the sixth principal meridian; portions of sections twenty-eight and thirty-three and all of sections four, five, six, seven, eight, nine, sixteen, seventeen, eighteen, nineteen, twenty, twenty-one, twenty-nine, thirty, thirty-one, and thirty-two, township eight south, range sixty-five west of the sixth principal meridian; portions of sections six, seven, eighteen, nineteen, twenty-nine, thirty, and thirty-one, and all of sections one, two, three, four, five, eight, nine, ten, eleven, twelve, thirteen, fourteen, fifteen, sixteen, seventeen, twenty, twenty-one, twenty-two, twenty-three, twenty-four, twenty-five, twenty-six, twenty-seven, twenty-eight, thirty-two, thirty-three, thirty-four, thirty-five and thirty-six, township eight south, range sixty-six west of the sixth principal meridian; a portion of section one, township eight south, range sixty-seven west of the sixth principal meridian; all of sections four, five, six, seven, eight, nine, sixteen, seventeen, eighteen, nineteen, twenty, twenty-one, twenty-eight, twenty-nine, thirty, thirty-one, thirty-two and thirty-three, township nine south, range sixty-five west of the sixth principal meridian; all of township nine south, range sixty-six west excepting portions of sections six and seven; portions of sections thirteen, twenty-three, twenty-four, twenty-five, and thirty-six, township nine south, range sixty-seven west of the sixth principal meridian; portions of sections twenty-eight and thirty-three, and all of sections four, five, six, seven, eight, nine, sixteen, seventeen, eighteen, nineteen, twenty, twenty-one, twenty-nine, thirty, thirty-one, and thirty-two, township ten south, range sixty-five west of the sixth principal meridian; portions of sections five, six, seven, eight, seventeen, eighteen, nineteen, twenty-nine, thirty, thirty-one, and all of sections one, two, three, four, nine, ten, eleven, twelve, thirteen, fourteen, fifteen, sixteen, twenty, twenty-one, twenty-two, twenty-three, twenty-four, twenty-five, twenty-six, twenty-seven, twenty-eight, thirty-two, thirty-three, thirty-four, thirty-five and thirty-six, township ten south, range sixty-six west of the sixth principal meridian; a portion of section one, township ten south range sixty-seven west of the sixth principal meridian.

(b) Lands may be included within the boundaries of the authority pursuant to section 25-8.5-119.

(c) Lands within the boundaries identified in paragraph (a) of this subsection (1) may be excluded from the authority pursuant to section 25-8.5-120.

(2) The authority shall maintain a current map, showing all lands that are included in the authority's boundaries.

## 25-8.5-105. Authority members.

(1) The following entities shall be members of the authority:

(a) Each county that has property within the authority's boundaries shall have one member;

(b) Each municipality that has property within the authority's boundaries shall have one member;

(c) The special districts that include in their service areas property within the Cherry Creek basin and that own and operate wastewater treatment services facilities in the Cherry Creek basin shall collectively be represented by a single member of the authority. For the purposes of this paragraph (c) , wastewater treatment services shall mean a wastewater treatment facility with a designed capacity to receive more than two thousand gallons of sewage per day.

(d) A total of seven members shall be appointed by the governor to represent sports persons, recreational users, and concerned citizens. A minimum of two of these appointees shall be residents of Colorado and shall be from bona fide sports persons' or recreational organizations that have members who use the reservoir. A minimum of two of these appointees shall be from bona fide citizen or environmental organizations interested in preserving water quality with members who use the reservoir or live within Cherry Creek basin. At least three of the appointed members shall have backgrounds in or professional training regarding water quality issues. A simple majority of the appointed members shall be appointed to four-year terms, the remainder shall be appointed to initial two-year terms, and the members appointed to fill the vacancies upon expiration of such two-year terms shall serve four-year terms. The governor may replace any appointed member with a new member by appointment every four years.

## 25-8.5-106. Board of directors.

(1) The governing body of the authority shall be a board of directors which shall exercise and perform all powers, rights, privileges, and duties invested or imposed by this article.

(2) Each authority member shall appoint one representative and two alternates to serve on the board. The representative and alternates for the special district authority member shall be chosen by unanimous consent of the special districts referenced in section 25-8.5-105 (1) (c) , or included under section 25-8.5-119. Any county, municipality, or special district that provides wastewater treatment services by contract with another entity that is a member of the authority shall not be entitled to a separate member on the board, and such a special district shall not be entitled to representation by the special district member.

(3) Directors shall be appointed for terms of two years. Notice of each appointment shall be given to the recording secretary for the authority.

(4) No director shall receive compensation as an employee of the authority. Reimbursement of actual expenses for directors shall not be considered compensation.

(5) An appointment to fill a vacancy on the board shall be made by the authority member for the remainder of the unexpired term.

(6) If a board member or designated alternate fails to attend two consecutive regular meetings of the board, the authority may submit a written request to the appointing authority member to have its representative attend the next regular meeting. If, following such request, said representative fails to attend the next regular board meeting, the board may appoint an interim representative from the authority member's jurisdiction to serve until the authority member appoints a new representative.

(7) An authority member, at its discretion, may remove from office any board member or designated alternate representing the authority member and appoint a successor.

(8) The board shall elect one of its members as chairman of the authority and one of its members as secretary-treasurer and shall appoint a recording secretary who may be a member of the board.

(9) The recording secretary shall keep in a visual text format that may be transmitted electronically a record of all of the authority's meetings, resolutions, certificates, contracts, bonds given by employees or contractors, and all corporate acts which shall be open to inspection of all interested parties.

(10) The secretary-treasurer shall keep strict and accurate accounts of all money received by and disbursed for and on behalf of the authority.

## 25-8.5-107. Voting.

(1) Each authority member, through its designated director or designated alternate acting in the director's place, shall be entitled to one vote.

(2) Board action upon proposed waste load allocations, site location or site plans selected pursuant to section 25-8-702, discharge permits secured pursuant to section 25-8-501, amendments to the authority's wastewater management plan, and all budget and funding decisions shall require an affirmative vote of a majority of all authority members. Any vote by the special district member on such board action shall reflect the majority of the represented special districts.

(3) All decisions of the board not enumerated in subsection (2) of this section shall be made and decided by a majority of the quorum. A quorum requires that at least fifty percent of all authority members be present.

(4) A director shall disqualify himself from voting on any issue in which he has a conflict of interest unless such director has disclosed such conflict of interest in compliance with section 18-

8-308, C.R.S., in which case such disclosure shall cure the conflict. A director shall abstain from voting if the director would obtain a personal financial gain from the contract or services being voted upon by the authority.

(5) Notwithstanding subsection (2) of this section, any vote regarding a change in the levy and collection of ad valorem taxes pursuant to section 25-8.5-111 (1) (p) (I) shall be limited to authority members representing municipalities or counties within the authority's boundaries.

## 25-8.5-108. Ex officio members.

(1) Ex officio members shall be provided with notice of the authority meetings. Ex officio members shall not serve on the board. Ex officio members are not voting members. The following shall be considered ex officio members:

(a) Every conservation district of which more than two-thirds of its territory is included within the authority's boundaries;

(b) Any other governmental or quasi-governmental agency designated as an ex officio member by the authority.

## 25-8.5-109. Meetings.

(1) The board shall fix the time and place at which its regular meetings shall be held and provide for the calling and holding of special meetings.

(2) Notice of the time and place designated for all regular meetings shall be posted at the office of the county clerk and recorder of each of the counties included within the authority. Such notices shall remain posted and shall be changed in the event that the time or place of such regular meetings is changed.

(3) Special meetings of the board shall be held at the call of the chairman or upon request of two board members. The authority shall inform all board members five calendar days before the special meeting and shall post notice in accordance with subsection (2) of this section at least three days before the special meeting of the date, time, and place of such special meeting and the purpose for which it is called.

(4) All business of the board shall be conducted only during said regular or special meetings, and all said meetings shall be open to the public, but the board may hold executive sessions as provided in part 4 of article 6 of title 24, C.R.S.

## 25-8.5-110. Powers of board - organization - administration.

(1) The board has the following powers relating to carrying on the affairs of the authority:

(a) To organize, adopt bylaws and rules of procedure, and select a chairman and chairman pro tempore;

(b) To make and pass resolutions and orders which are necessary for the governance and management of the affairs of the authority, for the execution of the powers vested in the authority, and for carrying out the provisions of this article;

(c) To fix the location of the principal place of business of the authority and the location of all offices maintained under this article;

(d) To prescribe by resolution a system of business administration, to create any and all necessary offices, to establish the powers and duties and compensation of all employees, and to require and fix the amount of all official bonds necessary for the protection of the funds and property of the authority;

(e) To appoint and retain employees, agents, and consultants to make recommendations, coordinate authority activities, conduct routine business of the authority, and act on behalf of the authority under such conditions and restrictions as shall be fixed by the board;

(f) To prescribe a method of auditing and allowing or rejecting claims and demands and a method for the letting of contracts on a fair and competitive basis for the construction of works, structures, or equipment or for the performance or furnishing of such labor, materials, or supplies as may be required for the carrying out of any of the purposes of this article.

## 25-8.5-111. Powers of authority - general and financial.

(1) In order to accomplish its purposes, the authority has the power to:

(a) Develop and implement, with such revisions as become necessary in light of changing conditions, plans for water quality controls for the reservoir, applicable drainage basin, waters, and watershed, to achieve and maintain the water quality standards. In particular, the authority shall submit, within two years after August 8, 2001, a plan to the water quality control commission that is intended to meet state water quality standards, including measures to mitigate the impacts of nonpoint source pollutants.

(b) Conduct pilot studies and other studies that may be appropriate for the development of potential water quality control solutions;

(c) Develop and implement programs to provide credits, incentives, and rewards within the Cherry Creek basin plan for water quality control projects;

(d) Recommend the maximum loads of pollutants allowable to maintain the water quality standards;

(e) Recommend erosion controls and urban runoff control standards and conduct educational programs regarding such controls in the basin;

(f) Recommend septic system maintenance programs;

(g) Incur debts, liabilities, and obligations;

(h) Have perpetual existence;

(i) Have and use a corporate seal;

(j) Sue and be a party to suits, actions, and proceedings;

(k) Enter into contracts and agreements affecting the affairs of the authority including, but not limited to, contracts with the United States and the state of Colorado and any of their agencies or instrumentalities, political subdivisions of the state of Colorado, corporations, and individuals;

(l) Acquire, hold, lease (as lessor or lessee) , and otherwise dispose of and encumber real and personal property;

(m) Acquire, lease, rent, manage, operate, construct, and maintain water quality control facilities or improvements for drainage, nonpoint sources, or runoff within or without the authority;

(n) Establish rates, tolls, fees, charges, and penalties except on agricultural land for the functions, services, facilities, and programs of the authority; except that the total annual revenue collected from said rates, tolls, fees, and charges, less the cost of said functions, services, facilities, and programs, shall not exceed thirty percent of the annual authority budget;

(o) Establish in cooperation with the department of natural resources fees for Cherry Creek reservoir users, which amounts shall be subject to the review and approval of the board of parks and outdoor recreation, which shall not unreasonably withhold approval. Said reservoir fees, including all users regardless of activity, however established, shall not in total exceed the amount that would be collected if the reservoir user fee was one dollar per reservoir user per year.

(p) (I) Levy and collect ad valorem taxes on and against all taxable property within the authority subject to the limitation that no mill levy for any fiscal year shall exceed one-half mill; however, ad valorem taxes greater than one-half mill can be levied by the authority if it is approved by the electors at an election held according to the procedures of part 8 of article 1 of title 32, C.R.S.

(II) No property tax shall be levied until the fees from the recreation users and the development fees are established.

(q) Issue and refund revenue and assessment bonds and pledge the revenues of the authority or assessments therefor to the payment thereof in the manner provided in part 4 of article 35 of title 31, C.R.S., and as provided in this article;

(r) Invest any moneys of the authority in securities meeting the investment requirements established in part 6 of article 75 of title 24, C.R.S.;

(s) Review and approve water quality control projects of any entity other than the authority within the boundaries of the authority;

(t) Except that the authority shall not have the power to regulate agricultural nonpoint source activities; such agricultural nonpoint source activities shall be subject only to the provisions of section 25-8-205 (5) ;

(u) Have and exercise all rights and powers necessary or incidental to or implied from the specific powers granted to the authority by this article. Such specific powers shall not be considered as a limitation upon any power necessary or appropriate to carry out the purposes and intent of this article.

(2) Nothing in subsection (1) of this section shall be construed as authorizing the authority to take any action or spend any moneys in a manner that is inconsistent with its statutory purpose to protect and preserve the water quality of Cherry Creek reservoir. Consistent therewith, the authority shall expend funds only pertaining to the water quality standards, control regulations, or similar regulations regarding the water quality of Cherry Creek and Cherry Creek reservoir if such expenditures are clearly consistent with improving, protecting, and preserving such water quality. The authority shall focus its efforts on improving, protecting, and preserving the water quality of Cherry Creek and Cherry Creek reservoir, and on achieving and maintaining the existing water quality standards.

(3) Of the revenues collected by the authority under paragraphs (n) , (o) , and (p) of subsection (1) of this section, a minimum of sixty percent on an annual basis shall be spent on construction and maintenance of pollution abatement projects in the Cherry Creek basin or on payments due under loans or other debt incurred and spent by the authority entirely upon such projects.

## 25-8.5-112. Power to issue bonds.

To carry out the purposes of this article, the board is authorized to issue revenue or assessment bonds of the authority. Bonds shall bear interest at a rate such that the net effective interest rate of the issue of bonds does not exceed the maximum interest rate set forth in the resolution adopted by the board authorizing the issuance of the bonds, payable semiannually, and shall be due and payable serially, either annually or semiannually, commencing not later than three years after date of issuance. The form and terms of said bonds, including provisions for their payment and redemption, shall be determined by the board. If the board so determines, such bonds may be redeemable prior to maturity upon payment of a premium not exceeding three percent of the principal thereof. Said bonds shall be executed in the name and on behalf of the authority, signed by the chairman of the board with the seal of the authority affixed thereto, and attested by the secretary of the board. Said bonds shall be in such denominations as the board shall determine, and the bonds and coupons shall bear the original or facsimile signature of the chairman of the board.

## 25-8.5-113. Revenue refunding bonds.

Any revenue bonds issued by the authority may be refunded by the authority, or by any successor thereof, in the name of the authority, subject to the provisions concerning their payment and to any other contractual limitations in the proceedings authorizing their issuance or otherwise appertaining thereto, by the issuance of bonds to refund, pay, and discharge all or any part of such outstanding bonds, including any interest on the bonds in arrears or about to become due, for the purpose of avoiding or terminating any default in the payment of the interest on and principal of the bonds, of reducing interest costs or effecting other economies, or of modifying or eliminating restrictive contractual limitations appertaining to the issuance of additional bonds or to any system appertaining thereto or for any combination of such purposes. Refunding bonds may be delivered in exchange for the outstanding bonds refunded or may be sold as provided in this article for an original issue of bonds.

## 25-8.5-114. Use of proceeds of revenue refunding bonds.

The proceeds of revenue refunding bonds shall either be immediately applied to the retirement of the bonds being refunded or be placed in escrow in any state or national bank within the state which is a member of the federal deposit insurance corporation to be applied to the payment of the bonds being refunded upon their presentation therefor; but, to the extent any incidental expenses have been capitalized, such refunding bond proceeds may be used to defray such expenses, and any accrued interest and any premium appertaining to a sale of refunding bonds may be applied to the payment of the interest thereon or the principal thereof, or both interest and principal, or may be deposited in a reserve therefor, as the board may determine. Any such escrow shall not necessarily be limited to proceeds of refunding bonds but may include other moneys available for its purpose. Any proceeds in escrow, pending such use, may be invested or reinvested in securities meeting the investment requirements established in part 6 of article 75 of title 24, C.R.S. Such proceeds and investments in escrow, together with any interest to be derived from any such investment, shall be in an amount at all times sufficient as to principal, interest, any prior redemption premium due, and any charges of the escrow agent payable therefrom to pay the bonds being refunded as they become due at their respective maturities or due at any designated prior redemption dates in connection with which the board shall exercise a prior redemption option. Any purchase of any refunding bond issued under this article shall in no manner be responsible for the application of the proceeds thereof by the authority or any of its officers, agents, or employees.

### 25-8.5-115. Facilities - comprehensive program.

(1) The authority, acting by and through the board, may acquire, construct, lease, rent, improve, equip, relocate, maintain, and operate water quality control facilities, any project, or any part thereof for the benefit of the authority and the inhabitants thereof, after the board has made such preliminary studies and otherwise taken such action as it determines to be necessary or desirable.
(2) (a) The authority shall develop a comprehensive program for the water quality control facilities specified in subsection (1) of this section. A comprehensive program may consist of one project or more than one project.
(b) A hearing on the proposed comprehensive program shall be scheduled, and notice of the hearing shall be given by publication and posted in the office of the county clerk and recorder of each member county. Upon closure of the hearing, the board may either require changes to be made in the comprehensive program or the board may approve or reject the comprehensive program as prepared.
(c) If any substantial changes to the comprehensive program are ordered at any time, a further hearing shall be held pursuant to notice which shall be given by publication.

### 25-8.5-116. Coordination with drainage and flood control measures.

(1) Any exercise by the authority of the powers granted by section 25-8.5-111 or 25-8.5-115 which affects drainage and flood control shall be consistent with and conform to the drainage and flood control program of the urban drainage and flood control district adopted pursuant to section 32-11-214, C.R.S., the resolutions, rules, regulations, and orders of the district issued pursuant to section 32-11-218 (1) (e) , C.R.S., and any flood plain zoning resolutions, rules, regulations, and orders of any public body having jurisdiction to adopt the same.
(2) Construction by the authority of drainage or water quality control facilities which might or will affect drainage or flood control within the boundaries of the urban drainage and flood control district shall not be undertaken until a proposal therefor has been presented to and approved by the board of directors of said district. Such proposal shall demonstrate compliance with the requirements of subsection (1) of this section, and the board shall apply the same standards of flood control and drainage criteria for approval thereof as it applies for review of proposals presented for approval pursuant to section 32-11-221, C.R.S. The provisions of section 32-11-221, C.R.S., shall apply to the presentation, consideration, and determination by said board of directors of any such proposal or modification thereof.

### 25-8.5-117. Transfer of powers.

(1) Upon the adoption of the board of directors of the urban drainage and flood control district and the board of directors of the authority created herein of a joint resolution delegating the agreed-

upon responsibility to the urban drainage and flood control district for carrying out and meeting, within the district's boundaries, the compliance requirements and the permitting requirements imposed with respect to storm water runoff quality by the federal "Water Quality Act of 1987" and any regulations and standards adopted pursuant thereto or pursuant to state law, all powers contained in this act to deal with water quality control and compliance relating to the agreed-upon aspects of storm water runoff and nonpoint sources of pollution, including financial powers and special assessment powers but not including ad valorem taxation powers, shall be transferred to the urban drainage and flood control district.

(2) Upon the transfer of powers as provided in subsection (1) of this section, any allocation of waste loads affecting storm water runoff or nonpoint sources of pollution proposed or adopted by the authority shall be effective only upon adoption thereof or concurrence therewith by the board of directors of the urban drainage and flood control district.

(3) If the urban drainage and flood control district accepts the responsibility and the transfer of powers as provided in subsection (1) of this section, after completion of a plan for water quality controls by the authority which involves storm drainage runoff or nonpoint sources and after commencement of implementation of such plan, the district shall be bound to carry out the plan as it relates to the storm water and nonpoint source powers transferred to it within the time requirements, if any, of the plan.

## 25-8.5-118. Power to levy special assessments.

(1) The board, in the name of the authority, for the purpose of defraying all the cost of acquiring or constructing, or both, any project or facility authorized by this article, or any portion of the cost thereof not to be defrayed with moneys available therefor from its own funds, any special funds, or otherwise, also has the power under this article:

(a) To levy assessments against all or portions of the property within the authority and to provide for collection of the assessments pursuant to part 6 of article 20 of title 30, C.R.S.;

(b) To pledge the proceeds of any assessments levied under this article to the payment of assessment bonds and to create liens on such proceeds to secure such payments;

(c) To issue assessment bonds payable from the assessments, which assessment bonds shall constitute special obligations of the authority and shall not be a debt of the authority; and

(d) To make all contracts, to execute all instruments, and to do all things necessary or convenient in the exercise of the powers granted in this article or in the performance of the authority's duties or in order to secure the payment of its assessment bonds.

(2) The authority shall give notice, by publication once in a newspaper of general circulation in the authority, to the owners of the property to be assessed, which shall include:

(a) The kind of improvements proposed;

(b) The number of installments and the time in which the cost of the project will be payable;

(c) A description of the properties which will be assessed;

(d) The probable cost per acre or other unit basis which, in the judgment of the authority, reflects the benefits which accrue to the properties to be assessed; except that no benefit shall accrue to agricultural lands;

(e) The time, not less than thirty days after the publication, when a resolution authorizing the improvements will be considered;

(f) A map of the properties to be assessed, together with an estimate and schedule showing the approximate amounts to be assessed, and a statement that all resolutions and proceedings are on file and may be seen and examined by any interested person at the office of the authority or other designated place at any time within said period of thirty days; and

(g) A statement that all complaints and objections by the owners of property to be assessed in writing concerning the proposed improvements will be heard and determined by the authority before final action thereon.

(3) The finding, by resolution, of the board that said improvements were ordered after notice given and after hearing held and that such proposal was properly initiated by the said authority shall be

conclusive of the facts so stated in every court or other tribunal.

(4) Any resolution or order regarding the assessments or improvements may be modified, confirmed, or rescinded at any time prior to the passage of the resolution authorizing the improvements.

## 25-8.5-119. Inclusion of property.

(1) Any municipality, county, or special district, or any portion thereof, shall be eligible for inclusion upon resolution of its governing body requesting inclusion in the authority and describing the property to be included. The authority, by resolution, may include such property on such terms and conditions as may be determined appropriate by the board.

(2) Upon receipt of a resolution requesting inclusion, the board shall cause an investigation to be made within a reasonable time to determine whether or not the municipality, county, or special district, or portion thereof, may feasibly be included within the authority, whether the municipality, county, or special district has any property which is tributary to the basin, waters, or watersheds governed by the authority, and the terms and conditions upon which the municipality, county, or special district may be included within the authority. If it is determined that it is feasible to include the municipality, county, or special district, or portion thereof, in the authority, and the municipality, county, or special district has property tributary to the basin, waters, or watersheds governed by the authority, the board by resolution shall set the terms and conditions upon which the municipality, county, or special district, or portion thereof, may be included within the authority and shall give notice thereof to the municipality, county, or special district. If the board determines that the municipality, county, or special district, or portion thereof, cannot feasibly be included within the authority or otherwise determines that the municipality, county, or special district should not be included within the authority, the board shall pass a resolution so stating and notifying the municipality, county, or special district of the action of the board. The board's determination that the county, municipality, or special district, or portion thereof, should not be included in the authority shall be conclusive.

(3) (a) If the governing body of the municipality, county, or special district desires to include the municipality, county, or special district, or portion thereof, within the authority upon the terms and conditions set forth by the board, the governing body shall adopt a resolution declaring that the public health, safety, and general welfare requires the inclusion of said municipality, county, or special district within the authority and that the governing body desires to have said municipality, county, or special district, or portion thereof, included therein upon the terms and conditions prescribed by the board. The governing body of such municipality, county, or special district, before final adoption of said resolution, shall hold a public hearing thereon, notice of which shall be given by publication in a newspaper of general circulation within such municipality, county, or special district, which shall be complete at least ten days before the hearing. Upon the final adoption of said resolution, the clerk of the governing body of such municipality, county, or special district shall forthwith transmit a certified copy of the resolution to the board and to the division of local government in the department of local affairs.

(b) After receipt of a copy of such resolution, the board shall pass and adopt a resolution including said municipality, county, or special district, or portion thereof, in the authority and shall cause a certified copy thereof to be transmitted to the division of local government and a certified copy to the governing body of the municipality, county, or special district.

(4) The director of said division, upon receipt of a certified copy of the resolution of the board, shall forthwith issue a certificate reciting that the municipality, county, or special district, or portion thereof, described in such resolution has been duly included within the authority according to the laws of the state of Colorado. The inclusion of such territory shall be deemed effective upon the date of the issuance of such certificate, and the validity of such inclusion shall not be contestable in any suit or proceeding which has not been commenced within thirty days from such date. The said division shall forthwith transmit to the governing body of such municipality, county, or special district and to the board five copies of such certificate, and the clerk of such

governing body shall forthwith record a copy of the certificate in the office of the clerk and recorder of each county in which such municipality, county, or special district, or portion thereof, is located and file a copy thereof with the county assessor of each such county. Additional copies of said certificate shall be issued by the division of local government upon request.

## 25-8.5-120. Exclusion of property.

(1) Any owner of property within the boundaries of the authority may petition to be excluded from the authority.

(2) In order for such property to be excluded, the board must determine that the property does not receive wastewater treatment services or have an on-site wastewater treatment system located within the authority and either:

(a) Was improperly included within the authority; or

(b) Is not tributary to the basin, waters, or watersheds governed by the authority or will not benefit from projects or improvements provided by the authority.

(3) Any petition for exclusion shall specify the property to be excluded and evidence that the property complies with the criteria of subsection (2) of this section.

(4) The authority shall provide notice of the date, time, and place of the authority's meeting to consider the petition for exclusion.

(5) The authority may approve, modify, or deny a petition for exclusion.

(6) If the authority approves a petition for exclusion of property, the authority shall file a copy of said resolution with the division of local government and with the county, municipality, or special district authority members which includes within its boundaries the excluded property, record a copy of the resolution in the office of the county clerk and recorder in the county in which said excluded property is located, and file a copy with the county assessor in such county.

# ARTICLE 9. WATER AND WASTEWATER TREATMENT FACILITY OPERATORS

## 25-9-101. Legislative declaration.

To assure adequate operation of water and wastewater facilities, and to preserve the public peace, health, and safety, this article 9 and any rules authorized pursuant thereto are enacted to provide for the examination, classification, and certification of water and wastewater facility operators and to establish minimum standards therefor based upon their knowledge and experience, to provide procedures for certification, to encourage career and technical education for such operators, to provide a penalty for the wrongful use of the title "certified operator", to require each water and wastewater facility to be under the supervision of a certified operator, to provide for the classification of all water and wastewater facilities in the state, and to provide a penalty for the operation of a water or wastewater facility without supervision of a certified operator.

## 25-9-102. Definitions.

As used in this article, unless the context otherwise requires:

(1) "Board" means the water and wastewater facility operators certification board.

(2) "Certificate" means the certificate of competency issued by the board stating that the operator named thereon has met the requirements for the specified operator classification of the certification program.

(3) "Certified operator" means the person who has responsibility for the operation of any water and wastewater facility covered under this article and is certified in accordance with the provisions of this article.

(4) "Department" means the Colorado department of public health and environment.

(4.3) "Division" means the water quality control division within the department of public health and environment.

(4.5) "Domestic wastewater treatment facility" means any facility or group of units used for the treatment of domestic wastewater or for the reduction and handling of solids and gases removed from such wastes, whether or not the facility or group of units is discharging into state waters. "Domestic wastewater treatment facility" specifically excludes on-site wastewater treatment systems.

(4.7) "Industrial wastewater treatment facility" means any facility or group of units used for the pretreatment, treatment, or handling of industrial waters, wastewater, reuse water, and wastes that are discharged into state waters. "Industrial wastewater treatment facility" includes facilities that clean up contaminated groundwater or spills; except that such term does not include facilities designed to operate for less than one year or facilities with in-situ discharge.

(4.8) "Small system" means a water or wastewater facility that serves a population of three thousand three hundred or less.

(4.9) "Wastewater collection system" means a system of pipes, conduits, and associated appurtenances that transports domestic wastewater from the point of entry to a domestic wastewater treatment facility. The term does not include collection systems that are within the property of the owner of the facility.

(5) "Wastewater treatment facility" means either a domestic wastewater treatment facility or an industrial wastewater treatment facility.

(5.3) "Water and wastewater facility" means a water treatment facility, wastewater treatment facility, water distribution system, or wastewater collection system.

(6) "Water distribution system" means any combination of pipes, tanks, pumps, or other facilities that delivers water from a source or treatment facility to the consumer.

(7) "Water treatment facility" means the facility or facilities within the water distribution system that can alter the physical, chemical, or bacteriological quality of the water.

## 25-9-103. Water and wastewater facility operators certification board - composition - repeal of article.

(1) There is hereby created the water and wastewater facility operators certification board, which constitutes a section of the division of administration of the department and consists of the following ten members:

(a) A certified water treatment or domestic wastewater treatment facility operator with the highest level of certification available in Colorado;

(b) A certified industrial wastewater treatment facility operator or other representative of a private entity that operates an industrial wastewater treatment facility;

(c) A city manager, manager of a special district, or utility manager in a city, county, or city and county that operates a domestic water or wastewater treatment facility;

(d) A representative of the department of public health and environment, who shall be an ex officio, nonvoting member;

(e) A certified water distribution or wastewater collection system operator with the highest level of certification available in Colorado;

(f) A representative of water or wastewater facilities serving rural areas; and

(g) Four members appointed to achieve geographical representation and to reflect the various interests in the water and wastewater facility certification program. At least one of such members shall reside west of the continental divide, and at least one shall reside in the rural portion of the eastern plains of Colorado.

(2) All members of the board shall be appointed by the governor. At least four of the voting members of the board shall be certified water or wastewater facility operators, including representatives of both the water and wastewater industries.

(3) (a) Except as otherwise provided in paragraph (b) of this subsection (3) , appointments are for terms of four years.

(b) The board shall be reconstituted as of July 1, 2004. The governor shall make initial appointments or reappointments to the reconstituted board so that two voting members' terms expire in 2005, two voting members' terms expire in 2006, two voting members' terms expire in 2007, and three voting members' terms expire in 2008.

(4) This article is repealed, effective September 1, 2020. Prior to the repeal, the water and wastewater facility operators certification board shall be reviewed as provided for in section 24-34-104, C.R.S.

## 25-9-104. Duties of board - rules.

(1) (a) The board shall elect a chair and secretary each year and shall establish rules in accordance with article 4 of title 24, C.R.S., setting forth the requirements governing certification for water and wastewater facility operators, including:

(I) Application for certification;

(II) Admission to the examinations;

(III) Setting and coordination of examination schedules;

(IV) Recording and issuing of certificates for the class of operator for which the applicant is found to be qualified;

(V) Renewal of certificates;

(VI) Issuance of certificates based on reciprocity;

(VII) Minimum standards of operator performance; and

(VIII) Standards for the accreditation of training programs.

(b) (Deleted by amendment, L. 2013.)

(2) (a) The board may promote and assist in regular training schools and programs designed to aid applicants and other interested persons to acquire the necessary knowledge to meet the certification requirements of this article.

(b) The board shall ensure that an office is maintained for contact with operators and employers.

(c) The board shall ensure, through the use of subject matter experts, that all certification examinations test for information that is relevant to the knowledge that is necessary to operate the level of facility for which certification is sought.

(3) (a) The board shall establish classes of:

(I) Water treatment facility operators;

(II) Domestic wastewater treatment facility operators;

(III) Industrial wastewater treatment facility operators;

(IV) Water distribution system operators;

(V) Wastewater collection system operators;

(VI) Operators for small systems; and

(VII) Other persons who require and qualify for multiple certifications.

(b) In establishing each classification, the board shall differentiate the various levels of complexity to be encountered in water and wastewater facility operation and the qualifications for certification for each class. The board shall set minimum education, experience, examination, and ongoing training requirements for each class.

(4) Except as provided in section 25-9-104.4, the board shall establish for each water and wastewater facility a minimum class of certified operators required for its supervision.

(5) (a) The board shall establish a procedure whereby any decision of the board, the division, or nonprofit corporation contracting with the board can be appealed to the board.

(b) The board may adopt rules as necessary to ensure the proper administration of the program.

(c) The board may promulgate rules to allow the division to immediately suspend or revoke a certification if immediate action is necessary to protect the public health or environment.

(6) The board may exercise other powers and duties as necessary within the scope of this article. The board shall promulgate rules to establish criteria for the discipline or reprimand of any water or wastewater facility operator and for the suspension or revocation of the certification of an operator. The criteria must include:

(a) Willfully or negligently violating, causing, or allowing the violation of rules promulgated under this article or failing to comply with this article;

(b) Submitting false or misleading information on any document provided to the department, the board, or any organization acting on behalf of the board;

(c) Using fraud or deception in the course of employment as an operator;

(d) Failing to conform with minimum standards in the performance of an operator's duties; and

(e) Engaging in dishonest conduct during an examination.

(6.5) (Deleted by amendment, L. 2013.)

(7) Members of the board serve without compensation but are entitled to reimbursement for their necessary expenses.

(8) The board may exercise its powers and perform its duties and functions as if it were transferred to the department by a type 1 transfer under the "Administrative Organization Act of 1968", article 1 of title 24, C.R.S.

## 25-9-104.2. Contracting - rules.

(1) The board may select and appoint one or more independent nonprofit corporations to carry out the administration of the program and examinations. The board may promulgate a rule establishing the scope and standards of the independent nonprofit corporation's duties. The contract must specifically address each duty or function required by law.

(2) To qualify for consideration to administer the duties of this section, a nonprofit corporation must have expertise in training and testing procedures as well as demonstrated knowledge of water and wastewater treatment, collection, and distribution systems.

(3) With the prior approval of the board for each agreement, a nonprofit corporation contracted by the board may enter into subsidiary agreements with other nonprofit corporations, educational institutions, and for-profit corporations to carry out the duties assigned by the board.

(4) The board is responsible for and retains the final authority for all actions and decisions carried out on behalf of the board by a nonprofit corporation, educational institution, or for-profit corporation. The board may modify, suspend, or reverse any action or decision of any nonprofit corporation, educational institution, or for-profit corporation.

## 25-9-104.3. Duties of the division - investigations.

The division shall investigate instances of possible misconduct by water and wastewater facility operators, report the results of any investigation to the board, and make recommendations regarding appropriate disciplinary action to the board.

## 25-9-104.4. Exemptions.

(1) The board may exempt wastewater facilities or classes of facilities from the requirement to operate under the supervision of a certified operator if the exemption does not endanger the public health or the environment. In determining whether to provide such an exemption, the board may consider the following criteria:

(a) Discharges of limited duration;

(b) The sensitivity of the receiving waters;

(c) The level of toxic pollutants in the discharge; and

(d) Situations where chemical, mechanical, or biological treatment techniques are not required to meet permit limits, including sedimentation ponds at mining operations for construction materials, as defined by section 34-32.5-103 (3) , C.R.S.

(2) The board may exempt water facilities or classes of facilities from the requirement to operate under the supervision of a certified operator if the exemption does not endanger public health or the environment. In determining whether to provide such an exemption, the board may consider:

(a) The classification of the facility as public or nonpublic under the Colorado primary drinking water regulation;

(b) The applicability of the Colorado primary drinking water regulation to the facility or class of facilities; and

(c) A distribution system having a minimal number of connections.

## 25-9-105. Water treatment facility operator.

(1) Persons who by specifically relevant examination, education, and experience are found to be qualified for certification as water treatment facility operators or water distribution system operators shall be certified as having the minimum qualifications required for each of the respective classes as established by the board by rules promulgated in accordance with article 4 of title 24, C.R.S.

(a) to (d) (Deleted by amendment, L. 2000, p. 771, § 5, effective May 23, 2000.)

## 25-9-106. Domestic wastewater treatment facility operator.

(1) Persons who by specifically relevant examination, education, and experience are found to be qualified for certification as domestic wastewater treatment facility operators or wastewater collection system operators shall be certified as having the minimum qualifications required for each of the respective classes as established by the board by rules promulgated in accordance with article 4 of title 24, C.R.S.

(a) to (d) (Deleted by amendment, L. 2000, p. 772, § 6, effective May 23, 2000.)

## 25-9-106.2. Industrial wastewater treatment facility operator.

(1) Persons who by specifically relevant examination, education, and experience are found to be qualified for certification as industrial wastewater treatment facility operators shall be certified as having the minimum qualifications required for each of the respective classes as established by the board by rules promulgated in accordance with article 4 of title 24, C.R.S.

(a) to (c) (Deleted by amendment, L. 2000, p. 773, § 7, effective May 23, 2000.)

## 25-9-106.3. Multiple facility operator.

Persons who by specifically related examination, education, and experience are found to be qualified for certification in more than one category of facility operators shall be certified as having the minimum qualifications required for such applicable multiple facility operator classes as the board may establish by rules promulgated in accordance with article 4 of title 24, C.R.S. Such classes of multiple facility operators shall be designed to minimize the number of separate examinations and separate operator certifications that must be held by persons working for small systems, persons in the private sector performing work for a municipality or industry, and other categories and classes where a multiple facility operator certification would be efficient and meet the goals of this article. Such multiple facility certifications may contain conditions established by the board restricting the certification to specific facilities, types of facilities, or activities.

## 25-9-106.5. Education and experience - substitution allowed.

Water and wastewater facility operator applicants must have a high school diploma or have successfully completed the high school equivalency examination, as defined in section 22-33-102 (8.5) , C.R.S.; except that experience or relevant training may be substituted for the high school diploma or successful completion of the high school equivalency examination. Education, training as established under section 25-9-104 (2) , and cross-experience may be substituted for experience requirements for certification as a water facility operator, as a water distribution system operator, as a domestic wastewater facility operator, as a wastewater collection system operator, as an industrial wastewater treatment facility operator, or as a multiple facility operator; except that at least fifty percent of any experience requirement must be met by actual on-site operating experience in a water facility or a wastewater facility, as the case may be. For the lowest classification of operator in each category, the board may establish rules allowing complete substitution of education for experience for any applicant who passes the applicable examination. For purposes of this section, "cross-experience" means that experience as a wastewater treatment facility operator may be substituted for experience requirements for certification as a water treatment facility operator and vice versa.

## 25-9-107. Certification procedure.

(1) Any individual possessing the required education and experience may apply for certification in the manner designated by the board on such forms as required and approved by the board. The application shall be accompanied by such fee as required by section 25-9-108. Those applicants who meet the minimum qualifications as established by rules of the board promulgated in accordance with article 4 of title 24, C.R.S., for certification shall be admitted for examination.

(2) When an individual desires certification in a field other than the field in which the individual has experience, the individual's experience shall be evaluated by the board or as directed by the board. The certificate issued is to be based upon the knowledge demonstrated by the applicant through examination and the individual's verified record of work experience in water and wastewater facility operation.

(3) Certificates shall be awarded by the board or at the direction of the board for a period of three years only to those applicants successfully meeting all of the requirements.

(4) (a) Certificates shall be renewed upon payment of the required renewal fee and a showing that the applicant for renewal has met the requirements established by the board for ongoing training.

(b) If any operator fails to renew the operator's certification before the expiration date of such certification, such certification is expired. If a certification expires because of failure to renew before the expiration date of such certification, the operator may renew the certification up to two years after the expiration date upon paying the required renewal fee and meeting the applicable ongoing training requirements for the certification being renewed. If an operator does not renew a certification within two years after the expiration date of such certification, the certification is automatically revoked and an applicant for recertification must meet all the requirements for certification as a new applicant.

(4.5) (Deleted by amendment, L. 96, p. 360, 8, effective July 1, 1996.)

(5) The board, upon application therefor, may issue a certificate, without examination, in a comparable classification to any person who holds a certificate in any state, territory, or possession of the United States or any country, providing the requirements for certification of operators under which the person's certificate was issued do not conflict with the provisions of this article and are of a standard not lower than that specified by regulations adopted under this article. Where there is a question as to the level of certification that should be granted, the board may authorize special examination or other procedures to confirm the appropriate certification level.

(6) to (8) (Deleted by amendment, L. 96, p. 360, § 8, effective July 1, 1996.)

## 25-9-108. Fees.

(1) Each application for certification shall be accompanied by a fee in the amount of fifteen dollars that is not refundable. The board shall adopt rules that set program fees in addition to the nonrefundable application fee in accordance with the provisions of article 4 of title 24, C.R.S., and such fees shall reflect the actual costs of administering the program as set forth in section 25-9-104 (1) . Such fees may be collected and retained by a nonprofit corporation selected and appointed by the board pursuant to section 25-9-104 (1) to pay for its actual costs to administer the program as approved by the board through duly adopted rules. However, any such nonprofit corporation shall remit a portion of the fee in the amount of five dollars for each new and renewal certificate to be issued to the department of the treasury pursuant to the provisions of section 24-36-103, C.R.S. With the approval of the board, all moneys may be paid to the nonprofit corporation and except for the five dollars for new and renewal certifications may be retained by the nonprofit corporation to defray program expenses. Alternatively, if certification and renewal fees are received directly by the board, all moneys shall be deposited with the department of the treasury pursuant to the provisions of section 24-36-103, C.R.S.

(2) Notwithstanding the amount specified for any fee in subsection (1) of this section, the board by

rule or as otherwise provided by law may reduce the amount of one or more of the fees if necessary pursuant to section 24-75-402 (3) , C.R.S., to reduce the uncommitted reserves of the fund to which all or any portion of one or more of the fees is credited. After the uncommitted reserves of the fund are sufficiently reduced, the board by rule or as otherwise provided by law may increase the amount of one or more of the fees as provided in section 24-75-402 (4) , C.R.S.

## 25-9-109. Use of title.

Only a person who has been qualified by the board as a certified operator and who possesses a valid certificate attesting to this certification in this state shall have the right and privilege of using the title "certified water treatment facility operator, class....", "certified domestic wastewater treatment facility operator, class....", "certified industrial wastewater treatment facility operator, class....", "certified wastewater collection system operator, class....", "certified water distribution system operator, class....", or "multiple facilities operator, class....".

## 25-9-110. Violations - penalty.

(1) It is unlawful for any person to represent himself or herself as a certified operator of any category and of any class without first being so certified by the board and without being the holder of a current valid certificate issued by the board. Any person violating the provisions of this subsection (1) is guilty of a misdemeanor and, upon conviction thereof, shall be punished by a fine of not more than three thousand dollars.

(2) (a) It is unlawful for any owner of a water treatment facility, a domestic or industrial wastewater treatment facility, a wastewater collection system, or a water distribution system in the state of Colorado to allow the facility to be operated without the supervision of a certified operator of the classification required by the board for the specific facility.

(b) Notwithstanding paragraph (a) of this subsection (2) , a sedimentary pond maintained in accordance with a permit issued by the division of reclamation, mining, and safety that does not require a permit issued by the water quality control division of the department of public health and environment shall not require the supervision of a certified operator.

(3) Whenever the division has reason to believe that a violation of subsection (2) of this section has occurred, the division shall cause written notice to be served personally or by certified mail, return receipt requested, upon the alleged violator or their agent for service of process. The notice shall state the provision of subsection (2) alleged to be violated and the facts alleged to constitute a violation and it may include specific action proposed to be required to cease the alleged violation. The division shall require the alleged violator to answer each alleged violation.

(4) Upon being served with any notice given under subsection (3) of this section, the alleged violator may request a public hearing. Such request shall be filed in writing with the division no later than thirty days after service of the notice. If such a request is made, a hearing shall be held within a reasonable time. Hearings held pursuant to this subsection (4) shall be conducted before the board in accordance with section 24-4-105, C.R.S. The determination of the board following a hearing shall be considered final agency action as to whether a violation has occurred.

(5) Any owner of a water treatment facility, a domestic or industrial wastewater treatment facility, a wastewater collection system, or a water distribution system in the state of Colorado who violates subsection (2) of this section shall be subject to a civil penalty of not more than three hundred dollars per day for each day during which such violation occurs. Any civil penalty collected under this section shall be credited to the general fund.

(6) Upon application of the division, any penalty for a violation of subsection (2) of this section shall be determined by the executive director of the department or his or her designee and may be collected by the division through a collection action instituted in a court of competent jurisdiction. The final decision of the executive director or his or her designee may be appealed to the board. A stay of any order of the division pending judicial review shall not relieve any person from any liability under this section, but the reason for the request for judicial review shall be considered in the determination of the amount of the penalty. In the event that such an action is instituted for the

collection of such penalty, the court may consider the appropriateness of the amount of the penalty if the party against whom the penalty was assessed raises the issue.

# ARTICLE 10. ON-SITE WASTEWATER TREATMENT SYSTEMS ACT

## 25-10-101. Short title.
This article shall be known and may be cited as the "On-site Wastewater Treatment Systems Act".

## 25-10-102. Legislative declaration.
(1) The general assembly declares it to be in the public interest to establish minimum standards and rules for on-site wastewater treatment systems in the state and to provide the authority for the administration and enforcement of those minimum standards and rules:
(a) To preserve the environment and protect the public health and water quality;
(b) To eliminate and control causes of disease, infection, and aerosol contamination; and
(c) To reduce and control the pollution of the air, land, and water.

## 25-10-103. Definitions.
As used in this article, unless the context otherwise requires: (1) "Absorption system" means a leaching field and adjacent soils or other system for the treatment of sewage in an on-site wastewater treatment system by means of absorption into the ground.
(2) "Applicant" means a person who submits an application for a permit for an on-site wastewater treatment system.
(3) "Cesspool" means an unlined or partially lined underground pit or underground perforated receptacle into which raw household wastewater is discharged and from which the liquid seeps into the surrounding soil. "Cesspool" does not include a septic tank.
(4) "Commission" means the water quality control commission created by section 25-8-201.
(5) "Department" means the department of public health and environment created by section 25-1-102.
(6) "Division" means the division of administration of the department.
(7) "Effluent" means the liquid flowing out of a component or device of an on-site wastewater treatment system.
(8) "Environmental health specialist" means a person trained in physical, biological, or sanitary science to carry out educational and inspectional duties in the field of environmental health.
(9) "Health officer" means the chief administrative and executive officer of a local public health agency, or the appointed health officer of the local board of health. "Health officer" includes a director of a local public health agency.
(10) "Local board of health" means any local, county, or district board of health.
(11) "Local public health agency" means any county, district, or municipal public health agency and may include a county, district, or municipal board of health or local agency delegated by a county, district, or municipal board of health to oversee OWTS permitting and inspection or an OWTS program.
(12) "On-site wastewater treatment system" or "OWTS" and, where the context so indicates, the term "system", means an absorption system of any size or flow or a system or facility for treating, neutralizing, stabilizing, or dispersing sewage generated in the vicinity, which system is not a part of or connected to a sewage treatment works.
(13) "Percolation test" means a subsurface soil test at the depth of a proposed absorption system or similar component of an on-site wastewater treatment system to determine the water absorption capability of the soil, the results of which are normally expressed as the rate at which one inch of

water is absorbed.

(14) "Permit" means a permit for the construction or alteration, installation, and use or for the repair of an on-site wastewater treatment system.

(15) "Person" means an individual, partnership, firm, corporation, association, or other legal entity and also the state, any political subdivision thereof, or other governmental entity.

(16) "Professional engineer" means an engineer licensed in accordance with part 1 of article 25 of title 12, C.R.S.

(17) "Septage" means a liquid or semisolid that includes normal household wastes, human excreta, and animal or vegetable matter in suspension or solution generated from a residential septic tank system. "Septage" may include such material issued from a commercial establishment if the commercial establishment can demonstrate to the department that the material meets the definition for septage set forth in this subsection (17) . "Septage" does not include chemical toilet residuals.

(18) "Septic tank" means a watertight, accessible, covered receptacle designed and constructed to receive sewage from a building sewer, settle solids from the liquid, digest organic matter, store digested solids through a period of retention, and allow the clarified liquids to discharge to other treatment units for final disposal.

(19) "Sewage" means a combination of liquid wastes that may include chemicals, house wastes, human excreta, animal or vegetable matter in suspension or solution, and other solids in suspension or solution, and that is discharged from a dwelling, building, or other establishment.

(20) "Sewage treatment works" has the same meaning as "domestic wastewater treatment works" under section 25-8-103.

(21) "Soil evaluation" means a percolation test, soil profile, or other subsurface soil analysis at the depth of a proposed soil treatment area or similar component or system to determine the water absorption capability of the soil, the results of which are normally expressed as the rate at which one inch of water is absorbed or as an application rate of gallons per square foot per day.

(22) "Soil treatment area" means the physical location where final treatment and dispersal of effluent occurs. "Soil treatment area" includes drainfields and drip fields.

(23) "State waters" has the meaning set forth under section 25-8-103.

(24) "Systems cleaner" means a person engaged in and who holds himself or herself out as a specialist in the cleaning and pumping of on-site wastewater treatment systems and removal of the residues deposited in the operation thereof.

(25) "Systems contractor" means a person engaged in and who holds himself or herself out as a specialist in the installation, renovation, and repair of on-site wastewater treatment systems.

## 25-10-104. Regulation of on-site wastewater treatment systems - state and local rules.

(1) The division shall develop, and recommend to the commission for adoption, rules setting forth minimum standards for the location, design, construction, performance, installation, alteration, and use of on-site wastewater treatment systems within Colorado. The commission may establish criteria for issuing variances in the rules.

(2) Every local board of health in the state shall develop and adopt detailed rules for on-site wastewater treatment systems within its area of jurisdiction. The rules must comply with the rules adopted by the commission pursuant to subsection (1) of this section and with sections 25-10-105 and 25-10-106. Before finally adopting such rules or any amendment to the rules, the local board of health shall hold a public hearing on the proposed rules or amendments. The local board of health shall give notice of the time and place of the hearing at least once, at least twenty days before the hearing, in a newspaper of general circulation within its area of jurisdiction. After the public hearing and before final adoption, the local board of health may make changes or revisions to the proposed rules or amendments, and no further public hearing is required regarding the changes or revisions. All rules and amendments must be transmitted to the department no later than five days after final adoption and become effective forty-five days after final adoption unless the department notifies the local board of health before the forty-fifth day that the rules or

amendments are not in compliance with this section or section 25-10-105 or 25-10-106.

(3) If a local board of health has not adopted rules in compliance with this section and submitted them to the commission, the commission shall promulgate rules for the areas of the state for which no complying rules have been adopted, except for areas serviced exclusively by a sewage treatment works. Rules for such areas of the state promulgated by the commission must comply with the rules adopted under subsection (1) of this section and sections 25-10-105 and 25-10-106. The rules must be the same for all the areas of the state for which the commission promulgates such rules, except as may be appropriate to provide for differing geologic conditions.

(4) A local board of health may adopt rules after action by the commission under subsection (3) of this section, if the rules comply with the procedural requirements of subsection (2) of this section and are no less stringent than those promulgated by the commission. Rules of the local board so adopted become effective only after they are transmitted to the division and the division determines that they comply with this section and sections 25-10-105 and 25-10-106.

(5) In promulgating rules under this article, the commission and local boards of health shall give consideration to the protection of public health and water quality.

## 25-10-105. Minimum standards - variances.

(1) Rules adopted by local boards of health under section 25-10-104 (2) or (4) or promulgated by the commission under section 25-10-104 (1) govern all aspects of the location, design, construction, performance, alteration, installation, and use of on-site wastewater treatment systems and must include minimum standards established by the commission.

(2) (a) A local board of health may grant variances to OWTS rules in accordance with the criteria adopted by the commission under this article.

(b) Applicants for a variance from OWTS rules have the burden of supplying the local board of health with information demonstrating that conditions exist that warrant the granting of the variance.

## 25-10-106. Basic rules for local administration.

(1) Local boards of health or the commission, as appropriate, shall adopt rules under section 25-10-104 that govern all aspects of the application for and issuance of permits, the inspection and supervision of installed systems, the issuance of cease-and-desist orders, the maintenance and cleaning of systems, and the disposal of waste material. The rules must, at a minimum, include provisions regarding:

(a) Procedures by which a person may apply for a permit for an on-site wastewater treatment system. The permit application must be in writing and must include any information, data, plans, specifications, statements, and commitments as required by the local board of health to carry out the purposes of this article.

(b) Review of the application and inspection of the proposed site by the local public health agency;

(c) Specification of studies to be performed and reports to be made by the applicant and the circumstances under which the studies or reports may be required by the local public health agency;

(d) Determination on behalf of the local public health agency by an environmental health specialist or a professional engineer after review of the application, site inspection, test results, and other required information, whether the proposed system complies with the requirements of this article and the rules adopted under this article;

(e) Issuance of a permit by the health officer or the health officer's designated representative if the proposed system is determined to be in compliance with this article and the rules adopted under this article;

(f) Review by the local board of health, upon request of an applicant, of applications denied by the local public health agency;

(g) The circumstances under which all applications are subject to mandatory review by the local public health agency to determine whether a permit shall issue;

(h) Final inspection of a system to be made by the local public health agency or its designated professional engineer after construction, installation, alteration, or repair work under a permit has been completed, but before the system is placed in use, to determine that the work has been performed in accordance with the permit and that the system is in compliance with this article and the rules adopted under this article;

(i) Inspection of operating systems at reasonable times, and upon reasonable notice to the occupant of the property, to determine if the system is functioning in compliance with this article and the rules adopted under this article. Officials of the local public health agency are permitted to enter upon private property for purposes of conducting such inspections.

(j) Issuance of a repair permit to the owner or occupant of property on which a system is not in compliance. An owner or occupant shall apply to the local public health agency for a repair permit within two business days after receiving notice from the local public health agency that the system is not functioning in compliance with this article or the rules adopted under this article or otherwise constitutes a nuisance or hazard to public health or water quality. The permit shall provide for a reasonable period of time within which the owner or occupant must make repairs, at the end of which period the local public health agency shall inspect the system to ensure that it is functioning properly. Concurrently with the issuance of a repair permit, the local public health agency may authorize the continued use of a malfunctioning system on an emergency basis for a period not to exceed the period stated in the repair permit. The period of emergency use may be extended, for good cause shown, if, through no fault of the owner or occupant, repairs may not be completed in the period stated in the repair permit and only if the owner or occupant will continue to make repairs to the system.

(k) (I) Issuance of an order to cease and desist from the use of any on-site wastewater treatment system or sewage treatment works that is found by the health officer not to be in compliance with this article or the rules adopted under this article or that otherwise constitutes a nuisance or a hazard to public health or water quality. Such an order may be issued only after a hearing is conducted by the health officer not less than forty-eight hours after written notice of the hearing is given to the owner or occupant of the property on which the system is located and at which the owner or occupant may be present, with counsel, and be heard. The order must require that the owner or occupant bring the system into compliance or eliminate the nuisance or hazard within a reasonable period of time, not to exceed thirty days, or thereafter cease and desist from the use of the system. A cease-and-desist order issued by the health officer is reviewable in the district court for the county in which the system is located and upon a petition filed no later than ten days after the order is issued.

(II) For the purposes of this paragraph (k) , any system or sewage treatment works that does not comply with any statute or rule of this title constitutes a nuisance.

(III) For the purposes of this paragraph (k) , a sewage treatment works does not include any sewage treatment facility with a discharge permit issued pursuant to section 25-8-501.

(l) Reasonable periodic collection and testing by the local public health agency of effluent samples from on-site wastewater treatment systems for which monitoring of effluent is necessary in order to ensure compliance with this article or the rules adopted under this article. The sampling may be required not more than two times a year, except when required by the health officer in conjunction with action taken pursuant to paragraph (k) of this subsection (1) . The local public health agency may charge a fee not to exceed actual costs, plus locally established mileage reimbursement rates for each mile traveled from the principal office of the local public health agency to the site of the system and return, for each sample collected and tested, and payment of such charges may be stated in the permit for the system as a condition for its continued use. Any owner or occupant of property on which an on-site wastewater treatment system is located may request the local public health agency to collect and test an effluent sample from the system. The local public health agency may, at its option, perform such collection and testing services, and is entitled to charge a fee not to exceed actual costs, plus locally established mileage reimbursement rates for each mile traveled from the principal office of the local public health agency to the site of the system and return, for each sample collected and tested.

(m) At the option of the local board of health, maintenance and cleaning schedules and practices adequate to ensure proper functioning of various types of on-site wastewater treatment systems. The local board of health may additionally require proof of proper maintenance and cleaning, in compliance with the schedule and practices adopted under this subsection (1), to be submitted periodically to the local public health agency by the owner of the system.

(n) Disposal of septage at a site and in a manner that does not create a hazard to the public health, a nuisance, or an undue risk of pollution.

## 25-10-107. Fees.

(1) A local board of health may set fees for permits. The permit fees may be no greater than required to offset the actual indirect and direct costs of the local public health agency's services. With respect to any permit, the local board of health shall set the fee for the permit so as to recover, as nearly as can be practically established, the costs associated with that permit, not to exceed one thousand dollars. A local board of health may also set fees for soil evaluation and other services as requested by the applicant. Such fees may be no greater than required to offset the actual indirect and direct costs of such services.

(2) Local boards of health may set fees for percolation tests and other soil evaluation services that are performed by the local public health agency. The fees may be no greater than required to offset the actual indirect and direct costs of such services.

(3) In addition to the fees established in this section, the division may assess a fee of twenty-three dollars for each permit authorized for a new, repaired, or upgraded on-site wastewater treatment system. Of that fee, the county in which the on-site wastewater treatment system is or will be located shall retain three dollars to cover the county's administrative costs and shall transmit twenty dollars to the state treasurer, who shall deposit that sum in the public and private utilities sector fund created in section 25-8-502 (1.5) (a) (V).

## 25-10-108. Performance evaluation and approval of systems employing new technology.

(1) A systems contractor, a professional engineer, or a manufacturer of on-site wastewater treatment systems that employ new technology may apply to the division for a determination of reliability of the system. The division may hold a public hearing to determine whether the particular design or type of system, based upon improvements or developments in the technology of sewage treatment, has established a record of performance reliability that would justify approval of applications for such systems by the health officer without mandatory review by the local board of health. If the division determines, based upon reasonable performance standards and criteria, that reliability has been established, the division shall so notify each local board of health, and applications for permits for the systems may thereafter be acted upon by the health officer, the health officer's designated representative, or the local board of health's designated representative, in the same manner as applications for systems described in section 25-10-106. The division shall not arbitrarily deny any person the right to a hearing on an application for a determination of reliability under this section.

(2) Except for designs or types of systems that have been approved by the division pursuant to subsection (1) of this section, the local public health agency may approve an application for a type of system not otherwise provided for in section 25-10-106, only if the system has been designed by a professional engineer and only if the application provides for the installation of a backup system, of a type previously approved by the division under subsection (1) of this section, in the event of failure of the primary system. A local public health agency shall not arbitrarily deny any person the right to consideration of an application for such a system and shall apply reasonable performance standards in determining whether to approve an application.

## 25-10-109. Licensing of systems contractors and systems cleaners.

(1) The local board of health may adopt rules that provide for the licensing of systems contractors.

The local public health agency may charge a fee, not to exceed actual costs, for the initial license of a systems contractor and for a renewal of the license. Initial licensing and renewals thereof shall be for a period of not less than one year. The local board of health may revoke the license of a systems contractor for violation of this article or the rules adopted under this article or for other good cause shown, after a hearing conducted upon reasonable notice to the systems contractor and at which the systems contractor may be present, with counsel, and be heard.

(2) The local board of health may adopt rules that provide for the licensing of systems cleaners, pursuant to section 25-10-104 (2) . The local public health agency may charge a fee, not to exceed actual costs, for the initial license of a systems cleaner and for the renewal of the license. Initial licensing and renewals thereof shall be for a period of not less than one year. The local board of health may suspend or revoke the license of a systems cleaner for violation of this article or the rules adopted under this article or for other good cause shown after a hearing conducted upon reasonable notice to the systems cleaner and at which the systems cleaner may be present, with counsel, and be heard.

## 25-10-110. Enforcement by local public health agencies and local boards of health.

The primary responsibility for the enforcement of this article and the rules adopted under this article lies with local public health agencies and local boards of health. If a local public health agency or local board of health substantially fails to administer and enforce this article and the rules adopted under this article, the department may assume any functions of the local public health agency or board of health as may be necessary to protect the public health and water quality.

## 25-10-111. Authority of local boards of health to deny permits for on-site wastewater treatment systems in unsuitable areas.

Nothing in this article preempts or affects the ability of a local board of health to prohibit issuance of OWTS permits, in accordance with applicable land use laws and procedures, for defined areas in which the local board of health determines that construction and use of additional on-site wastewater treatment systems may constitute a hazard to public health or water quality.

## 25-10-112. General prohibitions - rules.

(1) No city, county, or city and county shall issue to any person:

(a) A permit to construct or remodel a building or structure that is not serviced by a sewage treatment works until the local public health agency has issued a permit for an on-site wastewater treatment system; or

(b) A city, county, or city and county occupancy permit for the use of a building that is not serviced by a sewage treatment works until the local public health agency makes a final inspection of the on-site wastewater treatment system, as provided for in section 25-10-106 (1) (h) , and the local public health agency approves the installation.

(2) Construction of new cesspools is prohibited.

(3) A person shall not connect more than one dwelling, commercial, business, institutional, or industrial unit to the same on-site wastewater treatment system unless such multiple connection was specified in the application submitted and in the permit issued for the system.

(4) No person shall construct or maintain any dwelling or other occupied structure that is not equipped with adequate facilities for the sanitary disposal of sewage.

(5) All persons shall dispose of septage removed from systems in the process of maintenance or cleaning at an approved site and in an approved manner under this article.

## 25-10-113. Penalties.

(1) Any person who commits any of the following acts or violates this article commits a class 1

petty offense and shall be punished as provided in section 18-1.3-503, C.R.S.:

(a) Constructs, alters, installs, or permits the use of any on-site wastewater treatment system without first applying for and receiving a permit as required under this article;

(b) Constructs, alters, or installs an on-site wastewater treatment system in a manner that involves a knowing and material variation from the terms or specifications contained in the application, permit, or variance;

(c) Violates the terms of a cease-and-desist order that has become final under section 25-10-106 (1) (k) ;

(d) Conducts a business as a systems contractor without having obtained the license provided for in section 25-10-109 (1) in areas in which the local board of health has adopted licensing regulations pursuant to that section;

(e) Conducts a business as a systems cleaner without having obtained the license provided for in section 25-10-109 (2) in areas in which the local board of health has adopted licensing regulations pursuant to that section;

(f) Falsifies or maintains improper record keeping concerning system cleaning activities not performed or performed improperly; or

(g) Willfully fails to submit proof of proper maintenance and cleaning of a system as required by rules adopted pursuant to section 25-10-106.

(2) Upon a finding by the local board of health that a person is in violation of this article or of rules adopted and promulgated pursuant to this article, the local board of health may assess a penalty of up to fifty dollars for each day of violation. In determining the amount of the penalty to be assessed, the local board of health shall consider the seriousness of the danger to the health of the public caused by the violation, the duration of the violation, and whether the person has previously been determined to have committed a similar violation.

(3) A person subject to a penalty assessed pursuant to subsection (2) of this section may appeal the penalty to the local board of health by requesting a hearing before the appropriate body. The request must be filed within thirty days after the penalty assessment is issued. The local board of health shall conduct a hearing upon the request in accordance with section 24-4-105, C.R.S.

# ARTICLE 11. RADIATION CONTROL

# PART 1. GENERAL PROVISIONS

### 25-11-101. Definitions.

As used in this part 1, unless the context otherwise requires:

(1) "Byproduct material" means:

(a) Any radioactive material, except special nuclear material, yielded in, or made radioactive by, exposure to the radiation incident to the process of producing or using special nuclear material;

(b) The tailings or wastes produced by the extraction or concentration of uranium or thorium from ore processed primarily for its source material content, including discrete surface wastes resulting from uranium solution extraction processes. Underground ore bodies depleted by these solution extraction operations are not "byproduct material".

(c) (I) Any discrete source of radium-226 that is produced, extracted, or converted after extraction, before, on, or after August 8, 2005, for use for a commercial, medical, or research activity; or

(II) Any material that:

(A) Has been made radioactive by use of a particle accelerator; and

(B) Is produced, extracted, or converted after extraction, before, on, or after August 8, 2005, for use for a commercial, medical, or research activity; and

(d) Any discrete source of naturally occurring radioactive material, other than source material, that:

(I) The United States nuclear regulatory commission, in consultation with the administrator of the environmental protection agency, the secretary of energy, the secretary of homeland security, and the head of any other appropriate federal agency, determines would pose a threat similar to the threat posed by a discrete source of radium-226 to the public health and safety or the common defense and security; and

(II) Before, on, or after August 8, 2005, is extracted or converted after extraction for use in a commercial, medical, or research activity.

(1.5) "Civil penalty" means a monetary penalty levied against a licensee or registrant because of a violation of a statute, rule, license, or registration certificate. "Civil penalty" does not include any criminal penalty levied under section 25-1-114 or 25-11-107 (3) .

(2) "Department" means the department of public health and environment.

(2.5) "Mammographer" means a person who operates a machine source of radiation, commonly known as an "X-ray machine", in the conduct of a mammography exam.

(2.7) "Naturally occurring radioactive material" means any nuclide that is radioactive in its natural physical state and is not manufactured. "Naturally occurring radioactive material" does not include source material, special nuclear material, byproduct material, or by-products of fossil fuel combustion, including bottom ash, fly ash, and flue-gas emission by-products.

(3) "Radiation" means ionizing radiation, which includes gamma rays, X rays, alpha particles, beta particles, high-speed electrons, high-speed neutrons, high-speed protons, and other high-speed nuclear particles.

(4) "Radiation machine" means a device capable of producing radiation; except that "radiation machine" does not include a device with radioactive material as its only source of radiation.

(5) "Radioactive" means emitting radiation.

(6) "Radioactive material" means any material, whether solid, liquid, or gas, that emits radiation spontaneously.

(6.4) (a) "Source material" means uranium, thorium, or any combination of uranium and thorium in any physical or chemical form, including ores that contain, by weight, one-twentieth of one percent or more of uranium, thorium, or any combination of uranium and thorium.

(b) "Source material" does not include special nuclear material.

(6.7) (a) "Special nuclear material" means:

(I) Plutonium, uranium-233, uranium enriched in the isotope 233 or in the isotope 235, and any other material that the United States nuclear regulatory commission, pursuant to section 51 of the federal "Atomic Energy Act of 1954", as amended, 42 U.S.C. sec. 2071, determines to be special nuclear material; or

(II) Any material artificially enriched by any of the material specified in subparagraph (I) of this paragraph (a) .

(b) Notwithstanding any other provision of this subsection (6.7) , "special nuclear material" does not include source material.

(7) "Specific license" means a license issued to a person to use, manufacture, produce, transfer, receive, acquire, own, or possess quantities of, or devices or equipment utilizing, radioactive materials occurring naturally or produced artificially.

(8) "State board" means the state board of health created in section 25-1-103.

## 25-11-101.5. Coordination of regulatory interpretations regarding in situ leach uranium mining.

The general assembly recognizes that the proper and orderly regulation of in situ leach mining, as defined in section 34-32-103, C.R.S., for uranium ore has aspects that may involve more than one regulatory agency of state government and that the statutes that each agency is responsible for administering may, due to the use of terms of art and other technical words, phrases, and definitions, hold the potential of being interpreted inconsistently or to be held in conflict with each other. It is the intent of the general assembly that, with regard to in situ leach mining for uranium ore, the relevant agencies coordinate to the maximum extent practicable to resolve any such conflicts or inconsistencies.

## 25-11-102. Agreements for transfer of functions from federal government to state government.

(1) The governor, on behalf of this state, is authorized, from time to time, to enter into agreements with the federal government providing for the assumption by this state through the department, and the discontinuance by the federal government, of any responsibilities within the state of Colorado relating to the protection of persons and property from the hazards of radioactive materials and other sources of radiation.

(2) The governor, on behalf of this state, is authorized, from time to time, to enter into agreements with the federal government, other states, or interstate agencies whereby the department shall perform, on a cooperative basis with the federal government, other states, or interstate agencies, inspections or other functions relating to control of sources of radiation.

(3) No such agreement entered into pursuant to the provisions of subsections (1) or (2) of this section shall transfer to, delegate to, or impose upon the department any power, authority, or responsibility that is not fully consistent with the provisions of this article.

## 25-11-103. Radiation control agency - powers and duties.

(1) The department is designated as the radiation control agency of this state.

(2) Pursuant to rules adopted as provided in section 25-11-104, the department shall issue licenses pertaining to radioactive materials, prescribe and collect fees for such licenses, and require registration of other sources of radiation. No other agency or branch of this state has such power or authority.

(3) The department shall develop and conduct programs for evaluation and control of hazards associated with the use of radioactive materials and other sources of radiation, including criteria for disposal of radioactive wastes and materials to be considered in approving facilities and sites pursuant to part 2 of this article.

(4) The department may institute training programs for the purpose of qualifying personnel to carry out the provisions of this part 1 and may make said personnel available for participation in any program of the federal government, other states, or interstate agencies in furtherance of the purposes of this part 1.

(5) In the event of an emergency relating to any source of radiation that endangers the public peace, health, or safety, the department has the authority to issue such orders for the protection of the public health and safety as may be appropriate, including orders to lay an embargo upon or impound radioactive materials and other sources of radiation in the possession of any person who is not equipped to observe or who fails to comply with this part 1 or any rules promulgated under this part 1.

(6) The department or its duly authorized representatives has the power to enter at all reasonable times, in accordance with applicable state or federal regulations, into the areas in which sources of radiation are reasonably believed to be located for the purpose of determining whether or not the owner, occupant, or licensee is in compliance with or in violation of this part 1 and the rules promulgated under this part 1, and the owner, occupant, or person in charge of such property shall permit such entry and inspection.

(7) (a) In order to provide for the concentration, storage, or permanent disposal of radioactive materials consistent with adequate protection of the public health and safety, the state, through the department, may acquire by gift, transfer from another state department or agency, or other transfer any and all lands, buildings, and grounds suitable for such purposes. Any such acquisition shall be subject to the provisions of paragraph (h) of this subsection (7) .

(b) The state, through the department, may, by lease or license with private persons or corporations, provide for the operation of sites or facilities, for the purposes stated in paragraph (a) of this subsection (7) , in, under, and upon lands and grounds acquired under said paragraph (a) in accordance with rules and regulations established by the department; but no lease or license shall be authorized except with the prior approval of the state engineer. The department may permit the conduct thereon of other related activities involving radioactive materials not contrary to the public interest, health, and safety. Each such lease or license shall cover only one site or facility and shall provide for a term up to ninety-nine years, which shall be renewable. Each such lease or license shall provide for the payment to the state of a fee based upon the quantity of radioactive material stored in the lands covered thereby. Such fee shall be established at such rate that interest on the sum of all fees reasonably anticipated as payable under any lease or license shall provide an annual amount equal to the anticipated reasonable costs to the state of such maintenance, monitoring, and other supervision of the lands and facilities covered by such lease or license, following the term thereof, as are required in the interest of the public health and safety. In arriving at the rate of the fee, the department shall consider the nature of the material to be stored, the storage space available, estimated future receipts, and estimated future expenses of maintenance, monitoring, and supervision.

(c) Said lease shall include a payment in lieu of taxes which shall be paid over to local governmental units in compensation for loss of valuation for assessment. Said payment shall be adjusted annually to conform with current mill levies, assessment practices, and value of land and improvements.

(d) All fees provided in this section shall be paid quarterly, as accrued, to the department, which shall receipt for the same and shall transmit such payment to the state treasurer and take his receipt therefor.

(e) The department may require, as a condition to the issuance of any lease or license under paragraph (b) of this subsection (7) , that the lessee or licensee give reasonable security for the payment of the amount of all fees reasonably anticipated during the full term of such lease or license, and the department may also require, as a condition to the issuance of any lease or license, that the lessee or licensee post a bond or other security under such regulation as the department may prescribe to cover any tortious act committed during the term of the lease or license.

(f) Prior to the issuance of any lease or license under paragraph (b) of this subsection (7) , the department, at the expense of the applicant, shall hold a public hearing on the application, in the area of the proposed site or facility, after reasonable public notice.

(g) The operation of any and all sites and appurtenant facilities established for the purposes of paragraph (a) of this subsection (7) shall be under the direct supervision of the department and shall be in accordance with rules and regulations adopted under section 25-11-104.

(h) It is recognized by the general assembly that any site used for the concentration, disposal, or storage of radioactive material and the contents thereof will represent a continuing and perpetual responsibility involving the public health, safety, and general welfare and that ownership of said site and its contents must ultimately be reposed in a solvent government, without regard for the existence of any particular agency, instrumentality, department, division, or officer thereof. To this end and subject only to the terms of any lease or license issued under paragraph (b) of this subsection (7) , all lands, buildings, and grounds acquired by the state under paragraph (a) of this subsection (7) which are used as sites for the concentration, storage, or disposal of radioactive materials shall be owned in fee simple absolute by the state and dedicated in perpetuity to such purposes, and all radioactive material received at such facility, upon permanent storage therein, shall become the property of the state and shall be in all respects administered, controlled, and disposed of, including transfer by sale, lease, loan, or otherwise, by the state, through the department, unless the general assembly shall designate another agency, instrumentality, department, or division of the state so to act.

(8) The state board of health shall prescribe, revise periodically as appropriate, and provide for the collection of fees from any person for radiation control services provided by the department.

## 25-11-104. Rules to be adopted - fees - fund created.

(1) (a) The state board shall formulate, adopt, and promulgate rules as provided in subsection (2) of this section that cover subject matter relative to radiation machines and radioactive materials, including naturally occurring radioactive materials and other sources of radiation. The subject matter of the rules must include: Licenses and registration; records; permissible levels of exposure; notification and reports of accidents; technical qualifications of personnel; technical qualifications of mammographers; handling, transportation, and storage; waste disposal; posting and labeling of hazardous sources and areas; surveys; monitoring; security of materials; and financial assurance warranties.

(b) The state board may adopt rules concerning the disposal of naturally occurring radioactive materials at any time after the promulgation by the federal environmental protection agency or its successor of rules for the disposal of naturally occurring radioactive materials.

(c) Notwithstanding any provision of section 25-11-103 (7) (h) , it is not necessary that a governmental entity own any site that is used for the concentration, storage, or disposal of radioactive material if the owner of the site complies with rules promulgated by the board in accordance with this section. The rules must ensure the long-term protection of the public health and safety and may include financial assurance warranties pursuant to this part 1, deed annotations and restrictions, easement provisions, restrictive covenants, and adequate markers to warn of the presence of radioactive materials.

(2) Rules promulgated under this section must be consistent with United States nuclear regulatory commission requirements necessary to maintain agreement state status and final regulations proposed by the Conference of Radiation Control Program Directors, Inc., or its successor, under the title, "Suggested State Regulations for Control of Radiation"; except that, if the state board concludes on the basis of detailed findings that a substantial deviation from any of the suggested state regulations is warranted and that a substitute rule or no rule would effectively permit maximum utilization of sources of radiation consistent with the health and safety of all persons who might otherwise become exposed to the radiation, the state board need not maintain the suggested state regulation or may promulgate a substitute rule as the case may be.

(2.5) (Deleted by amendment, L. 2010, (HB 10-1149) , ch. 282, p. 1311, § 4, effective May 26, 2010.)

(3) The rules adopted pursuant to this part 1 shall never be construed to limit the kind or amount of radiation that may be intentionally applied to a person for diagnostic or therapeutic purposes by or under the direction of a duly licensed practitioner of the healing arts.

(4) (Deleted by amendment, L. 2010, (HB 10-1149) , ch. 282, p. 1311, § 4, effective May 26, 2010.)

(5) In adopting, amending, or repealing rules under this section, the board shall comply with article 4 of title 24, C.R.S.

(6) (a) The state board shall promulgate a fee schedule, in accordance with section 24-4-103, C.R.S., for radiation control services provided by the department. Radiation control services for which fees may be established include application processing for qualified inspectors, qualified experts, and service companies as defined by the state board, which fees shall be paid by the applicants or service companies; issuance of categories of specific licenses to accord with categories established by the nuclear regulatory commission and which shall include licenses for special nuclear material, source material, byproduct material, well logging and surveys and tracer studies, and for human use; and inspections of licensees as authorized by section 25-11-103 (6) . Licenses and fees shall, where appropriate, be in accordance with policies and priorities of the nuclear regulatory commission.

(b) The state board shall set fees that provide sufficient revenues to reimburse the state for the actual direct and indirect costs of the radiation control services specified in paragraph (a) of this subsection (6) . In so doing, the state board shall take into account any special arrangements between the state and the licensee, another state, or a federal agency whereby the cost of the service is otherwise recovered.

(c) All fees collected pursuant to this subsection (6) shall be transmitted to the state treasurer, who shall credit the same to the radiation control fund, which fund is hereby created. Moneys credited to the radiation control fund, in amounts determined annually by the general assembly by appropriation, shall be expended for radiation control services as provided in this subsection (6) .

(7) The state board shall promulgate rules as necessary to implement section 25-11-107 (5) .

(8) (a) The state board shall adopt rules requiring that all machine sources of radiation be inspected and certified by qualified inspectors as safe for the intended uses consistent with 42 U.S.C. sec. 263b and in compliance with the specifications of the state board and the equipment manufacturer. Rules shall include minimum specifications for radiation machines, minimum standards for the qualifications of individuals authorized to inspect and certify radiation machines, and procedures for inspection of radiation machines. If a qualified inspector determines that a radiation machine fails to meet the required specifications, the inspector shall notify the owner or operator immediately and shall notify the department within three days after the determination. A radiation machine that fails to meet the required specifications and is determined by a qualified inspector to be unsafe for human use shall not thereafter be used for human use until subsequent certification, and the qualified inspector shall affix an official noncertification sticker issued by the department indicating that the machine is not authorized for human use. A certification or noncertification sticker shall be affixed on each radiation machine in a location conspicuous to machine operators and to persons on whom the machine is used.

(a.5) and (b) (Deleted by amendment, L. 2010, (HB 10-1149) , ch. 282, p. 1311, § 4, effective May 26, 2010.)

(c) In establishing or revising specifications for each type of machine that is a source of radiation, the standards for approval of qualified inspectors, and the procedures for making inspections, the department shall consult with manufacturers of radiation equipment, health care providers and operators who use the equipment in diagnostic and therapeutic treatment of humans, and qualified inspectors and individuals.

(d) The general assembly hereby finds that the setting of minimum specifications for radiation machines and the establishment of minimum standards for qualified inspectors of those machines are matters of statewide concern. Therefore, no other state agency, political subdivision, or local government shall establish any other specifications for radiation machines or standards for radiation machine inspectors, or impose any fees therefor.

## 25-11-105. Radiation advisory committee.

(1) The governor shall appoint a radiation advisory committee of nine members, no more than four of whom shall represent any one political party and three of whom shall represent industry, three the healing arts, and three the public and private institutions of higher education. Members of the committee shall serve at the discretion of the governor and shall be reimbursed for necessary and actual expenses incurred in attendance at meetings or for authorized business of the board. The committee shall furnish to the department such technical advice as may be desirable or required on matters relating to the radiation control program.

(2) Repealed.

## 25-11-105.5. Mammography quality assurance advisory committee - repeal. (Repealed)


## 25-11-106. Injunction proceedings.

If, in the judgment of the department, any person has engaged in or is about to engage in an act or practice that constitutes a violation of this part 1 or of any license, registration, rule, or order issued under this part 1, the attorney general shall, at the request of the department, apply to the district court for an order enjoining the act or practice or for an order directing compliance with this part 1 and all rules and orders and the terms and conditions of a license or registration issued under this part 1.

## 25-11-107. Prohibited acts - violations - penalties - rules - cease-and-desist orders.

(1) Except as allowed by rule of the state board:

(a) No person shall acquire, own, possess, or use any radioactive material occurring naturally or produced artificially without having been granted a license therefor from the department; or

(b) Transfer to another or dispose of such material without first having been granted approval of the department therefor.

(2) Except as allowed by rule of the state board, no person shall knowingly use, manufacture, produce, transport, transfer, receive, send, acquire, own, or possess any source of radiation unless such person is licensed by or registered with the department. The exceptions promulgated by the state board shall include use of domestic television receivers, computer monitors, household microwave ovens, radiant heat devices, cellular telephones, incandescent gas mantles, and vacuum tubes.

(2.5) No person shall knowingly use any radiation machine to treat or diagnose any disease or conditions of the human body if the radiation machine is not certified for such treatment or diagnosis as provided in section 25-11-104 (8) .

(3) Any person who violates the provisions of subsection (1) , (2) , or (2.5) of this section is guilty of a misdemeanor and, upon conviction thereof, shall be punished by a fine of not less than one hundred dollars nor more than five hundred dollars, or by imprisonment in the county jail for not less than thirty days nor more than ninety days, or by both such fine and imprisonment.

(4) If a person does not pay the fee for radiation control services, the department may request the attorney general to commence a civil action against the person. If the court finds in such action that such person has not paid the fee for radiation control services, the court shall require such person to pay the fee together with a penalty not greater than twice the amount of the fee or one thousand dollars, whichever is greater. All civil penalties collected pursuant to this subsection (4) shall be transmitted to the state treasurer, who shall credit them to the general fund.

(5) (a) Any person who violates subsection (1) , (2) , or (2.5) of this section, any licensing or registration provision, any rule or order issued under this part 1, or any term, condition, or limitation of any license or registration certificate issued pursuant to this part 1 is subject to an administrative penalty not to exceed fifteen thousand dollars per day for each violation.

(b) If the department has reason to believe, based upon facts available to it, that a person has committed any of the violations designated in paragraph (a) of this subsection (5) , it shall send the person, within a reasonable time, a written notice of the violation specifying:

(I) The factual basis of each act or omission with which the person is charged; and

(II) The particular provision of the statute, rule, order, license, or registration certificate violated.

(c) (I) The department shall send the notice required by paragraph (b) of this subsection (5) by certified or registered mail, return receipt requested, to the last-known address of the alleged violator, or the department shall personally serve the notice of the violation upon the alleged violator or the alleged violator's agent.

(II) The alleged violator shall have thirty days following the receipt of the notice to submit a written response containing data, views, and arguments concerning the alleged violation and potential corrective measures.

(III) In addition, the alleged violator may request an informal conference with department personnel to discuss the notice of violation required by paragraph (b) of this subsection (5) . The alleged violator shall request the informal conference within fifteen days after receiving the notice, and the conference shall be held within the thirty days allowed for a written response.

(IV) After consideration of any written response and informal conference, the department shall issue a letter, within thirty days after the date of the informal conference or the receipt of a written response, whichever is later, affirming or dismissing the violation. Any remaining corrective measures that are necessary, and any administrative penalty determined to be appropriate, will be incorporated into an administrative order.

(c.3) In determining the amount of any administrative penalty, the department shall consider the factors in subparagraphs (I) to (X) of this paragraph (c.3) . The factors contained in subparagraphs (VII) , (VIII) , and (IX) of this paragraph (c.3) are mitigating factors and may be applied, with other factors, to reduce any administrative penalty. Such factors are:

(I) The seriousness of the violation;

(II) Whether the violation was intentional, reckless, or negligent;

(III) The impact on, or threat to, the public health or the environment as a result of the violation;

(IV) The degree of recalcitrance, if any, on the part of the violator;

(V) Whether the violator is a recidivist;

(VI) The economic benefit realized by the violator as a result of the violation;

(VII) The violator's voluntary, timely, and complete disclosure of the violation, if prior to the department's knowledge of the violation, and if all reports required pursuant to state environmental control laws have been submitted as required;

(VIII) The violator's full and prompt cooperation with the department following disclosure or discovery of a violation, including, when appropriate, entering into and implementing, in good faith, a legally enforceable agreement with the department to undertake compliance and remediation efforts;

(IX) The existence of a comprehensive regulatory compliance program or an audit program that the violator adopted in good faith and in a timely manner, which program includes measures determined by the department to be sufficient to identify and prevent future noncompliance; and

(X) Any other aggravating or mitigating circumstance.

(c.5) In accordance with article 4 of title 24, C.R.S., and based upon the factors enumerated in paragraph (c.3) of this subsection (5) , the state board shall adopt rules for determining administrative penalties imposed under this subsection (5) .

(c.7) The department may compromise, mitigate, or remit an administrative penalty imposed pursuant to this subsection (5) . The department may enter into a settlement agreement regarding any penalty or claim resolved under this part 1. The settlement agreement may include the payment or contribution of moneys to state or local agencies for other environmentally beneficial purposes.

(d) If the circumstances warrant, the department shall issue an order containing the elements of both the notice of violation specified in paragraph (b) of this subsection (5) and the letter described in subparagraph (IV) of paragraph (c) of this subsection (5) .

(e) (I) The letter issued pursuant to subparagraph (IV) of paragraph (c) of this subsection (5) and the order issued pursuant to paragraph (d) of this subsection (5) shall notify the alleged violator of the right to request a hearing within thirty days, which hearing shall be held in accordance with section 24-4-105, C.R.S., to determine any of the following:

(A) Whether the alleged violation exists or did exist;

(B) The reasonableness of the time set for abatement; and

(C) Whether the administrative penalty is reasonable in light of the statutory criteria on which it is based.

(II) The alleged violator shall address each alleged violation in the request for the hearing and shall specify which of the alleged violations the alleged violator is appealing. An allegation not addressed in the request for the hearing shall be deemed admitted.

(III) No person engaged in conducting the hearing or participating in a decision or an initial decision shall be responsible for or subject to the supervision or direction of any department employee engaged in the performance of an investigatory or prosecuting function for the department.

(IV) The final action of the department is subject to judicial review pursuant to section 24-4-106, C.R.S.

(f) and (g) (Deleted by amendment, L. 2010, (HB 10-1149) , ch. 282, p. 1315, § 6, effective May 26, 2010.)

(h) At the request of the department, the attorney general may institute a civil action to collect an administrative penalty imposed pursuant to this subsection (5) .

(i) Except as specified in paragraph (c.3) of this subsection (5) , all administrative penalties collected pursuant to this subsection (5) shall be transmitted to the state treasurer, who shall credit them to the general fund.

(j) For any site or facility licensed under part 2 of this article determined by the department to have caused a release to the groundwater that exceeds the basic standards for groundwater as established by the water quality control commission, until remediation has been completed, the licensee shall provide annual written notice of the status of the release and any remediation activities associated with the release, by certified or registered mail, return receipt requested, to the current address for each registered groundwater well within one mile of the release as identified in the corrective action monitoring program. Under no circumstances shall remediation be deemed complete until all groundwater wells affected by any release associated with the site or facility are restored to at least the numeric groundwater standards as established by the water quality control commission that apply to the historic uses of the wells. Prior to the application of any numeric groundwater standard different from the baseline standard contained in 10 CFR part 40, the standard must have been approved by the United States nuclear regulatory commission in accordance with section 274o of the federal "Atomic Energy Act of 1954", 42 U.S.C. sec. 2021 (o) . The licensee shall remediate any release affecting groundwater wells in the most expedited manner reasonably possible using best available active restoration and groundwater monitoring technologies.

(k) For any site or facility licensed under part 2 of this article, in addition to any reporting requirements provided in the license or rules, the licensee shall provide notice to the department as soon as practicable upon discovery of any spill or release involving toxic or radioactive materials and shall provide an initial written report within seven days after any such discovery. The department shall post all such written reports on the department's website as soon as practicable, and in no case later than seven days after receipt by the department.

(6) Any qualified inspector who incorrectly certifies a machine that is a source of radiation as meeting the applicable specifications as required in section 25-11-104 (8) is subject to disciplinary action in accordance with section 24-4-104, C.R.S.

(7) If the department has reasonable cause to believe that a violation of this part 1 or of a license, registration, rule, or order issued under this part 1 has occurred or is occurring, the department may issue a cease-and-desist order setting forth the provision alleged to be violated, the facts alleged to constitute the violation, and the time by which the violation must cease. Except for emergency orders issued to protect the public health or the environment, for which a person to whom the emergency order has been issued may request an immediate hearing pursuant to section 24-4-105 (12) , C.R.S., a person to whom a cease-and-desist order has been issued may petition the district court for the district in which the violation is alleged to have occurred or be occurring for a stay of the order. The court shall grant the request to stay if the person demonstrates that immediate and irreparable injury will result if the stay is not granted and that granting the stay will not result in serious harm to the public health, safety, or welfare or the environment.

## 25-11-108. Exemptions.

(1) Sections 25-11-103 and 25-11-104 do not apply to the following sources or conditions:

(a) Electrical or other equipment or material that is not intended primarily to produce radiation and that, by nature of design, does not produce radiation at the point of nearest approach at a weekly rate higher than one-tenth the appropriate limit generally accepted by the medical profession for any critical organ exposed. The production testing or production servicing of such equipment shall not be exempt.

(b) Radiation machines during process of manufacture or in storage or transit. The production testing or production servicing of such machines shall not be exempt.

(c) Repealed.

(d) Sound and radio waves and visible infrared and ultraviolet light.

(2) No exemptions under this section are granted for those quantities or types of activities which do not comply with the established rules and regulations promulgated by the atomic energy

commission or any successor thereto.

(3) Section 25-11-107 shall not apply to unmined minerals containing radioactive materials including such as are involved in mining operations.

(4) (Deleted by amendment, L. 2010, (HB 10-1149) , ch. 282, p. 1320, § 7, effective May 26, 2010.)

(5) Any person may file application for exemption under this section for activities including, but not limited to, licensed sources of radiation for educational or noncommercial public displays or scientific collections.

## 25-11-109. Provisional license. (Repealed)

## 25-11-110. Financial assurance warranties - definitions.

(1) As a part of any license, certificate, or authorization issued under this article and pursuant to regulations promulgated by the state board of health, the department may require financial assurance warranties.

(2) As used in this section, unless the context otherwise requires:

(a) "Decommissioning warranty" means a financial assurance arrangement provided by a person licensed, certified, or authorized pursuant to this article that is required to ensure decommissioning and decontamination of a facility and proper disposal of radioactive materials to meet the requirements of this part 1, the regulations promulgated pursuant thereto, or the license.

(b) "Financial assurance warranty" means a decommissioning warranty or a long-term care warranty.

(c) "Indirect costs" means those costs established annually in accordance with federal circular A-87, or any applicable successor document.

(d) "Long-term care warranty" means a financial assurance arrangement provided by a person licensed, certified, or authorized pursuant to this article that is required to cover the costs incurred by the department in conducting surveillance of a disposal site in perpetuity subsequent to the termination of the radioactive materials license for that site.

(3) (a) Financial assurance warranties may be provided by the licensee or by a third party or combination of persons.

(b) Any financial assurance warranty required pursuant to this section shall be in a form prescribed by the state board of health by regulation.

(c) The department may refuse to accept any financial assurance warranty if:

(I) The form, content, or terms of the warranty are other than as prescribed by the state board of health by regulation;

(II) The financial institution providing the financial assurance instrument is an off-shore, nondomestic institution or does not have a registered agent in the state of Colorado;

(III) The value of the financial assurance warranty offered is dependent upon the success, profitability, or continued operation of the licensed business or operation; or

(IV) The department determines that the financial assurance warranty cannot be converted to cash within thirty days after forfeiture.

(4) (a) The department shall determine the amount of financial assurance warranties required, taking into account the nature, extent, and duration of the licensed activities and the magnitude, type, and estimated cost for proper disposal of radioactive materials, decontamination, and decommissioning or long-term care.

(b) The amount of a decommissioning warranty shall be sufficient to enable the department to dispose of radioactive materials and complete decontamination and decommissioning of affected buildings, fixtures, equipment, personal property, and lands if necessary.

(c) The amount of the decommissioning warranty shall be based upon cost estimates of the total costs that would be incurred if an independent contractor were hired to perform the decommissioning, decontamination, and disposal work, and may include reasonable administrative costs, including indirect costs, incurred by the department in conducting or overseeing disposal, decontamination, and decommissioning and to cover the department's reasonable attorney costs that may be incurred in successfully revoking, foreclosing, or realizing the decommissioning warranty as authorized in section 25-11-111 (4) .

(d) The amount of a long-term care warranty must be enough that, with an assumed one percent annual real interest rate, the annual interest earnings will be sufficient to cover the annual costs of site surveillance by the department, including reasonable administrative costs incurred by the department, in perpetuity, subsequent to the termination of the radioactive materials license for that site.

(e) If the state of Colorado is the long-term caretaker for the disposal facility pursuant to section 25-11-103 (7) (h) , long-term care moneys shall be transferred, pursuant to section 25-11-113 (3) , to the long-term care fund, created in section 25-11-113, prior to license termination and shall be used by the department to perform site surveillance and to cover the department's administrative and reasonable attorney costs.

(f) The department is authorized to transfer a long-term care warranty to the United States department of energy or another federal agency if that agency will be the long-term caretaker for the disposal facility.

(5) (a) The department shall take reasonable measures to assure the continued adequacy of any financial assurance warranty and may annually or for good cause increase or decrease the amount of required financial assurance warranties or require proof of the value of existing warranties.

(b) The licensee shall submit an annual report to the department demonstrating proof of the value of existing warranties. The annual report shall describe any changes in operations, estimated costs, or any other circumstances that may affect the amount of the required financial assurance warranties, including any increased or decreased costs attributable to inflation.

(c) Public notice of the submittal of the licensee's annual report shall be posted on the department's website and published by the operator in the local paper of general circulation. Any person may submit written comments to the department concerning the adequacy of any financial assurance warranties. The act of submitting such comments does not provide a right to administrative appeal concerning the financial assurance warranties.

(d) The licensee shall have sixty days after the date of written notification by the department of a required adjustment to establish a warranty fulfilling all new requirements unless granted an extension by the department. If the licensee disputes the amount of the required financial assurance warranties, the licensee may request a hearing to be conducted in accordance with section 24-4-105, C.R.S.

(e) If the licensee requests a hearing, no new ore or other radioactive material may be brought on site for processing or disposal and no new radioactive material may be processed until the licensee's dispute over the financial assurance warranty is resolved, unless the licensee posts a bond in a form approved by the department equal to the amount in dispute.

(6) (a) Financial assurance warranties shall be maintained in good standing until the department has authorized in writing the discontinuance of such warranties.

(b) (I) If a financial warranty is provided by a corporate surety, the department shall require the surety to be A.M. Best rated "A-V" or better and listed on the United States treasury's federal register of companies holding certificates of authority as acceptable sureties on federal bonds; except that, the corporate surety shall notify the department and the licensee, in writing, as soon as practicable in the event its A.M. Best, or equivalent, rating deteriorates below an "A-V" rating or such corporate surety is removed from the department of the treasury's list of companies holding certificates of authority as acceptable sureties on federal bonds.

(II) The board may promulgate rules and regulations concerning other circumstances that may constitute an impairment of the warranties referenced in this article that would require reasonable notice to the department by the warrantor.

(III) A financial warrantor shall notify the department not less than ninety days prior to any cancellation, termination, or revocation of the warranty, unless the department has authorized in writing the discontinuance of such warranties.

## 25-11-111. Forfeiture of decommissioning warranties - use of funds.

(1) A decommissioning warranty shall be subject to immediate forfeiture whenever the department determines that any one of the following circumstances exist:

(a) The licensee has violated an emergency, abatement, or cease-and-desist order or court-ordered injunction or temporary restraining order related to decommissioning, decontamination, or disposal and, if decommissioning, decontamination, or disposal was required in such order, has failed to complete such decommissioning, decontamination, or disposal although reasonable time to have done so has elapsed; or

(b) The licensee is in violation of decommissioning, decontamination, or disposal requirements as specified in the license and the regulations and has failed to cure such violation although the licensee has been given written notice thereof pursuant to section 25-11-107 (5) and has had reasonable time to cure such violation; or

(c) The licensee has failed to provide an acceptable replacement warranty when:

(I) The licensee's financial warrantor no longer has the financial ability to carry out obligations under this article; or

(II) The department has received notice or information that the financial warrantor intends to cancel, terminate, or revoke the warranty; or

(d) The licensee has failed to maintain its financial assurance warranty in good standing as required by section 25-11-110 (6) (a) ; or

(e) An emergency endangering public health or safety has been caused by or resulted from the licensee's use or possession of radioactive materials.

(2) (a) Upon determining that a decommissioning warranty should be forfeited under subsection (1) of this section, the department shall issue to the licensee an order forfeiting the decommissioning warranty. The order shall contain written findings of fact and conclusions of law to support its decision and shall direct affected financial warrantors to deliver to the department the full amounts warranted by applicable decommissioning warranties within not more than thirty days after the date of the order.

(b) The licensee may request a hearing on the order of forfeiture that shall be conducted in accordance with section 24-4-105, C.R.S., and that, if the department alleges in the forfeiture order a violation of a license, regulation, or order, the hearing may be conducted in conjunction with a hearing requested under section 25-11-107 (5) . Any request for a hearing pursuant to this part 1 shall be made within twenty days after the date of the order of forfeiture and shall not affect the obligation to submit to the department funds from decommissioning warranties forfeited by such order unless a stay of forfeiture is granted by the department or by administrative or judicial order.

(3) The department may request the attorney general, and the attorney general is authorized, to commence legal proceedings necessary to secure or recover amounts warranted by decommissioning warranties. The attorney general shall have the power to collect, foreclose upon, present for payment, take possession of, or dispose of pledged property, and otherwise reduce to cash any financial assurance arrangement required by this article.

(4) (a) Decommissioning funds recovered by the department pursuant to this section shall be immediately deposited into the decommissioning fund created in section 25-11-113 and shall be used solely for the disposal of radioactive materials for the facility covered by the forfeited financial assurance warranties; the decommissioning and decontamination of buildings, equipment, personal property, and lands covered by the forfeited financial assurance warranties; and to cover the department's reasonable attorney and administrative costs associated with disposal, decommissioning, and decontamination for such facility.

(b) The department or its agent shall have a right to enter property of the licensee to dispose of radioactive materials, decommission, and decontaminate buildings, equipment, personal property, and lands. Upon completion of disposal, decommissioning, and decontamination activities, the department shall present to the licensee a full accounting and shall refund all unspent decommissioning warranty moneys, including interest.

(5) Licensees shall remain liable for the total actual cost of disposal of, decommissioning, and decontaminating affected buildings, equipment, personal property, and lands, less any amounts expended by the department pursuant to subsection (4) of this section, notwithstanding any discharge of applicable financial assurance warranties.

## 25-11-112. Forfeiture of long-term care warranty - use of funds.

(1) A long-term care warranty shall be subject to immediate forfeiture whenever the department determines that any one of the following circumstances exist:

(a) The licensee is in violation of long-term care requirements as specified in the license and the regulations and has failed to cure such violation although the licensee has been given written notice thereof pursuant to section 25-11-107 (5) and has had reasonable time to cure such violation; or

(b) The licensee has failed to provide an acceptable replacement warranty when:

(I) The licensee's financial warrantor no longer has the financial ability to carry out obligations under this article; or

(II) The department has received notice or information that the financial warrantor intends to cancel, terminate, or revoke the warranty; or

(c) The licensee has failed to maintain its financial assurance warranty in good standing as required by section 25-11-110 (6) (a) .

(2) (a) A long-term care warranty shall be subject to immediate use and expenditure by the department whenever the department determines that disposal, decommissioning, and decontamination requirements specified in the license conditions and regulations have been satisfied. The department shall give the licensee written notice of the department's intent to use the long-term care warranty for long-term care purposes. The notice shall contain findings of fact and conclusions of law to support its decision and shall direct affected financial warrantors to deliver to the department the full amounts warranted by applicable long-term care warranties within not more than thirty days after the date of the notice.

(b) The licensee may request a hearing on a notice under paragraph (a) of this subsection (2) that shall be conducted in accordance with section 24-4-105, C.R.S. Any request for a hearing under this subsection (2) shall be made within thirty days after the date of the notice and shall not affect the obligation to submit to the department funds from long-term care warranties unless a stay is granted by the department or by administrative or judicial order.

(3) The department may request the attorney general, and the attorney general is authorized, to commence legal proceedings necessary to secure or recover amounts warranted by long-term care warranties. The attorney general shall have the power to collect, foreclose upon, present for payment, take possession of, or dispose of pledged property, and otherwise reduce to cash any financial assurance arrangement required by this article.

(4) (a) Long-term care funds recovered by the department pursuant to this section shall be immediately deposited into the long-term care fund created in section 25-11-113 and shall be used solely for the long-term care for the facility covered by the financial assurance warranty and to cover the department's reasonable attorney and administrative costs associated with long-term care for such facility.

(b) The department or its agent shall have a right to enter property of the licensee to perform long-term care and monitoring. Upon completion of long-term care activities, the department shall present to the licensee a full accounting and shall refund all unspent warranty moneys, including interest.

## 25-11-113. Forfeitures - deposit - radiation control - decommissioning fund - long-term care fund.

(1) The department is hereby authorized to collect funds from forfeited decommissioning warranties and from long-term care warranties.

(2) (a) A fund to be known as the decommissioning fund is hereby created in the state treasury.

The fund shall be interest-bearing and invested to return the maximum income feasible as determined by the state treasurer and consistent with otherwise applicable state law. All moneys collected from decommissioning warranties pursuant to this section shall be transmitted to the state treasurer, who shall credit the same to the decommissioning fund. All moneys deposited in the fund and all interest earned on moneys in the fund shall remain in the fund for the purposes set forth in this article, and no part of the fund shall be expended or appropriated for any other purpose.

(b) The moneys in the fund shall be continuously appropriated for the purposes set forth in this part 1 and shall not be transferred to or revert to the general fund.

(3) Moneys in the decommissioning fund shall be available for use by the department for the sole purpose of disposing of radioactive materials and completing decontamination and decommissioning of affected buildings, fixtures, equipment, personal property, and lands, and to cover the department's reasonable attorney costs that may be incurred in successfully revoking, foreclosing, or realizing any decommissioning warranty, and reasonable administrative costs, including indirect costs, incurred by the department in conducting disposal, decontamination, and decommissioning.

(4) (a) A fund to be known as the long-term care fund is hereby created and established in the state treasury. Such fund shall be interest-bearing and invested to return the maximum income feasible as determined by the state treasurer and consistent with otherwise applicable state law. All moneys collected from long-term care warranties pursuant to this section shall be transmitted to the state treasurer who shall credit the same to the long-term care fund. All moneys deposited in the fund and all interest earned on moneys in the fund shall remain in the fund for the purposes set forth in this part 1 and no part thereof shall be expended or appropriated for any other purpose.

(b) Moneys in the long-term care fund shall be annually appropriated by the general assembly to the department in an amount sufficient to implement the provisions of this part 1.

(c) Moneys in the long-term care fund shall be available for use by the department for the sole purposes of:

(I) Performing annual site inspections to confirm the integrity of the stabilized waste system, environmental monitoring, and maintenance of the waste disposal site, including fixtures, cover, and equipment;

(II) Covering the department's reasonable attorney costs that may be incurred in successfully collecting or realizing any long-term care warranty, and reasonable administrative costs, including indirect costs, incurred by the department in conducting long-term care of the disposal facility.

## 25-11-114. Legislative declaration - public education regarding radon gas - assistance to low-income individuals for radon mitigation in their homes.

(1) The general assembly finds, determines, and declares that:

(a) Radon, an odorless, colorless, radioactive gas, is the leading cause of lung cancer deaths among nonsmokers in the nation and is the second leading cause of lung cancer deaths overall;

(b) Radon originates from the decay of naturally occurring uranium in Colorado granite, soil, and bedrock and can accumulate in structures at dangerous risk levels to humans;

(c) Indoor radon ranks among the most serious environmental health problems;

(d) Colorado ranks seventh in the nation for highest potential radon risk;

(e) All of Colorado's counties are at high risk for radon, and fifty percent of Colorado homes have radon levels that should be mitigated;

(f) An estimated five hundred Coloradans die from radon-induced lung cancer annually, causing more deaths than drunk driving, house fires, carbon monoxide, and drowning combined; and

(g) Increased education and awareness of the harmful effects of radon exposure will help save the lives of Coloradans and reduce the burden of health care costs from radon-induced lung cancer.

(2) The department shall establish a radon education and awareness program. As a part of the program, the department shall:

(a) Provide radon information and education statewide to citizens, businesses, and others in need of information;

(b) Work collaboratively with radon contractors and citizens to resolve questions and concerns regarding the installation of safe, healthy, and efficient radon mitigation systems; and

(c) Collaborate with local governments to provide information on best practices for radon mitigation strategies.

(3) Effective January 1, 2017, the department shall establish a radon mitigation assistance program to provide financial assistance to low-income individuals for radon mitigation in their homes. The state board of health shall set the program requirements, including eligibility requirements for financial assistance.

(4) The department shall use money in the hazardous substance response fund, established in section 25-16-104.6, to finance the radon education and awareness program and the radon mitigation assistance program.

# PART 2. RADIOACTIVE WASTE DISPOSAL

## 25-11-201. Definitions - scope.

(1) As used in this part 2, unless the context otherwise requires:

(a) "Disposal" means burial in soil, release through a sanitary sewerage system, incineration, or long-term storage with no intention of or provision for subsequent removal.

(b) "Facility" means a uranium or thorium mill, processing, or disposal facility required to be licensed pursuant to this article and a site for the facility.

(c) "Ore" means naturally occurring uranium-bearing, thorium-bearing, or radium-bearing material in its natural form prior to chemical processing, such as roasting, beneficiating, or refining, and specifically includes material that has been physically processed, such as by crushing, grinding, screening, or sorting.

(d) "Radioactive" means emitting alpha particles, beta particles, gamma rays, high-energy neutrons or protons, or other radioactive particles.

(e) "Radioactive waste" means low-level radioactive wastes containing source, special nuclear, or byproduct material that are acceptable for disposal in a land disposal facility. For the purposes of this paragraph (e), "low-level radioactive waste" means radioactive waste not classified as high-level radioactive waste, transuranic waste, spent nuclear fuel, or byproduct material, as that term is defined in section 25-11-101 (1) (b), (1) (c), and (1) (d).

(f) "Technologically enhanced naturally occurring radioactive material" or "tenorm" means naturally occurring radioactive material whose radionuclide concentrations are increased by or as a result of past or present human practices. "Tenorm" does not include:

(I) Background radiation or the natural radioactivity of rocks or soils;

(II) "Byproduct material" or "source material", as defined by Colorado statute or rule; or

(III) Enriched or depleted uranium as defined by Colorado or federal statute or rule.

(g) "Type 2 byproduct material" means the subcategory of byproduct material specified in section 25-11-101 (1) (b).

(2) Nothing in this part 2 applies to, includes, or affects:

(a) The following naturally occurring radioactive materials or tenorm:

(I) Residuals or sludges from the treatment of drinking water by aluminum, ferric chloride, or similar processes; except that the material may not contain hazardous substances that otherwise would preclude receipt;

(II) Sludges, soils, or pipe scale in or on equipment from oil and gas exploration, production, or development operations or drinking water or wastewater treatment operations; except that the material may not contain hazardous substances that otherwise would preclude receipt;

(III) Materials from or activities related to construction material mining regulated under article 32.5 of title 34, C.R.S.; or

(b) The treatment, storage, management, processing, or disposal of solid waste, which may include naturally occurring radioactive material and tenorm, either pursuant to a certificate of designation issued under article 20 of title 30, C.R.S., or at a solid waste disposal site and facility considered approved or otherwise deemed to satisfy the requirement for a certificate of designation pursuant to article 20 of title 30, C.R.S., or section 25-15-204 (6) .

## 25-11-202. Disposal of foreign radioactive waste prohibited.

The disposal of any radioactive waste which originates or has been used outside this state and has not been used in this state is prohibited except as provided in section 25-11-203.

## 25-11-203. Approval of facilities, sites, and shipments for disposal of radioactive waste.

(1) (a) No facility shall be constructed or site approved for the disposal of radioactive waste originating or used outside Colorado unless such facility or site has been approved as provided in subsection (3) of this section.

(b) (I) A facility shall not dispose of or receive for storage incident to disposal or processing at the facility radioactive material, except for nonprocessing operational purposes such as radioactive standards, samples for analysis, or materials contained in fixed or portable gauges, unless the facility has received a license, a five-year license renewal, or license amendment pertaining to the facility's receipt of radioactive material, in accordance with sections 24-4-104 to 24-4-105, C.R.S., for such receipt, storage, processing, or disposal of radioactive material and the license, license renewal, or license amendment approves that type of activity.

(II) Nothing in this paragraph (b) applies to a contract for the storage, processing, or disposal of less than the sum of one hundred ten tons of radioactive material per source or to a contract for a bench-scale or a pilot-scale testing project or a contract for less than a de minimis amount of radioactive material as determined by the department for storage, processing, or disposal.

(III) License amendments for the receipt of radioactive material at a facility are subject to subsections (2) and (3) of this section except when the material is from an approved source and the amendment would not result in a change in ownership, design, or operation of the facility. License amendments not subject to subsections (2) and (3) of this section are subject to subsection (4) of this section.

(2) (a) Any person desiring to have a facility or site referred to in subsection (1) of this section approved shall apply to the department of public health and environment for approval of such facility or site. The application shall contain such information as the department requires and shall be accompanied by an application fee determined by the board pursuant to the provisions of part 1 of this article.

(b) In addition to the requirements of paragraph (a) of this subsection (2) , each proposed license, five-year license renewal, or license amendment pertaining to the facility's receipt of any radioactive material must include a written application to the department and information relevant to the pending application, including:

(I) Transcripts of two public meetings hosted and presided over by a person selected upon agreement by the department, the board of county commissioners of the county where the facility is located, and the applicant. The applicant shall pay the reasonable, necessary, and documented expense of the meetings. The meetings shall not be held until the department determines that the application is substantially complete. The applicant shall provide the public with:

(A) Pursuant to part 1 of article 70 of title 24, C.R.S., at least two weeks' written notice before the first meeting and an additional two weeks' written notice before the second meeting;

(B) At both meetings, summaries of the facility's license to receive, store, process, or dispose of the radioactive material and the nature of the radioactive material, and an opportunity to be heard; and

(C) Access to make copies of a transcript of the meetings, and shall provide an electronic copy to the department in a manner that allows posting on the department's website within ten days after receipt from the transcription service.

(II) An environmental assessment as defined in paragraph (c) of this subsection (2) ;

(III) A response, if any, to the environmental assessment written by the board of county commissioners of the county in which the radioactive material is proposed to be received for storage, processing, or disposal at a facility and provided to the facility within ninety days after the first public meeting. Upon request of and documentation of the expenditure by the board, the applicant shall provide the board with up to fifty thousand dollars, as adjusted for inflation since 2003, which is available to the board for the reasonable and necessary expenses during the pendency of the application to assist the board in responding to the application, including to pay for an independent environmental analysis by a disinterested party with appropriate environmental expertise to assist the board in preparing its response. The board's response may consider whether the approval of the license, five-year license renewal, or license amendment pertaining to the facility's receipt or disposal of the radioactive material will present any substantial adverse impact upon the safety or maintenance of transportation infrastructure or transportation facilities within the county.

(c) As used in paragraph (b) of this subsection (2) , "environmental assessment" means a report and assessment submitted to the department by a facility upon and in connection with application for a license, a five-year license renewal, or license amendment pertaining to the facility's receipt of radioactive material, proposing to receive any radioactive material for storage, processing, or disposal at a facility that addresses the impacts of the receipt for storage, processing, or disposal of the radioactive material. The environmental assessment shall contain all information deemed necessary by the department, and shall include, at a minimum:

(I) The identification of the types of radioactive material to be received, stored, processed, or disposed of;

(II) A representative presentation of the physical, chemical, and radiological properties of the type of radioactive material to be received, stored, processed, or disposed of;

(III) An evaluation of the short-term and long-range environmental impacts of such receipt, storage, processing, or disposal;

(IV) An assessment of the radiological and nonradiological impacts to the public health from the application;

(V) Any facility-related impact on any waterway and groundwater from the application;

(VI) An analysis of the environmental, economic, social, technical, and other benefits of the proposed application against environmental costs and social effects while considering available alternatives;

(VII) A list of all material violations of local, state, or federal law at the facility since the submittal date of the previous license application or license renewal application;

(VIII) For an application for a license or license amendment pertaining to the facility's receipt of the radioactive material for storage, processing, or disposal at the facility, a demonstration that:

(A) There are no outstanding material violations of any state or federal statutes, compliance orders, or court orders applicable to the facility, and any releases giving rise to any such violation have been remediated;

(B) The operator, after a good-faith review of the facility and its operations, is not aware of any current license violation at the facility;

(C) There are no current releases to the air, ground, surface water, or groundwater that exceed permitted limits; and

(D) No conditions exist at the facility that would prevent the department of energy's receipt of title to the facility pursuant to the federal "Atomic Energy Act of 1954", 42 U.S.C. sec. 2113;

(IX) A list of all necessary permits and any changes to local land use ordinances that are needed to construct or operate the facility; and

(X) For sites or facilities placed on the national priority list pursuant to the federal "Comprehensive Environmental Response, Compensation, and Liability Act", 42 U.S.C. sec. 9605, a copy of the most recent five-year review and any associated updates that have been issued by the United States environmental protection agency.

(3) (a) Upon receipt of an application or notice as provided in subsection (2) of this section, the department of public health and environment shall notify the public and forward a copy of the application or notice to the governor and the general assembly, as appropriate.

(b) (I) No facility or site referred to in paragraph (a) of subsection (1) of this section shall be constructed or approved by the department of public health and environment unless the governor and the general assembly have approved such facility or site.

(II) The governor and the general assembly, in making their determination, shall consider criteria developed by the department of public health and environment for disposal of radioactive wastes pursuant to section 25-11-103 (3) in approving or disapproving the proposed facility or site.

(c) (I) In deciding whether to approve a license, five-year license renewal, or license amendment pertaining to the facility's receipt of radioactive material, the department shall consider the transcripts of the public meetings held pursuant to subparagraph (I) of paragraph (b) of subsection (2) of this section, the facility's license, any environmental assessment or analysis performed pursuant to this section, the facility's compliance with the financial assurance requirements of section 25-11-110, and the board of county commissioners' response to the environmental assessment prepared pursuant to subparagraph (III) of paragraph (b) of subsection (2) of this section. The department shall deny or approve the application as a whole.

(II) The department may order reasonable mitigation measures to address any substantial adverse impacts to public health or the environment or transportation infrastructure or transportation facilities within the county attributable solely to approval of the license, five-year license renewal, or license amendment pertaining to the facility's receipt of the radioactive material.

(III) The applicant shall demonstrate that if the license, five-year license renewal, or license amendment pertaining to the facility's receipt of the radioactive material is approved, then the receipt, storage, processing, and disposal of radioactive material will:

(A) Be conducted such that the exposures to workers and the public are within the dose limits of part 4 of the department's rules pertaining to radiation control for workers and the public;

(B) Not cause releases to the air, ground, or surface or groundwater that exceed permitted limits; and

(C) Not prevent transfer of the facility to the United States in accordance with 42 U.S.C. sec. 2113 upon completion of decontamination, decommissioning, and reclamation of the facility.

(IV) No facility may be permitted as a hazardous waste treatment, storage, or disposal facility under part 3 of article 15 of this title.

(V) (A) The department shall publish a determination as to whether an application submitted pursuant to paragraph (b) of subsection (2) of this section is substantially complete within forty-five days after receipt of the application.

(B) The department shall convene the first public meeting required by subparagraph (I) of paragraph (b) of subsection (2) of this section within forty-five days after publication of its determination that the application is substantially complete. The department shall convene the second such public meeting within thirty days after giving public notice of a draft decision as described in sub-subparagraph (C) of this subparagraph (V) .

(C) The department shall initiate a final public comment process by posting on the department's website an initial draft decision to approve, approve with conditions, or deny the application submitted under paragraph (b) of subsection (2) of this section, along with all required final technical and environmental impact analyses conducted by the department, all requests from the department seeking information from the applicant, all of the applicant's responses, all public comments, a draft license for any proposed approval, and any additional information that may assist the public review of the department's draft decision.

(D) After review of all final public comments, the department shall issue a final draft decision and provide affected parties, including the applicant in the case of approval with conditions or denial, an opportunity to request an adjudicatory hearing in accordance with section 24-4-105, C.R.S. If no party seeks a hearing, the final draft decision becomes final agency action. If any party seeks a hearing, resolution of all material issues of fact, law, or discretion presented by the record and the appropriate order, sanction, relief, or denial of the material issues must be through an initial decision of a hearing officer or administrative law judge. The applicant shall pay all reasonable, necessary, and documented expenses of the hearing. Upon issuance of the initial decision of the hearing officer or administrative law judge, and after any allowable appeal to the executive director, the department shall issue within a reasonable time a final decision to approve, approve with conditions, or deny the application. The final decision is subject to judicial review pursuant to section 24-4-106, C.R.S.

(4) (a) (I) At least ninety days before a facility proposes to receive, store, process, or dispose of radioactive material in a license application or amendment that is not subject to subsections (2) and (3) of this section and for which a material acceptance report has not already been filed with the department, the facility shall notify the department, and the department shall notify the public and the board of county commissioners of the county in which the facility is located, of the specific radioactive material to be received, stored, processed, or disposed of. The notice must include:

(A) A representative analysis of the physical, chemical, and radiological properties of the radioactive material;

(B) The material acceptance report that demonstrates that the radioactive material does not contain hazardous waste characteristics not found in uranium ore;

(C) A detailed plan for transport, acceptance, storage, handling, processing, and disposal of the material;

(D) A demonstration that the material contains technically and economically recoverable uranium, without taking into account its value as disposal material;

(E) The existing location of the radioactive material;

(F) The history of the radioactive material;

(G) A written statement by the applicant describing any preexisting regulatory classification of the radioactive material in the state of origin that describes all steps taken by the applicant to identify the classification;

(H) A written statement from the United States department of energy or successor agency that the receipt, storage, processing, or disposal of the radioactive material at the facility will not adversely affect the department of energy's receipt of title to the facility pursuant to the federal "Atomic Energy Act of 1954 ", 42 U.S.C. sec. 2113;

(I) Documentation showing any necessary approvals of the United States environmental protection agency; and

(J) An environmental assessment as defined in paragraph (c) of subsection (2) of this section, which may incorporate by reference relevant information contained in an environmental assessment previously submitted for the facility.

(II) For radioactive material that would otherwise be subject to the "Low-level Radioactive Waste Act", part 22 of article 60 of title 24, C.R.S., the facility's notice must also include written documentation that the Rocky Mountain low-level radioactive waste board has been notified that the radioactive material is being considered for disposal in the subject facility.

(b) Within thirty days after the department's receipt of notice pursuant to subparagraph (I) of paragraph (a) of this subsection (4) , the department shall determine whether the notice is complete.

(c) Once the department determines that the notice is complete, the department shall publish the notice on its website and provide a sixty-day public comment period for the receipt of written comments concerning the notice. A public hearing may be held, at the department's discretion, at the operator's expense.

(d) Within thirty days after the close of the written public comment period provided by paragraph (c) of this subsection (4) , the department shall approve, approve with conditions, or deny the receipt, storage, processing, or disposal as described in the notice based on whether the material proposed for receipt, storage, processing, or disposal at the facility complies with the facility's license and meets the standards established pursuant to subparagraph (III) of paragraph (c) of subsection (3) of this section.

# PART 3. DISPOSAL OF URANIUM MILL TAILINGS

## 25-11-301. Legislative declaration.

(1) The general assembly hereby finds and declares that the existence of uranium mill tailings at active and inactive mill operations poses a potential and significant radiation health hazard. This part 3 is therefore enacted to protect the public health, safety, and welfare by cooperating with the federal government in providing for the stabilization, disposal, and control of such tailings in a safe and environmentally sound manner to prevent or minimize other environmental impacts from such tailings.

(2) The general assembly recognizes the need for the state to expend such funds as are necessary to provide land annotation and site information for purposes of protecting prospective purchasers or users of mill sites designated for cleanup pursuant to public law 95-604. The general assembly therefore declares its intent to assist local governments with the identification, removal, storage, and disposal of tailing deposits associated with such designated mill sites for which remedial action is not taken pursuant to the federal "Uranium Mill Tailings Radiation Control Act of 1978".

## 25-11-302. Terms defined.

For the purposes of this part 3, the terms "processing site" and "residual radioactive material" shall have the meanings specified in section 101 (6) and (7) , respectively, of Public Law 95-604, as from time to time amended.

## 25-11-303. Authorization to participate - implementation.

(1) The general assembly hereby authorizes the department of public health and environment to participate in federal implementation of the "Uranium Mill Tailings Radiation Control Act of 1978", and for such purpose the department has the authority to:

(a) Enter into cooperative agreements with the secretary of energy to perform remedial actions at processing sites designated by the secretary;

(b) Obtain written consent from the record owner of a designated processing site to perform remedial actions at such site;

(c) Provide for reimbursement for the actual cost of any remedial action in accordance with the terms of Public Law 95-604;

(d) Repealed.

(e) Participate in the selection and performance of remedial actions in which the state pays a portion of the cost;

(f) Participate in the following activities for which the state may pay any portion or all of the costs:

(I) Land annotation and information gathering, identification, removal, and disposal of tailing deposits associated with mill sites designated for cleanup pursuant to public law 95-604 that remain outside of the disposal cells constructed for remedial purposes pursuant to the federal "Uranium Mill Tailings Radiation Control Act of 1978"; and

(II) The groundwater restoration phase of the federal "Uranium Mill Tailings Radiation Control Act of 1978".

## 25-11-304. Financial participation.

(1) The general assembly accepts the provisions of section 107 (a) of Public Law 95-604 requiring the state to pay ten percent of the actual cost of any remedial action and administrative costs from nonfederal moneys.

(2) The state of Colorado may receive a share of the net profits derived from the recovery of minerals from residual radioactive materials at any designated processing site within the state in

accordance with the provisions of section 108 (b) of Public Law 95-604.

## 25-11-305. Restriction - termination.
(1) Nothing in this part 3 shall supersede the provisions of part 1 of this article.
(2) The authority to participate in federal implementation of remedial actions at designated processing sites shall terminate at such time as the authority of the federal government to perform remedial action terminates under the provisions of section 112 (a) of Public Law 95-604.

# ARTICLE 12. NOISE ABATEMENT

## 25-12-101. Legislative declaration.
The general assembly finds and declares that noise is a major source of environmental pollution which represents a threat to the serenity and quality of life in the state of Colorado. Excess noise often has an adverse physiological and psychological effect on human beings, thus contributing to an economic loss to the community. Accordingly, it is the policy of the general assembly to establish statewide standards for noise level limits for various time periods and areas. Noise in excess of the limits provided in this article constitutes a public nuisance.

## 25-12-102. Definitions.
As used in this article, unless the context otherwise requires:
(1) "Commercial zone" means:
(a) An area where offices, clinics, and the facilities needed to serve them are located;
(b) An area with local shopping and service establishments located within walking distances of the residents served;
(c) A tourist-oriented area where hotels, motels, and gasoline stations are located;
(d) A large integrated regional shopping center;
(e) A business strip along a main street containing offices, retail businesses, and commercial enterprises;
(f) A central business district; or
(g) A commercially dominated area with multiple-unit dwellings.
(2) "db(A) " means sound levels in decibels measured on the "A" scale of a standard sound level meter having characteristics defined by the American national standards institute, publication S1. 4 - 1971.
(3) "Decibel" is a unit used to express the magnitude of a change in sound level. The difference in decibels between two sound pressure levels is twenty times the common logarithm of their ratio. In sound pressure measurements sound levels are defined as twenty times the common logarithm of the ratio of that sound pressure level to a reference level of $2 \times 10^{-5}$ N/m2 (Newton's/meter squared) . As an example of the effect of the formula, a three-decibel change is a one hundred percent increase or decrease in the sound level, and a ten-decibel change is a one thousand percent increase or decrease in the sound level.
(4) (a) "Industrial zone" means an area in which noise restrictions on industry are necessary to protect the value of adjacent properties for other economic activity but shall not include agricultural, horticultural, or floricultural operations.
(b) Nothing in paragraph (a) of this subsection (4) , as amended by House Bill 05-1180, as enacted at the first regular session of the sixty-fifth general assembly, shall be construed as changing the property tax classification of property owned by a horticultural or floricultural operation.
(5) "Light industrial and commercial zone" means:
(a) An area containing clean and quiet research laboratories;
(b) An area containing light industrial activities which are clean and quiet;

(c) An area containing warehousing; or

(d) An area in which other activities are conducted where the general environment is free from concentrated industrial activity.

(5.2) "Motorcycle" means a self-propelled vehicle with not more than three wheels in contact with the ground that is designed primarily for use on the public highways.

(5.4) "Motor vehicle" means a self-propelled vehicle with at least four wheels in contact with the ground that is designed primarily for use on the public highways.

(5.6) "Off-highway vehicle" means a self-propelled vehicle with wheels or tracks in contact with the ground that is designed primarily for use off the public highways. "Off-highway vehicle" shall not include the following:

(a) Military vehicles;

(b) Golf carts;

(c) Snowmobiles;

(d) Vehicles designed and used to carry persons with disabilities; and

(e) Vehicles designed and used specifically for agricultural, logging, firefighting, or mining purposes.

(6) "Residential zone" means an area of single-family or multifamily dwellings where businesses may or may not be conducted in such dwellings. The zone includes areas where multiple-unit dwellings, high-rise apartment districts, and redevelopment districts are located. A residential zone may include areas containing accommodations for transients such as motels and hotels and residential areas with limited office development, but it may not include retail shopping facilities. "Residential zone" includes hospitals, nursing homes, and similar institutional facilities.

(7) "SAE J1287" means the J1287 stationary sound test or any successor test published by SAE international or any successor organization.

(8) "SAE J2567" means the J2567 stationary sound test or any successor test published by SAE international or any successor organization.

(9) "Snowmobile" means a self-propelled vehicle primarily designed or altered for travel on snow or ice when supported in part by skis, belts, or cleats and designed primarily for use off the public highways. "Snowmobile" shall not include machinery used strictly for the grooming of snowmobile trails or ski slopes.

## 25-12-103. Maximum permissible noise levels.

(1) Every activity to which this article is applicable shall be conducted in a manner so that any noise produced is not objectionable due to intermittence, beat frequency, or shrillness. Sound levels of noise radiating from a property line at a distance of twenty-five feet or more therefrom in excess of the db(A) established for the following time periods and zones shall constitute prima facie evidence that such noise is a public nuisance:

| Zone | 7:00 a.m. to next 7:00 p.m. | 7:00 p.m. to next 7:00 a.m. |
|---|---|---|
| Residential | 55 db(A) | 50 db(A) |
| Commercial | 60 db(A) | 55 db(A) |
| Light industrial | 70 db(A) | 65 db(A) |
| Industrial | 80 db(A) | 75 db(A) |

(2) In the hours between 7:00 a.m. and the next 7:00 p.m., the noise levels permitted in subsection (1) of this section may be increased by ten db(A) for a period of not to exceed fifteen minutes in any one-hour period.

(3) Periodic, impulsive, or shrill noises shall be considered a public nuisance when such noises are at a sound level of five db(A) less than those listed in subsection (1) of this section.

(4) This article is not intended to apply to the operation of aircraft or to other activities which are subject to federal law with respect to noise control.

(5) Construction projects shall be subject to the maximum permissible noise levels specified for industrial zones for the period within which construction is to be completed pursuant to any applicable construction permit issued by proper authority or, if no time limitation is imposed, for a reasonable period of time for completion of project.

(6) All railroad rights-of-way shall be considered as industrial zones for the purposes of this article, and the operation of trains shall be subject to the maximum permissible noise levels specified for such zone.

(7) This article is not applicable to the use of property for purposes of conducting speed or endurance events involving motor or other vehicles, but such exception is effective only during the specific period of time within which such use of the property is authorized by the political subdivision or governmental agency having lawful jurisdiction to authorize such use.

(8) For the purposes of this article, measurements with sound level meters shall be made when the wind velocity at the time and place of such measurement is not more than five miles per hour.

(9) In all sound level measurements, consideration shall be given to the effect of the ambient noise level created by the encompassing noise of the environment from all sources at the time and place of such sound level measurement.

(10) This article is not applicable to the use of property for the purpose of manufacturing, maintaining, or grooming machine-made snow. This subsection (10) shall not be construed to preempt or limit the authority of any political subdivision having jurisdiction to regulate noise abatement.

(11) This article is not applicable to the use of property by this state, any political subdivision of this state, or any other entity not organized for profit, including, but not limited to, nonprofit corporations, or any of their lessees, licensees, or permittees, for the purpose of promoting, producing, or holding cultural, entertainment, athletic, or patriotic events, including, but not limited to, concerts, music festivals, and fireworks displays. This subsection (11) shall not be construed to preempt or limit the authority of any political subdivision having jurisdiction to regulate noise abatement.

(12) (a) Notwithstanding subsection (1) of this section, the public utilities commission may determine, while reviewing utility applications for certificates of public convenience and necessity for electric transmission facilities, whether projected noise levels for electric transmission facilities are reasonable. Such determination shall take into account concerns raised by participants in the commission proceeding and the alternatives available to a utility to meet the need for electric transmission facilities. When applying, the utility shall provide notice of its application to all municipalities and counties where the proposed electric transmission facilities will be located. The public utilities commission shall afford the public an opportunity to participate in all proceedings in which permissible noise levels are established according to the "Public Utilities Law", articles 1 to 7 of title 40, C.R.S.

(b) Because of the statewide need for reliable electric service and the public benefit provided by electric transmission facilities, notwithstanding any other provision of law, no municipality or county may adopt an ordinance or resolution setting noise standards for electric transmission facilities that are more restrictive than this subsection (12) . The owner or operator of an electric transmission facility shall not be liable in a civil action based upon noise emitted by electric transmission facilities that comply with this subsection (12) .

(c) For the purposes of this section:

(I) "Electric transmission facility" means a power line or other facility that transmits electrical current and operates at a voltage level greater than or equal to 44 kilovolts.

(II) "Rights-of-way for electric transmission facilities" means all property rights and interests obtained by the owner or operator of an electric transmission facility for the purpose of constructing, maintaining, or operating the electric transmission facility.

## 25-12-104. Action to abate.

Whenever there is reason to believe that a nuisance exists, as defined in section 25-12-103, any county or resident of the state may maintain an action in equity in the district court of the judicial district in which the alleged nuisance exists to abate and prevent such nuisance and to perpetually enjoin the person conducting or maintaining the same and the owner, lessee, or agent of the building or place in or upon which such nuisance exists from directly or indirectly maintaining or permitting such nuisance. Notwithstanding any other provision of this section, a county shall not maintain an action pursuant to this section if the alleged nuisance involves a mining operation or the development, extraction, or transportation of construction materials, as those terms are defined in section 34-32.5-103, C.R.S., a commercial activity, the commercial use of property, avalanche control activities, a farming or ranching activity, an activity of a utility, or a mining or oil and gas operation. When proceedings by injunction are instituted, such proceedings shall be conducted under the Colorado rules of civil procedure. The court may stay the effect of any order issued under this section for such time as is reasonably necessary for the defendant to come into compliance with the provisions of this article.

## 25-12-105. Violation of injunction - penalty.

Any violation or disobedience of any injunction or order expressly provided for by section 25-12-104 shall be punished as a contempt of court by a fine of not less than one hundred dollars nor more than two thousand dollars. Each day in which an individual is in violation of the injunction established by the court shall constitute a separate offense. The court shall give consideration in any such case to the practical difficulties involved with respect to effecting compliance with the requirements of any order issued by the court.

## 25-12-106. Noise restrictions - sale of new vehicles.

(1) Except for such vehicles as are designed exclusively for racing purposes, no person shall sell or offer for sale a new motor vehicle that produces a maximum noise exceeding the following noise limits, at a distance of fifty feet from the center of the lane of travel, under test procedures established by the department of revenue:

(a) Any motorcycle manufactured on or after July 1, 1971, and before January 1, 197388 db(A) ;

(b) Any motorcycle manufactured on or after January 1, 197386 db(A) ;

(c) Any motor vehicle with a gross vehicle weight rating of six thousand pounds or more manufactured on or after July 1, 1971, and before January 1, 197388 db(A) ;

(d) Any motor vehicle with a gross vehicle weight rating of six thousand pounds or more manufactured on or after January 1, 197386 db(A) ;

(e) Any other motor vehicle manufactured on or after January 1, 1968, and before January 1, 197386 db(A) ;

(f) Any other motor vehicle manufactured after January 1, 197384 db(A) .

(g) (Deleted by amendment, L. 2008, p. 2102, § 2, effective July 1, 2010.)

(2) Test procedures for compliance with this section shall be established by the department, taking into consideration the test procedures of the society of automotive engineers.

(3) Any person selling or offering for sale a motor vehicle or other vehicle in violation of this section is guilty of a misdemeanor and, upon conviction thereof, shall be punished by a fine of not less than fifty dollars nor more than three hundred dollars.

## 25-12-107. Powers of local authorities.

(1) Counties or municipalities may adopt resolutions or ordinances prohibiting the operation of motor vehicles within their respective jurisdictions that produce noise in excess of the sound levels in decibels, measured on the "A" scale on a standard sound level meter having characteristics established by the American national standards institute, publication S1.4 - 1971, and measured at a distance of fifty feet from the center of the lane of travel and within the speed limits specified in this section:

Speed limit

of more

Speed limitthan 35 mph

of 35 mphbut less

or lessthan 55 mph


(a) Any motor vehicle with a manufacturer's gross vehicle weight rating of six thousand pounds or more, any combination of vehicles towed by such motor vehicle, and any motorcycle other than a low-power scooter:
(I) Before January 1, 197388 db(A) 90 db(A)
(II) On and after January 1, 197386 db(A) 90 db(A)
(b) (Deleted by amendment, L. 2008, p. 2102, § 3, effective July 1, 2010.)

(2) The governing board shall adopt resolutions establishing any test procedures deemed necessary.
(3) This section applies to the total noise from a vehicle or combination of vehicles.
(4) For the purpose of this section, a truck, truck tractor, or bus that is not equipped with an identification plate or marking bearing the manufacturer's name and manufacturer's gross vehicle weight rating shall be considered as having a manufacturer's gross vehicle weight rating of six thousand pounds or more if the unladen weight is more than five thousand pounds.

## 25-12-108. Preemption.
Except as provided in sections 25-12-103 (12) and 25-12-110, this article shall not be construed to preempt or limit the authority of any municipality or county to adopt standards that are no less restrictive than the provisions of this article.

## 25-12-109. Exception - sport shooting ranges - legislative declaration - definitions.
(1) The general assembly hereby finds, determines, and declares that the imposition of inconsistent, outdated, and unnecessary noise restrictions on qualifying sport shooting ranges that meet specific, designated qualifications work to the detriment of the public health, welfare, and morale as well as to the detriment of the economic well-being of the state. The general assembly further finds, determines, and declares that a need exists for statewide uniformity with respect to exempting qualifying shooting ranges from the enforcement of laws, ordinances, rules, and orders regulating noise. As the gain associated with having a uniform statewide exemption for qualifying sport shooting ranges outweighs any gains associated with enforcing noise regulations against such ranges, the general assembly further declares that the provisions of this section, as enacted, are a matter of statewide concern and preempt any provisions of any law, ordinance, rule, or order to the contrary.
(2) As used in this section, unless the context otherwise requires:
(a) "Local government" means any county, city, city and county, town, or any governmental entity, board, council, or committee operating under the authority of any county, city, city and county, or town.
(b) "Local government official" means any elected, appointed, or employed individual or group of individuals acting on behalf of or exercising the authority of any local government.

(c) "Person" means an individual, proprietorship, partnership, corporation, club, or other legal entity.

(d) "Qualifying sport shooting range" or "qualifying range" means any public or private establishment, whether operating for profit or not for profit, that operates an area for the discharge or other use of firearms or other equipment for silhouette, skeet, trap, black powder, target, self-defense, recreational or competitive shooting, or professional training.

(3) Notwithstanding any other law or municipal or county ordinance, rule, or order regulating noise to the contrary:

(a) A local governmental official may not commence a civil action nor seek a criminal penalty against a qualifying sport shooting range or its owners or operators on the grounds of noise emanating from such range that results from the normal operation or use of the qualifying shooting range except upon a written complaint from a resident of the jurisdiction in which the range is located. The complaint shall state the name and address of the complainant, how long the complainant has resided at the address indicated, the times and dates on which the alleged excessive noise occurred, and such other information as the local government may require. The local government shall not proceed to seek a criminal penalty or pursue a civil action against a qualifying sport shooting range on the basis of such a noise complaint if the complainant established residence within the jurisdiction after January 1, 1985.

(b) No person may bring any suit in law or equity or any other claim for relief against a qualifying sport shooting range located in the vicinity of the person's property or against the owners or operators of such range on the grounds of noise emanating from the range if:

(I) The qualifying range was established before the person acquired the property;

(II) The qualifying range complies with all laws, ordinances, rules, or orders regulating noise that applied to the range and its operation at the time of its construction or initial operation;

(III) No law, ordinance, rule, or order regulating noise applied to the qualifying range at the time of its construction or initial operation.

## 25-12-110. Off-highway vehicles.

(1) An off-highway vehicle operated within the state shall not emit more than the following level of sound when measured using SAE J1287:

(a) If manufactured before January 1, 199899 db(A) ;

(b) If manufactured on or after January 1, 199896 db(A) .

(2) A snowmobile shall not emit more than the following level of sound when measured using SAE J2567:

(a) If manufactured on or after July 1, 1972, and before July 2, 197590 db(A) ;

(b) If manufactured on or after July 2, 197588 db(A) .

(3) (a) A person shall not sell or offer to sell a new off-highway vehicle that emits a level of sound in excess of that prohibited by subsection (1) of this section unless the off-highway vehicle complies with federal noise emission standards. A person shall not sell or offer to sell a new snowmobile that emits a level of sound in excess of that prohibited by subsection (2) of this section unless the snowmobile complies with federal noise emission standards.

(b) For the purposes of this section, a "new" snowmobile or off-highway vehicle means a snowmobile or off-highway vehicle that has not been transferred on a manufacturer's statement of origin and for which an ownership registration card has not been submitted by the original owner to the manufacturer.

(4) This section shall not apply to the following:

(a) A vehicle designed or modified for and used in closed-circuit, off-highway vehicle competition facilities;

(b) An off-highway vehicle used in an emergency to search for or rescue a person; and

(c) An off-highway vehicle while in use for agricultural purposes.

(5) A person who violates this section commits a class 2 petty offense and, upon conviction thereof, shall be punished by a fine of not more than one hundred dollars.

(6) No municipality or county may adopt an ordinance or resolution setting noise standards for off-highway vehicles or snowmobiles that are more restrictive than this section.

(7) (a) Nothing in this section shall be construed to modify the authority granted in section 25-12-103.

(b) Nothing in this section shall be construed to authorize the test to produce a less restrictive standard than the J1287 stationary sound test or the J2567 stationary sound test published by SAE international or any successor organization.

(8) The following shall be an affirmative defense to a violation under this section if the off-highway vehicle or snowmobile:

(a) Was manufactured before January 1, 2005;

(b) Complied with federal and state law when purchased;

(c) Has not been modified from the manufacturer's original equipment specifications or to exceed the sound limits imposed by subsection (1) or (2) of this section; and

(d) Does not have a malfunctioning exhaust system.

# ARTICLE 13. RECREATION LAND PRESERVATION

## 25-13-101. Short title.
This article shall be known and may be cited as the "Recreation Land Preservation Act of 1971".

## 25-13-102. Legislative declaration.
The purpose of this article is to establish minimum controls to prohibit the pollution of the air, water, and land, to prevent the degradation of the natural environment of recreational and mountain areas in this state in order to preserve and maintain the ecology and environment in its natural condition, to facilitate the enjoyment of the state and its ecology, nature, and scenery by the inhabitants and visitors of the state, and to protect their health, safety, and welfare.

## 25-13-103. Definitions.
As used in this article, unless the context otherwise requires:

(1) "Board" means the state board of health.

(2) "Campsite" means any specific area within organized campgrounds or other recreation areas which is used for overnight stays by an individual, a single camping family, a group, or any other similar entity.

(3) "Department" means the department of public health and environment.

(4) "Operator" means the person responsible for managing the organized campground or recreation area.

(5) "Organized campgrounds" means all federal, state, municipal, and county owned and designated roadside parks and campgrounds and privately owned campgrounds which are made available, either with or without a fee, to the public.

(6) "Person" means any private or public institution, corporation, individual, partnership, firm, association, or other entity.

(7) "Public accommodation facilities" means all motels, hotels, dude ranches, youth camps, and other similar facilities rented out to the public in areas used predominantly for recreation.

(8) "Recreation areas" means all public lands and surface waters of the state, other than organized campgrounds, used for picnicking, camping, and other recreational activities.

(9) "Refuse" means all combustible or noncombustible solid waste, garbage, rubbish, debris, and litter.

(10) "Sewage" means any liquid or solid waste material which contains human excreta.

(11) "Surface of ground" means any portion of the ground from the surface to a depth of six

inches.

(12) "Waters of the state" means all streams, lakes, rivers, ponds, wells, impounding reservoirs, watercourses, springs, drainage systems, and irrigation systems; all sources of water such as snow, ice, and glaciers; and all other bodies or accumulations of water, surface and underground, natural or artificial, public or private, located wholly or partly within or bordering upon this state and within the jurisdiction of this state.

## 25-13-104. Administration.

(1) Except as provided in section 25-13-111, the department shall administer the provisions of this article.

(2) The board shall promulgate reasonable rules and regulations to carry out the purposes of this article.

(3) The department shall furnish consulting services to county commissioners, municipalities, other governmental agencies, and private landowners regarding toilet facilities and procedures for refuse collection and disposal.

## 25-13-105. Unlawful acts.

(1) Except as otherwise provided in this article, it is unlawful for any person:

(a) Within the recreation areas of the state to discharge untreated sewage upon the surface of the ground or in any waters of the state;

(b) To deposit or bury refuse on the public lands or waters within this state, except within areas or receptacles designated by the operator for this purpose;

(c) To deposit refuse on private or public land in such a way that said refuse may be blown, carried, or otherwise transported from its point of deposit;

(d) To willfully mar, mutilate, deface, disfigure, or injure beyond normal use any rocks, trees, shrubbery, wild flowers, or other features of the natural environment in recreation areas of the state;

(e) To willfully cut down, uproot, break, or otherwise destroy any living trees, shrubbery, wild flowers, or natural flora in recreation areas of the state;

(f) To build fires unless in compliance with rules and regulations of the board, to abandon or to leave fires unattended, or to store flammable liquids in a container which is not of a type approved by the department in an organized campground or other recreation area subject to this article;

(g) In organized campgrounds or recreation areas to use any cleansing agents, whether organic or inorganic in nature, in waters of the state for any purpose, including but not limited to bathing, clothes washing, and similar activities, or to dispose of any water containing such agents on the surface of the ground within fifty feet of any waters of the state. Such water shall be disposed of in facilities provided by the operator or in the manner specified by the operator.

## 25-13-106. Sewage disposal.

(1) In organized campgrounds, all sewage shall be disposed of in facilities provided by the campground operator. The operator shall maintain such facilities in the manner prescribed by rules and regulations of the board.

(2) Sewage in recreation areas may be disposed of by burial at a depth greater than six inches at a distance of more than one hundred feet from any surface waters. Adequate precautions shall be taken to prevent the intrusion of such sewage and wastewater upon the environment in a manner which is unhealthful, injurious to the environment, or otherwise degrading to the environment.

(3) Public accommodation sewage and wastewater disposal facilities shall conform to such reasonable rules and regulations as may be promulgated by the board.

## 25-13-107. Refuse disposal.

(1) All persons shall dispose of refuse in containers which shall be provided for that purpose by operators of organized campgrounds. Organized campground operators shall keep the grounds free

of uncontained refuse and shall provide a sufficient number of secure waterproof containers, preferably metal, with flyproof tops for the disposal of refuse. The containers shall be emptied as often as necessary to maintain the organized campground free of uncontained refuse. The presence of uncontained refuse in excess of the capacity of the containers provided shall be prima facie proof that the numbers of containers or frequency of container emptying is inadequate and that the operator is in violation of this subsection (1) .

(2) Whenever containers for refuse are filled or are not available in campgrounds or recreation areas, all persons shall dispose of refuse in compliance with rules and regulations adopted by the board or operator or remove the refuse from the area for disposal in a manner not in violation of this article.

(3) Refuse in public accommodation facilities shall be disposed in the manner specified in such reasonable rules and regulations as may be promulgated by the board.

(4) Food wastes normally edible to human beings may be deposited on the surface of the ground if the quantity of such wastes does not result in an unhealthful or unpleasant aesthetic appearance by virtue of an unreasonable time required for decay of the waste or consumption of the waste by fauna of the area.

## 25-13-108. Water supplies.
All water supplied to the public in an organized campground shall conform to the requirements of standards adopted by the board, rules and regulations adopted by the board, or any higher local standards.

## 25-13-109. Group gatherings.
Any group of twenty-five or more persons assembled for a meeting, festival, social gathering, or other similar purpose in an organized campground or recreation area for a period which reasonably could have been anticipated to exceed ten hours shall make provision for sewage, wastewater, and refuse disposal in accordance with rules and regulations of the board. The organizers of and performers at any gathering in violation of this section shall be punished as provided in section 25-13-114.

## 25-13-110. Camping duration.
No person may camp in a campsite within recreation areas for a period exceeding two weeks. Any campsite may be closed by the department or other lawful authority for an indefinite period to permit recovery of the campsite to its natural state following excessive use and resulting environmental deterioration.

## 25-13-111. Enforcement.
This article shall be enforced by the department, the division of parks and wildlife, all county, district, and municipal public health agencies and boards of health, and any peace officer in this state.

## 25-13-112. Citizen's complaint.
Any person may initiate an action under the provisions of this article by signing a complaint, in accordance with the applicable rules of judicial procedure, that he has observed a violation of this article.

## 25-13-113. Construction.
No provisions of this article shall be construed to repeal or in any way invalidate more stringent actions, orders, rules, regulations, ordinances, resolutions, or quality standards established by any governmental entity or agency.

### 25-13-114. Penalty for violation.

Any person who violates any of the provisions of this article is guilty of a misdemeanor and, upon conviction thereof, shall be punished by a fine of not more than five hundred dollars.

# ARTICLE 14. CONTROL OF SMOKING

# PART 1. PROHIBITION AGAINST THE USE OF TOBACCO ON SCHOOL PROPERTY

### 25-14-101. Legislative declaration. (Repealed)

### 25-14-102. Definitions. (Repealed)

### 25-14-103. Smoking prohibited in certain public places. (Repealed)

### 25-14-103.5. Prohibition against the use of tobacco products and retail marijuana on school property - legislative declaration - education program - special account.

(1) The general assembly finds that many of the schools in this state permit the use of tobacco products in and around school property. The general assembly further finds that secondhand smoke generated by such activity and the negative example set and frequently imitated by our school children are detrimental to the health and well-being of such children as well as to school teachers, staff, and visitors. Accordingly, the general assembly finds and declares that it is appropriate to create a safe and healthy school environment by prohibiting the use of tobacco products on all school property.

(2) As used in this section, unless the context otherwise requires:

(a) "School" means a public nursery school, day care center, child care facility, head start program, kindergarten, or elementary or secondary school through grade twelve.

(b) "School property" means all property, whether owned, leased, rented, or otherwise used by a school, including, but not limited to, the following:

(I) All interior portions of any building used for instruction, administration, support services, maintenance, and storage and any other structure used by a school; except that such term shall not apply to a building primarily used as a residence;

(II) All school grounds surrounding any building specified in subparagraph (I) of this paragraph (b) over which the school is authorized to exercise dominion and control. Such grounds shall include any playground, athletic field, recreation area, and parking area; and

(III) All vehicles used by the school for the purpose of transporting students, workers, visitors, or any other persons.

(c) "Tobacco product" shall have the same meaning as set forth in section 18-13-121 (5) , C.R.S.

(d) "Use" means the lighting, chewing, smoking, ingestion, or application of any tobacco product.

(3) (a) (I) The board of education of each school district shall adopt appropriate policies and rules that mandate a prohibition against the use of all tobacco products and all retail marijuana or retail marijuana products authorized pursuant to article 43.4 of title 12, C.R.S., on all school property by

students, teachers, staff, and visitors and that provide for the enforcement of such policies and rules.

(II) Repealed.

(b) Signs regarding such prohibition and the consequences of violation shall be displayed prominently on all school property to ensure compliance no later than September 1, 1994.

(4) This section shall not be applicable to the use of a tobacco product in a limited classroom demonstration to show the health hazards of tobacco.

(5) The board of education of each school district is authorized to seek and accept gifts, donations, or grants of any kind from any private or charitable source or from any governmental agency to meet expenses required by this section. Such gifts, donations, and grants shall be accounted for separately, and, to the extent that such moneys are available, the board of education of each school district may maintain and operate an educational program designed to assist students, faculty, and staff to avoid and discontinue the use of tobacco products. Such program shall be offered at each school under the board's direction and control.

(6) This section shall not prohibit any school from enacting more stringent policies or rules than required by this section.

## 25-14-103.7. Control of smoking in state legislative buildings. (Repealed)


## 25-14-104. Optional prohibition. (Repealed)


## 25-14-105. Local regulations. (Repealed)


# PART 2. COLORADO CLEAN INDOOR AIR ACT

## 25-14-201. Short title.
This part 2 shall be known and may be cited as the "Colorado Clean Indoor Air Act".

## 25-14-202. Legislative declaration.
The general assembly hereby finds and determines that it is in the best interest of the people of this state to protect nonsmokers from involuntary exposure to environmental tobacco and marijuana smoke in most indoor areas open to the public, public meetings, food service establishments, and places of employment. The general assembly further finds and determines that a balance should be struck between the health concerns of nonconsumers of tobacco products and combustible marijuana and the need to minimize unwarranted governmental intrusion into, and regulation of, private spheres of conduct and choice with respect to the use or nonuse of tobacco products and combustible marijuana in certain designated public areas and in private places. Therefore, the general assembly hereby declares that the purpose of this part 2 is to preserve and improve the health, comfort, and environment of the people of this state by limiting exposure to tobacco and marijuana smoke.

## 25-14-203. Definitions.
As used in this part 2, unless the context otherwise requires:

(1) "Airport smoking concession" means a bar or restaurant, or both, in a public airport with regularly scheduled domestic and international commercial passenger flights, in which bar or restaurant smoking is allowed in a fully enclosed and independently ventilated area by the terms of

the concession.

(2) "Auditorium" means the part of a public building where an audience gathers to attend a performance, and includes any corridors, hallways, or lobbies adjacent thereto.

(3) "Bar" means any indoor area that is operated and licensed under article 47 of title 12, C.R.S., primarily for the sale and service of alcohol beverages for on-premises consumption and where the service of food is secondary to the consumption of such beverages.

(4) "Cigar-tobacco bar" means a bar that, in the calendar year ending December 31, 2005, generated at least five percent or more of its total annual gross income or fifty thousand dollars in annual sales from the on-site sale of tobacco products and the rental of on-site humidors, not including any sales from vending machines. In any calendar year after December 31, 2005, a bar that fails to generate at least five percent of its total annual gross income or fifty thousand dollars in annual sales from the on-site sale of tobacco products and the rental of on-site humidors shall not be defined as a "cigar-tobacco bar" and shall not thereafter be included in the definition regardless of sales figures.

(5) (a) "Employee" means any person who:

(I) Performs any type of work for benefit of another in consideration of direct or indirect wages or profit; or

(II) Provides uncompensated work or services to a business or nonprofit entity.

(b) "Employee" includes every person described in paragraph (a) of this subsection (5) , regardless of whether such person is referred to as an employee, contractor, independent contractor, or volunteer or by any other designation or title.

(6) "Employer" means any person, partnership, association, corporation, or nonprofit entity that employs one or more persons. "Employer" includes, without limitation, the legislative, executive, and judicial branches of state government; any county, city and county, city, or town, or instrumentality thereof, or any other political subdivision of the state, special district, authority, commission, or agency; or any other separate corporate instrumentality or unit of state or local government.

(7) "Entryway" means the outside of the front or main doorway leading into a building or facility that is not exempted from this part 2 under section 25-14-205. "Entryway" also includes the area of public or private property within a specified radius outside of the doorway. The specified radius shall be determined by the local authority or, if the local authority has not acted, the specified radius shall be fifteen feet.

(8) "Environmental tobacco smoke", "ETS", or "secondhand smoke" means the complex mixture formed from the escaping smoke of a burning tobacco product, also known as "sidestream smoke", and smoke exhaled by the smoker.

(9) "Food service establishment" means any indoor area or portion thereof in which the principal business is the sale of food for on-premises consumption. The term includes, without limitation, restaurants, cafeterias, coffee shops, diners, sandwich shops, and short-order cafes.

(10) "Indoor area" means any enclosed area or portion thereof. The opening of windows or doors, or the temporary removal of wall panels, does not convert an indoor area into an outdoor area.

(11) "Local authority" means a county, city and county, city, or town.

(11.5) "Marijuana" shall have the same meaning as in section 16 (2) (f) of article XVIII of the state constitution.

(12) "Place of employment" means any indoor area or portion thereof under the control of an employer in which employees of the employer perform services for, or on behalf of, the employer.

(13) "Public building" means any building owned or operated by:

(a) The state, including the legislative, executive, and judicial branches of state government;

(b) Any county, city and county, city, or town, or instrumentality thereof, or any other political subdivision of the state, a special district, an authority, a commission, or an agency; or

(c) Any other separate corporate instrumentality or unit of state or local government.

(14) "Public meeting" means any meeting open to the public pursuant to part 4 of article 6 of title 24, C.R.S., or any other law of this state.

(15) "Smoke-free work area" means an indoor area in a place of employment where smoking is

prohibited under this part 2.

(16) "Smoking" means the burning of a lighted cigarette, cigar, pipe, or any other matter or substance that contains tobacco or marijuana.

(17) "Tobacco" means cigarettes, cigars, cheroots, stogies, and periques; granulated, plug cut, crimp cut, ready rubbed, and other smoking tobacco; snuff and snuff flour; cavendish; plug and twist tobacco; fine-cut and other chewing tobacco; shorts, refuse scraps, clippings, cuttings, and sweepings of tobacco; and other kinds and forms of tobacco, prepared in such manner as to be suitable for chewing or for smoking in a cigarette, pipe, or otherwise, or both for chewing and smoking. "Tobacco" also includes cloves and any other plant matter or product that is packaged for smoking.

(18) "Tobacco business" means a sole proprietorship, corporation, partnership, or other enterprise engaged primarily in the sale, manufacture, or promotion of tobacco, tobacco products, or smoking devices or accessories, either at wholesale or retail, and in which the sale, manufacture, or promotion of other products is merely incidental.

(19) "Work area" means an area in a place of employment where one or more employees are routinely assigned and perform services for or on behalf of their employer.

## 25-14-204. General smoking restrictions.

(1) Except as provided in section 25-14-205, and in order to reduce the levels of exposure to environmental tobacco and marijuana smoke, smoking shall not be permitted and no person shall smoke in any indoor area, including, but not limited to:

(a) Public meeting places;

(b) Elevators;

(c) Government-owned or -operated means of mass transportation, including, but not limited to, buses, vans, and trains;

(d) Taxicabs and limousines;

(e) Grocery stores;

(f) Gymnasiums;

(g) Jury waiting and deliberation rooms;

(h) Courtrooms;

(i) Child day care facilities;

(j) Health care facilities including hospitals, health care clinics, doctor's offices, and other health care related facilities;

(k) (I) Any place of employment that is not exempted.

(II) In the case of employers who own facilities otherwise exempted from this part 2, each such employer shall provide a smoke-free work area for each employee requesting not to have to breathe environmental tobacco smoke. Every employee shall have a right to work in an area free of environmental tobacco smoke.

(l) Food service establishments;

(m) Bars;

(n) Limited gaming facilities and any other facilities in which any gaming or gambling activity is conducted;

(o) Indoor sports arenas;

(p) Restrooms, lobbies, hallways, and other common areas in public and private buildings, condominiums, and other multiple-unit residential facilities;

(q) Restrooms, lobbies, hallways, and other common areas in hotels and motels, and in at least seventy-five percent of the sleeping quarters within a hotel or motel that are rented to guests;

(r) Bowling alleys;

(s) Billiard or pool halls;

(t) Facilities in which games of chance are conducted;

(u) (I) The common areas of retirement facilities, publicly owned housing facilities, and, except as specified in section 25-14-205 (1) (k) , nursing homes, but not including any resident's private residential quarters or areas of assisted living facilities specified in section 25-14-205 (1) (k) .

(II) Nothing in this part 2 affects the validity or enforceability of a contract, whether entered into before, on, or after July 1, 2006, that specifies that a part or all of a facility or home specified in this paragraph (u) is a smoke-free area.

(v) Public buildings;

(w) Auditoria;

(x) Theaters;

(y) Museums;

(z) Libraries;

(aa) To the extent not otherwise provided in section 25-14-103.5, public and nonpublic schools;

(bb) Other educational and vocational institutions; and

(cc) The entryways of all buildings and facilities listed in paragraphs (a) to (bb) of this subsection (1) .

(2) A cigar-tobacco bar shall not expand its size or change its location from the size and location in which it existed as of December 31, 2005. A cigar-tobacco bar shall display signage in at least one conspicuous place and at least four inches by six inches in size stating: "Smoking allowed. Children under eighteen years of age must be accompanied by a parent or guardian."

## 25-14-205. Exceptions to smoking restrictions.

(1) This part 2 shall not apply to:

(a) Private homes, private residences, and private automobiles; except that this part 2 shall apply if any such home, residence, or vehicle is being used for child care or day care or if a private vehicle is being used for the public transportation of children or as part of health care or day care transportation;

(b) Limousines under private hire;

(c) A hotel or motel room rented to one or more guests if the total percentage of such hotel or motel rooms in such hotel or motel does not exceed twenty-five percent;

(d) Any retail tobacco business;

(e) A cigar-tobacco bar;

(f) An airport smoking concession;

(g) The outdoor area of any business;

(h) A place of employment that is not open to the public and that is under the control of an employer that employs three or fewer employees;

(i) A private, nonresidential building on a farm or ranch, as defined in section 39-1-102, C.R.S., that has annual gross income of less than five hundred thousand dollars; or

(j) Repealed.

(k) (I) The areas of assisted living facilities:

(A) That are designated for smoking for residents;

(B) That are fully enclosed and ventilated; and

(C) To which access is restricted to the residents or their guests.

(II) As used in this paragraph (k) , "assisted living facility" means a nursing facility, as that term is defined in section 25.5-4-103, C.R.S., and an assisted living residence, as that term is defined in section 25-27-102.

## 25-14-206. Optional prohibitions.

(1) The owner or manager of any place not specifically listed in section 25-14-204, including a place otherwise exempted under section 25-14-205, may post signs prohibiting smoking or providing smoking and nonsmoking areas. Such posting shall have the effect of including such place, or the designated nonsmoking portion thereof, in the places where smoking is prohibited or restricted pursuant to this part 2.

(2) If the owner or manager of a place not specifically listed in section 25-14-204, including a place otherwise exempted under section 25-14-205, is an employer and receives a request from an

employee to create a smoke-free work area as contemplated by section 25-14-204 (1) (k) (II) , the owner or manager shall post a sign or signs in the smoke-free work area as provided in subsection (1) of this section.

### 25-14-207. Other applicable regulations of smoking - local counterpart regulations authorized.

(1) This part 2 shall not be interpreted or construed to permit smoking where it is otherwise restricted by any other applicable law.

(2) (a) A local authority may, pursuant to article 16 of title 31, C.R.S., a municipal home rule charter, or article 15 of title 30, C.R.S., enact, adopt, and enforce smoking regulations that cover the same subject matter as the various provisions of this part 2. No local authority may adopt any local regulation of smoking that is less stringent than the provisions of this part 2; except that a local authority may specify a radius of less than fifteen feet for the area included within an entryway.

(b) The municipal courts or their equivalent in any city, city and county, or town have jurisdiction over violations of smoking regulations enacted by any city, city and county, or town under this section.

### 25-14-208. Unlawful acts - penalty - disposition of fines and surcharges.

(1) It is unlawful for a person who owns, manages, operates, or otherwise controls the use of a premises subject to this part 2 to violate any provision of this part 2.

(2) It is unlawful for a person to smoke in an area where smoking is prohibited pursuant to this part 2.

(3) A person who violates this part 2 is guilty of a class 2 petty offense and, upon conviction thereof, shall be punished by a fine not to exceed two hundred dollars for a first violation within a calendar year, a fine not to exceed three hundred dollars for a second violation within a calendar year, and a fine not to exceed five hundred dollars for each additional violation within a calendar year. Each day of a continuing violation shall be deemed a separate violation.

(4) All judges, clerks of a court of record, or other officers imposing or receiving fines collected pursuant to or as a result of a conviction of any persons for a violation of any provision of this part 2 shall transmit all such moneys so collected in the following manner:

(a) Seventy-five percent of any such fine for a violation occurring within the corporate limits of a city, town, or city and county shall be transmitted to the treasurer or chief financial officer of said city, town, or city and county, and the remaining twenty-five percent shall be transmitted to the state treasurer, who shall credit the same to the general fund.

(b) Seventy-five percent of any fine for a violation occurring outside the corporate limits of a city or town shall be transmitted to the treasurer of the county in which the city or town is located, and the remaining twenty-five percent shall be transmitted to the state treasurer, who shall credit the same to the general fund.

### 25-14-209. Severability.

If any provision of this part 2 or the application thereof to any person or circumstance is held invalid, such invalidity shall not affect other provisions or applications of this part 2 that can be given effect without the invalid provision or application, and to this end the provisions of this part 2 are declared to be severable.

# PART 3. TOBACCO USE BY MINORS

### 25-14-301. Possession of cigarettes or tobacco products by a minor prohibited

## - definitions.

(1) This section shall be known and may be cited as the "Teen Tobacco Use Prevention Act".

(2) (a) Possession of a cigarette or tobacco product by a person who is under eighteen years of age is prohibited.

(b) It shall not be an offense under paragraph (a) of this subsection (2) if the person under eighteen years of age was acting at the direction of an employee of a governmental agency authorized to enforce or ensure compliance with laws relating to the prohibition of the sale of cigarettes and tobacco products to minors.

(3) As used in this section, unless the context otherwise requires:

(a) "Cigarette" shall have the same meaning as set forth in section 39-28-202 (4) , C.R.S.

(b) "Possession" means that a person:

(I) Has or holds any amount of cigarettes or tobacco products anywhere on his or her person;

(II) Owns or has custody of cigarettes or tobacco products; or

(III) Has cigarettes or tobacco products within his or her immediate presence and control.

(c) "Tobacco product" shall have the same meaning as set forth in section 18-13-121 (5) , C.R.S.

(4) Nothing in this section shall be construed to prohibit any statutory or home rule municipality from enacting an ordinance that prohibits the possession of cigarettes or tobacco products by a person who is under eighteen years of age or imposes requirements more stringent than provided in this section.

(5) A violation of paragraph (a) of subsection (2) of this section is a noncriminal offense.

# ARTICLE 15. HAZARDOUS WASTE

# PART 1. GENERAL PROVISIONS

## 25-15-101. Definitions.

As used in this article, unless the context otherwise requires:

(1) "Commission" means the solid and hazardous waste commission created in part 3 of this article.

(2) "Department" means the department of public health and environment created by section 25-1-102.

(3) "Disposal" means the discharge, deposit, injection, dumping, spilling, leaking, or placing of any hazardous waste into or on any land or water so that such hazardous waste or any constituent thereof may enter the environment or be emitted into the air or discharged into any waters, including groundwaters.

(4) "Domestic sewage" means untreated sanitary wastes that pass through a sewer system.

(4.3) "Environmental covenant" means an instrument containing environmental use restrictions created pursuant to section 25-15-321.

(4.5) "Environmental remediation project" means closure of a hazardous waste management unit or solid waste disposal site or any remediation of environmental contamination, including determinations to rely solely or partially on environmental use restrictions to protect human health and the environment but excluding interim measures that are not intended as the final remedial action, that is conducted under any of the following:

(a) Subchapter III or IX of the federal "Resource Conservation and Recovery Act of 1976", 42 U.S.C. sec. 6921 to 6939e and 6991 to 6991i, as amended;

(b) Section 7002 or 7003 of the federal "Resource Conservation and Recovery Act of 1976", 42 U.S.C. sec. 6972 and 6973, as amended;

(c) The federal "Comprehensive Environmental Response, Compensation, and Liability Act of

1980", 42 U.S.C. sec. 9601 et seq., as amended;

(d) The federal "Uranium Mill Tailings Radiation Control Act of 1978", 42 U.S.C. sec. 7901 et seq., as amended;

(e) Part 1 of article 11 of this title, including any decommissioning of sites licensed under that part;

(f) Part 3 of article 11 of this title;

(g) Part 3 of article 15 of this title; and

(h) Article 20 of title 30, C.R.S.

(4.7) "Environmental use restriction" means a prohibition of one or more uses of or activities on specified real property, including drilling for or pumping groundwater; a requirement to perform certain acts, including requirements for maintenance, operation, or monitoring necessary to preserve such prohibition of uses or activities; or both, where such prohibitions or requirements are relied upon in the remedial decision for an environmental remediation project for the purpose of protecting human health or the environment.

(5) "Federal act" means the federal "Solid Waste Disposal Act", as amended by the federal "Resource Conservation and Recovery Act of 1976", as amended (42 U.S.C. sec. 6901, et seq.) .

(5.5) "Hazardous substance" means any substance that is defined as a hazardous substance, pollutant, or contaminant under the federal "Comprehensive Environmental Response, Compensation, and Liability Act of 1980", 42 U.S.C. sec. 9601 et seq., as amended, or its implementing regulations.

(6) (a) "Hazardous waste" means any material, alone or mixed with other materials, which has no commercial use or value, or which is discarded or is to be discarded by the possessor thereof, either of which because its quantity, concentration, or physical or chemical characteristics may:

(I) Cause, or significantly contribute to, an increase in mortality or an increase in serious irreversible, or incapacitating reversible, illness; or

(II) Pose a substantial present or potential hazard to human health or the environment when improperly treated, stored, transported, or disposed of, or otherwise managed.

(b) "Hazardous waste" does not include:

(I) Solid or dissolved material in discharges which are point sources subject to permits under section 402 of the "Federal Water Pollution Control Act", as amended;

(II) Source, special nuclear, or byproduct material as defined by the federal "Atomic Energy Act of 1954", as amended;

(III) (A) Agricultural, horticultural, or floricultural waste from the raising of crops or animals, including animal manures, that are returned to the soil as fertilizers or soil conditioners;

(B) Nothing in sub-subparagraph (A) of this subparagraph (III) , as amended by House Bill 05-1180, as enacted at the first regular session of the sixty-fifth general assembly, shall be construed as changing the property tax classification of property owned by a horticultural or floricultural operation.

(IV) Solid or dissolved material in domestic sewage;

(V) Irrigation return flows;

(VI) Inert materials deposited for construction fill or topsoil placement in connection with actual or contemplated construction at such location or for changes in land contour for agricultural and mining purposes, if such depositing does not fall within the definition of treatment, storage, or disposal of hazardous waste;

(VII) Any waste or other materials exempted or otherwise not regulated as a hazardous waste under the federal act, except as provided in section 25-15-302 (4) ;

(VIII) Indigenous waste from prospecting and mining operations which is disposed of in accordance with the requirements of an approved reclamation plan contained in a permit issued pursuant to article 32 of title 34, C.R.S., or article 33 of title 34, C.R.S.;

(IX) Waste from oil and gas activities, including but not limited to drilling fluids, produced water, and other wastes associated with the exploration, development, or production of crude oil, natural gas, or geothermal energy, which is disposed of in accordance with the requirements of the oil and gas commission pursuant to article 60 of title 34, C.R.S.

(c) Any material which would be hazardous waste subject to the provisions of this article except for the fact that it has commercial use or value may be subject to regulations promulgated by the commission when it is transported or stored prior to reuse.

(7) "Hazardous waste generation" means the act or process of producing hazardous waste.

(8) "Hazardous waste management" means the systematic control of the collection, source separation, storage, transportation, treatment, recovery, and disposal of hazardous waste.

(9) "Inert material" means non-water-soluble and nondecomposable inert solids together with such minor amounts and types of other materials as will not significantly affect the inert nature of such solids according to rules and regulations of the commission. The term includes but is not limited to earth, sand, gravel, rock, concrete which has been in a hardened state for at least sixty days, masonry, asphalt paving fragments, and other non-water-soluble and nondecomposable inert solids including those the commission may identify by regulation.

(10) "Manifest" means the document used for identifying the quantity, composition, origin, routing, and destination of hazardous waste during its transportation from the point of generation to the point of storage, treatment, or disposal.

(10.5) "Notice of environmental use restrictions" or "restrictive notice" means an instrument containing environmental use restrictions created pursuant to section 25-15-321.5.

(11) "Operation", when used in connection with hazardous waste management, means the use of procedures, equipment, personnel, and other resources to provide hazardous waste management.

(12) "Operator" means the person operating a hazardous waste management facility or site either by contract or permit.

(12.5) "Owner", as used in sections 25-15-317 to 25-15-326, means the record owner of real property and, if any, any other person or entity otherwise legally authorized to make decisions regarding the transfer of the subject property or placement of encumbrances on the subject property, other than by the exercise of eminent domain.

(13) "Person" means any individual, public or private corporation, partnership, association, firm, trust or estate; the state or any executive department, institution, or agency thereof; any municipal corporation, county, city and county, or other political subdivision of the state; or any other legal entity whatsoever which is recognized by law as the subject of rights and duties.

(13.5) "Remedial decision" means the administrative determination by the department, the United States environmental protection agency, or other appropriate government entity under the laws cited in subsection (4.5) of this section, that establishes the remedial requirements for the environmental remediation project.

(14) "Resource recovery", when used in connection with hazardous waste, means the operation of preparing and treating any such material or portion thereof for recycling or reuse or the recovery of material or energy.

(15) "Storage", when used in connection with hazardous waste, means the containment of hazardous waste, either on a temporary basis or for a period of years, in such a manner as not to constitute disposal of hazardous waste. The term "storage" does not apply to any hazardous waste generation if such waste is retained on the site by the generator in quantities or for time periods exempted by rules and regulations promulgated by the commission.

(16) "Transportation", when used in connection with hazardous waste, means the off-site movement of hazardous waste to any intermediate point or any point of storage, treatment, or disposal.

(17) "Treatment", when used in connection with an operation involved in hazardous waste management, means any method, technique, or process, including neutralization or incineration, designed to change the physical, chemical, or biological character or composition of a hazardous waste, so as to neutralize such waste or to render such waste less hazardous, safer for transport, amenable for recovery or reuse, amenable for storage, or reduced in volume.

(18) "Treatment, storage, or disposal site or facility" means a location at which hazardous waste is subjected to treatment, storage, or disposal and may include a facility where hazardous waste is generated.

### 25-15-102. Effective dates.
(1) Parts 1 and 2 of this article shall take effect July 1, 1981.
(2) Section 25-15-302 shall take effect January 1, 1982.
(3) Part 3 of this article, except section 25-15-302, shall take effect November 2, 1984.

### 25-15-103. Technical assistance.
The department may upon request provide technical advice to hazardous waste generators, to owners or operators of treatment plants, storage facilities, or disposal sites, and to counties and municipalities in which such facilities may be located in order to assure that appropriate measures are taken to protect the public health, safety, and welfare and the environment. The department may charge its actual costs of providing compliance assistance; except that, for company-specific compliance assistance, the department shall not charge fees for the first two hours in any given fiscal year.

### 25-15-104. Disposal service.
In order to encourage proper disposal of small quantities of hazardous wastes by individuals and local governmental agencies when such wastes cannot be reasonably handled by commercial services, the department may receive such hazardous wastes from such individuals or local governmental agencies and arrange for their proper detoxification, storage, reuse, or disposal. The department may impose a reasonable fee for such services to recover the actual costs thereof.

# PART 2. HAZARDOUS WASTE DISPOSAL SITES

### 25-15-200.1. Short title.
This part 2 shall be known and may be cited as the "State Hazardous Waste Siting Act".

### 25-15-200.2. Legislative declaration.
(1) The general assembly hereby finds that adverse public health and environmental impacts can result from the improper land disposal of hazardous waste and that the need for establishing safe sites with adequate capacity for the disposal of hazardous waste is a matter of statewide concern, and the provisions of this part 2 are therefore enacted to provide an effective method of establishing such sites.
(2) It is the intent of the general assembly that generators of hazardous waste be encouraged to use on-site and off-site alternative treatment methods to reduce the amount of hazardous waste that must be discharged into the environment and the associated hazards to the health and welfare of the citizens of this state. Alternative management technologies which detoxify, stabilize, and reduce the amount of hazardous waste that must be buried are available. For such purpose, the provisions of this part 2 are enacted to allow the development of safe alternative methods for the treatment of hazardous waste and to provide a means for the designation of hazardous waste disposal sites when such methods are unable to obviate the need for hazardous waste disposal on land. Whereas the state of Colorado may be responsible for the perpetual care of hazardous waste land disposal facilities, alternative technologies such as incineration, resource recovery, or physical, chemical, or biological degradation should be implemented to the maximum extent possible.

### 25-15-200.3. Definitions.
As used in this part 2, unless the context otherwise requires:
(1) Repealed.
(2) "Existing hazardous waste disposal site" means a hazardous waste disposal site which is in

active operation prior to July 1, 1981.

(3) "Governmental unit" means the state of Colorado, every county, city and county, municipality, school district, special district, and authority located in this state, every public body corporate created or established under the constitution or any law of this state, and every board, commission, department, institution, or agency of any of the foregoing or of the United States.

(4) (a) "Hazardous waste disposal" means any final action to abandon, deposit, inter, or otherwise discard hazardous waste after its use has been achieved or a use is no longer intended or any discharging of hazardous waste into the environment.

(b) The term includes the off-site surface impoundment of hazardous waste such as a holding, storage, settling, or aeration pit, pond, or lagoon, except as provided in paragraph (c) of this subsection (4) or section 25-15-201 (4) .

(c) The term does not include:

(I) (A) Recycling, reclaiming, incineration, processing, or other treatment of hazardous waste.

(B) For the purposes of this subparagraph (I) , the surface impoundment which is part of a sewage treatment works or feedlot operation shall be considered as treatment and not disposal.

(C) Any recycling, reclaiming, incineration, processing, or treatment facility shall be subject to all local land use regulations.

(II) The beneficial use, including use for fertilizer, soil conditioner, fuel, or livestock feed, of sludge from wastewater treatment plants if such sludge meets all applicable standards of the department.

(5) "Hazardous waste disposal site" means all contiguous land, including publicly-owned land, under common ownership which is used for hazardous waste disposal; except that such term shall not include any site which is in compliance with an approved reclamation plan contained in a permit issued pursuant to article 32 of title 34, C.R.S., or article 33 of title 34, C.R.S.

(6) "Publicly owned land" means any land owned by the federal government or any agency thereof or land owned by the state or any agency or political subdivision thereof.

## 25-15-201. Certificate required - disposal prohibited - exceptions.

(1) Any person who operates a hazardous waste disposal site shall first obtain a certificate of designation from the board of county commissioners if the site is in the unincorporated portion of any county, or from the governing body of a municipality if the site is in an incorporated area.

(2) Hazardous waste disposal by any person is prohibited except on or at a hazardous waste disposal site for which a certificate of designation has been obtained as provided in this part 2.

(3) Any existing hazardous waste disposal site which has obtained and possesses a certificate of designation pursuant to part 1 of article 20 of title 30, C.R.S., and which meets all applicable requirements and regulations under the federal act shall be deemed to have a certificate of designation issued pursuant to this part 2 and shall be fully subject to the provisions of this part 2 which apply to certificates of designation issued pursuant to this part 2.

(4) Notwithstanding the provisions of subsections (1) and (2) of this section, any person other than a governmental unit may dispose of his own hazardous waste on his own property, as long as such hazardous waste disposal site is part of that originally zoned or otherwise approved for the activity that generates the hazardous waste, the owner has notified the local government or the department of the types and methods of hazardous waste disposal, and such disposal complies with the rules and regulations of the commission issued pursuant to this part 2 and does not constitute a public nuisance. For the purposes of this part 2, the site of such hazardous waste disposal shall be an approved site for which obtaining a certificate of designation under the provisions of this part 2 shall be unnecessary. This subsection (4) shall not preclude any person from applying for a certificate of designation for the disposal of his own hazardous waste on his own property.

(5) Notwithstanding the provisions of subsections (1) and (2) of this section, any person who is engaged in mining operations pursuant to a permit issued by the mined land reclamation board or office of mined land reclamation which contains an approved plan of reclamation may dispose of hazardous waste generated by such operations within the permitted area for such operations. For

the purposes of this part 2, the site of such hazardous waste disposal shall be an approved site for which obtaining a certificate of designation under the provisions of this part 2 shall be unnecessary.

## 25-15-202. Application for certificate - review by department and Colorado geological survey - hearing.

(1) Any person desiring to operate a hazardous waste disposal site shall make application for a certificate of designation to the board of county commissioners of the county or to the governing body of the municipality in which such site is proposed to be located.

(2) The application shall be accompanied by a fee established by the board of county commissioners or the governing body of the municipality by resolution or ordinance, which fee shall not exceed fifty thousand dollars and which fee may be refunded in whole or in part. Fifty percent of such fee shall be transmitted to the department to offset the costs of the department's review pursuant to subsection (4) of this section, including possible costs of reimbursement to other state agencies which assist in such review. The application shall set forth the following: The location of the site; the types of waste to be accepted or rejected; the types of waste disposal; the method of supervision; and the anticipated access routes in the county in which the site is located. The application shall also contain such data as may reasonably be required by rules of the commission developed pursuant to section 25-15-208 to enable the department and the Colorado geological survey to perform their duties under subsection (4) of this section.

(3) The clerk of the county or municipality shall promptly notify the county commissioners and the governing body of any other county or municipality within twenty miles of a proposed hazardous waste disposal site of the filing of an application for a certificate of designation therefor.

(4) (a) Within ten working days of an application for a certificate of designation and prior to further consideration, the board of county commissioners or the governing body of the municipality, as the case may be, shall forward a copy of the application to the department and to the Colorado geological survey.

(b) The Colorado geological survey shall review each application received by it and make a recommendation to the department on the geological suitability of the proposed hazardous waste disposal site for land disposal of hazardous waste, based upon the geological, hydrological, climatological, geochemical, and geomorphological characteristics of the site. Such recommendation shall be submitted to the department within sixty days of the Colorado geological survey's receipt of the application.

(c) Within ninety days of its receipt of the application, the department shall make findings of fact on the technical merits of the application and provide such findings of fact to the board of county commissioners or the governing body of the municipality. The findings of fact shall at a minimum include:

(I) A determination as to whether the site could be designed and operated in compliance with applicable rules and regulations adopted by the commission pursuant to section 25-15-208;

(II) A determination as to whether the site is located within an area designated to be optimally suitable for hazardous waste disposal by the most recent study of the Colorado geological survey made pursuant to section 25-15-216 and, if not, as to whether the site is suitable for the land disposal of hazardous waste as demonstrated by reliable geologic, hydrologic, and other scientific data;

(III) A recommendation to the board of county commissioners or the governing body of a municipality, as the case may be, as to whether the application for a certificate of designation should be approved. A recommendation for approval may only be made upon affirmative findings of facts under subparagraphs (I) and (II) of this paragraph (c) .

(5) The application shall be considered by the board of county commissioners or the governing body of the municipality, as the case may be, at a public hearing to be held after notice. Such notice shall contain the time and place of the hearing and shall state that the matter to be

considered is the applicant's proposal for a hazardous waste disposal site. The notice shall be published in a newspaper having general circulation in the region in which the proposed hazardous waste disposal site is located at least ten but no more than thirty days prior to the date of the hearing.

## 25-15-203. Grounds for approval.

(1) The board of county commissioners or the governing body of the municipality, as the case may be, may approve an application for a certificate of designation only upon a finding of all of the following factors:

(a) The department has made a recommendation of approval pursuant to section 25-15-202 (4) (c) (III) .

(b) The site would not pose a significant threat to the safety of the public, taking into consideration:

(I) The density of population areas neighboring the site;

(II) The density of population areas adjacent to the portion of the delivery roads within a fifty-mile radius of the site;

(III) The risk of accidents during the transportation of waste to or at the site.

(c) The applicant has demonstrated a need for the facility by Colorado hazardous waste generators.

(d) The applicant has documented its financial ability to operate the proposed site.

(e) The applicant, taking into account its prior performance record, if any, in the treatment, storage, or disposal of hazardous waste, has documented sufficient reliability, expertise, and competency to operate and manage the proposed facility.

(f) The site conforms to officially adopted land use plans, policies, regulations, and resolutions.

(2) The board of county commissioners or the governing body of the municipality, as the case may be, shall notify the department of any approval of an application for a certificate of designation within five days after such approval.

## 25-15-204. Certificate.

(1) The certificate of designation shall identify the general types of waste which may be accepted or which shall be rejected.

(2) The certificate of designation shall be displayed in a prominent place at the hazardous waste disposal site.

(3) Repealed.

(4) The certificate of designation may provide such conditions as may reasonably be necessary for the safe operation of such site including but not limited to the provision by the site owner or operator of additional fire protection, security, or trained personnel for monitoring, inspections, and incident responses.

(5) Repealed.

(6) A certificate of designation issued pursuant to this part 2 shall be deemed to satisfy any requirement imposed by part 1 of article 20 of title 30, C.R.S., for a certificate of designation as a solid wastes disposal site and facility.

## 25-15-205. Permit required for operation - burial of liquids prohibited.

(1) Operation of a hazardous waste disposal site for which a certificate of designation has been issued shall not begin until the applicant obtains for such operation a federal permit issued under the federal act or a state permit issued under part 3 of this article.

(2) A certificate of designation for a hazardous waste disposal site shall not become effective until such time as the certificated facility has received a permit under section 3005 (c) of the federal act or the equivalent state permit.

(3) The burial of liquid hazardous waste both on-site and off-site is prohibited in this state. The commission may develop rules and regulations which phase out the land disposal of highly mobile, toxic, and persistent waste.

## 25-15-206. Substantial change in ownership, design, or operation.

(1) A substantial change in the ownership of a hazardous waste disposal site, including an assignment or a transfer of the certificate of designation therefor, or in the design or operation of a hazardous waste disposal site, as "substantial change" is defined in rules and regulations of the commission, shall be submitted to the board of county commissioners or the governing body of the municipality for its approval before such change shall become effective; except that, in the case of a hazardous waste disposal site which was designated by the council pursuant to section 25-15-217, as said section existed upon its repeal, such change shall be subject to approval by the department.

(2) Any approval of a substantial change under this section shall be made only upon the finding of all of the factors required in section 25-15-203.

(3) The application for approval of a substantial change under this section shall be accompanied by a fee established by the jurisdiction whose approval is required for such substantial change, which fee shall not exceed ten thousand dollars and which fee may be refunded in whole or in part. If the department is not the approving jurisdiction, up to fifty percent of such fee shall be transmitted to the department to offset the costs of the department's review pursuant to section 25-15-202 (4) , including possible costs of reimbursement to other state agencies which assist in such review.

## 25-15-206.5. Revocation or suspension of certificate.

(1) The jurisdiction which granted the certificate of designation may revoke or suspend the certificate of designation of any hazardous waste disposal site if it finds that:

(a) There was a material misrepresentation or misstatement of fact in the application for the certificate of designation;

(b) The hazardous waste disposal site is not being operated in substantial compliance with any term, condition, or limitation of its certificate of designation or any applicable rule or regulation adopted pursuant to this part 2; or

(c) The owner or operator of the site has failed to pay the annual fee to the county or municipality as required by section 25-15-214 (1) .

(2) The revocation or suspension of a certificate of designation shall not relieve the owner or operator of the hazardous waste disposal site from any legal liability.

## 25-15-207. Judicial review.

(1) The award, denial, revocation, or suspension of a certificate of designation by the board of county commissioners or by the governing body of the municipality shall be subject to judicial review in the district court for the judicial district in which the hazardous waste disposal site is located or is proposed to be located. Any request for such judicial review must be made within thirty days of such award, denial, revocation, or suspension. If the court finds no error, it shall affirm the action. If the court finds that the action is arbitrary and capricious, not in accord with the procedures or procedural limitations of this part 2, unsupported by substantial evidence when the record is considered as a whole, or otherwise contrary to law, then the court shall hold unlawful and set aside the action and remand the case to the board of county commissioners or to the governing body of the municipality for further proceedings as may be appropriate.

(2) In the case of any action or decision of the council or department pursuant to section 25-15-206, judicial review shall be in the district court for the judicial district within which the hazardous waste disposal site is or may be located and shall be in accordance with section 24-4-106, C.R.S.

## 25-15-208. Commission to promulgate rules and regulations - limitations.

(1) The commission may promulgate rules and regulations establishing criteria for the engineering design of hazardous waste disposal sites and for the location of such sites to the extent that site characteristics are integrally related to the safe engineering design of such sites. Such rules and

regulations shall take into account at least the following: Protection of surface and subsurface waters, suitable physical characteristics, distance from waste generation centers, access routes, distance from water wells, and final closure.

(2) The commission may also promulgate rules and regulations establishing what constitutes a substantial change in ownership, design, or operation of a hazardous waste disposal site under section 25-15-206.

(3) The rules and regulations promulgated by the commission pursuant to this section shall be based upon generally accepted scientific data.

### 25-15-209. Inventory required.

The operator of every hazardous waste disposal site shall maintain an inventory of the types of hazardous wastes accepted for disposal at such site, and a copy of such inventory shall be provided to any person upon request and upon payment of a reasonable charge for the costs of the reproduction. Upon a closure of the site, a final inventory shall be prepared and filed with the department where it shall remain available for public inspection and copying at a reasonable cost.

### 25-15-209.5. Inspection required.

A department employee shall inspect each off-site hazardous waste disposal site during times when hazardous wastes are ordinarily received. Such inspection shall be conducted at intervals determined by rule and regulation of the commission based on the volume and toxicity of the wastes being received. Such department employee shall be permitted reasonable access to disposal operations for the purpose of monitoring and inspecting such operations. Such department employee, whose salary and benefits shall be paid out of the department's share of the annual fee collected by the county or municipality pursuant to section 25-15-214 (1) , shall have training and experience in relevant aspects of hazardous waste management.

### 25-15-209.6. Performance audits.

Each designated and permitted hazardous waste disposal site shall be subject to a performance audit at least once every five years, for the purpose of reviewing the systems that provide assurance the site is protecting human health and the environment. Such performance audit shall be conducted by the department.

### 25-15-210. Sites deemed public nuisance - when.

Any hazardous waste disposal site that is found to be abandoned or that is operated or maintained in a manner so as to violate any of the provisions of this part 2 or any rule or regulation adopted pursuant thereto shall be deemed a public nuisance, and such violation may be enjoined by the district court for the judicial district wherein the violation occurred in an action brought by the department, the board of county commissioners of the county wherein the violation occurred, or the governing body of the municipality wherein the violation occurred.

### 25-15-211. Violation - criminal penalty.

Any person who violates any provision of this part 2 commits a class 3 misdemeanor and shall be punished as provided in section 18-1.3-501, C.R.S. Each day of violation shall be deemed a separate offense under this section. Except in regard to matters of statewide concern as expressed in section 25-15-200.2 (1) , nothing in this part 2 shall preclude or preempt a county, a city, a city and county, or an incorporated town from the enforcement of its local resolutions or ordinances or of its land use plans, policies, or regulations.

### 25-15-212. Violation - civil penalty - reimbursement of costs.

(1) Any person who violates any provision of this part 2 shall be subject to a civil penalty of not more than ten thousand dollars per day of violation. Such penalty shall be determined and

collected by the district court for the judicial district in which such violation occurs upon action instituted by the department, the board of county commissioners of the county in which the violation occurs, or the governing body of the municipality in which the violation occurs. In determining the amount of any such penalty, the court shall take into account the seriousness of the violation, whether the violation was willful or due to mistake, the economic impact of the penalty on the violator, and any other relevant factors. All penalties collected pursuant to this section shall be transmitted to the state treasurer and credited to the general fund. Except in regard to matters of statewide concern as expressed in section 25-15-200.2 (1) , nothing in this part 2 shall preclude or preempt a county, city, city and county, or an incorporated town from enforcement of its local resolutions or ordinances or of its land use plans, policies, or regulations. (2) If the violation for which a penalty has been assessed and paid into the general fund pursuant to this section results in a county, city, municipality, or town incurring costs to remove, contain, or otherwise mitigate the effects of the hazardous waste which was involved in the court action, such entity shall be entitled to reimbursement for its costs, which reimbursement shall not exceed the amount of the penalty collected. A claim for reimbursement shall be filed with the state treasurer. Reimbursement shall be paid by the state treasurer out of those funds attributable to such penalty.

## 25-15-213. County or municipal hazardous waste disposal site fund - tax - fees.

Any county or municipality that operates a county or municipal hazardous waste disposal site or sites is authorized to establish a county or municipal hazardous waste disposal site fund. The board of county commissioners of such county or the governing body of the municipality may levy a hazardous waste disposal site tax in addition to any other tax authorized by law, on the taxable property within said county or municipality, the proceeds of which shall be deposited to the credit of said fund and appropriated to pay the cost of land, labor, equipment, and services needed in the operation of county or municipal hazardous waste disposal sites. Any such county or municipality is also authorized, after a public hearing, to fix, modify, and collect service charges from users of county or municipal hazardous waste disposal sites for the purpose of financing the operations at those sites.

## 25-15-214. Hazardous waste disposal site fund - fees.

(1) Any hazardous waste disposal site which is issued a certificate of designation on or after July 1, 1981, or which receives approval for a substantial change in ownership as required in section 25-15-206 (1) on or after said date shall be required, contingent upon the issuance of a federal or state permit by the county or municipality in which it is located, to pay to the county or municipality in which it is located an annual fee for the purpose of offsetting the estimated direct costs of increased state, county, and municipal services created by the hazardous waste disposal site, including, but not limited to, the improvement and maintenance of roads and bridges, fire protection, law enforcement, monitoring by county or municipal health officials, and emergency preparation and response. The amount of the fee shall be two percent of the annual estimated gross revenue received by the hazardous waste disposal site. Out of the annual fee, the board of county commissioners or the governing body of the municipality shall provide for the reimbursement of governmental units for their estimated direct costs of increased services created by the hazardous waste disposal site. In the event that the site owner or operator fails to pay the annual fee, the board of county commissioners or the governing body of the municipality may suspend the site's certificate of designation until the annual fee has been paid.
(2) Any county or municipality is authorized to establish a hazardous waste disposal site fund. All fees collected pursuant to subsection (1) of this section shall be deposited to the credit of said fund and appropriated for the purposes for which collected.

## 25-15-215. Contracts with governmental units authorized.

(1) Any governmental unit may contract for the operation of a hazardous waste disposal site.

(2) Any city, city and county, county, or incorporated town acting by itself or in association with any other such governmental unit may establish and operate a hazardous waste disposal site under such terms and conditions as may be approved by the governing bodies of the governmental units involved. In the event such site is not operated by the governmental unit involved, any contract to operate such a site shall be awarded on a competitive bid basis if there is more than one applicant for a contract to operate such site.

(3) Any hazardous waste disposal site established in accordance with this section shall be required to obtain a certificate of designation pursuant to this part 2.

### 25-15-216. Colorado geological survey to designate optimally suitable areas.

Subject to available appropriations, the Colorado geological survey shall conduct a study of the geological suitability of areas of the state for hazardous waste disposal sites. Such study shall designate those areas of the state which the Colorado geological survey finds to be optimally suitable for hazardous waste disposal based upon detailed criteria relating to hydrology, geology, geochemistry, structural geology, geomorphology, climatology, and mineral resources. The designation of optimally suitable areas and the criteria utilized shall be produced in a publication available to the public at a reasonable cost.

### 25-15-217. Circumstances allowing state designation of a hazardous waste disposal site - conditions and limitations. (Repealed)

### 25-15-218. State hazardous waste siting council - composition. (Repealed)

### 25-15-219. Department to study need for disposal sites and feasibility of alternative technologies.

(1) The department shall conduct a study assessing the need for hazardous waste disposal sites in this state. Such study shall identify the volumes and types of hazardous wastes generated in this state and the appropriateness and feasibility of treatment and disposal technologies as alternatives to land disposal. To offset the cost of such study, the department is authorized to expend a maximum of sixty thousand dollars out of the annual appropriation to the department from the hazardous waste service fund pursuant to section 25-15-304.

(2) The department may also develop and submit to the general assembly proposed legislation to encourage the development and utilization of alternative technologies for hazardous waste management, which may include, by way of example, tax incentives for the purchase of equipment to implement alternative technologies.

### 25-15-220. Effect of 1983 amendments. (Repealed)

# PART 3. STATE HAZARDOUS WASTE MANAGEMENT PROGRAM

### 25-15-301. Powers and duties of department.

(1) The department shall be the entity in the state responsible for the regulation of hazardous waste management; however, the department may, in accordance with section 25-15-306, enter into agreements with local governments to conduct specified activities involving monitoring,

inspections, and technical services but not permit issuance or enforcement.

(2) Pursuant to rules and regulations as provided for in section 25-15-302, the department shall:

(a) Issue permits for treatment, storage, and disposal facilities, provide for the inspection of such operations, and enforce the limitations and conditions of such permits, including any conditions and schedules established to correct noncompliance; and

(b) Assure that all generators, transporters, storers, treaters, and disposers of hazardous waste have received appropriate identification by the department, use a manifest system, and provide periodic reports on wastes manifested.

(3) The department, by its duly authorized representatives, shall have the power to enter and inspect any property, premises, or place in which hazardous waste is reasonably believed to be located or in which relevant records may be located for the purpose of determining the compliance or noncompliance with any provision of this part 3, any rules and regulations promulgated pursuant to this part 3, or any order or permit, or term or condition thereof, issued pursuant to this part 3. Unless an emergency exists or the department has reason to believe that any unlawful activity is being conducted or will be conducted, the department shall provide prior notification of such inspection, which inspection shall be during normal business hours. If such entry or inspection is denied or not consented to and no emergency exists, the department is empowered to and shall obtain from the district court for the judicial district in which such property, premises, or place is located a warrant to enter and inspect any such property, premises, or place prior to entry and inspection. The district courts of this state are empowered to issue such warrants upon a showing that such entry and inspection is required to verify that the purposes of this part 3 are being carried out. Any information relating to proprietary processes or methods of manufacture or production obtained in the course of the inspection shall be kept confidential in accordance with section 24-72-204 (3) (a) (IV) , C.R.S., of the open records law. If samples are taken, the owner and operator of the premises from which such samples are taken shall be entitled to a receipt for such samples and, upon request, a sufficient portion to perform an analysis equivalent to that which the department may perform.

(4) (a) In the event of an emergency involving hazardous waste which presents an immediate and substantial threat to the public health and safety or the environment, the department shall have the authority to issue such orders as may be appropriate to protect the public health and safety or the environment, including emergency authorization to transport, treat, store, or dispose of hazardous waste.

(b) Any person against whom an emergency order is issued pursuant to this subsection (4) shall be entitled to an immediate hearing as provided in section 24-4-105 (12) , C.R.S.

(5) In order to provide for the essential long-term care of hazardous waste consistent with adequate protection of the public health and safety and the environment, the department may acquire by gift, purchase, transfer from another state department or agency, or other transfer any and all lands, buildings, and grounds that have been designated as a hazardous waste site and may lease such properties to others for hazardous waste management. Any such acquisition shall be subject to the provisions of section 25-15-303 (4) .

## 25-15-301.5. Additional powers of department - legislative declaration - report.

(1) The general assembly hereby finds, determines, and declares that the hazardous waste control program shall be implemented to protect human health and the environment in a manner that:

(a) Maintains program authorization by the federal government;

(b) Promotes a community ethic to reduce or eliminate waste problems;

(c) Is credible and accountable to industry and the public;

(d) Is innovative and cost-effective; and

(e) Protects the environmental quality of life for impacted residents as required by other provisions of this part 3 and rules promulgated in connection therewith.

(2) The department shall develop, implement, and continuously improve policies and procedures

for carrying out its statutory responsibilities at the lowest possible cost without jeopardizing the intent stated in subsection (1) of this section. At a minimum, these policies and procedures shall, to the extent practicable, include the following:

(a) Establish cost-effective level-of-effort guidelines for reviewing submittals including, but not limited to, permit applications and corrective action plans, to assure conformity with regulatory requirements, taking into consideration the degree of risk addressed and the complexity of the issues raised;

(b) Establish cost-effective level-of-effort guidelines for performing inspections that focus on major violations of regulatory requirements that pose an immediate and significant threat to human health and the environment;

(c) Streamline the corrective action process with features that include, without limitation, the following:

(I) Cost-effective level-of-effort guidelines for site investigations and remediation that focus on result-based outcomes and performance-based oversight by the department;

(II) Cost-effective level-of-effort guidelines for reviewing site investigation reports and corrective action plans;

(III) The use of enforceable institutional controls to avoid unnecessary cleanup costs; and

(IV) Realistic cleanup standards that address actual risk to human health and the environment on a site-specific basis and that take into account any applicable institutional controls.

(d) Establish cost-effective level-of-effort guidelines for enforcement activities;

(e) Establish schedules for timely completion of department activities including, but not limited to, submittal reviews, inspections and inspection reports, and corrective action activities;

(f) Establish a prioritization methodology for completing activities that focuses on actual risk to human health and the environment;

(g) Establish a preference for compliance assistance with at least ten percent of the annual budget amount being allocated to compliance assistance efforts;

(h) Establish a preference for alternative dispute resolution mechanisms to timely resolve disputed issues; and

(i) Establish a mechanism that continually values and provides incentives for further improvements in the policies and procedures of the department.

(3) Notwithstanding section 24-1-136 (11) (a) (I) , the department is directed to submit a report to the general assembly on or before February 1, 2002, and annually on or before each February 1 thereafter that describes the status of the hazardous waste control program, the department's efforts to carry out its statutory responsibilities at the lowest possible cost without jeopardizing the intent stated in subsection (1) of this section, and the department's implementation of the authority to accept environmental covenants created pursuant to section 25-15-321.

## 25-15-302. Solid and hazardous waste commission - creation - membership - rules - fees - administration.

(1) (a) There is hereby created in the department of public health and environment a solid and hazardous waste commission, referred to in this part 3 as the "commission", which shall exercise its powers and perform its duties and functions as if it were transferred to said department by a type 1 transfer. The commission shall consist of nine citizens of the state who shall be appointed by the governor, with the consent of the senate, for terms of three years each; except that, of the members appointed to take office initially, three shall be appointed for one-year terms, three shall be appointed for two-year terms, and three shall be appointed for three-year terms. Members of the commission shall be appointed so as to achieve geographical representation and to reflect the various interests in waste management in the state.

(b) Appointments to the commission shall be made so that all persons shall have appropriate scientific, technical, industrial, legal, public health, or environmental training or experience. Three members shall be from the regulated community. Three members shall be from the public at large. Three members shall be from government or the academic community; except that no member shall be an employee of the department. No more than five members of the commission shall be members of the same political party.

(c) The members of the commission shall disclose any potential conflicts of interest to the governor and the committee of reference of the general assembly prior to confirmation and shall disclose any potential conflicts of interest which arise during their terms of membership to the other commission members in a public meeting of the commission.

(d) Whenever a vacancy exists on the commission, the governor shall appoint a member for the remaining portion of the unexpired term created by the vacancy, subject to confirmation by the senate.

(e) The governor may remove any appointed member of the commission for malfeasance in office, for failure to attend meetings regularly, or for any cause that renders such member incapable or unfit to discharge the duties of such member's office.

(f) If any member of the commission is absent from two consecutive meetings or fails to attend at least seventy-five percent of the regularly scheduled meetings of the commission held in any one year and such absences were without sufficient cause as determined by the commission, the chairman of the commission shall notify the governor, who may remove such member and appoint a qualified person for the remaining portion of such member's term, subject to confirmation by the senate.

(g) Each member of the commission shall receive traveling and other necessary expenses actually incurred in the performance of such member's official duties as a member of the commission.

(h) The commission shall select from its own membership a chairman, a vice-chairman, and a secretary. The commission shall keep a record of its proceedings.

(i) The commission shall hold regular public meetings and may hold special meetings on the call of the chairman or vice-chairman at such other times as deemed necessary. Written notice of the time and place of each meeting shall be mailed to each member at least twenty days in advance of such meeting.

(j) (I) The commission shall hold an annual public meeting to hear public comment on hazardous waste issues within the state. At such meeting, the commission shall answer reasonable questions from the public concerning rules, regulations, appeals of penalties, and any other commission activities under the authority of this part 3 occurring during the previous year.

(II) Prior to the meeting required under subparagraph (I) of this paragraph (j) , the commission shall prepare and make available to the public a report which shall contain the following specific information:

(A) All rules and regulations promulgated by the commission during the previous year;

(B) All interpretive rules issued by the commission during the previous year;

(C) All appeals of penalties heard before the commission and the commission's determinations in such appeals; and

(D) Any other commission activities as appropriate.

(k) Each member of the commission shall have a vote. Two-thirds of the members of the commission shall constitute a quorum, and, except as otherwise provided in subsection (4) of this section, the concurrence of a majority of the members present at any meeting at which a quorum is present on any matter within its powers and duties shall be required for any determination made by the commission.

(2) The commission shall promulgate rules pertaining to hazardous waste in accordance with this part 3 and in accordance with the procedures and other provisions of article 4 of title 24, C.R.S. Such rules shall provide protection of public health and the environment and shall include:

(a) Criteria for establishing characteristics and listings of hazardous wastes, including mechanisms for determining whether any waste is hazardous for the purpose of this part 3;

(b) Regulations governing those wastes or combinations of wastes which are not compatible and which may not be stored, treated, or disposed of together;

(c) Regulations for the storage, treatment, and disposal of hazardous wastes, including regulations for the issuance of permits based on best engineering judgment, including but not limited to interim status, regulations concerning information required to be submitted to obtain such permits,

587

and regulations concerning the requirement of a permit prior to the construction of a treatment, storage, or disposal facility;

(d) Regulations for the operation and maintenance of hazardous waste treatment, storage, and disposal facilities, including such qualifications and requirements as to ownership, continuity of operation, training of personnel, and closure and postclosure care, as may be necessary or desirable;

(e) Regulations for the design and construction of treatment, storage, and disposal facilities;

(f) Regulations, promulgated in accordance with article 20 of title 42, C.R.S., providing procedures and requirements for:

(I) The use of a manifest during transportation of hazardous waste, applying equally to those persons transporting hazardous waste they have generated themselves and to persons who have contracted to transport hazardous waste for other parties, consistent with federal and state regulations on the transportation of hazardous wastes;

(II) Record keeping concerning the transportation of hazardous waste, including its source and destination;

(III) Notification and cleanup of spills or discharges during the transportation of hazardous waste;

(IV) Transportation of hazardous wastes only if such hazardous wastes are properly labeled and for restricting the transportation of all hazardous wastes only to permitted hazardous waste treatment, storage, or disposal facilities which the shipper designates on the manifest form;

(g) Regulations requiring reports and record-keeping requirements for hazardous waste management, including notification of accidents;

(h) Regulations establishing procedures for maintaining confidentiality relating to methods of manufacture or secret processes and establishing fees and financial assurance and ownership requirements, including bonds, required by this part 3;

(i) Regulations for issuing compliance orders and administrative penalties, for establishing compliance conditions and schedules, and for issuing, modifying, revoking and reissuing, or terminating permits; except that nothing in this paragraph (i) shall be interpreted to impair the department's authority to take such actions pending promulgation of such regulations;

(j) Regulations for the classification of sites in terms of wastes that can be received and managed thereon and hydrological, soil, and other siting characteristics for assuring long-term isolation of designated wastes from the environment;

(k) Regulations establishing standards applicable to generators of hazardous waste, including requirements for:

(I) Record-keeping practices that accurately identify the quantities of hazardous waste generated, the constituents of such hazardous waste which are significant in quantity or of potential harm to human health or the environment, and the disposition of such hazardous waste;

(II) Labeling practices for any container that is used for the storage, transportation, or disposal of hazardous waste so as to identify accurately such waste;

(III) The use of appropriate containers for hazardous waste;

(IV) The furnishing of information on the general chemical composition of hazardous waste to persons transporting, treating, storing, or disposing of such waste;

(V) The use of a manifest system and any other reasonable means necessary to assure that all hazardous waste generated is designated for treatment, storage, or disposal at a permitted facility;

(VI) The submission of reports;

(l) Regulations requiring contingency plans for effective action to minimize unanticipated damage from any treatment, storage, or disposal of any hazardous waste.

(3) The commission shall promulgate rules establishing categories of hazardous wastes and hazardous waste management practices based on degree of hazard considerations. Such rules may vary from category to category to reflect the degree of hazard involved in each such category. The commission's rules may also provide for general permits to be issued based on degree of hazard considerations.

(3.5) The commission shall promulgate rules pertaining to the assessment of fees to offset program costs from facilities that treat, store, or dispose of hazardous waste pursuant to a permit or interim status and from generators of hazardous waste in accordance with the following:

(a) On or after July 1, 2000, to July 1, 2002, the fees shall be as follows:

(I) The annual fees for facilities that treat, store, or dispose of hazardous waste pursuant to a permit or interim status shall be as set forth in 6 CCR 1007-3, section 100.31;

(II) The annual fee shall be one thousand nine hundred dollars for generators of hazardous waste who are subject to regulation under this part 3 during any calendar month of the year for which the annual fee is being assessed and who generate in each of any four calendar months in that year an amount greater than one thousand kilograms of hazardous wastes, one kilogram of acute hazardous wastes, or one hundred kilograms of any residue, contaminated soil, waste, or debris resulting from the clean-up of a spill, into or on any land or water, of any acute hazardous wastes;

(III) The annual fee shall be three hundred dollars for all other generators of hazardous waste that are subject to this part 3 during any calendar month of the year for which the annual fee is being assessed; except that no annual fee shall be assessed against those generators of hazardous waste who generate in every month of that year no more than one hundred kilograms of hazardous wastes, one kilogram of acute hazardous wastes, or one hundred kilograms of any residue, contaminated soil, waste, or debris resulting from the clean-up of a spill, into or on any land or water, of any acute hazardous wastes;

(IV) The document review and activity fee charged by the department shall be in accordance with 6 CCR 1007-3, section 100.32; except that the hourly charge shall be increased from eighty-five dollars to one hundred dollars;

(V) The document review and activity fee ceiling shall be in accordance with 6 CCR 1007-3, section 100.32; except that the department may, on a case-by-case basis and upon demonstration of need consistent with section 25-15-301.5, request a waiver of the ceiling from a facility subject to the document review and activity fee.

(b) On or after July 1, 2002, the commission may adjust the fees then in effect if the department has demonstrated that it has developed, implemented, and is continuing to improve policies and procedures for carrying out its statutory responsibilities at the lowest possible cost without jeopardizing the intent set out in section 25-15-301.5 (1) , and that, despite these efforts or as a result of these efforts, the fee adjustments are necessary; except that the adjusted fees shall be subject to the following limitations:

(I) Annual fees for facilities that treat, store, or dispose of hazardous waste pursuant to a permit or interim status shall be established at a level that will, when combined with an appropriate share of available federal grant moneys, generate revenues approximating the actual, reasonable program costs attributable to such facilities. Such annual fees shall take into account equitable factors including, without limitation, the quantity and degree of hazard of the hazardous waste involved and whether the hazardous waste is to be disposed of, stored, or treated.

(II) Annual fees for generators of hazardous waste who are subject to regulation under this part 3 during any calendar month of the year for which the annual fee is being assessed shall be established at a level that will, when combined with an appropriate share of available federal grant moneys, generate revenues approximating the actual, reasonable program costs attributable to generators with an appropriate differentiation between generators described in subparagraphs (II) and (III) of paragraph (a) of this subsection (3.5) ;

(III) The hourly charge for the document review and activity fees shall be established at a rate comparable to industry rates for performing similar tasks with maximum levels on document review and activity fees that reflect timely and cost-effective reviews; and

(IV) The overall fee structure shall be consistent with the trend in hazardous waste generation, treatment, storage, disposal, and corrective action in the state and with the authorized funding for the program.

(c) In addition to any other review provided in law, any rule adopted, or fee modified, by the commission pursuant to paragraph (b) of this subsection (3.5) may be reviewed by the joint budget committee of the general assembly upon its own motion or upon written request submitted within thirty days after the adoption of the rule by the commission. The joint budget committee shall review such rule for accuracy and compliance with the statutory provision set forth in this subsection (3.5) . Request may be made by any person regulated under this part 3. Any review by the joint budget committee shall be completed within ninety days after the date requested. Such rule shall not become effective until approved by the joint budget committee or upon the failure of the joint budget committee to take action within ninety days after the day of the request for review. Such rule may not result in a level of funding for the program that exceeds amounts appropriated or that will be appropriated by the general assembly.

(d) The department shall provide a receipt for the fees paid pursuant to this subsection (3.5) and shall transmit such payments to the state treasurer and take the treasurer's receipt therefor. The state treasurer shall credit all fees received to the hazardous waste service fund as provided in section 25-15-304.

(3.7) If the department determines that a facility is, and has been, treating, storing, or disposing of hazardous wastes without a permit or interim status, and that facility legally should have been operating pursuant to a permit or interim status, then, in addition to any other remedies the department may have, the department may assess a fee to offset program costs from that facility that is equivalent to the estimated annual fees, without interest, that such facility should have paid the department if the facility had been operating pursuant to a permit or interim status; except that such fee shall not be assessed under any one the following circumstances:

(a) The only hazardous waste being treated, stored, or disposed of is in-place contaminated media or debris, or contaminated structures;

(b) The treatment, storage, and disposal is part of a corrective action plan approved by the department; or

(c) The facility modified the facility's operations within one month after being notified in writing that the facility should be operating pursuant to a permit or interim status so that any treatment, storage, or disposal of hazardous wastes at the facility is no longer subject to a permit or interim status.

(4) (a) Except as provided in paragraph (b) of this subsection (4) , the rules promulgated by the commission pursuant to the provisions of this part 3 may be more stringent than the corresponding rules of the federal environmental protection agency promulgated pursuant to the federal act; however, more stringent rules including, without limitation, rules that list or define as a hazardous waste any waste or other material exempted or otherwise not regulated as a hazardous waste under the federal act may only be adopted if the commission makes a written finding, after a public hearing and based upon substantial evidence in the record that such rules are necessary to protect the public health and the environment of the state, and such findings and rules are approved by an affirmative vote of at least six members of the commission. Such findings and rules shall be accompanied by a commission opinion referring to and evaluating the public health and environmental information and studies contained in the record that form the basis for such findings and rules.

(b) The rules promulgated by the commission pursuant to the provisions of this part 3 concerning the regulation of mining and mineral processing wastes, including exploration, mining, milling, and smelting and the refining of waste, shall be identical to and no more inclusive than the regulations of the federal environmental protection agency promulgated pursuant to the federal act.

(c) (Deleted by amendment, L. 2000, p. 1068, § 3, effective July 1, 2000.)

(4.5) The commission shall adopt rules concerning solid waste disposal sites and facilities in accordance with part 1 of article 20 of title 30, C.R.S.

(4.6) The commission may adopt rules that specify types of composting facilities, by size, volume, or other suitable criteria that provide equivalent protection of public health and the environment that would not be required to obtain a certificate of designation in accordance with section 30-20-102, C.R.S.

(4.7) Repealed.

(5) The rules and regulations promulgated by the commission shall be subject to expiration in accordance with sections 24-4-103 (8) (c) and 24-4-108, C.R.S.

(6) The commission may advise and consult and cooperate with other agencies of the state, the

federal government, and other states and with groups, political subdivisions, and industries affected by the provisions of this article or by the policies or rules of the commission.

(7) (a) The commission may hold hearings. Such hearings shall be held pursuant to and in conformity with article 4 of title 24, C.R.S., and with this article.

(b) The commission shall adopt such rules governing procedures and hearings before the commission as may be necessary to assure that such procedures and hearings will be fair and impartial. Such rules shall be consistent with the pertinent provisions of article 4 of title 24, C.R.S. Such rules shall include a voting rule that excludes a member from voting on any matter arising under section 25-15-305, 25-15-308, or 25-15-309 if such member has a conflict of interest with respect to such matter.

(c) The disclosure of any information relating to secret processes or methods of manufacture or production which may be required, ascertained, or discovered by the commission shall be governed by the provisions of part 2 of article 72 of title 24, C.R.S.

(8) (a) Prior to promulgating any rule authorized by this article, the commission shall conduct a public hearing thereon as provided in section 24-4-103, C.R.S. Notice of any such hearing shall conform to the requirements of section 24-4-103, C.R.S.; except that such notice shall include a summary or the text of each proposed rule or rule revision. The commission may, if requested or when otherwise appropriate, lengthen the notice period to provide sufficient time for public review of a proposed rule or revision.

(b) Rules promulgated pursuant to this article shall take effect as provided in section 24-4-103 (5) or (6) , C.R.S.

(9) (a) The commission shall employ an administrator and shall delegate to such administrator such duties and responsibilities as it may deem necessary; except that no authority shall be delegated to such administrator to promulgate rules or to make determinations as provided in this part 3. Such administrator shall have appropriate practical, educational, technical, and administrative training or experience related to solid and hazardous waste management and shall be employed pursuant to section 13 of article XII of the Colorado constitution.

(b) Notice of meetings of the commission shall be published in the Colorado register at least twenty days prior to the date of such meeting and shall state the time, place, and nature of the subject matter to be considered at such meeting. The administrator shall maintain a mailing list of persons requesting to be included thereon and shall mail notice of any meeting of the commission to such persons at least twenty days prior to such meeting. Opportunity shall be afforded to interested persons to submit views orally or in writing on the proposals under consideration or to otherwise participate informally in a commission proceeding. For commission proceedings under this part 3 other than the review of administrative penalties pursuant to section 25-15-309, the department shall furnish such personnel to the commission as the commission may reasonably require.

## 25-15-303. Requirements for hazardous waste treatment, storage, and disposal sites and facilities - permits.

(1) Any site or facility for the treatment, storage, or disposal of hazardous waste shall be unlawful unless a permit is granted by the department for such site or facility. Each permit shall provide for a specified term and conditions for renewal and shall provide for modification upon the permittee's request or upon a finding that a substantial threat to the public health or safety or the environment exists at the site or facility. In issuing permits for disposal facilities the department shall consider the variations within this state in climate, geology, and such other factors as may be relevant to the management of hazardous wastes.

(2) A separate permit shall not be required, unless the permittee so requests, of a person otherwise subject to the requirements of this part 3 who is engaged in mining operations pursuant to a permit issued under the "Colorado Surface Coal Mining Reclamation Act", article 33 of title 34, C.R.S.

(3) Any person who possesses a federal permit or has federal interim status under section 3005 (c) of the federal act for the treatment, storage, or disposal of hazardous waste shall be deemed to

possess an identical permit or status with the department. Any such permit shall remain in effect until it expires or is suspended or revoked for failure to meet conditions in the permit or the requirements of this part 3.

(4) (a) Any deed for property which has been utilized for the disposal of hazardous waste and has received interim status or a permit under the federal act or a permit under this part 3 or has received a certificate of designation under part 2 of this article shall contain a notation that such property has been utilized for the disposal of hazardous waste.

(b) and (c) (Deleted by amendment, L. 92, p. 1244, § 7, effective August 1, 1992.)

(5) Repealed.

(6) Any operation conducted at sites acquired by the state for the express purpose of hazardous waste treatment, storage, or disposal shall be in accordance with a lease which shall provide for payments to the state based on the quantity of waste managed, and shall also require, in lieu of taxes, payments to be transferred to the local government having jurisdiction as compensation for loss of valuation and which shall be adjusted annually to conform with current mill levies, assessment practices, and value of land improvements.

(7) As a condition to the issuance of any permit under subsection (1) of this section, the department may require, in accordance with rules and regulations, that the permittee post a bond or provide other evidence of financial assurance so that the department may, if the permittee is unable or unwilling to do so, arrange to rectify any improper hazardous waste management technique committed during the term of the permit. If a bond is posted, a portion of the bond shall be refunded to the permittee upon proper closure of the permitted hazardous waste management activity if use of such portion of the bond is not required.

(8) Prior to the issuance of any permit under subsection (1) of this section, the department shall, in accordance with the "State Administrative Procedure Act", article 4 of title 24, C.R.S., give reasonable public notice and shall, upon sufficient interest, hold a public hearing on the application in the locality of the proposed site or facility.

## 25-15-304. Hazardous waste service fund created.

There is created in the state treasury a hazardous waste service fund, which shall consist of fees collected pursuant to section 25-15-302 (3.5) to reimburse the state for its annual program expenses incurred in the maintenance, monitoring, and other supervision of the lands and facilities used for the storage, treatment, and disposal of hazardous waste. Such moneys shall be appropriated annually to the department by the general assembly which shall review such expenditures to assure that they are used to accomplish the purposes of this section. All unappropriated balances in the hazardous waste service fund shall remain therein and shall not revert to the general fund.

## 25-15-305. Judicial review.

(1) (a) Any final rule issued by the commission shall be subject to judicial review in accordance with the provisions of this article and article 4 of title 24, C.R.S.

(b) Judicial review of any rules promulgated by the commission shall be filed in the district court for the second judicial district.

(2) (a) Except as provided in section 25-15-308, any final determination issued by the department pursuant to this part 3, including but not limited to, permit determinations, permit terms or conditions, determinations regarding closure plans, or determinations regarding permits, closure plans, or corrective action plans required by a compliance order, shall be subject to review in accordance with the provisions of this section and section 24-4-106, C.R.S. A hearing pursuant to section 24-4-105, C.R.S., shall not be required prior to the issuance of any final determination described in this paragraph (a) .

(b) Any proceeding for judicial review of any final determination of the department shall be filed in the district court for the district in which the site or facility is or may be located.

(c) Any proceeding for judicial review of any final determination of the department described in paragraph (a) of this subsection (2) shall be filed within thirty days after said determination has become effective. Such determination shall become effective upon issuance or upon such later date as is specified in such determination.

(d) The contested provisions of a determination under review and the uncontested provisions that are not severable from such contested provisions, as determined by the department, shall be stayed during the pendency of the judicial review of such determination. All other provisions of the department's determination under review shall be fully effective unless, upon application and a showing of good cause by a party to the judicial review, the court stays such other provisions. The stay of any portion of a determination pursuant to this paragraph (d) shall have no effect on the obligations of the person to whom such determination applies to comply with applicable laws, regulations, and valid existing orders. The commission shall promulgate regulations governing the continuance of existing, expiring, or superseded permits, closure plans, or corrective action plans during the time period of any appeal of such determination pursuant to this section.

(e) Upon motion of a party to the judicial review, and in the discretion of the court, the court may request an interpretive rule from the commission pertaining to any rule adopted pursuant to this part 3 which is at issue in the judicial review only in the event that there is no genuine issue of material fact, or in the event that the parties have stipulated to the material facts for the purposes of such interpretive rule. The court may adjust the schedule of the judicial review to accommodate the receipt of such information. Notwithstanding the provisions of section 24-4-103 (1) , C.R.S., in the event that an interpretive rule is requested by the court and the commission agrees to issue such an interpretation, notice to the public of the interpretive rule-making proceeding shall be given in accordance with the provisions of section 24-4-103, C.R.S. Such notice shall be provided within forty-five days following the receipt of the request. The commission shall receive written material, not to exceed fifteen pages in length, from any interested person no later than fifteen days following the date that notification is given. The commission shall issue the written interpretive rule no later than thirty days following the deadline for the receipt of any such written material. The legal effect of any such interpretive rule shall be determined in accordance with applicable law and is not presumed to be binding on any party to the judicial review.

## 25-15-306. Local control of facilities - authorization by department - allocation of fees.

The department may enter into an agreement with a county, a city and county, or a municipality within whose jurisdiction is located one or more hazardous waste treatment, storage, or disposal sites or facilities for such local government to provide inspection, monitoring, and emergency response for such sites and facilities. The department shall make available to any such local government a reasonable portion of the fees appropriated from the hazardous waste service fund for conducting such functions. The department shall have the power to reassume any such function granted a local government if it appears to the department that the appropriate expertise is unavailable or that the resources provided are not appropriately applied for the agreed purpose, or if the department and the local government mutually so agree.

## 25-15-307. Coordination with other programs.

(1) The department shall coordinate the hazardous waste program with all other programs within the department and with other agencies of federal, state, or local government which are related to hazardous waste.

(2) For the purposes of the administration and enforcement of this part 3, the department shall coordinate its activities with those of the Colorado state patrol relating to the transportation of hazardous materials. Rules and regulations of the commission relating to the transportation of hazardous waste shall be consistent with the rules and regulations of the Colorado state patrol on the transportation of hazardous materials promulgated pursuant to article 20 of title 42, C.R.S.

## 25-15-308. Prohibited acts - enforcement.

(1) On or after the date specified in section 25-15-102 (3) , no person shall:

(a) Dispose of any hazardous waste off-site at any facility that does not have state or federal interim status, a federal permit, or a permit granted by the department pursuant to section 25-15-303;

(b) Dispose of on-site, treat, or store any hazardous waste without having therefor either state or federal interim status, a federal permit, or a permit granted by the department pursuant to section 25-15-303;

(c) Substantially alter any hazardous waste treatment, storage, or disposal facility or site without first obtaining from the department a modification of an existing permit or a new permit.

(2) (a) Whenever the department finds that any person is or has been in violation of any permit, rule, regulation, or requirement of this part 3, the department may issue an order identifying the factual and legal elements of such violation with particularity and requiring such person to comply with any such permit, rule, regulation, or requirement and may request the attorney general to bring suit for injunctive relief or for penalties pursuant to section 25-15-309 or 25-15-310.

(b) Such orders may contain an administrative penalty assessment as provided in section 25-15-309. Issuance of an administrative order without a penalty assessment shall not preclude the department from subsequently seeking an administrative or civil penalty for the violations detailed in the order. A hearing pursuant to section 24-4-105, C.R.S., shall not be required prior to the issuance of an order pursuant to this section.

(c) Any order issued pursuant to this section shall be served upon the person who is the subject of such order by personal service or by registered mail, return receipt requested. Any such order may be prohibitory or mandatory in effect. Unless provided otherwise in such order, the order shall be effective immediately upon issuance.

(3) (a) Any appeal of an order issued by the department pursuant to this section shall be taken in accordance with the provisions of this section. Notice of appeal shall be filed by personal service or by registered mail, return receipt requested, with the office of administrative courts in the department of personnel, with the executive director of the department or the executive director's designee, and with the commission in the case of an appeal of an administrative law judge's determination concerning an administrative penalty assessment. Notice of appeal shall be filed no later than thirty calendar days after the effective date of the order which is the subject of the appeal.

(b) The filing of an appeal of any order shall stay the obligation to submit payment of any monetary penalty pursuant to such order. Such filing shall not negate the appellant's obligation to otherwise comply with the order. An appellant may seek a stay of any other provision of an order in accordance with this section. The issuance of a stay shall not prevent the department from subsequently imposing a penalty for any subsequent violation by an appellant.

(c) Any person appealing an order may make a motion that the administrative law judge stay the enforcement of such order. The administrative law judge may stay the enforcement of any portion of an order if the administrative law judge determines that the balance of equities favors the moving party. An administrative law judge shall consider the following factors in considering a request for a stay of an order:

(I) The probability of serious harm to the moving party if the motion for a stay is denied;

(II) The probability that no serious harm to the public health or the environment will occur if the motion for a stay is granted;

(III) The merits of the moving party's case on appeal; and

(IV) The public interest.

(d) The stay of any portion of an order shall have no effect on the recipient's obligations under applicable statutes, regulations, permits, and valid, existing orders.

(e) The administrative law judge shall expedite hearing and determinations in regards to a motion for a stay pursuant to this subsection (3) . The moving party shall have the burden of proof in any hearing regarding a motion for a stay.

(f) Any hearing held by an administrative law judge pursuant to this section shall be conducted in accordance with section 24-4-105, C.R.S., except as otherwise provided in this section. Except as provided in paragraph (e) of this subsection (3) , the department shall bear the burden of proof by a preponderance of the evidence in any hearing before an administrative law judge pursuant to this section.

(g) Upon motion of a party to the appeal, and in the discretion of the administrative law judge, an administrative law judge may request an interpretive rule from the commission pertaining to any rule which is at issue in the appeal only in the event that there is no genuine issue of material fact or in the event that the parties have stipulated to the material facts for the purposes of such interpretive rule. The administrative law judge may adjust the schedule of the appeal to accommodate the receipt of such information. Notwithstanding the provisions of section 24-4-103 (1) , C.R.S., in the event that an interpretive rule is requested by an administrative law judge and the commission agrees to issue such an interpretation, notice to the public of the interpretive rule-making proceeding shall be given in accordance with the provisions of section 24-4-103, C.R.S. Such notice shall be provided within forty-five days following the receipt of the request. The commission shall accept written material, not to exceed fifteen pages in length, that is received from any interested person no later than fifteen days following the date that notification is given. The commission shall issue the written interpretive rule no later than thirty days following the deadline for the receipt of any such written material. The legal effect of any such interpretive rule shall be determined in accordance with applicable law and is not presumed to be binding on any party to the appeal.

(h) Except as provided in paragraph (i) of this subsection (3) and notwithstanding the provisions of section 24-4-105 (15) , C.R.S., any appeal of the determination of the administrative law judge pursuant to this section or section 25-15-301 (4) (b) shall be taken to the district court in accordance with section 24-4-106, C.R.S.

(i) Questions raised upon appeal of the determination of an administrative law judge as to the amount of penalty assessed by an order issued pursuant to this section shall be heard by the commission based upon the record developed by the administrative law judge. Notwithstanding the provisions of section 24-4-103 (1) , C.R.S., in the event that the commission is requested to review the amount of a penalty, notice to the public of such penalty review shall be given in accordance with the provisions of section 24-4-103, C.R.S. Such notice shall be provided within forty-five days following receipt of such request for review of a penalty.

(4) (a) Any action pursuant to this part 3 shall commence within two years after the date upon which the department discovers an alleged violation of this part 3 or within five years after the date upon which the alleged violation occurred, whichever date occurs earlier; except that such limitation period is tolled during any period that the alleged violation is intentionally concealed. For the purposes of this section, "intentionally" shall have the meaning provided for such term in section 18-1-501 (5) , C.R.S.

(b) If any action has not been commenced within the limitation period provided by paragraph (a) of this subsection (4) in connection with any disposal of hazardous waste without either state or federal interim status, a federal permit, or a permit granted by the department pursuant to section 25-15-303, the department, within two years after the date upon which the department discovers such disposal, may issue an order pursuant to this section requiring action to remediate such disposal. The department is not authorized under these circumstances to seek any administrative, civil, or criminal penalties for such disposal of hazardous waste.

## 25-15-309. Administrative and civil penalties.

(1) Any person who violates the provisions of section 25-15-308 or who violates any compliance order of the department which is not subject to a stay pending judicial review and which has been issued pursuant to this part 3 shall, for each such violation, be subject to a penalty for each day during which such violation occurs or continues. The department may impose an administrative penalty of no more than fifteen thousand dollars per day per violation. In lieu of imposing an administrative penalty pursuant to this section, the department may seek a civil penalty for violation of state environmental law in the district court of the judicial district in which the

violation occurs. The district court may impose a civil penalty of no more than twenty-five thousand dollars per day per violation.

(2) The department shall not be precluded from referring a matter for criminal prosecution regardless of whether an order is issued pursuant to section 25-15-301 (4) (a) or 25-15-308. The department shall not impose both a civil penalty and an administrative penalty for any particular instance of a violation of this part 3.

(3) The department, the administrative law judge, the commission, or the court shall consider the factors contained in paragraphs (a) to (i) of this subsection (3) in determining the amount of any administrative or civil penalty for a violation of this part 3. The factors contained in paragraphs (f) , (g) , and (h) of this subsection (3) shall be mitigating factors and may be applied, together with other factors, to reduce penalties. Such factors are:

(a) The seriousness of the violation;

(b) Whether the violation was intentional, reckless, or negligent;

(c) The impact upon or the threat to the public health or the environment as a result of the violation;

(d) The degree, if any, of recalcitrance or recidivism upon the part of the violator;

(e) The economic benefit realized by the violator as a result of the violation;

(f) The voluntary and complete disclosure by the violator of such violation in a timely fashion after discovery and prior to the department's knowledge of the violation, provided that all reports required pursuant to state environmental law have been submitted as and when otherwise required;

(g) Full and prompt cooperation by the violator following disclosure of a violation, including, when appropriate, entering into in good faith and implementing a legally enforceable agreement to undertake compliance and remedial efforts;

(h) The existence of a regularized and comprehensive environmental compliance program or an environmental audit program that was adopted in a timely and good-faith manner and that includes sufficient measures to identify and prevent future noncompliance; and

(i) Any other aggravating or mitigating circumstances.

(4) Notwithstanding the provisions of subsection (3) of this section, the department may enter into settlement agreements regarding any penalty or claim resolved pursuant to this part 3. Any settlement agreement may include but is not necessarily limited to the payment or contribution of moneys to state or local agencies or for other environmentally beneficial purposes.

## 25-15-310. Criminal offenses - penalties.

(1) On or after the date specified in section 25-15-102 (3) , no person shall:

(a) Transport or cause to be transported any hazardous waste identified or listed pursuant to this article to a facility which does not have a permit under this article or the federal act;

(b) Treat, store, or dispose of any hazardous waste identified or listed pursuant to this article either without having obtained a permit as required by this article or the federal act or in knowing violation of any material condition or requirement of a permit or interim status requirement;

(c) Omit any material information or make any false material statement or representation in any application, label, manifest, record, report, permit, or other document filed, maintained, or used for purposes of compliance with this article or with the federal act or regulations promulgated under this article or the federal act;

(d) Destroy, alter, or conceal any record required to be maintained or fail to file any record required to be filed under regulations promulgated by the commission under this part 3 or pursuant to the federal act; or

(e) Treat, store, or dispose of any hazardous waste identified or listed pursuant to this article in violation of any material condition or requirement of a permit or interim status requirement.

(2) Except as provided in section 18-13-112, 29-22-108, or 42-20-113, C.R.S., any person acting with criminal negligence as defined in section 18-1-501 (3) , C.R.S., who violates any of the provisions of paragraph (a) , (c) , (d) , or (e) of subsection (1) of this section is guilty of a misdemeanor and, upon conviction thereof, shall be punished by a fine of not more than twenty-

five thousand dollars for each day of violation. If such conviction is for a violation committed after a previous conviction under this subsection (2) , the maximum fine shall be doubled.

(3) Any person who knowingly, as defined in section 18-1-501 (6) , C.R.S., violates any of the provisions of paragraph (a) , (b) , (c) , or (d) of subsection (1) of this section is guilty of a felony and, upon conviction thereof, shall be punished by a fine of not more than fifty thousand dollars for each day of violation, or by imprisonment not to exceed four years, or by both such fine and imprisonment. If said conviction is for a violation committed after a previous conviction of such person under this subsection (3) , the maximum punishment shall be doubled with respect to both fine and imprisonment.

(4) (a) (Deleted by amendment, L. 92, p. 1252, § 12, effective August 1, 1992.)

(b) Any generator who otherwise stores waste on-site in compliance with the requirements of 6 CCR 1007-3, section 262.34 (a) , as those requirements exist on July 1, 1988, but who knowingly exceeds the ninety-day storage period or any extension thereof is guilty of a misdemeanor and, upon conviction thereof, shall be punished as provided in subsection (2) of this section.

(5) The court shall consider the factors contained in paragraphs (a) to (i) of this subsection (5) in determining the amount of any criminal sanction to be imposed pursuant to this article. The factors contained in paragraphs (f) , (g) , and (h) of this subsection (5) shall be mitigating factors and may be applied, together with other factors, to reduce or eliminate sanctions or penalties. Such factors are:

(a) The seriousness of the violation;

(b) Whether the violation was intentional, reckless, or negligent;

(c) The impact upon or the threat to the public health or the environment as a result of the violation;

(d) The degree, if any, of recalcitrance or recidivism upon the part of the violator;

(e) The economic benefit realized by the violator as a result of the violation;

(f) The voluntary and complete disclosure by the violator of such violation in a timely fashion after discovery and prior to the department's knowledge of the violation, provided that all reports required pursuant to state environmental law have been submitted as and when otherwise required;

(g) Full and prompt cooperation by the violator following disclosure of a violation, including, when appropriate, entering into in good faith and implementing a legally enforceable agreement to undertake compliance and remedial efforts;

(h) The existence of a regularized and comprehensive environmental compliance program or an environmental audit program that was adopted in a timely and good-faith manner and that includes sufficient measures to identify and prevent future noncompliance; and

(i) Any other aggravating or mitigating circumstances.

## 25-15-311. Disposition of fines and penalties.

All receipts from penalties or fines collected under the provisions of sections 25-15-309 and 25-15-310 shall be credited to the general fund of the state.

## 25-15-312. Repeal. (Repealed)


## 25-15-313. Right to claim reimbursement.

(1) A public entity, political subdivision of the state, or unit of local government is hereby given the right to claim reimbursement from the parties or persons responsible for the hazardous waste abandonment or hazardous waste spill for costs resulting from action taken to remove, contain, or otherwise mitigate the effects of a hazardous waste abandonment or hazardous waste spill.

(2) As used in this section, "abandonment" means the act of leaving a thing with the intent not to retain possession of or assert ownership or control over it. The intent need not coincide with the act of leaving.

(3) Nothing contained in this section shall be construed to change or impair any right of recovery

or subrogation arising under any other provision of law.

(4) Claims for reimbursement made pursuant to this section shall be in accordance with article 22 of title 29, C.R.S.

## 25-15-314. Solid and hazardous waste commission funding.

(1) The commission is hereby authorized to promulgate rules regarding the following:

(a) (I) The establishment of fees to offset the reasonable costs actually associated with the operations of the commission. Such fees may be imposed upon generators and transporters of hazardous wastes and upon facilities that treat, store, or dispose of hazardous wastes. Such fees may be based upon a consideration of the quantity of hazardous wastes that is generated, transported, treated, stored, or disposed and the impact on small businesses. The fees imposed by this subparagraph (I) shall not exceed an amount equal to one-half of the appropriation made by the general assembly annually pursuant to section 25-15-315.

(II) In addition to the fees imposed pursuant to subparagraph (I) of this paragraph (a) , an amount equal to one-half of the appropriation made by the general assembly annually pursuant to section 25-15-315 shall be appropriated from the solid waste management fund created in section 30-20-118, C.R.S., to be expended for the commission's direct and indirect costs pursuant to this article.

(b) The establishment of a nominal filing fee to help defray reasonable administrative costs actually associated with processing petitions for interpretive rulings pursuant to sections 25-15-305 and 25-15-308. No filing fee established pursuant to the provisions of this paragraph (b) shall exceed one hundred dollars.

(2) All moneys collected pursuant to this section by the commission shall be transmitted to the state treasurer, who shall credit the same to the solid and hazardous waste commission fund created pursuant to section 25-15-315.

## 25-15-315. Solid and hazardous waste commission fund - creation.

There is hereby established in the state treasury a fund to be known as the solid and hazardous waste commission fund, which shall consist of moneys collected pursuant to section 25-15-314. All moneys in such fund shall be subject to annual appropriation by the general assembly to the department for the purpose of covering the reasonable costs actually associated with the operation of the solid and hazardous waste commission. All moneys in the solid and hazardous waste commission fund that are not appropriated shall remain in such fund and shall not be transferred or revert to the general fund at the end of any fiscal year. In accordance with section 24-36-114, C.R.S., all interest derived from the deposit and investment of moneys in the solid and hazardous waste commission fund shall be credited to the general fund.

## 25-15-316. Prior acts validated and rules continued.

(1) All acts, orders, and rules adopted by the state board of health under the authority of this article prior to August 1, 1992, that were valid prior to said date and not otherwise subject to judicial review shall, to the extent that they are not inconsistent with this article, be deemed and held to be legal and valid in all respects, as though issued by the commission under the authority of this article. No provision of this part 3 shall be construed to validate any actions, orders, or rules that were not valid when adopted by the board of health prior to such date.

(2) All acts, orders, and rules adopted by the state board of health under the authority of part 1 of article 20 of title 30, C.R.S., prior to July 1, 2006, that were valid prior to said date and not otherwise subject to judicial review shall, to the extent that they are not inconsistent with said provisions, be deemed and held to be legal and valid in all respects, as though issued by the commission under the authority of said provisions. No provision of this part 3 shall be construed to validate any actions, orders, or rules that were not valid when adopted by the board of health prior to such date.

## 25-15-317. Legislative declaration.

The general assembly declares that it is in the public interest to ensure that environmental remediation projects protect human health and the environment. The general assembly finds that environmental remediation projects may leave residual contamination at levels that have been determined to be safe for a specific use, but not all uses, and may incorporate engineered structures that must be maintained or protected against damage to remain effective. The general assembly finds that in such cases, it is necessary to provide an effective and enforceable means of ensuring the conduct of any required maintenance, monitoring, or operation, and of restricting future uses of the land, including placing restrictions on drilling for or pumping groundwater for as long as any residual contamination remains hazardous. The general assembly, therefore, declares that it is in the public interest to create environmental covenants and notices of environmental use restrictions because such covenants and restrictive notices are necessary for the protection of human health and the environment.

## 25-15-318. Nature of environmental covenants.

(1) An environmental covenant shall be perpetual unless by its terms it is limited to a specific duration, unless the department approves a request to terminate or modify it pursuant to section 25-15-319 (1) (h) , or unless it is terminated by a court of competent jurisdiction. An environmental covenant may not be extinguished, limited, or impaired through issuance of a tax deed or through adverse possession, nor may an environmental covenant be extinguished, limited, or impaired by reason of the doctrines of abandonment, waiver, lack of enforcement, or other common law principles relating to covenants, or by the exercise of eminent domain.

(2) Notwithstanding any other provision of law, including any common-law requirement for privity of estate, an environmental covenant shall run with the land and shall bind the owner of the land, the owner's successors and assigns, and any person using the land. An environmental covenant shall not be deemed unenforceable on the basis of:

(a) A lack of privity of contract;

(b) A lack of benefit to a particular parcel of land;

(c) Failure of the environmental covenant to expressly state that it runs with the land; or

(d) Any other inconsistency with common-law requirements applicable to common-law covenants.

(3) The requirements and restrictions of an environmental covenant are requirements under this part 3 but may only be enforced as provided in section 25-15-322. The creation of an environmental covenant does not trigger the application of any other requirement of this part 3.

(4) The department shall not acquire any liability under state law by virtue of accepting an environmental covenant, nor shall any named beneficiary of an environmental covenant acquire any liability under state law by virtue of being such a beneficiary.

## 25-15-318.5. Nature of a notice of environmental use restrictions.

(1) A notice of environmental use restrictions is an agency action based on the state's police power.

(2) A notice of environmental use restrictions is binding on current and subsequent owners of the affected land and any person using or possessing an interest in the land.

(3) The requirements and restrictions contained in a notice of environmental use restrictions are requirements under this part 3, but may be enforced only as provided in section 25-15-322. The creation of a notice of environmental use restrictions does not trigger the application of any other requirement of this part 3.

## 25-15-319. Contents of environmental covenants and notices of environmental use restrictions.

(1) Environmental covenants and notices of environmental use restrictions shall include provisions regarding:

(a) Duration and any conditions under which the environmental covenant or restrictive notice may be modified or terminated;

(b) Any environmental use restrictions relied on in the remediation decision for the environmental remediation project for the subject property;

(c) A requirement that the owner of the property subject to the environmental covenant or restrictive notice notify the department at least fifteen days in advance of any transfer of ownership of some or all of the real property subject to the environmental covenant or restrictive notice;

(d) A requirement that the owner of the property notify the department simultaneously with submitting any application to a local government for a building permit or change in land use;

(e) A requirement to allow the department right of entry at reasonable times with prior notice for the purpose of determining compliance with the terms of the environmental covenant or restrictive notice. Nothing in this section shall impair any other authority the department may otherwise have to enter and inspect property subject to the environmental covenant or restrictive notice.

(f) (I) For environmental covenants, inclusion of the following statement on the first page of the instrument creating the environmental covenant in fifteen-point, bold-faced type: "This property is subject to an environmental covenant held by the Colorado department of public health and environment pursuant to section 25-15-321, Colorado Revised Statutes."

(II) For restrictive notices, inclusion of the following statement on the first page of the restrictive notice in fifteen-point, bold-faced type: "This property is subject to a notice of environmental use restrictions imposed by the Colorado department of public health and environment pursuant to section 25-15-321.5, Colorado Revised Statutes."

(g) A requirement to incorporate, either in full or by reference, the environmental covenant or restrictive notice in any leases, licenses, or other instruments granting a right to use the property that may be affected by the environmental covenant or restrictive notice;

(h) Modification or termination of the environmental covenant or restrictive notice consistent with this subsection (1) . The owner of land subject to an environmental covenant or restrictive notice may request that the department approve modification or termination of the covenant or restrictive notice. The request shall contain information showing that the proposed modification or termination shall, if implemented, ensure protection of human health and the environment. The department shall review any submitted information and may request additional information. If the department determines that the proposal to modify or terminate the environmental covenant or restrictive notice will ensure protection of human health and the environment, it shall approve the proposal. No modification or termination of an environmental covenant or restrictive notice shall be effective unless it has been approved in writing by the department. Information to support a request for modification or termination may include one or more of the following:

(I) A proposal to perform additional remedial work;

(II) New information regarding the risks posed by the residual contamination;

(III) Information demonstrating that residual contamination has diminished;

(IV) Information demonstrating that an engineered feature or structure is no longer necessary;

(V) Information demonstrating that the proposed modification would not adversely impact the remedy and is protective of human health and the environment; and

(VI) Other appropriate supporting information; and

(i) Such other subjects as may be appropriate.

## 25-15-320. Environmental covenants - when required - waiver.

(1) No environmental covenant shall be required for any environmental remediation project that results in residual contamination levels that have been determined by the relevant regulatory agency to be safe for all uses and that does not incorporate any engineered feature or structure or require any monitoring, maintenance, or operation.

(2) Except as specified in subsections (3) and (4) of this section, an environmental covenant under this part 3 shall be required for any environmental remediation project in which the relevant regulatory authority makes a remedial decision on or after July 1, 2001, that would result in either or both of the following:

(a) Residual contamination at levels that have been determined to be safe for one or more specific uses, but not all uses; or

(b) Incorporation of an engineered feature or structure that requires monitoring, maintenance, or operation or that will not function as intended if it is disturbed.

(3) The department may waive the requirement for an environmental covenant in the following circumstances:

(a) If the department determines that it is authorized under another statute or decision of the Colorado supreme court to implement and enforce environmental use restrictions against the present and subsequent owners of real property remediated pursuant to an environmental remediation project and implements environmental use restrictions under such statute or decision; or

(b) For a parcel of land involved in an environmental remediation project that is owned by any person who is not being required to remediate the contamination, and:

(I) The owner of any such parcel does not grant an environmental covenant under this section;

(II) The county, city and county, or municipality having jurisdiction over the affected land has enacted an ordinance or resolution imposing the relevant environmental use restrictions; and

(III) The county, city and county, or municipality having jurisdiction and the department have entered into an intergovernmental agreement for oversight and enforcement of the local ordinance or resolution pursuant to section 29-1-203, C.R.S. Such agreement shall be binding and mutually enforceable. The department shall have such authority as may be provided in the intergovernmental agreement to bring suit for injunctive relief to enforce any local ordinance or resolution described in this subsection (3) , but only with respect to properties that are subject to the requirements of this section. Any intergovernmental agreement under this section shall require that, insofar as the local ordinance or resolution applies to properties that are subject to the requirements of this section, any amendments to the local ordinance or resolution shall incorporate such requirements as the department may recommend to ensure continued protection of human health and the environment.

(4) (a) When an environmental covenant is required under subsection (2) of this section, a restrictive notice may be substituted for the covenant as follows:

(I) An owner of a parcel of land involved in an environmental remediation project who is being required to remediate contamination may request that the department approve a proposed restrictive notice for such parcel or may request that the department issue a restrictive notice.

(II) The department may unilaterally issue a restrictive notice containing the provisions described in section 25-15-319 when an environmental covenant is required under subsection (2) of this section and the owner of the subject property fails to create a covenant or restrictive notice within thirty days after:

(A) The date of a remedial decision for an environmental remediation project that relies solely on environmental use restrictions to protect human health and the environment; or

(B) The completion of construction work for environmental remediation projects that require physical work.

(b) Prior to issuing a restrictive notice unilaterally under subparagraph (II) of paragraph (a) of this subsection (4) , the department shall make a good-faith attempt to reach agreement with the owner of the subject property regarding a consensual covenant or notice.

(c) The department may not issue a restrictive notice for a parcel of land involved in an environmental remediation project that is owned by a person who is not being required to remediate the contamination, unless such person consents in writing.

(5) The department may accept environmental covenants or issue restrictive notices in cases where such covenants or notices are not required, including approvals of voluntary cleanup plans or petitions for no action determinations under sections 25-16-306 and 25-16-307, but the owner of the remediated land nonetheless desires to create such a covenant or requests that the department issue such a notice. A covenant or notice created under this subsection (5) may be enforced as any other covenant or notice.

## 25-15-321. Creation, modification, and termination of an environmental covenant.

(1) An environmental covenant under this part 3 may be created only by the owner of the property through a written grant to the department by a deed or other instrument of conveyance specifically stating the intention of the grantor to create such a restriction under this article.

(2) The department is authorized to accept, refuse to accept, conditionally accept, hold, modify, and terminate environmental covenants.

(3) Instruments creating, modifying, or terminating an environmental covenant shall be recorded as any other instrument affecting title to and interests in real property.

(4) If the only uses allowed under the proposed environmental covenant are prohibited by existing ordinance or resolution, the department shall condition its acceptance of the covenant upon the applicant's demonstration that such applicant has obtained approval from the relevant authority that would allow for one or more of the proposed uses.

(5) Persons proposing to create, modify, or terminate an environmental covenant shall provide written notice of their intention to all persons holding an interest of record in the real property that will be subject to the environmental covenant, to all persons known to them to have an unrecorded interest in the property, and to all affected persons in possession of the property prior to such creation, modification, or termination, and shall provide the department with:

(a) A copy of the notice provided;

(b) A list of the persons to whom notice was given and the address or other location to which the notice was directed; and

(c) Such title information as the department may require.

(6) The department shall review and make a determination regarding all applications for creating, modifying, or terminating an environmental covenant within sixty days after receipt of such application, including the information described in subsection (5) of this section.

(7) Any determination by the department regarding a proposal to create, modify, or terminate an environmental covenant shall be subject to appeal in accordance with section 25-15-305.

## 25-15-321.5. Notice of environmental use restrictions - creation, modification, and termination.

(1) A person who proposes to create, modify, or terminate a restrictive notice shall provide written notice of the person's intention to all persons holding an interest of record in the real property that will be subject to the restrictive notice, to all persons known to the person to have an unrecorded interest in the property, and to all affected persons in possession of the property prior to such creation, modification, or termination and shall provide the department with:

(a) A copy of the notice provided;

(b) A list of the persons to whom notice was given and the address or other location to which the notice was directed; and

(c) Such title information as the department may require.

(2) Before issuing a notice of environmental use restrictions unilaterally, the department shall provide a copy of the proposed restrictive notice to all persons holding an interest of record in the real property that will be subject to the restrictive notice, all persons known to the department to have an unrecorded interest in such property, and all affected persons in possession of such property, and shall offer such persons a minimum of thirty days to comment on the proposed restrictive notice, unless notice has already been provided pursuant to subsection (1) of this section. In determining whether to issue the restrictive notice unilaterally, the department shall consider any comments received.

(3) The department shall review and make a determination regarding all requests to create, modify, or terminate a restrictive notice within sixty days after receipt of such request, including the information described in subsection (1) of this section.

(4) Upon issuance or approval of the restrictive notice, the department shall record the restrictive notice in the clerk and recorder's office for the county or counties in which the affected land is

situated. For approved restrictive notices, the department may allow the owner of the property to record the notice. No person may record a restrictive notice that does not have the department's written approval.

(5) The department may authorize any notice of environmental use restrictions created in accordance with this section to be replaced by an environmental covenant as described in section 25-15-319. The department may condition its authorization and approval of the termination of the notice of environmental use restrictions on the prior creation, department approval and acceptance, and effective recording of the environmental covenant.

(6) Modifications or terminations of restrictive notices shall be recorded as provided in subsection (4) of this section. No person may record a modification or termination of a restrictive notice that does not have the department's written approval.

(7) Any determination by the department to issue, approve, modify, or terminate a notice of environmental use restrictions shall be subject to appeal in accordance with section 25-15-305.

## 25-15-322. Enforcement - remedies.

(1) An environmental covenant or restrictive notice imposed at any environmental remediation project shall be enforceable as provided in this section, even if the environmental remediation project is not otherwise subject to this part 3.

(2) In the event of an actual or threatened failure to comply with an environmental covenant or restrictive notice, the department may issue an order under this section requiring compliance with the terms of the environmental covenant or restrictive notice and may request the attorney general to bring suit in district court to enforce the terms of the environmental covenant or restrictive notice, to enforce the order issued pursuant to this section, or to seek other appropriate injunctive relief. An administrative order issued under this subsection (2) shall be subject to appeal in accordance with section 25-15-308.

(3) If a court of competent jurisdiction determines that an environmental covenant or restrictive notice is void or otherwise unenforceable, the department may take such action as may be authorized by any other law.

(4) The grantor of an environmental covenant may file suit in district court to enjoin actual or threatened violations of the covenant. Any third-party beneficiary specifically named in an environmental covenant or restrictive notice may file suit in district court to enjoin actual or threatened violations of the covenant or restrictive notice. The person who requested creation of a restrictive notice may file suit in district court to enjoin actual or threatened violations of the restrictive notice.

(5) An affected local government, as defined in section 25-15-324, may file suit in district court to enjoin actual or threatened violations of any environmental covenant or restrictive notice that applies to land within its jurisdiction.

(6) (Deleted by amendment, L. 2008, p. 174, § 9, effective March 24, 2008.)

(7) A court of competent jurisdiction is authorized to issue orders requiring compliance with an environmental covenant or restrictive notice, to enjoin actual or threatened violations of environmental covenants or restrictive notices, and to grant such other injunctive relief as it may deem appropriate.

## 25-15-323. Registry of environmental covenants and notices of environmental use restrictions.

The department shall create and maintain a registry of all environmental covenants and notices of environmental use restrictions, including any modification or termination thereof.

## 25-15-324. Coordination with affected local governments.

(1) For purposes of this part 3, "affected local government" means every county, city and county, or municipality in which land subject to an environmental covenant or restrictive notice is located. The department shall provide each affected local government with a copy of every environmental

covenant and restrictive notice within such local government's jurisdiction and shall also provide a copy of any documents modifying or terminating such environmental covenant or restrictive notice.

(2) Whenever an affected local government receives an application affecting land use or development of land that is subject to an environmental covenant or restrictive notice and that may relate to or impact such covenant or restrictive notice, the affected local government shall notify the department of the application. The department shall evaluate whether the application is consistent with the environmental covenant or restrictive notice and shall notify the affected local government of the department's determination in a timely fashion, considering the time frame for the local government's review of the application.

## 25-15-325. Other interests not impaired.

Except as specifically provided in an environmental covenant or restrictive notice or pursuant to section 25-15-326, no transfer of a water right or any change of a point of diversion at any time, nor any interest in real property cognizable under statute, common law, or custom in effect in this state prior to July 1, 2001, nor any lease or sublease thereof at any time shall be impaired, invalidated, or in any way adversely affected by sections 25-15-317 to 25-15-326. All interests not transferred or conveyed in the environmental covenant shall remain in the grantor of the environmental covenant, including the right to engage in all uses of the lands affected by the environmental covenant that are not inconsistent with the environmental covenant and not expressly prohibited by the environmental covenant or by law.

## 25-15-326. Validation.

(1) Any document recorded by the owner of real property that restricts or requires certain uses or activities relating to such real property, including any restrictions on drilling for or pumping groundwater, to protect human health or the environment by limiting exposure to hazardous substances or by ensuring the integrity of a response action, shall be considered valid and enforceable by its terms, regardless of whether such document is denominated an easement, covenant, deed restriction, or some other instrument.

(2) The provisions of subsection (1) of this section shall apply only to:

(a) Documents that were required as part of an environmental remediation decision that was rendered prior to July 1, 2001; and

(b) Documents recorded in connection with a voluntary cleanup plan approved under section 25-16-306 or petition for a no action determination approved under section 25-16-307.

(3) Nothing in this section shall impair the validity or enforceability of an environmental covenant created under section 25-15-321.

## 25-15-327. Applicability.

The requirements of section 25-15-320 apply to remedial decisions made on or after July 1, 2001, that would create one or more of the conditions described in section 25-15-320 (2) .

## 25-15-328. Household medication take-back program - creation - liability - definitions - cash fund - rules.

(1) (a) The general assembly finds and declares that prescription drug misuse is a rampant problem in Colorado, in part due to the accidental and intentional abuse of leftover household medications. The general assembly further declares that citizen access to a disposal location to return unused household medications will reduce the availability of household medications for unintended or abusive purposes and will further protect the environment through proper disposal.

(b) It is the intent of the general assembly to establish a household medication take-back program to facilitate the safe and effective collection and proper disposal of unused medications.

(2) As used in this section:

(a) "Approved collection site" means a site approved by the department for the collection of unused household medications.

(b) "Carrier" means an entity approved by the department to transport unused household medications from approved collection sites to a disposal location.

(c) "Disposal location" means a site approved by the department where unused household medications are destroyed in compliance with applicable laws so that the household medications are in a nonretrievable state and cannot be diverted for illicit purposes.

(d) "Household medications" means controlled substances approved for collection by federal law, prescription drugs, and over-the-counter medications in the possession of an individual.

(3) Subject to available funds, the executive director of the department shall establish a household medication take-back program to collect and dispose of unused household medications. The program must allow for individuals to dispose of unused household medications at approved collection sites and for carriers to transport unused household medications from approved collection sites to disposal locations.

(4) A collection site, carrier, or disposal location is not subject to liability for incidents arising from the collection, transport, or disposal of household medications if the collection site, carrier, or disposal location complies with the household medication take-back program in good faith and does not violate any applicable laws.

(5) The household medication take-back cash fund is created in the state treasury for the direct and indirect costs associated with the implementation of this section. The fund consists of moneys appropriated or transferred to the fund by the general assembly and any gifts, grants, and donations from any public or private entity. The department shall transmit gifts, grants, and donations collected by the department to the state treasurer, who shall credit the moneys to the fund. The moneys in the fund are subject to annual appropriation by the general assembly.

(6) Nothing in this section:

(a) Affects the authority to collect and reuse medications pursuant to section 12-42.5-133, C.R.S.; or

(b) Prohibits the operation of existing medication take-back and disposal programs regulated by the department.

(7) The commission may promulgate rules for the implementation of this section.

# PART 4. INFECTIOUS WASTE

## 25-15-401. Legislative declaration.

(1) The general assembly hereby finds that there is a need for more clarity and uniformity regarding the definition of infectious waste and in the requirements for the handling, treatment, and disposal thereof and that the absence of such clarity and the inappropriate designation of general waste as infectious waste will result in further substantial and unnecessary costs, disparity, and confusion in the management of infectious waste, ultimately affecting many business and residential operations and facilities, including the operations and quality of care rendered by health care providers.

(2) For the purposes set forth in subsection (1) of this section, the provisions of this part 4 are enacted as a matter of statewide concern. The provisions of this part 4 shall not apply to infectious waste which is also deemed to be hazardous waste pursuant to section 25-15-101 (6) , nor shall infectious waste be deemed hazardous waste solely because it is characterized as infectious waste.

(3) The general assembly further finds that, because of the nature of infectious waste and the manner of its designation as provided in this part 4 and because this part 4 recommends portions of the guidelines of the United States environmental protection agency, no rules or regulations governing the generators of infectious waste are necessary for nor shall be applicable to the implementation of this part 4. This limitation shall not be construed to limit any other rule-making which is permitted under other authorizing statutes.

## 25-15-402. Infectious waste - definitions.

(1) For the purposes of this part 4 and statewide applicability:

(a) "Infectious waste" means waste capable of producing an infectious disease and requires the consideration of certain factors necessary for induction of disease. These factors include:

(I) Presence of a pathogen of sufficient virulence;

(II) Dose;

(III) Portal of entry;

(IV) Resistance of host.

(b) For a waste to be infectious, it must contain pathogens with sufficient virulence and quantity so that exposure to the waste by a susceptible host could result in disease. All the factors specified in paragraph (a) of this subsection (1) must be present simultaneously for disease transmission to occur and must be present in a manner which constitutes a substantial risk of infection to humans.

(2) (a) Infectious waste shall be designated as such by the generator in accordance with this part 4. Such designation shall not be based solely upon any source or type of waste but shall be based upon the factors specified in subsection (1) of this section.

(b) It is recommended by the general assembly that the following categories of waste, as published in the "EPA Guide for Infectious Waste Management", May 1986, by the United States environmental protection agency, be designated as infectious:

(I) Isolation wastes from persons diagnosed as having a disease caused by an organism requiring, pursuant to recommendations by the centers for disease control in the 1988 publication "Biosafety in the Microbiological and Biomedical Laboratory" (second edition) , biosafety level IV containment;

(II) Cultures and stocks of infectious agents and associated biologicals;

(III) Human blood and blood products and body fluids consisting of serum, plasma and other blood components, cerebrospinal fluid, synovial fluid, pleural fluid, peritoneal fluid, pericardial fluid, and amniotic fluid;

(IV) Human pathological/anatomical waste consisting of tissues and body parts that are discarded from surgical, obstetrical, autopsy, and laboratory procedures;

(V) Contaminated sharps;

(VI) Contaminated laboratory or research animal carcasses, body parts, and bedding.

## 25-15-402.5. Disposition of fetal tissue.

(1) As used in this section, unless the context otherwise requires, "fetal death" means death prior to the complete expulsion or extraction from its mother of a product of human conception, irrespective of the duration of pregnancy. The death is indicated by the fact that after such expulsion or extraction the fetus does not breathe or show any other evidence of life such as beating of the heart, pulsation of the umbilical cord, or definite movement of voluntary muscles.

(2) Nothing in this part 4 shall be deemed to prohibit the treatment of the remains from a fetal death pursuant to article 54 of title 12, C.R.S.

## 25-15-403. Generator management plan.

(1) Each generator of infectious waste shall develop and implement an on-site infectious waste management plan which is appropriate for the particular facility. Such plan shall include:

(a) The designation of infectious waste generated by the facility;

(b) The handling of infectious waste which includes segregation, identification, packaging, storage, transportation, treatment techniques for each waste type, if applicable, and disposal;

(c) Contingency planning for spills or loss of containment;

(d) Staff training and the designation of a person responsible for implementation of the management plan;

(e) If on-site treatment is not available, the management plan shall provide for appropriate off-site treatment or disposal.

(2) The management plan, including the documentation provided in section 25-15-404 (2) , shall be available for inspection to the hauler of any waste, to the disposal facility, and to the licensing or regulatory agency, if applicable, of the generator.

## 25-15-404. On-site disinfection.

(1) Any infectious waste which has been appropriately treated at the site of generation by the generator so as to render it noninfectious shall not thereafter be deemed infectious for purposes of handling or disposal.

(2) Appropriate treatment shall include any method of treatment which renders the infectious waste noninfectious. Use of a treatment method recommended by the United States environmental protection agency, as published in the "EPA Guide for Infectious Waste Management", May 1986, shall be conclusively presumed to be an appropriate treatment method. Any method of treatment shall include:

(a) Documentation by the generator that the method of treatment utilized for his operation is effective in rendering infectious waste noninfectious in such operation;

(b) Written standard operating procedures for the use of or implementation of the treatment method;

(c) Regular monitoring of the standard operating procedures and the effectiveness of such disinfective method.

(3) Upon request of the chairman of either the senate or house of representatives committees on health, environment, welfare, and institutions, or any successor committees, the department of public health and environment shall make a report to the senate and house of representatives committees on health, environment, welfare, and institutions, or any successor committees, on the current status, in view of scientific knowledge and technology, of the recommendations contained in the "EPA Guide for Infectious Waste Management", May 1986, and may make any additional recommendations it deems necessary.

## 25-15-405. Appropriate treatment and disposal - nonliability.

(1) A generator of infectious waste using an appropriate treatment method with appropriate documentation as provided in section 25-15-404 (2) and, in good faith, utilizing disposal facilities for such waste shall not be civilly or criminally liable for injuries or damages allegedly resulting from the infectious character of such waste; except that any generator who does not use an appropriate treatment method or any generator who fails to utilize disposal facilities in good faith shall not be relieved of civil or criminal liability.

(2) When any infectious waste has been appropriately treated, the generator shall either identify it as such or provide the hauler and disposal facility with a written statement that its general waste includes infectious waste which has been appropriately treated to render it noninfectious.

## 25-15-406. Penalty.

(1) (a) Any generator who knowingly removes, causes to be removed, or allows to be removed from the site of generation any infectious waste which he knew was not appropriately treated and not identified as untreated when such infectious waste was so removed from the site of generation shall be subject to the civil penalties set forth in paragraph (b) of this subsection (1) .

(b) Upon conviction of a first offense, a generator shall be subject to a civil penalty of not more than three thousand dollars per day for each day of violation, not to exceed fifteen thousand dollars. Upon conviction of a second or subsequent offense which occurs within five years of a previous conviction, a generator shall be subject to a civil penalty of three thousand dollars per day for each day of violation, not to exceed twenty-five thousand dollars.

(2) (a) Any person who knowingly hauls untreated infectious waste and recklessly spills or loses such waste or knowingly disposes of such waste at an unlawful site or disposal or treatment facility shall be subject to the civil penalties set forth in paragraph (b) of this subsection (2) .

(b) Upon conviction of a first offense, a person shall be subject to a civil penalty of not more than three thousand dollars per day for each day of violation, not to exceed fifteen thousand dollars. Upon conviction of a second or subsequent offense which occurs within five years of a previous conviction, a person shall be subject to a civil penalty of three thousand dollars per day, not to exceed twenty-five thousand dollars.

(3) All civil penalties set forth in this section shall be determined by a court of competent jurisdiction upon action instituted by the department of public health and environment.

### 25-15-407. Presumption of noninfectiousness.

It is conclusively presumed that any infectious waste which has been appropriately treated and documented in section 25-15-404 (2) either on the site or off the site is not infectious after it has been so treated.

# PART 5. HAZARDOUS WASTE INCINERATOR OR PROCESSOR SITES

### 25-15-501. Short title.

This part 5 shall be known and may be cited as the "State Hazardous Waste Incinerator or Processor Siting Act".

### 25-15-502. Definitions.

As used in this part 5, unless the context otherwise requires:

(1) "Existing hazardous waste incinerator" means a hazardous waste incinerator that was in active operation, as authorized by applicable federal and state laws and regulations, on or before August 21, 1991.

(1.5) "Existing hazardous waste processor" means a hazardous waste processing facility that was in active operation, regardless of the amount of hazardous waste treated annually, as authorized by applicable federal and state laws and rules, on or before March 22, 2002.

(2) "Governing body having jurisdiction" means the board of county commissioners if a hazardous waste incinerator or processor site is located in any unincorporated portion of a county and means the governing body of the appropriate municipality if a hazardous waste incinerator or processor site is located within an incorporated area.

(3) (a) "Hazardous waste incinerator" means:

(I) Any hazardous waste incinerator as defined in regulations of the commission promulgated pursuant to section 25-15-302; or

(II) Any boiler or industrial furnace that burns hazardous waste, as defined in subpart B of part 260 of title 40, code of federal regulations, as from time to time amended, until such time as the commission, pursuant to section 25-15-302, promulgates a definition of boiler or industrial furnace, at which time such state definition shall operate in lieu of the foregoing federal definition. Such term shall include, but is not limited to, any cement kiln, lime kiln, aggregate kiln, or blast furnace.

(b) The term "hazardous waste incinerator" excludes any facility for incineration of a hazardous waste performing on-site remediation pursuant to the federal "Comprehensive Environmental Response, Compensation, and Liability Act".

(4) (a) "Hazardous waste processing" means both of the following, except as provided in paragraph (b) of this subsection (4) :

(I) Any treatment method, technique, or process designed to change the physical, chemical, or biological character or composition of acute hazardous waste, as defined in rules of the commission promulgated pursuant to part 3 of this article, in order to neutralize such waste, reduce the volume of such waste, or render such waste less hazardous, safer for transport, amenable to recovery or use, or amenable to storage; and

(II) Any acute hazardous waste processing, as defined in rules of the commission promulgated pursuant to section 25-15-302.

(b) "Hazardous waste processing" does not include:

(I) The treatment of less than one thousand kilograms of acute hazardous waste per year;

(II) The treatment, storage, or disposal of hazardous waste pursuant to a certificate of designation issued under, or otherwise regulated by, part 2 of this article;

(III) The processing of hazardous waste that is not listed as acute hazardous waste in rules of the commission promulgated pursuant to part 3 of this article;

(IV) The processing of any hazardous waste pursuant to any record of decision, consent decree, or administrative order authorized by or made pursuant to applicable federal or state laws and rules, as amended or revised, or any record of decision issued pursuant to a periodic revision of a record of decision that was made on or before March 22, 2002;

(V) The performance of on-site processing or treatment of hazardous waste associated with efforts to clean up contaminated soil, groundwater, or surface water pursuant to federal or state environmental laws;

(VI) The processing of hazardous waste incidental to commercial manufacturing;

(VII) The treatment, storage, management, or processing of solid waste pursuant to a certificate of designation issued under article 20 of title 30, C.R.S.;

(VIII) The conduct of any activities pursuant to an approved reclamation plan contained in a permit issued under, or otherwise regulated by, article 32 or 33 of title 34, C.R.S.; or

(IX) The conduct of any activities regulated under article 60 of title 34, C.R.S.

(5) "Hazardous waste processor" means a facility that engages in hazardous waste processing subject to the requirement for a part B permit or interim status under rules of the commission promulgated pursuant to section 25-15-302.

(6) "Hazardous waste processor site" means a location where hazardous waste is:

(a) Processed; or

(b) Generated or stored by the owner of a hazardous waste processor or by an affiliate or customer of a hazardous waste processor who produces hazardous waste.

## 25-15-503. Certificate required - incineration or processing of hazardous waste prohibited - exceptions.

(1) Any person desiring to own or operate a hazardous waste incinerator or processor shall first obtain a certificate of designation from the governing body having jurisdiction over the area in which such proposed hazardous waste incinerator or processor site is located.

(2) Hazardous waste incineration or processing by any person is prohibited except on or at a hazardous waste incinerator or processor site for which a certificate of designation has been obtained as provided in this part 5.

(3) Notwithstanding the provisions of subsections (1) and (2) of this section and section 25-15-507, any existing hazardous waste incinerator or processor shall be an approved activity for which obtaining a certificate of designation under the provisions of this part 5 shall be unnecessary.

## 25-15-504. Application for certificate - review by governing body.

(1) Any person desiring to own or operate a hazardous waste incinerator or processor shall make application to the governing body having jurisdiction over the area in which such incinerator, incinerator site, processor, or processor site is or is proposed to be located for a certificate of designation.

(2) An application made pursuant to the provisions of subsection (1) of this section shall be accompanied by a fee to be established by the governing body having jurisdiction. Such fee shall be based on the reasonable anticipated costs that may be incurred by such governing body in the application review and approval process imposed by this article. Such fee shall be for the reasonable costs necessary in the application review and hearing process imposed by this article

and shall not exceed one hundred thousand dollars. The local governing body having jurisdiction shall provide an accounting of the actual costs incurred by such body in the application review and hearing process and shall refund any payment in excess of such costs within ninety days after completion of the certification process.

(3) An application made pursuant to the provisions of subsection (1) of this section shall set forth the location of the incinerator or processor site and incinerator or processor, the types of hazardous waste to be accepted or rejected, the types of incinerator or processor by-product disposal, the method of supervision, the anticipated access routes in the county in which the site is located, and such other information as may be required by the governing body having jurisdiction.

(4) The clerk of the governing body having jurisdiction shall promptly notify the county commissioners and the governing body of any other county or municipality within twenty miles of a proposed hazardous waste incinerator or processor upon the filing of any application for a certificate of designation for such incinerator, processor, or site.

## 25-15-505. Grounds for approval.

(1) A governing body having jurisdiction shall approve or disapprove an application for a hazardous waste incinerator or processor site certificate of designation within one hundred eighty days after receiving such application. Such governing body having jurisdiction may approve an application for a certificate of designation upon a finding of all of the following factors:

(a) That the proposed hazardous waste incinerator or processor site would not pose a significant threat to the health or safety of the public or the environment, taking into consideration:

(I) The density of population in the areas neighboring such proposed site;

(II) The density of population in the areas that are adjacent to any portion of delivery roads to such proposed site and that lie within a fifty-mile radius of such proposed site; and

(III) The risk of accidents occurring during the transportation of waste to or at the proposed site;

(b) That the applicant has documented such applicant's financial ability to operate the proposed hazardous waste incinerator or processor;

(c) That the applicant, taking into account such applicant's prior performance records, if any, in the treatment, storage, disposal, processing, or incineration of hazardous waste, has documented sufficient reliability, expertise, and competency to operate and manage the proposed hazardous waste incinerator or processor; and

(d) That the proposed site conforms to the comprehensive land use plans and relevant land use regulations of the governing body having jurisdiction; except that, to the extent the commission has promulgated a rule imposing a condition on incinerator or processor operation pursuant to section 25-15-302, such comprehensive land use plans and rules shall not impose a condition more stringent than that contained in such state rule.

(2) In considering an application for a proposed hazardous waste incinerator or processor, the governing body having jurisdiction shall take into account the effect that such hazardous waste incinerator or processor will have on the surrounding property, taking into consideration the types of processing to be used, wind and climatic conditions, and both the quality and quantity of public and private infrastructure necessary to facilitate the construction and subsequent operation of such incinerator, processor, or site.

(3) (a) Prior to the issuance of a certificate of designation for a hazardous waste incinerator or processor, the application, comprehensive land use plans, any relevant zoning ordinances, and any other pertinent information shall be presented to the governing body having jurisdiction at a public hearing to be held after notice. Such notice shall contain the date, time, and location of the hearing and shall state that the matter to be considered at such hearing is the applicant's application for a hazardous waste incinerator or processor. Such notice shall be published in a newspaper having general circulation in the county or municipality in which the proposed hazardous waste incinerator or processor site is located at least ten days but no more than thirty days prior to the date of such hearing. Any such notice shall be printed prominently in at least ten-point, bold-faced type. Such notice shall be posted at the proposed hazardous waste incinerator or processor site for

a period beginning at least thirty days before such public hearing and continuing through the date of such hearing.

(b) At any public hearing held pursuant to the provisions of paragraph (a) of this subsection (3) , the governing body having jurisdiction shall hear or receive any written or oral testimony presented by the applicant and by governmental entities and residents or any interested party concerning such proposed incinerator or processor site. All such testimony shall be considered by the governing body having jurisdiction in making a decision concerning such application.

(4) The governing body having jurisdiction shall notify the department of the approval or disapproval of any application for a hazardous waste incinerator or processor certificate of designation within five days after such approval or disapproval.

(5) The governing body having jurisdiction over a hazardous waste incinerator or processor may enact local procedural rules in order to implement the provisions of this part 5. If a local procedural rule conflicts with any of the provisions of this article, the provisions of this article shall control.

## 25-15-506. Certificate.

(1) A certificate of designation for a hazardous waste incinerator or processor site shall identify the general types of waste that shall be incinerated or processed and the types of waste that shall be rejected by such hazardous waste incinerator or processor site, subject to a more specific statement of waste to be rejected in the hazardous waste permit issued pursuant to part 3 of this article or the federal act.

(2) Such certificate of designation shall be displayed in a prominent place at the hazardous waste incinerator or processor site.

(3) Such certificate of designation may provide such conditions as may reasonably be necessary for the safe operation of such site. Such conditions may include but are not limited to the provision by the site owner or operator of additional fire protection, security, or trained personnel for monitoring, inspections, and incident responses.

(4) A certificate of designation issued pursuant to this part 5 shall be deemed to satisfy any requirement imposed by part 1 of article 20 of title 30, C.R.S., for a certificate of designation as a solid wastes disposal site and facility.

## 25-15-507. Substantial change in ownership, design, or operation.

(1) Any substantial change in the ownership of a hazardous waste incinerator or processor, including but not limited to an assignment or a transfer of the certificate of designation, or in the design or operation of a hazardous waste incinerator, incinerator site, processor, or processor site shall be submitted to the governing body having jurisdiction for its approval. Approval by the governing body having jurisdiction shall be required before such a substantial change may become effective. For the purposes of this section, "substantial change" shall have such meaning as is provided for such term in the rules of the commission promulgated pursuant to section 25-15-510.

(2) Except as provided in subsection (3) of this section, approval of a substantial change under this section shall be made if the governing body having jurisdiction finds all of the factors required by the provisions of section 25-15-505 (1) and has considered the factor provided in section 25-15-505 (2) .

(3) A substantial change involving only a change in ownership, including an assignment or transfer of the certificate of designation, shall be made if the governing body having jurisdiction finds the factors required in section 25-15-505 (1) (b) and (1) (c) .

(4) An application for approval of a substantial change under this section shall be accompanied by a fee established by the governing body having jurisdiction, which fee shall not exceed ten thousand dollars and which fee may be refunded in whole or in part.

## 25-15-508. Revocation or suspension of certificate.

(1) A governing body having jurisdiction that has granted a certificate of designation for a

hazardous waste incinerator or processor may revoke or suspend such certificate of designation if such governing body having jurisdiction finds that:

(a) There was a material misrepresentation or misstatement of fact in the application for such certificate of designation;

(b) Such hazardous waste incinerator or processor is not being operated in substantial compliance with any term, condition, or limitation of its certificate of designation or any applicable rule adopted pursuant to this part 5; or

(c) The owner or operator of such hazardous waste incinerator or processor has failed to pay the annual fee to the governing body having jurisdiction as required by the provisions of section 25-15-515 (1).

(2) The revocation or suspension of a certificate of designation shall not relieve the owner or operator of the hazardous waste incinerator or processor from any legal liability.

## 25-15-509. Judicial review.

The award, denial, revocation, or suspension of a certificate of designation by the governing body having jurisdiction shall be subject to judicial review in the district court for the judicial district in which the hazardous waste incinerator or processor is located or is proposed to be located. Any request for such judicial review shall be made within thirty days after such award, denial, revocation, or suspension. If the court finds that the governing body having jurisdiction has acted reasonably and in accordance with the procedures and procedural limitations of this part 5, the court shall affirm the action of the governing body having jurisdiction. If the court finds that the action is arbitrary and capricious, not in accord with the procedures or procedural limitations of this part 5, unsupported by substantial evidence when the record is considered as a whole, or otherwise contrary to law, then the court shall hold unlawful and set aside the action and shall remand the case to the governing body having jurisdiction for further proceedings as appropriate.

## 25-15-510. Rules - limitations.

(1) The commission may promulgate rules establishing what constitutes a substantial change in ownership, design, or operation of a hazardous waste incinerator or processor under the provisions of section 25-15-507.

(2) The regulations promulgated by the commission pursuant to this section shall be based upon generally accepted scientific data.

## 25-15-511. List of hazardous wastes - final inventory.

The operator of any hazardous waste incinerator or processor site shall maintain a list of the hazardous wastes accepted for incineration or processing at such site. Such list shall indicate the types of hazardous waste accepted for incineration or processing at such hazardous waste incinerator or processor and the location of such waste. A copy of such list shall be provided to any person upon request and upon payment of a reasonable charge for the costs of the reproduction of such list. Upon the closure of a hazardous waste incinerator or processor site, a final inventory of hazardous wastes shall be prepared and filed with the department. The department shall make any such final inventory available for public inspection and copying at reasonable cost.

## 25-15-512. Inspections of hazardous waste incinerator or processor sites.

(1) The department shall conduct inspections of each hazardous waste incinerator or processor site at intervals determined by rules of the commission based upon the volume and toxicity of the wastes being received at such site. Such inspections shall include, but are not limited to, inspections conducted during the reception of hazardous wastes, during the incineration of hazardous wastes, during the processing of hazardous wastes, and during the shipment of incineration or processing by-products. The department shall be permitted reasonable access to all operations at any hazardous waste incinerator or processor site for the purpose of monitoring and

inspecting such operations. Unless an emergency exists at such site, or unless the department has reason to believe that unlawful activity is being conducted or will be conducted at such site, the department shall provide prior notification of the inspection and shall conduct such inspection during normal business hours.

(2) The governing body having jurisdiction over any hazardous waste incinerator or processor site or the governing body of any other county or municipality having jurisdiction over such site pursuant to an intergovernmental agreement shall have physical and structural access to such site during the operating hours of such site for the purpose of periodic inspections by the agents of such governing body.

### 25-15-513. Violation - criminal penalty.

Any person who violates any provision of this part 5 commits a class 3 misdemeanor and shall be punished as provided in section 18-1.3-501, C.R.S.

### 25-15-514. Violation - civil penalty - reimbursement of costs.

(1) Any person who violates any provision of this part 5 shall be subject to a civil penalty of not more than ten thousand dollars per day of violation. Such penalty shall be determined and collected by the district court for the judicial district in which such violation occurs upon action instituted by the department or the governing body having jurisdiction. In determining the amount of any such penalty, the court shall take into account the seriousness of the violation, whether the violation was willful or due to mistake, the economic impact of the penalty on the violator, and any other relevant factors. All penalties collected pursuant to this section shall be transmitted to the state treasurer, who shall credit fifty percent of such moneys to the general fund and shall transmit the remaining fifty percent of such moneys to the governing body having jurisdiction.

(2) If the violation of the provisions of this part 5 for which a penalty has been assessed and paid into the general fund pursuant to the provisions of subsection (1) of this section results in a county, municipality, or other local government incurring costs to remove, contain, or otherwise mitigate the effects of the hazardous waste which was involved in the violation, such local government shall be entitled to reimbursement for such costs. A local government requesting reimbursement of such costs shall file a claim for reimbursement with the state treasurer. The state treasurer shall make reimbursements out of any funds attributable to the civil penalty imposed for such violation pursuant to the provisions of subsection (1) of this section.

### 25-15-515. Annual fees - commercial hazardous waste incinerator or processor funds.

(1) (a) The owner or operator of any hazardous waste incinerator or processor for which a certificate of designation has been issued pursuant to this article shall be required, contingent upon the issuance of federal or state permits, to pay the governing body having jurisdiction an annual fee for the purpose of offsetting the estimated direct costs necessitated by such hazardous waste incinerator or processor. The governing body having jurisdiction shall provide the owner or operator of such hazardous waste incinerator or processor with an accounting of the basis of such fees. Such costs may include but are not limited to the improvement and maintenance of roads and bridges; fire protection; law enforcement; monitoring by county or municipal health officials pursuant to the requirements of state law, rules, and the certificate of designation; and emergency preparation and response. The amount of such fee shall be no more than the greater of two percent of the annual estimated operating cost of or the annual estimated gross revenue received for the incineration or processing of hazardous wastes by the hazardous waste incinerator or processor. The governing body having jurisdiction may provide reimbursement out of such fee moneys to other governmental units for the reasonable direct costs to such governmental units of increased services necessitated by such hazardous waste incinerator or processor.

(b) In lieu of the annual fees imposed under paragraph (a) of this subsection (1), the governing body may request that the owner or operator of any hazardous waste incinerator or processor site make a lump-sum payment covering the total amount of fees imposed under this section. Such lump sum payment shall not be made unless the governing body having jurisdiction and the owner or operator of a hazardous waste incinerator or processor agree to such payment.

(2) In the event that the owner or operator of a hazardous waste incinerator or processor site fails to pay the annual fee imposed pursuant to the provisions of subsection (1) of this section, the governing body having jurisdiction may suspend the certificate of designation for such site until such annual fee has been paid.

(3) Any governing body having jurisdiction is authorized to establish a hazardous waste incinerator or processor fund. All fees collected pursuant to subsection (1) of this section shall be deposited to the credit of said fund and appropriated by the governing body for the purposes for which such fees are collected.

# ARTICLE 16. HAZARDOUS WASTE SITES

# PART 1. CLEAN-UP

### 25-16-101. Legislative declaration.

(1) The general assembly hereby finds and declares that the existence of facilities subject to the federal "Comprehensive Environmental Response, Compensation, and Liability Act of 1980", including old radium mill residue deposits, poses a potential and significant health hazard. This article is therefore enacted to protect the public health, safety, and welfare by cooperating with the federal government in providing for the disposal and control of such wastes in a safe and environmentally sound manner to prevent or minimize other environmental impacts from such wastes and by providing for the creation of a hazardous substance response fund to provide the necessary state's share of the response costs of cleaning up such sites.

(2) The general assembly also finds and declares that in order to further the purposes of section 30-20-100.5, C.R.S., it is necessary for a portion of the solid waste user fee imposed under section 25-16-104.5 to be used for the purposes specified in part 1 of article 20 of title 30, C.R.S.

### 25-16-102. Definitions.

As used in this article, unless the context otherwise requires:

(1) "Attended solid waste disposal site" means a site established pursuant to part 1 of article 20 of title 30, C.R.S., at which an attendant is present during the normal hours of operation on or after December 31, 1984. This term shall not include any site which is deemed to hold a certificate of designation, but for which such certificate is not required, pursuant to section 30-20-102 (4), C.R.S.; nor shall it include any site used by a person for disposal of solid waste on his own property pursuant to section 30-20-102 (3), C.R.S.

(1.5) "Commission" means the solid and hazardous waste commission created in section 25-15-302.

(2) "Department" means the department of public health and environment.

(3) "Federal act" means the federal "Comprehensive Environmental Response, Compensation, and Liability Act of 1980", as from time to time amended.

(4) "Hazardous substance" has the same meaning as that ascribed to it in the federal act.

(5) "National contingency plan" has the same meaning as that ascribed to it in the federal act and the OPA.

(5.3) "Oil" has the same meaning as that ascribed to it in the OPA.

(5.6) "OPA" means the federal "Oil Pollution Act of 1990", 33 U.S.C. sec. 2701 et seq., as amended.

(6) "Remedial action" has the same meaning as that ascribed to it in the federal act.

(7) "Removal" has the same meaning as that ascribed to it in the federal act.

(8) "Response" has the same meaning as that ascribed to it in the federal act.

(9) "Responsible party" has the same meaning as that ascribed to it in the federal act and the OPA.

(10) "Solid waste" has the same meaning as that ascribed to it in section 30-20-101 (6) , C.R.S.

(11) "Waste producer" means any legal person who contracts for the transportation of waste ultimately destined for an attended solid waste disposal site.

## 25-16-103. Authorization to participate - implementation.

(1) The general assembly hereby authorizes the department of public health and environment to participate in federal implementation of the federal act and the OPA and, for such purpose, the department has the authority to participate in the selection and performance of responses and remedial actions and to enter into cooperative agreements with the federal government providing for remedial actions and responses. The department, with the consent of the governor, has the authority to decline to participate with the federal government on remedial actions which the department determines are not in the interest of the state. Any cooperative agreements entered into under this article may provide assurances acceptable to the federal government that:

(a) The state will assure all future maintenance of the removal and remedial actions provided for the expected life of such actions;

(b) The state will assure the availability of an acceptable hazardous waste disposal facility for any necessary off-site storage, destruction, treatment, or secure disposition of the hazardous substances.

(2) Any state matching payment required by a cooperative agreement entered into pursuant to this section must be approved by the general assembly acting by bill.

## 25-16-104. Financial participation.

Subject to the provisions of section 25-16-103, the general assembly accepts the provisions of section 104 (c) (3) (C) of the federal act requiring the state to pay or assure payment of the necessary state share of response costs, as appropriated by the general assembly, including all future operation and maintenance costs. Any remedial action requiring state matching payment shall be explicitly approved by the general assembly acting by bill and shall be subject to appropriation.

## 25-16-104.5. Solid waste user fee - imposed - rate - direction - legislative declaration - repeal.

(1) Repealed.

(1.5) The general assembly hereby finds and declares that, for purposes of this section, a user fee is intended to be a charge imposed upon waste producers in addition to any charge specified by contract. Any such user fee imposed by this section shall be itemized and depicted on any bill, receipt, or other mechanism used for solid waste management services rendered to any person disposing of solid waste and shall be in addition to the costs of any other solid waste management services provided.

(1.7) (a) On or after July 1, 2010, the commission shall promulgate rules that establish a solid waste user fee upon each person disposing of solid waste at an attended solid waste disposal site. The operator of the site at the time of disposal shall collect the fee from waste producers or other persons disposing of solid waste. The effective date and amount of the fee shall be set by rule of the commission, and the amount shall be sufficient to offset:

(I) The department's direct and indirect costs associated with implementation of the solid waste management program under section 30-20-101.5, C.R.S.;

(II) The department's direct and indirect costs for the implementation of its responsibilities under the federal act, as described in this part 1, and to provide matching funds and cover future maintenance costs pursuant to section 25-16-103; and

(III) The anticipated payments to the department of law, pursuant to subparagraph (II) of paragraph (b) of this subsection (1.7) , for the direct and indirect costs of the department of law for the implementation of its responsibilities under the federal act, as described in this part 1, which costs are distinct from those described in subparagraph (II) of this paragraph (a) .

(b) (I) The portion of the fee collected for the costs described in subparagraph (I) of paragraph (a) of this subsection (1.7) shall be transmitted to the department for deposit into the solid waste management fund created in section 30-20-118, C.R.S.

(II) The portions of the fee imposed under this subsection (1.7) that are collected for the costs described in subparagraphs (II) and (III) of paragraph (a) of this subsection (1.7) shall be transmitted to the department for deposit into the hazardous substance response fund created in section 25-16-104.6. The department may expend money from the portion of the fee collected under subparagraph (III) of paragraph (a) of this subsection (1.7) to compensate the department of law for all or a portion of the expenses incurred for services rendered under the federal act and the OPA, as billed to the department by the department of law. The department may expend money from the fees collected under this subsection (1.7) to finance the radon education and awareness program, established in section 25-11-114 (2) , and the radon mitigation assistance program, established in section 25-11-114 (3) .

(c) The fee established by the commission under this subsection (1.7) shall not exceed fifty cents per cubic yard of solid waste, of which no more than three and one-half cents shall pay for the costs described in subparagraph (III) of paragraph (a) of this subsection (1.7) .

(d) The department shall give the operators of attended solid waste disposal sites written notice of changes to the solid waste user fees no later than ninety days before the effective date of the changes. Failure to provide the notice required by this paragraph (d) shall invalidate the rules that changed the fees.

(2) (a) Repealed.

(a.5) Notwithstanding any provision of law to the contrary, one hundred percent of the moneys collected pursuant to subparagraph (II) of paragraph (a) of subsection (1.7) of this section from persons disposing of solid waste at an attended solid waste disposal site where a local government solid waste disposal fee is imposed to fund hazardous substance response activities at sites designated on the national priority list pursuant to the federal act shall be transmitted to the owner of the solid waste disposal site to the extent that the moneys are used to fund the response activities at the sites on the national priority list. The balance of any moneys described under this paragraph (a.5) that are not used to fund such response activities shall be credited to the hazardous substance response fund created in section 25-16-104.6.

(b) At the end of each fiscal year, the state treasurer shall transfer any moneys in the solid waste management fund created in section 30-20-118, C.R.S., that exceed sixteen and one-half percent of the moneys expended from such fund during the fiscal year to the hazardous substance response fund created in section 25-16-104.6.

(3) to (3.7) Repealed.

(3.9) (a) Subject to subsection (1.5) of this section, in addition to any other user fee imposed by this section, on or after July 1, 2007, there is hereby imposed a user fee to fund the recycling resources economic opportunity program created in section 25-16.5-106.7. Such fee shall be collected by the operator of an attended solid waste disposal site at the time of disposal and shall be imposed and passed through to waste producers and other persons disposing of waste at the following rate or at an equivalent rate established by the department:

(I) Two cents per load transported by a motor vehicle that is commonly used for the noncommercial transport of persons over public highways;

(II) Four cents per load transported by a truck, as defined in section 42-1-102 (108) , C.R.S., that is commonly used for the noncommercial transport of persons and property over the public highways; and

(III) An amount, per cubic yard per load transported by any commercial vehicle or other vehicle not included in the vehicles described in subparagraph (I) or (II) of this paragraph (a) , in accordance with the following schedule:

(A) Through December 31, 2013, seven cents per cubic yard per load;

(B) From January 1, 2014, through December 31, 2014, nine cents per cubic yard per load;

(C) From January 1, 2015, through December 31, 2015, eleven cents per cubic yard per load; and

(D) On and after January 1, 2016, fourteen cents per cubic yard per load.

(b) Any user fee collected by the operator of a solid waste disposal site or facility pursuant to paragraph (a) of this subsection (3.9) shall be transmitted by the last day of the month following the end of each calendar quarter to the state treasurer, who shall credit one hundred percent of such moneys to the recycling resources economic opportunity fund created in section 25-16.5-106.5, to fund the recycling resources economic opportunity program pursuant to section 25-16.5-106.7.

(4) The department shall credit an amount equal to two and one-half percent of the money collected as fees by a solid waste disposal site or facility in order to defray the costs of such collection.

(5) Any operator who fails to collect or to transmit, within thirty days of the day specified in subsection (2) of this section, the fee imposed pursuant to this section is liable for payment of a civil penalty of ten percent of the total amount of fee money uncollected or untransmitted. Collection of such penalty and fee shall be in the manner provided for the collection and enforcement of taxes pursuant to article 21 of title 39, C.R.S.

(6) This section is repealed, effective July 1, 2026.

(7) Repealed.

## 25-16-104.6. Fund established - administration - revenue sources - use.

(1) (a) There is hereby established in the state treasury the hazardous substance response fund. The fund is composed of money that the general assembly may choose to appropriate from the general fund, money derived from the fee imposed pursuant to section 25-16-104.5, and any interest derived therefrom; money recovered from responsible parties pursuant to the federal act or the OPA that is not generated by the state litigating as trustee for natural resources pursuant to section 25-16-104.7; money recovered through litigation by the state pursuant to the federal act or the OPA that is designated for future response cost; and any other money derived from public or private sources that may be credited to the fund. Money in the fund shall be annually appropriated by the general assembly, subject to section 25-16-104, remains available for the purposes of this article, and does not revert to the general fund of the state at the end of any fiscal year. If the fund balance exceeds ten million dollars in any state fiscal year and the fund balance is not projected to fall below ten million dollars within twenty-four months, the department shall evaluate the need to reduce fees to bring the balance of the fund below ten million dollars, and shall present the evaluation to the commission.

(b) Repealed.

(c) Notwithstanding any provision of paragraph (a) of this subsection (1) to the contrary, on April 20, 2009, the state treasurer shall deduct seventeen million four hundred sixty-eight thousand five hundred seventeen dollars from the hazardous substance response fund and transfer such sum to the general fund.

(d) Notwithstanding any provision of paragraph (a) of this subsection (1) to the contrary, on June 1, 2009, the state treasurer shall deduct twelve million five hundred thousand dollars from the hazardous substance response fund and transfer such sum to the general fund.

(e) Notwithstanding any provision of paragraph (a) of this subsection (1) to the contrary, on July 1, 2009, the state treasurer shall deduct two million five hundred thousand dollars from the hazardous substance response fund and transfer such sum to the general fund.

(f) Notwithstanding any provision of paragraph (a) of this subsection (1) to the contrary, for the state fiscal year commencing July 1, 2010, the state treasurer shall make a one-time transfer from the hazardous substance response fund to the solid waste management fund created in section 30-20-118, C.R.S., of up to four hundred thousand dollars, to be used in connection with the department's solid waste management activities.

(2) The general assembly may appropriate up to two and one-half percent of the money in the

hazardous substance response fund for the department's costs of administration and its costs of collection of fees or civil penalties pursuant to section 25-16-104.5. In addition, the department is authorized, subject to appropriation by the general assembly, to use the money in the fund for the following purposes:

(a) To maintain an inventory of all sites and facilities at which hazardous substances have been disposed of in the state;

(b) To supply such state matching funds as may be needed to perform response actions at any site where action is being taken pursuant to the federal act;

(c) To provide any post-cleanup monitoring and maintenance required pursuant to the federal act;

(d) To provide for future response costs in connection with state activities at natural resource damage sites;

(e) To provide such state matching funds as may be needed to perform remediation activities at sites subject to remediation under the federal "Water Pollution Control Act", 33 U.S.C. sec. 1251 et seq., where such remediation activities would keep the site from being added to the national priorities list established pursuant to the federal act;

(f) To remediate sites:

(I) That do not have a responsible party that will perform a remediation;

(II) That have been determined to present a threat to human health or the environment; and

(III) Where the remediation will allow the redevelopment of the property for the public good;

(g) Repealed.

(h) To finance the radon education and awareness program, established in section 25-11-114 (2) , and the radon mitigation assistance program, established in section 25-11-114 (3) .

(2.5) Money in the hazardous substance response fund may be appropriated as follows:

(a) To finance any litigation arising under this part 1, the federal act, or the OPA on behalf of the state;

(b) For the enforcement of court-approved remedies under the federal act out of moneys in the hazardous substance response fund received for future response costs, excluding fines, under the federal act.

(2.7) (Deleted by amendment, L. 2007, p. 1503, § 1, effective May 31, 2007.)

(3) Before the department supplies hazardous substance response fund money as state matching funds for a particular site pursuant to paragraph (b) of subsection (2) of this section, the executive director of the department shall first make a written determination that no potentially responsible party or parties have offered to implement a proper removal and remedial action plan at such site at their own expense, consistent with the national contingency plan established pursuant to the federal act.

(4) It is the intent of the general assembly that state matching moneys be appropriated only from the hazardous substance response fund or the hazardous substance site response fund.

## 25-16-104.7. Natural resource damage recoveries - fund created - repeal.

(1) Except as provided in subsection (3) of this section, money recovered through litigation by the state acting as trustee of natural resources pursuant to the federal act or the OPA, and any interest derived therefrom, are credited to the natural resource damage recovery fund, which fund is hereby created. The department may expend the custodial money in the fund without further appropriation for purposes authorized by the federal act or the OPA, including the restoration, replacement, or acquisition of the equivalent of natural resources that have been injured, destroyed, or lost as a result of a release of a hazardous substance or oil. In addition, the department shall use the money in the natural resource damage recovery fund in a manner that is consistent with any judicial order, decree, or judgment governing the use of any particular recovery credited to the fund.

(2) Repealed.

(3) To the extent authorized by law, and consistent with a final judicial order or decree in any litigation by the state acting as trustee of natural resources pursuant to the federal act or the OPA,

any recovery of natural resource damage assessment or other costs, including litigation costs and fees, shall be credited to the fund from which such costs were originally paid.

(4) (a) Notwithstanding any other provision of law and except as provided in paragraph (b) of this subsection (4) , on June 30, 2010, and each June 30 thereafter, the state treasurer shall:

(I) Deduct an amount equal to sixty-two and three-tenths percent of the interest earned on those moneys in the natural resource damage recovery fund that were received in the settlement reached in the case denominated State of Colorado v. United States of America, Shell Oil Company, et al., Case No. 83 CV 2386, in the United States district court for the district of Colorado, and shall transfer such amount to the hazardous substance response fund created in section 25-16-104.6; and

(II) Deduct an amount equal to thirty-seven and seven-tenths percent of the interest earned on those moneys in the natural resource damage recovery fund that were received in the settlement reached in the case denominated State of Colorado v. United States of America, Shell Oil Company, et al., Case No. 83 CV 2386, in the United States district court for the district of Colorado, and shall transfer such amount to the general fund.

(b) The state treasurer shall continue to make the transfer specified in subparagraph (I) of paragraph (a) of this subsection (4) until the total amount transferred to the hazardous substance response fund and credited to the fund pursuant to paragraph (b.5) of this subsection (4) equals one million six hundred fifty-seven thousand five hundred seventy-seven dollars, at which time the state treasurer shall cease the transfers. The state treasurer shall continue to make the transfer specified in subparagraph (II) of paragraph (a) of this subsection (4) until the total amount transferred to the general fund and credited to the general fund pursuant to paragraph (b.5) of this subsection (4) reaches one million four thousand eight hundred seventy-three dollars, at which time the state treasurer shall cease the transfers.

(b.5) The department may accept moneys from public or private sources for the purpose of repaying the loans to the natural resource damage recovery fund from the hazardous substance response fund created in section 25-16-104.6 or the general fund. The department shall transmit these moneys to the state treasurer, who shall credit the moneys to the appropriate fund. This paragraph (b.5) is exempt from the provisions of part 13 of article 75 of title 24, C.R.S.

(c) This subsection (4) is repealed, effective July 1, 2020.

## 25-16-104.8. Report required. (Repealed)


## 25-16-104.9. Hazardous substance site response fund - creation - transfer - use - definition.

(1) As used in this section, "fund" means the hazardous substance site response fund created in subsection (2) of this section.

(2) The hazardous substance site response fund is created in the state treasury. The fund consists of any moneys transferred pursuant to section 24-75-220 (4) (a) (III.5) , C.R.S. The general assembly may appropriate moneys in the fund to the department for the purposes specified in section 25-16-104.

(3) Any moneys in the fund not expended may be invested by the state treasurer as provided by law. All interest and income derived from the investment and deposit of moneys in the fund are credited to the fund. Any unexpended and unencumbered moneys remaining in the fund at the end of a fiscal year remain in the fund and may not be credited or transferred to the general fund or any other fund.

## 25-16-105. Repeal of part - repeal of various sections. (Repealed)

# PART 2. RECOVERIES PURSUANT TO FEDERAL LAW - DISPOSITION

## 25-16-201. CERCLA recovery fund - creation - repeal of subsection. (Repealed)

# PART 3. VOLUNTARY CLEAN-UP AND REDEVELOPMENT ACT

## 25-16-301. Short title.
This part 3 shall be known and may be cited as the "Voluntary Clean-up and Redevelopment Act".

## 25-16-302. Legislative declaration.
(1) The general assembly hereby declares that the purpose of this part 3 is to provide for the protection of human health and the environment and to foster the transfer, redevelopment, and reuse of facilities and sites that have been previously contaminated with hazardous substances or petroleum products. The general assembly further declares that this program is intended to permit and encourage voluntary clean-ups of contaminated property by providing persons interested in redeveloping existing industrial sites with a method of determining what the clean-up responsibilities will be when they plan the reuse of existing sites. It is the further intent of the general assembly that this voluntary program operate in such a way as to:
(a) Eliminate impediments to the sale or redevelopment of previously contaminated property;
(b) Encourage and facilitate prompt clean-up activities; and
(c) Minimize administrative processes and costs.

## 25-16-303. Voluntary clean-up and redevelopment program - general provisions - fees - access to property during reviews.
(1) The program established in this part 3 shall be voluntary and may be initiated by:
(a) The submission to the department of an application for approval of a voluntary clean-up plan pursuant to section 25-16-304 for properties where remediation may be necessary to protect human health and the environment in light of the current or proposed use of the property; or
(b) The submission to the department of a no action petition pursuant to section 25-16-307 for properties where remediation is complete or not necessary to protect human health and the environment in light of the current or proposed use of the property.
(2) No person, financial institution, or other entity financing a commercial real estate transaction shall require a purchaser to participate in the voluntary program contained in this part 3, and no entity of Colorado state government regulating any person, financial institution, or other entity financing a commercial real estate transaction shall require evidence of participation in this program to be a component of standard real estate loan documentation.
(3) (a) The program contained in this part 3 is voluntary and may only be initiated by the owner of the subject real property.
(b) The provisions of this part 3 shall not apply to the following:
(I) Property that is listed or proposed for listing on the national priorities list of superfund sites established under the federal act;
(II) Property that is the subject of corrective action under orders or agreements issued pursuant to

the provisions of part 3 of article 15 of this title or the federal "Resource Conservation and Recovery Act of 1976", as amended;

(III) Property that is subject to an order issued by or an agreement with the water quality control division pursuant to part 6 of article 8 of this title;

(IV) A facility which has or should have a permit or interim status pursuant to part 3 of article 15 of this title for the treatment, storage, or disposal of hazardous waste; or

(V) Property that is subject to the provisions of part 2 of article 20.5 of title 8, C.R.S.

(4) (a) Each application for approval of a voluntary clean-up plan and each petition for a no action determination shall be accompanied by a filing fee determined by the department at a level sufficient to cover the direct and indirect costs of the department in processing applications for approval of voluntary clean-up plans and petitions for no action under this part 3, but such filing fee shall not exceed two thousand dollars.

(b) (I) The department shall establish and publish hourly rates for review charges performed by the department in connection with applications for approval of voluntary clean-up plans and petitions for no action under this part 3. Within thirty days after the department's approval or denial of a voluntary clean-up plan or no action petition, the department shall bill an applicant or petitioner for all direct and indirect charges of review of applications and petitions under this part 3 in accordance with the hourly rate structure established pursuant to this subparagraph (I). The department's charges shall be billed against the application fee paid pursuant to this subsection (4) in accordance with subparagraph (II) of this paragraph (b).

(II) (A) If the department bills charges in an amount less than the application fee, the department shall return any unused balance to the applicant or petitioner after the department's final determination in the matter has been made.

(B) If the department bills charges that exceed the application fee, the department may bill the applicant or petitioner for direct and indirect charges that the department incurs in excess of the application fee up to a maximum of an additional one thousand dollars.

(C) If the department determines that review of the application cannot be completed for three thousand dollars or less due to the size or complexity of the site, the department shall contact the applicant or petitioner prior to incurring additional charges. The applicant or petitioner shall then be given the opportunity to either negotiate an agreement containing an upper limit on the department's charges and complete the review, or withdraw the application and receive a refund of the unbilled balance of fees already paid to the department. Agreements negotiated pursuant to this sub-subparagraph (C) shall be in writing and shall be signed by authorized representatives of the parties.

(D) The department shall make its best efforts to determine whether the application review will exceed three thousand dollars within the first ten hours of review or, if the applicant or petitioner requests a pre-application conference, within ten business days after such conference.

(c) All moneys collected pursuant to this subsection (4) shall be transmitted to the state treasurer, who shall credit the same to the hazardous substance response fund, created in section 25-16-104.6 (1). Moneys collected pursuant to this subsection (4) shall be subject to annual appropriation by the general assembly only to defray the direct and indirect costs of the department in processing voluntary clean-up plans and petitions for no action determination as specified in this part 3.

(5) During the time allocated for review of applications for voluntary clean-up plans and petitions for no action determination under this part 3, the department shall, upon reasonable notice to the property owner, have access at all reasonable times to the subject real property.

## 25-16-304. Voluntary clean-up plan.

(1) Any person who owns real property which has been contaminated with hazardous substances or petroleum products may submit an application for the approval of a voluntary clean-up plan to the department under the provisions of this section.

(2) A voluntary clean-up plan shall include:

(a) An environmental assessment of the real property which describes the contamination, if any, on the property and the risk the contamination currently poses to public health and the environment;

(b) A proposal, if needed, to remediate any contamination or condition which has or could lead to a release which poses an unacceptable risk to human health or the environment, considering the present and any differing proposed future use of the property and a timetable for implementing the proposal and for monitoring the site after the proposed measures are completed;

(c) A description of applicable promulgated state standards establishing acceptable concentrations of constituents in soils, surface water, or groundwater and, for constituents present at the site for which such state standards do not exist, a description of proposed clean-up levels and any current risk to human health or the environment based upon the current or proposed use of the site.

## 25-16-305. Remediation alternatives.

(1) Remediation alternatives shall be based on the actual risk to human health and the environment currently posed by contaminants on the real property, considering the following factors:

(a) The present or proposed uses of the site;

(b) The ability of the contaminants to move in a form and manner which would result in exposure to humans and the surrounding environment at levels which exceed applicable promulgated state standards or, in the absence of such standards, which represent an unacceptable risk to human health or the environment;

(c) The potential risks associated with proposed clean-up alternatives and the economic and technical feasibility and reliability of such alternatives.

## 25-16-306. Approval of voluntary clean-up plan - time limits - contents of notice - conditions under which approval is void - expiration of approval.

(1) (a) The department shall provide formal written notification that a voluntary clean-up plan has been approved or disapproved within no more than forty-five days after a request by a property owner, unless the property owner and the department agree to an extension of the review to a date certain. Such review shall be limited to a review of the materials submitted by the applicant and documents or information readily available to the department. If the department fails to act on an application within the time limits specified in this subsection (1), the voluntary clean-up plan shall be deemed approved. If the department has received eight applications for review of voluntary clean-up plans or no action petitions in a calendar month, the department may notify any additional applicants in that month that their plan or petition will be considered the following month, and the forty-five day period for department review shall begin on the first day of the month following receipt of the plan or petition.

(b) The department shall approve a voluntary clean-up plan if, based on the information submitted by the property owner, the department concludes that the plan will:

(I) Attain a degree of clean-up and control of hazardous substances or petroleum products, or both, that complies with all promulgated applicable state requirements, regulations, criteria, or standards;

(II) For constituents not governed by subparagraph (I) of this paragraph (b), reduce concentrations such that the property does not present an unacceptable risk to human health or the environment based upon the property's current use and any future uses proposed by the property owner.

(c) In the event that a voluntary clean-up plan is not approved by the department, the department shall promptly provide the property owner with a written statement of the reasons for such denial. If the department disapproves a voluntary clean-up plan based upon the applicant's failure to submit the information required by section 25-16-304, the department shall notify the applicant of the specific information omitted by the applicant.

(d) The approval of a voluntary clean-up plan by the department applies only to conditions on the property and state standards that exist as of the time of submission of the application.

(2) Written notification by the department that a voluntary clean-up plan is approved shall contain the basis for the determination and the following statement:

Based upon the information provided by [insert name(s) of property owner(s) ] concerning property located at [insert address], it is the opinion of the Colorado Department of Public Health and Environment that upon completion of the voluntary clean-up plan no further action is required to assure that this property, when used for the purposes identified in the voluntary clean-up plan, is protective of existing and proposed uses and does not pose an unacceptable risk to human health or the environment at the site.

(3) (a) Failure of a property owner to materially comply with the voluntary clean-up plan approved by the department pursuant to this section shall render the approval void.
(b) Submission of materially misleading information by the applicant in the context of the voluntary clean-up plan shall render the department approval void.
(4) (a) If a voluntary clean-up plan is not initiated within twelve months and completed within twenty-four months after approval by the department, such approval shall lapse; except that the department may grant an extension of the time limit for completion of the voluntary clean-up plan.
(b) A property owner desiring to implement a voluntary clean-up plan after the time limits permitted in paragraph (a) of this subsection (4) shall submit a written petition for reapplication accompanied by written certification of a qualified environmental professional that the conditions on the subject real property are substantially similar to those that existed at the time of the original approval.
(c) Reapplications pursuant to paragraph (b) of this subsection (4) shall be subject to limited review by the department, which shall complete such review within thirty days of receipt of a petition for reapplication; except that any reapplication that involves real property, the condition of which has substantially changed since approval of the original voluntary clean-up plan, shall be treated as a new application and shall be subject to all the requirements of this part 3.
(5) (a) Within forty-five days after the completion of the voluntary clean-up described in the voluntary clean-up plan approved by the department, the property owner shall provide to the department a certification from a qualified environmental professional that the plan has been fully implemented.
(b) If the owner is applying for the tax credit provided in section 39-22-526 (1) , C.R.S., or to transfer a transferable expense amount pursuant to section 39-22-526 (2) , C.R.S., the owner shall submit to the department the certification along with an application pursuant to section 25-16-303. The certification shall, in addition to certifying that the plan has been fully implemented, disclose the costs of implementation and include supporting documentation of those costs. The department shall then certify the accuracy of the costs and issue the property owner a certificate stating that the clean-up has occurred and the costs of such clean-up. The property owner may submit this certificate to the department of revenue to claim a tax credit or transfer a transferable expense amount under section 39-22-526, C.R.S.

## 25-16-307. No action determinations.

(1) A property owner may file with the department a written petition to request a no action determination pursuant to this section. The department shall provide formal written notification that a no action petition has been approved or disapproved within no more than forty-five days after a request by a property owner, unless the property owner and the department agree to an extension of the review to a date certain. Such review shall be limited to a review of the materials submitted by the applicant and documents or information readily available to the department. If the department fails to act on a petition within the time limits specified in this subsection (1) , the no action petition shall be deemed approved. If the department has received eight applications for review of voluntary clean-up plans or no action petitions in a calendar month, the department may notify any additional applicants in that month that their plan or petition will be considered the following month, and the forty-five day period for department review shall begin on the first day of the month following receipt of the plan or petition.

(2) (a) The department shall issue a written determination approving a no action petition when:

(I) The environmental assessment described in section 25-16-308 performed by a qualified environmental professional indicates the existence of contamination which does not exceed applicable promulgated state standards or contamination which does not pose an unacceptable risk to human health and the environment; or

(II) The department finds that contamination or a release or threatened release of a hazardous substance or petroleum product originates from a source on adjacent or nearby real property if a person or entity responsible for such a source of contamination is or will be taking necessary action, if any, to address the contamination.

(b) The department shall provide formal written notification of a no action determination, which shall contain the basis for the determination and the following statement:

Based upon the information provided by [insert name(s) of property owner(s) ] concerning property located at [insert address], it is the opinion of the Colorado department of public health and environment that no further action is required to assure that this property, when used for the purposes identified in the no action petition, is protective of existing and proposed uses and does not pose an unacceptable risk to human health or the environment at the site.

(c) The approval of a no action petition by the department applies only to conditions on the property and state standards that exist as of the time of submission of the petition.

(3) Submission of materially misleading information by the applicant in the context of a no action petition shall render the department approval void.

(4) In the event that a no action petition is not approved by the department, the department shall promptly provide the property owner with a written statement of the reasons for such denial. If the department disapproves a no action petition based upon the applicant's failure to submit required information, the department shall notify the applicant of the specific information omitted.

## 25-16-308. Environmental assessment - requirements.

(1) The department may only accept environmental assessments under this part 3 that are prepared by a qualified environmental professional. A qualified environmental professional is a person with education, training, and experience in preparing environmental studies and assessments.

(2) The environmental assessment described in section 25-16-304 (2) (a) shall include the following information:

(a) The legal description of the site and a map identifying the location and size of the property;

(b) The physical characteristics of the site and areas contiguous to the site, including the location of any surface water bodies and groundwater aquifers;

(c) The location of any wells located on the site or on areas within a one-half mile radius of the site and a description of the use of those wells;

(d) The current and proposed use of on-site groundwater;

(e) The operational history of the site and the current use of areas contiguous to the site;

(f) The present and proposed uses of the site;

(g) Information concerning the nature and extent of any contamination and releases of hazardous substances or petroleum products which have occurred at the site including any impacts on areas contiguous to the site;

(h) Any sampling results or other data which characterizes the soil, groundwater, or surface water on the site; and

(i) A description of the human and environmental exposure to contamination at the site based upon the property's current use and any future use proposed by the property owner.

## 25-16-309. Coordination with other laws.

(1) Nothing in this part 3 shall absolve any person from obligations under any other law or regulation, including any requirement to obtain permits or approvals for work performed under a voluntary clean-up plan.

(2) If the United States environmental protection agency indicates that it is investigating a site which is the subject of an approved voluntary clean-up plan or no action petition, the department shall actively pursue a determination by the United States environmental protection agency that the property not be addressed under the federal act or, in the case of property being addressed through a voluntary clean-up plan, that no further federal action be taken with respect to the property at least until the voluntary clean-up plan is completely implemented.

### 25-16-310. Enforceability of voluntary clean-up plans and no action determinations.

(1) Voluntary clean-up plans are not enforceable against a property owner; except that, if the department can demonstrate that a property owner who initiated a voluntary clean-up under an approved plan has failed to fully and properly implement that plan, the department may require further action if the action is authorized by other laws or regulations of this state.

(2) Information provided by a property owner to support a voluntary clean-up plan or no action petition shall not provide the department with an independent basis to seek penalties from the property owner pursuant to state environmental statutes or regulations. If, pursuant to other state statutes or regulations, the department initiates an enforcement action against the property owner subsequent to the submission of a voluntary clean-up plan or no action petition regarding the contamination addressed in the plan or petition, the voluntary disclosure of the information in the plan or petition shall be considered by the enforcing authority to reduce or eliminate any penalties assessed to the property owner.

### 25-16-311. Repeal of part. (Repealed)

# ARTICLE 16.5. POLLUTION PREVENTION

### 25-16.5-101. Short title.

This article shall be known and may be cited as the "Pollution Prevention Act of 1992".

### 25-16.5-102. Legislative declaration - state policy on pollution prevention.

(1) The general assembly hereby finds and declares that:

(a) Colorado is blessed by natural beauty and an excellent quality of life, which should be maintained;

(b) The prevention of pollution will assist in maintaining quality of life in our state;

(c) There are resources and expertise in Colorado, including industry, government, and citizen groups, which can provide information and assistance to promote the cost-effective prevention of pollution;

(d) There are opportunities to reduce or prevent pollution through voluntary changes in procurement, production, operations, and use of raw materials throughout the state;

(e) The purpose of this article is to create a cooperative partnership among business, agriculture, the environmental community, and the department of public health and environment in which technical assistance, outreach, and education activities are coordinated and conducted to achieve pollution prevention and waste reduction and source reduction;

(f) The prevention of pollution is preferable to treatment and disposal of toxic substances and is the cornerstone of the future of environmental management.

(2) The general assembly, therefore, determines and declares that the state policy of Colorado shall be that pollution prevention is the environmental management tool of first choice. The state policy shall be that: Pollution should be prevented or reduced at the source by means including the

reduction in the production or use of hazardous substances; pollution that cannot be prevented should be recycled in an environmentally safe manner; pollution that cannot be prevented or recycled should be treated in an environmentally safe manner; and disposal or other releases into the environment should be employed only as a last resort and should be conducted in an environmentally safe manner.

## 25-16.5-103. Definitions.

As used in this article, unless the context otherwise requires:

(1) "Advisory board" means the pollution prevention advisory board created in section 25-16.5-104.

(2) "By-product" means all toxic or hazardous substances, other than a product, that are generated from production processes prior to recycling, handling, treatment, disposal, or release.

(3) "Department" means the department of public health and environment.

(4) "Federal act" means the federal "Emergency Planning and Community Right-to-know Act of 1986", 42 U.S.C. sec. 11001 et seq., Title III of the federal "Superfund Amendments and Reauthorization Act of 1986", Pub.L. 99-499, as amended.

(5) "Hazardous substance" or "toxic substance" means those chemicals defined as hazardous substances under section 313 of the federal "Superfund Amendments and Reauthorization Act of 1986" (SARA Title III) and sections 101(14) and 102 of the federal "Comprehensive Environmental Response, Compensation, and Liability Act" (CERCLA) , as amended.

(6) "Pollution prevention" means any practice which reduces the use of any hazardous substance or amount of any pollutant or contaminant prior to recycling, treatment, or disposal, and reduces the hazards to public health and the environment associated with the use or release or both of such substances, pollutants, or contaminants.

(7) "Production process" means a process, line, method, activity, or technique, or a series or combinations of such processes, necessary to and integral to making a product or providing a service, and does not include waste management activities.

(8) "Small and medium-sized business" means a business which has five hundred or fewer employees and which has gross annual sales of seventy-five million dollars or less.

(9) "Toxics use reduction" means changes in production processes, products, or raw materials that reduce, avoid, or eliminate the use of toxic or hazardous substances and the generation of hazardous by-products per unit of production, so as to reduce the overall risks to the health of workers, consumers, or the environment without creating new risks of concern.

(10) "Waste management" means the recycling, treatment, handling, transfer, controlled release, cleanup, and disposal of waste, and the containment of accidents and spills.

(11) "Waste reduction" and "source reduction" mean any practice which reduces the amount of any hazardous substances, pollutant, or contaminant entering any waste stream or otherwise being released into the environment (including fugitive emissions) prior to recycling, treatment, or disposal, and reduces the hazards to public health and the environment associated with the release of such substances, pollutants, or contaminants. The terms include equipment or technology modifications, process or procedure modifications, reformulation or redesign of products, substitution of raw materials, and improvements in housekeeping, maintenance, training, or inventory control. The term "source reduction" does not include any practice which alters the physical, chemical, or biological characteristics or the volume of a hazardous substance, pollutant, or contaminant through a process or activity which itself is not integral to and necessary for the production of a product or the providing of a service.

## 25-16.5-104. Pollution prevention advisory board - creation.

(1) There is hereby created in the department of public health and environment a pollution prevention advisory board for the purposes of providing overall policy guidance, coordination, and advice to the department on pollution prevention activities and for carrying out the duties specified in section 25-16.5-105. The advisory board shall consist of fifteen members to be appointed by the

governor. The members appointed shall include representatives of businesses, agriculture, environmental groups, academic institutions of higher education, community groups, and local governments. In addition, the governor shall appoint two representatives from state agencies to serve as ex-officio members of the advisory board, with at least one of such appointees to be from the department of public health and environment. In making the appointments, the governor shall provide for geographic diversity. The board shall elect its own chairperson. Members of the advisory board shall serve without compensation.

(2) Repealed.

## 25-16.5-105. Powers and duties of advisory board.

(1) The advisory board has the following powers and duties:

(a) To provide overall policy guidance, coordination, and advice in the development and implementation of the pollution prevention activities of the department;

(b) To support nonregulatory public and private efforts that promote the prevention of pollution in this state;

(c) To develop pollution prevention goals and objectives;

(d) To review environmental regulatory programs, laws, and policies to identify pollution prevention opportunities and incentives;

(e) To provide direction for pollution prevention outreach, education, training, and technical assistance programs;

(f) Repealed.

(g) To contract with a provider or providers, which may include the department, to provide pollution prevention activities as described in section 25-16.5-106;

(h) To award grants from the recycling resources economic opportunity fund, referred to in this section as the "fund", in accordance with the requirements of section 25-16.5-106.7 and to develop criteria for awarding grants from the fund in accordance with the provisions of section 25-16.5-106.7 (3) (b) . Grant awards shall be made, and the criteria for awarding grants shall be developed, in consultation with the pollution prevention advisory board assistance committee created in section 25-16.5-105.5 (2) , referred to in this section as the "committee".

(i) To commission such studies, using moneys in the fund, as the board, in consultation with the committee, deems necessary and appropriate;

(j) To receive and expend gifts, grants, and bequests from any source, public or private, specifically including state and federal moneys and other available moneys, to fund grants made available from the fund in accordance with the provisions of section 25-16.5-106.7;

(j.5) (Deleted by amendment, L. 2010, (HB 10-1018) , ch. 421, p. 2163, § 3, effective June 10, 2010.)

(k) (I) In consultation with the committee, to develop a formula for paying a rebate to any local government or to any nonprofit or for-profit entity that recycles any commodity. The rebate authorized by this paragraph (k) shall be paid on commodities recycled on a per-ton basis with differential rates for different commodities. For any one state fiscal year, the board, in consultation with the committee, has the discretion to determine the amount rebated pursuant to this paragraph (k) ; except that the amount shall not exceed one-fourth of the amount of moneys projected to be collected in the fund in the next state fiscal year. Any moneys of the amount so determined that are not spent on rebates remain in the fund to be expended for the same purposes and in the same manner as other moneys in the fund. Any rebate shall be paid out of moneys collected:

(A) Repealed.

(B) From the user fee imposed by section 25-16-104.5 (3.9) (a) to fund the recycling resources economic opportunity program created in section 25-16.5-106.7.

(II) Applications to the advisory board for any rebate may be submitted after the last day of the month following the end of each calendar quarter for recycling activities undertaken in such calendar quarter, beginning with the calendar quarter ending on December 31, 2007; except that the period for the first rebate payment shall cover July 1, 2007, through December 31, 2007.

(l) To make recommendations, as requested, on policy matters related to sustainable resource and discarded materials management; and

(m) (I) In accordance with the provisions of subsection (1) (m) (II) of this section, to submit an annual report to the department of local affairs, the department, and the Colorado energy office created in section 24-38.5-101.

(II) The annual report required by subparagraph (I) of this paragraph (m) shall include a calculation of the proportion of solid waste generated in the state in the previous year that was diverted to other uses and the number of jobs created and any other economic impacts resulting from grants made from the fund by the advisory board pursuant to paragraph (h) of this subsection (1) and section 25-16.5-106.7 (3) .

(2) (Deleted by amendment, L. 2010, (HB 10-1018) , ch. 421, p. 2163, § 3, effective June 10, 2010.)

## 25-16.5-105.5. Pollution prevention advisory board assistance committee - appointments - membership - definitions.

(1) As used in this section, unless the context otherwise requires:

(a) "Committee" means the pollution prevention advisory board assistance committee created in subsection (2) of this section.

(b) "Fund" means the recycling resources economic opportunity fund created in section 25-16.5-106.5 (1) .

(2) (a) There is hereby created in the department the committee that shall assist the advisory board in undertaking the powers and duties given to the board as specified in this article.

(b) The committee shall consist of thirteen members as described in paragraph (c) of this subsection (2) , each of whom shall be appointed by the executive director of the department no later than September 1, 2007.

(c) The members appointed to the committee shall include representatives of industry, nonprofit and community organizations, state agencies, and local governments in accordance with the following:

(I) One member of the committee shall be a representative of the department.

(II) One member of the committee shall be a representative of the Colorado office of economic development created in section 24-48.5-101 (1) , C.R.S.

(III) One member of the committee shall be a representative of the Colorado energy office created in section 24-38.5-101, C.R.S.

(IV) Two members of the committee shall represent counties that operate county solid waste or recycling facilities, one member of which shall represent a county that is predominately rural in character and the other of which shall represent a county that is predominately urban in character.

(V) Two members of the committee shall represent municipalities that operate municipal solid waste or recycling facilities, one member of which shall represent a municipality that is located in a county that is predominately rural in character and the other of which shall represent a municipality that is located in a county that is predominately urban in character.

(VI) The remaining six members of the committee shall be balanced equally to the extent practicable from among representatives of nonprofit and for-profit entities engaged in recycling or composting through the collection of recyclable material, the manufacturing of products containing recycled material, the marketing of products manufactured with recycling material, or other entities whose mission is directed to advance and promote recycling and composting through educational programs, technical assistance, research, or community outreach.

(d) The terms of members of the committee shall be for four years; except that the initial terms of seven of the members of the committee shall, in the discretion of the executive director of the department, be for two years. All appointments made following the expiration of the initial two-year terms shall be for four years. Members of the committee shall serve no more than three consecutive four-year terms on the committee. No more than six members of the committee shall be from the same political party.

(e) Any vacancy on the committee shall be filled for the unexpired term in the same manner as the original appointment. Any member of the committee may be removed by the executive director of the department at any time and for any reason.

(f) The committee shall elect a chairperson and vice-chairperson by majority vote of the members. The members of the committee shall serve without compensation; except that members of the committee shall receive a per diem amount of ninety-nine dollars for each day actually engaged in the duties of the committee and shall be reimbursed for necessary traveling and other reasonable expenses incurred in the performance of their official duties.

(3) The committee has the following powers and duties:

(a) To make recommendations to the advisory board in connection with the awarding of grants by the board from the fund pursuant to section 25-16.5-105 (1) (h) and to make recommendations to the board on the development of criteria to guide the board in making decisions concerning the awarding of grants pursuant to section 25-16.5-106.7 (3) (b) ;

(b) Repealed.

(c) To make recommendations to the advisory board in connection with the receipt or expenditure of gifts, grants, and bequests by the board pursuant to section 25-16.5-105 (1) (j) ;

(d) To make recommendations to the advisory board, as requested, on policy matters related to sustainable resource and discarded materials management;

(e) To determine whether and to what extent to pay rebates to entities recycling commodities, and to make recommendations to the advisory board on the formula created for paying the rebates, pursuant to section 25-16.5-105 (1) (k) ; and

(f) To make additional recommendations to the advisory board on such other matters as will further the purposes of this article.

## 25-16.5-106. Pollution prevention activities program.

(1) The advisory board shall contract with a provider or providers, which may include the department, to develop a pollution prevention activities program. The pollution prevention activities program shall be carried out to make pollution prevention the environmental management tool of first choice, and the provider which provides the services pursuant to contract shall have the following powers and duties:

(a) To provide education and training about pollution prevention to businesses that use or produce hazardous substances and their employees, local and state governments, and the general public. Such education and training may include pollution prevention techniques, total cost analysis of toxics use and pollution prevention techniques, economic evaluation methods of such techniques, and management and employee involvement and public involvement.

(b) To expand the pollution prevention technical library and resource center providing access to information on new products, production process techniques, and raw materials for production related to pollution prevention, technical reports, fact-sheets, case studies, articles, and other reference materials;

(c) To collect and evaluate information on toxics use reduction and waste reduction and the amount of hazardous substances used in Colorado as the basis for establishing pollution prevention priorities and measuring progress in achieving pollution prevention program objectives;

(d) To conduct an evaluation of pollution prevention activities in this state analyzing existing data to determine what priority should be given to different hazardous substances and production processes;

(e) To prepare a report with data on the amount of hazardous substances, pollutants, and contaminants used in Colorado and the amount of pollution released in Colorado prior to recycling, treatment, or disposal. Such report shall be developed from existing sources and updated every two years and used as a tool to measure the success of the pollution prevention activities program and the technical assistance program in Colorado.

(f) To develop other methods to measure the success of pollution prevention projects at facilities.

Methods shall be developed to measure the use of hazardous substances for production processes and the amount of waste prior to waste management practices.

(g) To cooperate with the advisory board in the performance of duties assigned to the board, including the review of environmental regulatory programs, laws, and policies for identifying pollution prevention opportunities and incentives;

(h) To coordinate with any of the academic institutions or other recipients of grants under the technical assistance program pursuant to section 25-16.5-107.

## 25-16.5-106.5. Recycling resources economic opportunity fund - creation - repeal.

(1) (a) The recycling resources economic opportunity fund is hereby created in the state treasury, referred to in this section as the "fund". The fund shall consist of:

(I) (A) Repealed.

(B) Effective July 1, 2011, moneys collected for the fund pursuant to section 25-16-104.5 (3.9) (a) and credited to the fund in accordance with section 25-16-104.5 (3.9) (b) .

(II) Any moneys appropriated to the fund by the general assembly; and

(III) All other moneys that may be available to the fund, including moneys made available from gifts, grants, or bequests.

(b) All interest derived from the deposit of moneys in the fund shall be credited to the fund. At the end of any fiscal year, all unexpended and unencumbered moneys in the fund shall remain in the fund and shall not be credited or transferred to the general fund or any other fund.

(2) Any moneys generated pursuant to subsection (1) of this section shall be annually appropriated to the department for allocation to the advisory board for the purpose of funding the recycling resources economic opportunity activities authorized by section 25-16.5-106.7, as well as any administrative costs associated therewith, including without limitation the grants authorized to be made under section 25-16.5-106.7 (3) and grant program oversight authorized by section 25-16.5-105.5 (3) . Such moneys may also be used to fund studies pursuant to section 25-16.5-105 (1) (i) .

(3) Moneys in the fund shall be used to pay for administrative costs incurred by the department in implementing the provisions of House Bill 07-1288 as enacted by the first regular session of the sixty-sixth general assembly.

(4) Except as otherwise provided in this section, no moneys in the fund shall be used for the administration, implementation, or enforcement of any state law or rule.

(4.5) Notwithstanding any provision of this section to the contrary, on April 20, 2009, the state treasurer shall deduct one million five hundred thousand dollars from the recycling resources economic opportunity fund and transfer such sum to the general fund.

(5) This section is repealed, effective July 1, 2026.

## 25-16.5-106.7. Recycling resources economic opportunity program - grants - definitions - repeal.

(1) As used in this section, unless the context otherwise requires:

(a) "Committee" means the pollution prevention advisory board assistance committee created in section 25-16.5-105.5.

(b) "Fund" means the recycling resources economic opportunity fund created in section 25-16.5-106.5 (1) .

(c) "Local government" means a county, home rule or statutory city, town, territorial charter city, or city and county.

(2) There is hereby created the recycling resources economic opportunity program. In connection with the program, the advisory board shall accept proposals from local governments requesting an award of a grant from moneys made available under the fund. Subject to the requirements of this subsection (2) , the board may award grants under this section to nonprofit or for-profit organizations or other entities where the application submitted by the organization or entity applying for grant moneys has been approved by the local government within the boundaries of

which the organization or entity is located. In awarding grants pursuant to this section, the board may consider proposals that have not been approved by a local government if the entity submitting the proposal provides documentation that the proposal will be beneficial to the community that would be affected by the grant award, the award otherwise satisfies the criteria specified in paragraph (b) of subsection (3) of this section, and the grant is made available for one of the purposes specified in subsection (4) of this section.

(3) (a) The advisory board may award grants from the fund to public and private entities, both nonprofit and for-profit, including without limitation the department and solid waste disposal sites and facilities and their local affiliates that collect the solid waste user fee pursuant to section 25-16-104.5 (3.9) .

(b) (I) In consultation with the committee, the advisory board shall develop criteria to guide it in making decisions concerning the awarding of grants to implement the purposes described in subsection (4) of this section. Such criteria shall include without limitation:

(A) The amount of moneys raised for the fund by the region of the state in which the applicant's project is located;

(B) The needs of the community submitting the proposal;

(C) The feasibility of the proposal and sustainability of the project that is the subject of the proposal;

(D) The economic and environmental benefits that would accrue from the proposal, including the creation of markets for recycled materials;

(E) Measurable results; and

(F) Adverse impacts on existing businesses.

(II) In developing the criteria specified in subparagraph (I) of this paragraph (b) , the advisory board shall determine priorities for the grants in consultation with the committee.

(4) The advisory board may award moneys from the fund to finance grants made available pursuant to subsection (2) of this section for the following purposes:

(a) Recycling, beneficial use, and reuse;

(b) Public-private partnerships that promote waste diversion, recycling, recycling markets, the beneficial use of discarded materials, or other recycling-related uses;

(c) Developing or expanding local economic infrastructure for the sustainable use of discarded materials;

(d) Providing local incentives to develop or expand markets for recycled products;

(e) Developing or expanding local recycling infrastructure;

(f) Undertaking sustainable resource education programs;

(g) Developing or implementing sustainable resource plans or programs for the use or collection of organic matter, household hazardous waste, electronic scrap material, or other discarded materials;

(h) Providing assistance in connection with the development or improvement of integrated waste management plans by local governments; and

(i) Repealed.

(j) Reducing waste tire stockpiles.

(5) Repealed.

(6) Any grant award made pursuant to this section is made complete by means of a contract entered into between the department and the grant recipient that specifies the conditions for the grant and the requirements and responsibilities of the grant recipient, as applicable.

(7) Repealed.

(8) This section is repealed, effective July 1, 2026.

## 25-16.5-107. Technical assistance program.

(1) The advisory board shall develop guidelines on how to allocate the portion of and shall select grant recipients for the moneys in the pollution prevention fund created in section 25-16.5-109 which is available under said section for making grants for the purpose of providing technical assistance to small and medium-sized businesses and to other generators or users of hazardous and

toxic substances. Grants may be made to academic institutions, trade associations, and environmental or engineering firms with knowledge of pollution prevention techniques and processes. The advisory board shall develop guidelines for awarding grants to provide technical assistance. In developing such guidelines, the advisory board shall determine priorities for such assistance, including an emphasis on reducing the production processes that use the largest amounts of hazardous substances and an emphasis on assisting small businesses. The advisory board shall select the grant recipients and shall determine the amount of the grant awarded to each recipient. The department shall then award the grants pursuant to this section through a contract entered into between the department and the grant recipient which details the conditions of the grant and the requirements and responsibilities of the grant recipient.

(2) For the purposes of this article, "technical assistance program" means the following types of activities:

(a) Providing technical assistance and outreach on pollution prevention to small and medium-sized businesses and to other generators or users of toxic substances;

(b) Providing on-site toxics use reduction and waste reduction assistance to small and medium-sized businesses and to other generators or users of toxic substances;

(c) Providing to businesses, trade associations, public entities, and to other generators or users of toxic substances information on the annual toxics use reduction and waste reduction that could be achieved by using pollution prevention techniques, the annual savings and implementation costs of such techniques, and the period of time necessary to recoup the money spent to implement the pollution prevention techniques;

(d) Providing on-site pollution prevention assessments of industrial plant production processes and waste generation, upon request of the affected businesses.

(3) Technical assistance programs shall be offered to small and medium-sized businesses and to public generators or users of toxic substances without charge.

(4) It is the intent of the general assembly that the technical assistance program not be used to document violations of or used in the enforcement of state laws or regulations.

## 25-16.5-108. Pollution prevention fees.

(1) (a) The department shall charge and collect pollution prevention fees from any reporting facility which is required to file a report with the department pursuant to the federal act as follows:

(I) Facilities required to report pursuant to section 11002 of the federal act shall pay an annual fee not to exceed ten dollars per reporting facility.

(II) Each facility required to report pursuant to section 11022 of the federal act shall be required to pay an annual fee not to exceed ten dollars for every hazardous substance located at the facility in excess of the thresholds adopted by the United States environmental protection agency.

(III) Each facility required to report pursuant to section 11023 of the federal act shall pay an annual fee not to exceed twenty-five dollars for every extremely hazardous substance located at the facility in excess of the thresholds adopted by the United States environmental protection agency.

(a.5) The department shall charge and collect pollution prevention fees from any federal agency from which, pursuant to federal Executive Order No. 12856, as published in 58 Fed. Reg. 41981 (1993) , the department has the authority to collect pollution prevention fees.

(b) Any retail motor fuel outlet which is required to report pursuant to the federal act shall pay one-half of the fee set forth in paragraph (a) of this subsection (1) .

(c) Any single reporting organization which owns or operates multiple reporting facilities shall not be required to pay more than a total of one thousand dollars for all pollution prevention fees required by this section.

(d) Agricultural businesses which are required to report under the federal act are not required to pay the pollution prevention fees set forth in this subsection (1) .

(e) It is the intent of the general assembly that the department of public health and environment collect all fees from any reporting facility required to report under the federal act, including the pollution prevention fee, in a single, centralized billing procedure.

(2) Any moneys collected pursuant to subsection (1) of this section shall be transmitted to the treasurer and credited to the pollution prevention fund created in section 25-16.5-109.

(3) (Deleted by amendment, L. 95, p. 182, § 4, effective April 7, 1995.)

### 25-16.5-109. Pollution prevention fund - created.

(1) There is hereby created in the state treasury the pollution prevention fund. Any moneys collected pursuant to section 25-16.5-108 shall be credited to such fund. In accordance with section 24-36-114, C.R.S., all interest derived from the deposit and investment of moneys in the fund shall be credited to the general fund. At the end of any fiscal year, all unexpended and unencumbered moneys in the fund shall remain therein and shall not be credited or transferred to the general fund or any other fund.

(2) The moneys generated from the pollution prevention fees pursuant to section 25-16.5-108 shall be annually appropriated to the department of public health and environment for allocation to the pollution prevention advisory board created in section 25-16.5-104 for contracting for pollution prevention activities programs as set forth in section 25-16.5-106 and for the purpose of making grants under the technical assistance program as set forth in section 25-16.5-107 and as directed by the pollution prevention advisory board created in section 25-16.5-104. None of the moneys in the fund shall be used for the enforcement of any state law or regulation.

### 25-16.5-110. Report to the general assembly. (Repealed)


# ARTICLE 17. WASTE DIVERSION AND RECYCLING


# PART 1. RECYCLING OF PRODUCTS


### 25-17-101. Legislative declaration.

(1) The general assembly hereby finds and declares that the recycling of materials and products is a matter of statewide concern and that such recycling should be promoted in cooperation with units of local government in light of its economic and environmental benefits. The general assembly further finds that the recycling of materials and products will decrease the amount of materials and products which is disposed of in landfills and will also spur economic development in the recycling industry in Colorado. It is the intent of the general assembly in adopting this act to encourage the development of the recycling industry and the development of markets for recycled materials and products.

(2) The general assembly further finds and declares that:

(a) Proper management of waste in all forms is necessary to protect the public health and environment for the citizens of this state;

(b) The diversion of waste from the waste stream by encouraging available, affordable, and innovative alternatives to disposal is a key strategy in any state-local waste management policy;

(c) A comprehensive, cooperative, and integrated approach to waste management is necessary to achieve the goal of diverting waste from the municipal waste stream;

(d) Such an approach should foster public and private initiatives to reduce and divert waste through: Source reductions; recycling, including the secondary use of waste material or products in all forms; composting as a recycling option for materials such as yard debris, food scraps, and soiled or otherwise unrecyclable paper which are not recovered using traditional recycling methods; and other waste management strategies and disposal alternatives; and

(e) The state's waste management policies should include a combination of tax incentives, procurement policies, and economic development incentives: To encourage government entities and businesses and individuals to reduce sources of waste, recycle, and compost; to encourage the development of the recycling industry; and to encourage the development of markets for reusable, recycled, and composted products and materials.

## 25-17-102. Definitions.

As used in this article, unless the context otherwise requires:

(1) "Cathode ray tube product" means an item of scientific equipment or a consumer electronic product that contains a glass tube used to provide an electronic visual display. The term includes, but is not limited to, televisions, computer monitors, and oscilloscopes.

(1.5) "Label" means one of the code labels described in section 25-17-103 that is molded into the bottom of a plastic container.

(2) "Plastic" means any material made of polymeric organic compounds and additives that can be shaped by flow.

(3) "Plastic bottle" means a plastic container that has a neck that is smaller than the body of the container, accepts a screw-type, snap-cap, or other closure, and has a capacity of sixteen fluid ounces or more but less than five gallons.

(4) "Rigid plastic container" means any formed or molded container other than a bottle, intended for single use, composed predominantly of plastic resin, and having a relatively inflexible finite shape or form with a capacity of eight ounces or more but less than five gallons.

## 25-17-103. Labeling and coding.

On or after July 1, 1992, no person shall distribute, sell, or offer for sale in this state any plastic bottle or rigid plastic container manufactured on or after July 1, 1992, unless the product is labeled with a code indicating the plastic resin used to produce the bottle or container. Plastic bottles or rigid plastic containers with labels and basecups of a different material shall be coded by their basic material. Such code shall consist of a number placed within a triangle of arrows and letters placed below the triangle of arrows. The triangle shall be equilateral, formed by three arrows with the apex of each point of the triangle at the midpoint of each arrow, rounded with a short radius. The arrowhead of each arrow shall be at the midpoint of each side of the arrow. The triangle, formed by the three arrows curved at their midpoints, shall depict a clockwise path around the code number. The numbers and letters used shall be as follows: 1=PETE (polyethylene terephthalate) , 2=HDPE (high density polyethylene) , 3=V (vinyl) , 4=LDPE (low density polyethylene) , 5=PP (polypropylene) , 6=PS (polystyrene) , 7=OTHER (includes multi-layer) .

## 25-17-104. Local government preemption.

No unit of local government shall require or prohibit the use or sale of specific types of plastic materials or products or restrict or mandate containers, packaging, or labeling for any consumer products.

## 25-17-105. Pilot program - recycled plastic and products - rules.

(1) The executive director of the department of local affairs may establish a pilot program for the purpose of encouraging private industry to engage in the research and development of new technologies for recycling plastics. The executive director of the department of local affairs may cooperate with any other entity of state government, including institutions of higher education, in developing the pilot program.

(2) The executive director of the department of local affairs may make grants or loans to private industry for the research and development authorized by subsection (1) of this section. Said grants and loans shall be made only to private industries for location or expansion in Colorado.

(3) The executive director of the department of local affairs is hereby authorized to accept any grants or loans from any public or private source for the purpose of encouraging plastics recycling.

None of such moneys shall be used for overhead or administrative costs of the department.
(4) The executive director of the department of local affairs may establish a pilot program for the purpose of encouraging private enterprises and state and local government entities to develop and implement waste diversion strategies or programs. The executive director of such department is hereby authorized to accept grants or loans from any public or private source for the purpose of implementing this section. The executive director may make grants or loans from such moneys to such entities for the development of waste diversion strategies.

## 25-17-105.5. Pilot program - cathode ray tube product recycling.

(1) The executive director of the department of public health and environment shall establish a cathode ray tube recycling pilot program, only if the department has received a grant, gift, or bequest pursuant to subsection (3) of this section that is sufficient to do so, for the purpose of:
(a) Minimizing the number of cathode ray tube products that are disposed of within Colorado, including through public education regarding:
(I) Why the disposal of cathode ray tube products in landfills should be minimized; and
(II) How to recycle cathode ray tube products;
(b) Developing local markets and business opportunities based on the recycling and reuse of cathode ray tube products;
(c) Encouraging private industry and public-private partnerships to undertake research and development of new technologies for the recycling, waste minimization, and disposal of cathode ray tube products;
(d) Providing businesses and individuals with easy access to cathode ray tube product recycling centers; and
(e) Leveraging public support of cathode ray tube recycling with private grants and in-kind contributions to the pilot program.
(2) The executive director of the department of public health and environment may make grants or loans to private industry and public-private partnerships for the purposes specified in subsection (1) of this section from any moneys in the cathode ray tube recycling fund, which fund is hereby created; except that said grants and loans shall be made only to entities that are located, or will be located, in Colorado.
(3) The executive director of the department of public health and environment is hereby authorized to request, receive, and expend grants, gifts, and bequests, specifically including federal moneys, and other moneys available from any public or private source, excluding appropriations from the general fund, for the purposes specified in subsection (1) of this section, subject to annual appropriation by the general assembly. The executive director shall transmit such moneys to the state treasurer, who shall credit the moneys to the cathode ray tube recycling fund.
(4) The general assembly shall make annual appropriations out of the cathode ray tube recycling fund to the department of public health and environment in an amount equal to the department's direct administrative costs in administering the cathode ray tube recycling pilot program and for purposes consistent with subsections (1) and (2) of this section, including developing and distributing public education materials.
(5) Repealed.

## 25-17-106. Repeal of part. (Repealed)


## 25-17-107. Electronic device recycling task force - report - cash fund - repeal. (Repealed)

# PART 2. STRATEGIES FOR MOTOR VEHICLE WASTE TIRES

## 25-17-201 to 27-17-208. (Repealed)

# PART 3. ELECTRONIC DEVICE RECYCLING

### 25-17-301. Short title.
This part 3 shall be known and may be cited as the "Electronic Recycling Jobs Act".

### 25-17-302. Definitions.
As used in this part 3, unless the context otherwise requires:

(1) "Commission" means the solid and hazardous waste commission created in section 25-15-302.

(2) "Consumer" means a person who has purchased an electronic device primarily for personal or home business use.

(3) (a) "Electronic device" means a device that is marketed by a manufacturer for use by a consumer and that is:

(I) A computer, peripheral, printer, facsimile machine, digital video disc player, video cassette recorder, or other electronic device specified by rule promulgated by the commission; or

(II) A video display device or computer monitor, including a laptop, notebook, ultrabook, or netbook computer, television, tablet or slate computer, electronic book, or other electronic device specified by rule promulgated by the commission that contains a cathode ray tube or flat panel screen with a screen size that is greater than four inches, measured diagonally.

(b) "Electronic device" does not include:

(I) A device that is part of a motor vehicle or any component part of a motor vehicle, including replacement parts for use in a motor vehicle;

(II) A device, including a touch-screen display, that is functionally or physically part of or connected to a system or equipment designed and intended for use in any of the following settings, including diagnostic, monitoring, or control equipment:

(A) Industrial;

(B) Commercial, including retail;

(C) Library checkout;

(D) Traffic control;

(E) Security, sensing, monitoring, or counterterrorism;

(F) Border control;

(G) Medical; or

(H) Governmental or research and development;

(III) A device that is contained within any of the following:

(A) A clothes washer or dryer;

(B) A refrigerator, freezer, or refrigerator and freezer;

(C) A microwave oven or conventional oven or range;

(D) A dishwasher;

(E) A room air conditioner, dehumidifier, or air purifier; or

(F) Exercise equipment;

(IV) A device capable of using commercial mobile radio service, as defined in 47 CFR 20.3, that does not contain a video display area greater than four inches, measured diagonally; or

(V) A telephone.

(4) "Landfill" means a solid wastes disposal site and facility, as that term is defined in section 30-20-101 (8) , C.R.S.

(5) "Peripheral" means a keyboard, mouse, or other device that is sold exclusively for external use with a computer and provides input or output into or from a computer.

(6) "Processing for reuse" means a method, technique, or process by which electronic devices that would otherwise be disposed of or discarded are instead separated, processed, and returned to their original intended purposes or to other useful purposes as electronic devices.

(7) "Recycle" or "recycling" means processing, including disassembling, dismantling, shredding, and smelting, an electronic device or its components to recycle a useable component, commodity, or product, including processing for reuse. "Recycling", with respect to electronic devices, does not include any process defined as incineration under applicable laws or rules.

(8) "State agency" means any department, commission, council, board, bureau, committee, institution of higher education, agency, or other governmental unit of the executive, legislative, or judicial branch of state government.

(9) (a) "Video display device" means:

(I) An electronic device with an output surface that displays or is capable of displaying moving graphical images or visual representations of image sequences or pictures that show a number of quickly changing images on a screen to create the illusion of motion; or

(II) An electronic device with a viewable screen of four inches or larger, measured diagonally, that contains a tuner that locks on to a selected carrier frequency or cable signal and is capable of receiving and displaying television or video programming via broadcast, cable, or satellite.

(b) "Video display device" includes a device that is an integral part of the display and cannot easily be removed from the display by the consumer and that produces the moving image on the screen. A video display device may use a cathode ray tube, liquid crystal display, gas plasma, digital light processing, or other image-projection technology.

(c) "Video display device" does not include a device that is part of a motor vehicle or any component part of a motor vehicle assembled by, or for, a vehicle manufacturer or franchised dealer, including replacement parts for use in a motor vehicle.

## 25-17-303. Landfill ban - rules.

By July 1, 2013, a person shall not dispose of an electronic device or a component of an electronic device in a landfill in this state; except that a board of county commissioners for a county that does not have at least two electronic waste recycling events per year or an ongoing electronic waste recycling program that serves residents of the county may, by majority vote of the commissioners and in compliance with the requirements of this section, exempt its residents from the ban established by this section. A county shall make a good-faith effort to secure the electronic waste recycling services before the board of commissioners may exempt the county's residents from the landfill ban. An exemption from the landfill ban is valid for two years, after which the board may vote on another two-year exemption after again making a good-faith effort to secure a vendor to provide the recycling services. A county is not required to pay for the recycling services. Counties that currently do not have such services are encouraged to work with the department of public health and environment and other entities, such as the Colorado association for recycling, or its successor organization, to find an electronics recycling vendor that will serve that county.

## 25-17-304. State electronic device recycling - rules.

(1) Effective July 1, 2013, each state agency shall recycle its electronic devices. The agency shall use only a recycler that is certified to a national environmental certification standard such as the R2 or e-steward standards or other comparable recycling or disposal standard; except that this certification requirement does not apply to processing for reuse conducted on behalf of state agencies as stipulated in section 17-24-106.6, C.R.S., by the division of correctional industries created in section 17-24-104, C.R.S. The commission may adopt rules to avoid the use of

certifications that are not comparable.

(2) Upon receipt of a device, a recycler that accepts an electronic device from a state agency shall provide the agency with appropriate documentation verifying the recycler's certification as required in subsection (1) of this section.

### 25-17-305. Immunity.

(1) A recycler is not liable for personal or financial data or other information that a consumer or state agency may leave on an electronic device that is collected, processed, or recycled unless the recycler acted in a grossly negligent manner.

(2) A waste hauler, as that term is defined in section 30-20-1001 (16), C.R.S., or owner or operator of a landfill or transfer station does not violate this part 3 if the hauler, owner, or operator has made a good-faith effort to comply with this part 3 by posting and maintaining, in a conspicuous location at the waste hauler's facility, transfer station, or the landfill, a sign stating that electronic devices will not be accepted at the facility, transfer station, or landfill.

### 25-17-306. Public education.

The department of public health and environment shall coordinate with existing public and private efforts regarding the development and implementation of a public education program about the recycling of electronic devices, the removal of data from an electronic device being offered for recycling, the benefits of electronic device recycling, how to find electronic device recyclers, and implementation of the landfill ban pursuant to section 25-17-303. The department shall perform these functions within its existing resources.

### 25-17-307. Charitable donations of electronic devices.

(1) A charitable organization, as defined in section 6-16-103 (1), C.R.S., may:

(a) Refuse to accept a donation of an electronic device; and

(b) Establish a surcharge for acceptance of a donation of an electronic device.

### 25-17-308. Rules.

The commission shall adopt rules necessary to implement this part 3.

# PART 4. ARCHITECTURAL PAINT STEWARDSHIP PROGRAMS

### 25-17-401. Short title.

This part 4 shall be known and may be cited as the "Architectural Paint Stewardship Act".

### 25-17-402. Legislative declaration.

(1) The general assembly hereby finds and declares that paint disposal creates environmental and public health problems, and these problems should be addressed through the implementation of environmentally sound management practices for recycling postconsumer architectural paint.

(2) To that end, it is the general assembly's intent to establish a system of paint stewardship programs that:

(a) Provides substantial cost savings to household hazardous waste collection programs;

(b) Significantly increases the number of:

(I) Postconsumer architectural paint collection sites; and

(II) Recycling opportunities for households, businesses, and other generators of postconsumer architectural paint; and

638

(c) Exemplifies the principles of a product-centered approach to environmental protection, often referred to as "product stewardship".

## 25-17-403. Definitions.

As used in this part 4, unless the context otherwise requires:

(1) (a) "Architectural paint" means an interior or exterior architectural coating sold in a container of five gallons or less.

(b) "Architectural paint" does not include industrial, original equipment manufacturer, or specialty coatings as those terms are defined by the commission by rule.

(2) "Commission" means the solid and hazardous waste commission created in section 25-15-302.

(3) "Curbside service" means a waste collection, recycling, and disposal service that provides pickup of covered architectural paint from residences, including single- and multi-family dwelling units, and small businesses in quantities that a residence or small business would reasonably generate.

(4) "Department" means the department of public health and environment created in section 24-1-119, C.R.S.

(5) "Distributor" means a person who has a contractual relationship with one or more producers to market and sell architectural paint to retailers.

(6) "Energy recovery" means a process by which all or part of architectural paint materials are processed in order to use the heat content or another form of energy from the materials.

(7) "Environmentally sound management practices" means policies that a producer or a stewardship organization implements to ensure compliance with all applicable environmental laws, including laws addressing:

(a) Record keeping;

(b) Tracking and documenting the disposal of architectural paint within and outside the state; and

(c) Environmental liability coverage for professional services and contractor operations.

(8) "Executive director" means the executive director of the department or the executive director's designee.

(9) "Paint stewardship assessment" means an amount that a producer participating in a paint stewardship program adds to the purchase price of a container of architectural paint sold in Colorado that covers the cost of collecting, transporting, and processing postconsumer architectural paint statewide.

(10) "Paint stewardship program" means a program created in accordance with section 25-17-405.

(11) "Postconsumer architectural paint" means unused architectural paint that the purchaser of the paint no longer wants.

(12) "Producer" means an original producer of architectural paint that sells, offers for sale, or distributes architectural paint within or into Colorado under either the producer's own name or a brand that the producer manufactures.

(13) "Recycling" means a process that transforms discarded products, components, or byproducts into new usable or marketable materials that may involve a change in the product's identity. "Recycling" does not mean energy recovery or energy generation by means of combusting discarded products, components, or by-products with or without other waste products.

(14) "Retailer" means a person that sells or offers for sale architectural paint within or into Colorado.

(15) "Reuse" means the return of a product that has already been used into the marketplace for use in the same manner as originally intended without a change in the product's identity.

(16) "Sell" means to transfer title for consideration, including remote sales conducted through sales outlets, catalogs, or online. "Sell" does not include sales or donations of architectural paint in the original container for reuse.

(17) "Stewardship organization" means a corporation, nonprofit organization, or other legal entity created or contracted by one or more producers to implement a paint stewardship program.

## 25-17-404. Paint stewardship program plan - assessment - rules - fees.

(1) Effective July 1, 2015, no producer shall sell, offer for sale, or distribute architectural paint in Colorado unless the producer is implementing or participating in a paint stewardship program approved by the executive director. The executive director may approve an earlier start date as part of his or her approval of a paint stewardship program plan submitted in accordance with subsection (2) of this section. A paint stewardship program must commence within ninety days after the executive director's approval of the paint stewardship program plan.

(2) One or more producers, or a stewardship organization contracted by one or more producers, shall submit for approval a paint stewardship program plan to the executive director by January 1, 2015. To be approved, a paint stewardship program plan must:

(a) Identify the following:

(I) A list of each producer participating in the program;

(II) The contact information for the producer or stewardship organization implementing the program; and

(III) A list of all brands covered by the program;

(b) Describe the manner in which the program will collect, transport, reuse, recycle, and process postconsumer architectural paint, including a description of the following:

(I) Energy recovery and disposal; and

(II) Standards to ensure the use of environmentally sound management practices, including collection standards;

(c) Describe the manner in which the program will collect postconsumer architectural paint. At a minimum, a program plan must establish collection practices that:

(I) Provide convenient collection sites throughout the state;

(II) To ensure adequate collection coverage, use demographic and geographic information modeling to determine the number and distribution of collection sites based on the following criteria:

(A) At least ninety percent of Colorado residents must have a permanent collection site within a fifteen-mile radius of their homes;

(B) An additional permanent site must be provided for every thirty thousand residents of an urbanized area, as defined by the United States census bureau, and distributed in a manner that provides convenient and reasonably equitable access for residents within each urbanized area, unless the executive director approves otherwise; and

(C) For the portion of Colorado residents who will not have a permanent collection site within a fifteen-mile radius of their homes, the plan must provide collection events at least once per year; and

(III) Include specific information on how to serve geographically isolated populations and a proposal for how to measure and report service to those populations. This information must include a description of how the program will work with existing recyclers and local governments that wish to continue to be involved in paint recycling and collection.

(d) Notwithstanding the requirements of subparagraphs (I) and (II) of paragraph (c) of this subsection (2) , the plan may, in lieu of providing collection sites for a specified geographic area or population, identify an available curbside service that provides access to residents that is at least as convenient and equitably accessible as a collection site;

(e) Describe how the paint stewardship program will incorporate and fairly compensate service providers for activities that may include:

(I) For services such as permanent collection sites, collection events, or curbside services, the coverage of costs for collecting postconsumer architectural paint and architectural paint containers;

(II) The reuse or processing of postconsumer architectural paint at a permanent collection site; and

(III) The transportation, recycling, and proper disposal of postconsumer architectural paint;

(f) Provide a list of the names, locations, and hours of operation for facilities accepting postconsumer architectural paint for recycling under the program;

(g) Identify one or more designated persons responsible for:

(I) Ensuring the program's compliance with this part 4 and the rules promulgated under this part 4; and

(II) Serving as a contact person for the department with respect to the paint stewardship program;

(h) Describe the manner in which the program will achieve the following goals:

(I) Reducing the generation of postconsumer architectural paint;

(II) Promoting the reuse of postconsumer architectural paint; and

(III) Using best practices that are both environmentally and economically sound to manage postconsumer architectural paint. These practices should follow a waste handling hierarchy, which provides a preference for source reduction, then reuse, followed by recycling, energy recovery, and finally waste disposal.

(i) Include an education and outreach program that must:

(I) Target consumers, painting contractors, and paint retailers;

(II) Reach all architectural paint markets served by the participating producers; and

(III) Include a methodology for evaluating the effectiveness of the education and outreach program on an annual basis, including methods for determining the percentage of consumers, painting contractors, and retailers who are aware of:

(A) Ways to reduce the generation of postconsumer architectural paint; and

(B) Opportunities available for the reuse and recycling of postconsumer architectural paint;

(j) (I) Demonstrate sufficient funding for the architectural paint stewardship program described in the plan through the imposition of a paint stewardship assessment that each producer shall charge retailers and distributors for each container of the producer's architectural paint sold in Colorado. Each producer shall remit the paint stewardship assessments collected to the paint stewardship program. Each retailer and distributor shall add the amount of the paint stewardship assessment to the purchase price of a container of the producer's architectural paint sold in Colorado. The paint stewardship program must not impose any fees on customers for the collection of post-consumer architectural paint.

(II) To ensure that a paint stewardship program's funding mechanism is equitable and sustainable, the funding mechanism must:

(A) Provide a uniform paint stewardship assessment that does not exceed the amount necessary to recover program costs; and

(B) Require that any funds generated by the aggregate amount of fees charged to consumers be placed back into the program.

(k) Include a proposed budget and a description of the process used to determine the paint stewardship assessment required by paragraph (j) of this subsection (2) .

(3) (a) The executive director shall review a paint stewardship program plan submitted in accordance with subsection (2) of this section for compliance with this part 4, including a review of the proposed paint stewardship assessment required by paragraph (j) of subsection (2) of this section, to ensure that the paint stewardship assessment does not exceed an amount necessary to recover program costs. The executive director shall approve or reject a plan in writing within ninety days after receipt of the plan. If a plan meets the criteria of subsection (2) of this section, the executive director shall approve the plan. If the executive director rejects a plan, the executive director shall include in the written rejection the reason or reasons for rejecting the plan.

(b) (I) If the executive director approves a paint stewardship program plan, the executive director shall add:

(A) The producer or group of producers participating in the paint stewardship program plan to a list of producers participating in an approved paint stewardship program plan; and

(B) The brands being sold by the producer or group of producers to a list of brands included in an approved paint stewardship program plan.

(II) The executive director shall publish the lists on the department's website, and he or she shall update the published lists as necessary.

(c) The executive director's rejection of a paint stewardship program plan constitutes a final agency action that may be appealed in accordance with the procedures set forth in section 24-4-

106, C.R.S.

(d) If the executive director's decision to reject a paint stewardship program plan is not appealed pursuant to section 24-4-106, C.R.S., or the executive director prevails on appeal, the producer, group of producers, or stewardship organization that submitted the paint stewardship program plan must submit a revised plan within ninety days after the date on which the executive director's decision was affirmed or, if no appeal was pursued, the date on which the time for appeal expired. The revised plan must provide the information required by subsection (2) of this section. The executive director shall approve or reject a revised plan under the procedure set forth in paragraph (a) of this subsection (3) . The executive director's rejection of a revised plan may be appealed in accordance with section 24-4-106, C.R.S.

(4) When submitting a paint stewardship program plan, a revised plan, or an annual report, as required by section 25-17-405, one or more producers or a stewardship organization contracted by one or more producers shall pay a paint stewardship program plan fee, revised plan fee, or annual report fee in an amount that the commission has established or adjusted by rule. In establishing or adjusting a fee by rule, the commission shall consult with the executive director and, as needed, with an association of producers.

(5) The aggregate amount of fees charged to consumers pursuant to this section shall be in an amount not to exceed the actual cost of the program.

## 25-17-405. Paint stewardship program requirements - annual reports - customer information.

(1) A paint stewardship program must be financed and either managed or contracted by a producer or group of producers. The program must be implemented statewide and include:

(a) The collection, transportation, reuse, recycling, and disposal of postconsumer architectural paint; and

(b) Initiatives to reduce the generation of postconsumer architectural paint.

(2) A paint stewardship program shall comply with any fire, hazardous waste, or other relevant ordinances or resolutions adopted by a local government.

(3) (a) On or after March 31 of the second year of a paint stewardship program's implementation, and annually thereafter, one or more participating producers, or a stewardship organization contracted by one or more producers, shall submit a report to the executive director describing the progress of the paint stewardship program. The paint stewardship program report must include the following information from the preceding calendar year:

(I) A description of the method or methods used to reduce, reuse, collect, transport, recycle, and process postconsumer architectural paint;

(II) The total volume, in gallons, and type of postconsumer architectural paint collected, with the data broken down by:

(A) Collection site; and

(B) Method of waste handling used to handle the collected postconsumer architectural paint, such as reuse, recycling, energy recovery, or waste disposal;

(III) The total volume, in gallons, of postconsumer architectural paint sold in Colorado by the producer or producers participating in the paint stewardship program;

(IV) For the education and outreach program implemented in compliance with section 25-17-404 (2) (i) :

(A) Samples of any materials distributed; and

(B) A description of the methodology used and the results of the evaluation conducted pursuant to section 25-17-404 (2) (i) (III) . The results must include the percentage of consumers, painting contractors, and retailers made aware of the ways to reduce the generation of postconsumer architectural paint, available opportunities for reuse of postconsumer architectural paint, and collection options for postconsumer architectural paint recycling.

(V) The name, location, and hours of operation of each facility added to or removed from the list developed in accordance with section 25-17-404 (2) (f) ;

(VI) Any proposed changes to the paint stewardship program plan. The executive director shall review any proposed changes set forth in the annual report in accordance with the review procedures for a revised plan, as set forth in section 25-17-404 (3) .

(VII) A copy of an independent third party's report auditing the paint stewardship program. The audit must include a detailed list of the program's costs and revenues.

(b) Notwithstanding section 24-1-136 (11) (a) (I) , the executive director shall annually compile the results of the reports received pursuant to subsection (3) (a) of this section into a general report describing the progress of the paint stewardship programs. The executive director shall annually present the report to the health and human services committee of the senate and the public health care and human services committee of the house of representatives, or their successor committees.

(4) As part of the education and outreach program set forth in section 25-17-404 (2) (i) , a producer shall distribute paint stewardship program information to all retailers offering the producer's architectural paint for sale. The information may include the following:

(a) Signage that is prominently displayed and easily visible to the consumer;

(b) Written materials that may be provided to the consumer at the time of purchase or delivery or both and templates of those materials for reproduction by the retailer; and

(c) Promotional materials including advertising materials that reference the architectural paint stewardship program.

## 25-17-406. Retail sales - requirements - paint stewardship assessment added to purchase price - customer information.

(1) The executive director, upon the executive director's own motion, may, and, upon a person's written complaint, shall, investigate a producer to determine whether, on the date that the producer's architectural paint was sold at retail, the producer or the producer's brand was listed on the department's website as part of an approved paint stewardship program. If the executive director determines that the producer's architectural paint was sold in violation of this part 4, the executive director may order the producer to cease and desist from distributing the architectural paint until the producer is in compliance with this part 4.

(2) For each container of architectural paint sold in Colorado, a retailer shall add the amount of the producer's paint stewardship assessment, established under section 25-17-404 (2) (j) , to the purchase price of the container of architectural paint.

(3) A retailer selling architectural paint or offering architectural paint for sale shall, at the time of sale of any of a producer's architectural paint, provide customers with information about the producer's paint stewardship program, as provided by the producer pursuant to section 25-17-405 (4) . If a retailer fails to disseminate information about the producer's paint stewardship program pursuant to this subsection (3) , but the retailer can demonstrate to the satisfaction of the executive director that the producer failed to provide the requisite education and outreach program information to the retailer, the retailer is neither liable nor prohibited from selling the producer's architectural paint.

## 25-17-407. Violations - enforcement - administrative penalty.

(1) In addition to other penalties prescribed by this part 4 or any other law, a producer or stewardship organization that violates this part 4 is liable for an administrative penalty assessment not to exceed one thousand dollars per day for the first violation and five thousand dollars per day for a second or subsequent violation.

(2) If a person is liable pursuant to subsection (1) of this section, the executive director shall serve by personal service or by certified mail an order that imposes an administrative penalty on the person who has been designated in the paint stewardship program plan as the contact person.

(3) The contact person may submit a written request to the executive director for a hearing by personal service or by certified mail within thirty calendar days after the date of the order. An administrative law judge from the office of administrative courts shall conduct the hearing in accordance with section 24-4-105, C.R.S.

(4) If a request for a hearing is filed, payment of any monetary penalty is stayed pending a final decision by the administrative law judge after the hearing on the merits. The department is not precluded from imposing an administrative penalty against the producer or stewardship program for subsequent violations of this part 4 committed during the pendency of the stay.

(5) The department bears the burden of proof by a preponderance of the evidence in a hearing held pursuant to this section.

(6) The executive director may enter into a settlement agreement with a producer or stewardship organization assessed an administrative penalty under this section.

(7) The executive director shall transfer any moneys collected under this section to the state treasurer, who shall deposit the moneys into the general fund.

### 25-17-408. Fees - cash fund - creation.

The executive director shall transmit all fees collected under section 25-17-404 (4) to the state treasurer, who shall credit them to the paint stewardship program cash fund, hereby created and referred to in this section as the "fund". The moneys in the fund are appropriated to the department for the purposes set forth in this part 4. All interest earned from the investment of moneys in the fund is credited to the fund. Any moneys not expended at the end of the fiscal year remain in the fund and do not revert to the general fund or any other fund.

### 25-17-409. Certificate of designation not required.

If a retailer or other facility serving as a postconsumer architectural paint collection site would not otherwise be required to obtain a certificate of designation as a solid wastes disposal site and facility pursuant to section 30-20-102, C.R.S., then the retailer or other facility need not obtain a certificate of designation.

### 25-17-410. Limited exemption from antitrust, restraint of trade, and unfair trade practices provisions.

If a producer or group of producers participating in a paint stewardship program or a stewardship organization contracted by one or more producers to implement a paint stewardship program engages in an activity performed solely in furtherance of implementing the paint stewardship program and in compliance with the provisions of this part 4, the activity is not a violation of the antitrust, restraint of trade, and unfair trade practices provisions of the "Unfair Practices Act", article 2 of title 6, C.R.S., or the "Colorado Antitrust Act of 1992", article 4 of title 6, C.R.S.

# ARTICLE 18. UNDERGROUND STORAGE TANKS

### 25-18-101 to 25-18-109. (Repealed)

# ARTICLE 18.5. ILLEGAL DRUG LABORATORIES

### 25-18.5-101. Definitions.

As used in this article, unless the context otherwise requires:

(1) "Board" means the state board of health in the department of public health and environment.

(2) "Certified industrial hygienist" means an individual who is certified by the American board of industrial hygiene or its successor.

(3) "Clean-up standards" means the acceptable standards for the remediation of an illegal drug laboratory involving methamphetamine, as established by the board under section 25-18.5-102.

(4) "Consultant" means a certified industrial hygienist or industrial hygienist who is not an employee, agent, representative, partner, joint venture participant, or shareholder of the contractor or of a parent or subsidiary company of the contractor, and who has been certified under section 25-18.5-106.

(5) "Contractor" means a person:

(a) Hired to decontaminate an illegal drug laboratory in accordance with the procedures established by the board under section 25-18.5-102; and

(b) Certified by the department under section 25-18.5-106.

(6) "Department" means the Colorado department of public health and environment.

(7) "Governing body" means the agency or office designated by the city council or board of county commissioners where the property in question is located. If there is no such designation, the governing body shall be the county, district, or municipal public health agency, building department, and law enforcement agency with jurisdiction over the property in question.

(8) "Illegal drug laboratory" means the areas where controlled substances, as defined by section 18-18-102, C.R.S., have been manufactured, processed, cooked, disposed of, used, or stored and all proximate areas that are likely to be contaminated as a result of the manufacturing, processing, cooking, disposal, use, or storage.

(9) "Industrial hygienist" has the same meaning as set forth in section 24-30-1402 (2.2) , C.R.S.

(10) "Property" means anything that may be the subject of ownership, including land, buildings, structures, and vehicles.

(11) "Property owner", for the purposes of real property, means the person holding record fee title to real property. "Property owner" also means the person holding title to a manufactured home.

## 25-18.5-102. Illegal drug laboratories - rules.

(1) The board shall promulgate rules in accordance with section 24-4-103, C.R.S., as necessary to implement this article, including:

(a) Procedures for testing contamination, evaluating contamination, and establishing the acceptable standards for cleanup of illegal drug laboratories involving methamphetamine;

(b) Procedures for a training and certification program for people involved in the assessment, decontamination, and sampling of illegal drug laboratories. The board may develop different levels of training and certification requirements based on a person's prior experience in the assessment, decontamination, and sampling of illegal drug laboratories.

(c) A definition of "assessment", "decontamination", and "sampling" for purposes of this article;

(d) Procedures for the approval of persons to train consultants or contractors in the assessment, decontamination, or sampling of illegal drug laboratories; and

(e) Procedures for contractors and consultants to issue certificates of compliance to property owners upon completion of assessment, decontamination, and sampling of illegal drug laboratories to certify that the remediation of the property meets the clean-up standards established by the board under paragraph (a) of this subsection (1) .

(2) The board shall establish fees for the following:

(a) Certification of persons involved in the assessment, decontamination, and sampling of illegal drug laboratories;

(b) Monitoring of persons involved in the assessment, decontamination, and sampling of illegal drug laboratories, if necessary to ensure compliance with this article; and

(c) Approval of persons involved in training for consultants or contractors under paragraph (d) of subsection (1) of this section.

(3) The board shall adopt rules for determining administrative penalties for violations of this article, based on the factors enumerated in section 25-18.5-107 (2) (g) .

## 25-18.5-103. Discovery of illegal drug laboratory - property owner - cleanup -

**liability.**

(1) (a) Upon notification from a peace officer that chemicals, equipment, or supplies of an illegal drug laboratory are located on a property, or when an illegal drug laboratory is otherwise discovered and the property owner has received notice, the owner of any contaminated property shall meet the clean-up standards for property established by the board in section 25-18.5-102; except that a property owner may, subject to paragraph (b) of this subsection (1), elect instead to demolish the contaminated property. If the owner elects to demolish the contaminated property, the governing body or, if none has been designated, the county, district, or municipal public health agency, building department, or law enforcement agency with jurisdiction over the property may require the owner to fence off the property or otherwise make it inaccessible for occupancy or intrusion.

(b) An owner of personal property within a structure or vehicle contaminated by illegal drug laboratory activity has ten days after the date of discovery of the laboratory or contamination to remove or clean the property according to board rules and paragraph (c) of this subsection (1). If the personal property owner fails to remove the personal property within ten days, the owner of the structure or vehicle may dispose of the personal property during the clean-up process without liability to the owner of the personal property for the disposition.

(c) A person who removes personal property or debris from a drug laboratory shall secure the property and debris to prevent theft or exposing another person to any toxic or hazardous chemicals until the property and debris is appropriately disposed of or cleaned according to board rules.

(2) (a) Except as specified in paragraph (b) of this subsection (2), once a property owner has received certificates of compliance from a contractor and a consultant in accordance with section 25-18.5-102 (1) (e), or has demolished the property, or has met the clean-up standards and documentation requirements of this section as it existed before August 7, 2013, the property owner:

(I) Shall furnish copies of the certificates of compliance to the governing body; and

(II) Is immune from a suit brought by a current or future owner, renter, occupant, or neighbor of the property for health-based civil actions that allege injury or loss arising from the illegal drug laboratory.

(b) A person convicted for the manufacture of methamphetamine or for possession of chemicals, supplies, or equipment with intent to manufacture methamphetamine is not immune from suit.

(3) (Deleted by amendment, L. 2013.)

## 25-18.5-104. Entry into illegal drug laboratories.

(1) If a structure or vehicle has been determined to be contaminated or if a governing body or law enforcement agency issues a notice of probable contamination, the owner of the structure or vehicle shall not permit any person to have access to the structure or vehicle unless:

(a) The person is trained or certified to handle contaminated property under board rules or federal law; or

(b) The owner has received certificates of compliance under section 25-18.5-102 (1) (e).

## 25-18.5-105. Drug laboratories - governing body - authority.

(1) Governing bodies may declare an illegal drug laboratory that has not met the clean-up standards set by the board in section 25-18.5-102 a public health nuisance.

(2) Governing bodies may enact ordinances or resolutions to enforce this article, including preventing unauthorized entry into contaminated property; requiring contaminated property to meet clean-up standards before it is occupied; notifying the public of contaminated property; coordinating services and sharing information between law enforcement, building, public health, and social services agencies and officials; and charging reasonable inspection and testing fees.

## 25-18.5-106. Powers and duties of department.

(1) The department shall implement, coordinate, and oversee the rules promulgated by the board in accordance with this article, including:

(a) The certification of persons involved in the assessment, decontamination, or sampling of illegal drug laboratories;

(b) The approval of persons to train consultants and contractors in the assessment, decontamination, or sampling of illegal drug laboratories.

## 25-18.5-107. Enforcement.

(1) A person that violates any rule promulgated by the board under section 25-18.5-102 is subject to an administrative penalty not to exceed fifteen thousand dollars per day per violation until the violation is corrected.

(2) (a) Whenever the department has reason to believe that a person has violated any rule promulgated by the board under section 25-18.5-102, the department shall notify the person, specifying the rule alleged to have been violated and the facts alleged to constitute the violation.

(b) The department shall either:

(I) Send the notice by certified or registered mail, return receipt requested, to the alleged violator's last-known address; or

(II) Personally serve the notice upon the alleged violator or the alleged violator's agent.

(c) The alleged violator has thirty days following receipt of the notice to submit a written response containing data, views, and arguments concerning the alleged violation and potential corrective actions.

(d) Within fifteen days after receiving notice of an alleged violation, the alleged violator may request an informal conference with department personnel to discuss the alleged violation. The department shall hold the informal conference within the thirty days allowed for a written response.

(e) After consideration of any written response and informal conference, the department shall issue a letter, within thirty days after the date of the informal conference or written response, whichever is later, affirming or dismissing the violation. If the department affirms the violation, the department shall issue an administrative order within one hundred eighty days after the time for a written response has expired. The administrative order must include any remaining corrective actions that the violator shall take and any administrative penalty that the department determines is appropriate.

(f) The department shall serve an administrative order under this article on the person subject to the order by personal service or by registered mail, return receipt requested, at the person's last-known address. An order may be prohibitory or mandatory in effect. The order is effective immediately upon issuance unless otherwise provided in the order.

(g) In determining the amount of an administrative penalty, the department shall consider the following factors:

(I) The seriousness of the violation;

(II) Whether the violation was intentional, reckless, or negligent;

(III) Any impact on, or threat to, the public health or environment as a result of the violation;

(IV) The violator's degree of recalcitrance;

(V) Whether the violator has had a prior violation and, if so, the nature and severity of the prior violation;

(VI) The economic benefit the violator received as a result of the violation;

(VII) Whether the violator voluntarily, timely, and completely disclosed the violation before the department discovered it;

(VIII) Whether the violator fully and promptly cooperated with the department following disclosure or discovery of the violation; and

(IX) Any other relevant aggravating or mitigating circumstances.

(3) If the department determines that a person has been grossly noncompliant with the rules promulgated by the board under section 25-18.5-102, the department may:

(a) Suspend or revoke the person's certification for the assessment, decontamination, or sampling of illegal drug laboratories; or

(b) Suspend or revoke the approval of a person to provide training for consultants or contractors performing assessment, decontamination, or sampling of illegal drug laboratories.

### 25-18.5-108. Illegal drug laboratory fund.

The illegal drug laboratory fund is hereby established in the state treasury. The department shall transfer the fees collected under section 25-18.5-102 (2) to the state treasurer who shall credit these fees to the fund. The general assembly shall appropriate the moneys in the fund for the implementation of this article. The treasurer shall credit to the fund all interest derived from the deposit and investment of moneys in the fund. The moneys in the fund stay in the fund at the end of the fiscal year and do not revert to the general fund or any other fund.

### 25-18.5-109. Judicial review.

The department's decisions are subject to judicial review in accordance with section 24-4-106, C.R.S.


# ARTICLE 18.7. INDUSTRIAL HEMP REMEDIATION PILOT PROGRAM


**25-18.7-101 to 25-18.7-105. (Repealed)**


# ENVIRONMENT - SMALL COMMUNITIES


# ARTICLE 19. SMALL COMMUNITY ENVIRONMENTAL FLEXIBILITY ACT


### 25-19-101. Short title.

This article shall be known and may be cited as the "Small Community Environmental Flexibility Act".

### 25-19-102. Legislative declaration.

(1) The general assembly hereby finds and determines that small communities throughout the state are struggling to identify adequate resources, particularly for infrastructure improvements, to comply with the numerous environmental requirements that have been established by federal and state laws.

(2) The general assembly further finds and determines that citizens in small communities, as well as all citizens of the state, are entitled to the benefits of appropriate measures for public health and environmental protection.

(3) The general assembly therefore declares that the provisions of this article are enacted to provide maximum flexibility for small communities to comply with the environmental laws of this state without diminishing the public health and environmental protection provided to the citizens of Colorado.

## 25-19-103. Definitions.

As used in this article, unless the context otherwise requires:

(1) "Department" means the department of public health and environment created by section 25-1-102.

(2) "Environmental priorities plan" means a plan prepared in accordance with section 25-19-104.

(3) "Integrated environmental compliance agreement" means an agreement entered into between a small community and the department pursuant to section 25-19-105.

(4) "Small community" means a municipality, county, or special district with a population of less than two thousand five hundred persons or a combination of two or more such municipalities, counties, or special districts working together pursuant to an intergovernmental agreement for purposes of participation in the program established pursuant to this article.

## 25-19-104. Environmental priorities plan.

(1) Any small community wishing to enter into an integrated environmental compliance agreement pursuant to section 25-19-105 shall submit to the department on or before July 1, 1998, an environmental priorities plan prepared in accordance with the provisions of this section; except that an environmental priorities plan may be submitted by a small community after July 1, 1998, if the department finds that the small community did not become aware of and could not have reasonably anticipated the environmental compliance concerns of the community in time to meet the deadline of July 1, 1998.

(2) An environmental priorities plan shall:

(a) Identify the environmental requirements enumerated in section 25-19-105 that pose an existing compliance problem or a near term compliance problem for the small community;

(b) Demonstrate the resource limitations that make it difficult for the small community to achieve and sustain compliance within the established statutory or regulatory deadlines;

(c) Set forth the small community's proposed environmental compliance priorities, including the identified actions to be taken, anticipated expenditures required for such actions, and a proposed schedule that would result in compliance with all individual environmental requirements as soon as practicable, within an overall period not to exceed ten years, without adversely impacting public health or the environment outside of the small community; and

(d) Describe the public process that has resulted in the formulation of the environmental compliance priorities for the small community.

(3) A small community participating in the program created by this article shall take reasonable steps to provide the public affected by its actions with a meaningful opportunity to participate in the preparation of an environmental priorities plan, through whatever combination of public meetings or hearings or opportunity for written input is most practical for the particular community.

(4) A small community participating in the program created by this article shall provide a copy of its proposed plan to any person who has so requested prior to the small community's submission of its plan to the department.

(5) The multimedia environmental integration advisory committee established pursuant to section 25-1-108 may, following notice to associations of political subdivisions eligible to participate in the program created by this article, develop guidance documents that provide more specific criteria for the preparation of an environmental priorities plan if the advisory committee determines that such criteria would further the purposes of this article.

(6) An environmental priorities plan submitted to the department shall be approved if the plan meets the requirements of this section and is consistent with any criteria for the preparation of such plans set forth in guidance documents developed by the multimedia environmental integration advisory committee.

## 25-19-105. Integrated environmental compliance agreements.

(1) The department is authorized to enter into integrated environmental compliance agreements with small communities in accordance with the provisions of this section.

(2) The environmental requirements that may be addressed in an integrated environmental compliance agreement are the requirements established by or pursuant to article 7, 8, 11, or 15 of this title, article 20.5 of title 8, C.R.S., or article 20 of title 30, C.R.S. An integrated environmental compliance agreement may address environmental requirements applicable to a solid waste disposal site and facility only if such site and facility receives twenty tons per day or less of solid waste.

(3) Any integrated environmental compliance agreement with a small community shall:

(a) Identify actions to be taken by the small community, including a schedule with interim deadlines, that will result in compliance with each of the applicable individual environmental requirements as soon as practicable, within an overall period not to exceed ten years;

(b) Be consistent with an approved environmental priorities plan for the small community;

(c) Contain a provision directing that the agreement will not take effect until the community's registered electors have approved any creation of a multiple-fiscal year debt or other financial obligation for which an election is required by section 20 of article X of the Colorado constitution and which is required to implement the terms of the agreement;

(d) Be structured as a formal enforcement agreement to ensure continued compliance or to resolve an existing compliance issue involving a small community; and

(e) Be enforceable pursuant to the provisions of the statutes governing the individual environmental requirements addressed in the agreement with respect to any of the agreement deadlines that are not met.

(4) A small community participating in the program created by this article shall provide a copy of its proposed agreement to any person who has so requested in writing prior to the small community's submission of its plan to the department. Before the agreement is approved by the department, the department shall allow at least twenty days within which any person may review and submit written comments on the agreement to the small community and the department.

(5) An integrated environmental compliance agreement may be amended by agreement of the small community and the department to address compliance concerns not anticipated at the time of the original agreement. The amended agreement shall require compliance with any new requirement added to the amended agreement as soon as practicable, within an overall period not to exceed ten years from the date of the amendment. The deadline for any requirement addressed in the original agreement may be extended as a part of the amendment of the agreement, but the deadline may not be extended beyond ten years after the date of the original agreement.

(6) An integrated environmental compliance agreement entered into under this article shall not be deemed to impair, modify, or otherwise affect prior agreements entered into between a small community and any entity other than the department.

(7) Any provision of an integrated compliance agreement implementing a requirement that, absent such agreement, would no longer be applicable as the result of repeal or modification of a statutory or regulatory requirement shall be unenforceable.

(8) No component of an integrated environmental compliance agreement that would result in an increased regulatory compliance burden on any other entity shall be approved without such entity's consent.

(9) Paragraph (e) of subsection (3) of this section notwithstanding, if requested by the small community, the department may file in district court a complaint and a proposed consent order embodying the requirements of the integrated environmental compliance agreement to require compliance with any applicable standard, limitation, or order.

## 25-19-106. Planning assistance.

The department of local affairs shall provide assistance to small communities in the preparation of environmental priorities plans upon request.

### 25-19-107. Mentoring.

The department, in cooperation with the department of local affairs, is authorized to identify opportunities for small communities with similar compliance problems to share information or for larger communities to work with small communities in addressing the technical and other issues involved in preparing an environmental priorities plan.

### 25-19-108. Implementation within existing resources.

Any department of state implementing any provision of this article shall do so without additional appropriations of state moneys and without additional personnel.

# SAFETY - DISABLED PERSONS

# ARTICLE 20. DUTIES OWED DISABLED PERSONS - IDENTIFICATION

### 25-20-101. Short title.

This article shall be known and may be cited as the "Uniform Duties to Disabled Persons Act".

### 25-20-102. Definitions.

As used in this article, unless the context otherwise requires:

(1) "Disabled condition" means the condition of being unconscious, semiconscious, incoherent, or otherwise incapacitated to communicate.

(2) "Disabled person" means a person in a disabled condition.

(3) "Emergency symbol" means the caduceus inscribed within a six-barred cross used by the American medical association to denote emergency information.

(4) "Identifying device" means an identifying bracelet, necklace, metal tag, or similar device bearing the emergency symbol and the information needed in an emergency.

(5) "Medical practitioner" means a person licensed or authorized to practice medicine pursuant to article 36 of title 12, C.R.S.

(6) "Peace officer" means any county sheriff, undersheriff, deputy sheriff, or coroner, any municipal police officer or marshal, or any Colorado state patrol officer.

### 25-20-103. Identifying devices for persons having certain conditions.

(1) A person who suffers from epilepsy, diabetes, a cardiac condition, or any other type of illness that causes temporary blackouts, semiconscious periods, or complete unconsciousness, or who suffers from a condition requiring specific medication or medical treatment, is allergic to certain medications or items used in medical treatment, wears contact lenses, has religious objections to certain forms of medication or medical treatment, or is unable to communicate coherently or effectively in the English language, is authorized and encouraged to wear an identifying device.

(2) Any person may carry an identification card bearing his name, type of medical condition, physician's name, and other medical information.

(3) By wearing an identifying device a person gives his consent for any peace officer or medical practitioner who finds him in a disabled condition to make a reasonable search of his clothing or other effects for an identification card of the type described in subsection (2) of this section.

### 25-20-104. Duty of peace officer.

(1) A peace officer shall make a diligent effort to determine whether any disabled person he finds

is an epileptic or a diabetic, or suffers from some other type of illness that would cause the condition. Whenever feasible, this effort shall be made before the person is charged with a crime or taken to a place of detention.

(2) In seeking to determine whether a disabled person suffers from an illness, a peace officer shall make a reasonable search for an identifying device and an identification card of the type described in section 25-20-103 (2) and examine them for emergency information. The peace officer may not search for an identifying device or an identification card in a manner or to an extent that would appear to a reasonable person in the circumstances to cause an unreasonable risk of worsening the disabled person's condition.

(3) A peace officer who finds a disabled person without an identifying device or identification card is not relieved of his duty to that person to make a diligent effort to ascertain the existence of any illness causing the disabled condition.

(4) A claim for relief against a peace officer does not arise from his making a reasonable search of the disabled person to locate an identifying device or identification card, even though the person is not wearing an identifying device or carrying an identification card.

(5) A peace officer who determines or has reason to believe that a disabled person is suffering from an illness causing his condition shall promptly notify the person's physician, if practicable. If the officer is unable to ascertain the physician's identity or to communicate with him, the officer shall make a reasonable effort to cause the disabled person to be transported immediately to a medical practitioner or to a facility where medical treatment is available. If the officer believes it unduly dangerous to move the disabled person, he shall make a reasonable effort to obtain the assistance of a medical practitioner.

## 25-20-105. Duty of medical practitioners.

(1) A medical practitioner, in discharging his duty to a disabled person whom he has undertaken to examine or treat, shall make a reasonable search for an identifying device or identification card of the type described in section 25-20-103 (2) and examine them for emergency information.

(2) A claim for relief against a medical practitioner does not arise from his making a reasonable search of a disabled person to locate an identifying device or identification card, even though the person is not wearing an identifying device or carrying an identification card.

## 25-20-106. Duty of others.

(1) A person, other than a peace officer or medical practitioner, who finds a disabled person shall make a reasonable effort to notify a peace officer. If a peace officer or medical practitioner is not present, a person who finds a disabled person may make a reasonable search for an identifying device, and, if the identifying device is found, may make a reasonable search for an identification card of the type described in section 25-20-103 (2) . If a device or card is located, the person making the search shall attempt promptly to bring its contents to the attention of a peace officer or medical practitioner.

(2) A claim for relief does not arise from a reasonable search to locate an identifying device or identification card as authorized by subsection (1) of this section.

(3) The duties imposed by this article are in addition to, and not in limitation of, other duties existing under the laws of this state.

## 25-20-107. Falsifying identification or misrepresenting condition.

Any person who, with intent to deceive, provides, wears, uses, or possesses a false identifying device or identification card of the type described in section 25-20-103 (2) is guilty of a misdemeanor and, upon conviction thereof, shall be punished by imprisonment in the county jail for not more than ninety days, or by a fine of not more than three hundred dollars, or by both such fine and imprisonment.

## 25-20-108. Uniformity of application and construction.

This article shall be so applied and construed as to make uniform the law with respect to the subject matter among those states which enact it.

# PREVENTION, INTERVENTION, AND TREATMENT SERVICES

# ARTICLE 20.5. PREVENTION, INTERVENTION, AND TREATMENT SERVICES FOR CHILDREN AND YOUTH

# PART 1. ADMINISTRATION

## 25-20.5-101. Legislative declaration.

(1) The general assembly hereby finds that:

(a) The state operates or state agencies provide funding for a wide variety of prevention, intervention, and treatment programs designed to assist youth in achieving an education, in making informed choices about their health and well-being, in avoiding the juvenile and criminal justice systems, and, generally, in becoming healthy, law-abiding, contributing members of society;

(b) These prevention, intervention, and treatment programs are operated by or funded through several departments within the executive branch, and this high degree of decentralization often makes communications between and among these departments and programs difficult;

(c) There is some overlap among prevention, intervention, and treatment programs, sometimes resulting in the potentially inefficient use of state resources which may result in the provision of fewer services to youth;

(d) The dispersion of prevention, intervention, and treatment programs among state departments makes it difficult for both state employees and the public to determine what programs are available and what services are provided through prevention, intervention, and treatment programs that are operated by or funded through state agencies;

(e) The term limitations placed on persons who serve in public office, including members of the general assembly, make it increasingly important that information concerning the existence, funding, and operation of prevention, intervention, and treatment programs for youth be readily accessible;

(f) In the area of prevention, intervention, and treatment services, there is a critical need for local and state programs to overcome barriers and the categorical requirements of various funding sources in order to design and implement programs that provide a more comprehensive response to the needs of Colorado youth;

(g) Research demonstrates that program coordination among multiple systems for the purpose of improving prevention, intervention, and treatment services results in significant positive outcomes;

(h) A unified, coordinated response to community-based programs for the delivery of prevention, intervention, and treatment services has proven to be an effective and efficient state response to local programs and their needs.

(2) The general assembly therefore finds that it is in the best interests of the youth and families of the state to create a single division in the department of public health and environment to operate

prevention and intervention programs and to oversee the provision of prevention, intervention, and treatment services through federally and state-funded prevention, intervention, and treatment programs to ensure collaboration among programs and the availability of a continuum of services for youth.

## 25-20.5-102. Definitions.

As used in this article, unless the context otherwise requires:

(1) "Department" means the department of public health and environment, created pursuant to section 25-1-102.

(2) "Division" means the prevention services division created in section 25-20.5-103.

(3) "Executive director" means the executive director of the department of public health and environment.

(4) "Prevention, intervention, and treatment program" means a program that provides prevention, intervention, or treatment services.

(5) "Prevention, intervention, and treatment services" means services that are designed to promote the well-being of youth and their families by decreasing high-risk behaviors, strengthening healthy behaviors, and promoting family stability.

(6) "State plan" means the state plan for delivery of prevention, intervention, and treatment services to youth throughout the state adopted by the division pursuant to section 25-20.5-105.

## 25-20.5-103. Prevention services division - creation.

(1) There is hereby created within the department of public health and environment a prevention services division. The division shall be headed by the director of prevention services appointed by the executive director of the department of public health and environment in accordance with section 13 of article XII of the state constitution.

(2) The division shall exercise its powers and perform its duties and functions specified in this article under the department of public health and environment as if it were transferred to the department by a type 2 transfer as such transfer is defined in the "Administrative Organization Act of 1968", article 1 of title 24, C.R.S.

## 25-20.5-104. Functions of division.

(1) The division has the following functions:

(a) On or before February 1, 2001, to submit to the executive director and to the governor for approval a state plan for delivery of prevention, intervention, and treatment services to youth throughout the state as provided in section 25-20.5-105, and to biennially review the state plan and submit revisions as provided by rule of the state board of health to the executive director and the governor for approval;

(b) To identify performance indicators for prevention, intervention, and treatment programs based on the standards adopted by the state board of health pursuant to section 25-20.5-106 (2) (d) , and to review, as provided in section 25-20.5-108, all prevention, intervention, and treatment programs operated by the division and by other state departments;

(c) To act as a liaison with communities throughout the state and assist the communities in their efforts to assess their needs with regard to prevention, intervention, and treatment services and to provide information to assist the communities in obtaining funding for appropriate prevention, intervention, and treatment programs;

(d) To provide technical assistance to communities and to entities that provide prevention, intervention, and treatment services;

(e) To operate the prevention and intervention programs specified in this article and such other prevention and intervention programs as may be created in or transferred to the division by executive order to be funded solely by nonstate moneys, including but not limited to reviewing applications submitted by entities to receive funding through said programs, awarding grants based on such applications, and notifying the state board of health of the grants awarded and the amounts of said grants;

(f) To solicit and accept grants from the federal government and to solicit and accept contributions, grants, gifts, bequests, and donations from individuals, private organizations, and foundations for the operation of any prevention and intervention programs under the authority of the division;

(g) To periodically review the federal funding guidelines for federal prevention, intervention, and treatment programs and to seek the maximum flexibility in the use of federal moneys in funding prevention, intervention, and treatment programs provided through the state plan;

(h) To seek such federal waivers as may be necessary to allow the division to combine federal moneys available through various federal prevention, intervention, and treatment programs and to combine said moneys with moneys appropriated by the general assembly to fund state prevention, intervention, and treatment programs to allow the greatest flexibility in awarding combined program funding to community-based prevention, intervention, and treatment programs;

(i) Repealed.

(2) In addition to any prevention and intervention programs created in or transferred to the division by executive order and any prevention and intervention programs transferred to the division by the executive director pursuant to subsection (4) of this section, the division shall operate the following prevention and intervention programs:

(a) to (e) (Deleted by amendment, L. 2013.)

(f) The school-based health center grant program created in part 5 of this article.

(3) In operating prevention and intervention programs, on receipt of an application for funding through any of said prevention and intervention programs, the division shall review the application and determine whether there are other prevention, intervention, and treatment programs operated by state agencies within this state through which funding may be available to the applicant. With the applicant's consent, the division shall forward a copy of the application to any such program for consideration.

(4) The executive director shall transfer any prevention and intervention programs operated by the department to the division, as he or she deems appropriate. The division shall collaborate with any other division within the department that operates a prevention, intervention, and treatment program in the same manner that it collaborates with other state agencies that operate prevention, intervention, and treatment programs.

## 25-20.5-105. State plan for delivery of prevention, intervention, and treatment services to youth - contents.

(1) On or before February 1, 2001, the division shall submit to the governor and the executive director for approval a state plan for delivery of prevention, intervention, and treatment services to youth throughout the state. The state plan shall apply to all prevention, intervention, and treatment programs that receive state or federal funds and are operated within the state. The state plan shall be designed to coordinate and provide direction for the delivery of prevention, intervention, and treatment services through the various prevention and intervention programs operated by the division and the prevention, intervention, and treatment programs operated by other state departments and to ensure collaboration among programs that results in a continuum of services available to youth throughout the state. At a minimum, the state plan shall:

(a) Target and prioritize community prevention, intervention, and treatment services needs throughout the state;

(b) Specify the standards for and measurable outcomes anticipated to be achieved by prevention, intervention, and treatment programs that receive state and federal funds and the outcomes to be achieved through the coordination of said prevention, intervention, and treatment programs;

(c) Identify all state- and community-based prevention, intervention, and treatment programs that are receiving state and federal funds during the fiscal years for which the plan is submitted and the schedule for review of said prevention, intervention, and treatment programs;

(d) Identify the methods by which the division shall encourage collaboration at the local level among public and private entities, including but not limited to private for-profit and nonprofit providers and faith-based services providers, in providing prevention, intervention, and treatment services;

(e) Include any other information required by rule of the state board of health.

(2) The division shall biennially review and revise the state plan as necessary to ensure the most efficient and effective delivery of prevention, intervention, and treatment services throughout the state. The division shall submit any revised state plan as provided by rule of the state board of health to the governor and the executive director for approval.

(3) In preparing the state plan and biennial revisions to the state plan, the division shall hold at least two public meetings to receive input from members of the public and from state agencies and entities operating prevention, intervention, and treatment programs.

(4) On or before March 15, 2001, the governor and the executive director shall submit copies of the approved state plan to the general assembly, to each state department that operates a prevention, intervention, and treatment program, and to each entity that will receive state or federal funds for the operation of a prevention, intervention, and treatment program during the fiscal years for which the state plan is prepared. The division shall provide copies of the approved state plan to any person upon request. The governor and the executive director shall submit copies of any approved revised state plans as provided by rule of the state board of health.

## 25-20.5-106. State board of health - rules - program duties.

(1) The state board of health created in section 25-1-103 shall promulgate rules as necessary for the operation of the division, including but not limited to rules establishing the time frames for review of the state plan and submittal of any revised state plan to the governor and the executive director and to the entities specified in section 25-20.5-105 (4) .

(2) The state board of health also shall adopt rules for the uniform operation of federally and state-funded prevention, intervention, and treatment programs. In adopting such rules, the board shall take into account prevention, intervention, and treatment programs' need for responsiveness and flexibility and their need for procedures and standards that will ensure the provision of programs that meet a high standard of excellence. At a minimum such rules shall include:

(a) Standardized procedures for the operation of prevention, intervention, and treatment programs, including but not limited to:

(I) The use of a system whereby entities may use a single application to seek funding from a variety of prevention, intervention, and treatment programs;

(II) The use of uniform application forms promulgated by rule of the state board of health;

(III) Uniform standards regarding the information to be submitted by entities applying for funding for community-based prevention, intervention, and treatment programs;

(IV) Uniform application dates to the extent possible for all prevention, intervention, and treatment programs;

(V) Uniform standards for selecting community-based prevention, intervention, and treatment programs that receive funding through state prevention, intervention, and treatment programs;

(VI) Uniform monitoring and reporting forms, including rules to ensure that no prevention, intervention, and treatment program is required to submit more than one annual report;

(VII) A standard database of service providers by location;

(VIII) Internet access to each prevention, intervention, and treatment program;

(IX) The ability to submit applications and report submissions through the internet; and

(X) The use of contracts to combine multiple state and federal funding sources provided by or through various state agencies as a single funding grant to a prevention, intervention, and treatment program;

(b) Uniform, minimum standards for prevention, intervention, and treatment programs, including but not limited to requirements that each prevention, intervention, and treatment program that receives state or federal funds:

(I) Provide research-based prevention, intervention, and treatment services that have been previously implemented in one or more communities with demonstrated success or that otherwise demonstrate a reasonable potential for success; and

(II) Provide outcome-based prevention, intervention, and treatment services, specifying the outcomes to be achieved; and

(III) Work collaboratively with other public and private prevention, intervention, and treatment programs in the community and with local governments, county, district, and municipal public health agencies, county departments of social services, and faith-based organizations in the community;

(c) Uniform standards and procedures for reviewing state and local prevention, intervention, and treatment programs that receive state or federal funds;

(d) Performance standards and measurable outcomes for state and local prevention, intervention, and treatment programs that receive state or federal funds;

(e) Criteria for determining whether a program operated by a state agency constitutes a prevention, intervention, and treatment program;

(f) A formula for calculating the amount forwarded to the division by each prevention, intervention, and treatment program to offset the costs incurred by the division in reviewing the programs.

(3) The state board of health shall act as the program board for the oversight of the prevention and intervention programs operated by the division.

(4) In addition to any other duties specified in law, the state board of health shall have the following duties:

(a) Repealed.

(b) To assist division personnel in working with communities and local elected officials to identify the communities' prevention, intervention, and treatment services needs;

(c) To assist division personnel in reviewing the performance of prevention, intervention, and treatment programs created in this article.

## 25-20.5-107. Memoranda of understanding - duties of executive director - program meetings.

(1) The executive director shall enter into a memorandum of understanding, as described in subsection (2) of this section, with each state agency that operates a prevention, intervention, and treatment program, as identified by the division pursuant to criteria adopted by rule of the state board of health.

(2) On or before July 1, 2001, each state agency that operates a prevention, intervention, and treatment program, as identified by the division based on criteria adopted by rule of the state board of health, shall enter into a memorandum of understanding with the executive director and the division through which, at a minimum, the state agency shall agree to:

(a) Comply with the rules for the operation of prevention, intervention, and treatment programs adopted by the state board of health pursuant to section 25-20.5-106;

(b) Upon receipt of a grant application, forward a copy of the application to other appropriate prevention, intervention, and treatment programs operated by state agencies for consideration and to collaborate in providing combined program grants to appropriate community-based prevention, intervention, and treatment programs;

(c) Comply with the prevention, intervention, and treatment program reporting requirements specified in section 25-20.5-108, and to forward a percentage of the program operating funds, as determined by rule, to the division to offset the costs incurred in reviewing the program;

(d) Seek such federal waivers as may be necessary to allow the agency to combine federal moneys available through various federal prevention, intervention, and treatment programs and to combine said moneys with moneys appropriated to fund state prevention, intervention, and treatment programs to allow the greatest flexibility in awarding combined program funding to community-based prevention, intervention, and treatment programs.

(3) Any state agency that fails to enter into and comply with a memorandum of understanding as

described in subsection (2) of this section shall be ineligible for state funding for operation of a prevention, intervention, and treatment program until such time as the agency enters into and complies with the memorandum of understanding.

(4) The governor is strongly encouraged to deny federal funding for prevention, intervention, and treatment programs to any state agency that fails to enter into and comply with a memorandum of understanding as described in subsection (2) of this section.

(5) Beginning July 1, 2001, the office of legislative legal services shall annually review all bills enacted during a regular or special legislative session and identify any bills that appear to create a prevention, intervention, and treatment program in a state agency other than the division. The office of legislative legal services shall notify the division in writing of the enactment of such bill. Upon receipt of such notice, the division shall determine whether the identified program meets the criteria for a prevention, intervention, and treatment program adopted by rule of the state board of health. If the division determines based on such criteria that the program is a prevention, intervention, and treatment program, it shall notify in writing the state agency in which the program is created of the requirements of this section.

(6) (a) The executive director shall meet at least annually with the governor, or his or her designee, and with the executive directors specified in paragraph (b) of this subsection (6) to review the activities and progress of the division and its interaction with the prevention, intervention, and treatment programs provided by other state agencies. The purpose of the meetings shall be to identify and streamline the prevention, intervention, and treatment programs operated by state agencies, as appropriate to achieve greater efficiencies and effectiveness for the state, for local communities, and for persons receiving services.

(b) The following executive directors shall attend the meetings required under this subsection (6) :

(I) (Deleted by amendment, L. 2002, p. 222, § 2, effective April 3, 2002.)

(II) The commissioner of education;

(III) and (IV) (Deleted by amendment, L. 2002, p. 222, § 2, effective April 3, 2002.)

(V) The executive director of the department of human services;

(VI) and (VII) (Deleted by amendment, L. 2002, p. 222, § 2, effective April 3, 2002.)

(VIII) The executive director of the department of public safety; and

(IX) The executive director of the department of transportation.

## 25-20.5-108. Prevention, intervention, and treatment program requirements - reports - reviews - annual review summary.

(1) Each state agency that operates a prevention, intervention, and treatment program, as identified by the division based on criteria adopted by rule of the state board of health, annually shall submit to the division the following information:

(a) The name of, statutory authority for, and funding source for each prevention, intervention, and treatment program operated by the state agency;

(b) The parameters of each prevention, intervention, and treatment program, including but not limited to the specific, measurable outcomes to be achieved by each prevention, intervention, and treatment program;

(c) The entities that are receiving funding through each prevention, intervention, and treatment program operated by the state agency, the amount awarded to each entity, and a description of the population served and prevention, intervention, and treatment services provided by each entity.

(2) (a) Except as otherwise provided in paragraph (b) of this subsection (2) , each state agency using state or federal moneys to fund local prevention and intervention programs shall submit an annual report concerning these programs to the division. The state board of health by rule shall specify the time frames, procedures, and form for submittal of the report and the information to be included in the report, which at a minimum shall include:

(I) A description of the prevention, intervention, and treatment program, including but not limited to the population served, the prevention, intervention, and treatment services provided, and the goals and specific, measurable outcomes to be achieved by the prevention, intervention, and treatment program;

(II) Evidence of the prevention, intervention, and treatment program's progress in meeting its stated outcomes and goals during the preceding fiscal year and in previous fiscal years, depending on how long the prevention, intervention, and treatment program has been in operation;

(III) The sources from which the prevention, intervention, and treatment program receives funding and the amount received from each source;

(IV) A list of any entities that are collaborating in the delivery of prevention, intervention, and treatment services through the program.

(b) If a community-based prevention, intervention, and treatment program is required to submit an annual report that is comparable to the report described in paragraph (a) of this subsection (2) to a state agency other than the division, the state agency, in lieu of submittal of a report by the prevention, intervention, and treatment program as required in paragraph (a) of this subsection (2) , shall forward a copy of the comparable report to the division in accordance with rules adopted by the state board of health. If a forwarded report does not include all of the information specified in paragraph (a) of this subsection (2) , the division shall obtain such information directly from the community-based prevention, intervention, and treatment program.

(3) (a) The division, in accordance with the time frames adopted by rule of the state board of health, but at least every four years, shall review, or cause to be reviewed under a contract entered into pursuant to subsection (5) of this section, each state and community-based prevention, intervention, and treatment program operated within this state that receives state or federal funds. The division may establish a schedule for the review of prevention, intervention, and treatment programs pursuant to this subsection (3) . The review shall be designed to determine whether the prevention, intervention, and treatment program is meeting its identified goals and outcomes and complying with all requirements of the agency overseeing the operation of the prevention, intervention, and treatment program and the applicable rules adopted by the state board of health pursuant to this article.

(b) If the division determines that a community-based prevention, intervention, and treatment program is not meeting or making adequate progress toward meeting the outcomes specified for the program or is otherwise failing to comply with statutory or regulatory requirements, the division shall revoke the grant issued to the program, if it was issued by the division, or recommend revocation to the state agency that issued the grant. The entity operating any program for which the grant is revoked may appeal as provided in the "State Administrative Procedure Act", article 4 of title 24, C.R.S.

(c) If the division determines that a state-operated prevention, intervention, and treatment program is not meeting or making adequate progress toward meeting the outcomes specified for the prevention, intervention, and treatment program or is otherwise failing to comply with statutory or regulatory requirements, the division shall recommend to the governor or to the general assembly, whichever is appropriate, that the prevention, intervention, and treatment program cease receiving state or federal funding.

(4) The division shall receive a percentage, as determined by rule, of the operating cost of each state prevention, intervention, and treatment program reviewed pursuant to this section to offset the costs incurred by the division in performing such review.

(5) The division may contract with one or more public or private entities to conduct the reviews of prevention, intervention, and treatment programs and assist in preparing the annual executive summary report as required in this section.

(6) The division shall annually prepare or oversee the preparation of an executive summary of the prevention, intervention, and treatment program reviews conducted during the preceding year and submit such summary to the governor, to each state department that operates a prevention, intervention, and treatment program, and to each entity that received state or federal funds for operation of a prevention, intervention, and treatment program during the fiscal year for which the summary is prepared. In addition, the division shall provide copies of the summary to any person upon request.

### 25-20.5-109. Programs not included.

(1) Notwithstanding any other provisions of this article 20.5 to the contrary, the following programs are not subject to the requirements of this article 20.5:

(a) Any juvenile programs operated by the division of youth services in the department of human services;

(b) Any program operated for juveniles in connection with the state judicial system;

(c) Any program pertaining to out-of-home placement of children pursuant to title 19, C.R.S.

### 25-20.5-110. Coordinated comprehensive community-based prevention and intervention services - pilot program - reports - repeal. (Repealed)

### 25-20.5-111. Colorado Homeless Youth Services Act. (Repealed)

# PART 2. TONY GRAMPSAS YOUTH SERVICES PROGRAM

### 25-20.5-201. to 25-20.5-205 (Repealed)

# PART 3. CANCER, CARDIOVASCULAR DISEASE, AND CHRONIC PULMONARY DISEASE PREVENTION, EARLY DETECTION, AND TREATMENT PROGRAM

### 25-20.5-301. Definitions.

As used in this part 3, unless the context otherwise requires:

(1) "Health disparities" means an unequal burden of cancer, cardiovascular disease, or chronic pulmonary disease impacting specific populations, including but not limited to racial and ethnic populations, minority populations, rural populations, urban populations, low-income populations, or any other underserved population.

(2) "Program" means the cancer, cardiovascular disease, and chronic pulmonary disease prevention, early detection, and treatment program created in section 25-20.5-302.

(3) "Review committee" means the cancer, cardiovascular disease, and chronic pulmonary disease program review committee created pursuant to section 25-20.5-303.

### 25-20.5-302. Program.

(1) There is hereby created, in the prevention services division of the department, the cancer, cardiovascular disease, and chronic pulmonary disease prevention, early detection, and treatment program for the purpose of assisting in the implementation of the state's strategic plans regarding cancer and cardiovascular disease. The program shall fund competitive grants to provide a cohesive approach to cancer, cardiovascular disease, and chronic pulmonary disease prevention, early detection, and treatment in Colorado. The division shall administer the program with the

goal of developing a comprehensive approach that will bring together stakeholders at the community and state level who are interested in impacting cancer, cardiovascular disease, or chronic pulmonary disease. Grant applications shall address at least one of the following program criteria:

(a) Translating evidence-based strategies regarding the prevention and early detection of cancer, cardiovascular disease, and chronic pulmonary disease into practical application in healthcare, workplace, and community settings;

(b) Providing appropriate diagnosis and treatment services for anyone who has abnormalities discovered in screening and early detection programs;

(c) Implementing education programs for the public and health care providers regarding the prevention, early detection, and treatment of cancer, cardiovascular disease, and chronic pulmonary disease; and

(d) Providing evidence-based strategies to overcome health disparities in the prevention and early detection of cancer, cardiovascular disease, and chronic pulmonary disease.

## 25-20.5-303. Cancer, cardiovascular disease, and chronic pulmonary disease program review committee.

(1) There is hereby created the cancer, cardiovascular disease, and chronic pulmonary disease program review committee. The review committee is established in the prevention services division of the department. The review committee is responsible for overseeing program strategies and activities and ensuring compliance with section 25-20.5-302.

(2) The review committee shall consist of the director of the disease prevention services division of the department, or the director's designee, and fifteen members appointed as follows:

(a) The executive director of the department or the executive director's designee.

(b) The executive director shall appoint three members, all of whom are department staff with expertise in cancer, cardiovascular disease, or chronic pulmonary disease.

(c) The state board shall appoint:

(I) One member who is a member of the state board;

(II) One member who is a chronic pulmonary disease professional;

(III) One member who is cardiovascular disease professional;

(IV) One member who is a cancer professional;

(V) Two members who are public health professionals;

(VI) One member who is a recognized expert in health disparities;

(VII) One member who represents the rural interest in regard to the prevention, early detection, and treatment of cancer, cardiovascular disease, and chronic pulmonary disease; and

(VIII) One member who is a primary care provider.

(d) The president of the senate shall appoint one member of the senate.

(e) The speaker of the house of representatives shall appoint one member of the house of representatives.

(3) (a) Except as provided in paragraph (b) of this subsection (3) , members of the review committee shall serve three-year terms; except that, of the members initially appointed to the review committee, five members appointed by the state board shall serve two-year terms. Members of the review committee appointed pursuant to paragraph (c) of subsection (2) of this section shall not serve more than two consecutive terms.

(b) The terms of the members appointed by the speaker of the house of representatives and the president of the senate and who are serving on March 22, 2007, shall be extended to and expire on or shall terminate on the convening date of the first regular session of the sixty-seventh general assembly. As soon as practicable after such convening date, the speaker and the president shall appoint or reappoint members in the same manner as provided in paragraphs (d) and (e) of subsection (2) of this section. Thereafter, the terms of members appointed or reappointed by the speaker and the president shall expire on the convening date of the first regular session of each general assembly, and all subsequent appointments and reappointments by the speaker and the president shall be made as soon as practicable after such convening date. The person making the original appointment or reappointment shall fill any vacancy by appointment for the remainder of an unexpired term. Members shall serve at the pleasure of the appointing authority and shall continue in office until the member's successor is appointed.

(4) The composition of the review committee shall reflect, to the extent practical, Colorado's ethnic, racial, and geographical diversity.

(5) The review committee shall elect from its membership a chair and a vice-chair of the committee.

(6) The division shall provide staff support to the review committee.

(7) Except as otherwise provided in section 2-2-326, C.R.S., members of the review committee shall serve without compensation but shall be reimbursed from moneys deposited in the prevention, early detection, and treatment fund created in section 24-22-117, C.R.S., for their actual and necessary expenses incurred in the performance of their duties pursuant to this part 3.

(8) If a member of the review committee has an immediate personal, private, or financial interest in any matter pending before the review committee, the member shall disclose the fact and shall not vote upon such matter.

## 25-20.5-304. Grant program.

(1) The program shall fund programs and initiatives that provide evidence-based education and intervention strategies for cancer, cardiovascular disease, and chronic pulmonary disease prevention, early detection, and treatment through a competitive grant program which shall be overseen by the review committee. The state board, upon recommendations of the review committee, shall adopt rules that specify, but need not be limited to, the following:

(a) The procedures and timelines by which an entity may apply for program grants;

(b) Grant application contents;

(c) Criteria for selecting the entities that shall receive grants and determining the amount and duration of the grants;

(d) Reporting requirements for entities that receive grants pursuant to this section; and

(e) The qualifications of an adequate proposal.

(2) The review committee shall review the applications received pursuant to this section and submit to the state board and the executive director of the department recommended grant recipients, grant amounts, and the duration of each grant. Within thirty days after receiving the review committee's recommendations, the executive director shall submit his or her recommendations to the state board. The review committee's recommendations regarding grants for projects impacting rural areas shall be submitted to the state board and the executive director of the department of local affairs. Within thirty days after receiving the review committee's recommendations, the executive director of the department of local affairs shall submit his or her recommendations to the state board. The state board shall have the final authority to approve the grants under this part 3. If the state board disapproves a recommendation for a grant recipient, the review committee may submit a replacement recommendation within thirty days. In making grant recommendations, the review committee shall follow the intent of the program as outlined in section 25-20.5-302. The state board shall award grants to the entities selected by the review committee, specifying the amount and duration of each grant award. In reviewing and approving grant applications, the review committee and the state board shall ensure that grants are distributed statewide and address the needs of Colorado's disparate populations, as well as the needs of both urban and rural residents of Colorado. Grants providing for treatment services shall not exceed ten percent of the total amount of grant funds distributed in any given year.

(3) (a) For the prevention, early detection, and treatment of cardiovascular disease, the review committee and the state board are encouraged to consider programs that address the major risk factors of cardiovascular disease including but not limited to blood pressure, cholesterol, and diabetes screenings.

(b) For the prevention, early detection, and treatment of cancer, the review committee and the state board are encouraged to consider programs to increase screening for cancer including but not limited to colorectal cancer screening.

(c) For the prevention, early detection, and treatment of chronic pulmonary disease, the review committee and the state board are encouraged to consider programs to expand the prevention, early detection, and treatment of chronic pulmonary diseases.

(4) A minimum of ten percent of the moneys awarded through the grant program shall be directed to projects impacting rural areas as part of the governor's rural healthcare initiative and a minimum of ten percent of the moneys awarded through the grant program shall be directed to each of the following three disease areas: Cancer; cardiovascular disease; and chronic pulmonary disease; except that, if the review committee determines that there are no adequate proposals in a given disease or geographic area for a particular grant cycle, the review committee may waive the ten percent requirement.

### 25-20.5-305. Evaluation.

Commencing with the 2006-07 fiscal year, and each fiscal year thereafter, the state board shall select a grant recipient to evaluate the effectiveness of the program and the health disparities grant program established pursuant to part 22 of article 4 of this title. Costs for the evaluation shall be adequately funded from the amount annually appropriated by the general assembly to the division from the prevention, early detection, and treatment fund.

### 25-20.5-306. Administration - limitation.

(1) Except as provided in subsection (2) of this section, the prevention services division of the department may receive up to five percent of the moneys annually appropriated by the general assembly to the division from the prevention, early detection, and treatment fund created in section 24-22-117, C.R.S., for the actual costs incurred in administering the program, including the hiring of sufficient staff within the division to effectively administer the program and the reimbursement of review committee members pursuant to section 25-20.5-303 (4) .

(2) For fiscal year 2011-12, and for any fiscal year in which a declaration of a state fiscal emergency is declared pursuant to section 21 (7) of article X of the state constitution, the prevention services division of the department may receive up to five percent of the moneys annually appropriated by the general assembly from the prevention, early detection, and treatment fund created in section 24-22-117, C.R.S., for the actual costs incurred in administering the program, including the hiring of sufficient staff within the division to effectively administer the program and the reimbursement of review committee members pursuant to section 25-20.5-303 (4) .

# PART 4. CHILD FATALITY PREVENTION ACT

### 25-20.5-401. Short title.

This part 4 shall be known and may be cited as the "Child Fatality Prevention Act".

### 25-20.5-402. Legislative declaration.

(1) The general assembly hereby finds and declares that protection of the health and welfare of the children of this state is an important goal of the citizens of this state, and the injury and death of infants and children are serious public health concerns that require legislative action. The general assembly further finds that the prevention of child abuse, neglect, and fatalities is a community responsibility; that professionals from disparate disciplines have responsibilities to children and have expertise that can promote the safety and well-being of children; and that multidisciplinary reviews of child abuse, neglect, and fatalities can lead to a greater understanding of the causes of,

and methods of preventing, child abuse, neglect, and fatalities.

(2) It is, therefore, the intent of the general assembly in enacting this part 4 to establish state and local multidisciplinary, multi-agency child fatality prevention review teams. The purpose of these teams is:

(a) For local or regional review teams, to review specific cases of child fatalities in the team's service area that occur from birth through seventeen years of age and involve unintentional injury, violence, motor vehicle incidents, child abuse or neglect, sudden unexpected infant death, suicide, or undetermined causes and to provide the state with individual case findings to develop a community approach to the systemic issues surrounding child fatalities;

(b) For the state review team, to review the individual case findings of the local and regional review teams and to create a report based on those findings to make specific recommendations regarding systemic trends across the state that may help prevent future child fatalities;

(c) To help the people of Colorado understand the incidence and causes of child fatalities and therefore encourage public action to prevent further child fatalities;

(d) To identify services provided by public, private, and nonprofit agencies to children and their families that are designed to prevent, and that are effective in preventing, child fatalities;

(e) To identify gaps or deficiencies that may exist in the delivery of services provided by public, private, and nonprofit agencies to children and their families that are designed to prevent child fatalities; and

(f) To make recommendations for, act as a catalyst for, and implement any changes to laws, rules, and policies that will support the safe and healthy development of the children in this state and prevent future child fatalities.

## 25-20.5-403. Definitions.

As used in this part 4, unless the context otherwise requires:

(1) "County department" means the county or district department of social services.

(2) "Local or regional review team" means a local or regional child fatality prevention review team established pursuant to section 25-20.5-404.

(3) "State review team" means the Colorado state child fatality prevention review team created pursuant to section 25-20.5-406.

(4) Repealed.

## 25-20.5-404. Local and regional review teams - creation - membership - authority.

(1) On or before January 1, 2015, each county or district public health agency established pursuant to section 25-1-506 shall establish, or arrange to be established, subject to available appropriations, a local child fatality prevention review team. County or district public health agencies may collaborate to form a regional child fatality prevention review team to fulfill the requirements of this section.

(2) Each local or regional review team shall consist of representatives of public and nonpublic agencies in the county or counties that provide services to children and their families and of other individuals who represent the community.

(3) (a) A local or regional review team must include representatives from the following entities located within the service area of the establishing county or district public health agency or agencies:

(I) Each county department;

(II) Local law enforcement agencies;

(III) The district attorney's office;

(IV) School districts;

(V) Each county department of public health;

(VI) Each coroner's office or county medical examiner's office; and

(VII) Each county attorney's office.

(b) A local or regional review team may include but is not limited to representatives from the following entities or groups located within the service area of the establishing county or district public health agency or agencies:

(I) Hospitals, trauma centers, or other providers of emergency medical services;

(II) Each county board of social services;

(III) Mental health professionals;

(IV) Medical professionals specializing in pediatrics;

(V) Each court-appointed special advocate program;

(VI) Child advocacy centers;

(VII) Private out-of-home placement providers;

(VIII) Victim advocates associated with law enforcement agencies; and

(IX) The community at large.

(4) Each local or regional review team has the authority to establish committees to review specific types of child fatalities.

## 25-20.5-405. Local review teams - duties - authority.

(1) The local or regional review team shall conduct individual, case-specific reviews of fatalities of children from birth through seventeen years of age occurring in the jurisdiction of the local or regional review team for the purpose of identifying prevention recommendations related, at a minimum, to the following causes of child fatality:

(a) Undetermined causes;

(b) Unintentional injury;

(c) Violence;

(d) Motor vehicle incidents;

(e) Child abuse or neglect as defined in section 19-1-103 (1) , C.R.S., including the death of a child who was previously unknown to the county department but whose death included circumstances related to child abuse or neglect, regardless of the official manner of death;

(f) Sudden unexpected infant death; or

(g) Suicide.

(2) With respect to each child fatality reviewed, the local or regional review team shall:

(a) Review the cause and manner of the child fatality as determined by the local coroner, pathologist, or medical examiner, and determine whether the local or regional review team concurs with the coroner's, pathologist's, or medical examiner's findings. Any information requested from the local coroner must be in compliance with section 30-10-606, C.R.S.

(b) In cases in which the local or regional review team does not concur with the cause or manner of death as determined by the local coroner, pathologist, or medical examiner, forward a report of the local or regional review team's analysis of the cause and manner of the child fatality to the local coroner, pathologist, or medical examiner for his or her consideration;

(c) Evaluate means by which the fatality might have been prevented;

(d) Report case review findings, as appropriate, to public and private agencies that have responsibilities for children and make prevention recommendations to these agencies that may help to reduce the number of child fatalities;

(e) (Deleted by amendment, L. 2013.)

(e.5) No later than two months after reviewing a case, enter information regarding the child fatality into a web-based data-collection system, utilized by the department;

(f) Submit to the state review team the following information:

(I) (Deleted by amendment, L. 2013.)

(II) A listing of any system issues identified through the review process and recommendations to the state review team and the appropriate agencies for system improvements and needed resources, training, and information dissemination where gaps and deficiencies may exist;

(III) Any changes, positive or negative, that appear to have resulted from implementation of previous recommendations made by the local or regional review team to the state review team and appropriate agencies; and

(IV) Examples of services known by the local or regional review team to be provided by public or private agencies to children and their families that are designed to prevent child fatalities and that are effective in preventing such fatalities.

(V) (Deleted by amendment, L. 2013.)

(g) Secure the most reliable information possible that is related to a child fatality to provide a thorough, comprehensive review of each child fatality; and

(h) Request capacity assistance as necessary from the department for the purpose of conducting a child fatality review.

(3) Each local or regional review team may, within existing appropriations and community resources, promote continuing education for professionals involved in investigating, treating, and preventing child abuse and neglect as a means of preventing child fatalities due to abuse or neglect and other child fatalities. The local or regional review team may also, within existing resources, promote public education related to preventing child fatalities related to abuse and neglect.

## 25-20.5-406. State review team - creation - membership - vacancies.

(1) There is hereby created the Colorado state child fatality prevention review team in the department of public health and environment.

(2) (a) On or before September 1, 2013, the governor shall appoint eighteen voting members of the state review team specified in this paragraph (a) , as follows:

(I) Two members who represent the county sheriffs within the state, one of whom represents a rural area of the state;

(II) Two members who represent the county coroners within the state;

(III) Two members who represent peace officers within the state who specialize in crimes against children;

(IV) Two members who represent the district attorneys within the state, one of whom represents a rural area of the state;

(V) Six members who represent members of the medical profession within the state who specialize in traumatic injury or children's health, including four physicians and two nurses;

(VI) One member who represents local fire department employees within the state;

(VII) One member who represents county attorneys within the state who practice in the area of dependency and neglect;

(VIII) One member who represents county commissioners within the state; and

(IX) One member who represents the office of Colorado's child protection ombudsman.

(b) The executive director of the department of human services shall appoint six voting members, as follows:

(I) Two members who represent the unit within the department of human services that is responsible for child welfare;

(II) Repealed.

(III) Two members who represent the office of behavioral health in the department of human services;

(IV) One member who represents the division of youth services; and

(V) One member who represents the directors of county departments of social services.

(c) The executive director of the department of public health and environment shall appoint eight voting members who represent the department of public health and environment, one of whom represents county or district public health agencies.

(d) The commissioner of education shall appoint one voting member who represents the department of education.

(e) The executive director of the department of public safety shall appoint one voting member who represents the department of public safety.

(f) A member of the department of public health and environment shall call a preliminary meeting of the members of the state review team specified in paragraphs (a) to (e) of this subsection (2) , and the voting members appointed pursuant to said paragraphs may, by a majority vote, select an additional twelve nonvoting members of the state review team as follows:

(I) Four members who represent injury prevention or safety specialists from hospitals within the state;

(II) One member who represents organizations specializing in auto safety or driver safety within the state;

(III) One member who represents sudden infant death specialists within the state;

(IV) One member who represents the state network of child advocacy centers within the state;

(V) One member who represents a state domestic violence coalition;

(VI) One member who represents the court-appointed special advocate program directors, described in section 19-1-203, C.R.S., within the state;

(VII) One member who represents the office of the child's representative, established in section 13-91-104, C.R.S.;

(VIII) One member who represents a private out-of-home placement provider; and

(IX) One member of the community with experience in childhood death.

(3) Members shall be appointed for three-year terms and shall be eligible for reappointment upon the expiration of the terms. Vacancies in the appointed membership shall be filled by the appointing entity.

## 25-20.5-407. State review team - duties - definitions.

(1) The state review team shall:

(a) Form committees to review a child fatality case, if a local or regional child fatality review team has not conducted such a review of the case, if the child fatality occurred in the state of Colorado and was related to one or more of the following causes:

(I) Undetermined causes;

(II) Unintentional injury;

(III) Violence;

(IV) Motor vehicle incidents;

(V) Child abuse or neglect, as defined in section 19-1-103 (1) , C.R.S.;

(VI) Sudden unexpected infant death; and

(VII) Suicide.

(b) Outline trends and patterns of child fatalities in Colorado;

(c) Identify and investigate risk factors that may lead to child fatalities;

(d) Characterize groups of children who are at risk for a child fatality;

(e) Evaluate the services offered and the system responses to children who are at risk of a child fatality and review recommendations of local or regional review teams, if any;

(e.5) Consider a review of all systemic child-related issues when evaluating services offered or system responses to children who are at risk of fatality. For purposes of this paragraph (e.5) ,"systemic child-related issues" means any issue involving one or more agencies.

(f) Take steps to improve the quality and scope of data obtained through investigations and review of child fatalities;

(f.5) Utilize a child fatalities data-collection system, using nationally developed public health guidelines, to ensure the proper identification of all potential child abuse or neglect fatalities;

(g) Report to the governor and to the public health care and human services committee and the judiciary committee of the house of representatives and the health and human services committee and the judiciary committee of the senate of the Colorado general assembly, or any successor committees, concerning any recommendations for changes to any law, rule, or policy that the state review team has determined will promote the safety and well-being of children. Notwithstanding section 24-1-136 (11) (a) (I) , the state review team shall report annually on or before July 1, 2014, and on or before July 1 each year thereafter. In its report, the state review team shall provide a list of system strengths and weaknesses identified through the review process and recommendations for preventive actions to promote the safety and well-being of children. The annual report must include an analysis of the state review team's recommendations from the previous year and state what policy changes, if any, were made to improve child safety and well-being. The state review team shall make the annual report publicly available and will conduct outreach efforts to educate members of the child protection community on report findings.

(h) Provide an annual summary to the department of human services outlining the trends and patterns of child abuse and neglect fatalities, including information regarding the findings from cases known and unknown to the county departments of social services;

(i) Collaborate with the department of human services child fatality review team, created pursuant to section 26-1-139, C.R.S., to make joint recommendations for the prevention of child fatalities;

(j) (Deleted by amendment, L. 2013.)

(k) Subject to available appropriations, administer moneys to county or district public health agencies to support local or regional review team activities;

(l) Provide training and technical assistance to local or regional review teams regarding the facilitation of a child fatality review process, data collection, evidence-based prevention strategies, and the development of prevention recommendations. The training and technical assistance for local or regional review teams must be provided through federally funded training programs for improving effectiveness in conducting child fatality reviews; except that, if such federally funded programs are unavailable, the state, subject to available appropriations, may provide the training and technical assistance. The training and technical assistance may also include, but need not be limited to:

(I) Strategies or assistance with convening and facilitating local and regional review teams;

(II) Establishing methods of notification after a child fatality has occurred; and

(III) Strategies for members of state, local, or regional review teams to address a conflict of interest in a child fatality review;

(m) Provide an annual data report to each local or regional review team summarizing its local or regional review data entered into the web-based data-collection system;

(n) Subject to available appropriations and community resources, distribute information to the public concerning risks to children and recommendations for promoting the safety and well-being of children;

(o) Serve as a link with child fatality review teams throughout the country and participate in national child fatality review team activities; and

(p) Perform any other functions necessary to enhance the capability of the state of Colorado to reduce and prevent childhood injuries and fatalities.

## 25-20.5-408. Access to records.

(1) Review team access to records. (a) Notwithstanding any other state law to the contrary but subject to the requirements of applicable provisions of federal law, the state review team and the local or regional review teams shall have access to all records and information in the possession of the department of human services and the county departments of social services that are relevant to the review of a child fatality, including records and information related to previous reports and investigations of suspected child abuse or neglect.

(b) Except as otherwise provided in paragraph (c) of this subsection (1), notwithstanding any other state law to the contrary, but subject to the requirements of applicable provisions of federal law, the state review team and the local or regional review teams shall have access to all other records and information that are relevant to a review of a child fatality and that are in the possession of a state or local governmental agency. These records include, but are not limited to, birth certificates, records of coroner or medical examiner investigations, and records of the department of corrections.

(c) Treatment records for behavioral, mental health, or substance use disorders may be accessed only with the written consent of appropriate parties in accordance with applicable federal and state law.

(2) Public access to records and information. (a) Open meetings. Meetings of the state review team

668

and local or regional review teams shall be subject to the provisions of section 24-6-402, C.R.S.

(b) Confidentiality. Each member of the state review team, each member of a local or regional review team, and each invited participant at a meeting shall sign a statement indicating an understanding of and adherence to confidentiality requirements. A person who knowingly violates confidentiality requirements commits a class 3 misdemeanor and, upon conviction, shall be punished as provided in section 18-1.3-501, C.R.S.

(c) Release of information. (I) Members of the state review team, members of the local or regional review teams, a person who attends a review team meeting, and a person who presents information to a review team may release information to governmental agencies as necessary to fulfill the requirements of this part 4.

(II) Members of the state review team, members of the local or regional review teams, a person who attends a review team meeting, and a person who presents information to a review team shall not be subject to examination, in any civil or criminal proceeding, concerning information presented to members of the review team or opinions formed by the review team based on that information. A person may, however, be examined concerning information reviewed by the state review team or a local or regional review team that is otherwise available to the public or that is required to be revealed by that person in another official capacity.

(III) Information, documents, and records of the state review team and the local or regional review teams shall not be subject to subpoena, discovery, or introduction into evidence in any civil or criminal proceeding; except that information, documents, and records that would otherwise be available from a person serving on the state review team or a local or regional review team or that would otherwise be required to be revealed by law shall not be immune from subpoena, discovery, or introduction into evidence solely because the information was presented at or became available due to a proceeding of the state review team or a local or regional review team.

(IV) Information received by the state review team or a local or regional review team that contains information exculpatory to a person charged with a criminal offense shall be subject to release pursuant to the rules of criminal procedure.

## 25-20.5-409. Administration - funding - cash fund.

(1) To the extent moneys are available, the state review team and the local or regional review teams may hire staff or consultants to assist them in completing their duties.

(2) Staff and consultants of the state review team or the local or regional review teams shall receive reimbursement for travel and expenses to offset the costs incurred in fulfilling their duties, which shall be paid from moneys appropriated to implement this part 4 and within the limits of those moneys.

(3) The division of prevention services in the department of public health and environment, on behalf of the state review team, is authorized to receive contributions, grants, services, and donations from any public or private entity for any direct or indirect costs associated with the duties of the state review team set forth in this part 4.

(4) All private and public funds received by the state review team through grants, contributions, and donations pursuant to this part 4 shall be transmitted to the state treasurer, who shall credit the same to the child fatality prevention cash fund, which fund is hereby created and referred to in this section as the "fund". The moneys in the fund shall be subject to annual appropriation by the general assembly for the direct and indirect costs associated with the implementation of this part 4. All moneys in the fund not expended for the purpose of this part 4 may be invested by the state treasurer as provided by law. All interest and income derived from the investment and deposit of moneys in the fund shall be credited to the fund. Any unexpended and unencumbered moneys remaining in the fund at the end of a fiscal year shall remain in the fund and shall not be credited or transferred to the general fund or another fund.

# PART 5. SCHOOL-BASED HEALTH CENTER GRANT PROGRAM

## 25-20.5-501. Legislative declaration.

(1) The general assembly hereby finds that:

(a) Access to school-based primary health care for children and adolescents has been shown to increase the use of primary care, reduce the use of emergency rooms, and result in fewer hospitalizations;

(b) High-risk students who use school-based health centers are more likely to stay in school and be available for instruction;

(c) School-based health centers are effective at managing health conditions, such as asthma;

(d) School-based health centers serve primarily low-income schools. The majority of students who attend schools with on-site health centers are from low-income families, are medically uninsured or underinsured, and qualify for free or reduced-cost school lunch.

## 25-20.5-502. Definitions.

As used in this part 5, unless the context otherwise requires:

(1) "School-based health center" means a clinic established and operated within a public school building, including charter schools and state-sanctioned high school equivalency examination programs associated with a school district, or on public school property by the school district. School-based health centers are operated by school districts in cooperation with hospitals, public or private health care organizations, licensed medical providers, public health nurses, community health centers, and community mental health centers. The term "school-based health center" includes clinics or facilities authorized to provide clinic services pursuant to section 25.5-5-301, C.R.S., or authorized to apply for and receive medical assistance payments under a contract entered into pursuant to section 25.5-5-318, C.R.S.

## 25-20.5-503. School-based health center grant program - creation - funding - grants.

(1) There is hereby created, in the prevention services division of the department of public health and environment, the school-based health center grant program, referred to in this part 5 as the "grant program", for the purpose of assisting the establishment, expansion, and ongoing operations of school-based health centers in Colorado. The grant program shall be funded by moneys annually appropriated by the general assembly specifically for said program.

(2) Operators of school-based health centers may apply for grants for the benefit of school-based health centers. The grant program shall provide grants for school-based health centers selected by the division. The division, in consultation with school-based health centers, shall develop criteria under which the grants are distributed and evaluated. In developing the criteria for grants, the division shall give priority to centers that serve a disproportionate number of uninsured children or a low-income population or both and may award grants to establish new school-based health centers, to expand primary health services, behavioral health services, or oral health services offered by existing school-based health centers, to expand enrollment in the children's basic health plan, or to provide support for ongoing operations of school-based health centers. None of the grants shall be awarded to provide abortion services in violation of section 50 of article V of the state constitution.

(3) The division shall specify and provide to potential grant recipients the following information:

(a) Procedures and timelines by which an operator of a school-based health center may apply for a grant;

(b) Grant application contents;

(c) Criteria for selection, reporting, evaluation, and other criteria as necessary;

(d) Criteria for determining the amount and duration of the grants;

(e) Reporting requirements for grant recipients; and

(f) Any other information the division deems necessary.

(4) Grant recipients shall submit reports to the division as outlined in the reporting requirements summarizing the use of the grant moneys.

(5) A grant awarded by the division shall be used for the school-based health center for the purposes stated in this part 5. The grants shall supplement existing funding sources for the school-based health center, such as federal funds, patient fees, public and private insurance, and grants and donations, including in-kind donations received from community hospitals, foundations, local governments, and private sources.

# PART 6. PRIMARY CARE OFFICE

**25-20.5-601 to 25-20.5-605. (Repealed)**

# PART 7. STATE HEALTH CARE PROFESSIONAL LOAN REPAYMENT PROGRAM

**25-20.5-701 to 25-20.5- 706. (Repealed)**

# HEALTH CARE

# ARTICLE 21. DENTAL CARE

**25-21-101 to 25-21-109. (Repealed)**

# ARTICLE 21.5. CHILDREN'S DENTAL ASSISTANCE ANDFLUORIDATION PROGRAM

**25-21.5-101. Short title.**

This article shall be known and may be cited as the "Colorado Oral Health Community Grants Program Act".

**25-21.5-102. Legislative declaration.**

(1) The general assembly hereby finds and declares that:

(a) Statewide, students miss seven million eight hundred thousand school hours each year due to oral pain. Nationwide, workers miss one hundred sixty-four million work hours each year due to dental issues.

(b) Forty percent of children in kindergarten and fifty-five percent of children in third grade have a history of dental decay.

(c) Children in low-income schools have twice as much untreated tooth decay and are twice as likely to have a history of cavities than children who are not in low-income schools.

(d) Among children, ninety percent of dental decay is in the pits and fissures of posterior permanent teeth.

(e) Children who have received dental sealants in a school-based program have, for a period of up to five years, sixty percent fewer new decayed pit and fissure surfaces in their posterior permanent teeth than children who have not received an application of dental sealants.

(f) Fluoride is nature's cavity fighter. Fluoride occurs naturally in almost all water sources. Since 1948, scientific research has shown that community water fluoridation can reduce the incidence of dental cavities.

(g) Community water fluoridation is the process of adjusting the level of fluoride found naturally in water to a level recommended to protect against dental decay. The centers for disease control named community water fluoridation as one of ten great public health achievements of the twentieth century.

(h) Water fluoridation is safe and provides the most cost-effective means to prevent tooth decay for persons of all ages and socioeconomic backgrounds.

(i) Water fluoridation is one of the most researched and cost-effective oral health interventions available, as the average cost of one dental filling can fund a lifetime of fluoridation, which is known to prevent eighteen to forty percent of cavities in both children and adults.

(2) The general assembly further finds that improving access to oral health care services and fluoridated water for all Coloradans, particularly low-income Coloradans, will reduce the burden of oral disease. Therefore, the Colorado oral health program dedicates itself to improving access to oral health care services by working with community stakeholders, professional organizations, and direct recipients of oral health care to remove barriers to access to oral health care.

(3) The purpose of this article is to promote the public health and welfare of Coloradans by providing a grant program to:

(a) Provide oral health services, including sealants, to school children; and

(b) Assist communities in attaining optimal levels of fluoride in drinking water provided by community water systems as a means of preventing dental decay.

## 25-21.5-103. Definitions.

As used in this article, unless the context otherwise requires:

(1) Repealed.

(2) "Department" means the department of public health and environment.

(3) Repealed.

## 25-21.5-104. Oral health community grants program.

(1) Subject to available appropriations, the department shall administer a grant program to assist communities with:

(a) Implementing population-based, evidence-based strategies, including administering school dental sealant programs, to prevent dental decay in children;

(b) Assisting water systems, operators, and personnel, including water districts, with adjusting the level of fluoride in drinking water to optimal levels as a means of preventing dental decay in both children and adults; and

(c) Other oral health evidence-based programs that the department identifies and deems eligible for assistance.

(2) Subject to criteria that the department may establish, including the types of providers to whom

the department may award grants, the department shall award grants in the following categories:
(a) Oral health services that target children who are eligible for free and reduced-price lunches under the "Richard B. Russell National School Lunch Act", 42 U.S.C. sec. 1751 et seq., or who attend school in a school district whose median household income is at or below two hundred thirty-five percent of the federal poverty line. Grants awarded in this category may support the following:
(I) School-based programs that are conducted completely within the school setting;
(II) School-linked programs that are connected with schools but deliver services off-site;
(III) School-linked programs that conduct dental screenings at schools; and
(IV) Hybrid programs that incorporate school-based and school-linked components.
(b) Fluoridation support services, including:
(I) Assistance in the design, purchase, installation, maintenance, and inspection of equipment designed to add fluoride to drinking water to achieve optimal levels for the prevention of tooth decay, as determined by the federal department of health and human services;
(II) Training of water treatment personnel in the proper operation of fluoridation equipment and current water fluoridation practices; and
(III) Monitoring of fluoride content by obtaining monthly samples of finished drinking water to assure the optimal level of fluoride to prevent dental decay.

**25-21.5-105. Copayment - eligibility - children's dental plan cash fund - payment schedule. (Repealed)**

**25-21.5-106. Dental advisory committee - creation - repeal. (Repealed)**

**25-21.5-107. Donated dental services - contract. (Repealed)**

**25-21.5-108. Fluoridation of community water supplies - grants - rules. (Repealed)**

**25-21.5-109. No general fund moneys. (Repealed)**

# ARTICLE 22. STATE LOAN REPAYMENT PROGRAM

**25-22-101 to 25-22-104. (Repealed)**

# ARTICLE 23. DENTAL LOAN REPAYMENT PROGRAM

## 25-23-101. Legislative declaration.

(1) The general assembly hereby finds that:

(a) Many dental professionals, particularly dentists, graduate with large debt levels that were used to finance their professional education;

(b) Dentimistry is provided predominantly through individual practices, which minimizes the opportunity for dental professionals to provide unreimbursed services while maintaining the costs of a practice and repaying their educational loans;

(c) Many Colorado communities encounter difficulty recruiting dental providers dedicated to serving underserved populations;

(d) Incentives to reduce the indebtedness of dental professionals will increase access to dental care for underserved populations.

(2) The general assembly also finds that, during the 2000 regular session, the general assembly expanded the children's basic health plan to include dental services and paid for such expansion out of the tobacco settlement moneys, but, due to a lack of dental providers, the inclusion of dental care services was made contingent upon an adequate number of dental providers being willing to provide services. The general assembly hereby finds that the loan repayment program created in this article would provide a method to develop the infrastructure and resources needed to provide dental services as part of the children's basic health plan.

(3) The general assembly, therefore, states that the purpose of this article is to encourage and enable dental professionals to provide care through the children's basic health plan and the medicaid program and to other underserved populations in Colorado by the use of a financial incentive program.

## 25-23-102. Definitions.

As used in this article, unless the context otherwise requires:

(1) "Board" means the state board of health.

(2) "Eligible dental professional" means a person who is:

(a) A dentist licensed in Colorado pursuant to article 35 of title 12, C.R.S.; or

(b) A dental hygienist licensed in Colorado pursuant to article 35 of title 12, C.R.S.

(3) "Loan repayment assistance" means financial assistance in paying all or part of the principal, interest, and other related expenses of a loan for professional education in either dentistry or dental hygiene, whichever is appropriate.

(4) "Master settlement agreement" means the master settlement agreement, the smokeless tobacco master settlement agreement, and the consent decree approved and entered by the court in the case denominated State of Colorado, ex rel. Gale A. Norton, Attorney General v. R.J. Reynolds Tobacco Co.; American Tobacco Co., Inc.; Brown & Williamson Tobacco Corp.; Liggett & Myers, Inc.; Lorillard Tobacco Co., Inc.; Philip Morris, Inc.; United States Tobacco Co.; B.A.T. Industries, P.L.C.; The Council For Tobacco Research--U.S.A., Inc.; and Tobacco Institute, Inc., Case No. 97 CV 3432, in the district court for the city and county of Denver.

(5) "Underserved population" includes but is not limited to:

(a) Individuals eligible for medical assistance under articles 4, 5, and 6 of title 25.5, C.R.S.;

(b) Individuals enrolled in the children's basic health plan pursuant to article 8 of title 25.5, C.R.S.;

(c) Individuals eligible for medical services pursuant to the Colorado indigent care program set forth in part 1 of article 3 of title 25.5, C.R.S.;

(d) Individuals who are provided services by a dental professional and who are charged fees on a sliding scale based upon income or who are served without charge.

## 25-23-103. State loan repayment program for dentists and dental hygienists serving underserved populations - creation - conditions.

(1) Subject to available appropriations, the department of public health and environment shall develop and maintain a state dental loan repayment program in which the state agrees to pay all or part of the principal, interest, and related expenses of the educational loans of each eligible dental

professional. The department of public health and environment shall operate the program in cooperation with other health professional loan repayment programs.

(2) A dental professional is eligible for loan repayment assistance if the dental professional meets at least one of the following criteria:

(a) The dental professional is employed by a federally qualified health center;

(b) The dental professional owns or is employed by a practice that remains open to new clients enrolled in the medicaid program or the children's basic health plan program;

(c) The dental professional owns or is employed by a practice that provides a significant level of service to underserved populations as defined in rule by the board; or

(d) The dental professional provides, on a pro bono basis, a significant level of service to underserved populations.

(3) Loan repayments shall be available to eligible dental professionals on an annual basis, however, an eligible dental professional shall enter into a contract, as a condition of qualifying for the loan repayment assistance, in which the dental professional agrees to provide care to underserved populations for a minimum of two years. The department of public health and environment shall enter into contracts with eligible dental professionals on or after April 1, 2002.

(4) The board may establish the total amount of annual financial assistance available under the loan repayment program to any dental professional in order to promote recruitment and retention of a dental professional. Any contracts for loan repayment shall include reasonable penalties for breach of contract. In the event of a breach of contract for a loan repayment entered into pursuant to this article, the department of public health and environment shall be responsible for enforcing the contract and collecting any damages or other penalties owed.

(5) Nothing in this article shall be interpreted to create a legal entitlement to loan repayment assistance. The amount of assistance available is limited by available appropriations.

(6) The department of public health and environment may apply for any available matching federal funds on behalf of an eligible dental professional and shall use such federal funds to provide all or part of the financing for loan repayment for an eligible dental professional.

(7) Repealed.

## 25-23-104. Dental loan repayment fund - acceptance of grants and donations.

(1) The state dental loan repayment program shall be funded by moneys appropriated by the general assembly specifically for said program, moneys transferred thereto pursuant to subsection (2) of this section, and any matching funds or contributions received from any public or private sources. Such funds shall be transmitted to the treasurer, who shall credit the same to the state dental loan repayment fund, which fund is hereby created. At the end of any fiscal year, all unexpended and unencumbered moneys in the fund shall remain therein and shall not be credited or transferred to the general fund or any other fund. Moneys in the fund shall be used to provide loan repayment assistance to eligible dental professionals. Moneys in the fund may also be used to pay for the administrative costs of the department of public health and environment to implement the loan repayment program; except that administrative costs shall not exceed ten percent.

(2) Pursuant to section 24-75-1104.5 (1.7) (m) , C.R.S., for fiscal year 2016-17 and for each fiscal year thereafter so long as the state receives moneys pursuant to the master settlement agreement, the state treasurer shall transfer to the state dental loan repayment fund one percent of the moneys received by the state pursuant to the master settlement agreement for the preceding fiscal year. The state treasurer shall transfer the amount specified in this subsection (2) from moneys credited to the tobacco litigation settlement cash fund created in section 24-22-115, C.R.S. Moneys in the fund are subject to annual appropriation by the general assembly for the purposes of this article. The amount appropriated pursuant to this subsection (2) is in addition to and not in replacement of any general fund moneys appropriated to the state dental loan repayment fund.

(3) The department of public health and environment is authorized to receive contributions, grants, and services from public and private sources to carry out the purposes of this article.

## 25-23-105. Board - rule-making authority.

The board is authorized to promulgate rules necessary to implement the loan repayment program authorized in this article, including determining the amount of financial assistance available; establishing the criteria in section 25-23-103 (2) for loan repayment assistance and the criteria for determining what constitutes a significant level of service to underserved populations for purposes of qualifying for loan repayment assistance; and establishing criteria for prioritizing the repayment of loans if there are insufficient moneys in the state dental loan repayment fund.

# ARTICLE 25. COLORADO HEALTH FACILITIES AUTHORITY

## 25-25-101. Short title.

This article shall be known and may be cited as the "Colorado Health Facilities Authority Act".

## 25-25-102. Legislative declaration.

(1) The general assembly hereby finds and declares that, for the benefit of the people of the state of Colorado and the improvement of their health, welfare, and living conditions:

(a) It is essential that the people of this state have adequate medical care and health facilities;

(b) It is important that medical care and health facilities are made readily available by networks and organizations of health institutions, whether such networks and organizations are located within the state of Colorado or have facilities located both within and outside the state of Colorado;

(c) It is a benefit to the people of the state of Colorado to serve such multistate institutions, as such service will create health care-related employment opportunities;

(d) It is essential that health institutions that have headquarters in Colorado or that operate or manage health facilities in Colorado, and affiliates of such health institutions, be provided with appropriate additional means to assist in the development and maintenance of public health, health care, hospitals, and related facilities wherever such health institutions are located in order that they can provide more adequate medical care and health facilities to the people of Colorado;

(e) It is the purpose of this article to provide a measure of assistance to enable health institutions in the state to refund or refinance outstanding indebtedness incurred for health facilities and to provide additional facilities and structures that are greatly needed to accomplish the purposes of this article; and

(f) The exemption of bonds and notes issued pursuant to this article from all taxation and assessments in the state of Colorado benefit only the residents of the state of Colorado.

(2) It is the intent of the general assembly to create the Colorado health facilities authority to lend money to health institutions and to authorize the authority to acquire, construct, reconstruct, repair, alter, improve, extend, own, lease, and dispose of properties so that the authority may be able to promote the health and welfare of the people of this state and develop health care-related employment opportunities for the people of this state. In enacting this article, it is the intent of the general assembly to vest the authority with the powers necessary to accomplish these purposes. However, it is not the intent of the general assembly to authorize the authority to operate a health facility.

(3) This article shall be liberally construed to accomplish the intentions expressed in this section.

## 25-25-103. Definitions.

As used in this article, unless the context otherwise requires:

(1) "Authority" means the Colorado health facilities authority created by this article.

(2) "Board" means the board of directors of the authority.

(3) "Bond", "note", "bond anticipation note", or "other obligation" means any bond, note, debenture, interim certificate, or other evidence of financial indebtedness issued by the authority pursuant to this article, including refunding bonds.

(4) "Bond resolution" means the resolution authorizing the issuance of, or providing terms and conditions related to, bonds issued under the provisions of this article and includes any trust agreement, trust indenture, indenture of mortgage, or deed of trust providing terms and conditions for such bonds.

(5) "Costs", as applied to facilities financed in whole or in part under the provisions of this article, means and includes the sum total of all reasonable or necessary costs incidental to:

(a) The acquisition, construction, reconstruction, repair, alteration, equipment, enlargement, improvement, and extension of such facilities; and

(b) The acquisition of all lands, structures, real or personal property, rights, rights-of-way, franchises, easements, and interest acquired, necessary, or used for, or useful for or in connection with, a facility; and

(c) All other undertakings that the authority deems reasonable or necessary for the development of a facility, including, without limitation, the cost of or for:

(I) Studies and surveys;

(II) Land title and mortgage guaranty policies;

(III) Plans, specifications, and architectural and engineering services;

(IV) Legal, accounting, organization, marketing, or other special services;

(V) Financing, acquisition, demolition, construction, equipment, and site development of new and rehabilitated buildings;

(VI) Rehabilitation, reconstruction, repair, or remodeling of existing buildings; and

(VII) All other necessary and incidental expenses, including working capital and an initial bond and interest reserve funds, together with interest on bonds issued to finance such facilities to the extent permitted under applicable federal tax law.

(6) (a) "Health facility" or "facility", in the case of a participating health institution, means any structure or building, whether such structure or building is located within the state or whether such structure or building is located outside the state if an out-of-state health institution that operates or manages such structure or building, or an affiliate of such institution, also operates or manages a health facility within this state, suitable for use as a hospital, clinic, nursing home, home for the aged or infirm, or other health care facility; laboratory; pharmacy; laundry; nurses', doctors', or interns' residences; administration building; research facility; maintenance, storage, or utility facility; auditorium; dining hall; food service and preparation facility; mental or physical health care facility; dental care facility; nursing school; medical or dental teaching facility; mental or physical health facilities related to any such structure or facility; or any other structure or facility required or useful for the operation of a health institution, including but not limited to offices, parking lots and garages, and other supporting service structures; and any equipment, furnishings, appurtenances, or other assets, tangible or intangible, including but not limited to assets related to the medical practice of a health care professional, that are necessary or useful in the development, establishment, or operation of a participating health institution; and the acquisition, preparation, and development of all real and personal property necessary or convenient as a site or sites for any such structure or facility.

(b) "Health facility" or "facility" does not include the following:

(I) Food, fuel, supplies, or other items that are customarily considered as a current operating expense or charges;

(II) Property used or to be used primarily for sectarian instruction or study or as a place for devotional activities or religious worship; or

(III) Property used or to be used primarily in connection with any part of a program of a school or department of divinity of any religious denomination.

(7) (a) "Health institution" means a limited liability company controlled directly or indirectly by one or more nonprofit entities, a private nonprofit hospital, corporation, association, or institution, or a public hospital or institution authorized or permitted by law, whether directly or indirectly

through one or more affiliates, to provide, operate, or manage one or more health facilities in this state or outside this state if such entity, or an affiliate of such entity, also operates or manages a health facility within this state.

(b) "Health institution" also includes a cooperative hospital service organization, as described in section 501 (e) of the "Internal Revenue Code of 1986", as amended, or a similar corporation, whether or not such corporation is exempt from federal income taxation pursuant to said section 501 (e) .

(c) (I) "Health institution" also includes a network of health care providers, however organized; an integrated health care delivery system; a joint venture or partnership between or among health care providers; a health care purchasing alliance; health insurers and third-party administrators that are participants in a system, network, joint venture, or partnership that provides health services; an organization whose primary purpose is to provide supporting services to one or more health institutions; or a health care provider or such other health care-related organization, or an affiliate of such organization, whose regional or national headquarters are located in this state.

(II) In order to be a health institution, a network, system, joint venture, partnership, alliance, provider, or organization described in subparagraph (I) of this paragraph (c) shall be a nonprofit entity or controlled by one or more nonprofit entities.

(7.5) "Participating health institution" means a health institution that undertakes the financing and construction or acquisition of health facilities or undertakes the refunding or refinancing of outstanding obligations in accordance with this article.

(8) "Refinancing of outstanding obligations" means liquidation, with the proceeds of bonds or notes issued by the authority, of any indebtedness of a participating health institution incurred prior to, on, or after July 1, 1977, to finance or aid in financing a lawful purpose of such health institution not financed pursuant to this article which would constitute a facility had it been undertaken and financed by the authority, or consolidation of such indebtedness with indebtedness of the authority incurred for a facility related to the purpose for which the indebtedness of the health institution was initially incurred.

(9) "Revenues" means, with respect to facilities, the rents, fees, charges, interest, principal repayments, and other income received or to be received by the authority from any source on account of such facilities.

## 25-25-104. Colorado health facilities authority - creation - membership - appointment - terms - vacancies - removal.

(1) There is hereby created an independent public body politic and corporate to be known as the Colorado health facilities authority. Said authority is constituted a public instrumentality, and its exercise of the powers conferred by this article shall be deemed and held to be the performance of an essential public function. The authority shall be a body corporate and a political subdivision of the state and shall not be an agency of state government and shall not be subject to administrative direction by any department, commission, board, or agency of the state.

(2) The governing body of the authority shall be a board of directors which shall consist of seven members to be appointed by the governor, with the consent of the senate. Such members shall be residents of the state. No more than four of the members shall be of the same political party. The members of the board first appointed shall serve for terms to be designated by the governor, expiring on June 30 of each year beginning in 1978 and ending in 1984. Persons holding office on June 15, 1987, are subject to the provisions of section 24-1-137, C.R.S. Thereafter, upon the expiration of the term of any member, his successor shall be appointed for a term of four years. Each member shall serve until his resignation or, in the case of a member whose term has expired, until his successor has been appointed and qualified. Any member shall be eligible for reappointment. The governor shall fill any vacancy by appointment for the remainder of an unexpired term. Any member appointed by the governor when the general assembly is not in regular session, whether appointed for an unexpired term or for a full term, shall be deemed to be duly appointed and qualified until the appointment of such member is approved or rejected by the

senate. Such appointment shall be submitted to the senate for its approval or rejection during the next regular session of the general assembly following the appointment.

(3) (a) Any member of the board may be removed by the governor for misfeasance, malfeasance, willful neglect of duty, or other cause, after notice and a public hearing, unless such notice and hearing shall be expressly waived in writing.

(b) Notwithstanding the provisions of paragraph (a) of this subsection (3) , a member shall be removed by the governor if such member fails, for reasons other than temporary mental or physical disability or illness, to attend three regular meetings of the board during any twelve-month period without the board having entered upon its minutes an approval for any of such absences.

## 25-25-105. Organization meeting - chair - executive director - surety bond - conflict of interest.

(1) A member of the board, designated by the governor, shall call and convene the initial organizational meeting of the board and shall serve as its chair pro tempore. At such meeting, appropriate bylaws shall be presented for adoption. The board's bylaws may provide for the election or appointment of officers, the delegation of certain powers and duties, and such other matters as the authority deems proper. At such meeting and annually thereafter, the board shall elect one of its members as chair and one as vice-chair. It shall appoint an executive director and, if desired, an associate executive director and any other officer designated by the board, who shall not be members of the board and who shall serve at its pleasure. They shall receive such compensation for their services as shall be fixed by the board.

(2) The executive director, the associate executive director, or any other person designated by the board shall keep a record of the board's proceedings and shall be custodian of all books, documents, and papers filed with the board, the minute books or journal, and the official seal of the authority. This person may make copies of the minutes and other records and documents of the board and may certify under the official seal of the authority that such copies are true copies. All persons dealing with the authority may rely on such certifications.

(3) The board may delegate, by resolution, to one or more of its members or to its executive director, associate executive director, or any other officer designated by the board, such powers and duties as it may deem proper.

(4) (a) Before the issuance of any bonds under this article, the executive director, associate executive director, and any other officer designated by the board shall each execute a surety bond in the penal sum of one hundred thousand dollars, and each member of the board shall execute a surety bond in the penal sum of fifty thousand dollars.

(b) In lieu of the surety bonds required by paragraph (a) of this subsection (4) , the chair of the board may execute a blanket bond covering each member, the executive director, the associate executive director, and the employees or other officers of the authority.

(c) Each surety bond shall be conditioned upon the faithful performance of the duties of the office or offices covered and shall be executed by a surety authorized to transact business in this state as surety. The cost of each such bond shall be paid by the authority.

(5) Notwithstanding any other law to the contrary, it shall not constitute a conflict of interest for a trustee, director, officer, or employee of any health institution, financial institution, investment banking firm, brokerage firm, commercial bank or trust company, architecture firm, insurance company, or other firm, person, or corporation to serve as a member of the board; except that such trustee, director, officer, or employee shall disclose such interest to the board and shall abstain from deliberation, action, and voting by the board in each instance where the business affiliation of any such trustee, director, officer, or employee is involved.

## 25-25-106. Meetings of board - quorum - expenses.

(1) Four members of the board shall constitute a quorum for the purpose of conducting business and exercising its powers. Action may be taken by the board upon the affirmative vote of at least

four of its members. A vacancy in the membership of the board shall not impair the right of a quorum of the board to exercise all the rights and perform all the duties of the board.

(2) Each meeting of the board for any purpose whatsoever shall be open to the public. Notice of meetings shall be as provided in the bylaws of the authority. One or more members of the board may participate in a meeting of the board or a committee of the board and may vote on resolutions presented at the meeting through the use of telecommunications devices, including, but not limited to, a conference telephone or similar communications equipment. Participation through telecommunications devices shall constitute presence in person at the meeting. The use of telecommunications devices shall not supersede any requirements for public hearing otherwise provided by law. Resolutions need not be published or posted, but resolutions and all proceedings and other acts of the board shall be a public record.

(3) Members of the board shall receive no compensation for services but shall be entitled to the necessary expenses, including traveling and lodging expenses, incurred in the discharge of their official duties. Any payments for expenses shall be paid from funds of the authority.

## 25-25-107. General powers of authority.

(1) In addition to any other powers granted to the authority by this article, the authority shall have the following powers:

(a) To have perpetual existence and succession as a body politic and corporate;

(b) To adopt and from time to time amend or repeal bylaws for the regulation of its affairs and the conduct of its business, consistent with the provisions of this article;

(c) To sue and be sued;

(d) To have and to use a seal and to alter the same at pleasure;

(e) To maintain an office at such place or places as it may designate;

(f) To determine, in accordance with the provisions of this article, the location and character of any facility to be financed under the provisions of this article; to acquire, construct, reconstruct, renovate, improve, alter, replace, maintain, repair, operate, and lease as lessee or lessor; to enter into contracts for any and all of such purposes and for the management and operation of a facility; and to designate a participating health institution as its agent to determine the location and character of a facility undertaken by such participating health institution under the provisions of this article and, as agent of the authority, to acquire, construct, reconstruct, renovate, replace, alter, improve, maintain, repair, operate, lease as lessee or lessor, and regulate the same, and, as agent of the authority, to enter into contracts for any and all of such purposes including contracts for the management and operation of such facility;

(g) To lease to a participating health institution any or all of the facilities upon such terms and conditions as the authority shall deem proper; to charge and collect rent therefor and to terminate any such lease upon the failure of the lessee to comply with any of the obligations thereof; and to include in any such lease, if desired, provisions that the lessee thereof shall have options to renew the term of the lease for such period or periods, at such rent, and upon such terms or conditions as shall be determined by the authority or to purchase any or all of the facilities, or provisions that, upon payment of all of the indebtedness incurred by the authority for the financing of such facilities, the authority will convey any or all of the facilities to the lessee or lessees thereof with or without consideration;

(h) To borrow money and to issue bonds, notes, bond anticipation notes, or other obligations for any of its corporate purposes and to fund or refund the same, all as provided for in this article;

(i) To establish rules and regulations and to designate a participating health institution as its agent to establish such rules and regulations, for the use of the facilities undertaken or operated by such participating health institution; to employ or contract for consulting engineers, architects, attorneys, accountants, construction and financial experts, superintendents, managers, and such other employees and agents as may be necessary in its judgment and to fix their compensation;

(j) To receive and accept from the federal government, the state of Colorado, or any other public agency loans, grants, or contributions for or in aid of the construction of facilities or any portion thereof, or for equipping the same, and to receive and accept grants, gifts, or other contributions from any source; and to use such funds only for the purposes for which they were loaned, contributed, or granted;

(k) To mortgage or pledge all or any portion of the facilities and the site or sites thereof, whether then owned or thereafter acquired, for the benefit of the holders of bonds issued to finance such facilities or any portion thereof;

(l) To make mortgage or other secured or unsecured loans to any participating health institution for the cost of the facilities in accordance with an agreement between the authority and such participating health institution; but no such loan shall exceed the total cost of such facilities as determined by such participating health institution and approved by the authority;

(m) To make mortgage loans or other secured or unsecured loans to a participating health institution; to refund outstanding obligations, mortgages, or advances issued, made, or given by such institution for the cost of its facilities, including the issuance of bonds and the making of loans to a participating health institution; and to refinance outstanding obligations and indebtedness incurred for facilities undertaken and completed prior to, on, or after July 1, 1977, when the authority makes a finding consistent with section 25-25-115 (1) ;

(n) To obtain, or aid in obtaining, from any department or agency of the United States or of this state or any private company, any insurance or guarantee as to, or of, or for the payment or repayment of interest or principal, or both, or any part thereof, on any loan, lease, or obligation or any instrument evidencing or securing the same, made or entered into pursuant to the provisions of this article; and, notwithstanding any other provisions of this article, to enter into any agreement, contract, or any other instrument whatsoever with respect to any such insurance or guarantee, to accept payment in such manner and form as provided therein in the event of default by a participating health institution, and to assign any such insurance or guarantee as security for the authority's bonds;

(o) To do all things necessary and convenient to carry out the purposes of this article;

(p) To charge to and equitably apportion among participating health institutions its administrative costs and expenses incurred in the exercise of the powers granted and duties conferred by this article;

(q) To make and execute contracts and all other instruments necessary or convenient for the exercise of its powers and functions under this article;

(r) To assist, coordinate, and participate with other issuers of tax-exempt bonds and public officials in other states in connection with financing on behalf of a multistate health institution;

(s) In connection with financing on behalf of a multistate health institution:

(I) To determine or agree upon who will be assisting, coordinating, or participating issuers of tax-exempt bonds in other states;

(II) To determine or agree upon what the terms or conditions of the financing will be with assisting, coordinating, or participating issuers of tax-exempt bonds in other states; and

(III) To charge fees to, apportion fees among, or agree upon fees with assisting, coordinating, or participating issuers of tax-exempt bonds in other states.

(2) The authority shall not have the power to operate the facilities as a business other than as a lessee or lessor. Notwithstanding anything contained in this subsection (2) to the contrary, the authority shall have the power to enter into leases which are annually renewable with a public hospital or institution. Any lease of the facilities entered into pursuant to the provisions of this article shall provide for rentals adequate to pay principal and interest on any bonds issued to finance such facilities as the same fall due and to create and maintain such reserves and accounts for depreciation as the authority shall determine to be necessary.

## 25-25-108. Acquisition of property.

The authority may, directly or by or through a participating health institution as its agent, acquire by purchase, lease, gift, devise, or otherwise such lands, structures, real or personal property, rights-of-way, franchises, easements, and other interests in lands, including lands lying under water and riparian rights which are located within or without the state, as it may deem necessary or convenient for the construction, acquisition, or operation of facilities, upon such terms as may be considered by the authority to be reasonable, and may take title thereto in the name of the authority or in the name of such participating health institution as its agent.

## 25-25-109. Notes.

The authority may issue from time to time its negotiable notes for any corporate purpose, including the payment of all or any part of the cost of any facility, and may renew from time to time any notes by the issuance of new notes, whether the notes to be renewed have or have not matured. The authority may issue notes partly to renew notes or to discharge other obligations then outstanding and partly for any other purpose. The notes may be authorized, sold, executed, and delivered in the same manner as bonds. Any resolution or resolutions authorizing notes of the authority or any issue thereof may contain any provisions which the authority is authorized to include in any resolution or resolutions authorizing bonds of the authority or any issue thereof, and the authority may include in any notes any terms, covenants, or conditions which it is authorized to include in any bonds. All such notes shall be payable from the proceeds of bonds or renewal notes or from the revenues of the authority or other moneys available therefor and not otherwise pledged, subject only to any contractual rights of the holders of any of its notes or other obligations then outstanding.

## 25-25-110. Bonds.

(1) The authority may issue from time to time its bonds in such principal amount as the authority shall determine for the purpose of financing all or a part of the cost of any health institutions or any facilities authorized by this article or for the refinancing of outstanding obligations. In anticipation of the sale of such bonds, the authority may issue bond anticipation notes and may renew the same from time to time. Such notes shall be paid from any revenues of the authority or other moneys available therefor and not otherwise pledged, or from the proceeds of the sale of the bonds of the authority in anticipation of which they were issued. The notes shall be issued in the same manner as bonds. Such notes and the resolution or resolutions authorizing them may contain any provisions, conditions, or limitations which a bond resolution of the authority may contain.

(2) The bonds may be issued as serial bonds, as term bonds, or as a combination of both types. All bonds issued by the authority shall be payable solely out of the revenues and receipts derived from the leasing, mortgaging, or sale by the authority of the facilities concerned or of any part thereof as designated in the resolutions of the authority under which the bonds are authorized to be issued or as designated in a trust indenture authorized by the authority, which trust indenture shall name a bank or trust company in Colorado, or outside of Colorado if it is determined by the authority to be in the best interests of the financing, such determination to be conclusive, as trustee, or out of other moneys available therefor and not otherwise pledged. Such bonds may be issued and delivered by the authority at such times and in such manner, may be in such form and denominations and include such terms and maturities, may be in fully registered form or in bearer form registerable either as to principal or interest or both, may bear such conversion privileges, may be payable in such installments and at such time or times not exceeding forty years after the date thereof, may be payable at such place or places whether within or without the state of Colorado, may bear interest at such rate or rates per annum as shall be determined by the authority or as shall be determined by any formula prescribed by the authority or as may be determined from time to time by a designated agent of the authority in accordance with specified standards and procedures and without regard to any interest rate limitation appearing in any other law, may be evidenced in such manner, may be in the form of coupon bonds that have attached thereto interest coupons bearing the facsimile signature of an authorized officer of the authority, and may contain such provisions not inconsistent with this article, all as shall be provided in the resolutions of the authority under which the bonds are authorized to be issued or as is provided in a trust indenture authorized by the authority. Notwithstanding anything in this subsection (2) to the

contrary, in the case of short-term notes or other obligations maturing not later than one year after the date of issuance thereof, the board may authorize the executive director, associate executive director, or any officer of the board to fix principal amounts, maturity dates, interest rates, and purchase prices of any particular issue of such short-term notes or obligations, subject to such limitations as to maximum term, maximum principal amount outstanding, and maximum net effective interest rates as the board shall prescribe by resolution, and such authorization shall remain effective for the period of time designated in the initial resolution regardless of whether the composition of the board changes in the interim unless sooner rescinded by the board.

(3) If deemed advisable by the authority, there may be retained in the resolutions or the trust indenture under which any bonds of the authority are authorized to be issued an option to redeem all or any part thereof as may be specified in such resolutions or in such trust indenture, at such price or prices, after such notice or notices, and on such terms and conditions as may be set forth in such resolutions or in such trust indenture and as may be briefly recited on the face of the bonds; but nothing in this article shall be construed to confer on the authority the right or option to redeem any bonds except as may be provided in the resolutions or in such trust indenture under which they are issued.

(4) The bonds or notes of the authority may be sold at public or private sale for such price or prices, in such manner, and at such times as may be determined by the authority, and the authority may pay all expenses, premiums, and commissions that it may deem necessary or advantageous in connection with the issuance thereof. The power to fix the date of sale of bonds and notes, to receive bids or proposals, to award and sell bonds and notes, and to take all other necessary action to sell and issue bonds and notes may be delegated to the executive director, associate executive director, or any officer of the board of the authority by resolution of the authority. Pending preparation of the definitive bonds, the authority may issue interim receipts or certificates, which shall be exchanged for the definitive bonds.

(5) (a) Issuance by the authority of one or more series of bonds for one or more purposes shall not preclude it from issuing other bonds in connection with the same facilities, any other facilities, or any other purpose under this article, but the resolutions or trust indenture under which any subsequent bonds may be issued shall recognize the terms and provisions of any prior pledge or mortgage made for any prior issue of bonds and the terms upon which such additional bonds may be issued and secured. Any outstanding bonds of the authority may at any time and from time to time be refunded or advance refunded by the authority by the issuance of its bonds for such purpose and in a principal amount as may be determined by the authority, which may include interest accrued or to accrue thereon with or without giving effect to investment income thereon and other expenses necessary to be paid in connection therewith. If deemed advisable by the authority, such bonds may be refunded or advance refunded for the additional purpose of paying all or any part of the cost of constructing and acquiring additions, improvements, extensions, or enlargements of a facility or any portion thereof.

(b) Any such refunding may be effected whether the bonds to be refunded shall have then matured or shall thereafter mature either by sale of the refunding bonds and the application of the proceeds thereof for the payment of the bonds to be refunded thereby or by the exchange of the refunding bonds for the bonds to be refunded thereby with the consent of the holders of the bonds to be so refunded, regardless of whether or not the bonds to be refunded were issued in connection with the same facilities or separate facilities or for any other purpose under this article and regardless of whether or not the bonds proposed to be refunded shall be payable on the same date or different dates or shall be due serially or otherwise. The proceeds of any such bonds issued for the purpose of refunding outstanding bonds may, in the discretion of the authority, be applied to the purchase or retirement at maturity or redemption of such outstanding bonds either on their earliest or any subsequent redemption date or upon the purchase or at the maturity thereof and may, pending such application, be placed in escrow to be applied to such purchase or retirement at maturity or redemption on such date as may be determined by the authority. Any such escrowed proceeds, pending such use, may be invested or deposited in securities or depositories meeting the requirements established in part 6 of article 75 of title 24, C.R.S. The interest, income, and profit, if any, earned or realized on any such investment may also, in the discretion of the authority, be applied to the payment of the outstanding bonds or notes to be so refunded or to the payment of principal and interest on the refunding bonds or for any other purpose under this article. After the terms of the escrow have been fully satisfied and carried out, any balance of such proceeds and interest, income, and profits, if any, earned or realized on the investments thereof may be returned to the authority for use by it in any lawful manner. The portion of the proceeds of any such bonds issued for the additional purpose of paying all or any part of the cost of constructing and acquiring additions, improvements, extensions, or enlargements of a facility may be invested or deposited in securities or depositories meeting the requirements established in part 6 of article 75 of title 24, C.R.S. The interest, income, and profits, if any, earned or realized on such investment may be applied to the payment of all or any part of such cost or may be used by the authority in any lawful manner. All such bonds shall be subject to the provisions of this article in the same manner and to the same extent as other bonds issued pursuant to this article.

## 25-25-111. Negotiability of bonds.

All bonds and the interest coupons applicable thereto are hereby declared and shall be construed to be negotiable instruments.

## 25-25-112. Security for bonds and notes.

(1) The principal of and interest on any bonds or notes issued by the authority may be secured by a pledge of, or security interest in, the revenues, rentals, and receipts out of which the same may be made payable or from other moneys available therefor and not otherwise pledged or used as security and may be secured by a trust indenture, mortgage, or deed of trust (including assignment of leases or other contract rights of the authority thereunder) covering all or any part of the facilities from which the revenues, rentals, or receipts so pledged or used as security may be derived, including any enlargements of and additions to any such facility thereafter made. The resolution under which the bonds are authorized to be issued and any such trust indenture, mortgage, or deed of trust may contain any agreements and provisions which shall be a part of the contract with the holders of the bonds or notes to be authorized as to:

(a) Pledging or providing a security interest in all or any part of the revenues of a facility or any revenue-producing contract or contracts made by the authority with any individual, partnership, corporation, or association or other body, public or private, to secure the payment of the bonds or notes or of any particular issue of bonds, subject to such agreements with noteholders or bondholders as may then exist;

(b) Maintenance of the properties covered thereby;

(c) Fixing and collection of mortgage payments, rents, fees, and other charges to be charged and the amounts to be raised in each year thereby, and the use and disposition of the revenues;

(d) Setting aside, creation, and maintenance of special and reserve funds and sinking funds and the use and disposition of the revenues;

(e) Limitations on the right of the authority or its agent to restrict and regulate the use of the facilities;

(f) Limitations on the purpose to which the proceeds of sale of any issue of bonds or notes then or thereafter to be issued may be applied, and pledging or providing a security interest in such proceeds to secure the payment of the bonds or notes or any issue of the bonds or notes;

(g) Limitations on the issuance of additional bonds, the terms upon which additional bonds may be issued and secured, and the refunding of outstanding bonds;

(h) The procedure, if any, by which the terms of any contract with bondholders or noteholders may be amended or abrogated, the amount of bonds or notes the holders of which must consent thereto, and the manner in which such consent may be given;

(i) Limitations on the amount of moneys derived from a facility to be expended for operating, administrative, or other expenses of the authority;

(j) Defining the acts or omissions to act which shall constitute a default in the duties of the authority to holders of its obligations and providing the rights and remedies of such holders in the event of a default;

(k) Mortgaging of a facility and the site thereof for the purpose of securing the bondholders or noteholders;

(l) Such other additional covenants, agreements, and provisions as are judged advisable or necessary by the authority for the security of the holders of such bonds or notes.

(2) Any pledge made by the authority shall be valid and binding from the time when the pledge is made. The revenues, moneys, or property so pledged and thereafter received by the authority shall immediately be subject to the lien of such pledge without any physical delivery thereof or further act, and the lien of such pledge shall be valid and binding as against all parties having claims of any kind in tort, contract, or otherwise against the authority, irrespective of whether such parties have notice thereof. Neither the resolution nor any other instrument by which a pledge is created need be recorded. Each pledge, agreement, lease, indenture, mortgage, and deed of trust made for the benefit or security of any of the bonds of the authority shall continue to be effective until the principal of and interest on the bonds for the benefit of which the same were made shall have been fully paid or provision for such payment duly made. In the event of default in such payment or in any agreements of the authority made as a part of the contract under which the bonds were issued, whether contained in the resolutions authorizing the bonds or in any trust indenture, mortgage, or deed of trust executed as security therefor, said payment or agreement may be enforced by suit, mandamus, the appointment of a receiver in equity, foreclosure of any mortgage and deed of trust, or any one or more of said remedies.

(3) In addition to the provisions of subsections (1) and (2) of this section, bonds of the authority may be secured by a pooling of leases, loans, or mortgages whereby the authority may assign its rights, as lessor, lender, or mortgagee, and pledge rents, loan payments, or mortgage payments under two or more leases, loans, or mortgages, with two or more participating health institutions as lessees, borrowers, or mortgagors, respectively, upon such terms as may be provided for in the resolutions of the authority or as may be provided for in a trust indenture or mortgage or deed of trust authorized by the authority.

## 25-25-113. Personal liability.

Neither the members of the authority nor any person executing the bonds or notes shall be liable personally on bonds or notes or be subject to any personal liability or accountability by reason of the issuance thereof.

## 25-25-114. Purchase.

The authority may purchase its bonds or notes out of any funds available therefor. The authority may hold, pledge, cancel, or resell such bonds or notes, subject to and in accordance with agreements with bondholders or noteholders.

## 25-25-115. Procedure concerning issuance of bonds.

(1) Notwithstanding any other provisions of this article, the authority may not undertake any facility authorized by this article unless, prior to the issuance of any bonds or notes, the board finds that the facility will enable or assist a health institution to fulfill its obligation to provide health facilities.

(2) (Deleted by amendment, L. 2007, p. 416, § 7, effective August 3, 2007.)

## 25-25-116. Trust agreement to secure bonds.

(1) In the discretion of the authority, any bonds issued under this article may be secured by a trust agreement between the authority and a corporate trustee or trustees. A corporate trustee may be any trust company or bank in Colorado. If the authority determines it to be in the best interests of the financing, a trust company or bank outside of Colorado may be a corporate trustee. The trust agreement or the resolution providing for the issuance of the bonds may pledge or assign the

revenues to be received or the proceeds of any contract or contracts pledged and may convey or mortgage the facilities or any portion of the facilities. The trust agreement or resolution providing for the issuance of the bonds may contain provisions for protecting and enforcing the rights and remedies of the bondholders that are reasonable, proper, and not in violation of law, including provisions that have been specifically authorized to be included in any resolution or resolutions of the authority authorizing the bonds.

(2) Any bank or trust company incorporated under the laws of this state that may act as depository of the proceeds of bonds or of revenues or other moneys may furnish such indemnifying bonds or pledge such securities as may be required by the authority. A trust agreement may set forth the rights and remedies of the bondholders and of the trustee or trustees and may restrict the individual right of action by bondholders. In addition, the trust agreement or resolution may contain such other provisions as the authority may deem reasonable and proper for the security of the bondholders. All expenses incurred in carrying out such trust agreement or resolution may be treated as a part of the cost of the operation of a facility.

## 25-25-117. Payment of bonds - nonliability of state.

Bonds and notes issued by the authority shall not constitute or become an indebtedness, a debt, or a liability of the state, the general assembly, or any county, city, city and county, town, school district, or other subdivision of the state, or of any other political subdivision or body corporate and politic within the state, and neither the state, the general assembly, nor any county, city, city and county, town, school district, or other subdivision of the state shall be liable thereon; nor shall such bonds or notes constitute the giving, pledging, or loaning of the faith and credit of the state, the general assembly, or any county, city, city and county, town, school district, or other subdivision of the state, or of any other political subdivision or body corporate and politic within the state but shall be payable solely from the funds provided for in this article. The issuance of bonds or notes under the provisions of this article shall not, directly, indirectly, or contingently, obligate the state or any subdivision thereof nor empower the authority to levy or collect any form of taxes or assessments therefor, or to create any indebtedness payable out of taxes or assessments therefor or make any appropriation for their payment, and such appropriation or levy is prohibited. Nothing in this section shall prevent or be construed to prevent the authority from pledging its full faith and credit or the full faith and credit of a participating health institution to the payment of bonds or notes authorized pursuant to this article. Nothing in this article shall be construed to authorize the authority to create a debt of the state within the meaning of the constitution or statutes of Colorado or to authorize the authority to levy or collect taxes or assessments; and all bonds issued by the authority pursuant to the provisions of this article are payable and shall state that they are payable solely from the funds pledged for their payment in accordance with the resolution authorizing their issuance or with any trust indenture, mortgage, or deed of trust executed as security therefor and are not a debt or liability of the state of Colorado. The state shall not in any event be liable for the payment of the principal of or interest on any bonds of the authority or for the performance of any pledge, mortgage, obligation, or agreement of any kind whatsoever which may be undertaken by the authority. No breach of any such pledge, mortgage, obligation, or agreement shall impose any pecuniary liability upon the state or any charge upon its general credit or against its taxing power.

## 25-25-118. Exemption from taxation - securities law.

The authority is hereby declared to be a public instrumentality of the state, performing a public function for the benefit of the people of the state for the improvement of their health and living conditions. Accordingly, the income or other revenues of the authority, all properties at any time owned by the authority, any bonds, notes, or other obligations issued under this article, the transfer thereof and the income therefrom, including any profit made on the sale thereof, and all mortgages, leases, trust indentures, and other documents issued in connection therewith shall be exempt at all times from all taxation and assessments in the state of Colorado. Bonds issued by the authority shall also be exempt from the "Colorado Securities Act", article 51 of title 11, C.R.S.

## 25-25-119. Rents and charges.

A sufficient amount of the revenues derived in respect of a facility, except such part of such revenues as may be necessary to pay the cost of maintenance, repair, and operation and to provide reserves and for renewals, replacements, extensions, enlargements, and improvements as may be provided for in the resolution authorizing the issuance of any bonds or notes of the authority or in the trust agreement securing the same, shall be set aside at such regular intervals as may be provided in such resolution or trust agreement in a sinking or other similar fund, which is hereby pledged to and charged with the payment of the principal of and the interest on such bonds or notes as the same shall become due and the redemption price or the purchase price of bonds retired by call or purchase as therein provided. Such pledge shall be valid and binding from the time when the pledge is made; and the rates, rents, fees, charges, and other revenues or other moneys so pledged and thereafter received by the authority shall immediately be subject to the lien of such pledge without any physical delivery thereof or further act, and the lien of any such pledge shall be valid and binding as against all parties having claims of any kind in tort, contract, or otherwise against the authority, irrespective of whether such parties have notice thereof. Neither the resolution, any trust agreement, any other agreement, nor any lease by which a pledge is created need be filed or recorded except in the records of the authority. The use and disposition of moneys to the credit of such sinking or other similar fund shall be subject to the resolution authorizing the issuance of such bonds or notes or of such trust agreement. Except as may otherwise be provided in such resolution or such trust agreement, such sinking or other similar fund may be a fund for all such bonds or notes issued to finance facilities at a particular health institution without distinction or priority of one over another; except that the authority in any such resolution or trust agreement may provide that such sinking or other similar fund shall be the fund for a particular facility at a health institution and for the bonds issued to finance a particular facility and may, additionally, permit and provide for the issuance of bonds having a lien in respect of the security authorized which is subordinate to other bonds of the authority, and, in such case, the authority may create separate sinking or other similar funds in respect of such subordinate lien bonds.

## 25-25-120. Fees.

(1) All expenses of the authority incurred in carrying out the provisions of this article shall be payable solely from funds provided under the authority of this article, and no liability shall be incurred by the authority beyond the moneys which are provided pursuant to this article; except that, for the purposes of meeting the necessary expenses of initial organization and operation until such date as the authority derives moneys from funds provided pursuant to this article, the authority may borrow such moneys as may be required for the necessary expenses of organization and operation. Such borrowed moneys shall be repaid within a reasonable time after the authority receives funds provided pursuant to this article.

(2) An initial planning service fee in an amount determined by the authority shall be paid to the authority by each health institution that applies for financial assistance to provide for its facilities. Such initial planning service fees shall be included in the cost of the facilities to be financed and shall not be refundable by the authority, whether or not any such application is approved, or, if approved, whether or not such financial assistance is accomplished. In addition to such initial fee, an annual planning service fee shall be paid to the authority by each participating health institution in an amount determined by the authority. Such fees shall be paid on dates or in installments as may be satisfactory to the authority. Such fees may be used for:

(a) (Deleted by amendment, L. 2007, p. 417, &sect 9, effective August 3, 2007.)

(b) Necessary administrative and operating expenses; and

(c) Reserves for anticipated future expenses.

(3) In addition, the authority may retain the services of any other public or private person, firm, partnership, association, or corporation to furnish services and data to be used by the authority in

determining the financial feasibility of any facilities for which application is being made or for such other services or surveys as the authority deems necessary to carry out the purposes of this article. The authority may negotiate the fee to be paid to a person or entity that provides these services to the authority.

## 25-25-121. Conveyance of title - release of lien.

When the principal of and interest on bonds issued by the authority to finance the cost of facilities or to refinance outstanding indebtedness of one or more participating health institutions, including any refunding bonds issued to refund and refinance such bonds, have been fully paid and retired or when adequate provision has been made to fully pay and retire the same, and all other conditions of the resolution, the lease, the trust indenture, and the mortgage, deed of trust, or other form of security arrangement, if any, authorizing and securing the same have been satisfied, the authority shall promptly do all things and execute such deeds, conveyances, and other documents as are necessary and required to release the lien of such mortgage, deed of trust, or other form of security arrangement in accordance with the provisions thereof and to convey its right, title, and interest in such facilities so financed, and any other facilities leased or mortgaged or subject to deed of trust or any other form of security arrangement to secure the bonds, to such participating health institution or institutions.

## 25-25-122. Investment of funds.

(1) The authority may invest the proceeds from the sale of a series of bonds or any funds related to the series in securities and other investments as may be provided in the proceedings under which the series of bonds are authorized to be issued, whether or not the investment or reinvestment is authorized under any other provision of law. Such investment or reinvestment may include, but is not limited to, the following:

(a) Bonds or other obligations of the United States;

(b) Bonds or other obligations, the payment of the principal and interest of which is unconditionally guaranteed by the United States;

(c) Obligations issued or guaranteed as to principal and interest by any agency or person controlled or supervised by and acting as an instrumentality of the United States pursuant to authority granted by the congress of the United States;

(d) Obligations issued or guaranteed by any state of the United States or any political subdivision of any such state;

(e) Prime commercial paper;

(f) Prime finance company paper;

(g) Bankers acceptances drawn on and accepted by commercial banks;

(h) Repurchase agreements fully secured by obligations issued or guaranteed as to principal and interest by the United States or by any person controlled or supervised by and acting as an instrumentality of the United States pursuant to authority granted by the congress of the United States;

(i) Certificates of deposit or time deposits issued by commercial banks or savings and loan associations that are insured by the federal deposit insurance corporation or its successor; or

(j) Such other securities and investments as may be authorized by resolution of the board if such securities and investments are rated within one of the three highest rating categories by a nationally recognized rating agency.

(2) The authority may invest any other funds in the securities as provided in this section and with such maturities as the authority shall determine if such maturities are on a date or dates prior to the time that, in the judgment of the authority, the funds so invested will be required for expenditure. The express judgment of the authority as to the time that any funds will be required for expenditure or be redeemable is final and conclusive.

## 25-25-123. Proceeds as trust funds.

All moneys received pursuant to this article, whether as proceeds from the sale of bonds, notes, or other obligations or as revenues or receipts, shall be deemed to be trust funds to be held and applied solely as provided in this article. Any officer, bank, or trust company with which such moneys are deposited shall act as trustee of such moneys and shall hold and apply the same for the purposes of this article, subject to such regulations as this article and the resolution authorizing the bonds, notes, or other obligations of any issue or the trust agreement securing such obligations shall provide.

## 25-25-124. Agreement of state not to limit or alter rights of obligees.

The state hereby pledges to and agrees with the holders of any bonds, notes, or other obligations issued under this article, and with those parties who may enter into contracts with the authority pursuant to the provisions of this article, that the state will not limit, alter, restrict, or impair the rights hereby vested in the authority to acquire, construct, reconstruct, maintain, and operate any facility or to establish, revise, charge, and collect rates, rents, fees, and other charges as may be convenient or necessary to produce sufficient revenues to meet the expenses of maintenance and operation thereof and to fulfill the terms of any agreements made with the holders of bonds, notes, or other obligations authorized and issued pursuant to this article and with the parties who may enter into contracts with the authority pursuant to this article. The state further agrees that it will not in any way impair the rights or remedies of the holders of such bonds, notes, or other obligations of such parties until such bonds, notes, and other obligations, together with interest thereon, with interest on any unpaid installment of interest and all costs and expenses in connection with any action or proceeding by or on behalf of such holders, are fully met and discharged and such contracts are fully performed on the part of the authority. Nothing in this article precludes such limitation or alteration if and when adequate provision is made by law for the protection of the holders of such bonds, notes, or other obligations of the authority or those entering into such contracts with the authority. The authority may include this pledge and undertaking for the state in such bonds, notes, or other obligations and in such contracts.

## 25-25-125. Enforcement of rights of bondholders.

Any holder of bonds issued pursuant to this article or any trustee under a trust agreement, trust indenture, indenture of mortgage, or deed of trust entered into pursuant to this article, except to the extent that their rights are restricted by any bond resolution, may, by any suitable form of legal proceedings, protect and enforce any rights under the laws of this state or granted by the bond resolution. Such rights include the right to compel the performance of all duties of the authority required by this article or the bond resolution; to enjoin unlawful activities; and, in the event of default with respect to the payment of any principal of, premium on, if any, and interest on any bond or in the performance of any covenant or agreement on the part of the authority in the bond resolution, to apply to a court having jurisdiction of the cause to appoint a receiver to administer and operate the project or projects, the revenues of which are pledged to the payment of principal of, premium on, if any, and interest on such bonds, with full power to pay, and to provide for payment of, principal of, premium on, if any, and interest on such bonds, and with such powers, subject to the direction of the court, as are permitted by law and are accorded receivers in general equity cases, but excluding any power to pledge additional revenues of the authority to the payment of such principal, premium, and interest.

## 25-25-126. Bonds eligible for investment.

All banks, bankers, trust companies, savings and loan associations, investment companies, and insurance companies and associations and all executors, administrators, guardians, trustees, and other fiduciaries may legally invest any sinking funds, moneys, or other funds belonging to them or within their control in any bonds issued pursuant to this article. Public entities, as defined in section 24-75-601 (1) , C.R.S., may invest public funds in such bonds only if said bonds satisfy the investment requirements established in part 6 of article 75 of title 24, C.R.S.

### 25-25-127. Account of activities - receipts for expenditures - report - audit.

(1) The authority shall keep an accurate account of its activities, receipts, and expenditures and shall annually make a report of its activities, receipts, and expenditures to the board, the governor, and the state auditor. The report shall be submitted within six months after the close of the authority's fiscal year and shall be in a form prescribed by the recipients of the report.

(2) The state auditor may investigate the affairs of the authority, severally examine the properties and records of the authority, and prescribe methods of accounting and the rendering of periodical reports in relation to facilities undertaken by the authority. This article and the expenditures of the authority shall be reviewed by the legislative audit committee every odd-numbered year.

### 25-25-128. Federal social security act.

The authority may take such action as it deems appropriate to enable its employees to come within the provisions and obtain the benefits of the federal "Social Security Act", as from time to time amended.

### 25-25-129. Powers of authority not restricted - law complete in itself.

This article shall not be construed as a restriction or limitation upon any powers which the authority might otherwise have under any laws of this state but shall be construed as cumulative of any such powers. No proceedings, referendum, notice, or approval shall be required for the creation of the authority or the issuance of any bonds or any instrument as security therefor, except as provided in this article; but nothing in this article shall be construed to deprive the state and its political subdivisions of their respective police powers over properties of the authority or to impair any power thereover of any official or agency of the state and its governmental subdivisions which may be otherwise provided by law.

### 25-25-130. Powers in addition to those granted by other laws.

The powers conferred by this article are in addition and supplementary to, and the limitations imposed by this article do not affect the powers conferred by, any other law, except as provided in this article. Facilities may be acquired, purchased, constructed, reconstructed, improved, bettered, and extended, and bonds may be issued under this article for said purposes notwithstanding that any other law may provide for the acquisition, purchase, construction, reconstruction, improvement, betterment, and extensions of like facilities or the issuance of bonds for like purposes, and without regard to the requirements, restrictions, limitations, or other provisions contained in any other law.

### 25-25-131. Annual report.

The authority shall submit to the governor within six months after the end of the fiscal year a report which shall set forth a complete and detailed operating and financial statement of the authority during such year. Also included in the report shall be any recommendations with reference to additional legislation or other action that may be necessary to carry out the purposes of the authority.

# ARTICLE 26. MULTIPHASIC HEALTH SCREENING

### 25-26-101. Short title.

This article shall be known and may be cited as "The Multiphasic Health Screening Act".

### 25-26-102. Legislative declaration.

The general assembly declares it to be in the interests of public health, safety, and welfare to protect the people of this state from the danger of uncertainty and confusion as to the responsibility for, and the rendering of, professional health care. The general assembly further declares that multiphasic health screening units provide to people certain health testing services which do not include diagnosis or treatment. Unless persons are aware of the nature and extent of such services, a false and injurious sense of security relating to personal health may result. Therefore, the general assembly finds that the protection of the public requires that multiphasic health screening units comply with certain minimum standards and practices.

### 25-26-103. Definitions.
As used in this article, unless the context otherwise requires:
(1) "Multiphasic health screening unit" means any fixed or mobile facility where diagnostic testing is performed, where specimens are taken from the human body for laboratory analyses, or where certain measurements such as height and weight determination, blood pressure determination, audio and visual tests, and electrocardiograms are made. The term does not include a facility licensed or certified in this state as a hospital, a home health agency, a clinical laboratory, or the office of a physician licensed to practice medicine in this state.

### 25-26-104. Immunity.
No cause of action in tort or contract shall accrue against any person on account of receipt by such person of an unsolicited referral arising from a test performed by a multiphasic health screening unit.

# ARTICLE 27. ASSISTED LIVING RESIDENCES

### 25-27-101. Legislative declaration.
(1) In order to promote the public health and welfare of the people of Colorado, it is declared to be in the public interest to establish minimum standards and rules for assisted living residences in the state of Colorado and to provide the authority for the administration and enforcement of such minimum standards and rules. These standards and rules shall be sufficient to assure the health, safety, and welfare of assisted living residents.
(2) The general assembly further finds that the department of public health and environment, as the executive branch agency assigned to administer and enforce minimum standards for assisted living residences, is in a position to provide technical assistance, educational materials, and training information to residences. The general assembly determines that a proactive approach by the department, acting as a mentor and educator for residences, will enhance the quality of care of residents of assisted living residences. Additionally, the general assembly finds that the department should explore whether risk-based inspections may be implemented to allocate resources more effectively and at the same time adequately protect the health and safety of the residents.
(3) Further, the general assembly determines and declares that, in administering and enforcing standards for assisted living residences, the department of public health and environment should focus on the outcome related to measures and treatment of residents.

### 25-27-102. Definitions.
As used in this article, unless the context otherwise requires:
(1) Repealed.
(1.3) "Assisted living residence" or "residence" means a residential facility that makes available to three or more adults not related to the owner of such facility, either directly or indirectly through

an agreement with the resident, room and board and at least the following services: Personal services; protective oversight; social care due to impaired capacity to live independently; and regular supervision that shall be available on a twenty-four-hour basis, but not to the extent that regular twenty-four-hour medical or nursing care is required. The term "assisted living residence" does not include any facility licensed in this state as a residential care facility for individuals with developmental disabilities, or any individual residential support services that are excluded from licensure requirements pursuant to rules adopted by the department of public health and environment.

(2) "Department" means the department of public health and environment of the state of Colorado.

(3) to (5) Repealed.

(6) "Local board of health" means any county, district, or municipal board of health.

(7) Repealed.

(8) (Deleted by amendment, L. 2002, p. 1317, § 2, effective July 1, 2002.)

(9) "Personal services" means those services that the operator and employees of an assisted living residence provide for each resident, including, but not limited to:

(a) An environment that is sanitary and safe from physical harm;

(b) Individualized social supervision;

(c) Assistance with transportation; and

(d) Assistance with activities of daily living, including but not limited to bathing, dressing, and eating.

(10) "Protective oversight" means guidance of a resident as required by the needs of the resident or as reasonably requested by the resident, including the following:

(a) Being aware of a resident's general whereabouts, although the resident may travel independently in the community; and

(b) Monitoring the activities of the resident while on the premises to ensure the resident's health, safety, and well-being, including monitoring the resident's needs and ensuring that the resident receives the services and care necessary to protect the resident's health, safety, and well-being.

(11) "State board" means the state board of health.

## 25-27-103. License required - criminal and civil penalties.

(1) On or after July 1, 2002, it is unlawful for any person, partnership, association, or corporation to conduct or maintain an assisted living residence without having obtained a license therefor from the department of public health and environment. Any person who violates this provision:

(a) Is guilty of a misdemeanor and, upon conviction thereof, shall be punished by a fine of not less than fifty dollars nor more than five hundred dollars;

(b) May be subject to a civil penalty assessed by the department of not less than fifty dollars nor more than one hundred dollars for each day the residence violates this section. The assessed penalty shall accrue from the date the residence is found by the department to be in violation of this section. The assessment, enforcement, and collection of the penalty shall be by the department in accordance with article 4 of title 24, C.R.S., for credit to the assisted living residence cash fund created pursuant to section 25-27-107.5. Enforcement and collection of the penalty shall occur following the decision reached in accordance with procedures set forth in section 24-4-105, C.R.S.

## 25-27-104. Minimum standards for assisted living residences - rules.

(1) On or before November 1, 2002, the state board shall promulgate rules pursuant to section 24-4-103, C.R.S., providing minimum standards for the location, sanitation, fire safety, adequacy of facilities, adequacy of diet and nutrition, equipment, structure, operation, provision of personal services and protective oversight, and personnel practices of assisted living residences within the state of Colorado. Such rules shall differentiate between homes of different sizes. In formulating such rules, the state board shall seek recommendations from the advisory committee established pursuant to section 25-27-110.

(2) Rules promulgated by the state board pursuant to subsection (1) of this section shall include, as

a minimum, provisions requiring the following:

(a) Compliance with all applicable zoning, housing, fire, sanitary, and other codes and ordinances of the city, city and county, or county where the residence is situated, to the extent that such codes and ordinances are consistent with the federal "Fair Housing Amendment Act of 1988", as amended, 42 U.S.C. sec. 3601 et seq.;

(b) Annual inspection of assisted living residences by the department or its designated representative;

(c) That the premises to be used are in fit, safe, and sanitary condition and properly equipped to provide good care to the residents;

(d) That the Colorado long-term care ombudsman, designated by the department of human services, have access to the premises and residents during reasonable hours for the purposes set out in the federal "Older Americans Act of 1965";

(e) Protection of the individual rights of residents either through a written board and care plan or by means of contracts executed with the residents, which board and care plan or contract shall meet the requirements stated in section 25-27-104.5;

(f) Responsibility of the assisted living residences for social supervision, personal services, and coordination with community resources as needed by the residents;

(g) That the administrator and staff of a residence meet minimum educational, training, and experience standards established by the state board, including a requirement that such persons be of good, moral, and responsible character. In making such a determination, the owner or licensee of a residence may have access to and shall obtain any criminal history record information from a criminal justice agency, subject to any restrictions imposed by such agency, for any person responsible for the care and welfare of residents of such residence.

(h) Intermediate enforcement remedies as authorized by section 25-27-106 (2) ;

(i) Written plans, to be submitted by residences to the department for approval, detailing the measures that will be taken to correct violations found as a result of inspections;

(j) The definition for high medicaid utilization facility as a basis for a modified fee schedule. A high medicaid utilization residence shall be a residence in which no less than thirty-five percent of the available beds are occupied by medicaid enrollees as indicated by the most complete claims data available.

(k) A modified fee schedule for residences that serve a disproportionate share of low-income residents. The board may adopt a standard for determining residences that serve a disproportionate share of low-income residents. Such standard may require a residence to submit documentation determined appropriate by the department for verification.

## 25-27-104.5. Requirements governing forfeiture of security deposits and rent.

If a lease provision in a resident care plan or in a contract signed by a resident of an assisted living residence results in or requires forfeiture of more than thirty days of rent if a resident moves due to a medical condition or dies during the term of the plan, then the plan shall be deemed to be against public policy and shall be void; except that inclusion of such a provision shall not render the remainder of the plan or contract void. A lease provision in a written board and care plan or in a contract that requires forfeiture of rent for thirty days after the resident moves due to a medical condition or dies does not violate this section. The provisions regarding forfeiture of rent shall appear on the front page of the plan or contract and shall be printed in no less than twelve-point bold-faced type. The provisions shall read as follows:

This lease agreement is for a month-to-month tenancy. The lessor shall not require the forfeiture of rent beyond a thirty-day period if the lessee moves due to a medical condition or dies during the term of the lease.

In circumstances in which the resident moves due to a medical condition or dies during the term of a plan or contract, the assisted living residence shall return that part of rent paid in excess of thirty days' rent after a patient moves or dies to the resident or the resident's estate. The assisted living residence may assess daily rental charges for any days in which the former or deceased resident's personal possessions remain in the resident's room after the time period for which the resident has paid rent and for the usual time to clean the room after the resident's personal possessions have been removed. For purposes of this section, "daily rental charges" means an amount not to exceed one-thirtieth of thirty days' rental amount plus reasonable expenses.

## 25-27-105. License - application - inspection - issuance.

(1) An application for a license to operate an assisted living residence shall be submitted to the department annually upon such form and in such manner as prescribed by the department.

(2) The department shall investigate and pass on each original application and each renewal application for a license. The department shall inspect or cause to be inspected the residences to be operated by an applicant for an original license before the license is granted and shall annually thereafter inspect or cause to be inspected the residences of all licensees. The department shall make such other inspections as it deems necessary to insure that the health, safety, and welfare of the residents are being protected. The residence shall submit in writing, in a form prescribed by the department, a plan detailing the measures that will be taken to correct any violations found by the department as a result of inspections undertaken pursuant to this subsection (2) .

(2.5) (a) On July 1, 2002, as part of an original application and on and after July 1, 2002, on the first renewal of an application for assisted living residences licensed before July 1, 2002, for a license, an owner, applicant, or licensee shall request from a criminal justice agency designated by the department criminal history record information regarding such owner, applicant, or licensee. The information, upon such request and subject to any restrictions imposed by such agency, shall be forwarded by the criminal justice agency directly to the department.

(a.5) On and after July 1, 2002, the department may require that an administrator request from a criminal justice agency designated by the department a criminal history record on such administrator. The information, upon such request and subject to any restrictions imposed by such agency, shall be forwarded by the criminal justice agency directly to the department.

(b) The information shall be used by the department in ascertaining whether the person applying for licensure has been convicted of a felony or of a misdemeanor, which felony or misdemeanor involves moral turpitude or involves conduct that the department determines could pose a risk to the health, safety, and welfare of residents of the assisted living residence. Information obtained in accordance with this section shall be maintained by the department.

(c) All costs of obtaining any information from a criminal justice agency pursuant to this section shall be borne by the individual who is the subject of such check.

(2.8) No license shall be issued or renewed by the department if the owner, applicant, or licensee of the assisted living residence has been convicted of a felony or of a misdemeanor, which felony or misdemeanor involves moral turpitude or involves conduct that the department determines could pose a risk to the health, safety, and welfare of the residents of the assisted living residence.

(3) Except as otherwise provided in subsection (4) of this section, the department shall issue or renew a license when it is satisfied that the applicant or licensee is in compliance with the requirements set out in this article and the rules promulgated thereunder. Except for provisional licenses issued in accordance with subsection (4) of this section, a license issued or renewed pursuant to this section shall expire one year from the date of issuance or renewal.

(4) The department may issue a provisional license to an applicant for the purpose of operating an assisted living residence for a period of ninety days if the applicant is temporarily unable to conform to all the minimum standards required under this article; except that no license shall be issued to an applicant if the operation of the applicant's residence will adversely affect the health, safety, and welfare of the residents of such residence. As a condition of obtaining a provisional license, the applicant shall show proof to the department that attempts are being made to conform and comply with applicable standards. No provisional license shall be granted prior to the submission of a criminal background check in accordance with subsection (2.5) of this section. A

provisional license shall not be renewed.

## 25-27-105.5. Compliance with local government zoning regulations - notice to local governments - provisional licensure.

(1) The department shall require any assisted living residence seeking licensure pursuant to this article to comply with any applicable zoning regulations of the municipality, city and county, or county where the residence is situated. Failure to comply with applicable zoning regulations shall constitute grounds for the denial of a license to a residence; except that nothing in this section shall be construed to supersede the provisions of sections 30-28-115 (2) , 31-23-301 (4) , and 31-23-303 (2) , C.R.S.

(2) The department shall assure that timely written notice is provided to the municipality, city and county, or county where an assisted living residence is situated, including the address of the residence and the population and number of persons to be served by the residence, when any of the following occurs:

(a) An application for a license to operate an assisted living residence pursuant to section 25-27-105 is made;

(b) A license is granted to an assisted living residence pursuant to section 25-27-105;

(c) A change in the license of an assisted living residence occurs; or

(d) The license of an assisted living residence is revoked or otherwise terminated for any reason.

(3) Notwithstanding the provisions of section 25-27-105 (4) , in the event of a zoning or other delay or dispute between an assisted living residence and the municipality, city and county, or county where the residence is situated, the department may grant a provisional license to the residence for up to one hundred twenty days pending resolution of the delay or dispute.

## 25-27-106. License denial, suspension, or revocation.

(1) When an application for an original license has been denied by the department, the department shall notify the applicant in writing of such denial by mailing a notice to the applicant at the address shown on his or her application. Any applicant believing himself or herself aggrieved by such denial may pursue the remedy for review provided in article 4 of title 24, C.R.S., if the applicant, within thirty days after receiving such notice, petitions the department to set a date and place for hearing, affording the applicant an opportunity to be heard in person or by counsel. All hearings on the denial of original licenses shall be conducted in conformity with the provisions and procedures specified in article 4 of title 24, C.R.S.

(2) (a) The department may suspend, revoke, or refuse to renew the license of any residence that is out of compliance with the requirements of this article or the rules promulgated thereunder. Such suspension, revocation, or refusal shall be done after a hearing thereon and in conformance with the provisions and procedures specified in article 4 of title 24, C.R.S.

(b) (I) The department may impose intermediate restrictions or conditions on a licensee that may include at least one of the following:

(A) Retaining a consultant to address corrective measures;

(B) Monitoring by the department for a specific period;

(C) Providing additional training to employees, owners, or operators of the residence;

(D) Complying with a directed written plan, to correct the violation; or

(E) Paying a civil fine not to exceed two thousand dollars in a calendar year.

(II) (A) If the department imposes an intermediate restriction or condition that is not a result of a life-threatening situation, the licensee shall receive written notice of the restriction or condition. No later than ten days after the date the notice is received from the department, the licensee shall submit a written plan that includes the time frame for completing the plan and addresses the restriction or condition specified.

(B) If the department imposes an intermediate restriction or condition that is the result of a life-threatening situation, the department shall notify the licensee in writing, by telephone, or in person during an on-site visit. The licensee shall implement the restriction or condition immediately upon receiving notice of the restriction or condition. If the department provides notice of a restriction or condition by telephone or in person, the department shall send written confirmation of the restriction or condition to the licensee within two business days.

(III) (A) After submission of an approved written plan, a licensee may first appeal any intermediate restriction or condition on its license to the department through an informal review process as established by the department.

(B) If the restriction or condition requires payment of a civil fine pursuant to this paragraph (b) , the licensee may request that the informal review be conducted in person. In addition, the licensee may request and the department shall grant a stay in payment of the fine until final disposition of the restriction or condition.

(C) In the event a licensee is not satisfied with the result of the informal review or chooses not to seek informal review, no intermediate restriction or condition on the licensee shall be imposed until after an opportunity for a hearing has been afforded the licensee pursuant to section 24-4-105, C.R.S.

(IV) (A) In the event that the department assesses a civil fine pursuant to this paragraph (b) , moneys received by the department shall be transmitted to the state treasurer, who shall credit the same to the assisted living residence improvement cash fund, which fund is hereby created.

(B) The general assembly shall make annual appropriations from the assisted living residence improvement cash fund for expenditures of the department pursuant to subparagraph (V) of this paragraph (b) .

(C) Notwithstanding any provision of section 24-36-114, C.R.S., to the contrary, all interest derived from the deposit and investment of moneys from the assisted living residence improvement cash fund created in sub-subparagraph (A) of this subparagraph (IV) shall remain in the assisted living residence improvement cash fund.

(V) Civil fines collected pursuant to this paragraph (b) shall be used for expenses related to:

(A) Continuing monitoring required pursuant to this paragraph (b) ;

(B) Education for licensees to avoid restrictions or conditions or facilitate the application process or the change of ownership process;

(C) Education for residents and their families about resolving problems with a residence, rights of residents, and responsibilities of residences;

(D) Providing technical assistance to any residence for the purpose of complying with changes in rules or state or federal law;

(E) Relocating residents to other facilities or residences;

(F) Maintaining the operation of a residence pending correction of violations, as determined necessary by the department;

(G) Closing a residence; or

(H) Reimbursing residents for personal funds lost, as determined necessary by the department.

(3) The department shall revoke or refuse to renew the license of a facility where the owner or licensee has been convicted of a felony or misdemeanor involving moral turpitude or involving conduct which the department determines could pose a risk to the health, safety, and welfare of the residents of such facility. Such revocation or refusal shall be made only after a hearing is provided in accordance with article 4 of title 24, C.R.S.

## 25-27-107. License fees - rules.

(1) Repealed.

(1.5) (a) No later than January 1, 2009, the state board shall promulgate rules establishing a schedule of fees sufficient to meet the direct and indirect costs of administration and enforcement of this article. The rules shall set a lower fee for facilities with a high medicaid utilization rate as defined by the state board. The rules shall be adopted in accordance with article 4 of title 24, C.R.S.

(b) Prior to setting a fee by rule pursuant to this subsection (1.5) , the department shall hold public stakeholder meetings on behalf of the state board to discuss issues pertaining to setting fees, including, without limitation, a phased-in fee schedule based upon expected licensing program costs, maximum yearly fee increases, risk-based assessments, and technical assistance that may be met by or in collaboration with the private sector.

(c) The department shall assess and collect, from assisted living residences subject to licensure, fees in accordance with the fee schedule established by the state board.

(d) (Deleted by amendment, L. 2010, (HB 10-1422), ch. 419, p. 2108, § 133, effective August 11, 2010.)

(2) The fees collected pursuant to this section shall be transmitted to the state treasurer, who shall credit the same to the assisted living residence cash fund created in section 25-27-107.5.

(3) Notwithstanding the amount specified for any fee in this section, the state board by rule or as otherwise provided by law may reduce the amount of one or more of the fees if necessary pursuant to section 24-75-402 (3), C.R.S., to reduce the uncommitted reserves of the fund to which all or any portion of one or more of the fees is credited. After the uncommitted reserves of the fund are sufficiently reduced, the state board by rule or as otherwise provided by law may increase the amount of one or more of the fees as provided in section 24-75-402 (4), C.R.S.

(4) Fees collected pursuant to subsection (1.5) of this section shall be used by the department, in addition to regulatory and administrative functions, to provide technical assistance and education to assisted living residences related to compliance with Colorado law. The department may contract with private entities to assist the department in providing such technical assistance and education.

## 25-27-107.5. Assisted living residence cash fund created.

(1) The fees collected pursuant to section 25-27-107, plus any civil penalty collected pursuant to section 25-27-103 (1) (b), shall be transmitted to the state treasurer, who shall credit the same to the assisted living residence cash fund, which fund is hereby created. The moneys in the fund shall be subject to annual appropriation by the general assembly for the direct and indirect costs of the department in performing its duties under this article. Notwithstanding subsection (2) of this section, at the end of any fiscal year, all unexpended and unencumbered moneys in the fund shall remain therein and shall not be credited or transferred to the general fund or any other fund.

(2) Notwithstanding subsection (1) of this section, on July 1, 2013, any moneys remaining in the fund from fees collected by the department for assisted living residence building and structure code plan reviews and inspections are transferred to the health facility construction and inspection cash fund created in section 24-33.5-1207.8, C.R.S.

## 25-27-108. Enforcement - ability to contract.

(1) The department is responsible for the enforcement of the provisions of this article and the regulations adopted thereunder.

(2) The department may contract with a local board of health to investigate and inspect the facilities to be licensed under this article and may accept reports on such investigations or inspections as a basis for licensing. The department may also contract with local boards of health to enforce the provisions of this article and the regulations adopted thereunder and is required to transfer license fees and additional fees collected in this article to the local boards of health if a contract is so negotiated.

## 25-27-109. List of licensed residences maintained by department.

The department shall maintain a current list of assisted living residences that have been licensed and shall make such list available to individuals upon request.

## 25-27-110. Advisory committee.

(1) There is hereby established an advisory committee to the department for the purposes of making recommendations to the department and reporting to the house and senate committees on health and human services, or any successor committees, concerning the rules promulgated by the

state board pursuant to this article, implementation of the licensing program, the impact of the program, and the effectiveness of enforcement. The advisory committee shall consist of not fewer than nine members to be appointed by the executive director of the department. The committee shall elect its own chairperson. Such members shall be representatives from assisted living residences, the Colorado commission on the aging, county, district, or municipal public health agencies, or local boards of health, and consumer and other agencies and organizations providing services to or concerned with residents of assisted living residences. Members of the advisory committee shall serve on a voluntary basis and shall serve without compensation.
(2) and (3) Repealed.

### 25-27-111. Rules.
The state board shall promulgate such rules as are necessary to implement this article pursuant to the provisions of article 4 of title 24, C.R.S.

### 25-27-112. Treatment - religious belief.
Nothing in this article shall authorize the department to impose any mode of treatment inconsistent with the religious faith or belief of any person.

### 25-27-113. Fees for providers with high medicaid utilization and disproportionate low-income residences.
(1) The general assembly hereby finds, determines, and declares that assisted living residences provide necessary services to many residents who receive medicaid benefits pursuant to articles 4, 5, and 6 of title 25.5, C.R.S. Because so many Coloradans benefit from assisted living centers that serve medicaid recipients, the general assembly hereby finds, determines, and declares that assisted living residences that have high medicaid utilization should receive a modified fee schedule for fees required by this article.
(2) Residences identified as high medicaid utilization residences by the department shall be subject to a modified fee schedule as determined by the board.
(3) Residences identified as servicing a disproportionate number of low-income residents may be subject to a modified fee schedule as determined by the board.

# ARTICLE 27.5. HOME CARE AGENCIES

### 25-27.5-101. Legislative declaration.
(1) In order to promote the public health and welfare of the people of Colorado, it is declared to be in the public interest to establish minimum standards and rules for home care agencies in the state of Colorado and to provide the authority for the administration and enforcement of such minimum standards and rules. These standards and rules shall be sufficient to assure the health, safety, and welfare of home care consumers.
(2) The general assembly further finds that the department of public health and environment, as the executive branch agency assigned to administer and enforce minimum standards for home care agencies, should explore whether risk-based inspections may be implemented to allocate resources more effectively and at the same time adequately protect the health and safety of the home care consumers. Risk shall be evaluated based on the home care agency's compliance history, quality performance measures, and other relevant factors set forth in rules promulgated by the state board of health.
(3) Further, the general assembly determines and declares that, in administering and enforcing standards for home care agencies, the inspections by the department should focus on home care consumer safety and outcomes.

## 25-27.5-102. Definitions.

As used in this article, unless the context otherwise requires:

(1) "Certified home care agency" means an agency that is certified by either the federal centers for medicare and medicaid services or the Colorado department of health care policy and financing to provide skilled home health or personal care services.

(1.3) "CMS" means the federal centers for medicare and medicaid services in the United States department of health and human services.

(1.5) "Community-centered board" means a community-centered board, as defined in section 25.5-10-202, C.R.S., that is designated pursuant to section 25.5-10-209, C.R.S., by the department of health care policy and financing.

(2) "Department" means the Colorado department of public health and environment.

(3) (a) "Home care agency" means any sole proprietorship, partnership, association, corporation, government or governmental subdivision or agency subject to the restrictions in section 25-1.5-103 (1) (a) (II) , not-for-profit agency, or any other legal or commercial entity that manages and offers, directly or by contract, skilled home health services or personal care services to a home care consumer in the home care consumer's temporary or permanent home or place of residence. A residential facility that delivers skilled home health or personal care services which the facility is not licensed to provide shall either be licensed as a home care agency or require the skilled home health or personal care services to be delivered by a licensed home care agency.

(b) "Home care agency" does not include:

(I) Organizations that provide only housekeeping services;

(II) Community and rural health networks that furnish home visits for the purpose of public health monitoring and disease tracking;

(III) An individual who is not employed by or affiliated with a home care agency and who acts alone, without employees or contractors;

(IV) Outpatient rehabilitation agencies and comprehensive outpatient rehabilitation facilities certified pursuant to Title XVIII or XIX of the "Social Security Act", as amended;

(V) Consumer-directed attendant programs administered by the Colorado department of health care policy and financing;

(VI) Licensed dialysis centers that provide in-home dialysis services, supplies, and equipment;

(VII) Subject to the requirements of section 25-27.5-103 (3) , a facility otherwise licensed by the department;

(VIII) A home care placement agency as defined in subsection (5) of this section;

(IX) Services provided by a qualified early intervention service provider and overseen jointly by the department of education and the department of human services; or

(X) A program of all-inclusive care for the elderly established in section 25.5-5-412, C.R.S., and regulated by the department of health care policy and financing and the CMS; except that PACE home care services are subject to regulation in accordance with section 25-27.5-104 (4) .

(4) "Home care consumer" means a person who receives skilled home health services or personal care services in his or her temporary or permanent home or place of residence from a home care agency or from a provider referred by a home care placement agency.

(5) "Home care placement agency" means an organization that, for a fee, provides only referrals of providers to home care consumers seeking services. A home care placement agency does not provide skilled home health services or personal care services to a home care consumer in the home care consumer's temporary or permanent home or place of residence directly or by contract. Such organizations shall follow the requirements of sections 25-27.5-103 (2) , 25-27.5-104 (1) (c) , and 25-27.5-107.

(5.3) "Manager" or "administrator" means any person who controls and supervises or offers or attempts to control and supervise the day-to-day operations of a home care agency or home care placement agency.

(5.5) "Owner" means a shareholder in a for-profit or nonprofit corporation, a partner in a partnership or limited partnership, a member in a limited liability company, a sole proprietor, or a person with a similar interest in an entity, who has at least a fifty-percent ownership interest in the business entity.

(5.7) "PACE home care services" means skilled home health services or personal care services:

(a) Offered as part of a comprehensive set of medical and nonmedical benefits, including primary care, day services, and interdisciplinary team care planning and management, by PACE providers to an enrolled participant in the program of all-inclusive care for the elderly established in section 25.5-5-412, C.R.S., and regulated by the department of health care policy and financing and the CMS; and

(b) Provided in the enrolled participant's temporary or permanent place of residence.

(6) "Personal care services" means assistance with activities of daily living, including but not limited to bathing, dressing, eating, transferring, walking or mobility, toileting, and continence care. It also includes housekeeping, personal laundry, medication reminders, and companionship services furnished to a home care consumer in the home care consumer's temporary or permanent home or place of residence, and those normal daily routines that the home care consumer could perform for himself or herself were he or she physically capable, which are intended to enable that individual to remain safely and comfortably in the home care consumer's temporary or permanent home or place of residence.

(6.3) "Qualified early intervention service provider" has the meaning set forth in section 27-10.5-702, C.R.S.

(6.7) "Service agency" means a service agency, as defined in section 25.5-10-202, C.R.S., that has received certification from the department of health care policy and financing as a developmental disabilities service agency under rules promulgated by the medical services board and is providing services pursuant to the supported living services waiver or the children's extensive support waiver of the home- and community-based services waivers administered by the department of health care policy and financing under part 4 of article 6 of title 25.5, C.R.S.

(7) "Skilled home health services" means health and medical services furnished to a home care consumer in the home care consumer's temporary or permanent home or place of residence that include wound care services; use of medical supplies including drugs and biologicals prescribed by a physician; in-home infusion services; nursing services; home health aide or certified nurse aide services that require the supervision of a licensed or certified health care professional acting within the scope of his or her license or certificate; occupational therapy; physical therapy; respiratory care services; dietetics and nutrition counseling services; medication administration; medical social services; and speech-language pathology services. "Skilled home health services" does not include the delivery of either durable medical equipment or medical supplies.

(8) "State board" means the state board of health.

## 25-27.5-103. Home care agency license required - home care placement agency registration required - civil and criminal penalties.

(1) On or after June 1, 2009, it is unlawful for any person, partnership, association, or corporation to conduct or maintain a home care agency that provides skilled home health services without having submitted a completed application for licensure as a home care agency to the department. On or after January 1, 2010, it is unlawful for any person, partnership, association, or corporation to conduct or maintain a home care agency that provides skilled home health services without having obtained a license therefor from the department. On or after January 1, 2010, it is unlawful for any person, partnership, association, or corporation to conduct or maintain a home care agency that provides in-home personal care services without having submitted a completed application for licensure as a home care agency to the department. On or after January 1, 2011, it is unlawful for any person, partnership, association, or corporation to conduct or maintain a home care agency that provides in-home personal care services without having obtained a license therefor from the department. Any person who violates this provision:

(a) Is guilty of a misdemeanor and, upon conviction thereof, shall be punished by a fine of not less than fifty dollars nor more than five hundred dollars; and

(b) May be subject to a civil penalty assessed by the department of up to ten thousand dollars for each violation of this section. The department shall assess, enforce, and collect the penalty in accordance with article 4 of title 24, C.R.S., for credit to the home care agency cash fund created in section 25-27.5-105. Enforcement and collection of the penalty shall occur following the decision reached in accordance with procedures set forth in section 24-4-105, C.R.S.

(1.5) It is unlawful for a community-centered board that is directly providing home care services or a service agency to conduct or maintain a home care agency that provides in-home personal care services without having obtained a license from the department. Any person who violates this subsection (1.5) is guilty of a misdemeanor and is subject to the civil and criminal penalties described in paragraphs (a) and (b) of subsection (1) of this section. Nothing in this section relieves an entity that contracts or arranges with a community-centered board or service agency and that meets the definition of a home care agency from the entity's obligation to apply for and operate under a license in accordance with this article.

(2) (a) (I) On or after June 1, 2015, it is unlawful for a person to conduct or maintain a home care placement agency unless the person has submitted a completed application for registration as a home care placement agency to the department, including evidence of general liability insurance coverage as required in subparagraph (II) of this paragraph (a) . On or after January 1, 2016, it is unlawful for a person to conduct or maintain a home care placement agency without a valid, current home care placement agency registration issued by the department. The department shall maintain a registry of all registered home care placement agencies and shall make the registry accessible to the public. While a home care placement agency must be registered by the department, a home care placement agency is not licensed or certified by the department and shall not claim or assert that the department licenses or certifies the home care placement agency.

(II) As a condition of obtaining an initial or renewal home care placement agency registration pursuant to this subsection (2) , a person applying for initial or renewal registration shall submit to the department, in the form and manner required by the department, proof that the person has obtained and is maintaining general liability insurance coverage that covers the home care placement agency and the providers it refers to home care consumers in an amount determined by the state board by rule pursuant to section 25-27.5-104 (1) (h) .

(b) A home care placement agency shall provide to its home care consumer clients, before referring a provider to the client, a written disclosure containing the information required in section 25-27.5-104 (1) (c) and in state board rules adopted pursuant to that section.

(c) A person who violates this subsection (2) :

(I) Is guilty of a misdemeanor and, upon conviction thereof, shall be punished by a fine of not less than fifty dollars nor more than five hundred dollars; and

(II) May be subject to a civil penalty assessed by the department of up to ten thousand dollars for each violation. The department shall assess, enforce, and collect the penalty in accordance with article 4 of title 24, C.R.S. The department shall transfer any penalties it collects to the state treasurer for deposit in the home care agency cash fund created in section 25-27.5-105.

(3) If a facility that is licensed pursuant to this title provides skilled home health or personal care services also provides the services outside the premises of the licensed facility, the facility license shall be amended to include the services, and the facility shall meet the requirements promulgated by the state board.

## 25-27.5-104. Minimum standards for home care agencies and home care placement agencies - rules - advisory committee.

(1) The state board shall promulgate rules pursuant to section 24-4-103, C.R.S., providing minimum standards for the operation of home care agencies and home care placement agencies within the state of Colorado that apply regardless of the source of payment for the home care services or the diagnosis of the home care consumer. In promulgating these rules, the state board shall establish different requirements appropriate to the various types of skilled home health and

personal care services, including differentiating requirements for providers that are substantially funded through medicare and medicaid reimbursement, providers for the program of all-inclusive care for the elderly established in section 25.5-5-412, C.R.S., providers that are already licensed under this title, and providers that are solely or substantially privately funded. This differentiation must include consideration of the requirements already imposed by other federal and state regulatory agencies and must require the department of health care policy and financing and the department to work jointly to resolve differing requirements. The rules must include the following:

(a) Inspection of home care agencies by the department or its designated representative;

(b) Minimum educational, training, and experience standards for the administrator and staff of an agency, including a requirement that such persons be of good, moral, and responsible character;

(c) Requirements for disclosure notices to be provided by home care agencies and home care placement agencies to home care consumers concerning the duties and employment status of the individual providing services. With regard to home care placement agencies, the rules must require a home care placement agency to disclose in writing, at a minimum, the following to each home care consumer client in the form and manner prescribed by the department before referring a provider to the client:

(I) That the home care placement agency is not the employer of any provider it refers to a home care consumer; and

(II) That the home care placement agency does not direct, control, schedule, or train any provider it refers;

(d) Intermediate enforcement remedies as authorized by section 25-27.5-108;

(e) A requirement and form for written plans, to be submitted by agencies to the department for approval, detailing the measures that will be taken to correct violations found as a result of inspections;

(f) Establishing occurrence reporting requirements pursuant to section 25-1-124;

(g) (I) Fees for home care agency licensure. Home care agency fees are payable to the home care agency cash fund. The annual fee must include a component that reflects whether a survey is planned for the year based on the agency's compliance history. The state board shall develop a methodology for establishing differentiating fees for licensure of home care agencies, including community-centered boards and service agencies, to reflect the differences in type, scope, and volume of services provided by the various types of home care agencies, including their volume of medicaid and medicare services, and that allows for reduced fees for home care agencies that are certified prior to initial license application. The department shall not charge a duplicate fee for survey work conducted pursuant to its role as state survey agency for the federal centers for medicare and medicaid services or the Colorado department of health care policy and financing.

(II) Notwithstanding section 25-3-105 (1) (a) (I) (B) , the state board may set and adjust licensure fees for home care agencies as appropriate based on the differentiating fee methodology developed by the state board pursuant to this paragraph (g) .

(h) Requirements for home care agencies to provide evidence of and maintain either liability insurance coverage or a surety bond in lieu of liability insurance coverage and for home care placement agencies to provide evidence of and maintain liability insurance coverage as required in section 25-27.5-103 (2) (a) (II) in amounts set through rules of the state board;

(i) Factors for home care agencies and home care placement agencies to consider when determining whether an applicant's conviction of or plea of guilty or nolo contendere to an offense disqualifies the applicant from employment or a referral. The state board may determine which offenses require consideration of the factors.

(j) Requirements for home care placement agencies to retain their records for a length of time determined by the state board to be available for inspection by the department pursuant to section 25-27.5-106 (2) (a) (III) ; and

(k) Fees for the registration of home care placement agencies to cover the direct and indirect costs associated with implementing the department's oversight of home care placement agencies.

(2) Rules promulgated by the state board are subject to judicial review in accordance with the

requirements of section 24-4-106, C.R.S.

(3) There is hereby established a home care advisory committee, which shall make recommendations to the department and the state board of health concerning the rules promulgated pursuant to this article and implementation of the licensing of home care agencies. The home care advisory committee shall be appointed by the executive director of the department. The advisory committee shall, at a minimum, consist of representatives from skilled home health services agencies, personal care services agencies, members of the disabled community who are home care consumers, seniors or representatives of seniors who are home care consumers, providers of medicaid services, providers of in-home support services, and representatives of the departments of health care policy and financing and human services. Members of the advisory committee shall serve at the pleasure of the appointing authority on a voluntary basis and shall serve without compensation.

(4) The department shall regulate a provider of PACE home care services for minimum standards for the operation of home care agencies as follows:

(a) For a PACE provider that serves only medicaid or medicare clients, if a full federal recertification survey required by the department of health care policy and financing is conducted at least every three years, the department shall accept the federal recertification survey in lieu of a separate survey for relicensure;

(b) The department shall not impose any requirement on a PACE provider that is more stringent than the federal and state medicaid PACE regulations, the three-way agreement entered into by the provider, CMS, and the department of health care policy and financing, and the PACE provider's policies and procedures;

(c) In reviewing a PACE provider's compliance with home care licensure, the department shall coordinate with the department of health care policy and financing regarding both license and certification requirements to ensure that the departments' similar regulations are congruently met;

(d) At the time that a PACE provider enrolls a PACE participant in a PACE program, the PACE provider shall give the client the department's contact information in writing to allow the client to report any complaints that may arise out of the client's PACE home care services. The department shall undertake any investigation arising from a complaint, other than a complaint alleging matters that are outside of the department's licensing authority.

(e) Under the department's licensing authority, the department has complete authority to enforce all home care requirements applicable to a PACE provider. If the department is unable to take corrective action congruently with the department of health care policy and financing, the department shall forward the proposed corrective action to and consult with the department of health care policy and financing before taking final action against a PACE provider.

## 25-27.5-105. Home care agency cash fund - created.

The department shall transmit the fees collected pursuant to section 25-27.5-104 (1) , plus any civil penalty collected pursuant to section 25-27.5-103 (1) (b) and (2) (c) (II) , to the state treasurer, who shall credit the fees and penalties to the home care agency cash fund, which fund is hereby created. The moneys in the fund are subject to annual appropriation by the general assembly for the direct and indirect costs of the department in performing its duties under this article. At the end of any fiscal year, all unexpended and unencumbered moneys in the fund remain in the fund and must not be credited or transferred to the general fund or any other fund.

## 25-27.5-106. License or registration - application - inspection - issuance - rules.

(1) A person applying for a home care agency license or a home care placement agency registration shall submit an application to the department annually upon a form and in a manner prescribed by the department.

(2) (a) (I) The department shall investigate and review each original application and each renewal application for a home care agency license or home care placement agency registration. The

department shall determine an applicant's compliance with this article and the rules adopted pursuant to section 25-27.5-104 before the department issues a license or registration.

(II) Except as provided in paragraph (a.5) of this subsection (2) , the department shall make inspections as it deems necessary to ensure that the health, safety, and welfare of the home care agency's or home care placement agency's home care consumers are being protected. Inspections of a home care consumer's home are subject to the consent of the home care consumer to access the property. The home care agency or home care placement agency shall submit in writing, in a form prescribed by the department, a plan detailing the measures that will be taken to correct any violations found by the department as a result of inspections undertaken pursuant to this subsection (2) .

(III) The department may inspect, as it deems necessary, a home care placement agency's records on weekdays between 9 a.m. and 5 p.m. to ensure that the home care placement agency is in compliance with the criminal history record check, general liability insurance, and disclosure requirements set forth in sections 25-27.5-103 (2) (b) , 25-27.5-104 (1) (c) and (1) (h) , and 25-27.5-107.

(a.5) Repealed.

(b) The department shall keep all medical information or documents obtained during an inspection or investigation of a home care agency, home care placement agency, or home care consumer's home confidential. All records, information, or documents so obtained are exempt from disclosure pursuant to sections 24-72-204, C.R.S., and 25-1-124.

(3) (a) With the submission of an application for a license or registration granted pursuant to this article or within ten days after a change in the owner, manager, or administrator, each owner of a home care agency or home care placement agency and each manager or administrator of a home care agency or home care placement agency must submit a complete set of his or her fingerprints to the Colorado bureau of investigation for the purpose of conducting a state and national fingerprint-based criminal history record check utilizing records of the Colorado bureau of investigation and the federal bureau of investigation. Each owner and each manager or administrator is responsible for paying the fee established by the Colorado bureau of investigation for conducting the fingerprint-based criminal history record check to the bureau. Upon completion of the criminal history record check, the bureau shall forward the results to the department. The department may acquire a name-based criminal history record check for an applicant who has twice submitted to a fingerprint-based criminal history record check and whose fingerprints are unclassifiable.

(b) The department shall use the information from the criminal history record check in ascertaining whether the person applying for licensure or registration has been convicted of a felony or of a misdemeanor, which felony or misdemeanor involves conduct that the department determines could pose a risk to the health, safety, or welfare of home care consumers of the home care agency or home care placement agency. The department shall maintain information obtained in accordance with this section.

(4) The department shall not issue a license or registration if the owner, manager, or administrator of the home care agency or home care placement agency has been convicted of a felony or of a misdemeanor, which felony or misdemeanor involves conduct that the department determines could pose a risk to the health, safety, or welfare of the home care consumers of the home care agency or home care placement agency.

(5) Except as otherwise provided in subsections (6) and (7) of this section, the department shall issue or renew a license or registration when it is satisfied that the applicant, licensee, or registrant is in compliance with the requirements set out in this article and the rules promulgated pursuant to this article. Except for provisional licenses issued in accordance with subsections (6) and (7) of this section, a license or registration issued or renewed pursuant to this section expires one year after the date of issuance or renewal.

(6) The department may issue a provisional license to an applicant for the purpose of operating a home care agency for a period of ninety days if the applicant is temporarily unable to conform to all of the minimum standards required under this article; except that no license shall be issued to

an applicant if the operation of the applicant's home care agency will adversely affect the health, safety, or welfare of the home care consumers of such home care agency. As a condition of obtaining a provisional license, the applicant shall show proof to the department that attempts are being made to conform and comply with applicable standards. No provisional license shall be granted prior to the completion of a criminal background check in accordance with subsection (3) of this section and a finding in accordance with subsection (4) of this section. A second provisional license may be issued, for a like term and fee, to effect compliance. No further provisional licenses may be issued for the current year after the second issuance.

(7) If requested by the Colorado department of health care policy and financing, the department may issue a provisional license for a period of ninety days to an agency that has applied to be a certified home care agency as defined in section 25-27.5-102. A provisional license shall not be granted prior to the completion of a fingerprint-based criminal history record check in accordance with subsection (3) of this section and a finding in accordance with subsection (4) of this section. A second provisional license may be issued, for a like term and fee, to effect compliance. No further provisional licenses may be issued for the current year after the second issuance.

## 25-27.5-107. Employee or referred service provider criminal history record check - rules.

The home care agency or home care placement agency shall require a person seeking employment or placement to submit to a criminal history record check before employment or referral to a consumer. The home care agency or home care placement agency or the person seeking employment with the home care agency shall pay the costs of the criminal history record check. The criminal history record check shall be conducted not more than ninety days before the employment or placement of the applicant.

## 25-27.5-108. License or registration denial - suspension - revocation.

(1) Upon denial of an application for an original license or registration, the department shall notify the applicant in writing of the denial by mailing a notice to the applicant at the address shown on his or her application. Any applicant aggrieved by the denial may pursue the remedy for review provided in article 4 of title 24, C.R.S., if the applicant, within thirty days after receiving the notice of denial, petitions the department to set a date and place for hearing, affording the applicant an opportunity to be heard in person or by counsel. All hearings on the denial of original licenses or registrations must be conducted in conformity with the provisions and procedures specified in article 4 of title 24, C.R.S.

(2) (a) The department may suspend, revoke, or refuse to renew the license or registration of a home care agency or home care placement agency that is out of compliance with the requirements of this article or the rules promulgated pursuant to this article. Before taking final action to suspend, revoke, or refuse to renew a license or registration, the department shall conduct a hearing on the matter in conformance with the provisions and procedures specified in article 4 of title 24, C.R.S.; except that the department may implement a summary suspension prior to a hearing in accordance with article 4 of title 24, C.R.S. If the department suspends, revokes, or refuses to renew a home care placement agency registration, the department shall remove the home care placement agency from the registry maintained by the department pursuant to section 25-27.5-103 (2) (a) (I) .

(b) (I) The department may impose intermediate restrictions or conditions on a licensed home care agency or registered home care placement agency that may include at least one of the following:

(A) Retaining a consultant to address corrective measures;

(B) Monitoring by the department for a specific period;

(C) Providing additional training to employees, owners, or operators of the home care agency or home care placement agency;

(D) Complying with a directed written plan to correct the violation; or

(E) Paying a civil fine not to exceed ten thousand dollars per calendar year for all violations.

(II) (A) If the department imposes an intermediate restriction or condition that is not a result of a serious and immediate threat to health or welfare, the department shall provide written notice of the restriction or condition to the licensed home care agency or registered home care placement agency. No later than ten days after the date the notice is received from the department, the licensed home care agency or registered home care placement agency shall submit a written plan that includes the time frame for completing the plan and addresses the restriction or condition specified.

(B) If the department imposes an intermediate restriction or condition that is the result of a serious and immediate threat to health, safety, or welfare, the department shall notify the licensed home care agency or registered home care placement agency in writing, by telephone, or in person during an on-site visit. The licensed home care agency or registered home care placement agency shall remedy the circumstances creating harm or potential harm immediately upon receiving notice of the restriction or condition. If the department provides notice of a restriction or condition by telephone or in person, the department shall send written confirmation of the restriction or condition to the licensed home care agency or registered home care placement agency within two business days.

(III) (A) After submission of an approved written plan, a licensed home care agency or registered home care placement agency may first appeal any intermediate restriction or condition on its license or registration to the department through an informal review process as established by the department.

(B) If the restriction or condition requires payment of a civil fine, the licensed home care agency or registered home care placement agency may request, and the department shall grant, a stay in payment of the fine until final disposition of the restriction or condition.

(C) If a licensed home care agency or registered home care placement agency is not satisfied with the result of the informal review or chooses not to seek informal review, the department shall not impose an intermediate restriction or condition on the licensed home care agency or registered home care placement agency until after the licensed home care agency or registered home care placement agency is afforded an opportunity for a hearing pursuant to section 24-4-105, C.R.S.

(IV) If the department assesses a civil fine pursuant to this paragraph (b) , the department shall transmit the fines to the state treasurer, who shall credit the fines to the home care agency cash fund created in section 25-27.5-105.

(V) The department shall use civil fines collected pursuant to this paragraph (b) for expenses related to:

(A) Continuing monitoring required pursuant to this paragraph (b) ;

(B) Education for licensed home care agencies or registered home care placement agencies to avoid restrictions or conditions or facilitate the application process or the change of ownership process;

(C) Education for home care consumers and their families about resolving problems with a home care agency or home care placement agency, rights of home care consumers, and responsibilities of home care agencies and home care placement agencies;

(D) Providing technical assistance to any home care agency or home care placement agency for the purpose of complying with changes in rules or state or federal law;

(E) Monitoring and assisting in the transition of home care consumers to other home care agencies or home care placement agencies, when the transition is a result of the revocation of a license or registration, or to other appropriate medical services; or

(F) Maintaining the operation of a home care agency or home care placement agency pending correction of violations, as determined necessary by the department.

(3) The department shall revoke or refuse to renew the license of a home care agency or the registration of a home care placement agency where the owner, licensee, or registrant has been convicted of a felony or misdemeanor involving conduct that the department determines could pose a risk to the health, safety, or welfare of the home care consumers of the home care agency or home care placement agency. The department may revoke or refuse to renew a license or registration only after conducting a hearing on the matter in accordance with article 4 of title 24,

### 25-27.5-109. Enforcement.
The department is responsible for the enforcement of this article and the rules adopted pursuant to this article.

### 25-27.5-110. Repeal of article - sunset review.
(1) This article is repealed, effective September 1, 2019.
(2) Before repeal, the department of regulatory agencies shall review the licensing of home care agencies and the registering of home care placement agencies as provided in section 24-34-104, C.R.S. In conducting its review and compiling its report pursuant to section 24-34-104 (5), C.R.S., the department of regulatory agencies shall segregate the data in the report based on the type of agency, specifying whether the agency is:
(a) A home care agency that provides skilled home health services;
(b) A home care agency that only provides personal care services; or
(c) A home care placement agency.

# ARTICLE 28. COLORADO HEALTH DATA COMMISSION

**25-28-101 to 25-28-111. (Repealed)**

# ARTICLE 29. DENVER HEALTH AND HOSPITAL AUTHORITY

### 25-29-101. Legislative declaration.
(1) The general assembly hereby finds and declares that:
(a) The city and county of Denver department of health and hospitals:
(I) Provides access to quality preventive, acute, and chronic health care for all the citizens of Denver regardless of ability to pay;
(II) Provides high quality emergency medical services to the citizens of Denver and the Rocky Mountain region;
(III) Fulfills public health functions as dictated by the Denver charter and the needs of the citizens of Denver;
(IV) Provides health education for patients and participates in the education of the next generation of health care professionals; and
(V) Engages in research which enhances its ability to meet the health care needs of patients of the Denver health system.
(b) In order to carry out its patient care and community service mission in an era of health care reform, it is necessary that the Denver health system be able to take whatever actions are necessary to enable its continuation as a system which provides the finest possible quality of health care.
(c) It is essential that the Denver health system be able to maximize its economic viability and productivity in order to avoid becoming increasingly dependent on city, state, and other

governmental subsidies.

(d) Both the quality and economic viability of the Denver health system will be difficult to maintain in the future under the present constraints imposed by government policy and regulation.

(e) The needs of the citizens of the state of Colorado and of the city and county of Denver will therefore be best served if the Denver health system is operated by a political subdivision charged with carrying out the mission and programs of the Denver health system.

(2) The general assembly further finds and declares that, after the transfer date, all new employees of the Denver health system shall be employees of the authority.

## 25-29-102. Definitions.

As used in this article, unless the context otherwise requires:

(1) "Authority" means the political subdivision and body corporate known as the Denver health and hospital authority created by this article.

(2) "Board" or "Board of directors" means the board of directors of the authority.

(3) "City" means the city and county of Denver as constituted under article XX of the state constitution.

(4) "City employee" means a person employed by the city and county of Denver, whether or not a classified employee.

(5) "Denver health system" means the programs, services, and facilities operated by the Denver department of health and hospitals prior to the transfer date.

(6) "Department" means the Denver department of health and hospitals.

(7) "Health system" means the Denver health system or the programs, services, and facilities operated by the authority after the transfer date.

(8) "Health system assets" means all property or rights in property, real and personal, tangible and intangible existing on the transfer date, used by or accruing to the department in the normal course of operations.

(9) "Health system liabilities" means all debts or other obligations, contingent or certain, owing on the transfer date, to any person or other entity, arising out of the operation of the Denver health system and including, without limitation, all debts for the purchase of goods and services, whether or not delivered, and obligations for the delivery of services, whether or not performed.

(10) "Mayor" means the mayor of the city and county of Denver.

(11) "Transfer date" means a date agreed to by the city and the authority for the transfer of Denver health system assets to and the assumption of health system liabilities by such authority.

## 25-29-103. Denver health and hospital authority.

(1) There is hereby created the Denver health and hospital authority, which shall be a body corporate and a political subdivision of the state, which shall not be an agency of the state or local government, and which shall not be subject to administrative direction or control by any department, commission, board, bureau, or agency of state or local government.

(2) Prior to July 1, 2016, the authority shall be governed by a nine-member board of directors, and on and after July 1, 2016, the authority shall be governed by an eleven-member board of directors. The board shall be responsible for the operation of the health system. The mayor shall appoint the members of the board whose appointments shall be conditioned upon confirmation by the Denver city council. Of the nine members first appointed, four shall serve a term of two years and five shall serve a term of five years. Thereafter, all members, including the two members first appointed for terms beginning on July 1, 2016, shall serve five-year terms. Actions of the board shall require the affirmative vote of the majority of the total membership of the board. The board shall annually elect a chairperson from among its members. Any member may be elected to serve successive terms as chairperson.

(3) Each member of the board of directors shall hold office until a successor is appointed and qualified. Any member shall be eligible for reappointment, but voting members shall not be eligible to serve more than two consecutive full terms. Members of the board shall receive no

compensation for such services but may be reimbursed for necessary expenses while serving on the board. Any vacancy in office shall be filled in the same manner provided for original appointments.

(4) (a) Repealed.

(b) On and after July 1, 2015, any member may be removed upon a unanimous vote of the board, excluding the member to be removed, and approval of the mayor. The decision to remove a board member pursuant to this paragraph (b) shall be based on the board's determination that the member to be removed has failed to perform his or her duties as a board member or has engaged in conduct detrimental to the hospital authority or the board. Prior to the removal of the member, the board shall provide written notice to the member. A member removed from the board pursuant to this paragraph (b) does not have the right to appeal the board's decision to remove the member from the board.

(5) No part of the revenues or assets of the authority shall inure to the benefit of, or be distributed to, members of the board of directors, officers of the authority, or any other private person or entity; except that the authority may make reasonable payments for expenses incurred on its behalf relating to any of its lawful purposes and the authority is also authorized and empowered to pay reasonable compensation for services rendered to or for its benefit relating to any of its lawful purposes.

(6) The authority and its corporate existence shall continue until terminated by law; except that no such law shall take effect so long as the authority has outstanding bonds, notes, or other obligations unless adequate provisions have been made for the payment of such outstanding debt.

## 25-29-104. Mission of authority - action of board of directors.

(1) The mission of the authority is to:

(a) Provide access to quality preventive, acute, and chronic health care for all the citizens of Denver regardless of ability to pay;

(b) Provide high quality emergency medical services to Denver and the Rocky Mountain region;

(c) Fulfill public health functions in accordance with the agreement entered into with the city pursuant to the authority granted in section 25-29-105 and the needs of the citizens of Denver;

(d) Provide for the health education of patients and to participate in the education of the next generation of health care professionals; and

(e) Engage in research to the extent that it enhances the ability of the authority to meet the health care needs of its patients.

(2) The board of directors shall not transfer assets of the authority or of the health system to any person or entity except for such grants or transfers as may be incidental to health system programs and which are consistent with the purposes of this article.

(3) Upon the dissolution of the authority, all assets of the authority, after the satisfaction of creditors, shall revert to the city.

(4) The business activities of the authority, including any joint ventures, shall be primarily in furtherance or in support of the duties and responsibilities of the health system as specified in subsection (1) of this section.

## 25-29-105. Transfer of health system assets and liabilities to authority.

(1) The authority is authorized to enter into agreements with the city for the purpose of leasing, conveying, or otherwise acquiring Denver's health system assets. Any such lease, conveyance, transfer, or other agreement to acquire such assets shall be on such terms as may be agreed upon by the parties and shall include consideration of the authority's agreement to assume Denver's health system liabilities.

(2) Any transfer of health system assets to the authority shall be conditioned upon the existence of a binding agreement between the city and the authority transferring management and operation of some or all of the Denver health system to the authority and by which the authority shall accept and agree to fulfill the mission specified in section 25-29-104 and the provisions of section 25-29-

107 concerning personnel.

(3) Any transfer of health system assets to the authority pursuant to this section shall be further conditioned upon the existence of a binding agreement between the authority and the city which provides that, effective on the transfer date and thereafter, the authority shall assume responsibility for and shall defend, indemnify, and hold the city harmless with respect to:

(a) All liabilities and duties of the city pursuant to contracts, agreements, and leases for commodities, services, and supplies utilized by the Denver health system, including real property leases;

(b) All claims related to the employment relationship between employees of the authority and the authority on and after the transfer date;

(c) All claims for breach of contract resulting from the authority's action or failure to act on and after the transfer date; and

(d) All claims related to the authority's errors and omissions including but not limited to medical malpractice; director and officer liability; workers' compensation; automobile liability; and premises, completed operations, and products liability.

## 25-29-106. Relationship between authority and city and county of Denver.

(1) On and after the transfer date, except for the power of the city and the mayor to appoint and remove members of the authority's board of directors, the city shall have no further control over the operation of the health system.

(2) The authority may enter into any agreement with the city including but not limited to contracts for:

(a) The provision of goods, services, and facilities in support of Denver's health system; and

(b) Insurance coverage for the authority and its employees for medical malpractice liability from any self-insurance trust fund controlled or maintained by the city.

(3) The authority shall comply with all of city regulatory laws, ordinances, and rules and regulations generally applicable to entities and property holders in the city.

## 25-29-107. Personnel.

(1) Any employee of the Denver health system who is an employee of the city on the transfer date may elect to remain a city employee or may elect to become an employee of the authority. An employee may elect to become an employee of the authority at any time on or after the transfer date but may not thereafter return to the city's personnel system while employed by the authority. No city employee shall be discriminated against in training, promotion, retention, assignment of duties, granting of rights and benefits, or any other personnel action. Promotion or a change in position shall not be contingent upon the employee becoming an employee of the authority.

(2) Any employee of the authority who elects to remain a city employee shall retain all rights and privileges which are applicable to such employee's position.

(3) In the case of any dispute involving a city employee who is a member of the city personnel system, the authority shall agree to accept resolution of all disciplinary appeals or other employment disputes governed by the city's system according to the rules and procedures applicable to members of the city's personnel system.

(4) Any city employee who elects to become an employee of the authority shall receive credit from the authority for sick leave and annual leave accrued while employed by the city, the cash equivalent of all or part of such leave, or a combination of credit or cash equivalent, all in accordance with a written agreement between the city and the authority.

(5) The authority shall establish and administer its own personnel program, including a wage and benefit structure, for authority employees.

## 25-29-108. Retirement benefits - rights of former city employees.

(1) Any former city employee who elects to become an employee of the authority shall be eligible for membership in the authority's retirement plan.

(2) The authority shall qualify its retirement plan under section 401 (a) of the "Internal Revenue Code of 1986", as amended, as a governmental plan under section 414 (d) of such code.

## 25-29-109. Records of board of directors.
Records of the authority are subject to the open records law under article 72 of title 24, C.R.S.

## 25-29-110. Meetings of board of directors.
(1) All meetings of the board of directors of the authority shall be subject to the provisions of section 24-6-402, C.R.S. No business of the board of directors shall be transacted except at a regular or special meeting at which a quorum consisting of at least a majority of the total membership of the board is present. Any action of the board shall require the affirmative vote of a majority of the total membership of the board.
(2) The board may elect to hold an executive session for the consideration of any documents or data protected from disclosure pursuant to section 25-29-109.

## 25-29-111. Disclosure of interests required.
Any member of the board of directors and any employee or other agent or advisor of the authority, who has a direct or indirect interest in any contract or transaction with the authority, shall disclose this interest to the authority. This interest shall be set forth in the minutes of the authority, and no director, employee, or other agent or advisor having such interest shall participate on behalf of the authority in the authorization of any such contract or transaction; except that the provisions of this section shall not be construed to prohibit any city employee who is a member of the board of directors who has no personal interest in the matter at hand from voting on the authorization of any such contract or transaction between the authority and the city. The status of a board member as a member of the department board, in and of itself, shall not be a conflicting interest.

## 25-29-112. General powers of authority.
(1) In addition to any other powers granted to the authority in this article, the authority shall have the following powers:
(a) To have the duties, privileges, immunities, rights, liabilities, and disabilities of a body corporate and political subdivision of the state;
(b) To have perpetual existence and succession;
(c) To adopt, have, and use a seal and to alter the seal at its pleasure;
(d) To sue and be sued;
(e) To enter into any contract or agreement not inconsistent with this article or the laws of this state and to authorize the chief executive officer to enter into contracts, execute all instruments, and do all things necessary or convenient in the exercise of the powers granted in this article and to secure the payment of bonds;
(f) To borrow money and to issue bonds evidencing the same;
(g) To purchase, lease, trade, exchange, or otherwise acquire, maintain, hold, improve, mortgage, lease, sell, and dispose of personal property, whether tangible or intangible, and any interest therein; and to purchase, lease, trade, exchange, or otherwise acquire real property or any interest therein, and to maintain, hold, improve, mortgage, lease, and otherwise transfer such real property, so long as such transactions do not interfere with the mission of the authority as specified in section 25-29-104;
(h) To acquire space, equipment, services, supplies, and insurance necessary to carry out the purposes of this article;
(i) To deposit any moneys of the authority in any banking institution within or without the state or in any depository authorized in section 24-75-603, C.R.S., and to appoint, for the purpose of making such deposits, one or more persons to act as custodians of the moneys of the authority, who shall give surety bonds in such amounts and form and for such purposes as the board of directors requires;

(j) To contract for and to accept any gifts, grants, and loans of funds, property, or any other aid in any form from the federal government, the state, any state agency, or any other source, or any combination thereof, and to comply, subject to the provisions of this article, with the terms and conditions thereof;

(k) To have and exercise all rights and powers necessary or incidental to or implied from the specific powers granted in this article, which specific powers shall not be considered as a limitation upon any power necessary or appropriate to carry out the purposes and intent of this article;

(l) To fix the time and place or places at which its regular and special meetings are to be held. Meetings shall be held on the call of the presiding officer, but no less than six meetings shall be held annually.

(m) To adopt and from time to time amend or repeal bylaws and rules and regulations consistent with the provisions of this article; except that article 4 of title 24, C.R.S., shall not apply to the promulgation of any policies, procedures, rules, or regulations of the authority;

(n) To appoint one or more persons as secretary and treasurer of the board and such other officers as the board of directors may determine and provide for their duties and terms of office;

(o) To appoint the authority's chief executive officer and such agents, employees, and professional and business advisers as may from time to time be necessary in its judgment to accomplish the purposes of this article, and to fix the compensation of such chief executive officer, employees, agents, and advisers, and to establish the powers and duties of all such agents, employees, and other persons contracting with the authority;

(p) To waive, by such means as the authority deems appropriate, the exemption from federal income taxation of interest on the authority's bonds, notes, or other obligations provided by the "Internal Revenue Code of 1986", as amended, or any other federal statute providing a similar exemption;

(q) To make and execute agreements, contracts, and other instruments necessary or convenient in the exercise of the powers and functions of the authority under this article, including but not limited to contracts with any person, firm, corporation, municipality, state agency, county, or other entity. All municipalities, counties, and state agencies are hereby authorized to enter into and do all things necessary to perform any such arrangement or contract with the authority.

(r) To arrange for guaranties or insurance of its bonds, notes, or other obligations by the federal government or by any private insurer, and to pay any premiums therefor;

(s) To engage in joint ventures, or to participate in alliances, purchasing consortia, health insurance pools, or other cooperative arrangements, with any public or private entity;

(t) To authorize officers or employees of the authority to incorporate a nonprofit corporation to be capitalized and controlled by the authority, or to serve in their official capacities on the governing body of a governmental or nongovernmental entity.

## 25-29-113. Bonds and notes.

(1) (a) The authority has the power and is authorized to issue from time to time its notes and bonds in such principal amounts as the authority determines to be necessary to provide sufficient funds for achieving any of its corporate purposes, including the payment of interest on notes and bonds of the authority, the establishment of reserves to secure such notes and bonds, and all other expenditures of the authority incident to and necessary or convenient to carry out its corporate purposes and powers.

(b) (I) The authority has the power, from time to time, to issue:

(A) Notes to renew notes;

(B) Bonds to pay notes, including the interest thereon, and, whenever it deems refunding expedient, to refund any bonds whether the bonds to be refunded have or have not matured; and

(C) Bonds partly to refund bonds then outstanding and partly for any of its corporate purposes.

(II) Refunding bonds issued pursuant to this paragraph (b) may be exchanged for the bonds to be refunded or sold and the proceeds applied to the purchase, redemption, or payment of such bonds.

(c) The authority has the power to provide for the replacement of lost, destroyed, or mutilated bonds or notes.

(d) Except as may otherwise be expressly provided by the authority, every issue of its notes and bonds shall be general obligations of the authority payable out of any revenues or moneys of the authority, subject only to any agreements with the holders of particular notes or bonds pledging any particular revenues.

(2) The notes and bonds shall be authorized by a resolution adopted by an affirmative vote of a majority of the members of the board of directors.

(3) Any resolution authorizing any notes or bonds or any issue thereof may contain provisions, which shall be a part of the contract with the holders thereof, as to:

(a) Pledging all or any part of the revenues of the authority to secure the payment of the notes or bonds or of any issue thereof, subject to such agreements with noteholders or bondholders as may then exist;

(b) Pledging all or any part of the assets of the authority to secure the payment of the notes or bonds or of any issue of notes or bonds, subject to such agreements with noteholders or bondholders as may then exist, such assets to include any grant or contribution from the federal government or any corporation, association, institution, or person;

(c) The setting aside of reserves or sinking funds and the regulation and disposition thereof;

(d) Limitations on the purpose to which the proceeds of sale of notes or bonds may be applied and pledging such proceeds to secure the payment of the notes or bonds or of any issue thereof;

(e) Limitations on the issuance of additional notes or bonds, the terms upon which additional notes or bonds may be issued and secured, and the refunding of outstanding or other notes or bonds;

(f) The procedure, if any, by which the terms of any contract with noteholders or bondholders may be amended or abrogated, the amount of notes or bonds the holders of which must consent thereto, and the manner in which such consent may be given;

(g) Limitations on the amount of moneys to be expended by the authority for operating expenses of the authority;

(h) Vesting in a trustee such property, rights, powers, and duties in trust as the authority may determine, which may include any or all of the rights, powers, and duties of the trustee appointed by the bondholders pursuant to this article, and limiting or abrogating the right of the bondholders to appoint a trustee under this article or limiting the rights, powers, and duties of such trustee;

(i) Defining the acts or omissions to act which shall constitute a default in the obligations and duties of the authority to the holders of the notes or bonds and providing for the rights and remedies of the holders of the notes or bonds in the event of such default, including as a matter of right the appointment of a receiver; except that such rights and remedies shall not be inconsistent with the general laws of this state and the other provisions of this article;

(j) Any other matters, of like or different character, which in any way affect the security or protection of the holders of the notes or bonds.

(4) The bonds or notes of each issue may, in the discretion of the board of directors, be made redeemable before maturity at such prices and under such terms and conditions as may be determined by the board of directors. Notes shall mature at such time as may be determined by the board of directors, and bonds shall mature at such time, not exceeding thirty-five years from their date of issue, as may be determined by the board. The bonds may be issued as serial bonds payable in annual installments or as term bonds or as a combination thereof. The notes and bonds shall bear interest at such rate, be in such denominations, be in such form, either coupon or registered, carry such registration privileges, be executed in such manner, be payable in such medium of payment and at such place, and be subject to such terms of redemption as such resolution may provide. The notes and bonds of the authority may be sold by the authority, at public or private sale, at such price as the board of directors shall determine.

(5) In case any officer whose signature or a facsimile of whose signature appears on any bonds or notes or coupons attached thereto ceases to be such officer before the delivery thereof, such signature or such facsimile shall nevertheless be valid and sufficient for all purposes the same as if the officer had remained in office until such delivery. The board of directors may also provide for

the authentication of the bonds or notes by a trustee or fiscal agent.

(6) Prior to the preparation of definitive bonds or notes, the authority may, under like restrictions, issue interim receipts or temporary bonds or notes until such definitive bonds or notes have been executed and are available for delivery.

(7) The authority, subject to such agreements with noteholders or bondholders as may then exist, has the power out of any funds available therefor to purchase notes or bonds of the authority, which shall thereupon be cancelled at a price not exceeding:

(a) If the notes or bonds are then redeemable, the redemption price then applicable plus accrued interest to the next interest payment thereon; or

(b) If the notes or bonds are not then redeemable, the redemption price applicable on the first date after such purchase upon which the notes or bonds become subject to redemption plus accrued interest to such date.

(8) In the discretion of the authority, the bonds may be secured by a trust indenture by and between the authority and a corporate trustee, which may be any trust company or bank having the power of a trust company within or without this state. Such trust indenture may contain such provisions for protecting and enforcing the rights and remedies of the bondholders as may be reasonable and proper and not in violation of law, including covenants setting forth the duties of the authority in relation to the exercise of its corporate powers and the custody, safeguarding, and application of all moneys. The authority may provide by such trust indenture for the payment of the proceeds of the bonds and the revenues to the trustee under such trust indenture or other depository and for the method of disbursement thereof, with such safeguards and restrictions as it may determine. All expenses incurred in carrying out such trust indenture may be treated as a part of the operating expenses of the authority. If the bonds are secured by a trust indenture, the bondholders shall have no authority to appoint a separate trustee to represent them.

(9) The authority shall not have outstanding, at any one time, bonds, not including bond anticipation notes, or bonds which have been refunded, in an aggregate principal amount exceeding one hundred twenty million dollars without the approval of the city acting by formal resolution of the Denver city council; however, this limitation shall not apply to bonds which are unsecured or secured solely by a pledge of the revenues of the authority and are not in any way secured by a pledge of any of the authority's other assets, including, without limitation, any buildings or real property, and which contain a statement that the bondholders shall not have any recourse against the authority's other assets for repayment of the bonds. Under no circumstances shall the city be liable for any indebtedness incurred by the authority. The general assembly specifically finds there is a substantial public purpose in limiting the indebtedness of the authority in the event the authority assets or the hospital assets are transferred back to or revert to the city.

(10) The authority has the power and is authorized to issue from time to time notes, bonds, and other securities which may be collateralized or otherwise secured in whole or in part by loans or participations or other interests in such loans or which may evidence loans or participations or other interests in such loans to provide net funds that are to be dedicated in whole or in part by resolution of the authority to the carrying out of one or more of the purposes of the authority. The interest on or from such notes, bonds, and other securities may be subject to or exempt from federal income taxation.

(11) Any notes, bonds, or other securities issued pursuant to this section, and the income therefrom, including any profit from the sale thereof, shall at all times be free from taxation by the state or any agency, political subdivision, or instrumentality of the state.

## 25-29-114. Remedies.

Any holder of bonds issued under the provisions of this article, or any coupons appertaining thereto and the trustee under any trust agreement or resolution authorizing the issuance of such bonds, except to the extent the rights under this article may be restricted by such trust agreement or resolution, may, either at law or in equity by suit, action, mandamus, or other proceeding, protect and enforce any and all rights under the laws of the state or granted under this article or under such agreement or resolution, or under any other contract executed by the authority pursuant to this article, and may enforce and compel the performance of all duties required by this article or by such trust agreement or resolution to be performed by the authority or by an officer thereof.

## 25-29-115. Negotiable instruments.

Notwithstanding any of the foregoing provisions of this article or any recitals in any bonds issued under the provisions of this article, all such bonds and interest coupons appertaining thereto shall be negotiable instruments under the laws of this state, subject only to any applicable provisions for registration.

## 25-29-116. Bonds eligible for investment.

Bonds issued under the provisions of this article are hereby made securities in which all insurance companies, trust companies, banking associations, savings and loan associations, investment companies, executors, administrators, trustees, and other fiduciaries may properly and legally invest funds, including capital in their control or belonging to them. Public entities, as defined in section 24-75-601 (1) , C.R.S., may invest public funds in such bonds only if said bonds satisfy the investment requirements established in part 6 of article 75 of title 24, C.R.S. Such bonds are hereby made securities which may properly and legally be deposited with and received by any state or municipal officer or any agency or political subdivision of the state for any purpose for which the deposit of bonds, notes, or obligations of the state is authorized by law.

## 25-29-117. Refunding bonds.

(1) The board of directors may provide for the issuance of refunding obligations of the authority for the purpose of refunding any obligations then outstanding which have been issued under the provisions of this article, including the payment of any redemption premium thereon and any interest accrued or to accrue to the date of redemption of such obligations, and for any corporate purpose of the authority.

(2) Refunding obligations issued as provided in subsection (1) of this section may be sold or exchanged for outstanding obligations issued under this article, and, if sold, the proceeds thereof may be applied, in addition to any other authorized purposes, to the purchase, redemption, or payment of such outstanding obligations. Pending the application of the proceeds of any such refunding obligations, with any other available funds, to the payment of the principal, the accrued interest, and any redemption premium on the obligations being refunded and, if so provided or permitted in the resolution authorizing the issuance of such refunding obligations or in the trust agreement securing the same, to the payment of any interest on such refunding obligations and any expenses in connection with such refunding, such proceeds may be invested in securities meeting the investment requirements established in part 6 of article 75 of title 24, C.R.S., which shall mature or which shall be subject to redemption by the holders thereof, at the option of such holders, not later than the respective dates when the proceeds, together with the interest accruing thereon, will be required for the purposes intended.

## 25-29-118. Nonliability of state for bonds.

Neither the state of Colorado nor the city shall be liable for bonds of the authority, and such bonds shall not constitute a debt of the state or the city. The bonds shall contain on the face thereof a statement to such effect.

## 25-29-119. Members of authority not personally liable on bonds.

Neither the members of the board of directors nor any authorized person executing bonds issued pursuant to this article shall be personally liable for such bonds by reason of the execution or issuance thereof.

## 25-29-120. Annual report.

The authority shall submit to the mayor of the city within six months after the end of the fiscal year a report which shall set forth a complete and detailed operating and financial statement of the authority during such year. Also included in the report shall be any recommendations with reference to additional legislation or other action that may be necessary to carry out the purposes of the authority.

## 25-29-121. Powers of authority - investments.

(1) The authority has the power:

(a) To invest any funds not required for immediate disbursement in property or in securities which meet the standard for investments established in section 15-1-304, C.R.S., provided such investment assists the authority in carrying out its public purposes; and to sell from time to time such securities thus purchased and held; and to deposit any securities in any trust bank within or without the state. Any funds deposited in a banking institution or in any depository authorized in section 24-75-603, C.R.S., shall be secured in such manner and subject to such terms and conditions as the board may determine, with or without payment of any interest on such deposit, including, without limitation, time deposits evidenced by certificates of deposit. Any commercial bank incorporated under the laws of this state which may act as depository of any funds of the authority may issue indemnifying bonds or may pledge such securities as may be required by the board of directors.

(b) Notwithstanding the provisions of paragraph (a) of this subsection (1), to contract with the holders of any of its notes or bonds as to the custody, collection, securing, investment, and payment of any moneys of the authority and of any moneys held in trust or otherwise for the payment of notes or bonds and to carry out such contract. Moneys held in trust or otherwise for the payment of notes or bonds or in any way to secure notes or bonds and deposits of such moneys may be secured in the same manner as moneys of the authority, and all banks and trust companies are authorized to give such security for such deposits.

## 25-29-122. Agreement of this state.

This state does hereby pledge to and agree with the holders of any notes or bonds issued under this article that this state will not limit or alter the rights hereby vested in the authority to fulfill the terms of any agreements made with the said holders thereof or in any way impair the rights and remedies of such holders until such notes and bonds, together with the interest thereon, with interest on any unpaid installments of interest, and all costs and expenses in connection with any action or proceeding by or on behalf of such holders are fully met and discharged. The authority is authorized to include this pledge and agreement of this state in any agreement with the holders of such notes or bonds.

## 25-29-123. This article not a limitation of powers.

Nothing in this article shall be construed as a restriction or limitation upon any other powers which the authority might otherwise have under any other law of this state, and this article is cumulative to any such powers. This article does and shall be construed to provide a complete, additional, and alternative method for the doing of the things authorized thereby and shall be regarded as supplemental and additional to powers conferred by other laws. However, the issuance of bonds, notes, and other obligations and refunding bonds under the provisions of this article need not comply with the requirements of any other state law applicable to the issuance of bonds, notes, and other obligations. No proceedings, notice, or approval shall be required for the issuance of any bonds, notes, or other obligations or any instrument as security therefor, except as is provided in this article.

## 25-29-124. Exemption from property taxation.

The authority shall be exempt from any general ad valorem taxes upon any property of the authority acquired and used for its public purposes. The authority may enter into agreements to pay annual sums in lieu of taxes to any county, municipality, or other taxing entity with respect to any real property which is owned by the authority and is located in such county, municipality, or other taxing entity.

### 25-29-125. General assembly retains authority to enact laws governing Denver health and hospital authority.

The general assembly expressly reserves its plenary legislative authority relating to the Denver health and hospital authority, including but not limited to the authority to enact laws relating thereto. Nothing in this part 5 or part 6 of this article or in section 11 of article II of the state constitution or in section 10 of article I of the federal constitution, relating to impairment of the obligation of contract, shall be construed to limit said legislative authority. Any contract or other obligation of the authority is expressly subject to the provisions of this section, and the parties to such contract or obligation shall not assert such contract or obligation as a bar to the general assembly's exercise of legislative authority relating to the Denver health and hospital authority.

### 25-29-126. Severability.

Any provision of this article declared to be unconstitutional or otherwise invalid shall not impair the remaining provisions of this article.


# ARTICLE 30. FEMALE GENITAL MUTILATION OUTREACH


### 25-30-101 to 25-30-104. (Repealed)


# ARTICLE 31. COLORADO NURSE HOME VISITOR PROGRAM


### 25-31-101 to 25-31-108. (Repealed)


# ARTICLE 32. POISON CONTROL ACT


### 25-32-101. Short title.

This article shall be known and may be cited as the "Poison Control Act".

### 25-32-102. Legislative declaration.

The general assembly hereby declares that it is in the interest of the public's health and well-being to continue to provide quality poison control services to the people of this state and that the provision of such services is a matter of statewide concern. It is the intent of the general assembly in enacting this article that such services be made available throughout the state on a consistent and prompt basis, by means of a toll-free telephone network, in order that illness or death that may result from the exposure of an individual to poisonous substances may be avoided. The general assembly finds that the provision of such poison control services may be accomplished on a more cost-efficient basis, at a savings to the taxpayer, if the duty of providing such services is placed with the department of public health and environment with authority to contract with a competitively priced service provider for the entire state.

## 25-32-103. Definitions.

As used in this article, unless the context otherwise requires:

(1) Repealed.

(2) "Department" means the department of public health and environment.

(3) "Poison control services" shall include the following services provided by an entity certified by the American association of poison control centers or its successor organization:

(a) Twenty-four-hour toll-free telephone service dedicated to disseminating information on prevention of poisoning and the care and treatment of individuals exposed to poisonous substances;

(b) Dissemination of poison information by persons who are trained in poison control education, and the prevention, triage, and treatment of poisoning and who meet the criteria established by and are certified by the American association of poison control centers, or its successor organization; and

(c) Supervision of poison control centers by a person who meets the criteria established by the American association of poison control centers, or its successor organization, and who shall be available twenty-four hours each day for consultation.

## 25-32-104. Poison control services - statewide poison control oversight board - duties. (Repealed)

## 25-32-105. Department - poison control services - duties - contract.

(1) The department has the following powers and duties with respect to the provision of poison control services on a statewide basis and for the dissemination of information as provided in this article:

(a) To solicit, receive, and review contract bids for the provision of poison control services and the dissemination of poison control information by means of a toll-free telephone network;

(b) (I) To contract with private, nonprofit, or public entities for the continuing provision of statewide poison control services and the continuing dissemination of poison control information to the citizens of the state by means of a toll-free telephone network, the provision of which services initially commenced on July 1, 1995. The department shall review the contract at least once each year and shall solicit and receive bids on the provision of poison control services no less than once every five years. This paragraph (b) shall apply to contract years commencing July 1, 1995, and thereafter.

(II) On or after January 1, 2016, to contract with private, nonprofit, or public entities for the continuing provision of statewide poison control services and the continuing dissemination of poison control information to the citizens of the state by means other than a toll-free telephone network, such as text messaging, instant messaging, and e-mail. The entity or entities shall coordinate these services with the toll-free telephone network described in subparagraph (I) of this paragraph (b) . The general assembly shall appropriate at least one million dollars for the fiscal year 2015-16 to the department for it to contract with an entity to build the infrastructure necessary for the services identified in this subparagraph (II) , and any unexpended and unencumbered moneys from the appropriation remain available for expenditure by the department in the next fiscal year without further appropriation. In addition, the general assembly may annually appropriate moneys from the marijuana tax cash fund created in section 39-28.8-501, C.R.S., or the proposition AA refund account created in section 39-28.8-604 (1) , C.R.S., to the department for the services identified in this subparagraph (II) .

(c) To provide, by contract and for adequate reimbursement, poison control services and the dissemination of poison control information to the citizens of other states by this state;

(d) To contract with an auditor for a performance or financial audit at the discretion of the department. A copy of such audit, when performed, shall be sent to the joint budget committee.

(2) Whenever the department of health care policy and financing is referred to or designated by any contract or other document in connection with the duties and functions transferred to the department of public health and environment, such reference or designation shall be deemed to apply to the department of public health and environment. All contracts entered into by the department of health care policy and financing prior to July 1, 2002, in connection with the duties and functions transferred to the department of public health and environment, are hereby validated, with the department of public health and environment succeeding to all the rights and obligations of such contracts. Any appropriation of funds from prior fiscal years open to satisfy obligations incurred under such contracts are hereby transferred and appropriated to the department of public health and environment for the payment of such obligations.

### 25-32-106. Release of medical information.

Notwithstanding any other provisions to the contrary, when a poison control service provider selected pursuant to section 25-32-105 determines that a medical emergency exists and that information concerning the patient's medical history is necessary to assist in the diagnosis or treatment of such patient, the patient's physician shall release to the poison control service provider such medical information concerning the patient as may be necessary to aid in the diagnosis or treatment of the patient. The poison control service provider receiving such information shall maintain the confidentiality of the information received.

# ARTICLE 33. FARMERS' MARKET NUTRITION PROGRAM WOMEN, INFANTS, AND CHILDREN

**25-33-101 to 25-33-104. (Repealed)**

# ARTICLE 34. COLORADO STROKE ADVISORY BOARD

**25-34-101 to 25-34-107. (Repealed)**

# ARTICLE 34.1. STROKE PREVENTION AND TREATMENT CASH FUND TRANSFER

**25-34.1-101. Transfer of balance of stroke prevention and treatment cash**

**fund - repeal. (Repealed)**

# ARTICLE 35. COLORADO CANCER DRUG REPOSITORY PROGRAM

## 25-35-101. Short title.
This article shall be known and may be cited as the "Colorado Cancer Drug Repository Act".

## 25-35-102. Definitions.
As used in this article, unless the context otherwise requires:

(1) "Cancer drug" means a prescription drug that is used to treat cancer or the side effects of cancer.

(2) "Department" means the department of public health and environment.

(3) "Dispense" shall have the same meaning as set forth in section 12-42.5-102 (11) , C.R.S.

(4) "Eligible patient" means an uninsured or underinsured cancer patient who meets the eligibility criteria established in rule by the state board.

(5) "Health care facility" means a hospital, hospice, or hospital unit that is required to be licensed pursuant to section 25-3-101.

(6) "Medical clinic" means a community health clinic required to be licensed or certified by the department pursuant to section 25-1.5-103.

(7) "Medical device" means an instrument, apparatus, implement, machine, contrivance, implant, in vitro reagent, or other similar or related article, including a component, part, or accessary that is:

(a) Recognized in the official national formulary, or the United States pharmacopoeia, or any supplement;

(b) Intended for use in the diagnosis of disease or other conditions, or in the cure, mitigation, treatment, or prevention of disease, in humans or animals; or

(c) Intended to affect the structure or any function of the human body or animals, that does not achieve any of its primary intended purposes through chemical action within or on the human body or animals, and that is not dependent upon being metabolized for the achievement of any of its primary intended purposes.

(8) "Pharmacist" means an individual licensed by this state pursuant to article 42.5 of title 12, C.R.S., to engage in the practice of pharmacy.

(9) "Program" means the Colorado cancer drug repository program created in section 25-35-103.

(10) "State board" means the state board of health.

## 25-35-103. Cancer drug repository - administration - donation - dispensing - cancer drugs - medical devices.
(1) There is hereby established the Colorado cancer drug repository program for the purpose of allowing a cancer patient or the patient's family to donate unused cancer drugs and medical devices to uninsured and underinsured cancer patients in the state of Colorado. The program shall be administered by the department.

(2) The program shall allow a cancer patient or the patient's family to donate unused cancer drugs or medical devices to a health care facility, medical clinic, or pharmacy that elects to participate in the program. A health care facility, medical clinic, or pharmacy that receives a donated cancer drug or medical device under the program may distribute the cancer drug to another eligible health care facility, medical clinic, or pharmacy for use under the program.

(3) A pharmacist may accept and dispense cancer drugs and medical devices donated under the program to eligible patients if all of the following requirements are met:

(a) (I) The cancer drug or medical device is in its original, unopened, sealed, and tamper-evident packaging or, if packaged in single-unit doses, the single-unit-dose packaging is unopened; or

(II) The pharmacist has determined that the cancer drug or medical device is safe for redistribution;

(b) The cancer drug bears an expiration date that has not expired;

(c) The cancer drug or medical device is not adulterated or misbranded, as determined by a pharmacist; and

(d) The cancer drug or medical device is prescribed by a practitioner, as defined in section 12-42.5-102 (32) , C.R.S., for use by an eligible patient and is dispensed by a pharmacist.

(4) A cancer drug or medical device donated under the program may not be resold. A health care facility, medical clinic, or pharmacy may charge an eligible patient a handling fee to receive a donated cancer drug or medical device, which fee may not exceed the amount specified in rule by the state board.

(5) Nothing in this section requires a health care facility, medical clinic, or pharmacy to participate in the program.

(6) A health care facility, medical clinic, or pharmacy that elects to participate in the program shall establish eligibility criteria for individuals to receive donated cancer drugs or medical devices. Dispensation shall be prioritized to cancer patients who are uninsured or underinsured. Dispensation to other cancer patients shall be permitted if an uninsured or underinsured cancer patient is not available.

### 25-35-104. Rules.

(1) The state board, in consultation with the state board of pharmacy, shall promulgate any rules necessary for the implementation and administration of the program. The rules shall include, at a minimum:

(a) Requirements for health care facilities, medical clinics, and pharmacies to accept and dispense donated cancer drugs and medical devices under the program, including but not limited to:

(I) Eligibility criteria; and

(II) Standards and procedures for a health care facility, medical clinic, or pharmacy to accept, safely store, and dispense donated cancer drugs and medical devices.

(b) and (c) Repealed.

(d) The maximum handling fee that a health care facility, medical clinic, or pharmacy may charge for distributing or dispensing donated cancer drugs or medical devices.

(e) Repealed.

### 25-35-105. Liability - prescription drug manufacturers.

Nothing in this article shall be construed to create or abrogate any liability on behalf of a prescription drug manufacturer for the storage, donation, acceptance, or dispensing of a cancer drug or medical device, or to create any civil cause of action against a prescription drug manufacturer, in addition to that which is available under applicable law.

# ARTICLE 36. SHORT-TERM GRANTS FOR INNOVATIVEHEALTH PROGRAMS

## 25-36-101. Short-term grants for innovative health programs - grant fund - creation - appropriation from fund - transfer of moneys for fiscal years 2007-

# ARTICLE 37. CONTRACTS WITH HEALTH CARE PROVIDERS

## 25-37-101. Applicability of article.
A person or entity that contracts with a health care provider shall comply with this article and shall include the provisions required by this article in the contract.

## 25-37-102. Definitions.
As used in this article, unless the context otherwise requires:
(1) "Category of coverage" means one of the following types of coverage offered by a person or entity:
(a) Health maintenance organization plans;
(b) Any other commercial plan or contract that is not a health maintenance organization plan;
(c) Medicare;
(d) Medicaid; or
(e) Workers' compensation.
(2) "CMS" means the federal centers for medicare and medicaid services in the United States department of health and human services.
(3) "CPT code set" means the current procedural terminology code, or its successor code, as developed and copyrighted by the American medical association, or its successor entity, and adopted by the CMS as a HIPAA code set.
(4) Repealed.
(5) "HCPCS" means the health care common procedure coding system developed by the CMS for identifying health care services in a consistent and standardized manner.
(6) "Health care contract" or "contract" means a contract entered into or renewed between a person or entity and a health care provider for the delivery of health care services to others.
(7) "Health care provider" means a person licensed or certified in this state to practice medicine, pharmacy, chiropractic, nursing, physical therapy, podiatry, dentistry, optometry, occupational therapy, or other healing arts. "Health care provider" also means an ambulatory surgical center, a licensed pharmacy or provider of pharmacy services, and a professional corporation or other corporate entity consisting of licensed health care providers as permitted by the laws of this state.
(8) "HIPAA code set" means any set of codes used to encode elements, such as tables of terms, medical concepts, medical diagnostic codes, or medical procedure codes, that have been adopted by the secretary of the United States department of health and human services pursuant to the federal "Health Insurance Portability and Accountability Act of 1996", as amended. "HIPAA code set" includes the codes and the descriptors of the codes.
(9) (a) "Material change" means a change to a contract that decreases the health care provider's payment or compensation, changes the administrative procedures in a way that may reasonably be expected to significantly increase the provider's administrative expense, replaces the maximum allowable cost list used with a new and different maximum allowable cost list by a person or entity for reimbursement of generic prescription drug claims, or adds a new category of coverage.
(b) "Material change" does not include:
(I) A decrease in payment or compensation resulting solely from a change in a published fee schedule upon which the payment or compensation is based and the date of applicability is clearly identified in the contract;
(II) A decrease in payment or compensation resulting from a change in the fee schedule specified

in a contract for pharmacy services such as a change in a fee schedule based on average wholesale price or maximum allowable cost;

(III) A decrease in payment or compensation that was anticipated under the terms of the contract, if the amount and date of applicability of the decrease is clearly identified in the contract;

(IV) An administrative change that may significantly increase the provider's administrative expense, the specific applicability of which is clearly identified in the contract;

(V) Changes to an existing prior authorization, precertification, notification, or referral program that do not substantially increase the provider's administrative expense; or

(VI) Changes to an edit program or to specific edits; however, the person or entity shall provide notice of the changes to the health care provider in accordance with paragraph (c) of this subsection (9) , and the notice shall include information sufficient for the health care provider to determine the effect of the change.

(c) If a change to the contract is administrative only and is not a material change, the change shall be effective upon at least fifteen days' notice to the health care provider. All other notices shall be provided pursuant to the contract.

(10) "National correct coding initiative" or "NCCI" means the system developed by the CMS to promote consistency in national correct coding methodologies and to control improper coding leading to inappropriate payment in medicare part B claims for professional services.

(11) "National initiative" means a collaborative effort led by or occurring under the direction of the secretary of the United States department of health and human services, which includes a diverse group of stakeholders, to create a level of understanding of the impact of coding edits on the industry and a uniform, standardized set of claim edits that meets the needs of the stakeholders in the industry.

(12) "Person or entity" means a person or entity that has a primary business purpose of contracting with health care providers for the delivery of health care services.

(13) "Pharmacy benefit manager" means an entity doing business in this state that contracts to administer or manage prescription drug benefits on behalf of any carrier that provides prescription drug benefits to residents of this state. "Pharmacy benefit manager" does not include the department of health care policy and financing created in section 25.5-1-104, C.R.S.

## 25-37-103. Health care contracts - required provisions - permissible provision.

(1) (a) A person or entity shall provide, with each health care contract, a summary disclosure form disclosing, in plain language, the following:

(I) The terms governing compensation and payment;

(II) Any category of coverage for which the health care provider is to provide service;

(III) The duration of the contract and how the contract may be terminated;

(IV) The identity of the person or entity responsible for the processing of the health care provider's claims for compensation or payment;

(V) Any internal mechanism required by the person or entity to resolve disputes that arise under the terms or conditions of the contract; and

(VI) The subject and order of addenda, if any, to the contract.

(b) The summary disclosure form required by paragraph (a) of this subsection (1) shall be for informational purposes only and shall not be a term or condition of the contract; however, such disclosure shall reasonably summarize the applicable contract provisions.

(c) If the contract provides for termination for cause by either party, the contract shall state the reasons that may be used for termination for cause, which terms shall not be unreasonable, and the contract shall state the time by which notice of termination for cause shall be provided and to whom the notice shall be given.

(d) The person or entity shall identify any utilization review or management, quality improvement, or similar program the person or entity uses to review, monitor, evaluate, or assess the services provided pursuant to a contract. The policies, procedures, or guidelines of such program applicable to a provider shall be disclosed upon request of the health care provider within fourteen days after the date of the request.

(2) (a) The disclosure of payment and compensation terms pursuant to subsection (1) of this section shall include information sufficient for the health care provider to determine the compensation or payment for the health care services and shall include the following:

(I) The manner of payment, such as fee-for-service, capitation, or risk sharing;

(II) (A) The methodology used to calculate any fee schedule, such as relative value unit system and conversion factor, percentage of medicare payment system, or percentage of billed charges. As applicable, the methodology disclosure shall include the name of any relative value system; its version, edition, or publication date; any applicable conversion or geographic factor; and any date by which compensation or fee schedules may be changed by such methodology if allowed for in the contract.

(B) The fee schedule for codes reasonably expected to be billed by the health care provider for services provided pursuant to the contract, and, upon request, the fee schedule for other codes used by or which may be used by the health care provider. Such fee schedule shall include, as may be applicable, service or procedure codes such as current procedural terminology (CPT) codes or health care common procedure coding system (HCPCS) codes and the associated payment or compensation for each service code.

(C) The fee schedule required in sub-subparagraph (B) of this subparagraph (II) may be provided electronically.

(D) A fee schedule for the codes described by sub-subparagraph (B) of this subparagraph (II) shall be provided when a material change related to payment or compensation occurs. Additionally, a health care provider may request that a written fee schedule be provided up to twice per year, and the person or entity must provide such fee schedule promptly.

(III) The person or entity shall state the effect of edits, if any, on payment or compensation. A person or entity may satisfy this requirement by providing a clearly understandable, readily available mechanism, such as through a website, that allows a health care provider to determine the effect of edits on payment or compensation before service is provided or a claim is submitted.

(b) Notwithstanding any provision of this subsection (2) to the contrary, disclosure of a fee schedule or the methodology used to calculate a fee schedule is not required:

(I) From a person or entity if the fee schedule is for a plan for dental services, its providers include licensed dentists, the fee schedule is based upon fees filed with the person or entity by dental providers, and the fee schedule is revised from time to time based upon such filings. Specific numerical parameters are not required to be disclosed.

(II) If the fee schedule is for pharmacy services or drugs such as a fee schedule based on use of national drug codes.

(3) When a proposed contract is presented by a person or entity for consideration by a health care provider, the person or entity shall provide in writing or make reasonably available the information required in subsections (1) and (2) of this section. If the information is not disclosed in writing, it shall be disclosed in a manner that allows the health care provider to timely evaluate the payment or compensation for services under the proposed contract. The disclosure obligations in this article shall not prevent a person or entity from requiring a reasonable confidentiality agreement regarding the terms of a proposed contract.

(4) Nothing in this article shall be construed to require the renegotiation of a contract in existence before the applicable compliance date in this article, and any disclosure required by this article for such contracts may be by notice to the health care provider.

(5) A contract subject to this article may include an agreement for binding arbitration.

## 25-37-103.5. Pharmacy benefit managers - contracts with pharmacies - maximum allowable cost pricing.

(1) (a) In each contract between a pharmacy benefit manager and a pharmacy, the pharmacy shall be given the right to obtain from the pharmacy benefit manager, within ten days after any request,

a current list of the sources used to determine maximum allowable cost pricing. The pharmacy benefit manager shall update the pricing information at least every seven days and provide a means by which contracted pharmacies may promptly review pricing updates in a format that is readily available and accessible.

(b) A pharmacy benefit manager shall maintain a procedure to eliminate products from the list of drugs subject to maximum allowable cost pricing in a timely manner in order to remain consistent with pricing changes in the marketplace.

(2) In order to place a prescription drug on a maximum allowable cost list, a pharmacy benefit manager shall ensure that:

(a) The drug is listed as "A" or "B" rated in the most recent version of the United States food and drug administration's approved drug products with therapeutic equivalence evaluations, also known as the orange book, or has an "NR" or "NA" rating or similar rating by a nationally recognized reference; and

(b) The drug is generally available for purchase by pharmacies in this state from a national or regional wholesaler and is not obsolete.

(3) Each contract between a pharmacy benefit manager and a pharmacy must include a process to appeal, investigate, and resolve disputes regarding maximum allowable cost pricing that includes:

(a) A twenty-one-day limit on the right to appeal following the initial claim;

(b) A requirement that the appeal be investigated and resolved within twenty-one days after the appeal;

(c) A telephone number at which the pharmacy may contact the pharmacy benefit manager to speak to a person responsible for processing appeals;

(d) A requirement that a pharmacy benefit manager provide a reason for any appeal denial and the identification of the national drug code of a drug that may be purchased by the pharmacy at a price at or below the benchmark price as determined by the pharmacy benefit manager; and

(e) A requirement that a pharmacy benefit manager make an adjustment to a date no later than one day after the date of determination. This requirement does not prohibit a pharmacy benefit manager from retroactively adjusting a claim for the appealing pharmacy or for another similarly situated pharmacy.

## 25-37-104. Material change in health care contract - written advance notice.

(1) A material change to a contract shall occur only if the person or entity provides in writing to the health care provider the proposed change and gives ninety days' notice before the effective date of the change. The writing shall be conspicuously entitled "notice of material change to contract".

(2) If the health care provider objects in writing to the material change within fifteen days and there is no resolution of the objection, either party may terminate the contract upon written notice of termination provided to the other party not later than sixty days before the effective date of the material change.

(3) If the health care provider does not object to the material change pursuant to subsection (2) of this section, the change shall be effective as specified in the notice of material change to the contract.

(4) If a material change is the addition of a new category of coverage and the health care provider objects, the addition shall not be effective as to the health care provider, and the objection shall not be a basis upon which the person or entity may terminate the contract.

## 25-37-105. Contract modification by operation of law.

Notwithstanding section 25-37-103 (3) , a contract may be modified by operation of law as required by any applicable state or federal law or regulation, and the person or entity may disclose this change by any reasonable means.

## 25-37-106. Clean claims - development of standardized payment rules and

code edits - task force to develop - legislative recommendations - short title - applicability. (Repealed)

## 25-37-107. Claim adjudication information - balance owing.

Upon completion of processing of a claim, the person or entity shall provide information to the health care provider stating how the claim was adjudicated and the responsibility for any outstanding balance of any party other than the person or entity.

## 25-37-108. Assignment of rights - requirements.

(1) A person or entity shall not assign, allow access to, sell, rent, or give the person's or entity's rights to the health care provider's services pursuant to the person's or entity's contract unless the person or entity complies with the requirements of this section.

(2) A person or entity may assign, allow access to, sell, rent, or give his, her, or its rights to the health care provider's services pursuant to the person's or entity's contract if one of the following situations exists:

(a) The third party accessing the health care provider's services under the contract is an employer or other entity providing coverage for health care services to its employees or members and such employer or entity has, with the person or entity contracting with the health care provider, a contract for the administration or processing of claims for payment or service provided pursuant to the contract with the health care provider;

(b) The third party accessing the health care provider's services under the contract is an affiliate of, subsidiary of, or is under common ownership or control with the person or entity; or, is providing or receiving administrative services from the person or entity or an affiliate of, or subsidiary of, or is under common ownership or control with the person or entity; or

(c) The health care contract specifically provides that it applies to network rental arrangements and states that it is for the purpose of assigning, allowing access to, selling, renting, or giving the person's or entity's rights to the health care provider's services.

(3) In addition to satisfying the requirements of subsection (2) of this section, a person or entity may assign, allow access to, sell, rent, or give his, her, or its rights under the contract to the services of the health care provider only if:

(a) The individuals receiving services under the health care provider's contract are provided with appropriate identification stating where claims should be sent and where inquiries should be directed; and

(b) The third party accessing the health care provider's services through the health care provider's contract is obligated to comply with all applicable terms and conditions of the contract; except that a self-funded plan receiving administrative services from the person or entity or its affiliates shall be solely responsible for payment to the provider.

## 25-37-109. Waiver of rights prohibited.

Except as permitted by this article, a person or entity shall not require, as a condition of contracting, that a health care provider waive or forego any right or benefit to which the health care provider may be entitled under state or federal law, rule, or regulation that provides legal protections to a person solely based on the person's status as a health care provider providing services in this state.

## 25-37-110. Provider declining service to new patients - notice - definition.

(1) Upon sixty days' notice, a health care provider may decline to provide service pursuant to a contract to new patients covered by the person or entity. The notice shall state the reason or reasons for this action.

(2) As used in this section, "new patients" means those patients who have not received services

from the health care provider in the immediately preceding three years. A patient shall not become a "new patient" solely by changing coverage from one person or entity to another person or entity.

## 25-37-111. Termination of contract - effect on payment terms - right to terminate - termination of pharmacy contracts.

(1) A term for compensation or payment shall not survive the termination of a contract, except for a continuation of coverage required by law or with the agreement of the health care provider.

(2) In addition to the right to terminate a contract in accordance with section 25-37-104 (2) based on a material change to the contract, a contract with a duration of less than two years shall provide to each party a right to terminate the contract without cause, which termination shall occur with at least ninety days' written notice. For contracts with a duration of two or more years, termination without cause may be as specified in the contract.

(3) A contract between a pharmacist or a pharmacy and a pharmacy benefit manager, such as a pharmacy benefit management firm as defined in section 10-16-102, C.R.S., shall be terminated if the federal drug enforcement agency or other federal law enforcement agency ceases the operations of the pharmacist or pharmacy due to alleged or actual criminal activity.

## 25-37-112. Disclosure to third parties - confidentiality.

A contract shall not preclude its use or disclosure to a third party for the purpose of enforcing the provisions of this article or enforcing other state or federal law. The third party shall be bound by the confidentiality requirements set forth in the contract or otherwise.

## 25-37-113. Article inapplicable - when.

(1) This article shall not apply to:

(a) An exclusive contract with a single medical group in a specific geographic area to provide or arrange for health care services; however, this article shall apply to contracts for health care services between the medical group and other medical groups;

(b) A contract or agreement for the employment of a health care provider or a contract or agreement between health care providers;

(c) A contract or arrangement entered into by a hospital or health care facility that is licensed or certified pursuant to section 25-3-101;

(d) A contract between a health care provider and the state or federal government or their agencies for health care services provided through a program for workers' compensation, medicaid, medicare, the children's basic health plan provided for in article 8 of title 25.5, C.R.S., or the Colorado indigent care program created in part 1 of article 3 of title 25.5, C.R.S.;

(e) Contracts for pharmacy benefit management, such as with a pharmacy benefit management firm as defined in section 10-16-102, C.R.S.; except that this exclusion shall not apply to a contract for health care services between a person or entity and a pharmacy, pharmacist, or professional corporation or corporate entity consisting of pharmacies or pharmacists as permitted by the laws of this state; or

(f) A contract or arrangement entered into by a hospital or health care facility that is licensed or certified pursuant to section 25-3-101, or any outpatient service provider that has entered into a joint venture with the hospital or is owned by the hospital or health care facility.

## 25-37-114. Enforcement.

(1) With respect to the enforcement of this article, including arbitration, there shall be available:

(a) Private rights of action at law and in equity;

(b) Equitable relief, including injunctive relief;

(c) Reasonable attorney fees when the health care provider is the prevailing party in an action to enforce this article, except to the extent that the violation of this article consisted of a mere failure to make payment pursuant to a contract;

(d) The option to introduce as persuasive authority prior arbitration awards regarding a violation of this article.

(2) Arbitration awards related to the enforcement of this article may be disclosed to those who have a bona fide interest in the arbitration.

## 25-37-115. Providers obligated to comply with law.

No provision of this article shall be used to justify any act or omission by a health care provider that is prohibited by any applicable professional code of ethics or state or federal law prohibiting discrimination against any person.

## 25-37-116. Copyrights protected.

Nothing in this article, including the designation of standards, code sets, rules, edits, or related specifications, divests copyright holders of their copyrights in any work referenced in this article.

# ARTICLE 38. PHYSICIAN AND DENTIST DESIGNATION AND DISCLOSURE

## 25-38-101. Short title.

This article shall be known and may be cited as the "Physician and Dentist Designation Disclosure Act".

## 25-38-102. Legislative declaration.

(1) The general assembly hereby finds, determines, and declares that:

(a) Health care entities have instituted or are instituting quantitative and qualitative designations of physicians and dentists;

(b) Physician and dentist designations are disclosed and represented to consumers and others as part of marketing, sales, and other efforts, and such designations may be used by consumers in selecting the physicians and dentists from whom they receive care;

(c) Designations are based on claims data, practice criteria or guidelines, and other criteria, not all of which are made known to consumers or to the physicians and dentists designated;

(d) Health care entities differ in the extent to which they provide access to some or all of the data, criteria, and methodologies;

(e) Regulatory agencies in other states have taken action against health care entities to require disclosure of designation information and to set certain criteria by which designations may be used;

(f) For the protection of consumers, physicians, and dentists and to avoid improper profiling of physicians and dentists, health care entities must ensure that they are using designations that are fair and accurate and must accord physicians and dentists the right to challenge and correct erroneous designations, data, and methodologies;

(g) Full disclosure of the data and methodologies by which physicians and dentists are designated will encourage, to the fullest extent possible, the accuracy, fairness, and usefulness of such designations. Disclosures will help keep patients from being exposed to inaccurate, misleading, and incorrect information about the nature and quality of the care of physicians and dentists. The disclosure required by this article will encourage the use of guidelines and criteria from well-recognized professional societies and groups using evidence-based and consensus practice recommendations. Disclosure will allow health care consumers and physicians and dentists an opportunity to better understand the criteria, basis, and methods by which physicians and dentists are evaluated, and disclosure will foster competition among health care entities to improve the way in which designations are used. Accordingly, the general assembly finds that requiring full disclosure of designation data and methodologies and setting certain minimum standards for making such designations will help improve the quality and efficiency of health care delivered in Colorado.

(h) The general assembly intends this article to serve as the initial stage of a multipart process to increase transparency of information about health care quality and costs in Colorado. Future actions may include, but are not limited to, creation of a multistakeholder work group, comprised of health care entities, health plans, businesses, consumer groups, and others as identified, to develop a system for aggregating cost and quality information across health care entities and consumers. The ultimate goal is to develop standardized quality reporting arrangements, consistent with national standards and subject to evaluation by an independent entity, that are accessible and meaningful to consumers and other stakeholders.

## 25-38-103. Definitions.

As used in this article, unless the context otherwise requires:

(1) "Carrier" shall have the same meaning as set forth in section 10-16-102, C.R.S.

(2) "Commissioner" means the commissioner of insurance.

(3) "Consumer" includes members of the public, health care consumers and potential health care consumers, purchasers of health insurance plans, or patients.

(3.5) "Dentist" means a dentist licensed under the "Dental Practice Act", article 35 of title 12, C.R.S.

(4) "Designation" means an award, assignment, characterization, or representation of the cost efficiency, quality, or other assessment or measurement of the care or clinical performance of any physician or dentist that is disclosed or intended for disclosure to the public or persons actually or potentially covered by a health plan, by use of a grade, star, tier, rating, profile, or any other form of designation. "Designation" does not include:

(a) Information that is derived solely from health plan member feedback such as satisfaction ratings; or

(b) Information for programs designed to assist health plan members with estimating a physician's or dentist's routine fees or costs.

(5) "Health care entity" means any carrier or other entity that provides a plan of health care coverage to beneficiaries under a plan.

(6) "Methodology" means the method by which a designation is determined, including, but not limited to, the use of algorithms or studies, evaluation of data, application of guidelines, or performance measures.

(7) "Physician" means any physician licensed under the "Colorado Medical Practice Act", article 36 of title 12, C.R.S.

## 25-38-104. Minimum requirements for designations - disclaimer required.

(1) Any designation of a physician or dentist shall include, at a minimum, the following:

(a) A quality of care component that may be satisfied by incorporating a practice guideline or performance measure pursuant to paragraph (f) of this subsection (1) , and a clear representation of the weight given to quality of care in comparison with other designation factors;

(b) Statistical analyses that are accurate, valid, and reliable and, where reasonably possible, that appropriately adjust for patient population, case mix, severity of patient condition, comorbidity, outlier events, or other known statistical anomalies;

(c) A period of assessment of data, pertinent to the designation, that shall be updated by the health care entity at appropriate intervals;

(d) If claims data are used in the designation process, accurate claims data appropriately attributed to the physician or dentist. When reasonably available, the health care entity shall use aggregated data to supplement its own claims data.

(e) The physician's or dentist's responsibility for health care decisions and the financial consequences of those decisions, which shall be fairly and accurately attributed to the physician or dentist;

(f) If practice guidelines or performance measures are used in the designation process:

(I) Practice guidelines or performance measures that are promulgated or endorsed by nationally recognized health care organizations that establish or promote guidelines and performance measures emphasizing quality of health care, such as the national quality forum or the AQA alliance, or their successors, or other such national physician or dentist specialty organizations, or the Colorado clinical guidelines collaborative or its successor;

(II) Practice guidelines or performance measures that are:

(A) Evidence-based, whenever possible;

(B) Consensus-based, whenever possible; and

(C) Pertinent to the area of practice, location, and characteristics of the patient population of the physician or dentist being designated.

(2) (a) Any disclosure of a designation to a physician, dentist, or consumer shall be accompanied by a conspicuous disclaimer written in bold-faced type. The disclaimer shall state that designations are intended only as a guide to choosing a physician or dentist, that designations should not be the sole factor in selecting a physician or dentist, that designations have a risk of error, and that consumers should discuss designations with a physician or dentist before choosing him or her.

(b) Failure to include the disclaimer makes the use of the designation a violation of this article.

## 25-38-105. Disclosure required upon request - information not proprietary.

(1) Upon request by or on behalf of the designated physician or dentist or the commissioner, a health care entity shall disclose to the requesting person a description of the methodology upon which the health care entity's designation is based and all data upon which the designation was based within forty-five days after receiving the request. The description shall be sufficiently detailed to allow the designated physician or dentist or the commissioner to determine the effect of the methodology on the data being reviewed. The disclosure of the data shall be made in a manner that is reasonably understandable and allows the physician, dentist, or commissioner to verify the data against his or her records. Where law or the health care entity's contractual obligations with a bona fide third party prevents disclosure of any of the data required to be disclosed by this section, the health care entity shall nonetheless provide sufficient information to allow the physician or dentist to determine how the withheld data affected the physician's or dentist's designation.

(2) After the disclosure of the description of the methodology provided for in subsection (1) of this section and upon further request by or on behalf of the designated physician or dentist or the commissioner, the health care entity shall provide the complete methodology within thirty days after such further request.

(3) The "Uniform Trade Secrets Act", article 74 of title 7, C.R.S., shall not be used by a health care entity to prevent it from complying with this section.

## 25-38-106. Notice of use or change of designation required - appeal process.

(1) At least forty-five days before using, changing, or declining to award a designation in an existing program of designation, a health care entity shall provide the physician or dentist with written notice of the designation decision. The written notice shall describe the procedures by which the physician or dentist may:

(a) Obtain the information pursuant to section 25-38-105, including all of the data upon which the designation was based or declined; and

(b) Request an appeal of the designation decision, including the opportunity for a face-to-face meeting pursuant to subparagraph (IV) of paragraph (a) of subsection (2) of this section.

(2) (a) Any health care entity providing designations of physicians or dentists shall establish procedures for the designated physician or dentist to appeal the designation, including a change in designation or a declination to award a designation in an existing program of designation. The procedures, in addition to the written notice provided for in subsection (1) of this section, shall provide for the following:

(I) A reasonable method by which the designated physician or dentist shall provide notice of his or her desire to appeal;

(II) If requested by the designated physician or dentist, disclosure of the methodology and data upon which the health care entity's decision is based;

(III) The name, title, qualifications, and relationship to the health care entity of the person or persons responsible for the appeal of the designated physician or dentist;

(IV) An opportunity to submit or have considered corrected data relevant to the designation decision and to have considered the applicability of the methodology used in the designation decision. If requested by the designated physician or dentist, the opportunity may be afforded by the health care entity in a face-to-face meeting with those responsible for the appeal decision at a location reasonably convenient to the physician or dentist or by teleconference. All data submitted to the entity by a designated physician or dentist is presumed valid and accurate. However, this presumption does not permit a health care entity to unreasonably withhold consideration of corrected or supplemented data pursuant to this subparagraph (IV) .

(V) The right of the physician or dentist to be assisted by a representative;

(VI) An opportunity, if so desired, to be considered as part of the appeal, an explanation of the designation decision that is the subject of the appeal by a person or persons deemed by the health care entity as responsible for the designation decision;

(VII) A written decision regarding the physician's or dentist's appeal that states the reasons for upholding, modifying, or rejecting the physician's or dentist's appeal.

(b) The appeal shall be made to a person or persons with the authority granted by the designating health care entity to uphold, modify, or reject the designation decision or to require additional action to ensure that the designation is fair, reasonable, and accurate.

(c) The appeal process shall be complete within forty-five days from the date upon which the data and methodology are disclosed unless otherwise agreed to by the parties to the appeal.

(3) No change or modification of a designation that is the subject of an appeal shall be implemented or used by the health care entity until the appeal is final.

(4) With respect to any designation previously disclosed publicly, the health care entity shall update any changes to such designation within thirty days after the appeal is final.

### 25-38-107. Enforcement.

(1) A health care entity shall not limit, by contract or other means, the right of a physician or dentist to enforce this article.

(2) This article may be enforced in a civil action, and any remedies at law and in equity shall be available.

(3) A violation of this article by a health care entity shall constitute an unfair or deceptive act or practice under part 11 of article 3 of title 10, C.R.S.

### 25-38-108. Severability.

If any provision of this article or its application to any person or circumstance is held invalid, the invalidity does not affect other provisions or applications of this article that can be given effect without the invalid provision or application, and to this end the provisions of this article are severable.

# ARTICLE 39. COLORADO ALZHEIMER'S COORDINATING COUNCIL

### 25-39-101 to 25-39-108. (Repealed)

# ARTICLE 40. UMBILICAL CORD BLOOD COLLECTION AND AWARENESS

## 25-40-101. Short title.
This article shall be known and may be cited as the "Colorado Cures Act".

## 25-40-102. Legislative declaration.
(1) The general assembly hereby finds and determines that:

(a) The national marrow donor program reports that researchers are studying umbilical cord blood, also known as cord blood, as a source of adult blood stem cells that can be used to treat leukemia, lymphoma, and other life-threatening diseases;

(b) For many patients with a life-threatening disease, a cord blood transplant may be the best and only hope for a cure;

(c) Cord blood is desirable for use in stem cell transplants because it has a large number of adult blood stem cells;

(d) Blood from each donated umbilical cord is frozen and made available for transplant, and if it cannot be used for transplant, the cord blood stem cells may be used for research;

(e) Cord blood donations are urgently needed to keep up with the demand for transplants and research; and

(f) Many women in good health may be eligible to voluntarily donate their children's cord blood but are unaware of its unique value or of the existence of donation programs.

(2) Therefore, it is the intent of the general assembly to create the adult stem cells cure fund for the purpose of advancing umbilical cord blood collection for public blood banks and promoting awareness across the state.

## 25-40-103. Adult stem cells cure fund - creation.
(1) There is hereby created in the state treasury the adult stem cells cure fund, referred to in this section as the "fund". The fund shall consist of gifts, grants, and donations transferred to the fund, which the department of public health and environment is authorized to accept, and any voluntary contributions to the fund pursuant to part 35 of article 22 of title 39, C.R.S.

(2) The department of public health and environment shall transfer any gifts, grants, and donations to the fund to the state treasurer, who shall credit the same to the fund. All interest derived from the deposit and investment of moneys in the fund shall be credited to the fund. All moneys remaining in the fund at the end of any fiscal year shall remain in the fund and shall not be deposited into any other fund. The moneys in the fund shall be annually appropriated by the general assembly to the department for the purposes of this article.

## 25-40-104. Standards for cord blood collection and donation - administrative costs.
(1) The department of public health and environment shall set standards for hospitals for the voluntary donation and collection of umbilical cord blood for hospitals that volunteer to participate in umbilical cord donation. The department is encouraged to take part in efforts to increase the number of umbilical cord donations to public blood banks and to promote public awareness of the availability of umbilical cord donation as an option for new mothers.

(2) The department may use up to five percent of the moneys appropriated from the adult stem cells cure fund, created in section 25-40-103, for administrative costs incurred in the implementation of this article. The department may use up to twenty-five percent of the moneys

appropriated to the department from the fund for umbilical cord collection awareness. The department shall work with public cord blood banks and shall use the remaining moneys appropriated to the department from the fund for activities in connection with umbilical cord blood collection for public cord blood banks.

# ARTICLE 41. RESTROOM ACCESS ACT

## 25-41-101. Restroom access - short title - definitions - retail establishments - liability - penalty.

(1) This article shall be known and may be cited as the "Restroom Access Act".

(2) As used in this article, unless the context otherwise requires:

(a) "Customer" means an individual who is lawfully on the premises of a retail establishment.

(b) "Eligible medical condition" means Crohn's disease, ulcerative colitis, any other inflammatory bowel disease, irritable bowel syndrome, or any other medical condition that requires immediate access to a toilet facility.

(c) "Retail establishment" means a place of business open to the general public for the sale of goods or services. "Retail establishment" does not include a filling station or service station that has an enclosed floor area of eight hundred square feet or less and that has an employee toilet facility located within that enclosed floor area.

(3) A retail establishment that has a toilet facility for its employees shall allow a customer to use the toilet facility during normal business hours if the toilet facility is reasonably safe and all of the following conditions are met:

(a) The customer requesting the use of the employee toilet facility suffers from an eligible medical condition or utilizes an ostomy device and offers a physician's note indicating the eligible medical condition or device;

(b) Three or more employees of the retail establishment are working at the time the customer requests use of the employee toilet facility;

(c) The employee toilet facility is not located in an area where providing access would create an obvious health or safety risk to the customer or an obvious security risk to the retail establishment; and

(d) A public restroom is not immediately accessible to the customer.

(4) A retail establishment or an employee of a retail establishment is not civilly liable for any act or omission in allowing a customer that has an eligible medical condition to use an employee toilet facility that is not a public restroom if the act or omission:

(a) Is not willful or grossly negligent;

(b) Occurs in an area of the retail establishment that is not accessible to the public; and

(c) Results in injury to or death of the customer or any individual other than an employee accompanying the customer.

(5) This article shall not be construed to require a retail establishment to make any physical changes to an employee toilet facility.

(6) A retail establishment or an employee of a retail establishment that violates this article is guilty of a petty offense and, upon conviction thereof, shall be punished by a fine of not more than one hundred dollars.

# ARTICLE 42. TAXING AUTHORITY OF UNIT OF GOVERNMENT HOSPITAL CARE PROVIDERS

## 25-42-101. Legislative declaration.

(1) The general assembly hereby finds and declares that:

(a) State and local governmental hospital care providers form a critical part of the health care delivery system in Colorado; and

(b) Federal programs require the state to further define a unit of government for certain state and local governmental hospital care providers.

## 25-42-102. Definitions.

As used in this article, unless the context otherwise requires:

(1) "Eligible elector" means an eligible elector as defined in section 32-1-103 (5) (a) (I) , C.R.S., of the taxing area of a unit of government hospital provider.

(2) "Qualified purchaser" means a person domiciled in Colorado who has been issued a direct payment permit number pursuant to section 39-26-103.5, C.R.S.

(3) "Taxing area" means:

(a) In the case of the Denver health and hospital authority, the city and county of Denver;

(b) In the case of a county hospital, the county in which the hospital is located;

(c) In the case of a hospital within a health service district, the health service district;

(d) In the case of the university of Colorado hospital authority, the counties of Adams, Arapahoe, Boulder, Douglas, and Jefferson and the city and county of Broomfield; and

(e) In the case of a municipal hospital, the county in which the hospital is located.

(4) "Unit of government hospital care provider" means:

(a) The Denver health and hospital authority created pursuant to section 25-29-103;

(b) The board of any county hospital created pursuant to section 25-3-301;

(c) A health service district within the meaning of section 32-1-103 (9) , C.R.S.;

(d) The university of Colorado hospital authority created pursuant to part 5 of article 21 of title 23, C.R.S.; or

(e) A municipally owned hospital created pursuant to section 31-15-711 (1) (e) , C.R.S.

## 25-42-103. Grant of taxing authority.

(1) Each unit of government hospital care provider, upon the affirmative action of its governing body, shall have the authority to levy and collect a sales tax as follows:

(a) Upon the approval of the eligible electors of the unit of government hospital care provider's taxing area at an election held in accordance with section 20 of article X of the state constitution and this article, the unit of government hospital care provider may levy a uniform sales tax throughout its entire taxing area upon every transaction or other incident with respect to which a sales tax is levied by the state pursuant to the provisions of article 26 of title 39, C.R.S.

(b) A sales tax imposed pursuant to paragraph (a) of this subsection (1) shall not be levied on:

(I) The sale of tangible personal property delivered by a retailer or a retailer's agent or to a common carrier for delivery to a destination outside the taxing area; or

(II) The sale of tangible personal property on which a specific ownership tax has been paid or is payable when such sale meets the following conditions:

(A) The purchaser does not reside in the taxing area or the purchaser's principal place of business is outside the taxing area; and

(B) The personal property is registered or required to be registered outside the taxing area under the laws of this state.

(c) The sales tax imposed pursuant to paragraph (a) of this subsection (1) shall be in addition to any other sales or use tax imposed pursuant to law.

(2) (a) The collection, administration, and enforcement of a sales tax imposed pursuant to subsection (1) of this section shall be performed by the executive director of the department of revenue in the same manner as that for the collection, administration, and enforcement of the state sales tax imposed pursuant to article 26 of title 39, C.R.S., including, without limitation, the

retention by a vendor of the percentage of the amount remitted to cover the vendor's expense in the collection and remittance of the sales tax as provided in section 39-26-105, C.R.S. The executive director of the department of revenue shall make monthly distributions of sales tax collections to the unit of government hospital care provider. The unit of government hospital care provider shall pay the net incremental cost incurred by the department of revenue in the administration and collection of the sales tax.

(b) (I) A qualified purchaser may provide a direct payment permit number issued pursuant to section 39-26-103.5, C.R.S., to a vendor or retailer that is liable and responsible for collecting and remitting any sales tax levied on a sale made to the qualified purchaser pursuant to the provisions of this article. A vendor or retailer that has received a direct payment permit number in good faith from a qualified purchaser shall not be liable or responsible for collection and remittance of any sales tax imposed on the sale that is paid for directly from the qualified purchasers' funds and not the personal funds of any individual.

(II) A qualified purchaser that provides a direct payment permit number to a vendor or retailer shall be liable and responsible for the amount of sales tax levied on a sale made to the qualified purchaser pursuant to the provisions of this article in the same manner as liability would be imposed on a qualified purchaser for state sales tax pursuant to section 39-26-105 (3) , C.R.S.

(3) A sales tax shall not be levied by a unit of government hospital care provider without first complying with this section and section 25-42-106.

### 25-42-104. Use of revenues derived from sales tax.

The revenues derived by a unit of government hospital care provider from the levy and collection of the sales tax authorized by this article shall be in addition to and shall not be used to replace any state funding that the unit of government hospital care provider or any other state or local government entity would otherwise be entitled to receive from the state. The unit of government hospital care provider may use said revenues for any purpose permitted by law or by the terms of its organizational documents.

### 25-42-105. Preservation of enterprise status of certain providers and activities.

The authority granted in this article shall be subject to affirmative action of the governing body of a unit of government hospital care provider to avail itself of this authority and shall be contingent upon electoral approval at an election held pursuant to sections 25-42-103 (1) (a) and 25-42-106. The enactment of this article shall not affect the treatment of any existing or future activity of a unit of government hospital care provider as an enterprise for purposes of section 20 of article X of the state constitution.

### 25-42-106. Call, notice, conduct, and determination of results of tax elections.

An election held pursuant to this article may be conducted under the provisions of either the "Uniform Election Code of 1992", articles 1 to 13 of title 1, C.R.S., or the "Colorado Municipal Election Code of 1965", article 10 of title 31, C.R.S.

### 25-42-107. Authority granted supplemental to other authority.

The authority granted by this article shall be in addition and supplemental to, and not in lieu of, the authority granted by other laws.

# ARTICLE 43. REQUIRED HEAD TRAUMA GUIDELINES

## 25-43-101. Short title.

This article shall be known and may be cited as the "Jake Snakenberg Youth Concussion Act".

## 25-43-102. Definitions.

As used in this article, unless the context otherwise requires:

(1) "Health care provider" means a doctor of medicine, doctor of osteopathic medicine, licensed nurse practitioner, licensed physician assistant, or licensed doctor of psychology with training in neuropsychology or concussion evaluation and management.

(2) "Public recreation facility" means a recreation facility owned or leased by the state of Colorado or a political subdivision thereof.

(3) "Youth athletic activity" means an organized athletic activity where the majority of the participants are eleven years of age or older and under nineteen years of age, and are engaging in an organized athletic game or competition against another team, club, or entity or in practice or preparation for an organized game or competition against another team, club, or entity. A "youth athletic activity" does not include college or university activities. "Youth athletic activity" does not include an activity that is entered into for instructional purposes only, an athletic activity that is incidental to a nonathletic program, or a lesson.

## 25-43-103. Organized school athletic activities - concussion guidelines required.

(1) (a) Each public and private middle school, junior high school, and high school shall require each coach of a youth athletic activity that involves interscholastic play to complete an annual concussion recognition education course.

(b) Each private club or public recreation facility and each athletic league that sponsors youth athletic activities shall require each volunteer coach for a youth athletic activity and each coach with whom the club, facility, or league directly contracts, formally engages, or employs who coaches a youth athletic activity to complete an annual concussion recognition education course.

(2) (a) The concussion recognition education course required by subsection (1) of this section shall include the following:

(I) Information on how to recognize the signs and symptoms of a concussion;

(II) The necessity of obtaining proper medical attention for a person suspected of having a concussion; and

(III) Information on the nature and risk of concussions, including the danger of continuing to play after sustaining a concussion and the proper method of allowing a youth athlete who has sustained a concussion to return to athletic activity.

(b) An organization or association of which a school or school district is a member may designate specific education courses as sufficient to meet the requirements of subsection (1) of this section.

(3) If a coach who is required to complete concussion recognition education pursuant to subsection (1) of this section suspects that a youth athlete has sustained a concussion following an observed or suspected blow to the head or body in a game, competition, or practice, the coach shall immediately remove the athlete from the game, competition, or practice.

(4) (a) If a youth athlete is removed from play pursuant to subsection (3) of this section and the signs and symptoms cannot be readily explained by a condition other than concussion, the school coach or private or public recreational facility's designated personnel shall notify the athlete's parent or legal guardian and shall not permit the youth athlete to return to play or participate in any supervised team activities involving physical exertion, including games, competitions, or practices, until he or she is evaluated by a health care provider and receives written clearance to return to play from the health care provider. The health care provider evaluating a youth athlete suspected of having a concussion or brain injury may be a volunteer.

(b) Notwithstanding the provisions of paragraph (a) of this subsection (4) , a doctor of chiropractic with training and specialization in concussion evaluation and management may evaluate and provide clearance to return to play for an athlete who is part of the United States olympic training program.

(c) After a concussed athlete has been evaluated and received clearance to return to play from a health care provider, an organization or association of which a school or school district is a member, a private or public school, a private club, a public recreation facility, or an athletic league may allow a registered athletic trainer with specific knowledge of the athlete's condition to manage the athlete's graduated return to play.

(5) Nothing in this article abrogates or limits the protections applicable to public entities and public employees pursuant to the "Colorado Governmental Immunity Act", article 10 of title 24, C.R.S.; volunteers and board members pursuant to sections 13-21-115.7 and 13-21-116, C.R.S.; or ski area operators pursuant to sections 33-44-112 and 33-44-113, C.R.S.

# ARTICLE 44. COMPREHENSIVE HUMAN SEXUALITY EDUCATIONGRANT PROGRAM

## 25-44-101. Definitions.

As used in this article, unless the context otherwise requires:

(1) "Age-appropriate" means topics, messages, and teaching methods suitable to a particular age or age group, based on developing cognitive, emotional, and behavioral capacity typical for the age or age group.

(2) "Cash fund" means the comprehensive human sexuality education grant program cash fund created in section 25-44-104.

(3) "Comprehensive human sexuality education" means medically accurate information about all methods to prevent unintended pregnancy and sexually transmitted infections, including HIV, the link between human papillomavirus and cancer, and other types of cancer involving the human reproductive systems, including prostate, testicular, ovarian, and uterine cancer. Methods must include information about the correct and consistent use of abstinence, contraception, condoms, other barrier methods, and other prevention measures. Additional contents of comprehensive human sexuality education must include:

(a) Encouraging family communication about sexuality;

(b) Teaching young people to avoid making unwanted verbal, physical, and sexual advances;

(c) Discussions and information on how to recognize and respond safely and effectively in situations where sexual or physical violence may be occurring or where there may be a risk for these behaviors to occur;

(d) Focusing on the development of safe relationships, including the prevention of sexual violence in dating; and

(e) Teaching young people how alcohol and drug use can affect responsible decision-making.

(4) "Culturally sensitive" means the integration of knowledge about individuals and groups of people into specific standards, requirements, policies, practices, and attitudes used to increase the quality of services. "Culturally sensitive" includes resources, references, and information that are meaningful to the experiences and needs of communities of color; immigrant communities; lesbian, gay, bisexual, and transgender communities; people with physical or intellectual disabilities; people who have experienced sexual victimization; and others whose experiences have traditionally been left out of sexual health education, programs, and policies.

(5) "Department" means the department of public health and environment, created and existing pursuant to section 25-1-101.5.

(6) "Evidence-based program" means a program that:

(a) Was evaluated using a rigorous research design, including:

(I) Measuring knowledge, attitude, and behavior;

(II) Having an adequate sample size;

(III) Using sound research methods and processes;

(IV) Replicating in different locations and finding similar evaluation results; and

(V) Publishing results in a peer-reviewed journal;

(b) Research has shown to be effective in changing at least one of the following behaviors that contribute to early pregnancy, sexually transmitted infections and disease, and HIV infection:

(I) Delaying sexual initiation;

(II) Reducing the frequency of sexual intercourse;

(III) Reducing the number of sexual partners; or

(IV) Increasing the use of condoms and other contraceptives.

(7) "Oversight entity" means the interagency youth sexual health team created in section 25-44-103.

(8) "Positive youth development" means an approach that emphasizes the many positive attributes of young people and focuses on developing inherent strengths and assets to promote health. Positive youth development is culturally sensitive, age-appropriate, inclusive of all youth, collaborative, and strength-based.

(9) "Program" means the comprehensive human sexuality education grant program created in section 25-44-102.

(10) "Public school" means a school of a school district, a district charter school, an institute charter school, a facility school, or a board of cooperative services, as defined in section 22-5-103.

(11) "State board" means the state board of health created pursuant to section 25-1-103.

## 25-44-102. Comprehensive human sexuality education grant program - creation - application for federal moneys - notification to schools - rules - repeal.

(1) There is hereby created in the department the comprehensive human sexuality education grant program. The purpose of the program is to provide moneys to public schools and school districts for use in the creation and implementation of comprehensive human sexuality education programs in their curriculum.

(2) Upon receipt of federal moneys or other appropriations to the cash fund, the department, in conjunction with the oversight entity, shall notify the school districts, the state charter school institute, and boards of cooperative services throughout the state of grants available through the program.

(3) Based on the recommendations of the oversight entity, the department shall award grants to public schools and school districts for periods of one to three years.

(4) Moneys distributed to public schools and school districts through the program must only be used for the provision of comprehensive human sexuality education programs that comply with the provisions of and meet or exceed the requirements for comprehensive human sexuality curriculum set forth in section 22-1-128, C.R.S., and developed pursuant to section 22-25-104 (3) , C.R.S.

(5) On or before December 1, 2013, or not more than ninety days after the department receives sufficient moneys to implement the program, whichever is later, the state board shall promulgate rules for the administration of this article, using the recommendations developed by the oversight entity pursuant to section 25-44-103 (2) (b) .

(6) (a) On or before January 30, 2017, and every year thereafter in which grants have been awarded pursuant to this article, the department shall submit a report concerning the outcomes of the program to the state board of education, the department of education, and the education committees of the senate and house of representatives, the health and human services committee of the senate, and the public health care and human services committee of the house of representatives, or any successor committees. The report must include, at a minimum:

(I) The number of public schools and school districts that received a grant under the program;

(II) The number of students reached and the curriculum utilized;

(III) The amount of each grant awarded;

(IV) The average amount of all grants awarded; and

(V) The source and amount of each gift, grant, or donation received by the department for the implementation of this article.

(b) Pursuant to section 24-1-136 (11) (a) (I) , this subsection (6) is repealed, effective July 2, 2020.

(7) Notwithstanding any other provision of this article, the department shall not be required to implement the provisions of this article until sufficient moneys have been received and transferred or appropriated to the cash fund.

(8) The provisions of this article shall not apply to students in kindergarten through third grade unless the content of the instruction relates to personal hygiene, healthy habits, respecting personal space and boundaries, interpersonal communication skills, and personal safety, as identified in the content standards developed by the department of education and adopted by the state board of education.

## 25-44-103. Comprehensive human sexuality education grant program - oversight entity - duties - application process.

(1) On or before July 1, 2013, the department shall convene the interagency youth sexual health team, referred to in this article as the "oversight entity". Membership of the oversight entity must include:

(a) The executive director of the department of public health and environment, or his or her designee;

(b) The executive director of the department of health care policy and financing, or his or her designee;

(c) The commissioner of education, or his or her designee;

(d) The executive director of the department of human services, or his or her designee; and

(e) A parent representative, appointed by the department of health.

(2) The oversight entity has the following duties:

(a) During the 2013-14 academic year and every academic year thereafter, to assess opportunities for available federal and state moneys to fund the program; except that the oversight entity shall not recommend applying for any federal or state moneys that promote abstinence as the sole behavioral method for youth or funding requiring adherence to the A-H guidelines of section 510 (b) of title V of the federal "Social Security Act", Pub. L. 104-193, which are inconsistent with the provisions of section 22-1-128, C.R.S. The oversight entity will provide information to the appropriate state departments concerning available federal and state moneys related to comprehensive human sexuality education funds for which a given department is eligible to apply.

(b) To develop policies and procedures for the implementation of the program and recommend such policies and procedures to the state board for adoption by rule pursuant to section 25-44-102. The policies and procedures must include, but are not limited to:

(I) A process by which public schools and school districts will be notified of available program funds for comprehensive human sexuality education.

(II) The procedures by which public schools and school districts may apply for grants pursuant to this article. Each grant application must, at a minimum, describe:

(A) How the applicant public school or school district will use any awarded grant moneys to provide comprehensive human sexuality education to its student population;

(B) How the proposed comprehensive human sexuality education program complies with section 22-1-128, C.R.S., and article 25 of title 22, C.R.S., and is evidence-based, culturally sensitive, and represents positive youth development principles;

(C) How many students the public school or school district expects to reach through the comprehensive human sexuality education program; and

(D) The length of time for which the applicant is requesting grant moneys;

(III) Criteria for the oversight entity to apply in selecting public schools and school districts that may receive grants and how to determine the amount of grant moneys to be awarded to each grant recipient. The criteria must include a requirement that the proposed comprehensive human sexuality education program complies with sections 22-1-128 and 22-25-104, C.R.S., and is evidence-based, culturally sensitive, and represents positive youth development principles.

(c) In conjunction with the department, to solicit grant applications from public schools and school districts;

(d) To review grant applications and, based on the criteria developed pursuant to paragraph (b) of this subsection (2) , make recommendations to the department concerning which public schools or school districts should receive grants and in what amount.

## 25-44-104. Comprehensive human sexuality education grant program cash fund - creation - funding through gifts, grants, and donations.

(1) There is hereby established in the state treasury the comprehensive human sexuality education grant program cash fund. The cash fund consists of moneys transferred thereto pursuant to subsection (3) of this section and any other moneys that may be made available by the general assembly. The moneys in the cash fund are continuously appropriated to the department for the direct and indirect costs associated with implementing this article. Any moneys not provided as grants may be invested by the state treasurer as provided in section 24-36-113, C.R.S. All interest and income derived from the investment and deposit of moneys in the cash fund must be credited to the cash fund. Any amount remaining in the cash fund at the end of any fiscal year must remain in the cash fund and must not be credited or transferred to the general fund or to any other fund.

(2) The department is authorized to expend a reasonable amount of the moneys received for the program for the direct and indirect costs associated with administering the program, unless otherwise provided by any provision related to the department's receipt of federal moneys that are applied to the grant program.

(3) (a) General fund moneys shall not be appropriated to the cash fund for the implementation of this article.

(b) The department may seek, accept, and expend public or private gifts, grants, and donations from public and private sources to implement this article; except that the department shall not accept a gift, grant, or donation that is subject to conditions that are inconsistent with the provisions of section 25-44-102 (2) or any other state law. The department shall transfer all public and private moneys received through gifts, grants, and donations to the state treasurer, who shall credit the same to the cash fund.

(c) Repealed.

# ARTICLE 45. ACCESS TO TREATMENTS FOR TERMINALLY ILL PATIENTS

## 25-45-101. Short title.

This article shall be known and may be cited as the "Right to Try Act".

## 25-45-102. Legislative declaration.

(1) The general assembly finds and declares that:

(a) The process of approval for investigational drugs, biological products, and devices in the United States protects future patients from premature, ineffective, and unsafe medications and treatments over the long run, but the process often takes many years;

(b) Patients who have a terminal illness do not have the luxury of waiting until an investigational drug, biological product, or device receives final approval from the United States food and drug administration;

(c) Patients who have a terminal illness have a fundamental right to attempt to pursue the preservation of their own lives by accessing available investigational drugs, biological products, and devices;

(d) The use of available investigational drugs, biological products, and devices is a decision that should be made by the patient with a terminal illness in consultation with the patient's health care provider and the patient's health care team, if applicable; and

(e) The decision to use an investigational drug, biological product, or device should be made with full awareness of the potential risks, benefits, and consequences to the patient and the patient's family.

(2) It is the intent of the general assembly to allow for terminally ill patients to use potentially life-saving investigational drugs, biological products, and devices.

## 25-45-103. Definitions.

As used in this article, unless the context otherwise requires:

(1) (a) "Eligible patient" means a person who has:

(I) A terminal illness, attested to by the patient's treating physician;

(II) Considered all other treatment options currently approved by the United States food and drug administration;

(III) Been unable to participate in a clinical trial for the terminal illness within one hundred miles of the patient's home address or not been accepted to the clinical trial within one week of completion of the clinical trial application process;

(IV) Received a recommendation from his or her physician for an investigational drug, biological product, or device;

(V) Given written, informed consent for the use of the investigational drug, biological product, or device or, if the patient is a minor or lacks the mental capacity to provide informed consent, a parent or legal guardian has given written, informed consent on the patient's behalf; and

(VI) Documentation from his or her physician that he or she meets the requirements of this paragraph (a) .

(b) "Eligible patient" does not include a person being treated as an inpatient in a hospital licensed or certified pursuant to section 25-3-101.

(2) "Investigational drug, biological product, or device" means a drug, biological product, or device that has successfully completed phase one of a clinical trial but has not yet been approved for general use by the United States food and drug administration and remains under investigation in a United States food and drug administration-approved clinical trial.

(3) "Terminal illness" means a disease that, without life-sustaining procedures, will soon result in death or a state of permanent unconsciousness from which recovery is unlikely.

(4) "Written, informed consent" means a written document signed by the patient and attested to by the patient's physician and a witness that, at a minimum:

(a) Explains the currently approved products and treatments for the disease or condition from which the patient suffers;

(b) Attests to the fact that the patient concurs with his or her physician in believing that all currently approved and conventionally recognized treatments are unlikely to prolong the patient's life;

(c) Clearly identifies the specific proposed investigational drug, biological product, or device that the patient is seeking to use;

(d) Describes the potentially best and worst outcomes of using the investigational drug, biological product, or device with a realistic description of the most likely outcome, including the possibility that new, unanticipated, different, or worse symptoms might result, and that death could be hastened by the proposed treatment, based on the physician's knowledge of the proposed treatment in conjunction with an awareness of the patient's condition;

(e) Makes clear that the patient's health insurer and provider are not obligated to pay for any care or treatments consequent to the use of the investigational drug, biological product, or device;

(f) Makes clear that the patient's eligibility for hospice care may be withdrawn if the patient begins curative treatment and care may be reinstated if the curative treatment ends and the patient meets hospice eligibility requirements;

(g) Makes clear that in-home health care may be denied if treatment begins; and

(h) States that the patient understands that he or she is liable for all expenses consequent to the use of the investigational drug, biological product, or device, and that this liability extends to the patient's estate, unless a contract between the patient and the manufacturer of the drug, biological product, or device states otherwise.

## 25-45-104. Drug manufacturers - availability of investigational drugs, biological products, or devices - costs - insurance coverage.

(1) A manufacturer of an investigational drug, biological product, or device may make available the manufacturer's investigational drug, biological product, or device to eligible patients pursuant to this article. This article does not require that a manufacturer make available an investigational drug, biological product, or device to an eligible patient.

(2) A manufacturer may:

(a) Provide an investigational drug, biological product, or device to an eligible patient without receiving compensation; or

(b) Require an eligible patient to pay the costs of, or the costs associated with, the manufacture of the investigational drug, biological product, or device.

(3) (a) Nothing in this article expands the coverage provided in sections 10-16-104 (20) or 10-16-104.6, C.R.S.

(b) A health insurance carrier may, but is not required to, provide coverage for the cost of an investigational drug, biological product, or device.

(c) An insurer may deny coverage to an eligible patient from the time the eligible patient begins use of the investigational drug, biological product, or device through a period not to exceed six months from the time the investigational drug, biological product, or device is no longer used by the eligible patient; except that coverage may not be denied for a preexisting condition and for coverage for benefits which commenced prior to the time the eligible patient begins use of such drug, biological product, or device.

(4) If a patient dies while being treated by an investigational drug, biological product, or device, the patient's heirs are not liable for any outstanding debt related to the treatment or lack of insurance due to the treatment.

## 25-45-105. Action against health care provider's license or medicare certification prohibited.

Notwithstanding any other law, a licensing board may not revoke, fail to renew, suspend, or take any action against a health care provider's license issued pursuant to title 12, C.R.S., based solely on the health care provider's recommendations to an eligible patient regarding access to or treatment with an investigational drug, biological product, or device, as long as the recommendations are consistent with medical standards of care. Action against a health care provider's medicare certification based solely on the health care provider's recommendation that a patient have access to an investigational drug, biological product, or device is prohibited.

## 25-45-106. Access to investigational drugs, biological products, and devices.

An official, employee, or agent of this state shall not block or attempt to block an eligible patient's access to an investigational drug, biological product, or device. Counseling, advice, or a recommendation consistent with medical standards of care from a licensed health care provider is not a violation of this section.

## 25-45-107. No cause of action created.

This article does not create a private cause of action against a manufacturer of an investigational drug, biological product, or device or against any other person or entity involved in the care of an eligible patient using the investigational drug, biological product, or device, for any harm done to the eligible patient resulting from the investigational drug, biological product, or device, so long as the manufacturer or other person or entity is complying in good faith with the terms of this article, unless there was a failure to exercise reasonable care.

### 25-45-108. Effect on health care coverage.
Nothing in this section affects the mandatory health care coverage for participation in clinical trials pursuant to section 10-16-106 (20) , C.R.S.

# ARTICLE 46. COLORADO COMMISSION ON AFFORDABLE HEALTH CARE

### 25-46-101 to 25-46-106. (Repealed)

# ARTICLE 47. USE OF EPINEPHRINE AUTO-INJECTORS BY AUTHORIZED ENTITIES

### 25-47-101. Definitions.
As used in this article:
(1) "Administer" means to directly apply an epinephrine auto-injector to the body of an individual.
(2) "Authorized entity" means an entity or organization, other than a school described in section 22-1-119.5, C.R.S., or a hospital licensed or certified pursuant to section 25-1.5-103 (1) (a) (I) (A) or (1) (a) (II) , at which allergens capable of causing anaphylaxis may be present. The term includes but is not limited to recreation camps, colleges and universities, day care facilities, youth sports leagues, amusement parks, restaurants, places of employment, ski areas, and sports arenas.
(3) "Emergency public access station" or "EPAS" means a locked, secure container used to store epinephrine auto-injectors for use under the general oversight of a medical professional, which allows a lay rescuer to consult with a medical professional in real time by audio, televideo, or other similar means of electronic communication. Upon authorization of the consulting medical professional, an EPAS may be unlocked to make an epinephrine auto-injector available.
(4) "Epinephrine auto-injector" means a single-use device used for the automatic injection of a premeasured dose of epinephrine into the human body.
(5) "Health care practitioner" means a person authorized by law to prescribe any drug or device, acting within the scope of his or her authority.
(6) "Medical professional" means a physician or other person authorized by applicable law to prescribe drugs in this state or another state.
(7) "Pharmacist" has the meaning set forth in section 12-42.5-102 (28) , C.R.S.
(8) "Provide" means to supply one or more epinephrine auto-injectors to an individual.

### 25-47-102. Stock supply of epinephrine auto-injectors - emergency administration.
(1) Notwithstanding any provision of law to the contrary:
(a) Prescribing to an authorized entity permitted. A health care practitioner may direct the

distribution of epinephrine auto-injectors from an in-state prescription drug outlet to an authorized entity for use in accordance with this article, and health care practitioners may distribute epinephrine auto-injectors to an authorized entity; and

(b) Authorized entities permitted to maintain supply. An authorized entity may acquire and stock a supply of epinephrine auto-injectors pursuant to a prescription issued in accordance with this section.

(2) Epinephrine auto-injectors must be stored:

(a) In a location that will be readily accessible in an emergency;

(b) According to the applicable instructions for use; and

(c) In compliance with any additional requirements that may be established by the department of public health and environment.

(3) An authorized entity shall designate employees or agents who have completed the training required by section 25-47-104 to be responsible for the storage, maintenance, control, and general oversight of epinephrine auto-injectors acquired by the authorized entity.

## 25-47-103. Use of epinephrine auto-injectors.

(1) An employee or agent of an authorized entity or other individual who has completed the training required by section 25-47-104 may use epinephrine auto-injectors prescribed pursuant to section 25-47-102 to provide or administer an epinephrine auto-injector to any individual whom the employee, agent, or other individual believes in good faith is experiencing anaphylaxis, regardless of whether the individual has a prescription for an epinephrine auto-injector or has previously been diagnosed with an allergy, or to provide an epinephrine auto-injector to a family member, friend, colleague, caregiver, or person with a similar relationship with the individual.

(2) The administration of an epinephrine auto-injector in accordance with this section is neither the practice of medicine nor of any other profession that requires licensure.

## 25-47-104. Training.

(1) An employee, agent, or other individual must complete an anaphylaxis training program before using an epinephrine auto-injector. The training must be conducted by a nationally recognized organization experienced in training laypersons in emergency health treatment or by an individual or entity approved by the department of public health and environment. The department of public health and environment may approve specific entities or individuals to conduct training or may approve specific classes by individuals or entities. The training may be conducted online or in-person and, at a minimum, must cover:

(a) How to recognize the signs and symptoms of severe allergic reactions, including anaphylaxis;

(b) The standards and procedures for the storage and administration of an epinephrine auto-injector; and

(c) Emergency follow-up procedures.

(2) The individual or entity that conducts the anaphylaxis training program shall issue a certificate, on a form developed or approved by the department of public health and environment, to each person who successfully completes the anaphylaxis training program.

## 25-47-105. Reporting.

An authorized entity that possesses and makes available epinephrine auto-injectors shall submit to the department of public health and environment, on a form developed by the department of public health and environment, a report of each incident on the authorized entity's premises that involves the administration of an epinephrine auto-injector pursuant to section 25-47-103. The department of public health and environment shall annually publish a report that summarizes and analyzes all reports submitted to it under this section.

## 25-47-106. Emergency public access stations - life-saving allergy medication.

(1) Notwithstanding any law to the contrary:

(a) A medical professional may prescribe a stock supply of epinephrine auto-injectors to any authorized entity for storage in an EPAS and may place a stock supply of epinephrine auto-injectors in an EPAS maintained by an authorized entity;

(b) A medical professional may consult the user of an EPAS and make the epinephrine auto-injectors stored in the EPAS available to the user; and

(c) Any person may use an EPAS to administer or provide an epinephrine auto-injector to an individual believed in good faith to be experiencing anaphylaxis or to provide an epinephrine auto-injector to a family member, friend, colleague, caregiver, or person with a similar relationship with the individual.

(2) The use of an EPAS in accordance with this article is neither the practice of medicine nor of any other profession that requires licensure.

### 25-47-107. Good samaritan protections - liability.

(1) The following individuals and entities are immune from criminal liability and from suit in any civil action brought by any person for injuries or related damages that result from an act or omission taken pursuant to this article:

(a) An authorized entity that possesses and makes available epinephrine auto-injectors or an EPAS and the entity's employees, agents, and other individuals;

(b) An authorized entity that does not possess or make available epinephrine auto-injectors or an EPAS and the entity's employees, agents, and other individuals;

(c) An individual or entity that conducts an anaphylaxis training program;

(d) An individual who prescribes or dispenses an epinephrine auto-injector;

(e) An individual who administers or provides an epinephrine auto-injector;

(f) A medical professional who consults the user of an EPAS and makes the epinephrine auto-injectors stored in the EPAS available to the user; or

(g) An individual who uses an EPAS.

(2) Immunity under subsection (1) of this section does not apply to acts or omissions that are grossly negligent or willful and wanton.

(3) This section does not eliminate, limit, or reduce any other immunity or defense that may be available under state law, including the protections set forth in section 13-21-108, C.R.S. Providing or administering an epinephrine auto-injector by an entity or individual is deemed emergency care or emergency assistance for purposes of section 13-21-108, C.R.S.

(4) An authorized entity located in this state that provides or administers an epinephrine auto-injector outside of this state is not liable for any resulting injuries or related damages if the authorized entity:

(a) Would not be liable for the injuries or related damages if the epinephrine auto-injector had been provided or administered in this state; or

(b) Is not liable for injuries or related damages under the law of the state where the authorized entity provided or administered the epinephrine auto-injector.

### 25-47-108. Health care professionals - hospitals - obligations under state and federal law.

Nothing in this article limits the obligations of a health care professional or hospital under state or federal law in prescribing, storing, or administering drugs or devices.

# ARTICLE 48. END-OF-LIFE OPTIONS

### 25-48-101. Short title.

The short title of this article is the "Colorado End-of-life Options Act".

## 25-48-102. Definitions.

As used in this article, unless the context otherwise requires:

(1) "Adult" means an individual who is eighteen years of age or older.

(2) "Attending physician" means a physician who has primary responsibility for the care of a terminally ill individual and the treatment of the individual's terminal illness.

(3) "Consulting physician" means a physician who is qualified by specialty or experience to make a professional diagnosis and prognosis regarding a terminally ill individual's illness.

(4) "Health care provider" or "provider" means a person who is licensed, certified, registered, or otherwise authorized or permitted by law to administer health care or dispense medication in the ordinary course of business or practice of a profession. The term includes a health care facility, including a long-term care facility as defined in section 25-3-103.7 (1) (f.3) and a continuing care retirement community as described in section 25.5-6-203 (1) (c) (I) , C.R.S.

(5) "Informed decision" means a decision that is:

(a) Made by an individual to obtain a prescription for medical aid-in-dying medication that the qualified individual may decide to self-administer to end his or her life in a peaceful manner;

(b) Based on an understanding and acknowledgment of the relevant facts; and

(c) Made after the attending physician fully informs the individual of:

(I) His or her medical diagnosis and prognosis of six months or less;

(II) The potential risks associated with taking the medical aid-in dying medication to be prescribed;

(III) The probable result of taking the medical aid-in-dying medication to be prescribed;

(IV) The choices available to an individual that demonstrate his or her self- determination and intent to end his or her life in a peaceful manner, including the ability to choose whether to:

(A) Request medical aid in dying;

(B) Obtain a prescription for medical aid-in-dying medication to end his or her life;

(C) Fill the prescription and possess medical aid-in-dying medication to end his or her life; and

(D) Ultimately self-administer the medical aid-in-dying medication to bring about a peaceful death; and

(V) All feasible alternatives or additional treatment opportunities, including comfort care, palliative care, hospice care, and pain control.

(6) "Licensed mental health professional" means a psychiatrist licensed under article 36 of title 12, C.R.S., or a psychologist licensed under part 3 of article 43 of title 12, C.R.S.

(7) "Medical aid in dying" means the medical practice of a physician prescribing medical aid-in-dying medication to a qualified individual that the individual may choose to self-administer to bring about a peaceful death.

(8) "Medical aid-in-dying medication" means medication prescribed by a physician pursuant to this article to provide medical aid in dying to a qualified individual.

(9) "Medically confirmed" means that a consulting physician who has examined the terminally ill individual and the individual's relevant medical records has confirmed the medical opinion of the attending physician.

(10) "Mental capacity" or "mentally capable" means that in the opinion of an individual's attending physician, consulting physician, psychiatrist or psychologist, the individual has the ability to make and communicate an informed decision to health care providers.

(11) "Physician" means a doctor of medicine or osteopathy licensed to practice medicine by the Colorado medical board.

(12) "Prognosis of six months or less" means a prognosis resulting from a terminal illness that the illness will, within reasonable medical judgment, result in death within six months and which has been medically confirmed.

(13) "Qualified individual" means a terminally ill adult with a prognosis of six months or less, who has mental capacity, has made an informed decision, is a resident of the state, and has satisfied the requirements of this article in order to obtain a prescription for medical aid-in-dying

medication to end his or her life in a peaceful manner.

(14) "Resident" means an individual who is able to demonstrate residency in Colorado by providing any of the following documentation to his or her attending physician:

(a) A Colorado driver's license or identification card issued pursuant to article 2 of title 42, C.R.S.;

(b) A Colorado voter registration card or other documentation showing the individual is registered to vote in Colorado;

(c) Evidence that the individual owns or leases property in Colorado; or

(d) A Colorado income tax return for the most recent tax year.

(15) "Self-administer" means a qualified individual's affirmative, conscious, and physical act of administering the medical aid-in-dying medication to himself or herself to bring about his or her own death.

(16) "Terminal illness" means an incurable and irreversible illness that will, within reasonable medical judgment, result in death.

## 25-48-103. Right to request medical aid-in-dying medication.

(1) An adult resident of Colorado may make a request, in accordance with sections 25-48-104 and 25-48-112, to receive a prescription for medical aid-in-dying medication if:

(a) The individual's attending physician has diagnosed the individual with a terminal illness with a prognosis of six months or less;

(b) The individual's attending physician has determined the individual has mental capacity; and

(c) The individual has voluntarily expressed the wish to receive a prescription for medical aid-in-dying medication.

(2) The right to request medical aid-in-dying medication does not exist because of age or disability.

## 25-48-104. Request process - witness requirements.

(1) In order to receive a prescription for medical aid-in-dying medication pursuant to this article, an individual who satisfies the requirements in section 25-48-103 must make two oral requests, separated by at least fifteen days, and a valid written request to his or her attending physician.

(2) (a) To be valid, a written request for medical aid-in-dying medication must be:

(I) Substantially in the same form as set forth in section 25-48-112;

(II) Signed and dated by the individual seeking the medical aid-in-dying medication; and

(III) Witnessed by at least two individuals who, in the presence of the individual, attest to the best of their knowledge and belief that the individual is:

(A) Mentally capable;

(B) Acting voluntarily; and

(C) Not being coerced to sign the request.

(b) Of the two witnesses to the written request, at least one must not be:

(I) Related to the individual by blood, marriage, civil union, or adoption;

(II) An individual who, at the time the request is signed, is entitled, under a will or by operation of law, to any portion of the individual's estate upon his or her death; or

(III) An owner, operator, or employee of a health care facility where the individual is receiving medical treatment or is a resident.

(c) Neither the individual's attending physician nor a person authorized as the individual's qualified power of attorney or durable medical power of attorney shall serve as a witness to the written request.

## 25-48-105. Right to rescind request - requirement to offer opportunity to rescind.

(1) At any time, an individual may rescind his or her request for medical aid-in-dying medication without regard to the individual's mental state.

(2) An attending physician shall not write a prescription for medical aid-in-dying medication

under this article unless the attending physician offers the qualified individual an opportunity to rescind the request for the medical aid-in-dying medication.

## 25-48-106. Attending physician responsibilities.

(1) The attending physician shall:

(a) Make the initial determination of whether an individual requesting medical aid-in- dying medication has a terminal illness, has a prognosis of six months or less, is mentally capable, is making an informed decision, and has made the request voluntarily;

(b) Request that the individual demonstrate colorado residency by providing documentation as described in section 25-48-102 (14) ;

(c) Provide care that conforms to established medical standards and accepted medical guidelines;

(d) Refer the individual to a consulting physician for medical confirmation of the diagnosis and prognosis and for a determination of whether the individual is mentally capable, is making an informed decision, and acting voluntarily;

(e) Provide full, individual-centered disclosures to ensure that the individual is making an informed decision by discussing with the individual:

(I) His or her medical diagnosis and prognosis of six months or less;

(II) The feasible alternatives or additional treatment opportunities, including comfort care, palliative care, hospice care, and pain control;

(III) The potential risks associated with taking the medical aid-in-dying medication to be prescribed;

(IV) The probable result of taking the medical aid-in-dying medication to be prescribed; and

(V) The possibility that the individual can obtain the medical aid-in-dying medication but choose not to use it;

(f) Refer the individual to a licensed mental health professional pursuant to section 25-48-108 if the attending physician believes that the individual may not be mentally capable of making an informed decision;

(g) Confirm that the individual's request does not arise from coercion or undue influence by another person by discussing with the individual, outside the presence of other persons, whether the individual is feeling coerced or unduly influenced by another person;

(h) Counsel the individual about the importance of:

(I) Having another person present when the individual self-administers the medical aid-in-dying medication prescribed pursuant to this article;

(II) Not taking the medical aid-in-dying medication in a public place;

(III) Safe-keeping and proper disposal of unused medical aid-in-dying medication in accordance with section 25-48-120; and

(IV) Notifying his or her next of kin of the request for medical aid-in-dying medication;

(i) Inform the individual that he or she may rescind the request for medical aid-in-dying medication at any time and in any manner;

(j) Verify, immediately prior to writing the prescription for medical aid-in-dying medication, that the individual is making an informed decision;

(k) Ensure that all appropriate steps are carried out in accordance with this article before writing a prescription for medical aid-in-dying medication; and

(l) Either:

(I) Dispense medical aid-in-dying medications directly to the qualified individual, including ancillary medications intended to minimize the individual's discomfort, if the attending physician has a current drug enforcement administration certificate and complies with any applicable administrative rule; or

(II) Deliver the written prescription personally, by mail, or through authorized electronic transmission in the manner permitted under article 42.5 of title 12, C.R.S., to a licensed pharmacist, who shall dispense the medical aid-in-dying medication to the qualified individual, the attending physician, or an individual expressly designated by the qualified individual.

## 25-48-107. Consulting physician responsibilities.

Before an individual who is requesting medical aid-in-dying medication may receive a prescription for the medical aid-in-dying medication, a consulting physician must:

(1) Examine the individual and his or her relevant medical records;

(2) Confirm, in writing, to the attending physician:

(a) That the individual has a terminal illness;

(b) The individual has a prognosis of six months or less;

(c) That the individual is making an informed decision; and

(d) That the individual is mentally capable, or provide documentation that the consulting physician has referred the individual for further evaluation in accordance with section 25-48-108.

## 25-48-108. Confirmation that individual is mentally capable - referral to mental health professional.

(1) An attending physician shall not prescribe medical aid-in-dying medication under this article for an individual with a terminal illness until the individual is determined to be mentally capable and making an informed decision, and those determinations are confirmed in accordance with this section.

(2) If the attending physician or the consulting physician believes that the individual may not be mentally capable of making an informed decision, the attending physician or consulting physician shall refer the individual to a licensed mental health professional for a determination of whether the individual is mentally capable and making an informed decision.

(3) A licensed mental health professional who evaluates an individual under this section shall communicate, in writing, to the attending or consulting physician who requested the evaluation, his or her conclusions about whether the individual is mentally capable and making informed decisions. If the licensed mental health professional determines that the individual is not mentally capable of making informed decisions, the person shall not be deemed a qualified individual under this article and the attending physician shall not prescribe medical aid-in-dying medication to the individual.

## 25-48-109. Death certificate.

(1) Unless otherwise prohibited by law, the attending physician or the hospice medical director shall sign the death certificate of a qualified individual who obtained and self-administered aid-in-dying medication.

(2) When a death has occurred in accordance with this article, the cause of death shall be listed as the underlying terminal illness and the death does not constitute grounds for post-mortem inquiry under section 30-10-606 (1) , C.R.S.

## 25-48-110. Informed decision required.

(1) An individual with a terminal illness is not a qualified individual and may not receive a prescription for medical aid-in-dying medication unless he or she has made an informed decision.

(2) Immediately before writing a prescription for medical aid-in-dying medication under this article, the attending physician shall verify that the individual with a terminal illness is making an informed decision.

## 25-48-111. Medical record documentation requirements - reporting requirements - department compliance reviews - rules.

(1) The attending physician shall document in the individual's medical record, the following information:

(a) Dates of all oral requests;

(b) A valid written request;

(c) The attending physician's diagnosis and prognosis, determination of mental capacity and that the individual is making a voluntary request and an informed decision;

(d) The consulting physician's confirmation of diagnosis and prognosis, mental capacity and that the individual is making an informed decision;

(e) If applicable, written confirmation of mental capacity from a licensed mental health professional;

(f) A notation of notification of the right to rescind a request made pursuant to this article; and

(g) A notation by the attending physician that all requirements under this article have been satisfied; indicating steps taken to carry out the request, including a notation of the medical aid-in-dying medications prescribed and when.

(2) (a) The department of public health and environment shall annually review a sample of records maintained pursuant to this article to ensure compliance. The department shall adopt rules to facilitate the collection of information defined in subsection (1) of this section. Except as otherwise required by law, the information collected by the department is not a public record and is not available for public inspection. However, the department shall generate and make available to the public an annual statistical report of information collected under this subsection (2) .

(b) The department shall require any health care provider, upon dispensing a medical aid-in-dying medication pursuant to this article, to file a copy of a dispensing record with the department. The dispensing record is not a public record and is not available for public inspection.

## 25-48-112. Form of written request.

(1) A request for medical aid-in-dying medication authorized by this article must be in substantially the following form:

Request for medication to end my life
 in a peaceful manner


I, am an adult of sound mind. I am suffering from , which my attending physician has determined is a terminal illness and which has been medically confirmed. I have been fully informed of my diagnosis and prognosis of six months or less, the nature of the medical aid-in-dying medication to be prescribed and potential associated risks, the expected result, and the feasible alternatives or additional treatment opportunities, including comfort care, palliative care, hospice care, and pain control.

I request that my attending physician prescribe medical aid-in-dying medication that will end my life in a peaceful manner if I choose to take it, and I authorize my attending physician to contact any pharmacist about my request.

I understand that I have the right to rescind this request at any time.

I understand the seriousness of this request, and I expect to die if I take the aid-in-dying medication prescribed.

I further understand that although most deaths occur within three hours, my death may take longer, and my attending physician has counseled me about this possibility. I make this request voluntarily, without reservation, and without being coerced, and I accept full responsibility for my actions.

Signed:

Dated:


Declaration of witnesses


We declare that the individual signing this request:

Is personally known to us or has provided proof of identity;

Signed this request in our presence;

Appears to be of sound mind and not under duress, coercion, or undue influence; and
I am not the attending physician for the individual.

witness 1/date
witness 2/date
Note: Of the two witnesses to the written request, at least one must not:
Be a relative (by blood, marriage, civil union, or adoption) of the individual signing this request;
be entitled to any portion of the individual's estate upon death; or own, operate, or be employed at
a health care facility where the individual is a patient or resident.
And neither the individual's attending physician nor a person authorized as the individual's
qualified power of attorney or durable medical power of attorney shall serve as a witness to the
written request.

## 25-48-113. Standard of care.

(1) Physicians and health care providers shall provide medical services under this act that meet or
exceed the standard of care for end-of-life medical care.
(2) If a health care provider is unable or unwilling to carry out an eligible individual's request and
the individual transfers care to a new health care provider, the health care provider shall coordinate
transfer of the individual's medical records to a new health care provider.

## 25-48-114. Effect on wills, contracts, and statutes.

(1) A provision in a contract, will, or other agreement, whether written or oral, that would affect
whether an individual may make or rescind a request for medical aid in dying pursuant to this
article is invalid.
(2) An obligation owing under any currently existing contract must not be conditioned upon, or
affected by, an individual's act of making or rescinding a request for medical aid-in-dying
medication pursuant to this article.

## 25-48-115. Insurance or annuity policies.

(1) The sale, procurement, or issuance of, or the rate charged for, any life, health, or accident
insurance or annuity policy must not be conditioned upon, or affected by, an individual's act of
making or rescinding a request for medical aid-in-dying medication in accordance with this article.
(2) A qualified individual's act of self-administering medical aid-in-dying medication pursuant to
this article does not affect a life, health, or accident insurance or annuity policy.
(3) An insurer shall not deny or otherwise alter health care benefits available under a policy of
sickness and accident insurance to an individual with a terminal illness who is covered under the
policy, based on whether or not the individual makes a request pursuant to this article.
(4) An individual with a terminal illness who is a recipient of medical assistance under the
"Colorado Medical Assistance Act", articles 4, 5, and 6 of title 25.5, C.R.S. shall not be denied
benefits under the medical assistance program or have his or her benefits under the program
otherwise altered based on whether or not the individual makes a request pursuant to this article.

## 25-48-116. Immunity for actions in good faith - prohibition against reprisals.

(1) A person is not subject to civil or criminal liability or professional disciplinary action for
acting in good faith under this article, which includes being present when a qualified individual
self-administers the prescribed medical aid-in-dying medication.
(2) Except as provided for in section 25-48-118, a health care provider or professional
organization or association shall not subject an individual to any of the following for participating
or refusing to participate in good-faith compliance under this article:
(a) Censure;
(b) Discipline;
(c) Suspension;

(d) Loss of license, privileges, or membership; or

(e) Any other penalty.

(3) A request by an individual for, or the provision by an attending physician of, medical aid-in-dying medication in good-faith compliance with this article does not:

(a) Constitute neglect or elder abuse for any purpose of law; or

(b) Provide the basis for the appointment of a guardian or conservator.

(4) This section does not limit civil or criminal liability for negligence, recklessness, or intentional misconduct.

## 25-48-117. No duty to prescribe or dispense.

(1) A health care provider may choose whether to participate in providing medical aid-in-dying medication to an individual in accordance with this article.

(2) If a health care provider is unable or unwilling to carry out an individual's request for medical aid-in-dying medication made in accordance with this article, and the individual transfers his or her care to a new health care provider, the prior health care provider shall transfer, upon request, a copy of the individual's relevant medical records to the new health care provider.

## 25-48-118. Health care facility permissible prohibitions - sanctions if provider violates policy.

(1) A health care facility may prohibit a physician employed or under contract from writing a prescription for medical aid-in-dying medication for a qualified individual who intends to use the medical aid-in-dying medication on the facility's premises. The health care facility must notify the physician in writing of its policy with regard to prescriptions for medical aid-in-dying medication. A health care facility that fails to provide advance notice to the physician shall not be entitled to enforce such a policy against the physician.

(2) A health care facility or health care provider shall not subject a physician, nurse, pharmacist, or other person to discipline, suspension, loss of license or privileges, or any other penalty or sanction for actions taken in good-faith reliance on this article or for refusing to act under this article.

(3) A health care facility must notify patients in writing of its policy with regard to medical aid-in-dying. A health care facility that fails to provide advance notification to patients shall not be entitled to enforce such a policy.

## 25-48-119. Liabilities.

(1) A person commits a class 2 felony and is subject to punishment in accordance with section 18-1.3-401, C.R.S. if the person, knowingly or intentionally causes an individual's death by:

(a) Forging or altering a request for medical aid-in-dying medication to end an individual's life without the individual's authorization; or

(b) Concealing or destroying a rescission of a request for medical aid-in-dying medication.

(2) A person commits a class 2 felony and is subject to punishment in accordance with section 18-1.3-401, C.R.S. if the person knowingly or intentionally coerces or exerts undue influence on an individual with a terminal illness to:

(a) Request medical aid-in-dying medication for the purpose of ending the terminally ill individual's life; or

(b) Destroy a rescission of a request for medical aid-in-dying medication.

(3) Nothing in this article limits further liability for civil damages resulting from other negligent conduct or intentional misconduct by any person.

(4) The penalties specified in this article do not preclude criminal penalties applicable under the "Colorado Criminal Code", title 18, C.R.S., for conduct that is inconsistent with this article.

## 25-48-120. Safe disposal of unused medical aid-in-dying medications.

A person who has custody or control of medical aid-in-dying medication dispensed under this article that the terminally ill individual decides not to use or that remains unused after the terminally ill individual's death shall dispose of the unused medical aid-in- dying medication either by:

(1) Returning the unused medical aid-in-dying medication to the attending physician who prescribed the medical aid-in-dying medication, who shall dispose of the unused medical aid-in-dying medication in the manner required by law; or

(2) Lawful means in accordance with section 25-15-328, C.R.S. or any other state or federally approved medication take-back program authorized under the federal "Secure and Responsible Drug Disposal Act of 2010", Pub.L.111-273, and regulations adopted pursuant to the federal act.

### 25-48-121. Actions complying with article not a crime.

Nothing in this article authorizes a physician or any other person to end an individual's life by lethal injection, mercy killing, or euthanasia. Actions taken in accordance with this article do not, for any purpose, constitute suicide, assisted suicide, mercy killing, homicide, or elder abuse under the "Colorado Criminal Code", as set forth in title 18, C.R.S.

### 25-48-122. Claims by government entity for costs.

A government entity that incurs costs resulting from an individual terminating his or her life pursuant to this article in a public place has a claim against the estate of the individual to recover the costs and reasonable attorney fees related to enforcing the claim.

### 25-48-123. No effect on advance medical directives.

Nothing in this article shall change the legal effect of:

(1) A declaration made under article 18 of title 15, C.R.S., directing that life-sustaining procedures be withheld or withdrawn;

(2) A cardiopulmonary resuscitation directive executed under article 18.6 of title 15, C.R.S.; or

(3) An advance medical directive executed under article 18.7 of title 15, C.R.S.

# ARTICLE 49. TRANSPARENCY IN HEALTH CARE PRICES

### 25-49-101. Short title.

[Editor's note:This section is effective January 1, 2018.]The short title of this article 49 is the "Transparency in Health Care Prices Act".

### 25-49-102. Definitions.

[Editor's note:This section is effective January 1, 2018.]As used in this article 49, unless the context otherwise requires:

(1) "Agency" means a government department or agency or a government-created entity.

(2) "CPT code" means the current procedural terminology code, or its successor code, as developed and copyrighted by the American Medical Association or its successor entity.

(3) "Health care facility" means a facility licensed or certified by the department of public health and environment pursuant to section 25-1.5-103. The term does not include a nursing care facility, assisted living residence, or home care agency.

(4) (a) "Health care price" means the price, before negotiating any discounts, that a health care provider or health care facility will charge a recipient for health care services that will be rendered. "Health care price" is the price charged for the standard service for the particular diagnosis and does not include any amount that may be charged for complications or exceptional treatment. The

health care price for a specific health care service may be determined from any of the following:
(I) The price charged most frequently for the health care service during the previous twelve months;
(II) The highest charge from the lowest half of all charges for the health care service during the previous twelve months; or
(III) A range that includes the middle fifty percent of all charges for the health care service during the previous twelve months.
(b) "Health care price" does not mean the amount charged if a public or private third party will be paying or reimbursing the health care provider or health care facility for any portion of the cost of services rendered.
(5) "Health care provider" means a person who is licensed, certified, or registered by this state to provide health care services or a medical group, independent practice association, or professional corporation providing health care services.
(6) (a) "Health care services" or "services" means services included in, or incidental to, furnishing to an individual:
(I) Medical, mental, dental, or optometric care or hospitalization; or
(II) Other services for the purpose of preventing, alleviating, curing, or healing a physical or mental illness or injury.
(b) "Health care services" includes services rendered through the use of telemedicine.
(7) "Health insurer" means a carrier, as defined in section 10-16-102 (8) , disability insurer, group disability insurer, or blanket disability insurer.
(8) (a) "Public or private third party" means a health insurer, self-insured employer, or other third party, including a third-party administrator or intermediary, responsible for paying all or a portion of the charges for health care services.
(b) "Public or private third party" does not mean:
(I) An employer of the recipient of the health care services that is not responsible for paying the charges for the health care services provided to the recipient;
(II) A person paying money from a health savings account, flexible spending account, or similar account; or
(III) A family member, charitable organization, or other person who is not responsible for, but pays charges for, health care services on behalf of the recipient of the services.
(9) "Punish" means to impose a penalty, surcharge, fee, or other additional cost or measure that has the same effect as a penalty or that discourages the exercise of rights under this article 49.
(10) "Recipient" means an individual who receives health care services from a health care provider or health care facility.

## 25-49-103. Transparency - charges for services rendered by health care providers.

[Editor's note:This section is effective January 1, 2018.](1) (a) (I) Except as provided in subsection (1) (a) (II) or (1) (a) (III) of this section, a health care provider shall make available to the public, in a single document, either electronically or by posting conspicuously on the provider's website if one exists, the health care prices for at least the fifteen most common health care services the health care provider provides. If the health care provider, in the normal course of his or her practice, regularly provides fewer than fifteen health care services, the health care provider shall make available the health care prices for the health care services the provider most commonly provides.
(II) A health care provider practicing in a solo practice or in a medical group, independent practice association, or professional corporation comprised of not more than six individual health care providers with the same license type may comply with the requirements of this section by making the health care prices described in subsection (1) (a) (I) of this section available in patient waiting areas.
(III) A health care provider who is a member of a professional corporation that contracts with a

single health maintenance organization, as defined in section 10-16-102 (35) , complies with this section if the professional corporation or its contracting health maintenance organization makes available to the public, in a single document, either electronically or by posting conspicuously on its website, the health care prices for at least the fifteen most common health care services that the health care provider or health maintenance organization would charge individuals who are not members of the health maintenance organization.

(b) The health care provider shall identify the services by:

(I) A common procedural terminology code or other coding system commonly used by the health care provider and accepted as a national standard for billing; and

(II) A plain English description.

(c) The health care provider shall update the document as frequently as the health care provider deems appropriate, but at least annually.

(2) The health care provider shall include:

(a) A disclosure specifying that the health care price for any given health care service is an estimate and that the actual charges for the health care service are dependent on the circumstances at the time the service is rendered; and

(b) The following statement or a statement containing substantially similar information:

If you are covered by health insurance, you are strongly encouraged to consult with your health insurer to determine accurate information about your financial responsibility for a particular health care service provided by a health care provider at this office. If you are not covered by health insurance, you are strongly encouraged to contact our billing office at (insert telephone number) to discuss payment options prior to receiving a health care service from a health care provider at this office since posted health care prices may not reflect the actual amount of your financial responsibility.

(3) A hospital-based health care provider that is not an employee of the hospital where the services are being delivered is not required to provide health care prices in the manner specified in this section for the health care services the health care provider renders in the hospital setting.

(4) Nothing in this section precludes a health care provider from informing a current or potential patient, upon request of the patient, of the health care price for a health care service that the health care provider renders.

## 25-49-104. Transparency - health care facility charges.

[Editor's note:This section is effective January 1, 2018.](1) (a) A health care facility shall make available to the public, in a single document, either electronically or by posting conspicuously on its website if one exists, the health care prices for at least:

(I) The fifty most used, diagnosis-related group codes or other codes for in-patient health care services used by the health care facility for billing or, if those codes are not used, the codes under another coding system for in-patient health care services commonly used by the facility and accepted as a national standard for billing; and

(II) The twenty-five most used out-patient CPT codes or health care services procedure codes used for billing or, if those codes are not used, the codes under another coding system for out-patient health care services commonly used by the facility and accepted as a national standard for billing.

(b) If a health care facility did not use fifty codes for in-patient health care services at least eleven times in the previous twelve months or did not use twenty-five codes for out-patient health care services at least eleven times in the previous twelve months, the health care facility shall make available the health care price for only those most common in-patient and out-patient health care services or procedure codes that the health care facility used at least eleven times in the previous twelve months.

(c) A health care facility shall include with the health care price provided pursuant to this subsection (1) a plain English description of the service for which the health care price is provided.

(d) The health care facility shall update the document as frequently as it deems appropriate, but at least annually.

(2) The health care facility shall include:

(a) A disclosure specifying that the health care price for any given health care service is an estimate and that the actual charges for the health care service are dependent on the circumstances at the time the service is rendered; and

(b) The following statement or a statement containing substantially similar information:

If you are covered by health insurance, you are strongly encouraged to consult with your health insurer to determine accurate information about your financial responsibility for a particular health care service provided at this health care facility. If you are not covered by health insurance, you are strongly encouraged to contact (insert office name and telephone number) to discuss payment options prior to receiving a health care service from this health care facility since posted health care prices may not reflect the actual amount of your financial responsibility.

(3) A health care facility may disclose the basis for its health care prices and may take into consideration all payer sources when determining a health care price.

## 25-49-105. No review of health care prices - no punishment for exercising rights - no impairment of contracts.

[Editor's note:This section is effective January 1, 2018.](1) Nothing in this article 49 requires a health care facility or health care provider to report its health care prices to any agency for review, filing, or other purposes, except as required by section 25-3-112, or for applications for health care professional loan repayment submitted pursuant to section 25-1.5-503. This article 49 does not grant any agency the authority to approve, disapprove, or limit a health care facility's or health care provider's health care prices or changes to its health care prices. The department of public health and environment is not authorized to take any action regarding or pursuant to this article 49.

(2) This article 49 is intended to make health care prices and payments, and participating in or exercising rights under this article 49, free from paperwork, punishment, reporting, and regulation to the fullest extent permissible under the state constitution and state and federal law. A person, entity, agency, or health insurer shall not punish a recipient, health care provider, health care facility, person, entity, or employer for participating directly in, exercising rights under, or complying with this article 49. The health care price for a given health care service that a health care provider or health care facility makes available to the public pursuant to this article 49 shall not be used as the basis for determining payment rates from a public or private third party for that health care service.

(3) Nothing in this article 49 impairs contracts between private parties.

# ARTICLE 50. CANCER CURE CONTROL

## 25-50-101. Definitions.

As used in this article 50, unless the context otherwise requires:

(1) "Cancer" means all malignant neoplasms regardless of the tissue of origin including malignant lymphoma and leukemia.

(2) "Department" means the department of public health and environment.

(3) "Licensed dentist" means a person licensed to practice dentistry under article 35 of title 12 by the Colorado dental board or its successor.

(4) "Licensed physician or osteopath" means a person licensed to practice medicine under article

## 25-50-102. Application of article.

The provisions of this article 50 shall not be construed in any manner to authorize any licensed physician, osteopath, or dentist to practice medicine or dentistry beyond the limits imposed by the applicable statutes of the state.

## 25-50-103. Powers and duties of department.

(1) The department shall:

(a) Prescribe reasonable rules with respect to the administration of this article 50;

(b) Investigate violations of the provisions of this article 50 and report the violations to the appropriate enforcement authority;

(c) Secure the investigation and testing of the content, method of preparation, efficacy, or use of drugs, medicines, compounds, or devices, held out by any individual, person, firm, association, or other entity in the state as of value in the diagnosis, treatment, or cure of cancer, prescribe reasonable regulations with respect to the investigation and testing, and make findings of fact and recommendations upon completion of any investigation and testing;

(d) Hold hearings in respect to the investigations made under the provisions of subsection (1) (c) of this section, and subpoena witnesses and documents. Prior to issuance of a cease-and-desist order under section 25-50-107, a hearing shall be held by the department. The person furnishing a sample under section 25-50-104 shall be given due notice of the hearing and an opportunity to be heard.

(e) Contract with independent scientific consultants for specialized services and advice.

## 25-50-104. Investigation by department.

On written request by the department, delivered personally or by mail, any individual, person, firm, association, or other entity that holds out either expressly or impliedly any drug, medicine, compound, or device as being of a value in the diagnosis, treatment, alleviation, or cure of cancer, shall furnish the department with a sample as the department may deem necessary for adequate testing of the drug, medicine, compound, or device and shall specify the formula of any drug or compound and name all ingredients by their common or usual names, and, upon like request by the department, shall furnish further necessary information as it may request as to the composition and method of preparation of and the manner in which the drug, compound, or device is of value in diagnosis, treatment, alleviation, or cure of cancer.

## 25-50-105. Failure to comply with request of department.

(1) If there is failure to either provide the sample, disclose the formula, or name the ingredients as required by this article 50, it shall be conclusively presumed that the drug, medicine, compound, or device that is the subject of the department's request has no value in the diagnosis, treatment, alleviation, or cure of cancer.

(2) Any individual, person, firm, association, or other entity that fails to comply with any of the provisions of this article 50, or with any order of the department validly issued under this article 50, is guilty of a misdemeanor and, upon conviction thereof, shall be punished as provided in section 18-1.3-505.

## 25-50-106. Unlawful acts.

(1) It is a misdemeanor for an individual, person, firm, association, or other entity, other than a licensed physician, licensed advanced practice nurse within his or her scope of practice, licensed osteopath, or licensed dentist to diagnose, treat, or prescribe for the treatment of cancer or to hold himself or herself out to any person as being able to cure, diagnose, treat, or prescribe for the treatment of the disease of cancer. A licensed chiropractor shall not treat cancer or prescribe for the treatment of cancer. A chiropractor may treat any person for human ailments within the scope

of his or her license even though the person has or may have cancer at the time, but if a chiropractor knows or has reason to believe that any patient has or may have cancer, he or she must refer the patient to a medical doctor or an osteopath.

(2) It is a misdemeanor for any individual, person, firm, association, or other entity willfully and falsely to represent a device, substance, or treatment as being of a value in the treatment, alleviation, or cure of cancer. Nothing in this section shall abridge the existent rights of the press. Any person who is convicted of a third or any subsequent violation of this article 50 commits a class 6 felony and shall be punished as provided in section 18-1.3-401.

## 25-50-107. Findings - cease-and-desist order.

(1) Following an investigation or testing of the content or composition of any drug, medicine, compound, or device held out either expressly or impliedly by any individual, person, firm, association, or other entity to be of value in the diagnosis, treatment, alleviation, or cure of cancer and after a hearing as provided in section 25-50-103, the department may direct that any such individual, person, firm, association, or other entity shall cease and desist any further holding out, either expressly or impliedly, that any such drug, medicine, compound, or device, or any substantially similar drug, medicine, compound, or device, is of value in the diagnosis or treatment of cancer.

(2) In the investigation or testing required by this article 50 to determine the value or lack of value of any drug, medicine, compound, or device in the diagnosis, treatment, or cure of cancer, the department, as it deems necessary or advisable, shall utilize the facilities and findings of its own laboratories or other appropriate laboratories, clinics, hospitals, and nonprofit cancer research institutes recognized by the national cancer institute within this state or the facilities and findings of the federal government or of the national cancer institute. The department may arrange, by contract, for investigation by and submission to it of findings, conclusions, or opinions of trained scientists in the appropriate departments of universities, medical schools, clinics, hospitals, and nonprofit cancer research institutes recognized by the national cancer institute and the submission to it of findings, conclusions, or opinions of other qualified scientists. Prior to the issuance of a cease-and-desist order under this section, the department shall make a written finding of fact based on the investigation that the drug, medicine, compound, or device so investigated has been found to be either definitely harmful or of no value in the diagnosis, treatment, alleviation, or cure of cancer, and the department shall be satisfied beyond a reasonable doubt that the written findings of fact are true.

## 25-50-108. Injunction.

(1) If an individual, person, firm, association, or other entity, after service upon him, her, or it of a cease-and-desist order issued by the department under section 25-50-107, persists in prescribing, recommending, or using the drug, medicine, compound, or device described in the cease-and-desist order, or a substantially similar drug, medicine, compound, or device, the district court in any county, on application of the department and when satisfied by a preponderance of the evidence that the written findings of fact required of the department by section 25-50-107 are true, may issue an order to show cause why there should not be issued an injunction or other appropriate order restraining the individual, person, firm, association, or other entity from holding out either expressly or impliedly the drug, medicine, compound, or device, or any substantially similar drug, medicine, compound, or device, as being of a value in the treatment, diagnosis, alleviation, or cure of cancer. After a hearing on the order to show cause, an injunction or other appropriate restraining order may be issued.

(2) Any person against whom an injunction has been issued, under subsection (1) of this section, may not undertake to use in the diagnosis, treatment, or cure of cancer any new, experimental, untested, or secret drug, medicine, compound, or device without first submitting it to the department for investigation and testing.

## 25-50-109. Investigation by executive director.

(1) The executive director shall investigate possible violations of this article 50 and report violations to the appropriate enforcement authority.

(2) County or district health officers, district attorneys, and the attorney general shall cooperate with the executive director in the enforcement of this article 50.

## 25-50-110. Reports of investigation.

The department, in accordance with the provisions of section 24-1-136, may publish reports based on its investigation or testing of any drug, medicine, compound, or device prescribed, recommended, or used by any individual, person, firm, association, or other entity; and, when the use of any drug, medicine, compound, or device constitutes an imminent danger to health or a gross deception of the public, the department may take appropriate steps to publicize the same.

## 25-50-111. Investigation not an endorsement.

The investigation or testing of any product shall not be deemed to imply or indicate any endorsement of the qualifications or value of the product. No person shall make any representation that investigation or testing under this article 50 constitutes any approval or endorsement of his, her, or its activities by the department. The investigation or testing of any product shall not be deemed to imply or indicate that the product is useless or harmful, and during testing no person shall make any representation, except to the department, that the product under test is discredited or that it has been found useless or harmful.

## 25-50-112. Exceptions.

(1) This article 50 shall not apply to the use of any drug, medicine, compound, or device intended solely for legitimate and bona fide investigational purposes by experts qualified by scientific training and experience to investigate the safety and therapeutic value thereof unless the department finds that the drug, medicine, compound, or device is being used in diagnosis or treatment for compensation and profit.

(2) The provisions of this article 50 shall not apply to any person who depends exclusively upon prayer for healing in accordance with the teachings of a bona fide religious sect, denomination, or organization, nor practitioner thereof.

(3) The provisions of this article 50 shall except any drug that is being clinically investigated as a cure, treatment, or aid to the diagnosis of cancer according to the regulations of the "Federal Food, Drug, and Cosmetic Act".

(4) (a) (I) The provisions of this article 50 shall not apply to the compound known as laetrile when manufactured in Colorado and prescribed by a licensed physician after fully disclosing to his or her patient the known adverse effects and reactions and the known reliability or unreliability in cancer treatment of the compound.

(II) In prescribing the use of laetrile, the licensed physician shall do so only upon a request by the patient.

(III) In complying with a patient's request concerning the use of laetrile, a licensed physician, pharmacist, hospital, or health care facility shall be immune from any civil or criminal liability for prescribing or administering laetrile as provided for in this subsection (4) , but nothing in this subsection (4) (a) (III) shall preclude any cause of action brought by a patient against a licensed physician, pharmacist, hospital, or health care facility that does not arise from the prescription or administration of laetrile in accordance with the provisions of this subsection (4) .

(b) It is the intent of the general assembly that the exception granted by this subsection (4) does not constitute an endorsement of the use of laetrile nor does it in any way encourage its use.

Made in the USA
Las Vegas, NV
28 February 2023